The PUB GUIDE 2020

The PUB GUIDE 2020

2,000 pubs for great beer and good food

AA

Published by AA Publishing, a trading name of AA Media Limited, whose registered office is Fanum House, Basing View, Basingstoke, Hampshire RG21 4EA.
Registered number 06112600.

21st edition published 2019

Assessments of AA inspected establishments are based on the experience of the Hotel and Restaurant inspectors on the occasion(s) of their visit(s) and therefore descriptions given in this guide necessarily dictate an element of subjective opinion which may not reflect or dictate a reader's own opinion on another occasion. See pages 10–13 for a clear explanation of how, based on our Inspectors' inspection experiences, establishments are graded. If the meal or meals experienced by an inspector or inspectors during an inspection fall between award levels the restaurant concerned may be awarded the lower of any award levels considered applicable.

The AA strives to ensure accuracy of the information in this guide at the time of printing. Due to the constantly evolving nature of the subject matter the information is subject to change.

The AA gratefully receives any advice from readers regarding any necessary updates.

For any queries relating to this guide, please email: **pubs@theaa.com**

Website addresses are included in some entries as specified by the respective establishment. Such websites are not under the control of AA Media Limited and as such AA Media Limited will not accept any responsibility or liability in respect of any and all matters whatsoever relating to such websites including access, content, material and functionality. By including the addresses of third party websites the AA does not intend to solicit business or offer any security to any person in any country, directly or indirectly.

If you would like to advertise in future editions of the guide, please contact **advertisingsales@theaa.com**

Image credits:
AA media wishes to thank the following pubs for the courtesy of using their images.

Abbreviations for the picture credits are as follows – (t) top; (b) bottom; (l) left; (r) right; (c) centre

6–7 The Highway Inn (Oxfordshire); 9 Sibton White Horse Inn (Suffolk); 10 Meikleour Arms (Perth & Kinross); 14 The Swan (Devon); 15 The Crafty Baa; 15 Nags Head; 15 The Pot Still; 16 The Pheasant at Buckland (Surrey); 17 Cholmondeley Arms (Cheshire); 18t 19t Cholmondeley Arms (Cheshire); 18b The Pheasant at Buckland (Surrey); 19t Cholmondeley Arms (Cheshire); 19b The Bridge Inn (Herefordshire); 20 The Bow Bar (Edinburgh).

Every effort has been made to trace the copyright holders, and we apologise in advance for any unintentional omissions or errors. We would be pleased to apply any corrections in a following edition of this publication.

Photographs in the gazetteer are provided by the establishments.

This book was compiled by the AA Lifestyle Guides team and Austin Taylor.

Pub descriptions were contributed by Jackie Bates, Phil Bryant and Mark Taylor.

AA Lifestyle Guides would like to thank Carly Bristow, Geoff Chapman, Phoebe Haynes, Liz Haynes, Lin Hutton, David Popey, Jacqui Savage, Katharine Stockermans, Austin Taylor and Stuart Walton for their help in the preparation of this guide.

Layout and cover design by Austin Taylor.

Printed in the UK by Bell & Bain.

ISBN: 978-0-7495-8188-6

A05670

Visit www.theaa.com/books/the-pub-guide-2020

CONTENTS

THE PUBS

Welcome to the 21st edition

We aim to bring you the country's best pubs, selected for their atmosphere, good beer and great food. Now at the grand old age of 21, this brand new edition of a well-established guide includes lots of old favourites, plus many new and interesting destinations for drinking and eating across the country.

The 21st edition – what's changed?

It might be better to ask what hasn't changed – back in the days of the first edition, in 1998, there were 60,500 pubs in the UK. Now that figure is fast falling below the 40,000 mark with around 18 closing every week. Indeed, we have seen many pubs that we've previously listed fall by the wayside during the creation of this new edition. There is some light at the end of the tunnel, however – AA inspectors and guide readers are recommending more and more pubs for inclusion, which means those that are left must be upping their game.

A place to stay

Pubs are vital focal points for their communities, and many have done all they can do to diversify with accommodation and food. For example, some of the pubs in this guide have hotel or B&B accommodation

rated by the AA – see pages 10–11 for details. Likewise, food is a far greater attraction to many pub goers these days than even the drink. Over 250 of the pubs in this guide have been awarded AA Rosettes for the quality of their cuisine and hundreds more have told us about their specialities and best dishes.

Who's in the guide?

We make our selection by seeking out pubs that are worth making a detour for – 'destination' pubs – where publicans show real enthusiasm for their trade and offer a good selection of well-kept drinks and great food. We also choose neighbourhood pubs which are supported by locals and prove attractive to passing drivers or walkers. Our selected pubs make no payment for their inclusion in the guide (although they can choose to enhance their entries with a photograph or two); they appear entirely at our discretion.

Pick of the Pubs

Some of the pubs included in the guide are particularly special, and we have highlighted these as Pick of the Pubs. For this edition, over 500 pubs have been selected using the personal knowledge of our editorial team, our AA Inspectors, and suggestions from our readers.

Tell us what you think

We welcome your feedback about the pubs included, and about the guide itself. We would also be chuffed to receive suggestions about good pubs you have visited that do not feature in this guide. See page 576 for details.

We hope you enjoy discovering your next favourite pub.

The AA Pub Guide team

Above Preparing a drink at the Highway Inn, Oxfordshire (see page 334).

Using the Pub Guide

To help us squeeze in as many great pubs as possible, we've used an array of symbols – the following explains all. We send an annual questionnaire to pubs and the information is based on their responses.*

1 Location
Pubs are listed by country and then alphabetically by county, then town or village location and then alphabetically within each location. There is an index by pub name at the back of the guide.

2 Pub name

3 AA ratings/designators/awards
The star rating under AA Hotel or B&B Schemes (see pages 10–11) followed by an accommodation category (i.e. INN) which shows the type of hotel or B&B. The AA Rosette award for food excellence is also shown (see pages 12–13).

4 Pick of the Pubs
See page 7.

5 Contact details and directions
Telephone number, address, website, and brief details on how to find the pub.

6 Description
A write-up about the pub, including key facilities and an idea of the food served. Generally, details of any accommodation is only mentioned if it is AA-rated.

7 Opening times
Times are given for when the pub is open, and closed.

8 Brewery and Company
⊕ indicates the name of the brewery to which the pub is tied, or the company that owns it. 'Free House' is shown if the pub is independently owned and run.

9 Real ales
indicates where more than 5 real ales are sold. These may be listed in the description.

10 Real ciders
indicates where more than 3 real ciders sold by the pub.

11 Wine by the glass
indicates where more than 8 wines are available by the glass.

1 TRENT
2 The Rose and Crown Inn, Trent
3 ★★★★★ INN PICK OF THE PUBS 4
Tel 01935 850776 | DT9 4SL
Web www.theroseandcrowntrent.co.uk 5
Dir Just off A30 between Sherborne and Yeovil.
This ivy-clad building once housed 14th-century workmen building the village church spire, but the beams and flagstone floors owe more to its days as a farmhouse in the 18th century. The inn has a lounge with a large open fire, whilst the main bar looks out over fields. At the bar, Wadworth's ales usually include 6X and Henry's Original IPA, with guests alongside. From the restaurant, you can survey the valley of the Trent Brook as you enjoy dishes from the regularly changing menu. Stylish dishes such as a fillet of pork loin, crushed peas, black pudding croquette potatoes, confit carrots and rosemary jus have resulted in the award of 2 AA Rosettes.
6
8
9
7 Open all day, all week 11–11 Wadworth 10
11 25 from £13.50 portions/menu
notice required
18 12 13 14 15 16 17

12 Meal prices
followed by a price indicates the minimum price of a main course. Service charges are not included and may be added by some establishments depending on the size of the group. Most pubs with restaurant facilities will have some form of service charge.

13 Child friendliness
indicates that the pub welcomes children and if they offer a children's menu and/or children's portions.

14 Dog friendliness
shows that the pub has told us they are happy to be described as dog friendly. There may be restrictions on where dogs are allowed, e.g. restaurant, garden etc – do contact the pub if unsure.

15 Wi-fi is available

16 Parking
Indicates if the pub has on-site parking.

17 Garden
shows if there is a garden

18 Coach parties
Indicates if coach parties are accepted and whether notice is required.

***Note**, 7–18 are omitted from an entry where a pub has not responded to us.

Photographs
Many pubs have chosen to enhance their entry by purchasing photographs.

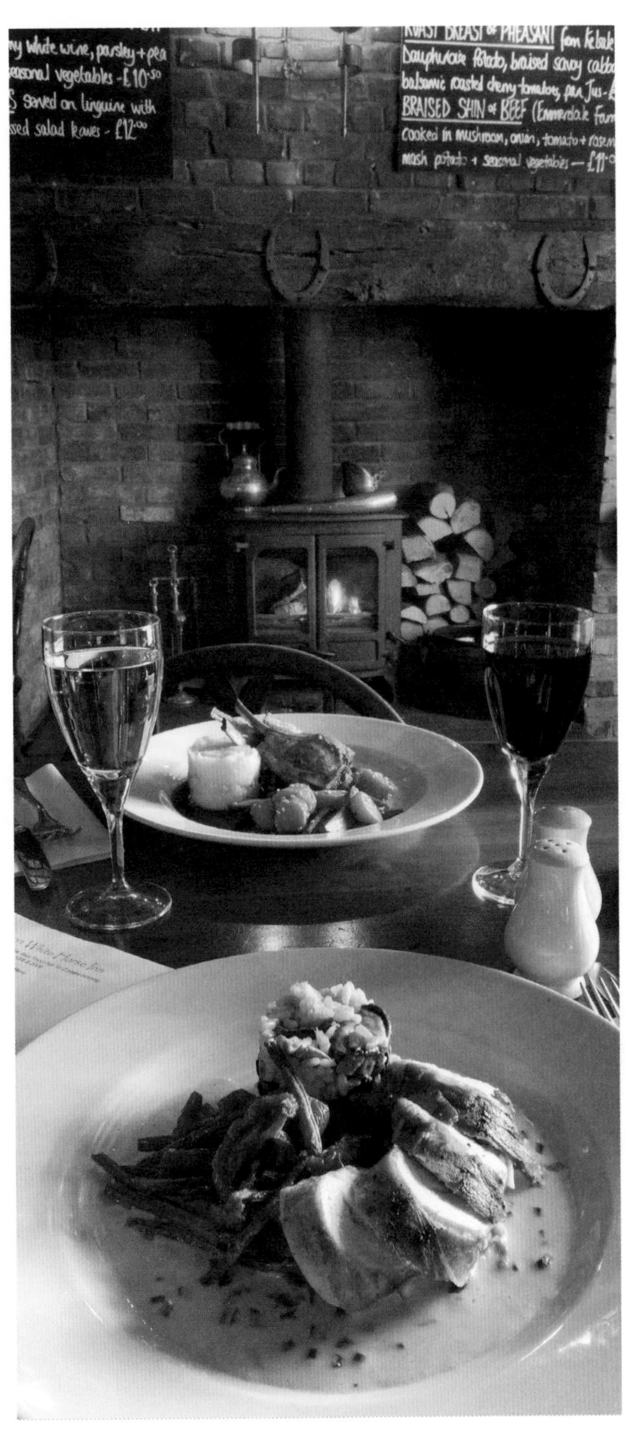

right A meal at the Sibton White Horse Inn, Suffolk (page 405).

Stay the night – AA accommodation ratings

Many of the pubs in this guide offer accommodation. Where a star rating appears next to an entry's name in the guide, the establishment has been inspected by the AA.

Accommodation inspections take place under common Quality Standards agreed between the AA, VisitEngland, VisitScotland and VisitWales. They ensure that the establishment meets the highest standards of cleanliness, with an emphasis on professionalism, proper booking procedures and prompt and efficient service. Some of the pubs in this guide offer accommodation but do not belong to an AA rating scheme; in this case reference to the accommodation is not included in their entry.

AA recognised establishments pay an annual fee that varies according to the classification and the number of bedrooms. The establishments receive an unannounced inspection from a qualified AA inspector who recommends the appropriate classification. Return visits confirm that standards are maintained; the classification is not transferable if an establishment changes owners.

below A room at the Meikleour Arms, Perth & Kinross (see page 535).

The annual *AA Hotel Guide* and *AA Bed & Breakfast Guide* give further details of the classification schemes. Details of the scheme behind AA recognised hotels, guest accommodation, restaurants and pubs are also available at theAA.com/hotel-services.

The accommodation shown in the *AA Pub Guide* falls under one of two AA accommodation ratings schemes.

AA guest accommodation scheme

The guest accommodation is classified on a scale of one to five black stars, with one star (★) being the most simple, and five being more luxurious. Gold stars (★) indicate the very best B&Bs, Guest Houses, Farmhouses, Inns, Restaurant with Rooms and Guest Accommodation in the 3, 4 and 5 star ratings. Establishments with silver stars (★) are highly recommended for their levels of hospitality, service and cleanliness within their star rating.

Guest accommodation ratings are followed by a category designator phrase, e.g. INN, that best describes it.

INN – Accommodation provided in a fully licensed establishment. The bar will be open to non-residents and food is provided in the evenings.

B&B – Bed and breakfast accommodation provided in a private house, run by the owner and with no more than six paying guests.

GUEST HOUSE – Accommodation provided for more than six paying guests and run on a more commercial basis than a B&B. Usually more services, for example dinner, provided by staff as well as the owner.

FARMHOUSE – B&B or guest house rooms on a working farm or smallholding.

RESTAURANT WITH ROOMS – Destination restaurant offering overnight accommodation. The restaurant is the main business and is open to non-residents. A high standard of food should be offered, at least five nights a week. A maximum of 12 bedrooms. Most Restaurants with Rooms have been awarded AA Rosettes for their food.

GUEST ACCOMMODATION – Any establishment which meets the entry requirements for the scheme can choose this designator.

AA hotel classification

Hotels are classified on a 5-point scale, with one star (★) being the simplest, and five stars offering a luxurious service at the top of the range. The AA's top hotels in Britain and Ireland are identified by red stars (★). Hotels with silver stars (★) are highly recommended for their standards of hotel keeping and quality of food within their star rating. In addition to the main Hotel HOTEL classification which applies to some pubs in this guide, there are other hotel categories which may be applicable to pubs, as follows:

TOWNHOUSE – A small, individual city or town centre property.

COUNTRY HOUSE HOTEL – Quietly located in a rural area.

SMALL HOTEL – Owner-managed with fewer than 20 bedrooms.

A – a small number of pubs have this symbol because they are Associate entries. They are rated by VisitEngland, VisitScotland and VisitWales and have joined the AA scheme on a marketing-only basis.

Inn of the Year

A brand new award for 2019, AA Inn of the Year celebrates the best guest accommodation which is also fully licensed. The Inn of the Year is awarded annually.

The Swan, Bampton, Devon

This classic English country inn is the oldest pub in Bampton and offers great cooking and friendly service. The inn also offers three spacious and comfortable rooms located on the top floor. The rooms have been renovated and decorated by local craftsmen and offer plenty of the quirky character you might expect from an old building. There's nothing contrived here and it's all built on hard graft and integrity. The rooms are full of extras and underpinned by care and pride. Owners Paul and Donna have poured their heart and soul into the pub and are proud to be recognised for their efforts.

See also page 121

below/right A glimpse of what's on the menu at the 2-Rosette The Swan, Bampton (see also page 121).

Pubs of the Year

The prestigious annual awards for the AA Pub of the Year for England, Scotland and Wales are selected with the help of our AA inspectors, and represent the very best of British pubs

Annual awards

The pubs of the year stand out for being great all-rounders, combining a convivial atmosphere, well-kept beers and ciders, excellent food, and of course, a warm welcome from the friendly and efficient hosts and their staff.

The awards are announced every September at the annual AA Hospitality Awards. We've yet to announce the 2019–20 winners at the time of going to press, but the current holders are:

AA Pub of the Year – England 2018–19:
The Crafty Baa, *see page 109*

AA Pub of the Year – Scotland 2018–19:
The Pot Still, *see page 526*

AA Pub of the Year – Wales 2018–19:
The Nags Head Inn, *see page 562*

That's the spirit

The growth of the spirit industry in the past few years has been phenomenal. **Stuart Walton** takes a look at how distilled drinks have made a spectacular comeback in forward-thinking pubs and bars

The diversification of the spirits market has been one of the most dynamic trends in the UK over the past twenty years. Indeed, so specialised has the whole sector become that the catchall category of 'spirits' is becoming increasingly meaningless. People want to drink niche products with a story, a sense of place, a unique selling point, a range of fascinating and often challenging flavours. And Britain's most interesting pubs and bars have matched this demand with revitalised lists of craft products, small-batch distillates, and premium bottlings of the familiar brands, so anyone innocently asking for a gin-and-tonic can expect to be asked which gin they would prefer. And which tonic.

This tendency is driven by a desire for variety, to find something different from the usual beer or house wine, but also the greater discernment that comes with drinking carefully. If it seems counter-intuitive to suggest that spirit sales should do well when conscientious consumers are counting their units, it's also the case that precisely because people are often drinking less, they want to drink better.

People want to drink niche products with a story, a sense of place, a unique selling point, a range of fascinating and often challenging flavours.

above A glass of Haymans at The Pheasant at Buckland's annual gin festival.

opposite Just a few of the 366 gins available at The Cholmondeley Arms in Cheshire.

Cocktails make a comeback in every generation, but their present ubiquity on bar lists, and on the drinks menus of aspirational restaurants, has been a major influence in the discovery of spirits. Modern recipes emphasise the inherent flavours of the base ingredients rather than drowning them with too many juices, syrups and fruit pulp, and they have rescued some of the more obscure spirit products from certain oblivion. Herbs and infusions add the same kind of fragrant character to a cocktail as foraged wild plants bring to contemporary cooking, while preserving the underlying personality of the spirit base.

If distilled drinks have once more come into their own, it is because they have finally

HAYMAN'S OLD TOM GIN
FLORAISON
Citadelle Reserve GIN
6
GIN
Chase
BOMBAY SAPPHIRE Distilled LONDON DRY GIN
HENDRICK'S GIN
BLOOM PREMIUM LONDON DRY GIN
ADNAMS
THE LONDON N°1
BOMBAY SAPPHIRE Distilled LONDON DRY GIN
THE BOTANIST ISLAY DRY GIN
N°209 GIN
SAFFRON GIN
HAYMAN'S 1820 GIN LIQUEUR
DEATH'S DOOR GIN
CHASE
Williams CHASE Elegant CRISP GIN
45% Vol 70cl e
BEEFEATER LONDON
Williams CHASE Elegant CRISP GIN
Gordon's THE ORIGINAL LONDON GIN
HOXTON GIN WARNING! GRAPEFRUIT AND COCONUT
Gordon's SLOE GIN
KRAHN
GIN MARE
1793 PLYMOUTH ENGLISH GIN
OPIHR
Bluecoat AMERICAN DRY GIN

been freed from their age-old confining association with a few market-leading brands, the familiar names seen on pub optics everywhere. To be sure, some of these brands have been in the vanguard of innovation, but they now have to take their place among the smaller producers with distinctive ideas. Adventurous drinkers have found the heady diversity of these products reflected across nearly all categories.

above A gin for every day of a leap year The Cholmondeley Arms.

below Gins on display at The Pheasant at Buckland's Surrey gin festival.

Gin

It's hard to imagine how unlikely the present gin scene would have seemed even a decade ago. All the on-trend youthful action in the white spirits sector was with vodka back then. Gin, with its peculiar apothecarial scent – brought home by British soldiers who'd fought in Holland during the Thirty Years' War, it essentially originated as a medicinal elixir – and cultural associations with gloom and ruin, forever seemed suitable only for those whose sun had long since gone over life's yardarm. Not now. The spirit's striking botanical aromas turn out to be its trump card, and there are craft gins, artisanal gins, rhubarb gins and Czech gins. Gin lists have transitioned from happy novelty to de rigueur, and the range of mixers from independent producers, with which they are teamed as judiciously as sommeliers match wines to food, has extended alongside them.

There is a gin for every day of a leap year at the Cholmondeley Arms in Cholmondeley, Cheshire (page 67) – from Adnams Copper

House to Manchester's Zymurgorium Mandarin. An annual gin festival is one of the high points of The Pheasant's calendar in Buckland, Surrey (page 409), while in the London Docklands, the premises of the Gun in Poplar (page 279) extend to a Gin Garden covered by a stretch marquee, where glasses are garnished with leaves from the pub's herb patch. At Michaelchurch Escley, the Bridge Inn (page 221) boasts its very own gin, crafted in the pub's micro-distillery.

There is a gin for every day of a leap year at the Cholmondeley Arms

above A glass of rhubarb and ginger gin at The Cholmondeley Arms.

below Hill Billy Red – one of The Bridge Inn's very own gins made at their tiny distillery in Herefordshire.

above Edinburgh's The Bow Bar was the AA Pub of the Year for Scotland in 2017.

Whisky

Before there were dozens of anything, there were dozens of single malts, primarily – though not exclusively – in their Scottish homeland. A serious appreciation of single malt begins with recognising the differences in regional styles, and is progressively refined by seeing the nuances in aromas, palate weight and wood influence between individual producers. More than any other niche spirit, single malt deserves to be savoured as it is, unmixed, un-iced, perhaps with just a dash of spring water to lift it.

Among the many Scottish pubs with fine selections of malts, we particularly commend those at the West Loch Hotel, Tarbert (page 520); the Clachaig Inn, Ballachulish, Glencoe (page 529); the George Hotel, Inveraray (page 519); the Inn on Loch Lomond, Luss (page 519); and, in the big cities, the Bow Bar (page 523) and Whiski Bar in Edinburgh (page 524), and the Pot Still in Glasgow. They may be a long way from home, but the extensive single malt listing at the NoBody Inn at Doddiscombsleigh, Devon (page 129), will set drinkers' compass needles wavering north.

Not all the running in the whisky stakes is being made by Scotland's finest. Triple-distilled Irish whiskey has its devotees. American whiskeys from Kentucky, Tennessee and further afield have carved a niche for their own sweetly smoky, wood-driven styles, and the growing presence of Japanese whiskies, a logical next step for aficionados of sake, is a development worth watching.

Vodka

Once popular among immature palates because it was considered (not quite accurately) to taste of nothing, vodka's first advance into the premium market was via speciality higher-strength bottlings. That was followed by a plethora of flavoured products, some based on the old traditional eastern European infusions, others more obviously designed to appeal to the cocktail crowd. In the latest development, the buzz is with vodkas that make a virtue of their places of origin, ultra-rectified products that have undergone multiple distillations, often by means of recherché processes such as filtration through diamond crystals or purifications with a breakfast melange of bread, milk and egg-white. The Rosendale in West Dulwich (page 285) has a handsome array of niche vodkas among its other distinguished spirit ranges. For the true taste of localism, vodka distilled in-house can be sampled at Number Twenty 2 in Darlington (page 160), or at the King's Arms at Wing, Rutland (page 354), where the own-made elderflower vodka makes a beguiling summer sip.

Rum

Rum has awaited its turn in the limelight longer than most spirits. If Bacardi white was once the world's biggest-selling colourless spirit, it did little to spur any investigation of anything more interesting, either among white or dark and golden rums. Very gradually, driven perhaps by Caribbean and South American tourism, that picture is changing. Premium bottlings of naval-strength spirit, rums blended with glutinous blackstrap molasses, and small-batch artisanal products from the Caribbean islands are breaking out here and there, but the biggest growth is in the category of spiced rum, a relatively recent development that makes all kinds of sense. Flavours of ginger, cardamom, allspice and even chilli inveigle themselves very attractively into the rolls of flavour delivered by cask-aged rum.

The Rosendale in West Dulwich treats rum with the same reverence it accords to premium vodkas, and Darlington's Number Twenty 2 also conjures a spiced rum from its own nano-distillery, while at the Boat Inn at Aboyne (page 516), there are locally distilled rums to keep out the northerly chill.

Tequila

From the Sunrises of the 1980s and the Slammers of the '90s, via a little nervous lime-squeezing and salt-licking, tequila finally wended its way towards a shaken dignity with the Margarita, a cocktail that bundled up the salt-and-lime performance into one capacious glass, along with a little Triple Sec to sweeten the edges. Like Martinis and Daiquiris, Margaritas now come in a wealth of modified forms, from salted caramel to blood orange, but the base spirit they all feature is a little hidden from view. Reposado tequilas, tinted and complexed from cask-ageing, are the way to a connoisseur's approach to tequila, with Añejo, the longest-aged spirits that have all the aromatic complexity of malt whisky, waiting at the summit.

Brandy

Finally, spare a thought for fine grape brandy, the forgotten elderly relative of the spirit family. At one time, no grand gastronomic occasion was complete without a final tot of cognac, and yet nobody for the time being can quite see the appeal. Served in the wrong glasses – those inelegant balloons that only emphasise the vicious prickle of 40 per cent alcohol over the drink's subtler aromatic characters – and often diluted with unrequested ice, it isn't hard to see why it has comparatively few followers. Bars with dozens of gins and malts quite often only have one or two standard brands of cognac, and nothing from the Armagnac region, or from further afield in Spain, Italy, Greece or South Africa. If ever there were a trend waiting to be ignited, here it is. ■

ENGLAND

BEDFORDSHIRE

BEDFORD

The Embankment

Tel **01234 261332** | **6 The Embankment, MK40 3PD**
Web **www.embankmentbedford.co.uk**
Dir ***From M1 junction 13, A421 to Bedford. Left onto A6 to town centre. Into left lane on river bridge. Into right lane signed Embankment. Follow around St Paul's Square into High Street, into left lane. Left onto The Embankment.***

This imposing pub sits behind an outdoor terrace overlooking the River Great Ouse on the edge of Bedford's beautifully landscaped Embankment gardens. Dating from 1891, the building has been renovated and its Victorian features brought back to life. Among its delights are the open fire, antique mirrors, vintage tablesand silk lampshades. Food choices range from deli boards to full meals such as Devon crab cakes, followed by venison haunch, juniper potato cake, glazed carrots and blackberry jus.

Open all day, all week Closed 25 Dec Charles Wells/ Peach Pubs 16 portions notice required

The Knife and Cleaver

Tel **01234 930789** | **The Grove, Houghton Conquest, MK45 3LA**
Web **www.theknifeandcleaver.com**
Dir ***A6 from Bedford towards Luton. In 5 miles right to Houghton Conquest. Or B530 from Bedford towards Ampthill left to Houghton Conquest.***

The Shuttleworth aeroplane collection and Bletchley Park are easily reached from this friendly pub. The bar and All Saints Restaurant welcome customers throughout the day, every day, whether for a pint of Wells Eagle IPA or something more substantial. Starters include sharing boards, or single starters of potted shrimps and cucumber on toast; among the mains are smoked haddock risotto; nut roast Wellington; and beef bourguignon. Apple and pecan pie for afters.

Open all day, all week Charles Wells 20 from £12 portions/menu notice required

The Park Pub & Kitchen

Tel **01234 273929** | **98 Kimbolton Road, MK40 2PA**
Web **www.theparkbedford.co.uk**
Dir ***M1 junction 14, A509 follow Newport Pagnell signs, then A422, A428 onto A6. Right into Tavistock Street (A600). Left into Broadway, 1st left into Kimbolton Road. Pub 0.5 mile.***

Built in the 1900s, this fine-looking pub is a stone's throw from Bedford Park. The smartly decorated exterior promises a similarly well cared for interior, and you won't be disappointed – fireplaces, flagstone floors and beamed ceilings combine to create a traditional welcoming atmosphere.

The Three Tuns

Tel **01234 354847** | **57 Main Road, Biddenham, MK40 4BD**
Web **www.thethreetunsbiddenham.co.uk**
Dir ***On A428 from Bedford towards Northampton 1st left signed Biddenham. Into village, pub on left.***

In a pretty village, a short distance from Bedford, this stone-built, thatched pub has a large garden with a patio and decking, and a separate children's play area. With a relaxed and friendly atmosphere, menus include breakfast fare.

BOLNHURST

The Plough at Bolnhurst

PICK OF THE PUBS

Tel **01234 376274** | **Kimbolton Road, MK44 2EX**
Web **www.bolnhurst.com**
Dir ***On B660, north of Bedford.***

This whitewashed 15th-century country inn, six miles north of Bedford has fresh, country-style decor coupled with thick walls, low beams and great open fires. The impressive choice of real ales and inspired wine list are matched by a menu prepared by Raymond Blanc-trained Martin Lee and his team of skilled chefs. The menu is driven by the freshest local and regional produce and the result is an ever-changing choice of unique dishes, which have gained The Plough an AA Rosette. Maybe try the roast John Dory fillet with aubergine purée, courgette, crispy garlic and anchovy potato; and look out for the cheeseboard, which offers a fantastic choice of British and Irish varieties.

Open Tue to Sat 12–3 6.30–11 (Sun 12–3) Closed 2 weeks Jan, Mon and Sun evening Free House 17 portions notice required

FLITTON

The White Hart

Tel **01525 862022** | **Brook Lane, MK45 5EJ**
Web **www.thewhitehartflitton.co.uk**
Dir ***In village centre, adjacent to church.***

Opposite the 13th-century church of St John The Baptist, this village pub was issued its first beer licence in 1822. Today's beers come from the B&T brewery in nearby Shefford, with meats from the local family butcher. Fresh fish and shellfish are the big thing here. A typical menu might include smoked salmon and prawn timbale, and roast rump of lamb with sauté potatoes.

Open 12–3 6–12 Closed 2–9 Jan, Sun evening and Mon Free House 18 portions notice required

HARROLD

The Muntjac

Tel **01234 721500** | **71 High Street, MK43 7BJ**
Web **www.muntjacharrold.co.uk**
This 17th-century, former coaching inn in a pretty village has a lot on offer. For starters, a bar with six hand-pulls with regularly changing real ales, craft lagers and 60 gins – probably the largest such collection in Bedfordshire.

KEYSOE

The Chequers

Tel **01234 708678** | **Pertenhall Rd, Brook End, MK44 2HR**
Dir ***On B660, 7 miles north of Bedford. 3 miles south of Kimbolton.***

This peaceful 15th-century country pub has been in the same safe hands for over a quarter of a century. No games machines, pool tables or jukeboxes disturb the simple pleasures of well-kept ales and great home-made food. The menu offers pub stalwarts like ploughman's; plain or toasted sandwiches; home-made steak and ale pie; chicken curry and rice; chilli con carne and a variety of grilled steaks; and a blackboard displays further choices.

Open all year 11.30–2.30 6.30–11 Closed Sun evening, Mon and Tue, Wed lunch Free House portions/menu notice required

IRELAND

The Black Horse

Tel **01462 811398** | **Ireland, SG17 5QL**
Web **www.blackhorseireland.com**
Dir ***From south M1 junction 12, A5120 to Flitwick. Onto A507 by Redbourne School. Follow signs for A1, Shefford (cross A6). Left onto A600 towards Bedford. Right at next roundabout, immediately left towards Ireland. Pub on left.***

'Pretty as a picture' pub in the hamlet of Ireland

Colourful flower baskets and window boxes decorate the outside of this family-run, 17th-century inn. The interior has been thoughtfully updated using natural materials, including a slate top bar, yet with the original low-beamed ceilings, slate floors, inglenook fireplaces and original artworks it still retains its character. With a pint or glass of wine, settle down in comfort to appreciate the seasonally inspired traditional British food, sometimes revealing European hints – bubble-and-squeak risotto with crispy egg, for example. Among the plentiful main dishes are Woburn Estate venison steak with celeriac purée, pickled chantenay carrots, crispy shallots and blackberry jus; pavé of sea-reared trout on butter bean and chorizo cassoulet; and vegetable suet pudding.

Open Mon to Sat 12–3 6–12 (Sun 12–6) Closed 25–26 Dec, 1 Jan Free House 16 from £10.50 portions/menu notice required

LEIGHTON BUZZARD

The Heath Inn ★★★ INN

Tel **01525 237816** | **76 Woburn Road, Heath and Reach, LU7 0AR**
Web **www.theheathinn.com**
Dir ***Phone for detailed directions.***

On the outskirts of Leighton Buzzard, this inn's cosy, wood-beamed bar has an open fire, and in summer there's a pretty courtyard garden with a children's play area to enjoy. Cask ales are well represented from the likes of Tring, Hopping Mad and Vale, ably supported by Westons cider, and draft lagers. Food served in the bar or restaurant follows traditional lines with ploughman's, jackets, sandwiches, paninis, grills and pub favourites like bangers and mash; gammon steak, chips and egg; or mushroom risotto.

Open all day, all week *Free House* *from £12* *portions/menu* Wi-fi *notice required*

NORTHILL

The Crown

Tel **01767 627337** | **2 Ickwell Road, SG18 9AA**
Web **www.crownnorthill.co.uk**
Dir ***In village centre, adjacent to church.***

A delightful 16th-century pub with smart, modern interior decor. Guest ales are very well kept and make delightful companions to almost anything on the menu. Dig into sharing deli boards or sandwiches, baguettes and paninis with fillings such as prawn and avocado, or topside of beef. Or how about mains such as seared sea trout fillet, Lyonnaise potatoes, wilted spinach and sorrel cream? The garden has plenty of tables for alfresco eating, and a children's play area.

Open all day, all week *Greene King* *9* *portions/menu* Wi-fi

OAKLEY

Bedford Arms

Tel **01234 822280** | **57 High Street, MK43 7RH**
Web **www.bedfordarmsoakley.co.uk**
Dir ***From A6 north of Bedford follow Oakley signs.***

Bounded on three sides by the River Ouse in the heart of a pretty village, this 16th-century inn is surrounded by beautiful countryside. Enjoy a pint in the cosy, traditional beamed bar or head to the large garden and decked alfresco dining area.

RAVENSDEN

The Horse & Jockey

Tel **01234 772319** | **Church End, MK44 2RR**
Web **www.horseandjockey.info**
Dir ***North of Bedford. Phone for detailed directions.***

Staff ensure a happy welcome at this quiet country pub, which sits atop a hill next to the village church. Visitors feel equally at home, enjoying a pint in the bar, or relaxing in the peaceful garden where birdsong is all that can be heard.

SALFORD

The Swan PICK OF THE PUBS

Tel **01908 281008** | **2 Warendon Road, MK17 8BD**
Web **www.swansalford.co.uk**
Dir ***M1 junction 13, follow signs to Salford.***

Located in a pretty village, the tile-hung, Edwardian-era Swan, run by an enthusiastic team, has a lively bar with comfy leather armchairs that make you feel instantly at home, as does the eating area, where the big French doors can be thrown open to the garden. Sandwiches, snacks and deli boards are available throughout the day. The pub has its own smokehouse so the likes of home-smoked pork loin and mackerel appear on the deli boards. Main courses include pumpkin and Swiss chard pancake with gruyère sauce; or slow-cooked venison bourguignon with parsnip and thyme purée. Puddings are very tempting – who could resist iced apple parfait and warm cinnamon fritter?

Open all day, all week 10am–11pm (Sun 10am–10.30pm) Closed 25 Dec *Free House* *14* *portions* Wi-fi

SOULDROP

The Bedford Arms

Tel **01234 781384** | **High Street, MK44 1EY**
Dir ***From Rushden take A6 towards Bedford. In 6 miles right into Stocking Lane. Pub 50 metres on right.***

A quiet village setting, deep in the Bedfordshire countryside adds to the appeal of this cosy 300-year-old pub. There's a beer garden, and a traditional, cottagey interior.

Open all year 12–3 5–11 (Fri to Sat 12–12 Sun 12–10) Closed Mon (excluding bank holidays) *Free House* *13* *from £9.50* *portions/menu* Wi-fi

STANBRIDGE

The Five Bells

Tel **01525 210224** | **Station Road, LU7 9JF**
Web **www.fivebellsstanbridge.co.uk**
Dir ***A505 from Leighton Buzzard towards Dunstable, turn left to Stanbridge.***

This whitewashed 400-year-old village inn has a bar that features lots of bare wood as well as comfortable armchairs and rustic wood and tiled floors. The modern decor extends to the bright, airy 75-cover dining room with its oak beams and paintings.

STUDHAM

The Bell in Studham

Tel **01582 872460** | **Dunstable Road, LU6 2QG**
Web **www.thebellinstudham.co.uk**
Dir ***M1 junction 9, A5 towards Dunstable. Left onto B4540 to Kensworth, B4541 to Studham.***

This 500-year-old, Grade II listed pub is surrounded by some of Bedfordshire's prettiest countryside, close to Whipsnade Zoo and Hemel Hempstead. The welcoming interior is full of beams and stacked logs ready for a winter fire. In summer, grab a table in the large garden and enjoy the panoramic views. From the menu expect sharing boards, home-made pies, roasts with all the trimmings, beer battered cod and triple cooked chips and even '99' ice creams. Authentic pizzas are cooked on the stone clay oven.

Open all day, all week Free House 10 from £9.25 portions notice required

See advertisement on page 28

SUTTON

The John O'Gaunt

Tel **01767 260377** | **30 High Street, SG19 2TP**
Web **www.johnogauntsutton.co.uk**
Dir ***From A1 at Biggleswade at roundabout take A6001, straight on at 2 roundaboutss, right onto B1040. Pub in village centre.***

First licensed in 1835, this 18th-century free house takes its name from the 1st Duke of Lancaster, son of King Edward III and local lord of the manor. Set back from the road, it's close to an ancient, double-arched packhorse bridge and ford across Potton Brook.

TILSWORTH

The Anchor

Tel **01525 211404** | **1 Dunstable Road, LU7 9PU**
Web **www.anchortilsworth.co.uk**
Dir ***Exit A5 at Tilsworth. In 1 mile pub on right at 3rd bend.***

Xenia, the Greek concept of hospitality, awaits you at this late 19th-century pub overlooking the village green. Among some amazing wallpapers and carpets, xenia here means home-made Greek cooking, Greek wines and, of course, ouzo. Menu translations reveal that lamb kleftiko is slow-cooked 'stolen' leg, and pastitsio is baked pasta, minced beef with béchamel sauce. But eating à la Grècque is optional, as chicken curry, fish and chips and much more testify. A large garden includes patio seating and a playground.

Open all day, all week 12–11 Greene King from £7.90 portions/menu

WOBURN

The Birch at Woburn – see page 29

The Black Horse

Tel **01525 290210** | **1 Bedford Street, MK17 9QB**
Web **www.blackhorsewoburn.co.uk**
Dir ***In town centre on A4012.***

An integral part of Woburn's attractive main street, this 18th-century former coaching inn – once one of 27 – reveals an elegant dining room, and a cosy bar lined with leather-upholstered settles. Seasonal menus offer Dorset chorizo with peppers, kale and free-range fried egg; sea bass and Bombay potatoes with Indian salad; slow-cooked blade of beef bourguignon with parsnip purée; and daily specials. It's Wednesday nights for grills, Thursdays for fish. The old coach yard is now a courtyard garden.

Open all day, all week 11–11 (Sat 11am–11.30pm) Closed 25 Dec Greene King/Peach Pubs portions notice required

WOBURN

The Birch at Woburn

Tel **01525 290295** | **20 Newport Road, MK17 9HX**
Web **www.birchwoburn.com**
Dir ***M1 junction 13, follow A4012 (Woburn) signs at roundabouts. From A4012 turn right at T-junction signed Woburn Sands (A5130). Pub on right.***

A reputation built on friendly service and good food

Close to Woburn Abbey and the Safari Park, this is a smart, family-run bar and restaurant. The contemporary bar has red walls, slate bar-top and strategic lighting, designed to help you relax and unwind. The equally contemporary restaurant is welcoming, with a menu offering baguettes, salads and dishes such as pan-fried Woburn Estate venison steak, with roast beetroot and shallots; roasted free-range chicken supreme, sautéed mushrooms and shallot purée; and vegetarian platter. On the evening menu are chargrilled swordfish steak with lobster and brandy bisque; confit English pork belly with caramelised apple purée; and Thai spiced red pepper and butternut squash risotto. Traditional roasts on Sundays, of course, and live music some Friday evenings.

Open 12–3 6–12 (Sun 12–6) Closed 25–26 Dec, 1 Jan, Sun evening and Mon Free House 14 from £12.95 portions/menu notice required

BERKSHIRE

ALDWORTH

The Bell Inn

Tel **01635 578272** | **RG8 9SE**
Dir ***Just off B4009 (Newbury to Streatley road).***

Beginning life as a manor hall in 1340, The Bell has reputedly been in the same family for 200 years. A 300-year-old, one-handed clock stands in the taproom 'keeping imperfect time', and the rack for the spit-irons and clockwork roasting jack can still be seen over the fireplace.

ASCOT

The Thatched Tavern

Tel **01344 620874** | **Cheapside Road, SL5 7QG**
Web **www.thethatchedtavern.co.uk**
Dir ***Follow Ascot Racecourse signs. Through Ascot 1st left (Cheapside). 1.5 miles, pub on left.***

En route to Windsor Castle, Queen Victoria's carriage was allegedly sometimes spotted outside this 400-year-old, flagstone-floored, low-ceilinged pub, while what the history books call 'her faithful servant' John Brown knocked a few back inside. The sheltered garden makes a fine spot to enjoy a Fuller's real ale, a glass of wine and, for lunch, perhaps Cumberland sausage sandwich or salt and pepper squid oriental salad. For something more substantial try Cornish crab linguine, then butternut squash, pine nut and ricotta Wellington with a heritage tomato salad.

Open all day, all week Mon to Sat 11–11 Sun 11am–10.30pm Free House 11 from £13.95 portions/menu Wi-fi

BOXFORD

The Bell at Boxford

Tel **01488 608721** | **Lambourn Road, RG20 8DD**
Web **www.bellatboxford.com**
Dir ***M4 junction 14, A338 towards Wantage. Right onto B4000 to crossroads, signed Boxford. Or from A34 junction 13 towards Hungerford, right at roundabout onto B4000. At crossroads right to Boxford. Pub signed.***

At the heart of the lovely Lambourn Valley, this country pub boasts a period main bar in the 17th-century part of the building, and the very occasional visit from Mr Merritt, the resident ghost. Alfresco dining on flower-laden heated terraces might feature hog roasts and barbecues. There's a good range of local ales, and Stowford Press cider on draught; all 60 wines are available by the glass. Feast on seafood specials (lobster is available in season); and mixed seafood salad.

Open all day, all week Free House 60 from £8.95 portions/menu notice required

BRAY

The Crown at Bray – see opposite

The Hind's Head – see page 32

COLNBROOK

The Ostrich

Tel **01753 682628** | **High Street, SL3 0JZ**
Web **www.theostrichcolnbrook.co.uk**
Dir ***M25 junction 14 towards Poyle. Right at 1st roundabout, over next 2 roundabouts. Left at sharp right bend into High Street. Left at mini-roundabout, pub on left.***

One of England's oldest pubs can be found surprisingly close to Heathrow and minutes from the M25. Dating from 1106, the vast and rambling Ostrich oozes history, with a heavily timbered façade, cobbled courtyard, wonky oak beams, massive fireplaces and crooked stairs. Yet the interior has acquired a contemporary style, so expect glass doors, a steel bar, chunky furnishings and vibrant colours. The menu of pub food embraces crispy thyme charred polenta; rustic fish pie; and beef Wellington.

Open all day, all week 7am–11pm (Sat 7.30am–11pm Sun 7.30am–10.30pm) Shepherd Neame 11 portions/menu notice required

COOKHAM

The White Oak PICK OF THE PUBS

Tel **01628 523043** | **The Pound, SL6 9QE**
Web **www.thewhiteoak.co.uk**
Dir ***From A4 east of Maidenhead take A4094 signed Cookham. Left into High Street (B4447) signed Cookham Rise/Cookham Dean. Pass through common. Left at mini-roundabout, pub on right.***

Like its sister pub, The Three Oaks at Gerrards Cross, this contemporary village inn and restaurant has been run with huge success by former London restaurateurs Henry and Katherine Cripps for the past decade. Diners at The White Oak can tuck into award-winning, daily-changing, modern British dishes, so perhaps start with dressed Devonshire crab, sourdough toast and mustard cress; or game and apple terrine, blackberry and apple chutney; then pan-roast halibut, poached lobster, lobster bisque and braised celery or roast partridge, rainbow chard and chilli polenta. To finish, perhaps try the creamed rice; caramelised pear and ginger crumble; or marmalade and vanilla cheesecake with vanilla ice cream.

Open all day, all week Greene King 24 portions/menu

COOKHAM DEAN

Uncle Tom's Cabin

Tel **01628 483339** | **Hills Lane, SL6 9NT**
Web **www.uncletomscookham.co.uk**
Dir ***Phone for detailed directions.***

The artist Stanley Spencer called Cookham, his birthplace and where he lived most of his life, 'a village in Heaven'. His museum is less than two miles away from this charming, low-beamed 17th-century pub, warmed, when nature demands, by open fires.

BRAY

The Crown at Bray ◎◎

Tel 01628 621936 | High Street, SL6 2AH
Web www.thecrownatbray.com/
Dir *M4 junction 8, A308(M) signed Maidenhead (Central). At next roundabout, right onto A308 signed Bray and Windsor. 0.5 mile, left onto B3028 signed Bray. In village, pub on left.*

Cosy, Thames-side village inn

PICK OF THE PUBS

Half-timbered outside, this Tudor building is a well-preserved reminder of days long gone, with heavy beams, open fires and all the trimmings. It's been an inn for several centuries; the name possibly derives from regular visits made by King Charles II when visiting Nell Gwynn nearby. Assignations today are firmly rooted in the desire to enjoy the dishes that have gained this Heston Blumenthal-owned pub two AA Rosettes for the distinctly traditional English menu. Diners (restaurant bookings essential, but not for bar meals) may commence with a starter such as Cornish mussels with garlic, apple, cider and parsley; setting the standard for mains like chargrilled Hereford sirloin steak with marrowbone sauce; or roast stone bass fillet with spinach, tomato, shallot and rocket; finishing with apple and plum crumble with vanilla ice cream. The enclosed courtyard is sheltered and there is a newly-designed garden and outdoor kitchen open from April each year.

Open all day, all week *Fat Duck Group* 19
portions/menu *notice required*

BRAY

The Hind's Head

Tel 01628 626151 | **High Street, SL6 2AB**
Web **www.hindsheadbray.com**
Dir ***M4 junction 8/9 take Maidenhead Central exit. Next roundabout take Bray/Windsor exit. 0.5 mile, B3028 to Bray.***

Old-English fare with a modern twist

PICK OF THE PUBS

This Heston Blumenthal establishment in Bray has become, not surprisingly, a gastronomic destination, yet the striking 15th-century building remains very much a village local. Its origins as a pub are a little obscure, but the bar's atmosphere created by beams and sturdy oak panelling, log fires, leather chairs, and Windsor & Eton seasonal ales is reassuringly traditional. The main restaurant is on the ground floor, while upstairs are two further dining areas: the Vicar's Room and the larger Royal Room. Having worked alongside the team in the Tudor kitchens at Hampton Court Palace, Heston elaborates on original British cuisine, reintroducing classic recipes from the pub's Tudor roots. Hash of snails; and terrine of pork and Cumbrian ham are indicative starters. Gutsy main courses vary from bone-in sirloin of veal or oxtail and kidney pudding to smoked pollock, cured salmon and prawns fish pie with 'sea and sand'. For seekers of plainer fare there are 28-day aged Hereford prime steaks. Quaking pudding, inspired by a 17th-century sweet jelly recipe, is an ever popular dessert favourite.

Open all week 11.30–11 (Sun 12–7 Mon 12–11) Closed 25 Dec Free House 15 menus notice required

The Fat Duck

High Street, Bray, Berkshire, SL6 2AQ

A three-star Michelin and 5-AA Rosette restaurant, the Fat Duck is legendary for its food, which is not only superbly well executed, but also imaginative and inspiring. This is food that appeals to all the senses and summons up memories, nostalgia and emotion. Visit the Fat Duck for a culinary journey like no other.

CURRIDGE

The Bunk Inn ★★★★ INN

Tel **01635 200400** | **RG18 9DS**
Web **www.thebunkinn.co.uk**
Dir ***M4 junction 13, A34 north towards Oxford. Take 1st slip road. At T-junction right signed Hermitage. In approximately 1 mile right at mini rounabout into Long Lane, 1st right signed Curridge.***

One of the oldest buildings in the village, this inn is cosy and welcoming. The snug remains a comfy focus for chatter or contemplation, and there's also an airy restaurant with eye-catching decor, and a heated patio. The chefs work with local suppliers to create dishes like glazed pork faggot with black pudding, baked potato purée, Savoy cabbage and honeyed parsnip.

Open all day, all week Upham Group 10 portions/menu notice required

EASTBURY

The Eastbury Plough

Tel **01488 71312** | **RG17 7JN**
Web **www.eastburyplough.com**
Dir ***M4 junction 14, A338 towards Wantage. In Great Shefford left into Church Street. 3 miles, pub on right.***

Eastbury is a pretty downland village, in the 'vale of the racehorse' and the Plough is a real local gem. You can eat and drink alfresco when the weather is good, or in the comfortable restaurant. If you'd just like a pint and sandwich there are excellent choices for both.

EAST GARSTON

Queens Arms

★★★★ INN PICK OF THE PUBS

Tel **01488 648757** | **RG17 7ET**
Web **www.queensarmseastgarston.co.uk**
Dir ***M4 junction 14, A338 towards Wantage. Turn left in Great Shefford for East Garston.***

The oldest part of this Lambourn Valley inn was a farmer's cottage in the 18th century; it was first licensed as an inn around 1856. In an area with 2,000 racehorses and more than 50 racing yards, this charming pub acts as a quasi-headquarters for British racing with owners, trainers and jockeys among its clientele. With a glass of Doom Bar or Aspall cider in hand, choose from the menu: ham hock and home-made chutney sandwich; a burger from the bar menu or pub favourites – fish pie or beer battered cod and chips. Alternatively try chicken parfait with toasted brioche, followed by roasted salmon fillet with new potatoes, mango salsa and salad.

Open all day, all week 11am to midnight (Sun 11–10) Free House 10 from £12 portions/menu notice required

FINCHAMPSTEAD

The Greyhound

Tel **0118 973 2269** | **Longwater Road, RG40 3TS**
Web **www.greyhoundfinchampstead.co.uk**
Dir ***On B3016.***

From the outside, a largely unchanged Victorian, red-brick building with attractive, bargeboard gables; the interior is an object lesson in how modern design can work successfully in a 19th-century shell. Although owned by Greene King, guest real ales from breweries such as Siren Craft in the village and Windsor & Eton are offered. Food-wise, honourable mentions go to oxtail and beef shin pie; duo of lamb; and seabass, squid, mussels and chorizo ragù. At lunch, there are simpler choices.

Open all day, all week Greene King 16 from £12.50 portions/menu

FRILSHAM

The Pot Kiln PICK OF THE PUBS

Tel **01635 201366** | **RG18 0XX**
Web **www.potkiln.org**
Dir ***From Yattendon follow Pot Kiln signs, cross over motorway. 0.25 mile, pub on right.***

Hidden down narrow lanes, this 18th-century pub (a former kiln-workers' beer house) can be a bit elusive, but when you find it, you'll find it was worth the effort. At the time of writing, it is closed for renovations, but it is due to re-open in July 2019.

HAMPSTEAD NORREYS

The White Hart

Tel **01635 202248 | Church Street, RG18 0TB**
Web **www.goodfoodatthewhitehart.co.uk**
Dir ***M4 junction 13, A34 signed Oxford. Left signed Hermitage. Through Hermitage. At T-junction left signed Hampstead Norreys. At mini-roundabout in village turn right. Pub on left.***

A charming building dating back to the 16th-century. Absolutely everything on the menu, from stocks and sauces to the desserts, is made from scratch. Meats come from an award-winning butcher and game-supplier down the road. Arrive on the last weekend in June for the beer festival.

HERMITAGE

The White Horse of Hermitage

Tel **01635 741141 | Newbury Road, RG18 9TB**
Web **www.whitehorsehermitage.com**
Dir ***5 miles from Newbury on B4009. From M4 junction 13 follow signs for Newbury Showground, right into Priors Court Road, left at mini-roundabout, pub approximately 50 yards on right.***

This family-friendly pub dates back at least 160 years, and has a solid reputation for its pub food, using the freshest and finest local produce to create a daily menu that typically includes burgers, steaks and other specials, all washed down with pints of Abbot Ale or Orchard Pig cider. The interior bar and restaurant are contemporary in decor, and outside you can choose between the Mediterranean-style patio or the large garden, which is equipped with swings and climbing frames for younger visitors.

Open all year, all day 11.30–11.30 (Sun 12–8) Closed Mon Greene King 9 from £10 portions/menu notice required

HOLYPORT

The Belgian Arms

Tel **01628 634468 | SL6 2JR**
Web **www.thebelgianarms.com**
Dir ***M4 junction 8, A308(M). At roundabout take A330 signed Ascot. At Holyport village green left signed Bray and Windsor. 1st left into Holyport Street. Belgian Arms on right.***

First World War German prisoners being marched past The Eagle, as it then was, would salute their national bird, so villagers who'd fought in Belgium decided to rename it. After a pint of Brakspear the seasonal menu might tempt you with Windsor Park game pie; Brixham cod with black garlic paste; or roast butternut squash Kerala curry. The beer garden stretches from the secluded patio to the village duck pond. First Friday of the month for live music.

Open all day, all week Mon to Thu 11–11 Fri to Sat 11am–midnight Sun 11–10 Brakspear 12 portions/menu

HUNGERFORD

The Pheasant Inn  INN

Tel **01488 648284 | Ermin Street, Shefford Woodlands, RG17 7AA**
Web **www.thepheasant-inn.co.uk**
Dir ***M4 junction 14, A338 towards Wantage. Left onto B4000 towards Lambourn.***

Welsh drovers following Roman Ermin Street would stop at what was originally the Board House. Today, the bar serves Ramsbury Gold ale and Symonds Founders Reserve cider. Food style is evidenced by starters of king prawn raviolo with pea shoots, tarragon and celeriac; and mains of pan-fried duck breast with pressed potatoes, creamed leeks, cranberries and roasted figs. For dessert, perhaps caramel pannacotta, pineapple and amaretti biscuits.

Open all day, all week Closed 25 Dec Free House 12 portions/menu

HURLEY

Dew Drop Inn

Tel **01628 315662 | Honey Lane, SL6 6RB**
Web **www.dewdrophurley.co.uk**
Dir ***M4 junction 8, A404(M). A4130 signed Hurley. At T-junction left (A4130 signed Hurley). At roundabout 1st left signed Burchetts Green. Right into Honey Lane. Pub at end (single track road) on right.***

Hidden away down a bridle path, there's hardly another building within sight of this dog-friendly Brakspear pub. Highwayman Dick Turpin allegedly hid his mount in the cellar. The legend explains why the menu lists a Turpin minced beef and pork burger. The pub cures its own bacon, makes its own sausages and sells eggs from its own hens.

Open all year Closed Mon Brakspear 9 portions/menu

The Olde Bell Inn PICK OF THE PUBS

Tel **01628 825881 | High Street, SL6 5LX**
Web **www.theoldebell.co.uk**
Dir ***M4 junction 8/9 follow Henley signs. At roundabout take A4130 towards Hurley. Right to Hurley, inn 800 yards on right.***

In the 12th century the inn was a guest house for pilgrims visiting Hurley's Benedictine priory, its nave surviving to become today's parish church. Although not medieval throughout, it has a good claim to be the country's longest-operating inn, and is full of nooks, crannies and crooked doors. Meals are served in both the bar and chic dining room, where the banquettes at some tables are softened by Welsh woollen blankets. Bar menu favourites are Cumberland sausages, mash and red onion marmalade; and beef and beer puff pastry pie, while likely to appear on the main menu are pork tenderloin with creamy Stilton and parmesan polenta; or pan-fried fillet of sea bass with sweet chilli escabeche. Guests are free to roam the charming estate.

Open all day, all week 11am to midnight (Sun 11–11) Free House 10 from £15 portions/menu

KNOWL HILL

Bird In Hand Country Inn

PICK OF THE PUBS

Tel **01628 826622 | Bath Road, RG10 9UP**
Web **www.birdinhand.co.uk**
Dir ***On A4, 5 miles west of Maidenhead, 7 miles east of Reading.***

Acquired and refurbished by Wadworth, the lovely old brick and beamed Bird in Hand dates back to the 14th century, and has its share of history; apparently George III was one past visitor. There's a sunny terrace for outdoor dining. Obviously Wadworth supply the ales, but the food is all homemade. Nibble on some Thai chilli nuts while you're waiting, and then start with ham hock terrine with pickled vegetables, or venison and Armagnac pâté with crostini; before wild mushroom linguine, smoked trout and beetroot salad with horseradish crème fraîche, or Thai green chicken and coconut curry. If you've room, there's plum frangipane tart or seasonal fruit crumble for afters.

Open all day, all week 12–11 Wadworth 20 portions/menu notice required

HURST

The Green Man

Tel **0118 934 2599 | Hinton Road, RG10 0BP**
Web **www.greenmanhurst.co.uk**
Dir ***From Wokingham on A321 towards Twyford. Right after Hurst Cricket Club cricket ground on right into Hinton Road.***

Ever-reliable village retreat

The Green Man is a homely half-timbered cottage pub situated close to the village cricket pitch. Older parts of the building predate its first licence granted in 1602; thick beams were recycled from Tudor warships and offer a memorable interior in this appealing rustic retreat. Brakspear Brewery bitter and seasonal ales continue to keep drinkers happy. Diners can anticipate a seasonally adjusted, solidly British menu with mains like grilled salmon with wild rice risotto; venison Wellington, black cabbage with port and blackcurrant gravy; or potato rösti with broccoli, roasted salsify and crisp duck egg. Sandwiches, jacket potatoes, and lighter meals are also available. The tree-shaded beer garden has serene country views.

Open all day, all week Brakspear 20 portions/menu

LITTLEWICK GREEN

The Cricketers

Tel **01628 822888** | **Coronation Road, SL6 3RA**
Dir ***West of Maidenhead on A4 (Bath Road). Left into Coronation Road, pub on right.***

In the idyllic village of Littlewick Green, overlooking the cricket pitch, this is as quintessentially British as pubs get. In summer, the lovely garden really comes into its own, but there's also a log fire and cosy seating inside for winter. Either way, you can expect a warm welcome and well-kept ales like Tanglefoot and First Call or Stowford Press cider. The kitchen keeps things simple with pub favourites of home-made lasagne; steak and ale pie; cottage pie; and home-cooked ham, egg, chips and peas.

Open all week 12–3 5–11 (Sat to Sun all day) Hall & Woodhouse 11 portions/menu

MARSH BENHAM

The Red House

Tel **01635 582017** | **RG20 8LY**
Web **www.theredhousepub.com**
Dir ***From Newbury A4 towards Hungerford. Pub signed, in approximately 3 miles. Left onto unclassified road to Marsh Benham.***

This trim thatched pub is just a stroll (dog walkers welcome) from the Kennet & Avon Canal. Indulge in a beer from the respected West Berkshire Brewery whilst enjoying views from the sheltered garden or sit beside the log fire choosing from the menu of experienced French chef-patron Laurent Lebeau. His essentially British menu might include Old Winchester cheese soufflé and steak and kidney pudding. There's also a thoughtful gluten-free menu. As for the wines, Laurent chooses well.

Open all day, all week Free House from £9.50 portions/menu notice required

MONEYROW GREEN

The White Hart

Tel **01628 621460** | **SL6 2ND**
Web **www.thewhitehartholyport.co.uk**
Dir ***2 miles south from Maidenhead. M4 junction 8/9, follow Holyport signs then Moneyrow Green. Pub by petrol station.***

The close proximity to the M4 makes this traditional 19th-century coaching inn a popular spot. The wood-panelled lounge bar is furnished with leather chesterfields, and quality home-made food and award-winning real ales can be enjoyed in a cosy atmosphere with an open fire.

NEWBURY

The Newbury PICK OF THE PUBS

Tel **01635 49000** | **137 Bartholomew Street, RG14 5HB**
Web **www.thenewburypub.co.uk**
Dir ***Phone for detailed directions.***

This popular 19th-century pub holds court in the pedestrianised town centre. Through its elegant portico a quirkily decorated bar reveals an open fire, real ales from Berkshire and Hampshire, and 26 wines sold by the glass. Beyond are the lounge, restaurant and heated roof terrace serving cocktails and oven-fired pizzas. An eclectic approach in the open kitchen results, for example, in whole plaice with pan-fried scallops, caper butter and skinny fries; and 12-hour haggis-stuffed lamb shoulder with cumin and celeriac potatoes, confit root vegetables and braised red cabbage purée. A new addition is the micro gin distillery-cum-rustic chic private dining room, offering five- and seven-course tasting menus.

Open all day, all week Lumber & Clarke 26 from £16.50 portions/menu notice required

OAKLEY GREEN

The Greene Oak

Tel **01753 864294** | **SL4 5UW**
Web **www.thegreeneoak.co.uk**
Dir ***M4 junction 8, A308(M) signed Maidenhead Central. At roundabout take A308 signed Bray and Windsor. Right into Oakley Green Road (B3024) signed Twyford. Pub on left.***

This neighbourhood pub near Windsor was taken over in 2018 by two chefs who met while working at the legendary Ivy restaurant. Needless to say, the cooking is of a high quality, with fish dishes a specialty and everything prepared from scratch including the cured ham. Choose one of three rotating cask ales at the solid oak bar, which also serves premium lagers and ciders and a wide range of wines.

Open all day, all week Mon to Sat 12–11, Sun 12–10 Greene King 26 from £14 portions/menu notice required

PALEY STREET

The Royal Oak Paley Street

 **PICK OF THE PUBS**

Tel **01628 620541 | Littlefield Green, SL6 3JN**
Web **www.theroyaloakpaleystreet.com**
Dir ***M4 junction 8/9a, A308(M) signed Maidenhead (Central). Take A330 to Ascot. In 2 miles turn right onto B3024 to Twyford. 2nd pub on left.***

From the outside you see a simple, white-painted, cottagey roadside pub, but perhaps an inner voice tells you not to pass by. Once inside, when you've taken in its time-honoured decor and furnishings, enhanced by contemporary artwork, you realise it was a good decision. Further reasons are the food, typical dishes being beetroot, blue cheese royale with savoury granola and red chicory; Cornish monkfish with red pepper purée, tempura mussels and chargrilled broccoli; and Crown Estate venison with braised shoulder, aubergine and blackberries. And there's a modern garden featuring large planters, white pebbles and a contemporary waterfall. Your host here, by the way, is Nick Parkinson, son of Sir Michael.

Open all week 12–3 6–11 (Sun 12–4) Fuller's 30 from £18 portions/menu

PEASEMORE

The Fox at Peasemore

PICK OF THE PUBS

Tel **01635 248480 | Hill Green Lane, RG20 7JN**
Web **www.foxatpeasemore.co.uk**
Dir ***M4 junction 13, A34 signed Oxford. Immediately left onto slip road signed Chieveley, Hermitage and Beedon. At T-junction left, through Chieveley to Peasemore. Left at phone box, pub signed.***

Right opposite the village cricket ground, the imposing Fox draws in spectators with the promise of great microbrewery beers from the likes of West Berkshire Brewery and artisan local ciders from Tutts Clump. The modern-rustic bar with its polished wooden floor, settles and log-burning stove is the place to consider the confident menu of tried and tested pub classics and contemporary British dishes. Robust favourites include pie of the day or haddock and chips; the carte presents an eclectic choice. Anticipate garlic baked scallops with cheddar cheese crust to start, or smoked chicken salad, followed by mixed game and juniper berry pie; whole roast poussin with chunky chips and marinated vine tomatoes; or seared sea bass with crushed new potatoes. Round things off with a honeycomb Eton mess, iced pistachio parfait, or a passion fruit crème brulée with chilli and pineapple salsa.

Open all year 12–3 6–11 (Sat to Sun 12–late) Closed Mon, Tue Free House 16 portions/menu notice required

READING

The Flowing Spring

Tel **0118 969 9878 | Henley Road, Playhatch, RG4 9RB**
Web **www.theflowingspringpub.co.uk**
Dir ***3 miles north of Reading on A4155 towards Henley.***

Unusually this 18th-century pub is on the first floor, which slopes steeply from one end of the bar to the other; the balcony overlooks the Chilterns. The pub has been recognised for its well-kept ales and cellar, and the menu of no-nonsense pub favourites.

The Shoulder of Mutton

Tel **0118 947 3908 | Playhatch, RG4 9QU**
Web **www.theshoulderplayhatch.co.uk**
Dir ***From Reading follow signs to Caversham, take A4155 to Henley-on-Thames. At roundabout left to Binfield Heath, follow brown pub sign, 1st pub on left.***

A pleasant walled cottage garden, beams and open fire grace this long-established local favourite in tiny Playhatch, close to Caversham Lakes and the River Thames. Beer lovers pop in for ales brewed just up the road by Loddon Brewery, whilst diners travel from afar.

RUSCOMBE

Buratta's at the Royal Oak

Tel **0118 934 5190 | Ruscombe Lane, RG10 9JN**
Web **www.burattas.co.uk**
Dir ***From A4 (Wargrave roundabout) take A321 to Twyford (signed Twyford/Wokingham). Straight on at 1st lights, right at 2nd lights onto A3032. Right onto A3024 (Ruscombe Road which becomes Ruscombe Lane). Pub on left on brow of hill.***

Originally a one-bar pub, the Royal Oak has been extended over the years and the cottage next door is now the kitchen. Visit for the à la carte sharing platters, mains menu and range of wines.

SHURLOCK ROW

The Shurlock Inn

Tel **0118 934 9094** | **The Street, RG10 0PS**
Web **www.theshurlockinn.co.uk**
Dir ***Phone for detailed directions.***

This lovely 17th-century pub was bought by a group of villagers a few years ago and hasn't looked back; the stylish interior has retained exposed timbers and an open fireplace. The large family garden and sheltered courtyard are a draw during the warmer months.

SINDLESHAM

The Walter Arms

Tel **0118 977 4903** | **Bearwood Road, RG41 5BP**
Web **www.thewalterarms.com**
Dir ***A329 from Wokingham towards Reading. 1.5 miles, left onto B3030. 5 miles, left into Bearwood Rd. Pub 200 yards on left.***

A typically solid Victorian building built about 1850 by John Walter III, grandson of the man who founded The Times newspaper. The idea was that it should be a working men's club for the workers on the Bearwood Estate, where Walter lived.

SONNING

The Bull Inn

Tel **0118 969 3901** | **High Street, RG4 6UP**
Web **www.bullinnsonning.co.uk**
Dir ***From Reading take A4 towards Maidenhead. Left onto B4446 to Sonning.***

Two minutes' walk from the River Thames in the pretty village of Sonning, this inn can trace its roots back 600 years; it can also boast visits by former owner Queen Elizabeth I and a mention in Jerome K Jerome's *Three Men in a Boat*.

STANFORD DINGLEY

The Bull Inn

Tel **0118 974 4582** | **RG7 6LS**
Web **www.thebullinnpub.com**
Dir ***M4 junction 12, A4 towards Newbury, A340 towards Pangbourne. 1st left to Bradfield. Through Bradfield, 0.3 mile left into Back Lane. At end left, pub 0.25 mile on left.***

Dating from the 15th century, this red-brick pub is still the hub of the lovely village of Stanford Dingley. The Tap Room bar is where the locals congregate. For simple rustic surroundings, eat in the Saloon; the Dining Room is more formal.

The Old Boot Inn

Tel **0118 974 5191** | **RG7 6LT**
Web **www.oldbootinnstanforddingley.co.uk**
Dir ***M4 junction 12, A4, A340 to Pangbourne. 1st left to Bradfield. Through Bradfield, follow Stanford Dingley signs.***

Oak beams and half-timbering feature inside this cottagey inn found in the peaceful Pang Valley. The rustic theme continues with log fires and an enormous beer garden rolling back to merge with pastureland backed by wooded hills. The modern conservatory restaurant is light and airy.

Open all day, all week 12–11 (Tue 5–11 Sat 12–11.30 Sun 12–9) Free House 10 from £13 portions/menu notice required

SUNNINGHILL

Dog & Partridge

Tel **01344 623204** | **92 Upper Village Road, SL5 7AQ**
Web www.**dogandpartridgesunninghill.co.uk**
Dir ***From either A329 or A330 into High Street. Into Truss Hill Road, 1st right into Upper Village Road, pub on left.***

If the weather's favourable, make for the courtyard garden, where the fountain gently burbles away as you ease into your Pinot Grigio, or a Windsor & Eton brewery real ale. At lunchtime, you'll find a selection of sandwiches, pies, jacket potatoes and pasta on offer.

WALTHAM ST LAWRENCE

The Bell

Tel **0118 934 1788** | **The Street, RG10 0JJ**
Web **www.thebellwalthamstlawrence.co.uk**
Dir ***On B3024 east of Twyford. From A4 turn at Hare Hatch.***

This 14th-century free house is renowned for its ciders and an ever-changing range of real ales selected from small independent breweries. Everything possible is made on site, including all charcuterie and preparation of game. Perhaps choose steamed mussels in cider, then bream and split-pea dhal; finish with beer ice cream.

Open all week 12–3 5–11 (Sat 12–11 Sun 12–10.30) Free House 19 portions/menu

WARFIELD

The Cricketers

Tel **01344 882910** | **Cricketers Lane, RG42 6JT**
Web **www.cricketerswarfield.co.uk**
Dir ***North-east of Bracknell.***

A white-painted, brick-built country pub dating back to the early 19th century, The Cricketers has been thoughtfully refurbished and extended. There's a patio for outdoor dining in the summer, and a large beer garden (say hello to resident ducks, Cheese and Quackers, if you see them).

WHITE WALTHAM

The Beehive ◎◎ PICK OF THE PUBS

Tel **01628 822877** | **Waltham Road, SL6 3SH**
Web **www.thebeehivewhitewaltham.com**
Dir ***M4 junction 8/9, A404, follow White Waltham signs.***

If choosing a pub involves ticking boxes, then The Beehive will keep you busy. Externally, it's 18th century, stands in a pleasant village, overlooks a cricket pitch and from its beer garden there are distant views of woods and rich pastureland. Inside, while contemporary in style, you just know it has always been the focus of village life. Real ales are from nearby breweries, and the bar also does snacks, such as rollmops and Scotch eggs. More box ticking will be required for award-winning chef Dominic Chapman's menu offering wild Berkshire rabbit and bacon pie with mash potato; roast Cornish cod, creamed Savoy cabbage, haricot beans, tarragon and bacon; and blackberry trifle.

Open all week 11–3 5–11 (Sat 11am–midnight Sun 12–10.30) Closed 25–26 Dec Enterprise Inns portions/menu notice required

WINKFIELD

The Winning Post ★★★★ INN

Tel **01344 882242** | **Winkfield Street, SL4 4SW**
Web **www.winningpostwinkfield.co.uk**
Dir ***M4 junction 6, A355. 3rd exit at roundabout into Imperial Road (B3175). Right at lights into Saint Leonards Road (B3022). At 2nd roundabout 2nd exit into North Street signed Winkfield. Through Winkfield, at sharp left bend turn right into Winkfield Street. Pub 200 yards on right.***

A short canter from Ascot and Windsor racecourses, this charming 18th-century pub has long been a favourite with the equine-inclined. The Winning Post is off the beaten track and surrounded by stunning Berkshire countryside but it's also a convenient pit stop for Heathrow Airport.

WOKINGHAM

The Broad Street Tavern

Tel **01189 773706** | **29 Broad Street, RG40 1AU**
Web **www.broadstreettavern.co.uk**
Dir ***In town centre, adjacent to Pizza Express.***

A handsome detached period building fronted by elegant railings, this town-centre pub offers a friendly atmosphere and spacious indoor and outdoor seating areas. Regular child-centric events are an intrinsic element of the pub's diary, which also includes two ale festivals and one for cider in the summer.

The Crooked Billet – see opposite

YATTENDON

The Royal Oak Hotel

PICK OF THE PUBS

Tel **01635 201325** | **The Square, RG18 0UG**
Web **www.royaloakyattendon.co.uk**
Dir ***M4 junction 12, A4 to Newbury, right at 2nd roundabout to Pangbourne then 1st left. From junction 13, A34 north 1st left, right at T-junction. Left then 2nd right to Yattendon.***

Yattendon was once important enough to have a castle, although it was largely destroyed by Parliamentary forces during the Civil War. The Royal Oak is part of a row of 16th-century cottages, with log fires in the bar, oak beams, and quarry-tiled and wooden floors in the lounge and dining rooms. French windows lead to a walled rear garden with a vine-laden trellis. Enjoy a pint of local Ramsbury Gold or Ringwood beer from the New Forest. Abundant local produce from top suppliers is used for seasonal dishes – just have a sandwich, or keep browsing and to discover much more. There's always something going on, with fortnightly quizzes, rib and crab nights, quarterly seafood weekends and masterclasses in cheese.

Open all day, all week Free House 10 from £16 portions/menu

WOKINGHAM

The Crooked Billet

Tel **0118 978 0438** | **Honey Hill, RG40 3BJ**
Web **www.crookedbilletwokingham.co.uk**
Dir ***Phone for detailed directions.***

A picture-book, weatherboarded old pub

A little tucked away, but once on the right leafy country lane you really can't miss this cute, white-painted little pub, where Brakspear's real ales are accompanied by two monthly guests. Typical dishes include slow-cooked duck leg, mash, spinach and redcurrant gravy; fish stew with pollack, red mullet, prawns, mussels and cockles in brown crab and tomato sauce; pan-roasted calves' liver with bacon, bubble-and-squeak and onion gravy; and mushroom and leek cottage pie, cauliflower cheese mash topping and buttered kale. Winter menus feature local game. Sandwiches and light meals, such as mussels steamed in cider with shallots and smoked bacon, are available at lunchtime. The main menu also applies on Sundays, when, of course, traditional roasts are a big draw. The cheeseboard is good enough to win a prize.

Open all day, all week Brakspear 9 portions/menu notice required

BRISTOL

BRISTOL

The Albion

Tel **0117 973 3522** | **Boyces Avenue, Clifton, BS8 4AA**
Web **www.thealbionclifton.co.uk**
Dir ***From A4 take B3129 towards city centre. Right into Clifton Down Road. 3rd left into Boyces Avenue.***

This handsome Grade II listed coaching inn dates from the 17th century. A popular place to enjoy St Austell Brewery ales and Thatchers ciders, you can order jugs of Pimm's in summer or sip mulled cider under heaters in the enclosed courtyard in the winter.

The Alma Tavern & Theatre

Tel **0117 973 5171** | **18–20 Alma Vale Road, Clifton, BS8 2HY**
Web **www.almatavernandtheatre.co.uk**
Dir ***Phone for detailed directions.***

In the heart of Clifton, this bustling Victorian pub has the unique added attraction of a small theatre upstairs. The team here continues to draw in the theatre crowd and maintain a pubby atmosphere for the locals, while also enticing others with their good food.

Highbury Vaults

Tel **0117 973 3203** | **164 St Michaels Hill, Cotham, BS2 8DE**
Web **www.highburyvaults.co.uk**
Dir ***A38 to Cotham from inner ring dual carriageway.***

A classic little city pub with the character of a Victorian drinking house; lots of nooks and crannies, dim lighting, impressive original bar and a cosmopolitan crowd of locals. Condemned Victorian prisoners took their last meals here; today's crowd are more fortunate, revelling in beers such as Bath Ales and chowing down on no-nonsense pub fare like chilli con carne; lasagne al forno; and fish pie. An added attraction is the model train that runs the length of the bar.

Open all day, all week 12–12 (Sun 12–11) Closed 25 Dec evening, 26 Dec lunch, 1 Jan lunch Young & Co's Brewery Wi-fi notice required

The Kensington Arms

Tel **0117 944 6444 | 35–37 Stanley Road, BS6 6NP**
Web **www.thekensingtonarms.co.uk**
Dir ***From Redland Rail Station into South Road, then Kensington Road. 4th right into Stanley Road.***

This Victorian corner pub in the backstreets of Bristol's affluent Redland district still attracts discerning local drinkers. The elegant dining room is packed with mismatched antique furniture, Victorian prints and views into the open kitchen.

BUCKINGHAMSHIRE

AMERSHAM

Hit or Miss Inn

Tel **01494 713109 | Penn Street Village, HP7 0PX**
Web **www.ourpubs.co.uk**
Dir ***M25 junction 18, A404 (Amersham to High Wycombe road) to Amersham. Past crematorium on right, 2nd left into Whielden Lane (signed Winchmore Hill). 1.25 miles, pub on right.***

Overlooking the cricket ground from which its name is taken, this is an 18th-century cottage-style dining pub with a beautiful garden for warmer days. Inside are fires, old beams, Badger ales and a warm welcome. Menu options include tempting sandwiches, baked potatoes and dishes like slow-cooked lamb shank with vegetable tagine. There are daily specials, Sunday roasts and a children's menu, too. Beer and cider festival in mid-July.

Open all day, all week 11–11 (Sun 12–10.30) Hall & Woodhouse 14 portions/menu Wi-fi P notice required

ASHENDON

The Hundred of Ashendon

Tel **01296 651296 | Lower End, HP18 0HE**
Web **www.thehundred.co.uk**
Dir ***Phone for detailed directions.***

The interiors of The Hundred boast polished wood floors, mismatched furniture and eclectic knick-knacks. Walkers, cyclists, families with children and dogs all receive the same warm welcome. A splendid array of real ales greets the thirsty, notably Side Pocket for a Toad from Tring Brewery.

Open 12–3.30 6–11 Closed 1–8 Jan, Mon Free House 10 portions/menu Wi-fi P notice required

AYLESBURY

The King's Head & Farmer's Bar

Tel **01296 718812 | Market Square, HP20 2RW**
Web **www.kingsheadaylesbury.co.uk**
Dir ***Access on foot only. From Market Square access cobbled passageway. Pub entrance under archway on right.***

A former coaching inn, dating from 1455, where Henry VIII reputedly wooed Anne Boleyn. These days, it's the award-winning brewery tap for the Chiltern Brewery, which prides itself on serving their beers, plus craft and guest ales, with care and a great deal of knowledge. Special beer celebrations are held throughout the year; wines come from The Rothschild Estate. Enjoy a drink in the ancient cobbled courtyard, or a lunch of home-cooked dishes – venison and wild mushroom Wellington, and pie of the day to name but two.

Open all day, all week 11–11 (Sun 12–10.30) Closed 25 Dec Free House 12 portions/menu Wi-fi notice required

BEACONSFIELD

The Royal Standard of England PICK OF THE PUBS

Tel **01494 673382 | Forty Green, HP9 1XT**
Web **www.rsoe.co.uk**
Dir ***A40 to Beaconsfield, right at church roundabout onto B474 towards Penn, left into Forty Green Road, 1 mile.***

Tucked away in The Chiltern Hills, this claims to be the oldest free house in England. It all started with the West Saxons, who brewed ale on this site using water from an old Romano-British well that remains under the kitchen to this day. Ancient blackened timbers, flagstone floors, leaded windows, battle standards, armour and dried hops greet your entry to an interior warmed in winter by open fires. Chiltern Ale and Windsor & Eton's Conqueror share bar space with farm ciders and a Herefordshire perry. Hearty mains include home-made pies, sausages and home-made chips; Welsh lamb shoulder, sauté potatoes and cabbage; and fish pie made with salmon, cod, smoked haddock and prawns. Specials, including local game, appear on a blackboard.

Open all day, all week 11–11 Free House 11 portions Wi-fi P

BLEDLOW

The Lions of Bedlow – see below

BOURNE END

The Garibaldi

Tel **01628 522092** | **Hedsor Road, SL8 5EE**
Web **www.garibaldipub.co.uk**
Dir ***From A4094 (in town centre) into Hedsor Road. Pub on left.***

Known locally as the 'Gari', this 19th-century pub is the hub of the village and a warm welcome is assured from Charmain and Jayson McAlpine. Local real ales including Marlow-brewed Rebellion Blonde are on offer at the bar, which also serves more than 20 wines by the glass. The menu might kick off with duck and pork parfait before moving on to home-made pie of the day; gammon steak with egg and fries or a South African-inspired bobotie. Look out for the Easter and August Bank Holiday beer festivals.

Open all week 12–3 5–11 (Fri to Sat 12–11 Sun 12–10) Free House 23 from £9.50 portions/menu notice required

BOVINGDON GREEN

The Royal Oak PICK OF THE PUBS

Tel **01628 488611** | **Frieth Road, SL7 2JF**
Web **www.royaloakmarlow.co.uk**
Dir ***A4155 from Marlow. 300 yards right signed Bovingdon Green. 0.75 mile, pub on left.***

'Dogs, children and muddy boots welcome' is the friendly motto at this little old whitewashed pub, standing in sprawling, flower-filled gardens. The inside is spacious yet cosy, with dark floorboards, heritage colours, rich fabrics, and a wood-burning stove. Have a pint of Rebellion from Marlow, or Mortimers Orchard draught cider from Westons in Herefordshire, or relax with an aperitif and choose something from the generous gin menu. The imaginative modern British and international menu is designed to appeal to all, beginning with 'small plates', such as Wobbly Bottom goats' cheese, garden honey ham hock terrine using honey from their own beehive. An exclusively European wine list has 33 by the glass.

Open all day, all week 11–11 (Sun 12–10.30) Closed 25–26 Dec Free House 33 from £12.50 portions/menu

BLEDLOW

The Lions of Bledlow

Tel **01844 343345** | **Church End, HP27 9PE**
Web **www.lionsofbledlow.co.uk**
Dir ***M40 junction 6, B4009 to Princes Risborough, through Chinnor into Bledlow.***

Good beers, good food and steam trains

Midsomer Murders and various period TV drama series have been filmed in this lovely, whitewashed, 16th-century free house. Its atmosphere of yesteryear is reinforced by the occasional steam train trundling past on the Chinnor & Princes Risborough heritage railway the other side of the village green. Ramblers who detour from the wooded Chilterns – and of course, everyone else – can expect a good range of real ales, often including Loddon, Tring and Wadworth, as well as ever-changing beers from much nearer. Also awaiting them will be generously filled baguettes, baps and burgers; home-made leek, spinach and crème fraîche tart; lamb rump stuffed with garlic and chervil; and smoked cod, bacon and brie fishcakes, as well as vegetarian dishes and daily-changing specials. Dogs also receive a warm welcome.

Open all week 11.30–3 6–11 (weekends all day) Free House 12 portions/menu

BRILL

The Pheasant ★★★★ INN

Tel **01844 239370** | **39 Windmill Street, HP18 9TG**
Web **www.thepheasant.co.uk**
Dir ***In village centre, by windmill.***

This friendly 17th-century hilltop country pub and restaurant has wonderful views of Brill Windmill and neighbouring counties. Enticing starter choices might be pan-fried mixed mushrooms with garlic and parsley; or antipasti to share. Then consider steak and pheasant ale pie, bangers and mash, or a Brill beef burger with Oxford Blue cheese. Head for the garden when the weather's good in the summer and book for a Thursday curry evening.

Open all day, all week 12–11 (Fri to Sat 12–12 Sun 12–10.30) Free House 9 from £12 portions/menu notice required

The Pointer ★★★★★

RESTAURANT WITH ROOMS | PICK OF THE PUBS

Tel **01844 238339** | **27 Church Street, HP18 9RT**
Web **www.thepointerbrill.co.uk**
Dir ***M40 junction 9, A41 towards Aylesbury. Right onto B4011 signed Thame. Follow signs to Brill.***

Brill stands high on a hill. Take a short walk from the pub to see the famous windmill and the fabulous views over Buckinghamshire and into Oxfordshire. Sit by the open fire in the front bar with a pint of Pointer, an artisanal English gin or one of the 13 wines by the glass. Suggestions from the short, ever-changing seasonal menu include home-cured Loch Duart salmon with cucumber and fennel sorbet as a starter, followed by Angus steak (from the owners' Chilton Home Farm) with wild mushrooms and roasted cherry tomatoes; winter game (also from the farm); haunch of venison with celeriac, blackberries and wild juniper; and risotto primavera. Next door is the pub's butcher's shop, selling fresh bread and pastries as well as meats.

Open all day Closed 1st week Jan, Mon Free House 13 portions/menu notice required

BUCKINGHAM

The Old Thatched Inn

Tel **01296 712584** | **Main Street, Adstock, MK18 2JN**
Web **www.theoldthatchedinn.co.uk**
Dir ***A413 from Buckingham towards Aylesbury. Approximately 4 miles left to Adstock.***

This lovely early 18th-century owner-operated thatched inn still boasts traditional beams and inglenook fireplace. The spacious interior consists of a formal conservatory and a bar with comfy furniture and a welcoming, relaxed atmosphere. Using the freshest, seasonal ingredients from local and regional suppliers, the menu takes in starters like smoked haddock and leek arancini; and pulled ham and cheese croquette; and mains like Cumberland sausage ring with creamed potatoes and braised red cabbage; pan-roasted chicken breast with lentil and root vegetable casserole; or home-made burger in a brioche bun.

Open all day, all week Closed 26 Dec Free House 16 from £11.95 portions/menu

BURNHAM

The Blackwood Arms

Tel **01753 645672** | **Common Lane, Littleworth Common, SL1 8PP**
Web **www.theblackwoodarms.net**
Dir ***Phone for detailed directions.***

Eagle-eyed fans of TV detective drama *Midsomer Murders* will immediately recognise this pub. Surrounded by lovely woodland, the pub is popular with walkers, cyclists and horse riders and it has a pretty garden. Well-kept ales such as Brakspear Bitter and Oxford Gold are dispensed in the bar. A typical meal might include pan-fried pigeon breasts with crumbed black pudding and raspberry pickled beets, or the mixed seafood grill in white wine sauce. Time a visit for the St George's Day beer festival.

Open all year, all day Closed Mon (except bank holiday) Brakspear 12 portions notice required

CHALFONT ST PETER

The Greyhound Inn PICK OF THE PUBS

Tel **01753 883404** | **SL9 9RA**
Web **www.thegreyhoundinn.net**
Dir ***M40 junction 1/M25 junction 16, follow signs for Gerrards Cross, then Chalfont St Peter.***

Over the centuries, this old coaching inn has welcomed many a traveller, Oliver Cromwell and Winston Churchill among them. Much of the pub's 14th-century character survives, particularly the massive beams, huge brick chimneys, and imposing panelled and flagstoned bar. Here you can join the villagers supping pints of Sharp's Doom Bar, watch the big game, and order a bar snack at half time. The restaurant specialises in English and continental dishes so perhaps start with the hot and cold Var salmon with asparagus and cream cheese dressing. Next may come a pub favourite such as a home-made burger with back bacon, cheese, fries and relish; or a simple grilled rump steak cooked to your liking.

Open all day, all week Mon to Wed 7am–11pm (Thu 7am to midnight Fri 7am–1am Sat 8am–1am Sun 8am–10.30pm) Enterprise Inns from £12.50 portions/menu notice required

CHESHAM

The Swan

Tel **01494 783075** | **Ley Hill, HP5 1UT**
Web **www.swanleyhill.com**
Dir ***1.5 miles east of Chesham by golf course.***

Set in the delightful village of Ley Hill, this beautiful 16th-century pub was once the place where condemned prisoners would drink a 'last and final ale' on the way to the nearby gallows. During World War II, both Glen Miller and Clark Gable cycled here from the Bovingdon Air Force for a pint. These days, it is a free house offering a warm welcome, real ales and good food. Look out for the summer beer festival in August.

Open all year 12–2.30 5.30–11 (Sun 12–4) Closed Mon Free House portions notice required

CUBLINGTON

The Unicorn

Tel **01296 681261** | **High Street, LU7 0LQ**
Web **www.theunicornpub.co.uk**
Dir ***2 miles north of A418 (between Aylesbury and Leighton Buzzard). In village centre.***

All the right elements of an English country pub are here: low-beamed bar, wooden floors, real fires, mismatched furniture and a minimum of four real ales, including XT from Long Crendon and Fuller's London Pride. You can expect dishes such as pumpkin and marrow curry; pan-fried sea bream; hand-made shortcrust pie of the day; Cublington pork sausages, mash, onion rings and sage gravy; and beer-battered whiting and hand-cut chips. There are barbecues on Saturday evenings from May to September.

Open all week 12–3 5–11 (Fri 10.30am–midnight Sat 9.30am–midnight Sun 12–7) Free House from £11 portions/menu notice required

CUDDINGTON

The Crown PICK OF THE PUBS

Tel **01844 292222** | **Spurt Street, HP18 0BB**
Web **www.thecrowncuddington.co.uk**
Dir ***From A418 between Thame and Aylesbury follow Cuddington signs. Pub in village centre.***

This thatched and whitewashed listed pub sits in the picturesque village of Cuddington. The Crown's atmospheric interior includes a locals' bar and several low-beamed dining areas lit by candles in the evening. Fuller's London Pride, Adnams and guest ales are on tap, and there's also an extensive wine list, with 12 by the glass. Look to the blackboard for daily specials or the set menu for good value options. A patio area provides outside seating.

DENHAM

The Falcon Inn ★★★★ INN

Tel **01895 832125** | **Village Road, UB9 5BE**
Web **www.falcondenham.com**
Dir ***M40 junction 1, follow A40/Gerrards Cross signs. Approximately 200 yards, right into Old Mill Road. Pass church on right. Pub opposite village green on left.***

Barely 17 miles away as the crow flies, central London seems light years away from this lovely 16th-century coaching inn opposite the village green. Expect well-kept Timothy Taylor and other real ales. Brasserie food includes pub classics and dishes like pan-fried seabass, tomato salsa, potato cake and seasonal veg; and steak and ale pie with chunky chips. Other attractions are a south-facing terraced garden and four bedrooms, two of which have original oak beams.

Open all day, all week Ei Group 10 portions/ menu notice required

DORNEY

The Palmer Arms

Tel **01628 666612** | **Village Road, SL4 6QW**
Web **thepalmerarms.com**
Dir ***From A4 take B3026, over M4 to Dorney.***

Built in the 15th century, with wooden beams and open fires, this family-friendly pub in the pretty conservation village of Dorney is just a stroll from the Thames Path and Boveney Lock. The interior is contemporary and the menu combines modern and classic British dishes.

EASINGTON

Mole and Chicken PICK OF THE PUBS

Tel **01844 208387** | **HP18 9EY**
Web **www.themoleandchicken.co.uk**
Dir ***M40 junction 8 or 8a, A418 to Thame. At roundabout left onto B4011 signed Long Crendon and Bicester. In Long Crendon right into Carters Lane signed Dorton and Chilton. At T-junction left into Chilton Road signed Chilton. Approximately 0.75 mile to pub.***

On the Oxfordshire–Buckinghamshire border, the pub was built in 1831 as housing for estate workers, later becoming the village store and beer and cider house. The far-reaching views from its high terraced garden are magnificent, while inside it's a combination of exposed beams, flagged floors and smart, contemporary furniture. Beechwood Bitter and Vale Wychert are on tap, alongside Aspall cider. From a British and eastern Mediterranean-influenced menu, a typical meal would be salt and pepper squid, aïoli, lime and coriander, then pan-fried liver, bacon and kidneys, creamed potatoes, cabbage and onion gravy; ending with warm chocolate fondant and honeycomb ice cream. Bar dishes include spaghetti, prawns, tomato, pesto and parmesan. And if you were wondering about the whimsical name – it recalls two long-gone landlords, 'Moley' and 'Johnny Chick'.

Open all day, all week Mon to Fri 7.30am–11pm (Sat to Sun 8am to midnight) Closed 25 Dec Free House from £12 portions/menu

FARNHAM COMMON

The Foresters

Tel **01753 643340** | **The Broadway, SL2 3QQ**
Web **www.theforesterspub.com**
Dir ***Phone for detailed directions.***

This handsome 1930s building has an interior where old meets new – crystal chandeliers and log fires, real ales and cocktails, glass-topped tables and wooden floors, chesterfields and velvet thrones. There are pleasant gardens at the front and to the rear.

FARNHAM ROYAL

The Emperor

Tel **01753 643006** | **Blackpond Lane, SL2 3EG**
Web **theemperorpub.co.uk**
Dir ***Phone for detailed directions.***

Just a short, easy stroll from the fabulous ancient woodland of Burnham Beeches nature reserve, this Victorian village inn seamlessly mixes contemporary comforts with the character of a mature local pub.

FRIETH

The Prince Albert

Tel **01494 881683** | **RG9 6PY**
Web **www.theprincealbert-pub.co.uk**
Dir ***4 miles north of Marlow. Follow Frieth road from Marlow. Straight across at crossroads on Fingest road. Pub 200 yards on left.***

There's no TV, jukebox or electronic games in this cottagey Chiltern Hills pub. What you get instead, surprise, surprise, is just good conversation, probably much as when it was built in the 1700s. In the bar, low beams, a big black inglenook stove, high-backed settles and lots of copper pots and pans; an alternative place to enjoy a pint of Brakspear is a seat in the garden, while admiring the woods and fields. A short, snack menu of pub favourites is available.

Open all day, all week 11–11 (Sun 12–10.30)
Brakspear 8 portions WI-FI

FULMER

The Black Horse

Tel **01753 663183** | **Windmill Road, SL3 6HD**
Web **www.theblackhorsefulmer.co.uk**
Dir ***M40 junction 1, A40 (Amersham). Then follow Beaconsfield and Gerrards Cross signs. Into Tatling End (over M25), left signed Fulmer (over M40). Pub on left after church.***

Dating back to the 17th century and originally a craftsman's cottage, The Black Horse is a great blend of old-world charm and contemporary decor, lovingly refurbished and extended. The village is close to Pinewood Studios, so who knows who you might see.

GERRARDS CROSS

The Three Oaks PICK OF THE PUBS

Tel **01753 899016** | **Austenwood Lane, SL9 8NL**
Web **www.thethreeoaksgx.co.uk**
Dir ***From A40 at lights take B416 (Packhorse Road) signed Village Centre. Over railway. Left signed Gold Hill into Austenwood Lane. Pub on right.***

On the edge of affluent Gerrards Cross, The Three Oaks is a stylish venue with a contemporary feel and relaxed vibe. Drop by for a pint of Rebellion Ale or one of 18 wines served by the glass and tuck into the cracking value set menus offered at lunch and dinner. A typical meal might start with crispy baby squid, bacon crumb, pickled fennel, bacon and maple mayonnaise; followed by suckling pig belly, spiced potato terrine, chorizo and pepper jam, sweetcorn, coriander and charred kale. If there's still room, finish with sticky toffee ice cream, pressed date cake, custard, sherry and treacle caramel sauce. There's a garden for alfresco dining.

Open all week 12–11 Enterprise Inns 18
portions/menu WI-FI

GREAT HAMPDEN

The Hampden Arms

Tel **01494 488255** | **HP16 9RQ**
Web **www.thehampdenarms.co.uk**
Dir ***M40 junction 4, A4010, right before Princes Risborough. Great Hampden signed.***

The large garden of this mock-Tudor free house on the wooded Hampden Estate sits beside the common, where you might watch a game of cricket during the season. The pub has a secure beer garden, ideal for private functions.

GREAT KINGSHILL

The Red Lion

Tel **01494 711262** | **Missenden Road, HP15 6EB**
Web **www.redlion-greatkingshill.co.uk**
Dir ***On A4128.***

Whoever built this former beer house clearly made good use of flints extracted from Chiltern Hills chalk. An early example, perhaps, of a 'source local' philosophy that continues both for food and real ales. Specials change daily.

GREAT MISSENDEN

The Nags Head – see page 48

GREAT MISSENDEN

The Nags Head

 INN

Tel 01494 862200 | London Road, HP16 0DG
Web www.nagsheadbucks.com
Dir *North of Amersham on A413, left at Chiltern hospital into London Road signed Great Missenden.*

Charming rural pub with excellent Anglo-French cooking

Famous children's author and long-term local resident Roald Dahl was a regular here, which is why you'll find many of his limited-edition prints in the dining room (his award-winning museum is in the village). And over the years many a prime minister, especially Sir Harold Wilson, has called in here en route to Chequers, the premier's official country house retreat not far away. Originally three late 15th-century cottages, whose inhabitants were known as 'bodgers', the Chilterns word for chairmakers in the surrounding beech woods; over time the properties became a popular coaching inn on the London road, which follows the Misbourne Valley. The owning Michaels family have restored it, just as they have their sister pub, the Bricklayers Arms in Flaunden, over the county border in Hertfordshire. Low oak beams and an inglenook fireplace set the scene for the bar and its real ales from local breweries in perhaps Brill, Prestwood or Tring. The Anglo-French fusion menu abounds with interesting dishes. In summer, relax under the pergola over a drink or a meal in the lovely garden and gaze out towards the hills. Maybe stay overnight in one of the six beautifully designed bedrooms.

Open all day, all week Closed 25 Dec *Free House* *19* *from £12.95* *portions* *notice required*

HEDGERLEY

The White Horse

Tel **01753 643225** | **SL2 3UY**
Dir ***Phone for detailed directions.***

Definitely a serious ale house

With parts dating back 500 years, this is a classic ale-drinker's paradise, or as the landlord describes it 'A perfectly preserved slice of unspoiled pubbery'. Inside, it's all ancient gas lamps – some are on the façade too – low beams and horseshoes, while outside there are plenty of colourful flower and window baskets, and cartwheels hanging from the whitewashed walls. An ever-changing selection of real ales from micro and artisan brewers is the norm, with traditional ales drawn from the cask and real ciders and Belgian bottled beers augmenting the range. A blackboard lists the day's lunchtime-only pub favourites, which take in a wide range of dishes from salads, quiches, sandwiches and ploughman's through to home-cooked curries, chilli, pastas, pies and steaks. A large well-kept rear garden hosts summer barbecues and a May beer festival.

Open all week 11–2.30 5–11 (Sat 11–11 Sun 12–10.30) Free House 10 from £7 portions

LACEY GREEN

The Whip Inn

Tel **01844 344060** | **Pink Road, HP27 0PG**
Web **www.thewhipinn.co.uk**
Dir ***1 mile from A4010 (Princes Risborough to High Wycombe road). Adjacent to windmill.***

Standing high above the Vale of Aylesbury in the heart of the Chiltern Hills, the beer garden of this 200-year-old pub overlooks the Lacey Green windmill. Ramblers on the Chiltern Way join locals in appreciating some of 800 different real ales offered each year.

LITTLE KINGSHILL

The Full Moon

Tel **01494 862397** | **Hare Lane, HP16 0EE**
Web **www.thefullmoon.info**
Dir ***South-west of Great Missenden, accessed from either A413 or A4128.***

A popular post-ramble refuelling stop, especially as both dogs and children are warmly welcomed inside, this pub has a wealth of wonderful walks through the Chiltern Hills radiating from its doorstep. It is noted for its tip-top Fuller's London Pride and the weekly-changing guest ales.

LITTLE MARLOW

The Queens Head

Tel **01628 482927** | **Pound Lane, SL7 3SR**
Web **www.marlowslittlesecret.co.uk**
Dir ***From A404 take Marlow exit towards Bourne End. Approximately 1 mile, right into Church Road. Approximately 100 metres right into Pound Lane.***

Dating from the 16th century, 'Marlow's little secret' is a pretty collection of buildings from three different periods, and its beamed, open fire-warmed interior feels immediately welcoming. Since it's just a tankard's throw from the Marlow Rebellion Brewery, expect IPA and from November to January, Roasted Nuts. Starters could include smoked haddock and crab cake; with mains like roast chicken with sweet potato hash, black pudding purée and glazed shallots.

Open all day, all week Closed 25–26 Dec Punch Taverns from £12.50 portions/menu notice required

LONG CRENDON

The Angel Inn PICK OF THE PUBS

Tel **01844 208268** | **47 Bicester Road, HP18 9EE**
Web **www.angelrestaurant.co.uk**
Dir ***M40 junction 7, A418 to Thame, B4011 to Long Crendon. Inn on B4011.***

Situated in the Vale of Aylesbury and close to the Chiltern Hills, the village of Long Crendon retains a real sense of history, with an old courthouse, picturesque rows of cottages and the gabled Angel Inn. This old coaching stop still displays much of its original character with ancient fireplaces and wattle-and-daub walls, alongside modern additions which include an airy conservatory. Refreshments centre on Vale Brewery's Wychert and the village's own XT Brewing Company's ales; the good wine list offers a dozen served by the glass. Hand-made dishes are cooked to order based on daily deliveries of fresh produce. Typical of these are pumpkin and sage ravioli; trio of Dingley Dell pork – roast fillet in Parma ham, crispy belly and braised cheek; and sticky toffee banana pudding.

Open all day Closed 1–2 Jan, Sun evening Free House 12 from £10.95 portions notice required

MARLOW

The Coach PICK OF THE PUBS

3 West Street, SL7 2LS
Web **www.thecoachmarlow.co.uk**
Dir ***From A404 to Marlow. Pub in town centre.***

This is one of celebrity chef Tom Kerridge's three Marlow pubs, co-run with his wife, Beth Cullen-Kerridge. Inside you'll find glazed wall tiles, soft leather furnishings and an open kitchen, where head chef Tom de Keyser manages the concise, reasonably priced, modern menu with headings of 'meat', 'no meat' and 'sweet'. From 'meat' perhaps choose beef biltong chilli, Monterey Jack and lime. From 'no meat' pick Cornish pollack Scotch egg with shellfish burger; or rotisserie beetroot, feta and horseradish. Finally, two 'sweet' options are banana custard, dates, honeycomb and pistachios; and orange and almond tart with olive oil ice cream. No table bookings here – it's first come, first served.

Open all day, all week Closed 25 Dec Enterprise Inns 20 from £7.50 portions

The Hand & Flowers

PICK OF THE PUBS

Tel **01628 482277** | **126 West Street, SL7 2BP**
Web **www.thehandandflowers.co.uk**
Dir ***M4 junction 9, A404 to Marlow, A4155 towards Henley-on-Thames. Pub on right.***

Celebrity chef Tom Kerridge and his sculptor wife Beth have surely achieved their aim in making this 18th-century pub the sort of place where they, and everyone else, would like to eat. Housing all the desired historic features – flagstone floors, old timbers and log fires – the bar offers real ale from Marlow's Rebellion brewery. Sourcing some ingredients from his own allotment, Tom's menus combine modern British and rustic French cooking, such as the duck liver parfait with orange chutney and toasted brioche starter. Mouth-wateringly descriptive mains include loin of Cotswold venison with parsnip purée, game and Stilton pie, poached pear and cacao crumble. Booking to eat here is essential and must be arranged months in advance – although it's always worth a call to check for cancellations.

Open 12–2.45 6.30–9.45 (Sun 12–3.15) Closed 24–26 Dec, 1 Jan (dinner), Sun evening Greene King 34 from £39.50 portions

The Kings Head

Tel **01628 476718** | **Church Road, Little Marlow, SL7 3RZ**
Web **www.kingsheadinlittlemarlow.co.uk**
Dir ***M40 junction 4, A4040 south, then A4155 towards Bourne End. Pub 0.5 mile on right. Or M4 junction 8/9, A404(M) signed High Wycombe. Then A4155 towards Bourne End. Pub 0.5 mile.***

Walking the Thames Path might well make you thirsty and hungry, in which event this charming 16th-century pub, now under new ownership, is the perfect place to satisfy both desires. The open-plan interior features original beams and log fires, and unsurprisingly makes local brew Marlow Rebellion one of its staple real ales. Pub classics include spaghetti with meatballs; battered haddock, chips and peas; fried chicken burger; and Caesar salad, with lighter meals, small plates and snacks at lunchtime.

Open all day, all week Enterprise Inns 13 portions/menu notice required

MOULSOE

The Carrington Arms

Tel **01908 218050** | **Cranfield Road, MK16 0HB**
Web **www.thecarringtonarms.co.uk**
Dir ***M1 junction 14, A509 to Newport Pagnell 100 yards, turn right signed Moulsoe and Cranfield. Pub on right.***

The family-run Carrington in the pretty village of Moulsoe combines tradition with modern hospitality. Real ales and a good wine list are a given, but the pub is most famous for its fresh meat counter where customers can talk through their selection with the chef.

NEWTON BLOSSOMVILLE

The Old Mill ★★★ INN

Tel **01234 881273** | **MK43 8AN**
Web **www.oldmill-newtonblossomville.co.uk**
Dir ***A509 north of Milton Keynes. Right to village. Or A428 from Bedford. In Turvey, turn left to village.***

A handsome inn in a village of thatched cottages in the tranquil Ouse Valley; The Old Mill is an ideal base to stay over. The beer range changes with the seasons, whilst the choice on the menu relies heavily on what's available from local suppliers.

NEWTON LONGVILLE

The Crooked Billet

Tel **01908 373936** | **2 Westbrook End, MK17 0DF**
Web **crookedbilletmk.co.uk**
Dir ***M1 junction 13, A421 towards Buckingham. 6 miles. At Bottledump roundabout 1st left signed Newton Longville. Pub on right in village.***

A thatched former farmhouse dating back to 1600, The Crooked Billet is located just south west of Milton Keynes. The pub has a real family feel for drinkers who can enjoy glasses of Abbot Ale or one of the wines served by the glass.

SEER GREEN

The Jolly Cricketers

Tel **01494 676308** | **24 Chalfont Road, HP9 2YG**
Web **www.thejollycricketers.co.uk**
Dir ***M40 junction 2, A355 signed Beaconsfield A40, Amersham. At Pyebush roundabout 1st exit, A40 signed Beaconsfield, Amersham, A355. At roundabout, A355 signed Amersham. Right into Longbottom Lane signed Seer Green. Left into Bottom Lane, right into Orchard Road, left into Church Road, right into Chalfont Road.***

Top notch food in a homely setting

This 19th-century, wisteria-clad free house in the heart of the picture-perfect Seer Green appeals to all-comers: locals chatting over pints of Marlow's Rebellion IPA, quiz addicts on Sunday nights, live music fans, beer festival-goers and dog-walkers. The modern, AA-Rosette menu could include local pigeon, sausage and smoked bacon terrine; or Wye Valley kipper fillet, potato farl, hen's egg and crème fraîche. Follow with slow-roast shoulder of lamb, white wine, root vegetables, butter beans; or grilled fillet of halibut, rösti, spinach, chorizo and lemon butter. For dessert, maybe treacle tart and clotted cream. Beer festivals are held on Easter weekend and the Summer Bank Holiday in August.

Open all day, all week Mon to Thu 12–11.30 (Fri to Sat 12–12 Sun 12–10.30) Free House 16 portions/menu

NORTH MARSTON

The Pilgrim

Tel **01296 670969 | 25 High Street, MK18 3PD**
Web **www.thepilgrimpub.co.uk**
Dir ***From Aylesbury take A413 towards Buckingham. In Whitchurch turn left and follow North Marston sign. Right to North Marston, approximately 1 mile to pub.***

A holy well in the village, reputedly the site of many miracles in the Middle Ages, was once reason enough for pilgrims to make the journey to North Marston. Now, Brett and Nadia Newman manage the kitchen and front of house respectively at this 300-year-old pub. They have worked hard to build local loyalty with their burgers, quizzes, curries and open mic evenings. The weekly-changing menus feature home-grown produce in dishes such as organic beef shin, spelt and local ale stew.

Open all year 12–3 5–11 (Fri 12–3 5–12 Sat 12–12 Sun 12–6) Closed Sun evening and Mon Free House 10 from £13 portions Wi-fi P notice required

SEER GREEN

The Jolly Cricketers – see page 51

SKIRMETT

The Frog PICK OF THE PUBS

Tel **01491 638996 | RG9 6TG**
Web **www.thefrogatskirmett.co.uk**
Dir ***Exit A4155 at Mill End, pub in 3 miles.***

An 18th-century coaching inn within the Chilterns Area of Outstanding Natural Beauty. Winter warmth is guaranteed in the charming public bar where oak beams, bare floorboards and leather seating combine with colourful textiles to create a welcoming atmosphere. Where better to settle with a pint of Leaping Frog or Henry's Original IPA? Alternatively, 15 wines are sold by the glass, or push the boat out and share a sparkler from the Hambleden vineyard just down the road. The menu offers deli boards and perhaps a starter of crisp fried south coast squid; or haggis, neeps and tatties, followed by fillet of pork Wellington; pie of the day; or slow-braised oxtail.

Open 11.30–3 6–11 Closed 25 Dec, Mon (Jan and Feb), Sun evening (Oct to Apr) Free House 15 portions/menu P

STOKE MANDEVILLE

The Bell

Tel **01296 612434 | 29 Lower Road, HP22 5XA**
Web **www.bellstokemandeville.co.uk**
Dir ***From south and east follow signs from Stoke Mandeville towards Stoke Mandeville Hospital, pub on left in 200 yards after primary school. From north and west pass Stoke Mandeville Hospital on left, pub approximately 1 mile on right.***

The Bell has a sign that reads 'Dogs, children and muddy boots welcome', thereby setting the tone of a visit to this traditional village pub. Physiotherapists at nearby Stoke Mandeville hospital have been known to set The Bell as an objective for newly mobile patients.

TURVILLE

The Bull & Butcher PICK OF THE PUBS

Tel **01491 638283 | RG9 6QU**
Web **www.thebullandbutcher.com**
Dir ***M40 junction 5, follow Ibstone signs. Right at T-junction. Pub 0.25 mile on left.***

The village of Turville is set in an Area of Outstanding Natural Beauty, and this Grade II listed, 16th-century inn, originally known as the 'Bullen Butcher', (a reference to Henry VIII's treatment of his second wife Anne Boleyn), enjoys beautiful country views. The Well Bar and the Windmill Lounge both feature original beams, open fires and a friendly, laid-back atmosphere. You can expect to find locally sourced produce on the menus, where hearty pub classics rub shoulders with less traditional offerings. The speciality is home-made pies, with a choice of pastry and accompaniments, while dinner might begin with grilled garlic king prawns, or ham hock terrine with piccalilli; before moving on to roasted butternut and gorgonzola ravioli with rocket salad and sage butter dressing.

Open all week summer 12–11 (Sat noon–1am) winter 12–3 5.30–11 Brakspear 36 menus Wi-fi P notice required

TURWESTON

The Stratton Arms

Tel **01280 704956** | **Main Street, NN13 5JX**
Dir ***From A43 (north-east of Brackley) take A422 towards Buckingham. Left to Turweston. Through village, pub on left.***

Like many of the other buildings in this rather straggly village, the pub is built of mellow local stone. Landlord Philip Caley offers a good range of ales – Bass, London Pride, Otter and more. His menu is full of classic tried and tested, home-made pub food, from chilli con carne with rice; wholetail scampi, chips and peas; to Barnsley chop and mash. Freshly baked pizzas can be taken home to eat. The River Great Ouse is at the end of the large garden.

Open all day, all week Enterprise Inns portions/menu Wi-fi notice required

WEST WYCOMBE

The George and Dragon Hotel

Tel **01494 535340** | **High Street, HP14 3AB**
Web **www.georgeanddragonhotel.com**
Dir ***On A40.***

West Wycombe was owned by the Dashwood family until the Wall Street Crash in 1929 forced them to sell it. It was bought by the Royal Society of Arts which, in 1934, after extensive repairs, handed the village, including the 14th-century inn, over to the National Trust, its owner ever since. Ever-reliable real ales include St Austell Tribute and Hook Norton Hooky Gold, while gins almost span the alphabet from Bathtub to Warner Edwards rhubarb. The varied menu offers home-made sweet potato, chickpea and herb falafel with tzatziki; chargrilled rare breed Dexter beefburger with applewood smoked Swiss cheese, and other grills; and seafood and prawn linguine with white wine velouté. A small range of sandwiches includes classic toasted club – chargrilled chicken, crispy bacon, egg, tomato and lettuce.

Open all day, all week 12–12 (Fri to Sat noon–1am Sun 12–11.30) Enterprise Inns 9 from £11.50 portions/menu Wi-fi notice required

WHEELER END

The Chequers Inn

Tel **01494 883070** | **Bullocks Farm Lane, HP14 3NH**
Web **thechequersinnwheelerend.co.uk**
Dir ***4 miles north of Marlow.***

This picturesque 16th-century inn, with its low-beamed ceilings, roaring winter fires and two attractive beer gardens, is ideally located for walkers on the edge of Wheeler End Common (families and dogs are welcome).

WOOBURN COMMON

Chequers Inn ★★★

HOTEL **PICK OF THE PUBS**

Tel **01628 529575** | **Kiln Lane, HP10 0JQ**
Web **www.chequers-inn.com**
Dir ***M40 junction 2, A40 through Beaconsfield towards High Wycombe. Left into Broad Lane, signed Taplow/Burnham/Wooburn Common. 2 miles to pub.***

The atmosphere of much of this 17th-century coaching inn is still firmly of the past, especially in the open-fired bar, where the hand-tooled oak beams and posts, and timeworn flagstone and wooden floors shrug off the passage of time. Contrast then the 21st-century chic lounge, with leather sofas and chairs, low tables and greenery while outside, sheltering the patio and flowery garden, stands a magnificent old oak tree. Beers are Rebellion IPA and Smuggler and there are 14 wines by the glass. The two AA-Rosette restaurant menu features ever-changing dishes such as calves' liver with olive oil mash, bacon and green beans; coconut crusted cod with wilted spinach and chorizo butter sauce; and Stilton and red onion tart.

Open all day, all week 12–12 Free House 14 from £13.95 portions/menu Wi-fi

CAMBRIDGESHIRE

ABBOTS RIPTON

The Abbot's Elm

Tel **01487 773773** | **PE28 2PA**
Web **www.theabbotselm.co.uk**
Dir ***From A141 follow Abbots Ripton signs.***

Situated in the village of Abbots Ripton, the exterior of this pub looks pretty much as it has done over the centuries but step inside and you'll find that the open-plan bar and restaurant are bathed in natural light.

BALSHAM

The Black Bull Inn ★★★★

INN **PICK OF THE PUBS**

Tel **01223 893844** | **27 High Street, CB21 4DJ**
Web **www.blackbull-balsham.co.uk**
Dir ***From south: M11 junction 9, A11 towards Newmarket, follow Balsham signs. From north: M11 junction 10, A505 signed Newmarket (A11), onto A11, follow Balsham signs.***

Here since the 16th century and still going strong, with a new dining area in the listed barn, featuring an oak-panelled, high-vaulted ceiling. The bar serves Adnams and Woodforde's East Anglian real ales and ciders, sandwiches, baguettes, burgers and home-made shortcrust pastry pies. The restaurant menu might offer pan-roasted pork tenderloin rolled in sage crumbs, parsnip purée, parsnip crisps, prunes and whisky sauce. Old favourites, sticky toffee pudding with butterscotch sauce and vanilla ice cream, and lemon meringue tart appear as desserts.

Open all day, all week Free House 20 portions/menu notice required

BARRINGTON

The Royal Oak

Tel **01223 870791** | **31 West Green, CB22 7RZ**
Web **www.royaloakbarrington.net**
Dir ***South-west of Cambridge.***

One of the oldest thatched and timbered pubs in England, this rambling 16th-century building overlooks a 30-acre village green. The smart interior is contemporary; and popular pub classics feature on the menu.

BOURN

The Willow Tree

Tel **01954 719775** | **29 High Street, CB23 2SQ**
Web **www.feastandfrolic.co.uk/the-willow-tree**
Dir ***From Royston on A1198, right on B1046 signed Bourn. Pub in village on right (8 miles from Cambridge).***

Just off Ermine Street, the old Roman road from London to York, is Shaina Galvin's mansard-roofed village pub. A white picket fence surrounds the street frontage, while in the large rear garden are the majestic eponymous willow tree, a heated terrace, a swing and deckchairs.

CAMBRIDGE

The Anchor Pub, Dining & River Terrace

Tel **01223 353554** | **Silver Street, CB3 9EL**
Web **www.anchorcambridge.com**
Dir ***Phone for detailed directions.***

Bordering Queens' College is a medieval lane, at the end of which stands this attractive pub, right by the bridge over the River Cam. Head for the riverside patio with a local real ale, or an Aspalls cider, and watch rookie punters struggling with their tricky craft – another definition of pole position, perhaps. A good choice of food includes flat-iron chicken, watercress salad, wild garlic butter and rosemary salt fries; plus a selection of steaks, and beer-battered fish and chips.

Open all day, all week Sun to Thu 11–11 (Fri to Sat 11am–midnight) Metropolitan Pub Company 15 menus notice required

The Old Spring

Tel **01223 357228** | **1 Ferry Path, CB4 1HB**
Web **www.theoldspring.co.uk**
Dir ***Just off Chesterton Road, (A1303) in city centre.***

A bustling pub in the leafy suburb of De Freville, just a short stroll from the River Cam. The bright and airy interior offers rug-covered wooden floors, comfy sofas and large family tables. Sip a pint of Elgood's Cambridge Bitter, one of the real ales on tap while choosing from over a dozen main courses plus specials – perhaps Cumberland sausage and mash.

Open all day, all week 11.30–11 (Sun 12–10.30) Greene King 20 portions/menu

The Punter

Tel **01223 363322 | 3 Pound Hill, CB3 0AE**
Web **www.thepuntercambridge.com**
Dir ***Phone for detailed directions.***

Two minutes' walk from the city centre, this former coaching house is popular with post-grads, locals and dog lovers alike who create a happy mood with their chatter and laughter. The interior is an eclectic mix of previously loved hand-me-downs, comfy sofas, sturdy school chairs, and pictures and paintings jostling for space on the walls. Drinkers can enjoy local ales but it seems it's the modern menu that draws people in – confit duck cassoulet with herb butter; and baked haloumi falafel with winter tabbouleh perhaps.

Open all day, all week Closed 25–27 Dec Punch Taverns 13 portions Wi-fi

COTON

The Plough

Tel **01954 210489 | 2 High Street, CB23 7PL**
Web **www.theploughcoton.co.uk**
Dir ***M11 junctions 12 or 13. Follow Coton signs.***

Nudging the cricket pitches and grassy recreation ground, this village pub attracts savvy diners escaping the hubbub of nearby Cambridge. The cool, chic interior creates a relaxing atmosphere in which to enjoy the modern menus. Lunchtime brings choices such as upmarket pizzas, a fish platter and baked camembert. Come the evening, expect dishes such as potted beef, piccalilli and toast; and glazed pork belly, burnt apple purée, smoked mash and hispi cabbage. In summer, children can happily play in the spacious garden.

Open all day, all week Enterprise Inns portions/ menu Wi-fi P *notice required*

DUXFORD

The John Barleycorn

PICK OF THE PUBS

Tel **01223 832699 | 3 Moorfield Road, CB22 4PP**
Web **www.johnbarleycorn.co.uk**
Dir ***Exit A505 into Duxford.***

Built in 1660, this thatched, former coach house became the John Barleycorn in the mid-19th century. The name first appeared in an old folksong as the personification of malting barley and the beer and whisky that results. During World War II the brave young airmen of Group Captain Douglas Bader's Duxford Wing drank here in what today is a softly-lit bar with a large brick fireplace, old tiled floor, cushioned pews and hop-adorned beams. Food is a big draw, whether sandwiches and jacket potatoes, the tzatziki and charcuterie grazing boards; smoked Gressingham duck cassoulet with Puy lentils and pancetta; chargrilled supreme of tuna marinated in lime and coriander, stir-fried pak choi and ginger and carrot broth; or Hereford and Limousin steaks. Finish with vanilla and strawberry crème brûlée.

Open all day, all week Greene King 12 from £10.95 menus Wi-fi P

ELSWORTH

The George and Dragon

Tel **01954 267236 | 41 Boxworth Road, CB23 4JQ**
Web **www.georgeanddragon-elsworth.co.uk**
Dir ***Follow Elsworth signs from either A428 or A14.***

If you're in Cambridge, Huntingdon or St Ives and fancy a meal out of town, then head here. Inside it's a good size, with beams and brass and a good real ale selection. Crusty baguettes, sandwiches, ploughman's and omelettes will satisfy your light lunch expectations.

ELY

The Anchor Inn ★★★★ INN

PICK OF THE PUBS

Tel **01353 778537 | Sutton Gault, CB6 2BD**
Web **anchor-inn-restaurant.co.uk**
Dir ***From A14, B1050 to Earith, take B1381 to Sutton. Sutton Gault on left.***

Today, low beams, dark wood panelling, scrubbed pine tables, gently undulating tiled floors, antique prints and log fires create the intimate character of this family-run free house. Twelve wines served by the glass and a selection of East Anglian real ales will be found in the bar. The kitchen is proud to source local ingredients for their modern British cuisine. Meals may be enjoyed on the terrace overlooking the river.

Open all day, all week 11.30–10.30 Closed 25–26 Dec evening Free House 12 from £13 portions/ menu Wi-fi P *notice required*

FEN DITTON

Ancient Shepherds

Tel **01223 293280** | **High Street, CB5 8ST**
Web **www.fenditton.pub**
Dir ***From A14 take B1047 signed Cambridge/Airport.***

Originally three cottages in the 16th century, the Ancient Order of Shepherds used to meet here to discuss ovine matters over a pint or three. Today's customers in the bars, dining room or beer garden are more likely to talk about whether to order seafood linguine; fish and chips; game (in season); a beef or halloumi burger; or maybe Niçoise salad. Real ales are from Adnams and Greene King. On the nearby River Cam, an eccentric rowing race called 'The Bumps' takes place.

Open all week 12–3 5–11 (Fri to Sat 12–11 Sun 12–10) Closed 25 Dec Free House 15 from £11.95 portions/menu notice required

FENSTANTON

King William IV

Tel **01480 462467** | **High Street, PE28 9JF**
Web **www.kingwilliam1vfenstanton.co.uk**
Dir ***On A14 between Hunstanton and Cambridge follow Fenstanton signs.***

This rambling 17th-century village pub features oak beams, old brickwork and a wonderful central fireplace. Lunchtime offerings include a range of hot and cold sandwiches, wraps and salads as well as a full menu. Occasionally, there's live music on a Sunday afternoon.

FORDHAM

White Pheasant

PICK OF THE PUBS

Tel **01638 720414** | **CB7 5LQ**
Web **www.whitepheasant.com**
Dir ***From Newmarket A142 to Ely, approximately 5 miles to Fordham. Pub on left in village.***

This 18th-century building stands in a fenland village. Take a pint of Adnams or a glass of wine while you peruse the menu – cooking is taken seriously here, with quality, presentation and flavour taking top priority; specials change daily. Starters may include poached salmon with tomatoes, pink grapefruit and pickled cucumber; or duck spring rolls with sweet chilli mayonnaise. Followed by sea trout with crab risotto, cavolo nero and dill oil; game pie with creamed potato and braised red cabbage; or venison sausage and mash with buttered kale. Desserts are tempting too – perhaps blackberry mousse with pear, red wine and flapjack. If you fancy something less sweet, the British cheese selection will fit the bill.

Open all year Tue to Sat 12–2.30 6.30–9.30 (Sun 12–3.30) Closed Sun evening and Mon Free House 12 from £14.50 portions notice required

GLINTON

The Blue Bell – see opposite

GRANTCHESTER

The Red Lion

Tel **01223 840121** | **33 High Street, CB3 9NF**
Web **www.redliongrantchester.co.uk**
Dir ***M11 junction 11, A1309 signed city centre. In Trumpington at lights into Maris Lane. At T-junction left into Grantchester Road; pass church in Grantchester on left, next right to pub. Or from M11 junction 12 follow Grantchester signs.***

Its village location, carefully trimmed thatch, and warm welcome for muddy boots and dogs make The Red Lion popular with Cambridge folk who fancy a Sunday stroll along the Cam's banks. Food served all day from midday onwards is based on British seasonal produce.

The Rupert Brooke

Tel **01223 841875** | **2 Broadway, CB3 9NQ**
Web **www.therupertbrooke.com**
Dir ***M11 junction 12, follow Grantchester signs.***

Named after the English poet who lived at the Old Vicarage, this is a stylish pub located alongside the River Cam. A couple of miles from the centre of Cambridge, it can be accessed via the river path, although some customers arrive by punt.

GREAT ABINGTON

Three Tuns INN

Tel **01223 891467** | **75 High Street, CB21 6AB**
Web **www.thethreetuns-greatabington.co.uk**
Dir ***A11 onto A1307 (Haverhill). Right signed Abington. Pub on left.***

A rashly shouted 'Oi!' here might well bring the chef running out from his kitchen, for that's his

GLINTON

The Blue Bell

Tel **01733 252285** | **10 High Street, PE6 7LS**
Web **www.thebluebellglinton.co.uk**
Dir ***Phone for detailed directions.***

Children- and dog-friendly village pub

Chef Will Frankgate and his wife Kelly run this charming 18th-century village pub that looks across an extensive front lawn to the village church. The bar stocks a good selection of real ales, draught and bottled beers and ciders, and sandwiches are served at lunchtime. On the periodically updated menus expect traditional pub classics, such as baked fisherman's pie; and partly-matured prime beef steak. Dinner in the Long Room just off the bar, could be pot-steamed Exmouth mussels; pan-roasted Skrei cod fillet; Stilton and radicchio salad; braised pork belly; battered fish and chips; or baked field mushroom with Mediterranean vegetables. On a warm summer's day, the contemporary, light-filled Garden Room's bi-fold doors open to reveal the adjoining outside eating area, so creating the perfect place to enjoy a relaxing meal.

Open all day, all week ⛁ *Greene King* 👪 *portions/menu* Ⓟ ❀ 🚌 *notice required*

name. The highly experienced Oi is from Thailand and his huge range of traditional Thai food embraces starters and soups; beef, chicken, duck, pork and prawn stir-fries; classic green, red, yellow, massaman, penang and jungle curries; and fish dishes, such as sea bass in chilli sauce. Among the 200 beers, many from local breweries, available in the bar is Austrian Stiegl lager on tap.

Open all week 12–2 6–11 (Fri to Sun 12–11) Closed 1 Jan ⛁ *Free House* 👪 🐕 Wi-fi Ⓟ ❀ 🚌 *notice required*

GREAT WILBRAHAM

The Carpenters Arms

Tel **01223 882093** | **10 High Street, CB21 5JD**
Web **www.carpentersarmsgastropub.co.uk**
Dir ***From A11 follow "The Wilbraham" signs. Into Great Wilbraham, right at junction, pub 150 yards on left.***

This warm and friendly country pub and restaurant is both a multiple award winner and the birthplace of Crafty Beers microbrewery, whence come the bar's Carpenters Cask and Sauvignon Blonde ales. Understandably, given that in the past the owners ran a restaurant in France, French dishes, such as cassoulet and tartiflette, partner pub favourites like decidedly British beer-battered fish and chips, and Sunday roasts. Also, unsurprisingly, there's French wines as well as New World choices.

Open 11.30–3 6.30–11 Closed 26 Dec, 1 Jan, 1 week Nov and 1 week Feb, Sun evening, Mon and Tue ⛁ *Free House* 🍽 *from £9.95* 👪 *portions/menu* Wi-fi Ⓟ ❀ 🚌 *notice required*

HARDWICK

The Blue Lion

Tel **01954 210328** | **74 Main Street, CB23 7QU**
Web **www.bluelionhardwick.co.uk**
Dir ***West of Cambridge. In village centre.***

A pub since 1737, The Blue Lion stands well back from Hardwick's main thoroughfare. The owners raise rare-breed sheep, which you might find on the menu; if not, start with roast sweet potato, warm houmous, red cabbage and pomegranate salad followed by 24-hour short-rib of beef with dauphinoise potato, and oxtail and Stilton shortbread; or Cajun gumbo chicken with chorizo and crayfish.

Open all day, all week ⛁ *Greene King* 🍷 *10* 🍽 *from £10.50* 👪 *portions/menu* 🐕 Wi-fi Ⓟ ❀ 🚌 *notice required*

HEMINGFORD GREY

The Cock Pub and Restaurant

PICK OF THE PUBS

Tel **01480 463609 | 47 High Street, PE28 9BJ**
Web **www.cambscuisine.co.uk**
Dir ***Between A14 junctions 25 and 26, follow village signs.***

A handsome 17th-century pub on the main street of the charming village of Hemingford Grey, The Cock stands among thatched, timbered and brick cottages. Although it's only a mile from the busy A14, it feels like a world away. Other than the peaceful location, the detour is well worth taking as the food on offer is excellent – the set lunch menu is a steal. Cooking is modern British, with the occasional foray further afield.

HINXTON

The Red Lion Inn ★★★★

INN PICK OF THE PUBS

Tel **01799 530601 | 32 High Street, CB10 1QY**
Web **www.redlionhinxton.co.uk**
Dir ***Northbound only: M11 junction 9, towards A11, left onto A1301. Left to Hinxton. Or M11 junction 10, A505 towards A11/Newmarket. At roundabout take 3rd exit onto A1301, right to Hinxton.***

This 16th-century, pink-washed free house and restaurant has a pretty walled garden and dovecote, and a patio overlooking the church. Four local real ales await your order in the low-ceilinged and wood-floored bar; three of them – Woodforde's Wherry, Crafty Sauvignon Blonde and own label Red & Black – are fixtures, the fourth a local guest brew. Over 20 wines are served by the glass. It's good to eat in the bar, but you might prefer the high-raftered, L-shaped restaurant, which is similarly furnished with high-backed settles. The menu gives a taste of the modern British approach to food, with braised pork cheeks with celeriac purée and remoulade for starters; mains such as pesto gnocchi with purple sprouting broccoli, tomato concasse and broad beans; and puddings like salted caramel tart.

Open all day, all week Free House 22 from £12 portions/menu Wi-fi notice required

HISTON

Red Lion

Tel **01223 564437 | 27 High Street, CB24 9JD**
Web **www.theredlionhiston.co.uk**
Dir ***M11 junction 14, A14 towards. Exit at junction 32 onto B1049 for Histon.***

A pub since 1836, this popular village local on Cambridge's northern fringe has been run by Mark Donachy for more than two decades. A dyed-in-the-wool pub man, Mark's real ales include Oakham Bishops Farewell, as well as Pickled Pig Porker's Snout cider.

HORNINGSEA

The Crown & Punchbowl

Tel **01223 860643 | CB25 9JG**
Web **thecrownandpunchbowl.co.uk**
Dir ***A14 junction 34, A14 towards Newmarket. Left onto B1047 signed Horningsea. Pub on left in Village.***

Dating back to 1764, this tiled and whitewashed former coaching inn stands next to a church in a little one-street village on the outskirts of Cambridge. The pub includes a beer garden at the front, a conservatory and modern kitchen.

KEYSTON

Pheasant Inn PICK OF THE PUBS

Tel **01832 710241 | Village Loop Road, PE28 0RE**
Web **www.thepheasant-keyston.co.uk**
Dir ***0.5 mile from A14, clearly signed, 10 miles west of Huntingdon, 14 miles east of Kettering.***

This pretty thatched pub was bought by the Hoskins family in 1964 and it has been serving good food ever since. Continuing that tradition are today's owners, Simon Cadge and Gerda Koedijk, while John Hoskins, a Master of Wine, compiles the wine list. There's a large oak-beamed bar, serving pints of Brewster's Hophead and Digfield Ales Barnwell Bitter, while at the rear, the Garden Room surveys a sunny patio. You might begin with chargrilled John Dory with chickpeas, grilled lemon and samphire, followed by braised Scotch beef with horseradish mash. Finish with damson cheesecake with plum sauce and toasted almonds.

Open 12–3 6–11 (Sun 12–5) Closed 2–16 Jan, Sun evening and Mon Free House 16 portions/menu Wi-fi notice required

MADINGLEY

The Three Horseshoes

PICK OF THE PUBS

Tel **01954 210221** | **High Street, CB23 8AB**
Web **www.cambscuisine.com/three-horseshoes**
Dir ***M11 junction 13, 1.5 miles from A14.***

Chimneys of mellow brick pierce the thick thatch of this cute village inn outside Cambridge. Between the main building and the beer garden, a conservatory restaurant bathes in dappled light cast by the mature trees that edge this plot in what must be one of the county's most charming villages. With beers from the likes of Adnams and 17 wines by the glass, the bar attracts a good following, and the food emerging from the kitchen takes the treat to another level. A starter of fettuccine with wild mushrooms and parmesan might lead on to roast partridge with Jerusalem artichoke purée, wild mushrooms and caramelised shallots. Menus change seasonally; children's portions are available.

Open all week 12–3 6–11 (Sun 12–10) Free House 17 portions/menu Wi-fi notice required

NEWTON

The Queen's Head

Tel **01223 870436** | **Fowlmere Road, CB22 7PG**
Dir ***6 miles south of Cambridge on B1368, 1.5 miles off A10 at Harston, 4 miles from A505.***

The same family has owned and operated this tiny and very traditional village pub for some 50 years. Unchanging and entirely unmarred by gimmickry, the bars with log fires, pine settles and old school benches, draw an eclectic clientele, from Cambridge dons to local farm workers. They all come for tip-top Adnams ale direct from the barrel, the friendly atmosphere and straightforward food. As well as pâtes and sausage rolls – at lunch, soup, sandwiches and Aga-baked potatoes; in the evening – soup, cold platters, and toast and beef dripping.

Open all week 11.30–2.30 6–11 (Sun 12–2.30 7–10.30) Closed 25–26 Dec Free House from £3.50 portions notice required

OFFORD D'ARCY

The Horseshoe Inn

Tel **01480 810293** | **90 High Street, PE19 5RH**
Web **www.theoffordshoe.co.uk**
Dir ***Between Huntingdon and St Neots. 1.5 miles from Buckden on A1.***

Behind this substantial, gabled old farmhouse, a long, grassy beer garden stretches to meadows fringing the Great Ouse Valley with its countless ponds and lakes. Tranquil territory in which to sup renowned East Anglian real ales, supplemented each mid-summer by a beer festival.

PETERBOROUGH

The Brewery Tap

Tel **01733 358500** | **80 Westgate, PE1 2AA**
Web **www.thebrewery-tap.com**
Dir ***Opposite bus station.***

Home to the multi-award winning Oakham Brewery and one of the largest brewpubs in Europe, this striking pub is located in the old labour exchange on Westgate. More than five real ales and a vast range of bottled beers are on offer and the kitchen is run by Thai chefs producing delicious and authentic Thai dishes. Look out for live music nights, and DJs on Saturdays.

Open all day, all week Closed 25–26 Dec, 1 Jan Free House 10 from £7.95 portions/menu Wi-fi

Charters Bar & East Restaurant

Tel **01733 315700** | **Upper Deck, Town Bridge, PE1 1FP**
Web **www.charters-bar.com**
Dir ***A1/A47 towards Wisbech, 2 miles to city centre and town bridge (River Nene). Barge moored at Town Bridge (west side).***

The largest floating real ale emporium in Britain, this 176-foot converted barge arrived from Holland in 1991 and is now a haven for real ale and cider lovers. Twelve handpumps dispense a continually changing repertoire of cask ales, craft and foreign beers, while entertainment, live music and an Easter beer festival are regular features.

Open all day, all week 12–11 (Fri to Sat noon–2am) Closed 25–26 Dec, 1 Jan Free House 11 Wi-fi notice required

REACH

Dyke's End

Tel **01638 743816** | **CB25 0JD**
Web **www.dykesend.co.uk**
Dir ***Phone for detailed directions.***

Located in the village centre, overlooking the green, this pub is owned by Frances Dylong-Fuller, and has a strong local following for its beers and great home cooking, made from locally-sourced ingredients. Dinner might begin with warm confit duck salad with oranges, walnuts, picked red onion and crispy parsnips, and followed by eight-hour slow-roasted Blythburgh pork belly with mustard mash and curly kale; or local game pie. Bring things to a satisfactory conclusion with autumn fruit crumble or sticky toffee pudding.

Open all week 12–3 6–11 (Sat to Sun 12–11) Free House portions/menu Wi-fi notice required

SPALDWICK

The George

Tel **01480 890293** | **5–7 High Street, PE28 0TD**
Web **www.thegeorgespaldwick.co.uk**
Dir ***In village centre. Just off A14 junction 18.5 miles west of Huntingdon.***

Dating from 1679, this former coaching inn is a successful pub and restaurant; it has moved with the times, yet retained its rustic charm and character. The bar serves local real ales and bar snacks, while the restaurant menu majors on all the pub favourites.

STAPLEFORD

The Rose at Stapleford

Tel **01223 843349** | **81 London Road, CB22 5DG**
Web **www.rose-stapleford.co.uk**
Dir ***Phone for detailed directions.***

The Rose is a traditional village pub close to Cambridge and Duxford Imperial War Museum. Expect a stylish interior, replete with low beams and inglenook fireplaces, and traditional unfussy menus majoring on local produce, fresh Lowestoft fish, and quality Scottish steaks.

STILTON

The Bell Inn Hotel

★★★ HOTEL PICK OF THE PUBS

Tel **01733 241066** | **Great North Road, PE7 3RA**
Web **www.thebellstilton.co.uk**
Dir ***From A1(M) junction 16 follow signs for Stilton. Hotel on main road in village centre.***

Built from local oolitic limestone and Collyweston stone slates, The Bell dates from 1642, although its origins are even older. Characters associated with it include, allegedly, the highwayman Dick Turpin, and, unquestionably, Clark Gable and Joe Louis. A lovely log fire warms the Village Bar, where you can choose from a number of wines by the glass, and its menu is shared with the elegant yet informal Bistro. In the Galleried Restaurant upstairs start maybe with Stilton pâté and passionfruit coulis, then continue with slow-cooked British beef brisket; duck breast with duck leg croquette; or roast cod, chorizo and chickpea cassoulet. Vegans have their own menu. Accommodation includes three Garden Rooms.

Open all week 12–2.30 6–11 (Sat 12–12 Sun 12–11) Closed 25 Dec Free House 13 from £13 portions/menu Wi-fi notice required

STRETHAM

Lazy Otter Pub Restaurant

Tel **01353 649780** | **Cambridge Road, CB6 3LU**
Web **www.lazy-otter.com**
Dir ***Phone for detailed directions.***

A pub here has served fenland watermen for several centuries; today's bustling incarnation is popular with leisure boaters on the River Ouse, which glides past the extensive beer garden. The restaurant offers dishes like steak and kidney pudding; ham, egg and chips; Somerset brie and beetroot tart; and a variety of gourmet burgers including wild boar and apple; and kangaroo. An annual beer and cider festival is held here.

Open all day, all week 7am–11pm (Sun 8.30am–10.30pm) Free House 10 portions/menu Wi-fi

The Red Lion

Tel **01353 648132** | **47 High Street, CB6 3LD**
Web **www.redlionstretham.com**
Dir ***Exit A10 between Cambridge and Ely into Stretham. Left into High Street, pub on right.***

Set in the Cambridgeshire fenlands just a short hop from Ely, this creeper-clad old coaching inn shares the village centre with the church and medieval cross. The courtyard beer garden is a popular spot on warm days, when beers from the likes of Wychwood hit the spot. The licensees have developed a well-liked menu of pub favourites and classic dishes which draws in locals and visitors to the conservatory-style restaurant. 'Piggy three ways' – sausage, chop and belly pork, mash and cabbage – is a popular dish.

Open all day, all week *Free House* *8* *from £9.95* *portions* Wi-fi *notice required*

THORNEY

Dog In A Doublet PICK OF THE PUBS

Tel **01733 202256** | **Northside, PE6 0RW**
Web **www.doginad.co.uk**
Dir ***On B1040 between Thorney and Whittlesey.***

This 16th-century, riverside pub stands beside one of the biggest lock gates in Europe. It's a real success story, with local ales and home-made cider drawing drinkers to the bar with its open fire, while the kitchen create British classics with a twist. There's a street food and bar snack menu of 'nibbling snacks' (Swedish juniper and sweet orange roll mops), 'munching snacks' (home-reared sausage hot dog in a blanket) and 'bowls' (Thai beef salad with lemongrass). Turning to the tempting main menu and there could be a starter of black sesame tempura whitebait with korma mayo; and 24-hour lamb shoulder, shepherd's pie sauce, potato purée, cheese and chive hash and pea medley.

Open all day, all week 5–11 (Fri to Sat 12–11 Sun 12–7 until Apr then 1–11 (Fri to Sat 12–11 Sun 12–7) *Free House* *20* *from £10* *portions/menu* Wi-fi *notice required*

UFFORD

The White Hart ★★★★ INN

Tel **01780 740250** | **Main Street, PE9 3BH**
Web **www.whitehartufford.co.uk**
Dir ***From Stamford take B1443 signed Barnack. Through Barnack, follow signs to Ufford.***

Salvaged old agricultural tools and other farming memorabilia embellish the bar of this 17th-century country inn. Among its four real ales is Grainstore Brewery's Red Kite, Aspall cider and 14 wines are by the glass, selected from an extensive cellar. The Orangery, The Pantry and the garden are three of the five dining areas, where options include Portobello mushroom bruschetta with poached hen's egg; slow-braised lamb shank, creamed potatoes and rich mint jus; and roasted vegetable Wellington, parsnip purée and fondant potato.

Open all day, all week Mon to Thu 9am–11pm (Fri to Sat 9am–midnight Sun 9–9) *Free House* *14* *from £11.95* *portions/menu* Wi-fi *notice required*

WHITTLESFORD

The Tickell Arms

Tel **01223 833025** | **North Road, CB22 4NZ**
Web **www.cambscuisine.com**
Dir ***M11 junction 10, A505 towards Saffron Walden. Left signed Whittlesford.***

Part of the Cambscuisine (that's cuisine from Cambridgeshire) group, this blue-washed village pub stands behind a neat, white picket fence; the car park is entered through wrought-iron gates. Inside the pub are elegant fireplaces, gilt mirrors and whimsical bowler hat-shaped lampshades.

CHESHIRE

ALDFORD

The Grosvenor Arms

PICK OF THE PUBS

Tel **01244 620228** | **Chester Road, CH3 6HJ**
Web **www.grosvenorarms-aldford.co.uk**
Dir ***On B5130, south of Chester.***

With its red brick and black and white timbering, this higgledy-piggledy Brunning & Price pub was designed by Victorian architect John Douglas, who designed around 500 buildings, many of them in Cheshire. The spacious, open-plan interior includes an airy conservatory and a panelled, book-filled library. Smoked haddock, salmon and cod gratin makes a tasty opener to beef rendang; chicken, ham hock and leek pie; pink-roasted duck breast; and Mexican vegetarian burger. A terrace leads into a small, pleasant garden, and on out to the village green.

Open all day, all week Free House 20 from £10.95 portions/menu WI-FI

ALLOSTOCK

The Three Greyhounds Inn
– see opposite

ASTON

The Bhurtpore Inn – see page 64

BROXTON

Egerton Arms

Tel **01829 782241** | **Whitchurch Road, CH3 9JW**
Web **www.egerton-arms.com**
Dir ***On A41 between Whitchurch and Chester.***

Handy for the castle-studded, wooded sandstone ridge that splits Cheshire in two, this gabled roadside restaurant, bar and grill offers diners and drinkers the best of the county's produce. Weetwood Brewery ales populate the bar, whilst the frequently-changing menu offers both pub grub and modern classics.

BUNBURY

The Dysart Arms **PICK OF THE PUBS**

Tel **01829 260183** | **Bowes Gate Road, CW6 9PH**
Web **www.brunningandprice.co.uk/dysart**
Dir ***Between A49 and A51, by Shropshire Union Canal.***

Pub group Brunning & Price care hugely about their properties, as is evident here. Named after local landowners, the Earls of Dysart, this classic village pub has open fires, lots of old oak, and properly filled bookcases – not a job lot from a jumble sale. Built in the mid-18th century, this was at one time simultaneously a farmhouse, abattoir and pub. Views from the garden take in two castles and the parish church.

BURLEYDAM

The Combermere Arms

Tel **01948 871223** | **SY13 4AT**
Web **www.brunningandprice.co.uk/combermere**
Dir ***From Whitchurch take A525 towards Nantwich, at Newcastle/Audlem/Woore sign, turn right at junction. Pub 100 yards on right.***

Local shoots, walkers and town folk frequent this classic 17th-century country inn. Full of character and warmth, it has three roaring fires and a wealth of oak, nooks and crannies, pictures and old furniture. There is a great choice of real ales.

BURWARDSLEY

The Pheasant Inn – see page 65

CHELFORD

Egerton Arms

Tel **01625 861366** | **Knutsford Road, SK11 9BB**
Web **www.chelfordegertonarms.co.uk**
Dir ***On A537 (Knutsford to Macclesfield road).***

The 16th-century Egerton Arms is efficiently and enthusiastically run by Jeremy Hague. Low beams, large fireplaces, eccentric antiques and a long bar with brass pumps characterise the interior. Local real ales are served in the bar, while the 100-seat restaurant offers a comprehensive menu full of pub classics. There's a deli adjoining the pub which sells a wide choice of artisan produce.

Open all day, all week 12–12 Free House 9 from £12 portions/menu WI-FI *notice required*

ALLOSTOCK

The Three Greyhounds Inn

Tel **01565 723455** | **Holmes Chapel Road, WA16 9JY**
Web **www.thethreegreyhoundsinn.co.uk**
Dir ***South from Allostock on A50. Right on B5082 signed Northwich. Over M6, pub on right.***

Cosy atmosphere and well-kept ales

This 300-year-old former farmhouse is a warren of atmospheric rooms, with exposed beams, rugs on wooden floors, log fires in brick fireplaces, candles on old tables, and heaps of quirky touches. Go there for a choice of five local ales – perhaps Shropshire Gold, Merlin's Gold, Weetwood's Eastgate, Tatton's Best and Almighty Allostock, over 50 brandies (ask to see their Brandy Bible), and a good selection of New and Old World wines. Turning to the food, maybe start with a snack of cauliflower fritters with garlic mayonnaise, or a Cheshire pork pie with piccallili; look out for the seafood trawler board (enough for two, or maybe even three); chicken, ham, leek and tarragon pie; sweet potato, chickpea and spinach curry; and root vegetable and pearl barley hotpot. Do book for a memorable Sunday lunch. Dogs are welcome in the bar area and garden. Classic vehicle owners can join the car club.

Open all day, all week 🛢 *Free House* 🍷 *15* 🍽 *from £11.95* 👪 *portions* Ⓟ ✿ 🚌 *notice required*

ASTON

The Bhurtpore Inn

Tel 01270 780917 | Wrenbury Road, CW5 8DQ
Web www.bhurtpore.co.uk
Dir *Just off A530 between Nantwich and Whitchurch. Follow Wrenbury signs at crossroads in village.*

Friendly traditional inn with real community spirit

PICK OF THE PUBS

A pub since at least 1778, when it was called the Queen's Head. It subsequently became the Red Lion, but it was Lord Combermere's success at the Siege of Bhurtpore in India in 1826 that inspired the name that has stuck. Simon and Nicky George came across it in 1991, boarded-up and stripped out. Simon is a direct descendant of Joyce George, who leased the pub from the Combermere Estate in 1849, so was motivated by his family history to take on the hard work of restoring the interior. Since then, 'award-winning' hardly does justice to the accolades heaped upon this hostelry. In the bar, 11 ever-changing real ales are available, mostly from local microbreweries, as are real ciders and continental draught lagers. An annual beer festival, reputedly Cheshire's largest, showcases around 130 real ales. The pub has also been shortlisted many times for the 'National Whisky Pub of the Year' award, and there is a soft drinks menu. Recognition extends to the kitchen too, where unfussy dishes of classic pub fare are prepared using hearty British ingredients.

Open Mon to Thu 12–11.30 (Fri to Sat 12–12, Sun 12–11) Free House

BURWARDSLEY

The Pheasant Inn

 INN

Tel 01829 770434 | CH3 9PF
Web www.thepheasantinn.co.uk
Dir *A41 (Chester to Whitchurch) left signed Tattenhall. Through Tattenhall to Burwardsley. In Burwardsley follow Cheshire Workshops signs.*

PICK OF THE PUBS

Popular pub with magnificent rural views

High on the sandstone ridge known as the Peckforton Hills stands Beeston Castle. Enjoying a similarly lofty position on its west-facing slopes overlooking the Cheshire Plain, is this 300-year-old former farmhouse and barn, where only five families have been licensees since it became an alehouse. Such is its elevation that you can see the Welsh hills and two cathedrals, Liverpool's 23 miles away and, much nearer, Chester's. Particularly familiar with the Pheasant are walkers and hikers on the Sandstone Trail long-distance footpath that links Frodsham on the Mersey with Whitchurch in Shropshire. On a fine day the obvious place to be is in the flower-filled courtyard or on the terrace, but when the weather dictates otherwise grab a space by the big open fire in the wooden-floored, heftily-beamed bar. Here you'll find four real ales, three from the Weetwood Brewery near Tarporley. The kitchen makes extensive use of local produce, while much of the seafood comes from Fleetwood in Lancashire. The daily-changing restaurant menu offers a wide choice of modern British and European dishes.Comfortable en suite accommodation is also available.

Open all day, all week *Free House* 12
portions/menu *notice required*

CHESTER

The Brewery Tap

Tel **01244 340999** | **52–54 Lower Bridge Street, CH1 1RU**
Web **www.the-tap.co.uk**
Dir ***From B5268 in Chester into Lower Bridge Street towards river.***

This historic pub is situated in part of Gamul House, named after Sir Francis Gamul, a wealthy merchant and mayor of Chester who built it in 1620. It is reputedly where Charles I stayed when his troops were defeated at Rowton Moor, shortly before the king's final flight to Wales. Relax with a Thirstquencher ale and enjoy hearty favourites such as pork and rabbit rillettes, prune purée, cornichons and toast; pearl barley risotto; and Spanish pig stomach and white bean stew.

Open all day, all week Closed 25–26 Dec Free House 14 from £10

Old Harkers Arms

Tel **01244 344525** | **1 Russell Street, CH3 5AL**
Web **www.brunningandprice.co.uk**
Dir ***Close to railway station, on canal side.***

Housed in a former Victorian chandler's warehouse beside the Shropshire Union Canal, the tall windows, lofty ceilings, wooden floors and bar constructed from salvaged doors make this one of Chester's more unusual pubs. The bar offers over 100 malt whiskies plus ales from a range of breweries. The daily-changing menu from light dishes such as smoked haddock and leek spring roll to main courses like slow-braised shoulder of lamb with dauphinoise potatoes.

Open all day, all week 10.30am–11pm (Sat 10am–11pm Sun 10am–10.30pm) Closed 25 Dec Free House 15 from £10.95

The Stamford Bridge

Tel **01829 740229** | **CH3 7HN**
Web **www.stamfordbridgeinn.co.uk**
Dir ***A51 from Chester towards Tarporley, left at lights, pub on left.***

This city-outskirts inn has extensive views from its beer garden across the Cheshire Plain. Inside, country-house formality meets cottage homeliness – heavy beams, open fires with precision-cut logs, and well-stocked bookshelves. Lunchtime offers sandwiches, wraps and focaccias, while evening diners can expect a good choice of fish dishes such as whole roasted sea bass, wild rice, pak choi and red Thai sauce; and meat dishes, perhaps toad in the hole; or venison loin; plus steaks, pies and vegetarian options such as tomato and roasted red pepper risotto.

Open all day, all week 12–10.30 (Fri to Sat 12–11 25 Dec 12–6 31 Dec 12–7) Hydes Brewery 14 from £9.95 portions/menu notice required

CHOLMONDELEY

The Cholmondeley Arms – see opposite

CHRISTLETON

Ring O'Bells

Tel **01244 335422** | **Village Road, CH3 7AS**
Web **www.ringobellschester.co.uk**
Dir ***3 miles from Chester between A51 towards Nantwich and A41 towards Whitchurch.***

Much of the appeal of this spruced-up village pub is the scope of events that draw drinkers and diners. Wine tastings, networking events, excellent offers and welcoming staff are just a few of the reasons why people keep on returning. The bar stocks real ale from Chester's Spitting Feathers brewery, as well as representatives from Cheshire Brew Brothers. Good use of local produce is evident on seasonal menus.

Open all day, all week Trust Inns from £8 portions/menu notice required

CHURCH MINSHULL

The Badger Inn

Tel **01270 522348** | **Cross Lane, CW5 6DY**
Web **www.badgerinn.co.uk**
Dir ***From A350 between Crewe and Middlewich follow Church Minshull signs.***

This brick-built, late 18th-century inn is popular with walkers and boaters from the nearby Shropshire Union Canal. Local ales from Weetwood and Tatton breweries keep the drinkers happy, with diners lured in by platters, salads, steaks and main courses such as home-made pie of the day, seasonal greens, and a choice of mash or chips; pea, asparagus and rocket risotto. Look out for the June beer festival on Fathers' Day weekend.

Open all day, all week Free House 11 portions/menu notice required

CHOLMONDELEY

The Cholmondeley Arms

Tel **01829 720300 | SY14 8HN**
Web **www.cholmondeleyarms.co.uk**
Dir ***On A49, between Whitchurch and Tarporley.***

Friendly inn with imaginative menus and 140 gins

PICK OF THE PUBS

Set in rolling Cheshire countryside virtually opposite Cholmondeley Castle on the A49, and still part of the Viscount's estate, this red-brick former schoolhouse is quirky and eclectic. It's surely one of England's more unusual pubs, the decor and artefacts, including family heirlooms, educational memorabilia, bell tower without and blackboards within add tremendously to the atmosphere of the cavernous interior. Owners Tim and Mary Bird have created a warm and inviting interior, with church candles on old school desks, fresh flowers, glowing log fires and a relaxing atmosphere. After exploring the local countryside, visiting the castle, or the fabulous ruins at Beeston, stapled to Cheshire's hilly sandstone spine, it's the perfect place to unwind, sup a pint of Cholmondeley Best or another local guest (only microbrewery beers from a 35-mile radius are stocked), or delve into the mindboggling list of 366 different gins, celebrated at the annual gin festival that takes place in July. Allow time to taste some of the best produce from Cheshire's burgeoning larder, including seasonal game from the estate. Please note that children under 10 are not allowed after 7pm in the bar, or 9pm in the garden.

Open all day, all week Cheshire Cat Pubs & Bars 16 from £12.95 portions notice required

CONGLETON

The Plough Inn Eaton

★★★★ INN

Tel **01260 280207 | Macclesfield Road, Eaton, CW12 2NH**
Web **www.theploughinncheshire.com**
Dir ***On A536 (Congleton to Macclesfield road).***

Brick-built around timber beams, the modest looks of this former coaching inn belie a multi-roomed interior with a large rear garden. The restaurant is in a galleried barn, reassembled here after a long agricultural existence in Wales. Seasonal menus may offer classic fish pie; lamb three ways; and Quorn and roasted red pepper burger, along with the internationally influenced blow-torched brie fondue; and South Indian-style beef curry. Spacious, well-equipped bedrooms are in a separate annexe.

Open all day, all week 12–11 (Fri to Sat 12–12) Free House 10 from £10 portions/menu

DELAMERE

The Fishpool Inn – see opposite

GAWSWORTH

Harrington Arms

Tel **01260 223325 | Church Lane, SK11 9RJ**
Web **www.harringtonarmsgawsworth.robinsonsbrewery.com**
Dir ***From Macclesfield take A536 towards Congleton. Turn left for Gawsworth.***

Part farmhouse, part pub, the little-changed interior comprises a main bar serving Robinsons real ales and quirky rooms with open fires and rustic furnishings. Memorable for its impression of timelessness, it dates from 1664 and has been licensed since 1710. On offer is good pub food made extensively from the wealth of local produce, so expect rump, sirloin and gammon steaks; fish and chips; vegetarian dishes; sandwiches; pizzas; burgers; plus daily specials and Sunday roasts. Early October sees an annual conker championship here.

Open all week 12–2.30 5–11.30 (Fri 12–2.30 4.30–12 Sat 12–11.30 Sun 12–11) Closed 25 Dec Robinsons 8 portions notice required

GOOSTREY

The Crown

Tel **01477 532128 | 111 Main Road, CW4 8DE**
Web **www.thecrownpubgoostrey.co.uk**
Dir ***In village centre. Follow Goostrey signs either from A50, or from A535 in Tremlow Green.***

A traditional pub set in the heart of the village of Goostrey, The Crown has been an integral part of community life since the 18th century. Beyond its red-bricked façade, the pub's interior retains much charm with old oak beams and real fireplaces.

GREAT BUDWORTH

George and Dragon

Tel **01606 892650 | High Street, CW9 6HF**
Web **www.georgeanddragonatgreatbudworth.co.uk**
Dir ***From M6 junction 19 or M56 junction 10 follow signs for Great Budworth.***

Painstakingly restored, this charming inn has many original features, including a stone tablet in the bar dated 1722 and inscribed 'Nil nimium cupito' ('I desire nothing to excess'). Regular real ales are Lees Bitter from Manchester and the pub's own Great Budworth Best Bitter. Start your meal with deep-fried Cheshire brie with cranberry and claret compôte; then move on to slow-cooked lamb shank; or cheese and onion pie.

Open all day, all week J W Lees 12 from £11.95 portions/menu notice required

HAUGHTON MOSS

The Nags Head

Tel **01829 260265 | Long Lane, CW6 9RN**
Web **www.nagsheadcheshire.co.uk**
Dir ***Exit A49 south of Tarporley at Beeston/Haughton sign into Long Lane. 2.75 miles to pub.***

Deep in the Cheshire countryside this half-timbered country inn is almost 400 years old and full of character, with a huge cruck frame and crackling fire adding rustic charm. The light, conservatory-inspired dining extension overlooks the tranquil garden. Great beers from Cheshire's Weetwood brewery are matched by the wide-ranging menu.

Open all day, all week 12–11 (Fri to Sat 12–12) Free House 10 portions/menu

DELAMERE

The Fishpool Inn

Tel **01606 883277** | **Fishpool Road, CW8 2HP**
Web **www.thefishpoolinn.co.uk**
Dir ***Phone for detailed directions.***

Striking village pub with quirky interior

PICK OF THE PUBS

Idyllically positioned on the edge of the Delamere Forest in the picturesque Cheshire countryside, this 18th-century pub seamlessly blends the traditional with the contemporary. The extensive refurbishment in the pub's recent past created an interior that impresses with its spaciousness. Scrubbed beams and pillars, pale floorboards, and roof windows augmented by downlighters and wall lamps together produce an unexpected light airiness. The decor is rich in furnishings such as chesterfield-style banquettes, solid wood tables and chairs, rugs, and Victorian tiles. Memorabilia from the Cheshire Polo Club, fishing rods and reels, decorated stags' heads, and even an upside-down skiff are just a few of the artefacts hanging from walls and ceilings in this engagingly quirky interior. The cellar keeps up to eight handpumps busy, with Weetwood's Cheshire Cat in permanent residence alongside a changing selection of local and seasonal real ales. An open-fronted kitchen produces modern British and popular European food, the latter in the form of thin-crust pizzas from the dedicated Wood Stone oven. Children have their own menu, dogs are welcome, and there's a pleasant garden to relax in.

Open all day, all week 11–11 Free House 14 portions/menu notice required

KETTLESHULME

Swan Inn

Tel **01663 732943** | **SK23 7QU**
Dir ***On B5470 between Whaley Bridge (2 miles) and Macclesfield (5 miles).***

Huddled in the shadow of the craggy Windgather Rocks in the Cheshire Peak District, the Swan is a glorious 15th-century village inn. The dining room offers an eclectic and international menu. Local craft ales such as Thornbridge keep ramblers and locals very contented.

KNUTSFORD

The Dog Inn PICK OF THE PUBS

Tel **01625 861421** | **Well Bank Lane, Over Peover, WA16 8UP**
Web **www.thedogpeover.co.uk**
Dir ***South from Knutsford take A50. Turn into Stocks Lane at The Whipping Stocks pub. 2 miles to inn.***

This row of cottages housed village industries before being joined together to form a public house in 1860. In summer, colourful flowerbeds, tubs and hanging baskets create quite a display, while the interior – rich with dark wood furniture and gleaming brass – generates year-round appeal. A range of cask-conditioned Cheshire ales from Weetwood in Tarporley is supported by a good selection of wines sold by the glass. The menu is strong on comfort food, such as fish and chips, along with more complex choices such as main courses of sticky sesame chilli beef with cashew nuts and noodle salad. Dessert offers things like sticky toffee pudding and lemon meringue sundae.

Open all day, all week 7am–11pm Free House 10 portions/menu

MARTON

The Davenport Arms

Tel **01260 224269** | **Congleton Road, SK11 9HF**
Web **www.pestorestaurants.co.uk**
Dir ***2 miles from Congleton on A34.***

Opposite the oldest half-timbered church still in use in Europe, the pub, originally a farmhouse, dates back to the 18th century. These days, the cooking is exclusively Italian, with the new owners offering an extensive menu of pizzas, pastas and main dishes such as meatballs in tomato, garlic and herb sauce; pork belly rubbed with fresh sage, paprika and garlic or boneless chicken thighs stuffed with Parma ham, spinach and mozzarella.

Open all year, all day 12–10.30 (Fri to Sat 12–11) Closed Mon lunch (excluding bank holidays) Free House 9 menus notice required

MOBBERLEY

The Bulls Head – see opposite

The Church Inn – see page 72

The Roebuck Inn – see page 73

MOULDSWORTH

The Goshawk

Tel **01928 740900** | **Station Road, CH3 8AJ**
Web **www.thegoshawkpub.co.uk**
Dir ***A51 from Chester onto A54. Left onto B5393 towards Frodsham. Into Mouldsworth, pub on left.***

This sturdy inn has a hint of Edwardian grandeur whilst benefiting from contemporary comforts, with print-clad walls and dado rails, comfy sofas and open fires. Its village setting makes the most of the area's delights. Local ales draw an appreciative crowd.

NANTWICH

The Thatch

Tel **01270 524223** | **Wrexham Road, Faddiley, CW5 8JE**
Web **www.thethatchnantwich.co.uk**
Dir ***From Nantwich follow Wrexham signs, inn on A534 in 4 miles.***

One of the oldest pubs in south Cheshire, and one of the prettiest, this black-and-white inn has a three-quarter acre garden, while inside there are plentiful oak beams and open fires. Enjoy a pint of Shropshire Gold with dishes such as lamb Henry, steak and ale pie, and cheddar and nut roast. Light bites and sandwiches are served until 6pm. Children can choose from their own menu.

Open all day, all week 12–11 (Sun 12–10.30) Enterprise Inns from £11.95 portions/menu

MOBBERLEY

The Bulls Head

Tel **01565 873395** | **Mill Lane, WA16 7HX**
Web **www.thebullsheadpub.co.uk**
Dir ***From Knutsford take A537, A5085 to Mobberley.***

A 200-year-old pub with lots going on

PICK OF THE PUBS

This little gem thrives as both a village local and also a destination eatery. One attraction is the range of seven real ales from Cheshire microbreweries within 35 miles of the pub – Dunham Massey, Merlin, Redwillow, Storm, Tatton and Wincle – but you'll need more than one visit to make acquaintance with them all. Yet another, Weetwood, brews Mobberley Wobbly (aka Mobb Wobb) for the pub; it's a pint of this that is enjoyed with the 'legendary' hand-crafted steak and ale pie with chips and 'not so mushy' peas. Smart, traditionally styled dining rooms ensure a comfortable and convivial setting for wholesome home-cooked food, including delicious The pub hosts two car clubs: the 'Three P' Club, which stands for 'Pub, Porsche and Pint', and for which you have to own, borrow or hire said German vehicle; and the Goodfellows, for which you must own anything but a Porsche. The clubs raise money for local charities including the village church. The pub garden comes into its own for the village fête and dog show held on the August Bank Holiday.

Open all day, all week 12–11 (Sun 12–10.30)
Cheshire Cat Pubs & Bars 16 *from £11.95*
portions *notice required*

MOBBERLEY

The Church Inn

Tel **01565 873178** | **WA16 7RD**
Web **www.churchinnmobberley.co.uk**
Dir ***From Knutsford take B5085 towards Wilmslow. In Mobberley left into Church Lane. Pub opposite church.***

Local produce drives the menu of this stylish village pub

PICK OF THE PUBS

Tim Bird and Mary McLaughlin have certainly put this old inn back on the map, together with their other pubs in the village, The Bulls Head and Roebuck Inn. The Church Inn has a stylish country appeal, pleasing locals and destination diners alike. On the edge of the village and opposite the 12th-century St Wilfrid's church, it is ideally situated between the bustling towns of Wilmslow and Knutsford and only eight miles from Manchester Airport. Surrounded by rolling Cheshire countryside, the attractive summer dining terrace and rear garden lead down to an old bowling green that boasts panoramic views across neighbouring fields. In the bar and boot room, a range of locally sourced ales includes Storm Brewery – Mallory's Mobberley Best, named after Mobberley-born mountaineer George Mallory; Tatton Brewery's Ale-Alujah may be making a guest appearance. A choice of intimate dining areas provide relaxed and comfortable seating for the perusal of the extensive menu, which includes country tavern favourites such as home-made venison burger, tobacco onions and rarebit and Massey's farm chips. Canines are more than welcome in the bar and the boot room; a bowl of dog biscuits, together with dog 'beer' (meat-based stock) to refresh them, are very thoughtful touches.

Open all day, all week Closed 25 Dec *Free House* *14* *portions* *notice required*

MOBBERLEY

The Roebuck Inn

Tel **01565 873939** | **Mill Lane, WA16 7HX**
Web **www.roebuckinnmobberley.co.uk**
Dir ***Off Town Lane, in centre of village, into Mill Lane.***

Smartly-renovated inn offering bistro dining

This Grade II listed building is the oldest pub in Mobberley and has been stylishly restored to the style of a "petit hotel", with a bar, bistro and pretty tiered garden. The food is prepared using fresh, local ingredients and features a smart contemporary menu of bistro classics. Fresh stone-baked pizzas are a hit; or you can go for one of the impressive sharing boards, enough for two or three people. If you're not one for sharing, something from the small plates selection might appeal – crab, spring onion and parsley cakes with Romesco sauce, maybe, or crushed avocado and fermented chilli with grilled sourdough. Main courses might include tempura monkfish, Thai sweet and sour sauce, and aromatic rice; or grilled lamb chops with roasted red peppers, bulgur wheat, garlic and harissa yogurt and pomegranate. When it comes to beer, they have a couple of local cask ales, Buck Bitter from Weetwood, and Dunham Massey Brewery's Deer Beer, as well as craft English lager, a choice of bottled beers and ciders, and an interesting wine list.

Open all day, all week Closed 25 Dec (for food and drink) Cheshire Cat Pubs & Bars 12 from £12 portions notice required

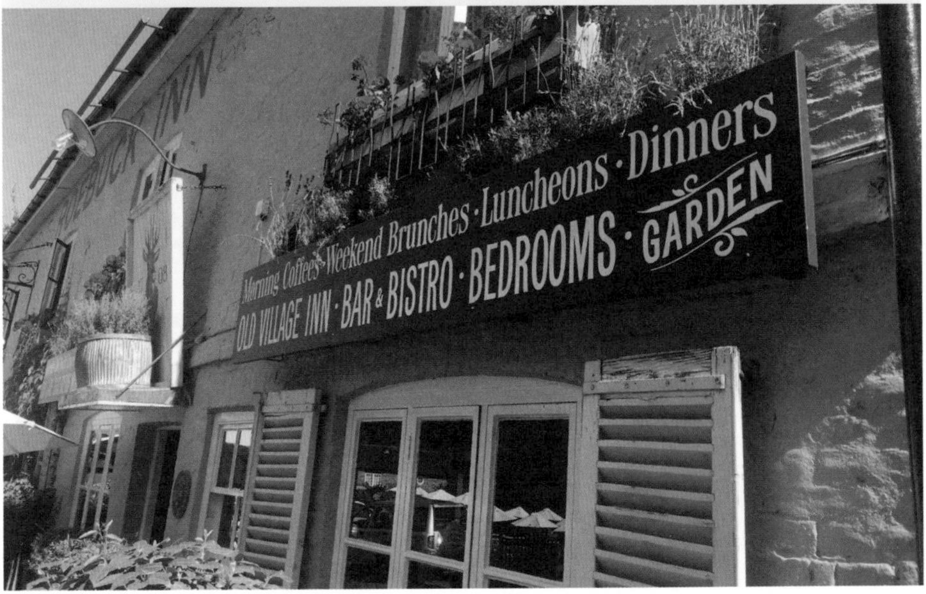

PARKGATE

The Boat House

Tel **0151 336 4187** | **1 The Parade, CH64 6RN**
Web **www.theboathouseparkgate.co.uk**
Dir ***On B5135, 3 miles from Heswall.***

The salt marshes begin right in front of The Boat House, so there's nothing to spoil the views of north Wales across the estuary. Once a thriving Deeside port, Parkgate's silted-up waters are now a nature reserve, although exceptionally high tides do still reach the pub walls.

The Ship

Tel **0151 336 3931** | **The Parade, CH64 6SA**
Web **www.the-shiphotel.co.uk**
Dir ***A540 from Chester towards Neston. Left onto B5134 to Neston town centre. At T-junction right onto B5136. Next left onto B5135 to Parkgate. Hotel 50 yards on right on The Parade.***

With 18th-century origins, The Ship was regularly visited by Lord Nelson and his mistress Lady Hamilton, who was born in nearby Neston. Real ale names to conjure with in the contemporary bar include Trapper's Hat from Wirral brewery, Brimstage and Weetwood Oast-House Gold from Cheshire. Home-made food might include garlic and herb-roasted lamb rump; Goan curry with scented lemon and coriander rice; steak and ale pie; aubergine, mixed bean, tomato and basil cassoulet, and specials.

Open all day, all week Free House 15 portions/menu WI-FI P notice required

PRESTBURY

The Legh Arms

Tel **01625 829130** | **The Village, SK10 4DG**
Web **www.legharmsprestbury.pub**
Dir ***On A538 (New Road).***

Trendy Prestbury is popular with Premiership footballers and they're lucky to have the gabled and part-timbered Legh Arms right on their doorstep. Fine ales from nearby Robinsons Brewery are served in the bar with its oak beams and roaring fires.

SPURSTOW

The Yew Tree Inn

Tel **01829 304384** | **Long Lane, CW6 9RD**
Web **www.bunburyyewtree.co.uk**
Dir ***400 metres from A49.***

Built by the Earl of Crewe, this is a sympathetically refurbished 19th-century pub. Inside, the original beams and open fires are a reminder of the pub's history, while the terrace is a more modern addition and perfect for summer dining.

STYAL

The Ship Inn

Tel **01625 444888** | **Altrincham Road, SK9 4JE**
Web **www.theshipstyal.co.uk**
Dir ***From B5166 north of Wilmslow, left signed Styal into Altrincham Road.***

Styal's history is closely bound to that of the local cotton industry; many of the Ship's customers call in after visiting nearby Quarry Bank Mill. The 350-year-old building was once a shippon, an ancient term for a farm's cattle shed.

SWETTENHAM

The Swettenham Arms

PICK OF THE PUBS

Tel **01477 571284** | **Swettenham Lane, CW12 2LF**
Web **www.swettenhamarms.co.uk**
Dir ***M6 junction 18 to Holmes Chapel, then A535 towards Jodrell Bank. 3 miles right (Forty Acre Lane) to Swettenham (Note: do not use postcode for Sat Nav; enter Swettenham Lane).***

A comfortable pub full of quiet corners, drawing an appreciative crowd with a generous selection of real ales, lagers and ciders and 14 wines by the glass. Diners might expect to find Cheshire gammon with fried duck egg and hand-cut chips; or Portobello mushroom, pepper, courgette and aubergine stack. Sandwiches and ploughman's are available from noon till 6pm, and there's a children's menu.

Open all week 11.30am–close Free House 14 from £13 portions/menu WI-FI P notice required

TARPORLEY

Alvanley Arms Inn – see page 76

WARMINGHAM

The Bear's Paw

★★★★★ INN

Tel **01270 526317** | **School Lane, CW11 3QN**
Web **www.thebearspaw.co.uk**
Dir ***M6 junction 18, A54, A533 towards Sandbach. Follow signs for village.***

Refined cooking and stylish accommodation

PICK OF THE PUBS

With its prominent central gable and some nods towards typical Cheshire black-and-white half-timbering, this stylish 19th-century gastro-inn has clearly had a lot of money spent on it. Acres – well it seems like acres – of reclaimed antique oak flooring, leather sofas surrounding a huge open fireplace, bookshelves offering plenty of choice for a good read, and more than 200 pictures and archive photos lining the oak-panelled walls. The bar, in which stands a carved wooden bear with a salmon in its mouth, offers a half dozen cask ales from local microbreweries, including the somewhat appropriate Beartown in Congleton, Weetwood in Tarporley, and Tatton in Knutsford, as well as Hereford Dry Cider. Whether you're sitting out front looking across to the churchyard or in the clubby interior, there's plenty of comfortable dining space in which to sample wholesome, locally sourced food from wide-ranging daily menus that expertly blend the classic with the modern. Great for sharing are the imaginative deli boards, which come laden with local cheeses, charcuterie or pickled and smoked fish, and don't miss the Sunday roast lunches.

Open all day, all week *Free House* *12*
portions/menu *notice required*

TARPORLEY

Alvanley Arms Inn ★★★★ INN

Tel **01829 760200 | Forest Rd, Cotebrook, CW6 9DS**
Web **www.alvanleyarms.co.uk**
Dir ***On A49, 1.5 miles north of Tarporley.***

Refurbished to a high standard, this lovely 16th-century former coaching inn has a traditional, oak-beamed bar where hand-pulled ales complement freshly prepared dishes, based on ingredients from local family businesses; the chef-patron makes his own bread from local Walk Mill flour. Dishes range from starters and light bites like baked honey figs to sandwiches, salads and pub classics. There are steaks from the grill and seafood treats like baked cod mornay or pan-fried stone bass.

Open all day, all week 12–11 Robinsons 12 portions/menu Wi-fi P notice required

The Swan, Tarporley

Tel **01829 733838 | 50 High Street, CW6 0AG**
Web **www.theswantarporley.co.uk**
Dir ***From junction of A49 and A51 into Tarporley. Pub on right in village centre.***

The 16th-century Swan has been the hub of Cheshire's picturesque Tarporley village for over 500 years. While locals stop by for a pint of the pub's own 16 Ale, the chef prepares local produce for the seasonal menus which change weekly.

WARMINGHAM

The Bear's Paw – see page 75

WRENBURY

The Dusty Miller

Tel **01270 780537 | CW5 8HG**
Web **www.robinsonsbrewery.com/dustymiller**
Dir ***Phone for detailed directions.***

This beautifully converted 18th-century corn mill is beside the Llangollen Canal in the rural village of Wrenbury. The pub's large arched windows offer views of passing boats, while a black-and-white lift bridge, designed by Thomas Telford, completes the picture-postcard setting.

CORNWALL & ISLES OF SCILLY

ALTARNUN

Rising Sun Inn

Tel **01566 86636 | PL15 7SN**
Web **www.therisingsuninn.co.uk**
Dir ***From A30 follow Altarnun signs onto unclassified road. Through Altarnun and Treween to T-junction. Inn 100 yards on left.***

It's still fine to arrive by horse at this inviting, 18th-century moorland inn – there's a hitching post in the car park. The specials board changes daily, but always focuses on seasonal and local produce. Home of the original 'Boxeater' steak.

BODINNICK

The Old Ferry Inn

Tel **01726 870237 | PL23 1LX**
Web **www.theoldferryinn.co.uk**
Dir ***From Liskeard on A38 to Dobwalls, left at lights onto A390. After 3 miles left onto B3359 signed Looe. Right signed Lerryn/Bodinnick/Polruan for 5 miles.***

Daphne du Maurier wrote many of her novels at 'Ferryside', the house next door to this 400-year-old inn by the River Fowey. You can watch people messing about in boats from one of the terraces, stay in the bar among the nautical memorabilia, or the stone-walled snug.

BOLINGEY

Bolingey Inn

Tel **01872 571626 | Penwartha Road, TR6 0DH**
Dir ***From B3285 in Perranporth at roundabout into Station Road. Approximately 0.5 mile right signed Bolingey. Pub 0.5 mile on right.***

In a previous life, the 17th-century Bolingey Inn was reputedly a count house for the vicinity's mines. 'More landlords than can be researched', the menu tells us, have served here since its change of use. Today, the Bolingey charms its clients with its atmosphere, serves four bitters from the likes of Sharp's and Fuller's, and prepares good home-cooked dishes. Fresh fish options appear on the specials board.

Open all year, all day Closed Mon (Nov to Mar) Punch Taverns from £14 portions/menu Wi-fi P notice required

BOSCASTLE

The Wellington – see page 78

CADGWITH

Cadgwith Cove Inn

Tel **01326 290513** | **TR12 7JX**
Web **www.cadgwithcoveinn.com**
Dir ***A3083 from Helston towards Lizard. Left to Cadgwith.***

A visit to this 300-year-old pub in the largely unspoilt fishing hamlet on the Lizard will illustrate why it once appealed to smugglers. Relics in the atmospheric bars attest to a rich seafaring history; the cove itself is just across the old pilchard cellar from its sunny front patio. Traditional favourites include fish and chips; seafood chowder; and vegetarian dish of the day. There are seafood buffets on Saturdays throughout the summer, and an October beer and cider festival too.

Open all day, all week Punch Taverns 9 from £13.70 portions/menu

CHAPEL AMBLE

The Maltsters Arms

Tel **01208 812473** | **PL27 6EU**
Web **www.themaltsters1.co.uk**
Dir ***A39 from Wadebridge towards Camelford. In 1 mile left signed Chapel Amble. Pub on right in village.***

In the pretty Cornish village of Chapel Amble and a short drive from Rock and Port Isaac, The Maltsters Arms oozes old-world charm and character, from slate floors and copper pots to 'mind-your-head' beams and open fires. This pub is at the heart of the community with a quiz night and must-book Sunday carvery. The traditional, home-cooked food includes burgers; battered fish and chips; grilled seabass fillets with samphire; and braised lamb shank, creamy garlic mash with red wine, rosemary jus.

Open all week 11–3 6–11 (Sun all day) Free House 10 portions/menu notice required

CONSTANTINE

Trengilly Wartha Inn

PICK OF THE PUBS

Tel **01326 340332** | **Nancenoy, TR11 5RP**
Web **www.trengilly.co.uk**
Dir ***Follow signs to Constantine, left towards Gweek until 1st sign for inn, left and left again at next sign, continue to inn.***

The name means 'a settlement above the trees', although this charming 600-year-old inn near the Helford River actually lies at the foot of a densely wooded valley. Since taking over, Will and Lisa Lea have created a popular local, which benefits from a pretty beer garden complete with vine-shaded pergola. In the black-beamed bar, regularly changing local real ales might include Penzance Potion No 9, served alongside Healey's Cornish Rattler cider. You can eat in the bar or the bistro, with most dishes likely to be sourced locally. Cornish mussels with white wine cream, onion and garlic sauce might be followed by chicken and leek pie.

Open all week 11–3 6–12 Free House 15 portions/menu notice required

CUBERT

The Smugglers' Den Inn

Tel **01637 830209** | **Trebellan, TR8 5PY**
Web **www.thesmugglersden.co.uk**
Dir ***From Newquay take A3075 to Cubert crossroads, then right, then left signed Trebellan, 0.5 mile to inn.***

A thatched 16th-century pub, just 15 minutes from Newquay and popular with locals and visitors alike. The pub comprises a long bar, family room, children's play area, courtyards and huge beer garden. Local ingredients are the cornerstone of the family-friendly menu.

BOSCASTLE

The Wellington 

INN 

Tel 01840 250202 | The Harbour, PL35 0AQ
Web www.wellingtonhotelboscastle.com
Dir *A30/A395 at Davidstow follow Boscastle signs. B3266 to village. Right into New Road.*

Popular pub and fine dining restaurant on the Cornish coast

PICK OF THE PUBS

This listed 16th-century coaching inn with its castellated tower sits on one of England's most stunning coastlines, at the end of a glorious wooded valley where the rivers Jordan and Valency meet; in 1852 it was renamed in honour of the Duke of Wellington. Known affectionately as 'The Welly' by both locals and loyal guests, it retains much of its original charm as in the traditional Long Bar, complete with minstrels' gallery, where a good selection of Cornish ales, ciders such as Cornish Rattler, and malt whiskies are to be found. Bar snacks here embrace sandwiches and soup of the day, along with small plates, plus specials from the blackboard. For fine dining, head to the award-winning restaurant on the first floor. The kitchen team prepares fresh local produce – none fresher or more local than the seafood landed by the boats in the harbour a few yards away. Children are well catered for with their own menu, and some adult main courses can be served in half-size portions.

Open all day, all week 11–11 Free House 8 portions/menu notice required

DULOE

The Plough

Tel **01503 262556** | **PL14 4PN**
Web **www.ploughduloe.co.uk**
Dir ***From A34 to Dobwalls, follow Duloe signs.***

Found in a quiet village midway between the bustling towns of Liskeard and Looe, this pub is set deep in the Cornish countryside. It's home to the Cornish Orchards Company, so no surprise to find its Gold ciders on tap alongside St Austell ales in The Plough's bar.

FEOCK

The Punchbowl & Ladle

Tel **01872 862237** | **Penelewey, TR3 6QY**
Web **www.punchbowlandladle.com**
Dir ***From Truro take A39 towards Falmouth, after Shell garage at Playing Place roundabout follow King Harry Ferry signs. 0.5 mile, pub on right.***

Close to the King Harry Ferry, parts of this lovely old pub date from the 15th century and rumour has it that the fireplace was used by smugglers to burn contraband. Settle down in the cosy low-beamed bar and enjoy typical dishes like braised beef and red wine stew, and pan-fried hake. In summer, head for the garden or patio with a glass of St Austell Proper Job.

Open all day, all week St Austell Brewery 16 from £11.95 portions/menu

FOWEY

The Ship Inn

Tel **01726 832230** | **Trafalgar Square, PL23 1AZ**
Web **www.shipfowey.co.uk**
Dir ***From A30 take B3269 and A390.***

One of Fowey's oldest buildings, the Ship was built in 1570 by John Rashleigh, who sailed to the Americas with Walter Raleigh. Given Fowey's riverside position, assume a good choice of fish, including River Fowey mussels as a starter or main; and grilled sardines in garlic. Other options include Mr Kittow's pork sausages and mash; spinach, asparagus and wild mushroom risotto.
St Austell ales, real fires and a long tradition of genial hospitality add the final touches.

Open all day, all week 11am–midnight (Fri to Sat 11am–1am) St Austell Brewery portions/menu Wi-fi notice required

GUNNISLAKE

The Rising Sun Inn

Tel **01822 832201** | **Calstock Road, PL18 9BX**
Web **www.therisingsuninngunnislake.com**
Dir ***From Tavistock take A390 to Gunnislake. Left after lights into Calstock Road. Inn approximately 500 metres on right.***

This two-roomed pub has fabulous views from the pretty terraced gardens of the Tamar Valley and the river flowing towards Plymouth. Gunnislake is just in Cornwall, so it's understandable that Dartmoor Brewery's Jail Ale and Legend draught beers are served.

GUNWALLOE

The Halzephron Inn

PICK OF THE PUBS

Tel **01326 240406** | **TR12 7QB**
Web **www.halzephron-inn.co.uk**
Dir ***3 miles south of Helston on A3083, right to Gunwalloe, through village. Inn on left.***

The name of the inn derives from Als Yfferin, Cornish for 'Cliffs of Hell', an appropriate description for this hazardous stretch of Atlantic coastline. Located high above Gunwalloe Cove, this 500-year-old, rugged stone inn commands an enviable position, with breathtaking views across Mount's Bay. On sunny days grab a front bench and enjoy a pint of Sharp's Doom Bar while looking out to St Michael's Mount. The two interconnecting bars feature cosy log fires, fishing memorabilia, and watercolours of local scenes. The best Cornish produce appears on the menu, including fresh seafood, and everything is homemade. Main courses include white crab in a thermidor sauce, baked with cheese; steak and ale pie; and medallions of pork fillet, black pudding in garlic and rosemary sauce.

Open all day, all week 11–11 (Sun 12–10.30) Free House 10 from £10 portions/menu Wi-fi notice required

GWEEK

Black Swan

Tel **01326 221502 | TR12 6TU**
Web **www.theblackswangweek.co.uk**
Dir ***In village centre.***

This delightful inn is located in the picturesque village of Gweek on the River Helford, a stone's throw from the National Seal Sanctuary. They're famous for their sirloin steaks, but also offer signature dishes of steak and Guinness pie with creamy mash, and Cajun chicken breast, chips and peas. There's a choice of regularly changing specials, too. Not to be missed is a selection of Cornish ales and guest ales.

Open all day, all week Punch Taverns 9 portions/menu notice required

HALSETOWN

The Halsetown Inn PICK OF THE PUBS

Tel **01736 795583 | TR26 3NA**
Web **www.halsetowninn.co.uk**
Dir ***On B3311, 1 mile from St Ives.***

Built in 1831, The Halsetown Inn is named after the village's architect and benefactor, James Halse. From the outside, little changes at this stone-built pub, but the interior reveals a more contemporary style although the open fires remain. A well stocked bar featuring local Skinner's ales also offers a robust cocktail and gin selection. Head chef Fraser Bruce and his team create a wide selection of vegetarian and vegan dishes alongside pub classics.

Open all week 12–3 5–close Closed 5 Jan to 16 Feb Punch Taverns 12 from £12.50 portions/menu notice required

HELFORD PASSAGE

The Ferryboat Inn

Tel **01326 250625 | TR11 5LB**
Web **ferryboatcornwall.co.uk**
Dir ***In village centre, 1st turn after Trebah Gardens.***

Dating back 300 years and overlooking the North Helford Passage, this waterside pub remains a family-run pub with a welcome as warm as its roaring open fire. Cornish and Devon ales and ciders dominate the pumps in the bar.

KINGSAND

The Halfway House Inn

Tel **01752 822279 | Fore Street, PL10 1NA**
Web **www.halfwayinnkingsand.co.uk**
Dir ***In town centre.***

This property is firmly in Cornwall; until 1844 the pub was partly in Devon because the stream running through the garden was the dividing line between the counties. The twin villages of Kingsand and Cawsand were once smuggling hotspots; something to think about over a pint of Sharp's Atlantic.

LANLIVERY

The Crown Inn PICK OF THE PUBS

Tel **01208 872707 | PL30 5BT**
Web **www.thecrowninncornwall.co.uk**
Dir ***Signed from A390. Follow brown sign approximately 1.5 miles west of Lostwithiel.***

In a moorland village above a tributary of the Fowey River is this former longhouse, with characteristic thick stone walls, low beams, granite and slate floors, open fires and an unusual bread oven. Much of the present building dates from the 12th century, when it housed the stonemasons constructing the nearby church. The pub has been extensively but sympathetically restored over the years; at one point the work uncovered a deep well, now covered by glass, under the porch. With the sea only a few miles away, expect a menu offering plenty of fresh fish and seafood, as well as other local produce. A popular main course is breast of chicken on a chorizo risotto with a chilli, lime and coriander dressing.

Open all day, all week Free House portions/menu notice required

LAUNCESTON

The Racehorse Inn

Tel **01566 786916** | **PL15 7PG**
Web **www.racehorseinn.co.uk**
Dir ***South of Launceston on B3254. Continue to North Hill village, midway between Lauceston and Liskeard.***

On the edge of Bodmin Moor, and handy for Launceston and Liskeard, this is a comfortable inn offering four Cornish guest ales, a takeaway menu of pizza and fish and chips, themed food nights and a menu focused on the best of local ingredients. Winter dishes might be Cornish gin and dill-cured salmon with beetroot, horseradish crème fraîche and G&T jelly; pheasant breast with creamed potatoes; pork cooked three ways, or an organic beef burger. Round it all off with a classic crème brûlée.

Open 12–3 5.30–10.30 Closed 1st 2 weeks Jan, Mon Free House 12 from £14 portions notice required

LOOE

The Ship Inn ★★★ INN

Tel **01503 263124** | **Fore Street, PL13 1AD**
Web **www.staustellbrewery.co.uk/pub/east-looe/ship-hotel**
Dir ***In town centre.***

This lively St Austell Brewery-owned pub stands on a corner in the heart of this charming old fishing town, a minute's walk from the working harbour. Locals and tourists join together in the appreciation of a pint of Tribute, and select their favourites from the menu – a burger or hot baguette for some, while others go for steak and ale pie or hunter's chicken. A quiz is held on Mondays throughout the year, live bands play regularly, and well-equipped bedrooms are available for those wanting to tarry awhile.

Open all day, all week St Austell Brewery portions/menu

MEVAGISSEY

The Ship Inn

Tel **01726 843324** | **Fore Street, PL26 6UQ**
Web **www.theshipinnmeva.co.uk**
Dir ***7 miles south of St Austell.***

This 400-year-old inn stands just a few yards from Mevagissey's picturesque fishing harbour, so the choice of fish and seafood dishes comes as no surprise on a menu of home-cooked dishes. The popular bar has low-beamed ceilings, flagstone floors and a strong nautical feel.

MITCHELL

The Plume of Feathers

PICK OF THE PUBS

Tel **01872 510387** | **TR8 5AX**
Web **www.theplumemitchell.co.uk**
Dir ***From A30 follow Mitchell signs.***

From the impressive pillared porch at this sturdy old Cornish inn, John Wesley preached the benefits of Methodism to farmers and miners in the 1750s. Elements of the old place still survive, with low beams, a wood-burning stove and a natural well in the bar blending with the contemporary artworks on display. The airy conservatory is an appealing place in which to dine. Local Cornish produce takes centre stage on the modern British menu and there's always a good showing of fish and locally reared meats. To start, chicken, ham and pistachio terrine; advancing then to mains like herb-crusted hake, chorizo, tomato and bean cassoulet. The raised, tree-shaded beer garden is a tranquil retreat.

Open all day, all week 9am–11pm/midnight (25 Dec 11–4) Free House from £12 menus notice required

MYLOR BRIDGE

The Pandora Inn PICK OF THE PUBS

Tel **01326 372678** | **Restronguet Creek, TR11 5ST**
Web **www.pandorainn.com**
Dir ***From Truro/Falmouth follow A39, left at Carclew, follow signs to pub.***

Enjoying a spectacular setting on the edge of Restronguet Creek, parts of the Pandora date back to the 13th century and flagstone floors, low-beamed ceilings and thatched roof iremain. While the setting is unchanged, today the pub offers 21st-century comfort, quality and attention to detail in everything – from the food and service, to the decor and furniture. Alongside an excellent wine list and the local ales from St Austell Brewery, chef John Poole uses the freshest local and seasonal produce, including fish and shellfish bought from boats landing at the Pandora's own pontoon. Dine on that very pontoon, at a table by the water's edge, or in one of the series of little rooms inside.

Open all day, all week 10.30am–11pm St Austell Brewery 20 from £10.95 portions/menu

See advertisement opposite

NEWQUAY

The Lewinnick Lodge Bar & Restaurant

Tel **01637 878117** | **Pentire Headland, TR7 1NX**
Web **www.lewinnicklodge.co.uk**
Dir ***From Newquay take Pentire Road, 0.5 mile, pub on right.***

Lewinnick Lodge perches on the cliff top of the Pentire Headland, enjoying a timeless panorama of sea views. This is a destination eatery, but real ales, local cider, crisp wines and premium lagers are all on offer in the bar. Wraps and baps and gourmet burgers can be ordered, but fresh seafood, much of it from Cornish waters, is the menu's key attraction. Meats from the county include slow-roasted lamb and beef.

Open all day, all week Free House 8 from £12 portions/menu

PAR

The Britannia Inn & Restaurant ★★★★ INN

Tel **01726 812889** | **St Austell Road, PL24 2SL**
Web **www.britanniainn.com**
Dir ***On A390 between Par and St Austell, adjacent to Cornish Market World.***

Solidly built 16th-century free house, where Sharp's Doom Bar, St Austell Tribute and Healey's Cornish Rattler wave the county flag. The three dining areas offer prime-cut Cornish steaks and other locally sourced dishes, typically grilled Cornish hake with chorizo, fennel, olives and peppers; and Cajun-spiced salmon steak with garlic mayonnaise. The Sunday carvery is popular.

Open all day, all week Free House 9 portions/menu notice required

The Royal Inn ★★★★ INN

Tel **01726 815601** | **66 Eastcliffe Road, PL24 2AJ**
Dir ***A3082 Par, follow brown tourist signs for 'Newquay Branch line' or railway station. Pub opposite rail station.***

A visit by Edward VII to a local copper mine gave this much-extended 19th-century inn its name, and it was originally frequented by travellers and employees of the Great Western Railway. The pub is on the Atlantic Coast Line of the 'Rail Ale Trail', and an open-plan bar serves rotating guest ales. There are small plates, sandwiches and mains available in the bar, while the restaurant menu might offer sea bream with lemon and parsley.

Open all day, all week 11–11 (Sun 12–10.30) Free House 13 portions/menu notice required

PENZANCE

The Coldstreamer Inn

Tel **01736 602092** | **Gulval, TR18 3BB**
Web **thecoldstreamer.co.uk**
Dir ***From Penzance take B3311 towards St Ives. In Gulval right into School Lane. Pub in village centre.***

A change of hands and a refurbishment have taken place at this stone-built village inn on a hillside outside Penzance. With a wood-burner pumping out the heat, the interior is cosy, contemporary and welcoming. Glimpses of Mount's Bay reward drinkers on the terrace.

The Pandora Inn

Restronguet Creek, Mylor Bridge, Falmouth, Cornwall TR11 5ST

Tel: 01326 372678 **Web:** pandorainn.com **Email:** info@pandorainn.com

en you visit the *Pandora*, it's easy to forget you're in the 21st century. Its spectacular setting on the edge of ronguet Creek is timeless. Parts of the Inn date back to the 13th Century and, with its flagstone floors, low-ned ceilings and thatched roof it's not difficult to believe that little has changed since that time.

le the *Pandora*'s wonderful setting remains unchanged, everything else in this cosy traditional inn is 21st ury comfort and quality.

licans John Milan and Steve Bellman have ı at the helm of the *Pandora* since 1999. Their ntion to detail in everything – from the food service to the décor and furniture – has blished the *Pandora* as a multi award-winning that aims to give customers an enjoyable and norable experience whenever you visit.

ngside an extensive wine list and local real ales ı St Austell Brewery, Chef John Poole uses the nest, local, seasonal produce including fish and fish bought from boats landing at the *Pandora*'s pontoon. Dine on that pontoon, at a table at vater's edge or in one of the cosy rooms with fires inside.

The Dolphin Tavern ★★★ INN

Tel **01736 364106 | Quay Street, TR18 4BD**
Web **www.dolphintavern.com**
Dir ***From rail station follow road along harbour. Tavern on corner opposite Scilonian Ferry Terminal.***

Sir Walter Raleigh is said to have smoked the first pipe of tobacco in England at this lovely 16th-century pub, part of which was once used as a courtroom by Judge Jeffreys. These days, the Dolphin offers great home-made food accompanied by a full range of St Austell beers, plus accommodation. Fresh, locally caught fish features on the daily specials board, and the menu offers a tempting selection of meat (a house speciality – sizzling Cornish rump steak and chips), vegetarian and children's dishes.

Open all day, all week Closed 25 Dec ⊕St Austell Brewery 🍷 10 portions/menu Wi-fi notice required

The Turks Head Inn

Tel **01736 363093 | Chapel St, TR18 4AF**
Web **www.turksheadpenzance.co.uk**
Dir ***Phone for detailed directions.***

This popular side-street local is the oldest pub in Penzance, dating from around 1233, and was the first in the country to be given the Turks Head name. Enjoy hearty pub food in the sunny flower-filled garden. Don't miss the annual beer festival.

PERRANUTHNOE

The Victoria Inn PICK OF THE PUBS

Tel **01736 710309 | TR20 9NP**
Web **www.victoriainn-penzance.co.uk**
Dir ***Exit A394 (Penzance to Helston road), signed Perranuthnoe.***

Its history spans nine centuries, so this striking pink-washed village inn could be Cornwall's oldest public house. Decorated with seafaring memorabilia, its typically Cornish stone-walled interior attracts families strolling up from Perran Sands and walkers from the South West Coast Path. Real ales, lager and cider – all from Cornwall – enjoy pride of place. Enjoy the Mediterranean-style patio garden in clement weather. Dishes are modern British, making good use of locally sourced produce.

PHILLEIGH

Roseland Inn

Tel **01872 580254 | TR2 5NB**
Web **www.roselandinn.co.uk**
Dir ***From Truro take A39 towards Falmouth. Left onto B3289 towards St Mawes. Left at sharp right bend for Philleigh. Or take King Harry Ferry from Feock (Trelissick) to St Mawes/Roseland peninsula. Onto B3289. At right bend turn left signed Philleigh, 1.5 miles to pub on left.***

Owner Phil Heslip and chef Brian Green take pride in the quality of the home-prepared modern British cooking at this highly appealing, rural 16th-century inn. The character of the interior owes much to the low-beamed ceilings, brassware, paintings and prints.

POLKERRIS

The Rashleigh Inn

Tel **01726 813991 | PL24 2TL**
Web **www.therashleighinnpolkerris.co.uk**
Dir ***From A3082 between Fowey and Par follow Polkerris signs.***

Once a coastguard station, this 300-year-old pub on the road to Polkerris Beach faces west, so watching the sun set over St Austell Bay is a delight. In the bar there's a good selection of real ales from the south-west, real cider, and locally-produced organic soft drinks.

PORT GAVERNE

Port Gaverne

★★★★★ ◎◎ INN PICK OF THE PUBS

Tel **01208 880244 | PL29 3SQ**
Web **www.portgavernehotel.co.uk**
Dir ***Signed from B3314, south of Delabole via B3267, east of Port Isaac.***

This delightful 17th-century inn in pretty Port Gaverne overlooks the secluded cove where women once loaded sea-bound ketches with slate from Delabole's quarry. The slate industry is long gone, but the inn is right on the South West Coast Path, handy for walkers ready for a thirst-quenching Cornish-brewed Skinner's Betty Stogs real ale, Rattler cider or a refreshing glass of wine, in the slate-floored, low-beamed bar or small beer garden. Local produce includes plenty of fresh fish; Porthilly mussels; and Port Isaac lobster thermidor. Not everything is from the Atlantic, of course, so look out for braised venison, juniper and ale pie, smoked butter mash and red cabbage; or charcoal-grilled pork T-bone steak with peppercorn sauce. Finish with blueberry and ginger steamed pudding and custard.

Open all day, all week Free House 16 portions/ menu

PORTHLEVEN

The Ship Inn

Tel **01326 564204** | **TR13 9JS**
Web **www.theshipinnporthleven.co.uk**
Dir ***From Helston follow signs to Porthleven (B3304), 2.5 miles. On entering village continue to harbour. Follow road to other side of harbour. 1st left to inn.***

Dating from the 17th century, this smugglers' inn is built into the cliffs, and is approached by a flight of stone steps. In summer there's nothing better than sitting with a glass of ale and watching the fishing boats coming and going in the picturesque Porthleven harbour. In winter, a log fires warms the interior. Beer mats and brasses adorn the ceiling and walls. The food is kept simple – fish pies, steak, mussels, crab and catch of the day.

Open all day, all week 11am–11.30pm (Fri to Sun 11am–midnight) Free House 8 portions

PORT ISAAC

The Slipway

Tel **01208 880264** | **Harbour Front, PL29 3RH**
Web **www.portisaachotel.com**
Dir ***From A39 take B3314 signed Port Isaac. Through Delabole and Pendoggett, right onto B3267. 2 miles to Port Isaac, pass Co-op on right, 100 metres into Back Hill (one way) to harbour (Note: no parking by pub; car park at top of village).***

This 16th-century, one-time ship's chandlery could hardly be closer to Port Isaac's tiny harbour, so no wonder it has a reputation for seriously good fresh fish and seafood. Cornish Orchards cider, and real ales from Sharp's breweries are on hand pump in the bar.

Open all day, all week Closed 25 Dec Free House menus

PORTREATH

Basset Arms

Tel **01209 842077** | **Tregea Terrace, TR16 4NG**
Web **www.bassetarms.com**
Dir ***From Redruth take B3300 to Portreath. Pub on left near seafront.***

Built as a pub to serve harbour workers, at one time this early 19th-century Cornish stone cottage served as a mortuary for ill-fated seafarers, so there are plenty of ghost stories. Tin-mining and shipwreck photographs adorn the low-beamed interior of the bar where you can wash down a meal with a pint of Skinner's real ale. The menu makes the most of local seafood, such as seafood stew, but also provides a wide selection of alternatives, including steak and ale pie.

Open all day, all week 11–11 (Fri to Sat 11am–midnight Sun 11–10.30) Free House portions/ menu notice required

10 TOP CORNWALL PUBS WITH ACCOMMODATION

The following pubs are rated as part of the AA Guest Accommodation scheme (see page 10–11 for more information).

Port Gaverne ★★★★★ INN
Port Gaverne, *see page 84*

The Britannia Inn & Restaurant ★★★★ INN Par, *see page 82*

The New Inn ★★★★ INN Tresco (Isles of Scilly), *see page 90*

The Wellington ★★★★ INN Boscastle, *see page 78*

The Crooked Inn ★★★★ INN Saltash, *see page 89*

Driftwood Spars ★★★★ GUEST ACCOMMODATION St Agnes, *see page 86*

The Royal Inn ★★★★ INN Par, *see page 82*

The Dolphin Tavern ★★★ INN Penzance, *see page 84*

The Sloop Inn ★★★ INN St Ives, *see page 87*

The Ship Inn ★★★ INN Looe, *see page 81*

ROCK

The Mariners

Tel **01208 863679** | **PL27 6LD**
Web **www.themarinersrock.com**
Dir ***On seafront.***

With a great seafront location, views across the Camel Estuary, The Mariners is now a Sharps pub and a major refurbishment at the time of going to press promises great things, especially as the new venture will be helmed by top chef Paul Ainsworth. One to watch.

RUAN LANIHORNE

The Kings Head

Tel **01872 501263** | **TR2 5NX**
Web **www.kingsheadruan.co.uk**
Dir ***3 miles from Tregony Bridge on A3078.***

Set deep in the beautiful Roseland countryside, this traditional pub has a warm and welcoming atmosphere. Roaring winter fires, beamed ceilings and mulled wine contrast with summer days relaxing on the terrace with a pint of Betty Stogs or Cornish Orchards cider. The seasonal dishes use the best local produce. Look out for the signature dish of Ruan duck three ways – confit leg, pan-fried breast and drakes pudding.

Open 12–2.30 6–11 Closed 29 Oct to 7 Dec, Sun evening, Mon Free House 9 from £13 menus

ST AGNES

Driftwood Spars – see below

ST EWE

The Crown Inn

Tel **01726 843322** | **PL26 6EY**
Web **www.staustellbrewery.co.uk/pub/st-ewe/crown-inn**
Dir ***From St Austell take B3273. At Tregiskey crossroads turn right. St Ewe signed on right.***

A mile away from the Lost Gardens of Heligan, this attractive 16th-century village inn is the ideal place to refuel, whether by the fire in the traditional bar or in the flower-festooned garden. Sandwiches, jacket potatoes and small portions of main dishes are available at lunchtime.

ST AGNES

Driftwood Spars ★★★★

GUEST ACCOMMODATION

Tel **01872 552428** | **Trevaunance Cove, TR5 0RT**
Web **www.driftwoodspars.co.uk**
Dir ***A30 onto B3285, through St Agnes, down hill, left at Peterville Inn, follow Trevaunance Cove sign.***

Great 16th-century find near coastal path

PICK OF THE PUBS

This whitewashed, three-storey building has fulfilled many functions, not least as a smugglers' rendezvous – secret tunnel and all. The roof timbers are spars from a wreck (hence the name), and assorted furnishings, open fires and dressed stone walls provide additional character in the warren of rooms, including the summer-only, ocean-facing seaview bistro. Up to six hand-pulled real ales, including those from the on-site microbrewery, are served, as are Rattler Cornish cider and a few English wines. A seasonal bar menu features baked Cornish brie with ciabatta; Cornish mussels cooked in Driftwood beer with fennel; Thai green vegetable curry with basmati rice. Beer festivals are in mid March, early May and at the end of October.

Open all day, all week 11–11 (Fri to Sat 11am–1am 25 Dec 11am–2pm) Free House 11 from £10.95 portions/menu notice required

ST IVES

The Queens ★★ HOTEL

Tel **01736 796468** | **2 High Street, TR26 1RR**
Web **www.queenshotelstives.com**
Dir ***From roundabout on A30 take A3074 signed St Ives. Through Carbis Bay. In St Ives pass entrance to rail station on right, pass church on corner on right. Road becomes High Street. Pub on left (opposite Boots the Chemist).***

There's an easy-going mix of chic and contemporary design with a nod to times past in this thriving hostelry at the heart of the old town. It's worth the stroll from the harbour or the beaches to discover this late-Georgian building, where local art works vie for attention with local cider, Cornish beers and a great menu. Lunch might be Tribute beer-battered fish 'n' chips; or home-cooked honey-roast ham, free-range eggs and chips.

Open all day, all week St Austell Brewery 13 portions/menu notice required

The Sloop Inn ★★★ INN

Tel **01736 796584** | **The Wharf, TR26 1LP**
Web **www.sloop-inn.co.uk**
Dir ***On St Ives harbour by middle slipway.***

A trip to St Ives wouldn't be complete without visiting this 700-year-old pub perched right on the harbourside. Slate floors, beamed ceilings and nautical artefacts dress some of the several bars and dining areas, whilst the cobbled forecourt is an unbeatable spot for people-watching.

ST IVES

The Watermill

Tel **01736 757912** | **Lelant Downs, Hayle, TR27 6LQ**
Web **www.watermillincornwall.co.uk**
Dir ***Exit A30 at junction for St Ives/A3074, turn left at 2nd mini-roundabout.***

A stunning panorama across open countryside

In extensive gardens on the old St Ives coach road, with glorious valley views towards Trencrom Hill, this cosy, family-friendly pub and restaurant was built in the 18th century as Lelant Mill. Although it ceased milling in the early 1900s, the old machinery is still in place and the mill stream still turns the original iron waterwheel. Downstairs is the old beamed bar with a wood-burning stove, while upstairs in the open-beamed loft is an atmospheric restaurant where a full menu, including light bites and children's favourites, is available both at lunchtime and in the evening. You'll find plenty to appeal among the burgers, pub classics, pastas, chargrills and salads; if not, a daily specials board adds to the options. There's a beer festival in June each year.

Open all day, all week 12–11 (Sun 12–10.30)
Free House portions/menu

ST KEW

St Kew Inn

Tel **01208 841259** | **Churchtown, PL30 3HB**
Web **www.stkewinn.co.uk**
Dir ***From Wadebridge north on A39. Left to St Kew.***

Visit this 15th-century, stone-built pub in summer and you will be rewarded with flower tubs and creepers enhancing its pretty façade, whilst traditional features inside include a huge open fire. Cornish St Austell beers and Rattler cider are the prime refreshments, while menus proffer carefully sourced British dishes, often featuring local fish and seafood. Choose between four eating areas – five if you include the garden – when ordering your lunchtime snack. Evening dishes might include seared seafood gratin; and chicken, bacon and mushroom pie.

Open all week 11–3 5.30–11 (summer all day) St Austell Brewery portions/menu

ST MAWES

The Victory Inn PICK OF THE PUBS

Tel **01326 270324** | **Victory Hill, TR2 5DQ**
Web **www.victoryinn.co.uk**
Dir ***A3078 to St Mawes. Pub adjacent to harbour.***

Tucked away near the harbour, this friendly fishermen's local is named after Nelson's flagship. Wines are all carefully chosen, as are the real ales from Cornwall's own Roseland, Sharp's and Skinner's breweries. Whether you eat downstairs in the traditional bar, or in the modern and stylish first-floor restaurant with its white walls, white linen and wicker chairs, the approach to food is modern. Start with duck spring roll, Asian salad and hoisin sauce, perhaps followed by Doom Bar-battered cod, chips, crushed peas and tartare sauce or lamb chop with dauphinoise potatoes, roasted sweet potato purée, mixed greens and chorizo and mushroom brandy cream. There is outside seating with views over the harbour.

Open all year, all day Closed Sun evening in winter Punch Taverns 11 from £10 portions/menu

ST MAWGAN

The Falcon Inn PICK OF THE PUBS

Tel **01637 860225** | **TR8 4EP**
Web **www.thefalconinnstmawgan.co.uk**
Dir ***From A30 (8 miles west of Bodmin) follow signs to Newquay Airport. Turn right 200 metres before airport terminal into St Mawgan, pub at bottom of hill.***

You'll find this wisteria-clad, stone-built inn in what is known as both the Vale of Lanherne and the Vale of Mawgan. Built in 1758, or perhaps even earlier, it has been The Falcon since about 1880, named after the nearby estate's coat of arms. Inside, flagstones and log fires; outside a cobbled courtyard and an attractive garden with a magnificent magnolia tree. Rotating real ales are predominantly Cornish, although outsiders do get a look in; there's also a dozen wines by the glass and an impressive range of spirits. Snacks and light meals appear at lunchtime, along with rump steaks; battered fish fillets; and sweet potato and butternut squash ravioli, which are also available as dinner choices.

Open all week 11–3 5.30–11 (Fri to Sat 11–11 Sun 12–11) Free House 12 portions/menu notice required

ST MERRYN

The Cornish Arms PICK OF THE PUBS

Tel **01841 532700** | **Churchtown, PL28 8ND**
Web **www.rickstein.com**
Dir ***From Padstow follow signs for St Merryn, up hill, pub on right.***

St Merryn, just outside Padstow, is home to this ancient pub, part of the Stein portfolio. Situated across the road from the parish church and overlooking a peaceful valley, it remains very much the village boozer. It oozes character, with slate floors, beams and roaring log fires, and they've kept the food offering equally traditional. Start with grilled Mount's Bay sardines, or half pint of prawns, continue with traditional battered fish and chips; or curries inspired by Rick's travels; and end with sticky toffee pudding with clotted cream. Wash it down with a glass of Chalky's Bite. Check with the pub for details of special seasonal offers throughout the year.

Open all day, all week 11.30–11 St Austell Brewery 12 portions/menu

ST TUDY

St Tudy Inn

Tel **01208 850656 | PL30 3NN**
Web **www.sttudyinn.com**
Dir ***Follow St Tudy signs from A39 between Camelford and Wadebridge. Pub in village centre.***

Emily Scott, one of Cornwall's most admired female chefs, owns this much-loved village pub. The building's exterior stonework and interior warm terracotta decor create a welcoming ambience. Emily's short and sweet menus with no-nonsense pricing indicate treats in store.

SALTASH

The Crooked Inn ★★★★ INN

Tel **01752 848177 | Stoketon Cottage, Trematon, PL12 4RZ**
Web **www.crooked-inn.co.uk**
Dir ***Phone for detailed directions.***

Overlooking the lush Lyher Valley, this delightful inn is set in 10 acres of lawns and woodland, just 15 minutes from Plymouth, and once housed staff from Stoketon Manor, whose ruins lie on nearby. The menu offers something for everyone – Mediterranean meze; confit of belly pork; and home-made soup of the day; mains include rack of roasted ribs; or warm Manuka smoked duck salad. There's a children's playground and a treehouse.

Open all day, all week 11–11 (Sun 12–10.30) Closed 25 Dec Free House 9 portions/menu

SCILLY ISLES – *SEE TRESCO*

TORPOINT

Edgcumbe Arms PICK OF THE PUBS

Tel **01752 822294 | Cremyll, PL10 1HX**
Web **www.edgcumbearms.co.uk**
Dir ***Phone for detailed directions.***

Close to the foot ferry from Plymouth, this inn next to Mount Edgcumbe Country Park offers fabulous views from its bow window seats and waterside terrace, which take in Drakes Island, the Royal William Yard and the marina. Real ales from St Austell and quality home-cooked food are served in a series of characterful rooms. The same extensive menu is offered throughout and dishes are a mixture of international and traditional British pub.

TREBARWITH

The Mill House Inn – see page 90

The Port William

Tel **01840 770230 | Trebarwith Strand, PL34 0HB**
Web **www.theportwilliam.co.uk**
Dir ***From A39 onto B3314 signed Tintagel. Right onto B3263, follow Trebarwith Strand signs, then brown Port William signs.***

This former harbourmaster's house lies directly on the coastal path, 50 yards from the sea, which means the views of the Trebarwith Strand are amazing, and there is an entrance to a smugglers' tunnel. Obviously there's quite an emphasis on fresh fish, but there's no shortage of other options.

TREBURLEY

The Springer Spaniel

Tel **01579 370424 | PL15 9NS**
Web **www.thespringerspaniel.co.uk**
Dir ***On A388 halfway between Launceston and Callington.***

Set above the valley of the River Inny in the pretty hamlet of Treburley, a few miles south of Launceston, this 18th-century pub is dedicated to serving top-notch ales, ciders and food. The tree-shaded garden to the rear is a pleasant place to relax.

TREGADILLETT

Eliot Arms

Tel **01566 772051 | PL15 7EU**
Web **www.theeliotarms.co.uk**
Dir ***From Launceston take A30 towards Bodmin. Then follow brown signs to Tregadillett.***

The extraordinary decor in this charming creeper-clad coaching inn, dating back to 1625, includes Masonic regalia, horse brasses and grandfather clocks. Customers can enjoy real fires in winter. Food is based on locally sourced meat and fresh fish and shellfish caught off the Cornish coast.

TREBARWITH

The Mill House Inn

Tel **01840 770200 | PL34 0HD**
Web **www.themillhouseinn.co.uk**
Dir ***From Tintagel take B3263 south, right after Trewarmett to Trebarwith Strand. Pub 0.5 mile on right.***

Family-friendly inn with good food

PICK OF THE PUBS

Set in seven acres of woodland on the north Cornish coast, the Mill House is half a mile from the surfing beach at Trebarwith Strand, one of the finest in Cornwall. The log fires in this atmospheric stone building warm the residents' lounge and slate-floored bar, where wooden tables and chapel chairs help create a relaxed, family-friendly feel. Real ales are supplied by Tintagel brewery, and the ciders are Cornish Orchards and Healey's Cornish Rattler. Lunches, evening drinks and barbecues are served out on the attractive terraces, while dinner in the Millstream Restaurant might involve Boscastle beef fillet, pulled beef cheek croquette, sweet potato, autumn greens, and crispy parsnips with red wine and port jus. Regular live entertainment features local musicians.

Open all day, all week 11–11 (Fri to Sat 11am–midnight Sun 12–10.30) Free House from £12 portions/menu notice required

TRESCO (ISLES OF SCILLY)

The New Inn ★★★★ INN

PICK OF THE PUBS

Tel **01720 422849 | New Grimsby, TR24 0QQ**
Web **www.tresco.co.uk**
Dir ***By New Grimsby Quay.***

Just a few steps away from this old inn is the first of a string of white-sand beaches that garland this sub-tropical island in the Atlantic. Very much at the heart of Tresco's community, the pub hosts three ale and cider festivals during the summer months, and live music throughout the year. You can expect a hearty welcome at the bar, which is partly created from shipwreck salvage. Delicious Scillonian provender from both land and sea are the mainstays of the pub's menu. The 'surf and turf' combination of Bryher lobster and chargrilled Tresco beefsteak is a no-brainer, while the savoury delicacy of a Cornish pork and Tresco partridge sausage roll may suffice for the smaller appetite.

Open all day, all week (Apr to Oct), phone for winter opening times Free House 14 from £9.50 portions/menu Wi-fi

TRURO

Old Ale House

Tel **01872 271122 | 7 Quay Street, TR1 2HD**
Web **www.skinnersbrewery.com**
Dir ***In town centre.***

As a Skinner's Brewery tap, this heavily beamed pub close to the old riverside quays is renowned for its impressive range of ales and ciders. There are 20 keg lines offering a wide choice of beers and over 100 spirits. Go for a pint of Betty Stogs or Porthleven IPA and check out the live music on Mondays and Saturdays. Food isn't served here but customers can bring their own.

Open all day, all week 11–11 (Fri to Sat 11am–1am Sun 12–10.30) Free House 9 Wi-fi notice required

VERYAN

The New Inn

Tel **01872 501362** | **TR2 5QA**
Web **www.newinn-veryan.co.uk**
Dir ***From St Austell take A390 towards Truro, in 2 miles left to Tregony. Through Tregony, follow signs to Veryan.***

This lovely unspoiled pub started life as a pair of cottages in the 16th century. In the centre of a pretty village on the Roseland Peninsula, The New Inn has open fires, a beamed ceiling, a single bar serving St Austell ales and a delightfully warm, welcoming atmosphere.

WADEBRIDGE

The Quarryman Inn

Tel **01208 816444** | **Edmonton, PL27 7JA**
Web **www.thequarryman.co.uk**
Dir ***From A39 (west of Wadebridge) follow Edmonton sign (opposite Royal Cornwall Showground).***

Close to the famous Camel Trail, this family-owned free house was originally a group of 18th-century slate workers' cottages, built around a courtyard. The pub's menus change frequently, but the house speciality is hake, monkfish, prawns and mussels Thai-style green curry, cooked and served in a copper cataplana. Also popular are chargrilled, sizzling, prime Cornish steaks served on a platter with mushrooms, tomatoes, onions and chips. Enjoy one of the good range of beers and ciders in the slate courtyard.

Open all day, all week 12–11 Closed 25 Dec Free House from £10 portions/menu notice required

WIDEMOUTH BAY

Bay View Inn

Tel **01288 361273** | **Marine Drive, EX23 0AW**
Web **bayviewinn.co.uk**
Dir ***Adjacent to beach.***

Dating back around 100 years, this welcoming, family-run pub was a guest house for many years before becoming an inn in the 1960s. True to its name, it has fabulous views of the Atlantic. It has three dining areas: Driftwood Restaurant, Surf Restaurant, and Beach Hut Restaurant.

ZENNOR

The Tinners Arms PICK OF THE PUBS

Tel **01736 796927** | **TR26 3BY**
Web **www.tinnersarms.co.uk**
Dir ***Take B3306 from St Ives towards St Just. Zennor approximately 5 miles.***

Close to the South West Coast Path, the Tinners Arms is popular with walkers who along with other visitors enjoy the timelessness of its stone floors, low ceilings, cushioned settles, open fires and refreshimg Cornish real ales or Burrow Hill cider from Somerset. Built in 1271 for the masons working on St Senara's church next door (famous for its Mermaid Chair), the only pub in the village has no TV, jukebox or fruit machine, nor can a mobile phone signal reach it. Menus are based on ingredients from local suppliers, and a winter supper might feature moules marinière; grilled goats' cheese and couscous salad; venison and chorizo stew, with creamy mash and curly kale; and winter berry crumble with ice cream or custard. Sandwiches, ploughman's and light meals are available at lunchtime.

Open all day, all week Free House 10 portions/menu

CUMBRIA

ALLITHWAITE

The Pheasant Inn

Tel **015395 32239** | **Flookburgh Road, LA11 7RQ**
Web **www.thepheasantallithwaite.com**
Dir ***From A590 onto B5277, follow signs for Grange-over-Sands. Continue on B5277, after 2 miles on sharp left bend.***

Run by the Jones family, this free house close to the Cumbrian Coastal Way is situated in the pretty south Lakeland village of Allithwaite and boasts views across Morecambe Bay. The bar offers a wide selection of local ales including Loweswater Gold and guest beers from the likes of Hawkshead and Bowness Bay breweries. At lunchtime, the emphasis is on hot and cold sandwiches and platters, but things move up a gear in the evening with favourites like slow-roasted lamb shoulder and red wine gravy.

Open all day, all week Free House 9 from £10.95 portions/menu

AMBLESIDE

Drunken Duck Inn PICK OF THE PUBS

Tel **015394 36347** | **Barngates, LA22 0NG**
Web **www.drunkenduckinn.co.uk**
Dir ***From Kendal on A591 to Ambleside, then follow Hawkshead sign. In 2.5 miles inn sign on right, 1 mile up hill.***

When a 19th-century landlady found her ducks blotto in the road after a beer leak 'contaminated' their feed, she thought they were dead and began plucking them. When they came round, she was so full of remorse she knitted them warm woollen waistcoats. The inn stands at a crossroads above Ambleside with splendid views towards Windermere, and ales from the on-site Barngates brewery are served on a slate counter in the characterful oak-floored, hop-hung bar. Add candlelight and a log fire, and what more could you want? The menu offers a Lancashire cheese and smoked haddock soufflé; lamb rump and shoulder, potato terrine, salt-baked carrot and salsa verde; and parkin, poached grapes and salted caramel ice cream. Behind lies a tranquil garden with its own tarn.

Open all day, all week Closed 25 Dec Free House 12 menus Wi-fi

Wateredge Inn

Tel **015394 32332** | **Waterhead Bay, LA22 0EP**
Web **www.wateredgeinn.co.uk**
Dir ***M6 junction 36, A591 to Ambleside, 5 miles from Windermere station.***

The Wateredge Inn was converted from two 17th-century fishermen's cottages, and now offers a stylish bar and restaurant. With large gardens and plenty of seating running down to the lakeshore, the inn has been run by the same family for over 30 years. The lunch menu offers sandwiches, salads and pub classics, while dinner dishes range from Cumberland sausage, mash, apple sauce and rich gravy to a fish pie with salmon, prawns, cod and smoked haddock. Specials and a children's menu are also available.

Open all day, all week 10.30am–11pm Closed 23–26 Dec Free House 9 from £11.95 portions/menu Wi-fi

APPLEBY-IN-WESTMORLAND

Tufton Arms Hotel PICK OF THE PUBS

Tel **017683 51593** | **Market Square, CA16 6XA**
Web **www.tuftonarmshotel.co.uk**
Dir ***In town centre.***

This imposing, gabled building sits at the foot of Appleby's main street, close to the River Eden below the curvaceous fells of the wild North Pennines. There's a soothingly elegant, country house feel to the public rooms, with astonishing attention to detail producing a timeless atmosphere and contemporary comforts. At the heart of the hotel, overlooking a cobbled mews courtyard, is the Conservatory Fish Restaurant, where the kitchen team's cuisine is complemented by a serious wine list.

BASSENTHWAITE LAKE

The Pheasant – see opposite

BEETHAM

The Wheatsheaf at Beetham

PICK OF THE PUBS

Tel **015395 64652** | **LA7 7AL**
Web **www.wheatsheafbeetham.com**
Dir ***On A6, 5 miles north of M6 junction 35.***

What became today's Wheatsheaf was built in 1609, since when many owners have contributed to the look and feel of this impressive corner-site pub. Now newly refurbished in soothing tones of grey and creamy-white, it continues to appeal not just to villagers, but to the many visitors intent on exploring the splendid surrounding countryside, perhaps to make a secret wish at nearby Fairy Steps. Local ales, award-winning craft beers and a wide-ranging wine and spirits collection offer a great choice as accompaniment to, for instance, devilled kidneys as a starter, with fish – delivered daily from Fleetwood – and chips, lamb shank pie or maybe vegan falafel burger with minted houmous to follow. Sandra's sticky toffee pudding is a firm favourite.

Open all day, all week 10am–11pm Free House 18 from £10.95 portions/menu Wi-fi notice required

BASSENTHWAITE LAKE

The Pheasant

Tel 01767 76234 | CA13 9YE
Web www.the-pheasant.co.uk
Dir *A66 to Cockermouth, 8 miles north of Keswick on left.*

Accomplished food in peaceful Lake District setting

PICK OF THE PUBS

At the foot of the Sale Fell and close to Bassenthwaite Lake, this 17th-century former coaching inn occupies a peaceful spot in the Lake District and is surrounded by lovely gardens. Once a farmhouse, the pub today combines the role of traditional Cumbrian hostelry with that of an internationally renowned, modern hotel. Even so, you still sense the history the moment you walk through the door – the legendary foxhunter John Peel, whose "view halloo would awaken the dead", according to the song, was a regular here. In the warmly inviting bar, with polished parquet flooring, panelled walls and oak settles, hang two of Cumbrian artist and former customer Edward H Thompson's paintings. Here, you can order a pint of Coniston Bluebird or Hawkshead Bitter, or cast your eyes over the extensive selection of malt whiskies. The high standard of food is well known for miles around; meals are served in the attractive beamed restaurant, bistro, bar and lounges overlooking the gardens. Treat the family to afternoon tea with home-made scones and rum butter. The Pheasant can get pretty busy, so booking ahead for meals may be required.

Open all day, all week Closed 25 Dec *Free House* 12 *from £13.50* *portions/menu*

BOOT

Brook House Inn PICK OF THE PUBS

Tel **019467 23288** | **CA19 1TG**
Web **www.brookhouseinn.co.uk**
Dir ***M6 junction 36, A590 follow Barrow signs. A5092, then A595. Pass Broughton-in-Furness, right at lights to Ulpha. Cross river, next left signed Eskdale to Boot. (Note: not all routes to Boot are suitable in bad weather conditions).***

Few locations can rival this: Lakeland fells rise behind the inn to England's highest peak, while golden sunsets illuminate tranquil Eskdale. Footpaths wind to nearby Stanley Ghyll's wooded gorge with its falls and red squirrels, and the charming La'al Ratty narrow-gauge railway steams to and from the coast. Up to seven real ales are kept, including Langdale from Cumbrian Legendary Ales, and an amazing selection of 175 malt whiskies, plus 25 gins. Home-made food might include a warming bowl of home-made soup, or grilled goats' cheese rarebit with Eskdale relish, followed by local Cumberland sausage; beef and beer pie; or smoked haddock on mashed potato with leeks. This great community pub also takes a full role in the famous Boot Beer Festival each June.

Open all day, all week Closed 25 Dec Free House 10 portions/menu

BORROWDALE

The Langstrath Country Inn

Tel **017687 77239** | **CA12 5XG**
Web **www.thelangstrath.com**
Dir ***From Keswick take B5289, through Grange and Rosthwaite, left to Stonethwaite. Inn on left after 0.5 mile.***

Sitting in the stunning Langstrath Valley in the heart of the Lakes and on the coast-to-coast and Cumbrian Way walks, this lovely family-run, 16th-century inn was originally a miner's cottage. It is an ideal base for those attempting England's highest peak, Scafell Pike, and the restaurant is ideally positioned to maximise the spectacular views. Here hungry ramblers can enjoy high-quality Lakeland dishes based on local ingredients. Local cask-conditioned ales include some from the Keswick Brewery.

Open all day 12–10.30 Closed Dec and Jan, Mon Free House 9 from £14.75 portions/menu notice required

BOWLAND BRIDGE

Hare & Hounds Country Inn

PICK OF THE PUBS

Tel **015395 68785** | **LA11 6NN**
Web **www.hareandhoundsbowlandbridge.co.uk**
Dir ***M6 junction 36, A590 signed Barrow. Right onto A5074 signed Bowness and Windermere. Approximately 4 miles at sharp left bend and follow Bowland Bridge sign.***

Just three miles from Lake Windermere with exceptional views of the surrounding fells, this 17th-century coaching inn's black slate floors, stacked logs, old pine tables and mis-matched chairs give it plenty of atmosphere. Frequently changing real ales come from local breweries, while the home-cooked menu and daily specials might indclude Cartmel Valley burger and fries, or beer-battered haddock and chunky chips. For something more sophisticated, consider grilled sirloin steak with green peppercorn sauce, or beetroot and red wine risotto with grilled goats' cheese. Homely desserts include Bramley apple crumble with vanilla ice cream. The terrace or garden will beckon on fine days.

Open all day, all week 12–11 Closed 25 Dec Free House portions/menu

BRAITHWAITE

Coledale Inn

Tel **017687 78272** | **CA12 5TN**
Web **www.coledale-inn.co.uk**
Dir ***M6 junction 40, A66 signed Keswick. Approximately 18 miles. Exit A66, follow Whinlatter Pass and Braithwaite sign, left on B5292. In Braithwaite left at pub sign, over stream bridge to inn.***

Originally a woollen mill, the refurbished Coledale Inn dates from around 1824 and has had stints as a pencil mill and a private house before becoming the inn it is today. The interior is attractively designed, whilst footpaths leading off from the large gardens make it ideal for exploring the nearby fells. Two homely bars serve a selection of local ales while traditional lunch and dinner menus are served in the dining room.

Open all day, all week Free House 8 portions/menu notice required

The Royal Oak

Tel **017687 78533** | **CA12 5SY**
Web **www.royaloak-braithwaite.co.uk**
Dir ***M6 junction 40, A66 towards Keswick, approximately 18 miles (bypass Keswick), exit A66 left onto B5292 to Braithwaite. Pub in village centre.***

Surrounded by high fells and beautiful scenery, The Royal Oak is set in the centre of the village and is the perfect base for walkers. The interior is all oak beams and log fires, and the menu offers hearty pub food, such as slow-roasted pork belly and apple flavoured mash; and giant Yorkshire pudding filled with Cumberland sausage casserole, all served alongside local ales, such as Sneck Lifter or Cumberland Ale.

Open all day, all week Closed 25 Dec Marston's 9 portions/menu WiFi P

BRAMPTON

Blacksmiths Arms ★★★★ INN

Tel **016977 3452** | **Talkin, CA8 1LE**
Web **www.blacksmithstalkin.co.uk**
Dir ***M6 junction 43, A69 east. 7 miles, straight on at roundabout, follow signs to Talkin Tarn then Talkin Village.***

With cartwheels lined up outside, this former smithy has northern Cumbria's wildly beautiful countryside on its doorstep. Four real ales are always available and there's a beer garden. The menu of good, traditional home cooking makes extensive use of fresh local produce for dishes like smoked haddock and spring onion fishcakes; steak and ale pie; Barnsley double lamb chop; and spinach and ricotta cannelloni. At lunchtime a choice of sandwiches, paninis and baked potatoes is offered.

Open all day, all week 12-12 Free House 16 from £7.95 WiFi *portions/menu* P

CARTMEL

The Masons Arms

Tel **015395 68486** | **Strawberry Bank, LA11 6NW**
Web **www.masonsarmsstrawberrybank.co.uk**
Dir ***M6 junction 36, A590 towards Barrow. Right onto A5074 signed Bowness/Windermere. 5 miles, left at Bowland Bridge. Through village, pub on right.***

A charmingly decorated pub with a stunning location overlooking the Winster Valley and beyond, The Masons Arms has an atmospheric interior with low, beamed ceilings, old fireplaces and quirky furniture. Waiting staff manoeuvre through the busy bar, dining rooms and heated, covered terraces.

CLIFTON

George and Dragon, Clifton
– see page 96

COCKERMOUTH

The Trout Hotel ★★★★ HOTEL

Tel **01900 823591** | **Crown Street, CA13 0EJ**
Web **www.trouthotel.co.uk**
Dir ***In town centre.***

Until he was eight, the poet William Wordsworth lived next door, although in those days this 17th-century building was a private house. Much remains to remind us of its heritage: stone walls, exposed beams, marble fireplaces, restored plasterwork, period stained-glass, and a carefully-preserved oak staircase.

CONISTON

The Black Bull Inn & Hotel

PICK OF THE PUBS

Tel **015394 41335** | **1 Yewdale Road, LA21 8DU**
Web **www.conistonbrewery.com**
Dir ***M6 junction 36, A590. 23 miles from Kendal via Windermere and Ambleside.***

Beside a stream, or beck as they say round here, stands this traditional Lakeland pub. Its bare stone walls, oak beams, log-burning stove and part-slate floor all contribute to its appeal, while of further interest, at least to beer drinkers, is its own microbrewery's Bluebird Bitter, commemorating Donald Campbell's attempts on the world water speed record; it also brews Old Man Ale, named for the local 2,634-ft mountain. Those out walking all morning or all day can look forward to sandwiches or filled jacket potatoes. Chances are they'll want something heartier, such as roast rib of beef with Yorkshire pudding and gravy; poached sole fillets with dill and cucumber cream; or roast loin and belly of pork with sage and onion stuffing, crackling and gravy.

Open all day, all week Closed 25 Dec Free House 10 portions/menu WiFi P *notice required*

CLIFTON

George and Dragon, Clifton ★★★★ INN

Tel **01768 865381** | **CA10 2ER**
Web **www.georgeanddragonclifton.co.uk**
Dir ***M6 junction 40, A66 towards Appleby-in-Westmorland, A6 south to Clifton.***

Historic pub majoring on local produce

This lovely pub is more peaceful today than it was in 1745, when the retreating army of 'Bonnie' Prince Charlie was defeated in the nearby village of Clifton. The pub is set on the historic Lowther Estate near Ullswater. Meticulously renovated by owner Charles Lowther, this is a traditional inn with contemporary comforts, and the appealing menu majors on the bountiful produce of the estate. Beef is from pedigree Shorthorns; pork from home-reared rare breed stock; while game and most fish is local. Settle in with a pint of Hawkshead Bitter and secure a starter of Estate venison pie with a fruit chutney followed by. perhaps, Rough Fell lamb and cockle suet pudding, spring onion mash, braised leek and lamb sauce.Sharing plates, salads, sandwiches and burgers all vie for space on the menu. There is a secluded courtyard and garden.

Open all day, all week Closed 26 Dec Free House 17 from £9 portions/menu

CROSTHWAITE

The Punch Bowl Inn – see opposite

ENNERDALE BRIDGE

Shepherds Arms Hotel – see page 98

ELTERWATER

The Britannia Inn PICK OF THE PUBS

Tel **015394 37210** | **LA22 9HP**
Web **www.thebritanniainn.com**
Dir ***In village centre.***

Walks and mountain-bike trails head off in all directions from the door of this free house in the Langdale Valley. Built as a farmhouse more than 500 years ago, the whitewashed building has been an inn for some 200 years and the bar is a series of small, cosy rooms with low-beamed oak ceilings and winter coal fires. You'll find guest beers, as well as the house special brewed by Coniston; an even wider selection of real ales is available during the two-week beer festival in mid-November. Dinner might be grilled haggis with home-made plum jam; or chicken, ham and leek pie. Dine in the garden for views of the village and tarns.

Open all day, all week 10.30am–11pm Free House portions/menu Wi-fi

FAUGH

The String of Horses Inn

Tel **01228 670297** | **CA8 9EG**
Web **www.stringofhorses.com**
Dir ***M6 junction 43, A69 towards Hexham. In approximately 5 miles right at 1st lights at Corby Hill/Warwick Bridge. 1 mile, through Heads Nook, in 1 mile sharp right. Left into Faugh. Pub on left down hill.***

Close to Hadrian's Wall in the peaceful village of Faugh, this traditional 17th-century Lakeland inn may be tucked away but it's just 10 minutes from Carlisle. There are oak beams, wood panelling, old settles and log fires in the restaurant, where imaginative pub food (Creole sticky prawn rice; chicken fajitas; chilli lasagne) is on offer, and in the bar, where you'll find real ales from the Allendale and Hesket breweries.

Open all year Tue to Sun 6–11 Closed Mon Free House 8 menus Wi-fi notice required

CROSTHWAITE

The Punch Bowl Inn

★★★★★  

Tel 015395 68237 | LA8 8HR
Web www.the-punchbowl.co.uk
Dir *M6 junction 36, A590 towards Barrow, A5074, follow Crosthwaite signs. Pub by church.*

Luxury Lake District inn and restaurant

PICK OF THE PUBS

Very much a destination dining inn, the Punch Bowl stands alongside the village church in the delightfully unspoilt Lyth Valley. The slates on the bar floor, which were found beneath the old dining room, complement the Brathay slate bar top and antique furnishings. Ales from Cumbrian microbreweries include Tag Lag from Barngates Brewery, and Swan Blonde. The restaurant has comfortable leather chairs, polished oak floorboards and an eye-catching stone fireplace. Two rooms off the bar add extra space for eating or relaxing with a pint and the daily paper in front of an open fire. The head chef and his team focus on the best local and seasonal produce with ingredients sourced extensively from the area's estates, farms and coastal villages. Desserts are accomplished and tempting – blackberry soufflé, vanilla ice cream and blackberry sauce; or lemon tart with damson sorbet for example. In addition to a good list of dessert wines, champagne is available by the glass. Individually designed and furnished guest rooms featuring freestanding roll-top baths can be booked.

Open all day, all week *Free House* 12
portions/menu P

ENNERDALE BRIDGE

Shepherds Arms Hotel

Tel **01946 861249** | **Kirkland Road, CA23 3AR**
Web **www.shepherdsarms.com**
Dir ***From A66 at Cockermouth take A5086 to Egremont. 7.3 miles, left towards Ennerdale. Through Kirkland down to Ennerdale Bridge.***

A popular destination for coast-to-coast walkers

You don't have to be walking the 192 miles from St Bees to Robin Hood's Bay to swap travellers' tales in the two-fire bar, but you'll probably meet those who are. The hotel was once a village-centre farmhouse that also dispensed beer to the local farmers and travellers. Today, it serves an excellent array of Cumbrian ales, alongside traditional home cooking, starting at lunchtime with sandwiches, snacks and main meals such as steak and ale pie, and finishing in the evening with fresh lobster; Lakeland lamb and beef; chicken and chorizo cassoulet; baked salmon with chilli salsa; and, one of several vegan options, Mediterranean bean casserole. Walkers may order a packed lunch for the final push to St Bees, or the more daunting climb east. Further seating is available at the rear.

Open all day, all week (winter times may vary) Closed 25–26 Dec Free House portions notice required

GRASMERE

The Travellers Rest Inn – see opposite

GREAT SALKELD

The Highland Drove Inn

PICK OF THE PUBS

Tel **01768 898349** | **CA11 9NA**
Web **www.kyloes.co.uk**
Dir ***M6 junction 40, A66 eastbound, A686 to Alston. 4 miles, left onto B6412 for Great Salkeld and Lazonby.***

On an old drove road, this 300-year-old country inn recalls the long-vanished days when hardy Highland cattle were driven across open water from Scotland's Western Isles to markets in England. A reputation for high-quality food might suggest it's a destination pub, but it's more than that, because locals love it. The attractive brick and timber bar is furnished with old tables and settles; the more formal dining takes place upstairs in the hunting lodge-style restaurant.

HAWKSHEAD

Kings Arms

Tel **015394 36372** | **The Square, LA22 0NZ**
Web **www.kingsarmshawkshead.co.uk**
Dir ***M6 junction 36, A590 to Newby Bridge, right at 1st junction past roundabout, over bridge, 8 miles to Hawkshead.***

In the heart of this Lakeland village, made famous by Beatrix Potter who lived nearby, this 16th-century inn throngs in summer. In colder weather, bag a table by the fire in the traditional carpeted bar, take a pint of Hawkshead Bitter and tuck into lunchtime food such as Cumberland sausage, mash and onion gravy, or evening meals along the lines of potted rabbit with pickled vegetables followed by steak and Hawkshead ale pie.

Open all day, all week 11am to midnight Free House 10 from £12.75 portions/menu Wi-fi notice required

GRASMERE

The Travellers Rest Inn

Tel **015394 35604** | **Keswick Road, LA22 9RR**
Web **www.lakedistrictinns.co.uk**
Dir ***A591 to Grasmere, pub 0.5 mile north of Grasmere.***

A pub for more than 500 years with old world charm

The name makes perfect sense when you arrive. Facing Fell Crag and with Rydal Crag to its rear, it stands alone a little way out of picturesque Grasmere, making it an ideal base for touring the ever-beautiful Lake District. William Wordsworth, who lived in Grasmere for 14 years, called it "the loveliest spot that man hath ever found"; he would probably still think so. Oak beams, inglenooks and winter fires inside, and beer gardens with dramatic views of the fells outside, prove a powerful draw. Along with much-loved real ales like Jennings' Sneck Lifter, there's an extensive cellar of fine wines and a fair few malt whiskies. Traditional home-cooked food is offered from a wide-ranging menu, which at lunchtime offers small, medium and large plates, examples respectively being Ploughman's Lakeland Board, chicken supreme stuffed with feta, spinach and sun dried tomatoes, and home-made steak and kidney pudding. In the evening, begin with confit duck leg salad; then crusted rack of lamb; or aubergine, tomato and vegetable parmigiana bake. Or you may want to seek inspiration from the steak menu. Last, but by no means least, are Cumbrian sticky toffee pudding, and a platter of local cheeses to finish.

Open all day, all week 12–11 Free House 10 from £12.95 portions/menu P notice required

The Queen's Head Inn & Restaurant ★★★★ INN

PICK OF THE PUBS

Tel **015394 36271** | **Main Street, LA22 0NS**
Web **www.queensheadhawkshead.co.uk**
Dir ***M6 junction 36, A590 to Newby Bridge, 1st right, 8 miles to Hawkshead.***

Home to William Wordsworth and Beatrix Potter, the liberally whitewashed village of Hawkshead, with its cobbled alleyways and squares, is one of the Lakes' most picturesque. Standing right in the centre of the village, this lively, black-and-white timbered inn has been part of local life since the early 17th century. No great surprise then to find a timeless interior of low beams, wood panelling and slate floors. Real ales travel up from Robinsons of Stockport, while the food owes much to truly local sources. Start with braised pork cheek and creamed parsnip then follow with slow-roasted shoulder of Lakeland lamb with pea purée and curly kale; or pan-fried cod supreme risotto with Jerusalem artichoke crisps. Pub classics and pizzas get a fair billing too. For dessert – good old sticky toffee pudding.

Open all day, all week 11am–11.45pm (Sun 12–11.45) Closed 25 Dec Robinsons 11 from £9.95 portions/menu notice required

The Sun Inn ★★★★ INN

Tel **015394 36236** | **Main Street, LA22 0NT**
Web **www.suninn.co.uk**
Dir ***Northbound on M6 junction 36, A591 to Ambleside, B5286 to Hawkshead. Southbound on M6 junction 40, A66 to Keswick, A591 to Ambleside, B5286 to Hawkshead.***

This listed 17th-century coaching inn is at the heart of the charming Hawkshead village and makes a great base for exploring the Lakes. The wood-panelled bar has low, oak-beamed ceilings, and hill walkers and others will enjoy the log fires, real ales and locally sourced food. Choices range from crispy confit rabbit wontons, to venison terrine with cured ham and chestnuts for starters; and for mains from sharing curry platter, to Cumbrian lamb shoulder with lamb and mint jus.

Open all day, all week 10am to midnight Free House portions/menu

KENDAL

The Punch Bowl ★★★★ INN

Tel **015395 60267** | **Barrows Green, LA8 0AA**
Web **www.thepunchbowla65.co.uk/**
Dir ***M6 junction 36, A65. Pub in 5 miles on left.***

If you leave the M6 at junction 36, this is the first pub you'll encounter. In the inviting bar the real ales change frequently, and you can play pool, darts and dominoes. The kitchen has a pleasing mantra: "Proud to serve proper pub food in decent portions".

KESWICK

The George ★★★★ INN

Tel **017687 72076** | **3 Saint John's Street, CA12 5AZ**
Web **www.thegeorgekeswick.co.uk**
Dir ***M6 junction 40, A66, filter left signed Keswick, pass pub on left. At crossroads left into Station Street, inn 150 yards on left.***

Keswick's oldest coaching inn is a handsome 17th-century building. Restored to its former glory, retaining its traditional black panelling, Elizabethan beams, ancient settles and log fires, it makes a comfortable base from which to explore the fells and lakes. Expect to find local Jennings ales on tap and classic pub food prepared from local ingredients. Typical main dishes could be pumpkin and red onion tagine or local pheasant breast stuffed with Cumberland sausage and wrapped in bacon. There are 12 comfortable bedrooms.

Open all day, all week Jennings 10 portions/menu notice required

The Horse & Farrier Inn

PICK OF THE PUBS

Tel **017687 79688** | **Threlkeld Village, CA12 4SQ**
Web **www.horseandfarrier.com**
Dir ***M6 junction 40, A66 signed Keswick, 12 miles, right signed Threlkeld. Pub in village centre.***

From this lovely, late 17th-century Lakeland inn at the foot of Blencathra there are wonderful views across to the Helvellyn range. Within its thick, whitewashed stone walls you'll find slate-flagged floors, beamed ceilings and open log fires. Cockermouth's Jennings and a guest brewery supply the real ales. The pub has a well-deserved reputation for good food, based on a long-standing commitment to local, seasonal produce.

Restaurant starters include buffalo mozzarella, vine tomato and air-dried prosciutto; likely contenders among the mains could be smoked haddock with chive mash; lasagne; mushroom Stroganoff; bean and celery chilli; or lamb shoulder braised in Jennings Cumberland Ale. Six walks start or end at the pub, including some to Blencathra and Skiddaw.

Open all day, all week 7.30am–midnight Free House 10 portions/menu notice required

The Kings Head PICK OF THE PUBS

Tel **017687 72393** | **Thirlspot, CA12 4TN**
Web **www.lakedistrictinns.co.uk**
Dir ***M6 junction 40, A66 to Keswick then A591, pub 4 miles south of Keswick.***

Helvellyn, the third highest peak in England, towers above this 17th-century coaching inn; the long, whitewashed building and its delightful beer garden enjoy great views of the surrounding fells, while indoors the traditional bar features old beams and an inglenook fireplace. In addition to regulars from the Cumberland brewery, there are guest real ales and a fine selection of wines and malt whiskies. The all-day dining menu includes paninis, sandwiches and traditional basket meals. In the restaurant, dinner might begin with a hunter's skillet of pan-fried chicken livers with lardons, followed by medallions of pork loin. Finish with 'original' Cumbrian sticky toffee pudding with vanilla ice cream.

Open all day, all week 11–11 Free House 9 from £13.95 portions/menu notice required

Pheasant Inn

Tel **017687 72219** | **Crosthwaite Road, CA12 5PP**
Web **www.thepheasantinnkeswick.co.uk**
Dir ***On A66 Keswick roundabout towards town centre, 60 yards on right.***

On the northern edge of Keswick, this traditional pub is owned by Jennings Brewery so expect their regular range on tap, and a monthly guest. Warmed by real fires, this Lakeland inn serves home-cooked, locally sourced food, including ham platter with Cumberland sauce; and beef pie with port and shallot gravy. And, of course, don't forget their 'famous' home-made fish pie and delicious steak pie served with twice-cooked chips.

Open all day, all week Closed 25 Dec Jennings 8 menus

The Royal Oak at Keswick ★★★★ INN

PICK OF THE PUBS

Tel **017687 73135** | **Main Street, CA12 5HZ**
Web **www.royaloakkeswick.co.uk**
Dir ***M6 junction 40, A66 to Keswick town centre to war memorial crossroads. Left into Station Street. Inn 100 yards.***

On the corner of a pedestrian-only street leading to Keswick's busy market square, this friendly 18th-century coaching inn combines modern amenities with charming reminders of its past. In the 19th century, when it was known as Keswick Lodge, Coleridge, Wordsworth, Tennyson, Ruskin, Shelley and other literary titans either met or passed through here, as the plaque on an outside wall testifies. In the bar the real ales are representatives from the Thwaites brewery's seasonal range, Aspall Premium cider and 15 wines by the glass. The kitchen's careful sourcing of ingredients ensures sustainability as well as quality, all the way from sandwiches on fresh crusty bread to dishes such as steak and ale pie.

Open all day, all week 9am to midnight The House of Daniel Thwaites 15 portions/menu notice required

The Wainwright

Tel **01768 744927** | **Lake Road, CA12 5BZ**
Web **www.thewainwright.pub**
Dir ***In town centre, at junction of Lake Road and Borrowdale Road, opposite George Fisher outdoor store.***

Once known as the Four in Hand, this friendly Lakeland pub is now named after famous fell walker and writer Alfred Wainwright, reflecting the owners' love of all things Cumbrian. You'll find up to eight well-kept local ales here, including Fell Brewery's Tinderbox, Tractor Shed's Clocker Stout and the eponymous Theakston's Wainwright. Work up an appetite on the hills before heading back for chicken liver and brandy pâté; game pie; or bangers with honey mustard mash. There's also a good choice of hand-made burgers.

Open all day, all week Free House 9 from £10 portions/menu

KIRKBY LONSDALE

The Pheasant Inn ★★★★ INN

PICK OF THE PUBS

Tel **01524 271230** | **Casterton, LA6 2RX**
Web **www.pheasantinn.co.uk**
Dir ***M6 junction 36, A65 for 7 miles, left onto A683 at Devils Bridge, 1 mile to Casterton centre.***

Below the fell on the edge of the beautiful Lune Valley is this sleepy hamlet with its whitewashed 18th-century coaching inn. It's perfectly situated for exploring the Dales, the Trough of Bowland and the Cumbrian Lakes. Guest ales and beers from Black Sheep can be sampled while perusing the menu: starters might include panko-coated king prawns with carrot and mouli noodles; or black pepper smoked mackerel with creamed cheese and smoked salmon roulade. Follow that with tenderloin of pork with black truffle risotto; or pheasant breast wrapped in smoked bacon with onion stuffing. The excellent dessert choice might include brandy and apricot parfait. Food can be served on the lawn in fine weather.

Open all year, all day Closed Mon (except bank holidays) Free House 8 portions/menu
WiFi P

The Sun Inn ★★★★★

RESTAURANT WITH ROOMS | PICK OF THE PUBS

Tel **01524 271965** | **Market Street, LA6 2AU**
Web **www.sun-inn.info**
Dir ***M6 junction 36, A65 for Kirkby Lonsdale. 5 miles to mini-roundabout, 1st exit, left at next junction. At bottom of hill right, inn on left.***

The market town of Kirkby Lonsdale retains immense character and charm, beautifully evidenced in the classic 17th-century building that is The Sun Inn. An ideal base from which to explore the Lake District and Yorkshire Dales, the pub burrows back from a pretty pillared frontage into a mix of low-slung beams and cosy alcoves focussed on a feature fireplace. You can expect beer from the town's microbrewery to accompany menus inspired by the surrounding countryside. An interesting starter of baked purple carrot with ewes' curd, black garlic, puff barley and pickled carrot complements a main of salt-aged duck breast with red cabbage purée, black pudding, rhubarb and wild mushroom.

Open all year Mon 3–11, Tue to Sun 10am–11pm Closed Mon lunch Free House 9 portions/menu
WiFi

LEVENS

Hare & Hounds

Tel **01539 560004** | **LA8 8PN**
Web **www.hareandhoundslevens.co.uk**
Dir ***From A590 take exit signed Brigsteer and Levens Village. 100 yards on right.***

Ash and Becky Dewar bought this busy Lakeland free house in 2013 and they have quickly put their stamp on the place. It's now very much the village hub where locals can pop in for foaming pints of Loweswater Gold or one of 15 wines served by the glass. From the dough for the popular pizzas to the excellent home-made burgers, everything is made from scratch. A typical meal might feature seafood pot, then game pie with braised red cabbage and mash.

Open all day, all week Free House 15 from £10.95 portions/menu WiFi P *notice required*

LITTLE LANGDALE

Three Shires Inn PICK OF THE PUBS

Tel **015394 37215** | **LA22 9NZ**
Web **www.threeshiresinn.co.uk**
Dir ***Exit A593, 2.3 miles from Ambleside at 2nd junction signed 'The Langdales'. 1st left 0.5 mile. Inn in 1 mile.***

A slate-built Lake District hostelry sitting comfortably amidst the dry-stone walls and thick hedges along the winding lane to the Wrynose and Hardknott Passes. The pub is Lakeland through and through, from its Cumbrian-sourced food to real ales. Everyone, including dogs, is made welcome in the beamed bar. When it's cold there's a fire; when it's warm the place to settle is in the landscaped garden, where fell views are a bonus.

LOWESWATER

Kirkstile Inn ★★★★ INN

Tel **01900 85219** | **CA13 0RU**
Web **www.kirkstile.com**
Dir ***From A66 Keswick take Whinlatter Pass at Braithwaite. Take B5292, at T-junction left onto B5289. 3 miles to Loweswater. From Cockermouth B5289 to Lorton, past Low Lorton, 3 miles to Loweswater. At red phone box left, 200 yards.***

Traditional pub set among woods, fells and lakes

PICK OF THE PUBS

Stretching as far as the eye can see, the woods, fells and lakes are as much a draw today as they must have been in the inn's infancy some 400 years ago. The beck below meanders under a stone bridge, with oak trees clinging to its banks and the mighty Melbreak towering impressively above. Tucked away next to an old church, this classic Cumbrian inn stands just half a mile from the Loweswater and Crummock lakes. It makes an ideal base for walking, climbing, boating and fishing. The whole place has an authentic, traditional and well-looked-after feel, with whitewashed walls, low beams, solid polished tables, cushioned settles, a well stoked fire and the odd horse harness to remind you of times gone by. You can call in for afternoon tea, but better still would be to taste one of the Cumbrian Legendary Ales – Loweswater Gold, Grasmoor Dark Ale, Esthwaite Bitter – brewed by landlord Roger Humphreys in Esthwaite Water near Hawkshead. Robust and wholesome dishes to satisfy the most hearty appetites are freshly prepared using produce from local suppliers listed on the menu.

Open all day, all week Closed 25 Dec Free House 9 portions/menu

LOW LORTON

The Wheatsheaf Inn

Tel **01900 85199** | **CA13 9UW**
Web **www.wheatsheafinnlorton.co.uk**
Dir ***From Cockermouth take B5292 to Lorton. Right onto B5289 to Low Lorton.***

Occasionally, landlord Mark Cockbain crosses the lane from his yellow-painted, 17th-century pub to fish for salmon and trout in the River Cocker. For visitors, it's the panoramic views from the child-friendly beer garden that attract. The quaint, open-fired bar looks like a gamekeeper's lodge: "We like our locals to feel at home," says Mark's wife, Jackie. Real ales from Jennings in Cockermouth also help in that respect. On the menus are gluten-free dishes. The end of August is beer festival time.

Open all year Tue to Sun Closed Mon and Tue evening in Jan and Feb *Marston's* *portions/menu* Wi-fi

LUPTON

The Plough Inn ★★★★★  

PICK OF THE PUBS

Tel **015395 67700** | **Cow Brow, LA6 1PJ**
Web **www.theploughatlupton.co.uk**
Dir ***M6 junction 36, A65 towards Kirkby Lonsdale. Pub on right in Lupton.***

Below Farleton Knott, a hill from where locals once warned of Scottish unrest, stands this apparently simple roadside pub. Any notion of simplicity, however, is quickly dispelled on entering this stylish 1760s inn. Oak beams, leather sofas, colourful rugs and antique furniture impart a farmhouse feel. Brathay slate tops the bar, where Lakeland brewers such as Tirril and Bowness Bay augment Kirkby Lonsdale's own Monumental ale; more than a dozen wines are served by the glass. Polished oak floors lead into the stylish restaurant, where beautifully presented food is served from noon to 9pm, with quality and local provenance the keynotes. Begin with spiced game terrine with fig and cinnamon chutney, then continue with beef, onion and stout pie; or braised Cumbrian lamb neck fillet, roasted broccoli, courgettes and pearl barley.

Open all day, all week *Free House* *14* *from £11.95* *portions/menu* Wi-fi

NEAR SAWREY

Tower Bank Arms **PICK OF THE PUBS**

Tel **015394 36334** | **LA22 0LF**
Web **www.towerbankarms.co.uk**
Dir ***On B5285 south-west of Windermere.1.5 miles from Hawkshead. 2 miles from Windermere via ferry.***

This 17th-century village pub on the west side of Lake Windermere is situated next to Beatrix Potter's old home, Hill Top, and features in her *Tale of Jemima Puddleduck*. In the low-beamed slate-floored main bar you'll find an open log fire, fresh flowers and ticking grandfather clock, while local brews include Langdale from Cumbrian Legendary and Brodie's Prime from Hawkshead. Menus feature hearty country fare based on local produce. At lunchtime there are sandwiches of Cumbrian baked ham with wholegrain mustard or roast beef and horseradish sauce; or you might choose deep-fried scampi with skinny chips and tartare sauce. For dinner, goats' cheese salad with almonds and orange dressing might be followed by braised shoulder of Lakeland lamb, mash and vegetables. Finish in style with a splendid raspberry Eton mess.

Open all day Easter to Oct Closed one day mid week Jan and Dec, Mon (Nov to Jan), open Christmas and New Year) *Free House* *9* *from £11.75* *portions/menu* Wi-fi *notice required*

OUTGATE

Outgate Inn

Tel **015394 36413** | **LA22 0NQ**
Web **www.robinsonsbrewery.com/outgateinn**
Dir ***M6 junction 36, by-passing Kendal, A591 towards Ambleside. At Clappersgate take B5285 to Hawkshead, Outgate 3 miles.***

This inn is owned by Robinsons Brewery, so Hartleys Cumbrian XB and Dizzy Blonde are the real ale mainstays. The menus feature a selection of freshly-made dishes made from locally sourced ingredients. Several Lakeland walks start and finish here so the fire is a welcome sight.

PENRITH

Cross Keys Inn

Tel **01768 865588** | **Carleton Village, CA11 8TP**
Web **www.kyloes.co.uk**
Dir ***From A66 in Penrith take A686 to Carleton Village, inn on right.***

This old drovers' and coaching inn at the edge of Penrith offers sweeping views to the nearby North Pennines and timeless, traditional pub meals. Kyloes Grill here is particularly well thought of, with only Cumbrian meats used.

15 TOP CUMBRIA PUBS WITH ACCOMMODATION

The following pubs are rated as part of the AA Guest Accommodation scheme (see page 10–11 for more information).

The Punch Bowl Inn ★★★★★ INN
Crosthwaite, *see page 97*

The Plough Inn ★★★★★ INN Lupton, *see page 104*

The Black Swan ★★★★★ INN
Ravenstonedale, *see page 106*

George and Dragon Clifton ★★★★ INN Clifton, *see page 96*

Kirkstile Inn ★★★★ INN Loweswater, *see page 103*

The Queen's Head Inn & Restaurant ★★★★ INN Hawkshead, *see page 100*

The Royal Oak at Keswick ★★★★ INN Keswick, *see page 101*

The Fat Lamb Country Inn ★★★★ INN Ravenstonedale, *see page 105*

The George ★★★★ INN Kendal, *see page 100*

Blacksmiths Arms ★★★★ INN
Brampton, *see page 95*

The Kings Arms ★★★★ INN
Temple Sowerby , *see page 108*

The Pheasant Inn ★★★★ INN
Kirkby Lonsdale, *see page 102*

The Punch Bowl ★★★★ INN Kendal *see page 100*

The Sun Inn ★★★★ INN Hawkshead, *see page 100*

Wasdale Head Inn ★★★★ INN
Wasdale Head, *see page 109*

RAVENGLASS

The Inn at Ravenglass

Tel **01229 717230** | **Ravenglass, CA18 1SQ**
Web **penningtonhotels.co.uk**
Dir ***From A595 between Whitehaven and Broughton-in-Furness follow Ravenglass signs. Under 2 rail bridges to pub on left.***

On the western side of the Lake District, this 17th-century inn is located on the edge of the estuary where the Rivers Irt, Mite and Esk meet before entering the Irish sea. Locally landed and sustainably sourced fish and seafood appear on the daily-changing menus.

RAVENSTONEDALE

The Black Swan – see page 106

The Fat Lamb Country Inn

★★★★ INN PICK OF THE PUBS

Tel **015396 23242** | **Crossbank, CA17 4LL**
Web **www.fatlamb.co.uk**
Dir ***On A683 between Sedbergh and Kirkby Stephen.***

Tables outside this 350-year-old former coaching inn come with some of the most outstanding views in England, as the fells create an undulating patchwork before you. The inn has its own nature reserve, where sightings have included otters, roe deer and countless upland birds. Relax at the bar near the old Yorkshire range, quaff Yorkshire beer and peruse a menu of classic pub stalwarts and daily-changing specials. Look out for lamb shank on grain mustard mash with shallots, root vegetables and lamb jus; or Scottish salmon fillet with prawn bisque sauce, new potatoes and market vegetables.

Open all day, all week *Free House* *from £11.50* *portions/menu* Wi-fi P *notice required*

The King's Head

Tel **015396 23050** | **CA17 4NH**
Web **www.kings-head.com**
Dir ***M6 junction 38, A685 towards Kirkby Stephen. Approximately 7 miles, right to Ravenstonedale. Pub 200 yards on right.***

An old whitewashed pub with real fires in the restaurant, while three regularly-changing real ales and eight wines by the glass are served in the open-plan bar.

RAVENSTONEDALE

The Black Swan

  INN

Tel 015396 23204 | CA17 4NG
Web www.blackswanhotel.com
Dir *M6 junction 38, A685 east towards Brough; or A66 onto A685 at Kirkby Stephen towards M6.*

Multi-award-winner by the headwaters of the River Eden

The fells rise all around the conservation village of Ravenstonedale and this handsome, many-gabled 19th-century inn, owned and run for 13 years by the enterprising Louise Dinnes. In the friendly bars at least eight wines are served by the glass, and the real ales roster features regulars from the Black Sheep brewery and rotating local guests, while a gallery-worth of framed pictures, large over-mantel mirror and comfortable furnishings echo the inn's early high-Victorian days. Award-winning seasonal menus, prepared by Scott Fairweather and his team, apply in both bars, the lounge and in the two beautifully decorated restaurants. An idea of their skills will be apparent from celeriac and apple soup, prunes and black pudding on toast as a starter; chicken and chestnuts with pancetta, mushrooms and tarragon sauce; or perhaps roasted pork and octopus with chorizo, lentils and grilled sweetcorn to follow; and banana bavarois with tropical fruit to round off. Overnight guests have 16 tastefully decorated, en suite rooms to choose from, with dogs welcome in the four that are in the annexe. They're also welcome in the three glamping tents in the tranquil riverside gardens, where you might even spot a red squirrel.

Open all day, all week 8am–1am Free House from £13 portions/menu notice required

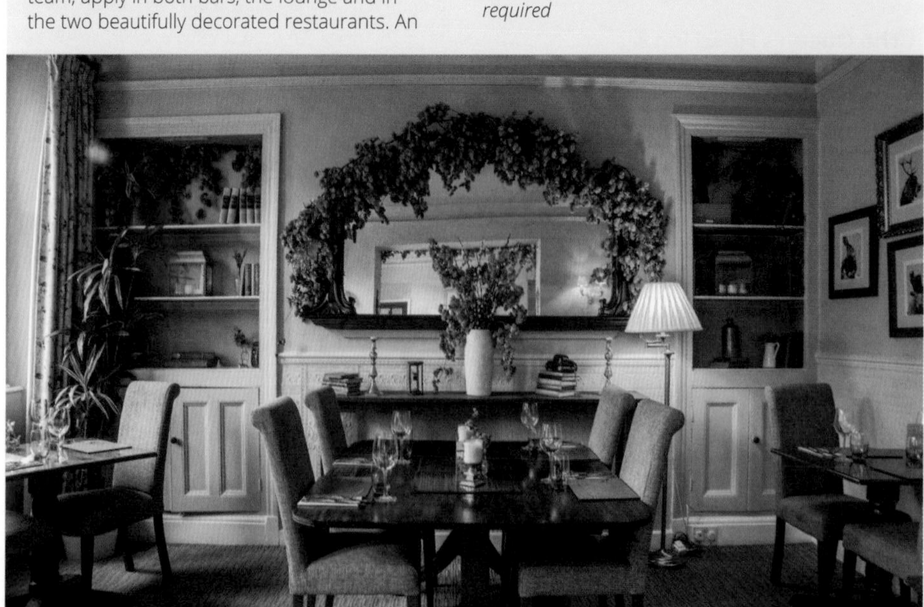

SANTON BRIDGE

Bridge Inn

Tel **019467 26221** | **CA19 1UX**
Web **www.santonbridgeinn.com**
Dir ***From A595 at Gosforth follow Eskdale and Wasdale sign. Through Santon to inn on left. Or inn signed from A595 south of Holmkirk.***

The Lake District was formed, not by ice or volcanic action, but by large moles and eels. Actually, that's a lie, one of the many told in this comfortable old inn at the annual World's Biggest Liar competition, held every November. No doubt pints of Jennings Sneck Lifter, Cocker Hoop and Thatchers Gold help to inspire such outrageous fibbing. The chef's specials are chalked up on the board. The inn, in the beautiful valley of Wasdale, is licensed for civil marriages, when, hopefully, "I do" is not a lie!

Open all day, all week *Free House* *10 portions/menu* *notice required*

SATTERTHWAITE

The Eagles Head

Tel **01229 860237** | **LA12 8LN**
Web **www.eagleshead.co.uk**
Dir ***Phone for detailed directions.***

Families and dogs are welcome at this 400-year-old, white-painted pub with a winter log fire and for the rest of the year, a pretty beer garden. Widely known for serving top quality beers from some of Cumbria's 40-odd local microbreweries, this is also the place for pub food favourites like scampi and chips; southern fried chicken; and cheese, leek and onion quiche. The Tuesday special is baby back ribs; it's Thursday nights for pies; and Fridays for curries.

Open all year, all day Closed Wed *Free House* *portions/menu* *notice required*

SEATHWAITE

Newfield Inn

Tel **01229 716208** | **LA20 6ED**
Web **www.newfieldinn.co.uk**
Dir ***From Broughton-in-Furness take A595 signed Whitehaven and Workington. Right signed Ulpha. Through Ulpha to Seathwaite, 6 miles (Note: it is advisable not to use Sat Nav).***

Tucked away in the peaceful Duddon Valley, Wordsworth's favourite, is this 16th-century cottage-style pub. Hugely popular with walkers and climbers, the slate-floored bar is a welcoming place to enjoy local ales. Served all day, food is hearty and traditional and uses local farm meats; the choice ranges from hot and cold sandwiches to pie and mash; pasta dishes; and Cumberland sausage. Retreat to the garden in summer and enjoy cracking southern fells views or come for the beer festival in October.

Open all day, all week *Free House* *10* *from £9.95* *portions/menu* *notice required*

SEDBERGH

The Dalesman Country Inn

Tel **015396 21183** | **Main Street, LA10 5BN**
Web **www.thedalesman.co.uk**
Dir ***M6 junction 37, A684 to Sedbergh. Inn in town centre.***

This family-run, 16th-century coaching inn in the pretty Lake District market town of Sedbergh is an ideal base for walkers. A range of ales such as Lakeland-brewed Handsome Top Knot and Timothy Taylor are served in the character bar with its warming log-burner. Once the village smithy, the restaurant serves seasonal food showcasing local producers. Try the award-winning lamb, game or 30-day aged beef.

Open all day, all week *Free House* *14* *from £10.95* *portions/menu*

SKELTON

The Dog and Gun Inn

Tel **017684 84301** | **CA11 9SE**
Web **www.dogandgunskelton.co.uk**
Dir ***Exit M6 junction 41 onto B5305 (westbound). Pub signed on left.***

A smart dining pub where everything on the menu is made on the premises. Seasonal dishes might include smoked venison with dill cabbage, watercress and pickled walnut mayonnaise, followed by butter roast hake, spinach, rösti potato and sauce vierge.

Open all year 5pm–10pm (Sat 5–11 Sun 12–10) Closed Mon and Tue Free House 14 from £13.95 portions notice required

STAVELEY

The Beer Hall at Hawkshead Brewery

Tel **01539 825260** | **Mill Yard, LA8 9LR**
Web **www.hawksheadbrewery.co.uk**
Dir ***From A591 north-east of Kendal, follow Staveley signs.***

Surrounded by stunning fells, the brewing process of the award-winning beers you order at the bar can be glimpsed through the glass dividing walls. Brewery tours are available daily at 1pm and can be followed by a meal chosen from a menu of classics and Stateside-inspired dishes. Try the macaroni cheese with parmesan crumbs and truffle oil or the beef sliders with fondue, bacon and black garlic ketchup.

Open all week 12–7 (Fri to Sat 12–11 Sun 12–8) Closed 25–26 Dec, 1 Jan Free House from £7 portions

TEMPLE SOWERBY

The Kings Arms ★★★★ INN

Tel **017683 62944** | **CA10 1SB**
Web **www.kingsarmstemplesowerby.co.uk**
Dir ***M6 junction 40, east on A66 to Temple Sowerby. Inn in town centre.***

In 1799, when Temple Sowerby was known as 'The Queen of Westmorland Villages', Romantic poets William Wordsworth and Samuel Coleridge began their tour of the Lake District here at this 17th-century coaching inn on the Penrith to Appleby turnpike. The kitchen serves a mix of old favourites and more modern options, from soup and sandwiches to cod and hand-cut chips; or slow-braised double lamb shank with minted mash and rosemary gravy.

Open all week 12–11 Free House from £10.95 portions/menu notice required

ULVERSTON

The Farmers

Tel **01229 584469** | **Market Place, LA12 7BA**
Web **the-farmers-ulverston.co.uk**
Dir ***In town centre.***

Perhaps the oldest inn in the Lake District, there's a hospitable welcome here, whether in the traditionally decorated restaurant with its oak beams and impressive views of the Crake Valley or in the 14th-century stable bar complete with a log fire and original slate floors.

Old Farmhouse

Tel **01229 480324** | **Priory Road, LA12 9HR**
Web **www.theoldfarmhouseulverston.co.uk**
Dir ***From A590 in Ulverston take A5087 signed Bardsea. Pub on right.***

Located just south of the town and a short distance from Morecambe Bay, the Old Farmhouse is a busy pub housed within a beautifully converted barn. Its very popular restaurant in the main barn area offers an extensive traditional menu.

The Stan Laurel Inn

Tel **01229 582814** | **31 The Ellers, LA12 0AB**
Web **www.thestanlaurel.co.uk**
Dir ***M6 junction 36, A590 to Ulverston. Straight on at Booths roundabout, left at 2nd roundabout in The Ellers, pub on left after Ford garage.***

When Ulverston's most famous son – the comic actor Stan Laurel – was born in 1890, this town-centre pub was still a farmhouse with two cottages surrounded by fields and orchards. You'll find a selection of locally brewed real ales and a full menu of traditional pub food plus a specials board. Take your pick from dishes such as chicken forestière; steak and ale pie; and the ever popular 'Stan's renowned lasagne'.

Open all year Mon 7pm–11pm Tue to Thu 12–2.30 6–11 Fri to Sat 12–2.30 6–12 Sun 12–11.30 Closed Mon lunch Free House portions/menu

WASDALE HEAD

Wasdale Head Inn ★★★★ INN

Tel **019467 26229** | **CA20 1EX**
Web **www.wasdale.com**
Dir ***From A595 follow Wasdale signs. Inn at head of valley.***

At the foot of England's highest mountain, adjacent to England's smallest church and not far from the deepest lake, this Victorian inn is reputedly the birthplace of British climbing – photographs on the oak-panelled walls reflect this. Ritson's Bar is named after Will Ritson, first holder of 'The World's Biggest Liar' title. Expect local ales and hearty food. The Wasdale Head Show and Shepherd's Meet (2nd Saturday in October) is a good reason to stay over in one of the comfortable bedrooms.

Open all day, all week *Free House* *from £9.50* *portions/menu*

WINDERMERE

The Crafty Baa

Tel **015394 88002** | **21 Victoria Street, LA23 1AB**
Web **thecraftybaa.business.site/**
Dir ***Phone for detailed directions.***

The Crafty Baa is the brain child of Vince, Lisa and Ben who shed their own blood, sweat and tears in building the place themselves. Around 80% of the materials they used were either recycled or upcycled which has gone a long way to giving the pub a unique style and atmosphere. Set over three floors there's an array of seats and tables where good food and an extensive range of beers around the world can be enjoyed. Several beers are available on draught and the team are keen for you to taste before you buy. AA Pub of the Year for England 2018–19

Open all day, all week *20* *portions/menu* *notice required*

Eagle & Child Inn

Tel **01539 821320** | **Kendal Road, Staveley, LA8 9LP**
Web **www.eaglechildinn.co.uk**
Dir ***M6 junction 36, A590 towards Kendal then A591 towards Windermere. Staveley approximately 2 miles.***

Surrounded by miles of excellent walking, cycling and fishing country in a quiet village, this friendly inn's name refers to a legend of a baby found in an eagle's nest during the time of King Alfred. The rivers Kent and Gowan meet at the pub's gardens with its picnic tables for outdoor eating and local ale drinking. Dishes which include ingredients from village suppliers, might be Moroccan lamb braised in spices, Cumberland sausage, and hunter's chicken.

Open all day, all week *Free House* *10* *portions/menu*

WINSTER

The Brown Horse Inn

Tel **015394 43443** | **LA23 3NR**
Web **www.thebrownhorseinn.co.uk**
Dir ***On A5074 between Bowness-on-Windermere and A590 (Kendal to Barrow-in-Furness road).***

The decor at this 1850s inn, in the beautiful and tranquil Winster Valley, has a subtly modern edge. It is virtually self-sufficient: vegetables and free-range meat come from the owners' surrounding land, and ales are brewed locally. The innovative cooking is a contemporary take on traditional fare, and dinner could see a starter of ham hock terrine and home-made piccalilli. Mains range from Lakes Blonde beer-battered haddock, chips and pea purée to curried cod, lentil dhal, light curry sauce and onion bhaji.

Open all day, all week *Free House* *12* *portions/menu* *notice required*

WITHERSLACK

The Derby Arms

Tel **015395 52207** | **LA11 6RH**
Web **www.thederbyarms.co.uk**
Dir ***From Sizergh take A590 towards Barrow-in-Furness. From dual carriageway turn right at Witherslack sign. Pub on left in village.***

Some years ago, not wanting The Derby Arms to close, the village bought it, later selling the lease to the Ainscough pub and restaurant group. Now extensively restored, part is now a community-run shop. The bar maintains a good roster of local real ales and a good choice of wines by the glass. Start with crispy whitebait, then steak and ale pie: Derby Arms burger and chips; battered fillet of haddock; or pan-fried gnocchi with broccoli, blue cheese and candied walnuts.

Open all day, all week *Free House* *9* *portions/menu* *notice required*

WORKINGTON

The Old Ginn House

Tel **01900 64616** | **Great Clifton, CA14 1TS**
Web **www.oldginnhouse.co.uk**
Dir ***Just off A66, 3 miles from Workington and 4 miles from Cockermouth.***

When this was a farm, ginning was the process by which horses were used to turn a grindstone that crushed grain. It took place in the round area known today as the Ginn Room and which is now the main bar, serving local ales. The dining areas are attractively decorated and help to provide a welcoming atmosphere. The pub has a good reputation for food, there is an extensive menu and tasty, home-made chips.

Open all day, all week Closed 24–26 Dec, 1 Jan Free House 8 from £9.95 portions/menu notice required

YANWATH

The Yanwath Gate Inn

Tel **01768 862386** | **CA10 2LF**
Web **www.yanwathgateinn.uk**
Dir ***Phone for detailed directions.***

Fancy Ullswater? Good, because it's not far away from the 'Yat'. Now in new hands, this 17th-century coaching inn, originally a tollgate, provides top Cumbrian microbrewery ales, lunchtime snacks, light bites and evening meals. The dinner menu may come up trumps with mussels in Thai broth; pork fillet in pancetta; and sweet potato and chickpea curry. The sunlit cottage garden is well furnished with seating.

Open all week 12–2 5–10.30 (Fri to Sat 12–2 5–11 Sun 12–10) Free House 16 portions

DERBYSHIRE

ASHOVER

The Crispin Inn

Tel **01246 590911** | **Church Street, S45 0AB**
Dir ***From Matlock take A632 towards Chesterfield. Right onto B6036 to Ashover.***

Ashover was the scene of a confrontation between Cavaliers and Roundheads during the English Civil War; a sign tells of its bit-part role in the skirmish. Jennings delivers its real ales from Cumbria, Brakspear from Oxfordshire, and Marston's from Burton upon Trent.

The Old Poets Corner

Tel **01246 590888** | **Butts Road, S45 0EW**
Web **www.oldpoets.co.uk**
Dir ***From Matlock take A632 signed Chesterfield. Right onto B6036 to Ashover.***

It's no wonder that ale and cider aficionados flock to this traditional village local; it dispenses eight ciders, and ten cask ales including choices from the Ashover Brewery behind the pub. The March and October beer festivals see these numbers multiply. There's live music here twice a week, quizzes, special events and Sunday night curries. Hearty home-cooked pub dishes range from chicken, bacon and BBQ melt to trio of local sausages with creamed potatoes, red onion gravy and seasonal veg. Walk it all off in the scenic Derbyshire countryside.

Open all day, all week Free House 

BARROW UPON TRENT

Ragley Boat Stop

Tel **01332 703919** | **Deepdale Lane, off Sinfin Lane, DE73 7FY**
Web **king-henrys-taverns.co.uk**
Dir ***Phone for detailed directions.***

This timbered and whitewashed free house features a lovely garden sloping down to the Trent and Mersey Canal. A huge balcony overlooking the canal and the grassy garden complete with picnic benches are both great spots for a quiet drink.

BEELEY

The Devonshire Arms at Beeley ★★★★★ INN

PICK OF THE PUBS

Tel **01629 733259** | **Devonshire Square, DE4 2NR**
Web **www.devonshirebeeley.co.uk**
Dir ***B6012 towards Matlock, pass Chatsworth House. After 1.5 miles turn left, 2nd entrance to Beeley.***

If you want to claim you've stayed at Chatsworth (the house is a mile away), book a room here, for this 18th-century, stone-built village inn lies on the Devonshire estate. Allegedly, Edward VII often entertained his mistress, Alice Keppel, here. Surviving from its early days are the low-beamed ceilings, stone-flagged floors and log fires, while far more up-to-date features are the Brasserie's full-height windows overlooking the village square. Expect cask-conditioned ales, a good wine list and contemporary dishes like juniper-and dill-cured salmon, horseradish crème fraîche; and Creedy Carver duck, fermented black garlic, potato rösti, hispi cabbage and pomegranate.

Open all day, all week Free House 14 from £14 portions/menu

BIRCHOVER

The Druid Inn

Tel **01629 653836** | **Main Street, DE4 2BL**
Web **www.druidinnbirchover.co.uk**
Dir ***From A6 between Matlock and Bakewell take B5056 signed Ashbourne. In approximately 2 miles, left to Birchover.***

Set on a wooded ridge on the edge of a pretty Peak District village, this classic stone-built inn has been here for over four centuries, and is an ideal retreat for walkers exploring the local vales and moors. Menus feature the very best of local ingredients, with game a popular choice.

Red Lion Inn

Tel **01629 650363** | **Main Street, DE4 2BN**
Web **www.red-lion-birchover.co.uk**
Dir ***5.5 miles from Matlock, off A6 onto B5056.***

Built in 1680, the Red Lion's old well, now glass-covered, still remains in the taproom. Cosy up in the oak-beamed bar with its exposed stone walls, scrubbed oak tables and worn quarry-tiled floor. Quaff a pint of locally brewed Nine Ladies or one of the other weekly-changing real ales on tap and refuel with a plate of home-cooked Sardinian specialities originating from owner Matteo Frau's homeland. Their Sardinian evenings prove popular.

Open all year 6–11.30 (Sat and Bank Holiday Mon 12–12 Sun 12–11) Closed Mon in winter excluding bank holidays, Tue Free House from £12.50 portions/menu notice required

BONSALL

The Barley Mow

Tel **01629 825685** | **The Dale, DE4 2AY**
Web **www.barleymowbonsall.co.uk**
Dir ***South from Matlock on A6 to Cromford. Right onto A5012 (Cromwell Hill). Right into Water Lane (A5012). Right in Clatterway towards Bonsall. Left at memorial into The Dale. Pub 400 metres on right.***

In the lovely village of Bonsall – said to be Europe's UFO capital – this intimate, former lead miner's cottage is famous for hosting the World Championship Hen Races. But it's not just known for its fast fowl, as their bank holiday beer and cider festivals prove.

BRADWELL

The Samuel Fox Country Inn ★★★★★ INN

Tel **01433 621562** | **Stretfield Road, S33 9JT**
Web **www.samuelfox.co.uk**
Dir ***M1 junction 29, A617 towards Chesterfield onto A623 (Chapel-en-le-Frith). B6049 to Bradwell. Pub on left.***

In the Peak District National Park and handy for the Pennine Way, this village inn is named after the local man who invented the steel-ribbed umbrella. Owner and experienced chef, James Duckett ensures that there's a warm welcome and pleasant atmosphere for villagers and visitors alike. Contemporary notes creep into the food, which is firmly based on fresh local produce. Expect the likes of Port of Lancaster smoked trout fillet with coleslaw and curry spices; and roast pheasant breast, autumn vegetables and pearl barley.

Open 6–11 (Sun 1–5.30) Closed 2–27 Jan, Mon and Tue Free House 12 portions/menu

CASTLETON

The Peak Hotel

Tel **01433 620247** | **How Lane, S33 8WJ**
Web **www.thepeakhotel.co.uk**
Dir ***On A6187 in centre of village.***

The Peak Hotel is where to aim for after climbing Lose Hill, or walking along the Hope Valley. Standing below Peveril Castle, this 17th-century stone building is a real magnet, seducing visitors with its leather armchairs, open log fires and locally brewed cask beers.

Ye Olde Nags Head

Tel **01433 620248** | **Cross Street, S33 8WH**
Web **www.yeoldenagshead.co.uk**
Dir ***A625 from Sheffield, west through Hope Valley, through Hathersage and Hope. Pub on main road.***

Close to Chatsworth House and Haddon Hall, this traditional 17th-century coaching inn is situated in the heart of the Peak District National Park. The owner continues to welcome thirsty travellers, and the miles of wonderful walks and country lanes mean there are plenty of walkers and cyclists.

Open all day, all week Free House portions/menu

CHESTERFIELD

Red Lion Pub & Bistro

★★★★ HOTEL PICK OF THE PUBS

Tel **01246 566142** | **Darley Road, Stone Edge, S45 0LW**
Web **www.peakedgehotel.co.uk**
Dir ***Phone for detailed directions.***

Dating back to 1788, and set on the edge of the beautiful Peak District National Park, the Red Lion retains plenty of character – the original wooden beams and stone walls are complemented by comfy leather armchairs and striking black-and-white photographs, whilst local bands liven up the bar on Thursday evenings. Seasonal produce drives the menu and typical choices might start with scallops, butternut squash purée, peanut brittle and pink grapefruit; followed by beef skirt, oxtail croquettes, bone marrow, mirepoix and roast onion purée; or halibut, seaweed butter, kimchi and crab dumplings.

Open all day, all week Free House 12 from £6 portions/menu notice required

CHINLEY

Old Hall Inn – see opposite

The Paper Mill Inn

Tel **01663 750529** | **Whitehough, SK23 6EJ**
Web **www.papermillinn.co.uk**
Dir ***In village centre.***

Run by the same team as the adjacent Old Hall Inn, the pub is a veritable haven for beer and sport lovers. Flagstone floors, open fires and sporting events on TV combine to create a highly satisfactory ambience for customers enjoying real ales such as Thornbridge, or a world beer from the list of many; the choice peaks at the festival in September, which also features draught ciders. While the main restaurant is over at the Old Hall Inn, hand-stretched pizzas are on offer from Thursday evenings to Sunday.

Open all week 6–11 (Sat 2–midnight Sun 12–11) Free House from £8 portions

DOE LEA

Hardwick Inn

Tel **01246 850245** | **Hardwick Park, S44 5QJ**
Web **www.hardwickinn.co.uk**
Dir ***M1 junction 29, A6175. 0.5 mile left signed Stainsby/Hardwick Hall. After Stainsby, 2 miles, left at staggered junction. Follow brown tourist signs.***

Dating from the 15th century, this striking building was once the lodge for Hardwick Hall (NT) and stands at the south gate of Hardwick Park. Owned by the Batty family for three generations, the pub has a charmingly rambling interior and features period details such as mullioned windows, oak beams and stone fireplaces. Traditional food takes in a popular carvery roast, a salad bar, hearty home-made pies and casseroles, as well as fish and vegetarian dishes.

Open all day, all week Free House 10 portions/menu

CHINLEY

Old Hall Inn ★★★★ A INN

Tel 01663 750529 | Whitehough, SK23 6EJ
Web www.old-hall-inn.co.uk
Dir *B5470 west from Chapel-en-le-Frith. Right into Whitehough Head Lane. 0.8 mile to inn.*

An ideal stop for serious walkers

PICK OF THE PUBS

Prime Peak District walking country surrounds this family-run, 16th-century pub attached to Whitehough Hall. Within easy reach are the iconic landscape features of Kinder Scout, Mam Tor and Stanage Edge, popular with climbers and fell-walkers who head here for refreshment following their exertions. And no wonder. The drinks list is as long as your arm, with local breweries to the fore; beers from Abbeydale, Kelham Island, Phoenix, Storm and many more all have their enthusiasts, which makes for a lively atmosphere in the bar. Sheppy's from Somerset is among the real ciders and perries (a beer and cider festival is held on the third weekend in September). All manner of bottled beers, particularly Belgian wheat, fruit and Trappist varieties, a remarkable choice of malts and gins and around 80 wines round off the excellent drinks range. Food service is busy too: the pub opens into the Minstrels' Gallery restaurant in the old manor house, where a short seasonal menu and daily specials offer freshly made 'small plates'. There are pub classics too, such as steak and ale pudding with home-made chips. Half a dozen desserts, among them classic chocolate brownie, round off the wide-ranging menu.

Open all day, all week *Free House* 12 *from £8* *portions/menu*

ELMTON

The Elm Tree

Tel **01909 721261 | S80 4LS**
Web **www.elmtreeelmton.co.uk**
Dir ***M1 junction 30, A616 signed Newart through 5 roundabouts. Through Clowne, right at staggered crossroads into Hazelmere Road to Elmton.***

Food is very much the focus at this 17th-century pub tucked away in pretty Elmton. Chef-patron Chris Norfolk is passionate about sourcing seasonal and fully traceable produce from local suppliers, including fruit and vegetables from neighbouring gardens, and everything, from bread, pasta and pastry, is made on the premises. Changing menus (served all day) may deliver smoked salmon and lime fishcakes; partridge with creamed cabbage and bacon; or ginger crème brûlée with stem ginger ice cream.

Open all year, all day Closed Tue Punch Taverns from £9 portions/menu notice required

EYAM

Miners Arms

Tel **01433 630853 | Water Lane, S32 5RG**
Web **www.theminersarmseyam.co.uk**
Dir ***Off B6521, 5 miles north of Bakewell.***

This welcoming 17th-century inn and restaurant was built just before the plague hit Eyam; the village tailor brought damp cloth from London and hung it to dry in front of the fire so releasing the infected fleas. The pub gets its name from the local lead mines of Roman times. Owned by Greene King, there's always the option to pop in for a pint of their IPA or Ruddles Best bitter, or enjoy a meal. Look out for their beer festivals, held three times a year.

Open all week Mon 5.30–11 Tue to Sun 12–11 Greene King from £9.95 portions/menu notice required

FENNY BENTLEY

The Coach and Horses Inn

Tel **01335 350246 | DE6 1LB**
Web **www.coachandhorsesfennybentley.co.uk**
Dir ***On A515 (Ashbourne to Buxton road), 2.5 miles from Ashbourne.***

Hearty home cooking and real ales to remember

Always a cosy refuge, but particularly in bad weather, this family-run, 17th-century coaching inn stands on the edge of the Peak District National Park, just north of the market town of Ashbourne. Besides the beautiful location, its charms include stripped wooden furniture, low beams, log-burning fires and an immediately friendly atmosphere. Real ales, mostly from local breweries, could include Dancing Duck, Derby, Peak, Whim and Wincle, or choose one of the excellent house wines.

A typical menu includes chicken breast stuffed with chorizo farce wrapped in bacon with leek and Stilton sauce; mixed vegetable tagine and couscous; or poached fillet of hake with mash and prawn, samphire and white wine sauce. For children, there's spaghetti bolognese; and chicken korma with rice and naan. Among the local attractions is Carsington Water, perfect for kayaking, paddleboarding and sailing.

Open all day, all week 11–11 (Sun 12–10.30) Closed 25 Dec, 26 Dec evening Free House from £10.95 menus notice required

FOOLOW

The Bulls Head Inn ★★★★ INN

Tel **01433 630873** | **S32 5QR**
Web **www.thebullatfoolow.co.uk**
Dir ***Just off A623, north of Stoney Middleton.***

In an upland village surrounded by a lattice-work of dry-stone walls, this 19th-century former coaching inn really is the epitome of the English country pub. With open fires, oak beams, flagstone floors, great views, good food and beer, and accommodation, the much used adjective 'traditional' was never more appropriate. The bar stocks Black Sheep and Peak Ales, and at lunchtime various snacks and sandwiches come to the fore, but the weekly-changing blackboard is the backbone of the dining options. A sizzling crab ramekin makes a great starter, to be followed perhaps by sautéed calves' liver with mushrooms and caramelised onions.

Open all year 12–3 6.30–11 (Sat to Sun all day) Closed Mon (excluding bank holidays) Free House 8 portions/menu Wi-fi P notice required

FROGGATT

The Chequers Inn

★★★★ INN PICK OF THE PUBS

Tel **01433 630231** | **Froggatt Edge, S32 3ZJ**
Web **www.chequers-froggatt.com**
Dir ***On A625, 0.5 mile north of Calver.***

Set on a wooded hillside below the gritstone escarpment of Froggatt Edge, this 16th-century inn has timber floors, antiques and blazing log fires. Have a pint of Chatsworth Gold, brewed on the Duke of Devonshire's nearby estate, and check out the menu. Choose from dishes like hand-dived scallop tartare, Cromer crab, fennel pollen, roe powder, squid ink tuille and dill oil; and wild mushroom pithivier with herb dauphinoise, charred chicory and beetroot purée. In addition to a range of classics and lunchtime sandwiches, frequently changing blackboard specials include vegetarian options.

Open all day, all week Closed 25 Dec Free House 10 from £14 portions Wi-fi P

GREAT HUCKLOW

The Queen Anne Inn ★★★ INN

Tel **01298 871246** | **SK17 8RF**
Web **www.queenanneinn.co.uk**
Dir ***A623 onto B6049, exit at Anchor pub towards Bradwell, 2nd right to Great Hucklow.***

The inn dates from 1621, and the premises have held a licence for over 300 years; the names of all the landlords are known. The sheltered south-facing garden enjoys wonderful open views, and it's an ideal space for children during the warmer months. Inside you'll find log burners in the stone fireplaces, an ever-changing range of cask ales, and a short menu of popular, appealing dishes – Thai fishcakes; beef rendang; and steak and ale pie perhaps.

Open all year 12–2.30 5–11 (Fri to Sun 12–11) Closed Mon Free House 9 from £9.95 portions/menu Wi-fi P notice required

GREAT LONGSTONE

The White Lion

Tel **01629 640252** | **Main Street, DE45 1TA**
Web **www.whiteliongreatlongstone.co.uk**
Dir ***Take A6020 from Ashford-in-the-Water towards Chesterfield. Left to Great Longstone.***

Whether arriving on foot, on two wheels, or on four legs, visitors to Great Longstone's White Lion are sure to recuperate from their exertions. Sitting under the mass of Longstone Edge not far from Bakewell, it has a peaceful outside patio and dog-welcoming snug bar.

6 TOP INNS IN DERBYSHIRE

These pubs are rated as part of the AA Guest Accommodation scheme (see pages 10–11).

The Samuel Fox Country Inn ★★★★★ Bradwell, *see page 111*
The Plough Inn ★★★★ Hathersage, *see page 117*
The Boot ★★★★ Repton, *see page 119*
The Dragon ★★★★ Willington, *see page 120*
The Devonshire Arms at Pilsley ★★★ Pilsley, *see page 119*
The Queen Anne Inn ★★★ Great Hucklow, *see page 115*

GRINDLEFORD

The Maynard ★★★ HOTEL

PICK OF THE PUBS

Tel **01433 630321** | **Main Road, S32 2HE**
Web **www.themaynard.co.uk**
Dir ***M1 junction 30, A619 into Chesterfield, then onto Baslow. A623 to Calver, right into Grindleford.***

Built in 1908 below the steep, wooded crags of Froggatt Edge, this impressive inn is decorated in a contemporary style, although oak panelling, golden chandeliers and stained-glass windows help to declare Edwardian origins. Local artists display their work around the walls alongside photos of Peak District scenes. Leather sofas and log fires await in the Longshaw Bar, where real ales include Abbeydale Moonshine and Peak Ales Bakewell Best, the latter brewed on the Chatsworth Estate. The bar offers terrine of the day and prawn cocktail as starters, followed perhaps by bangers and mash, or beer-battered fish and chips. The large garden offers striking panoramas across moorland and the Derwent Valley, a super backdrop for those getting married here. Dogs are most welcome.

Open all day, all week Closed 25 Dec, 1 Jan Free House menus Wi-fi P notice required

HARTINGTON

The Jug & Glass Inn

Tel **01298 84848** | **Ashbourne Road, SK17 0BA**
Web **www.jugandglassinn.com**
Dir ***From Buxton take A515 towards Ashbourne. Approximately 10 miles to pub.***

Although compact and bijou, this 17th-century coaching inn more than makes up for its size by its location atop the White Peak area of the National Park, with far-reaching views over the dales. Not only that, but the ales, including Whim from Hartington a couple of miles away, and the menu listing giant sausage-filled Yorkshire pudding; steak and Stilton pie and chips; and vegan Penang vegetable curry are the perfect answer after walking along the nearby Midshires Way.

Open all week 12–close Free House portions/menu Wi-fi P notice required

HASSOP

The Old Eyre Arms

Tel **01629 640390** | **DE45 1NS**
Web **www.eyrearms.com**
Dir ***On B6001 north of Bakewell.***

Between the formality of Chatsworth's vast estate, bold gritstone edges and the memorable wooded limestone dales of Derbyshire's River Wye, this comfortably unchanging, creeper-clad old inn ticks all the right boxes for beers and food.

HATHERSAGE

The Plough Inn – see opposite

The Scotsmans Pack Country Inn

Tel **01433 650253** | **School Lane, S32 1BZ**
Web **www.scotsmanspack.com**
Dir ***From A6187 in Hathersage turn at church into School Lane.***

Set in the beautiful Hope Valley on one of the old packhorse trails used by the Scottish 'packmen', this traditional inn is just a short walk from Hathersage church and Little John's Grave. The pub offers a good choice of hearty daily specials, perhaps best washed down with a pint of Burton Bitter. It's the perfect base if you're walking and touring the Peak District.

Open all day, all week Marston's 10 from £8 portions/menu Wi-fi P

HAYFIELD

The Royal Hotel

Tel **01663 742721** | **Market Street, SK22 2EP**
Web **www.theroyalathayfield.com**
Dir ***From A624 follow Hayfield signs.***

Up in the High Peak, below the windswept plateau of Kinder Scout, this hotel dates from 1755. Relax with a pint of Thwaites Original or Howard Town Twenty Trees in the oak-panelled bar, the Cricket Room or the Ramblers Bar. On the menu – chicken satay skewers with sticky rice and prawn crackers. There's also a sandwich menu and Sunday roasts.

Open all day, all week Mon to Thu 11–11 (Fri to Sat 11am–11.30pm Sun 11–10.30) Free House 10 from £9.50 portions/menu Wi-fi P notice required

HOGNASTON

The Red Lion Inn

Tel **01335 370396 | Main Street, DE6 1PR**
Web **www.redlionhognaston.uk**
Dir ***From Ashbourne take B5035 towards Wirksworth. Approximately 5 miles follow Carsington Water signs. Turn right to Hognaston.***

In 1997, to attend a wedding, John F Kennedy's son and his wife stayed at this whitewashed, 17th-century village pub overlooking Carsington Water. With beams, bare brick, old photos, bric-à-brac, antique furniture and open fires, traditional character isn't hard to find. Settle with a pint, perhaps from the Wincle Brewery in Cheshire, and start considering the menu, on which might appear smoked fish chowder; oven-roasted sea bass with beurre blanc sauce; chicken Kiev; lamb rump; and wild mushroom arancini.

Open all week 12–2.30 6–11 (Sun 12–11) Free House 11 portions/menu Wi-fi P notice required

HOPE

The Old Hall Hotel

Tel **01433 620160 | Market Place, S33 6RH**
Web **www.oldhallhotelhope.co.uk**
Dir ***On A6187 in town centre.***

For generations this early 16th-century building was the Balguy family seat. In 1730 it became The Cross Daggers inn, then in 1876 it was renamed The Hall Hotel. Main menus promise dishes such as slow-cooked pork belly, grain mustard mash, spring cabbage and black pudding. For lunch there's also soup and sandwiches, hot ciabattas and light bites. On bank holidays, the Hope Valley Beer and Cider Festival draws the crowds.

Open all day, all week Heineken/Theakston 10 from £11.95 portions/menu Wi-fi P notice required

HATHERSAGE

The Plough Inn

 INN

Tel **01433 650319 | Leadmill Bridge, S32 1BA**
Web **www.theploughinn-hathersage.co.uk**
Dir ***M1 junction 29, take A617 west, A619, A623, then B6001 north to Hathersage.***

Stylish, riverside pub with extensive menu choices

PICK OF THE PUBS

The 16th-century Plough stands in nine acres by the River Derwent. Inside, smart red tartan carpets harmonise well with the open fires and wooden beams of the bar, where you'll find hand-pulled local ales and wines from a well-stocked cellar. From the extensive bar menu come cod fillet in a real ale batter with a choice of hand-cut chunky chips or fries, and garden or mushy peas; beef and ale pudding with a choice of potatoes and minted garden peas; and grills, pastas, pizzas, salads and sandwiches. The restaurant menu pushes the boat out and roast meats are only part of the Sunday line-up, with fillet of bream on rice noodles in a galangal broth; and liver and bacon, champ potato and onion gravy also on offer. Overnight guests can stroll through the landscaped grounds before a good night's rest.

Open all day, all week 11–11 (Sun 12–10.30) Closed 25 Dec Free House 19 portions/menu P

HURDLOW

The Royal Oak

Tel **01298 83288 | SK17 9QJ**
Web **www.peakpub.co.uk**
Dir ***From A515 between Buxton and Ashbourne follow Hurdlow signs.***

Situated in the southern Peak District, this warm-hearted, friendly hostelry welcomes one and all, at any time of day. Tired ramblers and cyclists head straight for the pumps, where five real ales include locals such as Whim Hartington, Thornbridge and Peak Ales.

INGLEBY

The John Thompson Inn & Brewery

Tel **01332 862469 | DE73 7HW**
Web **www.johnthompsoninn.com**
Dir ***From A38 between Derby and Burton upon Trent take A5132 towards Barrow upon Trent. At mini-roundabout right onto B5008 (signed Repton). At roundabout 1st exit into Brook End. Right into Milton Road. Left, left again to Ingleby.***

A pub since 1968, this 15th-century former farmhouse took its name from licensee and owner John Thompson. Now run by son Nick, it is a traditional brewpub set in idyllic countryside beside the banks of the River Trent with views of the neighbouring National Forest.

LITTLE HAYFIELD

Lantern Pike

Tel **01663 747590 | 45 Glossop Road, SK22 2NG**
Web **lanternpikeinn.co.uk**
Dir ***On A624 between Glossop and Chapel-en-le-Frith.***

The stunning views from the beer garden of the wooded Peak District hills are reason enough to seek out this fine pub set in a tiny mill village at the edge of the Kinder Scout moors and below Lantern Pike hill, site of an Armada beacon.

LITTON

Red Lion Inn

Tel **01298 871458 | SK17 8QU**
Web **www.theredlionlitton.co.uk**
Dir ***Just off A623 (Chesterfield to Stockport road), 1 mile east of Tideswell.***

This tiny, terraced pub has served locals and visitors to this pretty White Peak village for two centuries. The warren of hobbit-sized rooms ooze character – log-fires, low beams, murmuring chit-chat and happy ramblers add to the timeless atmosphere. Beers from local microbreweries such as Peak Ale and Abbeydale major on the bar, whilst diners can happily chomp away on good pub food. Sandwiches are available until 6pm. Space constraints mean that children under six cannot be accommodated inside the pub.

Open all day, all week *Enterprise Inns* *10* *from £12* Wi-fi

MATLOCK

The Red Lion

Tel **01629 584888 | 65 Matlock Green, DE4 3BT**
Web **www.theredlionmatlock.co.uk**
Dir ***From Chesterfield, A632 into Matlock, on right just before junction with A615.***

This friendly, family-run free house makes a good base for exploring local attractions like Chatsworth House, Carsington Water and Dovedale. Spectacular walks in the beautiful local countryside will help you work up an appetite for bar lunches, or great tasting home-cooked dishes in the comfortable restaurant.

MONYASH

The Bulls Head

Tel **01629 812372 | Church Street, DE45 1JH**
Web **www.thebullsheadmonyash.co.uk**
Dir ***South of Buxton on A515, turn left onto B5055 signed Monyash.***

A beautiful Peak District pub that's been welcoming visitors for centuries, and was probably established to serve the weekly market. These days the market is only once a year, but you can still expect a friendly welcome. The cosy bar is the heart of the operation.

PILSLEY

The Devonshire Arms at Pilsley ★★★ INN

Tel **01246 565405** | **High Street, DE45 1UL**
Web **www.devonshirepilsley.co.uk**
Dir ***From A619, in Baslow, at roundabout take 1st exit onto B6012. Follow signs to Chatsworth, 2nd right to Pilsley.***

Set in an estate village amidst the rolling parkland that surrounds Chatsworth House, this fabulous old stone pub is an ideal base for visiting Matlock Bath and Castleton. There are open fires, Peak Ales from the estate's brewery and meats, game and greens from the adjacent estate farm shop. After a day's exploration, tuck into braised lamb Henry, mint mash, pea and caper sauce, followed by sticky toffee pudding.

Open all day, all week Free House 11 from £13.95 portions/menu

REPTON

The Boot   INN

PICK OF THE PUBS

Tel **01283 346047** | **12 Boot Hill, DE65 6FT**
Web **www.thebootatrepton.co.uk**
Dir ***From junction A50 and A38 follow Repton and Willington (B5008) signs. In Willington follow Repton sign. Under railway bridge. At cross in Repton left into Brook End, pub on right.***

The Boot's first occupant in the 17th century was a cobbler who hung a boot outside to attract customers; while mending their footwear he'd offer them a glass of ale. Today, there's no point bringing your shoes in for new soles, but ale is most certainly still offered – Clod Hopper, Tuffer's Old porter and Golden Boot are all brewed on site in the inn's microbrewery. The Boot makes a good choice for a drink, a meal and overnight luxury accommodation, if you're looking to stay in this lovely part of the country. The team provide first-class meals, beginning with a champagne breakfast. There's a beer festival in August.

Open all day, all week Free House 12 from £12.95 portions/menu

ROWSLEY

The Grouse & Claret

Tel **01629 733233** | **Station Road, DE4 2EB**
Web **www.grouseclaretpub.co.uk**
Dir ***On A6 between Matlock and Bakewell.***

Popular with local anglers, this 18th-century pub takes its name from a fishing fly. Situated at the gateway to the Peak District National Park, it is handy for visits to the stately homes of Haddon Hall and Chatsworth House. Dogs are welcome in outside areas.

SHARDLOW

The Old Crown Inn

Tel **01332 792392** | **Cavendish Bridge, DE72 2HL**
Web **www.oldcrownshardlow.co.uk**
Dir ***M1 junction 24, A50 signed Stoke and Shardlow. Take slip road signed B6540. At roundabout right, follow Shardlow sign. Left at Cavendish Bridge sign to inn.***

Up to nine real ales are served at this family-friendly pub on the River Trent. Built as a coaching inn in the 17th century, it retains a warm and atmospheric interior. Several hundred water jugs hang from the ceilings, while the walls display an abundance of brewery and railway memorabilia. Food is lovingly prepared by the landlady; main meals focus on pub classics such as home-made steak and kidney pie; and ham, eggs and chips, plus a good choice of baguettes, sandwiches and jacket potatoes.

Open all week 11am–11.30pm (Mon 3–11 Fri to Sat 11am–12.30am Sun 11–11) Marston's portions/menu notice required

SHIRLEY

The Saracen's Head

Tel **01335 360330 | Church Lane, DE6 3AS**
Web **www.saracens-head-shirley.co.uk**
Dir ***A52 from Ashbourne towards Derby. Right in 4 miles to Shirley.***

Overlooking the front garden and village street, the 1791-built Saracen's Head takes its name from the family crest of Sewallis de Scyrle (pronounced Shirley), a Holy Land crusader. All dishes are made on the premises from local, ethical sources. Starting with fresh crab and avocado mayonnaise salad, it's an easy move to, say, Goan fish and tiger prawn curry with steamed rice; or cod loin, cheddar and garlic crust and fresh tomato sauce. For a quintessential country pub experience, visit on a Sunday at lunchtime.

Open all week 11–3 6–11 (Sun 11–10.30) Greene King from £10 portions notice required

STANTON IN PEAK

The Flying Childers Inn

Tel **01629 636333 | Main Road, DE4 2LW**
Web **www.flyingchilders.com**
Dir ***From A6 (between Matlock and Bakewell) follow Youlgrave signs. Onto B5056 to Ashbourne. Follow Stanton in Peak signs.***

Above this instantly likeable, charmingly old-fashioned village pub looms Stanton Moor, and it was named after a champion racehorse owned by the 4th Duke of Devonshire. Log fires warm the cosy, beamed interior, where settles and magpie-furniture fit an absolute treat. The lunchtime-only menu is small but perfectly formed: home-made soups, casseroles, filled cobs, toasties and hearty ploughman's, all with locally sourced ingredients. Local real ales, a beer garden and a great welcome for canine companions, too.

Open all week Mon and Tue 7pm–11pm, Wed to Fri 12–2 7–11, Sat and Sun 12–3 7–11 Free House

TIDESWELL

The George

Tel **01298 872840 | Commercial Road, SK17 8NU**
Web **www.georgeinn-tideswell.co.uk**
Dir ***A619 to Baslow, A623 towards Chapel-en-le-Frith, 0.25 mile.***

Well placed for exploring the Peak District National Park and visiting Chatsworth, this delightful stone-built coaching inn is in the shadow of the village church, the 'Cathedral of the Peak'. The simple menu focuses on traditional pub classics – lunchtime sandwiches and mains might include grilled salmon steak with dill butter, new potatoes and mixed salad; or sweet honey- and mustard-glazed ham with chips and peas. Home-made apple and fruit crumble comes with custard, cream or ice cream.

Open all day, all week Closed 1st week Jan Greene King 8 portions/menu notice required

WILLINGTON

The Dragon

Tel **01283 704795 | 11 The Green, DE65 6BP**
Web **www.thedragonatwillington.co.uk**
Dir ***From junction of A50 and A38 follow Willington and Repton signs onto B5008. At crossroads in Willington left into The Green. Pub on left.***

Full of charm and character, the 150-year-old Dragon sits in the heart of the village, beside the Trent & Mersey Canal. The pub has been sympathetically extended, renovated and restored, with a new 70-seater restaurant complementing the fine beer garden, courtyard and bar. Classic and contemporary dishes are served all day, with booking advised in the evening and at weekends. There's a beer festival in August, plus themed evenings and community events.

Open all day, all week Free House 10 from £11.95 portions/menu notice required

WOOLLEY MOOR

The White Horse Inn

Tel **01246 590319** | **Badger Lane, DE55 6FG**
Web **www.thewhitehorsewoolleymoor.co.uk**
Dir ***From A61 at Stretton take B6014, then B6036 Woolley Moor.***

This 200-year-old pub sits in two acres of gardens amidst beautiful countryside. The building's interior has been meticulously updated, with exposed solid stone walls, precisely laid flagstone floors, polished tables and chairs in both the bar area and bright garden conservatory. Peak Ales are well kept but this is primarily a food destination. Cauliflower and Stilton soup makes a flavoursome starter, to be followed perhaps by crispy pork belly with spring onion mash and smoked bacon sauce; or butternut squash, pea and rosemary risotto.

Open 12-3 5.30-11 (Sun 12-5) Closed 2-21 Jan, Mon lunch Free House 13 portions notice required

YOULGREAVE

The Farmyard Inn

Tel **01629 636221** | **DE45 1UW**
Web **www.farmyardinn.co.uk**
Dir ***Phone for detailed directions.***

This old farmhouse, which became an inn in 1829, looks south across Bradford Dale and its picturesque stretches of tree-hung, crystal-clear water. Warm and friendly, the bar offers two guest real ales and a selection of wines by the glass.

DEVON

ASHBURTON

The Rising Sun

Tel **01364 652544** | **Woodland, TQ13 7JT**
Web **www.therisingsunwoodland.co.uk**
Dir ***From A38 east of Ashburton follow Woodland and Denbury signs. Pub on left, approximately 1.5 miles.***

This former drovers' pub is in the hands of the capable Ward family who welcome everyone including families, and visitors with dogs. Surrounded by gorgeous countryside, and with a large garden in which to enjoy a pint of Dartmoor Jail Ale, it's on the edge of the Dartmoor National Park. Renowned for their pies, chips and specials board, they also offer light snacks at lunchtime and a great children's menu.

Open all year Tue to Sat 12-3 6-11 (Sun 12-4 5.30-11) Closed Mon (excluding bank holidays) Free House portions/menu notice required

AVONWICK

The Turtley Corn Mill

PICK OF THE PUBS

Tel **01364 646100** | **TQ10 9ES**
Web **www.turtleycornmill.com**
Dir ***From A38 at South Brent/Avonwick junction, take B3372, then follow signs for Avonwick, 0.5 mile.***

Set among six acres of gardens and fields on the edge of Dartmoor, including a lake complete with ducks and its own small island, this sprawling old free house was originally a corn mill. The interior is light and fresh with old furniture and oak and slate floors. The daily-changing modern British menus are based on local produce from around the pub's idyllic location. Choices from a sample menu start with terrine of pork, apple and black pudding; or salad of heritage beetroot and goats' curd; continue with smoked haddock and chive fishcakes; or red wine braised oxtail with mustard, mash and vegetables; and wind up with poached apricot open tart, or cappuccino pannacotta.

Open all day, all week Closed 25 Dec Free House 10 portions

BAMPTON

The Swan ★★★★ INN

PICK OF THE PUBS

Tel **01398 332248** | **Station Road, EX16 9NG**
Web **theswan.co**
Dir ***M5 junction 17, A361 towards Barnstaple. At roundabout north-west of Tiverton take A396 to Bampton.***

Originally used as accommodation by masons and other such craftsmen enlarging the church in 1450, this inn has a contemporary style despite its considerable age; the bread oven and original fireplace remain. The inn is popular with walkers and cyclists as it is just six miles from Exmoor National Park, so it's a pretty good idea to make for The Swan after being out and about in the fresh air.

BEER

Anchor Inn

Tel **01297 20386** | **Fore Street, EX12 3ET**
Web **www.oldenglishinns.co.uk**
Dir ***A3052 towards Lyme Regis. At Hangmans Stone take B3174 into Beer. Pub on seafront.***

A traditional inn overlooking the bay in this picture-perfect Devon village, this pretty pub is perfectly situated for walking the Jurassic coastline. Fish caught by local boats features on the menu, and tempting mains might include roasted pork belly with black treacle and bourbon glaze.

BEESANDS

The Cricket Inn   

PICK OF THE PUBS

Tel **01548 580215** | **TQ7 2EN**
Web **www.thecricketinn.com**
Dir ***From Kingsbridge take A379 towards Dartmouth. At Stokenham mini-roundabout turn right to Beesands.***

Over the years, the inn has survived storms, a World War II bomb that destroyed the adjacent cottages and killed seven villagers, and a mud slide that passed through from back to front. Mercifully catastrophe free since then, it concentrates on maintaining its reputation as a favoured foodie pub, providing starters such as salt and pepper prawns; and chicken parfait with red onion marmalade and walnut salad. Memorable mains include Josper-grilled whole fresh fish, lobster and chargrills, not to mention chef's signature seafood pancake in a rich creamy sauce. New England-style bedrooms look east over the bay.

Open all week all day Apr to Oct (Nov to Mar Mon to Fri 11–3 6–10.30 Sat 11–10.30 Sun 11–5) Closed 25 Dec Heavitree 12 from £12.50 portions/menu Wi-fi P

BICKLEIGH

Fisherman's Cot

Tel **01884 855237** | **EX16 8RW**
Web **www.marstonsinns.co.uk**
Dir ***Phone for detailed directions.***

This well-appointed thatched inn stands by Bickleigh Bridge over the River Exe. With food served all day and beautiful gardens, The Waterside Bar is the place for doorstep sandwiches, pies, snacks and afternoon tea, while the restaurant incorporates a carvery (on Sunday) and carte menus.

BISHOPSTEIGNTON

Cockhaven Arms – see opposite

BLACKAWTON

The George Inn  INN

Tel **01803 712342** | **Main Street, TQ9 7BG**
Web **www.blackawton.com**
Dir ***From Totnes on A381 through Halwell. Left onto A3122 towards Dartmouth, turn right to Blackawton at Forces Cross.***

In the South Hams village of Blackawton, The George gained its name during George III's reign, but it was rebuilt after a fire in 1939, after which it became the rallying point for the forced evacuation of the parish in World War II. Now a family-friendly and dog-friendly pub with comfortable accommodation, it's a place to relax with a real ale or cider and choose from a traditional menu, based on local produce.

Open all week 12–3 5–11 (Sun 12–3 7–10.30, Sun 12–3 in Jan) Free House 12 portions/menu Wi-fi P

BRAMPFORD SPEKE

The Lazy Toad **PICK OF THE PUBS**

Tel **01392 841591** | **EX5 5DP**
Web **www.thelazytoad.co.uk**
Dir ***From Exeter take A377 towards Crediton 1.5 miles, right signed Brampford Speke.***

Dating from the late 18th century, when the village farrier and wheelwright worked here, this oak-beamed Grade II listed pub offers ales from the likes of Otter and the Exeter Brewery, Sandford Orchards ciders, and wines from Sharpham near Totnes. A smallholding behind the pub supplies vegetables, fruits and herbs for the short, daily-changing menus. These offer starters such as rolled ham hock, spinach and grain mustard roulade, home-made chutney, and walnut toast; and mains of deep-fried herbed skate wings, cubed roast potatoes and tartare dressing.

Open all year 12–3 6–10 (Sun 12–4) Closed Sun evening, Mon Free House 8 from £9.95 portions/menu P

BRANSCOMBE

The Fountain Head

Tel **01297 680359** | **EX12 3BG**
Web **www.fountainheadinn.com**
Dir ***From Seaton on A3052 towards Sidmouth left at Branscombe Cross to pub.***

This 500-year-old forge and cider house is a true rural survivor, in a peaceful village just a short walk from the coastal path. The traditional worn flagstones, crackling log fires, rustic furnishings, village-brewed beers from Branscombe Vale, and the chatty atmosphere charm locals and visitors alike. Hearty pub food includes home-made chicken liver and wild mushroom pâté; and venison, vegetable and red wine pie. There's a spit-roast and barbecue every Sunday evening July to September, and a midsummer beer festival.

Open all week 11–3 6–11 (Sun 12–10.30) Free House portions/menu notice required

The Masons Arms

Tel **01297 680300** | **EX12 3DJ**
Web **www.masonsarms.co.uk**
Dir ***Exit A3052 towards Branscombe, down hill, Masons Arms at bottom of hill.***

Just a 10-minute stroll from the beach, the gardens of this inn have sea views across a valley. Creeper-clad, it dates from 1360 when it was a cider house. Slate floors, stone walls, and a huge fireplace all add to the time-warp charm.

BRENDON

Rockford Inn

Tel **01598 741214** | **EX35 6PT**
Web **www.therockfordinn.co.uk**
Dir ***A39 through Minehead follow signs to Lynmouth. Left to Brendon.***

Standing alongside the East Lyn River in the tucked-away Brendon Valley, this traditional 17th-century free house stands at the heart of Exmoor and is handy for several walking routes. Eat in the garden in warm weather, or head inside to the open fire.

BISHOPSTEIGNTON

Cockhaven Arms

★★★★ INN

Tel **01626 775252** | **TQ14 9RF**
Web **www.cockhavenarms.co.uk**
Dir ***From A380 onto A381 towards Teignmouth. Follow brown signs for pub.***

Long-standing inn serving pub classics

Overlooking the Teign Estuary, this friendly pub, dating from the 16th century, but with later additions, is to be found below Haldon Moor in the quiet village of Bishopsteignton. Downstairs it retains much of its historic character, although it has been opened up to create a lovely bar and restaurant with log fires, and plenty of original features, including the gallery landing, beams and fireplaces. Menus are strong on local produce and pub classics,

and you really ought to book for Sunday lunch. At lunchtime choose from sharing platters, ciabattas, sandwiches and classics like ham, egg and chips. In the evening you might start with prawn and crayfish cocktail, followed by vegetable hotpot; or duck breast with dauphinoise potatoes, orange and dark cherry sauce. The refurbished bedrooms are all named after sailing craft.

Open all day, all week Free House 14 from £11.50 portions/menu notice required

BROADHEMBURY

The Drewe Arms

Tel **01404 841267** | **EX14 3NF**
Web **www.drewearmsinn.co.uk**
Dir ***M5 junction 28, A373 towards Honiton. Left to Broadhembury.***

Tucked away in the Blackdown Hills, but only five miles from Honiton, this ancient building has a delightfully quirky interior with original beams, sisal flooring and wood-burning stove. Otter Amber and Branscombe Vale Branoc are among the five Devon ales dispensed from the convivial bar.

BUCKLAND MONACHORUM

Drake Manor Inn

Tel **01822 853892** | **The Village, PL20 7NA**
Web **www.drakemanorinn.co.uk**
Dir ***From A386 (Plymouth) turn left before Yelverton, follow signs to Buckland Monachorum. Left into village, on left next to church.***

Dating back to the 12th century, when it was home to the masons working on nearby St Andrew's church, this ancient inn is run by Mandy Robinson, who prides herself on running a 'proper pub', with a menu of traditional, locally-sourced delights. Start with ham hock terrine, followed by local mussels in beer broth; or a trio of local sausages, mash and red onion gravy. There's a lovely cottage garden to the side of the pub, and a wood-burner blazing in the winter.

Open all week Mon to Thu 11.30–2.30 6.30–11 (Fri to Sat 11.30–11.30 Sun 12–11) Punch Taverns 9 from £7 portions/menu

BUTTERLEIGH

The Butterleigh Inn

Tel **01884 855433** | **EX15 1PN**
Web **www.butterleighinn.co.uk**
Dir ***M5 junction 28, B3181 signed Cullompton. In Cullompton High Street right signed Butterleigh. 3 miles to pub.***

Set in a delightful village in the heart of the rolling Devon countryside, the 400-year-old Butterleigh is a traditional free house. There is a mass of local memorabilia throughout this friendly local, where customers can choose from a selection of changing real ales including Dartmoor Jail Ale and ciders including Sandford Orchards' Devon Scrumpy. Expect home-made dishes such as home-made burgers; steak and ale pie; fish specials; and curry of the week. On fine days, the garden is very popular.

Open all year 12–2.30 6–11 (Fri to Sat 12–2.30 6–12 Sun 12–3) Closed Sun evening, Mon lunch Free House 9 from £10 portions

CADELEIGH

The Cadeleigh Arms

Tel **01884 855238** | **EX16 8HP**
Web **www.thecadeleigharms.com**
Dir ***South of Tiverton on A396 to Bickleigh. Turn right onto A3072 signed Crediton, continue over humpback bridge. Turn right to Cadeleigh.***

Just nine miles from Exeter, this rural village pub is set high in the hills above the River Exe. So tucked away is The Cadeleigh Arms that as you sup your pint of Exeter Brewery Avocet ale or Sandford Orchard cider on the terrace, the only sound you might hear is the distant moo of cows. In winter, a table near the log burner is the place to tuck into seasonal dishes using local produce.

Open all year 12–3 6–11.30 Closed Mon Free House 10 from £11.95 portions/menu notice required

8 DEVON PUBS WITH ACCOMMODATION

The following pubs are rated as part of the AA Guest Accommodation scheme (see page 10–11 for more information).

Cary Arms & Spa ★★★★★ INN Torquay, *see page 142*
The Cricket Inn ★★★★ INN Beesands, *see page 122*
The Oxenham Arms and Restaurant ★★★★ INN South Zeal, *see page 138*
Rising Sun ★★★★ INN Lynmouth, *see page 133*
The Rock Inn ★★★★ INN Haytor Vale, *see page 130*
The Swan ★★★★ INN Bampton, *see page 121*
Cockhaven Arms ★★★★ INN Bishopsteignton, *see page 123*
Red Lion ★★★★ INN Clovelly, *see page 125*

CHAGFORD

The Chagford Inn

Tel **01647 433109** | **7 Mill Street, TQ13 8AW**
Web **www.thechagfordinn.com**
Dir ***From A30 at Whiddon Down follow Chagford signs onto A382. Right onto B3206 signed Chagford.***

Set within the glorious Dartmoor National Park, this blue-washed pub has an artistic bent with regular exhibitions of new artists and also life drawing classes. Close links with neighbouring farms means a steady supply of quality local meat, and the kitchen adopts a nose-to-tail philosophy.

CHALLACOMBE

Black Venus Inn

Tel **01598 763251** | **EX31 4TT**
Web **www.blackvenusinn.co.uk**
Dir ***On B3358.***

Named after an extinct breed of sheep, this 16th-century, stone-built pub occupies a wonderful location in the Exmoor National Park. Surrounded by many excellent walks, the low-beamed pub welcomes dogs and children, particularly in the school summer holidays when the pub opens all day. This is a pub passionate about beer so there's always two local cask ales on tap – among them Cotleigh Golden Seahawk and Exmoor Fox – to accompany robust dishes such as home-made chilli con carne; beef and ale pie; plus daily specials and fresh fish.

Open all week 12–2.30 5.30–11 Closed 25–26 Dec Free House 10 portions/menu Wi-fi

CHULMLEIGH

The Red Lion Hotel

Tel **01769 580384** | **1 East Street, EX18 7DD**
Web **www.theredlionchulmleigh.co.uk**
Dir ***From A377 onto B3096 signed Chulmleigh. In village centre.***

Chulmleigh is a thriving little community with the Red Lion at its heart, an ideal place from which to explore north Devon. It is stylishly decorated with old settles, comfortable armchairs and scrubbed wooden tables, complemented by the fine flagstone floors.

CLOVELLY

Red Lion ★★★★ INN

PICK OF THE PUBS

Tel **01237 431237** | **The Quay, EX39 5TF**
Web **www.clovelly.co.uk**
Dir ***From Bideford roundabout, A39 to Bude, 10 miles. At Clovelly Cross roundabout right. Park at Visitor Centre. Walk to hotel at bottom of hill.***

This charming whitewashed hostelry sits right on the quay in Clovelly, the famously unspoilt 'village like a waterfall', which descends down broad steps to a 14th-century harbour. Originally a beer house for fishermen and other locals, the Red Lion has plenty of character and offers Cornish ales such as Sharp's Doom Bar in its snug bar. Alternatively, you could settle in the Harbour Bar, and sample the home-cooked food, the modern seasonal menu specialising in fresh seafood, which is landed daily right outside the door. Choose pan-fried fillet of sea bass with cream bean cassoulet, or opt for medallions of wild venison, or beetroot risotto served with parsnip chips.

Open all day, all week Free House portions/menu Wi-fi *notice required*

CLYST HYDON

The Five Bells Inn

Tel **01884 277288** | **EX15 2NT**
Web **www.fivebells.uk.com**
Dir ***B3181 towards Cullompton, right at Hele Cross towards Clyst Hydon. 2 miles turn right, then sharp right at left bend at village sign.***

Early in the 20th century the village rector objected to the pub being next door to his church, so he had it moved into this old thatched farmhouse. Today, local boy James has returned to his roots to run it with his wife, Charlie. Their ever-changing menus specialise in classics like Brixham fish pie, and spiced aubergine caponata, while on the specials menu could be pan-fried stone bass; Creedy Carver duck breast; and cured Loch Duart salmon. The large garden is delightful.

Open all year 12–3 6–11 (Sat 12–11 Sun 12–10) Closed Sun evening and Mon (Oct to Feb) Free House 19 from £12 portions Wi-fi *notice required*

COCKWOOD

The Anchor Inn

Tel **01626 890203** | **EX6 8RA**
Web **www.anchorinncockwood.com**
Dir ***From A379 between Dawlish and Starcross follow Cockwood sign.***

This 450-year-old inn overlooks a small landlocked harbour on the River Exe and was once the haunt of smugglers. In summer, customers spill out onto the verandah and harbour wall, while real fires, nautical bric-à-brac and low beams make the interior cosy in winter.

COLEFORD

The New Inn ★★★★ INN

PICK OF THE PUBS

Tel **01363 84242** | **EX17 5BZ**
Web **www.thenewinncoleford.co.uk**
Dir ***From Exeter take A377, 1.5 miles after Crediton left for Coleford, 1.5 miles to inn.***

The attractive 13th-century building with thatched roof makes a perfect home for this friendly inn. The ancient slate-floored bar with its old chests and polished brass blends effortlessly with fresh white walls, original oak beams and simple wooden furniture in the dining room. Set beside the River Cole, the garden is perfect for alfresco summer dining. Menus change regularly, and special events such as 'posh pies week' or 'sea shanty evening' take place throughout the year. Home-made bar food includes a range of soups, omelettes and platters, while dinner might be roast guinea fowl breast, redcurrant sauce with raspberry and Madeira; seasonal game pie; or aubergine moussaka with tomato and fresh basil. The pub's talking Amazon Blue parrot, called Captain, has been a famous fixture here for some 30 years.

Open all week 12–3 6–11 (Sun 12–3 6–10.30) Closed 25–26 Dec Free House 15 from £10.50 portions/menu Wi-fi notice required

CREDITON

The Lamb Inn ★★★★ INN

Tel **01363 773676** | **The Square, Sandford, EX17 4LW**
Web **www.lambinnsandford.co.uk**
Dir ***Phone for detailed directions.***

This 16th-century coaching inn is full of character, with plenty of period detail and a delightful sheltered garden. Four local beers take pride of place in the bar, and the short, regularly-changing menus might feature pork belly and crackling.

Open all day, all week 9am–close Free House 10 from £6.95 portions/menu Wi-fi

DARTMOUTH

Royal Castle Hotel – see page 128

DODDISCOMBSLEIGH

The NoBody Inn – see page 129

DOLTON

Rams Head Inn – see opposite

EAST ALLINGTON

The Fortescue Arms

Tel **01548 521215** | **TQ9 7RA**
Web **www.thefortescuearms.com**
Dir ***Phone for detailed directions.***

Named after a local landowner, this 19th-century pub retains the charms of yesteryear with wooden tables, flagstone floors and beamed ceilings. Open fires burn in winter, warming the informal candlelit interior where a range of local ales is served.

EAST DOWN

Pyne Arms

Tel **01271 850055** | **EX31 4LX**
Web **www.pynearms.co.uk**
Dir ***Follow East Down and pub signs from A39 between Blackmoor Gate and Barnstaple.***

Just seven miles from Barnstaple, the Pyne Arms is a popular stop for walkers visiting nearby Arlington Court (NT) and Exmoor National Park. The pub was renovated in recent years, retaining its character and long tradition of feeding visitors well.

DOLTON

Rams Head Inn

Tel 01805 804255 | South Street, EX19 8QS
Web www.ramsheadinn.co.uk
Dir *8 miles from Torrington on A3124.*

Making quite a mark on Devon's culinary landscape

Tastefully refurbished by previous owners, Dolton's 17th-century inn is now owned by top French chef Nicolas Boucher from the Vendée and his partner, Vanessa. In their tastefully furnished bar you'll be able to try well-kept real ales and lagers and Nicolas's hand-picked wines, demonstrating ample proof of his passionate interest in the matter. On the menu spicy Calabrian 'nduja Scotch egg joins a strong modern British cast that also includes grilled John Dory and pollack; pan-fried rack of pistachio- and mustard-crust lamb; and vegetarian pie of the day. To finish with something suitably French, ask for liquorice crème brûlée served with sablé biscuit. In summer there's a delightful, sun-trap garden area, while wood-burning stoves in winter make staying in the smartly furnished bar areas a no-brainer.

Open all day, all week Free House from £10.50 portions/menu notice required

EAST PRAWLE

The Pigs Nose Inn

Tel 01548 511209 | TQ7 2BY
Web www.pigsnoseinn.co.uk
Dir ***From Kingsbridge take A379 towards Dartmouth. After Frogmore turn right signed East Prawle. Approximately 5 miles to pub in village centre.***

This inn was once a smugglers' haunt and owners today demonstrate their adherence to old-fashioned values by banning juke boxes and games machines, and by their provision of a 'knitting corner', games and toys. Devon-sourced real ales are served straight from the barrel in the wonderfully cluttered bar. Food here is never a 'minuscule blob on an oversized square plate', but is good helpings of traditional pub grub, such as chicken curry; scampi and chips; cod and chips; and vegetarian Mediterranean pasta. There's also a dogs' menu.

Open all week 12–3 6–11.30 Free House from £9 portions/menu Wi-fi notice required

EXETER

The Hour Glass

Tel 01392 258722 | 21 Melbourne Street, EX2 4AU
Web www.hourglassexeter.co.uk
Dir ***M5 junction 30, A370 signed Exeter. At Countess Weir roundabout 3rd exit onto Topsham Road (B3182) signed City Centre. In approximately 2 miles left into Melbourne Street.***

This distinctively shaped backstreet pub has built a reputation for its friendly service and inventive food, not to mention its rotating local ales and great choice of ciders. Expect beams, wood floors, an open fire and resident cats in the bar.

DARTMOUTH

Royal Castle Hotel

★★★ HOTEL

Tel 01803 833033 | 11 The Quay, TQ6 9PS
Web www.royalcastle.co.uk
Dir *In town centre, overlooking inner harbour.*

A fine place to eat and drink

PICK OF THE PUBS

An iconic building in the centre of this bustling sailing honeypot, the Royal Castle Hotel commands a prime site overlooking the Dart estuary. Indication of its rich history is outlined on a sign over the entrance, 'This old coaching inn has been famous since Drake first sailed'. Originally four Tudor houses built on either side of a narrow lane, now forming the lofty hallway, this handsome old coaching inn offers plenty of original features in the shape of period fireplaces, spiral staircases, priest holes and oil paintings. The traditional Galleon Bar and the contemporary Harbour Bar, both dog friendly, always have log fires lit in the cooler months. Choose either for a light lunch or a main meal, with real ales from Devon breweries Dartmoor and Otter, and carefully selected wines served by the glass. In June, July and August the full bar menu is served upstairs in the Grill Room, with its hard-to-beat river views. In the evening, this is a great setting to enjoy well-prepared dishes, such as Brixham crab mayonnaise and avocado; pan-fried turbot fillet; saddle and roasted rack of lamb; and Mediterranean vegetable and ricotta cheese lasagne. All the well-appointed bedrooms come with a complimentary parking service.

Open all day, all week 8am–11pm Free House 25 from £13.50 portions/menu notice required

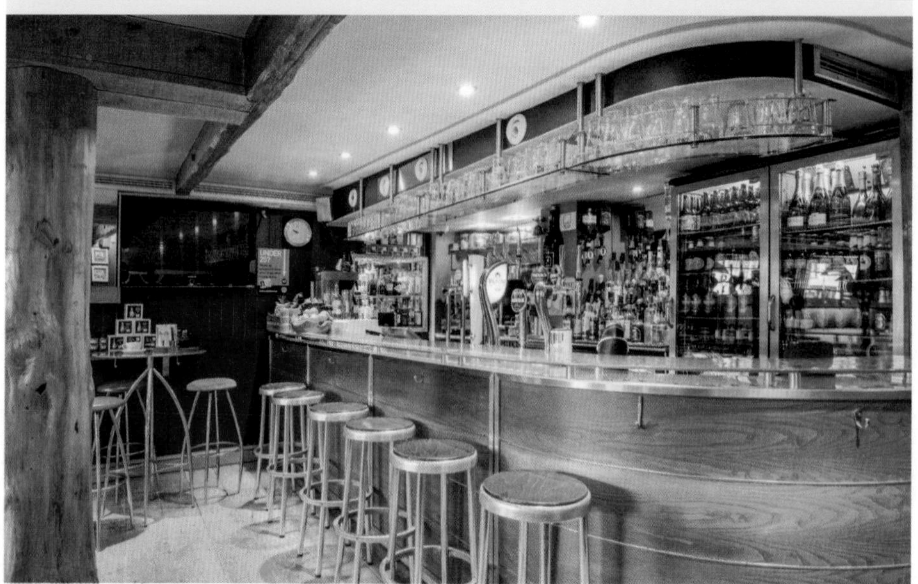

DODDISCOMBSLEIGH

The NoBody Inn

★★★★ INN

Tel 01647 252394 | EX6 7PS
Web www.nobodyinn.co.uk
Dir *3 miles south-west of Exeter Racecourse (A38).*

All the old-world charm you could want

PICK OF THE PUBS

For over 400 years, this fine old building has stood in the rolling countryside between the Haldon Hills and the Teign Valley. Remodelling over the centuries has reflected its several roles, including a long spell as a centre for parish affairs and meeting place until in 1838 Pophill House, as it was then known, formally became The New Inn. Among the five landlords since was the poor chap in 1952 whose body undertakers mistakenly left in the mortuary, so that his funeral went ahead with an empty coffin – which is how the inn acquired its name. Inside, providing all the expected old-world charm, there are low ceilings, blackened beams, an inglenook fireplace and antique furniture. The bar serves 30-odd wines by the glass, selected from a range of more than 250 bins, some quite rare, and the shelves groan under the weight of a mind-boggling 280 whiskies, mostly malts. Branscombe Vale brewery supplies NoBody's Bitter, with other Devon and Cornwall guest ales adding to the choice. Crisp white napkins define the restaurant, where the seasonally changing menus, awarded an AA Rosette, rely extensively on fine Devon produce.

Open all day, all week 11–11 (Sun 12–10.30)
Free House 31 from £9.95 portions

EXTON

The Puffing Billy PICK OF THE PUBS

Tel **01392 877888** | **Station Road, EX3 0PR**
Web **www.thepuffingbilly.co.uk**
Dir ***A376 signed Exmouth, through Ebford. Follow signs for pub, right into Exton.***

The whitewashed building might be 16th century and the 19th-century name refers to the nearby railway line, but the food is absolutely 21st century. Taken over in 2015 by the St Austell Brewery, the traditional exterior disguises the crisp, clean lines and finish within, where reliable West Country beers such as Branscombe Vale Branoc, along with an appealing menu, combine to make The Puffing Billy a favourite destination dining bar. The home-cooked dishes are seasonal and locally sourced so along with pub classics you can expect the likes of baked fig, Parma ham, parmesan crisp, rocket and sherry vinaigrette; and Darts Farm 28-day dry aged 10oz rump steak.

Open all day, all week St Austell Brewery 15 portions/menu Wi-fi notice required

GEORGEHAM

The Rock Inn

Tel **01271 890322** | **Rock Hill, EX33 1JW**
Web **www.therockgeorgeham.co.uk**
Dir ***From A361 at Braunton follow Croyde Bay signs. Through Croyde, 1 mile to Georgeham. Pass shop and church. Turn right (Rock Hill), inn on left.***

Handy for the famous surfing beaches at Woolacombe, this old inn is also a lovely watering hole for walkers and cyclists. Its friendly atmosphere, comprising a mix of happy banter from the locals and gentle jazz played at lunchtime, adds to the enjoyment.

HAYTOR VALE

The Rock Inn 

INN PICK OF THE PUBS

Tel **01364 661305** | **TQ13 9XP**
Web **www.rock-inn.co.uk**
Dir ***A38 from Exeter, at Drum Bridges roundabout take A382 for Bovey Tracey, 1st exit at 2nd roundabout (B3387), 3 miles left to Haytor Vale.***

Just inside Dartmoor National Park, below the Haytor Rocks, this beamed and flagstoned 18th-century coaching inn occupies a stunning location in wonderful walking country. The traditional interior is full of character, with settles, prints and paintings, a grandfather clock, and two crackling fireplaces. After a day's exercise, healthy appetites can be satisfied with some robust and contemporary British cooking. From the fixed-price dinner menu, carrot and tarragon soup could be followed by pan-fried salmon fillet with samphire, and rounded off with sticky toffee pudding, caramel sauce and the county's famous clotted cream. West Country cheeses are a particular feature, as are Devon Mist or Ashridge Devon Gold ciders from the bar. In fair weather, eat or drink alfresco in the courtyard or in the peaceful garden across the lane.

Open all day, all week 11–11 (Sun 12–10.30) Closed 25–26 Dec Free House 12 from £14.95 portions/menu Wi-fi

HONITON

The Holt PICK OF THE PUBS

Tel **01404 47707** | **178 High Street, EX14 1LA**
Web **www.theholt-honiton.com**
Dir ***Phone for detailed directions.***

Successfully run by brothers Joe and Angus McCaig, this popular split-level establishment is just where the High Street crosses a stream called The Gissage. The downstairs bar is stocked with the full range of Otter beers from nearby Luppitt, ciders from Honiton's own Norcotts, and Joe's wine selection; for the candlelit restaurant, head upstairs. The cooking is modern British, with regularly changing menus showcasing local suppliers in a big way and making good use of meats and fish from Angus's smokehouse. Tapas is served at lunchtime and in the evening, and daily specials supplement main dishes such as Thai red curry with smoked tofu, sweet potato, coconut, coriander and jasmine rice; and seared wild venison haunch served with dauphinoise potato, celeriac, chocolate oil and port jus.

Open 11–3 5.30–12 Closed 25–26 Dec, Sun and Mon Free House 9 portions Wi-fi

The Railway

Tel **01404 371007** | **Queen Street, EX14 1HE**
Web **www.therailwayhoniton.co.uk**
Dir ***From High Street into New Street (Lloyds bank on corner). 1st left into Queen Street (follow road to right). Pub on left. Or from A35 (at Copper Castle) into Pine Park Road. 1st right (Pine Park Road), over railway bridge, pub on right.***

The Railway dates back to 1869, when it was built as a cider house for thirsty GWR workers. It offers visitors a warm, family-friendly atmosphere and there's an appealing menu.

IDDESLEIGH

The Duke of York PICK OF THE PUBS

Tel **01837 810253** | **EX19 8BG**
Web **www.dukeofyorkdevon.co.uk**
Dir ***Phone for detailed directions.***

In a tiny village of pretty cottages, this thatched, cob and stone inn is where local author Michael Morpurgo embarked on his novel *War Horse*, following conversations in front of the fire with a First World War veteran. Another literary link is Henry Williamson's *Tarka the Otter*; the Tarka Trail now passes the pub door. An enticing range of real ales includes Bays Topsail from Paignton, and Winkleigh cider. Around 640 years old, the interior is full of character: ancient beams and pillars, huge inglenooks and timeworn furniture. The short menu typically offers a three-course meal of smoked duck breast with avocado and mixed leaf salad; whole brill stuffed with prawns, and rich white wine and parsley sauce; and Dunstaple Farm ice cream. There's a beer festival in August.

Open all day, all week 11–11 Free House 10 portions/menu Wi-fi notice required

KILMINGTON

The Old Inn

Tel **01297 32096** | **EX13 7RB**
Dir ***From Axminster on A35 towards Honiton. Pub on left in 1 mile.***

This thatched Devon longhouse dates from 1650, when it was a staging house for changing post horses. Today's weary travellers will find a cosy, beamed interior with a relaxed atmosphere, crackling log fires, and a fine range of local ales on tap. Order a pint of Otter or Thatchers Gold to accompany a traditional pub meal, perhaps a jacket potato with a choice of toppings. The south-facing garden is the venue for the Spring Bank Holiday beer festival in late May.

Open all day, all week 8am–11pm Free House 10 portions/menu Wi-fi notice required

KINGSBRIDGE

The Crabshell Inn

Tel **01548 852345** | **Embankment Road, TQ7 1JZ**
Web **www.thecrabshellinn.com**
Dir ***A38 towards Plymouth, follow signs for Kingsbridge.***

Beside the gorgeous Kingsbridge Estuary on an old quay, this waterside pub offers glorious views of vessels, wildlife and paddleboarders. More restful is the practice of supping Devonshire beers from the likes of Dartmoor Brewery or an ultra-local farm cider, whilst contemplating the menu of gourmet pizzas created here. The daily menu is equally impressive; local scallops with squash purée, polenta chips and bacon crumb being a case in point.

Open all day, all week 8.30am–11pm (check website for seasonal variations) Free House from £20 portions/menu Wi-fi notice required

KINGSKERSWELL

Bickley Mill Inn PICK OF THE PUBS

Tel **01803 873201** | **TQ12 5LN**
Web **www.bickleymill.co.uk**
Dir ***From Newton Abbot take A380 towards Torquay. Left, follow Stoneycombe signs. Then follow Bickley Mill signs.***

Located in an idyllic Devon valley, this beautifully restored 13th-century flour mill has a unique appeal among pubs close to the beaches on the English Riviera and the wilderness of Dartmoor. Sitting beside the cosy log fire or watching the trickle of the stream in the tree-shaded garden, it's hard to believe this tranquil setting is only a short hop from the tourist-filled resort of Torquay. Sticking to local suppliers, Torbay's Bays Brewery ales appear on the pumps and Devon produce dominates the menu.

Open all day, all week Free House 12 portions/menu Wi-fi notice required

KINGS NYMPTON

The Grove Inn PICK OF THE PUBS

Tel **01769 580406** | **EX37 9ST**
Web **www.thegroveinn.co.uk**
Dir ***2.5 miles from A377 (Exeter to Barnstaple road). 1.5 miles from B3226 (South Molton road). Follow brown pub signs.***

Commanding the crossroads in a peaceful village, The Grove has all the requisites of a typical Devon pub – thatched roof, whitewashed exterior, beamed ceilings, flagstone floors, winter log fires and even on occasions, Morris dancers. The kitchen takes full advantage of fresh produce from nearby farms and the coast for dishes such as tagine of north Devon goat served with herbed couscous; fresh West Country mackerel fillets in real ale batter with chips and peas; or half a spit-roast chicken with red wine and rosemary sauce and chips. All wines, even fizz, are served by the glass, beers come from regional breweries and there's a collection of 65 single malts from around the world. Dogs are allowed in the bar. A beer and cider festival takes place in July.

Open all year 12–3 6–11 (Sun 12–4 7–10 some bank holidays 12–4) Closed Mon Free House 31 portions/menu Wi-fi notice required

KINGSTON

The Dolphin Inn

Tel **01548 810314** | **TQ7 4QE**
Web **dolphininnkingston.co.uk**
Dir ***From A379 (Plymouth to Kingsbridge road) take B3233 signed Bigbury-on-Sea, at crossroads straight on to Kingston. Follow brown inn signs.***

Situated between the coast and Dartmoor, church stonemasons lived here in the 15th century, and later it was taken over by fishermen and their families. Warmed by inglenook fireplaces, the inn is close to the Erme estuary and the surfing beaches of the South Hams. Real ales and Thatchers cider are served alongside dishes as Cornish scallops with smoked pancetta followed by slow-roasted pork belly with apple and ginger.

Open all week 12–3 6–11 (Sun 12–3 7–10.30) Punch Taverns portions/menu Wi-fi P

KNOWSTONE

The Masons Arms

PICK OF THE PUBS

Tel **01398 341231** | **EX36 4RY**
Web **www.masonsarmsdevon.co.uk**
Dir ***Follow Knowstone signs from A361.***

A thatched 13th-century inn on the edge of Exmoor, where excellent food and drink are preceded by a genuinely warm welcome. Villagers and visiting walkers mix happily in the low-beamed bar, where pints of Cotleigh Tawny Owl and Sam's Poundhouse cider are supped around the warmth of the huge fireplace. The bright rear dining room offers long views, an extraordinary ceiling mural, and a sophisticated menu. Typical of choices are terrine of rabbit, bacon and leek; loin of venison with red wine pear and blue cheese gratin; and pineapple and shortbread, with rum and ginger. No under 5s in dining room in the evening.

Open 12–2 6–11 Closed 1st week Jan, Feb half term and last week Aug, Sun, Mon Free House 10 from £25.50 Wi-fi P

LIFTON

The Arundell Arms ★★★

HOTEL PICK OF THE PUBS

Tel **01566 784666** | **PL16 0AA**
Web **www.arundellarms.com**
Dir ***1 mile from A30 dual carriageway, 3 miles east of Launceston.***

This former coaching inn has a 250-year-old cock-fighting pit in the garden, and from the car park you can see the window bars of the cells of the neighbouring former police station. The Courthouse Bar dispenses the aptly named Dartmoor Jail Ale, and Ashridge cider; sensibly priced wines come from around the world. Holding two AA Rosettes for many years, Devon-born Master Chef of Great Britain Steve Pidgeon's restaurant makes excellent use of produce from local shoots and estates, as well as from the hotel's kitchen garden and the villagers; he'll cook fish caught by guests, too. Menus might feature pan-fried grey mullet; roast best-end of English lamb; fillet of Aylesbury duck; and vegetable croustade provençale.

Open all week 12–3 6–11 Free House 9 portions/menu Wi-fi P notice required

LUSTLEIGH

The Cleave Public House

Tel **01647 277223 | TQ13 9TJ**
Web **www.thecleavelustleigh.co.uk**
Dir ***From Newton Abbot take A382, follow Bovey Tracey signs, then Moretonhampstead signs. Left to Lustleigh.***

Set on the edge of Dartmoor National Park, and dating from the 16th century, this thatched pub has a traditional snug bar, with beams, granite flooring and log fire; to the rear, formerly the old railway station waiting room, is now a light and airy dining area leading to a lovely cottage garden. The pub/bistro has gained a reputation for an interesting and varied, daily-changing menu.

Open all day, all week 11.30–11 (Sun 12–7) Heavitree 8 from £8.50 portions/menu

LUTON (NEAR CHUDLEIGH)

Elizabethan Inn

Tel **01626 775425 | Fore Street, TQ13 0BL**
Web **www.elizabethaninn.co.uk**
Dir ***Between Chudleigh and Teignmouth.***

Known locally as the Lizzie, this smart, welcoming 16th-century free house attracts diners and drinkers alike. There's a great selection of West Country ales to choose from, as well as local Reddaway's Farm cider.

LYNMOUTH

Rising Sun ★★★★ INN

PICK OF THE PUBS

Tel **01598 753223 | Harbourside, EX35 6EG**
Web **www.risingsunlynmouth.co.uk**
Dir ***M5 junction 25 follow Minehead signs. A39 to Lynmouth.***

Set beneath Countisbury Cliffs, the highest in England, and overlooking Lynmouth's tiny harbour and bay, this 14th-century thatched smugglers' inn has all the uneven oak floors, crooked ceilings and thick walls you could wish for. Literary associations are plentiful: R D Blackmore wrote some of his wild Exmoor romance, *Lorna Doone*, here; the poet Shelley is believed to have honeymooned in the garden cottage, and Coleridge stayed here too. Immediately behind rises Exmoor Forest and National Park, home to red deer, wild ponies and birds of prey. Game and seafood are in plentiful supply, seen in dishes such as braised pheasant with pancetta, quince and Braunton greens; and roast shellfish – crab, mussels, clams and scallops in garlic, ginger and coriander.

Open all day, all week 11am–midnight Closed 25 Dec Free House 13 from £14 portions

MARLDON

The Church House Inn

Tel **01803 558279 | Village Road, TQ3 1SL**
Web **www.churchhousemarldon.com**
Dir ***From Torquay ring road follow signs to Marldon and Totnes, follow brown signs to pub.***

Built as a hostel for the church stonemasons, this ancient country inn dates from 1362. Rebuilt in 1740, it retains many period features, including beautiful Georgian windows. These days it has an uncluttered, contemporary feel with additional seating in the garden. The menu might include pan-fried tiger prawns with spaghetti, asparagus and broad beans; or slow-cooked lamb shoulder with apricots, cinnamon and sultanas.

Open all week 11–2.30 5.30–11 (Fri to Sat 11–2.30 5.30–11.30 Sun 12–3 5.30–10.30) Free House 12 from £15 portions

MEAVY

The Royal Oak Inn

Tel **01822 852944 | PL20 6PJ**
Web **www.royaloakinn.org.uk**
Dir ***B3212 Yelverton to Princetown. Right at Dousland to Meavy, past school. Pub opposite village green.***

This traditional 15th-century inn is situated by a village green within Dartmoor National Park. Flagstone floors, oak beams and a welcoming open fire set the scene at this free house, popular with cyclists and walkers. Local cask ales, ciders and fine wines accompany the carefully sourced ingredients on a menu ranging from lunchtime light bites to good pub classics. A beer and cider festival takes place on the Summer Bank Holiday .

Open all day, all week Free House 12 portions/menu notice required

MODBURY

California Country Inn

PICK OF THE PUBS

Tel **01548 821449** | **California Cross, PL21 0SG**
Web **www.thecaliforniainn.co.uk**
Dir ***On B3196 (north-east of Modbury).***

Just outside Modbury, which became Europe's first plastic bag-free town a few years ago, is a rural crossroads where the 14th-century 'Cali' now stands. It's where 19th-century, would-be emigrants caught the Plymouth stagecoach before sailing to the New World. How many, we can only wonder, regretted leaving behind the familiarity of the pub's ancient beams, exposed stone walls, huge fireplace and its beer, probably then brewed on the spot? Today's real ales, Dartmoor, St Austell and Sharp's, come from a little further away, while the award-winning wine list includes some from nearby Sharpham Vineyard. On the menu are prime Devon fillet and rump steaks; home-made beef lasagne; extra-large breaded wholetail scampi; and curry of the day. There's a children's menu too.

Open all day, all week Free House 12 from £9.95 portions/menu

MORETONHAMPSTEAD

The Horse

Tel **01647 440242** | **George Street, TQ13 8PG**
Web **www.thehorsedartmoor.co.uk**
Dir ***In village centre.***

Once virtually derelict, The Horse is an object lesson in pub revival, as its beautiful dining room, Mediterranean-style courtyard and stunning barn conversion testify. The chesterfield-furnished bar offers Devon-brewed real ales and ciders, and the same menu as the restaurant, which could mean antipasto to share; tapas choices; or hand-rolled gourmet pizzas. The courtyard smokery is responsible for smoked pastrami, salmon and salt beef. Other choices might be moules frites; or chargrilled 21-day-hung Dartmoor rib-eye.

Open Tue to Sat 12–2.30 5–12 (Sun and Mon 5–12) Closed 25 Dec Free House 12 portions/menu notice required

NEWTON ABBOT

The Wild Goose Inn

Tel **01626 872241** | **Combeinteignhead, TQ12 4RA**
Web **wildgoosedevon.com**
Dir ***From A380 at Newton Abbot roundabout take B3195 (Shaldon road) signed Milber, 2.5 miles to village, right at pub sign.***

An integral part of the village street scene, this former farmstead was first licensed as the Country House Inn in 1840; then, in the 1960s, when geese began intimidating customers, it acquired a new name. Dartmoor Brewery's Jail Ale and Sandford Orchards Devon Mist cider represent the county in the bar. On offer is home-made pub food that includes smoked trout with rock samphire at lunchtime, and in the evening guinea fowl supreme, truffled polenta and cauliflower.

Open all year 12–3 5.30–11 (Sun 12–3 7–11) Closed Mon (autumn/winter only) Free House 11 from £13 portions/menu

NEWTON ST CYRES

The Beer Engine

Tel **01392 851282** | **EX5 5AX**
Web **www.thebeerengine.co.uk**
Dir ***From Exeter take A377 towards Crediton. Signed from A377 towards Sweetham. Pub opposite rail station, over bridge.***

Just a stone's throw from Exeter in the picturesque village of Newton St Cyres, Devon's oldest brewpub can be found in a 19th-century coaching inn. The cosy bar is a welcoming place for drinkers, diners and dogs alike, with five home-brewed ales on the hand pumps. Classic pub dishes are available every day with a wide selection to suit all tastes and appetites. Typically, home-made Scotch eggs and steak and ale pie, or look to the seasonally-changing specials board. It gets busy, so booking is recommended.

Open all day, all week Mon to Sat 11–11 (Sun and bank holidays 12–9) Closed 25–27 Dec, 1 Jan Free House 9 from £9.95 portions notice required

NOSS MAYO

The Ship Inn PICK OF THE PUBS

Tel **01752 872387** | **PL8 1EW**
Web **www.nossmayo.com**
Dir ***5 miles south of Yealmpton. From Yealmpton take B3186, then follow Noss Mayo signs.***

Surrounded by wooded hills, Noss Mayo lies on the south bank of the tidal Yealm, and the waterside location means you can, if you wish, sail to this superbly renovated pub. Log fires, wooden floors, old bookcases and dozens of local pictures characterise the interior. The cellar keeps a good range of beers, and whether eating in the bar, panelled library or out by the river, the daily-changing menus include starters like chicken liver pâté with red onion marmalade and toast; and mains such as seared scallops with bacon and sautéed potatoes; or oven-baked cod with smoked haddock and saffron chowder. For chicken curry and rice; steak and kidney pie; or ploughman's and baguettes, see the bar menu. Dogs are allowed downstairs only.

Open all day, all week Free House 13 from £12.95 portions

OTTERY ST MARY

The Talaton Inn

Tel **01404 822214** | **Talaton, EX5 2RQ**
Web **www.talatoninn.com**
Dir ***A30 to Fairmile, then follow signs to Talaton.***

This well-maintained, timber-framed, 16th-century inn is run by a brother and sister partnership. There is a good selection of real ales (Otter Ale, Otter Amber) and malts, and a fine collection of bar games. The regularly-changing evening blackboard menu might include beer battered calamari or seasoned whitebait; home-cooked ham with eggs and chunky chips; or a choice of steaks. There is a patio for summer dining, plus bingo, quizzes, and themed food nights. In winter, tables must be booked for Wednesday evenings.

Open all year 12–3 7–11 Closed Mon, Sun evening Free House portions/menu notice required

PLYMTREE

The Blacksmiths Arms

Tel **01884 277474** | **EX15 2JU**
Dir ***From A373 (Cullompton to Honiton road) follow Plymtree signs. Pub in village centre.***

A traditional free house with exposed beams and log fire, it has a reputation for serving quality food using local ingredients and is known for generous portions of classics like game pie and local steaks, as well as curries, sharing platters and fish dishes.

RATTERY

Church House Inn

Tel **01364 642220** | **TQ10 9LD**
Web **www.thechurchhouseinn.co.uk**
Dir ***1 mile from A38 (Exeter to Plymouth road) and 0.75 mile from A385 (Totnes to South Brent road).***

Some customers at the Church House Inn encounter the wandering spirit of a monk; fortunately for the owners, he seems to be friendly. Tracing its history as far back as 1028, this venerable inn burgeons with brasses, bare beams, large fireplaces and other historic features.

RINGMORE

The Journey's End Inn

Tel **01548 810205** | **TQ7 4HL**
Web **www.thejourneysendinn.co.uk**
Dir ***From Exeter take A38 towards Plymouth. Left onto A3121 signed Modbury. Left onto A379 signed Modbury. From Modbury High Street follow Ringmore and St Anne's Chapel signs. In St Anne's Chapel at Old Chapel Inn (on right) turn right signed Ringmore. Inn's car park opposite church on left. Walk 200 yards downhill to pub.***

A short walk from the coastal path at Ayrmer Cove, this 13th-century village inn was built by monks and the original fireplaces are still used during the winter months. There are five different areas for drinkers and diners, plus a large beer garden. Look out for the selection of wok-fried eg noodle dishes.

ROBOROUGH

The New Inn

Tel **01805 603247 | EX19 8SY**
Web **www.thenewinnroborough.co.uk**
Dir ***From Great Torrington take B3227 signed South Molton. Right signed Kingscott, through Kingscott to Roborough. Or from A377 (west of Portsmouth Arms) follow High Bickington and Burrington signs. At crossroads left signed Roborough. Pub on right.***

Magda and James Berry run this handsome thatched inn that has been part of daily life in this idyllic village since the 16th century. Whether you choose a spot near the log fire or out on the sunny patio in summer, this rural inn offers a really friendly welcome.

ROCKBEARE

Jack in the Green Inn

PICK OF THE PUBS

Tel **01404 822240 | London Road, EX5 2EE**
Web **www.jackinthegreen.uk.com**
Dir ***M5 junction 29, A30 (dual carriageway) towards Honiton. Left onto B3174 (old A30) to Rockbeare.***

The Jack has a well-deserved reputation for upmarket modern British food, but this family-friendly roadside pub also offers good West Country brews on tap. The smart interior with its low beamed rooms, soft brown leather chairs and a wood-burning stove creates a contemporary pub atmosphere. In the restaurant, the aim is to serve the best seasonal Devon produce in stylish surroundings. A three-course 'Totally Devon' selection could start with goats' cheese mousse, baby figs in rum and warm walnut bread. Next may come breast of Pipers Farm chicken with smoked celeriac purée, buttered cabbage and truffle hazelnut pesto, and last but not least lemon verbena crème brûlée with peach sorbet; or Devon blue cheese with biscuits and fig jam.

Open all week 11–3 5.30–11 (Sun 12–11) Closed 25 Dec to 5 Jan Free House 12 portions/menu notice required

SALCOMBE

The Victoria Inn

Tel **01548 842604 | Fore Street, TQ8 8BU**
Web **www.victoriainn-salcombe.co.uk**
Dir ***In town centre, overlooking estuary.***

Tim and Liz Hore's dog-friendly pub has something unique among Salcombe's licensed premises – a large garden with sun terraces, children's play area and even chickens. Where better to sit and enjoy a warm summer evening with a drink in hand? Inside, there is a mix of traditional seating and comfy sofas, and a roaring open fire in winter. The menu is built around the owners' appreciation of the high-quality produce on their doorstep, both from the sea and the surrounding countryside.

Open all day, all week 11.30–11 Closed 25 Dec St Austell Brewery 20 portions/menu

SHEBBEAR

The Devil's Stone Inn

Tel **01409 281210 | EX21 5RU**
Web **www.devilstoneinn.com**
Dir ***From Okehampton turn right opposite White Hart, follow A386 towards Hatherleigh. At roundabout outside Hatherleigh take Holsworthy road to Highampton. Just after Highampton right, follow signs to Shebbear.***

Reputedly one of England's most haunted pubs, The Devil's Stone Inn was a farmhouse before it became a coaching inn some 400 years ago. The pub's name comes from the village tradition of the turning the Devil's Stone (situated opposite the pub), which happens every year on 5th November. It is especially a haven for fly-fishermen, with beats, some of which the pub owns, on the middle and upper Torridge. Locally sourced and home-cooked food and a selection of real ales and ciders are offered.

Open all week 12–3 6–11 (Fri to Sun all day from 12) Free House from £8.95 portions/menu notice required

SIDBURY

The Hare & Hounds

Tel 01404 41760 | Putts Corner, EX10 0QQ
Web www.hareandhounds-devon.co.uk
Dir *From Honiton take A375 signed Sidmouth. In approximately 0.75 mile, pub at Seaton Road crossroads.*

Local ales and 17th-century charm

Good local ales might well be what attracts people to this whitewashed, 17th-century free house. Or maybe it's the comfortable beamed, log-fire-warmed interior and large garden with children's play area, with fantastic views down the valley to the sea at Sidmouth. Yet again, perhaps the spur is the best cuts of Devon meat from the daily carvery, or the extensive menu of snacks and freshly prepared classic pub dishes, such as beef in red wine; pork and mushroom bake; chargrilled steaks; breaded plaice; and aromatic vegetable burger. Devon folklore has it that the large stone at the front of the building dances at night when it hears the parish church bells ring, and that it rolls down the valley to drink from the River Sid.

Open all day, all week 10am–11pm (Sun 11–10.30) Closed 25 Dec evening, 26 Dec Heartstone Inns Ltd 10 from £10 portions/menu notice required

SLAPTON

The Tower Inn

Tel 01548 580216 | Church Road, TQ7 2PN
Web www.thetowerinn.com
Dir *Exit A379 south of Dartmouth, left at Slapton Sands.*

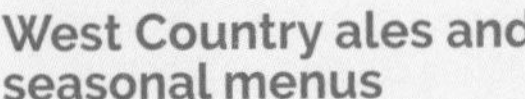

West Country ales and seasonal menus

Tucked away behind the church in this unspoilt Devon village, the ancient ivy-clad tower (which gives this charming 14th-century inn its name) looms hauntingly above the pub, all that remains of the old College of Chantry Priests. Six hundred years on and this truly atmospheric village pub continues to welcome guests and the appeal, other than its peaceful location, is the excellent range of real ales on tap and the good choice of modern pub grub prepared from locally sourced ingredients. Stone walls, open fires, low beams, scrubbed oak tables and flagstone floors characterise the welcoming interior. There's a splendid landscaped rear garden, perfect for alfresco meals.

PICK OF THE PUBS

Open all week 12–3 6–11 (Sun 12–4 also open Fri and Sat from 5 and Sun evening at peak times) Closed 1st 2 weeks Jan) menu

SOURTON

Bearslake Inn

Tel **01837 861334** | **Lake, EX20 4HQ**
Web **www.bearslakeinn.com**
Dir ***A30 onto A386. South of Sourton on left.***

A delightfully cosy thatched inn, set in a lovely village, the Bearslake Inn is a traditional Devon longhouse, and dates back in parts to the 13th century. You can enjoy a pint of local Otter Bitter in the bar, and the restaurant, with its crisp white-clothed tables, is a smart venue for the home-cooked food. Seared scallops with chorizo and pea purée might be followed by venison haunch with braised red cabbage.

Open all year, all day Closed Sun evening Free House 8 portions/menu WiFi P notice required

SOUTH POOL

The Millbrook Inn – see opposite

SOUTH ZEAL

The Oxenham Arms and Restaurant ★★★★ INN

Tel **01837 840244** | **EX20 2JT**
Web **www.theoxenhamarms.com**
Dir ***From A30, follow signs for A382 Moreton Hampstead/Winkleigh/Torrington. Over mini-roundabout towards South Zeal, after 2 miles, right into village, opposite village shop and post office.***

On the northern edge of Dartmoor, this inn's previous guests have included Charles Dickens, Sir Francis Drake and Admiral Lord Nelson. Incorporating a 5,000-year-old granite standing stone and a 12th-century monastery, this post-medieval manor house has such a rich history that the pub runs tours of the building. Whether simply for a pint of locally brewed Merry Monk or a meal in one of the six different dining areas, this ancient pub covers all bases. Time a visit for the beer festival during the second weekend of August.

Open all day, all week Closed 1st 2 weeks Jan Free House 10 from £8.95 portions/menu WiFi P notice required

SPREYTON

The Tom Cobley Tavern

PICK OF THE PUBS

Tel **01647 231314** | **EX17 5AL**
Web **www.tomcobleytavern.co.uk**
Dir ***From A30 at Whiddon Down take A3124 towards North Tawton. 1st right after services, 1st right over bridge.***

Close to the village green in this village of cob and thatch cottages, guests in the tree-shaded beer garden here can enjoy views across to the distant moors of northern Dartmoor. It was from this pub in 1802 that Thomas Cobley and his companions set forth for Widecombe Fair, an event immortalised in song; his cottage still stands in the village. The inn's unspoilt main bar has a roaring log fire, cushioned settles, and benefits from a stillage where an impressive selection of Devon microbrewery beers are always on tap. Time-honoured hearty English fare is the mainstay of the menus, and there's a good selection of vegetarian and vegan dishes. Chicken, ham, leek and tarragon pie; steak and ale pie; or steak and kidney suet pudding are popular choices.

Open all year 12–3 6–11 (Sun 12–4 7–10.30 Mon 6–10.30 Fri to Sat 12–3 6–12) Closed Mon lunch Free House portions/menu WiFi P notice required

STOKE FLEMING

The Green Dragon Inn

Tel **01803 770238** | **Church Road, TQ6 0PX**
Dir ***From A379 (Dartmouth to Kingsbridge coast road) follow brown pub sign, into Church Road. Pub opposite church.***

Opposite the village church, this South Hams pub has many seafaring connections, being only two miles from Dartmouth. The interior is decorated in a seafaring theme with charts and sailing pictures. Local beers such as Otter and Exmoor slake the thirst of walkers, whilst the great-value menu can satisfy the largest of appetites with hearty baguettes; wild boar terrine; venison burgers; trawlerman's fish pie; Thai green curry or a West Country sirloin steak.

Open 12–3 5–11 (Fri to Sat 12–11 Sun 12–8.30) Closed 26 Dec, Mon lunch Heavitree 10 portions/menu WiFi P notice required

SOUTHPOOL

The Millbrook Inn

★★★★ INN

Tel **01548 531581** | **South Pool, TQ7 2RW**
Web **www.millbrookinnsouthpool.co.uk**
Dir ***A379 from Kingsbridge to Frogmore. In Frogmore right signed South Pool. 2 miles to village.***

Innovative dishes from a new kitchen duo

PICK OF THE PUBS

Near to Southpool Creek, which leads to the Kingsbridge Estuary, is this quaint, white-painted, 16th-century village pub. It attracts small boat-owners from all along the south Devon coast, especially at high tide, when they can moor within walking distance. Open fires warm the two traditionally decorated, flagstone-floored and beamed bars, where South Hams brewery ales such as Wild Blonde, and Salcombe brewery's Lifesaver await. Newly at the helm are Dave Gobbett and his Canadian partner-in-cuisine Iain Dawson, who are stamping their mark on it with new, and sometimes surprising dishes, notably their signature pan-roasted skate wing with chorizo vinaigrette, charred broccoli and Jerusalem artichoke; and a dessert called Singapore gin-sling upside-down cake with Limoncello curd and frozen Cointreau yogurt. Other possibilities are tandoori-crusted scallops, parsnip purée and seaweed; seared calves' liver, bone-marrow mash and caramelised onion fritters; burgers, steaks and other choice cuts of meat. Children are bound to like to sound of Mad Dog's sausage, chips and peas. Stay over in a self-contained apartment in The Loft.

Open all day, all week 12–11 (Sun 12–10.30)
Free House portions/menu notice required

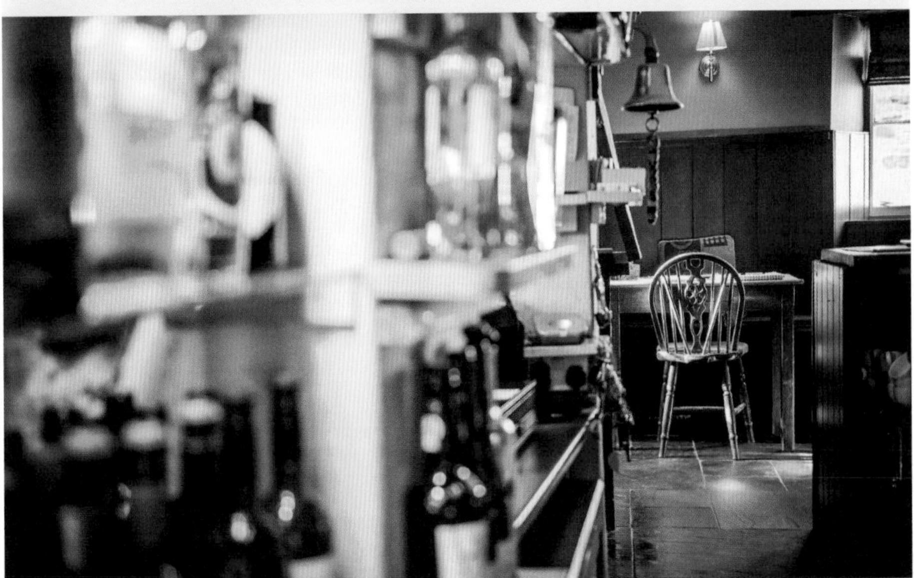

STOKENHAM

The Tradesman's Arms

★★★★ INN

Tel **01548 580996 | TQ7 2SZ**
Web **www.thetradesmansarms.com**
Dir ***Signed from A379 between Kingsbridge and Dartmouth.***

This part-thatched, 14th-century pub stands in the pretty village of Stokenham and was previously a brewhouse and cottages. One mile from stunning Slapton Sands, tables in the garden overlook the village green and church, with a log-burning fire warming the beamed bar where local ales such as Otter keep the drinkers happy. Bar meals and sandwiches are supplemented by a full menu that includes prawn cocktail and steak and ale pie.

Open all week 11–3 6–11 Free House 8 from £11.50 portions/menu notice required

TAVISTOCK

The Cornish Arms

Tel **01822 612145 | 15–16 West Street, PL19 8AN**
Web **www.thecornisharmstavistock.co.uk**
Dir ***Phone for detailed directions.***

Historically the last coaching inn before reaching Cornwall, The Cornish Arms is run by John and Emma Hooker. Whether inside the contemporary but cosy interior or out in the garden, guests will find a wide-ranging and unpretentious menu of pub favourites, from roast loin of venison, pork belly, parsnip and spiced prune; to blue cheese and walnut tart, soft poached egg and new potatoes. The bar is well stocked with ales including St Austell's Trelawny and ciders such as Cornish Rattler.

Open all day, all week St Austell Brewery 10 from £13 portions/menu notice required

Peter Tavy Inn

Tel **01822 810348 | Peter Tavy, PL19 9NN**
Web **www.petertavyinn.co.uk**
Dir ***From Tavistock take A386 towards Okehampton. In 2 miles right to Peter Tavy.***

It is thought this inn was originally built in the 15th century as a Devon longhouse for the stonemasons rebuilding the village church. On the western flanks of Dartmoor, it is likely that it became a pub by the early 17th century. It is now as much a draw for its range of local real ales and ciders as it is for its food, much of it sourced locally. The pies are popular main dishes, but other choices could be venison casserole or chicken curry.

Open all week 12–3 6–11 (Sun 12–3 6–10.30); all day Easter to Autumn Closed 25 Dec Free House 9 portions/menu

THURLESTONE

The Village Inn

★★★★ HOTEL

Tel **01548 563525 | TQ7 3NN**
Web **www.thurlestone.co.uk**
Dir ***Take A379 from Plymouth towards Kingsbridge, at Bantham roundabout take B3197, right signed Thurlestone, 2.5 miles.***

Run for the past century by the Grose family, who also own the neighbouring Thurlestone Hotel, this 16th-century inn's interior is smart with traditional touches including timbers salvaged from wrecked Spanish Armada warships. The menu offers freshly prepared sandwiches and salads; signature dishes such as fish pie and venison bourguignon; and daily specials including fish from Brixham and Plymouth markets. Dartmoor Jail Ale and Thurlestone Rocks are among the ales on tap. Children and dogs are welcome.

Open all week 11.30–3 6–10.30 (Fri 11.30–3 5–10.30 Sat to Sun, summer and school holidays all day) Free House 16 portions/menu notice required

TIPTON ST JOHN

The Golden Lion

Tel 01404 812881 | EX10 0AA
Web www.goldenliontipton.co.uk
Dir *Phone for detailed directions.*

PICK OF THE PUBS

Mediterranean slant to excellent menus

Michelle and Francois Teissier have been at the helm of this welcoming Devon village pub since 2003. So many things contribute to its traditional feel – the low wooden beams and stone walls, the winter log fire, the art deco prints and Tiffany lamps, not to mention the paintings by Devonian and Cornish artists. And there's the bar, of course, where locally brewed Otter ales are served. Chef-patron Franky (as everyone calls him) trained in classical French cooking at a prestigious establishment in the Loire Valley. As he sums up: 'our aim is to create a friendly, inviting village pub offering great value, high-quality food made from the freshest ingredients; with our combination of rustic French dishes and traditional British food with a Mediterranean twist, there's something for everyone!' Outside there is a grassy beer garden and walled terrace area.

Open all year Tue to Sat 12–2.30 6–11 (Sun 12–2.30) Closed Sun evening, Mon Heavitree 12 from £12.50 portions/menu notice required

TOPSHAM

Bridge Inn PICK OF THE PUBS

Tel 01392 873862 | Bridge Hill, EX3 0QQ
Web www.cheffers.co.uk
Dir ***M5 junction 30 follow Sidmouth signs, in approximately 400 yards right at roundabout onto A376 towards Exmouth. In 1.8 miles cross mini-roundabout. Right at next mini-roundabout to Topsham. 1.2 miles, cross River Clyst. Inn on right.***

This 'museum with beer' is substantially 16th century, and most of the fabric is local stone, while the old brewhouse at the rear is traditional Devon cob. Five generations of the Gibbings family have run it since 1897, and it remains eccentrically and gloriously old fashioned. Usually around eight real ales are served straight from their casks, the actual line-up varying by the week. Traditional, freshly prepared lunchtime bar food includes granary ploughman's, pasties and sandwiches, all made with local ingredients. Queen Elizabeth II visited in 1998; it is believed this is the only time she has officially stepped inside an English pub.

Open all week 12–2 6–10.30 (Fri to Sat 12–2 6–11 Sun 12–2 7–10.30) Free House

The Globe

Tel 01392 873471 | 34 Fore Street, EX3 0HR
Web www.theglobetopsham.co.uk
Dir ***M5 junction 30, A379 to Topsham. At roundabout take B3182. In Topsham at mini-roundabout straight ahead into Fore Street. Pub approximately 500 yards on left.***

Rich textures and colours meet the eye on entering this old inn, close to the River Exe. You can enjoy a pint of Tribute in the comfortable fire-warmed bar, while the wood-panelled Elizabethan restaurant's menu showcases locally grown, reared or caught ingredients. Perhaps chargrilled West Country rump and fillet steaks; pan-roasted sea bass fillet, potato gnocchi, mussels, roasted fennel and tomato butter; or pork tenderloin with pancetta, celeriac and baby cider apples. Daily-changing specials make the most of West Country produce too.

Open all day, all week St Austell Brewery 10 portions/menu notice required

TORCROSS

Start Bay Inn

Tel **01548 580553** | **TQ7 2TQ**
Web **www.startbayinn.co.uk**
Dir ***Between Dartmouth and Kingsbridge on A379.***

Located on the beach and with a freshwater reserve on its other side, the patio of this 14th-century inn overlooks the sea. The fishermen working from Start Bay deliver their catch direct to the kitchen. The former landlord continues to dive for scallops.

TORQUAY

Cary Arms & Spa 

INN PICK OF THE PUBS

Tel **01803 327110** | **Babbacombe Beach, TQ1 3LX**
Web **www.caryarms.co.uk**
Dir ***On entering Teignmouth, at bottom of hill at lights, right signed Torquay/A379. Cross river. At mini-roundabout follow Babbacombe signs. Pass Babbacombe Model Village, through lights, left into Babbacombe Downs Road, left into Beach Road.***

Right on the beach, the whitewashed Cary Arms is a real find in Babbacombe Bay. This 'boutique inn' is so much more than just a pub; unwind in the beamed bar with its original stone walls, perhaps with a pint of Otter Ale in hand, contemplating the stunning views across the bay, and sample the delicious food from the daily-changing menu. The watchwords in the kitchen are freshness and seasonality, underpinned by a respect for local ingredients. Pan-fried Brixham scallops, pea purée and crispy Parma ham might be followed by Dunterton Farm steak, Otter Ale and mushroom pie, dauphinoise potatoes and red wine jus; and trio of Gribbles sausages with mash and red onion jus. If it's a glorious summer's day, eat in the terraced gardens leading to the water's edge.

Open all week 12–4 6–11 Free House 11 portions/menu Wi-fi

TOTNES

The Durant Arms PICK OF THE PUBS

Tel **01803 732240** | **Ashprington, TQ9 7UP**
Web **www.durantarms.co.uk**
Dir ***From Totnes take A381 towards Kingsbridge, 1 mile, left for Ashprington.***

Dating from 1725, this village pub continues to go from strength to strength after its relaunch a couple of years ago. The stylish bar 'in all its solid-oak glory' has a wood-burning stove and the original stone-flag floor – here you'll find West Country ales and ciders, and award-winning Luscombe organic soft drinks and wines from Sharpham Vineyard just down the hill. Ingredients sourced from in and around Totnes appear on a seasonal menu listing home-cooked dishes such as chargrilled wood pigeon breast, salt-baked beetroot and redcurrant reduction; wild venison and red wine sausages and wholegrain mustard mash; and 8oz rump and frites. Dessert might be sticky stout cake and butterscotch sauce; or salted caramel, fruit and nut tart. Simple snacks, sandwiches and salads are available at lunchtime.

Open all year 11–3 6–11 Closed Mon (out of season) Free House 12 portions/menu Wi-fi *notice required*

Royal Seven Stars Hotel – see opposite

Steam Packet Inn

Tel **01803 863880** | **St Peter's Quay, TQ9 5EW**
Web **www.steampacketinn.co.uk**
Dir ***Exit A38 towards Plymouth, 18 miles. A384 to Totnes, 6 miles. Left at mini-roundabout, pass Morrisons on left, over mini-roundabout, 400 yards on left.***

Named after the passenger, cargo and mail steamers that once plied the Dart, this riverside pub (alongside which you can moor your boat) offers great views, particularly from the conservatory restaurant and heated waterside patio, where there is plenty of seating. A real log fire warms the bar in the colder months. The choices at lunch and dinner might include smaked mackerel and horseradish fishcakes; crab and king prawn linguini; or roast belly pork with black pudding mash, plus daily fish specials on the blackboard. Look out for the three-day beer festival in mid May, occasional live music and summer barbecues.

TOTNES

Royal Seven Stars Hotel

★★★ HOTEL

Tel 01803 862125 | The Plains, TQ9 5DD
Web www.royalsevenstars.co.uk
Dir *From A382 signed Totnes, left at 'Dartington' roundabout. Through lights towards town centre, through next roundabout, pass Morrisons car park on left. 200 yards on right.*

A welcoming atmosphere and friendly service

One of the most prominent buildings in town, this fine, Grade II listed, late 17th-century inn overlooks the bridge over the River Dart. It even has a grand ballroom in addition to the two character bars: the saloon, traditionally where locals gather and where a log fire chucks out the heat in the cooler months; and the more contemporary Bar 7, with an alfresco terrace, slate floors, and comfy leather sofas. Food is served all day, starting with breakfast, followed by an enticing all-day bar menu of home-cooked meals and specials. Real ales include Hunter's from Ipplepen and Bays from Paignton. In Bar 7, the modern British menu might include River Exe mussels as a starter, and mains such as grilled meats; battered cod fillet with triple-cooked chips; Moroccan vegetable and chickpea tagine; and seafood linguine. The restaurant, called TQ9 after the hotel's postcode, and adjoining Champagne Bar are in the old stables, where seasonal menus offer Brixham-landed fish of the day; roast chicken supreme; and home-made potato gnocchi, as well as weekly changing specials. The individually-styled bedrooms are appointed with high-quality furnishings. Leading straight up from the hotel is steep Fore Street, spanned by the East Gate Arch.

Open all day, all week *Free House* *26*
portions/menu P

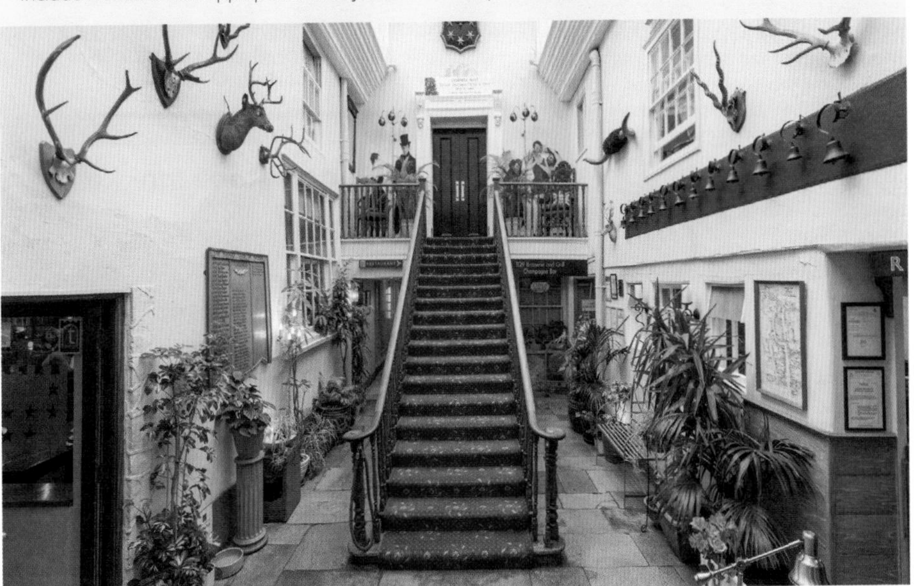

The White Hart Bar & Restaurant

Tel **01803 847111 | Dartington Hall, TQ9 6EL**
Web **www.dartington.org/visit/food-drink/white-hart**
Dir ***A38 onto A384 towards Totnes. Turn at Dartington church into Dartington Hall Estate.***

Surrounded by landscaped gardens and woodland paths, the White Hart is part of the splendid 14th-century Dartington Hall, home of a famous arts trust. Ancient tapestries, open fires, flagstones, Gothic chandeliers and limed oak settles characterise the interior. Devonshire and Cornish real ales and Dartington's own cider are available in the bar; outside there's a patio. Local sourcing is evident on the menu. Desserts are few but delicious, and Thursday night is curry night.

TRUSHAM

Cridford Inn PICK OF THE PUBS

Tel **01626 853694 | TQ13 0NR**
Web **www.thecridfordinn.co.uk**
Dir ***From A38 exit at junction for Teign Valley, right, follow Trusham signs for 4 miles.***

If you like ancient inns, put this former Devon longhouse, now in fresh hands, on your itinerary. Built in AD 825 it was once a nunnery (which explains the ghostly nun, although not the equally ethereal cavalier), and later a Domesday Book-recorded farm. It's a free house, so the dog-friendly bar offers a good choice of real ales and ciders, plenty of wines by the glass, and over 80 gins. The oak-beamed restaurant, with medieval stained-glass windows, prides itself on such dishes as confit duck leg with cavolo nero and roasted carrots; and fish pie with cod, smoked haddock, tiger prawns and scallop roe, topped with mashed potato and cheddar cheese. Grab a garden table for great views.

Open all day, all week 11–11 (Sun 12–10.30) Free House 13 from £10 portions WI-FI P notice required

TUCKENHAY

The Maltsters Arms

Tel **01803 732350 | TQ9 7EQ**
Web **www.tuckenhay.com**
Dir ***A381 from Totnes towards Kingsbridge. 1 mile, at hill top turn left, follow signs to Tuckenhay, 3 miles.***

An 18th-century inn standing just where tidal Bow Creek tapers to an end. Predictably, it was once a malthouse, malt being one of many commodities handled on the wide quay, now a lovely place to sit with a pint and admire the wooded river banks.

TYTHERLEIGH

Tytherleigh Arms

★★★★ INN

Tel **01460 220214 | EX13 7BE**
Web **www.tytherleigharms.com**
Dir ***Between Chard and Axminster on A358.***

On the borders of Devon, Dorset and Somerset, this 16th-century former coaching inn has been refurbished extensively but retains plenty of original features including huge fires to warm you up as you sup a pint of Otter or Branscombe ale. Much of the menu revolves around local produce, whether it's braised lamb shoulder, pan-roasted gurnard or root vegetable gratin. Pub classics, sandwiches and salads are served at lunchtime.

Open 12–2.30 6–9.30 Closed 25–26 Dec, 8–23 Jan, Sun evening – winter Free House 10 from £12.95 portions WI-FI P

WIDECOMBE IN THE MOOR

The Rugglestone Inn

PICK OF THE PUBS

Tel **01364 621327 | TQ13 7TF**
Web **www.rugglestoneinn.co.uk**
Dir ***From village centre take road by church towards Venton. Inn down hill on left.***

Originally a cottage, this Grade II listed building was converted to an inn around 1832. Cosy little rooms and comforting wood-burners encourage appreciative visitors and locals alike to tarry awhile and sup ales such as Dartmoor Legend; farmhouse ciders such as Ashridge are stillaged behind the snug bar and tapped straight from the barrel. The filling fare is a decent mix of classic pub staples and savoury dishes.

WOODBURY SALTERTON

The Digger's Rest – see below

YEALMPTON

Rose & Crown PICK OF THE PUBS

Tel **01752 880223** | **Market Street, PL8 2EB**
Web **www.theroseandcrown.co.uk**
Dir ***Phone for detailed directions.***

Close to the pretty Yealm Estuary and the seductive wilderness of southern Dartmoor, there's a cool, airy, bistro-like atmosphere in this classy dining pub. Sample beers from the St Austell Brewery stable, perhaps in the walled courtyard garden. The menu offers traditional classics with a focus on quality and local suppliers. A choice of pub favourites such as curry of the day or home-made burger runs alongside starters such as Yealmpton artichoke soup; or pan-fried south Devon scallops. Mains include five-spiced crispy duck leg with egg noodles; and blue cheese and walnut tart.

Open all day, all week St Austell Brewery from £10 portions/menu notice required

DORSET

ASKERSWELL

The Spyway Inn ★★★★ INN

Tel 01308 485250 | DT2 9EP
Dir ***From A35 follow Askerswell sign, then follow Spyway Inn sign.***

With a new husband and wife team at the helm, the Spyway focuses on local ales and ciders, while well-behaved four-legged customers may be given a doggy treat. The menu casts its culinary net far and wide with, for example, Sri Lankan king prawn curry; and grilled Moroccan hake, but from home territory are traditional lamb hotpot; venison, wild mushroom and red wine suet pudding; and chicken, ham and leek pie. The extensive beer garden has wonderful views.

Open all year 12–3 6–close Closed Mon daytime (winter) Free House 10 from £10.95 portions/menu notice required

WOODBURY SALTERTON

The Digger's Rest

Tel **01395 232375** | **EX5 1PQ**
Web **www.diggersrest.co.uk**
Dir ***2.5 miles from A3052. Signed from Westpoint Showground.***

Picturesque thatched pub offering the best seasonal produce

Welcoming drinkers for more than 500 years, this pretty free house is just a few minutes' drive from the Exeter junction of the M5. Originally a cider house, its vintage can be identified from the thatched roof, thick stone and cob walls, heavy beams and log fire. These days, real cider is still well represented by Westons and Symonds. Real ales feature Otter Ale from Devon with guest appearances of other West Country brews such as Exeter Avocet. Wine fans will appreciate the list

created by the independent wine merchant, Tanners of Shrewsbury. The menus make the best of seasonal produce with English and West Country organic produce used wherever possible. Menus feature fish landed at Brixham and Looe, West Country beef hung for 21 days and pork from a farm just up the road. The May beer and cider festival is worth a visit.

Open all week 11–3 5.30–11 (Sat 11–11 Sun 12–10.30) Free House 10 from £11 portions/menu notice required

BOURTON

The White Lion Inn

Tel **01747 840866** | **High Street, SP8 5AT**
Web **www.whitelionbourton.co.uk**
Dir ***Off A303, opposite B3092 to Gillingham.***

Dating from 1723, the White Lion is a beautiful stone-built, creeper-clad Dorset inn. The bar is cosy with beams, flagstones and an open fire. Here you will find a range of real beers and ciders, and menus drawing on the wealth of quality local produce.

BUCKHORN WESTON

Stapleton Arms PICK OF THE PUBS

Tel **01963 370396** | **Church Hill, SP8 5HS**
Web **www.thestapletonarms.com**
Dir ***3.5 miles from Wincanton in village centre.***

Clean, modern lines within belie the Georgian exterior of this progressive village inn. It sits on the edge of Blackmore Vale in Thomas Hardy's rolling Dorset countryside, classic walking country enjoyed by many of the inn's patrons. Hand-pulled pints from Plain Ales brewery in Salisbury and regional guests are complemented by a comprehensive range of world bottled beers. The pub's stylish and unstuffy attitude creates a welcoming and relaxing ambience in which to enjoy these drinks. For more of Dorset's larder, look no further than the menu, overflowing with fresh and local produce, ethically raised and delivered with minimum food miles. Light bites, sandwiches and classic dishes appear on the lunch menu.

Open all week 12–3 6–11 (Sun 12–10.30) Free House 20 portions/menu notice required

CATTISTOCK

Fox & Hounds Inn

Tel **01300 320444** | **Duck Street, DT2 0JH**
Web **www.foxandhoundsinn.com**
Dir ***On A37, between Dorchester and Yeovil, follow signs to Cattistock.***

Expect a bar full of locals, families, dogs and even chickens under foot at this attractive pub. Situated in a picturesque village, the 17th-century inn has a welcoming and traditional atmosphere engendered by ancient beams, open fires in winter and huge inglenooks, one with an original bread oven. Palmers ales are on tap, along with various ciders, while home-made meals embrace Dorset charcuterie boards; fresh fish, 'proper' double crusted pies and excellent steaks. Regular events include folk music and poetry.

Open all year 12–2.30 6–11 (Sun 12–10) Closed Mon lunch Palmers portions notice required

CERNE ABBAS

The New Inn

Tel **01300 341274** | **14 Long Street, DT2 7JF**
Web **www.thenewinncerneabbas.co.uk**
Dir ***Take A352 from Dorchester to Cerne Abbas. Pub in village centre.***

In the past, the pretty village of Cerne Abbas was famous for brewing – at one time there were 16 pubs here – and the one that remains is this beautifully restored 16th-century coaching inn. There's a mix of contemporary dishes and pub classics on offer, and weekdays are dominated by themed nights, from burgers and tapas to steak and fish. The owners have a background in wine so expect a superb list alongside local Palmers ales.

Open all day, all week 12–11 Closed 25–26 Dec Palmers 12 from £13.50 portions/menu

CHEDINGTON

Winyard's Gap Inn

Tel **01935 891244** | **Chedington Lane, DT8 3HY**
Web **www.winyardsgap.com**
Dir ***5 miles south of Crewkerne on A356.***

Situated beside National Trust woodlands in a corner of the Dorset Area of Outstanding Natural Beauty, this old inn's garden commands an extraordinary view across Somerset. The two counties provide the wherewithal for the August cider festival here, whilst beers from Exmoor and Otter breweries adorn the bar, with its solid rustic seating and tables and a log-burner for the winter months. Perhaps choose their impressive 'Ultimate Ploughman's' showcasing cheeses from the area.

Open all week 11.30–3 6–11 (Sat to Sun 11.30–11) Closed 25–26 Dec Free House 12 from £11 portions/menu notice required

CHETNOLE

The Chetnole Inn

Tel **01935 872337** | **DT9 6NU**
Web **www.thechetnoleinn.co.uk**
Dir ***A37 from Dorchester towards Yeovil. Left at Chetnole sign.***

This is a bright and airy village inn deep in Hardy country. Plenty of walks thread their way through the rich countryside. The flagstone-floored snug, bar and restaurant make an ideal setting for the West Country meats and Bridport-landed seafood that fill the British menu.

CHIDEOCK

The Anchor Inn ★★★★ INN

PICK OF THE PUBS

Tel **01297 489215** | **Seatown, DT6 6JU**
Web **www.theanchorinnseatown.co.uk**
Dir ***From A35 in Chideock turn opposite church and follow single track road for 0.75 mile to beach.***

Locals know it as the 'sea town of Chideock', although to call a pub and a few cottages a town is perhaps a bit ambitious. This former smugglers' haunt lies on a long shelving pebble beach, part of the Jurassic Coast, surrounded by National Trust land. It's separated from the waves by the South West Coast Path as it drops down to sea level from Golden Cap, the highest point on England's south coast. A large sun terrace and cliffside beer garden overlooking Lyme Bay help to make the Anchor a popular destination, but there's a good-size car park, just as the road morphs into shingle. Filled rolls, meat and veggie platters are on the menu alongside a selection of fresh fish (on the specials board), a Smuggler's Burger and steak. Desserts are tempting or try the local cheese board. Real ales are all from Palmers of Bridport.

Open all day, all week 10am–11pm (24 Dec 10–5, 26 Dec 11–5, 31 Dec 10–5) Closed 25 Dec Palmers portions/menu Wi-fi

See advertisement on page 148

CHURCH KNOWLE

The New Inn

Tel **01929 480357** | **BH20 5NQ**
Web **www.thenewinn-churchknowle.co.uk**
Dir ***From Wareham take A351 towards Swanage. At Corfe Castle right for Church Knowle. Pub in village centre.***

The Estop family have been here for over three decades – landlord Maurice being only the fourth licensee in 170 years. The inn's old-world charm includes inglenook fireplaces and a brick alcove once the farmhouse oven. Son and head chef Matthew Estop makes much of locally caught fish and seafood as well as local meats. Real ales include Dorset Jurassic and guests, with draught ciders too, but don't expect a wine list, because customers can browse for the right bottle in the 'Wine Shack'.

Open 10–3 6–11 (10–3 5–11 summer) Closed Mon (Jan to Feb) Free House 10 from £10.95 portions/menu Wi-fi notice required

CRANBORNE

The Inn at Cranborne

Tel **01725 551249** | **5 Wimborne Street, BH21 5PP**
Web **www.theinnatcranborne.co.uk**
Dir ***On B3078 between Fordingbridge and Wimborne Minster.***

This 17th-century former coaching inn is a must-visit destination in Cranborne Chase, nearly 400 square miles of rolling chalk downland. Badger Best shares bar space with Dorset and Somerset ciders. Choose a table near one of the wood-burning stoves for something hearty from the daily-changing menu, which includes an abundance of local produce. Go for retro prawn cocktail followed by steak, mushroom and ale pie.

Open all day, all week Hall & Woodhouse 10 portions/menu Wi-fi notice required

THE VERY BEST DISHES WITH EXCEPTIONAL, LOCAL DORSET PRODUCE

The local producers are a constant source of inspiration to our m at *The Anchor Inn* and we feel the spirit of Dorset really shi through. Home to so many interesting and dedicated people w grow and nurture plants and animals, West Dorset is a wonde place in which to run a kitchen.

Our Head Chef, Cameron Farquharson, is incredibly talentec conjuring up dishes using the region's exceptional fish, shell game, farm meats and artisanal foods.

Our award-winning menu suits all tastes from the walker seel refueling to the serious gourmet looking to settle in for a bow super fresh shellfish washed down with a bottle of fantastic wine

We have a beautiful selection of fresh fish and what better p to enjoy the fruits of the sea than on the doorstep of the beau ocean? Meat-eaters fear not! We equally have a fabulous select of hearty and delicious meat dishes for all of you land lovers toc there really is something for everyone.

AWARD-WINNING LOCAL REAL ALES

The local producers are a constant source of inspiration to our m at *The Anchor Inn* and we feel the spirit of Dorset really shi through. Home to so many interesting and dedicated people w grow and nurture plants and animals, West Dorset is a wonde place in which to run a kitchen.

We're a stickler for standards and work meticulously to main our Cask Marque seal of approval and you'll taste it in every drop of refreshing goodness. We stock a varied selection of real from Palmers Brewery in Bridport, an exciting wine list with a wh range of options alongside the well known premium brand sp and some local favourites too.

Come, relax and have a refreshing beverage with us at *The Anchor*

EAST MORDEN

The Cock & Bottle PICK OF THE PUBS

Tel 01929 459238 | BH20 7DL
Web www.cockandbottlemorden.co.uk
Dir *From A35 (west of Poole) turn right onto B3075, pub 0.5 mile on left.*

The low-beamed ceilings and wealth of nooks and crannies are a reminder that parts of this Dorset longhouse were built around 400 years ago. The simply furnished locals' bar is comfortably rustic, and the fine range of real ales from Hall & Woodhouse is also available in the lounge bar, while a modern restaurant at the back completes the picture. The ever-changing menu ranges from light lunches and bar meals to pub favourites. Choices might include a starter of crispy duck and green onion spring roll, cucumber and sweet and sour sauce. Moving on, rabbit pie; steak and kidney pudding; and lamb shank are typical main course options, and home-made desserts like dark and white chocolate terrine make a fitting finale.

Open all year 11.30–2.30 6–11 (Sun 12–3) Closed Sun evening Hall & Woodhouse portions/menu

FARNHAM

The Museum Inn

★★★★ INN PICK OF THE PUBS

Tel 01725 516261 | DT11 8DE
Web www.museuminn.co.uk
Dir *From Salisbury take A354 to Blandford Forum, 12 miles. Farnham signed on right. Pub in village centre.*

In the 19th century this part-thatched country pub on Cranborne Chase served visitors to General Augustus Pitt-Rivers' small archaeological and anthropological museum, now relocated to Oxford. The interior features the original inglenook fireplace, flagstone floors, a fashionable mismatch of furniture and a book-filled sitting room. If you're passionate about your real ales or ciders, the bar will oblige with Sixpenny 6D Best, Flacks Double Drop and Aspall cider. Local estates and farms supply many of the ingredients for dishes awarded two AA Rosettes. Pitt-Rivers also created Larmer Tree Gardens, a public pleasure garden, on his Rushmore Estate near Tollard Royal.

Open all day, all week 12–11 (Sun 12–10.30) Free House 12 portions/menu notice required

EVERSHOT

The Acorn Inn  INN

Tel 01935 83228 | 28 Fore Street, DT2 0JW
Web www.acorn-inn.co.uk
Dir *From A37 between Yeovil and Dorchester, follow Evershot and Holywell signs, 0.5 mile to inn.*

Surrounded by unspoilt rolling countryside

In *Tess of the d'Urbervilles*, Thomas Hardy called this pretty, 16th-century inn the 'Sow and Acorn'. He'd still recognise it, especially its unusual porch, old beams, low ceilings, oak panelling, flagstone floors and carved Hamstone fireplaces. Run by Richard and Natalie Legg, the inn is a big draw locally, with two lively bars stocking real ales from Devon and Dorset breweries and brewpubs, local cider and an impressive stock of 28 gins. There are quiz nights and occasional yard-of-ale-drinking

challenges too. In the softly lit restaurant, you'll find sustainability and seasonality govern the menu. A fish specials board changes daily, while lunch and bar menus offer sandwiches, honey and mustard ham with egg and triple-cooked chips, burgers and ploughman's. The pub also features a lovely old skittle alley and a pleasant beer garden.

Open all day, all week 11am–11.30pm Free House 39 from £14 portions/menu notice required

FERNDOWN

The Kings Arms

Tel **01202 577490** | **77 Ringwood Road, Longham, BH22 9AA**
Web **www.thekingsarms-longham.co.uk**
Dir ***On A348.***

The Kings Arms has gained a good local reputation for its British classics, especially beef, and other locally-sourced dishes prepared here. From their main menu come a variety of steaks, including a 100-day aged, grain-fed rib-eye, and a Chateaubriand for sharing.

FONTMELL MAGNA

The Fontmell ★★★★ INN

Tel **01747 811441** | **SP7 0PA**
Web **www.thefontmell.com**
Dir ***Halfway between Shaftesbury and Blandford Forum, on A350.***

On the A350, between Shaftesbury and Blandford Forum is The Fontmell, a stylish and comfortable country pub, complete with a stream flowing between the bar and the dining room. Most visitors and guests cannot resist chef Tom Shaw's frequently changing menus which feature flavour-packed meals such as roasted butternut squash with goats' curd, honey and pickled golden raisins; followed by pan-fried hake with Galician stew, and River Fowey mussels; and finishing with black cherry soufflé, dark chocolate, griottine cherry and clotted cream. From Monday to Thursday a classics menu is available alongside the à la carte.

Open all day, all week Closed 27–28 Dec, 2–10 Jan
Free House 13 from £10 portions/menu
Wi-fi

See advertisement on opposite page

GILLINGHAM

The Kings Arms Inn

Tel **01747 838325** | **East Stour Common, SP8 5NB**
Web **www.kingsarmseaststour.com**
Dir ***4 miles west of Shaftesbury on A30.***

Scottish touches – paintings by artist Mavis Makie, quotes by Robert Burns, the presence of haggis, skirlie and cranachan on the menus, and a wide choice of single malts – reflect the origin of this inn's landlord. A 200-year-old, family-run village free house where Victorian fireplaces sit comfortably alongside modern wooden furniture and subtly coloured fabrics. On offer is an extensive choice of dishes ranging from Puy lentil and mixed vegetable burger to steak and kidney baked suet pudding. Look out for the £8 pub lunch specials.

Open all week 12–3 5.30–11.30 (Sat to Sun 12–12)
Free House portions/menu Wi-fi
notice required

8 TOP DORSET PUBS WITH ACCOMMODATION

The following pubs are rated as part of the AA Guest Accommodation scheme (see page 10-11 for more information).

The Kings Arms ★★★★★ INN Sherborne, *see page 156*
The Anchor Inn ★★★★ INN Chideock, *see page 147*
The Museum Inn ★★★★ INN Farnham, *see page 149*
The Acorn Inn ★★★★ INN Evershot, *see page 149*
The Brace of Pheasants ★★★★ INN Plush, *see page 154*
The Fontmell ★★★★ INN Fontmell Magna, *see page 150*
The Hambro Arms ★★★★ INN Milton Abbas, *see page 152*
The Coppleridge Inn ★★★ INN Motcombe, *see page 153*

HINTON ST MARY

The White Horse Inn

Tel **01258 472723** | **DT10 1NA**
Web **www.thewhitehorsehinton.co.uk**
Dir ***From A357 in Sturminster Newton take B3092 (over bridge) signed Gillingham. At crossroads in Hinton St Mary turn right, pub on left.***

This 400-year-old pub is very much the hub of a timeless English village. The White Horse Inn is as dog-friendly as they get – pub dog Pepper is sure to greet you and your canine companions. Food is traditional, good value and sourced from local farms and suppliers whenever possible. Time a visit for the summer beer festival when the White Horse Craft Brewery comes into its own.

Open all year 12–3 6–11 Closed Sun evening, Mon
Free House 9 from £10 portions Wi-fi P
notice required

ROSETTES AND STARS

Stay the night

Many of the pubs in this guide have been inspected and rated for their hotel or guest accommodation by the AA.

To find out more about the accommodation ratings see pages 10–11.

Eat well

Rosette awards appear where the restaurant at the pub has been inspected for the quality of their cuisine.

To find out more about the Rosette award scheme see pages 12-13.

IWERNE COURTNEY OR SHROTON

The Cricketers

Tel 01258 860421 | DT11 8QD
Web www.heartstoneinns.co.uk
Dir *7 miles south of Shaftesbury on A350, turn right after Iwerne Minster. 5 miles north of Blandford Forum on A360, past Stourpaine, in 2 miles left into Shroton. Pub in village centre.*

PICK OF THE PUBS

Award-winning free house in secluded gardens

Euan and Lizzie Cunningham's genuine hospitality make this a real community local and it's a popular pit-stop for walkers on the Wessex Way. It's a dog friendly pub too. In the light, open-plan interior, the real beers are Butcombe and Otter Bitter, while wine drinkers will find up to nine by the glass; there's no separate restaurant. The menu changes seasonally and makes use of home-cooked, locally sourced ingredients to offer starters or light options. Sandwiches are available at lunchtime, and on Sunday a choice of roast meats is always on offer; specials are forever changing. There are occasional barbecues in the summer.

Open all week 12–3 6–11 (Sun 12–10.30 summer times may vary) Free House 9 from £11 portions/menu notice required

IWERNE MINSTER

The Talbot Hotel – see opposite

LYME REGIS

The Mariners

Tel 01297 442753 | Silver Street, DT7 3HS
Web www.hotellymeregis.co.uk
Dir *A35 onto B3165 (Lyme Road). The Mariners is pink building opposite road to The Cobb (Pound Road).*

Once a coaching inn, this restored property in the heart of the town is steeped in Lyme's fossil history, having once been home to the Philpot sisters, famed as collectors in the early 19th century. Beatrix Potter is said to have stayed here.

MILTON ABBAS

The Hambro Arms ★★★★ INN

Tel 01258 880233 | DT11 0BP
Web www.hambroarms.com
Dir *From A354 (Dorchester to Blandford road), exit at Milborne St Andrew to Milton Abbas.*

Many Dorset picture-postcards feature the 36 near-identical, late 18th-century thatched cottages of Milton Abbas, replacements for a nearby hamlet demolished by the privacy-seeking, landowning Earl of Dorchester. Built at the same time, this whitewashed pub thrives – its bar and outside tables are perfect for a lunchtime snack, and the elegant Library Restaurant offers a full carte. Perhaps choose home-made smoked mackerel and crab pâté, and cider-braised saddle of rabbit with wild mushroom, tarragon and cream sauce. Catch the July beer festival.

Open all week 11–11 Free House from £10.50 portions/menu

IWERNE MINSTER

The Talbot Hotel

Tel **01747 811269** | **Blandford Road, DT11 8QN**
Web **www.talbot-iwerne.co.uk**
Dir ***North of Blandford Forum on A350.***

Pub classics and well-kept beers

An impressive half-timbered brick building with a parquet-floored bar and dining room, the Talbot enjoys a lovely setting between Blandford Forum and Shaftesbury, handily placed for anyone undertaking the popular Wessex Ridgeway Trail (which takes you from Ashmore to Lyme Regis, with some wonderful views along the way). You'll find Butcombe, Otter bitter and Bath Gem on the handpumps, along with weekly-changing guest ales. Begin a meal with breaded whitebait or pan-fried garlic mushrooms, before moving on to an 8oz steak and chips; gammon, egg and chips; lamb

shank with potatoes, peas and gravy; or Whitby wholetail scampi. Make sure you save room for dessert, maybe sticky toffee pudding or Eton Mess.

Open all week 5–11 (Sat and Sun 12–11) Free House 10 from £9

MOTCOMBE

The Coppleridge Inn ★★★ INN

Tel **01747 851980** | **SP7 9HW**
Web **www.coppleridge.com**
Dir ***Take A350 towards Warminster for 1.5 miles, left at brown tourist sign. Follow signs to inn.***

About 30 years ago Chris and Di Goodinge took over this 18th-century farm and converted it into a pub. As well as retaining the flagstone floors and log fires, they kept the 15 acres of meadow and woodland, where they raise their own cattle. The bar offers a wide range of real ales, as well as a decent choice of food – maybe seared scallops with black pudding followed by chicken stuffed with pancetta.

Open all day, all week Free House 10 from £11 portions/menu notice required

NETTLECOMBE

Marquis of Lorne

Tel **01308 485236** | **DT6 3SY**
Web **www.themarquisoflorne.co.uk**
Dir ***From A3066 (Bridport-Beaminster road) approximately 1.5 miles north of Bridport follow Loders and Mangerton Mill signs. At junction left past Mangerton Mill, through West Milton. 1 mile to T-junction, straight over. Pub up hill, approximately 300 yards on left.***

In a picturesque hamlet and close to the market town of Bridport, the Marquis of Lorne has beautiful views. Built as a farmhouse in the 16th century and converted into a pub in 1871, it is now run by Steve and Tracey Brady. They have renewed the focus on local produce throughout the globally-inspired menus, and locally brewed Palmers ales are on tap. Look out for special dinner evenings. The attractive gardens are family friendly, too.

Open all week 12–2.30 6–11 Palmers 9 from £10 portions/menu notice required

PIDDLEHINTON

The Thimble Inn

Tel **01300 348270 | DT2 7TD**
Web **www.thimbleinn.co.uk**
Dir ***Take A35 westbound, right onto B3143, Piddlehinton in 4 miles.***

This 18th-century pub and restaurant is run by French-trained chef Mark Ramsden and his wife Lisa. The stunning interior features antique furniture, sandstone and oak floors and a glass-covered well. Its patio overlooks the River Piddle, or Puddle, as prim Victorians preferred to call it. Mark uses the best local produce for dishes such as ham hock and smoked chicken terrine; Blue Vinny and spinach risotto; and whole roasted partridge, poached quince, braised red cabbage, mash, and juniper and red wine jus.

Open all week 11.30–3 6–11 (Sat to Sun 11.30–11) Palmers 10 from £11.95 portions/menu notice required

PIDDLETRENTHIDE

The Poachers Inn

Tel **01300 348358 | DT2 7QX**
Web **www.thepoachersinn.co.uk**
Dir ***6 miles north from Dorchester on B3143. At church end of village.***

Located in the pretty little village of Piddletrenthide in the heart of Thomas Hardy country, this 17th-century riverside pub is perfectly situated for exploring west Dorset and the Jurassic Coast. The kitchen makes good use of Dorset suppliers to create both classic pub meals and contemporary alternatives for the extensive menu. Relax with a glass of ale in the beer garden, which even has a swimming pool to enjoy throughout the summer.

Open all day, all week 8am–midnight Free House 9 from £8.95 portions/menu notice required

PLUSH

The Brace of Pheasants

★★★★ INN

Tel **01300 348357 | DT2 7RQ**
Web **www.braceofpheasants.co.uk**
Dir ***A35 onto B3143, 5 miles to Piddletrenthide, then right to Mappowder and Plush.***

Tucked away in the hills, this pretty, 16th-century, thatched village inn is an ideal place to start or end a walk. With its welcoming open fire, oak beams and fresh flowers, it's the perfect place to enjoy the selection of real ales and ciders and 18 wines offered by the glass. Food options might include warm crab, caramelised leek and saffron tartlet or garlic and herb marinated venison steak with port and redcurrant sauce. The inn offers eight en suite bedrooms.

Open all week 12–3 7–11 Closed 25 Dec Free House 18 from £11.95 portions notice required

POOLE

The Plantation

Tel **01202 701531 | 53 Cliff Drive, Canford Cliffs, BH13 7JF**
Web **www.the-plantation.co.uk**
Dir ***From A35 between Poole and Bournemouth into Archway Road (leads to Canford Cliffs Road). At mini-roundabout left into Haven Road, right into Cliff Drive.***

Within the Poole conservation area and close to some of Bournemouth's best beaches, The Plantation has light and airy interiors in classic colonial style. At the bar you'll find Orchard Pig's range of bottled ciders, while short menus showcase high quality, fresh, local and seasonal ingredients. A typical three-course choice could be treacle-cured salmon, horseradish, rye and apple cracker; glazed beef cheek with tongue ragù, confit potato, shiitakes and port sauce; and gingerbread, blackberry and eggnog trifle.

Open all day, all week Free House 15 portions/menu notice required

POWERSTOCK

Three Horseshoes Inn

PICK OF THE PUBS

Tel **01308 485328** | **DT6 3TF**
Web **www.threeshoesdorset.co.uk**
Dir ***3 miles from Bridport off A3066 (Beaminster road).***

This pretty late-Victorian inn is owned by Palmers, a part-thatched brewery in nearby Bridport. The food owes much to the kitchen's devotion to seasonal, locally sourced ingredients, some from the garden and some foraged from surrounding hedgerows. Daily-changing menus lean towards game in winter and fresh fish in summer, but inventiveness is present all year round. For mains, try wild boar sausages, braised red cabbage and Apple Bee Cider gravy; or roast hake fillet with brown shrimp and lemon butter. Check the blackboards for the dessert choices.

Open all year 12–3 6–11 (Sun 12–6) Closed Mon lunch (winter only) Palmers 12 portions/menu Wi-fi notice required

PUNCKNOWLE

The Crown Inn

Tel **01308 897711** | **Church Street, DT2 9BN**
Web **www.thecrowninndorset.co.uk**
Dir ***From A35 through Litton Cheney to Puncknowle. Or from Swyre on B3157 follow Puncknowle signs.***

This picturesque 16th-century pub was once the haunt of smugglers on their way from nearby Chesil Beach to visit prosperous customers in Bath. There's a traditional, welcoming atmosphere within the rambling, child- and dog-friendly bars with their log fires, comfy sofas and low beams.

SHAPWICK

The Anchor Inn

Tel **01258 857269** | **West Street, DT11 9LB**
Web **www.anchorshapwick.co.uk**
Dir ***From Wimborne or Blandford Forum take B3082. Pub signed.***

For the Anchor, rescued by a village collective a few years back, 'our landlords are our neighbours'. This independence pays off, with menus featuring produce sourced from within a 20-mile radius of the village.

SHERBORNE

The Kings Arms – see page 156

STRATTON

Saxon Arms

Tel **01305 260020** | **DT2 9WG**
Web **www.thesaxon-stratton.co.uk**
Dir ***3 miles north-west of Dorchester on A37. Pub between church and village hall.***

Popular with villagers as much as visiting fishermen, cycling clubs and ramblers, this handsome, thatched flint-stone free house is ideally situated for riverside walks. Flagstone floors, a wood-burning stove and solid oak beams create a comfortable setting for the friendly welcome, range of well-kept real ales and simple, carefully cooked food. Menu choices might include wild boar, pork, red onion and herb meatballs and a fish platter. There's also a deli counter and a selection of baguettes and jackets.

Open all week 11–3 5.30–late (Fri to Sun 11am–late) Free House 15 portions/menu Wi-fi notice required

STUDLAND

The Bankes Arms Hotel

Tel **01929 450225** | **Watery Lane, BH19 3AU**
Web **www.bankesarms.com**
Dir ***B3369 from Poole, take Sandbanks chain ferry, or A35 from Poole, A351 then B3351.***

Standing above the wide sweep of Studland Bay, this 16th-century creeper-clad inn was once a smugglers' dive. Nowadays the pub hosts an annual four-day festival in mid-August, featuring live music and some 200 beers and ciders. Fresh fish and seafood salads are a speciality.

SHERBORNE

The Kings Arms

★★★★★ INN

Tel 01963 220281 | North Road, Charlton Horethorne, DT9 4NL
Web www.thekingsarms.co.uk
Dir *On A3145, north of Sherborne. Pub in village centre.*

Enjoyable food in elegantly converted country pub

PICK OF THE PUBS

The Kings Arms was first licensed in 1813, and while it retains its original grand frontage, owners Sarah and Tony Lethbridge, have completely transformed the interior into a chic country pub and modern restaurant with boutique-style bedrooms. First port of call for most, of course, is usually the bar, where you'll find Butcombe real ales and Lawrence's cider from nearby Corton Denham. Of the 50 wines, 15 are sold by the glass. Stay in the bar if you're looking for a light snack in relaxed surroundings, otherwise go through a light, airy atrium to the more formal self-contained, Georgian-mirrored dining room, where black and brown leather, high-backed chairs are set round chunky wooden tables. From here, doors open on to an extensive dining terrace overlooking the countryside. The cooking style is traditional and modern British with world influences and everything is made in-house, including breads, pastas and ice creams. The charcoal grill is kept busy with pork, rib-eye and venison steaks, although there are plenty of alternatives such as free-range Creedy Carver duck leg; pan-fried hake; and beetroot risotto on the menu. Children's dishes include salmon fishcake with hand-cut chips, and tagliatelle with roasted tomato sauce.

Open all day, all week Closed 25–26 Dec Free House 15 from £13 portions/menu

SYDLING ST NICHOLAS

The Greyhound Inn PICK OF THE PUBS

Tel **01300 341303** | **26 High Street, DT2 9PD**
Web **www.dorsetgreyhound.co.uk**
Dir ***From A37 (Yeovil to Dorchester road), exit at staggered crossroads signed Sydling St Nicholas and Cerne Abbas.***

Deep in Thomas Hardy country, this 18th-century pub is tucked away among pastel-hued flint and stone houses. With many lovely walks starting from the pub, the staff are accustomed to welcoming muddy-booted families and wet dogs. Relax in the open-plan bar with a pint of Trelawny, a glass of Sandford Orchards Devon Red craft cider, or one of the 18 wines sold by the glass. Next, choose where to eat: the bar, with its open fire; the conservatory with scrubbed wood tables and a deep chesterfield; the restaurant with an exposed well; or the suntrap front terrace. The food is modern British, and menus change daily. Look to the specials list for fresh fish, the pub's strength; it's ordered the night before from the quaysides in Weymouth and Bridport.

Open all week 11–3 5.30–late (Sun 12–late, summer and bank holiday hours may vary) Free House 18 portions/menu Wi-fi P

TARRANT MONKTON

The Langton Arms PICK OF THE PUBS

Tel **01258 830225** | **DT11 8RX**
Web **www.thelangtonarms.co.uk**
Dir ***A31 from Ringwood, or A357 from Shaftesbury, or A35 from Bournemouth.***

Located in countryside immortalised by Thomas Hardy, The Langton Arms is a lovely 17th-century thatched inn. Inside are two bars, each of which is a relaxing place to savour a pint from the ever-changing range of outstanding local ales and ciders. Traditional pub dishes are served in the bars, as well as in the Stables restaurant and conservatory. Expect choice West Country fare made from local produce – sourced in Dorset whenever possible, including beef from the owners' own herd at Rawston Farm. Children, if you can persuade them to leave the fully-equipped play area, are spoilt for choice with their own menu or smaller portions from the adult carte.

Open all day, all week 11–11 (Sun 12–10.30 summer 12–5 winter) Free House 10 portions/menu Wi-fi P *notice required*

TRENT

The Rose and Crown Inn, Trent

★★★★★ INN PICK OF THE PUBS

Tel **01935 850776** | **DT9 4SL**
Web **www.theroseandcrowntrent.co.uk**
Dir ***Just off A30 between Sherborne and Yeovil.***

This ivy-clad building once housed 14th-century workmen building the village church spire, but the beams and flagstone floors owe more to its days as a farmhouse in the 18th century. The inn has a lounge with a large open fire, whilst the main bar looks out over fields. At the bar, Wadworth's ales usually include 6X and Henry's Original IPA, with guests alongside. From the restaurant, you can survey the valley of the Trent Brook as you enjoy dishes from the regularly changing menu. Stylish dishes such as a fillet of pork loin, crushed peas, black pudding croquette potatoes, confit carrots and rosemary jus have resulted in the award of 2 AA Rosettes.

Open all day, all week 11–11 Wadworth 25 from £13.50 portions/menu Wi-fi P *notice required*

WEST BEXINGTON

The Manor House

Tel **01308 897660** | **DT2 9DF**
Web **www.manorhoteldorset.com**
Dir ***On B3157, 5 miles east of Bridport. In Swyre turn opposite The Bull Inn into 'No Through Road'.***

Overlooking the Jurassic Coast's most famous feature, Chesil Beach, parts of this 16th-century manor house are thought to date from the 11th century. It offers an inviting mix of flagstones, Jacobean oak panelling, roaring fires and a cosy cellar bar serving Otter ales and locally sourced dishes. Eat in the Manor Restaurant or in the Cellar Bar. With a drink in hand study the chalkboards displaying modern British dishes; perhaps smoked mackerel pâté followed by roasted vegetable lasagne. The large free car park is a bonus.

Open all week 11.30–3 6–10 Closed 1st 2 weeks Jan Free House 10 from £15 portions/menu Wi-fi P *notice required*

WEST LULWORTH

Lulworth Cove Inn

Tel **01929 400333** | **Main Road, BH20 5RQ**
Web **www.lulworth-coveinn.co.uk**
Dir ***From A352 (Dorchester to Wareham road) follow Lulworth Cove signs. Inn at end of B3070, opposite car park.***

Many smugglers' stories can be heard about this inn located just steps away from Lulworth Cove's famous horseshoe bay. The pub was once a distribution point for the mail service arriving by stagecoach but now it's frequented by ramblers sating their appetites from the extensive menu.

WEST STOUR

The Ship Inn

Tel **01747 838640** | **SP8 5RP**
Web **www.shipinn-dorset.com**
Dir ***On A30, 4 miles west of Shaftesbury (4 miles from Henstridge).***

Picturesque Dorset countryside surrounds this coaching inn built in 1750, and now popular with walkers. The main bar has a traditional flagstone floor, low ceiling and log fire, while the lounge bar has stripped oak floorboards and chunky farmhouse furniture.

WEYMOUTH

The Old Ship Inn

Tel **01305 812522** | **7 The Ridgeway, DT3 5QQ**
Web **www.theoldshipupwey.co.uk**
Dir ***3 miles from Weymouth town centre, at bottom of The Ridgeway.***

Thomas Hardy refers to this 400-year-old pub in his novel *Under the Greenwood Tree*, and copper pans, old clocks and a beamed open fire create a true period atmosphere. Expect a good selection of real ales of tap, perhaps Dorset Jurassic, St Austell Proper Job and Sharp's Doom Bar, with Addlestones cloudy cider as an alternative. A frequently changing menu of good home-cooked pub food offers, for example, crispy whitebait; grilled goats' cheese bruschetta; pork belly braised in Addlestones cider with black pudding and dauphinoise potatoes.

Open all year Tue to Fri 12–3 5–11 Sat 12–11 Sun 12–10 Closed Mon Punch Taverns 13 portions

WORTH MATRAVERS

The Square and Compass

Tel **01929 439229** | **BH19 3LF**
Web **www.squareandcompasspub.co.uk**
Dir ***Between Corfe Castle and Swanage. From B3069 follow signs for Worth Matravers.***

Beers and ciders from the pub's own microbrewery come straight from the barrel here and food is limited to pasties and pies. Little has changed at this pub for the past century, during which time it has been run by the same family. It's tucked away and boasts a simple interior with no bar, just a serving hatch and a museum of local artefacts and fossils from the nearby Jurassic Coast. In October, there's a beer and pumpkin festival, and in early November, a cider festival.

Open all week 12–3 6–11 (summer and Fri to Sun 12–11) Free House

COUNTY DURHAM

AYCLIFFE

The County

Tel **01325 312273** | **13 The Green, Aycliffe Village, DL5 6LX**
Web **www.thecountyaycliffevillage.com**
Dir ***A1(M) junction 59, off A167 into Aycliffe Village.***

Prettily perched on the village green, this inn's smart restaurant and terrace are lovely places to eat, as is the homely bar where you can sup a pint of Black Sheep or Cocker Hoop. With superb local produce on the doorstep, this pub offers seasonally changing menus.

BARNARD CASTLE

The Morritt Hotel ★★★★

COUNTRY HOUSE HOTEL | PICK OF THE PUBS

Tel **01833 627232** | **Greta Bridge, DL12 9SE**
Web **www.themorritt.co.uk**
Dir ***From A1(M) at Scotch Corner take A66 towards Penrith, in 9 miles exit at Greta Bridge. Hotel over bridge on left.***

With a grand Georgian creeper-clad exterior, country house character and contemporary comforts inside, this classic coaching inn has commanded a bridge over the River Greta for three centuries. Charles Dickens visited; he likely based a scene in *Nicholas Nickelby* here. In the bar, an eye-catching mural of Dickensian characters was painted by 'Guinness' artist Jack Gilroy; the practice of promoting local artists continues, with regularly changing works of art on display. Bar meals such as fish pie or braised shoulder of pork are served in the Dickens Bar and Bistro; Gilroy's Dining Room might offer a wood pigeon starter followed by sea bass with crispy chicken wing and French peas. Local real ales seal the deal.

Open all day, all week 7am–11pm (Sun 7am–10.30pm) Free House 12 portions/menu

The Old Well Inn

Tel **01833 690130 | 21 The Bank, DL12 8PH**
Web **www.theoldwellinn.co.uk**
Dir ***On A67.***

Dating back to the 16th century, this black-and-white timber-fronted pub is next to Barnard Castle itself and there is a well beneath the main bar. The castle wall borders the pub's beer garden, where you can enjoy one of the seven cask ales – Timothy Taylor Landlord, perhaps – and ciders in the summer. At other times of the year, grab a seat by the large open fire and order from the globally-inspired menu – traditional pub classics sit happily alongside the home-made Indian curries.

Open all day, all week Free House portions/menu notice required

Three Horseshoes

Tel **01833 631777 | 5–7 Galgate, DL12 8EQ**
Web **www.three-horse-shoes.co.uk**
Dir ***In town centre on A67.***

In the centre of the historic market town of Barnard Castle, this is an ideal base for walkers exploring the nearby Teesdale Valley and the North Pennines. The Green family successfully run this popular 17th-century coaching inn.

CASTLE EDEN

Castle Eden Inn

Tel **01429 835954 | Stockton Road, TS27 4SD**
Dir ***Phone for detailed directions.***

The village of Castle Eden was mentioned in the Domesday Book (although it seems there is no evidence that there was a castle there at the time) and the inn dates from the 18th century. The events calendar includes a beer festival.

CHESTER-LE-STREET

The Lambton Worm

Tel **0191 387 1162 | 52 North Road, DH3 4AJ**
Web **sonnet43pubs.com/lambton-worm/**
Dir ***A1(M) junction 63, A693 towards Stanley. At next roundabout take A167 signed Birtley. Pub on left.***

All six of Sonnet 43's core beers are on tap at The Lambton Worm. 'Sonnet 43' is Elizabeth Barrett Browning's best-known poem and the inspiration behind the operation here; the pub seeks to answer the poem's opening question 'How do I love thee?' in its approach to food, drink and accommodation. The ales are paired with dishes of 'good honest food that makes the heart sing'. Braised beef brisket, for example, followed by home-made rice pudding.

Open all day, all week Sonnet 43 Brewhouse 16 portions/menu notice required

The Moorings Hotel

Tel **0191 370 1597 | Hett Hill, DH2 3JU**
Web **www.themooringsdurham.co.uk**
Dir ***A1(M) junction 63 to Chester-le-Street. Take B6313. Hotel on left.***

Handy both for the fascinating open air museum at Beamish and the historic heart of Chester-le-Street, this thriving hotel bar attracts much custom from ramblers and riders enjoying the glorious countryside. Thirsts are quenched by beers from the respected microbrewery at Beamish.

COTHERSTONE

The Fox and Hounds

Tel **01833 650241 | DL12 9PF**
Web **www.cotherstonefox.co.uk**
Dir ***4 miles west of Barnard Castle. From A66 onto B6277, pub signed.***

A 360-year-old coaching inn at the heart of beautiful Teesdale. Beams, open fires, thickly cushioned wall seats and local photos set the scene inside. Enjoy a pint of Black Sheep Best Bitter or Thatchers cider and tuck into dishes made from the best local ingredients: black pudding and Black Sheep ale pie perhaps.

Open all week 12–2.30 6–11 (Sun 12–2.30 6–10.30) Closed 25–26 Dec Free House 8 from £9.25 portions/menu notice required

COXHOE

The Italian Farmhouse

Tel **0191 377 3773 | DH6 4HX**
Web **www.theitalianfarmhouse.co.uk**
Dir ***Phone for detailed directions.***

Landlord Mark Hird runs what used to be the Clarence Villa. It remains the home of Sonnet 43 Brewhouse, named for "How do I love thee?", the famous poem by Elizabeth Barrett Browning, who was born locally in 1806. As you might expect from the name, menus focus on Italian cuisine.

DARLINGTON

Number Twenty 2

Tel **01325 354590 | 22 Coniscliffe Road, DL3 7RG**
Web **www.villagebrewer.co.uk**
Dir ***In town centre, off A67.***

The rather ordinary front door opens to reveal a classic Victorian pub where up to 13 ales are pulled during busy periods. Even more interesting is the output from the onsite microbrewery and nano-distillery producing beers, gin, vodka and spiced rum. Add to all this, continental beers, wines and fine spirits and you have a drinker's paradise. Soak it all up with light bites, soups, burgers and toasted sandwiches.

Open all day Closed 25–26 Dec, 1 Jan and Bank Holiday Mon, Sun Free House 22 WI-FI

DURHAM

Victoria Inn

Tel **0191 386 5269 | 86 Hallgarth Street, DH1 3AS**
Web **www.victoriainn-durhamcity.co.uk**
Dir ***In city centre.***

This unique, listed inn has scarcely changed since it was built in 1899 – not a jukebox, pool table or TV to be found; just small rooms warmed by coal fires and a congenial atmosphere. Five minutes' walk from the cathedral, it has been carefully nurtured by the Webster family for over 40 years. You'll find a few simple snacks to tickle the taste buds, but it's the cracking, well-kept local ales that are the main attraction.

Open all day, all week 11–11 Free House WI-FI P

FIR TREE

Duke of York Inn

Tel **01388 767429 | DL15 8DG**
Web **www.dukeofyorkfirtree.com**
Dir ***On A68, 12 miles west of Durham. From Durham take A690 west. Left onto A68 to Fir Tree.***

On the tourist route (A68) to Scotland, the Duke of York is a former drovers' and coaching inn dating from 1749. Look out for Camerons Black Sheep to accompany the traditional food served all day. There are light bites, sandwiches and omelettes plus main menu choices such as the signature dish of chicken in creamy leek and pancetta sauce with crushed potatoes.

Open all day, all week Camerons Brewery from £8.50 portions/menu WI-FI P

FROSTERLEY

The Black Bull Inn

Tel **01388 527784 | DL13 2SL**
Web **www.blackbullfrosterley.com**
Dir ***From A68 onto A689 towards Stanhope. Left into Frosterley. Inn adjacent to railway station.***

Uniquely, this family-run, independent country pub has its own church bells – not to mention a great range of real ales to enjoy after a spot of bell-ringing. Located next to Weardale steam railway station, it has cosy, music-free rooms.

HESLEDEN

The Ship Inn ★★★★ INN

Tel **01429 836453 | High Hesleden, TS27 4QD**
Web **www.theshipinn.net**
Dir ***From A19 at Castle Eden take B1281 towards Blackhall Colliery. Turn right signed Hesleden. Pub on left.***

It took six years of hard work for the Crosbys to breathe new life into this once-derelict 1910 pub. The bar's seven changing real ales are of considerable appeal; so too are its freshly prepared, locally sourced dishes, among which favourites are main courses of sirloin steak and chargrilled rump of Yorkshire lamb. On Tuesdays to Fridays there are Early Bird two-course specials.

Open all year 6–11 (Sat 12–3 6–11 Sun 12–8) Closed Mon, Tue to Fri lunch Free House from £10.95 portions/menu WI-FI P *notice required*

HURWORTH-ON-TEES

The Bay Horse PICK OF THE PUBS

Tel **01325 720663 | 45 The Green, DL2 2AA**
Web **www.thebayhorsehurworth.com**
Dir ***From A66 at Darlington Football Club roundabout follow Hurworth sign.***

Refurbished in 2016, this 15th-century coaching inn retains considerable character, enhanced by carefully chosen period furnishings. Although real ale devotees make a beeline for bar pumps dispensing the likes of Hambleton Stallion, the thoroughly modern cooking of talented chef-proprietors Jonathan Hall and Marcus Bennett continues to draw the crowds in the two dining areas. At dinner, expect starters like creamed moules marinière, cider, Bramley apples, pancetta and thyme, and mains such as pan-fried hake, black squid, crab, giant couscous, sweet potato, yogurt and bouillabaisse. Finish with dark chocolate and caramel bar, peanut butter ice cream, macerated cinnamon cherries and cherry foam. There's a good vegetarian choice too.

Open all day, all week Closed 25 Dec Free House 16 from £20 menus

The Otter & Fish

Tel **01325 720019 | 1 Strait Lane, DL2 2AH**
Web **www.otterandfish.co.uk**
Dir ***Phone for detailed directions.***

Overlooking the River Tees in the picturesque village of Hurworth, this pub has been family owned and run for 10 years or so. The place has a relaxed and welcoming, contemporary style, with an emphasis on good food and great service. Traditional bar meals are available, as well as a full carte, offering plenty of choice, from sea bass fillets with seafood risotto; or Chinese-style pork fillet, pak choi and egg fried rice; to stuffed red pepper with spring onion and spinach risotto and provençale sauce.

Open all week Free House portions/menu notice required

MICKLETON

The Crown

Tel **01833 640381 | DL12 0JZ**
Web **www.thecrownatmickleton.co.uk**
Dir ***B6277 from Barnard Castle. Approximately 6 miles to Eggleston. Follow Mickleton signs.***

This old stone inn stands on Mickleton's main street, surrounded by the heather-covered moors of the North Pennines Area of Outstanding Natural Beauty. Candlelight and a log-burning stove illuminate the interior. Enjoy a well-kept pint from breweries, such as Cumberland, Thwaites and Jennings. The menu might catch your eye with roast chicken ballotine, new potatoes, braised lettuce and smoked bacon; twice-cooked Simpson's Aberdeen Angus beef steak and chunky chips; and apple and blackberry crumble with fresh vanilla custard. The dog-friendly garden is a real treat.

Open all day 11am to midnight Closed 1st 2 weeks Jan, Mon (May to Sep), Tue and Wed (Oct to Apr) Free House portions notice required

NEWTON AYCLIFFE

The Hammer & Pincers

Tel **01325 314873 | Preston le Skerne, (off Ricknall Lane), DL5 6JH**
Web **www.thehammers.co**
Dir ***Exit A167 (dual carriageway) at Gretna Green pub signed Great Stanton, Stillington and Bishopton, into Ricknall Lane. The Hammer & Pincers 0.5 mile.***

Regulars at the former Blacksmiths Arms swiftly simplified its new name to The Hammers. Traditional, home-cooked meals begin with a selection of small plates and tapas – duck pancakes, and trio of fishcakes, for example – at three for a tenner. In addition to pub classics, also worthy of an honourable mention are the chef's specials, which might include beef, root vegetable and Guinness casserole; slow-cooked belly pork; and scampi with dressed salad. Touring caravans are welcome.

Open 11.30–2.30 5.30–11 (Sun 12–10.30) Closed 1 Jan, Mon Free House 10 from £7.90 portions/menu notice required

SEAHAM

The Seaton Lane Inn

 INN

Tel **0191 581 2038** | **Seaton Lane, SR7 0LP**
Web **www.seatonlaneinn.com**
Dir ***South of Sunderland on A19 take B1404 towards Houghton-le-Spring. In Seaton turn left for pub.***

Just a five-minute drive from the coast and close to Sunderland, this boutique-style inn offers four real ales to keep the regulars happy, served from the central bar. With a traditional bar area as well as a stylish restaurant and lounge, there are plenty of dining options, and locally sourced seafood makes a strong appearance on the menu. The pub has built a formidable reputation for Sunday roasts.

Open all day, all week 7am to midnight *Free House* 10 *portions/menu* Wi-fi P

SHINCLIFFE

Seven Stars Inn

Tel **0191 384 8454** | **DH1 2NU**
Web **www.sevenstarsinn.co.uk**
Dir ***A1(M) junction 61, A177 towards Durham. Approximately 2 miles to Shincliffe. Pub in village centre.***

In a peaceful village a short hop from Durham's historic city centre, the family-run Seven Stars has been refreshing travellers since it was built as a coaching inn in 1724. The cosy traditional bar with open fire offers ales from the Durham Brewery.

STANLEY

The Stables Pub and Restaurant

Tel **01207 288750** | **Beamish Hall Hotel, Beamish, DH9 0YB**
Web **www.beamish-hall.co.uk**
Dir ***A693 to Stanley. Follow signs for Beamish Hall Country House Hotel and Beamish Museum. Left at museum entrance. Hotel on left 0.2 mile after golf club. Pub within hotel grounds.***

The stone-floored, beamed bar is the perfect spot to sample the pub's own real ales, brewed on site at their microbrewery. The beer festival will get you even more closely acquainted, while a cider festival is held during the second weekend of December.

WHORLTON

Fernaville's Rest

Tel **01833 627341** | **DL12 8XD**
Web **www.fernavilles.com**
Dir ***Phone for detailed directions.***

This stone-built, traditional inn is known for its food. Kick off with tempura sea bass, katsu sauce and salad; followed by lamb and black pudding shepherd's pie, or the Fernaville's burger with fries; finish with forced rhubarb and ginger beer trifle.

Open all day, all week *Free House* *from £9.50* *portions/menu* Wi-fi P *notice required*

WINSTON

The Bridgewater Arms

Tel **01325 730302** | **DL2 3RN**
Web **www.thebridgewaterarms.com**
Dir ***Exit A67 between Barnard Castle and Darlington, onto B6274 into Winston.***

Set in a former schoolhouse, this Grade II listed pub is decorated with original photographs of the building and its pupils. It prides itself on offering high quality, simple meals made with local produce, particularly seafood. Look out for salt and pepper chilli squid; smoked haddock risotto; roast rack of spring lamb, leek and potato cake and rosemary gravy; or pan-fried wild turbot fillet with tiger prawn, pancetta and wild garlic risotto.

Open 12–2.30 6–close Closed 23–28 Dec, 1 Jan, Sun and Mon *Free House* 15 *portions* P

ESSEX

AYTHORPE RODING

Axe & Compasses

Tel **01279 876648** | **Dunmow Road, CM6 1PP**
Web **www.theaxeandcompasses.co.uk**
Dir ***From A120 follow signs for Dunmow.***

This weather-boarded, 17th-century pub creates a 'nostalgic pub experience'. In the bar, ales from brewers such as Adnams, are backed by Westons ciders. The kitchen team uses the best seasonal produce. There's a daily breakfast menu too.

BELCHAMP ST PAUL

The Half Moon

Tel **01787 277402** | **Cole Green, CO10 7DP**
Web **www.halfmoonbelchamp.co.uk**
Dir ***From Braintree take A131 towards Halstead. Left onto A1017 to Great Yeldham. In Great Yeldham follow 'The Belchamps' signs. Approximately 4 miles to pub.***

Many pubs claim to be quintessentially English; this one deserves the claim. Dating from the 1520s, many of its original features, including low beams, leaded windows and an open fire have survived. Locally sourced, freshly-made food maintains an ever-changing seasonal menu offering such dishes as steak and kidney pudding; and wild boar and apple sausages. Essex-brewed beers are in the bar and again in August for the bank holiday beer and cider festival.

Open all week 12–3 6–11 (Sat to Sun 12–11) Free House 8 from £8.95 portions/menu notice required

BROXTED

The Prince of Wales

Tel **01279 850256** | **Brick End, CM6 2BJ**
Web **www.princeofwalesbroxted.co.uk**
Dir ***M11 junction 8, A120 towards Braintree, follow Stansted Airport signs. At 2nd roundabout follow Broxted sign. Right, through Molehill Green. Right at T-junction to pub on left.***

A friendly, traditional village inn with cosy log fires, offering up to six real ales from local breweries (Bishop Nick Ridley's Rite, maybe, or Heresy), and serving home-cooked pub grub all day. The Sunday roasts are popular. There's a great garden for summer days.

BURNHAM-ON-CROUCH

Ye Olde White Harte Hotel

Tel **01621 782106** | **The Quay, CM0 8AS**
Web **www.whiteharteburnham.co.uk**
Dir ***Along high street, right before clocktower, right into car park.***

Situated on the waterfront overlooking the River Crouch, the hotel dates from the 17th century and retains many original features. Enjoy fresh, local produce dishes in The Waterside Restaurant, the bar or on their private jetty. A typical menu starts with ham hock terrine; or baked, creamy mushrooms, then continues with lamb steak with shallot and red wine gravy; or pan-fried skate wing; finish with profiteroles and hot chocolate sauce.

Open all day, all week Free House from £9.50 portions notice required

CASTLE HEDINGHAM

The Bell Inn PICK OF THE PUBS

Tel **01787 460350** | **St James Street, CO9 3EJ**
Web **www.hedinghambell.co.uk**
Dir ***On A1124 north of Halstead, right to Castle Hedingham.***

A 15th-century coaching inn in the charming village of Castle Hedingham, The Bell has been run by the Ferguson family for over 50 years. Exposed stone walls, heavy beams and real log fires create a welcoming atmosphere in which to enjoy a Mighty Oak Maldon Gold, Adnams Southwold Bitter or one of the guest ales. The Turkish chef puts his stamp on the menu, with Mediterranean fish nights on Mondays, and Turkish stone-baked pizzas on Wednesdays, Thursdays and Fridays. The annual July beer festival showcases up to 40 ales, and there's live music every Friday night and jazz on the last Sunday of the month.

Open all week 12–3 5.30–11 (Fri to Sat 12–12 Sun 12–11) Closed 25 Dec evening Gray & Sons from £9 portions/menu notice required

CHRISHALL

The Red Cow

Tel **01763 838792** | **11 High Street, SG8 8RN**
Web **www.theredcow.com**
Dir ***M11 junction 10, A505 towards Royston. 2 miles, pass pet crematorium, 1st left signed Chrishall. 3.5 miles, pub in village centre.***

Conveniently positioned between Saffron Walden and Royston, this 500-year-old thatched pub is very much the busy hub of the local community. Ales such as Nelson's Revenge and Aspall ciders are locally brewed or from East Anglia. The seasonally-changing restaurant carte typically offers home-made pie of the day. The pub's social calendar is full to bursting, with music particularly high on the agenda.

Open all year 12–3 6–12 (Sat 12–12 Sun 12–11) Closed Mon Free House 10 portions/menu notice required

CLAVERING

The Cricketers PICK OF THE PUBS

Tel **01799 550442 | CB11 4QT**
Web **www.thecricketers.co.uk**
Dir ***M11 junction 10, A505 east, A1301, B1383. At Newport take B1038.***

Aged 19, Trevor Oliver, already married to Sally, became one of England's youngest licensees. In 1976 they arrived at this delightful 16th-century inn, he in the kitchen and she front-of-house and book-keeper. Two babies came too – Anna-Marie and Jamie (yes, that Jamie) so, who knows, maybe he'll be visiting his parents the day you visit, for he and his sister supply vegetables, salad leaves and herbs from their certified organic garden nearby. Food shows the famous Oliver focus on flavour, with all the fish fresh from Billingsgate market, meat hung and butchered on site, and bread and pasta made every morning. Daily specials complement a menu that offers lamb shank with slow-braised root vegetables; 'Jamie's' chicken katsu curry; vegetable Wellington, and plenty to tempt children. Terrace dining is an appealing option.

Open all day, all week Closed 25–26 Dec Free House 17 from £9.95 portions/menu notice required

COLCHESTER

The Rose & Crown Hotel

★★★ HOTEL

Tel **01206 866677 | East Street, CO1 2TZ**
Web **www.rose-and-crown.com**
Dir ***M25 junction 28, A12 north. Follow Colchester signs.***

Just a short stroll from Colchester Castle, this beautiful 14th-century, timber-framed building is said to be the oldest hotel in the oldest town in England. The Tudor bar, with its roaring fire, is a great place to relax, while food is served in the Oak Room or the Tudor Room brasserie, an informal alternative serving classic bar food. Typical dishes might be pulled lamb samosa with coriander and honey yogurt, and pan-fried sea bass with pistachio nut crust, seared cucumbers and sesame and saffron potato.

Open all week 10–2.30 5–11 Free House from £15.50 portions

COPFORD GREEN

The Alma

Tel **01206 210607 | CO6 1BZ**
Web **www.thealma.org.uk**
Dir ***From roundabout junction of A12 and A120 follow Colchester signs. At next roundabout follow Copford sign (B1408). In Copford right into School Road. Pub 0.75 mile on left.***

The staff at The Alma warmly welcome their guests, with or without their children and dogs. A Greene King house, there are always four ales and various lagers to choose from; its beer credentials are confirmed by the Spring Bank Holiday weekend festival. Crowd-pleasing dishes include hand-made pie, mash and veg; salmon fillet, creamed peas and new potatoes; and a comprehensive burger menu. Children are well catered for with their own menu or smaller portions from the main menu.

Open all week 12–3 5–close Greene King from £6.99 portions/menu

DANBURY

The Griffin

Tel **01245 699024 | 64 Main Road, CM3 4DH**
Web **www.thegriffindanbury.com**
Dir ***A12 onto A414 towards Maldon. Pub at top of hill on left in Danbury.***

A 400-year-old, black and white timber-framed inn on one of Essex's few high hills, whose attractive exterior prepares visitors for the wealth of scrubbed beams inside, some possibly dating from when the nearby church was being built. At lunchtime are baguettes, wraps, jacket potatoes, sharers and light meals, such as quesadilla with chunky chips. And from the main menu, guinea fowl with hasselback potatoes; fillet of sea bass, fennel and rösti; and duo of courgette cassoulet.

Open all year, all day Closed Mon Free House 12 from £9.50 portions/menu notice required

DEDHAM

Marlborough Head Inn

Tel **01206 323250** | **Mill Lane, CO7 6DH**
Web **www.themarlboroughdedham.co.uk**
Dir ***East of A12, north of Colchester.***

Tucked away in glorious Constable Country, this 16th-century building was once a clearing-house for local wool merchants. In 1660, after a slump in trade, it became an inn. Today it is as perfect for a pint as it is for a good home-cooked family meal.

Open all day, all week 11.30–11 Free House 18 from £12 portions/menu Wi-fi notice required

The Sun Inn  INN

PICK OF THE PUBS

Tel **01206 323351** | **High Street, CO7 6DF**
Web **www.thesuninndedham.com**
Dir ***From A12 follow signs to Dedham for 1.5 miles, pub on High Street.***

With its smart yellow-painted exterior and exposed timbers, this lovely old inn has two informal bars, an open dining room and a snug oak-panelled lounge. So take your pick of where to enjoy your chosen refreshment, be it a pint of Adnams Broadside or Aspall Harry Sparrow cider; for wine drinkers, two dozen plus are served by the glass. Locally sourced seasonal ingredients drive the daily-changing menu of Mediterranean-style dishes Choose from dishes like rigatoni pasta with pork ribs, sausage, featherblade of beef; and line-caught sea bass, cuttlefish in tomato sauce, squid ink cracker and mayonnaise. In summer, head to the suntrap terrace and walled garden overlooked by the church tower.

Open all day, all week 11–11 Closed 25–27 Dec Free House 25 portions/menu Wi-fi

FEERING

The Sun Inn

Tel **01376 570442** | **Feering Hill, CO5 9NH**
Web **www.suninnfeering.co.uk**
Dir ***On A12 between Colchester and Witham. Village 1 mile.***

This pretty Grade II listed building dates from 1527 and has the heavily carved beams and inglenook fireplaces to prove it. The traditional bar, which sells Shepherd Neame's real ales plus guest and seasonal brews, has no TV or games machines. As well as a range of real ales on tap, there is an extensive menu of home-cooked food. Warm pigeon salad might be followed by ox cheek, creamed chive potato, button mushrooms and baby onions. A large garden and courtyard make for popular alfresco options in the summer.

Open all week (Sat to Sun all day) Shepherd Neame 13 portions Wi-fi notice required

FINGRINGHOE

The Whalebone

Tel **01206 729307** | **Chapel Road, CO5 7BG**
Web **www.thewhaleboneinn.co.uk**
Dir ***Phone for detailed directions.***

This Grade II listed, 18th-century free house enjoys beautiful views from the top of the Roman River Valley. Wooden floors, exposed beams, bespoke furniture, a roaring fire and unique artwork combine to create a feeling of character. Hearty British fare is prepared from local ingredients.

FULLER STREET

The Square and Compasses
– see page 166

FYFIELD

The Queen's Head

Tel **01277 899231** | **Queen Street, CM5 0RY**
Web **www.queensheadfyfield.co.uk**
Dir ***M11 junction 7, A414 towards Chelmsford. In Chipping Ongar at roundabout left to Fyfield on B184.***

With a history dating back to the 15th century, The Queen's Head is a traditional free house with log fires and a riverside garden. Ales from Adnams are backed up by Aspall cider, a large selection of lagers and a wide choice of wines.

GOLDHANGER

The Chequers Inn

Tel **01621 788203** | **Church Street, CM9 8AS**
Web **www.thechequersgoldhanger.co.uk**
Dir ***From B1026, 500 metres to village centre.***

Built in 1410, The Chequers can be found next to the church in picturesque Goldhanger. The pub name comes from a chequerboard used by the tax collector in the pub many, many years ago. It reputedly has the 'lowest' bar in Britain.

FULLER STREET

The Square and Compasses

Tel **01245 361477** | **CM3 2BB**
Web **www.thesquareandcompasses.co.uk**
Dir ***From A131 (Chelmsford to Braintree) take Great Leighs exit, enter village, right into Boreham Road. Left signed Fuller Street and Terling. Pub on left.***

Facing green fields in a picturesque hamlet

This beautifully restored village pub stands in lovely countryside just 10 minutes outside Chelmsford. Originally two farm cottages dating from 1652, the atmospheric free house still retains its original beams, inglenook fireplaces and antique furnishings. In The Taproom you can expect a good selection of food, beers, ciders and perries, and well-behaved dogs are welcome. Both here and in The Dining Room you'll enjoy top-quality local beef and lamb, wild game from the surrounding estates, and fresh local fruit and vegetables, often supplied by villagers. Fresh line-caught fish comes from the Essex coast, and crab from Cromer. As well as pub classics, including home-cooked, hand-carved ham with eggs, the daily-changing specials might include crab cake with lime and chilli; and roast chump of lamb marinated in thyme and garlic.

Open all day, all week 11.30–11.30 Free House 14 portions

GREAT TOTHAM

The Bull at Great Totham

 RESTAURANT WITH ROOMS

PICK OF THE PUBS

Tel **01621 893385** | **2 Maldon Road, CM9 8NH**
Web **www.thebullatgreattotham.co.uk**
Dir ***Exit A12 at Witham junction to Great Totham.***

The Bull, overlooking the cricket green, is a 16th-century coaching inn and proud holder of two AA Rosettes. It offers not far short of 20 fine wines by the glass, real ales from Adnams and London Pride, and a bar menu of classics like filled baguettes, sausage and mash, and beer-battered cod tail. Named after the ancient tree in the lavender-filled garden is the fine-dining Willow Room. Musical and themed dining evenings and other events are held frequently.

Open all day, all week Free House 20 portions/menu notice required

HASTINGWOOD

Rainbow & Dove

Tel **01279 415419** | **Hastingwood Road, CM17 9JX**
Web **www.rainbowanddove.com**
Dir ***Just off M11 junction 7.***

Dating back to at least the 16th century, the Rainbow & Dove was a farmhouse, staging post, village shop and post office before it became a pub. English Heritage has given it Grade II historical building status. There are cask-conditioned real ales, a selection of craft gins and whiskies and a good wine list. Menus revolve around fresh, seasonal produce and the owners have their own smallholding where rare and traditional pigs, goats, geese, chickens and quail are reared.

Open all year 11.30–3 6–11 (Sun 12–7 Mon 11.30–3.30) Closed Sun evening, Mon evening Free House 10 portions/menu notice required

HATFIELD BROAD OAK

The Duke's Head

Tel **01279 718598** | **High Street, CM22 7HH**
Web **www.thedukeshead.co.uk**
Dir ***M11 junction 8, A120 towards Great Dunmow. Right into B183 to Hatfield Broad Oak. Pub on left at 1st bend in village.***

Standing behind a white-painted picket fence, this 185-year-old pub's proprietors are Justin and Liz Flodman. Spacious, with two fires, the pub's customers can enjoy good wines by the glass, real ales from Essex and surrounding counties, and Justin's seasonal, modern British food.

Open all day, all week Closed 25–26 Dec Enterprise Inns 25 portions/menu notice required

HATFIELD HEATH

The Thatcher's

Tel **01279 730270** | **Stortford Road, CM22 7DU**
Web **www.thethatcherspub.com**
Dir ***In village on A1060 (Bishop's Stortford road).***

White-painted weatherboarding outside, inside some mighty stout timbers supporting the oak beams in the convivial bar, warmed by a wood-burning stove tucked into a cavernous inglenook. Eleven wines are offered by the glass, with real ales coming from, among others, Harvey's Sussex brewery. Dishes, all prepared in-house, range from white-meat crab remoulade, and lamb kofta with couscous, to slow-cooked ox cheek, and Suffolk chicken supreme. Toasties and sandwiches with fries add to the choices.

Open all day, all week 11.30–11 Free House 11 from £10 portions/menu notice required

HORNDON ON THE HILL

Bell Inn PICK OF THE PUBS

Tel **01375 642463** | **High Road, SS17 8LD**
Web **www.bell-inn.co.uk**
Dir ***M25 junction 30 or 31 follow Thurrock signs.***

In the same family since 1938, this 15th-century coaching inn is steeped in history. The hot cross buns hanging from the king post supporting the ancient roof timbers are an unusal tradition, hung every year by the oldest willing villager and commemorating the time, 100 years ago, when the pub changed hands on Good Friday. In the bar, regular brews like Crouch Vale Brewers Gold are backed by a selection of changing guest ales. The lunchtime bar menu offers sandwiches and light meals but booking is essential in the restaurant, where the daily-changing menu is driven by seasonal produce. Start with hickory-smoked duck with cauliflower purée; followed by roasted pork fillet, sautéed chorizo and pearl barley.

Open all day, all week 11–11 (Sun 12–10.30) Closed 25–26 Dec Free House 16 from £13.95 portions

INGATESTONE

The Red Lion

Tel **01277 352184** | **Main Road, Margaretting, CM4 0EQ**
Dir ***From Chelmsford take A12 towards Brentwood. Margaretting in 4 miles.***

Emphatically a traditional inn and not a restaurant (although it does sell quality food), the 17th-century Red Lion is best described as a 'quintessential English pub'. The bar is decorated in burgundy and aubergine, the restaurant in coffee and cream.

LANGHAM

The Shepherd

Tel **01206 272711** | **Moor Road, CO4 5NR**
Web **www.shepherdlangham.co.uk**
Dir ***A12 from Colchester towards Ipswich, take 1st left signed Langham.***

In the pretty village of Langham, deep in Constable Country on the Suffolk/Essex border, this Edwardian pub is a stylish free house, open all day and with a relaxing, family-friendly feel. Real ales are on offer, alongside an extensive list of wines.

LITTLE BURSTEAD

The Dukes Head

Tel **01277 651333 | Laindon Common Road, CM12 9TA**
Web **www.thedukesheadlittleburstead.co.uk**
Dir ***From Basildon take A176 (Noah Hill Road) north towards Billericay. Left into Laindon Common Road to Little Burstead. Pub on left.***

Smart interiors and a friendly team characterise the atmosphere in this large hostelry. Chunky wood tables, leather-upholstered stools and relaxing armchairs surround the open fire in the bar area, where the ales vie for selection with an excellent range of wines served by the glass.

LITTLEBURY

The Queens Head Inn Littlebury

Tel **01799 520365 | High Street, CB11 4TD**
Web **www.thequeensheadinn.net**
Dir ***M11 junction 9A, B184 towards Saffron Walden. Right onto B1383, south towards Wendens Ambo.***

This beautiful, family-run former coaching inn with open fires, exposed beams and one of only two remaining full-length settles in England is very much at the centre of the local community. The chefs prepare good home-made dishes and fish is a major focus.

LITTLE CANFIELD

The Lion & Lamb

Tel **01279 870257 | CM6 1SR**
Web **lionandlamb.co.uk**
Dir ***M11 junction 8, B1256 towards Takeley and Little Canfield.***

Ideal for business or leisure, this former coaching inn was built on what used to be the main east coast road. Now a traditional country pub and restaurant, it's a popular stop for travellers on the way to Stansted Airport.

LITTLEY GREEN

The Compasses

Tel **01245 362308 | CM3 1BU**
Web **www.compasseslittleygreen.co.uk**
Dir ***Phone for detailed directions.***

Joss Ridley left London and a top job so he could snap up this pub to revive the family link with the former Ridley Brewery, and he hasn't looked back. It stands in a sleepy hamlet and thrives selling tip-top ales straight from the barrel.

MANNINGTREE

The Mistley Thorn PICK OF THE PUBS

Tel **01206 392821 | High Street, Mistley, CO11 1HE**
Web **www.mistleythorn.com**
Dir ***From Ipswich A12 junction 31 onto B1070, follow signs to East Bergholt, Manningtree and Mistley. From Colchester A120 towards Harwich. Left at Horsley Cross. Mistley in 3 miles.***

This 18th-century coaching inn overlooks the Stour Estuary at almost its widest point. During 2016 a major refurbishment introduced a new exhibition kitchen and enlarged the dining area. There's no doubt that diners comprise the majority of customers, but Adnams ales and a choice of 17 wines served by the glass can be enjoyed at the bar in the relaxed and casual ambience. Fresh and locally-sourced ingredients are the highlights of the daily-changing menu, with an emphasis on seafood, the likes of Mersea rock oysters served with shallot and ginger mignonette; and chargrilled dayboat squid 'a la plancha' with chilli, garlic, lemon oil and herbs. Non-fishy alternatives include chargrilled Suffolk Red Poll beef with hand-cut, skin-on fries; and home-made potato gnocchi with spinach, hazelnut pesto and pine nuts.

Open all week 12–2.30 6.30–9.30 (Fri 6–9.30 Sat to Sun all day) Free House 17 portions/menu
WiFi P

MARGARETTING TYE

The White Hart Inn

Tel **01277 840478** | **Swan Lane, CM4 9JX**
Web **www.thewhitehart.uk.com**
Dir ***From A12 junction 15, B1002 to Margaretting. At crossroads in Margaretting left into Maldon Road. Under rail bridge, left. Right into Swan Lane, follow Margaretting Tye signs. Follow to pub on right.***

Parts of this pub, sitting proudly on a green known locally as Tigers Island, are 250 years old. Landlady Liz and her team revel in offering a great choice of the best regional and local beers and ciders. The pub's interior oozes character.

MATCHING TYE

The Fox Inn

Tel **01279 731335** | **The Green, CM17 0QS**
Web **www.thefoxinn.com**
Dir ***From A414 in Harlow take B183 towards Sheering. At 2nd roundabout 2nd exit (Churchgate Street). At T-junction left (The Matchings). Over motorway. Pub on right in village centre.***

A licensed establishment since 1809, this pub has a lofty, timbered restaurant with a huge open fireplace spanned by a wide bressumer beam that supports a hefty brick chimney. The menus strike all the right notes for those who like their food both simply prepared and described, thus lamb's liver, bacon, mash and onion gravy; gammon, eggs and chips; baked salmon fillet, new potatoes and mixed vegetables; and home-made vegetable lasagne. Adnams Southwold and Shepherd Neame Spitfire are among the real ales.

Open all week 11.30–3.30 6–11.30 (Sun 12–11) Closed 26–27 Dec Free House 12 from £7.95 portions/menu Wi-fi P notice required

MESSING

The Old Crown

Tel **01621 815575** | **Lodge Road, CO5 9TU**
Dir ***From Chelmsford: A12 junction 23, B1024 (Kelvedon). In Kelvedon right onto B1023 (Maldon). Left to Messing. From Colchester: A12 junction 24, B1024 (Kelvedon) left onto B1023.***

After many years as regulars, Malcolm and Penny Campbell took over this lovely old pub a few years back. The Old Crown calls itself a 'bistro pub' and proves very popular with walkers and cyclists. Dogs are welcome in the bar and the atmosphere throughout is warm and cosy, with open fires in the winter and outside tables in summer. The food is all home cooked and sourced locally whenever possible, and there's a delicatessen on site. There's plenty of choice on the handwritten menus.

Open all day, all week Free House from £14.50 portions Wi-fi P notice required

MOUNT BURES

The Thatchers Arms

Tel **01787 227460** | **Hall Road, CO8 5AT**
Web **www.thatchersarms.co.uk**
Dir ***From A12 onto A1124 towards Halstead. Right immediately after Chappel Viaduct. 2 miles, pub on right.***

There's something for all comers at this cheery pub in the Stour Valley, a perfect rural setting for celebrations of all types in a function room and private patio. Challenge the quoits beds in the beer garden, or ramble on paths that Constable may once have walked.

MOUNTNESSING

The George & Dragon

Tel **01277 352461** | **294 Roman Road, CM15 0TZ**
Web **www.thegeorgeanddragonbrentwood.co.uk**
Dir ***In village centre.***

This 18th-century coaching inn successfully blends bold artwork, colourful leather chairs and chunky modern tables with preserved original wooden floors, exposed beams and brick fireplaces.
In this relaxed and convivial setting tuck into Mediterranean-inspired British dishes from an extensive menu that should please all tastes.

NEWNEY GREEN

The Duck Pub & Dining

Tel **01245 421894** | **CM1 3SF**
Web **www.theducknewneygreen.co.uk**
Dir ***From Chelmsford take A1060 (Sawbridgeworth). Straight on at mini-roundabout, 4th left into Vicarage Road (signed Roxwell and Willingate), left into Hoe Street, becomes Gravelly Lane, left to pub.***

Formed from two agricultural cottages, this 17th-century inn is situated in the tiny hamlet of Newney Green. The friendly Duck offers up to six real ales, including weekly guests, and menus that reflect the region's produce. Choose from the extensive menu in the beamed dining room; start with spiced duck pancakes, then move on to mains like steak and ale pie; or ham, egg and chips. Soak up the sun in the pleasant garden with its children's play area.

Open all year, all day Closed Mon, Tue, Wed Free House 14 portions/menu

PATTISWICK

The Compasses at Pattiswick

PICK OF THE PUBS

Tel **01376 561322** | **Compasses Road, CM77 8BG**
Web **www.thecompassesatpattiswick.co.uk**
Dir ***A120 from Braintree towards Colchester. After Bradwell 1st left to Pattiswick.***

Set in the heart the beautiful north Essex countryside, and only a mile from the A120, this dining pub developed from two farm workers' cottages more than a century ago. Flagstone floors, eclectic furniture and a relaxing colour palette all create a stylish interior; the welcome is genuine and the kitchen sources quality produce from local suppliers for the well-cooked food – from classic pub favourites such as fish and chips, through to more complex dishes. A roaring log fire makes a welcoming sight in winter after a long walk, while in summer the large garden is inviting. Families are very well catered for here, with a play area and toy box.

Open all week 12–3 5.30–11 (Sat 12–3 5.30–12 Sun 12–4) Free House 10 portions/menu notice required

PELDON

The Peldon Rose

Tel **01206 735248** | **Colchester Road, CO5 7QJ**
Dir ***On B1025 (Mersea Road), just before causeway.***

Since the 14th century the Rose has faced The Strood, the approach road to Mersea Island. It was once popular with smugglers, who wouldn't have any trouble recognising the bar today, with its beams and leaded windows. A well-deserved reputation for food begins with regularly-changing menus offering good-quality, traditional pub dishes, as well as pan-fried duck on pea fricassée; and cashew Stroganoff with rice. A conservatory leads to the garden.

Open all day, all week Free House from £10.95 portions notice required

PURLEIGH

The Bell

Tel **01621 828348** | **The Street, CM3 6QJ**
Web **www.purleighbell.com**
Dir ***Between Chelmsford and Burnham-on-Crouch on B1010. (5 miles south of Maldon). In Purleigh, pub on top of hill adjacent to church.***

A direct ancestor of George Washington is believed to have lived here in 1634 when he was the local rector. The building was old even then, going back to the 14th century. Purleigh Hill on which it stands offers sweeping views south.

RICKLING GREEN

The Cricketers Arms

Tel **01799 543210** | **CB11 3YG**
Web **www.thecricketersarmsricklinggreen.co.uk**
Dir ***M11 junction 10, A505 east. 1.5 miles, right onto B1301, 2.2 miles, right onto B1383 at roundabout. Through Newport to Rickling Green. Right into Rickling Green Road, 0.2 mile to pub, on left.***

Well-placed for Saffron Walden and Stansted Airport, this inn enjoys a peaceful position overlooking the village green and cricket pitch in sleepy Rickling Green. The bar and dining rooms have a comfortable, contemporary feel, with squashy sofas by the fire providing the perfect winter refuge.

SAFFRON WALDEN

The Crown Inn  INN

Tel **01799 522475** | **Little Walden, CB10 1XA**
Web **www.thecrownlittlewalden.co.uk**
Dir ***2 miles from Saffron Walden on B1052.***

The Crown's rural situation just outside the pretty market town of Saffron Walden makes it a good choice for families wanting to tire out children and dogs on one of the many walks in the surrounding countryside. Mums and dads can return for a well-earned glass of Adnams Broadside or a glass of wine, and hungry children can choose from the half dozen options on their dedicated menu. The short but reasonably priced menus embrace all the classic pub grub dishes. Live jazz on Wednesday evenings.

Open all week 11.30–2.30 6–11 (Sun 12–10.30) Free House portions/menu notice required

Old English Gentleman – see page 172

STANSTED MOUNTFITCHET

The Cock Public House

Tel **01279 812964** | **30 Silver Street, CM24 8HD**
Web **www.thecockatstansted.co.uk**
Dir ***Phone for detailed directions.***

The Cock sits on a busy road running through Stansted Mountfitchet, but today's locals are given just the same warm welcome as their ancestors received when it opened for business back in the 1800s. The pub hosts quizzes, live music and charity events.

STISTED

The Dolphin

Tel **01376 321143** | **CM77 8EU**
Web **www.thedolphinpub.co.uk**
Dir ***On A120 between Braintree and Coggeshall.***

The Dolphin was originally four cottages dating from the 16th century, one of which was an alehouse. Midway between Braintree and Colchester, The Dolphin makes a great refreshment stop, serving food and drink all day, every day. Greene King ales, Aspall's cider, popular home-cooked pub fare, warming log fires and friendly staff are all attributes here. Children have their own menu, washed down with unlimited squash. On the à la carte menu there's pan-fried lamb's liver and bacon; and locally-sourced beef is grilled to your liking.

Open all day, all week Greene King portions/menu notice required

STOCK

The Hoop – see page 173

WENDENS AMBO

The Bell

Tel **01799 540382** | **Royston Road, CB11 4JY**
Web **www.thebellinnpub.co.uk**
Dir ***Phone for detailed directions.***

First mentioned in 1576 as a farm, evidence of its great age is everywhere, particularly the fine Elizabethan chimney stack. Other attributes include acres of gardens, a willow-edged pond, a woodland walk, play equipment, open fires and a resident ghost.

WIDDINGTON

Fleur de Lys

Tel **01799 543280** | **CB11 3SG**
Web **www.thefleurdelys.co.uk**
Dir ***M1 junction 9A, follow Newport (B1383) signs. After Newport turn left signed Widdington. 2 miles to pub on left.***

Terracotta-painted, low-beamed, and with a fine inglenook fireplace, the Fleur is over 500 years old. A games room is essential in a pub, say the landlords, which is why you'll find one here, accommodating a dartboard, full-size pool table, table football and jukebox. Regional brews such as Woodforde's Wherry and Adnams are usually accompanied by guest ales and Rosie's Pig cloudy cider. Huge doorstep sandwiches are served with hand-cut chips, while the fish and chips has been dubbed 'whale and chips', so make sure you're hungry.

Open 12–3 6–11 (Mon 6.30–11 Tue 6–11 Fri to Sat 12–11.30 Sun 12–10) Closed 1 Jan, Mon lunch and Tue lunch Free House 8 from £12.50 portions

SAFFRON WALDEN

Old English Gentleman

Tel **01799 523595** | **11 Gold Street, CB10 1EJ**
Web **www.oldenglishgentleman.co.uk**
Dir ***M11 junction 9a, B184 signed Saffron Walden. Left at High Street lights into George Street, 1st right into Gold Street (one-way system).***

A well-mannered town-centre pub

Regulars call this 19th-century, town-centre pub the OEG, an informality which the top-hatted dandy on the sign over the front door might be a little sniffy about. Ancient beer taps line a wall of the traditional, wooden-floored central bar, which opens out to a spacious area with tables and seating with a log-burner in the dining area, and air conditioning; outside is a patio garden, which can often be a sun-trap, but heated if not. Resident ales Adnams Southwold and Woodforde's Wherry are backed up by changing guests, Adnams dry-hopped lager and Aspall cider, a portfolio that earns full customer approval. Throughout the week the kitchen prepares hearty main meals, light lunches, salads, paninis, hand-cut sandwiches and deli boards, and on Sundays, roasts and a variety of light bites and salads. In more detail, this translates as Scottish smoked salmon with crème fraîche; and lamb patties in flatbread as starters, then mains of 'giant' couscous halloumi salad; crispy Belgian beer-battered catch of the day; corned beef hash; and OEG Aberdeen Angus beef burger. Possible alternatives to the Sunday roast meat-of-the-day are Moroccan aubergine and chickpea casserole; and pie of the week.

Open all day, all week 🍷10 👪

STOCK

The Hoop

Tel **01277 841137 | 21 High Street, CM4 9BD**
Web **www.thehoop.co.uk**
Dir ***On B1007 between Chelmsford and Billericay.***

Traditional pub with a focus on food

This weather-boarded 15th-century free house on Stock's village green began life as weavers' cottages before being converted to an ale house more than four centuries ago. Nowadays it's every inch the traditional country pub, offering a warm welcome, authentic interiors including fine brick fireplaces, and a pleasing absence of music and fruit machines. There's an emphasis on food here, with dishes ranging from toad-in-the-hoop to pan-fried calves' liver with crispy bacon, creamy mash and home-cooked onion rings. You could finish with treacle tart and ice cream, or hot chocolate fondant with salted caramel ice cream. The annual beer festival (late May) has been going from strength to strength for over 30 years; you'll have over 100 real ales to choose from, not to mention fruit beers, perries and more.

Open all day, all week Free House 14 portions

WOODHAM MORTIMER

Hurdlemakers Arms

Tel **01245 225169 | Post Office Road, CM9 6ST**
Web **www.hurdlemakersarms.co.uk**
Dir ***From Chelmsford A414 to Maldon (Danbury). 4.5 miles, through Danbury into Woodham Mortimer. Over 1st roundabout, 1st left, pub on left. Behind golf driving range.***

This family-run pub slumbers contentedly in tranquil countryside just inland from Maldon's creeks and sea-marshes. Posts and beams inside hint at the age of the building, which is much older than its first licence in 1837. There's an enormous garden here, dappled with ancient fruit trees; an ideal location for their June beer festival. Year-round treats on the bar include beers from Dark Star and Wibblers, who also provide the local cider. The consummate menu covers all bases.

Open all day, all week 12–11 (Sun 12–9) Gray & Sons 8 portions/menu Wi-fi

ROSETTES AND STARS

Stay the night

Many of the pubs in this guide have been inspected and rated for their hotel or guest accommodation by the AA.

To find out more about the accommodation ratings see pages 10–11.

Eat well

Rosette awards appear where the restaurant at the pub has been inspected for the quality of their cuisine.

To find out more about the Rosette award scheme see pages 12-13.

GLOUCESTERSHIRE

ALDERTON

The Gardeners Arms

Tel **01242 620257** | **Beckford Road, GL20 8NL**
Web **www.gardenersarms.biz**
Dir ***M5 junction 6, A46 towards Evesham. At roundabout take B4077 signed Stow. Left to Alderton.***

Operating as a pub since the 16th century, this pretty, family-run, thatched free house is popular with walkers, cyclists and car clubs. You can play boules in the large beer garden, and traditional games in the stone-walled bar, where Cotswold Way numbers among the real ales.

ALMONDSBURY

The Swan Hotel

Tel **01454 625671** | **14 Gloucester Road, BS32 4AA**
Web **www.swanhotelbristol.com**
Dir ***M5 junction 16, A38 to Almondsbury.***

Dating back in part to the 16th century, this former coaching inn on the outskirts of Bristol enjoys a fine hilltop setting with views of the Bristol Channel. The daily menu might kick off with lamb koftas with minted yogurt, and you could follow that with a steak – perhaps an 8oz ribeye, or 12oz rump – or maybe confit belly pork, fondant potato, crackling, beetroot and blue cheese emulsion; a fish finger bun; or hake fillet with squid ink pasta. There's a beer and cider festival in July.

Open all day, all week Marston's 18 portions/menu Wi-fi P notice required

AMBERLEY

The Amberley Inn ★★★★ INN

Tel **01453 872565** | **Culver Hill, GL5 5AF**
Web **www.theamberleyinn.co.uk**
Dir ***From A46 follow signs for Amberley, up Culver Hill, in village centre on left.***

This 19th-century inn is located in a Cotswold village on the edge of the National Trust-owned Minchinhampton Common. Original oak-panelled rooms, mullioned windows and roaring log fires provide a timeless setting to enjoy pints of Stroud-brewed Tom Long ale or Old Rosie cider. The pub's close proximity to Gatcombe Park Estate ensures a consistent supply of top-quality meat for the appealing menus. Typical dishes are crispy aromatic duck salad with plum sauce; and garlic and rosemary marinated rump of lamb with dauphinoise potatoes.

Open all day, all week Free House 12 portions/menu Wi-fi P notice required

BARNSLEY

The Village Pub – see opposite

BERKELEY

The Malt House – see page 176

BIBURY

Catherine Wheel 

Tel **01285 740250** | **Arlington, GL7 5ND**
Web **www.catherinewheel-bibury.co.uk**
Dir ***On B4425, west of Bibury.***

The beautiful Cotswold-stone building, stable courtyard and orchard date back to the 15th century but plenty of historical features remain. This former blacksmith's has changed hands many times since it opened as an inn in 1856 but a warm welcome, a good selection of accredited ales such as Hook Norton and quality food remain its hallmarks. The appetising menu might include smoked haddock and chive fishcake; and whole Bibury trout along with classics such as steak and red wine pie; and Gloucester Old Spot sausages and mash.

Open all day, all week 9am–11pm Free House 9 from £11 portions/menu Wi-fi P notice required

BIRDLIP

The Golden Heart

Tel **01242 870261** | **Nettleton Bottom, GL4 8LA**
Web **www.thegoldenheart.co.uk**
Dir ***On A417, 8 miles from Cheltenham. Pub at base of dip in Nettleton Bottom.***

Once a drovers' resting place, this lovely 17th-century Cotswold-stone inn boasts stunning views of the valley from the terraced gardens. The main bar is divided into four cosy areas with log fires and settles. Excellent local ales and ciders are backed by a good selection of wines, while the kitchen is committed to using local produce.

Open all day, all week Free House 10 portions/menu Wi-fi P

BARNSLEY

The Village Pub

★★★★★ INN

Tel **01285 740421** | **GL7 5EF**
Web **www.thevillagepub.co.uk**
Dir ***On B4425, 4 miles north-east of Cirencester.***

Non-touristy traditional local in an Area of Outstanding Natural Beauty

Part of the Calcot Collection, The Village Pub's interior is warmly furnished and decorated, as befits the flagstones, oak floorboards, exposed timbers and open fireplaces. Also contributing to its appeal is a contemporary approach to English pub food, holder of an AA Dinner Award, with regularly-changing, largely locally-sourced menus. Vegetables, for example, come from 17th-century Barnsley House across the road. A carefully curated board of British cheeses might include Cotswold-made Simon Weaver Brie or award-winning Perl Las blue cheese from Wales. Bar snacks of quail and black pudding Scotch eggs or onion bhaji and pickle go well with a pint of North Cotswold Shagweaver or Mortimers Orchard cider, or perhaps one of the many wines served by the glass from a concise but interesting list.

Open all day, all week all week 7am–11pm
Free House portions notice required

BISLEY

The Bear Inn

Tel **01452 770265** | **George Street, GL6 7BD**
Web **www.bisleybear.co.uk**
Dir ***Phone for detailed directions.***

There has been a pub here for almost 400 years. Stories and legends abound here and there is even a priest hole halfway up the inglenook fireplace. The pub's original character and charm is still evident. There are weekly pie specials and Tuesday night curries.

BLAISDON

The Red Hart Inn

Tel **01452 830477** | **GL17 0AH**
Web **www.redhartinn.co.uk**
Dir ***Take A40 (north-west of Gloucester) towards Ross-on-Wye. At lights left onto A4136 signed Monmouth. Left into Blaisdon Lane to Blaisdon.***

This dog-friendly pub exudes the charm of a village local, all flagstones, log fire and low beams. Guest ales whet the whistle, whilst diners will appreciate the quality pork raised by the pub's owners. Locally sourced produce appears on the menu and daily specials such as braised Hereford beef in ale and dumplings. The large garden is ideal for families in summer, as is the more secluded patio.

Open all week 12–3 6–11.30 (Sun 12–3.30 6.30–11)
Free House from £10 portions/menu Wi-fi
notice required

BERKELEY

The Malt House ★★★ INN

Tel **01453 511177** | **Marybrook Street, GL13 9BA**
Web **www.themalthouse.uk.com**
Dir ***M5 junction 13/14, A38 towards Bristol. Pub on main road towards Sharpness.***

Close to a variety of historic attractions

The little town of Berkeley is where you'll find 12th-century Berkeley Castle, scene of the imprisonment and eventual murder of King Edward II in 1327, and still home to the Berkeley family, who've lived there since 1153. The town is also home to a museum devoted to immunologist Edward Jenner, who pioneered the smallpox vaccine and was born here in 1749. The Malt House is a traditional and popular free house, usefully located for walkers on the Severn Way that runs along the river's highly scenic estuary shoreline, as well as for visitors to the nearby Slimbridge Wetland Centre. Once ensconced in the copiously beamed old bar, consider a menu rich with classic and modern British dishes, represented by a starter of black pudding glazed with Stilton; and main courses of pork steak with forestière sauce; sizzling chilli beef; halibut steak with lime and butter; and roasted vegetable lasagne, one of several vegetarian options. In addition, are grilled steaks, curries, a sausage board, daily specials and a busy Sunday carvery. Comfortable bed and breakfast accommodation is available for those wishing to stay in the area.

Open all week Mon to Thu 6–11 (Fri 5–12 Sat 12–12 Sun 12–3) Free House portions/menu notice required

BLEDINGTON

The Kings Head Inn

★★★★ INN PICK OF THE PUBS

Tel **01608 658365** | **The Green, OX7 6XQ**
Web **www.kingsheadinn.net**
Dir ***On B4450, 4 miles from Stow-on-the-Wold.***

Facing the village green, this stone-built pub dates back to the 15th century; it's been called the quintessential Cotswolds inn. It's axiomatic that people make pubs – on both sides of the bar. They certainly do here. On one side, long-term owners Archie and Nicola Orr-Ewing; on the other, their customers, drawn by a reputation for well-kept real ales and top-quality food. Original structure survives in the low-beamed ceilings, flagstone floors, exposed stone walls and an inglenook fireplace. In the bar you'll find Hooky Bitter, Purity Gold and Wye Valley alongside local lagers; 11 wines are served by the glass. Among choices in the restaurant are deep-fried Windrush goats' cheese salad; vodka-and-tonic soft-shell crab; wood pigeon tart; seafood and saffron risotto; and Tamworth pork and black pudding burger.

Open all day, all week Closed 25-26 Dec Free House 11 portions/menu Wi-fi P

BOURTON-ON-THE-HILL

Horse and Groom ★★★★ INN

PICK OF THE PUBS

Tel **01386 700413** | **GL56 9AQ**
Web **www.horseandgroom.info**
Dir ***2 miles west of Moreton-in-Marsh on A44.***

This handsome Grade II listed Cotswold stone pub is both a serious dining destination and a friendly place for a drink. The building combines a contemporary feel with plenty of original period features and the mature garden is a must-visit in summer with its panoramic hilltop views. With committed local suppliers backed up by the pub's own abundant vegetable patch, the kitchen has plenty of good produce to work with.

Open all week 12–11 (Sun 12–10.30) Free House 14 portions Wi-fi P *notice required*

BROCKHAMPTON

Craven Arms Inn

Tel **01242 820410** | **GL54 5XQ**
Web **www.thecravenarms.co.uk**
Dir ***From Cheltenham take A40 towards Gloucester. In Andoversford, at lights, left onto A436 signed Bourton and Stow. Left, follow signs for Brockhampton.***

This set-back, gabled old village inn glows with mellow honeyed stone; log fires, beams and mullioned windows add to the charm of its setting beneath the gently undulating horizon of the Cotswolds. Drinkers appreciate the selection of real ales; ciders and perry from regional orchards.

CHELTENHAM

The Gloucester Old Spot

Tel **01242 680321** | **Tewkesbury Road, Piff's Elm, GL51 9SY**
Web **www.thegloucesteroldspot.co.uk**
Dir ***On A4019 on outskirts of Cheltenham towards Tewkesbury.***

With its quarry tile floors, roaring log fires, farmhouse furnishings and real ales such as Wye Valley, this free house ticks all the boxes. Local ciders and perries are on offer at the bar, and the baronial dining room takes its inspiration from the local manor. The lovely gardens are just the place for enjoying a drink or lunch.

Open all day, all week Closed 25–26 Dec Free House portions/menu Wi-fi P *notice required*

The Royal Oak Inn

Tel **01242 522344** | **The Burgage, Prestbury, GL52 3DL**
Web **www.royal-oak-prestbury.co.uk**
Dir ***From town centre follow signs for Winchcombe/ Prestbury and Racecourse. In Prestbury follow brown signs for inn from Tatchley Lane.***

Close to the racecourse, this 16th-century pub offers well-kept cask ales and delicious food in the snug, the comfortable dining room or the heated patio. Menus and blackboard specials might list roast lamb chump with mustard and rosemary crust; and a spicy chickpea burger. There is a beer and sausage festival on the Spring Bank Holiday and a cider festival on the Summer Bank Holiday.

Open all day, all week Butcombe 14 from £13 portions/menu Wi-fi P *notice required*

Sandford Park Alehouse

Tel **01242 574517** | **GL50 1DZ**
Web **www.spalehouse.co.uk**
Dir ***South-east end of High Street.***

The large garden of this handsome Grade II listed pub backs on to Sandford Park with its landscaped gardens and lido. A pub that takes its beers very seriously, there are 10 hand pumps and 16 taps set aside for ale, not to mention around 100 bottled beers. The beer theme continues with the food, which might include Flemish stew of beef shin, slowly cooked in Belgian brown ale; or haddock fried in Belgian beer batter.

Open all day, all week Closed 25–26 Dec, 1 Jan Free House 10 from £7.95 notice required

CHIPPING CAMPDEN

The Bakers Arms

Tel **01386 840515** | **Broad Campden, GL55 6UR**
Web **www.bakersarmscampden.com**
Dir ***1 mile from Chipping Campden.***

Ease into the compact bar here, squeeze into a space near the eye-catching inglenook and live the Cotswold dream, with local Stanney Bitter mirroring the colour of the mellow thatched cottages in this delightful picture-postcard hamlet. The patio, terrace and garden are all ideal for warm summer evenings.

6 GLOUCESTERSHIRE PUBS WITH ACCOMMODATION

The following pubs are rated as part of the AA Guest Accommodation scheme (see page 10–11 for more information).

The Feathered Nest Country Inn ★★★★★ INN Nether Westcote, *see page 184*

The Porch House ★★★★★ INN Stow-On-The-Wold, *see page 188*

The Slaughters Country Inn ★★★★★ INN Lower Slaughter, *see page 183*

The Village Pub ★★★★★ INN Barnsley, *see page 175*

The Ebrington Arms ★★★★ INN Ebrington, *see page 181*

The Green Dragon Inn ★★★★ INN Cowley, *see page 182*

The Kings ★★★★ @@@

RESTAURANT WITH ROOMS | PICK OF THE PUBS

Tel **01386 840256** | **The Square, GL55 6AW**
Web **www.kingscampden.co.uk**
Dir ***Phone for detailed directions.***

Packed with character, this sympathetically restored, 16th-century building surveys the square in one of England's most appealing market towns. Good then to find on entering the bar – in addition to the real ales, of course – are the daily papers, traditional pub games and a fine range of snacks, baguettes and sandwiches. The Jackrabbit Restaurant, with golden-stone walls, beamed ceilings and a huge candlelit fireplace sets the scene for such culinary delights as roasted cod loin with braised barley, chicken wing, smoked squash and barbecued leeks; poached guinea fowl breast with slow-cooked leg, celeriac and bacon; roast loin of Cornish hake with oat-crumbed mussels, saffron potatoes and bouillabaisse.

Open all day, all week 7am–11pm (Sat to Sun 8am–11pm) Free House 10 portions/menu notice required

The Noel Arms ★★★★ INN

PICK OF THE PUBS

Tel **01386 840317** | **High Street, GL55 6AT**
Web **www.noelarmshotel.com**
Dir ***On High Street, opposite Town Hall.***

The Noel Arms is one of the oldest hotels in the Cotswolds (Charles II stayed here once, or so it's said), a place where traditional appeal has been successfully preserved and interwoven seamlessly with contemporary comforts. It was through the carriage arch that packhorse trains used to carry bales of wool, the source of Chipping Campden's prosperity, to Bristol and Southampton. Absorb these details of the hotel's history while sipping a pint of North Cotswold Brewery's Windrush Ale in front of the log fire in Dover's Bar; read the papers over a coffee and pastry in the coffee shop; and enjoy brasserie-style food in the restaurant. Curry is a big thing here, with the Curry Club (held on the last Thursday evening of the month) proving extremely popular.

Open all day, all week Free House 10 portions/menu

The Seagrave Arms

★★★★ INN PICK OF THE PUBS

Tel **01386 840192** | **Friday Street, Weston Subedge, GL55 6QH**
Web **www.seagravearms.co.uk**
Dir ***From Moreton-in-Marsh take A44 towards Evesham. 7 miles, right onto B4081 to Chipping Campden. Left at junction with High Street. 0.5 mile, straight on at crossroads to Weston Subedge. Left at T-junction.***

Built as a farmhouse around 1740, this handsome Grade II listed Cotswold stone building is approached between a display of neatly trimmed, globe-shaped bushes in stone planters. In the bar you'll find real ales from Hook Norton and the same menu is served in the bar and the two AA Rosette restaurant, with a garden and sheltered courtyard offering alfresco dining options. Local sourcing and sustainability are the basic tenets behind compact seasonal menus.

The Volunteer Inn

Tel **01386 840688** | **Lower High Street, GL55 6DY**
Web **www.thevolunteerinn.net**
Dir ***From Shipston-on-Stour take B4035 to Chipping Campden.***

The beautiful, honey-coloured Cotswold stone glowing on Chipping Campden's main street continues within; the convivial, log-fire warmed stone-floored bar a welcoming retreat for guests hunting through the town's antique shops or pausing on a stroll along the Cotswold Way.

CIRENCESTER

The Crown of Crucis

PICK OF THE PUBS

Tel **01285 851806** | **Ampney Crucis, GL7 5RS**
Web **www.thecrownofcrucis.co.uk**
Dir ***On A417 to Lechlade, 2 miles east of Cirencester.***

Five minutes' drive out of Cirencester will bring you to this 16th-century former coaching inn; it overlooks a cricket green, and Ampney Brook meanders past its lawns. Its name is derived from the 'crucis' or ancient cross in the churchyard. Although modernised, the interior still feels old, and the traditional beams and log fires create a warm, friendly atmosphere. Atlantic and Wickwar are among the real ales, along with some 17 wines served by the glass. Sandwiches, salads, pastas and grills are served from midday, while in the evening the restaurant's dinner menu proffers popular pub dishes such as starters of breaded whitebait with salad and tartare sauce; followed by a dish from the chargrill stove: pan-fried calves' liver with crispy bacon, bubble-and-squeak cake and Madeira sauce.

Open all day, all week Closed 25 Dec Free House 17 portions/menu notice required

CLEEVE HILL

The Rising Sun

Tel **01242 676281** | **GL52 3PX**
Web **www.oldenglish.co.uk**
Dir ***On B4632, 4 miles north of Cheltenham.***

On a clear day you can see south Wales from this Victorian property on Cleeve Hill, which also boasts views across Cheltenham and the Malverns. Settle in the bar or out in the garden, which is well furnished with trestle tables and benches.

COATES

The Tunnel House Inn

PICK OF THE PUBS

Tel **01285 770702** | **Tarlton Road, GL7 6PW**
Web **www.tunnelhouse.com**
Dir ***A433 from Cirencester towards Tetbury, 2 miles, right towards Coates, follow brown inn signs.***

This inn was built in the 1770s to cater for navvies constructing the Thames & Severn Canal, and leggers who propelled the barges through the Sapperton Tunnel. The eclectic design of the interior has changed little over the last 30 years despite the pub being in new hands – witness the stuffed otters and weasels, redundant dentists' chairs, copper pans and old advertising signs. Nothing too out of the ordinary on the menu though, as demonstrated by fish, chips and marrowfat mushy peas; Gloucester Old Spot sausage and mash; honey-roast ham, eggs and chips; grilled fillet of sea bass; and steaks and salads. Relax in the garden while the children safely play.

Open all day, all week 12–11 Free House 8 portions/menu

COLD ASTON

The Plough Inn

Tel **01451 822602 | GL54 3BN**
Web **www.coldastonplough.com**
Dir ***In village centre.***

Nick and Laura Avery successfully run the 17th-century Plough, whose Cotswold flagstones, oak beams and big open fire make it look and feel very welcoming. Rotating real ales, such as local Stroud Budding, are served from casks, and there are real ciders, too. Try devilled lamb's kidneys on toast; local Windrush Farm lamb chop; or beer-battered haddock, chips and crushed peas; then hot chocolate fondant. A charcoal oven cooks perfect steaks and fish.

Open all day, all week 10am–11pm Free House 12 from £13.50 portions/menu Wi-fi P notice required

COLEFORD

The Dog & Muffler Inn – see below

COLESBOURNE

The Colesbourne Inn

Tel **01242 870376 | GL53 9NP**
Web **www.thecolesbourneinn.co.uk**
Dir ***Midway between Cirencester and Cheltenham on A435.***

This handsome, stone-built inn is just a short meadow walk from the source of the Thames; you can sit in the two-acre grounds with a pint of Wadworth 6X or Swordfish and savour the glorious country views. Dating back to 1827, the inn oozes historic charm and character with its original beams and roaring log fires aplenty. The seasonal menus combine traditional pub classics, including fish and chips, with modern ideas.

Open all day, all week Wadworth 20 portions Wi-fi P notice required

COWLEY

The Green Dragon Inn – see page 182

COLEFORD

The Dog & Muffler Inn

Tel **01594 832444 | Joyford, Berry Hill, GL16 7AS**
Dir ***Phone for detailed directions.***

Lovely garden with views

Set in the ancient and beautiful Forest of Dean, where wild boar and deer roam free, The Dog & Muffler was once a cider house with its own orchard and cider press; the press can still be seen in the large garden. It's a little off the beaten track, and as you approach, it rather hides itself between a weeping willow and a cypress. Once there, though, this one-time favourite watering hole of *Pennies From Heaven* dramatist Dennis Potter is a delight, as you mingle with locals supping pints of Wye Valley ale or one of several ciders. The seasonally-changing menu offers dishes such as liver and bacon; barbecued pork loin with bourbon sauce; duck with Morello cherry and red wine sauce; caramelised shallot tarte Tatin with marinated goats' cheese; and their prize-winning pies.

Open all year 12–3.30 6–11.30 Closed Mon Free House 14 from £9.95 portions/menu P notice required

CRANHAM

The Black Horse Inn

Tel **01452 812217** | **GL4 8HP**
Dir ***A46 towards Stroud, follow signs for Cranham.***

Near the Cotswold Way and the Benedictine Prinknash Abbey, in a small village surrounded by woodland and commons, this inn is popular with walkers, the cricket team and visiting Morris dancers. Traditional pub food is served as well as a lunchtime bar menu.

DURSLEY

The Old Spot Inn PICK OF THE PUBS

Tel **01453 542870** | **Hill Road, GL11 4JQ**
Web **www.oldspotinn.co.uk**
Dir ***From Tetbury on A4135 (or Uley on B4066) into Dursley, round Town Hall. Straight on at lights towards bus station, pub behind bus station. Or from Cam to lights in Dursley immediately prior to pedestrianised street. Right towards bus station.***

This classic 18th-century free house is a real ale champion, so it's worth a visit to savour the tip-top brews on hand pump. The pub sits smack on the Cotswold Way, and is formed from three terraced farm cottages known as 'pig row'. The Ale festival held in May also showcases ciders, and fans of fermented apple juice enjoy the weekly alternating choice at the bar.

Open all day, all week 12–11 Free House 8 portions notice required

EBRINGTON

The Ebrington Arms

★★★★ INN PICK OF THE PUBS

Tel **01386 593223** | **GL55 6NH**
Web **www.theebringtonarms.co.uk**
Dir ***From Chipping Campden on B4035 towards Shipston on Stour. Left to Ebrington signed after 0.5 mile.***

The large inglenook fireplaces of this charming old pub recall the building's days as the village bakery. Built in 1640, it's an award-winning Cotswold gem with an abundance of character thanks to the heavy beams and original flagstones in both the bar and Old Bakehouse dining room. Drinkers are spoilt for choice as the pub brews three of its own beers: Yubberton Yubby, Yawnie and Goldie, which sit alongside others such as Stroud's and Hogans cider, as well as more than a dozen whiskies. Recognised with two AA Rosettes, the pub's menu offers the likes belly of pork, spring cabbage, chorizo and creamed potato, with pistachio iced parfait, almond and blackberry to finish.

Open all day, all week noon to close Free House 9 portions/menu notice required

FRAMPTON MANSELL

The Crown Inn ★★★★ INN

PICK OF THE PUBS

Tel **01285 760601** | **GL6 8JG**
Web **www.thecrowninn-cotswolds.co.uk**
Dir ***A419 halfway between Cirencester and Stroud.***

Right in the heart of the village, the Crown is surrounded by the peace and quiet of the Golden Valley. Once a simple cider house, it's a classic 17th-century Cotswold-stone inn full of old-world charm, with honey-coloured stone walls and open fireplaces where logs blaze in winter. Gloucestershire beers, such as Stroud Organic and Laurie Lee's Bitter, are usually showcased alongside others from the region, and a good choice of wines by the glass is served in the restaurant and three inviting bars. Fresh local food with lots of seasonal specials is what you'll find on the menu – start with a tasty smoked haddock, leek and pearl barley risotto with a poached egg, followed by curried chicken Kiev with home-made mango chutney and cauliflower biryani.

Open all day, all week 12–11 Closed 25 Dec Free House 13 from £12 portions

GLOUCESTER

Queens Head

Tel **01452 301882** | **Tewkesbury Road, Longford, GL2 9EJ**
Web **queensheadlongford.co.uk**
Dir ***On A38 (Tewkesbury to Gloucester road) in Longford.***

This pretty 250-year-old half-timbered pub and restaurant is just out of town, but cannot be missed in summer when it is festooned with hanging baskets. The owners believe in giving their diners high-quality, freshly prepared food that is great value for money.

COWLEY

The Green Dragon Inn

★★★★ INN

Tel **01242 870271 | Cockleford, GL53 9NW**
Web **www.green-dragon-inn.co.uk**
Dir ***Phone for detailed directions.***

Cotswolds inn featuring Mouseman furniture

With a pretty rose and creeper-covered Cotswold-stone façade, this building was recorded as an inn in 1675. However, it was 1710 before Robert Jones, a churchwarden, became the first landlord, splitting his time between pews and pulling pints for the next 31 years. Today ,the secluded patio overlooking a lake is the obvious spot to head for in summer. Step inside the stone-flagged Mouse Bar and you'll notice that each piece of English oak furniture features a carved mouse, the trademark of Robert Thompson, the Mouseman of Kilburn. He may have died in 1955, but North Yorkshire craftsmen continue the tradition. A range of lunchtime sandwiches is on offer, while the comfortable, individually furnished en suite bedrooms, and the St George's Suite, make the Green Dragon the ideal base for exploring the Cotswolds.

Open all day, all week Closed 24 and 25 Dec evening and 1 Jan evening *Free House* *12* *from £12.95* *menus*

GREAT BARRINGTON

The Fox Inn PICK OF THE PUBS

Tel **01451 844385 | OX18 4TB**
Web **www.foxinnbarrington.com**
Dir ***From Burford take A40 towards Northleach. In 3 miles right signed The Barringtons, pub approximately 0.5 mile on right.***

With a garden overlooking the River Windrush, this busy old former coaching house is a perfect base for lovely walks and cycle rides in summer. The pub is popular with race-goers visiting Cheltenham, and the bar offers a range of well-kept Donnington beers. The conservatory dining bar and alfresco eating area contribute to the friendly and relaxed atmosphere. The menu might offer slow-cooked knuckle of Cotswold lamb with rosemary sautéed potatoes and seasonal vegetables, and vegetarians are well catered for, with typical dishes including brie, spinach and cranberry Wellington. Barbecues and pig roasts are held in summer.

Open all day, all week 11am–close *Donnington Brewery* *portions* Wi-fi

HAM

The Salutation Inn

Tel **01453 810284 | GL13 9QH**
Web **www.the-sally-at-ham.com**
Dir ***South of Berkeley towards Stone.***

Landlord Peter Tiley says "What makes the Sally so special isn't the range of quality ales and ciders, the heritage pub games, the humble bar snacks, the cosy bars with log fires, or the genuine community spirit. It's something intangible".

HINTON

The Bull at Hinton

Tel **0117 937 2332 | SN14 8HG**
Web **www.thebullathinton.co.uk**
Dir ***From M4 junction 18, A46 to Bath, 1 mile turn right 1 mile, down hill. Pub on right.***

Just 20 minutes from Bath and Bristol, this 17th-century, stone-built former farmhouse and dairy is packed with character, with beams in the bar and dining room, flagstone floors, inglenook fireplaces, old pews and big oak tables. Meals are prepared using local ingredients and home-grown produce.

LECHLADE ON THAMES

The Trout Inn

Tel **01367 252313** | **St Johns Bridge, GL7 3HA**
Web **www.thetroutinn.com**
Dir ***A40 onto A361 then A417. From M4 junction 15, A419, then A361 and A417 to Lechlade.***

Built by the workmen constructing a new bridge over the Thames in 1220, The Trout became an inn in 1472, and its flagstone floors and beams reflect its history. There's an extensive menu, with smaller portions for children, who also have their own separate menu. The large garden often hosts live jazz, an annual steam week and a beer festival, (both in June), plus a Riverfolk festival in July.

Open all day, all week 11–11 Enterprise Inns 15 portions/menu Wi-fi P notice required

LEIGHTERTON

The Royal Oak

Tel **01666 890250** | **1 The Street, GL8 8UN**
Web **www.royaloakleighterton.co.uk**
Dir ***M4 junction 18, A46 towards Stroud. After Dunkirk continue on A46. Right signed Leighterton.***

Set in a picture-postcard Cotswold village, this pub thrives as a popular dining venue. The contemporary bar and dining room successfully blends antiques with modern furnishings. Food is classic British and everything is made on the premises from local ingredients.

LONGHOPE

The Glasshouse Inn

Tel **01452 830529** | **May Hill, GL17 0NN**
Web **www.glasshouselodges.co.uk**
Dir ***From A40 approximately 8 miles south-east of Ross-on-Wye, follow signs for May Hill. Through May Hill to pub on left.***

The Glasshouse gets its name from Dutch glassmakers who settled locally in the 16th century but its origins go back to 1450. It's located in a fabulous rural setting with a garden and an elegant interior. The inn serves a range of real ales including Butcombe and Sharp's Doom Bar, plus home-cooked dishes such as fish pie; and steak and kidney served in Yorkshire puddings.

Open all year 11.30–3 7–11 (Sun 12–3) Closed Sun evening, Mon, Tue lunch Free House 11 Wi-fi P

LOWER SLAUGHTER

The Slaughters Country Inn

★★★★★ INN PICK OF THE PUBS

Tel **01451 822143** | **GL54 2HS**
Web **www.theslaughtersinn.co.uk**
Dir ***Between Stow-on-the-Wold and Bourton-on-the-Water on A429 follow 'The Slaughters' signs.***

Formerly Washbourne Court, and once a crammer school for Eton, this handsome inn stands close to the River Eye. Well positioned for exploring the Cotswolds, Bourton-on-the-Water is within walking distance and Cheltenham is only a 30-minute drive away. The spacious beamed bar and stone mullioned windows are a good example of how to successfully balance the appealing qualities of a 17th-century building with the demands of the 21st century. Food ranges from sandwiches and light bites to a chargrilled Hereford flat iron steak with watercress and fries. In between might come braised ham hock croquette with parsley mayonnaise and sauce gribiche; followed by roast cod with wet polenta, samphire and chorizo, with caper confit. A final flourish might be cherry cheesecake and pistachio ice cream.

Open all day, all week Free House 9 from £12.50 portions/menu Wi-fi P notice required

MARSHFIELD

The Catherine Wheel

Tel **01225 892220** | **39 High Street, SN14 8LR**
Web **www.thecatherinewheel.co.uk**
Dir ***M4 junction 18, A46 signed Bath. Left onto A420 signed Chippenham. Right signed Marshfield.***

On the edge of the Cotswolds, this mainly 17th-century inn has the expected exposed brickwork and large open fireplaces offset by a simple, stylish decor. The patio is a lovely spot for a summertime pint of Butcombe Bitter or Thatchers cider.

MEYSEY HAMPTON

The Masons Arms

Tel **01285 850164** | **28 High Street, GL7 5JT**
Web **www.masonsarmsmeyseyhampton.com**
Dir ***6 miles east of Cirencester off A417, beside village green.***

Sitting proudly on the village green in the heart of a Cotswolds village, this 17th-century, stone-built inn used to be owner Paul Fallows' local pub. Now running it, he has transformed it into a bustling community pub with a warming log fire in the large inglenook, and well-kept Arkell's ales and Thatchers ciders in the convivial beamed bar. Good value home-made food includes coconut and chilli steamed mussels; and pan-roasted duck breast, mustard mash and cherry jus.

Open all day, all week 8.30–3 5–11 (Sat to Sun all day) Arkell's 12 portions/menu Wi-fi notice required

MINCHINHAMPTON

The Weighbridge Inn – see opposite

NETHER WESTCOTE

The Feathered Nest Country Inn ★★★★★ INN

PICK OF THE PUBS

Tel **01993 833030** | **OX7 6SD**
Web **www.thefeatherednestinn.co.uk**
Dir ***A424 between Burford and Stow-on-the-Wold, follow signs.***

The views over the Evenlode Valley from this old malthouse in picturesque Nether Westcote are marvellous. Thoughtfully designed, the inn retains its original character, especially in the log-fired bar, where rotating local real ales – maybe Severn Vale's Nibley or Prescott's Hill Climb – can be found. Local produce forms the backbone of the modern British menus, with herbs and vegetables grown in the kitchen garden. The seasonal carte's take on classic combinations includes salmon with beetroot, black garlic and dill; chicken, girolles, sweetcorn and almond; sticky toffee pudding, clotted cream, lemon and pecans. Look out for the events that run throughout the year, including jazz evenings, flower workshops and a vintage car rally.

Open all day Closed 25 Dec, Mon, Tue, Wed Free House 19 portions/menu Wi-fi P

NEWENT

Kilcot Inn ★★★★ INN

Tel **01989 720707** | **Ross Road, Kilcot, GL18 1NA**
Web **www.kilcotinn.com**
Dir ***M50 junction 3, B4221 signed Newent. Approximately 2 miles to pub on left.***

A restored country inn on the borders of Gloucestershire and Herefordshire, the Kilcot offers the best traditions of hospitality, food and drink. From the selection of local real ales and ciders on tap to the high quality produce used in the dishes, there is something for everyone.

Open all day, all week Closed 26 Dec and 1 Jan Free House from £14.50 portions/menu Wi-fi P notice required

NORTH CERNEY

The Bathurst Arms – see page 186

NORTHLEACH

The Wheatsheaf Inn

Tel **01451 860244** | **West End, GL54 3EZ**
Web **theluckyonion.com/property/the-wheatsheaf**
Dir ***Just off A40 between Oxford and Cheltenham.***

A beautiful 17th-century Cotswold-stone inn on the square of the pretty former wool town of Northleach, The Wheatsheaf is everything anyone could wish for, with flagstone floors, beams, log fires and a vibrant, smartened-up feel throughout.

OLDBURY-ON-SEVERN

The Anchor Inn

Tel **01454 413331** | **Church Road, BS35 1QA**
Web **www.anchorinnoldbury.co.uk**
Dir ***From south: A38 through Thornbury.***

The stone-built Anchor is almost 500 years old, and you can see some of its more recent history in the old photos and bric à brac in the bar. There are guest real ales, Ashton ciders, perries and 16 wines by the glass. On the good-value menus you'll find baked lasagne; Kashmiri lamb curry; Spanish fish stew; chicken and ham pie; and butternut squash, red onion and cranberry tagine.

Open all week Mon to Thu 11.30–2.30 6–10.30 (Fri to Sat 11.30–11 Sun 12–10) Free House 16 menus Wi-fi P notice required

MINCHINHAMPTON

The Weighbridge Inn

Tel **01453 832520** | **GL6 9AL**
Web **www.weighbridgeinn.co.uk**
Dir ***On B4014 between Nailsworth and Avening.***

Recommended for its freshly made pies

PICK OF THE PUBS

Parts of this whitewashed free house date back to the 17th century, when it stood adjacent to the original packhorse trail between Bristol and London. While the trail is now a footpath and bridleway, the road in front (now the B4014) became a turnpike in the 1820s. The innkeeper at the time ran both the pub and the weighbridge for the local woollen mills – serving jugs of ale in between making sure tolls were paid. Associated memorabilia and other rural artefacts from the time are displayed around the inn, which has been carefully renovated to retain original features, like exposed brick walls and cosy open log fires. Up in the restaurant, which used to be the hayloft, the old roof timbers reach almost to the floor. The inn prides itself on its decent ales and ciders, and the quality of its food, with everything cooked from scratch.The Weighbridge is also the home of 'the famous 2 in 1 pies', one half containing a filling of your choice from a selection of seven (such as steak and mushroom, or chicken, ham and leek) and topped with pastry, the other half home-made cauliflower cheese – all baked to order. The pub has a peaceful, sheltered garden, the perfect place to while away a summer's afternoon.

Open all day, all week 12–10 (Fri to Sat 12–11, Sun 12–10.30) Closed 25 Dec Free House 15 from £11.95 portions/menu notice required

NORTH CERNEY

The Bathurst Arms

Tel **01285 832150** | **GL7 7BZ**
Web **www.bathurstarms.co.uk**
Dir ***Just off A435.***

Smart and characterful Cotswold inn

This distinctive pale pink pub sits in the pretty village of North Cerney, which has a Grade I listed church and is set in the Churn Valley, deep in the Cotswolds Area of Outstanding Natural Beauty. Now refurbished, it's a stylish, charming and cosy place, with wooden and tiled floors, exposed stone walls, mismatched furniture, fine panelling and several very impressive stone fireplaces, complete with woodburners. Menus might offer wild boar terrine with toast and chutney, followed by lamb shank with mashed potato and gravy; or roast chicken breast with port and fig sauce. Save room for pudding – perhaps carrot or chocolate fudge cake with cream, ice cream or custard; profiteroles; or caramel and peanut tart. Children have their own menu, and there's a large garden for alfresco drinking and dining.

Open all day, all week Free House 10 from £11 portions/menu notice required

PAINSWICK

The Falcon Inn  INN

Tel **01452 814222** | **New Street, GL6 6UN**
Web **www.falconpainswick.co.uk**
Dir ***On A46 in centre of Painswick, opposite St Mary's church.***

Dating from 1554, this pub spent more than 200 years as a courthouse in this old wool town, and occupies a lovely spot, opposite the church with its iconic yew trees. Expect a good choice of local real ales, including Hook Norton, Wye Valley HPA and various guest ales. A typical dinner might start with a Greek-inspired sharing platter before moving on to blade of beef and bean cassoulet with dauphinoise potatoes.

Open all day, all week 10am–11pm Parsnip Inns Ltd 10 portions/menu Wi-fi notice required

POULTON

The Falcon Inn PICK OF THE PUBS

Tel **01285 851597** | **London Road, GL7 5HN**
Web **www.falconinnpoulton.co.uk**
Dir ***From Cirencester 4 miles east on A417 towards Fairford.***

Slap-bang in the middle of this pretty Cotswold village, with its lovely stone cottages, the Falcon is a charming old pub, run with passion and enthusiasm. You can expect genuine dedication to local produce, ensuring a reliable pint of real ale from some of the area's independent breweries, enjoyed in a pub that marries contemporary comforts with age-old tradition. The fresh, vibrant menu changes every month to make the most of what's available locally. The set price lunch menu is great value, while the à la carte offers more options. Kick things off with mixed game terrine followed by braised beef cheek. There's a good range of steaks as well, and for dessert you could go for peanut parfait, caramelised banana and chocolate sorbet.

Open Tue to Sat 12–3 5–11 (Sun 12–4) Closed 25 Dec, Mon Free House 11 menus Wi-fi

SAPPERTON

The Bell at Sapperton

PICK OF THE PUBS

Tel **01285 760298** | **GL7 6LE**
Web **www.bellsapperton.co.uk**
Dir ***From A419 between Cirencester and Stroud follow Sapperton signs.***

The Cotswold stone exterior of this village inn has been quietly mellowing for over 300 years. Still gently maturing are the beamed ceilings, unrendered walls, polished flags, bare boards and open fireplaces inside. The menu also displays variety, with nibbles and sharing boards to start. Meals are served in four cosy dining areas, each with its own individual character. A secluded rear courtyard and a landscaped front garden make fine-weather alfresco dining a pleasure.

SELSLEY

The Bell Inn ★★★★  

Tel **01453 753801** | **Bell Lane, GL5 5JY**
Web **www.thebellinnselsley.com**
Dir ***Phone for detailed directions.***

In the picturesque village of Selsley, close to the busy market town of Stroud, The Bell dates back to the 16th century but it has changed with the times and is now a destination dining pub. The kitchen looks to the immediate area for its ingredients, so expect a starter of beetroot and Cerney goats' curd salad with pea shoots to kick off a meal, perhaps followed by rump fillet of local beef with rösti potato, purple sprouting broccoli and shallots. Flourless orange and grapefruit cake with home-made ice cream makes for a satisfying finale. Ales from nearby Uley brewery keep local drinkers happy, as do the 70 gins on offer.

Open all year Mon to Thu 11–3 5–11 (Fri to Sat 11–11 Sun 11–5) Summer – open all day Closed Sun evening Free House portions/menu notice required

SHEEPSCOMBE

The Butchers Arms

Tel **01452 812113** | **GL6 7RH**
Web **www.butchers-arms.co.uk**
Dir ***1.5 miles south of A46 (Cheltenham to Stroud road), north of Painswick.***

Rural Cotswold gem with stunning views

Tucked into the western scarp of the Cotswolds and reached via narrow winding lanes, pretty Sheepscombe radiates all of the mellow, sedate, bucolic charm you'd expect from such a haven. The village pub, dating from 1670 and a favourite haunt of *Cider with Rosie* author Laurie Lee, lives up to such expectations and then some. Views from the gardens are idyllic whilst within is all you'd hope for: log fires, clean-cut rustic furnishings, village chatter backed up by beers from Prescotts of Cheltenham, Wye Valley and Otter, as well as Westons Stowford Press and Rosie's Pig ciders. The fulfilling menus here include locally sourced meats. Following a sympathetic extension, there is now more room to enjoy the delights of this lovely pub.

PICK OF THE PUBS

Open all week 11.30–2.30 6.30–11 (Sat 11.30–11.30 Sun 12–10.30) Free House 10 from £10 portions/menu

SOMERFORD KEYNES

The Bakers Arms

Tel **01285 861298** | **GL7 6DN**
Web **www.thebakersarmssomerford.co.uk**
Dir ***Exit A419 signed Cotswold Water Park. Cross B4696, 1 mile, follow signs for Keynes Park and Somerford Keynes.***

The beautiful Bakers Arms dates from the 17th century and was formerly the village bakery; it still has its low-beamed ceilings and inglenook fireplace. Only a stone's throw from the Thames Path and Cotswold Way, the pub is a convenient watering hole for walkers. The home-cooked food on offer runs along the lines of baguettes, light lunches and pub favourites – home-made vegetable curry; and 8oz Forest of Dean boar burger with rosemary salted chips. The mature gardens, with discreet children's play areas, are ideal for alfresco dining, .

Open all day, all week 12–11 Enterprise Inns from £13 portions/menu notice required

SOUTHROP

The Swan

Tel **01367 850205** | **GL7 3NU**
Web **www.thyme.co.uk/dining/the-swan-at-southrop**
Dir ***Follow Southrop signs from A361 between Lechlade and Burford.***

Overlooking the green, The Swan is the village focal point. Ivy covers the external walls, while those in the stone-floored bar and restaurant are painted white, soft grey-blue or left unrendered.

STANTON

The Mount Inn

Tel **01386 584316** | **Old Snowshill Road, WR12 7NE**
Web **www.themountinn.co.uk**
Dir ***Follow Stanton signs from B4632 between Broadway and Winchcombe.***

In a tranquil, picture-perfect hillside setting at the top of a no-through-road Cotswold village, memorable views from the patio here stretch west to the crinkly top of Bredon Hill in the Vale of Evesham, with shimmering glimpses of the distant Black Mountains.

STOW-ON-THE-WOLD

The Bell at Stow

Tel **01451 870916** | **Park Street, GL54 1AJ**
Web **www.thebellatstow.com**
Dir ***In town centre on A436.***

This ivy-clad stone pub in lovely Stow offers a warm welcome to all. Open-plan with flagstone floors, beamed ceilings and log fires, it's a relaxed setting to enjoy a pint of Young's Special. Seafood dominates the daily-changing specials boards.

The Porch House  INN

PICK OF THE PUBS

Tel **01451 870048** | **Digbeth Street, GL54 1BN**
Web **www.porch-house.co.uk**
Dir ***A429 into Stow, off main square at end of Digbeth Street.***

In the centre of Stow-on-the-Wold, this stone-built inn claims to be the oldest pub in England. Parts of the building date back to AD 947, when it is believed to have been a hospice built by the order of Aethelmar, Duke of Cornwall. The Porch has a relaxed feel, especially in the bar which dispenses a range of real ales, including several from the pub's brewery owners, Brakspear.

STROUD

Bear of Rodborough Hotel

★★★ HOTEL **PICK OF THE PUBS**

Tel **01453 878522** | **Rodborough Common, GL5 5DE**
Web **www.cotswold-inns-hotels.co.uk/the-bear-of-rodborough**
Dir ***From M5 junction 13 follow signs for Stonehouse then Rodborough.***

Set in the rolling grassland of Rodborough Common, with far-reaching views of the Stroud Valley and Severn Vale, this 17th-century former alehouse takes its name from the bear-baiting that used to take place nearby. Head to the bar for a pint of Wickwar before checking out the bar menu – a wide choice includes afternoon tea, sharing platters and ploughman's, plus classics like fisherman's pie and chargrilled steaks. The Library Restaurant is more formal; perhaps rump of lamb and braised shoulder, dauphinoise potatoes, wilted spinach and rosemary jus.

Open all day, all week 10am–11pm Free House 10 portions/menu notice required

Toni's Kitchen at Bisley House

Tel **01453 751328** | **Middle Street, GL5 1DZ**
Web **www.toniskitchen.co.uk**
Dir ***From A419 roundabout follow hospital signs. 1st right into Field Road. 3rd left into Whitehall (leads to Middle Street). Pub on right.***

Dating from Victorian times, this bar takes its regular real ales from Stroud Brewery, but the food is authentically Italian. Start with chicken tortellini in its own broth and follow it with fritto misto of squid, octopus, lemon sole and prawns with lemon mayonnaise. Leave room for the chocolate nemesis cake. On the extensive wine list are bins from France, Italy and Spain, chosen to complement the dishes' Mediterranean flavours.

Open all day 12–10 (Fri to Sat 12–11) Closed 25–26 Dec 1 Jan, Mon and Tue Free House from £14 portions/menu Wi-fi notice required

TETBURY

Gumstool Inn – see below

The Priory Inn PICK OF THE PUBS

Tel **01666 502251** | **London Road, GL8 8JJ**
Web **www.theprioryinn.co.uk**
Dir ***M4 junction 17, A429 towards Cirencester. Left into B4014 to Tetbury. Over mini-roundabout into Long Street, pub 100 yards after corner on right.***

An enormous 'walk-around' open log fire greets visitors to this thriving place. Its high exposed beams date from the 16th century, when it was the stable-block and grooms' cottages for the neighbouring priory. Local microbreweries, typically Uley and Cotswold Lion, supply the real ales; a white wine and a sparkling rosé come from a vineyard in Malmesbury; and damson brandy, sloe gin and quince liqueur are made on the banks of the River Severn.

TETBURY

Gumstool Inn

Tel **01666 890391** | **Calcot & Calcot Spa, GL8 8YJ**
Web **www.calcot.co**
Dir ***3 miles west of Tetbury at A4135 and A46 junction.***

Stylish dining-pub with good wine choices

Now a stylish and popular free house that's part of Calcot & Calcot Spa, this stone farmhouse was originally built by Cistercian monks in the 14th century. Part of the Calcot Collection, the buzzy and comfortable Gumstool Inn has a proper country-pub atmosphere and stocks a good selection of West Country ales such as Butcombe Bitter, as well as Mortimers Orchard cider. An excellent choice of more than 20 wines is offered by the glass or bottle. The food here is top-notch and there is a pronounced use of local suppliers and seasonal produce. A typical meal might feature among the main courses: truffled chicken Kiev, wild mushrooms, parsley mash and seasonal greens. Leave a space for the apple and rhubarb crumble with ice cream or the old-fashioned but comforting treacle tart.

Open all day, all week Free House 24 from £15 portions/menu notice required

The Royal Oak Tetbury

Tel **01666 500021 | 1 Cirencester Road, GL8 8EY**
Web **www.theroyaloaktetbury.co.uk**
Dir ***From town centre at mini-roundabout by Market House (yellow building) into Chipping Street. Pass car park on right. Royal Oak on right at bottom of hill.***

The carved bar front, an art deco piano and a vintage jukebox catch the eye here, as do the upcycled furnishings and cosy booths. Beer drinkers have a good choice of thoughtfully chosen craft brews, both national and regional. Diners in the 'restaurant in the rafters' can study 300-year-old construction methods while enjoying beer-battered sustainable fish; free-range meats and poultry; Texas barbecued pork ribs; or maybe something vegan. A courtyard and gardens add to the drinking and eating spaces.

Open all day, all week Closed 1st week Jan Mon to Thu Free House 10 from £12 portions/menu notice required

Snooty Fox Hotel

★★★ SMALL HOTEL

Tel **01666 502436 | Market Place, GL8 8DD**
Web **www.snooty-fox.co.uk**
Dir ***In town centre opposite covered market hall.***

Occupying a prime spot in the heart of Tetbury, this 16th-century coaching inn and hotel retains many of its original features. Sit in front of the log fire with a pint of St Austell's Tribute ale and take a look at the interesting menu.

Open all day, all week Free House 14 from £12 portions/menu notice required

WINCHCOMBE

The Lion Inn  

Tel **01242 603300 | 37 North Street, GL54 5PS**
Web **www.thelionwinchcombe.co.uk**
Dir ***In town centre (parking in Chandos Street).***

A buzzy, welcoming watering hole in the pretty town of Winchcombe, The Lion Inn has 15th-century origins, and care has been taken to maintain the building's quirky charms. Lovers of wine and real ale are spoilt for choice in the spacious and relaxed bar.

GREATER MANCHESTER

CHORLTON CUM HARDY

The Horse & Jockey

Tel **0161 860 7794 | Chorlton Green, M21 9HS**
Web **www.joseph-holt.com/pubs/view/horse-and-jockey**
Dir ***M60 junction 7, A56 towards Stretford. Right onto A5145 towards Chorlton. After lights, 2nd right into St Clements Road. Pub on left on green.***

This Tudor pub has been a much-loved part of the scenery here in leafy Chorlton for 500 years, and is now a family-friendly local offering a relaxed atmosphere, its own microbrewery and lots of local and community activities.

DELPH

The Old Bell Inn  

Tel **01457 870130 | 5 Huddersfield Road, OL3 5EG**
Web **www.theoldbellinn.co.uk**
Dir ***M62 junction 22, A672 to Denshaw junction (signed Saddleworth). Left onto A6052 signed Delph. Through Delph to T-junction. Left onto A62, pub 150 yards on left.***

Did highwayman Dick Turpin rest here en route to the gallows in York? Possibly. More certain is that in 1835 a young Queen Victoria stayed here when visiting that city. If you're dining, starters might include home-made chicken liver parfait; tempura cauliflower florets with curried mayonnaise; and prawn cocktail. Moving on to mains you may find seasonal fish and seafood pie; spiced Yorkshire lamb rump; and seared salmon fillet. Finish with a slate of fine cheese from Lancashire, Yorkshire and Europe.

Open all day, all week Free House 10 portions/menu notice required

DIDSBURY

The Metropolitan

Tel **01614 453145** | **2 Lapwing Lane, M20 2WS**
Web **www.themetropolitanwestdidsbury.co.uk**
Dir ***M60 junction 5, A5103, right into Barlow Moor Road, left into Burton Road. Pub at crossroads. Right into Lapwing Lane for car park.***

Didsbury station on a long-closed line into Manchester has long vanished, but its imposing railway hotel, now 'The Met', remains, proudly declaring its Victorian heritage through its decorative floor tiling, ornate windows and huge, antique-filled rooms. Customers, mainly young and cosmopolitan, come partly for the local cask ales, continental beers, 28 wines by the glass and adventurous spirits collection, and partly for dishes like smoked haddock fishcakes, Frosty's sausages and Thai-spiced tofu skewers. Family Sunday lunch is a big draw, too.

Open all day, all week 10am–11pm (Wed to Thu 10am–11.30pm Fri to Sat 10am to midnight Sun 10am–11pm) Closed 25 Dec Enterprise Inns 28 from £10 portions/menu Wi-fi notice required

LITTLEBOROUGH

The White House

Tel **01706 378456** | **Blackstone Edge, Halifax Road, OL15 0LG**
Web **www.thewhitehousepub.co.uk**
Dir ***On A58, 8 miles from Rochdale, 9 miles from Halifax.***

Known as The White House for over 100 years, this 17th-century coaching house is on the Pennine Way, 1,300 feet above sea level – it has panoramic views of the moors and Hollingworth Lake far below. Not surprising then, that it attracts walkers and cyclists who rest up and sup on Black Sheep and Theakston Best Bitter. A simple menu of pub grub ranges from sandwiches and salads, to grills, international and vegetarian dishes, and traditional mains such as home-made steak and kidney pie, and haddock and prawn Mornay.

Open all week Mon to Sat 12–3 6–10 (Sun 12–10.30) Closed 25 Dec Free House portions/menu Wi-fi

MANCHESTER

Marble Arch

Tel **0161 832 5914** | **73 Rochdale Road, M4 4HY**
Web **www.marblebeers.com**
Dir ***In city centre (Northern Quarter).***

A listed building famous for its sloping floor, glazed brick walls and barrel-vaulted ceiling, the Marble Arch is a fine example of Manchester's Victorian heritage. Part of the award-winning organic Marble Brewery, the pub was built in 1888 by celebrated architect Alfred Darbyshire for Manchester brewery B&J McKenna. An established favourite with beer aficionados and offering six regular ales and eight seasonal house beers, the pub has a well-considered menu of pub favourites and ever-changing specials including Sunday lunches. The Marble Arch hosts its own beer festivals

Open all day, all week Closed 25 Dec Free House Wi-fi

MARPLE BRIDGE

Hare & Hounds

Tel **0161 427 4042** | **19 Mill Brow, SK6 5LW**
Web **www.hareandhoundsmillbrow.co.uk**
Dir ***From A626 in Marple Bridge (at lights at river bridge) follow Mellor signs into Town Street. 1st left into Hollins Lane. Right at T-junction into Ley Lane. Pub 0.25 mile on left.***

Tucked away in a secluded hamlet in the hills fringing the Peak District, this comfortable community local first opened its doors in 1805. It retains much of the character of days gone by and is a popular stop with ramblers exploring the countless paths threading the ridges, moors and wooded cloughs hereabouts. Roaring winter fires take away the chill, while in summer you could settle down outside with a glass of Stockport-brewed Robinsons beer and anticipate freshly cooked food.

Open all year Mon to Tue 5–10 (Wed to Thu 5–12 Fri 12–3 5–12 Sat 12–12 Sun 12–10) Closed Mon to Thu lunch Robinsons 10 portions Wi-fi

OLDHAM

The White Hart Inn

Tel 01457 872566 | 51 Stockport Road, Lydgate, OL4 4JJ
Web www.thewhitehart.co.uk
Dir *From Manchester A62 to Oldham. Right onto bypass, A669 through Lees. In 500 yards past Grotton, at brow of hill right onto A6050.*

From a pint and a sandwich to tasting menus

PICK OF THE PUBS

There's been a pub here since 1788, when brewing took place in its huge cellars. It has also served as a police station and lock-up, schoolhouse and weaver's cottage, while in World War II its hilltop location made it ideal as a lookout point, and the cellars were used as a bomb shelter. Manchester and the Cheshire plain are spread out below, and on a good day you can even see Snowdonia. Owner Charles Brierley has, by harmonising the period charm of its beams, exposed stonework and open fireplaces with contemporary decor, turned it into today's success story. Among the cosmopolitan dishes in The Brasserie are natural Colchester oysters; Loch Fyne smoked salmon, passionfruit and radish; honey-roast duck leg with Sarawak pepper, English plums, pak choi and potato cake; and truffle tagliatelle. Or for a five- or seven-course tasting menu with complementary wine flight, head for the elegant Dining Room. Sunday's set lunch includes a traditional roast, a fish or vegetarian dish. Twelve of the luxury, individually styled bedrooms are in the original building, with a further four spacious family rooms in The Cottage next door.

Open all day, all week Closed 26 Dec, 1 Jan
Free House 9 menus

MELLOR

Oddfellows Arms

Tel **0161 449 7826** | **73 Moor End Road, SK6 5PT**
Web **www.oddfellowsmellor.com**
Dir ***In Mellor village centre.***

A pub since 1803, the 'Oddies' was taken over by a group of regulars who set about restoring it to its 17th-century splendour. Situated in the High Peak National Park, the pub boasts two log burners, oak floors and a stylish upstairs dining room. In the bar, cask ales such as Abbeydale Deception keep the drinkers happy, but the excellent food using local produce attracts diners from far and wide.

Open all day Closed 25 Dec, Mon Free House 13 from £10.95 portions/menu Wi-fi notice required

OLDHAM

The Roebuck Inn

Tel **0161 624 7819** | **Strinesdale, OL4 3RB**
Web **www.the-roebuck-inn.co.uk**
Dir ***From Oldham Mumps Bridge take Huddersfield Road (A62), right at 2nd lights into Ripponden Road (A672), 1 mile right at lights into Turfpit Lane, 1 mile.***

A thousand feet up on the edge of Saddleworth Moor, this traditionally styled inn provides a menu with plenty of choice. Among the options are steak, kidney and ale suet pudding. Beers come from a variety of local breweries.

The White Hart Inn – see opposite

SALFORD

The King's Arms

Tel **0161 839 3605** | **11 Bloom Street, M3 6AN**
Web **www.kingsarmssalford.com**
Dir ***Phone for detailed directions.***

Redevelopment has swept away much of old Salford but this striking street-corner edifice survives intact. It's a grass-roots venue renowned for festivals and creative exhibitions. Performances continue almost non-stop in the busy function room, refreshed by the bar's six guest ales and two draught ciders. Aunty Hilda's Kitchen serves a short list of home-made favourites from tea-time to supper between Wednesday and Saturday.

Open all day, all week Free House portions/menu Wi-fi notice required

STOCKPORT

The Arden Arms

Tel **0161 480 2185** | **23 Millgate, SK1 2LX**
Web **www.robinsonsbrewery.com/ardenarmsstockport**
Dir ***M60 junction 27 to town centre. Across mini-roundabout, at lights turn left. Pub on right of next roundabout behind Asda.***

This late-Georgian coaching inn just has to be seen. Essentially unchanged since a 1908 brewery makeover, it retains its classic multi-roomed layout, fine curved wooden bar, tiled floors and tiny snug. Out back is a cobbled courtyard, used for music gigs on summer Saturdays.

HAMPSHIRE

ALTON

The Anchor Inn ★★★★

INN **PICK OF THE PUBS**

Tel **01420 23261** | **Lower Froyle, GU34 4NA**
Web **www.anchorinnatlowerfroyle.co.uk**
Dir ***From A31 follow Bentley signs.***

A 16th-century, tile-hung farmhouse forms the nucleus of the Anchor. The stylish interior is all low ceilings, exposed beams, wooden floors and open fires, suggesting that little has changed for decades. In the intimate snug and saloon bar you'll find Marston's beers taking pride of place. Menus feature regularly changing, locally sourced dishes; perhaps octopus carpaccio, crispy pig's ears, pickled grapes and spiced tomato, followed by hay-baked hake, sweet potato, asparagus, roasted palm hearts and red wine jus; or roasted cauliflower and truffle tortellini, cocoa bean cassoulet and confit shallot. For dessert, how about rhubarb pannacotta, salsa, pistachio tuile and rhubarb soup; or chocolate cake, raspberry sorbet and popcorn?

Open all day, all week Free House 9 portions/menu Wi-fi

AMPFIELD

White Horse at Ampfield

Tel **01794 368356** | **Winchester Road, SO51 9BQ**
Web **www.whitehorseampfield.co.uk**
Dir ***From Winchester take A3040, then A3090 towards Romsey. Ampfield in 7 miles. Or M3 junction 13, A335 (signed Chandler's Ford). At lights right onto B3043, follow Chandler's Ford Industrial Estate then Hursley signs. Left onto A3090 to Ampfield.***

Background music in the 16th-century, timber-framed White Horse? Certainly not, although what you might well hear is a faint noise as crib players slap down their cards, the crackle of logs burning in the two large inglenooks and the murmur of conversation. If you're eating, check the daily Skipper's Catch board for its fresh, sustainable south coast fish, and the main menu for Romsey chalk-stream cold smoked trout. Also listed could be rabbit and bacon pie; Lucknow Express Indian railway mutton curry; confit of Burgundy duck leg; and steaks, ribs and burgers. At least two roasts on Sundays, as well as goats' cheese, beetroot and horseradish pie.

Open all day, all week 11–11 (Sun 12–9) Greene King 14 from £12 portions/menu notice required

AMPORT

The Hawk Inn ★★★★ INN

Tel **01264 710371** | **SP11 8AE**
Web **www.hawkinnamport.co.uk**
Dir ***From Andover towards Thruxton on A303 exit signed Hawk Conservancy and Amport. 1 mile to Amport. Or A303 onto A343 (south of Andover) follow Abbots Ann and Amport signs.***

On warmer days, the terrace area of The Hawk Inn is a draw, with fine views towards Pill Hill Brook. In the light and spacious interior of adjoining rooms, the bar offers local real ale.

BALL HILL

The Furze Bush Inn

Tel **01635 253228** | **Hatt Common, East Woodhay, RG20 0NQ**
Web **www.furzebushinn.co.uk**
Dir ***From Newbury take A343 (Andover Road), pub signed.***

A popular rural free house, this is a perfect place for refreshment following a day at the Newbury Races, walking the Berkshire Downs or visiting Highclere Castle. The bar menu features a good range of favourites, such as belly of pork, black pudding and bubble-and-squeak; and Moroccan-spiced lamb shank with apricot couscous and vegetable tagine. There's a large front garden, a children's play area and a patio with parasols – perfect for summer drinking.

Open all day, all week Closed 25 Dec Free House 9 menus

BAUGHURST

The Wellington Arms

PICK OF THE PUBS

Tel **0118 982 0110** | **Baughurst Road, RG26 5LP**
Web **www.thewellingtonarms.com**
Dir ***From A4, east of Newbury, through Aldermaston. At 2nd roundabout 2nd exit signed Baughurst, left at T-junction, pub 1 mile.***

Hidden down a maze of lanes in peaceful countryside between Basingstoke and Newbury, the stylish 'Welly' was once used as a hunting lodge by the Duke of Wellington. Inside are wooden tables, tiled floors and an obvious attention to detail. Daily chalkboard menus offer plenty of interest and imagination and much of the produce is organic and local or home grown, since they are dedicated to keeping down the food miles. Salad leaves, herbs and vegetables are grown in the pub's polytunnel and raised vegetable beds, free-range eggs come from their rare-breed and rescue hens, and there are also pedigree Jacob sheep, Tamworth pigs and five beehives. The dining room is small, so booking is certainly advisable. The well-tended garden acts as an extension for diners when the sun shines.

Open all year 12–3 6–11 (Sun 12–3) Closed Sun evening Free House 12 from £26.50 portions

BEAULIEU

The Drift Inn

Tel **023 8029 2342** | **Beaulieu Road, SO42 7YQ**
Web **www.driftinn.co.uk**
Dir ***From Lyndhurst take B3056 (Beaulieu Road) signed Beaulieu. Cross railway line, inn on right.***

This inn is surrounded by the glorious New Forest National Park. The word 'drift' refers to the centuries-old, twice a year, round-up of the 3,000-plus free-wandering ponies. Beers from Ringwood on the western side of the forest and a guest ale are served in the bar.

BISHOP'S WALTHAM

The Hampshire Bowman

Tel **01489 892940** | **Dundridge Lane, SO32 1GD**
Web **www.hampshirebowman.com**
Dir ***From Bishop's Waltham on B3035 towards Corhampton. Right signed Dundridge. 1.2 miles to pub.***

A true rural local, set in 10 acres beside a country lane in rolling downland, this unassuming Victorian pub remains delightfully old fashioned. In the beamed, simply furnished bar you'll find time-honoured pub games and barrels of beer on racks behind the bar. Ale-lovers come for foaming pints of Bowman Ales Swift One or West Berkshire's Good Old Boy, or a glass of heady Black Dragon cider, best enjoyed in the rambling orchard garden. Soak it up with traditional bar meals.

Open all day, all week *Free House* *10* *portions/menu* *notice required*

BOLDRE

The Hobler Inn

Tel **01590 623944** | **Southampton Road, Battramsley, SO41 8PT**
Web **www.thehobler.co.uk**
Dir ***From Brockenhurst take A337 towards Lymington. Pub on main road.***

On the main road between Brockenhurst and Lymington, The Hobler has a large grassed area and trestle tables ideal for families visiting the New Forest. The Hobler Inn is more London wine bar with its stylish leather furniture than a village local.

The Red Lion PICK OF THE PUBS

Tel **01590 673177** | **Rope Hill, SO41 8NE**
Web **www.redlionboldre.co.uk**
Dir ***M27 junction 1, A337 through Lyndhurst and Brockenhurst towards Lymington, follow Boldre signs.***

Mentioned in the Domesday Book, The Red Lion sits at the crossroads in the ancient village of Boldre. The rambling interior contains cosy, beamed rooms, log fires and rural memorabilia; the rooms glow with candlelight on antique copper and brass. Expect a genuinely warm welcome and traditional values, with Ringwood ales on offer at the bar. The kitchen places an emphasis on traditional meals made using the very best of the forest's produce. Typical starters include home-made venison Scotch egg; crispy lime and coconut prawns; and baked camembert, then home-made steak and ale pie; pork tenderloin wrapped in Parma ham and stuffed with apricot and sage; and pan fried halloumi with asparagus, sautéed potatoes and sweet peppers. In the summer, you can eat outside on the herb patio.

Open all week 12–3 5.30–11 (Sat 12–11 Sun 12–10.30) Closed 25 Dec *Free House* *15* *portions* *notice required*

BRAISHFIELD

The Wheatsheaf

Tel **01794 368652** | **SO51 0QE**
Web **www.thewheatsheafbraishfield.co.uk**
Dir ***On A3090 from Romsey towards Winchester, left for Braishfield.***

Close to the Test Valley Way, The Wheatsheaf welcomes walkers, cyclists and especially dogs. Your four-legged friends will appreciate the barrel of treats on the bar while you sample a pint of St Austell Tribute or Flack's Double Drop. The pub has lovely gardens and great views, and there's always something going on – live music and 'jam' nights, quiz nights, theme nights, and 'pie nite' where there's a choice of nine or more home-made pies. In the summer there are barbecues and an annual bottled cider festival.

Open all day, all week *Enterprise Inns* *10* *portions/menu* *notice required*

BRAMBRIDGE

The Dog & Crook

Tel **01962 712129 | Church Lane, SO50 6HZ**
Web **thedogandcrook.co.uk**
Dir ***M3 junction 12, A335 towards Eastleigh. At next roundabout into Allbrook Hill signed Brambridge. Right, follow brown pub sign.***

Worth a visit when in the Winchester/Southampton area, the 18th-century Dog & Crook provides a wide choice of food. You might begin with Welsh rarebit and buttered leeks, pick a main from the special fish menu, and end with the sponge pudding of the day.

BRANSGORE

The Three Tuns Country Inn

PICK OF THE PUBS

Tel **01425 672232 | Ringwood Road, BH23 8JH**
Web **www.threetunsinn.com**
Dir ***1.5 miles from A35 Walkford junction, 3 miles from Christchurch, and 1 mile from Hinton Admiral railway station.***

A thatched 17th-century inn set in a south-facing garden, surrounded by fields, trees and grazing ponies, just beyond the edge of the New Forest National Park. Food is served in all five public areas, including the comfortable, fire-warmed lounge bar offering Ringwood beers and cider from Burley. Look for slow-roasted Avon Tyrell pork served with compressed apple, dauphinoise potatoes and a cider and mustard sauce, or specials of seafood linguine nero; warm octopus in lemon and thyme. A cider festival takes place during the summer holidays, as well as a food festival in June, followed by a beer festival at the end of September.

Open all day, all week 11–11 (Sun 12–10.30, bank holidays 12–9.15) Free House 9 from £12.95 portions/menu notice required

BROOK

The Bell Inn 

Tel **023 8081 2214 | SO43 7HE**
Web **www.bellinn-newforest.co.uk**
Dir ***M27 junction 1, B3079 signed Brook. Inn 1 mile on right.***

This fine red brick building, set in a charming village, has an airy, contemporary look that makes the most of the open fires, flagstone floor and spacious, elegant rooms. Relax in the bar with a pint of something local – there are ales from Ringwood and Romsey's Flack Manor Brewery – and an indulgent bar snack before choosing from the menu.

Open all day, all week Free House from £12.50 portions/menu notice required

BROUGHTON

The Tally Ho

Tel **01794 301280 | High Street, SO20 8AA**
Web **www.thetallyhobroughton.co.uk**
Dir ***From crossroads on A30 between Stockbridge and Salisbury take B3084 signed Broughton. Follow pub signs in village.***

For walkers and cyclists on the Clarendon Way between Winchester and Salisbury, the 300-year-old Tally Ho couldn't be better located. It's been a pub since 1832, and now belongs to top record producer, Chris Thomas. Real ales, among them Ringwood and Cheddar, are on tap as perfect accompaniments to the seasonal dishes. Top quality, locally raised meats include buffalo, pork, lamb and venison, with pan-seared halibut appealing to fish lovers. There's create-your-own pizza nights on Thursdays, and roasts on Sundays.

Open all day, all week Free House 10 portions/menu notice required

6 HAMPSHIRE PUBS WITH ACCOMMODATION

The following pubs are rated as part of the AA Guest Accommodation scheme (see page 10–11 for more information).

The Bell Inn ★★★★ INN Brook, *see page 196*
The Mayflower ★★★★ INN Lymington, *see page 207*
The Old Vine ★★★★ INN Winchester, *see page 216*
The Woolpack Inn ★★★★ INN Northington, *see page 208*
The Kings Head ★★★★ INN Hursley, *see page 204*
The Three Cups Inn ★★★★ INN Stockbridge, *see page 213*

BURLEY

The Burley Inn

Tel **01425 403448** | **BH24 4AB**
Web **www.theburleyinn.co.uk**
Dir ***4 miles south-east of Ringwood.***

A great base from which to explore the tracks, paths and rides of the surrounding New Forest National Park, this imposing Edwardian edifice, in neat grounds behind picket fencing, is one of a small local chain of dining pubs combining the best local real ales – Flack's Double Drop being one – with homely, traditional pub grub from an extensive menu. Toast wintery toes before log fires or relax on the patio, whilst idly watching free-roaming livestock amble by on the village lanes.

Open all day, all week Closed 25 Dec Free House 10 portions

CADNAM

Sir John Barleycorn

Tel **023 8081 2236** | **Old Romsey Road, SO40 2NP**
Web **www.sir-john-barleycorn.co.uk**
Dir ***From Southampton M27 junction 1 into Cadnam.***

The name of this friendly thatched establishment comes from a folksong celebrating the transformation of barley to beer. The menu has something for everyone with quick snacks and sandwiches, a children's menu and dishes like pan-fried sea bass fillet with prawn and spinach risotto.

CHALTON

The Red Lion

Tel **023 9259 2246** | **PO8 0BG**
Web **www.fullers.co.uk**
Dir ***Just off A3 between Horndean and Petersfield. Follow signs for Chalton.***

Said to be the oldest pub in Hampshire, dating back to 1147, when it was built to house craftsmen constructing St Michael's church opposite. It retains an olde worlde English charm. A large purpose-built dining room is kept busy serving plates of pub grub.

CHARTER ALLEY

The White Hart Inn

Tel **01256 850048** | **White Hart Lane, RG26 5QA**
Web **www.whitehartcharteralley.com**
Dir ***M3 junction 6, A339 towards Newbury. Right signed Ramsdell. Right at church, then 1st left into White Hart Lane.***

When this free house opened in 1819, on the northern edge of the village overlooking open farmland and woods – just as today – it must have delighted the woodsmen and coach drivers visiting the farrier next door. Real ale pumps lined up on the herringbone-patterned, brick-fronted bar dispense brews from the likes of Hop Back and Harvey's breweries. The regularly changing menu features many pub favourites – steak and Stilton pie; slow-roasted pork belly; and beer-battered cod and chips.

Open Mon and Tue 7–11 Wed 12–2.30 7–11 Thu and Fri 12–2.30 5.30–11 Sat 12–3 6.30–11 Sun 12–3 Closed 25 Dec to 3 Jan, Mon lunch, Tue lunch, Sun evening Free House 9 from £11.50 portions/menu notice required

CHAWTON

The Greyfriar

Tel **01420 83841** | **Winchester Road, GU34 1SB**
Web **www.thegreyfriar.co.uk**
Dir ***Just off A31 near Alton. Access to Chawton via A31/A32 junction. Follow Jane Austen's House signs. Pub opposite.***

This welcoming 16th-century pub stands across the road from Jane Austen's House Museum in the lovely village of Chawton. Fuller's-owned, The Greyfriar offers London Pride and HSB along with an appealing seasonal menu that might include duck breast with plum, crispy fennel gnocchi and soy and orange reduction, finishing with banana sticky toffee pudding and rum sauce. When the weather allows, head outside to the sunny, south-facing garden.

Open all day, all week 12–11 (Sun 12–10.30) Closed 25 Dec Fuller's 9 from £12 portions/menu notice required

CHERITON

The Flower Pots Inn

Tel **01962 771318** | **SO24 0QQ**
Web **www.flowerpotsf2s.com**
Dir ***A272 towards Petersfield, left onto B3046, pub 0.75 mile on right.***

Known almost universally as The Pots, this pub was once a farmhouse and home to the head gardener of nearby Avington Park. These days, local beer drinkers know the pub well for its award-winning Flowerpots Bitter and Goodens Gold, brewed across the car park in the microbrewery. Simple home-made food includes hearty filled baps, toasted sandwiches, jacket potatoes, cheese and meat ploughman's and different hotpots. A large, safe garden, with a covered patio, allows children to let off steam (under 13s are not allowed in the bar).

Open all week 12–2.30 6–11 (Sun 12–3 7–10.30) Free House

The Hinton Arms

Tel **01962 771252** | **Petersfield Road, SO24 0NH**
Web **www.hintonarms.co.uk**
Dir ***A272 between Petersfield and Winchester.***

Weary walkers, cyclists, well-behaved children and dogs are all very welcome at this privately-owned bar and restaurant. So too are those interested in the English Civil War keen to follow the trail to the nearby site of the 1644 Battle of Cheriton. Food is a high point, especially the game and fresh fish; portions are reputedly generous. Seasonal menus cover all bases, with dishes such as Malaysian chicken korma; gammon steak and eggs; and sausages and mash. Their real ale policy favours those brewed in Hampshire.

Open all week 10–3 6–11 (Sat to Sun 10am–11pm) Free House 12 portions/menu notice required

CLANFIELD

The Rising Sun Inn

Tel **023 9259 6975** | **North Lane, PO8 0RN**
Web **www.risingsunclanfield.co.uk**
Dir ***A3(M) then A3 towards Petersfield. Left signed Clanfield. Follow brown inn signs.***

It might look old, but the flint-faced Rising Sun was actually built in the 21st century. There's a choice of real ales and ciders, as well as a good selection of single malt whiskies, while the menu focuses on pub favourites – beer-battered cod; pan-fried lamb's liver, bacon and onion gravy; and ham, egg and chips. Tuesday night is steak night, curries are on Thursday and it's Friday for music.

Open all day, all week Enterprise Inns 15 from £10.95 portions/menu notice required

CROOKHAM VILLAGE

The Exchequer

Tel **01252 615336** | **Crondall Road, GU51 5SU**
Web **www.exchequercrookham.co.uk**
Dir ***M3 junction 5, A287 towards Farnham for 5 miles. Left to Crookham Village.***

Amongst the quiet villages of north Hampshire in the beautiful setting of Crookham Village, this free house is just a stone's throw from the A287. They serve carefully chosen wines and local ales straight from the cask, and a great seasonal menu with dishes featuring local produce.

DENMEAD

The Fox & Hounds – see opposite

DROXFORD

The Bakers Arms PICK OF THE PUBS

Tel **01489 877533** | **High Street, SO32 3PA**
Web **www.thebakersarmsdroxford.com**
Dir ***10 miles east of Winchester on A32 between Fareham and Alton. 7 miles south-west of Petersfield.***

This is an unpretentious, white-painted pub with abundant country charm – the staff are friendly and the locals clearly love the place. The Bowman Brewery a mile away supplies the bar with Swift One and Wallops Wood, so why look any further afield, asks owner Adam Cordery. Pick from a list of hot filled baguettes, while over the big log fire a blackboard lists the main dishes. Among these will be the day's pie, burgers, sausages or steaks; and maybe roasted game with dauphinoise potatoes, red cabbage, celeriac purée and elderberry gravy; Bakers fish pie with gratinated cheese and potato topping, served with vegetables or dressed leaves; and Devon crab thermidor with skinny fries, slaw and lemon mayonnaise.

Open all year 11.45–3 6–11 (Sun 12–5) Closed Sun evening Free House 11 portions notice required

DENMEAD

The Fox & Hounds

Tel 023 9226 5984 | School Lane, PO7 6NA
Web www.foxandhounds-pub.co.uk
Dir *Phone for directions.*

A reputation for delicious food

A charming Victorian, family-run country pub on the edge of the village, with lovely farmland views, The Fox & Hounds was saved from demolition by the local community. Inside it's relaxed and friendly with 'country kitsch' vintage and modern decor, and a log burner, and for decent weather there's a sheltered patio garden with vines and clematis climbing a twinkling-light-covered pergola. Well-kept national and locally brewed real ales and craft beers change on a regular basis. The pub grows its own strawberries, gooseberries, rhubarb and raspberries, while a small allotment provides herbs from mint to sorrel, a variety of vegetables and edible flowers. On the British pub classics and modern British specials menu, you'll always find a hearty hand-made pie or traditional pub fish and chips, and dishes such as Thai green chicken curry; braised ribs; and pan-fried salmon. Among chef's blackboard specials – sesame chicken, spicy carrot and apple slaw salad; sea bass with saffron potatoes, creamed spinach and spiced shellfish butter; and spinach and wild mushroom cobbler. There's no children's menu as such, but the kitchen will happily provide smaller portions from the main menu. A quiz is held every other Sunday evening.

Open all day, all week *Free House* *from £10* *portions* *notice required*

DUMMER

The Queen Inn

Tel **01256 397367** | **Down Street, RG25 2AD**
Web **thequeeninndummer.com**
Dir ***From M3 junction 7 follow Dummer signs.***

Dine by candlelight at this 16th-century, low-beamed inn with a huge open log fire and enjoy the real ale portfolio of Doom Bar, Otter and guests, and a comprehensive menu. There are two roasts on Sundays as well as a specials board.

The Sun Inn

Tel **01256 397234** | **Winchester Road A30, RG25 2DJ**
Web **www.suninndummer.com**
Dir ***M3 junction 7, A30 (Winchester Road) towards Basingstoke. Left onto A30 towards Winchester. Inn on right.***

The Sun has stood for many years alongside the main coaching route from London to Exeter, today's A30. Passing traffic is not a problem since most West Country travellers now use the M3, accessible from nearby junction 7. A lovely garden lies at the back.

DURLEY

The Robin Hood

Tel **01489 860229** | **Durley Street, SO32 2AA**
Web **www.therobinhooddurley.co.uk**
Dir ***Phone for detailed directions.***

The Robin Hood is a friendly, welcoming place, with a cosy seating area, not one but two open fires and loos which are hidden behind a false bookcase door. The garden is huge, with a play area for children that includes a pirate ship.

EAST BOLDRE

Turfcutters Arms

Tel **01590 612331** | **Main Road, SO42 7WL**
Web **www.the-turfcutters-new-forest.co.uk**
Dir ***From Beaulieu take B3055 towards Brockenhurst. Left at Hatchet Pond onto B3054 towards Lymington, turn left, follow signs for East Boldre. Pub approximately 0.5 mile.***

Five miles south of Beaulieu, this New Forest pub, easily recognised by its white picket fence, attracts cyclists, ramblers, dog-walkers and locals. In winter the open fires warm the cockles, while the lovely garden comes into its own in summer.

EAST END

The East End Arms PICK OF THE PUBS

Tel **01590 626223** | **Main Road, SO41 5SY**
Dir ***From Lymington towards Beaulieu (past Isle of Wight ferry), 3 miles to East End.***

On the southern edge of the New Forest National Park, just a short stroll from the Solent and close to the delightful village of Buckler's Hard, The East End Arms is a happy mix of community village inn and restaurant, with daily-changing menus drawing on local produce. The inviting Foresters Bar is pleasingly old-fashioned, with flagstone floors and roaring fire adding to the pleasure of a gravity-drawn pint of ale, or a bottle of Thatchers cider. The bright and airy restaurant is decorated with photographs of musicians, reflecting the past of the pub's owner, Dire Straits' bass player John Illsley. Starters such as ham hock and pigeon terrine could be followed by garlic and thyme roast poussin with wild mushrooms, Savoy cabbage and Parmentier potatoes.

Open all week 11.30–3 5–11 (Fri to Sat 11.30–11 Sun 12–10.30) Free House portions WI-FI

EAST MEON

Ye Olde George Inn

Tel **01730 823481** | **Church Street, GU32 1NH**
Web **www.yeoldegeorgeinn.net**
Dir ***South of A272 (Winchester to Petersfield road). 1.5 miles from Petersfield turn left opposite church.***

In the beautiful countryside of the Meon Valley, the setting for this delightful 15th-century coaching inn is hard to beat. If you want heavy beams, inglenook fireplaces and wooden floors, look no further – they're all here, creating an ideal atmosphere for enjoying a pint of Badger Best Bitter or Westons cider. The kitchen team make everything in house for their monthly-changing menus (except the local farm-made ice cream). There are tables outside on the pretty patio.

Open all week 11–3 6–11 (Sun 11–10) Closed 25 Dec, 26 Dec evening, 1 Jan evening Hall & Woodhouse 9 portions/menu WI-FI *notice required*

EASTON

The Chestnut Horse

Tel **01962 779257 | SO21 1EG**
Web **www.thechestnuthorse.com**
Dir ***M3 junction 9, A33 towards Basingstoke, then B3047. 2nd right, 1st left.***

This gem of a 16th-century pub has an abundance of traditional English character and atmosphere. Old tankards hang from the low-beamed ceilings in the two bar areas, and a large open fire is the central focus through the winter months.

EMSWORTH

The Sussex Brewery

Tel **01243 371533 | 36 Main Road, PO10 8AU**
Web **www.sussexbrewery.co.uk**
Dir ***On A259, east of Emsworth towards Chichester.***

No prizes for guessing that this pub was once a brewery. Today, there is a pride in offering good, honestly-priced food and drinks served by friendly staff in a happy atmosphere. Young's ales sit beside guests, with Thatchers cider served too. Locally-made sausages with creamy mash, caramelised onions and gravy is a popular choice. Other dishes might include fish and chips, calves' liver and bacon, steak and kidney suet pudding, and vegetarian tartiflette. Sharing platters and light bites are also available.

Open all day, all week 11am–11.30pm (Sun 11–10.30) Young & Co.'s Brewery 11 portions/menu Wi-fi notice required

EVERSLEY

The Golden Pot PICK OF THE PUBS

Tel **0118 973 2104 | Reading Road, RG27 0NB**
Web **www.golden-pot.co.uk**
Dir ***Between Reading and Camberley on B3272 approximately 0.25 mile from Eversley cricket ground.***

Set beside meadows in the Long River valley, this creeper-clad pub, a jigsaw of interlinked cottages, has the charm of ages past. Three centuries of tradition ooze from the run of public spaces and 'The Pottery' restaurant suite. A double-sided warming fire connects the bar and restaurant, while outside the Snug and Vineyard, surrounded by colourful tubs and hanging baskets, are just the ticket for summer relaxation. The inspiring menu here is equally eclectic.

EVERSLEY CROSS

The Chequers

Tel **0118 402 7065 | RG27 0NS**
Web **www.thechequerseversleycross.co.uk**
Dir ***On B3272 (west of Yateley) in village centre.***

Belonging to the Peach Pubs group, which pursues the tenet of 'small is beautiful', The Chequers welcomes all-comers from breakfast onwards. Quality is the focus for all aspects of the operation, from ales such as Hogs Back to a carte packed with seasonal goodies.

EXTON

The Shoe Inn

Tel **01489 877526 | Shoe Lane, SO32 3NT**
Web **www.theshoeexton.co.uk**
Dir ***On A32 between Fareham and Alton.***

On warmer days, you can enjoy views of Old Winchester Hill from the garden of this popular pub in the heart of the Meon Valley. Food is key – local ingredients are used wherever possible. The bar offers weekly changing guest ales.

FREEFOLK

The Watership Down Inn
– see page 202

HANNINGTON

The Vine at Hannington

Tel **01635 298525 | RG26 5TX**
Web **thevineathannington.co.uk**
Dir ***Follow Hannington signs from A339 between Basingstoke and Kingsclere.***

Given the nature of North Hampshire's rolling chalk downland, you can expect rambling and cycling devotees to patronise this gabled Victorian inn. A wood-burning stove heats the spacious, traditionally furnished bar areas and conservatory. There is a large, secure garden with a children's play area.

FREEFOLK

The Watership Down Inn

Tel **01256 892254** | **RG28 7NJ**
Web **www.watershipdowninn.com**
Dir ***From Whitchurch take B3400 towards Basingstoke. Pub in 1.5 miles.***

Uniquely named village free house

The former Freefolk Arms took on its current name after the late Richard Adams, who lived in nearby Whitchurch, found fame in 1972 with his rabbity adventure tale. The unexpectedly famous hill itself lies just to the north of the inn. From the pub car park a few steps lead up through the garden into the quarry-tiled bar, where local brews, perhaps Cheriton, Itchen Valley, or Triple fff, will be ready and waiting. Among dishes here, and in the conservatory overlooking the garden, expect real ale-battered fresh haddock; pan-seared Hampshire venison; and mildly spiced mixed vegetable coconut curry. Home-made dessert options might include baked New York-style lemon and lime cheesecake, and caramelised white chocolate blondie. The River Test, famous for its trout, rises and flows nearby.

Open all week 12–3 6–11 (Fri to Sun all day) Free House 10 from £12.75 menus notice required

HAVANT

The Wheelwright's Arms

Tel **023 9247 6502** | **27 Emsworth Road, PO9 2SN**
Web **www.wheelwrightshavant.co.uk**
Dir ***A27 into Emsworth Road towards Havant. Pub on right.***

The Upham Group are owners of this handsome, twin-gabled pub. Local and seasonal produce always features on the menus, in dishes like pan-fried chalk stream trout with olive oil mash, crab bon bon and confit carrot, and over-65s can choose from the Pounds & Penny Farthings menu at lunchtime, Monday–Thursday.

HAWKLEY

The Hawkley Inn ★★★★ INN

Tel **01730 827205** | **Pococks Lane, GU33 6NE**
Web **www.hawkleyinn.co.uk**
Dir ***From A3 (Liss roundabout) towards Liss on B3006. Right at Spread Eagle, in 2.5 miles left into Pococks Lane.***

An inn sign saying 'Free Hoose' owes something to the moose head hanging above one of the fires. Enjoy the relaxed atmosphere, quirky decor and well-kept, local real ale; a festival takes place over June's first weekend. If not eating, you can just enjoy your drink in the appealing outside space. Menus change daily, on offer are pub classics and vegetarian specials with an emphasis on fresh, local produce, particularly fish and game.

Open all week Mon to Fri 12–3 5.30–11 (Sat to Sun all day) Free House 17 from £11 portions notice required

HERRIARD

The Fur & Feathers

Tel **01256 510510** | **Herriard Road, RG25 2PN**
Web **www.theherriardinn.co.uk**
Dir ***From Basingstoke take A339 towards Alton. After Herriard follow pub signs. Turn left to pub.***

Purpose-built 120 years ago for local farm workers, this high-ceilinged Victorian pub is light and airy, with log-burning fires at each end of the bar. Four ales are rotated, and you'll find modern British cooking and local ingredients on the menu. Start with Alresford watercress soup or the baked Tunworth cheese sharing platter; move on to pan-fried hake with roasted vine tomatoes and truffle mash, or Gressingham duck breast with orange and rhubarb sauce, Savoy cabbage and dauphinoise potatoes. There's a home-made burgers' menu too.

Open Tue to Thu 11–3 5.30–10 (Fri to Sat 12–11 Sun 12–6) Closed 1 week Jan, Sun evening, Mon Free House 28 from £14.95 portions/menu notice required

HIGHCLERE

The Yew Tree

RESTAURANT WITH ROOMS

Tel **01635 253360 | Hollington Cross, Andover Road, RG20 9SE**
Web **www.theyewtree.co.uk**
Dir ***M4 junction 13, A34 south, 4th junction on left signed Highclere/Wash Common, turn right towards Andover A343, inn on right.***

After visiting nearby Highclere Castle, where *Downton Abbey* was filmed, have lunch here. Or vice versa. Either way, enjoy its high standards of food and service, starting in the bar with tartan high back seats and comfy leather chairs.

HORDLE

The Mill at Gordleton

 INN

Tel **01590 682219 | Silver Street, SO41 6DJ**
Web **www.themillatgordleton.co.uk**
Dir ***M27 junction 1 towards Lyndhurst. Follow signs to Brockenhurst and Lymington on A337. Continue on A337, under railway bridge. Straight on at mini-roundabout, turn right signed Hordle just before Monkey House Inn. On right in 1.5 miles.***

Handy for the New Forest, Gordleton is now a lovely pub, with wonderful riverside gardens that include a number of sculptures – take the Art Walk to explore. Everything is made on site, including bread and ice cream, and plenty of produce is grown in the kitchen garden. Dinner might kick off with scallop and Lymington crab thermidor then a steak from the grill; or perhaps pan-roasted cod loin, mashed potato, rainbow kale and shellfish butter sauce to follow.

Open all day, all week Upham Pub Company 14 portions/menu notice required

HOUGHTON

The Boot Inn

Tel **01794 388310 | SO20 6LH**
Web **www.thebootinn-houghton.co.uk**
Dir ***Phone for detailed directions.***

Situated on the River Test, one of the world's best fly-fishing waters, the Boot enjoys a tranquil location. There's an 18th-century, timber-framed bar and its restaurant aims to serve good food without earning the gastro pub sobriquet. In the bar you can choose baguettes, salads, or the likes of sausages, mash, peas and onion gravy; while the restaurant might offer whitebait; grilled haloumi, rice with sweet and sour sauce; or smoked haddock mornay with prawns, mange tout and mash.

Open all week 10–3 6–11 Free House 10 from £12 portions/menu notice required

HURSLEY

The Dolphin Inn

Tel **01962 775209 | SO21 2JY**
Web **www.dolphinhursley.co.uk**
Dir ***Phone for detailed directions.***

Like most of the village, this old coaching inn once belonged to the Hursley Estate, which is now owned by IBM. It was built between 1540 and 1560, reputedly using timbers from a Tudor warship called HMS *Dolphin*. In the beamed bars you'll find Ringwood Razorback and Fuller's London Pride plus Thatchers and Orchard Thieves ciders. In addition to sandwiches, baguettes and jacket potatoes, favourites include sausage and mash; mushroom and cashew nut Stroganoff; and beer battered cod and chips.

Open all day, all week Mon to Sat 11–11 (Sun 12–10.30) Enterprise Inns 12 portions/menu

The Kings Head ★★★★ INN

PICK OF THE PUBS

Tel **01962 775208 | Main Road, SO21 2JW**
Web **www.kingsheadhursley.co.uk**
Dir ***On A3090 between Winchester and Romsey.***

A picturesque drive out of Winchester brings you to this creeper-clad Georgian coaching inn. Ales include Flack Manor, and there's a 25-strong gin list. Lunchtime small plates may include asparagus ravioli with Old Winchester cheese shavings. For dinner, a partridge and rabbit vol-au-vent with roasted Hursley pear purée could be followed by slow-roasted haunch of Hampshire venison. Round off with crème caramel with rum-soaked golden raisins and candied orange peel.

Open all day, all week 7.30am–11pm Cirrus Inns 10 portions/menu Wi-fi notice required

HURSTBOURNE TARRANT

The George and Dragon

★★★★ INN

Tel **01264 736277 | The Square, SP11 0AA**
Web **www.georgeanddragon.com**
Dir ***On A343 in village centre.***

On the old coach road between Newbury and Andover, is the 16th-century George and Dragon. The big bay window is where travellers would eat and drink while keeping an eye out for their coach, well known for its all-too-brief stops. House beer is Betteridge's brewed about a hundred metres away, the cider is Black Rat, and carefully chosen wines are available by the glass.

Open all day, all week Free House 12 portions/menu Wi-fi notice required

LEE-ON-THE-SOLENT

The Bun Penny

Tel **023 9255 0214 | 36 Manor Way, PO13 9JH**
Web **www.bunpenny.co.uk**
Dir ***From Fareham take B3385 to Lee-on-the-Solent. Pub 300 yards before High Street.***

Classic country free house close to the water

A short walk from the waterfront, this former farmhouse occupies a prominent position on the road into Lee-on-the-Solent. Every inch a classic country free house, it has a large patio area at the front and an extensive back garden that's ideal for summer relaxation, while real fires and cosy corners are welcome in winter. St Austell beer is sold alongside ales from the local breweries. A typical meal might be a home-made deep filled shortcrust pie; a pub favourite like slow-cooked pork belly with apple and Calvados compôte; or one of the fresh fish dishes. Sandwiches, wraps, salads and omelettes are offered too.

Open all day, all week 11–11 (Fri 11am–midnight Sun 12–10) Free House 13 portions/menu notice required

LISS

The Jolly Drover

★★★★ INN

Tel 01730 893137 | London Road, Hillbrow, GU33 7QL
Web www.thejollydrover.co.uk
Dir *From station in Liss at mini-roundabout right into Hill Brow Road (B3006) signed Rogate, Rake, Hill Brow. At junction with B2071, pub opposite.*

Just out of town at the top of the hill

This pub was built in 1844 by a drover, Mr Knowles, to offer cheer and sustenance to other drovers on the old London road. For over 20 years it has been run by Anne and Barry Coe, who welcome all-comers to enjoy the large log fire, secluded garden, a choice of real ales and home-cooked food. The same menu is served in the bar and restaurant. Dishes include roast beef and Yorkshire pudding; 'Hodgepodge Pie' (pork, veal and lamb); chicken breast with bacon and Stilton sauce; and grilled whole plaice with white wine and parsley sauce. Gluten-free and vegetarian choices are also available.

Open all week 10.30–3 5.30–11 (Sun 12–4) Closed 25–26 Dec, 1 Jan Enterprise Inns 10 portions notice required

LITTLETON

The Running Horse – see page 206

LOVEDEAN

The Bird in Hand

Tel 023 9259 1055 | 269 Lovedean Lane, PO8 9RX
Web www.lovedeanbirdinhand.co.uk
Dir *A3(M) junction 2, A3 signed Portsmouth. At next roundabout left (A3/Portsmouth). Right into Lovedean Lane (signed Lovedean). Pub on left.*

At the start of World War II, locals at this 200-year-old rural inn are rumoured to have drunk beer out of the FA Cup, which was despatched here for safe-keeping by the then-holders, Portsmouth. Overlooking gently rolling Hampshire countryside, the pub's multiple menus have broad appeal.

LOWER SWANWICK

The Navigator

★★★★ GUEST ACCOMMODATION

Tel 01489 572123 | 286 Bridge Road, SO31 7EB
Web www.thenavigatorswanwick.co.uk
Dir *M27 junction 8, A3024 signed Bursledon. 1st exit at next roundabout onto A27 (Bridge Road). Cross river, pub 300 yards on left.*

With its prime location on the magnificent marina at Lower Swanwick, The Navigator's ambience reflects the strong sea-faring traditions of this area. The food ticks all the boxes too, so a sample dinner menu, for example, details pan-fried scallops wrapped in pancetta, crispy chorizo and celeriac purée; and braised blade of beef, carrot purée, buttered kale, fondant potato and red wine jus.

Open all day, all week Upham Group 10 portions/menu Wi-fi notice required

LITTLETON

The Running Horse

★★★★ 

Tel **01962 880218** | **88 Main Road, SO22 6QS**
Web **www.runninghorseinn.co.uk**
Dir ***3 miles from Winchester, 1 mile from Three Maids Hill, signed from Stockbridge Road.***

Upmarket village pub and restaurant

Belonging to the Upham Group, this judiciously restored and rejuvenated, mid-1850s country pub lies in a favoured village to the north-west of Winchester. Before its acquisition it had been run by a succession of landlords, many of whom had opted "for a leisurely lifestyle in lovely Littleton after hectic years in busy Southampton pubs". A bit of a generalisation, perhaps, but fear not, things are different today as the pub's new lease of life came with a thoroughly professional team – and it shows. The light, spacious interior proves just what a good designer can achieve: contrasting wall colours, wooden flooring, bookcases crammed with old tomes, and a large hatch revealing the kitchen. Ales are local and cider fans will find Black Rat and Symonds, and wine drinkers a good selection by the glass. Two AA Rosettes prove the continuing high quality and careful preparation of the food – all from trusted local suppliers. An open area at the front features a cosy thatched cabana, and at the rear are tables and benches, beyond which overnight accommodation borders onto the garden.

Open all day, all week *Free House* 12
portions/menu *notice required*

LOWER WIELD

The Yew Tree PICK OF THE PUBS

Tel **01256 389224** | **SO24 9RX**
Web **www.the-yewtree.org.uk**
Dir ***A339 from Basingstoke towards Alton. Turn right for Lower Wield.***

The Yew Tree is set in wonderful countryside, and the enthusiastic landlord's simple mission statement promises 'Good honest food; great local beers; fine wines (lots of choice); and, most importantly, good fun for one and all'. There are 20 guest ale brewers on rotation, including Bowman Ales, Flowerpots and Hogs Back. Most of the food is sourced from Hampshire or neighbouring counties, and the menu reflects the seasons while keeping regular favourites 'to avoid uproar'. Sample dishes include Cumberland sausages, parsley mash and onion gravy; or Thai sweet potato, chickpea mushroom and bean curry with basmati rice. There is an annual cricket match and sports day in summer, and quizzes in the winter months.

Open Tue to Sat 12–3 6–11 (Sun all day) Closed 1st 2 weeks Jan, Mon Free House 14 portions/menu Wi-fi P

LYMINGTON

The Mayflower ★★★★ INN

Tel **01590 672160** | **SO41 3QD**
Web **www.themayflowerlymington.co.uk**
Dir ***Phone for detailed directions.***

A red-brick Edwardian pub overlooking the Lymington slipway and river, The Mayflower makes good use of its coastal position with a nautical theme throughout the bar, restaurant and bedrooms. Diners can tuck into modern British dishes conjured from local Hampshire and south coast ingredients. You might kivk off with warm mackerel salad with pickled beetroot, horseradish cream andcroutons, or mussels with white wine and garlic; follwoed by pie of the day with mash and gravy, or mushroom Wellington

Open all day, all week Free House 16 from £13.95 portions/menu Wi-fi P *notice required*

LYMINGTON

The Walhampton Arms

Tel **01590 673113** | **Walhampton Hill, SO41 5RE**
Web **walhamptonarmslymington.co.uk**
Dir ***From Lymington take B3054 towards Beaulieu. Pub in 2 miles.***

From model dairy farm to model pub

In the 19th-century, Home Farm, with its distinctive cupola, was a model dairy supplying the now broken-up Walhampton Estate. The old farm buildings, arranged in a quadrangle, have outwardly changed little but the interior is very different, since it is now this friendly and relaxing New Forest pub, although still with a distinct rustic look. It serves real ales from nearby Ringwood, and guest ales from local microbreweries. Those with a penchant for pub favourites, will find them here, including home-made pies; ale-battered fish and chunky chips; and trio of Old English sausages. But if you want something a little more, shall we say, refined then roast rump of lamb with Tuscan potatoes; luxury fish pie; or gnocchi pomodoro might be right up your culinary street. Sunday is carvery day.

Open all day, all week 11–11 (Sun 12–10.30) Free House 10 from £10 portions/menu P *notice required*

LYNDHURST

New Forest Inn

Tel **023 8028 4690** | **Emery Down, SO43 7DY**
Web **www.thenewforestinn.co.uk**
Dir ***M27 junction 1 follow signs for A35/Lyndhurst. In Lyndhurst follow signs for Christchurch, turn right at Swan Inn towards Emery Down.***

New Forest ponies occasionally wander into this traditional local, a distraction that only serves to enhance its friendly atmosphere. There's incumbents Fortyniner, Flack's Double Drop and Aspall cider on tap. The menu showcases a multitude of items. The beer festival is in July.

The Oak Inn

Tel **023 8028 2350** | **Pinkney Lane, Bank, SO43 7FD**
Web **www.oakinnlyndhurst.co.uk**
Dir ***From Lyndhurst signed A35 to Christchurch, follow A35 for 1mile, left at Bank sign.***

At the heart of the National Park, patrons enjoying Gales ales in the garden of this bare-boarded, bric-à-brac full country pub may idly watch local residents' pigs snuffling for acorns, New Forest ponies grazing or even fallow deer fleetingly flitting amidst the trees.

MAPLEDURWELL

The Gamekeepers – see opposite

MARCHWOOD

The Pilgrim Inn

Tel **023 8086 7752** | **Hythe Road, SO40 4WU**
Web **www.pilgriminnmarchwood.co.uk**
Dir ***M27 junction 2, A326 towards Fawley. Follow brown sign for inn, turn left into Twiggs Lane. At T-junction right into Hythe Road. Pub on right.***

What is now the Pilgrim was originally three 18th-century cottages, but although considerably expanded, altered and refurbished since, its thatched roof, exposed beams, stone walls and log fire still create an inviting atmosphere and welcoming, homely feel. There is a family-friendly menu of classic pub favourites.

NEW ALRESFORD

The Bell Inn

Tel **01962 732429** | **12 West Street, SO24 9AT**
Web **www.bellalresford.com**
Dir ***In village centre.***

A well-restored former coaching inn in Alresford's Georgian main street, where Hampshire real ales hold their own against contenders from Cornwall and Devon, and 18 wines are available by the glass. The bar dining area and candlelit restaurant offer grilled lamb and chicken skewers; and prawn cocktail to start; steak and kidney pie, mash, and greens; and pea and mint risotto. There's a good value two-course menu available at various times during the week. Station Road, opposite the inn, leads to the famous Watercress Line railway.

Open all year, all day Closed Sun evening Free House 18 from £11 portions/menu Wi-fi notice required

NORTHINGTON

The Woolpack Inn

★★★★ INN **PICK OF THE PUBS**

Tel **01962 734184** | **Totford, SO24 9TJ**
Web **www.thewoolpackinn.co.uk**
Dir ***From Basingstoke take A339 towards Alton. Under motorway, turn right (across dual carriageway) onto B3036 signed Candovers and Alresford. Pub between Brown Candover and Northington.***

Set in lovely Hampshire countryside, this brick and flint drovers' inn has a sense of calm modernity while still retaining the classic feel of a country pub. Standing in a tiny hamlet in the peaceful Candover Valley, The Woolpack welcomes walkers and their dogs, families, cyclists and foodies. Ales change weekly, and there's an upmarket wine list. Eat in the traditional bar, where tiled floors and a roaring log fire create a relaxing atmosphere; alternatives are the smart dining room or the terrace. Main courses include home-farmed partridge, parsnip purée, cabbage and bacon, black pudding, game chips; or maple-glazed duck leg, butternut squash purée and pak choi.

Open all day, all week Free House 13 portions/menu Wi-fi P notice required

OLD BASING

Bartons Mill – see opposite

MAPLEDURWELL

The Gamekeepers

Tel 01256 322038 | Tunworth Road, RG25 2LU
Web www.thegamekeepers.co.uk
Dir *M3 junction 6, A30 towards Hook. Right across dual carriageway after The Hatch pub. Pub signed.*

Charming 19th-century village pub with a large garden

Converted from a cottage into a beer house in around 1854, The Gamekeepers took on its current name in 1973 and 30 years later its present owners, Phil and Sandra Costello, arrived. Standing alone down a leafy lane in a village comfortably beyond Basingstoke's eastern limits, the weatherboarded pub has plenty of character, with a low-beamed, flagstone-floored interior and a covered well. The bar offers a choice of Hampshire-brewed real ales, Norcotts real cider from Devon, and 10 wines by the glass. You'll find a typical starter of ham hock terrine, followed by mains including chargrilled venison loin or pan-roasted Creedy Carver duck breast. To round off, perhaps choose sticky toffee pudding with cream, or the excellent Hampshire cheeseboard.

Open all week Mon to Fri 11–2.30 5.30–11 (Sat 11–11 Sun 11–10) Closed 31 Dec, 1 Jan *Free House* 10 *from £15.95* *portions/menu* *notice required*

OLD BASING

Bartons Mill

Tel 01256 331153 | Bartons Lane, RG24 8AE
Web www.bartonsmillpubanddining.co.uk
Dir *Phone for directions, follow brown signs.*

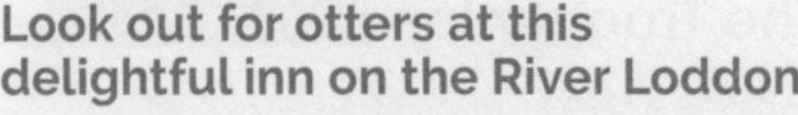

Look out for otters at this delightful inn on the River Loddon

A splendid converted mill in a lovely riverside location, with loads of outside space and plenty of tables for alfresco dining. Inside, the pub is full of character and a plethora of original features, dating back in part to the late 17th century – it was a working mill until the 1960s. There are Wadworth ales on the bar, including 6X, Swordfish and IPA, while the seasonal menus might offer seared scallops on cauliflower purée with pancetta and toasted pistachios, followed perhaps by home-cooked honey-glazed ham with free-range eggs, slow-roasted tomatoes and chips, or chargrilled pork ribeye steak with apple fritters, dauphinoise potatoes and cider sauce. Alternatively, share the Cornish smoked fish board with mackerel, trout and oak-smoked salmon, along with beetroot and horseradish chutney and rustic breads. There are also 12 en-suite rooms available.

Open all day, all week 11–11 (Sat 10am–11pm Sun 10am–10.30pm) *Wadworth* *from £12* *portions/menu* *notice required*

The Crown

Tel **01256 321424 | The Street, RG24 7BW**
Web **www.thecrownoldbasing.com**
Dir ***M3 junction 6 towards Basingstoke. At roundabout right onto A30. 1st left into Redbridge Lane, to T-junction. Right into The Street, pub on right.***

Just outside Basingstoke in the picturesque village of Old Basing, The Crown offers reliable and popular national ales backed by a good wine list. Here, they take great pride in the fact that every dish is prepared from scratch in the pub's kitchen. On the main menu, a typical choice could be crisp belly of lamb with cauliflower purée and spiced lentils. Lemon posset or warm coffee and walnut sponge both make for a delicious finale.

Open 12–3 5–11 (Fri to Sat 12–12 Sun 12–7) Closed 1 Jan, Mon lunch Enterprise Inns portions/menu notice required

OTTERBOURNE

The White Horse

Tel **01962 712830 | Main Road, SO21 2EQ**
Web **www.whitehorseotterbourne.co.uk**
Dir ***M3 junction 12, A335 1st exit at 1st roundabout and 2nd exit at next 2 roundabouts, via Otterbourne Hill into Main Road. Restaurant on left.***

Cosy and eclectically furnished, with exposed brick, open fires and plenty of period detail, The White Horse is set in a village between Winchester and Chandlers Ford, handy for the M3. The menu might tempt you to start with offerings like crispy paprika squid, or whole-baked camembert with garlic sourdough. Main courses include vegan options like spiced chickpea, coconut and sweet potato stew; plus chalk stream trout en papillote or slow-braised ox cheek and fillet steak. Finish with amaretti and fig cheesecake.

Open all day, all week Ideal 14 portions/menu notice required

OVERTON

The White Hart ★★★★ INN

Tel **01256 771431 | London Road, RG25 3NW**
Web **www.whitehartoverton.co.uk**
Dir ***Phone for detailed directions.***

An integral part of village life in Overton for more than five centuries, the stylishly restored White Hart is an ideal pitstop for visitors to nearby Basingstoke. Menus feature pub classics as well as dishes like Goan fish curry; pork medallions with Stilton, and dry aged steaks.

Open all day, all week 7am–11pm Upham Pub Company 16 from £10.95 portions/menu notice required

OVINGTON

The Bush PICK OF THE PUBS

Tel **01962 732764 | SO24 0RE**
Web **www.thebushinn.co.uk**
Dir ***A31 from Winchester towards Alton and Farnham, approximately 6 miles, left to Ovington. 0.5 mile to pub.***

On the banks of the River Itchen, in the pretty village of Ovington, this rose-covered pub is tucked down a track that's part of the historic Pilgrim's Way running from Winchester to Canterbury. Small rooms off the bar are characterised by subdued lighting, dark-painted walls, sturdy tables and chairs, high-backed settles, and trout-fishing and other rustic artefacts. Add the comforting log fire and one of Wadworth's real ales and the result is, well, pub heaven.

PETERSFIELD

The Trooper Inn PICK OF THE PUBS

Tel **01730 827293 | Alton Road, Froxfield, GU32 1BD**
Web **www.trooperinn.com**
Dir ***From A3 follow A272 Winchester signs towards Petersfield (Note: do not take A272). 1st exit at mini-roundabout for Steep. 3 miles, pub on right.***

It calls itself the 'Pub on the Hill' and, at an elevation of 220 metres, it's entitled to, although it sits in a dip. Allegedly a recruiting centre during the run-up to WWI, it backs on to Ashford Hangers National Nature Reserve. Inside are winter log fires, a spacious bar and a charming restaurant with a vaulted ceiling and wooden settles.

Hampshire real ales Ballards and Ringwood Best are served in the bar, and the menu offers a wide range of tempting dishes – breaded whitebait; duck and apricot pâté; Angus rump steak; aubergine bake; and The Trooper's speciality, slow-roasted lamb shank. Among the desserts are sticky toffee pudding and blackberry and cassis trifle.

Open 12–3 6–11 Closed Christmas and New Year (contact pub for details), Sun evening and Mon to Wed lunch (except bank holiday Mon lunch) Free House portions/menu notice required

RINGWOOD

The Railway

Tel **01425 473701** | **35 Hightown Road, BH24 1NQ**
Web **therailway.co**
Dir ***From A31 (north of Ringwood) follow Ringwood signs onto B3347. At next roundabout 2nd exit signed Winkton. At next roundabout 2nd exit into Christchurch Road. 2nd right into Hightown Road.***

This family-run pub has a traditional and unspoilt feel with locals huddled around the bar drinking Hampshire-brewed Ringwood Best. With a beautiful garden complete with play area and vegetable patch, The Railway is family-friendly and younger visitors get to choose from their own menu.

ROCKBOURNE

The Rose & Thistle

Tel **01725 518236** | **SP6 3NL**
Web **www.roseandthistle.co.uk**
Dir ***Follow Rockbourne signs from either A354 (Salisbury to Blandford Forum road) or A338 at Fordingbridge.***

A spectral presence is occasionally abroad here; hardly surprising that the spirit of a former landlord is loathe to leave such an idyllic thatched pub at the fringe of the New Forest. For mortal visitors it's the lure of the local beers, top-notch home cooking and the shrubby cottage garden that will detain them. A lunchtime snack might be crayfish tail sandwich with avocado and salad; or a Welsh rarebit; but for something more substantial choose steak and kidney steamed suet pudding; confit pork belly, celeriac and honey purée and caramelised apple segments; or roasted red pepper and haloumi burger.

ROMSEY

The Three Tuns PICK OF THE PUBS

Tel **01794 512639** | **58 Middlebridge Street, SO51 8HL**
Web **www.the3tunsromsey.co.uk**
Dir ***From Romsey bypass (A27) follow town centre sign. Left into Middlebridge Street.***

Five minutes from Romsey's Market Square, close to a stone bridge with the River Test flowing beneath it, this 370-year-old pub has a traditional feel with low oak beams and open fireplaces. Enjoy a pint of Romsey's own Flack Manor Double Drop ale or one of the 40 gins available as you scan the simple British menu made up of seasonal classics and sharing platters. For a starter, maybe Scotch egg of the day; followed by the daily Three Tuns pie or Romsey trout with crispy mussels. Puddings might feature warm black treacle tart or carrot cake with orange ice cream.

Open all day, all week Closed 25 Dec Enterprise Inns 11 from £12.50 portions

ROTHERWICK

The Coach and Horses

Tel **01256 768976** | **The Street, RG27 9BG**
Web **www.coachandhorses-rotherwick.co.uk**
Dir ***Follow brown signs from A32 (Hook to Reading road).***

Close to the church in Rotherwick – a picturesque village that has appeared in TV's *Midsomer Murders* – parts of this smart, cream-washed inn date back to the 17th century. With log fires in winter, exposed brickwork and red-and-black tiled or wooden floors, the interior is pleasingly traditional. The south-facing garden is a draw in the summer as a place for a relaxed pint of Badger Fursty Ferret or a sensibly priced meal.

Open all year 12–3 5–11 (Sat 12–11 Sun 12–6) Closed Sun evening and Mon Hall & Woodhouse 10 from £9.95 portions notice required

SELBORNE

The Selborne Arms

Tel **01420 511247 | High Street, GU34 3JR**
Web **www.selbornearms.co.uk**
Dir ***From A3 take B3006, pub in village centre.***

A huge chimney, known as a baffle entry, seemingly blocks your way to accessing this 17th-century pub. You must turn left or right, it doesn't matter which, for either way you'll find homely bars with hop-strewn beams, a huge fireplace, Bowman Ales Swift One, Ringwood Fortyniner, local guest ales and Mr Whitehead's cider. The menu will please those who enjoy, for example, local hand-made pork sausages and mash; home-made steak and kidney pie; and locally-smoked duck breast salad.

Open all week 11–3 6–11 (Sat 11–11 Sun 12–11) Free House 11 portions/menu notice required

SILCHESTER

Calleva Arms

Tel **0118 970 0305 | Little London Road, The Common, RG7 2PH**
Web **www.callevaarms.co.uk**
Dir ***A340 from Basingstoke, signed Silchester.***

The ancient walls of Calleva Atrebatum (Silchester Roman City Walls and Amphitheatre) are some of the best preserved in Britain. The ruins are not far away from this 19th-century Fuller's pub overlooking the common and cricket pitch. Two bar areas, with a log-burner in the middle, lead to a pleasant conservatory and pretty garden. The full lunch and evening menu includes baguettes, jacket potatoes; home-made steak and ale pie; ham, double egg and chips; and fish of the day.

Open all day, all week Fuller's 11 portions notice required

STEEP

Harrow Inn PICK OF THE PUBS

Tel **01730 262685 | GU32 2DA**
Web **www.theharrowinnsteep.co.uk**
Dir ***From A272 in Petersfield into Inmans Lane (diagonally opposite garage) to Sheet. In Sheet turn left opposite church into School Lane, over A3 by-pass bridge. Inn signed on right.***

This 16th-century, tile-hung gem is situated in a lovely rural location and has changed little over the years. The McCutcheon family has run it since 1929; sisters Claire and Nisa, both born and brought up here, are the third generation with their names over the door. Tucked away off the road, it comprises two tiny bars – the 'public' is Tudor, with beams, tiled floor, inglenook fireplace, scrubbed tables, and a 'library'; the saloon is Victorian. Beers are dispensed from barrels, there is no till and the toilets are across the road. Food is in keeping: ham and pea soup; hot Scotch eggs; cheddar ploughman's; and various quiches. The large garden has plenty of tables surrounded by country-cottage flowers and fruit trees. Quiz nights raise huge sums for charity.

Open all year 12–2.30 6–11 (Sat 11–3 6–11 Sun 12–3 7–10.30) Closed Sun evening in winter Free House from £11.60

STOCKBRIDGE

The Greyhound on the Test

★★★★ RESTAURANT WITH ROOMS

Tel **01264 810833 | 31 High Street, SO20 6EY**
Web **www.thegreyhoundonthetest.co.uk**
Dir ***In village centre.***

Hampshire's famous fly-fishing river runs right behind this early 19th-century free house on Stockbridge's wide, picturesque high street. The wood-floored interior is laid out with interestingly styled tables and chairs under a beamed ceiling. Very much a dining pub, The Greyhound has two AA Rosettes, so expect high quality in dishes such as buffalo carpaccio; braised ox cheek; roasted venison, faggot and pan haggerty; monkfish bouillabaisse; and roasted squash, chickpea and coconut curry.

Open all day, all week Closed 25–26 Dec Free House 12 from £15 portions notice required

Mayfly

Tel **01264 860283 | Testcombe, SO20 6AZ**
Web **www.mayflyfullerton.co.uk**
Dir ***Between A303 and A30, on A3057. Between Stockbridge and Andover.***

Standing right on the banks of the River Test, the Mayfly is an iconic drinking spot and very popular place. Inside the beamed old farmhouse with its traditional bar and bright conservatory you'll find a choice of draught ciders and up to six real ales.

The Peat Spade Inn

★★★★ INN PICK OF THE PUBS

Tel **01264 810612 | Longstock, SO20 6DR**
Web **www.peatspadeinn.co.uk**
Dir ***Phone for detailed directions.***

Owned by the successful Upham Pub Company, The Peat Spade stands very close to the River Test, famous as one of the best fly-fishing rivers in England. A gabled, red-brick Victorian building, its unusual windows overlook a peaceful village lane and thatched cottages. The short, daily-changing menu lists dishes reliant on local and regional suppliers. Among them at lunchtime may be dry-aged beefburger, wild mushrooms, truffle mayonnaise, fries and mixed leaves; Ale-battered hake and chips; or handpicked Portland crab on toast. The dinner menu might offer pan-fried fillet of salmon, pink fir potatoes, peas, samphire, cucumber and wasabi butter sauce; and slow-cooked rump of lamb, belly croquette, dauphinoise potatoes, baby carrots and rosemary jus. Outside is an enclosed, sheltered terrace.

Open all day, all week 11–11 (Sun 11–10.30) Free House 11 from £14 portions/menu Wi-fi notice required

The Three Cups Inn ★★★★

Tel **01264 810527 | High Street, SO20 6HB**
Web **www.the3cups.co.uk**
Dir ***M3 junction 8, A303 towards Andover. Left onto A3057 to Stockbridge.***

It's said that the name of this 15th-century, timber-framed pub comes from an Old English phrase for a meeting of three rivers, but there's only one here – The Test, world-famous as 'the birthplace of modern fly fishing'. You might even spot a brown trout or two while sitting on the patio in the charming rear garden. There's a log fire to warm the low-beamed bar, where you'll find local ales Itchen Valley and Flowerpots. Menus feature modern European and traditional dishes – maybe seared fillets of sole; heritage carrot and tarragon gnocchi; or wild boar and apple sausages – and the restaurant has an AA Rosette. Suites provide excellent overnight accommodation.

Open all day, all week 12–11 Free House 12 portions/menu Wi-fi notice required

SWANMORE

The Rising Sun

Tel **01489 896663 | Hill Pound, SO32 2PS**
Web **www.risingsunswanmore.co.uk**
Dir ***M27 junction 10, A32 through Wickham towards Alton. Left into Bishop's Wood Road, right at crossroads into Mislingford Road to Swanmore.***

Run by Ben and Amy Chester-Sterne, this 17th-century coaching inn is tucked away in the heart of the beautiful Meon Valley. Roaring fires, low beams and plenty of nooks and crannies provide a high comfort factor in winter. Time a visit for the beer festival in mid-September.

TANGLEY

The Fox Inn

Tel **01264 730276 | SP11 0RU**
Web **www.foxinntangley.co.uk**
Dir ***From roundabout (junction of A343 and A3057) in Andover follow station signs (Charlton Road). Through Charlton and Hatherden to Tangley.***

Curiously, among the team at The Fox Inn, is a former chef to the Thai Royal Family who now dedicates his skills to providing a startling menu to pub-goers who adventure along the country lanes to this 300-year-old brick and flint pub. There are far-reaching views across sloping fields, while the inside is largely furnished in a casual-contemporary style featuring an unusual log-end bar design, where guests may enjoy a wide choice of genuine Thai dishes and some fine local beers.

Open all day, all week 12–11 (Sun 12–10.30) Closed 25 Dec Free House 12 portions/menu Wi-fi notice required

THRUXTON

The White Horse Inn & Restaurant

Tel **01264 772401** | **Mullens Pond, SP11 8EE**
Web **www.whitehorsethruxton.co.uk**
Dir ***South of Thruxton, A303. Phone for detailed directions.***

There's plenty of Grade II listed atmosphere in this Test Valley pub, thought to date from around 1450. Local beers in the spacious bar might include Romsey's Flack Manor Flack's Double Drop, and King John from Andwell, near Basingstoke.

TICHBORNE

The Tichborne Arms

PICK OF THE PUBS

Tel **01962 733760** | **SO24 0NA**
Web **www.tichbornearms.co.uk**
Dir ***Follow pub signs from B3046, south of A31 between Winchester and Alresford.***

Not as old as its thatched roof might suggest, this village pub was built in the mid-20th century to replace its burnt-down predecessor. Antiques, prints and other artefacts decorate the bar, so there's plenty to look at as you relax with a pint of Hop Back or Red Cat real ale. The short daily menus may feature fillet of sea bream with creamy prawn sauce; or medallions of pork tenderloin; as well as at least one vegetarian option. A beer festival takes place in the tree-shaded garden over the Summer Bank Holiday weekend in August.

Open all week Mon to Fri 11.45–3 (Tue to Thu 6–10.30, Fri 6–11, Sat 11.45–11, Sun 12–7.30) Free House 10 portions Wi-fi P notice required

TWYFORD

The Bugle Inn

Tel **01962 714888** | **Park Lane, SO21 1QT**
Web **www.bugleinntwyford.co.uk**
Dir ***M3 junction 11, B3335, 1.5 miles to Twyford.***

This charming 18th-century coaching inn was sold for development in 2002 but rescued after the villagers stepped in. It re-opened six years later and has never looked back. A selection of snacks and sandwiches is available at lunchtime, or you can choose from the main menu.

UPPER CLATFORD

Crook & Shears

Tel **01264 361543** | **SP11 7QL**
Web **www.crookandshears.co.uk**
Dir ***Phone for detailed directions.***

Old photographs show the thatched and whitewashed exterior looking much as it did 100 years ago, when the Crook & Shears first became a pub; parts of the building date to the 17th century, when it was probably built as a farmhouse. The interiors ooze character.

UPPER FROYLE

The Hen & Chicken Inn

Tel **01420 22115** | **GU34 4JH**
Web **www.henandchicken.co.uk**
Dir ***2 miles from Alton towards Farnham on A31. Adjacent to petrol station. Signed from A31.***

Highwaymen, hop-pickers and high clergy have all supped and succoured here in this noble, three-storey Georgian road house. They'd still recognise some of the comfortably traditional interior and maybe the little wooden barn in the garden. The reliable country menu is strong on local produce.

WARNFORD

The George & Falcon

★★★★ INN

Tel **01730 829623** | **Warnford Road, SO32 3LB**
Web **www.georgeandfalcon.com**
Dir ***M27 junction 10, A32 signed Alton. Approximately 10.5 miles to Warnford.***

The lively little River Meon slides past the garden of this imposing inn, first recorded over 400 years ago. The cosy, fire-warmed snug is the place to settle with a pint of Ringwood Fortyniner and reflect on a grand winter walk on nearby Old Winchester Hill; or discover the terrace and consider the enticing modern choices including those on the good value, set menus – scallops, celeriac and hazelnut; salmon with jasmine rice, wasabi mayo; beef bourguignon; game faggots. Six en suite bedrooms complete the scene.

Open all year, all day 11–11 (Oct to Mar 11–3 6–11) Closed Mon lunch (Oct to Mar only) Marston's 9 portions/menu Wi-fi P notice required

WELL

The Chequers Inn

Tel **01256 862605** | **RG29 1TL**
Web **www.chequers-well.com**
Dir ***From Odiham High Street into King Street, becomes Long Lane. 3 miles, left at T-junction, pub 0.25 mile on top of hill.***

A lovely country pub with a multitude of low beams testifying to its 15th-century origins. Paul and Nichola Sanders have a proven track record of running successful pubs and their forte is preparing classic English dishes and daily specials based on fresh fish, steaks and duck, and serving well-kept pints of Hall & Woodhouse ales. Eat and drink by a log fire, out front under sheltered grapevines, or on the decked area in the rear garden, overlooking the countryside.

Open all week 12–3 6–11 (Sat to Sun all day) Hall & Woodhouse 23 portions notice required

WEST MEON

The Thomas Lord ★★★★ INN

PICK OF THE PUBS

Tel **01730 829244** | **High Street, GU32 1LN**
Web **www.thethomaslord.co.uk**
Dir ***M3 junction 9, A272 towards Petersfield, right at crossroads onto A32, 1st left.***

Thomas Lord, the eponymous founder of Lord's Cricket Ground, retired to the pretty village of West Meon in 1830 and is buried in the churchyard. This beautifully restored pub has a bar decorated with cricketing memorabilia and it's an agreeable setting for well-kept seasonal and guest ales, or a chilled glass of white chosen from the sophisticated range of wines. Herbs, salads and vegetables are grown in the pub's own garden; otherwise the kitchen is supplied by local farms and small-scale producers. A typical meal might start with pigeon, Waldorf salad, candied walnut, celery, apple and blue cheese, followed by beef sirloin, beef dripping mash, braised shallot, shallot purée and sautéed kale.

Open all day, all week Free House 12 portions notice required

WEST WELLOW

The Rockingham Arms

PICK OF THE PUBS

Tel **01794 324798** | **Canada Road, SO51 6DE**
Web **www.rockinghamarms.co.uk**
Dir ***M27 junction 2, A36 towards Salisbury. In Wellow left into Canada Road.***

Built in 1840, this cosy village pub on the edge of Canada Common, a National Heritage area, is just within the New Forest. While its age is still evident from the outside, the thoughtfully modernised interior retains few clues. Real ales include Ringwood Best and Dancing Cows Pony, with 20 wines by the glass. Sandwiches – Portland crab, for example – and snacks are available at lunchtime, as is 'pie of the day'; Malaysian fish curry with coconut rice (with a vegan option); pan-fried calves' liver with crisp pancetta; and baked Alaska with Kirsch-infused cherries to follow. Ample supplies of dog biscuits are kept in a jar on the bar.

Open all day, all week Free House 20 from £12.50 menus

WHITCHURCH

The White Hart

Tel **01256 892900** | **Newbury Street, RG28 7DN**
Web **www.whiteharthotelwhitchurch.co.uk**
Dir ***On B3400 in town centre.***

Strategically located where the old London to Exeter and Oxford to Southampton roads cross, this was Swindon brewery Arkell's first Hampshire pub. Dating from 1461, its rich history includes patronage by the late Lord Denning, Master of the Rolls, who was born in a house opposite.

WICKHAM

Greens Restaurant & Bar

Tel **01329 833197** | **The Square, PO17 5JQ**
Web **www.greensrestaurant.co.uk**
Dir ***M27 junction 10, A32 to Wickham.***

It's hard to miss Greens' black-and-white timbered building, standing prominently on a corner of Wickham's medieval market square, the second largest in England. Proprietors for 30 years still proudly use their original slogan – 'Nothing is too much trouble'.

WINCHESTER

The Black Boy

Tel **01962 861754** | **1 Wharf Hill, SO23 9NQ**
Web **www.theblackboypub.com**
Dir ***Off Chesil Street (B3300).***

This old-fashioned, whitewashed pub in the ancient capital of Wessex is a decidedly beer-led hostelry. As well as three regular regional ales from the Cheriton, Alfred's and Hop Back breweries, The Black Boy offers two Hampshire guests, perhaps from Bowman or Itchen Valley. The interior has quirky decor with all manner of objects hanging from the ceiling, while the short, traditional daily menu on the blackboard could include sandwiches, as well as home-made burgers and fish and chips. There is a sheltered garden with patio heaters.

Open all day, all week *Free House* Wi-fi

The Golden Lion

Tel **01962 865512** | **99 Alresford Road, SO23 0JZ**
Web **www.thegoldenlionwinchester.co.uk**
Dir ***From Union Street in town centre follow 'All other routes' sign. At roundabout 1st exit into High Street. At roundabout 1st exit into Bridge Street (B3404) signed Alton/Alresford, (becomes Alresford Road).***

This 1932-built pub on the outskirts of Winchester is well known for its wonderful floral displays in the summer months. Brid and Derek Phelan are strong on Irish charm and pride themselves on offering good, home-cooked food. Typically, you can tuck into steak and ale pie; home-cooked gammon steak (topped with egg or pineapple), chips and peas; a choice of burgers. Vegetarian options, a short vegan menu and gluten-free options are also available. The pub has a large beer garden too.

Open all week Mon to Sat 11.30–3 5.30–11 (Sun 12–10.30) Wadworth 8 from £10.95 portions/menu Wi-fi P *notice required*

The Green Man

Tel **01962 866809** | **53 Southgate Street, SO23 9EH**
Web **www.greenmanwinchester.co.uk**
Dir ***Phone for detailed directions.***

With its retro-furnished bar, Jayne Gillin's Green Man is one of her five city bars and restaurants, all showing her enviable talent for trendy makeovers. Upstairs is an Edwardian-style dining room, while The Outhouse, formerly the skittle alley, is now a cool, 1930s industrial-style function room.

The Old Vine ★★★★ INN

Tel **01962 854616** | **8 Great Minster Street, SO23 9HA**
Web **www.oldvinewinchester.com**
Dir ***M3 junction 11, follow Saint Cross and City Centre signs. 1 mile, right at Green Man pub right into Saint Swithun Street, bear left into Symonds Street (one-way). Right into Great Minster Street (Note: for Sat Nav use SO23 9HB).***

Directly opposite Winchester's Cathedral and City Museum, this elegant Grade II listed pub was built on Saxon foundations in the 18th century. There are four guest beers in the oak-beamed bar, where you can eat sandwiches, salads and light bites. A typical meal could include cottage pie or pan-fried calves' liver with Madeira and onion gravy. At the back of the pub you'll find a flower-filled patio.

Open all day, all week Closed 25 Dec Enterprise Inns 11 from £12.50 Wi-fi

The Wykeham Arms

PICK OF THE PUBS

Tel **01962 853834** | **75 Kingsgate Street, SO23 9PE**
Web **www.wykehamarmswinchester.co.uk**
Dir ***Near Winchester College and Winchester Cathedral.***

It's hard to convey just how much character The Wyk has. It's more than a pub; it's a Winchester institution. Beyond the cathedral from the High Street, with Winchester College as a neighbour, this 270-year-old building is entered from the pavement through curved, etched-glass doors straight into two bars. Both have open fires and are furnished with old pine tables and redundant college desks. Everywhere are portraits and prints, pewter tankards and miscellaneous ephemera.

Open all day, all week Fuller's 26 from £12.50 Wi-fi P

HEREFORDSHIRE

AYMESTREY

The Riverside at Aymestrey

★★★★ INN PICK OF THE PUBS

Tel **01568 708440** | **HR6 9ST**
Web **www.riversideaymestrey.co.uk**
Dir ***On A4110, 18 miles north of Hereford.***

Built in 1580, this character inn started catering to passing sheep drovers in 1700; it's midway along the Mortimer Trail, just by the ford across the River Lugg. The wood-panelled interior with low beams and log fires makes a cosy setting for a pint of Wye Valley Butty Bach or Hobsons Best; ciders include Westons and Robinsons. The pub's vegetable, herb and fruit garden is the source of many ingredients for the seasonal menus – Shropshire pressed pork and black pudding, pear and parsley broth might precede freshwater trout, fennel and English white wine sauce; celeriac ribbons, cracked wheat, cream, rosemary and Wigmore cheese; or slow-braised beef, oxtail sauce, smoked mash and kale.

Open all year Tue to Sat 11–3 6–11 (Sun 12–3 Mon 6–11) Closed Mon lunch Free House 16 portions notice required

BREDWARDINE

The Red Lion ★★★ INN

Tel **01981 500303** | **HR3 6BU**
Web **www.redlion-hotel.com**
Dir ***Take A438 from Hereford towards Eardisley. Follow signs for Bredwardine.***

Handy for both Hereford and Hay-on-Wye, the 17th-century Red Lion is tucked away in the sleepy hamlet of Bredwardine, set against a backdrop of fields and cider orchards. Once a coaching inn, the lounge was used as the courtroom for the circuit judge, although these days the only judgement being passed is on the well-kept Butty Bach beer and Gwatkin cider, and the highly-regarded food. A starter of smooth duck liver pâté might precede lamb shank in a rich red wine and rosemary sauce.

Open all week 12–2.30 6.30–11 Free House portions

BROMYARD DOWNS

The Royal Oak

Tel **01885 482585** | **HR7 4QP**
Web **www.royaloakbromyard.com**
Dir ***From A44 at Bromyard take B4203 towards Stourport-on-Severn. Approximately 1.5 miles, pub signed.***

A 300-year-old, black-and-white free house, 200 metres above sea level and the only pub left on the lovely Bromyard Downs. Breweries not too far away supply Shropshire Lad, Black Pear and Pure Gold real ales. A look at the menu reveals a comforting list of home-made dishes, including steak and kidney pie; and beef chilli. Curries make a good showing too, with Thai green, chicken tikka masala and vegetable balti. Batting for the fish team are breaded wholetail scampi; plaice goujons; and battered haddock.

Open 12–3 6–10/11 Closed 25 Dec, Sun evening and Mon Free House 9 portions/menu notice required

CAREY

Cottage of Content

Tel **01432 840242** | **HR2 6NG**
Web **www.cottageofcontent.co.uk**
Dir ***From crossroads on A49 between Hereford and Ross-on-Wye, follow Hoarwithy signs. In Hoarwithy branch right, follow Carey signs.***

Lost among narrow lanes in delightfully bucolic countryside close to the meandering River Wye, this pretty streamside inn (with lovely views from the garden) has been licensed for 530 years. Now, as then, local ciders and beers flow from the bar, which boasts a log fire, flagged floors and heavy timbering. Making the most of the county's produce, the concise menu might offer goats' cheese and red onion marmalade tartlet; followed by griddled Hereford fillet steak with all the trimmings.

Open 12–2 6.30–11 (times vary summer and winter) Closed 1 week Feb, 1 week Oct, Sun evening, Mon (Tue winter only) Free House from £12.50 portions/menu notice required

CLIFFORD

The Castlefields

Tel **01497 831554 | HR3 5HB**
Web **www.thecastlefields.co.uk**
Dir ***On B4352 between Hay-on-Wye and Bredwardine.***

After hours spent browsing in nearby Hay-on-Wye, the 'Town of Books', a 10-minute drive will get you to this family-run, 16th-century former coach house. Wednesday is curry night and traditional roasts are served on Sundays. Doom Bar and Butty Bach will be found in the bar.

COLWALL

The Wellington Inn

Tel **01684 540269 | Chances Pitch, WR13 6HW**
Web **www.thewellingtoninnmalvern.co.uk**
Dir ***Between Ledbury and Malvern on A449.***

The Wellington sits in an Area of Outstanding Natural Beauty – its garden enjoys panoramic views of unspoilt countryside and magnificent sunsets. The ethos is to keep the bar for drinkers, and to seat diners in one of the three dedicated eating areas.

EARDISLEY

The Tram Inn

Tel **01544 327251 | Church Road, HR3 6PG**
Web **www.thetraminn.co.uk**
Dir ***On A4111 at junction with Woodeaves Road.***

The long-closed tramway that once ran near here is remembered in this 16th-century inn, one of Eardisley's many traditional, black-and-white-timbered buildings. Wood-burners warm the bar, where Wye Valley's Butty Bach is likely to be on tap. As for the food, there's a menu dedicated to the nine varieties of filled baguettes, while the daily version might list coarse chicken and pork pâté; Butty-battered fillet of hake and chips; and local honey-baked ham, with, to finish, warm pear and almond frangipane tart.

Open all year 12–3 6–12 (Fri to Sat 12–3 6–12.30 Sun 12–3 7–11) Closed Mon (excluding bank holidays) Free House portions Wi-fi P notice required

EWYAS HAROLD

The Temple Bar Inn

★★★★ INN

Tel **01981 240423 | HR2 0EU**
Web **www.thetemplebarinn.co.uk**
Dir ***From Pontrilas on A465 take B4347 to Ewyas Harold. 1 mile turn left into village centre. Inn on right.***

Just a few miles from the Welsh border, The Temple Bar Inn is a popular pit-stop for walkers and cyclists exploring the Black Mountains and Herefordshire Trail. Painstakingly restored by the Jinman family, this handsome building was first licensed in the 1850s but it had also been a court house, corn exchange, school room and stable. It's now very much the hub of the community, with locals popping in for pints of real ale including Wye Valley's Butty Bach or foodies enjoying well-executed dishes.

Open all week 11–3 5–close (Sat to Sun and bank holiday 11am–close) Closed 25 Dec Free House from £7.50 portions Wi-fi P notice required

GARWAY

Garway Moon Inn

Tel **01600 750270 | HR2 8RQ**
Web **www.garwaymooninn.co.uk**
Dir ***From Hereford south on A49. Right onto A466, right onto B4521. At Broad Oak turn right to Garway.***

A family-run free house dating back to 1750, overlooking the peaceful, picturesque common. Ask at the bar for three circular walks which will take you to a Knights Templar church, Skenfrith Castle, and panoramic views. A good selection of real ales includes Butcombe and Wye Valley Brewery, with Westons cider also on tap. Traditional pub food is based on high quality local ingredients – many of the producers are regulars in the bar.

Open all week Mon 5–10 Tue 5–10.30 (Wed to Thu 12–3 5–10.30 Fri 12–3 5–11) Sat 12–11 Sun 12–9 Free House 8 portions/menu Wi-fi P notice required

HAREWOOD END

Harewood End Inn

Tel 01989 730637 | HR2 8JT
Web www.theharewoodend.com
Dir *On A49 between Hereford and Ross-on-Wye.*

Harewood End consists of little more than this old coaching inn, its wood-walled and wood-floored interior decorated with old enamel signs. Menus offer plenty of choice at both lunchtime and dinner, with several chargrills on the menu, and 'old faithfuls', including pasta al forno; mustard-roast ham; and chef's curry special. Among the fish choices is beer-battered hake, while for something different again try jerk pork-and-pineapple skewers. The lovely shady garden is perfect on fine summer days.

Open all year 12-3 6-10.30 (Fri to Sat 12-3 6-11 Sun 12-3.30 6-10) Closed Mon Free House from £9.99 portions/menu notice required

HOARWITHY

The New Harp Inn

Tel 01432 840900 | HR2 6QH
Web www.thenewharpinn.co.uk
Dir *From Ross-on-Wye take A49 towards Hereford. Turn right for Hoarwithy.*

The New Harp's slogan reads: 'Kids, dogs and muddy boots all welcome' – and it's certainly popular with locals, fishermen, campers and visitors to the countryside. Situated on the River Wye in an Area of Outstanding Natural Beauty, the pub has extensive gardens and a real babbling brook. Begin your visit with a local real ale or the home-produced cider. Dishes include king prawns in filo pastry with sweet chilli mayo; steak and ale pie, made with Herefordshire beef; and beer-battered Cornish fish and triple-cooked chips.

Open all day, all week 12-11 Free House from £10 portions/menu

KILPECK

The Kilpeck Inn

Tel 01981 570464 | HR2 9DN
Web kilpeckinn.com
Dir *From Hereford take A465 south. In 6 miles at Belmont roundabout left towards Kilpeck. Follow church and inn signs.*

A warm welcome awaits at this lovely old inn

A few minutes' walk from Kilpeck's famous Romanesque church, this 250-year old whitewashed pub is run by chef-patron Ross Williams. A champion of local and seasonal produce, Ross sources as much as possible from nearby artisan and award-winning suppliers. The bar stocks local real ales from Wye Valley Brewery and draught cider from Robsinson's in Tenbury, as well as a wide selection of Herefordshire gins. A typical menu might include pheasant breast with pearl barley, wild mushrooms and crispy kale, or rack of Welsh lamb roasted with a wild garlic and pine nut crust.

Open 12-3 5.30-11 (Sat 12-11 Sun 12-5) Closed 25 Dec, Mon lunch Free House portions/menu notice required

KINGTON

The Stagg Inn and Restaurant

PICK OF THE PUBS

Tel **01544 230221 | Titley, HR5 3RL**
Web **www.thestagg.co.uk**
Dir ***Between Kington and Presteigne on B4355.***

This well-established and celebrated rural gastro pub stands where the wooded ridges of west Herefordshire nudge the Welsh border. Locals congregate in the small bar to chat, snack and drink beers from Ludlow and Wye Valley, and Herefordshire real ciders. The rambling layout incorporates several dining areas, where a starter of Hereford snails, Monmouth ham, mushroom and parsley might be followed by local lamb – rump and slow-cooked shoulder; or seabass fillet, shrimps, samphire, courgettes and new potatoes. A specials board extends the options, while Sunday's set lunch could introduce you to Herefordshire beef, with roast topside served with roast potatoes and Yorkshire pudding. Nearby Chase Distillery provides gins and spirits for cocktails.

Open 12–3 6.30–11 Closed 25–27 Dec, 2 weeks Nov, 1 week Feb and 1 week Jun, Mon and Tue Free House 12 portions/menu Wi-fi

LEDBURY

The Talbot

Tel **01531 632963 | 14 New Street, HR8 2DX**
Web **www.talbotledbury.co.uk**
Dir ***From A449 in Ledbury into Bye Street, 2nd left into Woodley Road, over bridge to junction, left into New Street. Pub on right.***

With parts dating back to 1550, the interior of this higgledy-piggledy coaching inn oozes character. Holes caused by musket shot fired during a Civil War skirmish are just one quirky talking point of the gabled building, where Wadworth's beers slake the thirst. Indulge in starters like prawn and smoked salmon cocktail followed by spicy Goan chicken curry. If the weather permits, sit in the sun-trap, courtyard garden.

Open all day, all week Wadworth 15 portions Wi-fi

The Trumpet Inn

Tel **01531 670277 | Trumpet, HR8 2RA**
Web **www.trumpetinnledbury.co.uk**
Dir ***4 miles from Ledbury, at junction of A438 and A417.***

A very striking, ancient half-timbered inn which has stood at this rural crossroads for upwards of 600 years. The name recalls Georgian times when stagecoach guards blew a horn to warn of their approach. A warm welcome remains at the heart of today's pub.

LEOMINSTER

The Grape Vaults

Tel **01568 611404 | Broad Street, HR6 8BS**
Dir ***Phone for detailed directions.***

This unspoilt, 15th-century pub is so authentic that even its fixed seating is Grade II listed. Its many charms include a small, homely bar complete with a coal fire. A good selection of real ale is a popular feature and includes microbrewery offerings. The unfussy food encompasses favourites like cottage pie, lasagne, chicken curry and various fresh fish and vegetarian choices. There are also plenty of jackets, baguettes, omelettes and other lighter meals available.

Open all day, all week 11–11 Free House 10 portions Wi-fi

MADLEY

The Comet Inn

Tel **01981 250600 | Stoney Street, HR2 9NJ**
Dir ***6 miles from Hereford on B4352.***

Set at a crossroads deep in rural Herefordshire, the space-age parabolic dishes of the Madley Earth Station and the distant smudge of the Black Mountains provide contrasting skylines visible from the large grounds of this convivial local. Now refurbished, it still retains much of the character of the old cottages from which it was converted 150 years ago. Enjoy home-cooked food in the conservatory off the main bar. In winter, sit beside a roaring fire and in summer enjoy the large, well-kept garden.

Open all week Mon to Thu 6–11 (Fri to Sun and bank holidays 12–11) Free House portions/menu notice required

MICHAELCHURCH ESCLEY

The Bridge Inn

Tel **01981 510646** | **HR2 0JW**
Web **www.thebridgeinnmichaelchurch.co.uk**
Dir ***From Peterchurch take B4348 towards Hereford, turn right in Vowchurch to Michaelchurch Escley. At T-junction in village turn left.***

An ideal base for exploring the Golden Valley, Hay-on-Wye, the Brecon Beacons and Offa's Dyke, this delightful riverside inn exudes a warm welcome. It's a lovely setting to enjoy cask-conditioned ales and local ciders, as well as gin from the on-site micro-distillery. A typical meal might feature duck rillettes followed by lamb shoulder tagine. Over the August Bank Holiday weekend, there's a beer and cider festival.

Open all week 12–3 5.30–10 (Sat and Sun all day) Free House 20 from £11.50 portions/menu Wi-fi notice required

PEMBRIDGE

New Inn

Tel **01544 388427** | **Market Square, HR6 9DZ**
Dir ***From M5 junction 7 take A44 west through Leominster towards Llandrindod Wells.***

Formerly a courthouse and jail, and close to the site of the last battle of the War of the Roses, this 14th-century black and white timbered free house has been under the same ownership for 35 years. Worn flagstone floors and winter fires characterise the cosy bar, and in summer customers spill out into the pub's outdoor seating area on the Old Market Square. Home-cooked English fare, using local produce, is on offer.

Open 11–2.30 6–11 (summer 11–3 6–11) Closed 1st week Feb, Tue lunch Free House 10 from £10 portions Wi-fi notice required

STAPLOW

The Oak Inn PICK OF THE PUBS

Tel **01531 640954** | **HR8 1NP**
Web **www.oakinnstaplow.co.uk**
Dir ***M50 junction 2, A417 to Ledbury. At roundabout take 2nd exit onto A449, then A438 (High Street). Take B4214 to Staplow.***

Set in bucolic Herefordshire countryside amidst orchards and hopyards, The Oak enjoys an enviable location close to Ledbury. Ramblers can enjoy a walk along the former Herefordshire and Gloucestershire Canal before retiring to the lovingly extended cottage-style pub, complete with log-burning stoves and flagstone floors. Beers from Ledbury and Wye Valley breweries adorn the bar, whilst local cider adds interest. Dishes from the starter menu include warm Hereford Hop cheese and onion tart with a spiced apple chutney, followed perhaps with a main of Herefordshire steak and kidney pie with rich local ale gravy and horseradish short-crust pastry.

Open all day, all week Free House portions/menu Wi-fi

SYMONDS YAT [EAST]

The Saracens Head Inn – see page 222

TILLINGTON

The Bell Inn Tillington

Tel **01432 760395** | **HR4 8LE**
Web **www.thebelltillington.com**
Dir ***From A4103 (north Hereford) follow Tillington sign.***

This traditional, village pub has been run since 1988 by the Williams family. With two bars, one with an open fire and a screen for sporting events, dining room, extensive gardens and patio, it offers something for everybody. Served alongside Herefordshire ales are sandwiches, light lunches, and dishes such as 10oz sirloin steak; and baked salmon. If you have a sweet tooth, why not go for the Mars Bar cheesecake or salted caramel and chocolate tart.

Open all day, all week Free House menus Wi-fi notice required

WALFORD

The Mill Race – see page 222

SYMONDS YAT [EAST]

The Saracens Head Inn

★★★★ INN

Tel **01600 890435** | **HR9 6JL**
Web **www.saracensheadinn.co.uk**
Dir *A40 onto B4229, follow Symonds Yat East signs, 2 miles.*

Former cider mill in an unrivalled location

Occupying a stunning position on the east bank of the River Wye, The Saracens Head can be reached by the inn's own ferry, which still operates by hand, just as it has for the past 200 years. There's a relaxed atmosphere throughout the 16th-century inn, from the bar (serving Wye Valley ales), the cosy lounge and stylish dining room, and two sunny terraces overlooking the Wye. If you come at lunchtime, try beer-battered haddock; lamb, rosemary and red onion burger with celeriac remoulade, gentleman's relish and home-made chips; or pan-seared polenta cake with mushroom veloute, wild mushrooms, wild rocket and vegetarian parmesan. Complete your meal with one of the home-made desserts on the blackboard. A stay in one of the ten en suite bedrooms is a must if you're exploring this area.

Open all day, all week Closed 25 Dec Free House 10 portions/menu

WALFORD

The Mill Race

Tel **01989 562891** | **HR9 5QS**
Web **www.millrace.info**
Dir *B4234 from Ross-on-Wye to Walford. Pub 3 miles on right.*

Contemporary pub in the Wye Valley

On the borders of Herefordshire, Gloucestershire and Monmouthshire, The Mill Race is just upriver from the famously picturesque gorge at Symonds Yat. On the bank opposite the pub, and visible from the terrace, are the ruins of Goodrich Castle. Comfortable booths in the beamed and flagstoned, wood-burner warmed bar area, are tailor-made for conviviality, and there's also a separate restaurant. By working closely with farms, vineyards and artisan distilleries, the best produce of the Wye Valley and surrounding area ends up on the plate as, perhaps, Thai green curry; moules marinière; pork saltimbocca; and butternut squash risotto, not overlooking rump, rib-eye and sirloin steaks, light bites and sandwiches. Catch one of the occasional open mic nights.

Open 12–2.30 6–10 (Sat 12–10 Sun 12–6) Closed 29 Jan to 13 Feb, Mon to Tue Free House 15 from £12 portions/menu notice required

WALTERSTONE

Carpenters Arms

Tel **01873 890353** | **HR2 0DX**
Web **www.thecarpentersarmswalterstone.com**
Dir ***Exit A465 between Hereford and Abergavenny at Pandy.***

On the edge of the Black Mountains and overlooked by Offa's Dyke, this 300-year-old pub has plenty of character; it's been owned by the Watkins family for three generations. You'll find beams, antique settles and an open fire that burns all winter; the perfect, cosy setting for enjoying a pint of Ramblers Ruin. Popular food options include a steak with pepper or Stilton sauce; crispy battered cod; and vegetarian lasagne. There are a few tables outside – a suntrap in summer.

Open all week 12–3 7–11 Closed 25 Dec Free House from £12 portions notice required

WELLINGTON HEATH

The Farmers Arms

Tel **01531 634776** | **Horse Road, HR8 1LS**
Web **www.farmersarmswellingtonheath.co.uk**
Dir ***Take B4214 from Ledbury towards Bromyard. Right signed Wellington Heath.***

You'll find this friendly place just outside Ledbury, in the village of Wellington Heath, surrounded by beautiful countryside – it's good walking country if you want to work up an appetite. Inside you'll find pale walls, mis-matched furniture and home-cooked food.

WOOLHOPE

The Crown Inn

Tel **01432 860468** | **HR1 4QP**
Web **www.crowninnwoolhope.co.uk**
Dir ***B4224 to Mordiford, left after Moon Inn. Pub in village centre by church.***

The Crown Inn is popular with walkers and well supported by locals and visitors alike. Excellent food and drink are a priority here, with good ales as well as 24 local ciders and perries. There is an outside summertime bar in the garden on Saturday nights.

HERTFORDSHIRE

ALDBURY

The Greyhound Inn

Tel **01442 851228** | **19 Stocks Road, HP23 5RT**
Web **www.greyhoundaldbury.co.uk**
Dir ***Phone for detailed directions.***

The village's ancient stocks and duck pond are popular with film-makers who frequently use Aldbury as a location, allowing the pub's customers the chance to witness every clap of the clapperboard. In the oak-beamed restaurant, the comprehensive menu includes salads and platters, as well as pan-fried sea bass fillet with potato wedges; Thai chicken curry or local venison steak, fondant potato and redcurrant jus. The bar snacks are a local legend, especially when accompanied by Badger Dorset Best or Tanglefoot ale.

Open all day, all week 11.30–11 (Sun 12–10.30) Closed 25 Dec Hall & Woodhouse 13 portions/ menu WiFi notice required

Valiant Trooper

Tel **01442 851203** | **Trooper Road, HP23 5RW**
Web **www.valianttrooper.co.uk**
Dir ***A41 at Tring junction, follow rail station signs 0.5 mile, at village green turn right, 200 yards on left.***

Named in honour of the Duke of Wellington, this old pub has been enjoyed by lucky locals for centuries. Located in the quintessential Chilterns village of Aldbury, beneath the beech woods of Ashridge Park, you'll find six real ales in the bar.

ARDELEY

Jolly Waggoner

Tel **01438 861350** | **SG2 7AH**
Web **www.jollywaggoner.co.uk**
Dir ***From Stevenage take B1037, through Walkern, in 2 miles right to Ardeley.***

All meat on the Jolly Waggoner's menu, including heritage varieties and rare breeds, is traditionally reared at Church Farm across the road, together with over 100 different vegetables, fruits and herbs. As Church Farm runs this 500-year-old pub, the food on offer is truly local.

ASHWELL

Bushel & Strike

Tel **01462 742394** | **15 Mill Street, SG7 5LY**
Web **www.bushelandstrike.co.uk**
Dir ***Opposite church in village centre.***

That it was built in 1854 as a pub and brewery may account for the name, two bushels making a strike. Today it's a Charles Wells brewery house, with a monthly guest ale. Cooking with charcoal is the guiding principle in the kitchen and the local award-winning butcher's meats are all barbecued, including dry-aged Aberdeen Angus steaks, baby back ribs and jerk burgers. For non-meat eaters, there's grilled Mediterranean vegetable and halloumi skewers, and beer-battered cod. Stocks and sauces are home-made – try their chimichurri.

Open all day, all week Charles Wells 12 from £9 portions/menu Wi-fi P notice required

AYOT GREEN

The Waggoners

Tel **01707 324241** | **Brickwall Close, AL6 9AA**
Web **www.thewaggoners.co.uk**
Dir ***Ayot Green on unclassified road off B197, south of Welwyn.***

Close to the large, traditional village green and with good English real ales flowing in the beamed bar, it comes as rather a surprise that the menu has a strong French bent to it. The Gallic owners create inspired cuisine at their former waggoners' and coaching inn in the low Hertfordshire hills. Menus may include crab and cod pancake with creamy mushroom velouté; and braised lamb shank, prunes and dauphinoise potatoes. The wine list stretches to 100 bins.

Open all day, all week Punch Taverns 50 from £12.50 portions Wi-fi P notice required

BISHOP'S STORTFORD

Water Lane Bar and Restaurant

Tel **01279 211888** | **31 Water Lane, CM23 2JZ**
Web **www.waterlane.co**
Dir ***From A1250 in town centre at mini-roundabout into North Street. 2nd left into Barrett Lane (one way). At T-junction left into Water Lane.***

Just off the main street, the old Hawkes Brewery, founded in 1780, has been totally refurbished, with contemporary fixtures and fittings now enhancing the original features. It's a dog-free zone that warmly welcomes families.

BRAUGHING

The Golden Fleece – see opposite

BROOKMANS PARK

Brookmans

Tel **01707 664144** | **Bradmore Green, AL9 7QW**
Web **www.brookmanspub.co.uk**
Dir ***A1000 from Hatfield towards Potters Bar. Right signed Brookmans Park. Through Bradmore Green. Pub on right.***

Built as a hotel in the 1930s, Brookmans may no longer offer a bed for the night but it remains the social hub of the village. Leather upholstery and silk lampshades add a touch of class to the bar.

BUNTINGFORD

The Sword Inn Hand

★★★★ INN

Tel **01763 271356** | **Westmill, SG9 9LQ**
Web **www.theswordinnhand.co.uk**
Dir ***Off A10, 1.5 miles south of Buntingford.***

This atmospheric old inn still has its original oak beams, flagstone floors and open fireplace; outside is a large garden and pretty patio. There's a varied selection of real ales from the likes of Woodforde's and Timothy Taylor, and fresh produce is delivered daily for a good selection of bar snacks. A typical evening menu might include black pudding Scotch egg.

Open all week 12–3.30 5–11 (Fri to Sat all day Sun 12–6) Free House 9 portions/menu Wi-fi P

BRAUGHING

The Golden Fleece

Tel 01920 823555 | 20 Green End, SG11 2PG
Web www.goldenfleecebraughing.co.uk
Dir *A10 north from Ware. At roundabout right onto B1368 signed Braughing. Approximately 1 mile to village.*

A successfully revitalised village favourite

Experienced pub landlords Pete and Jess Tatlow both grew up in these parts, and bought this unloved 17th-century, former coaching inn at auction and then renovated it. Their hard work has clearly paid off as the pub has gained a good reputation. Jess changes her menu every month, but popular dishes are brought back time and time again. A staple, and big favourite, is the 'smokey', flaked smoked haddock topped with tomato concasse, which comes as both a starter or a main. Also dual purpose, and appearing on a sample monthly menu are tiger prawn kedgeree; salad of baba ghanoush; and pan-fried lamb and bulgur wheat patties. Mains include roast breast of chicken on creamy champ with whisky and mushroom cream sauce; mince of the week (see the specials board); and sirloin and fillet steaks. A separate menu lists vegetarian and vegan dishes. Pete selects the perfect real ales and craft beers as company for the much-loved Adnams Southwold. The monthly tapas night is a popular fixture on the last Wednesday of each month, and a beer festival is held in May. The pub has a safe garden at the back with patio tables and chairs plus children's play equipment.

Open all week 11.45–3 5.30–11 (Fri 11.45–3 5.30–midnight Sat 11.30am–midnight Sun 12–10) Closed 25 Dec Free House 15 from £15.95 portions/menu notice required

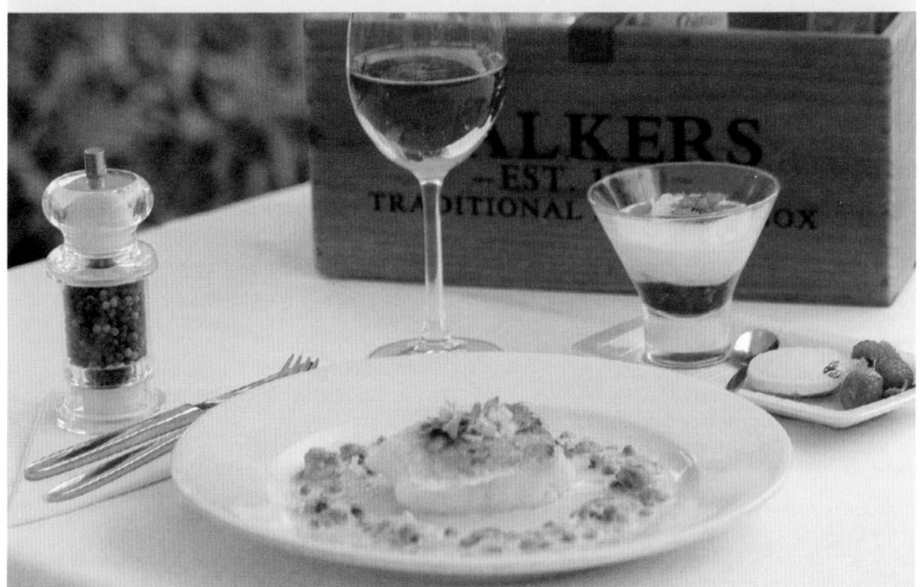

BUSHEY

The Horse & Chains

Tel **020 8421 9907 | 79 High Street, WD23 1BL**
Web **www.thehorseandchains.co.uk**
Dir ***Phone for detailed directions.***

First referred to in 1698, its location halfway up a hill was ideal for waggoners and their horses needing refreshment. Although redesigned, its great age remains evident, particularly the big open fireplace that dwarfs its modern wood-burner. If more than a sandwich, bar snack or sharing platter is called for, then maybe confit duck leg cassoulet with creamy mash; or oven-baked cod with Devon crab risotto will do the trick. Theme nights include fish (Mondays), mussels (Tuesdays), tapas, and Greek.

Open all day, all week Enterprise Inns 19 portions/menu Wi-fi notice required

The King Stag

Tel **0208 950 2988 | 15 Bournehall Road, WD23 3EH**
Web **www.thekingstag.com**
Dir ***From Bushey High Street turn into Melbourne Road. At mini-roundabout turn left into Herkomer Road. Follow road, turn left into Bournehall Road.***

This family-run pub is a welcoming community hub, with regular knitting and mother and baby groups, as well as 'Stagstock', the annual beer and music festival. Extremely dog-friendly, they even have a special menu for your four-legged companions, as well as an annual dog show. From the (human) menu you could share a mezze board, before moving on to pan-fried fillet of bream; the King Stag beef burger; or Cumberland sausage and mash.

Open all day, all week Greene King 11 from £12.50 portions/menu Wi-fi notice required

COTTERED

The Bull at Cottered

Tel **01763 281243 | SG9 9QP**
Web **www.thebullcottered.co.uk**
Dir ***On A507 in Cottered between Buntingford and Baldock.***

The four key things that sum up this member of the Greene King portfolio – low beams, antique furniture, cosy fires and teamwork. Then, of course, there's the brasserie-style food – everything that can be, is home made. You can eat in one of two traditional bars with open fires, in the pretty beamed dining room, or in the large, well-kept gardens and patio area. Look out for regular music evenings (mainly tribute acts).

Open all week 12–3 6.30–11 (Sun 12–10.30) Greene King from £7 portions Wi-fi notice required

DATCHWORTH

The Tilbury PICK OF THE PUBS

Tel **01438 815550 | Watton Road, SG3 6TB**
Web **www.thetilbury.co.uk**
Dir ***A1(M) junction 7, A602 signed Ware and Hertford. At Bragbury End right into Bragbury Lane to Datchworth.***

This pub in a little village south of Stevenage goes from strength to strength thanks to brothers James and Tom Bainbridge and a very experienced and welcoming team. They're all passionate about sourcing the best ingredients for the exciting modern British dishes. You could opt for a pub classic such as game cottage pie, or look to the à la carte choices – pheasant breast, wild mushrooms and pickled mustard seeds; braised rabbit, carrot cake and jus; or goats' cheese fondant, kale, braised baby onions, peas and lettuce. A set menu is available at both lunch and dinner.

Open all year 12–2.30 5.30–11 (Sat noon to 2am Sun 12–5) Closed Sun evening and Mon Brakspear 14 portions/menu Wi-fi notice required

EPPING GREEN

The Beehive

Tel **01707 875959 | SG13 8NB**
Dir ***B158 from Hertford towards Hatfield. Left signed Little Berkhamsted. Left at war memorial signed Epping Green.***

Weatherboarded under a tiled roof, this family-run pub has held a liquor licence for over 200 years. Hanging baskets and window boxes adorn the frontage, while the interior feels traditional to the core, with black beams, a log-burner and ornamental brasses. Fresh fish dishes are a speciality here, although meateaters, vegetarians and coeliacs have good choices too. On the beer pumps are Greene King and a changing guest ale.

Open all week Mon to Sat 12–3 5.30–11 (Sun 12–10.30) Free House 12 portions Wi-fi notice required

FLAUNDEN

The Bricklayers Arms

Tel 01442 833322 | Hogpits Bottom, HP3 0PH
Web www.bricklayersarms.com
Dir *M25 junction 18, A404 (Amersham road). Right at Chenies for Flaunden.*

Country inn with Anglo-French cuisine

The creeper-clad Bricklayers Arms evolved from early 18th-century cottages that, in 1832, the former Benskin's brewery had part-converted into an alehouse. Additional conversions took place in the 1970s, with remaining outbuildings and barn becoming the restaurant more recently. Like The Nags Head 10 miles away in Flaunden, it's owned by the Michaels family. Featuring in many films and TV programmes, the pub is a favourite with locals, walkers, horse-riders and, well, just about everyone, an obvious reason being the array of locally brewed real ales and locally sourced produce. Past the ivy-covered façade is an immaculate interior, with low beams, exposed brickwork, open fires and candlelight, although on a warm, sunny day a drink or a meal in the terraced, flower-filled garden would be hard to beat. Traditional English and French cooking in the award-winning AA Rosetted restaurant is masterminded by head chef Claude Paillet. With nearly 140 wines and champagnes to browse, the ideal accompaniment for your meal will jump off the page.

Open all day, all week 12–11.30 (Sun 12–9 25 Dec 12–3) Free House 20 portions

HEMEL HEMPSTEAD

Alford Arms PICK OF THE PUBS

Tel **01442 864480 | Frithsden, HP1 3DD**
Web **www.alfordarmsfrithsden.co.uk**
Dir ***From Hemel Hempstead on A4146, 2nd left at Water End. 1 mile, left at T-junction, right in 0.75 mile. Pub 100 yards on right.***

With a flower-filled garden overlooking the green in the untouched hamlet of Frithsden, this pretty Victorian pub is surrounded by National Trust woodland and has historic Ashridge Park on its doorstep. Tring Brewery's Side Pocket for a Toad shares bar space with Sharp's Doom Bar and Chiltern Brewery's Beechwood Bitter. The seasonal menus and daily specials are a balance of modern British with more traditional dishes, all prepared from fresh local produce whenever possible. There's a great choice of light dishes or 'small plates', from salmon and spring onion fishcake with wasabi avocado, to glazed honey and balsamic black figs. Equally imaginative 'big plates' include chicken ballotine with leg hash, hispi cabbage and truffle cream sauce; pan-fried polenta gnocchi with chilli roast butternut squash, watercress and pumpkin seed pesto.

Open all day, all week 11–11 (Sun 12–10.30) Closed 26 Dec Salisbury Pubs Ltd 33 from £12.50 portions/menu

HERONSGATE

The Land of Liberty, Peace and Plenty

Tel **01923 282226 | Long Lane, WD3 5BS**
Web **www.landoflibertypub.com**
Dir ***M25 junction 17, follow Heronsgate signs. 0.5 mile, pub on right.***

Named after a Chartist settlement established in Heronsgate in 1847, this free house is believed to have the second longest pub name in the British Isles. A traditional pub with a large garden and covered decked area, the cosy single bar has a buzz of conversation.

HERTFORD HEATH

The College Arms

Tel **01992 558856 | 40 London Road, SG13 7PW**
Web **www.thecollegearmshertfordheath.com**
Dir ***From A10 onto A1170 towards Hoddesdon. At roundabout left towards Ware. At next roundabout left signed Hertford Heath.***

With links to the old East India Company College, now Haileybury College, the pub backs on to woodland, making it an ideal halfway house for walkers. Thoughtful renovation is particularly evident inside, where exposed brickwork, large rugs and gentlemen's-club-style wingback chairs are harmoniously juxtaposed.

HEXTON

The Raven

Tel **01582 881209 | SG5 3JB**
Web **www.emeryinns.com**
Dir ***5 miles west of Hitchin. 5 miles north of Luton, just outside Barton-le-Clay.***

This neat 1920s pub is named after Ravensburgh Castle in the neighbouring hills. Comfortable bars witness the serving of four weekly-changing guest ales, perhaps Fuller's London Pride or Greene King IPA, while outside a large garden with a heated terrace and a play area ensure family friendliness. Extensive menus and blackboard specials embrace pub classics, salads, jackets, baguettes and wraps, vegetarian options, fish dishes and 'combination' meat plates like ribs and/or steak with Cajun chicken, and surf 'n' turf.

Open all day, all week Free House 24 from £9.95 portions/menu notice required

HITCHIN

Hermitage Rd.

Tel **01462 433603 | 20–21 Hermitage Road, SG5 1BT**
Web **www.hermitagerd.co.uk**
Dir ***From lights on B656 in town centre into Hermitage Road.***

Once a ballroom and nightclub, this is not your typical town-centre pub. Although original features survive, like the high vaulted ceiling and arched windows, the stage once graced by Sixties pop stars is now a dining area. Also part of the transformation is the open-plan kitchen.

The Highlander

Tel **01462 454612 | 45 Upper Tilehouse Street, SG5 2EF**
Web **www.highlanderhitchin.co.uk**
Dir ***From Hitchen centre take A505 towards Luton. Pub on right.***

Close to Hitchin's historic town centre, with rustic charm intact, open fire, and secluded garden with terrace, The Highlander continues to thrive in the capable hands of the Prutton family, who have run this Grade II listed pub for nearly 40 years.

HUNSDON

The Fox and Hounds

PICK OF THE PUBS

Tel **01279 843999 | 2 High Street, SG12 8NH**
Web **www.foxandhounds-hunsdon.co.uk**
Dir ***From A414 between Ware and Harlow take B180 in Stanstead Abbotts north to Hunsdon.***

Eye-catching features at this family-run free house include the unusual white-tiled bar-back, and a striking poster reading 'Nous sommes les soiffards', which, tactfully translated, suggests a fondness for drink. Chef James and wife Bianca run things, and together they've created an easy-going place where Adnams and local ales hold court at the bar, and lunch and dinner can be taken in the elegant, chandeliered dining room. James uses a Josper charcoal oven to cook squid, black beans, Nduja and gremolata; and Longhorn côte de boeuf for two, but you could also try the calves' liver, potato cake, crispy pancetta and onions. Finish with a black fig and almond tart with crème fraîche. Outside is a tree-shaded garden with a covered terrace.

Open 12–4 6–11 Closed 25–27 Dec, Sun evening, Mon and bank holiday evenings and Tue after bank holidays Free House 9 from £12 portions/menu

LITTLE HADHAM

The Nags Head

Tel **01279 771555 | The Ford, SG11 2AX**
Web **www.nagsheadlittlehadham.co.uk**
Dir ***M11 junction 8, A120 towards Puckeridge and A10. Left at lights in Little Hadham. Pub 1 mile on right.***

The small beamed rooms, one with an old bake-oven, conjure up images of how this country inn might have looked when it was built in 1595. The new owners offer several real ales and a menu featuring grilled Cornish mackerel; truffled mac 'n' cheese; hand-carved English ham; and onglet steak from Lancashire. Toasties and wholetail scampi are lunchtime favourites. A courtyard garden has now opened and there are tables on the forecourt.

Open all week 12–3 5.30–11 (Fri to Sun 12–11) Greene King from £12 portions/menu

LITTLE WYMONDLEY

Hermit of Redcoats

Tel **01438 747333 | Titmore Green, SG4 7JR**
Dir ***A1(M) junction 8 into Stevenage Road signed Little Wymondley. 1st left signed Todd's Green. At roundabout left under road bridge. At next roundabout 2nd exit. Pub on right.***

The hermit was James Lucas, who died in 1874. After meeting Lucas, Charles Dickens wrote 'Tom Tiddler's Ground', a story based on him. At the front, a picket fence encloses a pergola, tables and chairs; inside, painted quotations on the walls and old bottles on the mantelpiece.

PERRY GREEN

The Hoops Inn

Tel **01279 843568 | SG10 6EF**
Web **www.hoops-inn.co.uk**
Dir ***From Ware on B1004 towards Bishop's Stortford right onto unclassified road to Perry Green.***

The slightly surreal aspect of the villagescape here is courtesy of renowned sculptor Henry Moore, past resident of the parish, whose vast works dot the area. A subtle blend of cottagey and chic ensure the pub, part of the Moore Foundation Charity, caters for most tastes. The new licensee here maintains a commitment to real ale and has also tweaked the menus to offer a blend of traditional and modern dishes. Sunday roasts are a speciality.

Open all day, all week Mon to Tue 5–close Wed to Sun 12–11 Free House 10 portions/menu notice required

POTTEN END

Martins Pond

Tel **01442 864318** | **The Green, HP4 2QQ**
Web **www.martinspond.co.uk**
Dir ***A41 onto A416 signed Chesham, follow signs to Berkhamsted town centre. At lights straight over into Lower Kings Road. Pass station, into Station Road. Left at pub on opposite side of village green.***

The unusual name refers to the village green where this welcoming pub is located. A section of Grim's Dyke, an ancient bank-and-ditch earthwork, is clearly visible nearby. By comparison, the pub is relatively new, but there's been a public house here since the 17th century.

POTTERS CROUCH

The Holly Bush

Tel **01727 851792** | **AL2 3NN**
Web **www.thehollybushpub.co.uk**
Dir ***Village accessed from A4147 and A405.***

There is a delightfully welcoming atmosphere at this picturesque 17th-century pub, tucked away in a peaceful hamlet near St Albans. Wooden benches and tables, antique dressers, log fires and exposed beams set the interior style and there's a large enclosed garden too. Both traditional and modern pub fare is offered. At lunch – ploughman's, baked potatoes, garden salads, deli platters, burgers and toasted sandwiches; while on the evening menu there might be dishes like lamb koftas, feta cheese salad and pittas, tzatziki and olives.

Open all week 12–2.30 6–11 (Sun 12–3) Fuller's portions WiFi P notice required

ST ALBANS

Great Northern

Tel **01727 730867** | **172 London Road, AL1 1PQ**
Web **www.greatnorthernpub.co.uk**
Dir ***On A1081, close to the city centre.***

Although the current owners took over in 2015, this building has been an inn since 1839. Whether it's in the stylish, airy bar or separate restaurant, the focus is on high quality food, real ales from the likes of Mad Squirrel and Black Sheep breweries, traditional ciders and global wines. The seasonal menu mixes traditional pub classics with contemporary dishes, all created from local produce. Head to the large sun-trap garden when the weather allows.

Open all week 4–11.30 (Fri to Sat noon–12.30am Sun 12–11) Closed 25–26 Dec, 1 Jan Free House 16 from £10.50 portions WiFi notice required

SARRATT

The Cock Inn

Tel **01923 282908** | **Church Lane, WD3 6HH**
Web **www.cockinnsarratt.co.uk**
Dir ***M25 junction 18, A404 signed Chorleywood, Amersham. Right, follow signs to Sarratt. Pass church on left, pub on right.***

Standing opposite the Norman church in the picturesque village of Sarratt, this traditional inn dates back to the 17th century. In the heart of the Chess Valley, an area favoured by walkers, the pub retains plenty of vintage character, down to the low beams, inglenook fireplace and a restaurant in the ancient timbered barn. Enjoy a pint of Badger ale with pub favourites like sausage and mash or the curry of the day.

Open all day, all week Hall & Woodhouse 9 portions/menu WiFi P notice required

THERFIELD

The Fox and Duck

Tel **01763 287246** | **The Green, SG8 9PN**
Web **www.thefoxandduck.co.uk**
Dir ***From Royston take A505 towards Baldock. At roundabout left signed Therfield. 1st right signed Therfield.***

A quintessential country pub with plenty of original features – flagstone floors and exposed beams – The Fox and Duck is right on the village green in picturesque Therfield and ideally situated for walking the Icknield Way, which passes directly outside. Ramblers and walking groups use the pub as a start and finish point, calling in for a pint of IPA or one of the rotating guest ales. Food wise, there's a bar menu and a carte and you can mix and match from either.

Open all year 12–3 5.30–11.30 (Sat to Sun all day) Closed Mon (excluding bank holidays) Greene King 18 portions/menu WiFi P

WATTON-AT-STONE

The Bull

Tel **01920 831032 | High Street, SG14 3SB**
Web **www.thebullwatton.co.uk**
Dir ***A602 from Stevenage towards Ware. At roundabout follow Watton-at-Stone sign. Right at mini-roundabout (Datchworth and Walkern) into High Street. Pub on right.***

The owners here make sure that this inn extends warm hospitality to all-comers. Families gather for Christmas carols around the huge inglenook fireplace, Morris dancers entertain in summer, and beer and cider festivals are hosted in May and October. Menus feature simple dishes using seasonal, local ingredients.

WELWYN

The Wellington ★★★★★ INN

Tel **01438 714036 | High Street, AL6 9LZ**
Web **www.wellingtonatwelwyn.co.uk**
Dir ***A1(M) junction 6 to Welwyn.***

In the attractive village of Welwyn, this 13th-century coaching inn offers six comfortable bedrooms alongside great food. Inside, it's cosy and stylish but when the weather allows, grab a table on the terrace or enjoy a drink by the river at the bottom of the garden. There is plenty of choice when it comes to food, from lunchtime sandwiches and wraps to sharing plates and ambitious modern British dishes listed on the 'clipboard' menus and blackboard specials. There's a notable 37 wines by the glass.

Open all day, all week Greene King 37 portions/menu Wi-fi P notice required

WEST HYDE

The Oaks

Tel **01895 822118 | Old Uxbridge Road, WD3 9XP**
Web **www.theoakspub.co.uk**
Dir ***From roundabout on A412 between Rickmansworth and Denham into Chalfont Lane. At T-junction right, pub on left.***

Surrounded by a white picket-fence, The Oaks stands on a corner, with lakes and woodland behind; handy for an outing from Harefield, Chalfont St Peter, Rickmansworth or Denham. Expect to find St Austell and Rebellion IPA on hand pump along with guest ales. A typical meal could be hot and sticky pork ribs followed by haddock in cider batter, chips, peas and tartare sauce; a rump or sirloin steak; or Cumberland sausages and mash. Snacks include fish finger sandwiches and chicken satay skewers.

Open all day, all week Enterprise Inns 16 from £9.95 portions/menu Wi-fi P notice required

WESTON

The Cricketers

Tel **01462 790273 | Damask Green Road, SG4 7DA**
Web **www.thecricketersweston.co.uk**
Dir ***Phone for detailed directions.***

The warmest of welcomes is assured at The Cricketers, whether for adults with or without children, muddy boots and dogs. The open fire, range of ales and Symonds cider, and menu of home-cooked pub food meld into the pub's relaxed ambience.

WILLIAN

The Fox ★★★★

RESTAURANT WITH ROOMS | PICK OF THE PUBS

Tel **01462 480233 | SG6 2AE**
Web **www.foxatwillian.co.uk**
Dir ***A1(M) junction 9 towards Letchworth, 1st left to Willian, pub 0.5 mile on left.***

Sitting opposite the village pond and right next to the church, this imposing 18th-century pub is an award-winning destination, attracting locals, walkers and cyclists alike. A clean, crisp look defines the interior, while the laid-back bar, restaurant atrium, enclosed courtyard and two beer gardens are all pleasant places to settle down with East Anglian ales such as Adnams Southwold Bitter. There's lots of choice on the modern British menus – from bar snacks such as venison croquettes with pickled red cabbage and brown sauce, to main courses of Toulouse sausages with root vegetable and lentil ragù; or braised shoulder of lamb with roast potatoes and seasonal veg. Look out for 'bin end' wine deals and the popular themed food nights that take place throughout the year.

Open all day, all week Free House 12 from £5.95 portions/menu Wi-fi P notice required

ISLE OF WIGHT

ARRETON

The White Lion

Tel **01983 528479** | **Main Road, PO30 3AA**
Web **www.whitelionarreton.com**
Dir ***On A3056 (Blackwater to Shanklin/Sandown road).***

A 200-year-old coaching inn in the heart of Arreton village. Reliable ales are the top refreshments, while prices on the wine list are commendably affordable. Food ranges from paninis and sandwiches to light bites and children's choices, and then on to pub classics.

BEMBRIDGE

The Crab & Lobster Inn

Tel **01983 872244** | **32 Forelands Field Road, PO35 5TR**
Web **www.crabandlobsterinn.co.uk**
Dir ***From High Street in Bembridge, 1st left after Boots into Forelands Road. At right bend, left into Lane End Road, 2nd right into Egerton Road. At T-junction left into Howgate Road. Road bears right and becomes Forelands Field Road, follow brown inn signs.***

This inn is bedecked with flower baskets in summer, and the stunning coastal location means the raised deck and patio is the perfect place to sup locally brewed Goddards bitter whilst watching yachts and fishing boats out in the Solent. Locally caught seafood is one of the pub's great attractions, with dishes such as dressed crab; cold seafood platter; and moules marinière. There are, of course, pub favourites, seasonal and vegetarian dishes too, and sandwiches at lunchtime.

Open all day, all week 12–10.30 (Sun 12–10) Enterprise Inns 12 portions/menu

The Pilot Boat Inn

Tel **01983 872077** | **Station Road, PO35 5NN**
Web **www.thepilotboatinn.com**
Dir ***Follow B3395 (Embankment Road) around harbour. Pub on junction with Station Road.***

With a startling, quirky look of a beached ark, this lively pub makes the most of its setting beside Bembridge Harbour, with an ever-varying choice of daily seafood specials progressing straight from creel to galley. Morris dancers may brighten up a summer's afternoon.

The Spinnaker ★★★★ INN

Tel **01983 872840** | **1 Steyne Road, PO35 5UH**
Web **www.thespinnakeriow.co.uk**
Dir ***From A3055 onto B3395 towards Bembridge. After roundabout road becomes Steyne Road, pub on right.***

The Spinnaker is a warmly glowing beacon of hospitality on the island's east coast. Goddard's, the island brewer, furnishes the bar with Fuggle-Dee-Dum, just as the island's farmers and fishermen deliver most of the fresh produce used by the kitchen. Pub favourites such as butter-fried steaks from island herds are a cut above the norm, and a meal ends well with lemon meringue tart or a selection of Isle of Wight cheeses. Fourteen refurbished and fully-equipped, en suite bedrooms complete the picture here.

Open all day, all week Free House 12 portions/menu notice required

BONCHURCH

The Bonchurch Inn

Tel **01983 852611** | **Bonchurch Shute, PO38 1NU**
Web **www.bonchurch-inn.co.uk**
Dir ***Signed from A3055 in Bonchurch.***

Tucked away in a secluded Dickensian-style courtyard and little changed since the 1840s, this small inn is in a quiet, off-the-road location. Food is available lunchtime and evenings in the bar; choices range from sandwiches and salads to plenty of daily-fresh fish and traditional meat dishes, plus a specials board. Italian specialities are a prominent feature on account of the owners' heritage. Vegan and vegetarian dishes are made to order.

Open all week 12–3 6.30–11 Closed 25 Dec Free House from £10.95 portions/menu

COWES

Duke of York Inn ★★★ INN

Tel **01983 295171** | **Mill Hill Road, PO31 7BT**
Web **www.dukeofyorkcowes.co.uk**
Dir ***In town centre.***

A former coaching inn close to Cowes town centre, ferry terminals and marina, the Duke of York has been run by the Cass family for over 40 years. Fuggle-Dee-Dum from the island's Goddards Brewery is one of several real ales, while quality home-cooked food includes oven-baked sea bass, and traditional battered cod, along with bangers and mash, spaghetti bolognaise, and BBQ pork ribs. There are daily blackboard specials, vegetarian choices and Sunday roasts.

Open all day, all week *Enterprise Inns* *portions/menu*

FISHBOURNE

The Fishbourne ★★★★ INN

Tel **01983 882823** | **Fishbourne Lane, PO33 4EU**
Web **www.thefishbourne.co.uk**
Dir ***From East Cowes ferry terminal to roundabout. 3rd exit signed Ryde and Newport. At T-junction left onto A3021 signed Ryde and Newport. At next roundabout 1st exit signed Newport. At next roundabout 1st exit onto A3054 signed Ryde. Left at lights into Fishbourne Lane signed Portsmouth. Pass ferry terminal to pub.***

Time your ferry crossing carefully and, since it's down the same cul-de-sac as the Wightlink terminal, you'll be able to visit this mock-Tudor dining pub. A design-savvy approach to furnishing is apparent in the spacious bar, where there are smart leather sofas, and in the elegant dining area; lunchtime sees sandwiches, ciabattas, seafood specialities, as well as old favourites like fish and chips, and sausages and mash. The en suite bedrooms are stylishly decorated.

Open all day, all week *Free House* *12* *from £10.95* *portions/menu*

FRESHWATER

The Red Lion

Tel **01983 754925** | **Church Place, PO40 9BP**
Web **www.redlion-freshwater.co.uk**
Dir ***In Old Freshwater follow signs for All Saints Church.***

Its two big gables and red-brick walls give no indication of its great age but the pub's origins go back to the 11th century. Beers served include Fuggle-Dee-Dum and Sharp's Doom Bar in the shiny-flagstoned bar, where settles and sofas partner well-scrubbed pine tables.

GODSHILL

The Taverners PICK OF THE PUBS

Tel **01983 840707** | **High Street, PO38 3HZ**
Web **www.thetavernersgodshill.co.uk**
Dir ***Phone for detailed directions.***

Godshill is surely the island's prettiest village, and The Taverners fits the heritage jigsaw perfectly. With its beams, slab flooring, log fires and scrubbed rustic furnishings it's the archetypical village inn. Real ales and village-made cider are stalwarts in the bar, while meat and dairy products all come from Isle of Wight farmers, fish are from local waters, island fruit and vegetables are used when in season, and much else is locally caught, shot or foraged. Time-honoured pub grub is a given, including beef and ale pie with a suet crust; the daily-changing specials might include farmhouse-style terrine with piccalilli and toasted soda bread; followed by wild garlic and potato frittata, asparagus and pea shoots. For pudding try the warm gingerbread cake, butterscotch sauce, rhubarb and vanilla ice cream.

Open 11–11 (Sun 11–5) Closed 1st 3 weeks Jan, Sun evening *Punch Taverns* *10* *from £10.75* *portions/menu* *notice required*

HULVERSTONE

The Sun Inn at Hulverstone

Tel **01983 741124** | **Main Road, PO30 4EH**
Web **www.sunhulverstone.co.uk**
Dir ***Between Mottistone and Brook on B3399.***

All flagstones, floorboards, beams, settles and wood-burners, this lovely ancient thatched pub occupies an enviable position in the gently rolling countryside towards the western tip of the island. With fabulous English Channel views from the pleasant garden here, customers can enjoy a wide variety of ales and choose from a menu that has something for everyone. Expect to find moules marinière, home-made Ventnor crab cakes; seafood mixed grill; vegetable lasagne; and 10oz rump steak with all the trimmings, whilst the specials board highlights the pie of the day. Gluten free-dishes are marked on the menu. There's regular live music on Wednesdays, Fridays, Saturdays and Sundays.

Open all day, all week *Enterprise Inns* *10* *portions/menu* *notice required*

NINGWOOD

Horse & Groom

Tel **01983 760672 | Main Road, PO30 4NW**
Web **www.horse-and-groom.com**
Dir ***On A3054 (Yarmouth to Newport road).***

Just a couple of miles west of Yarmouth on the Newport road, this large landmark pub is certainly family-friendly. There's a pleasant garden with a large children's play area, and an extensive and well-priced kids' menu. Food is served daily from noon until 9pm.

NITON

Buddle Inn

Tel **01983 730243 | St Catherines Road, PO38 2NE**
Web **www.characterinns.co.uk/the-buddle-inn**
Dir ***From Ventnor take Whitwell Road (signed Niton). In Whitwell left after church into Kemming Road (signed Niton). In Niton, left opposite Norris (shop), right into St Catherines Road.***

With the English Channel on one side and the coastal path on the other, this 16th-century, former cliff-top farmhouse and smugglers' inn is one of the island's oldest hostelries. The interior is traditional while the home-made food is hearty.

NORTHWOOD

Travellers Joy

Tel **01983 298024 | 85 Pallance Road, PO31 8LS**
Web **www.travellersjoycowes.co.uk**
Dir ***Phone for detailed directions.***

Just inland from Cowes, this 300-year-old alehouse's broad appeal attracts people in cars, on bikes, and on foot. However they arrive, the real ale drinkers among them always enjoy setting the world to rights over Island Wight Gold, Old Peculier, or one of the other three beers on offer. The real cider collection is good, too. Home-cooked food includes speciality pies (Wednesday nights for pies), a range of daily-changing specials, and Sunday roasts.

Open all day, all week 12–12 Free House 9 portions/menu notice required

SEAVIEW

The Boathouse ★★★★ INN

Tel **01983 810616 | Springvale Road, PO34 5AW**
Web **www.theboathouseiow.co.uk**
Dir ***From Ryde take A3055. Left onto A3330, left into Puckpool Hill. Pub 0.25 mile on right.***

The powder-blue-painted Boathouse overlooks the eastern Solent, and the setting really is spectacular. Well-kept ales and an extensive global wine list complement specials boards that make the most of freshly landed local fish. Other choices include lunchtime baguettes and sandwiches; Isle of Wight reared rump and rib-eye steaks; whole cracked crab salad; cold seafood platter for two; and the Boathouse fisherman's pie. Sea views are available in some of the stylish en suite bedrooms.

Open all day, all week 9am–11pm (varies with season) Heineken Star Pubs 13 from £11.95 portions/menu

Seaview Hotel ★★★ HOTEL

PICK OF THE PUBS

Tel **01983 612711 | High Street, PO34 5EX**
Web **www.seaviewhotel.co.uk**
Dir ***B3330 from Ryde, left signed Puckpool, along seafront, hotel on left.***

One of life's great pleasures has to be sitting on the terrace outside the Seaview, sipping beer from Wight brewers like Yates and drinking in the views over the racing dinghies to one of the Solent's remarkable sea forts. Warm and welcoming, The Pump Bar is perfect for ladies who lunch, old friends spinning yarns, or families chilling out; its decor reflects the seaside location with a fascinatingly quirky selection of nautical memorabilia. Seafood features strongly on the menu, with a smoked haddock Scotch egg with curry mayonnaise starter or Ale of Wight fish and chips ticking all the right boxes. Salt-beef hash, spinach, fried egg and HP sauce; poached pigs' cheeks, Savoy cabbage and mash; and cheddar and stout rarebit with a fried egg and pickled red onion are typical of the choices.

Open all day, all week 10am–11pm Free House 11 from £9.50 portions/menu

SHORWELL

The Crown Inn PICK OF THE PUBS

Tel **01983 740293** | **Walkers Lane, PO30 3JZ**
Web **www.thecrowninnshorwell.co.uk**
Dir ***Left at top of Carisbrooke High Street. Shorwell approximately 6 miles.***

A traditional country pub in the pretty village of Shorwell, a short hop south-west from Newport. The rear garden boasts a children's play area, bounded by a spring-fed stream where trout, ducks and moorhens can be spotted. Parts of the Crown date from the 17th century, although its varying floor levels suggest many subsequent alterations. The most recent building work has increased the floor area significantly, but the pub's character has been preserved with log fires burning and antique furniture in abundance. Real ales include Goddards, brewed on the island, while cider comes from Healey's Farm in Cornwall. The kitchen makes good use of locally sourced lamb, beef, game and fish in daily specials.

Open all day, all week 12–3 5–close (Tue, Fri to Sat 12–close Sun 12–5; summer 12–close all week) Enterprise Inns 10 from £9.95 portions/menu notice required

WHIPPINGHAM

The Folly

Tel **01983 297171** | **Folly Lane, PO32 6NB**
Web **www.greeneking-pubs.co.uk/pubs/isle-of-wight/folly/**
Dir ***Phone for detailed directions.***

The Folly stands beside the River Medina and you can travel here from Cowes on the pub's own waterbus. In the bar are timbers from the hull of old barges. The menus offer a wide choice of lighter bites as well as classic pub grub.

KENT

APPLEDORE

The Black Lion

Tel **01233 758206** | **15 The Street, TN26 2BU**
Web **www.blacklion-pub.com**
Dir ***M20, junction 10, take A2070 to Brenzett. In Brenzett, at roundabout take 3rd exit, straight over next roundabout follow road to Appledore. Pub on right.***

In the historic village of Appledore, this free house has a rotating selection of ales and ciders, as well as plenty of wines by the glass. The Black Lion has developed a great reputation for its food, especially local fish.

BADLESMERE

The Red Lion

Tel **01233 740309** | **Ashford Road, Badlesmere Lees, ME13 0NX**
Web **www.redlionbadlesmere.com**
Dir ***M2 junction 6, A251 towards Ashford. Approximately 5 miles to Badlesmere Lees.***

A farmhouse for nearly 200 years before it became an inn in 1728, today's pub is known for its well-stocked cellar of changing, locally brewed beers, and for its totally gluten-free kitchen. There's even a gluten-free ale. To follow, say, a 'beetroot and feta salad, perhaps chunky pork chop with sage and garlic; oven-roasted spiced red snapper; or potato gnocchi with oyster mushrooms. Children have their own menu. A wheat-free Yorkshire pud accompanies all Sunday roasts.

Open all day, all week 12–10 (Fri to Sat 12–11 Sun 12–7) Free House 10 portions/menu notice required

BEARSTED

The Oak on the Green

Tel **01622 737976** | **Bearsted Green, ME14 4EJ**
Web **www.oakonthegreen.com**
Dir ***In village centre.***

Kentish hops drape the beams in this lively old pub, which dates from 1665 and is known for its good menu and unusual real ales. The oak-shaded terrace overlooks a corner of the immense village green and cricket pitch, great for those long summer evenings.

BENENDEN

The Bull at Benenden

PICK OF THE PUBS

Tel **01580 240054** | **The Street, TN17 4DE**
Web **www.thebullatbenenden.co.uk**
Dir ***From A229 onto B2086 to Benenden. Or from Tenterden take A28 south towards Hastings. Right onto B2086.***

A quintessential Wealden village location for the 17th-century Bull with its huge chimney and chinoiserie windows, Admire the bar's enormous inglenook fireplace, nooks and crannies and antique furniture, and check out the guest ale that accompanies brews from Larkins of Kent, Harvey's of Sussex, Biddenden-brewed cider and Kentish white wines. Sandwiches and ploughman's head the traditional pub-grub menu, on which you'll also find the Bull's much-admired home-made pies, suet puddings and burgers; scallops and mushrooms in white wine cream; and beer-battered haddock.

Open all day, all week 12-12 Free House 9 portions/menu notice required

BIDBOROUGH

The Kentish Hare

PICK OF THE PUBS

Tel **01892 525709** | **95 Bidborough Ridge, TN3 0XB**
Web **www.thekentishhare.com**
Dir ***Phone for detailed directions.***

The smart building, saved from demolition a few years ago, is distinctive – grey walls, a hare motif and white weatherboarding on the outside lead to a stylish modern interior. In the bar, you'll find house-brewed real ale The Kentish Hare alongside Harvey's Sussex, and Jake's Orchard cider; plus an excellent choice of wines by the glass. From the bar menu, devilled whitebait could precede Speldhurst sausages, mash and gravy. A la carte choices start with 'little dishes' such as whipped goats' cheese with beetroot, linseed and pickled shallots, followed by the 'main event' of sage gnocchi with butternut squash, parmesan and pickled wild mushrooms.

Open 11-3 5-11 (Sat 11-11 Sun 11-4) Closed 2-9 Jan, Sun evening and Mon Free House 30 from £15 portions/menu

BIDDENDEN

The Three Chimneys

PICK OF THE PUBS

Tel **01580 291472** | **Hareplain Road, TN27 8LW**
Web **www.thethreechimneys.co.uk**
Dir ***From A262 midway between Biddenden and Sissinghurst, follow Frittenden signs. (Pub visible from main road). Pub immediately on left.***

This 15th-century timbered pub is a classic. Atmosphere is provided by low beams, wood-panelling, worn brick floors, log fires and evening candlelight. Bar snacks are served all day, and the kitchen offers dishes like warm mushroom, bacon, brie and caramelised onion tart; or parcels of deep-fried breadcrumbed brie with an apple and celery salad and fruity Cumberland sauce. Continue with Wilkes pork and sage sausages, mash, spring greens with port and red onion gravy. Harvey's and Adnams ales and the heady (8.4 per cent ABV) Biddenden cider are tapped direct from the cask..

Open all day, all week 11.30-11 Free House 10 portions

BRABOURNE

The Five Bells Inn

Tel **01303 813334** | **The Street, TN25 5LP**
Web **www.ramblinns.com/the-five-bells-brabourne**
Dir ***5 miles east of Ashford.***

Environmental responsibility is important to the owners of this old village inn. Locally sourced wood supplies 25% of the energy here, whilst most of the food and drink is traceable locally. The on-site deli and shop is a trove of all things comestible and Kentish.

BROOKLAND

The Woolpack Inn

Tel **01797 344321** | **Beacon Lane, TN29 9TJ**
Web **www.woolpackinnbrookland.co.uk**
Dir ***From A259 between Rye and Brenzett follow Midley sign into lane to pub on left.***

Named after the wool smugglers of yesteryear, this inn has old-fashioned appeal. A perfect stop for ramblers then, with or without children and dogs. There's nothing passé about the quality of the Shepherd Neame ales at the bar, and the copious menu reflects today's popular tastes.

CANTERBURY

The Dove Inn PICK OF THE PUBS

Tel **01227 751085** | **Plum Pudding Lane, Dargate, ME13 9HB**
Web **www.dovedargate.co.uk**
Dir ***6 miles from Canterbury; 4 miles from Whitstable. Phone for detailed directions.***

About half-way between Faversham and Whitstable, this single-gabled ,18th-century village inn stands amid wooded hills and fruit orchards – this is the Garden of England, after all. Its matchboarded, wooden-floored interior is warmed by a log-burner, creating agreeably comfortable surroundings in which to enjoy a Shepherd Neame ale and hearty food, sourced from local ingredients. Outside is a gorgeous cottage garden complete, appropriately, with dovecote and doves; and a pitch for summer games of 'bat and trap', an old pub game that survives in Kent.

Open all year, all day Closed Mon and Sun evening Shepherd Neame 20 portions Wi-fi notice required

Duke of Cumberland

Tel **01227 831396** | **The Street, Barham, CT4 6NY**
Web **www.dukeofcumberland.co.uk**
Dir ***A2 from Canterbury towards Dover. Follow Barham signs. In village centre into The Street. Pub 200 yards on left.***

A traditional country inn, the Duke of Cumberland was built in 1749 and has been licensed to sell ale since 1766. It's named after the commander of the English army victorious at Culloden, although no one knows exactly why. You'll find a good choice of ales in the bar, including Greene King IPA and Harvey's Sussex Best. If you're peckish, there's a sandwich selection, or go all out with crispy whitebait followed by chicken fajitas, or a burger. There's a great children's play area.

Open all day, all week 12–11 (Fri to Sat 12–12 Jan to Feb Mon to Fri 12–3 5.30–11) Punch Taverns portions/menu Wi-fi notice required

The Granville

Tel **01227 700402** | **Street End, Lower Hardres, CT4 7AL**
Web **thegranvillecanterbury.co.uk**
Dir ***On B2068, 2 miles from Canterbury towards Hythe.***

As well as a striking feature central fireplace/flue, this light and airy pub not far from Canterbury displays an interesting series of roll-over art exhibitions and installations. Ample parking, a patio and large beer garden where summer barbecues take place make this good for families and dogs.

CHILHAM

The White Horse

Tel **01227 730355** | **The Square, CT4 8BY**
Dir ***Take A28 from Canterbury then A252, in 1 mile turn left.***

The White Horse is situated opposite Chilham Castle in the 15th-century village square that is a delightfully haphazard mix of gabled, half-timbered houses, shops, and inns dating from the late Middle Ages – it's often used as a film location. This 'chocolate box' inn offers a wide selection of real ales from breweries like Sharp's and Adnams. The modern cooking is based on fresh local produce. The menu offers ploughman's, sandwiches and dishes like bangers and wholegrain mustard mash, chilli con carne and crayfish linguine.

Open all day, all week 12–12 (Tue to Thu 12–11) Closed 25 Dec evening Enterprise Inns 10 from £9.95 portions/menu Wi-fi notice required

CHIPSTEAD

George & Dragon

Tel **01732 779019** | **39 High Street, TN13 2RW**
Web **www.georgeanddragonchipstead.com**
Dir ***Phone for detailed directions.***

The delights of this 16th-century village gastro pub are easily summarised: the welcoming open fires, the heavy oak beams and solid furnishings; the splendidly beamed upstairs restaurant; and the tree-house-inspired private dining room. Then there's Westerham Brewery's specially-produced George's Marvellous Medicine ale.

CRANBROOK

The George Hotel

Tel **01580 713348 | Stone Street, TN17 3HE**
Web **www.thegeorgehotelkent.co.uk**
Dir ***From A21 follow signs to Goudhurst. At large roundabout take 3rd exit to Cranbrook (A229). Hotel on left.***

One of Cranbrook's landmark buildings, the 14th-century George Hotel traditionally served visiting buyers of locally-made Cranbrook cloth. Magistrates held court here for over 300 years, and today the sophisticated interior mixes period features with contemporary decor. The brasserie menu offers a take on classic English cuisine.

CRUNDALE

The Compasses Inn

Tel **01227 700300 | Sole Street, CT4 7ES**
Web **www.thecompassescrundale.co.uk**
Dir ***Phone for detailed directions.***

Set in the beautiful countryside, this traditional inn dates from the 14th century. Owners Donna and Robert Taylor (she's front of house, he's in the kitchen) describe it as 'a muddy wellies and fine food' kind of place, with a modern British menu. Have a pint of Whitstable Bay Pale Ale in the bar and then peruse the menu where you might find roast stone bass with Jerusalem artichoke purée, braised oxtail and red wine sauce; or pork belly, parsnip purée, Morteau sausage and fermented red cabbage.

Open all year 12–3 6–11 (Sat all day Sun 12–6) Closed Mon and Tue Shepherd Neame 14 from £18.95 portions

DARTFORD

The Rising Sun Inn ★★★ INN

Tel **01474 872291 | Fawkham Green, Fawkham, Longfield, DA3 8NL**
Web **www.risingsun-fawkham.com**
Dir ***0.5 mile from Brands Hatch Racing Circuit and 5 miles from Dartford.***

Standing on the green in a picturesque village not far from Brands Hatch, this 16th-century building has been a pub since 1702. Inside, you will find a bar full of character, complete with inglenook log fire, and Inglenooks restaurant where home-made traditional house specials and a large fresh fish menu, using the best local produce, are served. There is also a front patio and garden for alfresco dining in warmer weather, plus comfortable en suite bedrooms if you would like to stay over.

Open all day, all week Free House 9 from £8.90 portions notice required

FAVERSHAM

Albion Taverna

Tel **01795 591411 | 29 Front Brents, ME13 7DH**
Web **www.albiontaverna.com**
Dir ***Phone for detailed directions.***

Located next to the Shepherd Neame Brewery near the Faversham swing bridge, the Albion Taverna looks directly onto the attractive waterfront area. The colourful menu is a combination of Mexican and English dishes. There is an annual hop festival in early September.

Shipwright's Arms PICK OF THE PUBS

Tel **01795 590088 | Hollowshore, ME13 7TU**
Web **www.theshipwrightsathollowshore.co.uk**
Dir ***A2 through Ospringe then right at roundabout. Right at T-junction then left opposite Davington School, follow signs.***

The creekside Shipwright's Arms was first licensed in 1738, when the brick and weather-boarded pub's remote location on the Swale Marshes made it a popular haunt for ne'er-do-wells; it's been favoured by sailors and fishermen ever since. Best reached on foot or by boat, the effort in getting here is well rewarded, as this charming and unspoilt tavern oozes character. Step back in time in the comfortable bars, which boast original timbers, built-in settles, wood-burning stoves and a wealth of maritime artefacts. Locally-brewed Goacher's ales are tapped straight from the cask, and make for a perfect match with simple, traditional bar food such as baguettes and jacket potatoes. Alternatively look to the specials board for fresh fish, or the carte for the likes of beef casserole and moules frites.

Open all year 11–3 6–10 (Sat 11–10 Sun 12–10) Closed Mon Free House 12 portions/menu

GOODNESTONE

The Fitzwalter Arms

Tel **01304 840303** | **The Street, CT3 1PJ**
Web **www.fitzwalterarms.co.uk**
Dir ***In village centre.***

This appealing pub was built in 1589 as the bailiff's lodge for the Goodnestone estate and gardens, to which it still belongs. Known as 'the Fitz' to locals, it welcomes many muddy boots and dogs as people discover this and other beautiful buildings in the village or finish a long walk. Log fires, wooden floors, exposed brick walls and beams adorned with Kentish hops characterise the interior; Shepherd Neame ales are ideally conditioned by chalk cellars.

Open all year 11–11 (Mon 3–9 Sun 11–10) Closed Mon lunch Shepherd Neame 10 portions/menu Wi-fi notice required

GOUDHURST

Green Cross Inn

Tel **01580 211200** | **TN17 1HA**
Web **www.greencrossinn.co.uk**
Dir ***A21 from Tonbridge towards Hastings left onto A262 towards Ashford. 2 miles, Goudhurst on right.***

In an unspoiled corner of Kent, close to Finchcocks Manor, and originally built to serve the Paddock Wood to Goudhurst railway line, this thriving dining pub specialises in fresh seafood. Arrive early to bag a table in the dining room, prettily decorated with fresh flowers.

The Star & Eagle ★★★★ INN

PICK OF THE PUBS

Tel **01580 211512** | **High Street, TN17 1AL**
Web **www.starandeagle.com**
Dir ***Just off A21 towards Hastings. Take A262 into Goudhurst. Pub at top of hill adjacent to church.***

From The Star & Eagle's lofty position in this Wealden hill village, some of the orchards and hop fields that originally earned Kent the sobriquet 'Garden of England' stretch out below. The rambling inn dates from the 14th century, when surviving vaulted stonework suggests it may have been part of a monastery. Four centuries later the infamous Hawkhurst Gang of smugglers and thieves drank and plotted here, until angry villagers finally sent them packing. Always on offer in the bar are Harvey's Sussex from its brewery in Lewes, guest ales, Biddenden cider and 14 wines by the glass. Suitably armed with a full glass, choose between fine traditional and European dishes prepared by head chef Scott Smith and team in the big-beamed, split-level restaurant.

Open all day, all week 11–11 (Sun 12–3 6.30–10.30) Free House 14 portions/menu Wi-fi P

GRAVESEND

The Cock Inn

Tel **01474 814208** | **Henley Street, Luddesdowne, DA13 0XB**
Web **www.cockluddesdowne.com**
Dir ***Phone for detailed directions.***

Set in the beautiful Luddesdowne Valley, this 'over-18s only' free house dates from 1713 and has two traditional beamed bars with wood-burning stoves and open fires. Always available are eight well-kept real ales and German lagers, and there isn't a fruit machine, jukebox or TV in sight, although traditional games like bar billiards and shove ha'penny are played. Submarine rolls and basket meals are served at lunchtimes.

Open all week 4–11 (Fri to Sat 12–11, Sun 12–10.30) Closed 25 Dec, 1 Jan Free House P

HALSTEAD

Rose & Crown

Tel **01959 533120** | **Otford Lane, TN14 7EA**
Dir ***M25 junction 4, A21, follow London (south-east), Bromley and Orpington signs. At Hewitts Roundabout 1st exit onto A224 signed Dunton Green. At roundabout 3rd exit into Shoreham Lane. In Halstead left into Station Road, left into Otford Lane.***

This handsome Grade II listed pub, situated in the lee of the North Downs, is all a good village pub should be; traditional pub games including bat and trap, family friendly, supporting local microbreweries and a welcoming base for walks into the peaceful countryside on the doorstep.

HAWKHURST

The Great House PICK OF THE PUBS

Tel **01580 753119** | **Gills Green, TN18 5EJ**
Web **www.elitepubs.com/the_greathouse**
Dir ***Just off A229 between Cranbrook and Hawkhurst.***

Tucked away along a lane in a tranquil hamlet, this eye-catching weatherboarded Kentish inn is over 400 years old, and displays equally appealing character in the range of rooms that cater well both for drinkers – beers from the ever-reliable Harvey's Brewery are stocked – and diners. With beams and trusses, open fires and stone floors, country furniture and very eclectic decor, there's a relaxed atmosphere here. The menus combine classic English dishes with a dash of French brasserie-style cooking. Offering starters like wood pigeon and figs; mains run to Kentish wild boar burger with fried duck egg, streaky bacon, apple relish and chips; or beer-battered fish and chips. Accompanying a meal can be Kentish cider and wines, and the pub hosts a beer festival every year.

Open all day, all week 11.30–11 Free House 20 from £12.50 menus

HODSOLL STREET

The Green Man

Tel **01732 823575** | **TN15 7LE**
Web **www.greenmanpub.com**
Dir ***Between Brands Hatch and Gravesend off A227.***

Alex and Steph, who now run this 300-year-old free house, abide by two time-honoured principles – to provide decent real ales (which they do) and well-prepared food. Take, for example, old favourites like liver and bacon, and home-made pies, or specials such as pan-fried scallops and black pudding, with pork belly in cider jus to follow. Dogs are welcome in the large beer garden, which incorporates a children's play area. Events include quiz, poker and live music nights.

Open all week 11–2.30 6–11 (Fri to Sun all day) Free House 8 portions/menu

HOLLINGBOURNE

The Dirty Habit PICK OF THE PUBS

Tel **01622 880880** | **Upper Street, ME17 1UW**
Web **www.thedirtyhabit.net**
Dir ***M20 junction 8, follow A20 signs, then Hollingbourne signs on B2163. Through Hollingbourne, pub on hill top on right.***

There's been a pub on this site since the 11th century, and it was once frequented by pilgrims plodding from Winchester to the shrine of Thomas à Becket at Canterbury. The building retains much period charm – look, for instance, at the long Georgian oak bar and panelling, and the Victorian furniture, all beautifully restored by skilled local craftsmen. Harvey's of Lewes is one of the real ales on tap, and there's cider from Aspall too. The kitchen prepares dishes such as fish, tapas and meat sharing boards; Rye Bay cod fillet with Jerusalem artichoke; local venison burger, 'nduja sausage, smoked cheddar, red cabbage and chips; king prawn linguine; and chocolate, orange and Cointreau tart.

Open all day, all week Enterprise Inns 28 from £12.50 menus

The Windmill

Tel **01622 889000** | **32 Eyhorne Street, ME17 1TR**
Web **www.thewindmillhollingbourne.co.uk**
Dir ***M20 junction 8, A20 towards Lenham. Straight on at 1st roundabout, left at 2nd roundabout into Eyhorne Street.***

The Windmill, found in the beautiful village of Hollingbourne, is one of chef Richard Phillips' collection of pubs and restaurants. Full of distinctive character and very much part of the local community, it's the ideal place for a relaxing lunch, a quiet drink (Doom Bar, Hoppin' Robin or Flintlock Pale Ale are on offer) or a more formal dinner. On the menu – pan-fried scallops, cauliflower purée, beignets, coriander and pickled cauliflower, followed by roast Gressingham duck breast with sweet chilli lentils and potato rösti.

Open all day, all week Enterprise Inns from £15 portions/menu notice required

HYTHE

The Three Mariners

Tel 01303 260406 | 37 Windmill Street, CT21 6BH
Dir *From A259, turn onto Stade Street towards seafront. Turn right onto Windmill Street. Pub at end of road on left.*

This white painted pub is an 'old-fashioned back street boozer', with traditional decor, a little courtyard garden and bright hanging baskets. Canine guests are welcome, and ales might include York Brewery Guzzler and Range Ales Black Ops. There's regular live music.

Open all week 12–11 (Mon 4–10) Closed 25 Dec Free House notice required

ICKHAM

The Duke William ★★★★ INN

Tel 01227 721308 | The Street, CT3 1QP
Web www.thedukewilliamickham.com
Dir *A257 Canterbury to Sandwich. In Littlebourne left opposite The Anchor, into Nargate Street. 0.5 mile right into Drill Lane, right into The Street.*

Famed as it is for hops, the Garden of England hosts some fine microbreweries and you can sample a selection of locally produced ales at the Duke's bar, The focus on 'local' applies equally to the ingredients for the kitchen's menus. A typical three-course choice could be smoked chicken terrine, lardons, curly endive and leek mayonnaise; fillet of cod, lentil dahl, curried shallots and warm banana bread, toffee sauce and clotted cream.

Open all day, all week Free House 9 portions/menu Wi-fi notice required

IVY HATCH

The Plough at Ivy Hatch

PICK OF THE PUBS

Tel 01732 810517 | High Cross Road, TN15 0NL
Web www.theploughivyhatch.co.uk
Dir *Exit A25 between Borough Green and Sevenoaks, follow Ightham Mote signs.*

Straddling a fork in the road through the village is this 17th-century, tile-hung free house, run by self-styled 'dynamic duo', Dale and James. Judging by their line-up of craft beers, they clearly know a thing or two – Beavertown Neck Oil is one, for instance – as indeed they also do about wines, judging by their world-spanning selection. It's open for breakfast, brunch and more until 4pm all week, so turn up in time and treat yourself to a Big Pig (essentially a full house); smoked salmon on toast; a 'posh' panko fish sandwich; ham, egg and chips; or a 'super' salad.

Open all day, all week 11–11 (Sun 12–6) Closed 26 Dec Free House 10 portions/menu Wi-fi P notice required

LAMBERHURST

The Vineyard PICK OF THE PUBS

Tel 01892 890222 | Lamberhurst Down, TN3 8EU
Web www.elitepubs.com/the_vineyard
Dir *From A21 follow brown Vineyard signs onto B2169 towards Lamberhurst. Left, continue to follow Vineyard signs. Straight on at crossroads, pub on right.*

Built more than 300 years ago, this pub is next door to one of England's oldest vineyards and there's a carefully chosen wine list and 20 served by the glass. Leather sofas, wingback and parlour chairs mix easily with the rustic look and chunky wooden furniture, whilst the eye is taken by a mural illustrating the well-established wine-making craft in the area. Fans of the hop are rewarded with firkins from microbreweries such as Old Dairy. From the kitchen comes a pleasing mix of top-notch traditional English and regional French brasserie dishes: seared king scallops with spiced apple to start, maybe, then wild duck breast with fondant potato, baby veg, kale and juniper jus; or king prawn linguine, finishing with banana sticky toffee pudding.

Open all day, all week 11.30–11 Free House 20 from £12.50 menus Wi-fi P

LEYSDOWN-ON-SEA

The Ferry House Inn

★★★★ INN

Tel **01795 510214** | **Harty Ferry Road, ME12 4BQ**
Web **www.theferryhouseinn.co.uk**
Dir ***From A429 towards Sheppey. At roundabout take B2231 to Eastchurch. From Eastchurch High Street into Church Road. At roundabout into Rowetts Way signed Leysdown. Right into Harty Ferry Road to village.***

Named for the ferry that crossed the Swale to the mainland until the onset of World War II, this 16th-century pub stands in three acres of terraced lawns. The views over the water to Faversham, Whitstable and the North Downs alone are worth the journey, while its open log fires, wooden beams and solid oak floors add to the tally. Foodwise, game comes from the Harty Estate, beef and lamb from their family farm in Eastchurch and fresh produce from the inn's kitchen garden.

Open all day Mon to Fri 11–11 (Sat all day, Sun 11–5) Closed 24–30 Dec, Sun evening Free House portions/menu Wi-fi notice required

LINTON

The Bull Inn

Tel **01622 743612** | **Linton Hill, ME17 4AW**
Web **www.thebullatlinton.co.uk**
Dir ***South of Maidstone on A229 (Hastings road).***

Built in 1674, this part-timbered, former coaching inn stands high on the Greensand Ridge, with wonderful views over the Weald. The award-winning garden includes two oak gazebos and a large decked area for alfresco bistro dining and afternoon tea. Inside, there's an imposing inglenook fireplace, lots of beams and a bar serving Shepherd Neame ales. The wide-ranging seasonal menu offers everything from hearty sandwiches, pub classics, daily-delivered seafood and home-made desserts.

Open all day, all week 11am–11.30pm (Sun 12–10.30) Shepherd Neame from £14.95 portions/menu Wi-fi

MAIDSTONE

The Black Horse Inn

★★★★ INN

Tel **01622 737185** | **Pilgrim's Way, Thurnham, ME14 3LD**
Web **www.wellieboot.net**
Dir ***M20 junction 7, A249, right into Detling. Turn opposite Cock Horse Pub into Pilgrim's Way.***

Candlelit dinners a speciality

Below the North Downs on the ancient Pilgrim's Way from Winchester to Canterbury, this 18th-century pub is a joy. In the bar, hops hang from ceilings, open log fires blaze and nooks and crannies wait to be discovered. A fine selection of Kentish real ales comes from its four hand-pumps, alongside more widely known brews, and Biddenden cider, while Chapel Down in Tenterden supplies not only wines, but Curious Brew, a lager

re-fermented with champagne yeast. A meal in the cosy, candlelit restaurant could be a fish or meat sharing plate; roast beef and Yorkshire pudding; pan-fried calves' liver with bubble-and-squeak; tournedos Rossini with Madeira sauce: slow-roasted belly and stuffed loin of pork with black pudding mash and cider and apple sauce; or a vegetarian option. Specials change daily.

Open all day, all week Closed 25 Dec Free House 21 from £9.95 portions/menu notice required

LOWER HALSTOW

The Three Tuns

Tel **01795 842840 | The Street, ME9 7DY**
Web **www.thethreetunsrestaurant.co.uk**
Dir ***From A2 between Rainham and Newington turn left, follow Lower Halstow sign. At T-junction right signed Funton and Iwade. Pub on right.***

Built in 1468 and licensed to sell ale since 1764, this traditional fire-warmed bar is paradise for lovers of local real ales and cider. Three Tun Best Bitter is brewed for the pub by Kent Brewery, and you'll also find Goacher's Real Mild and Dudda's Tun Kentish Cider, while Summer Bank Holiday sees the Kentish Ale and Cider Festival, with a hog-roast, seafood and live music.

Open all day, all week Free House 10 portions/ menu notice required

MAIDSTONE

The Black Horse Inn – see opposite

MARKBEECH

The Kentish Horse

Tel **01342 850493 | Cow Lane, TN8 5NT**
Web **www.kentishhorsemarkbeech.co.uk**
Dir ***3 miles from Edenbridge and 7 miles from Tunbridge Wells.***

Britain's only Kentish Horse honours Invicta, the county's prancing white stallion. Popular with ramblers and cyclists, the locals rate it too, partly because Chiddingstone-brewed Larkins and Lewes-brewed Harvey's are available, with guest ales on high days and holidays.

MATFIELD

The Poet at Matfield

Tel **01892 722416 | Maidstone Road, TN12 7JH**
Web **www.thepoetatmatfield.co.uk**
Dir ***From Tonbridge on A21 towards Hastings left onto B2160 signed Paddock Wood. Approximately 1.5 miles to pub on left in Matfield.***

Named after poet Siegfried Sassoon, who was born in this quintessentially English village just outside Tunbridge Wells, this Grade II listed pub is more than 350 years old. The pub retains its original character with the beams and antiques, but comfortable leather chesterfield sofas and armchairs add an elegant edge. Harvey's Sussex Best Bitter and guest ales can be found at the bar.

Open all year, all day Closed Mon Enterprise Inns 12 portions notice required

OARE

The Three Mariners

Tel **01795 533633 | 2 Church Road, ME13 0QA**
Web **www.thethreemarinersoare.co.uk**
Dir ***M2 junction 7, A2 towards Sittingbourne. Through Ospringe. At roundabout right onto B2045 (Western Link). At T-junction left signed Oare. 2nd pub on right.***

Dating back to the late 18th century, the Grade II listed Three Mariners occupies an enviable position in the village. With the Saxon Shore Way, the Swale Heritage Trail and the marshes close by, the pub is popular with walkers. Log fires warm the bar in winter, whilst the sunny terrace is a real draw in summer. Enjoy a pint of local Shepherd Neame or Whitstable Bay Pale Ale and order from the interesting modern, menus.

Open all day, all week 12–11 (Sun 12–10) Shepherd Neame 13 portions/menu notice required

PENSHURST

The Bottle House Inn – see page 244

PLUCKLEY

The Dering Arms

PICK OF THE PUBS

Tel **01233 840371 | Station Road, TN27 0RR**
Web **www.deringarms.com**
Dir ***M20 junction 8, A20 to Ashford. Right onto B2077 at Charing to Pluckley.***

There's a touch of Victorian Gothic about this eye-catching pub, built originally as a hunting lodge, with its creeper-clad stone gables and arched windows. Inside there are open fires, bare boards, and scrubbed tables. It's a popular destination for seafood lovers – half a pint of shell-on prawns could be followed by grilled skate wing with caper butter; or whole crab salad. Drinkers are rewarded with a fine selection of Kentish ales and ciders.

Open Tue to Fri 11.30–3.30 6–11 (Sat 9am–11pm Sun 12–4) Closed 26–27 Dec, Sun evening, Mon Free House 11 from £14.95 portions

PENSHURST

The Bottle House Inn

Tel 01892 870306 | Coldharbour Road, TN11 8ET
Web www.thebottlehouseinnpenshurst.co.uk
Dir *A264 west from Tunbridge Wells onto B2188 north. After Fordcombe left towards Edenbridge and Hever. Pub 500 yards after staggered crossroads.*

Historic pub off the beaten track

During 1492, the year Columbus landed in America, the uniquely named Bottle House was being built as an estate farmhouse, which helps to put its great age in context. Down a country lane, it wasn't until 1806 that it was granted a licence to sell ale and cider, later also becoming a shop, a farrier's and a cobbler's. In 1938 a refurbishment exposed hundreds of old bottles, hence the name. Later improvements have included sandblasting ancient oak beams back to their natural colour, exposing brickwork and painting walls in neutral shades. At the copper-topped bar counter there's a contingent of beers from Kentish breweries Larkins, Tonbridge, Westerham and Whitstable, with Sussex-brewed Weltons joining the line-up, as well as 19 wines by the glass. The menus in the stylish dining room capitalise on the abundant supply of local produce, so the chef's recommendations change accordingly. When the weather's favourable, there's a good-sized patio area with umbrellas.

Open all day, all week 11–11 (Sun 11–10.30) Closed 25 Dec Free House 19 from £10.95 portions/menu notice required

RIVER

The Royal Oak

Tel **01843 829433** | **36 Lower Road, CT17 0QU**
Web **www.royaloakriver.co.uk**
Dir ***Phone for detailed directions.***

Two 18th-century flint cottages that became a pub more than 150 years ago, this charming, friendly place offers monthly guest ales from local breweries like Breakwater or Romney Marsh as well as regulars from Adnams, and an impressive gin selection.

Open all year, all day 12–11 Closed Mon Free House 10 from £7.95 portions/menu notice required

ROLVENDEN

The Bull

Tel **01580 241212** | **1 Regent Street, TN17 4PB**
Web **www.thebullinnrolvenden.co.uk**
Dir ***Just off A28, approximately 3 miles from Tenterden.***

This handsome, tile-hung village inn dates, in part, back to the 13th century and is located close to the walled garden that inspired Frances Hodgson Burnett's classic tale *The Secret Garden*. Handy, too, for steam trains of the Kent and East Sussex Railway, there's a welcome focus on local beers and produce, with a heart-warming, pubby menu. Look out for warm chicken and chorizo salad and wild boar sausages with wholegrain mustard mash and tomato confit. The lovely beer garden overlooks the village cricket ground.

Open all day, all week Free House 12 portions/menu notice required

SELLING

The Rose and Crown – see page 246

SHIPBOURNE

The Chaser Inn

Tel **01732 810360** | **Stumble Hill, TN11 9PE**
Web **www.whitingandhammond.co.uk**
Dir ***North of Tonbridge take A227 towards Shipbourne. Pub on left.***

Once a haunt for stars such as Richard Burton and Elizabeth Taylor, The Chaser Inn is an informal, relaxed village inn, next to the church and overlooking the common. There is a lovely beer garden and the covered courtyard comes into its own in the winter months.

SISSINGHURST

The Milk House

Tel **01580 720200** | **The Street, TN17 2JG**
Web **www.themilkhouse.co.uk**
Dir ***In village centre.***

In picturesque Sissinghurst, this 16th-century, former hall house is very much the hub of the village. With its timber beams and Tudor fireplace, the pub has considerable charm with locals supping pints of Kentish-brewed Old Dairy Brewery ale mingling with destination diners tempted by the acclaimed food. Most of the produce comes from a 20-mile radius, and dishes such as pink peppercorn-crusted venison, parsnip and horseradish dauphinoise; or pan-fried John Dory, lemon beurre blanc, sautéed potatoes sit happily alongside innovative home-made pizzas and a top-notch children's menu.

Open all day, all week Enterprise Inns 18 portions/menu

SMARDEN

The Chequers Inn PICK OF THE PUBS

Tel **01233 770217** | **The Street, TN27 8QA**
Web **www.thechequerssmarden.com**
Dir ***From Maidstone take A229. Left through Sutton Valence and Headcorn. Left signed Smarden. Pub in village centre.***

The former weavers' village of Smarden has around 200 buildings of architectural and historical interest, one of which is the clapboarded 14th-century Chequers Inn. Its beautiful landscaped garden features a large carp pond and an attractive south-facing courtyard. Ales brewed by Harvey's, Sharp's, Fuller's, Wadworth and the Old Dairy Brewery are served in the low-beamed bars. Seasonal ingredients are sourced locally for the menus of traditional and modern food. Typical of the restaurant choices are potted ham with piccalilli; home-made Scotch egg; whole lemon sole, lemon and caper butter, green vegetables and new potatoes; and pie of the day. If you're hungry on a Sunday, the roast is served between 12 and 5 pm.

Open all day, all week Free House portions

SELLING

The Rose and Crown

Tel **01227 752214** | **Perry Wood, ME13 9RY**
Web **www.roseandcrownperrywood.co.uk**
Dir ***From A28 right at Badgers Hill, left at end. 1st left signed Perry Wood.***

In Kent's Area of Outstanding Natural Beauty

One night in 1889, Hammond John Smith, a local farmer, was drinking in this rambling, low-beamed 16th-century inn, with two others, when an increasingly fierce argument about who could cut an acre of corn the fastest ultimately led to his murder. The reason for mentioning this is that his ghost still occasionally gets up to mischief here, which sounds like a very good reason to visit. Packed with character imparted by the inglenooks, horse brasses and corn dollies, the bar offers Harvey's, Adnams and a guest real ale, plus Westons cider. Descend to the restaurant for home-cooked fish pie; lamb shank; steak and kidney pudding; wild mushroom risotto; or a selection of burgers, any of which Belgian cinnamon waffles would follow perfectly. The flower-festooned garden is tailor-made for summer eating and drinking.

Open 12–3 6.30–11 (Sat 12–4.30, Sun 12–6) Closed 25–26 Dec evening, 1 Jan evening, Mon (excluding bank holidays) Free House from £7.95 portions/menu notice required

SPELDHURST

George & Dragon PICK OF THE PUBS

Tel **01892 863125** | **Speldhurst Hill, TN3 0NN**
Web **www.speldhurst.com**
Dir ***Phone for detailed directions.***

This venerable building has surveyed the heart of the village for at least 800 years. Its gables, pitched roof, cruck frame and immense chimney recall another age. Roaring fires dismiss a winter chill, whilst outdoor areas are pleasing places to sit after an exploration of the High Weald Area of Outstanding Natural Beauty. Much of the food is equally parochial in provenance – Ashdown Forest, the Downs and cheeses from Sussex amongst areas championed.

Open all day, all week 12–11 Free House 9 from £12.50 portions/menu notice required

STALISFIELD GREEN

The Plough Inn

Tel **01795 890256** | **ME13 0HY**
Web **www.theploughinnstalisfield.co.uk**
Dir ***From A20 (dual carriageway) west of Charing follow Stalisfield Green signs. Approximately 2 miles to village.***

The Plough Inn is a splendid, 15th-century Wealden hall house situated by the green in an unspoilt hamlet high up on the North Downs. A real country pub, it enjoys far-reaching views across the Swale estuary and is worth seeking out for the array of Kentish drinks – microbrewery beers, ciders and juices – and a choice of dishes on the constantly changing menus and blackboard specials. Menus could include partridge escabeche, then slow-cooked pork belly and black pudding, and finally damson gin cheesecake with Hobnob ice cream.

Open all week 12–3 5–11 (Sat 12–11 Sun 12–6) Free House 13 from £13 portions/menu notice required

STOWTING

The Tiger Inn

Tel **01303 862130 | TN25 6BA**
Web **www.tigerinn.co.uk**
Dir ***Phone for detailed directions.***

Lost down winding lanes in a scattered North Downs hamlet, the 250-year-old Tiger Inn oozes traditional character and rural charm. The front bar is delightfully rustic and unpretentious, with stripped oak floors, two warming wood-burning stoves, cushioned pews and scrubbed pine tables.

TUDELEY

The Poacher & Partridge

Tel **01732 358934 | Hartlake Road, TN11 0PH**
Web **www.thepoacherandpartridge.co.uk**
Dir ***A21 south onto A26 east, at roundabout turn right. After 2 miles turn sharp left into Hartlake Road, 0.5 mile on right.***

Set amongst Kentish orchards, this pretty country pub has a rustic, down-to-earth feel with sturdy old wood furniture and unique features such as a beautiful old wine cellar and deli kitchen. Outside, you'll discover a large garden, with a children's play area, ideal for a refreshing summer pint of Harvey's from the wide selection of local ales and ciders. Traditional English, continental and wood-fire dishes appear on the menu, perhaps vegan tacos; seared king scallops; wood-fired sourdough pizzas; wild duck breast, dauphinoise, cavolo nero; vegan ramen; and almond and pear tart for dessert.

Open all day, all week 11.30–11 Free House 30 from £12.50 portions/menu notice required

TUNBRIDGE WELLS (ROYAL)

The Crown Inn

Tel **01892 864742 | The Green, Groombridge, TN3 9QH**
Web **www.thecrowngroombridge.com**
Dir ***Take A264 west of Tunbridge Wells, then B2110 south.***

In the 18th century, this charming free house was the infamous headquarters for a gang of smugglers who hid their casks of tea in the passages between the cellar and Groombridge Place, later home to Sir Arthur Conan Doyle. Doyle made this 16th-century pub his local and today, its low beams and an inglenook fireplace are the setting for some great food and drink. Eat alfresco during the summer months.

Open all day, all week Free House portions/menu notice required

Sankey's

Tel **01892 511422 | 39 Mount Ephraim, TN4 8AA**
Web **www.sankeys.co.uk**
Dir ***Phone for detailed directions.***

A respected family business in the Tonbridge area for over 50 years, Sankey's houses a unique collection of enamel signs, family memorabilia and antique church pews. But the focal points are the large open fire and the bar. Here, you will need time to peruse the 23 draught options, which include ales from the town's brewery such as Coppernob. A mouth-watering selection of pub favourites will soak up your refreshment, or head down to the old cellars to the Seafood Brasserie.

Open all day, all week Free House 12 portions/menu

WAREHORNE

Woolpack Inn

Tel **01233 732900 | Church Lane, TN26 2LL**
Web **www.woolpackinnwarehorne.com**
Dir ***Phone for detailed directions.***

With a history of smuggling, this lovely old white-painted inn with its mellow red-tiled roof was once a farmhouse. Inside, there's an eclectic sense of style and you'll find all sorts of fascinating things to look at. Produce is sourced from the region, with fish from the local boats. The menu offers fish sharing platters, great home-made burgers, and pizzas, while the beers come from local breweries – Harvey's, Tunbridge and Goachers. There are numerous annual events, from live music to the scallop festival each January.

Open all day, all week Free House 27 from £13 portions notice required

WESTERHAM

Grasshopper on the Green

Tel **01959 562926** | **The Green, TN16 1AS**
Web **www.grasshopperonthegreen.com**
Dir ***M25 junction 5, A21 towards Sevenoaks, then A25 to Westerham. Or M25 junction 6, A22 towards East Grinstead, A25 to Westerham.***

Overlooking Westerham's pretty green, the more-than-800-year-old Grasshopper takes its name from the coat of arms of local merchant Thomas Gresham, founder of London's Royal Exchange in 1565. The bar's low-beamed ceilings, hung with antique jugs, and its winter log fire are particularly appealing, as are Westerham brewery's Grasshopper and British Bulldog real ales. House specials include home-made steak and ale pie and the 'Winston Whopper' home-made burger. Ask long-term hosts Neale and Anne Sadlier for directions to Chartwell (NT), Sir Winston Churchill's former home.

Open all day, all week Free House 12 from £8.95 portions/menu notice required

WEST MALLING

The Farm House PICK OF THE PUBS

Tel **01732 843257** | **97 The High Street, ME19 6NA**
Web **www.thefarmhouse.biz**
Dir ***M20 junction 4, south on A228. Right to West Malling. Pub in village centre.***

Well positioned in the heart of the Kentish market town of West Malling, with a pretty walled garden overlooking 15th-century stone barns, this handsome Elizabethan building offers a friendly welcome, whether stopping for refreshment in the stylish bar or eating in one of its two dining areas. Local seasonal ingredients are expertly used in menus with a strong French influence. So, wine may be called for – choose from 20 sold by the glass. In addition to the tapas or sharing boards typical starters are beetroot-cured sea trout. Main courses vary from pub favourites such as a selection of steaks, to celeriac, fennel and apple gratin; and Kentish venison burger. Puddings could be chocolate and orange tart; and spiced apple and pear crumble. Sandwiches are served until 6pm.

Open all day, all week 10am–11pm Enterprise Inns 20 from £12.50 menus

WEST PECKHAM

The Swan on the Green

Tel **01622 812271** | **The Green, ME18 5JW**
Web **www.swan-on-the-green.co.uk**
Dir ***From A228 from West Malling towards Tonbridge, at roundabout take B2016 (Wrotham). At crossroads left to West Peckham. Pub opposite church.***

First licensed over 330 years ago, The Swan on the Green's microbrewery has revived the 18th-century principles of 'pure ale', using only natural and, when possible, local ingredients for its eight craft ales; these are colourfully celebrated during the pub's October beer festival.

WHITSTABLE

Pearson's Arms – see opposite

The Sportsman

Tel **01227 273370** | **Faversham Road, Seasalter, CT5 4BP**
Web **www.thesportsmanseasalter.co.uk**
Dir ***On coast road between Whitstable and Faversham, 3.5 miles west of Whitstable.***

There's been a pub here since at least 1642, while in the Middle Ages monks were supplying the kitchens of Canterbury Cathedral with the best the area had to offer. These days they like to keep that stuff to themselves, and it's a real destination restaurant. You can still get a pint of Whitstable Bay Pale Ale in the bar, however, before checking the menu. There are oysters (of course) or maybe mussel and bacon chowder; main courses might take in seared thornback ray with brown butter and cockles.

Open all week Mon 12–3 6–10.30, Tue to Sat 12–3 6–11 (Sun 12–10) Closed 25–26 Dec, 1 Jan Shepherd Neame 15 from £21.95 portions

WROTHAM

The Bull – see opposite

WHITSTABLE

Pearson's Arms

Tel 01227 773133 | Sea Wall, CT5 1BT
Web www.pearsonsarmsbyrichardphillips.co.uk
Dir *In town centre. On one-way system, left at end of High Street.*

Seafront pub serving modern British cuisine

Live music on Tuesdays and Sundays is one reason why this white-painted, clapboarded, beach-facing pub is so popular. It was built for workers constructing the long-vanished railway line between Whitstable and Canterbury – now the seven-mile Crab and Winkle Way. Carefully selected cask ales are generally from local breweries, but American pale ales push the boundaries a bit further. The food is sourced as locally as possible, so it would be disrespectful to Whitstable not to start with its famous rock oysters with pickled shallots. But if oysters aren't for you, try mussels cooked in Kentish white wine, then to follow, braised beef bourguignon; grilled calves' liver; pan-fried whole Dover sole; or spiced butternut squash shortcrust pastry pie. Finish with a plate of the county's cheeses. Vegetarians and vegans are by no means overlooked.

Open all day 12–12pm (Sun 12–10)

WROTHAM

The Bull ★★★★ INN

Tel 01732 789800 | Bull Lane, TN15 7RF
Web www.thebullhotel.com
Dir *M20 junction 2, A20 (signed Paddock Wood, Gravesend and Tonbridge). At roundabout 3rd exit onto A20 (signed Wrotham, Tonbridge, Borough Green, M20 and M25). At roundabout take 4th exit into Bull Lane (signed Wrotham).*

Ancient pub featuring micro-beers

PICK OF THE PUBS

World War II pilots once relaxed at this 14th-century coaching inn – stamps on the restaurant ceiling mark downed German planes. These days, guest ales from microbreweries such as Old Dairy are supported by a vast wine list offering 23 by the glass. A smoker (imported from Texas) and Big Green Egg BBQ are the workhorses of the kitchen and the bar menu offers the likes of Korean fried chicken wings and smoked pork ribs. From the main menu, a starter of chicken liver parfait, spiced pear pickle and saffron fruit bread, might precede bream fillet, borlotti bean paprika cream, black pudding and cavolo nero. Finish with raspberry sherry trifle and lemongrass custard.

Open all day, all week Free House 23 portions/menu notice required

LANCASHIRE

ALTHAM

The Walton Arms

Tel **01282 774444 | Burnley Road, BB5 5UL**
Web **www.thewaltonarms.co.uk**
Dir ***M65 junction 8, A678, pub between Accrington and Padiham.***

Fully renovated in the summer of 2018, this stone-built dining pub is located on an ancient highway in the Calder Valley. Oozing history, pilgrims to Whalley Abbey called at the inn here when Henry VII was king. Beams and brasses, rustic furniture and stone floors welcome today's drinkers and diners lured in by the extensive selection of cask ales, fine wines and quality spirits alongside a comprehensive food menu.

Open all year 12–2.30 5.30–11 (Sun 12–10.30) Closed Mon J W Lees 16 from £8.95 portions/menu notice required

ARKHOLME

The Red Well Inn

Tel **01524 221008 | Kirkby Longsdale Road, LA6 1BQ**
Web **www.theredwellinn.com**
Dir ***Phone for detailed directions.***

On the border of Forest of Bowland Area of Outstanding Natural Beauty, The Red Well Inn occupies a picturesque setting just outside the village of Arkholme within the Lune Valley. Just 20 minutes from the Lake District National Park, the pub enjoys a semi-rural position with a large beer garden to the rear. Bowland Brewery ales are on offer, with a similarly regional focus on the daily-changing menus.

Open all day, all week Free House from £10.95 portions/menu notice required

BARLEY

Barley Mow ★★★★ INN

Tel **01282 690868 | BB12 9JX**
Web **barleymowpendle.co.uk**
Dir ***M65 junction 13, at roundabout exit onto A682. Left into Pasture Lane, right into Ridge Lane, continue on Barley New Road. Turn right.***

Owned by the Seafood Pub Company, the Barley Mow is located at the start and end of a lovely walk on Pendle Hill, after which you should be in need of a glass of Wainwright ale and a hearty meal.

The Pendle Inn

Tel **01282 614805 | Barley Lane, BB12 9JX**
Web **www.pendle-inn.co.uk**
Dir ***M65 junction 13, A6068 signed Fence. In Fence follow brown pub signs. Through Newchurch-in-Pendle to Barley. Pub on left in village.***

The brooding, whaleback shape of Pendle Hill looms up behind this imposing, stone-built inn. They specialise in home-made Lancashire pub favourites here, such as steak and ale pies; battered Fleetwood haddock; and chicken Sinatra with wild rice. Equally, thoughts might turn to double-stack chicken burger; or Cumberland sausages and mash, or with egg and chips. Burnley's Moorhouse brewery and Marston's supply some of the bar's six cask ales, while all the wines are available by the glass.

Open all week 12–3 5–9 Jan to Mar (summer all day) Free House 9 from £10 portions/menu notice required

BASHALL EAVES

The Red Pump Inn

Tel **01254 826227 | Clitheroe Road, BB7 3DA**
Web **www.theredpumpinn.co.uk**
Dir ***From Clitheroe take B6243 to Bashall Eaves.***

The Ribble Valley and the Forest of Bowland are hardly short of high-quality pubs and restaurants. The Red Pump's USP is its lack of pretentiousness – it aims to keep things simple and serve 'seriously good' food. Steak is the speciality here – dry-aged for about 40 days, the meat originates from Longhorn, Shorthorn and Galloway cattle carefully reared on grass. Three cask ales in the Snug include Bowland and Moorhouses brews.

Open all day Closed 1–16 Jan, Mon to Tue Free House 8 from £10 portions/menu

BILSBORROW

Owd Nell's Tavern

Tel **01995 640010 | Guy's Thatched Hamlet, Canal Side, PR3 0RS**
Web **www.guysthatchedhamlet.co.uk**
Dir ***M6 junction 32 north on A6. In approximately 5 miles follow brown tourist signs to Guy's Thatched Hamlet.***

This authentic tavern sits by the Lancaster Canal within Guy's Thatched Hamlet. Flagged floors, low beamed ceilings and whitewashed walls add to the ambience, as do well-kept cask ales including the pub's own Owd Nell's Canalside Bitter and Moorhouse Pendle Witch.

BLACKBURN

The Clog and Billycock

PICK OF THE PUBS

Tel **01254 201163 | Billinge End Road, Pleasington, BB2 6QB**
Web **www.theclogandbillycock.com**
Dir ***M6 junction 29 to M65 junction 3, follow Pleasington signs.***

The unusual name refers to the preferred attire of an early 20th-century landlord, a billycock being a felt hat. Brunning & Price took over this 150-year-old village pub on Blackburn's western fringes in April 2018 and it was refurbished soon afterwards. The open fire and flagged stone floors have been retained, with a garden dining room and sun trap terrace being added along with a private dining room. The central bar dispenses six cask ales, as well as around 50 wines, gins and malts. The kitchen has a seasonal focus with dishes like game suet pudding and celeriac mash, and roasted hake with smoked paprika and pancetta cassoulet.

Open all day, all week 10am–11pm (Sun 10am–10.30pm) Free House 14 menus
Wi-fi P

The Millstone, Mellor

★★★★★ INN **PICK OF THE PUBS**

Tel **01254 813333 | Church Lane, Mellor, BB2 7JR**
Web **www.themillstonemellor.co.uk**
Dir ***M6 junction 31, A59 towards Clitheroe, past British Aerospace. Right at roundabout signed Blackburn/Mellor. Next roundabout 2nd left. At top of hill on right.***

This handsome coaching inn stands in an old village at the edge of Mellor Moor above Blackburn. With the beautiful Ribble Valley and Forest of Bowland Area of Natural Beauty to the north and Pendle Hill nearby, it's little wonder that this inn is a popular place. It's very much a village inn at the heart of the community and the skills of the kitchen has an innovative take on classic dishes. Warm up by the log fire in the well-appointed bar or relax in the oak-panelled Miller's restaurant and ponder the attractive menu options. Choose from one of the starters or sharing boards. Mains reflect the strong tradition of good pub food, with a home-made beef burger and thick cut chips, and Bowland steak, kidney and Wainwright ale pudding proving very popular options. Leave room for a delicious dessert.

Open all day, all week House of Daniel Thwaites 15 from £7 portions/menu Wi-fi P

BLACKO

Moorcock Inn

Tel **01282 614186 | Gisburn Road, BB9 6NG**
Web **www.moorcockinnblacko.com**
Dir ***M65 junction 13, A682, inn halfway between Blacko and Gisburn.***

Beyond the folly of Blacko Tower, high on the road towards Gisburn on the Upper Admergill area, lies this family-run, 18th-century inn with traditional log fires, splendid views towards the Pendle Way and locally brewed cask ales in the bar.

BURNLEY

White Swan at Fence

Tel **01282 611773** | **300 Wheatley Lane Road, Fence, BB12 9QA**
Web **www.whiteswanatfence.co.uk**
Dir ***Phone for detailed directions.***

The only Lancashire pub owned by Yorkshire brewery Timothy Taylor's, the White Swan takes its real ales as seriously as its award-winning food. Expect perfectly kept pints of Landlord and Boltmaker served in the cosy bar. In the kitchen, chef Tom Parker keeps things concise on the good-value set menus and à la carte. Regional produce comes to the fore in dishes like Dexter beef fillet, celeriac, foraged mushrooms and red wine. Make sure you leave room for garden apple crumble and vanilla custard.

Open Tue to Thu 12–3 5–11 (Fri to Sat 12–12 Sun 12–10.30) Closed 1st week Jan, Mon Timothy Taylor 13 from £18 portions Wi-fi P

BURROW

The Highwayman

Tel **01524 273338** | **LA6 2RJ**
Web **www.brunningandprice.co.uk/highwayman**
Dir ***M6 junction 36, A65 to Kirkby Lonsdale. A683 south. Burrow approximately 2 miles.***

Sitting in Lancashire but only a few miles from the Cumbrian and Yorkshire borders, The Highwayman is a stylishly appointed 18th-century coaching inn with craggy stone floors, warm wooden furniture and log fires.

CARNFORTH

The Longlands Inn and Restaurant

Tel **01524 781256** | **Tewitfield, LA6 1JH**
Web **www.longlandshotel.co.uk**
Dir ***Phone for detailed directions.***

Although very definitely Lancastrian, this traditional country inn is only minutes away from the Cumbria border. With its nooks and crannies, old beams and uneven floors, this family-run, dog-friendly inn stands next to Tewitfield Locks on the Lancaster Canal. The bar, with local ales on tap, also includes a wide range of spirits and wines. Otherwise look to the restaurant for good country cooking and local produce; stone-baked pizzas to 28 day-aged steaks, cured in-house and cooked on a chargrill; plus brasserie inspired dishes. Children are most welcome.

Open all day, all week Free House 9 portions/menu Wi-fi P *notice required*

CHORLEY

The Yew Tree Inn

Tel **01257 480344** | **Dill Hall Brow, Heath Charnock, PR6 9HA**
Web **www.yewtreeinnanglezarke.co.uk**
Dir ***Take A6 from Chorley towards Manchester. In Anderton, at lights, left into Babylon Road. Over M61, 1st left signed Anglezarke. Pub on right.***

This stone-built country inn stands at the fringe of Bolton's remarkable lakeland; a string of reservoirs wrapped around the foot of the West Pennine Moors. Beers come from the local Blackedge Brewery, and it's a popular destination dining pub, with hearty British dishes to the fore – lamb hotpot with braised red cabbage; or roast partridge with roast roots and damson sauce. Log fires warm the light interior of this rural retreat; while Good Friday sees a beer and cider festival here.

Open all year 12–3 5.30–9 (Fri 12–9 Sat 12–10.30 Sun 12–7) Closed Mon Free House 15 portions/menu Wi-fi P

see advertisement on opposite page.

CLAUGHTON

Fenwick Arms Steak and Seafood Pub ★★★★ INN

Tel **01524 221157** | **Hornby Road, LA2 9LA**
Web **www.fenwickarms.co.uk**
Dir ***M6 junction 34, A683. Follow Kirkby Lonsdale signs. Approximately 5 miles to pub on left.***

Joycelyn Neve founded her Seafood Pub Company on the back of her family's long-standing maritime associations. This 250-year-old inn, with open fires, low-beamed ceilings and oak floors, combines its traditional role with that of specialist fish, seafood and steak restaurant. Top quality produce arrives daily from the family business in Fleetwood; try the salt and pepper squid; or Goan king prawn and chicken curry. Excellent dry-aged Lancashire steaks are cooked on the Robata grill.

Open all day, all week Free House 24 from £10.50 portions Wi-fi P *notice required*

YEW TREE INN
ANGLEZARKE

CLITHEROE

The Assheton Arms ★★★★★

 RESTAURANT WITH ROOMS

PICK OF THE PUBS

Tel **01200 441227 | Downham, BB7 4BJ**
Web **asshetonarms.com**
Dir ***A59 to Chatburn, then follow Downham signs.***

A pub since 1872, this was originally a farmhouse brewing beer for its workers. The current name honours Ralph Assheton, Lord Clitheroe, for his contribution during World War II. Now it's owned by the Seafood Pub Company, which refreshed the stylish restaurant while preserving its traditional village inn credentials. You'll find a great choice of real ales, including Moorhouse's White Witch, and local sourcing is key, with fresh fish and seafood supplied daily.

Open all day, all week 7.30am–11pm (Sat 8am–midnight, Sun 8am–10.30pm) Free House 10 portions/menu notice required

ELSWICK

The Ship at Elswick

Tel **01995 672777 | High Street, PR4 3ZB**
Web **www.theshipatelswick.co.uk**
Dir ***M55 junction 3, A585 signed Fleetwood. Right onto Thistleton Road (B5269). 1 mile to pub.***

In a quiet village on the Fylde and handy both for Blackpool and the quieter resorts of Cleveleys and Fleetwood, this former farmhouse is now a reliable village local and dining inn. Lancashire produce is showcased – Fleetwood supplies some of the fish featured on the traditional menu.

ENTWISTLE

The Strawbury Duck

Tel **01204 852013 | Overshores Road, BL7 0LU**
Web **www.thestrawburyduck.co.uk**
Dir ***At crossroads in Edgworth follow Entwistle rail station signs. Left signed The Strawbury Duck and Entwistle Station. Over reservoir, over railway bridge to pub.***

Way up in the hills between the Entwistle and Wayoh reservoirs, The Strawbury Duck has long been a landmark pub. Although magnificently modernised, it hasn't said farewell to its old beams, open fire and comfortable chairs. No surprise to find an ale called Strawbury Duck in the bar, nor indeed Bowland Pheasant Plucker. Pub classics like home-made pie, and Southern fried chicken in a basket vie for attention with pub-raised, rare-breed Saddleback sausage and mash; and chargrilled steaks. The beer garden has sweeping views.

Open all day, all week Free House portions/menu notice required

FENISCOWLES

Oyster & Otter PICK OF THE PUBS

Tel **01254 203200 | 631 Livesey Branch Road, BB2 5DQ**
Web **www.oysterandotter.co.uk**
Dir ***M65 junction 3, right at lights, right at mini-roundabout into Livesey Branch Road.***

This clapboard and stone-fronted pub is run by a former Fleetwood fish wholesaler who comes from a long line of North Sea and Irish Sea trawlermen. His daughter studied the coastal food industry in South America before becoming head of operations here. This may look more New England than Lancashire mill-town but the menu gets inspiration from all over the world.

Open all day, all week The House of Daniel Thwaites 9 portions/menu notice required

FORTON

The Bay Horse Inn PICK OF THE PUBS

Tel **01524 791204 | LA2 0HR**
Web **www.bayhorseinn.com**
Dir ***M6 junction 33 take A6 towards Garstang, turn left for pub. Pub approximately 1 mile from M6.***

There's good Lancashire beer on offer, from Moorhouse's in Burnley, and mismatched furniture and a handsome stone fireplace with roaring winter log fire characterise the pub, offering a glimpse of the small coaching inn it once was. The kitchen makes full use of the wealth of produce the county has to offer. The concise menu might tempt with a starter of treacle-cured salmon with fennel salad, beetroot mayonnaise, crispy egg; progress then to Goosnargh duck legs, cider lentils, sauté potatoes, kale, and round off with warm orange and almond cake with vanilla ice cream.

Open 12–3 6–12 Closed 1 week Jan, 1 week Nov, Mon to Tue (except bank holiday lunch) Free House 8 from £15 portions

GREAT ECCLESTON

Farmers Arms

Tel **01995 672018** | **Halsalls Square, PR3 0YE**
Web **www.greatecclestonpub.co.uk**
Dir ***M55 junction 3, A585, A586 to Great Eccleston. From High Street into Chapel Street, pub on left.***

This two-storey pub-restaurant belongs to the Seafood Pub Company. It was set up by Joycelyn Neve who decided to capitalise on her family's long-standing involvement with deep-sea fishing. Naturally, there's plenty of seafood on the menu.

HEYSHAM

The Royal ★★★★ INN

Tel **01524 859298** | **Main Street, LA3 2RN**
Web **www.theroyalheysham.co.uk/eat/**
Dir ***A589 follow signs for Heysham Village, then brown tourist signs for St Peter's Church. The Royal is next to church.***

This newly-refurbished, white-painted village pub is ideally placed for exploring Morecambe Bay, and dates in part to the 16th century. In the early 1900s it was famous for its nettle beer, but these days you'll be able to sink a pint of Thwaites or Theakston's Wainwright.

Open all day, all week The House of Daniel Thwaites 15 from £10 portions/menu

LANCASTER

The Borough

Tel **01524 64170** | **3 Dalton Square, LA1 1PP**
Web **www.theboroughlancaster.co.uk**
Dir ***Phone for detailed directions.***

This Grade II Georgian pub, in the city centre, has a Victorian frontage, wooden floors, chunky tables, warm green hues and masses of light from a huge bay window. Dishes on the menu use top-notch ingredients from local suppliers.

The Sun Hotel and Bar

PICK OF THE PUBS

Tel **01524 66006** | **LA1 1ET**
Web **www.thesunhotelandbar.co.uk**
Dir ***6 miles from M6 junction 33.***

The oldest building in Lancaster, The Sun was first licensed as 'Stoop Hall' in 1680 as the town's premier coaching inn. Generals from the occupying Jacobite Army lodged here in 1745, and the artist JMW Turner stayed whilst making sketches of Heysham in 1812. The experienced kitchen brigade prepares sea bass niçoise; baby carrot and fennel risotto; and sausages and mash. There is a patio for alfresco dining in warmer weather, regular quiz nights and an annual beer festival in the summer.

Open all day, all week 7.30am–late (Sat 8am–late Sun 8.30am–late) Closed 25 Dec Free House 14 from £11 portions/menu notice required

Toll House Inn ★★★★ INN

PICK OF THE PUBS

Tel **01524 599900** | **Penny Street, LA1 1XT**
Web **www.tollhouseinnlancaster.co.uk**
Dir ***In city centre.***

Right in the centre of the city, this listed inn was once a Corporation Toll House. Demolished in 1901, it was then rebuilt as two separate pubs, which Thwaites Brewery joined together again in 2007 to create a grand 28-room inn with a bar. Its wonderfully high ceilings make it feel light and modern, although period features can be seen everywhere, from the listed staircase to the stained-glass windows. The atmosphere is quirkily elegant, and the seasonal menus make the most of excellent Lancashire produce.

Open all day, all week 9am to midnight The House of Daniel Thwaites 15 from £10.50 portions/menu notice required

The White Cross

Tel **01524 33999** | **Quarry Road, LA1 4XT**
Web **www.thewhitecross.co.uk**
Dir ***South on one-way system, left after Town Hall. Over canal bridge, on right.***

Set in a 130-year-old former cotton mill warehouse on the edge of the Lancaster Canal, The White Cross is a short stroll from the city centre. A regularly-changing selection of up to 14 cask ales includes beers from Copper Dragon, Timothy Taylor and Theakston breweries, but food is an equal draw at this popular waterfront venue. Look out for starters like poached duck egg Royale, then follow with Cajun-marinated chicken fillet burger.

Open all day, all week Enterprise Inns 13 portions/menu notice required

LANESHAW BRIDGE

The Alma Inn ★★★★ INN

Tel **01282 857830** | **Emmott Lane, BB8 7EG**
Web **www.thealmainn.com**
Dir ***M65, A6068 towards Keighley. At Laneshaw Bridge left into Emmott Lane. 0.5 mile, inn on left.***

With magnificent views to Pendle Hill from the paved patio, this stone inn deep in the Lancashire countryside is a great find. The rambling interior has real fires and stone floors, and it's popular for weddings. Reliable beers from Moorhouse's are behind the bar, and the wide-ranging contemporary menu features starters like devilled crab, salmon and brown shrimps; with mains of pies, puddings and pasta as well as dry-aged beef with slow-roast tomatoes.

Open all day, all week *Free House* *19* *portions/menu* Wi-fi *notice required*

LITTLE ECCLESTON

The Cartford Inn – see opposite

LONGRIDGE

Derby Arms ★★★★ INN

Tel **01772 782370** | **Chipping Road, PR3 2NB**
Web **www.derbyarmslongridge.co.uk**
Dir ***Phone for detailed directions.***

A delightful village inn owned by Joycelyn Neve's Seafood Pub Company, with a central bar leading into three dining rooms, two with feature fireplaces. A tap room is set aside for bar games. Its very ownership dictates fish by the boatload.

NEWTON-IN-BOWLAND

Parkers Arms PICK OF THE PUBS

Tel **01200 446236** | **BB7 3DY**
Web **www.parkersarms.co.uk**
Dir ***From Clitheroe take B6478 through Waddington to Newton-in-Bowland.***

In a beautiful hamlet amidst the rolling hills of the Trough of Bowland, this Georgian dining inn is just yards from the River Hodder and enjoys panoramic views over Waddington Fell. It celebrates its location by serving the best Lancashire produce; ales from the local breweries, meats raised on nearby moorland, vegetables from Ribble Valley farms and fresh fish from nearby Fleetwood. The simple, but elegant, modern dishes on the daily-changing, seasonal menu include Goosnargh corn-fed chicken and leek pie; slow-braised shin of Bowland beef in ale with creamed mash; and fillet of sea bass with pea gnocchi and lemon reduction. Pudding could be 'Wet Nelly', a classic north-west dessert originally created for Lord Nelson in Liverpool and reworked by co-owner Kathy Smith.

Open all year 12–3 6–close (Sat to Sun and bank holidays 12–close) Closed Mon (Tue in winter)
Free House *portions/menu* Wi-fi *notice required*

PARBOLD

The Eagle & Child PICK OF THE PUBS

Tel **01257 462297** | **Maltkiln Lane, Bispham Green, L40 3SG**
Web **www.ainscoughs.co.uk**
Dir ***M6 junction 27, A5209 to Parbold. Right onto B5246. 2.5 miles, Bispham Green on right.***

This thriving village inn is set in the tranquil valley of the River Douglas and close to some lovely rambles on Parbold Hill. A pub that caters admirably for all-comers, the emphasis is on high-quality modern cooking using locally sourced seasonal produce. On the menu Eagle & Child smokies on toasted granary bloomer is a typical opening gambit. From there you might progress to 28-day dry-aged 10oz steak with a choice of sauces; or pumpkin and sage ravioli; and steak, ale and mushroom pie with suet pastry, mushy peas and chunky chips. The traditionally styled pub is a popular village local, with an ever-changing array of beers from local microbreweries and farmhouse ciders, while the annual Early May Bank Holiday beer festival attracts up to 2,000 people to a huge marquee.

Open all day, all week 12–11 (Sun 12–10.30)
Free House *10* *portions/menu* Wi-fi *notice required*

PENDLETON

The Swan with Two Necks

Tel **01200 423112** | **BB7 1PT**
Web **www.swanwithtwonecks.co.uk**
Dir ***Exit A59 between Clitheroe and Worston follow Pendleton signs, 0.5 mile to pub.***

Dating back to 1722, The Swan with Two Necks is a traditional village inn tucked away in the pretty

LITTLE ECCLESTON

The Cartford Inn

Tel 01995 670166 | PR3 0YP
Web www.thecartfordinn.co.uk
Dir *North of A586 (west of Great Eccleston).*

A 17th-century inn with eclectic interiors and excellent food

Set in an idyllic location adjoining a toll bridge across the Wyre, this award-winning 17th-century coaching inn enjoys extensive views over the countryside towards the Trough of Bowland and the Lake District. The inn's stylish and contemporary interior is an appealing blend of striking colours, natural wood and polished floors, and an eclectic selection of furniture adds a comfortable and relaxed feel to the bar lounge. There are coffees from Guatemala, El Salvador, Ethiopia and Sumatra; while teas range from Irish breakfast, to a decaf Ceylon, green chai, or hedgerow tisane. There's a choice of eating areas – the Riverside Lounge, Fire Lounge and alcove, and outside on the terrace – where you can enjoy an imaginative range of dishes based on quality ingredients from local suppliers.

Open all day Closed 25 Dec, Mon lunch ⊕ *Free House* 👪 *portions/menu* Ⓟ ✿

village of Pendleton. The pub is renowned for its ales and ciders, so be sure to try the likes of ales from Reedley Hallows and Prospect breweries along with the good value home-cooked food. Open log fires warm the pub in winter and there's a lovely beer garden for warmer months.

Open all year 12–3 6–11 (Sat 12–11, Sun 12–10.30) Closed Mon lunch ⊕ *Free House* 🍺 🍎 🍷 *14* 👪 *portions/menu* 🐕 Wi-fi Ⓟ ✿ 🚌 *notice required*

RAMSBOTTOM

Eagle + Child – see page 258

Irwell Works Brewery Tap

Tel 01706 825019 | Irwell Street, BL0 9YQ
Web www.irwellworksbrewery.co.uk
Dir *Phone for detailed directions.*

Situated in Irwell's former Steam Tin, Copper and Iron Works, the building dates from 1888. It was used as an engineering works until 2002 and was derelict for almost a decade before being restored to house the brewery. Showcasing the full range of ales, from the hoppy Costa del Salford to the golden Steam Plate best bitter, the pub offers simple lunches but the focus is the ale and it's a popular pitstop for beer lovers on the East Lancashire Railway 'Rail Ale Trail'.

Open all year, all day 12–11 (Sat to Sun 11am to midnight) Closed Mon ⊕ *Free House* 🍺 🍎 👪 🐕 Wi-fi 🚌 *notice required*

SLAIDBURN

Hark to Bounty Inn

Tel 01200 446246 | Townend, BB7 3EP
Web www.harktobounty.co.uk
Dir *Phone for detailed directions.*

Located in the pretty village of Slaidburn is in the Forest of Bowland, an Area of Outstanding Natural Beauty, the Hark to Bounty is perfect for walking, fishing, bird-watching and cycling. Have a pint of Theakston's Old Peculier and check out the pub classics on the menu.

RAMSBOTTOM

Eagle + Child

Tel **01706 557181** | **3 Whalley Road, BL0 0DL**
Web **www.eagle-and-child.com**
Dir ***M66 junction 1, A56 towards Edenfield. Pub on left in outskirts of Ramsbottom.***

A pub with a social purpose

With the wholehearted support of Thwaites Brewery, supplier of its cask ales, the pub has won many local and national food awards; Top Bunk is the house ale. Landlord Glen Duckett specialises in what he calls 'Grandma's favourite classics', so look out for Double Bomber cheese and onion pie served in an old enamel pie dish; or beer-battered haddock fillet. He also offers 'more refined' plates, including local rabbit and Bury black pudding boudin; fillet of Cornish lemon sole; and pressed Bowland ox cheek. There's a vegan menu too, and snacks in the bar. A work in progress is the 'incredible edible' beer garden which is inspiring children and indeed the pub's clientele to grow, cook and eat delicious high-quality produce with minimum food miles. When finished it will contain an outdoor kitchen and bar, vegetable and compost beds, fruit shrubs, mini-orchard with chickens, children's play area and more. From the Orangery dining room there's a terrific view across the Irwell. The pub is a refreshment stop on the East Lancs Rail Trail from Heywood to Rawtenstall. An objective of Glen's is to attract marginalised 16–25-year-olds into careers in the pub, catering and hospitality trades.

Open all day, all week *The House of Daniel Thwaites* *10* *portions/menu* *notice required*

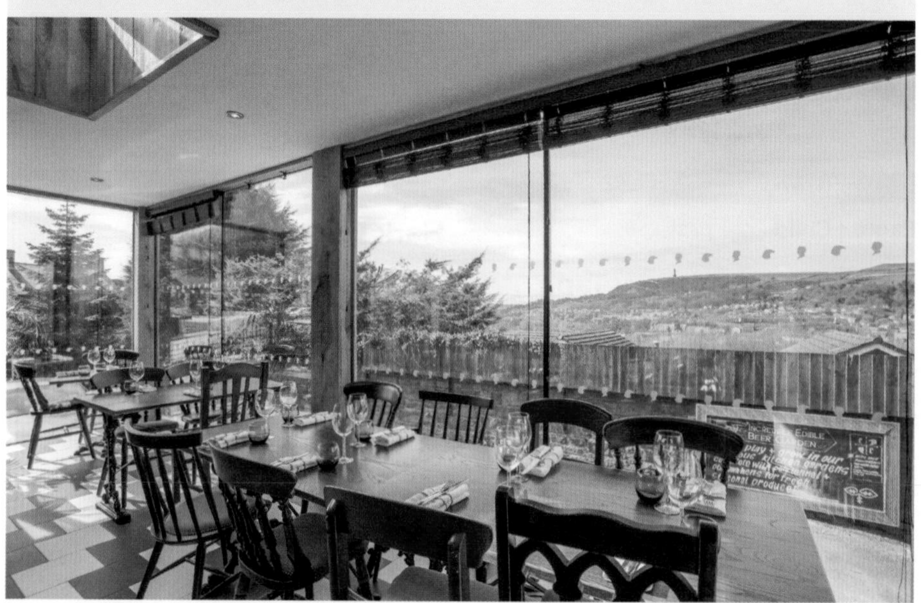

TOCKHOLES

The Royal Arms

Tel **01254 705373 | Tockholes Road, BB3 0PA**
Dir ***M65 junction 4, follow Blackburn signs. Right at lights, 1st left. Up hill left at Three B's Brewery into Tockholes Road. Pub in 1 mile on left.***

High in the West Pennine Moors is this appealing old stone pub situated in a tiny fold of mill-workers' cottages. There's an engaging hotchpotch of furnishings in the fire-warmed, flagstoned and beamed rooms. Take a glass of ale out to tables on the lawn and study the regularly-changing menu of home-cooked goodies, such as lamb kleftico, and braised steak in red wine. There are walks from the door – drop into Roddlesworth Woods or you can climb to the imposing Jubilee Tower on nearby Darwen Hill.

Open all year 12–11 (Sun 12–10.30) Closed Mon Free House from £6.95 portions/menu notice required

WADDINGTON

Higher Buck

Tel **01200 423226 | The Square, BB7 3HZ**
Web **www.higherbuck.com**
Dir ***From A671 at roundabout onto B6478 (Well Terrace) signed Waddington. Continue to village, in square on right at junction.***

Located beneath Waddington Fell and surrounded by open moorland, the Higher Buck occupies an idyllic spot in an unspoilt part of rural Lancashire. Dating back to the 19th century, this traditional pub has a modern approach to its food. Wellgate smoked salmon with pickled cucumber might be followed by venison Wellington, triple-cooked chips, roast parsnips and red wine sauce; or baked plaice fillet, clams, smoked bacon, tenderstem broccoli and new potatoes. Wash it down with a glass of well-kept Thwaites Original.

Open all day, all week Thwaites 14 from £13 portions/menu notice required

The Lower Buck

Tel **01200 423342 | Edisford Road, BB7 3HU**
Web **www.thelowerbuck.com**
Dir ***From A671 onto B6478 (Well Terrace) signed Waddington. In Waddington at crossroads left into Waddow View. At T-junction right signed Bashall Eaves. At next T-junction right, pub on left.***

Look for St Helen's church and you'll find The Lower Buck just behind it. The 250-year-old pub is run with an emphasis on warmth of welcome, excellent ales – with award-winning Bowland AONB among them – and a classic pub menu. Choose Bowand Bakery pies; or a hearty dish of Lancashire hotpot; or maybe the Cowman's of Clitheroe Cumberland sausage and mash.

Open all day, all week Free House 13 portions/menu notice required

Waddington Arms

Tel **01200 423262 | West View, Waddington Road, BB7 3HP**
Web **www.waddingtonarms.co.uk**
Dir ***In village centre.***

Close to the A59, this former coaching inn occupies an enviable position in the heart of the Ribble Valley. Take a pint of Bowland Hen Harrier while you look at the menu. Strong on local specialities, the menu offers Lancashire cheese and brioche crusted hake with shellfish and caper sauce; and Cowmans pork and leek sausages, creamy mash and crispy onion rings.

Open all day, all week Free House 14 portions/menu notice required

See advertisement on page 260

WEST BRADFORD

Three Millstones

Tel **01200 443339 | Waddington Road, BB7 4SX**
Web **www.3millstones.co.uk**
Dir ***From A59 between Wiswell and Gisburn follow Waddington signs. At roundabout 2nd exit signed West Bradford (over railway crossing, then River Ribble), at T-junction in Waddington left. Pub on left.***

Dating back to the 19th century, this Grade II listed building is one of the oldest in this picturesque village. With two real fires and a bar dispensing local ales such as Worsthorne Chestnut Mare, it has a warm and relaxed atmosphere.

Eat, Drink Sleep.

Located beside an ancie stone bridge over a babbling brook at the heart of the picture postca village of Waddington, the Waddington Arms is the hub of this vibrant little community and an ideal base for a multitude of walks – from a gentle countryside amble, to pretty riverside walks or challenging hikes up into the fells to the north of the village.

Fabulous food from well thought out menus is served for lunch and dinne seven days a week and six beautiful bedrooms provid a comfortable base for exploring the Ribble Valley by car or on foot.

Waddington, Clitheroe, Lancashire, BB7 3HP
01200 423262 | www.waddingtonarms.co.uk

WHALLEY

The Three Fishes PICK OF THE PUBS

Tel 01254 826888 | Mitton Road, Mitton, BB7 9PQ
Web www.thethreefishes.com
Dir *M6 junction 31, A59 to Clitheroe. Follow Whalley signs, B6246, 2 miles.*

Mitton is small – a few houses, the church and this 400-year-old pub, flagship of Ribble Valley Inns. It takes its name from the 'three fishes pendant' on the coat of arms of the last abbot of Whalley Abbey a few miles away. The removal of internal walls has created a long, contemporary space, with padded seating at well-spaced tables and a bar with tall chairs, while at one end is an open fire, at the other, a sofa and armchairs. The menu features steaks, Lancashire hotpot, fish and chips, and cheese and onion pie, with Sicilian stew of red mullet, mussels, cod and baby squid an alternative to such traditional pub favourites. Roasts on Sundays and no corkage charge on your own wine on Mondays.

Open all day, all week 12–11 (Sun 12–10.30) Free House 11 menus Wi-fi

WHEELTON

The Dressers Arms

Tel 01254 830041 | Briers Brow, PR6 8HD
Web www.dressersarms.co.uk
Dir *M61 junction 8, A674 to Blackburn. Follow sign for pub on right.*

This long, low, creeper-festooned old gritstone building is crammed with local photos, collectables and artefacts spread through a clutch of separate drinking areas, warmed by roaring fires in winter. Its appeal is enhanced by the choice of ales and a reliable raft of home-made pub grub: perhaps a beef and onion sandwich; beef lasagne; chilli con carne; braised lamb shank; sea bass risotto; a T-bone steak; or grilled aubergine, courgette and pepper stack.

Open all day, all week Free House 20 portions/menu Wi-fi

WHITEWELL

The Inn at Whitewell

Tel 01200 448222 | Forest of Bowland, BB7 3AT
Web www.innatwhitewell.com
Dir *From B6243 follow Whitewell signs.*

Historic inn with spectacular views

PICK OF THE PUBS

This must be one of the most idyllically located inns in England, in the heart of the glorious Forest of Bowland. Here the partly 13th-century inn slumbers by a tiny Georgian chapel, with slippery paths down to stepping stones across the River Hodder. All around the high moors, pastures and estates burst with provisions destined for the inn's kitchen. The engaging multi-roomed interior is liberally decorated with antiques, ephemera and pictures; there's also an independent wine shop. A light lunch could comprise potted Cornish crab with avocado purée. At dinner, try Goosnargh corn-fed chicken with potato cake, caramelised onions and red wine jus, or the kitchen's signature fish pie and beer-battered haddock, chips and choice of peas will do the trick. Ramblers dropping in from the heights will delight in beers from Timothy Taylor and Hawkshead, enjoyed on the terrace with fabulous fell views.

Open all day, all week 10am–1am Free House 16 portions notice required

LEICESTERSHIRE

BARROW UPON SOAR

The Blacksmiths Arms

Tel **01509 413100 | 2–4 Church Lane, LE12 8PP**
Web **www.blacksmiths1753.co.uk**
Dir ***From A6 follow signs for Barrow upon Soar. In centre of village.***

Just five minutes from Quorn and Loughborough, the pretty riverside village of Barrow upon Soar is a bit of a gem, and The Blacksmiths Arms, set on the bustling main street, is a warm and welcoming setting for some excellent gastro pub dining.

BLABY

The Bakers Arms

Tel **0116 278 7253 | The Green, LE8 4FQ**
Web **www.thebakersarms.com**
Dir ***From A426 (south of Leicester) at roundabout (with Northfield Park on left) into Sycamore Street. 2nd left into Wigston Road. Pub on left.***

When neighbouring All Saints Church was under construction in 1485 its builders needed a hostel, so they built what about half a millennium later became The Bakers Arms. Bar snacks are written on blackboards; restaurant dishes include duck liver parfait; Gloucestershire pork cheeks; steak suet pudding; and sweet potato and red lentil burgers. It's an Everard's house, so expect the Leicester brewery's Tiger and Beacon real ales, while also from the county comes Bottle Kicking cider.

Open all day, all week Everards 14 from £12.95 portions

BRAYBROOKE

The Swan

Tel **01858 462754 | 18 Griffin Road, LE16 8LH**
Web **www.swanbraybrooke.co.uk**
Dir ***South of Market Harborough on A508, turn left signed Braybrooke. In village.***

A lovely thatched pub in a pleasant village setting, The Swan is a friendly place with a focus on food. It's open for breakfast, if you fancy a full English or eggs Benedict, while lunch might bring brie, tomato and olive tartlet followed by beer-battered haddock and chips. In the evening, you could share a baked camembert, or keep the tempura black king prawns to yourself, while mains might include chicken supreme, spinach and baby mushroom sauté, garlic potato cake and truffled pea purée.

Open all year 12–3 6–close (Sat to Sun all day) Closed Mon Everards from £14 portions

BREEDON ON THE HILL

The Three Horseshoes

Tel **01332 695129 | Main Street, DE73 8AN**
Web **www.thehorseshoes.com**
Dir ***5 miles from M1 junction 23a. Pub in village centre.***

Originally a farrier's, the buildings here are around 250 years old; the pub's been here for at least a century; while a farm shop and a chocolate workshop occupy the smithy and stables in the courtyard. Inside, numerous original features, old beams, antique furniture and sea-grass matting create a warm and welcoming atmosphere. A typical menu presents mains such as beef, mushroom and red wine casserole; and cod with garlic roast vegetables.

Open 11.30–2.30 5.30–11 (Sun 12–3) Closed 25–26 and 31 Dec to 1 Jan, Sun evening and Mon Free House portions

BRUNTINGTHORPE

The Joiners

Tel **0116 247 8258 | Church Walk, LE17 5QH**
Web **www.thejoinersarms.co.uk**
Dir ***4 miles from Lutterworth.***

Yesteryear's modest village pub is today's popular eating place, thanks to Stephen and Tracy Fitzpatrick and their dedicated team. You'll find stripped oak beams, flagstone floors, an open fire and candles. Menus change constantly, with ingredients sourced from wherever Stephen thinks best – beef from Scotland, seafood from Cornwall, black pudding from Clonakilty. Vegetarians might like the butternut squash and sage risotto. Every Tuesday there's a three-course, fixed-price 'Auberge Supper' (booking is essential).

Open all year 12–2 6.30–11 Closed Mon Free House 16 from £14.50 notice required

BUCKMINSTER

Tollemache Arms

Tel **01476 860477** | **48 Main Street, NG33 5SA**
Web **www.tollemache-arms.co.uk**
Dir ***4 miles from A1, between Colsterworth and Melton Mowbray on B676.***

An imposing 19th-century, stone-built country inn with a reputation for warm hospitality and good home cooking. Flower-decorated tables, old pews and an open fire characterise the rustic yet contemporary ambience.

COLEORTON

George Inn

Tel **01530 834639** | **Loughborough Road, LE67 8HF**
Web **www.thegeorgecoleorton.com**
Dir ***A42 junction 13 onto A512.***

A traditional, beamed local offering a straightforward proposition: good honest food, three well-kept cask ales, and an extensive wine list. Start with crayfish and prawn cocktail, followed by beef lasagne; vegetable dansak curry; or something from the grill. Gluten- and dairy-free options are also available. On the walls are prints of paintings by Sir George Beaumont, who died at nearby Coleorton Hall in 1827.

Open all year 12–3 5.30–11 (Fri to Sat 12–11 Sun 12–8) Closed Mon Free House 12 portions/menu Wi-fi P

CROXTON KERRIAL

The Geese and Fountain

Tel **01476 870350** | **1 School Lane, NG32 1QR**
Web **www.thegeeseandfountain.co.uk**
Dir ***On A607 between Melton Mowbray and Grantham.***

The Geese and Fountain is named after two features of the village – the natural spring 'fountain' and the flocks of geese reared for three generations by the Botterill family. The geese, along with other locally farmed produce, often appear on the pub's menu, as does an ever-changing selection of five hand-pulled local ales and ciders. The locally sourced food is straightforward and generous.

Open all day, all week Free House 10 from £11 portions/menu Wi-fi P *notice required*

EVINGTON

The Cedars

Tel **01162 730482** | **Main Street, LE5 6DN**
Web **king-henrys-taverns.co.uk**
Dir ***From Leicester take A6 towards Market Harborough. Left at lights, onto B667 to Evington. Pub in village centre.***

At The Cedars you can choose to eat in the restaurant with its panoramic windows overlooking the fountain and pond, dine alfresco in the gardens, or just enjoy a drink in the lounge bar with its leather sofas and relaxed atmosphere.

GILMORTON

Grey Goose

Tel **01455 552555** | **Lutterworth Road, LE17 5PN**
Web **www.greygoosegilmorton.co.uk**
Dir ***From A426 in Lutterworth into Gilmorton Road signed Gilmorton. Over M1. Pub on left in village.***

Close to the A426, the Grey Goose is a light and airy, contemporary pub popular with families. Real ales and ciders are joined by a large selection of wines by the glass in the bar with its log-burning fire, although the emphasis here is as much about the food.

GRIMSTON

The Black Horse

Tel **01664 812358** | **3 Main Street, LE14 3BZ**
Dir ***Phone for detailed directions.***

At the foot of the hill dropping from the medieval church, The Black Horse commands the sloping green in this peaceful village outside Melton Mowbray. The trim, flowery garden, alfresco dining area and rich, warm interior reflect this village setting, where Leicestershire produce dominates the menu.

HUNGARTON

The Black Boy

Tel **0116 259 5410** | **Main Street, LE7 9JR**
Web **www.theblackboyhungarton.co.uk**
Dir ***From Leicester take A47 towards Peterborough. In Thurnby left at lights into Station Road signed Scraptoft. At T-junction right signed Beeby. In Beeby at crossroads right signed Hungarton. Pub on right in village.***

About 200 years old, The Black Boy is set in beautiful countryside and is a magnet for walkers; dogs, though, must be kept outside. The bar hosts a varied selection of beers, some with very low ale miles such as Langton's Inclined Plane (named after the Foxton boat lift), and Grainstore's Ten Fifty from Rutland. Look to the chalkboard for the week's home-cooked dishes. Typical are goats' cheese and red onion tart and lamb's liver with bacon, mash and onion gravy.

Open all week 12–3 6–11 (Mon 6–11 Sun 12–5) Free House 9 portions/menu notice required

KNOSSINGTON

The Fox & Hounds

Tel **01664 452129** | **6 Somerby Road, LE15 8LY**
Web **www.thefoxandhounds-knossington.co.uk**
Dir ***4 miles from Oakham in Knossington.***

High-quality food and helpful, friendly service are the hallmarks of this 500-year-old pub. Set in the leafy village of Knossington close to Rutland Water, the building retains lots of traditional features, and the large rear garden and sitting area are ideal for alfresco summer dining.

LEICESTER

The Rutland & Derby

Tel **0116 262 3299** | **Millstone Lane, LE1 5JN**
Dir ***Phone for detailed directions.***

Everything here seems carefully considered, and nothing is without some special quality. Handy for city-centre attractions, the pub is worth seeking out for a craft ale such as Everards, a glass of wine from the 20 on offer, or a carefully prepared cocktail. Attention to detail is evident too in the food. Ethically sourced ingredients feature in flavoursome dishes such as beef goulash; a duck Scotch egg; and smoked bratwurst in a pretzel bun. Hand-stretched and stone-cooked flatbreads are their speciality.

Open all year, all day Closed Sun Free House 20 portions notice required

LONG WHATTON

The Falcon Inn

Tel **01509 842416** | **64 Main Street, LE12 5DG**
Web **www.falconlongwhatton.co.uk**
Dir ***M1 junction 24, A6 (Derby Road) to Kegworth. Left into Whatton Road to Long Whatton.***

The Falcon is located in the heart of a pretty village and is convenient for access from the M1. It is a family-friendly, traditional English country pub with lots of character, from the teacup lights to the chairs 'made of suits and ties'.

The Royal Oak  

PICK OF THE PUBS

Tel **01509 843694** | **26 The Green, LE12 5DB**
Web **www.theroyaloaklongwhatton.co.uk**
Dir ***M1 junction 24, A6 to Kegworth. Right into Whatton Road (becomes Kegworth Lane) to Long Whatton. From Loughborough, A6 towards Kegworth. Left onto B5324, right into Hathern Road leading to The Green.***

Ideally situated in a picturesque village close to Loughborough and East Midlands Airport, The Royal Oak is an award-winning pub, offering high quality, locally sourced food. Charnwood ales, brewed just four miles down the road, are on offer in the smart bar, and the carefully selected wine list has 15 by the glass. In the stylish AA Rosette restaurant diners can expect some tough decisions – fresh mussels cooked with chorizo, tomato, garlic and parsley; Mediterranean sharing platter; duck leg confit with Toulouse sausage or a pub classic such as home-made burger of the day. Leave room for desserts like warm treacle tart; or chocolate mousse cake. An annual summer beer festival offers 30 real ales and 10 ciders. The impeccably furnished guest bedrooms are in a separate building.

Open all day, all week Free House 15 from £12.75 portions/menu

LUTTERWORTH

The Man at Arms

Tel **01455 552540 | The Green, Bitteswell, LE17 4SB**
Web **king-henrys-taverns.co.uk**
Dir ***From Lutterworth take Lutterworth Road towards Ullesthorpe. Turn left at small white cottage. Pub on left after college on village green.***

Close to the market town of Lutterworth, this large village pub is named after a bequest by the Dowse Charity to the nearby village of Bitteswell in return for providing a 'man at arms' for times of war.

MOUNTSORREL

The Swan Inn

Tel **0116 230 2340 | 10 Loughborough Road, LE12 7AT**
Dir ***On A6 between Leicester and Loughborough.***

Originally built as two terraced cottages in 1688, this Grade II listed free house stands on the banks of the River Soar and has a secluded riverside garden. Exposed beams, flagstone floors and roaring winter log fires characterise the cosy bar and dining areas.

MOWSLEY

The Staff of Life PICK OF THE PUBS

Tel **0116 240 2359 | Main Street, LE17 6NT**
Web **www.staffoflifeinn.co.uk**
Dir ***M1 junction 20, A4304 to Market Harborough. Left in Husbands Bosworth onto A5199. In 3 miles turn right to pub.***

This pub has been in the same hands for over a decade during which time it has been very well looked after. Were they to return, the former residents of this well-proportioned Edwardian house would be amazed by the transformation of their home into such an appealing community local. The bar has high-backed settles, flagstone floors and a large wood-burning stove. Look up to the ceiling see, not quite where you'd expect it, the wine cellar. Children under 12 years are not allowed on Friday and Saturday evenings.

REDMILE

The Windmill

Tel **01949 842281 | 4 Main Street, NG13 0GA**
Web **www.thewindmillinnredmile.co.uk**
Dir ***From A52 between Bingham and Grantham follow signs for Redmile. Pub in village centre.***

Located in the centre of Redmile, within walking distance of Belvoir Castle, The Windmill featured in the TV series *Auf Wiedersehen Pet* and still draws fans of the show. A comfortable lounge bar with a fireplace is a cosy place to enjoy a pint.

SADDINGTON

The Queens Head

Tel **0116 240 2536 | Main St, LE8 0QH**
Web **www.queensheadsaddington.co.uk**
Dir ***M1 junction 20, A4304 signed Market Harborough. At Husbands Bosworth left onto A5199 signed Leicester. In 4 miles right signed Saddington. Pub in village centre.***

Set in the rolling hills of south Leicestershire with views over Saddington Reservoir, this spacious, family-friendly pub promises a welcoming and relaxing atmosphere. Everards and a brace of guest ales, plus 11 wines by the glass and guest ciders, are the prime refreshments, while the work of Chris Lewis-Sharman in the kitchen pleases all-comers. Children have their own menu, and there's plenty of room for them to play outside.

Open all week 12–11 (Sun 12–10 Mon 12–2.30 5.30–10 Tue 12–2.30 5.30–11) Everards 11 portions/menu Wi-fi notice required

SHAWELL

The White Swan PICK OF THE PUBS

Tel **01788 860357** | **Main Street, LE17 6AG**
Web **www.whiteswanshawell.co.uk**
Dir ***M6 junction 1, A426, at roundabout into Gibbet Lane (by garage) to Shawell. Or M1 junction 19, A5 towards Nuneaton. Under M6, at roundabout into Gibbet Lane (by garage).***

Between Rugby and Lutterworth, in the pretty village of Shawell, the pub is just a few minutes from the M1, making it a perfect place to stop for a pint of local Dow Bridge Gladiator ale or Aspall cider. Chef Rory McClean used to cook in some of London's most notable restaurants and his modern British food is worth a detour. A starter of sesame marinated beef fillet with wasabi avocado mousse might precede cod loin with artichoke, runner beans and saffron cream. Finish with blackberry parfait or chocolate delice. The fixed-price lunch menu might feature lobster ravioli or braised beef, beetroot and horseradish mash.

Open all day, all week Closed 26 Dec to 6 Jan Free House 37 from £15 portions/menu notice required

SILEBY

The White Swan

Tel **01509 814832** | **Swan Street, LE12 7NW**
Web **www.whiteswansileby.co.uk**
Dir ***From Leicester A6 towards Loughborough, right for Sileby; or take A46 towards Newark-on-Trent, left for Sileby.***

Behind the unassuming exterior of this 1930s building, you'll find a refurbished free house of character. Menus change weekly, and there are blackboard specials, too. Favourites include duck and vegetable pancakes with pea and mint soup; roast duck breast in black cherry sauce; and home-made pies including beef, ale and mushroom. Desserts include chocolate brownie or chocolate tiffin. Sunday lunch is also a popular event and dogs are welcome in the snug bar.

Open Tue to Sat 6–10, Sun 12–3 Closed 1–5 Jan, Sun evening and Mon (Tue to Sat lunch) Free House 8 portions/menu

SOMERBY

Stilton Cheese Inn

Tel **01664 454394** | **High Street, LE14 2QB**
Web **www.stiltoncheeseinn.co.uk**
Dir ***From A606 between Melton Mowbray and Oakham follow signs to Pickwell and Somerby. Enter village, 1st right to centre, pub on left.***

Village pub surrounded by beautiful countryside

An attractive, mellow sandstone building dating from the 17th century, whose interior frequently prompts customers to liken a visit to stepping back in time. Its reputation for good hearty food stems from dishes such as deep-fried fillet of cod; home-made cottage pie; grilled beef and gammon steaks; chilli con carne; macaroni cheese, and regularly changing specials. Stilton comes as a cheese option for a ploughman's, and for a steak sauce topping.

In addition to the food, also attracting custom is the wide selection of wines by the glass or mini-bottle, and locally brewed real ales from Belvoir, The Grainstore, Newby Wyke and others. Furthermore, there's a choice of 25-plus malt whiskies.

Open all week 12–3 6–11 (Sun 12–3 7–11) Free House 15 from £7.50 portions/menu notice required

SUTTON CHENEY

Hercules Revived – see page 268 and advertisement above

SWITHLAND

The Griffin Inn

Tel **01509 890535** | **174 Main Street, LE12 8TJ**
Web **www.griffininnswithland.co.uk**
Dir ***From A46 into Anstey. Right at roundabout to Cropston. Right at crossroads, 1st left, 0.5 mile to Swithland. Follow brown signs for inn.***

Parts of this welcoming, traditional, family-run country inn date back to the 15th century. There are three cosy bar areas serving a range of real ales, two dining rooms, a skittle alley, large patio and 'secret' garden with a stream. Menus offer unfussy, internationally inspired food.

THORPE LANGTON

The Bakers Arms

Tel **01858 545201** | **Main Street, LE16 7TS**
Web **www.thebakersarms.co.uk**
Dir ***Take A6 south from Leicester then left signed 'The Langtons', at rail bridge continue to crossroads. Straight on to Thorpe Langton. Pub on left.***

A pretty, thatched pub set in an equally pretty village, The Bakers Arms has the requisite low beams, rug-strewn quarry-tiled floors, large pine tables and open fires. Its weekly-changing menu of modern pub food has gained it a keen local following. Expect dishes like crevettes with asparagus, soft boiled eggs and garlic mayonnaise; and confit of duck with red pepper and ginger marmalade. Fish lovers should be sure to visit on a Thursday. The area is popular with walkers, riders and mountain bikers.

Open 6.30–11 (Sat 12–2.30 6.30–11 Sun 12–2.30) Closed 1–7 Jan, Sun evening, Mon *Free House* 9
Wi-fi P

SUTTON CHENEY

Hercules Revived

Tel 01455 699336 | Main Street, CV13 0AG
Web www.herculesrevived.co.uk
Dir *Phone for detailed directions.*

Revitalised village inn serving traditional food

Named after an 18th-century racehorse, this pub has undergone its own revival; there's a relaxed and informal bar area serving well-kept ales and a range of gins, plus a cosy and elegant upstairs restaurant with comfortable, stylish seating. The map wall is particularly impressive. Look out for the brand-new Woodshed, too – an outdoor dining area with a wood-fired pizza oven, open early evenings in the spring and summer every Monday and Friday, and during the day on a Saturday. Back indoors, the talented chefs make everything fresh on site and offer an extensive selection of traditional food with a modern twist. Creamed garlic mushrooms on seeded toast or trio of salmon (smoked, poached, gravad lax) might precede chicken Kiev; pork belly, wild mushroom and tarragon sausage, mashed potato and bacon and red wine jus; or a 10oz rib-eye with field mushrooms, chunky chips, rocket and cherry tomatoes. Leave room for the classic date and sticky toffee pudding or strawberry cheesecake with strawberry salad. Various events, from a gin festival to a kids' pizza-making workshop in the summer, ensure things are never dull here, so make sure you check out the website to see what's going on.

Open all day, all week *Free House* 12 *from £12.95* *portions* *notice required*

WELHAM

The Old Red Lion

Tel 01858 565253 | Main Street, LE16 7UJ
Web www.king-henrys-taverns.co.uk
Dir *North-east of Market Harborough take B664 to Weston by Welland. Left to Welham.*

The airy, split-level, contemporary interior of today's pub blends well with vestiges of its origins as a coaching inn. Polished floorboards, leather seating and open fire are a welcome retreat for ramblers drifting in from the area's popular walking routes. Views from the windows stretch across this rural corner of Leicestershire where the River Welland meanders through rich pastureland. One of a small chain of local dining pubs, the menu covers all bases and the beers include Marston's Pedigree.

Open all day, all week 11.30–11 Free House 15 portions/menu Wi-fi P

WOODHOUSE EAVES

The Curzon Arms

Tel 01509 890377 | 44 Maplewell Road, LE12 8QZ
Web thecurzonarms.com
Dir *M1 junction 23, A512 towards Loughborough. Right signed Nanpantan. Through Nanpantan to Woodhouse Eaves.*

Traditional and lounge bars, a restaurant, wood-burning stoves, wooden floors, a large terrace and a beer garden just about sum up this Charnwood Forest pub. Other essentials are the four rotating real ales, hand-picked wines and satisfyingly seasonal British food.

The Wheatsheaf Inn

Tel 01509 890320 | Brand Hill, LE12 8SS
Web wheatsheafinn.net
Dir *M1 junction 22, follow Quorn signs.*

Once frequented by quarrymen, this 18th-century stone inn is located on the edge of Woodhouse Eaves village, close to the Great Central steam railway. Local produce drives the menu, while a carefully curated list of wines includes many offered by the glass.

WYMESWOLD

The Windmill Inn

Tel 01509 881313 | 83 Brook Street, LE12 6TT
Web www.thewindmillwymeswold.com
Dir *From A46 north of Six Hills left onto A606 signed Wymeswold. In village left into Church Lane, left into Brook Street. Or from M1 junction 24, A6 signed Loughborough and Kegworth, A6006 to Wymeswold.*

It may be a traditional village inn but the Windmill has a contemporary feel in both the bar and restaurant, with a mix of wood and stone tiled floors, wood-burners, warm heritage colours and comfortable seating creating the informal scene.

WYMONDHAM

The Berkeley Arms

Tel 01572 787587 | 59 Main Street, LE14 2AG
Web berkeley-arms.co.uk
Dir *In town centre.*

This appealing, stone-built Berkeley Arms is dedicated to sourcing fresh, local produce for the daily-changing menus. Well thought out two- and three- course Sunday lunches are a feature.

▶ LINCOLNSHIRE

BARNOLDBY LE BECK

The Ship Inn

Tel 01472 822308 | Main Road, DN37 0BG
Web www.the-shipinn.com
Dir *M180 junction 5, A18 past Humberside Airport. At Laceby Junction roundabout (A18 and A46) straight over follow Skegness/Boston signs. Approximately 2 miles turn left signed Waltham and Barnoldby le Beck.*

Set in a picturesque village on the edge of the Lincolnshire Wolds, this 300-year-old inn has always attracted an interesting mix of customers, from Grimsby's seafarers to aviators from the county's World War II airstrips. The bar is filled with maritime bric-à-brac and serves a grand choice of ales such as Black Sheep or Batemans XB, and there's also a beautiful garden. Seafood is a speciality but never fear, meat lovers have plenty of choice too.

Open 12–3 6–11 (Fri to Sat 12–3 6–12 Sun 12–5) Closed 25 Dec, Sun evening, Mon 9 portions Wi-fi P *notice required*

BASTON

White Horse Baston

Tel **01778 560923 | 4 Church Street, PE6 9PE**
Web **www.thewhitehorsebaston.co.uk**
Dir ***From Peterborough take A15 towards Sleaford. After Market Deeping turn right signed Baston, 2nd right into Church Street, pub on right.***

Local farmer Mark Richardson bought what for 40 years had been The Spinning Wheel. He transformed it, importing beams from an old barn, floorboards to form a ceiling, and a decorative piece of sycamore trunk for the Snug. His farm supplies the meat.

BELCHFORD

The Blue Bell Inn

Tel **01507 533602 | 1 Main Road, LN9 6LQ**
Web **www.bluebellbelchford.co.uk**
Dir ***From Horncastle take A153 towards Louth. Right signed Belchford.***

Pantiles on the roof, white walls reflecting the sun, this family-run free house stands on the Viking Way long-distance path from the Humber to Rutland Water. Diners from all over the county are attracted by its many culinary temptations and anyone just after a glass of wine or pint of Wainfleet-brewed Batemans XXXB, Greene King IPA or a guest beer, will find plenty of armchairs to sink into.

Open all week 11.30–2.30 6.30–11 (Sun 12–10.30) Closed 2nd and 3rd week Jan Free House from £9.50 portions/menu

BURTON COGGLES

The Cholmeley Arms

Tel **01476 550225 | Village Street, NG33 4JS**
Web **www.thecholmeleyarms.co.uk**
Dir ***From A1 at Colsterworth onto A151 towards Corby Glen. Left onto B1176 signed Burton Coggles.***

The inn is part of the Easton Estate, whose 'lost' walled gardens are worth visiting. The Prince of Wales visited the inn and associated farm shop in connection with His Royal Highness's Pub is the Hub initiative.

CAYTHORPE

Red Lion

Tel **01400 272632 | High Street, NG32 3DN**
Web **www.redlioncaythorpe.org.uk**
Dir ***South-east of Newark-on-Trent.***

Old world charm combines with contemporary comforts in this stylishly refurbished 17th-century inn. Grab one of the comfortable armchairs by the open fire and enjoy a glass of Adnams ale as you agonise over menu choices. Pub classics may be one way to go, or you could kick off with pan-fried crevettes with garlic and chilli dipping oil followed by duck breast with sweet potato mash and asparagus.

Open all year 12–3 6–11 (Sun 12–4) Closed Sun evening Punch Taverns 9 portions notice required

COLEBY

The Bell at Coleby

Tel **01522 813778 | 3 Far Lane, LN5 0AH**
Web **www.thebellatcoleby.com**
Dir ***7 miles south of Lincoln on A607 towards Grantham.***

Down a quiet cul-de-sac just off The Viking Way, Paul Vidic's friendly dining pub has three elegant yet informal dining areas. Paul is passionate about the food he creates, and his accomplished menu offers starters such as duck rillettes with sticky fig chutney and rustic toast; and typical mains of panache of halibut, turbot and John Dory; roast rack of lamb; and pasta with leeks and creamed wild mushrooms.

Open all year 5.30–11 (Sun 12–3) Closed Mon to Tue Free House 12 from £14.95

CONINGSBY

The Lea Gate Inn

Tel **01526 342370 | Leagate Road, LN4 4RS**
Web **www.the-leagate-inn.co.uk**
Dir ***From Coningsby take A153 towards Horncastle. Right onto B1192 signed Boston. Pub on left.***

Dating from 1542, this was the last of the Fen Guide Houses that provided shelter before the treacherous marshes were drained. Among the oak-beamed pub's features are a priest's hole, a very old inglenook fireplace, extensive gardens and a yew tree dating from the 1600s.

CORBY GLEN

Woodhouse Arms

Tel **01476 552452 | 2 Bourne Road, NG33 4NS**
Web **www.thewoodhousearms.co.uk**
Dir ***From A1 between Stamford and Grantham onto A151 signed Bourne and Corby Glen.***

The village of Corby Glen is a lovely setting for this cosy, welcoming pub, which has alfresco dining for the summer and roaring fires in the winter. In the bright and airy restaurant, you might pick Italian meatballs, tomato and basil sauce.

DRY DODDINGTON

Wheatsheaf Inn

Tel **01400 281458 | NG23 5HU**
Web **www.thewheatsheafinndrydoddington.com**
Dir ***From A1 between Newark-on-Trent and Grantham. Turn into Doddington Lane for Dry Doddington.***

This pantile-roofed inn looks across the green to the village church with its leaning tower. Picnic settles around the pub entrance encourage resting for a while with a pint in hand – Abbot Ale, Timothy Taylor Landlord and guest ales are all on hand pump inside.

EPWORTH

The Old School Inn

Tel **01427 875835 | 10 Battle Green, DN9 1JT**
Web **www.theoldschoolinnepworth.co.uk**
Dir ***Phone for detailed directions.***

Full of history, this stylish pub was once, as you can probably guess, the village school. There's plenty of atmosphere, with an open fire, large landscaped gardens and a warm welcome. On Wednesday evenings you can eat in the bar, otherwise the restaurant is the setting.

FULBECK

The Hare & Hounds

Tel **01400 273322 | The Green, NG32 3JJ**
Web **www.hareandhoundsfulbeck.com**
Dir ***On A607, north of Grantham.***

A 17th-century, Grade II listed pub overlooking Fulbeck's historic church and pretty village green, a log fire in the bar of The Hare & Hounds keeps the chills away in winter. On warmer days, a pleasant outside eating area awaits.

GEDNEY DYKE

The Chequers

Tel **01406 366700 | PE12 0AJ**
Web **www.the-chequers.co.uk**
Dir ***From A17 between Holbeach and Sutton Bridge left at roundabout onto B1359 (signed Gedney Dyke).***

You can just sit at the spotless bar and enjoy a pint of Woodforde's Wherry, but chances are most people arriving here will have booked a table. The contemporary decor, crisp white napery and smartly dressed front of house staff all indicate a quality food destination.

GOSBERTON

The Black Horse

Tel **01775 840995 | 66 Siltside, Gosberton Risegate, PE11 4ET**
Dir ***From Spalding take A16 towards Boston. Left onto A152. At Gosberton take B1397 to Gosberton Risegate. Pub set back from road.***

This lovely creeper-clad hostelry is tucked away in a village outside Spalding. Huddle up to the wood-burning stove with a pint of Black Sheep or Fuller's London Pride while perusing the menu. All the favourites are here, from starters of whitebait or prawn cocktail, to main plates of scampi with chips and peas, or pie of the day. Chef's home-made cheesecake with fruit coulis and honeycomb ice cream rounds things off nicely.

Open all year Tue to Sat 12–2 5.30–11, Sun 12–10.30 Closed Mon Free House 8 portions Wi-fi P

GREAT LIMBER

The New Inn PICK OF THE PUBS

Tel **01469 569998 | 2 High Street, DN37 8JL**
Web **www.thenewinngreatlimber.co.uk**
Dir ***From roundabout on A180 follow Brigg and Humber Airport signs. Pass airport, pub on right in Great Limber.***

Fifteen minutes from Grimsby, in the heart of the Brocklesby Estate, this Grade II listed inn has been welcoming travellers and locals for almost 240 years. The stylish decor has country-style chic and lots of period detail. The enthusiasm of the kitchen shows in modern British dishes using classical techniques. In the evening, a starter of ham hock terrine, pineapple chutney and crispy egg might be followed by a loin and glazed cheek of Saddleback pork, apple tarte Tatin, turnip and confit onion. The bar is a delightful place to enjoy a pint of Coastal Country Gold or one of 16 glasses served by the glass. At lunchtime, sandwiches are also on offer.

Open all week 11.30–11 (Mon 6–11) Free House 16 portions/menu Wi-fi P

HOUGH-ON-THE-HILL

The Brownlow Arms

★★★★★ INN

Tel **01400 250234 | High Road, NG32 2AZ**
Web **www.thebrownlowarms.com**
Dir ***From A607 (Grantham to Sleaford road), Hough-on-the-Hill signed from Barkston.***

This 17th-century stone inn is named after former owner Lord Brownlow, and it still looks, inside and out, every inch the country house it once was. Enjoy a pint of Timothy Taylor Landlord in the convivial bar while browsing the menu. The landscaped terrace invites outdoor drinking and dining, although please note that children must be eight or over to enter the pub, and only at lunchtime from Wednesday to Saturday.

Open Wed to Sat 12–2.30 Tue to Sat 6pm–11pm Sun 12–3 Closed 25–26 Dec, Mon, Sun evening Free House 10 from £16.95 Wi-fi P

INGHAM

The Inn on the Green

Tel **01522 730354 | 34 The Green, LN1 2XT**
Web **www.innonthegreeningham.co.uk**
Dir ***From Lincoln take A15 signed Scunthorpe. Left into Ingham Lane signed Ingham, Cammeringham. Right onto B1398 (Middle Street), left to Ingham.***

Excellent pub food on the village green

An inn for over 180 years, this lovely old limestone building is so close to RAF Scampton that drinkers enjoying a quiet pint in the garden may find themselves suddenly startled by the Red Arrows practicing above. On the corner of a pretty village green, the Grade II listed pub exudes character. Enjoyable, seasonal dishes such as traditional pork haslet with sweet pickled vegetables; and grilled plaice fillet, tiger prawn and pea risotto with chilli and lemon sauce are complemented by ales from Grantham, over 30 gins and a dozen whiskies. For those looking for a hearty start to the weekend, the pub serves breakfast on the last Saturday of each month.

Open all year, all day 12–11 (Sun 12–10.30) Closed Mon Free House 10 from £8.95 portions/menu P notice required

KIRKBY LA THORPE

Queens Head

Tel **01529 305743** | **Church Lane, NG34 9NU**
Web **www.thequeensheadinn.com**
Dir ***Follow brown tourist signs for pub from A17 (dual carriageway).***

Heavy beams, open log fires, antique furnishings and original watercolours – this destination dining pub fulfils the brief when it comes to traditional character. Food is all prepared on site, from breads to desserts, and local ingredients get star billing on the extensive, seasonal menus. Perhaps choose roast wood pigeon breast with black pudding fritters; home-made steak and kidney suet pie; or sea bass, red pepper mash and chorizo. Wash it down with wine from a well-considered list or an ale from Batemans brewery.

Open all week 12–3 6–11 (Sun 12–11) Free House 12 from £12 portions/menu notice required

KIRTON IN LINDSEY

The George

Tel **01652 640600** | **20 High Street, DN21 4LX**
Web **www.thegeorgekirton.co.uk**
Dir ***From A15 take B1205, turn right onto B1400.***

Lincoln and the Wolds are within easy reach of this extensively restored yet traditional pub. The 18th-century former coaching inn serves locally brewed ales and seasonally changing menus. Customers can dine in the comfortable bar area or in the informal restaurant.

LINCOLN

The Pyewipe

Tel **01522 528708** | **Saxilby Road, LN1 2BG**
Web **www.pyewipe.co.uk**
Dir ***From Lincoln on A57 towards Worksop, pub signed in 0.5 mile on left.***

There's a great view of nearby Lincoln Cathedral from the grounds of this waterside inn, which takes its name from the local dialect word for lapwing. Set in four wooded acres beside the Fossedyke Navigation, it serves real ales and home-made dishes from locally sourced produce. There is a beer garden and riverside patio.

Open all day, all week 11–11 Free House 10 portions/menu

The Victoria

Tel **01522 541000** | **6 Union Road, LN1 3BJ**
Web **www.victoriapub.net**
Dir ***From city outskirts follow signs for Cathedral Quarter. Pub 2 minutes walk from all major up-hill car parks. Adjacent to West Gate of Lincoln Castle.***

Situated right next to the West Gate entrance of the castle and a short stroll from Lincoln Cathedral, a long-standing drinkers' pub with a range of real ales, including three changing guest beers, ciders and perries. As well as the fantastic views of the castle, the pub also offers home-prepared food including hot sandwiches and filled rolls. Facilities include a large beer garden.

Open all day, all week 11am–midnight (Fri to Sat 11am–1am Sun 12–12) Batemans from £6.95 portions notice required

Wig & Mitre PICK OF THE PUBS

Tel **01522 535190** | **32 Steep Hill, LN2 1LU**
Web **www.wigandmitre.com**
Dir ***At top of Steep Hill, adjacent to cathedral and Lincoln Castle car parks.***

Just yards from the magnificent edifice of Lincoln Cathedral, this two-storey pub has a pedigree nearly as long; parts of it date back over 700 years. It's the ideal place for a quick pick-me-up snack, drink or leisurely meal from breakfast to evening. Notably music-free; instead you'll find a reading room, eclectic decor and furnishings, while own-brewed beers and those from local breweries slake the thirst. The daily-changing set menu adds modern twists to traditional dishes. Seared scallops come with chorizo, marinated new potatoes and tomato and dill dressing; or lobster thermidor with hand-cut chips and melange of vegetables may be listed. Daily blackboard specials considerably extend the choice and include vegetarian and gluten-free options. Gourmet evenings (pre-booking essential) are regularly held.

Open all day, all week 8.30am–11pm Closed 25 Dec Free House 24 portions/menu notice required

LITTLE BYTHAM

The Willoughby Arms

Tel **01780 410276** | **Station Road, NG33 4RA**
Web **www.willoughbyarms.co.uk**
Dir ***B6121 (Stamford to Bourne road), at junction follow signs to Careby and Little Bytham, inn 5 miles on right.***

This beamed, traditional stone country inn started life as the booking office and waiting room for Lord Willoughby's private railway line. These days it has a fresher look whilst retaining its traditional charms. Expect a good selection of real ales with great, home-cooked food.

MARKET RASEN

The Advocate Arms ★★★★★

 RESTAURANT WITH ROOMS

Tel **01673 842364** | **2 Queen Street, LN8 3EH**
Web **www.advocatearms.co.uk**
Dir ***In town centre.***

This 18th-century, three-storey corner property in the town centre has a stylishly contemporary veneer. Until 11am there's a wide choice of breakfasts, including kippers and eggs Benedict, then for lunch there are sandwiches (smoked salmon and beetroot mayo), three free-range egg omelettes, salads (chicken, asparagus and croûtons) and light bites (soufflé of the day), or more substantial main meals. These may include smoked lamb carpaccio; baked cod provençal; and blood orange and plum tart.

Open all day, all week Free House 12 portions/menu Wi-fi P notice required

PARTNEY

Red Lion Inn

Tel **01790 752271** | **PE23 4PG**
Web **www.redlioninnpartney.co.uk**
Dir ***On A16 from Boston, or A158 from Horncastle.***

A welcome sight for walkers and cyclists due to its location, many inevitably more than ready for pint of Batemans or a guest ale. The pub's solid reputation for home-cooked food can be attributed to dishes such as their 16oz Grimsby haddock and chips; 10oz rib-eye steak and chunky chips; and BBQ baby back pork ribs. A formidable selection of desserts includes puddings, sponges, sundaes and cheesecake.

Open all year 6–10.30 (Sat to Sun 12–2 6–10.30) Closed Mon Free House from £9.95 portions/menu P notice required

RAITHBY

Red Lion Inn

Tel **01790 753727** | **PE23 4DS**
Web **www.redlioninn.pub**
Dir ***A158 from Horncastle, through Hagworthingham, right at top of hill signed Raithby.***

This traditional beamed village pub, parts of which date back 300 years, is situated on the edge of the Lincolnshire Wolds, a great place for walking and cycling. Inside is a wealth of character with log fires providing a warm welcome in winter.

SCAMPTON

Dambusters Inn

Tel **01522 531333** | **23 High Street, LN1 2SD**
Dir ***4 miles north of Lincoln on B1398.***

Packed with artefacts, the pub hails the achievements of RAF Bomber Command's 617 Squadron, The Dambusters. In 1999, when this 200-year-old farmhouse became a pub, three survivors of that mission pulled the first pints. It's home to landlord Greg's microbrewery, whose real ales are among the seven on offer. Grimsby haddock appears on the menu, alongside scampi with hand-cut chips. RAF Scampton, home of the Red Arrows, is next door, and their training flights may occasionally rattle the glasses.

Open all year, all day 12–11 (Tue 12–10.30 Sun 12–7.30) Closed Mon Free House 9 portions Wi-fi P notice required

Informal hospitality at its best. The beautiful 19th century pub, run by Slawek Mikolajczyk, is nestled at the heart of the South Ferriby community and offers a traditional yet unique approach to food and drink. Priding itself on using locally sourced ingredients, including vegetables grown from its own field; it does not compromise on quality.

Offering panoramic, picturesque views of the Humber from the restaurant, guests at the Hope & Anchor can enjoy exceptional pub food whilst watching the local wildlife or staring into the stunning sunset. The bar area has cosy armchairs and a beautiful fire to keep you warm through the winter months. Summer sees the extensive beer garden filled with people enjoying a perfectly pulled pint in the refreshing breeze coming from the Humber.

Steaks are a speciality. Sourced from the Lake District, the Belted Galloway is their cattle of choice due to their superior quality. The steaks are stored in the state of the art MaturMeat cabinet and cooked on a charcoal Josper giving the meat a superbly smoky flavour.

We welcome a broad range of guests who appreciate the simple, yet satisfying things in life, whether it be a "cheeky" pint after a dog walk, sailing in via the Humber, or just to enjoy great wine and great food. Bedrooms are now available 7 nights per week from £95, exceptional corporate rates available.

For more information on our special offers please sign up to our monthly newsletter via our website.

The Hope and Anchor Pub, Sluice Road, South Ferriby, North Lincolnshire DN18 6JQ

Tel: 01652 635334 **E:** info@thehopeandanchorpub.co.uk

W: www.thehopeandanchorpub.co.uk **Facebook:** www.facebook.com/hopeandanchorsouthferriby

SOUTH FERRIBY

Hope and Anchor ★★★★ @@

RESTAURANT WITH ROOMS

Tel 01652 635334 | Sluice Road, DN18 6JQ
Web www.thehopeandanchorpub.co.uk
Dir *From A15 onto A1077 signed South Ferriby. In South Ferriby follow Winterton sign. Pub on right before River Ancholme.*

Tucked amidst creeks and moorings where the River Ancholme meets the Humber Estuary, with panoramic views from the patio and restaurant, this appealingly updated 19th-century inn, with much exposed brickwork and a log-burning stove, is a popular stop for birdwatchers and dog-walkers. Lincolnshire-brewed beers hit the spot and a happy mix of seasonal cuisine and traditional pub grub celebrates local produce; Lincolnshire pheasant with creamed sprouts and polenta may feature. Charcoal-grilled steaks are the speciality of the house; the Belted Galloway meat is matured in an ageing-cabinet onsite.

Open all day Closed 28–30 Dec, 1–8 Jan, Mon Free House 9 portions/menu notice required

See advertisement on page 275

SOUTH RAUCEBY

The Bustard Inn & Restaurant @ PICK OF THE PUBS

Tel 01529 488250 | 44 Main Street, NG34 8QG
Web www.thebustardinn.co.uk
Dir *A15 from Lincoln. Right onto B1429 for Cranwell, 1st left after village, straight across A17 to South Rauceby.*

Unable to resist the temptation, the owners have named their own-label real ale Cheeky Bustard. It's just one of the beers in the flagstone-floored bar of this pleasingly restored pub. In the restaurant, diners enjoy Moroccan spiced monkfish with braised lentils and spiced broccoli fritters; or deep-fried gorgonzola and walnut gnocchi with roasted butternut squash, spinach and nutmeg cream, with walnut dressing. The restaurant opens to a lovely courtyard, and there's a private dining area for up to 12 people. Live jazz features too.

Open 12–3 5.30–11 (Sat 12–11 Sun 12–3.30) Closed 1 Jan, Sun evening, Mon Free House 15 portions/menu notice required

SOUTH WITHAM

Blue Cow Inn

Tel 01572 767887 | High Street, NG33 5QB
Dir *Between Stamford and Grantham on A1.*

The pub was renamed 'blue' by erstwhile owner the Duke of Buckminster nearly 400 years ago, on account of his political allegiance to his king. Low beams, flagstone floors and dressed-stone walls characterise the ancient interior, with crackling log fires to take the edge off the fenland breezes. Snacks, salads and sandwiches are offered, as well as pub favourites. Time a visit for Thursday steak night or the Sunday carvery.

Open all day, all week 11–11 Free House 13 from £8.75 portions/menu notice required

STAMFORD

The Bull & Swan at Burghley

★★★★ @ INN

Tel 01780 766412 | High Street, St Martin's, PE9 2LJ
Web www.thebullandswan.co.uk
Dir *A1 onto B1081 (Carpenters Lodge junction). Signed Stamford and Burghley. 1 mile, pub on right.*

Commanding a prime position on one of historic Stamford's most stunning streets, this gabled coaching inn has an AA Rosette for its food. Dining is to the fore but beer lovers aren't short-changed, with local brewers The Grainstore one reliable supplier to the bar. Try the crispy whitebait in Bloody Mary sauce; or seared scallops with black pudding and pink apple, then move on to Norfolk Black turkey with all the trimmings.

Open all day, all week Free House 11 portions/menu

The George of Stamford

★★★★ @ HOTEL PICK OF THE PUBS

Tel 01780 750750 | 71 St Martins, PE9 2LB
Web www.georgehotelofstamford.com
Dir *From Peterborough take A1 north. Onto B1081 for Stamford, down hill to lights. Hotel on left.*

One of England's most renowned old coaching inns, it shares a stunning streetscape of imposing silver-limestone houses and villas tumbling down to the River Welland. The George, with its extraordinary gallows sign (erected as a welcome to some and a warning to others), was built in 1597 to extend an earlier inn, elements of which survive in the crypt and walled garden. The York Bar menu offers sandwiches, ploughman's, toasties and light dishes such as smoked Scottish salmon with capers. In the slightly more formal Garden Room expect the likes of seared calves' liver, parsley mash and red onion marmalade; steak and kidney pudding; or push the boat out and opt for the Grand Brittany platter comprising half lobster, crab, oyster, king prawn, mussels, clams, shell-on prawns and whelks.

Open all day, all week 11–11 (Sun 12–11) Free House 24 from £12.60 portions

The Tobie Norris PICK OF THE PUBS

Tel 01780 753800 | 12 St Pauls Street, PE9 2BE
Web www.kneadpubs.co.uk
Dir *From A1 to Stamford on A6121, becomes West Street, then East Street. After right bend right into St Pauls Street.*

Named after the man who bought it in 1617 for use as a bell foundry, this splendidly restored and renovated medieval hall house dates back to 1280. London Pride and JHB are permanent fixtures in the bar, while guest ales are rotated regularly. Having started with a plate of pigs in blankets with rosemary potatoes, your main course could be game casserole with herb dumplings; sag aloo pie; lamb kofta or beetroot falafel; or beer-battered haddock and chips. Stone-baked pizzas are cooked in ovens imported from Italy, their toppings ranging from spicy beef brisket to duck. Puddings include lemon posset and banana sticky toffee pudding. A large enclosed patio is ideal on warmer days. Note that, lunchtimes apart, there's a strict over 18s-only policy.

Open all day, all week 12–11 (Fri to Sat 12–12) Free House 18 portions

SUSWORTH

The Jenny Wren Inn

Tel 01724 784000 | East Ferry Road, DN17 3AS
Dir *Phone for detailed directions.*

This beamed and wood-panelled former farmhouse overlooking the River Trent has buckets of character. Ale lovers can enjoy the likes of Lancaster Bomber and Roosters Buckeye and the inn gains much praise for its food, to be enjoyed in the ground-floor lounge with open fire. Steaks, burgers and salads, steak and ale pie, vegetable lasagne and fish pie all make an appearance on the extensive menu.

Open all week (Tue to Sun 10am–11pm Mon 6–11) Free House portions/menu

TEALBY

The Kings Head

Tel 01673 838347 | 11 Kingsway, LN8 3YA
Web www.thekingsheadtealby.co.uk
Dir *At lights in Market Rasen take B1203 (Jameson Bridge Street) to Tealby.*

Dating from around 1367, The Kings Head stands in an ample garden in a pretty village where former resident and songwriter Bernie Taupin was apparently inspired by the colour of the Lincolnshire stone to pen 'Goodbye Yellow Brick Road' for his mate, Elton John.

THEDDLETHORPE ALL SAINTS

Kings Head Inn

Tel 01507 339798 | Mill Road, LN12 1PB
Web www.kingsheadinn.com
Dir *From A1031 between Mablethorpe and Theddlethorpe, turn left into Mill Road. Pub on right.*

Just a couple of miles from the beach and close to a nature reserve, this thatched 16th-century inn really is a sight for sore eyes. Inside are charming bars with traditional furnishings and very low ceilings. All food is locally sourced and vegetables are home grown.

WEST DEEPING

The Red Lion

Tel 01778 347190 | 48 King Street, PE6 9HP
Web www.redlionwestdeeping.co.uk
Dir *Between Stamford and Market Deeping on A1175 follow West Deeping and pub signs.*

This 16th-century, stone-built ,former cow barn is set in the heart of picturesque West Deeping. An open fire, exposed brickwork and beams add to the character of the pub, as does the friendly ghost of an old man who's reputed to once have lived there.

WOODHALL SPA

Village Limits Country Pub, Restaurant & Motel

Tel **01526 353312** | **Stixwould Road, LN10 6UJ**
Web **www.villagelimits.co.uk**
Dir ***At roundabout on main street in Woodhall Spa follow Petwood Hotel signs. Pub 500 yards past Petwood Hotel.***

Handily placed for the southern hills of the Lincolnshire Wolds, and 80 years of aircraft heritage at nearby RAF Coningsby, this friendly pub is on the outskirts of the Edwardian spa town. It excels at offering meals which champion the best of locally sourced ingredients.

WOOLSTHORPE

The Chequers Inn

★★★★ INN PICK OF THE PUBS

Tel **01476 870701** | **Main Street, NG32 1LU**
Web **www.chequersinn.net**
Dir ***Approximately 7 miles from Grantham. 3 miles from A607, follow heritage signs for Belvoir Castle.***

Leicestershire, Lincolnshire and Nottinghamshire all meet not far from this 17th-century coaching inn overlooking the village cricket pitch, and you can see Belvoir Castle, a mile or so away. Five real fires warm the interior, and a well-stocked bar does a good line in real ales. Dine in the Snug & Bar, the contemporary Dining Room or the Bakehouse Restaurant, which still features the oven from village bakery days. On the menu you might find grilled mackerel fillet, aubergine purée, cucumber, olive and celery salsa; and pan-fried duck breast, beetroot and spring onion mash, with confit orange and braised chicory. Representing the pub classics category are home-made pies; beer-battered fish and chips; and sausages, mash and onion gravy.

Open all day, all week Free House 32 from £7.99 portions/menu Wi-fi notice required

LONDON

LONDON E1

The Culpeper ★★★★

RESTAURANT WITH ROOMS PICK OF THE PUBS

Tel **020 7247 5371** | **40 Commercial Street, E1 6LP**
Web **www.theculpeper.com**
Dir ***Nearest tube stations: Aldgate East and Liverpool Street.***

This Victorian street-corner pub is named after 17th-century Spitalfields herbalist, physician and astrologer Nicholas Culpeper. The pub's huge windows help to illuminate original features in the large, open interior, and from the bar a curving staircase leads up to a more formal first-floor eating area and kitchen, which makes good use of herbs and vegetables grown in a rooftop greenhouse. The short, daily-changing menu might offer deep-fried black pudding balls with red-eye mayonnaise as a starter; then braised lamb shoulder pie with greens and salsa verde; and chocolate and orange lava cake, with praline and goats' curd sorbet. Real East End beer Truman's Runner might well be among those on hand pump, and 10 wines are by the glass.

Open all day, all week Closed 24–30 Dec Enterprise Inns 10 Wi-fi

Town of Ramsgate

Tel **020 7481 8000** | **62 Wapping High Street, E1W 2PN**
Web **www.townoframsgate.co.uk**
Dir ***Nearest tube station: Wapping.***

With wood panelling, snob screens, leaded windows and a secluded terrace with views across the river, the oldest Thames-side pub makes the most of its heritage and setting. Its robust past includes use by press-gangs and a visit by the ill-fated Captain Bligh on his way to view HMS *Bounty*. Today's guests are ensured a far more positive outcome, with traditional pub meals including a hand-made cheese and bacon burger; a sharing sausage platter with chips, Yorkshire pudding and gravy; and chicken and leek pie.

Open all day, all week 12–12 (Sun 12–11) Free House 13 Wi-fi notice required

LONDON E2

Marksman

Tel **020 7739 7393** | **254 Hackney Road, E2 7SJ**
Web **www.marksmanpublichouse.com**
Dir ***Nearest tube station: Bethnal Green.***

This impressive Victorian pub has been quenching the thirsts of generations of Eastenders. It's come up in the world more recently, but beer is still an important part of the offering, sourced from the Hackney Brewery. The upstairs dining room is a contrastingly modern space with a calm, contemporary atmosphere. You might tickle your tastebuds with half a dozen Falmouth oysters before getting stuck in to pig's head pie; braised squid; hake with mussels and sea beet; or guinea fowl, tarragon and chanterelle pie for two.

Open all day, all week Free House 10 from £16 portions Wi-fi

LONDON E9

The Empress PICK OF THE PUBS

Tel **020 8533 5123** | **130 Lauriston Road, Victoria Park, E9 7LH**
Web **www.empresse9.co.uk**
Dir ***From Mile End Station turn right into Grove Road, leads into Lauriston Road.***

A mid-Victorian corner pub with Gothic Revival windows and lofty ceilings, the long bar at The Empress serves ale and cider from venerable East End brewer, Truman's. Neighbourhood suppliers are important here, with fish from Jonathan Norris, bread from the E5 Bakehouse and coffee from Climpson & Sons. Among the dishes on the modern European menu might be burrata, sweet tomato, black sesame and salsa verde; quail with roasted roots, and onglet steak with chips and parsley aïoli. The short list of desserts could include pistachio financier and vanilla ice cream. A well as Sunday roasts, there's a popular weekend brunch menu and a cracking meal deal is offered on Monday evenings.

Open all day, all week Closed 25–26 Dec Free House 16 portions/menu Wi-fi notice required

LONDON E14

The Grapes

Tel **020 7987 4396** | **76 Narrow Street, Limehouse, E14 8BP**
Web **thegrapes.co.uk**
Dir ***Phone for detailed directions.***

In *Our Mutual Friend*, Charles Dickens immortalised this old Thames-side pub as the Six Jolly Fellowship Porters. While he might well recognise the wood-panelled, Victorian long bar and The Dickens Snug, where as a child he reputedly danced on a table, much of surrounding Limehouse has changed beyond recognition.

The Gun PICK OF THE PUBS

Tel **020 7519 0075** | **27 Coldharbour, Docklands, E14 9NS**
Web **www.thegundocklands.com**
Dir ***From West Ferry Road into Marsh Wall to mini-roundabout. Turn left, over bridge, 1st right into Coldharbour. Nearest tube stations: Canary Wharf, South Quay and Blackwall.***

In a wise move, Fuller's bought this rare surviving Thames-side pub a few years ago. It acquired its name when a cannon was fired to mark the 1802 opening of adjacent West India Import Dock (look for the whimsical cannonball hole in the pub sign). Allegedly, Lord Nelson often met Lady Hamilton here, although dockers were its mainstay until 1980. Deceptively small from the street, it's actually big enough to house a bar, formal restaurant, covered terrace and a discreet Gin Garden. Updated pub classics include rabbit loin wrapped in bacon; sea bream with polenta; braised shin of beef cobbler; and the appropriately named lamb cannon, all served by smart staff in white shirts, ties and black Gun aprons.

Open all week 12–12 (Sun 12–10) Closed 25–26 Dec Fullers & Griffin 22 from £16 portions/menu Wi-fi notice required

LONDON EC1

The Bleeding Heart Tavern

PICK OF THE PUBS

Tel **020 7242 8238** | **19 Greville Street, EC1N 8SQ**
Web **bleedingheart.co.uk**
Dir ***Close to Farringdon tube station, at corner of Greville Street and Bleeding Heart Yard.***

Dating from 1746 when drunkenness and debauchery were rife in the area, this historic tavern once offered a straw-lined back room where inebriated customers could sleep things off. Nowadays, early morning visitors can enjoy full English breakfasts, with croissants and baguettes from its own bakery. Drinks-wise, holding court are traditional ales from Adnams, Aspall cider and an impressive wine list with 450 global choices.

Open Mon to Fri 7am–11pm Closed bank holidays, 10 days at Christmas, Sat to Sun Free House

The Eagle

Tel **020 7837 1353** | **159 Farringdon Road, EC1R 3AL**
Web **www.theeaglefarringdon.co.uk**
Dir ***Nearest tube stations: Angel and Farringdon. Pub at north end of Farringdon Road.***

A trailblazer in the 1990s, this paved the way for everything we now expect from stylish gastro pubs. The lofty interior includes a wooden-floored bar and dining area, a mishmash of vintage furniture, and an open-to-view kitchen that produces a creatively modern, twice-daily changing menu and tapas selection.

The Jerusalem Tavern

Tel **020 7490 4281** | **55 Britton St, Clerkenwell, EC1M 5UQ**
Web **www.stpetersbrewery.co.uk**
Dir ***100 metres north-east of Farringdon tube station; 300 metres north of Smithfield.***

Owned by Suffolk's St Peter's Brewery, this tavern has close links to Samuel Johnson, Oliver Goldsmith, David Garrick and the young Handel. The current premises date from 1720. Its dimly lit Dickensian bar, with bare boards, rustic wooden tables, old tiles, candles, open fires and cosy corners, makes for a classic pub in every sense. It offers the full range of cask and bottled beers from St Peter's Brewery, as well as simple pub fare.

Open all day 12–11 Closed 25 Dec to 1 Jan, Sat to Sun St Peter's Brewery

The Peasant

PICK OF THE PUBS

Tel **020 7336 7726** | **240 Saint John Street, EC1V 4PH**
Web **www.thepeasant.co.uk**
Dir ***Nearest tube station: Farringdon. Pub on corner of Saint John Street and Percival Street.***

One of the first gastro pubs, standing opposite tree-shaded gardens in the heart of Clerkenwell. With imposing brickwork and a balustrade outside, the eye-catching interior emphasises the pub's Victorian grandeur, with decorative tiling, plasterwork ceiling, mosaic floor and great horseshoe mahogany bar. The first-floor restaurant continues the theme, with bold chandeliers and a quirky collection of arty circus memorabilia. A good selection of real ales includes beers from Crouch Vale brewery, whilst Bounders cider quenches a sharper thirst. The bar menu indulges most tastes, squid tempura and chilli aïoli; pheasant burger; and Denham Estate sausages, mash and caramelised onion gravy. The restaurant has a set menu (2 or 3 courses) of modern European-inspired dishes – coq au vin, pancetta, mash and mixed greens catches the eye.

Open all day, all week Closed 24 Dec to 2 Jan, bank holidays Free House 15 portions notice required

Ye Olde Mitre

Tel **020 7405 4751** | **1 Ely Court, Ely Place, EC1N 6SJ**
Web **www.yeoldemitreholborn.co.uk**
Dir ***From Chancery Lane tube station exit 3 to Holborn Circus, left into Hatton Garden. Pub in alley between 8 and 9 Hatton Garden.***

Built in 1546, extended in 1781, in the shadow of the palace of the Bishops of Ely, this quirky historic corner pub is in tucked away in Ely Court, off Hatton Garden. It is often used as a film location. Choose from at least six real ales and a range of bar snacks and 'English tapas' in the magnificent wood-panelled rooms. Please note, this pub is closed at weekends and bank holidays. There are beer festivals in May, August and December.

Open all day Closed 25 Dec, 1 Jan, bank holidays, Sat to Sun (except 1st weekend Aug) Fuller's 8

LONDON EC2

The Princess of Shoreditch

Tel **020 7729 9270** | **76–78 Paul Street, EC2A 4NE**
Web **www.theprincessofshoreditch.com**
Dir ***Nearest tube station: Old Street.***

Dating back to 1742, this popular place is a lively pub with three rotating ales on hand pump, around 40 bottled beers and canned craft beers and a range of wines. On the pub menu there's steamed Scottish mussels in chilli, garlic and parsley; and shepherd's pie with roasted root vegetables. The 42-seater candlelit dining room, accessed via a spiral staircase, is where the regularly-changing menu might feature 35-day aged Hereford rib of beef to share with maple glazed carrots and buttered kale, followed by spiced sultana ice cream, honeycomb and orange jelly.

Open all day, all week Closed 24–26 Dec Enterprise Inns 17 portions Wi-fi

LONDON EC4

The White Swan Pub and Chophouse PICK OF THE PUBS

Tel **020 7242 9696** | **108 Fetter Lane, Holborn, EC4A 1ES**
Web **www.thewhiteswanlondon.com**
Dir ***Nearest tube station: Chancery Lane. From station towards St Paul's Cathedral. At HSBC bank left into Fetter Lane. Pub on right.***

Styling itself as a 'pub and chophouse', the new interior of this City pub successfully blends the classic with the contemporary – exposed brickwork, taxidermy, butchers' tiles and vintage champagne racks contrast with polished concrete and on-trend Edison bulb lighting. The building comprises a traditional ground-floor bar, a galleried mezzanine, and a first-floor dining room. For its cosmopolitan selection of bottled beers and lagers, Adnams on tap, Addlestones cider and a dozen wines by the glass.

LONDON N1

The Albion

Tel **020 7607 7450** | **10 Thornhill Road, Islington, N1 1HW**
Web **www.the-albion.co.uk**
Dir ***From Angel tube station, cross road into Liverpool Road past Sainsbury's, continue to Richmond Avenue. Left. At junction with Thornhill Road turn right. Pub on right.***

This is a Georgian gem of a pub in the Barnsbury conservation area of Islington that continues to serve good food using top-notch British produce. In winter, log fires warm the pub, with the large walled garden and wisteria-covered pergola drawing the crowds in summer.

The Charles Lamb

Tel **020 7837 5040** | **16 Elia Street, Islington, N1 8DE**
Web **www.thecharleslamb.co.uk**
Dir ***From Angel station turn left, at junction of City Road turn left. Pass Duncan Terrace Gardens, left into Colebrooke Row. 1st right.***

Named after the writer, who lived in Islington in the 1830s, this is a cracking neighbourhood pub. Locals beat a path to the door for microbrewery ales and the hearty, home-cooked comfort food. Traditional pub food is the order of the day.

The Drapers Arms PICK OF THE PUBS

Tel **020 7619 0348** | **44 Barnsbury Street, N1 1ER**
Web **www.thedrapersarms.com**
Dir ***Turn right from Highbury and Islington station, into Upper Street. Barnsbury Street on right opposite Shell service station.***

Standing beside an attractive, tree-lined Georgian terrace and backed by a tranquil patio garden, this popular neighbourhood local was founded in the 1830s by one of London's trade guilds, and today combines fine dining with an appealing range of real ales and cider. Choose a beer from Dark Star or Windsor & Eton breweries, or one of 16 wines by the glass, and prepare to tackle the ever-changing menu. Exceptional starters may include devilled duck hearts, dripping pancake and watercress, followed by mackerel, pickled plums, chicory and mustard. You'll also find classics like steaks, beef pie, and roast pork, apple sauce and crackling sandwich.

Open all day, all week Closed 25–26 Dec Free House 16 from £10.50 portions Wi-fi

The Pig and Butcher

Tel **020 7226 8304** | **80 Liverpool Road, Islington, N1 0QD**
Web **www.thepigandbutcher.co.uk**
Dir ***Nearest tube station: Angel.***

Before The Pig and Butcher was built in the mid-1800s, the fields here were grazed by livestock on its way to Smithfield. Owner, Jack Ross and head chef, Jon Snodgrass embrace this history by receiving carcasses direct from the farm and then butchering on site. Rare breeds such as White Park cattle, Iron Age pigs and Hebridean lamb are specialities, along with game and vegetables from Kent and south coast fish. In winter, meats are brined, cured, smoked and braised, while summer sees the charcoal grill glowing.

Open all week 5–11 (Thu 5–12 Fri to Sat 12–12 Sun 12–11) Closed 24–26 Dec Enterprise Inns 22 from £15.50 portions

Smokehouse

Tel **020 7354 1144** | **63–69 Canonbury Road, N1 2DG**
Web **www.smokehouseislington.co.uk**
Dir ***Phone for detailed directions.***

Situated in Islington's prestigious Canonbury district, this successful gastro pub smokes, barbecues and roasts on Big Green Eggs, an Ole Hickory Pits Smoker and a Robata grill. Using the finest ingredients sourced from small, family-owned farms, the Smokehouse offers a refined take on barbecue dishes. Expect to find a range of 20 craft beers on tap and a further 60 by the bottle; the wine list showcases only wines from small, family-owned vineyards.

Open Mon to Wed 5–11 (Thu to Fri 5 to midnight Sat 11am to midnight Sun and bank holidays 12–10.30) Closed 24–26 Dec, Mon to Fri lunch (excluding bank holidays) Free House 15 from £17 portions notice required

LONDON N6

The Flask PICK OF THE PUBS

Tel **020 8348 7346** | **77 Highgate West Hill, N6 6BU**
Web **www.theflaskhighgate.com**
Dir ***Nearest tube stations: Archway or Highgate.***

High on Highgate Hill, The Flask may now be a gastro pub with a big reputation but its name was made long ago when Dick Turpin frequented it. This Grade II listed pub, dating back to 1663 and made famous by Byron, Keats, Hogarth and Betjeman, has become a London landmark. It retains much of its character and cosy atmosphere and a maze of small rooms is served by two bars.

The Red Lion & Sun

Tel **020 8340 1780** | **25 North Road, Highgate Village, N6 4BE**
Web **www.theredlionandsun.com**
Dir ***Nearest tube station: Highgate.***

A short walk from Hampstead Heath and Highgate Cemetery, there has been a pub on this site since the 16th century. Now an award-winning gastro pub with two beer gardens and alfresco hog roasts in summer, a wood-burning fire in the bar adds to the comfort factor.

LONDON NW1

The Chapel

Tel **020 7402 9220** | **48 Chapel Street, NW1 5DP**
Web **www.thechapellondon.com**
Dir ***By A40 Marylebone Road and Old Marylebone Road junction. Off Edgware Road by tube station.***

The Chapel has a bright, open-plan interior of stripped floors and pine furniture, and boasts one of central London's largest enclosed pub gardens – great for the children to let off steam. Daily-changing menus feature internationally influenced dishes, as well as Mediterranean antipasti and canapés

The Prince Albert

Tel **020 7485 0270** | **163 Royal College Street, NW1 0SG**
Web **www.princealbert.pub**
Dir ***From Camden tube station follow Camden Road. Right into Royal College Street, 200 metres on right.***

Picnic tables furnish the small paved courtyard, while The Prince Albert's wooden floors and bentwood furniture make a welcoming interior for customers and their four-legged friends. Real ales there are, but you may fancy a refreshing glass of wine and there's plenty of choice.

LONDON NW6

The Salusbury Pub and Dining Room

Tel **020 7328 3286 | 50–52 Salusbury Road, NW6 6NN**
Web **www.thesalusbury.co.uk**
Dir ***100 metres left from Queen's Park tube and train station (5 minutes walk from Brondesbury Station).***

A stone's throw from Queen's Park tube, this pub serves the local community well, admitting dogs and children and serving kiddy-sized portions too. Main dishes are robust and classically British. Food and drinks can be enjoyed on the patio.

LONDON NW8

The New Inn

Tel **020 7722 0726 | 2 Allitsen Road, St John's Wood, NW8 6LA**
Web **www.newinnlondon.co.uk**
Dir ***Exit A41 by St John's Wood tube station into Acacia Road, last right, to end on corner.***

Colourful flower baskets and troughs break the lines of this street-corner pub, where pavement tables are a popular retreat for locals supping Abbot Ale, Aspall cider or a choice from the extensive wine list. Well-placed for nearby Regent's Park and Lord's Cricket Ground.

LONDON SE1

The Anchor & Hope

Tel **020 7928 9898 | 36 The Cut, SE1 8LP**
Web **www.anchorandhopepub.co.uk**
Dir ***Nearest tube station: Southwark.***

One of the forerunners of the gastro pub movement, The Anchor & Hope is a short walk from Waterloo train station and The Old Vic. The deep red walls and mismatched furniture add a Bohemian touch and although the food is the driving force here, they offer a well-kept pint of Tribute. The food is taken seriously and the seasonal menu changes daily, with an emphasis on quality produce, organic vegetables and seafood from day boats. Duck hearts on toast and braised pig's cheeks typify the dishes.

Open all day, all week 11–11 (Mon 5pm–11pm Sun 12–5) Closed 24 Dec to 2 Jan Charles Wells 12 from £11.80

The Garrison PICK OF THE PUBS

Tel **020 7089 9355 | 99–101 Bermondsey Street, SE1 3XB**
Web **www.thegarrison.co.uk**
Dir ***From London Bridge tube station, east towards Tower Bridge 200 metres, right into Bermondsey Street. Pub in 100 metres.***

This green-tiled, street-corner pub refreshed generations of workers at the Surrey Docks. The docks are no more, Bermondsey has gone up-market, and The Garrison, too, has moved with the times. The pub's 21st-century restyling comprises an idiosyncratic mix of decorative themes and it's busy from breakfast through to the evening. Start the day with avocado on sourdough toast, porridge, or pancakes. At lunch there are 'small plates' – pumpkin, goats' curd and radicchio salad, say, or larger dishes like lentil, apple and walnut Wellington. Desserts may include Bramley apple and blackberry crumble. In the evening check out the smoked haddock and leek brandade with croûton soldiers, followed by seared hake with curried celeriac, Swiss chard, crab bisque and lemon pickle. Menus change every couple of months; ales rotate more frequently.

Open all day, all week 8am–11pm (Fri 8am to midnight Sat 9am to midnight Sun 9am–10.30pm) Closed 25 Dec Free House 17 from £15 portions Wi-fi

The George Inn

Tel **020 7407 2056 | 77 Borough High Street, SE1 1NH**
Web **www.greeneking-pubs.co.uk**
Dir ***From London Bridge tube station, take Borough High Street exit, left. Pub 200 yards on left.***

The coming of the railway meant demolishing part of London's sole surviving example of a 17th-century, galleried coaching inn but it still features some very old woodwork, like the simple wall seats. Pub grub is the order of the day.

The Market Porter

Tel **020 7407 2495** | **9 Stoney Street, Borough Market, London Bridge, SE1 9AA**
Web **www.themarketporter.co.uk/**
Dir ***Close to London Bridge Station, overlooking Borough Market.***

Harry Potter fans will recognise this Borough Market pub as the 'Third Hand Book Emporium' in one of the films. The pub is blessed with a great atmosphere and the exceptional choice of real ales includes the resident Harvey's, and guest ciders. Classic British and modern European dishes include hot smoked salmon Scotch eggs, a pie and chicken Kiev. On weekdays the pub opens at 6am. Children welcome before 6pm.

Open all day, all week 6am–9am, 11–11 (Sat 12–11 Sun 12–10.30) Closed 25–26 Dec, 1 Jan Free House 10 from £12.50 portions notice required

LONDON SE5

The Camberwell Arms

Tel **020 7358 4364** | **65 Camberwell Church Street, SE5 8TR**
Web **www.thecamberwellarms.co.uk**
Dir ***Nearest tube stations: Brixton and Oval.***

More elegant than its neighbours in a lively shopping street, this late Victorian pub is frequented by an enthusiastic crowd of drinkers and diners. Attractions include the wood-floored bar, its craft beers, organic and biodynamic wines, Breton cider and a generous lunch menu.

The Crooked Well

Tel **020 7252 7798** | **16 Grove Lane, Camberwell, SE5 8SY**
Web **www.thecrookedwell.com**
Dir ***Nearest tube station: Denmark Hill.***

Set up by three friends, each with stacks of restaurant experience in the kitchen or front of house, this Victorian, street corner pub has rapidly earned some worthy plaudits for its food. Regularly involved with community events, it offers mums' (and dads') mornings, jazz nights and more.

LONDON SE10

Greenwich Union Pub

Tel **020 8692 6258** | **56 Royal Hill, SE10 8RT**
Web **www.greenwichunion.com**
Dir ***From Greenwich DLR and main station exit by main ticket hall, turn left, 2nd right into Royal Hill. Pub 100 yards on right.***

In the heart of Greenwich's bustling Royal Hill, this pub's comfortable leather sofas and flagstone floors help to keep its original character intact. Interesting craft beers from the award-winning Meantime Brewing Company and a beer garden make this a popular spot.

North Pole Bar & Restaurant

PICK OF THE PUBS

Tel **020 8853 3020** | **131 Greenwich High Road, Greenwich, SE10 8JA**
Web **www.northpolegreenwich.com**
Dir ***Right from Greenwich rail station, pass Novotel. Pub on right.***

The name originated with the Victorian obsession for polar exploration, and the building dates from 1849. This stylish, contemporary venue offers a complete night out under one roof, with a bar, restaurant and basement club, while outside, the beer garden (which is also home to a shisha lounge) has seating for well over 100 people. Refreshments range from international beers such as Staropramen to cocktails, while the all-day bar menu features tapas, platters, sandwiches, grills and salads. The Piano restaurant attracts both visitors and loyal locals with its seasonally changing, modern European à la carte and brasserie menus: smoked salmon and prawn roulade; chicken liver parfait with grape and onion marmalade; a vegan dish of stuffed aubergine; and spatchcock chicken, corn salad and skin-on chips. Please note, a dress code applies.

Open all day, all week noon–2am Free House 9 portions/menu notice required

LONDON SE16

The Mayflower

Tel **020 7237 4088** | **117 Rotherhithe Street, SE16 4NF**
Web **www.mayflowerpub.co.uk**
Dir ***Phone for detailed directions.***

Named after the famous ship that set sail from Rotherhithe in 1620 with the Pilgrim Fathers on board, this historic Thameside pub has original fireplaces and timber floors as well as wonderful river views from the upstairs restaurant and the jetty outside. Choose the pie of the day from the specials board and try a pint of Scurvy Ale, one of several beers on tap.

Open all day, all week Closed 26 Dec Free House 12 portions Wi-fi notice required

LONDON SE18

Dial Arch

Tel **020 3130 0700** | **Dial Arch Buildings, The Warren, Royal Arsenal, SE18 6GH**
Web **www.dialarch.com**
Dir ***Nearest station: Woolwich Arsenal.***

In the heart of the swanky Royal Arsenal Riverside development alongside the Thames, this pub occupies a historic and elegant Georgian building. A range of Young's ales are dispensed from the long bar, and food is served throughout, including on the attractive terrace.

LONDON SE21

The Rosendale

Tel **020 8761 9008** | **65 Rosendale Road, West Dulwich, SE21 8EZ**
Web **www.therosendale.co.uk**
Dir ***Nearest station: West Dulwich.***

Part of a group of very successful south London pubs, The Rosendale likes to keep things simple but interesting, so you might find Timothy Taylor Landlord and also Harvey's Sussex classic bitter, several real ciders, and a mind-boggling range of rums, tequilas and vodkas. Traditional British food, using top-quality ingredients, takes in dishes like confit duck leg, squash terrine, spinach and apricot jus; and artisan pizzas.

Open all day, all week Closed 26 Dec Free House 27 from £12 portions/menu Wi-fi

LONDON SE23

The Dartmouth Arms

Tel **020 8488 3117** | **7 Dartmouth Road, Forest Hill, SE23 3HN**
Web **www.thedartmoutharms.com**
Dir ***100 metres from Forest Hill Station.***

The original patrons of today's stylish pub would have been boatmen from the Croydon Canal, which ran behind the pub until 1836. Georgian features remain in this popular meeting place, where good beers like Golden from Brockley Brewery quench the thirst.

LONDON SW1

The Alfred Tennyson

Tel **020 7730 6074** | **10 Motcomb Street, SW1X 8LA**
Web **thealfredtennyson.co.uk**
Dir ***Nearest tube station: Knightsbridge.***

Previously The Pantechnicon Rooms, inspired by the early 19th-century, Greek revival-style building a hundred yards away, this poetically renamed pub is very, very Belgravia. For a drink, a quick breakfast, lunch or supper, stay in the casual ground-floor bar; for something more formal ascend to the dining room.

8 TOP LONDON PUBS FOR FOOD

The following pubs have been awared AA Rosettes for the quality of their cuisine. (See page 12–13 for more information).

The Empress E9, *see page 279*
The Harwood Arms SW6 *see page 287*
The Wigmore ★★★★★ HOTEL W1, *see page 291*
The Culpeper ★★★★ RESTAURANT WITH ROOMS E1, *see page 291*
The Anchor & Hope SE1, *see page 283*
The Bleeding Heart EC1, *see page 280*
Fox & Grapes SW19, *see page 290*
Angelsea Arms W6, *see page 291*

The Buckingham Arms

Tel **020 7222 3386** | **62 Petty France, SW1H 9EU**
Web **www.youngs.co.uk**
Dir ***Nearest tube station: St James's Park.***

This elegant Young's pub retains much of its old charm including etched mirrors and period light fittings in the bar. Close to Buckingham Palace, it is popular with pretty much everyone: tourists, business people, politicians, media types and real ale fans.

The Nags Head PICK OF THE PUBS

Tel **020 7235 1135** | **53 Kinnerton Street, SW1X 8ED**
Dir ***Phone for detailed directions.***

This pub was built in the early 19th century for below-stairs staff and stable hands working in this quiet Belgravia mews near Harrods. With its Dickensian frontage and an interior like a well-stocked bric-à-brac shop, The Nags Head stubbornly resists any contemporary touches. It's a mobile-free zone, and you are politely requested to hang coats and bags on the hooks provided. Compact and bijou, it boasts wooden floors, low ceilings and panelled walls covered with photos, drawings, and mirrors; other adornments include helmets, model aeroplanes and penny-slot machines. The atmosphere is best described as 'entertaining' if you're in the right mood. The full Adnams range is served, along with a good value menu of traditional pub grub – real ale sausages, roast of the day; and chilli con carne.

Open all day, all week 11–11 Free House

The Orange Public House & Hotel

Tel **020 7881 9844** | **37 Pimlico Road, SW1W 8NE**
Web **theorange.co.uk**
Dir ***Nearest tube station: Victoria or Sloane Street.***

The Orange comprises a number of light and airy adjoining rooms, which have a rustic Tuscan feel. Well-heeled locals quaff local ales and Italian wines while selecting from menus of modern European dishes. The pub is recognised for its approach to sustainability.

The Thomas Cubitt

Tel **020 7730 6060** | **44 Elizabeth Street, SW1W 9PA**
Web **www.thethomascubitt.co.uk**
Dir ***Nearest tube stations: Victoria and Sloane Square.***

Norfolk-born builder Thomas Cubitt developed Belgravia as a stuccoed rival to swanky Mayfair. This exclusive, corner pub draws a discerning crowd to its country-house-style interior featuring open fireplaces, detailed panelling and a superb hand-made, oak counter. Glass doors open out on to tables on the street.

The Wilton Arms

Tel **020 7235 4854** | **71 Kinnerton Street, SW1X 8ED**
Dir ***Between Hyde Park Corner and Knightsbridge tube stations.***

Known locally as The Village Pub, this early 19th-century hostelry is distinguished by fabulous flower-filled baskets and window boxes in the summer. High settles and bookcases create cosy, individual seating areas in the air-conditioned interior, and a conservatory covers the old garden. Shepherd Neame ales, including Spitfire, accompany traditional pub fare – soup, sandwiches, burgers, sausages and home-made pies and curries.

Open all day, all week 11–11 (Sun 12–10.30
Shepherd Neame 8 portions WiFi

LONDON SW3

Coopers Arms

Tel **020 7376 3120** | **87 Flood Street, Chelsea, SW3 5TB**
Web **www.youngs.co.uk**
Dir ***From Sloane Square tube station, into King's Road. Approximately 1 mile west, opposite Waitrose, turn left. Pub half way down Flood Street.***

Just off the King's Road and close to the river, this pub sees celebrities rubbing shoulders with the aristocracy and blue-collar workers. The stuffed Canadian moose brings a character of its own to the bar, where at least five real ales grace the pumps. Food is served both in the main bar area and in the first-floor Albert Room. The menu offers a range of modern British classics, including beef and bone marrow burger and a pie of the day.

Open all day, all week 12–11 (Sun 12–10.30)
Young & Co.'s Brewery 15 portions/menu
WiFi

LONDON SW4

The Stonhouse

Tel **020 7819 9312** | **165 Stonhouse Street, SW4 6BJ**
Web **www.thestonhouse.co.uk**
Dir ***Nearest tube station: Clapham Common.***

Mark Reynolds bought The Stonhouse in 2015 and has taken it back to a free house after years of pub company ownership. Tucked discreetly away between Clapham's Old Town and its busy High Street, this impressively transformed corner local has an elegant bar.

LONDON SW6

The Atlas **PICK OF THE PUBS**

Tel **020 7385 9129** | **16 Seagrave Road, Fulham, SW6 1RX**
Web **www.theatlaspub.co.uk**
Dir ***2 minutes walk from West Brompton tube station.***

Just around the corner from West Brompton tube, The Atlas is one of only a handful of London pubs to have a walled garden. This traditional, relaxed local remains true to its cause with a spacious bar area split into eating and drinking sections. Typical menus might feature starters such as burrata and fig salad with pink peppercorns, pesto, mixed leaves and foccacia, while tempting mains also demonstrate Italian influences in dishes such as penne with Italian sausage ragù; or roast monkfish with prosciutto and sage, sautéed potatoes, tomatoes, peas and oregano.

Open all day, all week 12–11 Closed 24–31 Dec Free House 15 portions notice required

The Harwood Arms

PICK OF THE PUBS

Tel **020 7386 1847** | **Walham Grove, SW6 1QP**
Web **www.harwoodarms.com**
Dir ***Phone for detailed directions.***

The combined talents of chef Brett Graham and TV chef Mike Robinson have transformed this neighbourhood pub in leafy Fulham into a top dining venue. They're passionate about the provenance and seasonality of their ingredients; the pub is renowned for its game and wild food. The inspired British cooking makes it worthy of two AA Rosettes, but the Harwood remains a proper pub, with microbrewery ales on tap, and a vibrant and friendly atmosphere. You'll find bar snacks like venison rissoles with Oxford sauce, or crispy garlic potatoes, and there's a short daily-changing menu.

Open all day 12–11 (Mon 6.15–11) Closed 24–26 Dec Enterprise Inns 15 portions/menu notice required

The Jam Tree

Tel **020 3397 3739** | **541 King's Road, SW6 2EB**
Web **www.thejamtree.com**
Dir ***Nearest tube station: Imperial Wharf or Fulham Broadway.***

Antique mirrors, personalised artworks, old chesterfields and mismatched furniture give the interior a decidedly individual look. There is a modern British menu.

The Malt House

Tel **020 7084 6888** | **17 Vanston Place, Fulham, SW6 1AY**
Web **www.malthousefulham.co.uk**
Dir ***Nearest tube station: Fulham Broadway.***

Situated just five minutes from Fulham Broadway tube station, this 18th-century building still has its old name – The Jolly Maltster – on a gable-end. The kitchen's policy is to source ingredients from independent local suppliers; starters might include London gin-cured salmon gravad lax, with beetroot gel and quails' eggs; and for mains, roasted hake in Serrano ham, saffron risotto, charred broccoli, lemon, chilli and garlic; and slow-cooked charred spring lamb shoulder.

Open all day, all week Closed 25 Dec Brakspear 12 from £12 portions/menu notice required

The Sands End Pub

Tel **020 7731 7823** | **135–137 Stephendale Road, Fulham, SW6 2PR**
Web **www.thesandsend.co.uk**
Dir ***From Wandsworth Bridge Rd (A217) into Stephendale Road. Pub 300 yards at junction with Broughton Road.***

A much-loved neighbourhood gem with the feel stylish country pub. Expect to find scrubbed farmhouse tables, wooden floors, locals quaffing pints of real ale, chalkboard menus listing terrific bar snacks (the Scotch eggs are legendary).

The White Horse

Tel **020 7736 2115** | **1–3 Parson's Green, Fulham, SW6 4UL**
Web **www.whitehorsesw6.com**
Dir ***140 metres from Parson's Green tube station.***

Overlooking Parson's Green, the late 18th-century, coaching inn and Victorian gin palace is a substantial sandstone pub. It's a destination for lovers of British pub food and interesting real ales and wines, with a restaurant in the former coach house, an upstairs bar and a luxurious private dining area. Every dish on the menu comes with a recommended beer to drink, and there are always at least 135 bottled beers available from around the world.

LONDON SW8

Canton Arms

Tel **020 7582 8710** | **177 South Lambeth Road, SW18 1PX**
Web **www.cantonarms.com**
Dir ***Nearest tube: Stockwell and Vauxhall. Pub on corner of South Lambeth Road and Aldebert Terrace.***

The Canton Arms can be found midway between Stockwell and Vauxhall tube stations. Pavement trestle tables are much sought after on summers' evenings by office workers. The pub's interior is typical of its kind, with dark walls, mismatched furniture and well-trodden floorboards. Pints of Timothy Taylor Landlord and Skinner's Betty Stogs are dispensed at the darkwood bar. Chalkboards abound, displaying everything from snacks to specials – smoked rare breed pork chop included.

Open all day Closed 24 Dec to 2 Jan, Mon lunch Enterprise Inns from £13 Wi-fi

LONDON SW11

The Bolingbroke Pub & Dining Room

Tel **020 7228 4040** | **172–174 Northcote Road, SW11 6RE**
Web **www.thebolingbroke.com**
Dir ***Nearest tube stations: Clapham South and Clapham Junction.***

This refined dining pub stands in a road known colloquially as 'Nappy Valley', due to its popularity with well-heeled young families. Named after the first Viscount Bolingbroke, who managed to be both brilliant politician and reckless rake, the pub caters admirably for children and adults alike. Expect modern British fare along the lines of beetroot and goats' cheese tarte Tatin with balsamic glaze followed by braised beef cheeks with haggerty potatoes and red cabbage.

Open all day, all week Closed 25–27 Dec Free House 13 portions/menu Wi-fi notice required

The Fox & Hounds PICK OF THE PUBS

Tel **020 7924 5483** | **66 Latchmere Road, Battersea, SW11 2JU**
Web **www.thefoxandhoundspub.co.uk**
Dir ***From Clapham Junction exit into High Street, turn left, through lights into Lavender Hill. After post office, left at lights. Pub 200 yards on left.***

From the moment you step through the door of this archetypal Victorian corner pub, you'll feel like one of the locals. This is one of those timeless pubs that London still has in abundance, its style simple with bare wooden floors, an assortment of furniture, walled garden, extensive patio planting and a covered, heated seating area. Regulars head here for the good selection of real ales and an international wine list. Fresh ingredients arrive daily from the London markets, enabling the Mediterranean-style menu and specials to change accordingly; all prepared in the open-to-view kitchen. So, you might start with burrata and fig salad, leaves and foccacia. Follow with pot-roast guinea fowl, tomatoes and rosemary, roasted shallots, polenta croûtons. A traditional British lunch is served on Sundays.

Open 12–3 5–11 (Mon 5–11 Fri to Sat 12–11 Sun 12–10.30) Closed 24–28 Dec, Mon lunch Free House 14 portions Wi-fi notice required

LONDON SW12

The Avalon

Tel **020 8675 8613** | **16 Balham Hill, SW12 9EB**
Web **www.theavalonlondon.com**
Dir ***Nearest tube station: Clapham South.***

Named after the mythical isle of Arthurian legend, the attractions of this Balham member of the Renaissance Group of south London pubs are far from fairytale. For example, there's a three-tiered rear garden that really comes alive on sunny summer days.

LONDON SW13

The Brown Dog

Tel **020 8392 2200 | 28 Cross Street, Barnes, SW13 0AP**
Web **www.thebrowndog.co.uk**
Dir ***Phone for detailed directions.***

It would be odd, perhaps, if The Brown Dog did not welcome canines, albeit the resident dog isn't brown. The pub also welcomes children, which is perhaps more surprising, given its location in the exclusive back streets of Barnes and the gastro nature of its operation.

LONDON SW14

The Victoria PICK OF THE PUBS

Tel **020 8876 4238 | 10 West Temple Sheen, East Sheen, SW14 7RT**
Web **www.victoriasheen.co.uk**
Dir ***Nearest station: Mortlake.***

In a great location just a couple of minutes from the wide open spaces of Richmond Park, The Victoria is a friendly, welcoming place. There is a bright and airy conservatory dining room, plus a sunny courtyard and a leafy garden with a safe children's play area. And of course, as it's run by TV chef Paul Merrett, you can expect award-winning culinary delights.

Open all day, all week Enterprise Inns 28 portions/menu Wi-fi *notice required*

LONDON SW15

Prince of Wales

Tel **020 8788 1552 | 138 Upper Richmond Road, Putney, SW15 2SP**
Web **www.foodandfuel.co.uk/our-pubs/prince-of-wales-putney**
Dir ***From East Putney station turn left, pub on right. From Putney Station, left into High Street, left into Upper Richmond Road; pub on left.***

Just two minutes from East Putney tube station, this Victorian corner pub attracts a mix of drinkers and foodies. In the cosy front bar, you can enjoy a pint or head to the rear dining room with its skylight and eclectic country-style decor.

The Spencer

Tel **020 8788 0640 | 237 Lower Richmond Road, Putney, SW15 1HJ**
Web **www.thespencerpub.com**
Dir ***Corner of Putney Common and Lower Richmond Road, opposite Old Putney Hospital.***

This landmark pub occupies a lofty position on green and leafy Putney Common, close to the Thames. The beer garden is part of the common and the pub's picnic benches are hotly contested by those in search of an alfresco lunch. A light, bright and airy interior belies the rather traditional look of the place. Meals are traditional favourites embracing salads, pasta, burgers, and shepherd's pie. The extensive breakfast menu is popular with early morning dog walkers and cyclists; the New Yorker – a golden waffle with two fried eggs and crispy bacon rashers – will set you up for the day.

Open all day, all week Mon to Sat 9am to midnight (Sun 11–11) Free House 20 portions/menu Wi-fi

LONDON SW18

The Earl Spencer PICK OF THE PUBS

Tel **020 8870 9244 | 260–262 Merton Road, Southfields, SW18 5JL**
Web **www.theearlspencer.com**
Dir ***Exit Southfields tube station, into Replingham Road, left at junction with Merton Road, to junction with Kimber Road.***

This grand Edwardian pub is a popular drinking and dining venue, especially during Wimbledon Fortnight, but that still leaves 50 other weeks for its attractions to work their magic. The log fires and polished wood furnishings contribute, but for many it's the great choice of drinks – real ales and lagers including Belleville Amber and Meantime London Lager, ciders and global wines, of course, but not forgetting the Merton Mule, a cocktail of vodka, ginger beer, ginger ale and crushed lime. Another big draw is the daily-changing menu on which everything is homemade. Start with pork rillette, celeriac remoulade, cornichons and toast. For a main course, poached sea trout, smoked garlic and pea purée and Jersey Royals makes an enjoyable spring treat.

Open all week 4–11 (Fri to Sat 11am to midnight Sun 12–10.30) Enterprise Inns 17 from £12.50 Wi-fi

The Roundhouse

Tel **020 7326 8580** | **2 Northside, Wandsworth Common, SW18 2SS**
Web **www.theroundhousewandsworth.com**
Dir ***Phone for detailed directions.***

Between Clapham Junction and Wandsworth, The Roundhouse has the ambience of a friendly local, with a round, black walnut bar, open kitchen, and eclectic art on the walls. Ales come from two local microbreweries, including Sambrook's Wandle – an ale named after a nearby river.

LONDON SW19

Fox & Grapes

Tel **020 8619 1300** | **9 Camp Road, Wimbledon Common, SW19 4UN**
Web **www.foxandgrapeswimbledon.co.uk**
Dir ***Just off Wimbledon Common.***

Success from day one was more or less assured by the pedigree of chefs here, with a large open-plan interior of parquet flooring, wood panelling, and wooden tables. Enjoy a pint of Doom Bar or consult the small selection of sustainable, organic and biodynamic wines.

LONDON W1

The Carpenters Arms

Tel **020 7723 1050** | **12 Seymour Place, W1H 7NE**
Web **www.thecarpentersarmspub.co.uk**
Dir ***Nearest tube station: Marble Arch.***

A traditional London pub with a green and gold frontage and hanging baskets, this is the ideal place to watch the match, with a good choice of rotating guest ales. To eat – a Pieminister pie, maybe British beef steak and craft ale, free-range chicken and Wiltshire ham, or goats' cheese, sweet potato and red onion, served with gravy, mash and gravy, or mash, peas and gravy.

Open all day, all week Closed 25–26 Dec, 1 Jan
Free House *from £7.50* Wi-fi
notice required

French House

Tel **020 7437 2477** | **49 Dean Street, Soho, W1D 5BG**
Web **www.frenchhousesoho.com**
Dir ***Nearest tube stations: Piccadilly Circus; Tottenham Court Road; Covent Garden. Pub at Shaftesbury Avenue end of Dean Street.***

This legendary Soho watering hole was known as the Maison Francais a hundred years ago; it was patronised by General de Gaulle during the Second World War, and later by Dylan Thomas, Francis Bacon, Dan Farson and many other louche Soho habitués. These days it still boasts a tiny, atmospheric bar serving only half pints. There is a second bar upstairs.

The Grazing Goat

Tel **020 7724 7243** | **6 New Quebec Street, W1H 7RQ**
Web **www.thegrazinggoat.co.uk**
Dir ***Behind Marble Arch tube station, off Seymour Street.***

Just minutes away from Oxford Street and Marble Arch, this classy, six-storey pub is full of period features including open fireplaces, oak floors and solid oak bars. The name is not mere whimsy; goats did once graze around here.

The Portman

Tel **020 7723 8996** | **51 Upper Berkeley Street, W1H 7QW**
Web **www.theportmanmarylebone.com**
Dir ***From Marble Arch into Great Cumberland Place, 3rd left into Upper Berkeley Street.***

Tucked between today's hustle of Oxford Street and the elegant shops of Marylebone, prisoners once stopped here for a final drink on their way to the gallows at Tyburn Cross. These days, this friendly central London pub is the perfect place for weary shoppers and tourists to refuel on seasonal, British classics served all day, 365 days a year. Fish and chips, monkfish stew, and the pie of the day are popular choices in the ground-floor pub but for fine dining there's a restaurant upstairs.

Open all day, all week *Free House* 15 Wi-fi
from £11 *portions/menu* *notice required*

The Wigmore

★★★★★ HOTEL

Tel **020 7965 0198 | 15 Langham Place, Marylebone, W1B 3DE**
Web **the-wigmore.co.uk**
Dir ***Nearest tube station: Oxford Circus.***

A rather splendid modern British pub on Regent Street, with a menu overseen by Michel Roux Jr and a fine selection of cask ales and craft beers. Have a pint of the house brew, Saison, from Bermondsey's Brew by Numbers while you check out the menu. Try the masala-spiced Scotch egg with dahl relish; fat chips with Bloody Mary salt; or slow-cooked pork collar with polenta, chard and cider sauce.

Open 12–12 (Thu to Sat noon to 1am) Closed 25–26 and 30 Dec, 1–3 Jan, Sun Free House 18 from £11

LONDON W4

The City Barge

Tel **020 8994 2148 | 27 Strand on the Green, W4 3PH**
Web **www.citybargechiswick.com**
Dir ***Phone for detailed directions.***

Slap bang next to the Thames in Chiswick, The City Barge dates in part to the 14th century. With three open fires, old prints on the walls and photographs of the river and the famous Thames barges, it's certainly full of character.

The Swan PICK OF THE PUBS

Tel **020 8994 8262 | 1 Evershed Walk, 119 Acton Lane, Chiswick, W4 5HH**
Web **www.theswanchiswick.co.uk**
Dir ***At end of Evershed Walk.***

A friendly dining-pub, The Swan is a perfect choice for all seasons. Its welcoming wood-panelled interior is cosy in winter, and the large lawned garden and patio are popular in summer. Good food is at the heart of the operation; the menu of modern, mostly Mediterranean cooking has a particularly Italian influence. Start perhaps with burrata and fig salad with pink peppercorns, pesto, mixed leaves and foccacia; next could be calves' liver and crispy pancetta with Puy lentils, rainbow chard, balsamic vinegar and crème fraîche. A short choice of desserts may include pear tart with ginger ice cream. It's a cuisine that lends itself to tasty vegetarian options: an excellent example is a starter of butternut squash, parsnip crisps, golden raisins and smoked cheddar with leaves.

Open all week 5–11.30 (Fri 4–11.30 Sat 12–11.30 Sun 12–10.30) Closed 24–27 Dec Free House 12 portions/menu

LONDON W5

The Grove

Tel **020 85672439 | The Green, Ealing, W5 5QX**
Web **www.thegrovew5.co.uk**
Dir ***Nearest tube station: Ealing Broadway.***

Now in new hands, the well-positioned Grove lies between Ealing Broadway's shops and the famous film studios. In addition to the bar and restaurant there's an outdoor dining area and a large terrace. Beer festivals are held in February and October.

LONDON W6

Anglesea Arms PICK OF THE PUBS

Tel **020 8749 1291 | 35 Wingate Road, W6 0UR**
Web **www.angleseaarmspub.co.uk**
Dir ***Phone for detailed directions.***

Built in 1866, this traditional Victorian corner pub is thriving in the hands of Richard and George Manners, whose experience with six other London pubs has stood them in good stead. The Arms' reputation has grown steadily, thanks to a rotating choice of real ales in the bar, a global wine list and a concise menu of carefully prepared food. The ambience too plays its part; the bar's sofas make for cosy drinking, there's an intimate dining area at the rear, and an outdoor terrace. British and continental ingredients are mixed to great effect. A typical three-course choice could begin with borlotti bean and pancetta soup, with focaccia; followed by roasted red partridge, smoked pumpkin and quince jam; and finish with chocolate torte, pink peppercorns and blackcurrant sorbet.

Open all week 5–11 (Fri to Sat 12–11 Sun 12–10.30) Closed 24–26 Dec Free House 20 from £17 portions/menu

The Dartmouth Castle

PICK OF THE PUBS

Tel **020 8748 3614** | **26 Glenthorne Road, Hammersmith, W6 0LS**
Web **www.thedartmouthcastle.co.uk**
Dir ***Nearest tube station: Hammersmith. 100 yards from Hammersmith Broadway.***

The Dartmouth Castle is very much a place to relax in, serving a good range of refreshments and plates of very appealing food. It's a child-free zone after 7pm too, adding to its appeal for those seeking a quiet evening pint. Sambrook's make their mark with ales such as Wandle; alternatives are Cornish Orchards cider amidst a generous choice of cosmopolitan bottled ciders, beers and lagers; more than a dozen wines are sold by the glass. From the menu, expect imaginative flavours in starters such as fried squid with paprika; or chicken and chorizo croquettes. Move on to a main course of pan-roast duck breast with sweet potato hash or grilled Italian sausages, and finish with apple and mixed berries crumble.

Open all day, all week Closed Easter, 23 Dec to 2 Jan
Free House 15 from £14

The Hampshire Hog

Tel **020 8748 3391** | **225-227 King Street, W6 9JT**
Web **www.thehampshirehog.com**
Dir ***Nearest tube stations: Hammersmith and Ravenscourt Park.***

Located between Chiswick and Hammersmith, this corner gastro pub may be Victorian on the outside but it's stylishly contemporary within, with wood floors, white walls and an airy conservatory. With three additional private dining rooms and outdoor tables, there are plenty of options.

The Stonemasons Arms

Tel **020 8748 1397** | **54 Cambridge Grove, W6 0LA**
Web **www.stonemasons-arms.co.uk**
Dir ***From Hammersmith tube station into King Street, 2nd right into Cambridge Grove, pub at end.***

This family-friendly pub wraps round the end of a terrace of elegant houses in leafy Hammersmith. Handy for leading cultural venues and good transport links, the curious rustic-Georgian ambience of the pub is enhanced by a rolling display of artworks by local artists.

LONDON W8

The Scarsdale

Tel **020 7937 1811** | **23A Edwardes Square, Kensington, W8 6HE**
Web **www.fullers.co.uk**
Dir ***From Kensington High Street tube station turn left. 0.5 mile (10 minutes walk) left into Edwardes Square after Odeon Cinema.***

The Scarsdale is a 19th-century free-standing building with colourful hanging baskets and window boxes spilling into the small terraced patio, in a leafy road just off Kensington High Street. The Frenchman who developed the site was supposedly one of Bonaparte's secret agents.

The Windsor Castle

Tel **020 7243 8797** | **114 Campden Hill Road, W8 7AR**
Web **www.thewindsorcastlekensington.co.uk**
Dir ***From Notting Hill tube station into Bayswater Road towards Holland Park. Left into Campden Hill Road.***

One legend has it that Windsor Castle could be seen from the upstairs windows when this eponymous pub was built in the 1830s. Such stories add to the fascination of this pub, where wood panelling separates three areas inexplicably called Campden, Private and Sherry. Enjoy a pint of Timothy Taylor Landlord or Aspall cider as you choose from a menu that might include steak and smoked cheddar pie; pan-fried sea bass with saffron dill mash; or fish and chips.

Open all week 12–11 (Sat 10am–11pm Sun 12–10.30)
Mitchells & Butlers 21 from £10.75 portions/menu notice required

LONDON W9

The Waterway

Tel **020 7266 3557** | **54 Formosa Street, W9 2JU**
Web **www.thewaterway.co.uk**
Dir ***From Warwick Avenue tube station into Warwick Avenue, turn left into Formosa Street.***

Enjoying a fabulous location on Regent's Canal, The Waterway offers great alfresco opportunities all year round with its all-weather outdoor terrace, elevated barbecue and rotisserie. An extensive wine list and cocktail menu complements a comprehensive food menu that includes grilled meats, gourmet burgers and signature dishes such as lobster and crayfish roll or burrata and pomegranate salad. Decadent desserts come in form of gooey chocolate brownie and pecan pie.

Open all day, all week 11am to midnight (Sat 10am to midnight Sun 10am–11pm) Enterprise Inns 16 portions/menu

LONDON W12

Princess Victoria

Tel **020 8749 5886** | **217 Uxbridge Road, W12 9DH**
Web **www.princessvictoria.co.uk**
Dir ***Nearest tube station: Shepherd's Bush Market.***

This grand building dates from 1829, but it was a rebuild in 1872 that produced its grand 'gin palace' appearance. Gin's still a big deal here, with over 100 available, and it's an atmospheric place to sample them.

LONDON W14

The Albion

Tel **020 7603 2826** | **121 Hammersmith Road, West Kensington, W14 0QL**
Web **www.thealbionpub.com**
Dir ***Near Kensington Olympia and Barons Court tube stations.***

If you've been wandering around Olympia head across the road to The Albion for a pint of London Pride or one of the many wines by the glass. It takes its name from HMS *Albion* and has the look and feel of an old ship.

The Cumberland Arms

PICK OF THE PUBS

Tel **020 7371 6806** | **29 North End Road, Hammersmith, W14 8SZ**
Web **www.thecumberlandarmspub.co.uk**
Dir ***From Kensington Olympia tube station turn left. At T-junction right into Hammersmith Road. 3rd left into North End Road, 100 yards pub on left.***

At the heart of cosmopolitan Hammersmith and handy for Olympia, this eye-catching diners' pub, generously dressed with colourful hanging baskets and boxes, is a popular place for people-watching. Head indoors, where mellow furniture and stripped floorboards characterise the style. Friendly staff, a comprehensive wine list and well-kept ales (St Austell Tribute, Skinner's Betty Stogs, Exmoor Gold) are the draw for those seeking after-work refreshment. It's also a great place for food. Starters include pork and chorizo terrine with spiced pineapple chutney and brioche toasts; or bruscetta al pomodoro. Among the mains are penne with Italian sausage ragù; salmon and dill fishcakes; and pan-fried sea bream fillet with king prawn, chorizo croquette and sautéed spinach.

Open all day, all week 12–11 (Sun 12–10.30 Thu to Fri 12–12) Closed 24 Dec to 1 Jan Free House 16 from £14 portions WiFi notice required

LONDON WC1

The Bountiful Cow **PICK OF THE PUBS**

Tel **020 7404 0200** | **51 Eagle Street, Holborn, WC1R 4AP**
Web **www.thebountifulcow.com**
Dir ***230 metres north-east from Holborn tube station, via Procter Street. Walk through 2 arches into Eagle Street. Pub between High Holborn and Red Lion Square.***

This public house devoted to beef in all its glory is set across floors crowded with framed pictures of cows, bullfights, cowgirls, diagrams of meat cuts and posters of cow-themed films. Jazzy but discreet music adds to an atmosphere halfway between funky bistro and stylish saloon. The well kept ales are from Adnams or guest breweries, and the short wine list includes several gutsy reds. The meat is sourced from a trusted Smithfield Market supplier. Starters of duck rillettes and toast might be followed by one of the popular burgers or steaks, or perhaps chargrilled sea bass fillets on crushed fennel seeds with creamy mash.

Open all day 12–11 (Sat 12–10.30) Closed 25–26 Dec, 1 Jan, bank holidays, Sun Free House WiFi notice required

The Easton

Tel **020 7278 6530** | **22 Easton Street, WC1X 0DS**
Web **www.eastonclerkenwell.co.uk**
Dir ***Nearest tube stations: Farringdon; Angel; Kings Cross.***

Near the famous Sadlers Wells Theatre and a short distance from Farringdon tube, this pub with pavement benches is also just a stroll away from EC1's Exmouth Market. Timothy Taylor, Truman's and Hackney Pale Ale are the top real ales. Menus are modern and hearty – maybe start with glazed pig cheeks with beetroot piccalilli and follow that with beef and ale pie or a 10 oz chargrilled steak with chunky chips.

Norfolk Arms

Tel **020 7388 3937** | **28 Leigh Street, WC1H 9EP**
Web **www.norfolkarms.co.uk**
Dir ***Nearest tube stations: Russell Square, King's Cross St Pancras and Euston.***

Set amidst the elegant terraces of Bloomsbury, this eye-catching, partly tile-fronted Victorian pub brings a taste of Spain and the Med to this cosmopolitan corner of London. Its gastro pub credentials are greatly enhanced by the extensive tapas menu that draws an appreciative clientele.

The Perseverance

Tel **020 7405 8278** | **63 Lambs Conduit Street, WC1N 3NB**
Web **www.theperseverance.co.uk**
Dir ***Nearest tube station: Russell Square.***

Specialising in craft beers and lagers, including some from local London breweries like Meantime, Reunion Ales, Beavertown and Portobello Brewing Co, The Perseverance is a striking three-storey brick pub near Russell Square. Known for their excellent homecooked pizzas – try the chorizo, or one of the veggie options, they also offer 'beer food' – salt and pepper squid, a vegetable pakora, spicy cheese fries, or a fish finger sandwich.

Open all day, all week Closed 24–26 Dec, 31 Dec and 1 Jan Free House 12 from £8 WI-FI notice required

LONDON WC2

The Seven Stars PICK OF THE PUBS

Tel **020 7242 8521** | **53 Carey Street, WC2A 2JB**
Web **www.thesevenstars1602.co.uk**
Dir ***From Temple tube station turn right. 1st left into Arundel Street. Right into Strand (walking). Left into Bell Yard. 1st left into Carey Street.***

The Seven Stars may never have seen better days in its 415 years of existence. Since this Grade II listed pub was taken over 17 years ago, delicate and undisruptive primping has produced nothing but accolades. Strengthened by its personalities and ambience, The Seven Stars is considered the ideal pub – food is simple but well executed, ales are kept perfectly, wines are few but very good, and the staff are welcoming and efficient.

The Sherlock Holmes

Tel **020 7930 2644** | **10 Northumberland Street, WC2N 5DB**
Web **www.sherlockholmespub.com**
Dir ***From Charing Cross tube station into Villiers Street. Through 'The Arches' (runs underneath Charing Cross station) straight across Craven Street into Craven Passage to Northumberland Street.***

Painted black with etched glass windows and colourful hanging baskets, this traditional corner pub is chock-full of Holmes memorabilia, including photographs of Conan Doyle, mounted pages from manuscripts, and artefacts and pieces recording the adventures of the Master Detective.

GREATER LONDON

CARSHALTON

The Sun

Tel **020 8773 4549** | **4 North Street, SM5 2HU**
Web **www.thesuncarshalton.com**
Dir ***From A232 (Croydon Road) between Croydon and Sutton, turn into North Street signed Hackbridge (B277). Pub on right at crossroads.***

This imposing corner-plot pub has an enclosed walled garden area that houses a wood-fired pizza oven. Both wet and food sides of the business are increasingly popular; six real ales, such as Wimbledon, Surrey Hills and Dark Star attract beer lovers – there's a summer beer festival, too. The tempting menu encourages diners to tarry a while in the modish interior. Commence perhaps with roasted cauliflower soup with truffle oil and Welsh rarebit; then beer-battered haloumi (or cod) with minted peas and chips.

Open all day, all week Free House 14 portions/menu notice required

CHELSFIELD

The Bo-Peep

Tel **01959 534457** | **Hewitts Road, BR6 7QL**
Web **www.thebopeep.com**
Dir ***M25 junction 4 (Bromley exit). At roundabout follow Well Hill sign. Pub approximately 500 yards on right.***

Turn off the ever hectic M25 and within just five minutes you could be enjoying the tranquillity of this 14th-century inn. The low timber beams and inglenook in the bar offer plenty of character, and Adnams, Sharp's Doom Bar, and Westerham (when possible) are on tap. Just about everything is home cooked and typical dishes include pork belly, black pudding with cider jus; and Thai-spiced salmon, noodles and stir-fry vegetables. On sunny days, there's a large garden with views to admire.

Open all day, all week *Enterprise Inns* *12*
portions Wi-fi

The Five Bells PICK OF THE PUBS

Tel **01689 821044** | **BR6 7RE**
Web **www.thefivebells-chelsfieldvillage.co.uk**
Dir ***M25 junction 4, A224 towards Orpington. In approximately 1 mile turn right into Church Road. Pub on left.***

The Five Bells is a whitewashed Grade II listed building that dates from the late 17th century and takes its name from the magnificent bells at the church just up the road. There are two bars: the dog-friendly front bar boasting an original inglenook fireplace; the other is the dining room, leading out to the patio and extensive garden, complete with a children's play area. The seasonal menu complements the real ales and wines on offer: maybe start with duck pancakes and hoisin sauce, or a traditional prawn cocktail, followed by beer-battered cod and chips; freshly-made pie of the day; or lamb cutlets. Sandwiches and baguettes are available too, and beer festivals take place at Easter and in October along with regular live music and quizzes.

Open all day, all week *Enterprise Inns* *13*
portions/menu Wi-fi *notice required*

HAREFIELD

The Old Orchard

Tel **01895 822631** | **Park Lane, UB9 6HJ**
Web **www.brunningandprice.co.uk/oldorchard**
Dir ***M25 junction 17, follow Harefield signs. Before Harefield follow pub signs.***

An early 20th-century country house that became a B&B in the Sixties, a Seventies' dance venue and then a restaurant, until Brunning & Price bought and transformed it. The outside looks good, and the inside can hold its head high, with open fires and a decent bar.

RICHMOND UPON THAMES

The White Swan

Tel **020 8940 0959** | **26 Old Palace Lane, TW9 1PG**
Web **www.whiteswanrichmond.co.uk**
Dir ***Nearest tube station: Richmond.***

Tucked away from Richmond's bustling high street, The White Swan dates back to 1777. Whether it's for a pint of Timothy Taylor Landlord in the cosy bar or a meal in the dining room or suntrap garden, this is a pub to suit every occasion.

SURBITON

The Grove

Tel **020 8399 1662** | **9 Grove Road, KT6 4BX**
Web **www.thegrovekt6.co.uk**
Dir ***Phone for detailed directions.***

In a pleasant setting in leafy 'Surbiton Village', this imposing three-storey building has a spacious bar and extensive dining area as well as a large beer garden. A small plate menu might offer crab Scotch egg, devilled whitebait or flat iron chicken.

TWICKENHAM

The White Swan

Tel **020 8744 2951** | **Riverside, TW1 3DN**
Web **www.whiteswantwickenham.co.uk**
Dir ***Phone for detailed directions.***

The White Swan is so close to the Thames that the garden has been under water during particularly high tides. Twickenham Naked Ladies is one of the ales on offer at this free house, alongside three rotating guests and a good selection of wines by the glass.

MERSEYSIDE

BARNSTON

Fox and Hounds

Tel **0151 648 7685** | **107 Barnston Road, CH61 1BW**
Web **the-fox-hounds.co.uk**
Dir ***M53 junction 4, A5137 to Heswall, onto A551 signed Barnston.***

Friendly village inn serving classic pub grub

On the Wirral peninsula in quaint Barnston, the Fox and Hounds was built in 1911 but there has been a pub on this site since the 16th century when its clientele would have been thirsty farm workers. The pub's Edwardian character is retained in both the lounge and bar areas via leaded windows, pitch-pine woodwork and an open fire. As well as a range of real ales including Trappers Hat brewed just over a mile away at Brimstage and cider made in north Wales, the choice of 60-plus malts certainly appeals to whisky aficionados. Expect dishes like steak and Guinness pie, wild rabbit stew and cottage pie, along with sharing plates, paninis and open sandwiches.

Open all day, all week 11–11 (Sun 11–10.30) Free House 20 from £12 portions/menu notice required

GREASBY

Irby Mill

Tel **0151 604 0194** | **Mill Lane, CH49 3NT**
Web **www.irbymill.co.uk**
Dir ***M53 junction 3, A552 signed Upton and Heswall. At lights onto A551 signed Upton and Greasby. At lights left into Arrowe Brook Road. At roundabout 3rd exit into Mill Lane.***

An eye-catching, solid, sandstone-block built old miller's cottage just a short jog from the airy heights of Thurstaston Common at the heart of The Wirral Peninsula. One of the area's best choices of real ales meets an exceptional, very pubby menu strong on Wirral produce – 'Muffs' sausage and mash comes with black pudding, peas, mushrooms, gravy and onion rings. Popular with ramblers and Sunday diners, there's a suntrap grassy garden for summer; a log fire for the winter.

Open all day, all week Star Pubs & Bars 12 from £9.95 portions/menu Wi-fi notice required

HESWALL

The Jug and Bottle

Tel **0151 342 5535** | **Mount Avenue, CH60 4RH**
Web **www.the-jugandbottle.co.uk**
Dir ***From A540 in Heswall. At lights into The Mount, 1st left into Mount Avenue.***

In the heart of Heswall, on the spectacular Wirral Peninsula with its views towards Liverpool and north Wales, 'The Jug' (as the locals call it) is tucked away off the main road but convenient for the M56. With two open fires and surrounded by gardens, this traditional country pub offers a warm welcome, and serves good food and a range of real ales including local Brimstage Trapper's Hat. Typical dishes are fisherman's pie; and braised oxtail suet pudding.

Open all day, all week Free House portions/menu Wi-fi

HIGHTOWN

The Pheasant Inn

Tel **0151 929 2106 | 20 Moss Lane, L38 3RA**
Web **www.thepheasanthightown.co.uk**
Dir ***From A565 take B5193, follow signs to Hightown.***

This attractive pub with a whitewashed wooden exterior is a former alehouse with a sunny garden. It's just minutes from Crosby Beach. The menu is changed twice a year and there's also the legendary Sunday platter, fish suppers on 'Fin and Fizz' Fridays, and retro dining evenings.

LIVERPOOL

The Monro

Tel **0151 707 9933 | 92 Duke Street, L1 5AG**
Web **www.themonro.com**
Dir ***Phone for detailed directions.***

In 1746, merchant John Bolton built himself a finely-proportioned house, which today is this popular city pub. Bolton later entered history as a combatant in Liverpool's last recorded duel. The elegance of the interior would surely make him feel very nostalgic.

NORFOLK

BAWBURGH

Kings Head – see below

BLAKENEY

The Kings Arms

Tel **01263 740341 | Westgate Street, NR25 7NQ**
Web **www.blakeneykingsarms.co.uk**
Dir ***From Holt or Fakenham take A148, then B1156 for 6 miles to Blakeney.***

Tucked away in a popular fishing village close to north Norfolk's coastal path (Peddars Way), this thriving free house is the perfect refreshment stop following an invigorating walk, time spent birdwatching, or a boat trip to the nearby seal colony. Open all day and run by the same family for 43 years, it serves an excellent selection of real ales, including Norfolk-brewed Woodforde's Wherry that is backed by menus featuring locally caught fish and seasonal seafood.

Open all day, all week Closed 25 Dec evening Free House 10 portions/menu

BAWBURGH

Kings Head ★★★★ INN

Tel **01603 744977 | Harts Lane, NR9 3LS**
Web **www.kingsheadbawburgh.co.uk**
Dir ***From A47 take B1108 west towards Watton. Right signed Bawburgh.***

PICK OF THE PUBS

Worth finding after exploring nearby Norwich

Old English roses and lavender fragrance the lanes in front of this low, rambling 17th-century pub, set in a cosy village of flint and brick cottages beside the River Yare. Behind the roadside brick house rambles an eye-catching half-timbered cottage, complete with bulging walls, wooden floors and log fires. Leather sofas and a vaguely rustic mix of furnishings add to the charm which attracts customers keen to engage with Pamela and Anton Wimmer's enticing menu of pub favourites and something

that little bit special. The busy kitchen team relies on East Anglian suppliers for virtually all the ingredients; grilled pigeon breast, salted popcorn, sweetcorn purée and toasted seeds is a typically uplifting starter. There's plenty of seafood on the monthly-changing menu – witness the steamed salmon with warm salad of green beans, courgettes and peas. Gluten free options and daily specials add to the choices.

Open all day, all week Closed some evenings over Christmas/New Year Free House 11 from £13 portions/menu notice required

The White Horse ★★★★ INN

PICK OF THE PUBS

Tel **01263 740574 | 4 High Street, NR25 7AL**
Web **adnams.co.uk/**
Dir ***From A148 (Cromer to King's Lynn road) onto A149 signed to Blakeney.***

Since the 17th century, this former coaching inn has been tucked away among Blakeney's flint-built fishermen's cottages, a short, steepish amble up from the harbour. The tastefully appointed, Adnams-stocked bar is stylish yet informal, the conservatory is naturally bright – both are eating areas, where the same menu and daily specials apply. For a light lunch choose perhaps a sandwich; a seasonal salad; or an Adnams Broadside and Walsingham cheddar croquette with rainbow beetroot and dressed watercress. For something a bit more substantial, how about a White Horse classic – Norfolk loin of lamb, slow cooked bon bon, smoked carrot purée, heritage carrots, dauphinoise potatoes, curly kale and red wine jus?

Open all day, all week 11–11 (Sun 11–10.30 Adnams from £12.50 portions/menu

BLICKLING

Buckinghamshire Arms

Tel **01263 732133 | NR11 6NF**
Web **www.bucksarms.co.uk**
Dir ***From A140 at roundabout (south of Aylsham) into Norwich Road signed Aylsham. Through Aylsham centre, follow to Blickling. Pub on right (adjacent to Blickling Hall).***

Visitors to Blickling Hall often discover 'the Bucks' right next door. It's owned by the National Trust, leased by Colchester Inns, and run by a friendly team. The relaxed and unassuming ambience is in definite contrast to the stately pile a few minutes' walk away.

BRANCASTER

The Ship Hotel

Tel **01485 210333 | Main Road, PE31 8AP**
Web **www.shiphotelnorfolk.co.uk**
Dir ***On A149 in village centre.***

This family-friendly pub is set in a prime coastal location close to Brancaster Beach. The modern food is inspired by produce supplied by local farmers and fishermen. Be tempted by pan-fried squid, black garlic, chilli, lime, coriander and vermicelli noodles, or dressed crab. Wash it down with a pint Old Bustard in the gorgeous bar with its wood-burning stoves and nautical feel.

Open all day, all week Free House 20 portions/menu notice required

BRANCASTER STAITHE

The Jolly Sailors

Tel **01485 210314 | PE31 8BJ**
Web **www.jollysailorsbrancaster.co.uk**
Dir ***On A149 (coast road) midway between Hunstanton and Wells-next-the-Sea.***

Focal point of the village, the 18th-century 'Jolly' is the brewery tap for the Brancaster microbrewery, both being run by father and son team, Cliff and James Nye. In the Harbour Snug you can look out over the water, read local books, and play darts and board games. Pub food is typified by open-fired pizzas (make-your-own, eat in or take away), plus blackboard and the smokehouse choices. The beach-themed ice cream hut in the garden is an attraction in the summer.

Open all day, all week 12–11 Closed 25 Dec Free House 12 portions/menu notice required

The White Horse

★★★ HOTEL PICK OF THE PUBS

Tel **01485 210262 | PE31 8BY**
Web **www.whitehorsebrancaster.co.uk**
Dir ***A149 (coast road), midway between Hunstanton and Wells-next-the-Sea.***

This gem overlooks the glorious tidal marshes, with views across to Scolt Head Island National Nature Reserve;. Scrubbed pine tables and high-backed settles in the bar create a welcoming atmosphere, while alfresco dining in the sunken front garden is a popular warm-weather option, perhaps accompanied by a pint of Adnams Ghost Ship. The extensive menu in the airy conservatory restaurant (with two AA Rosettes) champions local seafood. On the menu are Brancaster mussels, garlic cream, white wine and shallots and a main of Staithe Smokehouse smoked cod, mashed potato, spinach, poached egg and cockle hollandaise.

Open all day, all week 11–11 (Sun 12–10.30) (open from 9am for breakfast) Free House 12 portions/menu notice required

BRISLEY

The Brisley Bell

Tel **01362 705024** | **The Green, NR20 5DW**
Web **www.thebrisleybell.co.uk**
Dir ***East of Brisley on B1145. On village green.***

Facing a lovely common where the village cricket team still plays during the summer, this renovated 17th-century pub retains plenty of original charm, down to the croquet lawn and large beer garden. In the colder months, roaring fires and a pint of ale are just the tonic after a long walk. Combining classic English cooking with global influences, the menu makes good use of fresh, seasonal and local produce and has good gluten free choices.

Open all year, all day Closed Mon Free House 20 portions/menu notice required

BURSTON

The Crown

Tel **01379 741257** | **Mill Road, IP22 5TW**
Web **www.burstoncrown.com**
Dir ***North-east of Diss.***

Steve and Bev Kembery have transformed their 16th-century pub by the green into a cracking community pub, drawing locals in for top-notch ale and food, organising the village fête, hosting three beer festivals a year, and offering a weekly busker's night and regular theme nights.

CASTLE ACRE

The Ostrich Inn ★★★★ INN

Tel **01760 755398** | **Stocks Green, PE32 2AE**
Web **www.ostrichcastleacre.com**
Dir ***From A1065 north of Swaffham follow Castle Acre signs. Pub in village centre, near church.***

The Ostrich has stood on Castle Acre's green for over four centuries – even the walls and ceilings that defied the ancient spirit level and plumb line are a delight. The decor is rich and warm, the bar bright. From a winter menu come duck and sweet potato hash cake with soft poached egg; and Ostrich Ale-battered haddock, chunky chips, mushy peas with tartare sauce. A June beer festival is held in the beautiful garden, which even finds room for a sandpit and a beach hut.

Open all day, all week Free House 11 from £10.95 portions/menu

CLEY NEXT THE SEA

The George PICK OF THE PUBS

Tel **01263 740652** | **High Street, NR25 7RN**
Web **www.thegeorgehotelatcley.co.uk**
Dir ***On A149 through Cley next the Sea, approximately 4 miles from Holt.***

An ornithological focal point for many years, The George's beer garden backs on to the salt marshes of the north Norfolk coast, a renowned paradise for birdwatchers. Close to the famous Cley Windmill and Blakeney Harbour, The George is a welcoming place, offering several real ales at the bar, including Yetman's. You can snack in the lounge bar or dine in the light, painting-filled restaurant. The daily-changing dishes offer the best of local ingredients, and fish and seafood is a real strength. Starters include potted pheasant, orange jelly, toasted ciabatta and mixed leaves, with pan-seared sea bass fillets, pea and smoked tomato pearl barley risotto, brown shrimp and dill velouté one of the typical main courses. Dogs are welcome in the bar and front restaurant.

Open all day, all week 10.30am–11.30pm Free House 11 menus notice required

CROMER

The Red Lion Food and Rooms ★★★★ INN

Tel **01263 514964** | **Brook Street, NR27 9HD**
Web **www.redlion-cromer.co.uk**
Dir ***From A149 into Cromer, on one-way system, pass church on left. 1st left after church into Brook Street. Pub on right.***

Guests can gaze through the inn's front windows directly over the beach to the pier. Fishing boats drawn up on the shingle bank may provide the wherewithal for the pub's renowned seafood dishes – try the fish chowder or Cromer crab. The playful menu has suggestions for wines to accompany dishes, whilst beer-lovers will delight at a choice that includes cutting edge local breweries like Wolf and Cromer's own Poppyland. Some of the bedrooms have sea views.

Open all day, all week Closed 25–26 Dec Free House 10 portions/menu notice required

EATON

The Red Lion

Tel **01603 454787** | **50 Eaton Street, NR4 7LD**
Web **www.redlion-eaton.co.uk**
Dir ***Off A11, 2 miles south of Norwich city centre.***

This beamed 17th-century coaching inn has bags of character, thanks to its Dutch gable ends, panelled walls, suit of armour and inglenook fireplaces. The terrace enables customers to enjoy one of the real ales outside. Everyone will find something that appeals on the extensive menus.

FAKENHAM

The Wensum Lodge Hotel

Tel **01328 862100** | **Bridge Street, NR21 9AY**
Web **www.wensumlodge.co.uk**
Dir ***In town centre.***

Dating from around 1700, this building was originally the grain store for the adjoining mill. It's an ideal base for cycling, birdwatching, fishing and horse racing, the pub serves a range of real ales that are complemented by home-cooked food, with baguettes, jacket potatoes and an all-day breakfast on the light bite menu.

Open all day, all week Free House portions/menu

FLEGGBURGH

The Kings Arms

GUEST ACCOMMODATION

Tel **01493 368333** | **Main Road, NR29 3AG**
Web **www.kingsarmsfleggburgh.com**
Dir ***From A47 east of Norwich onto A1064 signed Caister-on-Sea. In Fleggburgh, on left.***

This fine red-brick country pub, ideally located for exploring the Norfolk Broads, is well known for offering a well-kept pint of Timothy Taylor Landlord or Adnams Ghost Ship in the bar, while the seasonal food on the menus might include Cromer crab, north Norfolk mussels, or Norfolk beef. There's always a good choice of local fish – perhaps pan-roasted fillet of North Sea cod – along with meatier options like rump of spring Suffolk lamb, or roasted loin of Bunwell red deer.

Open all day, all week Free House 9 from £11.95 portions/menu notice required

GREAT HOCKHAM

The Eagle

Tel **01953 498893** | **Harling Road, IP24 1NR**
Web **www.hockhameagle.com**
Dir ***From Thetford take A1075 to Great Hockham. Right into Harling Road. Pub on left.***

A traditional country pub in the picturesque village of Great Hockham, close to Thetford Forest and just 10 minutes from the motor racing circuit at Snetterton. Children and dogs are welcome, and as well as seating out the front there's an enclosed rear courtyard.

14 NORFOLK AND SUFFOLK PUBS WITH ACCOMMODATION

The following pubs are rated as part of the AA Guest Accommodation scheme (see page 10–11 for more information).

The Bull Inn ★★★★★ INN Mildenhall, Suffolk, *see page 403*
Elveden Inn ★★★★★ INN Elveden, Suffolk, *see page 401*
The Packhorse Inn ★★★★★ INN Newmarket, Suffolk, *see page 404*
Kings Head ★★★★ INN Bawburgh, Norfolk, *see page 297*
The Red Lion Food and Rooms ★★★★ INN Cromer, Norfolk, *see page 299*
The Rose & Crown ★★★★ INN Snettisham, Norfolk, *see page 305*
Sibton White Horse Inn ★★★★ INN Sibton, Suffolk, *see page 405*
Wiveton Bell ★★★★ INN Wiveton, Norfolk, *see page 308*
Cherry Tree Inn ★★★★ INN Woodbridge, Suffolk, *see page 409*
The Blue Boar Inn ★★★ Great Ryburgh, Norfolk, INN *see page 301*
The Old Cannon Brewery ★★★ INN Bury St Edmunds, Suffolk, *see page 399*
The Crown ★★★ SMALL HOTEL Stoke-By-Nayland, Suffolk, *see page 407*
The White Horse ★★★ HOTEL Brancaster Staithe, Norfolk, *see page 298*
The Westleton Crown ★★★ HOTEL Westleton, Suffolk, *see page 408*

GREAT MASSINGHAM

The Dabbling Duck

Tel **01485 520827** | **11 Abbey Road, PE32 2HN**
Web **www.thedabblingduck.co.uk**
Dir ***From King's Lynn take either A148 or B1145 then follow Great Massingham signs. Or from Fakenham take A148 signed King's Lynn. Or from Swaffham take A1065 towards Cromer, then B1145 signed King's Lynn.***

A thriving community local, The Dabbling Duck is a cracking place, set on Great Massingham's glorious green. The cosy bar, with its comfy leather sofas and wood-burner, is the ideal place for bar snacks and a pint – maybe Adnams Ghost Ship – or a gin from the gin list. Head through to the relaxed, informal library for dishes like Cromer crab, fish and chips, burgers, or a Goan curry with coconut rice. Dogs are very welcome – they even have their own menu.

Open all day, all week 8am–11pm Free House from £10.50 portions/menu notice required

GREAT RYBURGH

The Blue Boar Inn ★★★ INN

Tel **01328 829212** | **NR21 0DX**
Web **www.blueboar-norfolk.co.uk**
Dir ***From Fakenham take A1067 towards Norwich. Approximately 4 miles right to Great Ryburgh.***

A popular, character, listed village inn, with quarry-tile floors, beams and a vast inglenook, spread through a jumble of levels marking the alterations over the centuries. It was used as a recruiting station during the Napoleonic Wars; all that's required of today's visitors is to enjoy the local Yetman's beers and indulge in the varied, Norfolk-based menu, which may include cassoulet of chicken leg and sausage, or pot roast half guinea fowl.

Open all year 6–11 (Sun 12–6) Closed Tue Free House 8 portions/menu

HEVINGHAM

Marsham Arms Coaching Inn

Tel **01603 754268** | **Holt Road, NR10 5NP**
Web **www.marshamarms.co.uk**
Dir ***On B1149 (north of Norwich Airport), 2 miles, through Horsford towards Holt.***

Victorian philanthropist and landowner Robert Marsham built the Marsham Arms as a roadside hostel for poor farm labourers, and some original features, including the wooden beams and large open fireplace are still evident. Real ales are served straight from the barrel.

HEYDON

Earle Arms

Tel **01263 587376** | **The Street, NR11 6AD**
Web **www.theearlearms.com**
Dir ***Signed between Cawston and Corpusty on B1149 (Holt to Norwich road).***

H, the landlord and chef, is responsible for the horseracing memorabilia throughout this 16th-century, Dutch-gabled free house on the village green. As part-owner of a racehorse, he will gladly give you a tip, but says it's probably best not to go nap on it. The privately owned conservation village of Heydon is often used for filming, and many a star of the big and small screen has enjoyed the Earle's off-the-pier-fresh seafood, game from local estates and locally reared meats. A beer festival is held in May.

Open all year 11–3 6–11 (Sun all day) Closed Mon Free House 16 portions/menu notice required

HOLT

The Pigs

Tel **01263 587634** | **Norwich Road, Edgefield, NR24 2RL**
Web **www.thepigs.org.uk**
Dir ***From Norwich A140 (Airport). Pass airport on right, left onto B1149 at roundabout. Approximately 16 miles to Edgefield.***

This 17th-century country inn on the edge of a lovely village has been transformed into a thriving local and celebration of all things Norfolk. The tranquil setting at the fringe of the village allows for a peaceful garden, while a versatile menu utilises forgotten cuts of locally sourced meat.

HUNSTANTON

The Ancient Mariner Inn

★★★★ HOTEL

Tel **01485 536390 | Golf Course Road, Old Hunstanton, PE36 6JJ**
Web **www.traditionalinns.co.uk**
Dir ***Exit A149, 1 mile north of Hunstanton. Turn left at sharp right bend by pitch and putt course.***

Summer evenings can be spectacular here; when the sun sets across the sands of The Wash, the light matches the golds of the real ales enjoyed by drinkers in the peaceful gardens, up to seven beers may be on tap. Equally enticing is the menu of modern pub classics such as trio of local sausages; beef lasagne; or slow-roast lamb shank; daily fish specials boost the choice. The stylish hotel rooms are popular with visitors to this beautiful Area of Outstanding Natural Beauty.

Open all day, all week Free House 10 from £12.75 portions/menu notice required

The King William IV Country Inn & Restaurant ★★★★ INN

Tel **01485 571765 | Heacham Road, Sedgeford, PE36 5LU**
Web **www.thekingwilliamsedgeford.co.uk**
Dir ***A149 to Hunstanton, right at Norfolk Lavender in Heacham onto B1454, signed Docking. 2 miles to Sedgeford.***

Tucked away in the village of Sedgeford, this free house has been an inn for over 175 years. It's conveniently close to the north Norfolk coastline and the Peddars Way. Made cosy by winter log fires, it has four dining areas, plus a covered terrace where you can enjoy a local crab salad in the summer. You'll find four real ales on tap, and extensive menus (including one for vegetarians) to please everyone. Events include quiz Mondays, curry Tuesdays and pie Wednesdays.

Open all year, all day 11–11 (Sun 12–10.30) Closed Mon lunch (excluding bank holidays) Free House 10 from £11.95 portions/menu notice required

ITTERINGHAM

The Walpole Arms

Tel **01263 587258 | NR11 7AR**
Web **www.thewalpolearms.co.uk**
Dir ***From Aylsham towards Blickling. After Blickling Hall take 1st right to Itteringham.***

Dining pub with inventive food

Owned by a local farming family, this renowned rural dining venue is tucked away down narrow lanes on the edge of sleepy Itteringham, close to the National Trust's Blickling Hall. Its oak-beamed bar offers local Woodforde's and Adnams ales on tap, while menus champion top-notch meats and produce from the family farm and local artisan producers. Typical dishes include poached duck egg with spinach, black pudding crumb and butter sauce; the Walpole Pigs board – ham hock terrine, pork rillette fritter, pork belly and black pudding with pickled pear, apple jelly and focaccia; and beef ribs with sauté potatoes and carrots. Leave room for vanilla crème brûlée; baked Alaska; or sticky toffee pudding.

Open all week 12–3 6–11 (Sat 12–11 Sun 12–5) Free House 20 from £13 portions/menu notice required

HUNWORTH

The Hunworth Bell PICK OF THE PUBS

Tel **01263 711151** | **The Green, NR24 2AA**
Web **www.hunworthbell.co.uk**
Dir ***From Holt take B1110. 1st right to Hunworth.***

Formerly known as The Hunny Bell, this lovely country pub is set in the heart of the stunning Stody Estate, just two miles from the charming town of Holt. An interesting selection of local ales and wines is complemented by a menu showcasing the best produce Norfolk has to offer, whether it's the bar bites or à la carte. Start with the butter-poached smoked salmon, celeriac and apple, followed by pork chop, baby jacket potatoes, black pudding bon bons and burnt apple jus. Leave room for the caramelised white chocolate and vanilla cheesecake, Bailey's fudge and brandy snap. Children get to choose from their own menu including wholetail scampi, fries and peas.

Open all day, all week *Free House* 18 *portions/menu* WI-FI P *notice required*

ITTERINGHAM

The Walpole Arms – see opposite

KING'S LYNN

The Stuart House Hotel, Bar & Restaurant

Tel **01553 772169** | **35 Goodwins Road, PE30 5QX**
Web **www.stuarthousehotel.co.uk**
Dir ***Follow signs to town centre, pass under Southgate Arch, immediate right, in 100 yards turn right.***

In a central, but nevertheless quiet location, this establishment, in attractive grounds, is one of the town's favoured eating and drinking places. Top-notch East Anglian ales and traditional snacks are served in the bar, and there's a separate restaurant menu typically featuring Norfolk sausages, creamy mash and red onion gravy; and pan-fried sea bass fillet with herbed sauté potatoes. Daily specials, like everything else, are home cooked from fresh, local produce. Lunch is only by arrangement for parties of 12 or more.

Open all week 5–11 *Free House* *from £9.99* WI-FI P *notice required*

LARLING

Angel Inn PICK OF THE PUBS

Tel **01953 717963** | **NR16 2QU**
Web **www.angel-larling.co.uk**
Dir ***5 miles from Attleborough; 8 miles from Thetford.***

On the edge of Breckland and Thetford Forest Park, this welcoming 17th-century former coaching inn has been run by the Stammers family for more than a century. In the beamed public bar, a jukebox and fruit machine add to the traditional feel, while the oak-panelled lounge bar has dining tables with cushioned wheel-back chairs, a wood-burner and a collection of water jugs. Five ales, including Crouch Vale Brewers Gold, are served, as well as more than a hundred whiskies. Menus make good use of local ingredients, with lighter snacks including sandwiches, jacket potatoes, ploughman's, burgers and salads. Typically among the mains are tiger prawn balti; lamb chops with mint sauce; or Stilton and mushroom bake. Look out for the August festival, with over 100 real ales.

Open all day, all week 10am–midnight *Free House* 10 *from £8.95* *portions/menu* WI-FI P

LETHERINGSETT

The Kings Head PICK OF THE PUBS

Tel **01263 712691** | **Holt Road, NR25 7AR**
Web **www.kingsheadnorfolk.co.uk**
Dir ***On A148, 1 mile from Holt. Pub on corner.***

From the outside this looks to be a grand, manor-like building, but step through the door and find elegant, rustic-chic decor throughout the rambling dining areas, with an eclectic mix of old dining tables, and squashy sofas and leather chairs fronting blazing winter log fires. The atmosphere is informal, the beer on tap is Woodforde's Wherry, and the modern British food is prepared from top-notch local ingredients. Look out for pan-fried sea bass fillet with crushed new potatoes, greens and brown shrimp butter; wild mushroom risotto; and beer-battered haddock with garden peas and hand-cut chips. There are superb alfresco areas including an excellent children's garden and a terrace with benches and brollies.

Open all day, all week 11–11 *Free House* 15 *portions/menu* WI-FI P

MORSTON

The Anchor PICK OF THE PUBS

Tel **01263 741392 | The Street, NR25 7AA**
Web **www.morstonanchor.co.uk**
Dir ***On A149 (Blakeney Road) in village centre.***

A dream come true for former school buddies Harry Farrow and Rowan Glennie, who reunited to buy and refurbish this popular pub. Norfolk breweries Winter's and Woodforde's, and Suffolk's Adnams provide the real ales, and the restaurant features East Anglian produce, particularly fish and game. Try chunky smoked haddock and brown shrimp chowder with sourdough bread, followed by roasted loin of venison with Anna potatoes, beetroot purée, spinach, piccolo parsnips and jus. Or there's the vegetarian home-made cheddar gnocchi, butternut squash, wild mushrooms and rocket and pine nut pesto. Round off with local apple and rhubarb crumble and home-made custard. Sixteen wines are sold by the glass, although bottles won't break the bank.

Open all week 9am–late Free House 16 menus

MUNDFORD

Crown Hotel

Tel **01842 878233 | Crown Road, IP26 5HQ**
Web **www.the-crown-hotel.co.uk**
Dir ***A11 to Barton Mills onto A1065 through Brandon to Mundford.***

Roofed with traditional Norfolk pantiles, this historic inn on the edge of Thetford Forest dates from 1652. Originally a hunting lodge, it has also served as a magistrate's court. Today it's a popular pub with two restaurants, the Old Court and the Club Room.

NORWICH

Adam & Eve

Tel **01603 667423 | Bishopsgate, NR3 1RZ**
Dir ***Behind Anglican Cathedral, adjacent to Law Courts.***

Licensed since 1249, this enchanting, brick-and-flint built inn sits beneath trees on the fringe of Norwich Cathedral grounds. It's a refreshing step back in time, free of electronic diversions. The beers are from Woodforde's and Wolf breweries; some spirits found here include ghosts of long-gone former locals. Expect no-nonsense, quality pub classics like large filled Yorkshire pudding, trawlerman's pie, home-made curry or chilli. The hanging basket displays are stunning.

Open all day, all week 11–11 (Sun 12–10.30) Closed 25–26 Dec, 1 Jan Enterprise Inns 11 notice required

Ribs of Beef

Tel **01603 619517 | 24 Wensum Street, NR3 1HY**
Web **www.ribsofbeef.co.uk**
Dir ***From Tombland (in front of cathedral) turn left at Maids Head Hotel. Pub 200 yards on right on bridge.***

On record as an alehouse back in the 18th century, this building has been used variously as an antiques shop, electrical store and fashion boutique, before Roger and Anthea Cawdron took over some 30 years ago. The pub is popular for its range of cask ales, excellent wines and varied menu of traditional English food using locally sourced produce. Sit outside on the jetty during the warmer months and enjoy the fabulous river views. There's live music on Sundays.

Open all day, all week 11–11 (Fri to Sat 11am–1am) Free House 9 from £9.50 portions/menu notice required

SALTHOUSE

The Salthouse Dun Cow

Tel **01263 740467 | Coast Road, NR25 7XA**
Web **www.salthouseduncow.com**
Dir ***On A149 (coast road). 3 miles east of Blakeney.***

In a quiet coastal village within an Area of Outstanding Natural Beauty, this traditional brick and flint pub probably originated as a cattle barn built around 1650. Today, it overlooks some of Britain's finest salt marshes, so expect to share it with birdwatchers and walkers.

SHERINGHAM

The Two Lifeboats

Tel **01263 823144 | 2 High Street, NR26 8JR**
Web **www.thetwolifeboatssheringham.com**
Dir ***In town centre.***

Once the local Fisherman's Mission building and a coffee shop, this seafront pub was named in honour of the two lifeboats that rescued a crew of eight from a Norwegian brig. Have a pint alongside locals or enjoy home-cooked dishes.

SNETTISHAM

The Rose & Crown

★★★★ INN PICK OF THE PUBS

Tel **01485 541382** | **Old Church Road, PE31 7LX**
Web **www.roseandcrownsnettisham.co.uk**
Dir ***10 miles north from King's Lynn on A149 signed Hunstanton. At Snettisham roundabout take B1440 to Snettisham. Left into Old Church Road, inn on left.***

Built in the 14th century for craftsmen working on the beautiful village church, this pub's rose-hung façade conceals twisting passages and hidden corners, heavy oak beams, uneven red-tiled floors and inglenooks. Three charming bars offer Adnams, Ringwood and Woodforde's real ales on tap and 26 wines by the glass. Locally supplied produce includes shellfish and samphire from Brancaster, beef from salt marsh-raised cattle, game shot by men in wellies who drink in the back bar, local asparagus and strawberries, and herbs from village allotments. Lunch and dinner menus typically offer duck and pork belly rillette, burnt orange and fig chutney; mackerel fillet, cucumber and cashews; pan-fried sea bass fillet, salt and vinegar mash and warm fruit de mer dashi broth; and chocolate truffle tart with raspberry sorbet.

Open all day, all week Free House 26 portions/menu Wi-fi P

STANHOE

The Duck Inn

Tel **01485 518330** | **Burnham Road, PE31 8QD**
Web **www.duckinn.co.uk**
Dir ***Phone for detailed directions.***

Ideally located for exploring the coast and countryside of north Norfolk, The Duck Inn is a real food-lover's paradise, showcasing the best of the region's produce. Have a pint of Adnams Ghost Ship or Elgood's Cambridge Bitter while you check out the menu.

STOKE HOLY CROSS

The Wildebeest PICK OF THE PUBS

Tel **01508 492497** | **82–86 Norwich Road, NR14 8QJ**
Web **www.thewildebeest.co.uk**
Dir ***From A47 take A140, left to Dunston. At T-junction turn left, pub on right.***

Set in a village just far enough out of Norwich to enjoy tranquillity, The Wildebeest is a haven of refined eating and drinking. The interior is a feast in itself, rich with beams, aged floorboards, solid wood tables and dark ochre leather-clad dining chairs. Settle on a bar stool for a pint of Adnams Southwold or Greene King Abbot Ale; or select a wine from the dozen sold by the glass while perusing the menu. Brancaster mussels and diver-caught scallops come from the Norfolk coast, and a typical main course might be pan-roast salt marsh lamb, parmesan and rosemary polenta, braised carrots, Swiss chard and red wine jus. Finish with a blood peach soufflé, vanilla-poached peach and thyme biscotti.

Open all week 11.30–3 6–11 (Sat to Sun all day) Closed 25–26 Dec Free House 12 portions Wi-fi P

STOW BARDOLPH

The Hare Arms PICK OF THE PUBS

Tel **01366 382229** | **PE34 3HT**
Web **www.theharearms.co.uk**
Dir ***From King's Lynn take A10 to Downham Market. After 9 miles village signed on left.***

Peacocks roam the garden of this ivy-clad pub named after the Hare family, who purchased Stow Bardolph estate in 1553 and still play an important part locally. Owners Pat and Deborah Palmer have retained the old-world charm of this former coaching inn, with fascinating memorabilia on display throughout the music-free, L-shaped bar, where guest ales partner those of Greene King. There's plenty to contemplate on the menu, so take your time choosing between, perhaps, slow-cooked beef ribs in BBQ sauce or steak and pork belly with grilled black pudding. Vegetarian options may include Moroccan bean burger. Gluten-free menus are available.

Open all week 11–2.30 6–11 (Sat and bank holiday Mon 11–11 Sun 12–10.30) Closed 25–26 Dec, 31 Dec evening, 1 Jan Greene King 12 from £11.95 portions/menu Wi-fi P *notice required*

THOMPSON

Chequers Inn

Tel **01953 483360** | **Griston Road, IP24 1PX**
Web **www.thompsonchequers.co.uk**
Dir ***Exit A1075 between Watton and Thetford.***

Breckland pub well off the beaten track

PICK OF THE PUBS

If you can't place Breckland, it's that region of gorse-covered sandy heath straddling south Norfolk and north Suffolk. Within its boundaries you'll find this splendid, long and low, thatched 17th-century inn, and worth finding it is for its peaceful location and unspoilt charm. In the 18th century manorial courts were held here, dealing with rents, letting of land, and petty crime. It's more fun here today. Beneath its steeply-raked thatch lies a series of low-ceilinged, interconnecting rooms served by a long bar at which the principal real ales are Adnams Southwold Bitter, Greene King IPA and Wolf Ale. The overall impression of the interior is of skew-whiff wall timbers, squat doorways, open log fires, rustic old furniture and farming implements. You'll find picnic tables in the large rear garden, where dogs are welcome. The inn is an ideal base for walking the Peddars Way and the Great Eastern Pingo Trail – a string of lakelets (the pingos) left behind after the last ice age.

Open all week 11–3 6–11 (Sun all day) Free House 8 portions/menu notice required

THORNHAM

The Orange Tree PICK OF THE PUBS

Tel 01485 512213 | High Street, PE36 6LY
Web www.theorangetreethornham.co.uk
Dir *Phone for detailed directions.*

Once the haunt of smugglers, this 400-year-old whitewashed inn has evolved over the years into the stylish family-run country pub it is today. Standing in the centre of the village opposite the church, it's a useful stop for walkers on the Peddars Way. Develop an appetite with a stroll to the local staithe, where working boats still come and go through the creeks of Brancaster Bay, before returning for a pint of East Anglian-brewed ale. The kitchen makes the most of freshly landed local seafood but it's not just the fish that justifies their claim that the restaurant is the jewel in The Orange Tree's crown; the pub has a long-established relationship with local suppliers, and most of the meat is sourced from Norfolk farms.

Open all day, all week Punch Taverns 29 portions/menu

TITCHWELL

Titchwell Manor Hotel

★★★★ HOTEL PICK OF THE PUBS

Tel 01485 210221 | PE31 8BB
Web www.titchwellmanor.com
Dir *A149 between Brancaster and Thornham.*

Elegant, bold, contemporary; descriptions both of the interior of the substantial Victorian farmhouse here and the brasserie-style cuisine that has gained three AA Rosettes for Eric Snaith and his team. In an enviable situation at the heart of north Norfolk's heritage coast, with bird-watching and rambling opportunities strung along the bays and salt marshes fringing the fields opposite. Your first choice from an autumn menu could be Norfolk quail terrine, honey soused veg and prune as a starter. Typical main dishes are sea trout fillet, parsley, lardo and smoked mousse; loin and belly of Houghton venison, roast pumpkin, chocolate and salsify. Desserts complete the treats here – perhaps lemon and cucumber tart; or poached rhubarb and honeycomb bavarois.

Open all day, all week Free House 17 portions/menu notice required

WARHAM ALL SAINTS

Three Horseshoes

Tel 01328 710547 | NR23 1NL
Web www.warhamhorseshoes.co.uk
Dir *From Wells A149 to Cromer, then right onto B1105 to Warham.*

An inn for people who love pubs with character

One of Norfolk's many cracking pubs, this nearly 300-year-old, brick and flint, pantile-roofed example retains a traditional serving hatch, clay pamment-tiled floors and other original features. Family owned and run, its reputation stems in part from its well-kept ales, some served straight from the cask, and its pies and puddings. Eat and drink at scrubbed tables in the bar and dining rooms, or in the sheltered, unusually large walled garden – a great place for children and dogs. From a short menu, possible

choices include sausage-meat-filled Warham plough pudding, with bacon and herbs; dry-hopped, beer-battered fish, chips and minted mushy peas; and summer vegetable curry with rice and poppadoms. Sunday prospects, apart from roast meats, are nut roasts and steak and kidney pudding.

Open all day, all week 11–11 Free House from £11 portions/menu notice required

WIVETON

Wiveton Bell

  INN

Tel 01263 740101 | Blakeney Road, NR25 7TL
Web www.wivetonbell.com
Dir *A149 from Blakeney towards Cley next the Sea. Right into Wiveton Road signed Cley Spy. Approximately 1 mile to pub.*

Tranquil country pub championing local fish and game

Immaculately spruced-up though it is, and while rightly renowned for its cuisine, the Bell remains faithful to its roots as a traditional village pub. This means that, even in full walking gear (dog in tow) you are welcome to drift in for just a pint of Woodforde's Wherry or Norfolk Moon Gazer, and nobody will suggest you should be better dressed, or have left Rex in his basket. In a village pub so close to the unspoilt salt marshes of the north Norfolk coast – an Area of Outstanding Natural Beauty – and just 10 minutes' walk from Blakeney nature reserve, that's a wise approach. Built in the 18th century, it features earthy, heritage-coloured walls, stripped beams, chunky tables and oak floors, with further character imbued by local artworks lining the walls of the bar and conservatory dining room. On a winter's evening head for the tables close to the inglenook fireplace. On a Sunday there's an excellent choice of roasts, but booking is essential.

Open all day, all week 12–11 Closed 25 Dec
Free House 14 portions/menu

WELLS-NEXT-THE-SEA

The Crown Hotel PICK OF THE PUBS

Tel **01328 710209 | The Buttlands, NR23 1EX**
Web **www.crownhotelnorfolk.co.uk**
Dir ***10 miles from Fakenham on B1105.***

Owned by TV chef Chris Coubrough, this 17th-century former coaching inn overlooks a tree-lined green. Contemporary decor blends effortlessly with the bar's ancient beams and other old-world charms. The menus offer modern British and internationally influenced dishes, and a selection of options include starters like venison and black pudding Scotch egg; or marinated chicken wings, salmon belly, smoked chicken and peanut salad and a chorizo and crab spring roll; and mains like potato gnocchi sautéed with butternut, pecan, sage and goats' cheese; or plaice fillets and prawns poached in lime leaf and chilli broth with noodles and seasonal greens. There could be cinnamon apple puff with ice cream; or kiwi and passionfruit Pavlova with fruit coulis for afters.

Open all day, all week *Free House* *20* *from £15.95* *portions/menu* Wi-fi

WINTERTON-ON-SEA

Fishermans Return

Tel **01493 393305 | The Lane, NR29 4BN**
Web **www.fishermansreturn.com**
Dir ***8 miles north of Great Yarmouth on B1159.***

This dog-friendly, 350-year-old brick and flint built free house stands close to long beaches and National Trust land, making it the ideal spot to finish a walk. Guest ales support Woodforde's Norfolk Nog and Wherry behind the bar. There is a beer festival in August.

WIVETON

Wiveton Bell – see opposite

WOODBASTWICK

The Fur & Feather Inn

Tel **01603 720003 | Slad Lane, NR13 6HQ**
Web **www.woodfordes.com/brewery-tap**
Dir ***From A1151 (Norwich to Wroxham road), follow brown signs for Woodforde's Brewery. Pub adjacent to brewery.***

A weeping willow and duckpond; a creeper-clad façade beneath rolling reed-thatched roof; oh, and a brewery right next door. This pub-lovers' nirvana gets better, with an interior wrested from a brace of artisan's cottages free of electronic entertainment. The top-notch locally made burgers are renowned.

NORTHAMPTONSHIRE

ASHBY ST LEDGERS

The Olde Coach House Inn

Tel **01788 890349 | CV23 8UN**
Web **www.oldecoachhouse.co.uk**
Dir ***M1 junction 18 follow A361/Daventry signs. Village on left.***

This mellow stone inn sits amidst thatched cottages in the lovely estate village here; until a century ago it was a farmhouse. Today it's an engaging mix of contemporary and rustic, with a strong emphasis on comfort; deep leather furnishings tempt you to linger by log fires.

AYNHO

The Great Western Arms

Tel **01869 338288 | Station Road, OX17 3BP**
Web **www.great-westernarms.co.uk**
Dir ***From Aynho take B4031 (Station Road) west towards Deddington. Turn right to pub.***

The Great Western Railway company may have disappeared in 1948, but its name lives on in this foliage-covered inn situated between the line it built to Birmingham and the Oxford Canal. It's a Hook Norton pub, so expect the brewery's range of ales to be well represented.

BRIXWORTH

The Coach & Horses

Tel **01604 880329** | **Harborough Road, NN6 9BX**
Web **www.coachandhorsesbrixworth.co.uk**
Dir ***From A508 follow signs to Brixworth. On main road through village.***

In the picturesque village of Brixworth and close to Earl Spencer's Althorp House estate, the Coach and Horses dates back to the 1700s. Today, the licensees of 30 years offer traditional pub dishes based on local ingredients; blackboard specials add to the choices.

CHARWELTON

Fox & Hounds

Tel **01327 260611** | **Banbury Road, NN11 3YY**
Web **www.foxandhoundscharwelton.co.uk**
Dir ***M40 junction 11 onto A361 signed Daventry. In Charwelton, on right.***

A fine example of what can be achieved when a village sees its pub as an asset, the Fox & Hounds was bought by the community in 2015, since when it has been completely refurbished. It also operates as the village shop.

CRICK

The Red Lion Inn

Tel **01788 822342** | **52 Main Road, NN6 7TX**
Web **www.redlioncrick.eu.pn**
Dir ***M1 junction 18, A428, 0.75 mile, follows signs for Crick from roundabout.***

A gabled, thatched, coaching inn of mellow ironstone standing beside the pretty main street just a stone's throw the ancient church. Exposed beams, low ceilings and open fires characterise this free house, family-run for over 35 years. Local beers, plus those from Adnams, and classic pub meals are the order of the day. Faggots in onion gravy; breaded haddock, chips and peas; and lasagne, hash browns and salad are typical dishes. There's a children's menu or they can eat smaller portions of the main menu dishes.

Open all week 11–2.30 6–11 (Sun 12–3 7–11) Free House from £5.95 portions/menu Wi-fi P

DUDDINGTON

Royal Oak

Tel **01780 444267** | **High Street, PE9 3QE**
Web **www.theroyaloakduddington.com**
Dir ***From Peterborough take A47 towards Leicester. Approximately 14 miles to Duddington.***

Built of locally quarried limestone, the interior of the family-run Royal Oak has been given a heritage-respecting makeover. The bar's leather chairs and sofas offer as ideal a place as any for a pint of Grainstore's GB Best, perhaps, or Ossett Silver King. Main menu attractions at lunchtime could be their chicken, ham hock and leek pie; or beef and red wine stew. In the evening a more expansive menu offers 21-day-aged Scottish rib-eye steak with hand-cut chips.

Open all week 11–3 6–11 (Fri to Sat 11–11 Sun 11–10) Free House 12 portions/menu Wi-fi P *notice required*

EAST HADDON

The Red Lion PICK OF THE PUBS

Tel **01604 770223** | **Main Street, NN6 8BU**
Web **www.redlioneasthaddon.co.uk/**
Dir ***Just off A428.***

There's something about the yellow Northamptonshire stone and thatched roof of Nick Bonner and Ren Aveiro's Red Lion that declares 'classic English village pub'. Classic ideas in the food too, from a starter of ham hock and black pudding fritter with piccalilli mayonnaise; or whipped goats' cheese, beetroot and walnut salad with sloe gin dressing, to mains of roasted hake with gnocchi and spicy tomato and chorizo casserole; or slow-cooked lamb shoulder, Greek-style salad and mint yogurt. Home-made doughnuts with warm jam sauce will prove more than tempting for dessert. As an accompaniment, a reasonably priced glass of Pinot Grigio or Malbec, or maybe a pint of Bombardier.

Open all day, all week Sun to Fri 11–10, Sat 11–11 Charles Wells 14 portions/menu Wi-fi P *notice required*

FARTHINGHOE

The Fox

Tel **01295 713965** | **Baker Street, NN13 5PH**
Web **www.foxatfarthinghoe.co.uk**
Dir ***M40 junction 11, A422, towards Brackley. Approximately 5.5 miles to Farthinghoe.***

This Charles Wells pub has a well-furnished beer garden to the front, and an interior gleaming with scrubbed and polished wood, mismatched chairs and well-worn floorboards. Customer service is friendly and welcoming.

FARTHINGSTONE

The Kings Arms

Tel **01327 361604** | **Main Street, NN12 8EZ**
Web **www.farthingstone.org.uk**
Dir ***M1 junction 16, A45 towards Daventry. At Weedon take A5 towards Towcester. Turn right signed Farthingstone.***

Tucked away in perfect walking country, this stone-built, 300-year-old free house is close to Canons Ashby, run by the National Trust. The pub's quirky garden is full of interesting recycled items, decorative trees and shrubs, and pleasantly secluded corners.

FOTHERINGHAY

The Falcon Inn

Tel **01832 226254** | **PE8 5HZ**
Web **www.thefalcon-inn.co.uk**
Dir ***From A605 between Peterborough and Oundle follow Fotheringhay signs.***

This attractive 18th-century, stone-built pub stands in gardens overlooking the stunning church. It's a real local, the Tap Bar regularly used by the village darts team, their throwing arms lubricated by pints of Fool's Nook ale. The menus in both the bar and charming conservatory restaurant rely extensively on locally sourced ingredients. In the spring, restaurant offerings are oriental duck salad with coriander dressing, followed by pie of the day with chips and peas. Hopefully, there'll still be room for caramelised lemon tart.

Open all day 12–11 (Sun 12–4 Jan to May) Closed 7–17 Jan, Sun evening Jan to May Free House 14 from £13 portions/menu Wi-fi notice required

GREAT EVERDON

The Plough Inn

Tel **01327 361606** | **High Street, NN11 3BL**
Web **theploughinneverdon.com**
Dir ***In village centre.***

Pub? Or antiques showroom? You decide. But after enjoying one of the many lovely walks around the village, the Plough's customers enjoy the relaxed ambience created by all the vintage furniture, collectables and plants on sale from barns in the garden.

HINTON-IN-THE-HEDGES

Crewe Arms

Tel **01280 705801** | **Sparrow Corner, NN13 5NF**
Web **www.crewearms.co.uk**
Dir ***From A422 between Banbury and Brackley follow Hinton-in-the-Hedges signs.***

A warm welcome is guaranteed at this dog-friendly pub, which dates from the 15th century. There's a cosy interior warmed by log fires in winter, and the two small gardens are often populated by the village cricket team on summer weekends. As well as beautifully conditioned ales, reasonably-priced home-made favourites could feature steak and ale pie and buttery mash, followed by poached strawberry and clotted cream tart.

Open all week Mon to Thu 4–11 Fri to Sat 12–11 Sun 12–10.30 Free House 10 from £10 portions Wi-fi notice required

KILSBY

The George

Tel **01788 822229** | **Watling Street, CV23 8YE**
Web **www.thegeorgeatkilsby.co.uk**
Dir ***M1 junction 18, follow A361 and Daventry signs. Pub at roundabout junction of A361 and A5.***

A warm welcome and great local atmosphere characterise this village pub, which has a traditional public bar and a high-ceilinged wood-panelled lounge opening into a smarter but relaxed area with solidly comfortable furnishings. The lunch bar menu includes sandwiches, filled baguettes and a selection of home-made dishes.

LITTLE BRINGTON

The Saracens Head

Tel **01604 770640** | **Main Street, NN7 4HS**
Web **www.thesaracensatbrington.co.uk**
Dir ***M1 junction 16, A45 to Flore. In Flore 1st right signed the Bringtons. Straight on at crossroads to Little Brington, pub on left.***

This 17th-century building of mellow ironstone slumbers in a tiny village where lucky locals enjoy a changing range of beers that includes some from local microbreweries. It's a popular stop too, for horse riders.

LITTLE HOUGHTON

Four Pears

Tel **01604 890900** | **28 Bedford Road, NN7 1AB**
Web **www.thefourpears.com**
Dir ***From Northampton take A428 towards Bedford. Left signed Little Houghton.***

In a peaceful, ironstone-built village just outside Northampton, this 400-year-old hostelry was rescued from closure by local residents a few years ago. The fresh, contemporary design owes little to the past. Rather; tip-top real ales are supped in the smart, light bar area.

NASSINGTON

The Queens Head Inn

★★★★ INN PICK OF THE PUBS

Tel **01780 784006** | **54 Station Road, PE8 6QB**
Web **www.queensheadnassington.co.uk**
Dir ***Exit A1 at Wansford, follow Yarwell and Nassington signs. Through Yarwell. Pub on left in Nassington.***

The sun-trap garden of this striking Collyweston-stone inn slopes to a meander of the River Nene. Savvy boaters moor up here to join customers who drive miles to engage with a menu that has gained AA-Rosette recognition. Fires warm the interior in winter and you can dine alfresco on the patio. Settle into the comfy, beamed interior with a glass of Oakham JHB beer and contemplate a choice of invigorating classics exampled by roasted pheasant with honeyed parsnips and creamed cabbage, or pan-fried sea trout with fennel, sauerkraut and salsa verde. The trump card is a notable range of luxury steaks. The Queen Head's diary is always full and includes events such as seafood week and the Great British game week. Sumptuous accommodation is also available here.

Open all day, all week 11–11 (Sat 11am–midnight Sun 12–11) Free House 8 portions/menu notice required

NORTHAMPTON

Althorp Coaching Inn

Tel **01604 770651** | **Main Street, Great Brington, NN7 4JA**
Web **www.althorp-coaching-inn.co.uk**
Dir ***From A428 pass main gates of Althorp House, left before rail bridge. Great Brington 1 mile.***

This 16th-century stone coaching inn occupies a lovely position in the village of Great Brington on the Althorp Estate. A courtyard is surrounded by stable rooms, and the enclosed flower garden is a peaceful spot in which to sample one of the ales and ciders. The restaurant specialises in traditional cooking based on local produce. Moules mariniére might be followed by braised blade of beef, creamy mash and cabbage.

Open all day, all week Sun to Thu 11–11 (Fri to Sat 11am to midnight) Free House 15 portions/menu notice required

The Hopping Hare

★★★★ INN PICK OF THE PUBS

Tel **01604 580090** | **18 Hopping Hill Gardens, Duston, NN5 6PF**
Web **www.hoppinghare.com**
Dir ***Take A428 from Northampton towards West Haddon. Left into Hopping Hill Gardens, pub signed.***

The mildly eccentric pub signage reflects the 'hopping' element; as it's hard to explain, a visit will clarify. In the bar, several national real ales accompany Saxby's cider, made on a local farm, and around 11 wines by the glass. For his modern British dishes, head chef Grant Wentzel hand-picks his suppliers, so knows how his meats were reared, his fish caught, and his vegetables grown. The result: pan-fried pigeon breast, beetroot, pickled girolles and toasted hazelnuts, followed by slow-roasted Bedfordshire pork belly, croquette and loin, pressed potato, sage and onion purée and red wine jus, followed by a home-made treacle tart. Sandwiches, omelettes and salads are also available.

Open all day, all week Free House 11 portions/menu notice required

OLD

The White Horse

Tel **01604 781297** | **Walgrave Road, NN6 9QX**
Web **www.whitehorseold.co.uk**
Dir ***From A43 (between Kettering and Northampton) follow Walgrave signs. Through Walgrave to Old.***

Whimsical sayings ("The road to success is under construction"), leather sofas, stacked logs and a book exchange characterise the interior of this stylishly designed steam-driven mill. Micro-brewed real ales rarely need to travel far, as for instance Gun Dog from Woodford Halse, and Whistling Kite from Kettering. Foodwise – seasonal dishes plus favourites such as a classic fish and chips, burgers and steaks from the grill. A doggy bag is willingly offered if you can't finish. A beer and cider festival on Summer Bank Holiday weekend.

Open all year 12–3 5–11 (Fri to Sat 12–11 Sun 12–7) Closed Mon (excluding bank holidays) Free House 11 portions/menu notice required

PAULERSPURY

Barley Mow

Tel **01327 811086** | **53 High Street, NN12 7NA**
Web **www.barleymow.pub**
Dir ***From A5 between Milton Keynes and Towcester follow Paulerspury signs (at BP Garage). 0.75 mile to pub on left.***

The description 'idyllic rural spot' may be a tad overworked, but it certainly applies to the Barley Mow in Paulerspury. Surrounded by thatched cottages and beautiful farmland views, it's been the village centre watering hole since at least the 17th century.

SIBBERTOFT

The Red Lion PICK OF THE PUBS

Tel **01858 880011** | **43 Welland Rise, LE16 9UD**
Web **www.redlionwinepub.co.uk**
Dir ***From Market Harborough take A4304, through Lubenham, left through Marston Trussell to Sibbertoft.***

Now refurbished, the interior of this friendly 300-year-old free house is an appealing blend of contemporary and classic decor, with oak beams, leather upholstery and woodburners. Andrew and Sarah Banks have built a loyal following here thanks to their special passion for wine: over 200 bins appear on the list, 20 labels are served by the glass, and an annual wine festival is a high point in the pub's busy calendar. After tasting, all wines can be bought at take-home prices, avoiding the guesswork of supermarket purchases. The monthly-changing and reasonably priced menu is served throughout, and could feature devilled whitebait, or pork belly and black pudding bites; fish pie with cheesy mash or an 8oz sirloin with hand-cut chips; and caramelised orange cheesecake or treacle sponge and custard.

Open all week 5–11 (Sat 12–3 6–11 Sun 12–6) Free House 20 from £7 portions/menu notice required

STAVERTON

The Countryman – see page 314

STOKE BRUERNE

The Boat Inn – see page 314

THORNBY

The Red Lion

Tel **01604 740238** | **Welford Road, NN6 8SJ**
Web **www.redlionthornby.co.uk**
Dir ***A14 junction 1, A5199 towards Northampton. Pub on left in village.***

Weary A14 travellers should earmark this 400-year-old village pub that's just a mile from junction 1. In winter months a log fire warms the traditional interior and its wall of pictures of the pub from bygone days. It's hospitably run by Simon and Louise Cottle, who consult the locals on their choice of four ales; Vale of Welton cider is here too. The menu of freshly prepared dishes includes home-made bread. The glorious summer garden hosts a beer festival on the last weekend in July.

Open all day, all week 12–11 (Mon 5–10 Sun 12–10) Free House portions/menu notice required

STAVERTON

The Countryman

Tel 01327 311815 | Daventry Road, NN11 6JH
Web www.thecountrymanstaverton.co.uk
Dir *On A425 between Daventry and Southam.*

Affordable food at the only pub in the village

Built of traditional Northamptonshire ironstone, this pretty 17th-century coaching inn retains plenty of original character, courtesy of log fires and beamed ceilings. A wide choice of ales, perhaps one from Church End or Wychwood, keeps beer fans in the L-shaped bar happy, while the seasonal menu showcases regional produce. As well as traditional pub classics like steak and ale pie, fish and chips and chicken carbonara, there's curry spiced duck breast; rolled shoulder of lamb; grilled fillet of sea bream; wild mushroom and chestnut 'cottage pie' and banana shallot tarte Tatin. Desserts include brioche and butter pudding with orange anglaise; and white chocolate and Baileys profiteroles topped with mini marshmallows, chocolate sauce and toasted almonds. The Jurassic Way long-distance footpath between Banbury and Stamford passes through the village.

Open all week Mon 12–3 6–10.30 Tue to Sat 12–3 6–11 (Sun 12–10) Closed 1–16 Jan Free House 9 portions/menu notice required

STOKE BRUERNE

The Boat Inn

Tel 01604 862428 | NN12 7SB
Web www.boatinn.co.uk
Dir *In village centre, just off A508 and A5.*

Family-run free house on the Grand Union Canal

Trim thatch topping a long, low building of golden limestone makes this canal-side pub stand out at the heart of the canal system. The busy locks here, together with the National Canal Museum directly opposite, are reflected in the decor; lots of old photos, paintings and ephemera. A wide choice of beers will satisfy a thirst, whilst food can be enjoyed in bars, bistro or elegant restaurant. Traditional pub grub is the foundation of robust bar meals; the carte menu in Woodwards Restaurant includes fillet of sea bass with balsamic stir-fried vegetables; slow-cooked rump of lamb; and mushroom and tarragon strudel with Madeira sauce.

Open all day, all week 9am–11pm (Sun 9am–10.30pm) Free House 10 portions/menu notice required

TITCHMARSH

The Wheatsheaf at Titchmarsh

Tel **01832 732203** | **1 North Street, NN14 3DH**
Web **www.the-wheatsheaf.pub**
Dir ***A14 junct 13, A605 towards Oundle, right to Titchmarsh. Or from A14 junction 14 follow signs for Titchmarsh.***

The Wheatsheaf is a stone-built country pub in a small village in the Northamptonshire countryside. Since its stylish refurbishment, this free house has gained a reputation for its ales and locally-sourced food, which combines pub classics with more adventurous dishes on the specials board. Typical dishes include lamb rack, crushed peas, dauphinoise potatoes, chard and merlot sauce; and a vegan beetroot bourguignon. Wash it down with craft beers from local breweries.

Open all year 12-3 5-11 (Fri to Sat 12-11 Sun 12-7) Closed Mon Free House 9 portions/menu notice required

TOWCESTER

The Folly Inn

Tel **01327 354031** | **London Road, NN12 6LB**
Web **www.follyinntowcester.co.uk**
Dir ***On A5 opposite Towcester Racecourse.***

Sitting beside the A5 opposite Towcester Racecourse, the Folly beckons with its picture-postcard looks, flower-filled hanging baskets and coaching lamps. The interior reveals all the hallmarks of a proper diners' pub, with neatly laid tables in a clean and fresh setting. Lunchtime classics include roast pork belly and crackling, while dinners feature Perkins Lodge Farm steaks. If a glass of ale in the extensive rear garden is all that's required, two local ales are on tap.

Open all year 12-2.30 6-9.30 (Sun 12-7.30) Closed Mon Free House 10 from £15 portions/menu

The Saracens Head

Tel **01327 350414** | **219 Watling Street, NN12 6BX**
Web **www.saracenshead-towcester.co.uk**
Dir ***M1 junction 15A, A43 towards Oxford. Take A5 signed Towcester.***

This imposing building dates back over 400 years, and is featured in Charles Dickens' first novel, *The Pickwick Papers*. The same home comforts that Dickens enjoyed have been updated, and discerning customers will find excellent service in the restored pub. Dishes include slow-cooked pork belly; or a selection of meat and fish pies; plus traditional pub classics. Finish with chocolate fudge cake or a knickerbocker glory. Sandwiches, jackets, wraps and ciabattas are all available too.

Open all day, all week 11-11 (Fri to Sat 11am-midnight) Greene King/Old English Inns 13 portions/menu

UPPER BODDINGTON

Plough Inn

Tel **01327 260364** | **32 Warwick Avenue, NN11 6DH**
Web **www.ploughinnboddington.co.uk**
Dir ***Phone for detailed directions.***

Just one mile from the tranquillity of Boddington reservoir with its fishing and sailing club, this charming 18th-century thatched coaching inn is also convenient for Silverstone. Set within lovely Northamptonshire countryside, the Plough is at the heart of village life in Upper Boddington.

WESTON

The Crown PICK OF THE PUBS

Tel **01295 760310** | **Helmdon Road, NN12 8PX**
Web **www.thecrownweston.co.uk**
Dir ***Accessed from A43 or B4525.***

This delightful 16th-century inn is a true community pub, with a reputation for its family- and dog-friendly attitude, its excellent beers and a range of high-quality, locally-sourced dishes. A seasonal menu might well feature the likes of twice baked cheddar cheese soufflé, blushed tomato, red onion and walnut salad; and cheddar, leek and feta sausages with spring onion mash and red onion gravy.

WOODNEWTON

The White Swan

Tel **01780 470944** | **22 Main Street, PE8 5EB**
Web **www.whiteswanwoodnewton.co.uk**
Dir ***Phone for detailed directions.***

With dedication and strong local support, the 19th-century White Swan really is making a name for itself. Beer drinkers will find Sharp's Doom Bar and Fuller's London Pride. Young ones can choose from their own dedicated menu.

NORTHUMBERLAND

ALNWICK

The Hogs Head Inn ★★★ INN

Tel **01665 606576** | **Hawfinch Drive, NE66 2BF**
Web **www.hogsheadinnalnwick.co.uk**
Dir ***From south: A1 onto A1068 signed Alnwick. 3rd exit at roundabout. Under A1, right at BP garage. From north: A1 onto A1068 signed Alnwick. 1st left, right at BP garage (Note: older Sat Nav systems may not recognise pub's postcode).***

Named after the pub featured in the Harry Potter books, this inn is just minutes from Alnwick Castle, which appeared as Hogwarts in the first two films. This is an ideal base for exploring Northumberland, and food at this family-friendly pub is served all day.

AMBLE

The Amble Inn ★★★ INN

Tel **01665 613333** | **Sandpiper Way, NE65 0FF**
Web **www.theambleinnamble.co.uk**
Dir ***Phone for detailed directions.***

This brand-new, purpose-built pub opened in January 2019 and is a stylish place to eat and drink. The menu offers a good selection of classics, pizza, steak and burgers, and there's a variety of draught beers, with rotating local cask ales.

Open all day, all week *Free House* *12*
from £8.95 *portions/menu* Wi-fi
notice required

The Wellwood

Tel **01665 714646** | **High Street, NE65 0LD**
Web **wellwoodarms.pub**
Dir ***At junction of A1068 and High Street in Amble.***

On the stunning Northumberland coast in an Area of Outstanding Natural Beauty, The Wellwood started life as a farmhouse and it's the oldest building in Amble. Walkers and locals mingle in the bar, while diners have very different options, with a restaurant, dining room and carvery.

Open all day, all week *Punch Taverns* *10*
portions/menu Wi-fi *notice required*

BARDON MILL

Twice Brewed Inn

Tel **01434 344534** | **Military Road, NE47 7AN**
Web **www.twicebrewedinn.co.uk**
Dir ***On B6318, 4 miles from Haltwhistle.***

If you're exploring Hadrian's Wall, you'll already know how stunning the scenery is, and Steel Rig, one of the most dramatic parts of the wall, is a fine place to find a pub. They welcome cyclists, walkers, and dogs – and anyone who fancies a pint of their own Sycamore Gap or Ale Caesar, or a bite to eat. A classic pub menu might feature steak and ale pie; sausage and mash; scampi and chips or shepherd's pie, all carefully made from locally-sourced produce.

Open all day, all week Closed 25 Dec *Free House*
portions/menu Wi-fi

BARRASFORD

The Barrasford Arms – see opposite

BEADNELL

The Craster Arms ★★★★ INN

Tel **01665 720272** | **The Wynding, NE67 5AX**
Web **www.crasterarms.co.uk**
Dir ***Exit A1 at Brownieside signed Preston. Left at T-junction signed Seahouses. Right signed Beadnell village. Pub on left.***

In the 15th century, the English hereabouts built small fortified watch towers to warn against Scottish invasions – this was one of them. Since becoming a pub in 1818, its role has widened to offer not just food, drink and accommodation, but live entertainment, including the Crastonbury music festival (an RNLI fundraiser), and a beer and cider festival (last weekend in July). Food is wide-ranging from sandwiches and salads, and evening dishes like braised lamb shank; and Thai green chicken curry.

Open all day, all week 11–11 *Punch Taverns*
portions/menu Wi-fi

BLANCHLAND

The Lord Crewe Arms ★★★

COUNTRY HOUSE HOTEL | PICK OF THE PUBS

Tel **01434 677100 | DH8 9SP**
Web **www.lordcrewearmsblanchland.co.uk**
Dir ***From Hexham take B6306 to Blanchland. Approximately 10 miles.***

High in the Durham Dales, Blanchland is an exquisite little estate village of honey-coloured limestone houses. The Lord Crewe was originally part of Blanchland Abbey. Although the abbey was dissolved in 1539, the buildings didn't become an inn until the 1720s when it was popular with lead miners from the moors. Part of the group that includes Calcot Manor, Barnsley House, The Village Pub and The Painswick in Gloucestershire, you can expect the team to know exactly how to create an enjoyable experience in a historic setting. The bar is in the vaulted crypt, a hugely atmospheric space offering Northumbrian ales, including the inn's own appropriately named Lord Crewe Brew.

Open all day, all week 11–11 Free House 9 portions/menu Wi-fi notice required

CARTERWAY HEADS

The Manor House Inn

PICK OF THE PUBS

Tel **01207 255268 | DH8 9LX**
Web **www.themanorhouseinn.com**
Dir ***A69 west from Newcastle, left onto A68 then south for 8 miles. Inn on right.***

A 30 minute drive from Newcastle or Durham will get you to this former coaching inn, an 18th-century building with stone walls, low-beamed ceiling and a massive timber support in the bar. From its lofty position, there are great views of both the Derwent Valley and reservoir. Most produce is local and includes game and wild fish from hereabouts. Suggested dishes include toasted walnut, red wine poached pear and Stilton salad; and premium Cumberland sausage and mash, garden peas and rich onion gravy; and crispy real ale-battered cod with home-made chips.

Open all day, all week 12–11 (Sun 12–10.30) Closed 25–26 Dec, 1st Mon in Jan Enterprise Inns 12 from £13 portions/menu Wi-fi notice required

BARRASFORD

The Barrasford Arms

★★★★ INN

Tel **01434 681237 | NE48 4AA**
Web **www.barrasfordarms.co.uk**
Dir ***From A69 at Hexham take A6079 signed Acomb and Chollerford. In Chollerford by church turn left signed Barrasford.***

Restaurant and country pub with rooms

With quite a few awards to their credit since arriving here in 2017, Michael and Victoria Eames maintain a traditional pub atmosphere in this 19th-century, stone-built village pub. It overlooks Haughton Castle and the Tyne Valley, and Hadrian's Wall isn't far away. Nor for that matter are the Allendale, First and Last and High House Farm breweries, which may well be on tap in the bar. Much of the produce is grown in

the pub's garden to accompany lunch of, say, black pudding Scotch egg, followed by cottage pie; or maple roast vegetable tart. At dinner, after starting with cured trout fishcake, the main course could be local pheasant breast with bacon croquette; a 200-gram rib-eye or rump steak; or North Sea hake and chips. Single, double and family accommodation is available.

Open all year, all day Closed Mon Free House from £12.50 portions/menu notice required

FALSTONE

The Pheasant Inn

★★★★ INN

Tel 01434 240382 | Stannersburn, NE48 1DD
Web www.thepheasantinn.com
Dir *A69, B6079, B6320, follow signs for Kielder Water.*

Perfect base for Northumbrian adventures

In the early 17th century, long, long before nearby Kielder Water and Kielder Forest were created, agricultural workers drank at a beer-house in Stannersburn. This ivy-clad country inn is that beer-house, now finding itself where the Northumberland National Park meets the Border Forest Park, and surrounded by verdant valleys, high moors and tranquil woodlands. It's well positioned too for cycle tracks, a sculpture trail, an observatory, endless walks and wildlife watching, including red squirrels. What you see today is what Walter, Irene and Robin Kershaw have achieved since they acquired it, then rather run down, over 32 years ago. Most spaces in the two bars have been filled with historic Northumberland memorabilia, and on the exposed stone walls that support the blackened beams are photos of yesteryear's locals. The daily-changing traditional British menu makes the most of what Northumbria has to offer. Excellent beers from Wylam Brewery and Timothy Taylor may cloud the mind, but not the dark night skies, which make the area a mecca for astronomers. There is a tranquil stream-side garden.

Open 11–3 6–11 Closed 25–27 Dec, Mon to Tue (Nov to Feb) Free House from £8.50 portions/menu

CHATTON

Percy Arms ★★★★ INN

Tel **01668 215244** | **Main Road, NE66 5PS**
Web **www.percyarmschatton.co.uk**
Dir ***From A1 between Warenford and Belford, onto B6348 signed Chatton.***

This beautifully appointed pub, with an underlying theme of game birds and animals, reflects the owner's refined approach to styling. The dog-friendly, L-shaped bar is filled with chesterfields, tartan-covered chairs, hunting-scene drapes, horns, horseshoes, riding crops and wellies, all within range of an open fire.

Open all day, all week Free House from £10.95 portions/menu notice required

CORBRIDGE

The Angel of Corbridge

Tel **01434 632119** | **Main Street, NE45 5LA**
Web **www.theangelofcorbridge.com**
Dir ***0.5 mile off A69, signed Corbridge.***

A handsome, white-painted inn overlooking the widest part of Main Street. Formerly the King's Head, it was extended in the 18th century and dates back to 1529. The lounge has a log fire, but the real hub is the bar, and all-day food is available.

CRASTER

The Jolly Fisherman

Tel **01665 576461** | **Haven Hill, NE66 3TR**
Web **www.thejollyfishermancraster.co.uk**
Dir ***Exit A1 at Denwick. Follow Seahouses signs, then 1st sign for Craster.***

When the pub opened in 1847, Craster was a thriving fishing village, and the charm of this historic stone-flagged, low-beamed pub remains undimmed. When it's cold, relax by an open fire; at any time admire impressive Dunstanburgh Castle from the delightful beer garden.

EGLINGHAM

The Tankerville Arms

Tel **01665 578444** | **15 The Village, NE66 2TX**
Web **www.tankervillearms.com**
Dir ***Follow Eglingham signs from A697 (between Powburn and Wooperton) or from Alnwick take B6346 to Eglingham, approximately 8 miles.***

The picturesque Northumbrian village of Eglingham is handily located for walkers exploring the Cheviot Hills. Menus feature pub classics like gammon with a fried duck egg and chunky chips.

ELLINGHAM

The Pack Horse Inn

Tel **01665 589292** | **NE67 5HA**
Web **www.packhorseinn-ellingham.co.uk**
Dir ***From A1 follow Ellingham signs.***

A lovely old stone-built inn with a collection of nearly 200 jugs hanging from the exposed beams in the bar. The daily-changing evening menu offers dishes like steak and ale pie with chips; or smoked haddock and mustard rarebit.

FALSTONE

The Pheasant Inn – see opposite

FELTON

The Northumberland Arms ★★★★ INN

Tel **01670 787370** | **The Peth, West Thirston, NE65 9EE**
Web **www.northumberlandarms-felton.co.uk**
Dir ***Take A1 from Morpeth towards Alnwick. Turn right, follow Felton signs.***

A coaching inn in a picturesque village beside the River Coquet, built in the 1820s by Hugh Percy, 3rd Duke of Northumberland, as a place for horses to rest and guests to freshen up before being received at Alnwick Castle. Northumbrian brewed beers are served in the bar, and the kitchen sources local ingredients for dishes such as warm mackerel with Niçoise salad; and Northumberland sausage, wholegrain mustard mash, crispy onions and ale gravy.

Open all day, all week Free House portions/menu notice required

HAYDON BRIDGE

The General Havelock Inn

Tel **01434 684376** | **Ratcliffe Road, NE47 6ER**
Dir ***On A69, 7 miles west of Hexham.***

Built in the 1760s and named after a 19th-century British Army officer, this riverside inn is a popular place. In a converted stone barn, the restaurant overlooks the river where otters can often be spotted. The real ales are all sourced locally – Cullercoats Shuggy Boat Blonde and Great North East Rivet Catcher are but two. Local ingredients are the foundation of the dishes here; in summer, the patio area is covered by a marquee.

Open all year 12–2.30 7–12 (Sun 12–10.30) Closed Mon Free House 15 portions notice required

HEDLEY ON THE HILL

The Feathers Inn PICK OF THE PUBS

Tel **01661 843607** | **NE43 7SW**
Web **www.thefeathers.net**
Dir ***A695 towards Gateshead. In Stocksfield right into New Ridley Road. Left at Hedley on the Hill sign to village.***

This 200-year-old, stone-built free house is set high above the Tyne Valley, with splendid views across the Cheviot Hills. It's worth the detour for the rotating choice of microbrewery ales; relax and sup Wylam Red Kite or Northumberland Pit Pony beside a welcoming wood-burning stove. Old oak beams, rustic settles and stone walls decorated with local photographs set the informal scene. There's a good selection of traditional pub games like shove ha'penny and bar skittles; you'll find a good collection of cookery books as well. The impressive daily menu makes use of the freshest local ingredients – including game from local shoots and Longhorn beef – to create great British classics as well as regional dishes.

Open all week 12–11 (Mon to Wed 6–11 Sun 12–10.30) Free House portions

HEXHAM

Battlesteads Hotel & Restaurant ★★★ HOTEL

PICK OF THE PUBS

Tel **01434 230209** | **Wark, NE48 3LS**
Web **www.battlesteads.com**
Dir ***10 miles north of Hexham on B6320 (Kielder road).***

Hadrian's Wall lies to the south of this converted 18th-century farmhouse, and Britain's darkest night skies are overhead. There are three dining options: the bar serving, among others, Nel's Best real ale from High House Farm brewery, and Sandford Orchards cider; the conservatory, overlooking the walled herb, salad leaf, fruit and vegetable garden; and the softly-lit main restaurant, decorated with old railway travel posters. Among the modern British dishes are venison bourguignon; baby leek and smoked brie pie; and autumn vegetable tagine with bulgur wheat and harissa. Desserts include the ever popular whisky and marmalade bread and butter pudding. Check with them for the summer beer festival date.

Open all day, all week Closed 25 Dec Free House 15 portions notice required

Dipton Mill Inn PICK OF THE PUBS

Tel **01434 606577** | **Dipton Mill Road, NE46 1YA**
Web **www.diptonmill.co.uk**
Dir ***2 miles south of Hexham on HGV route to Blanchland, B6306 (Dipton Mill Road).***

Surrounded by farmland and woods and not far from Hadrian's Wall, this former farmhouse has a pretty millstream running right through the gardens. The Dipton Mill is home to Hexhamshire Brewery ales, which include Devil's Water and Whapweasel, plus Blackhall English Stout. All dishes are prepared from local produce where available, and a wide range of sandwiches includes a gourmet selection. Lunch or dinner could start with smoked salmon and prawns, or soup, and mains might include haddock baked with tomatoes and basil, or lamb steak braised in wine and mustard. A good selection of veggie options includes a tomato, bean and vegetable casserole.

Open 12–2.30 6–11 (Sun 12–3) Closed 25 Dec, Sun evening Free House 10 from £6.50 portions notice required

Miners Arms Inn

Tel **01434 603909** | **Main Street, Acomb, NE46 4PW**
Web **www.theminersacomb.com**
Dir ***2 miles west of Hexham on A69.***

The Greenwell family took over this 18th-century village pub near Hadrian's Wall a few years ago, and it's very much a family business with David and Elwyn helped by their son and two daughters. Visitors can enjoy the open-hearth fire, the sunny beer garden, or simply sit out front soaking up life in this peaceful village. Among the choice of ales, local Wylam Gold Tankard is always available. The theme nights prove popular.

Open all week 5–12 (Sat 3–12 Sun 12–12pm) Free House portions/menu notice required

Rat Inn PICK OF THE PUBS

Tel **01434 602814** | **Anick, NE46 4LN**
Web **www.theratinn.com**
Dir ***2 miles from Hexham. At Bridge End (A69) roundabout, take exit signed Oakwood. Inn 500 yards on right.***

Facing a small, triangular green in a tiny hamlet of stone cottages, the terraced, tree-shaded garden of this convivial old drovers' inn looks out over the River Tyne as it curves round to the Roman town of Corbridge. Enjoy a glass of High House Farm Nel's Best or Wylam Gold Tankard in the flagstone-floored, beamed bar. The bar itself is fashioned from a great oak sideboard; chamberpots hang from the ceiling and a cast-iron range may blaze away. The daily-changing menu might offer beetroot, goats' curd, fennel and apple salad and hazelnut; pan-fried whole plaice, samphire and caper butter; or rich beef mince on goose fat toast, watercress and pickled red cabbage.

Open all day, all week Free House portions Wi-fi P

LONGFRAMLINGTON

The Anglers Arms PICK OF THE PUBS

Tel **01665 570271** | **Weldon Bridge, NE65 8AX**
Web **www.anglersarms.com**
Dir ***Take A697 north of Morpeth signed Wooler and Coldstream. 7 miles, left to Weldon Bridge.***

Since the 1760s, this part-battlemented, three-storey, former coaching inn has commanded the picturesque Weldon Bridge over the River Coquet. It belongs to John and Julie Young, whose knick-knacks and curios, pictures and fishing memorabilia are liberally distributed within. On the bar top, pump badges declare the availability of Timothy Taylor Landlord, Theakston Best Bitter and Greene King brews. A comprehensive menu suggests, for example, pigeon salad, black pudding, rocket and truffle oil, followed by Tournedos surf and turf – prime fillet steak with scallops, garlic sauce and skinny fries; or glazed ham hock with grilled tomatoes, onion rings and cheese sauce. The carefully tended half-acre of garden is perfect for outdoor eating and includes a children's play park.

Open all day, all week 11–11 (Sun 12–10.30) Free House from £12.95 portions P *notice required*

The Granby Inn ★★★★ INN

Tel **01665 570228** | **NE65 8DP**
Web **www.thegranbyinn.co.uk**
Dir ***In village centre.***

Once a coaching inn, this family-run pub just north of Morpeth is perfectly situated for exploring the stunning Northumbrian coast and the ancient town of Alnwick. Dating back around 250 years, The Granby Inn prides itself on being a traditional pub for a pint in the cosy bar, but the food attracts diners from all over, too. Local sourcing extends to meat from a nearby butcher and fish from North Shields, all of which turns up in dishes such as home-made cottage pie; and smoked haddock and potato crumble.

Open all day, all week 11.30–9 (Sun 12–9) Closed 25–26 Dec and 1 Jan Free House from £10.75 portions/menu Wi-fi P *notice required*

LONGHORSLEY

Linden Tree ★★★★ HOTEL

Tel **01670 500033 | Linden Hall, NE65 8XF**
Web **www.macdonald-hotels.co.uk/lindenhall**
Dir ***From A1 onto A697, 1 mile north of Longhorsley.***

The friendly and informal Linden Tree stands within the 450 acres that surround Linden Hall, an impressive Georgian mansion that is a popular golf and country club. A sunny patio makes a relaxed setting for lunch in summer and the brasserie-style menu makes good use of local and Scottish produce. Platters for sharing, sandwiches and grills are available too. Round off a long day with a nightcap in the golfers' lounge.

Open all day, all week Mon to Sat 11–11 (Sun 11–10.30) Free House 9 portions/menu notice required

LOW NEWTON BY THE SEA

The Ship Inn

Tel **01665 576262 | The Square, NE66 3EL**
Web **www.shipinnnewton.co.uk**
Dir ***From A1 at Alnwick north-east towards Seahouses. Then follow Newton by the Sea signs.***

A pretty, late-1700s inn overlooking a sandy beach. Their real ales – Sea Coal, Sea Wheat, Ship Hop Ale, Sandcastles at Dawn and Dolly Day Dream are brewed next door. The barrels are rolled all of 15 feet to the cellar; from here they are pumped to the small bar, where plenty of locally caught fresh and smoked fish, toasted sandwiches, ploughman's, cheddar cheese and salad stotties (a local flat roll or bap-like loaf), and hand-picked crab are also offered.

Open all week (seasonal variations, phone or see website for details) Closed 24–26 Dec Free House

LUCKER

The Apple Inn

Tel **01668 213824 | NE70 7JL**
Web **www.theappleinnlucker.com**
Dir ***At Warenford on A1 follow Lucker signs. After memorial at Lucker follow signs to pub.***

Larger villages than tiny Lucker have lost their pub, but the Apple is in good hands. Beer drinkers in the wooden-floored bar enjoy Alnwick Brewery's Amber and Gold real ales, while diners in the tartan-carpeted restaurant might choose seared scallops, black pudding and crispy pork belly; and a trio of Northumberland sausages with creamy champ. Some children might prefer toad-in-the-hole or battered fish and chips. There's plenty of room for eating and drinking outside too.

Open all day, all week Free House from £11.95 portions/menu notice required

MILFIELD

The Red Lion Inn

Tel **01668 216224 | Main Road, NE71 6JD**
Web **www.redlionmilfield.co.uk**
Dir ***On A697, 9 miles south of Coldstream (6 miles north of Wooler).***

Dating back to the 1700s, sheep drovers from the northern counties stayed at this stone building before it was used as a stopover for the mail stagecoach en route from Edinburgh and London. Well placed for salmon and trout fishing and for shooting on the Northumberland estates.

MORPETH

St Mary's Inn ★★★★★ INN

Tel **01670 293293 | Saint Mary's Lane, St Mary's Park, NE61 6BL**
Web **www.stmarysinn.co.uk**
Dir ***From A1 into Stannington into Church Road. At T-junction right into Green Lane, into St Mary's Park.***

Occupying the site of a former hospital, this eponymously named pub continues the caring tradition – with hospitality. In-patients have been known to make a speedy recovery while relaxing by the real fires and enjoying the pub's cosy corners. Four real ales, including an ale brewed especially by Rigg and Furrow Brewery, and a huge range of whiskies are dispensed at the oak bar. All-day sustenance ranges from good old-fashioned bar snacks such as pork quavers with mustard dip to steak and ale pie.

Open all day, all week Free House 10 portions/menu

NETHERTON

The Star Inn

Tel **01669 630238** | **NE65 7HD**
Dir ***7 miles from Rothbury.***

Little has changed at this timeless gem since the Wilson-Morton family took over in 1917. Lost in superb remote countryside north of Rothbury, The Star Inn retains many period features and the bar is like stepping into someone's living room, comfortable and quiet, with no intrusive fruit machines or piped music. Don't expect any food though, just bottled beer, served from a hatch in the entrance hall. This inn is a real find – best to check the days of the week when it's open, though.

Open all year Tue to Wed and Sun 7.30pm–10.30pm (Fri to Sat 7.30pm–11pm) Closed Mon, Thu Free House notice required

NEWBROUGH

Red Lion Inn

Tel **01434 674226** | **Stanegate Road, NE47 5AR**
Web **www.redlionnewbrough.co.uk**
Dir ***From Hexham take A69 towards Haydon Bridge. Follow Fourstones and Newbrough signs. Through Fourstones to pub on right.***

Part 12th century, this stone-built former coaching inn sympathetically accommodates 21st-century needs. The bar area is spacious, with original wood and stonework, open log fires and comfortable chairs. An outside seating area looks over the surrounding countryside.

NEWTON

Duke of Wellington Inn

  INN

Tel **01661 844446** | **NE43 7UL**
Web **www.thedukeofwellingtoninn.co.uk**
Dir ***From Corbridge take A69 towards Newcastle. 3 miles to village.***

This early 19th-century coaching inn overlooks the Tyne Valley, and has stunning views and is a handy base for exploring the National Park and Hadrian's Wall. The building's original oak and stone construction is complemented by modern furniture and fabrics.

Open all day, all week 8am–11pm Free House 12 portions/menu Wi-fi notice required

NEWTON-ON-THE-MOOR

The Cook and Barker Inn

★★★★ INN PICK OF THE PUBS

Tel **01665 575234** | **NE65 9JY**
Web **www.cookandbarkerinn.co.uk**
Dir ***0.5 mile from A1 south of Alnwick.***

For spectacular views of the North Sea coast and the Cheviot Hills, head for the Farmer family's creeper-covered, flower-adorned, stone-built pub and restaurant. Phil Farmer also runs Hope House Farm eight miles away, source of the free-range Aberdeen beef and lamb that feature on the various menus; there's also a seafood selection. A suggested dinner starter of crispy tempura shredded pork, black pudding, crispy pancetta and free-range poached egg with watercress and apple matchstick salad might be followed by either Hope Farm slow-cooked Texel lamb, roasted roots, rosemary potatoes and red wine jus; or king prawn ravioli with chilli, tomato and basil emulsion. Real ale drinkers can expect – indeed, should be pleased – to find Atlantic Hop on the bar, as well as Black Sheep.

Open all day, all week 12–11 Free House from £9.95 portions Wi-fi notice required

8 NORTHUMBERLAND PUBS WITH ACCOMMODATION

The following pubs are rated as part of the AA Guest Accommodation scheme (see page 10–11 for more information).

Duke of Wellington Inn ★★★★★ INN Newton, see page 323

St Mary's Inn ★★★★★ INN Morpeth, see page 322

The Northumberland Arms ★★★★ INN Felton, see page 319

The Olde Ship Inn ★★★★ INN Seahouses, see page 324

Percy Arms ★★★★ INN Chatton, see page 319

The Pheasant Inn ★★★★ INN Falstone, see page 318

The Cook and Barker Inn ★★★★ INN Newton-On-The-Moor, see page 323

The Craster Arms ★★★★ INN Beadnell, see page 316

PONTELAND

The Blackbird

Tel **01661 822684 | North Road, NE20 9UH**
Web **www.theblackbirdponteland.co.uk**
Dir ***From A696 in Ponteland, at mini-roundabout into North Road, on left.***

Ponteland Castle was destroyed by the Scots in 1388 – and the ruins were incorporated into a Tudor manor house that eventually became The Blackbird. Restoration in the 1930s revealed a fine fireplace and an ancient tower, which you can see today. They brew their own Blackbird Bitter and have frequently-changing guest beers as well as dozens of gins. On the menu you can expect to find dishes like smoked mackerel and spring onion croquettes; seared calves' liver; or pan-fried salmon with clam risotto.

Open all day, all week Closed 25 Dec Free House 10 from £10.95 portions/menu Wi-fi notice required

SEAHOUSES

The Bamburgh Castle Inn

★★★ INN

Tel **01665 720283 | NE68 7SQ**
Web **www.bamburghcastleinn.co.uk**
Dir ***A1 onto B1341 to Bamburgh, B1340 to Seahouses, follow signs to harbour.***

With its prime location on the quayside giving wraparound sea views as far as the Farne Islands, this is surely one of the best situated pubs anywhere along Northumberland's stunning coast. Dating back to the 18th century, the inn offers a superb bar and dining areas plus seating outside. Children and dogs are welcome, and imaginative pub dishes of locally sourced food represent excellent value. Typical dishes are slow-cooked beef brisket; black pudding and caramelised onion pork burger; and cheese and pesto penne pasta and feta.

Open all day, all week Free House 11 portions/menu Wi-fi notice required

The Olde Ship Inn

PICK OF THE PUBS

Tel **01665 720200 | 9 Main Street, NE68 7RD**
Web **www.seahouses.co.uk**
Dir ***Lower end of main street above harbour.***

Built around 1745, this stone-built inn with rooms is set above the bustling old harbour of Seahouses. The interior is lit through stained-glass windows and the main saloon bar is full of character, its wooden floor made from ships' decking. A range of whiskies is supplemented by a good selection of real ales, such as Hadrian Border Farne Island and Black Sheep. The inn's corridors and boat gallery are full of antique nautical artefacts, ranging from a figurehead to all manner of ship's brasses and dials. Bar food includes locally caught seafood and home-made soups. In the evenings, starters like pork terrine with apricot and gherkins might be followed by fish and chips; chicken and mushroom casserole; or fresh crab salad.

Open all day, all week 11–11 (Sun 12–11) Free House 10 from £9.75 portions/menu Wi-fi

SLAGGYFORD

The Kirkstyle Inn

Tel **01434 381559 | CA8 7PB**
Web **www.kirkstyleinn.co.uk**
Dir ***Just off A689, 6 miles north of Alston.***

Slaggyford has no shop or school, but when the South Tynedale Railway, currently being restored, reaches the village it will again have a station and its first trains since 1976. Thankfully, it already has the 18th-century Kirkstyle Inn, blessed with wonderful views of the river. In winter, a log fire heats the bar, where among the real ales are Great Corby ale and a summer brew named after the inn. There's a menu of popular dishes.

Open all year 12–3 6–11 Closed Mon and Tue in winter Free House from £9.95 portions Wi-fi notice required

WARDEN

The Boatside Inn

Tel **01434 602233** | **NE46 4SQ**
Web **www.theboatsideinn.com**
Dir ***From A69 west of Hexham, follow signs to Warden Newborough and Fourstones.***

Standing beneath Warden Hill at the confluence of the North and South Tyne rivers, the refurbished Boatside is surrounded by woodland footpaths and bridleways, and has fishing rights on the river. Cullercoats, Wylam and Mordue ales are on offer in the bar with its log fire and dart board. Meals are served in the conservatory, restaurant or snug, and include sharing platters (Tex mex; from the sea; and butchers block).

Open all day, all week 11–11 (Sun 11–10.30) Free House from £8.95 portions/menu notice required

WARENFORD

The White Swan PICK OF THE PUBS

Tel **01668 213453** | **NE70 7HY**
Dir ***100 yards east of A1, 10 miles north of Alnwick.***

Formerly on the Great North Road, and now a stone's throw from the A1, this 200-year-old coaching inn stands near the original toll bridge over the Waren Burn. The Dukes of Northumberland once owned the pub, and its windows and plasterwork still bear the family crests. Inside, you'll find thick stone walls and an open fire for colder days; in summer, there's a small sheltered seating area outside, with further seats in the adjacent field. The modern British dishes might include pheasant and black pudding terrine with black grape, apricot and cumin chutney; and seared duck breast, apple and hazelnut fricassée with anise velouté. Vegetarians are well catered for, with interesting dishes like baked tower of aubergine, courgette, onion, sweet pepper and mushroom with beetroot sorbet and blue cheese.

Open all day, all week 12–11 Free House 26 from £11.95 portions/menu

NOTTINGHAMSHIRE

BEESTON

The Victoria

Tel **0115 925 4049** | **Dovecote Lane, NG9 1JG**
Web **www.victoriabeeston.co.uk**
Dir ***M1 junction 25, A52 east. Turn right at Nurseryman pub, right opposite Rockaway Hotel into Barton Street, 1st left, adjacent to railway station.***

This free house combines a welcoming atmosphere with great food and a wide choice of traditional ales and ciders, continental beers and lagers, many wines by the glass and single malt whiskies. The Victoria dates from 1899 when it was built next to Beeston Railway Station, and the large, heated patio garden is still handy for trainspotting. Check out the dates of the annual beer festivals – Easter, last two weeks in July, and in October.

Open all day, all week 10.30am–11pm (Fri to Sat 10.30am–midnight Sun 12–11) Closed 26 Dec Free House 25 portions

BLIDWORTH

The Black Bull ★★★★  INN

Tel **01623 490222** | **Main Street, NG21 0QH**
Web **www.blackbullblidworth.co.uk**
Dir ***M1 junction 27, A608 east, left at Derby roundabout, right onto B6020. Into Blidworth, 1st right after St Marys Church.***

On the edge of Sherwood Forest in the ancient village of Blidworth, The Black Bull has been an ale house and inn since the early 1700s. After a century of brewery ownership, the pub returned to private hands in 2012, since when a sympathetic refurbishment has seen the return of a real ale tap room serving local brews such as Shipstones Original and Navigation Patriot. The restaurant has won awards for its innovative, locally sourced menu.

Open all day, all week Free House 8 from £11.95 portions/menu notice required

Fox & Hounds

Tel **01623 792383 | Blidworth Bottoms, NG21 0NW**
Web **www.foxblidworth.co.uk**
Dir ***From Ravenshead towards Blidworth on B6020, right to Blidworth.***

A fusion of blues, creams, reds and smart furniture and fabrics give this pub a modern feeling without taking away the traditional country-style character that stems from its early 19th-century origins. The Greene King ales are reliable as ever, and the menu delivers well-priced dishes of popular home-made favourites.

CAR COLSTON

The Royal Oak

Tel **01949 20247 | The Green, NG13 8JE**
Web **www.royaloakcarcolston.co.uk**
Dir ***From Newark-on-Trent on A46 follow Mansfield, then Car Colston signs. From roundabout north of Bingham on A46 follow Car Colston sign. Left at next roundabout signed Car Colston.***

Some experts attribute origins as a hosiery factory to this 200-year-old inn, citing as evidence its unusual vaulted brick ceiling, undoubtedly capable of supporting weighty textile machinery above. Much older is the centurion, perhaps from the nearby Roman-British town of Margidunum, whose ghost you may run into. Normally on bar duty is owner Richard Spencer, dispensing his carefully tended real ales, while Vicky, his wife (a dab hand chef) is in the kitchen preparing dishes such as her very popular steak pies.

Open all day, all week Marston's 12 from £8.25 portions WiFi notice required

CAUNTON

Caunton Beck PICK OF THE PUBS

Tel **01636 636793 | NG23 6AB**
Web **www.wigandmitre.com**
Dir ***6 miles north west of Newark on A616 to Sheffield.***

Tucked away deep in the rich farmlands of the Trent Valley, this beckside village inn is one of a small chain of quality dining pubs owned by the Hope family. Fans of the hop can expect a glass of Black Sheep alongside further guest ales; wine-lovers have a choice of 24 by the glass. Beams, oak floorboards and rustic furnishings characterise the traditional-style interior; outside is a sheltered terrace and lawned garden. The modern, mostly pan-European main menu changes regularly, and starters might be local pigeon breast with spiced roasted pumpkin, celeriac remoulade and popped wild rice; leading to confit pork belly with a black pudding bon bon, caramelised apple purée and Parmentier potatoes; or pan-seared sea bass. A daily-changing set menu is also available and gourmet evenings are held.

Open all day, all week 9am–10.30pm Closed 25 Dec Free House 24 portions/menu WiFi

COLSTON BASSETT

The Martin's Arms – see opposite

EDWINSTOWE

Forest Lodge ★★★★ INN

Tel **01623 824443 | 4 Church Street, NG21 9QA**
Web **www.forestlodgehotel.co.uk**
Dir ***A614 towards Edwinstowe, onto B6034. Inn opposite church.***

This 18th-century coaching inn stands on the edge of Sherwood Forest and has been sympathetically restored by the Thompson family to include stylish accommodation and a comfortable restaurant and bar. Award-winning cask ales are always on tap in two beamed bars warmed by open fires. An impressive baronial-style dining hall is an ideal setting for wholesome fare that changes to reflect the seasons. Dishes include beef and ale pie and home-made beef chilli.

Open all week 11.30–3 5.30–11 (Fri 11.30–3 5–11 Sun 12–3 6–10.30) Free House from £5.75 portions/menu WiFi notice required

COLSTON BASSETT

The Martin's Arms

Tel **01949 81361 | School Lane, NG12 3FD**
Web **www.themartinsarms.co.uk**
Dir ***Exit A46 between Leicester and Newark.***

Traditional 18th-century pub with seasonally inspired menus

PICK OF THE PUBS

Set in the pretty village of Colston Bassett in the Vale of Belvoir, this striking Grade II listed building occupies a quintessentially English spot on the corner of a leafy cul-de-sac close to an old cross. At the heart of village life since the 18th century, the pub takes its name from Henry Martin, MP for Kinsale in County Cork, who was the local squire in the early 19th century. Overlooked by the church spire, the one-acre garden even incorporates a croquet lawn. Close to National Trust land, the pub is surrounded by ancient trees in the estate parkland to which it belonged until 1990, when the current owners, Jack Inguanta and Lynne Strafford Bryan, bought it, undertaking to maintain its character and unique atmosphere. This they have clearly managed to do, since much of the interior will transport you straight back in time, especially the Jacobean fireplaces and the period furnishings. The bar has an impressive range of real ales, while another local 'brew' is elderflower pressé from Belvoir Fruit Farms. With head chef Paul Tingay at the helm, bread, preserves, sauces, terrines, soups, pasta and much, much more are all made on site.

Open all week 12–3 6–11 (Sun 12–4 7–11) Closed 25 Dec evening and 26 Dec evening Free House 22 from £15 portions notice required

FARNDON

The Farndon Boathouse ◎◎

PICK OF THE PUBS

Tel **01636 676578** | **Off Wyke Lane, NG24 3SX**
Web **www.farndonboathouse.co.uk**
Dir ***From A46 roundabout (south-west of Newark-on-Trent) take Fosse Way signed Farndon. Right into Main Street signed Farndon. At T-junction right into Wyke Lane, follow Boathouse signs.***

Should you arrive here on a mystery tour, you might not guess that the tranquil, wooded view from the terrace of this modern bar and restaurant is the River Trent. The setting is perfect for this old-boathouse-styled pub, with wood cladding, chunky exposed roof trusses and stone floors. The food champions home cooking and local sourcing, with herbs and salad leaves from the pub garden, and meats, fish and cheeses often smoked in-house. Wide-ranging menus offer four different sharing boards; a starter or main called The Mussel Pot; pizzas, burgers, and steaks; and other choices like pan-fried sea bass fillet, beetroot and watercress risotto and salsa verde. There are pie nights, monthly ladies' nights and live music every Sunday evening.

Open all day, all week 10am–11pm Free House 20 portions/menu WI-FI P *notice required*

HARBY

Bottle & Glass

Tel **01522 703438** | **High Street, NG23 7EB**
Web **www.wigandmitre.com**
Dir ***South of A57 (Lincoln to Markham Moor road).***

The Bottle & Glass, with flagged floors and heavy beams, has a microbrewery producing four different ales that are offered along with Black Sheep real ale and a generous 24 wines by the glass. Starters on the short, seasonal lunch and dinner menu might include twice-baked soufflé; grilled cod chermoula with herb tabouleh and houmous; and slow-cooked lamb shank with bubble-and-squeak. On sunny days stake an early claim for a terrace table.

Open all day, all week Mon to Fri 10am–11pm Sat to Sun 9am–11pm Closed 25 Dec Free House 24 portions/menu WI-FI P

KIMBERLEY

The Nelson & Railway Inn

Tel **0115 938 2177** | **12 Station Road, NG16 2NR**
Dir ***M1 junction 26, A610 to Kimberley.***

This popular village pub dating from the 17th-century with Victorian additions sits next door to the Hardys & Hansons Brewery that supplies many of the beers. Sadly, the two nearby railway stations that once made it a railway inn are now derelict.

LAXTON

The Dovecote Inn

Tel **01777 871586** | **Cross Hill, NG22 0SX**
Web **www.thedovecoteinnlaxton.co.uk**
Dir ***Exit A1 at Tuxford through Egmanton to Laxton.***

Like most of the village of Laxton, the 18th-century Dovecote Inn is Crown Estate property, belonging to the Royal Family. There's a delightful beer garden with views of the church, while the interior has a bar as well as three cosy wining and dining rooms. The seasonally changing menus and daily changing specials board could include twice-baked beetroot soufflé; Lancashire cheese and onion pie; crusted mackerel fillets; and plum clafoutis. The gourmet themed nights are extremely popular and booking is essential.

Open all week 11.30–3 5.30–11 (Sat 11.30–11 Sun 12–9) Free House 24 from £11 portions/menu WI-FI P *notice required*

MORTON

The Full Moon Inn **PICK OF THE PUBS**

Tel **01636 830251** | **Main Street, NG25 0UT**
Web **www.thefullmoonmorton.co.uk**
Dir ***A617 from Newark towards Mansfield. Past Kelham, left to Rolleston and follow signs to Morton.***

All pantiles, pale bricks and creeper, this long-established inn stands at the village centre just a short hop from the magnificent Minster at nearby Southwell. Within, it's a contemporary and comfortable pub, with exposed old beams and brickwork retained from the original 18th-century cottages, scattered with reclaimed panelling and furniture. It's a relaxing locale in which to chill out with a glass of wine or a pint of real ale. It's both child and dog-friendly, with a grassy, tree-shaded garden an additional bonus for summer days. Good pub tucker features on the menus: braised blade of beef, parmesan mash, peas, crumbled bacon and red wine jus; celeriac and spinach risotto, soft hen's egg and watercress; and beer-battered haddock, chunky chips, pea purée and tartare sauce.

Open all week 10–3 5.30–11 (Sat to Sun 10–11) Free House 14 from £7.95 portions/menu notice required

NEWARK-ON-TRENT

The Prince Rupert

Tel 01636 918121 | 46 Stodman Street, NG24 1AW
Web www.kneadpubs.co.uk/the-prince-rupert
Dir *5 minutes walk from castle, on entry road to Market Square.*

Full of charm and character, the 15th-century Prince Rupert is one of Newark's most historic pubs. Expect old beams, wood floors, crackling log fires and cosy corners in the series of small downstairs rooms; make sure you explore upstairs, as the ancient architectural features are stunning.

NOTTINGHAM

The Hand and Heart

Tel 0115 958 2456 | 65–67 Derby Road, NG1 5BA
Web www.thehandandheart.co.uk
Dir *On A610 (2 minutes walk from Canning Circus).*

This Georgian building was a brewery before becoming a pub in Victorian times. Beer was brewed in the converted stables and stored in the sandstone cave below, which is now an atmospheric restaurant. Famous for its excellent selection of real ales, The Hand and Heart holds two beer festivals a year, and in the bar, you can sample Round Heart from the Dancing Duck Brewery as well as the Maypole Brewery's Little Weed, and six changing guest ales. A tempting menu is offered.

Open all day, all week 4–midnight (Fri to Sat 9am–1am Sun 12–10.30) Closed 25–26 Dec and 1 Jan Free House 18

Ye Olde Trip to Jerusalem

PICK OF THE PUBS

Tel 0115 947 3171 | 1 Brewhouse Yard, Castle Road, NG1 6AD
Web www.greeneking-pubs.co.uk/pubs/nottinghamshire/ye-olde-trip-to-jerusalem
Dir *In town centre.*

Castle Rock, upon which stands Nottingham Castle, is riddled with caves and passageways cut into the sandstone. The builders of this unusual pub – one of Britain's oldest – founded in AD 1189 – made the most of this, incorporating some of the caves into the design of the inn. The name recalls that soldiers, clergy and penitents gathered here before embarking on crusade to the Holy Land. Beers from the Nottingham Brewery feature strongly, accompanying a reliable menu of old favourites like slow-cooked pork belly and Scottish scampi, to sharing plates, lighter mains and fish such as oven-baked cod, crayfish and spinach fishcakes. Several annual beer festivals are held.

Open all day, all week 11–11 (Fri to Sat 11am to midnight) Closed 25 Dec Greene King 13 portions notice required

RUDDINGTON

The Ruddington Arms

Tel 0115 984 1628 | 56 Wilford Road, NG11 6EQ
Web www.theruddingtonarms.com
Dir *From A52 (south of Nottingham) onto A60 signed Ruddington.*

Five miles south of Nottingham, this refurbished pub has built up a reputation for its locally-sourced products, whether it's the pints of quirkily-named Ruddy Good Ale or the regionally-inspired food. Toasted sandwiches, melts and light bites are served throughout the afternoon, with the carte served lunchtimes and evenings. Typical dishes include Lincolnshire Poacher and spinach soufflé; grilled salt hake chowder, mussels, clams, bacon and black cabbage; or slow-cooked pork belly, pickled red cabbage, onion purée, roast sweet potato and plums.

Open all day, all week Star Pubs & Bars from £11.50 portions/menu notice required

SOUTHWELL

The Hearty Goodfellow

Tel **01636 919176 | NG25 0HQ**
Web **www.heartygoodfellowpub.co.uk**
Dir ***From Newark-on-Trent take A617 towards Mansfield. At lights left to Southwell. Pub on right on A612.***

Close to the picturesque centre of Southwell, a stone's throw from the Minster and racecourse. Inside, a warm and caring welcome embraces one and all, including children and dogs. Settle back with a pint of Sunchaser, the house beer. Light bites include a posh fish-finger sandwich; for a 'Hearty' alternative, look to the home-made short-crust beef and ale pie. Children eat proper food too, choosing either from a Little Darlings menu or smaller portions from the main menu.

Open all week Mon to Thu 11–3 5–11 (Fri to Sun 11am–midnight) Everards 11 from £6.95 portions/menu Wi-fi notice required

STAUNTON IN THE VALE

The Staunton Arms

Tel **01400 281218 | NG13 9PE**
Web **www.stauntonarms.co.uk**
Dir ***Phone for detailed directions.***

A 200-year-old listed pub in the Vale of Belvoir, The Staunton Arms is a welcoming place, with well-kept cask ales sourced from local and regional breweries. You can eat in the bar or the more formal restaurant, choosing from the same menus. There's the option of lighter dishes – smoked salmon and scrambled egg on toast, perhaps, while for those with a bigger appetite, there's the pub's own beef and ale pie with mash or hand-cut chips; butternut squash ravioli; or pork tenderloin.

Open all day, all week Free House 17 from £11.50 portions/menu Wi-fi notice required

TUXFORD

The Fountain

Tel **01777 872854 | 155 Lincoln Road, NG22 0JQ**
Web **www.thefountainhotel.co.uk**
Dir ***Phone for detailed directions.***

The Fountain makes a convenient pit-stop off the A1(M) for frazzled parents and hungry children, especially with its large beer garden and playroom. Unpretentious pub grub at reasonable prices is the deal, but a 'fresh is best' attitude and support for local growers drive the inn's ethos nonetheless, with draught ales from nearby Welbeck Abbey Brewery. Great stone-baked pizzas and meal deals appear on the kids' menu, but grown-ups head for the steaks, BBQ ribs and home-made steak and ale pie.

Open all week Free House 12 from £7.50 portions/menu Wi-fi notice required

The Mussel & Crab

Tel **01777 870491 | Sibthorpe Hill, NG22 0PJ**
Web **www.musselandcrab.com**
Dir ***From Ollerton/Tuxford junction of A1 and A57. North on B1164 to Sibthorpe Hill. Pub 800 yards on right.***

Bruce and Allison Elliott-Bateman have turned this quirky pub in landlocked Nottinghamshire into a renowned seafood restaurant. Beautifully fresh fish and seafood, therefore, dominate the menu, with over a dozen blackboards offering ever-changing fish dishes, as well as 'things that don't swim'. You could select po'pei mussels, followed by lobster thermidor, twice-baked soufflé or locally shot pheasant.

Open all week 11–3 6–11 Free House 16 menus

UPTON

Cross Keys

Tel **01636 813269 | Main Street, NG23 5SY**
Web **www.crosskeysatupton.co.uk**
Dir ***From A617 west of Newark-on-Trent onto A612 towards Southwell. Pub in village centre.***

Open fires, cosy alcoves, beamed ceilings and candles in the evenings – that's the Cross Keys. Co-owner Steve Hussey, with partner Alison Ryan, is also head brewer/owner at Maythorne's Mallard microbrewery, which supplies the real ales, with Somerset's Broadoak providing cider and perry.

OXFORDSHIRE

ABINGDON-ON-THAMES

The Brewery Tap

Tel **01235 521655** | **40–42 Ock Street, OX14 5BZ**
Web **www.thebrewerytap.net**
Dir ***Phone for detailed directions.***

This predominantly late 17th-century pub has been in the aptly-named Heritage family for nearly 25 years. Flagstone floors and open fireplaces characterise the interior and there's a changing line-up of six guest ales along with a good choice of ciders. Bar snacks range from grilled jalapeño peppers to pork crackling, while classic dishes like home-made pies and the 'Made in America' dishes prove ever popular. Sunday roasts are a big thing, followed between 5pm and 7pm by live music. Beer and cider festivals in March and October.

Open all day, all week Redstar Pub Co 12 portions/menu

ASHBURY

The Rose & Crown

Tel **01793 710222** | **3 High Street, SN6 8NA**
Web **www.roseandcrowninn.co.uk/newrc**
Dir ***Take B4000 from Shrivenham signed Sevenhampton. At crossroads in Ashbury turn right, pub on left. Or from Lambourn take B4000 to Ashbury. Left at crossroads to pub.***

In the heart of the historic village of Ashbury, The Rose & Crown dates back to the 16th century when it was a coaching inn. It retains plenty of original features including open fires and the patio terrace is a real draw in the summer.

BANBURY

The Wykham Arms

Tel **01295 788808** | **Temple Mill Rd, Sibford Gower, OX15 5RX**
Web **www.wykhamarms.co.uk**
Dir ***Between Banbury and Shipston-on-Stour off B4035.***

A beautiful thatched pub in a hilly village on the edge of The Cotswolds. With roses round the door and a cosy courtyard for long summer evenings, it's the idyllic rural inn. With a brace and more of real ales, including local brewers, proprietors and classically trained chefs Damian and Debbie Bradley skilfully produce a regularly-changing menu of contemporary dishes. Typical dishes – Shetland salmon pavé with red wine risotto and fennel, leek compôte; and pork belly confit with bubble-and-squeak.

Open 12–3 6–11 (Sat to Sun all day) Closed 25 Dec, Mon (excluding bank holidays) Free House 20 portions notice required

Ye Olde Reindeer Inn

Tel **01295 270972** | **47 Parsons Street, OX16 5NA**
Web **www.ye-olde-reinedeer-inn-banbury.co.uk**
Dir ***1 mile from M40 junction 11, in town centre just off market square. Car park access via Bolton Road.***

Cotswold-brewed beers from the renowned Hook Norton Brewery draw in a lively local clientele to this historic pub right at the core of old Banbury, just a stone's throw from the Cross of nursery-rhyme fame. Enjoy good, solid pub grub in the traditional interior.

BEGBROKE

The Royal Sun

Tel **01865 374718** | **2 Woodstock Road West, OX5 1RZ**
Web **theroyalsunbegbroke.com**
Dir ***From Oxford take A44 towards Woodstock. Approximately 5 miles to Begbroke.***

A stone-built inn, dating from the 17th century, and handy for Woodstock and Blenheim Palace. Sir Winston Churchill and the Duke of Marlborough used to ride to the pub for a drink – and if it was good enough for them, then surely it's good enough for anyone.

BESSELS LEIGH

The Greyhound

Tel **01865 862110** | **OX13 5PX**
Web **www.brunningandprice.co.uk/greyhound**
Dir ***On A420 between Oxford and Fyfield.***

The best efforts to date the Cotswold-stone Greyhound suggest it's around 400 years old, when it was a coaching inn and forge. A plaque records how 19th-century landlord Alfred White began here what survives as Britain's oldest church-bell-hanging company.

BLACK BOURTON

The Vines

Tel **01993 843559** | **Burford Road, OX18 2PF**
Web **www.vinesblackbourton.co.uk**
Dir ***A40 at Witney onto A4095 to Faringdon, 1st right after Bampton to Black Bourton.***

Stylish village retreat with modern British food

Built of Cotswold stone, The Vines is discreetly set back from the road behind a screen of bushes. Inside, spacious and smartly decorated and furnished, it belongs to Ahdy and Karen Gerges, who maintain its excellent reputation. Leather sofas in the spacious lounge area by the log fire are the perfect place for a pint of Old Hooky from the Hook Norton brewery about 24 miles away, or maybe you'd prefer to drift patio-wards with a glass of wine for a game of Aunt Sally, a time-honoured pub game involving throwing sticks at an old woman's head (wooden of course). The menu lists imaginative, internationally influenced, modern British dishes, all freshly prepared from locally sourced produce. A good selection of Old and New World wines is always available. Food and drink can be served in the garden.

Open all year Closed lunch all week, Sun evening Free House portions/menu notice required

BLOXHAM

The Elephant & Castle

Tel **01295 720383** | **OX15 4LZ**
Web **www.bloxhampub.co.uk**
Dir ***Take A361 from Banbury towards Chipping Norton, 1st left after shops in Bloxham.***

Locals play Aunt Sally or shove-ha'penny in this 15th-century coaching inn's large bar, whilst the lounge boasts a bar-billiards table and a large inglenook fireplace. External features include the arch of a former turnpike when at night the pub gates were closed, and no traffic could get over the toll bridge. The menu offers favourites like scampi, crispy cod and vegetarian shepherd's pie. The bar serves seasonal and guest ales as well as Westons ciders. The beer festival in June is part of the Bloxfest Music Festival.

Open all week 10–3 6–12 (Fri 10–3 5–2am Sat 10am–2am Sun 10am–midnight) Hook Norton from £6 portions/menu

BRIGHTWELL BALDWIN

The Nelson PICK OF THE PUBS

Tel **01491 612497** | **OX49 5NP**
Web **www.thenelsonbrightwell.co.uk**
Dir ***Off B4009 between Watlington and Benson.***

As you approach The Nelson down the lane, look for the union flags flying patriotically outside. Its quiet position makes it a great getaway for a country walk before opening time. The interior is full of fresh flowers, and tables lit by candles in the evening are warmed by a splendid inglenook fireplace. In summer, the pretty terraced garden with its weeping willow is popular for alfresco eating and drinking. All food is freshly cooked, using local produce where possible – check out the dates of the annual crab and lobster festival. If refreshment is all that's required, ales from Rebellion Brewery, Marlow and around 20 wines served by the glass complete the drinks line-up.

Open 12–3 6–11 (Sun 12–4) Closed 25 Dec, Sun evening Free House 20 portions notice required

BRIGHTWELL-CUM-SOTWELL

The Red Lion

Tel **01491 837373** | **The Street, OX10 0RT**
Web **www.redlionbrightwell.co.uk**
Dir ***From A4130 (Didcot to Wallingford road) follow Brightwell-cum-Sotwell signs. Pub in village centre.***

This picture-postcard thatched and timbered 16th-century village pub is not only pretty but also a cracking community local. Behind the bar, beers come from the likes of West Berkshire, and Loddon breweries, while a choice of wine comes from the very local Brightwell Vineyard.

BROUGHTON

Saye and Sele Arms

Tel **01295 263348** | **Main Road, OX15 5ED**
Web **www.sayeandselearms.co.uk**
Dir ***From Banbury Cross take B4035 to Broughton. Approximately 3 miles.***

Sheltered by a spinney fringing the grounds buffering the extraordinary moated medieval Broughton Castle, this inn, parts of which date back 700 years, is named after the titled family who still call the manor home. Age-polished flagstones, wizened beams and gleaming brasses greet customers.

BURCOT

The Chequers

Tel **01865 407771** | **OX14 3DP**
Web **www.thechequers-burcot.co.uk**
Dir ***On A415 (Dorchester to Abingdon road) between Clifton Hampden and Dorchester.***

Once a staging post for boats on the Thames, this 400-year-old, thatched and timber-framed pub is run by chef-patron Steven Sanderson. Locals supply game during the winter months, and neighbours' gardens and allotments also yield their bounty. In the kitchen, Steven devises straightforward British classics for his seasonal menus, using carefully chosen meats along with, fish from Devon and Cornwall markets, mussels from the Norfolk coast, and oysters from Scotland and Jersey.

Open all year, all day 12–11 (Sun 12–8) Closed Mon Free House 10 from £15 portions/menu notice required

BURFORD

The Angel at Burford

 INN

Tel **01993 822714** | **14 Witney Street, OX18 4SN**
Web **www.theangelatburford.co.uk**
Dir ***Phone for detailed directions.***

This welcoming Hook Norton house continues to lure real ale drinkers with pints of perfectly kept Hooky, but it also draws the food crowd. The menu offers an all-day bar menu, including a charcuterie board, sandwiches and burgers, alongside the main carte.

The Highway Inn – see page 334

Inn for All Seasons PICK OF THE PUBS

Tel **01451 844324** | **Little Barrington, OX18 4TN**
Web **www.innforallseasons.com**
Dir ***3 miles west of Burford on A40.***

Almost 800 square miles of the Cotswolds Area of Outstanding Natural Beauty open up hard by this handsome, stone-built 16th-century pub. Like many old inns it started out somewhat differently, in this case as quarrymen's cottages, before the dawn of the coaching age offered new opportunities. Inside, find an abundance of oak beams, flagstone floors, big fireplaces, leather chairs and conversation-piece memorabilia. Given the inn's name, expect winter, spring etc menus, on which might appear, for example, pork and cranberry schnitzel, baked gnocchi, and Thai curry, and daily fish from Devon and Cornwall. Ten wines are available by the glass, with real ales from local-ish breweries, such as Wye Valley.

Open all day, all week Free House 10 from £11.95 portions

BURFORD

The Highway Inn

★★★★ INN

Tel **01993 823661 | 117 High Street, OX18 4RG**
Web **www.thehighwayinn.co.uk**
Dir ***From A40 onto A361.***

In the heart of pretty Burford, gateway to The Cotswolds

The essentials of modern hospitality have, over time, been introduced to Scott Williamson's 15th-century inn, but its historic character remains undiluted, with an abundance of dressed stone, bric-à-brac, cosy corners, winding corridors and open fires, lit every day between October and April. Tables out front on the High Street, and a secluded medieval courtyard garden with its own log fire provide additional dining and drinking spaces. The Duck & Pinot private cellar can be hired for celebrations and corporate entertaining. Beers on hand-pump come from Hook Norton and a guest brewery, and cider and lagers from Cotswold Brew Co. in Bourton-on-the-Water. High quality, seasonal dishes always include such pub classics as pie of the day, fish and chips and excellent steaks. Among the more refined dinner options are chorizo- and black pudding-stuffed pork tenderloin; gamekeepers' stew; and pearl barley and wild mushroom risotto. On the weekend lunch menu expect home-made steak and Guinness pie; scampi and chips; and Highway classic burger, with roasts on Sundays, of course. Coffee and Tia Maria pannacotta, and sticky date and toffee sponge are stalwarts of the dessert section. Bring the kids, the dog and the bikes.

Open all day, all week Mon to Sat 10am–11pm (Sun 12–11) Free House from £10 portions/menu notice required

The Lamb Inn

★★★ SMALL HOTEL PICK OF THE PUBS

Tel 01993 823155 | Sheep Street, OX18 4LR
Web www.cotswold-inns-hotels.co.uk/lamb
Dir *M40 junction 8, follow A40 and Burford signs, 1st turn, down hill into Sheep Street.*

In a tranquil side street in this attractive Cotswolds town, the 15th-century Lamb is a dyed-in-the-wool, all round award-winner. A welcoming atmosphere is generated by the bar's flagstone floor, log fire, cosy armchairs, gleaming copper, brass and silver. In fact, old-world charm and stylish interiors are a feature throughout. Take, for example, the elegant columns and mullioned windows of the courtyard-facing restaurant. An extensive cellar holds over 100 wines.

Open all day, all week Free House 16 portions/menu notice required

The Mermaid

Tel 01993 822193 | 78 High Street, OX18 4QF
Web www.themermaidburford.co.uk
Dir *In Burford from A40 roundabout onto A361 signed Chipping Norton. Pub in centre of High Street by pedestrian crossing.*

With a history dating back to the 14th century, an interior with character is only to be expected, and The Mermaid certainly does not disappoint. Part of the building once housed a bakery, and today the baker's fireplace still radiates a warmth to match the welcome extended to guests, their children and dogs. Add in the crooked beams, flagstone floors, a candle-lit first-floor restaurant, a choice of four real ales and quality home-cooked food, and it's no wonder the pub is popular. Gluten-free menus are available.

Open all day, all week Greene King 10 portions/menu notice required

BURFORD

The Maytime Inn

★★★★ INN

Tel 01993 822068 | Asthall, OX18 4HW
Web www.themaytime.com
Dir *Phone for detailed directions.*

Pleasing combination of traditional ambience and eclectic food

Dominic Wood (with help from Alfie the dog) heads up the young and passionate team in this 17th-century countryside pub that once had its own smithy. The church is worth a visit, and the manor often hosts public events. There's a large selection of over 100 gins, well-conditioned cask ales including Otter Ale and Paradigm Fake News, craft beers and ciders plus around 20 wines by the glass. The ambitious kitchen uses the finest, fresh, local ingredients to create mains such as kedgeree

with poached egg; and wild boar burger with skinny chips. If you are looking for something a touch more 'pub classic', there's also a daily pie with creamy mash, seasonal veg and gravy; or beer-battered haddock, hand-cut chips, tartare sauce and peas. Either way, you will want to leave room for one of the home-made desserts, which tick all the right boxes when it comes to comfort food.

Open all day, all week Free House 20 from £14 portions notice required

CAULCOTT

Horse & Groom

Tel 01869 343257 | Lower Heyford Road, OX25 4ND
Web www.horseandgroomcaulcott.co.uk
Dir *From Bicester on B4030, through Middleton Stoney. On left in Caulcott.*

A lovely, thatched coaching inn set in the heart of north Oxfordshire and well known for the Bastille Day beer festival held every July. It's a cosy, welcoming place, dating back to the 16th century, with Black Sheep Best bitter on tap and an interesting, seasonally-changing menu. There's a dedicated sausage menu, too – maybe try the gluten-free Creole Jazz; Toulouse garlic; or wild boar with cider and Calvados – all served with chips or mash and baked beans or peas.

Open 12–3 6–11 (Sun 12–3) Closed 25 Dec to 2 Jan (31 Dec closed daytime), Mon and Sun evening Free House from £12 portions

CHALGROVE

The Red Lion Inn PICK OF THE PUBS

Tel 01865 890625 | The High Street, OX44 7SS
Web www.redlionchalgrove.co.uk
Dir *B480 from Oxford ring road, through Stadhampton, left then right at mini-roundabout. At Chalgrove Airfield right into village.*

The medieval village of Chalgrove is tranquil these days but that wasn't the case in 1643 when Prince Rupert clashed with John Hampden's Parliamentarian forces during the first Civil War. The stream-side beer garden of this old inn overlooks the compact green at the heart of the village, where thatched cottages slumber not far from the church which is, unusually, the owner of the pub. In the bar, select from the great range of draught beers complementing the appealing menu. The choice may include roulade of smoked salmon with cream cheese and chives, an appetiser for lemon sole fillets 'simply grilled in a little butter', or slow-cooked pork belly with braised vegetables and roast gravy. Finish with sticky toffee pudding or warm treacle tart.

Open all week 11–3 6–12 (Fri to Sat 11–3 6–1am Sun all day) Free House 11 portions/menu notice required

CHARLBURY

The Bull Inn PICK OF THE PUBS

Tel 01608 810689 | Sheep Street, OX7 3RR
Web www.bullinn-charlbury.com
Dir *M40 junction 8, A40, A44 follow Woodstock/ Blenheim Palace signs. Through Woodstock take B4437 to Charlbury, pub at crossroads in town.*

Presiding over Charlbury's main street, this handsome, stone-fronted, 16th-century free house, is a conveniently short hop from Woodstock, Blenheim Palace and other attractions of the Cotswolds. Inside the decor is beautiful and refreshingly homely. Outside, their vine-covered terrace is a lovely backdrop for a drink or meal in summer. The bar offers Bull Bitter and weekly guest ales. The changing menu adapts to the seasons and what's available at the markets that week. That said, you can always rely on the infamous Bull burger, a pie of the week, fish and chips and other pub classics to always be available.

Open all day, all week Free House 14 menus

10 TOP OXFORDSHIRE PUBS WITH ACCOMMODATION

The following pubs are rated as part of the AA Guest Accommodation scheme (see page 10–11 for more information).

Old Swan ★★★★★ INN Witney, *see page 350*
The Angel at Burford ★★★★ INN Burford, *see page 333*
The Kingham Plough ★★★★ INN Kingham, *see page 342*
The Maytime Inn ★★★★ INN Burford, *see page 335*
The Swan Inn ★★★★ INN Swinbrook, *see page 348*
The Horse & Groom Inn ★★★★ INN Milcombe, *see page 344*
The Baskerville ★★★★ INN Lower Shiplake, *see page 343*
Bear and Ragged Staff ★★★★ INN Cumnor, *see page 338*
The Fat Fox Inn ★★★★ INN Watlington, *see page 349*
The Fox & Hounds ★★★★ INN Uffington, *see page 349*

CHASTLETON

The Greedy Goose

Tel 01608 646551 | Salford Hill, GL56 0SP
Web www.thegreedygoosemoreton.co.uk
Dir *From Chipping Norton towards Moreton-in-Marsh on A44, pub at crossroads junction with A436.*

With no immediate neighbours, The Greedy Goose looks lonely, but it knows how to attract customers. The interior, all intriguingly patterned walls, swathes of polished wood flooring, elegant striped-fabric chairs and much else point to the talents of an interior design pro.

CHECKENDON

The Highwayman

PICK OF THE PUBS

Tel 01491 682020 | Exlade Street, RG8 0UA
Web www.thehighwaymaninn-checkendon.co.uk
Dir *On A4074 (Reading to Wallingford road).*

The wooded hills of the Chilterns, criss-crossed by bridleways and footpaths, form a delightful backdrop to this attractive old building. Bare brick and beams predominate in the airy interior, interspersed by alcoves and warmed by log-burning stoves in this much updated 16th-century inn, where contented regulars sup beers from the nearby Loddon brewery. The eclectic menu is strong on locally sourced raw materials. The speciality here is pies; chicken, mushroom and bacon pie; or game pie may tempt as a follow-up to a starter of crispy calamari with lime, chilli and coriander. Alternatively try grilled sea bass, brown shrimps, market vegetables, and saffron potatoes and herb butter; or a steak from the Royal Windsor Estate.

Open 12–3 6–11 (Sun 12–6) Closed 25 Dec, Mon Free House 11 portions Wi-fi P notice required

CHINNOR

The Sir Charles Napier

PICK OF THE PUBS

Tel 01494 483011 | Spriggs Alley, OX39 4BX
Web www.sircharlesnapier.co.uk
Dir *M40 junction 6, B4009 to Chinnor. Right at roundabout to Spriggs Alley.*

Despite being tucked away down rural Oxfordshire lanes, this sublime flint-and-brick destination dining inn is just 10 minutes from the M40 and is definitely worth seeking out. Locally-felled timber fuels the fires in the bars, while hedgerow and field-sourced herbs, fungi, berries and game feature on the menus. You can eat inside, on the vine-covered terrace or under the cherry trees and watch red kites soaring overhead. Once you've negotiated the extensive wine list take a look at the blackboards and seasonally inspired menus. Look out for dishes such as saddle of venison, roast celeriac and blackberries; wild mushroom risotto and shaved ceps; and pork belly, creamed cabbage, pickled walnuts and apple.

Open 12–4 6–12 (Sun 12–6) Closed 25–26 Dec, Mon, Sun evening Free House 12 from £19.50 portions/menu Wi-fi P

CHURCH ENSTONE

The Crown Inn

PICK OF THE PUBS

Tel 01608 677262 | Mill Lane, OX7 4NN
Web www.crowninnenstone.co.uk
Dir *From A44 at Enstone (15 miles north of Oxford) onto B4030 signed Church Enstone.*

If log fires in an inglenook, traditional bar and beamed dining room sound like your type of pub then look no further. Similarly if you'd enjoy a pint of bitter or glass of Pinot Grigio in a secluded garden or terrace overlooking thatched, honey-coloured stone cottages, then this 17th-century inn will tick even more boxes. It also has a reputation for good food.

Open all week 12–3 6–11 (Sat 12–11 Sun 12–6) Closed 26 Dec and 1 Jan Free House 11 from £11 portions Wi-fi P

CUMNOR

Bear and Ragged Staff

★★★★ INN PICK OF THE PUBS

Tel **01865 862329** | **28 Appleton Road, OX2 9QH**
Web **www.bearandraggedstaff.com**
Dir ***A420 from Oxford, right onto B4017 signed Cumnor.***

In typically tranquil Oxfordshire countryside, this 16th-century, stone-built dining pub feels a world away from the busy Newbury and Swindon roads that pass just a mile away. The heart of the pub is Tudor, with ancient fireplaces, flagstone floors and mullioned windows with carved lintels all adding to the atmosphere. There's a comfortable conservatory and south-facing terrace, bedrooms are full of character, and the food has been awarded an AA Rosette.

Open all day, all week Mon to Thu 7am–11pm Fri to Sat 7am to midnight Sun 7.30am–10.30pm Closed 25 Dec Greene King 16 from £14 portions notice required

The Vine Inn

Tel **01865 862567** | **11 Abingdon Road, OX2 9QN**
Web **www.vineinncumnor.com**
Dir ***A420 from Oxford, right onto B4017.***

A vine does indeed clamber over the whitewashed frontage of this 18th-century village pub. In 1560, nearby Cumnor Place was the scene of the suspicious death of the wife of Lord Robert Dudley, favourite of Elizabeth I. There's a selection of rotating real ales in the bar, and a typical starter includes traditional ham hock terrine; and smoked haddock fishcake, followed by local sausages and mash; chilli con carne or one of the burger choices. Children love the huge garden.

Open all year 12–3 6–11 (Fri to Sun all day) Closed Mon Heineken Brewery 9 portions/menu notice required

DEDDINGTON

Deddington Arms PICK OF THE PUBS

Tel **01869 338364** | **Horsefair, OX15 0SH**
Web **www.deddington-arms-hotel.co.uk**
Dir ***M40 junction 11 to Banbury. Follow signs for hospital, then towards Adderbury and Deddington, on A4260.***

Overlooking Deddington's pretty market square, this striking 16th-century former coaching inn boasts a wealth of timbering, flagstone floors, numerous nooks and crannies, crackling winter log fires and sought-after window seats in the beamed bar. Here you can savour a glass of Hook Norton or Somersby cider while perusing the menu. Eat in the bar or head for the elegant dining room. The cheese selection tempts with notable products from around the UK.

DORCHESTER-ON-THAMES

The George PICK OF THE PUBS

Tel **01865 340404** | **25 High Street, OX10 7HH**
Web **www.georgehoteloxfordshire.co.uk**
Dir ***From M40 junction 7, A329 south to A4074 at Shillingford. Follow Dorchester signs. From M4 junction 13, A34 to Abingdon then A415 east to Dorchester.***

The 15th-century George stands on the picturesque high street. Believed to be one of the country's oldest coaching inns, it has been a haven for many an aristocrat. Oak beams and inglenook fireplaces characterise the interior, while the restaurant offers a secret garden with a waterfall. The Potboys Bar, named after the Abbey bell-ringers, is a traditional taproom serving beer from one of the six breweries that make up The George's roll of honour.

Open all day, all week 7am–midnight Chapmans Group from £12.50 portions/menu

DUNS TEW

The White Horse

Tel **01869 340272 | OX25 6JS**
Web **www.dunstewwhitehorse.co.uk**
Dir ***Take A4260 from Banbury towards Adderbury. Right signed Duns Tew. Pub on left in village. Or from M40 junction 10, A43, B430 to Ardley. Right signed Somerton. Through Somerton and North Aston to crossroads. Straight across signed Duns Tew.***

A beautiful Cotswold stone pub, dating from the 17th century and full of wonderful period features – panelling, beams and open fires. Newly refurbished with love and care, The White Horse is welcoming and friendly. You'll find three real ales and top-quality British produce.

EAST HENDRED

Eyston Arms

Tel **01235 833320 | High Street, OX12 8JY**
Web **www.eystonarms.co.uk**
Dir ***Just off A417 (Wantage to Reading road).***

Owned, appropriately, by the Eyston family, who have lived in the village since 1443, this old inn stands just north of The Ridgeway. The pub greets its customers with a huge log fire, flagstone floor, simple polished tables, leather chairs and cartoons of its regulars. The bar stocks real ales from Wadworth and Hook Norton. Chef Maria Jaremchuk's ever-changing menus may feature a massaman vegetarian curry; and beef and venison burgers, while carefully cultivated contacts with south coast fishermen mean excellent fish specials.

Open all day, all week 11–3 6–11 (Fri to Sat 11–11 Sun 11–9) Free House 20 from £15.50 portions Wi-fi P

FARINGDON

The Lamb at Buckland

PICK OF THE PUBS

Tel **01367 870484 | Lamb Lane, Buckland, SN7 8QN**
Web **www.lambatbuckland.com**
Dir ***Just off A420, 3 miles east of Faringdon.***

So often the word 'Cotswold' prefixes 'stone', but today it can also appear on the labels of the gin, vodka and lager available at the 17th-century Lamb, because they're all made in nearby Bourton-on-the-Water. Local produce is paramount; not just in terms of the drinks, but also the real ales, the game shot by a pub regular, and the many vegetables grown in the kitchen garden. Typical dishes include butternut squash and sage arancini with rocket and parmesan salsa; gin-cured salmon with fennel and lemon salad; and whole oven-roasted West Country partridge, served carved with rösti potato, leek gratin with pancetta and rosemary crumble. Among the desserts are chocolate and peanut butter iced parfait with chocolate sauce; and poached pineapple Eton mess. Steak Night is every Wednesday.

Open all year all week 11.30–3 6–11 Closed Sun evening, Mon Free House 12 portions Wi-fi P

The Trout Inn **PICK OF THE PUBS**

Tel **01367 870382 | Buckland Marsh, SN7 8RF**
Web **www.troutinn.co.uk**
Dir ***A415 from Abingdon signed Marcham, through Frilford to Kingston Bagpuize. Left onto A420. 5 miles, right signed Tadpole Bridge. Or M4 (eastbound) junction 15, A419 towards Cirencester. 4 miles, onto A420 towards Oxford. 10 miles, left signed Tadpole Bridge.***

The Trout is inevitably popular with boaters, and walkers from the Thames Path that runs along the bank opposite the pub's garden, a pleasant space clearly intended for those nursing a pint of locally brewed Abingdon Bridge, Ramsbury Bitter or Wayland Smithy, or a chilled Pinot Grigio. Maintaining the menu requires fish and seafood to arrive daily from Cornwall, game from area shoots, and fruit, herbs and vegetables from local growers.

FILKINS

The Five Alls **PICK OF THE PUBS**

Tel **01367 860875 | GL7 3JQ**
Web **www.thefiveallsfilkins.co.uk**
Dir ***Between Lechlade and Burford, just off A361.***

The Five Alls, in picture-postcard Filkins, oozes warmth and style, with rugs on stone floors, flickering candles on old dining tables, and a leather chesterfield fronting the log fire – the perfect spot to relax with a pint and the papers. The bar bustles with locals, walkers and cyclists tucking into proper bar snacks, while the concise modern British menu, bursting with quality, locally sourced ingredients, draws diners from far and wide across the Cotswolds.

FRINGFORD

The Butchers Arms

Tel **01869 277363 | OX27 8EB**
Dir ***4 miles from Bicester on A4421 towards Buckingham.***

Flora Jane Thompson, author of Lark Rise to Candleford, was born at Juniper Hill, a couple of miles from this pretty, creeper-covered pub, and her first job was in the Post Office in Fringford. Handpumps dispense Doom Bar, Hooky and Black Sheep, while the chalkboard menus offer a good traditional selection including home-made pies; liver, bacon and onions; king prawns; and mussels. There's a senior citizens lunch offer six days a week. You can watch the cricket from the patio and there's a June beer festival.

Open all day, all week Punch Taverns from £10 portions/menu Wi-fi P notice required

FYFIELD

The White Hart

PICK OF THE PUBS

Tel **01865 390585 | Main Road, OX13 5LW**
Web **www.whitehart-fyfield.com**
Dir ***7 miles south Oxford, just off A420 (Oxford to Swindon road).***

This 500-year-old chantry house is steeped in history and has been a pub since 1580 when St John's College in Oxford leased it to tenants but reserved the right to 'occupy it if driven from Oxford by pestilence' – this has never been invoked! The building is breathtaking and boasts a grand hall with a 15th-century arch-braced roof, original oak beams, flagstone floors, and huge stone-flanked windows. A splendid 30ft-high minstrels' gallery overlooks the restauran, where menus might feature roast rump of Cotswold lamb with crispy sweetbreads, smoked celeriac, and Appleton wild garlic.

Open 12–3 5–11(Sat 12–11 Sun 12–10.30) Closed Mon (excluding bank holidays Free House 14 portions/menu Wi-fi P notice required

GORING

The Miller of Mansfield

Tel **01491 872829 | High Street, RG8 9AW**
Web **www.millerofmansfield.com**
Dir ***From Pangbourne take A329 to Streatley. Right on B4009, 0.5 mile to Goring.***

A beautiful focal point for the village

PICK OF THE PUBS

It may date from the 18th century, but Nick and Mary Galer have transformed The Miller of Mansfield into a thoroughly modern inn. Enjoying a prime spot in upmarket Goring, this former coaching inn's location on the Oxfordshire/Berkshire border makes it an ideal pitstop for exploring the rolling Chilterns countryside. A typical dinner might begin with fallow deer tartare with sourdough, button mushrooms and horseradish followed by local partridge, sprout tops, ceps, chestnut purée and stout sauce. Local ales like Hook Norton Old Hooky, English wines and an extensive gin list befit the modern take on Georgian inn life.

Open all day, all week Closed 27–29 Dec Enterprise Inns 14 from £17 portions/menu notice required

GREAT TEW

The Falkland Arms PICK OF THE PUBS

Tel **01608 683653** | **OX7 4DB**
Web **www.falklandarms.co.uk**
Dir ***Off A361, 1.25 miles, signed Great Tew.***

Named after Lucius Carey, 2nd Viscount Falkland, who inherited the manor of Great Tew in 1629, this venerable creeper-clad inn has wooden floors, exposed beams, high-backed settles, low stools and an inglenook fireplace, and the Wadworth ales vary from the well-known such as 6X, to various seasonal brews. The menu mixes modern with traditional, and attention is paid to the provenance of ingredients. Small plates include faggots and mashed potatoes with onion gravy. The butcher's board presents pork pie, chicken liver pâté, honey-roast ham, Scotch egg, chutney and rustic bread. Expect to find poached salmon or pan-seared chicken breast among the main courses. Finish with bread and butter pudding.

Open all day, all week 12–11 Wadworth 35 from £11 portions notice required

HAMPTON POYLE

The Bell PICK OF THE PUBS

Tel **01865 376242** | **OX5 2QD**
Web **www.thebelloxford.co.uk**
Dir ***From north: exit A34 signed Kidlington, over bridge. At mini-roundabout turn right, left to Hampton Poyle (before slip road to rejoin A34). From Kidlington: at roundabout (junction of A4260 and A4165) take Bicester Road (Sainsbury's on left) towards A34. Left to Hampton Poyle.***

A centuries-old inn conveniently sited for Oxford, Bicester Village shopping outlet and Blenheim Palace. The charms of its oak beams and time-worn flagstone floors are complemented by the dining area with an open kitchen featuring an eye-catching wood-burning oven that produces rustic pizzas and other dishes. These, along with burgers and salads, are served in the bar at any time. There are plenty of other dishes to choose from including hot smoked salmon with pickled samphire; and roasted beetroot risotto. Finish with passionfruit meringue pie. Should you have a well-behaved dog, they're welcome to join you in the bar or out on the delightful south-facing terrace.

Open all day, all week 7am–11pm Free House 30 from £11.25 portions notice required

HARWELL

The Hart of Harwell

Tel **01235 834511** | **High Street, OX11 0EH**
Web **www.thehartofharwell.com**
Dir ***In village centre, accessed from A417 and A4130.***

Several old wells were found during renovations of this 15th to 16th-century pub – one now serves as a dining table which byou can peer down while eating. The bar's stable of Greene King real ales is supplemented by regularly-changing guests.

HENLEY-ON-THAMES

The Cherry Tree Inn

PICK OF THE PUBS

Tel **01491 680430** | **Stoke Row, RG9 5QA**
Web **www.thecherrytreeinn.co.uk**
Dir ***B481 towards Reading and Sonning Common 2 miles, follow Stoke Row sign.***

Located at one of the highest points in the Chilterns, the inn was originally three brick-and-flint cottages dating back to the 18th century. Modern, comfortable furnishings blend effortlessly with original flagstone floors, beamed ceilings and fireplaces. Brakspear's Bitter and seasonal ales are on draught in the bar where there is also a good range of gins and wines by the glass. Start with the game terrine, followed by chicken and chorizo tagliatelle, mushrooms, peas and cream sauce.

Open all day, all week Brakspear 14 from £12.95 portions/menu notice required

The Little Angel

Tel **01491 411008** | **Remenham Lane, RG9 2LS**
Web **www.thelittleangel.co.uk**
Dir ***M4 junctions 8/9, A404, A4130 to Henley, then towards Maidenhead. Pub on left.***

This large pub, just over the famous bridge from the town, underwent a major refurbishment in 2019, and gets pretty packed, especially at weekends. Brakspear ales are backed up with an exceptional modern menu. Try sautéed tiger prawns, harissa and garlic butter followed by roasted lamb rump, beetroot fondant, baby carrots, shallot purée and port sauce. Sundays are 'unbelievably busy' so booking is essential.

Open all day, all week 11–11 (Fri to Sat 11am to midnight Sun 12–10) Brakspear 11 from £10 portions/menu notice required

The Three Tuns

Tel **01491 410138** | **5 The Market Place, RG9 2AA**
Web **www.thethreetunshenley.com**
Dir ***In town centre. Parking nearby.***

Successfully run by Mark and Sandra Duggan, The Three Tuns is one of the oldest pubs in town and a bustling drinking and dining spot. The cosy, matchboarded front bar has scrubbed tables, an open fire and Brakspear Brewery prints from a bygone era.

The White Hart PICK OF THE PUBS

Tel **01491 641245** | **High Street, Nettlebed, RG9 5DD**
Web **www.tmdining.co.uk**
Dir ***On A4130 between Henley-on-Thames and Wallingford.***

Royalist and parliamentary soldiers frequently lodged in taverns during the English Civil War; this 15th-century inn reputedly billeted troops loyal to the King. During the 17th and 18th centuries the area was plagued by highwaymen. Today, the beautifully restored property is favoured by a stylish crowd who appreciate the chic bar and restaurant. Heading the beer list is locally-brewed Brakspear, backed by popular internationals. Food comprises typically English dishes interspersed with South African offerings.

HETHE

The Muddy Duck PICK OF THE PUBS

Tel **01869 278099** | **Main Street, OX27 8ES**
Web **www.themuddyduckpub.co.uk**
Dir ***From Bicester towards Buckingham on A4421 left signed Fringford. Through Fringford, right signed Hethe, left signed Hethe.***

The stone-built Muddy Duck is a sympathetic combination of old and new; it's family-owned and run by a close-knit team who are reassuringly big on friendly, efficient service. Real ales are likely to include old favourites Hooky, Landlord and Tribute, and the pub is a lively, welcoming place to enjoy a pint by the open fire, along with nibbles such as sweet and salty pork crackling sticks. For more of a dining experience, take a reassuring peek through the kitchen viewing window before checking out the menu.

Open all week 11–11 Free House 12 from £14 portions Wi-fi P

HIGHMOOR

Rising Sun

Tel **01491 640856** | **Witheridge Hill, RG9 5PF**
Web **www.risingsunwitheridgehill.com**
Dir ***From Henley-on-Thames take A4130 towards Wallingford. Take B481, turn right to Highmoor.***

Next to the green in a Chilterns' hamlet, you approach this 17th-century pub through the garden. Inside, you'll find richly coloured walls, low-beamed ceilings and open fires. Chalkboards tell you which guest ales are accompanying Brakspear Bitter, or Westons Wyld Wood Organic.

KINGHAM

The Kingham Plough

★★★★ INN PICK OF THE PUBS

Tel **01608 658327** | **The Green, OX7 6YD**
Web **www.thekinghamplough.co.uk**
Dir ***B4450 from Chipping Norton to Churchill. 2nd right to Kingham, left at T-junction. Pub on right.***

Set on the village green, The Kingham Plough is the epitome of the idyllic English inn. The bar area hosts two open fires and serves an enticing menu offering home-made bar food such as garlic snails and wild mushrooms on chargrilled sourdough, and local ales from the likes of North Cotswold brewery. Upstairs, in the refurbished dining room, the menu showcases the very best local ingredients in dishes such as a venison loin and venison boudin noir, beetroot and spelt risotto or, in summer, confit sea trout with smoked trout Scotch quail egg, cucumber, samphire and oyster mayonnaise.

Open all day, all week Closed 25 Dec Free House from £20 portions/menu Wi-fi P

The Wild Rabbit 

RESTAURANT WITH ROOMS

PICK OF THE PUBS

Tel **01608 658389** | **Church Street, OX7 6YA**
Web **www.thewildrabbit.co.uk**
Dir ***In centre of village.***

From the family behind nearby Daylesford Organic, The Wild Rabbit has already been dubbed 'the poshest pub in Britain' due to its A-list celebrity customers. The 18th-century Cotswold inn has stripped back walls, open fires and simple handcrafted furniture. Local Hook Norton is one of seven beers on tap, and the impeccably sourced wine list displays more than a dozen served by the glass. Three AA Rosettes have been awarded for the seasonal menu which features Daylesford's organic produce. Kick off with Scottish mackerel with heritage beetroot and English wasabi; followed by roast cauliflower with couscous; or Wootton Estate venison.

Open all day, all week Closed 1st week Jan Free House 17 from £22.50 portions/menu

KIRTLINGTON

The Oxford Arms

Tel **01869 350208** | **Troy Lane, OX5 3HA**
Web **www.oxford-arms.co.uk**
Dir ***Take either A34 or A44 north from Oxford, follow Kirtlington signs.***

Dating from 1862, this attractive dining pub prides itself on providing a warm welcome. In summer, head to the patio for alfresco dining near the kitchen garden that produces herbs, salad leaves and soft fruits. Inside, freshly-cut flowers and church candles on the tables adds a rustic touch. Everything in the kitchen is made from scratch from local produce. Two worthy dishes are pork pie with spiced apple chutney; and loin of pork with chickpeas, chorizo and tomato.

Open 12–2 6.30–9 Closed 25 Dec evening, 26 Dec, Bank Holiday Mon evening, Wed, Sun evening Heineken 13

LONG HANBOROUGH

The George & Dragon

Tel **01993 881362** | **133 Main Road, OX29 8JX**
Web **www.thegeorgeanddragonwitney.co.uk**
Dir ***On A4095 between Woodstock and Witney.***

A thatched and beamed 17th-century Cotswold stone pub with plenty of traditional charm and a lovely enclosed garden. Well-kept real ales like Eagle IPA are accompanied by 'British tapas' snacks – smoky bacon Scotch egg or home-made steak and mushroom pie. Finish with chocolate and orange pudding with salted caramel ice cream. There's also a gluten-free menu, plenty of vegetarian options and Thursday is pie night.

Open all day, all week Closed 25 Dec Charles Wells 12 portions/menu notice required

LOWER SHIPLAKE

The Baskerville

★★★★ INN

Tel **0118 940 3332** | **Station Road, RG9 3NY**
Web **www.thebaskerville.com**
Dir ***Just off A4155, 1.5 miles from Henley-on-Thames towards Reading, follow signs at War Memorial junction.***

Relaxed pub in Thames-side village

This family-run, traditional village inn on the Thames Path is just two minutes from the river itself. The dog-friendly bar is adorned with sporting memorabilia and home to four real ales from the nearby Loddon and Rebellion breweries. Food-wise, the cuisine is modern British and European with a menu that evolves with the seasons using fresh, locally sourced produce. With everything cooked to order, the

restaurant is very busy, so booking is advisable. Lunch and evening menus include three pub classics and at lunch open sandwiches and lighter bites are on offer. Also available are bar snacks (not Sundays) and a childrens' menu ,and they happily cater for vegetarians and vegans. The wine list extends to over 70 bins; there are over 50 malt whiskies and 10 gins.

Open all day, all week 11–11 (Sun 12–10.30) Closed 1 Jan Free House 13 from £15 portions/menu

MARSH BALDON

Seven Stars

Tel **01865 343337** | **The Green, OX44 9LP**
Web **www.sevenstarsonthegreen.co.uk**
Dir ***From Oxford ring road onto A4074 signed Wallingford. Through Nuneham Courtenay. Left, follow Marsh Baldon signs.***

After several closures, the exasperated Marsh Baldon residents dug deep into their pockets and bought the historic 350-year-old pub on the pretty village green. Today, the Seven Stars has a smart interior, local ales on tap and a modern pub menu offering a good range of dishes prepared from fresh local ingredients. For summer, there's a gorgeous garden and a beer festival. The area has several interesting walks and Oxford Arboretum is a five-minute stroll away.

Open all day, all week Free House 9 from £8 portions/menu notice required

MIDDLETON STONEY

The Jersey Arms

Tel **01869 343234** | **OX25 4AD**
Web **www.jerseyarms.com**
Dir ***M4 junction 9 or 10, A34 onto B340.***

Just three minutes from the Bicester Village shopping outlet and 10 minutes from Oxford itself, The Jersey Arms is a perfect spot for refreshments after grabbing a few bargains or sightseeing in the university city. The kitchen offers a seasonal menu of hearty dishes which changes throughout the week, from classic pub grub to a board of daily chef's specials. Wash it down with one of the real ales on offer.

Open all day, all week Free House portions/menu

MILCOMBE

The Horse & Groom Inn

★★★★ INN

Tel **01295 722142** | **OX15 4RS**
Web **www.thehorseandgroominn.co.uk**
Dir ***From A361 between Chipping Norton and Bloxham follow Milcombe signs. Pub at end of village.***

The 17th-century Horse & Groom still has many traditional elements such as stone floors, a wood-burning stove and delightful snug area, but is very much in the 21st century otherwise. The contemporary dining room offers daily-changing menus that are bursting with dishes created from local produce. Start off with chicken liver pâté, followed by a steak; Thai red chicken and pepper curry; or cripsy chilli pork. Vegetarians have some interesting choices too – beer-battered haloumi; or Thai red sweet potato, red pepper and spinach curry.

Open 12–3 6–11 (Sun 12–5) Closed 25 Dec evening and 26 Dec, Sun evening Punch Taverns 11 from £12.50 portions/menu notice required

MILTON

The Plum Pudding

Tel **01235 834443** | **44 High Street, OX14 4EJ**
Web **www.theplumpuddingmilton.co.uk**
Dir ***From A34 (Milton Interchange) follow Milton signs. 1st left (signed Milton) into High Street.***

The name 'Plum Pudding' derives from the nickname of the Oxford Sandy and Black pig, one of the oldest British breeds and bred in this area. The dog-friendly bar of this pub stocks local and regional ales such as Loose Cannon, and the Plum Pudding's pork specialities may include gammon steak, fried free-range egg, fresh pineapple and chips, and different varieties of specially-made sausages. Alternatives such as filled baguettes and sandwiches, home-made beefburger, aged steaks, and beer-battered cod and chips appear on the menu.

Open all week 11.30–2.30 5–11 (Fri to Sun all day) Free House portions notice required

MURCOTT

The Nut Tree Inn

PICK OF THE PUBS

Tel **01865 331253** | **Main Street, OX5 2RE**
Web **www.nuttreeinn.co.uk**
Dir ***M40 junction 9, A34 towards Oxford. Left onto B4027 signed Islip. At Red Lion turn left. Right signed Murcott, Fencott and Charlton-on-Otmoor. Pub on right in village.***

Local lad Mike North grew up dreaming of owning this thatched 15th-century free house overlooking the pond. Some 10 years ago his dream came true, and the oak beams, wood-burners and unusual carvings are the setting for a range of ales. Mike and his team have built an enviable destination dining reputation for their food. A typical menu promises parfait of Cotswold chicken livers with Nut Tree garden apple compôte, followed by crown roasted breast of partridge, leg meat 'pastilla', seared foie gras and Crozier Blue cheese; pear and walnut gâteau ends an excellent meal.

Open all year, all day Closed Sun evening Free House 16 portions notice required

NORTH HINKSEY VILLAGE

The Fishes

Tel **01865 249796** | **OX2 0NA**
Web **www.fishesoxford.co.uk**
Dir ***From A34 southbound (dual carriageway) left at junction after Botley Interchange, signed North Hinksey and Oxford Rugby Club. From A34 northbound exit at Botley Interchange and return to A34 southbound, then follow as above.***

A short walk from Oxford city centre, this attractive tile-hung pub stands in three acres of tranquil wooded grounds running down to Seacourt Stream, with a decking area, an outdoor tipi and a large garden. Providing plenty of shade, these grounds are ideal for barbecues and picnics.

NORTHMOOR

The Red Lion PICK OF THE PUBS

Tel **01865 300301** | **OX29 5SX**
Web **www.theredlionnorthmoor.com**
Dir ***A420 from Oxford. At 2nd roundabout take 3rd exit onto A415. Right after lights into Moreton Lane. At end turn right, pub on right.***

A pretty 17th-century pub in the middle of the village, going from strength to strength under the watchful eye of experienced publicans Ian and Lisa Neale, who have transformed the pub's land into a productive kitchen garden. The tempting modern menus might offer Densham's pork and sage sausages, mash potato, honey-roasted carrots, gravy; fillet of brill, girolle mushrooms, sweetcorn purée, grilled potatoes and pancetta; or The Red Lion burger with chunky chips.

Open all year 11–3 5.30–11 (Sat 11–11 Sun 12–6) Closed Mon Free House 11 from £10.50 portions/menu notice required

OXFORD

The Magdalen Arms

Tel **01865 243159** | **243 Iffley Road, OX4 1SJ**
Web **www.magdalenarms.co.uk**
Dir ***On corner of Iffley Road and Magdalen Road.***

Just a short stroll from Oxford city centre, this bustling food pub is run by the same team as Waterloo's hugely influential Anchor & Hope gastro pub. There is a similar boho feel to the place with its dark red walls, vintage furniture and the nose-to-tail menu. Expect the likes of twice-baked goats' cheese soufflé; Hereford steak and ale suet crust pie; and marmalade Bakewell tart and vanilla ice cream. Real ales are complemented by a vibrant modern wine list.

Open all day Closed 24–27 Dec, 1 Jan, Mon lunch Star Pubs & Bars 16 from £10 portions/menu notice required

The Old Bookbinders Ale House

Tel **01865 553549** | **17–18 Victor Street, Jericho, OX2 6BT**
Web **oldbookbinders.co.uk**
Dir ***From St Giles into Beaumont Street. At lights right into Walton Street. 6th left into Cranham Street. At end left into Canal Street, pub on left.***

Built in 1869 for workers from Oxford University Press, 'The Bookies' featured in the first episode of *Inspector Morse*, and more recently in The Hairy Bikers' *Pubs That Built Britain* series. Its quirky decoration includes a train set on the ceiling and a barrel of 'help-yourself' monkey nuts. The menu offers snails in garlic butter; seared sea bass with French beans and crushed new potatoes; and a range of sweet and savoury crêpes.

Open all day, all week 12–11 Greene King 10 from £10.50 portions notice required

The Punter

Tel **01865 248832 | 7 South Street, Osney Island, OX2 0BE**
Web **www.thepunteroxford.co.uk**
Dir ***Phone for detailed directions.***

If feeling famished on your tour of Oxford, then seek out this rustically-cool pub on Osney Island in the heart of the city – it enjoys a magnificent and very tranquil spot beside the river. The decor is eclectic and interesting, with much to catch the eye, from rugs on flagstone floors and mismatched tables and chairs to bold artwork on the whitewashed walls. Come for a relaxing pint of Punter Ale or refuel on something tempting from the daily menu.

Open all day, all week *Greene King* *12* *portions* Wi-fi

The Rickety Press

Tel **01865 424581 | 67 Cranham Street, OX2 6DE**
Web **www.thericketypress.com**
Dir ***Phone for detailed directions.***

The Rickety Press is run by the same three old school friends as The Rusty Bicycle in east Oxford. Deceptively spacious, there's a large conservatory restaurant, a snug and a bar serving Arkell's real ales, handpicked wines, coffees and teas.

The Rusty Bicycle

Tel **01865 435298 | 28 Magdalen Road, OX4 1RB**
Web **www.therustybicycle.com**
Dir ***From Oxford ring road (A4142) take A4158 (Iffley Road) towards city centre. Right into Magdalen Road.***

You can't miss the hanging sign – look for a 1950s grocer's bike swinging high above Magdalen Road's pavement. Inside is decidedly eccentric and Edwardian. This is a community pub in a very cosmopolitan part of the city, with the ambition of catering for all-comers.

Turf Tavern

Tel **01865 243235 | 4 Bath Place, off Holywell Street, OX1 3SU**
Web **www.greeneking-pubs.co.uk/pubs/oxfordshire/turf-tavern**
Dir ***Phone for detailed directions.***

This jewel of a pub is not easy to find, through hidden alleyways, which adds to its allure. Previously called the Spotted Cow, it became the Turf in 1842, probably in deference to its gambling clientele; it has also had brushes with literature, film and politics. Craft beers from Beavertown and a wide selection of gins complement the seasonal menus.

PISHILL

The Crown Inn PICK OF THE PUBS

Tel **01491 638364 | RG9 6HH**
Web **www.thecrowninnpishill.co.uk**
Dir ***A4130 from Henley-on-Thames, right onto B480 to Pishill.***

A pretty 15th-century coaching inn, The Crown began life in medieval times, serving ale to the thriving monastic community, then providing refuge to Catholic priests escaping Henry VIII's tyrannical rule. The bar is supplied by mostly local breweries, typically Brakspear. Lunch and dinner are served from Wednesdays through to Sunday lunchtime and may be enjoyed inside, where there are three log fires, or in the picturesque garden overlooking the valley.

RAMSDEN

The Royal Oak PICK OF THE PUBS

Tel **01993 868213 | High Street, OX7 3AU**
Dir ***B4022 from Witney towards Charlbury, right before Hailey, through Poffley End.***

Built of Cotswold stone and facing Ramsden's fine parish church, this former 17th-century coaching inn is a popular refuelling stop for walkers exploring nearby Wychwood Forest and visitors touring the pretty villages and visiting Blenheim Palace. Whether you are walking or not, the cosy inn oozes traditional charm and character, with its beams, warm fires and stone walls, and landlords provide a very warm welcome. A free house, it dispenses beers sourced from local breweries.

SHILTON

Rose & Crown

Tel **01993 842280** | **OX18 4AB**
Web **www.shiltonroseandcrown.com**
Dir ***From A40 at Burford take A361 towards Lechlade on Thames. Right, follow Shilton signs on left. Or from A40 east of Burford take B4020 towards Carterton.***

A traditional Cotswold-stone inn dating back to the 17th century, whose two rooms retain their original beams and are warmed by a wood-burner and an open log fire. In the bar, Hook Norton Old Hooky might well partner Young's Bitter and Ashton Press cider. As their pedigrees might lead you to expect, chef-landlord Martin Coldicott and head chef Mike Evans, prepare above average, but simply presented food. You may eat and drink in the garden if the weather's nice. Children are permitted at lunch.

Open all week 11.30–3 6–10 (Sat 11.30–10 Sun and bank holidays 11.30–9) Free House 10 from £11 portions Wi-fi

SHIPTON-UNDER-WYCHWOOD

The Shaven Crown Hotel

Tel **01993 830500** | **High Street, OX7 6BA**
Web **www.theshavencrown.co.uk**
Dir ***On A361, halfway between Burford and Chipping Norton.***

This 14th-century coaching inn was built by the monks of Bruern Abbey as a hospice for the poor. Elizabeth I used it as a hunting lodge before giving it to the village in 1580. Light meals are served in the bar, while the restaurant offers modern English dishes.

SOUTH STOKE

Perch & Pike

Tel **0141 872415** | **The Street, RG8 0JS**
Web **www.perchandpike.co.uk**
Dir ***Phone for detailed directions.***

South Stoke is a pretty village, home to this lovely 17th-century flintstone inn. There are beams and flagstone floors in the bar, with log fires on cold days and a fine selection of real ales, including Brakspear Bitter and Ringwood Boondoggle. You can eat outside in the garden on sunny days, or in the stylish converted barn whatever the weather. At lunchtime there's wraps, sandwiches and jacket potatoes, while in the evening you could share a charcuterie platter then enjoy fish and chips or home-made steak and ale pie.

Open all week 11.30–3 5–11 (Sat 11.30–11 Sun 11.30–close) Brakspear 20 portions/menu Wi-fi notice required

STANFORD IN THE VALE

The Horse & Jockey

Tel **01367 710302** | **25 Faringdon Road, SN7 8NN**
Web **www.horseandjockey.org**
Dir ***On A417 between Faringdon and Wantage.***

A wealth of exposed stone, leather-clad armchairs, and dark wood dining furniture characterise the interior of this stylish 16th-century inn. Children and dogs are made as welcome as their parents, and with a range of pizzas on the menu kids are unlikely to leave hungry.

STEEPLE ASTON

The Red Lion

Tel **01869 340225** | **South Side, OX25 4RY**
Web **www.redlionsteepleaston.co.uk**
Dir ***0.5 mile off A4260 (Oxford Road). Follow brown tourist signs for pub.***

In an elevated position in the village, this Hook Norton brewery pub offers a number of options: in front of the fire in the bar; in the comfortably furnished, oak-beamed Garden Room; or head for the pretty suntrap terrace, not least for its view of the delightful Cherwell Valley. In addition to generous Sunday roasts, other dishes include thin-crust, stone-baked pizzas; Aberdeen Angus burgers; steaks; light lunches, and sandwiches. Children and dogs are welcome.

Open all week 12–3 5.30–11 (Sat 12–11 Sun 12–5) Hook Norton 11 portions Wi-fi notice required

STOKE ROW

Crooked Billet PICK OF THE PUBS

Tel **01491 681048** | **RG9 5PU**
Web **www.thecrookedbillet.co.uk**
Dir ***From Henley towards Oxford on A4130. Left at Nettlebed for Stoke Row.***

Down a narrow, winding lane, lined with beech and oak trees, this mid 17th-century pub was one of notorious highwayman Dick Turpin's hideouts. Many of its finest features are unchanged, including the low beams, tiled floors, open fires and the absence of a bar – beer is drawn directly from casks in the cellar. Local produce and organic fare are the kitchen's mainstays, with set lunches typified by seared Cornish sardines, tomato and anchovy salsa, samphire and green herb oil; slow-roast local Saddleback pork belly, creamed mash potato, pickled red cabbage, broccoli and jus; and lemon tart, raspberry coulis and cream.

Open all week 12–3 7–12 (Sat to Sun 12–12)
Brakspear 10 portions

STONESFIELD

The White Horse

Tel **01993 891063** | **The Ridings, OX29 8EA**
Web **www.whitehorsestonesfield.com**
Dir ***From Oxford take A44 towards Chipping Norton. After Woodstock left signed Charlbury. Through Stonesfield to T-junction, pub opposite.***

Originally built as two mine-workers' cottages, this Cotswold-stone free house dates back to the 19th century and is situated in the village of Stonesfield, handy for exploring Woodstock, Blenheim Palace, and Oxford. The atmosphere is warm and welcoming at this family and dog-friendly, contemporary country pub.

SWERFORD

The Boxing Hare

Tel **01608 683212** | **Banbury Road, OX7 4AP**
Web **www.theboxinghare.co.uk**
Dir ***Between Banbury and Chipping Norton on A361.***

Known as The Masons Arms until Antony and Stacey took over in 2017, this fine old pub is a real dining destination, offering dishes like roast rump of Cotswold lamb with dauphinoise potatoes; or butter-poached haddock with spinach, mash and a poached egg.

SWINBROOK

The Swan Inn ★★★★  INN

PICK OF THE PUBS

Tel **01993 823339** | **OX18 4DY**
Web **www.theswanswinbrook.co.uk**
Dir ***A40 towards Cheltenham, left to Swinbrook.***

The Swan is the perfect English country pub – it stands by the River Windrush near the cricket pitch in the idyllic village of Swinbrook, overlooking unspoilt Cotswold countryside. It gets even better inside: the two cottage-style front rooms, replete with worn flagstones, crackling log fires, low beams and country furnishings, lead through to a cracking bar and classy conservatory extension. First-class pub food includes main courses of pork belly, potato and sage rösti, celeriac, red cabbage and apple gel; and cider battered haddock, mushy peas, chips and tartare-sauce. You won't want to leave, so book one of the stunning en suite rooms in the restored barn.

Open all day, all week 11–11 Closed 25 Dec
Free House 9 portions Wi-fi

TETSWORTH

The Old Red Lion

Tel **01844 281274** | **40 High Street, OX9 7AS**
Web **www.theoldredliontetsworth.co.uk**
Dir ***From Oxford ring road at Headington take A40. Follow A418 signs (over M40). Right onto A40 signed Milton Common and Tetsworth.***

An airy, contemporary pub with traditional flourishes, ideal for day trippers heading for the nearby Chilterns. Birdwatchers seeking red kites can stop by, whilst cricketers on the adjacent village green pitch can call from mid-morning onwards. Not content with two restaurant areas and a bustling bar to run, the owners also host a village shop here. Beers from local microbreweries hit the spot, whilst timeless pub grub meals like sausage and mash fill the gap. Summer barbecues are always popular, and there's a mini beer festival every Easter.

Open all day, all week Free House 8 portions/menu Wi-fi

THAME

The James Figg

Tel **01844 260166 | 21 Cornmarket, OX9 2BL**
Web **www.thejamesfiggthame.co.uk**
Dir ***In town centre.***

This pub's traditional interior of dark wood floors and a double-sided open fire also houses a curving bar that stocks ales such as Purity Mad Goose. 'Simple and tasty' possibilities are burger and chips; pizzas; beer-battered fish and chips; and 'proper' ham, egg and chips. Beyond The Stables function room you'll find a private garden. The pub's name? James Figg, born in Thame in 1684, was the bare-knuckle boxer who Jack Dempsey called the 'father of modern boxing'.

Open all day, all week 11am–midnight Closed 25 Dec Free House 10 from £11 portions Wi-fi P

The Thatch

Tel **01844 214340 | 29–30 Lower High Street, OX9 2AA**
Web **www.thethatchthame.co.uk**
Dir ***From roundabout on A418 into Oxford Road signed town centre. Follow into Thame High Street. Pub on right.***

Originally a row of cottages in the heart of Thame's high street, this thatched pub remains a cosy warren of rooms. If you make it past the bar without being tempted by coffee or a pint of XT 3, you'll find yourself in the restaurant overlooking the garden.

TOOT BALDON

The Mole Inn PICK OF THE PUBS

Tel **01865 340001 | OX44 9NG**
Web **www.themoleinn.com**
Dir ***5 miles south-east from Oxford city centre off B480.***

The lovely 300-year-old Mole, with stripped beams, solid white walls, terracotta floors and leather sofas is a true destination pub for those homing in on its Hook Norton real ales and house specials, notably spicy fishcakes, made from daily-delivered fish, and Thai shredded duck. Steaks are hung for a minimum of 28 days, lamb is local, and free-range, rare-breed Blythburgh pigs produce the pork. Venison and game come from various estates and local shoots. Vegetarians will head for shallot tarte Tatin with chicory, candied walnuts and cheese fondue perhaps. Go into the landscaped gardens – it's well worthwhile. To answer the obvious question about the village name, 'toot' was Old English for a look-out place.

Open all day, all week 12–12 (Sun 12–11) Closed 25–26 Dec Free House 11 from £16.95 portions/menu Wi-fi P

UFFINGTON

The Fox & Hounds ★★★★ INN

Tel **01367 820680 | High Street, SN7 7RP**
Web **www.uffingtonpub.co.uk**
Dir ***From A420 (south of Faringdon) follow Fernham or Uffington signs.***

Amidst the thatched cottages and 13th-century church in the charming village of Uffington, The Fox & Hounds boasts unrivalled views of The Ridgeway and the Uffington White Horse. Writer John Betjeman once lived across the road from the pub. This is a traditional free house with a range of well-kept real ales; the home-cooked food includes a vegetarian menu, pub favourites and daily specials; the Sunday roasts are ever popular. Stay over in one of the comfortable en suite rooms.

Open all day, all week 11–11 (Sun 12–10.30) Free House portions/menu Wi-fi P *notice required*

WATLINGTON

The Fat Fox Inn ★★★★ INN

Tel **01491 613040 | 13 Shirburn Street, OX49 5BU**
Web **www.thefatfoxinn.co.uk**
Dir ***In town centre.***

At the foot of the Chiltern Hills, parts of this building date back to Tudor times, although much of it is Georgian. An inglenook fireplace with wood-burning stove warms the bar, where locals can enjoy a pint of Brakspear Oxford Gold or one of 16 wines by the glass. South Oxfordshire producers supply the kitchen with seasonal ingredients for the short, daily-changing menu. Confit pork belly, seared scallops and celeriac might precede duck breast, potato fondant, feta, poached egg, artichoke and balsamic jus.

Open all day, all week Brakspear 16 portions Wi-fi P *notice required*

WEST HANNEY

Plough Inn

Tel **01235 868987 | Church Street, OX12 0LN**
Web **theploughatwesthanney.co.uk**
Dir ***From Wantage take A338 towards Oxford. Plough Inn in 1 mile.***

Thatched with four 'eyebrows', the Plough dates from around 1525, when it was a row of cottages. The landlord enjoys responsibility for such things as choosing the six rolling real ales and organising the popular Easter, Spring and Summer bank holiday beer festivals.

WITNEY

The Fleece

Tel **01993 892270 | 11 Church Green, OX28 4AZ**
Web **www.fleecewitney.co.uk**
Dir ***In town centre.***

Overlooking, as the address suggests, the green in front of St Mary's church, this fine Georgian pub was where, in the late 1940s, Dylan Thomas enjoyed a drink or two when he was living nearby. Then, it was also Clinch's brewery; today it's a Peach Pub.

Old Swan ★★★★★ INN

Tel **01993 774441 | Minster Lovell, OX29 0RN**
Web **www.oldswan.co.uk**
Dir ***Northbound: M40 junction 8, A40 (southbound M40 junction 9, A34) towards Oxford. From Oxford ringroad follow Cheltenham signs. 14 miles, follow Carterton and Minster Lovell signs. Through Minster Lovell, right at T-junction, 2nd left signed Old Swan***

Idyllically situated alongside the River Windrush, this 600-year-old inn was a favourite of Sir Winston Churchill, whose ancestral home is nearby Blenheim Palace. From the beautiful gardens to the charming beamed bar with its open fires and cosy nooks and crannies it's a bit of a stunner. Simple, seasonal food on the carefully constructed menus might include pig's cheek and spring onion terrine; followed by beer-battered fish of the day and triple-cooked chips.

Open all week 12.30–3 6.30–9 (Fri to Sat 12.30–3 6.30–9.30) Free House 16 portions/menu Wi-fi

WOLVERCOTE

Jacobs Inn

Tel **01865 514333 | 130 Godstow Road, OX2 8PG**
Dir ***From A40 roundabout into Godstow Road signed Wolvercote. Over railway line, pub on left in village.***

This comfortable, relaxed pub near Oxford is as welcoming and friendly as you please. Bring the kids and the dog and settle down with a pint (the choice of ales changes daily) while you peruse the menu. Great local produce features (they keep their own pigs) and there's a large garden with a pizza kitchen in the summer. Start with smoked salmon and anchovy terrine, or duck rillettes; then tuck into rump of lamb with minted gravy perhaps.

Open all day, all week Closed 25 Dec Marston's 10 from £12 portions/menu Wi-fi *notice required*

The Trout Inn

Tel **01865 510930 | 195 Godstow Road, OX2 8PN**
Web **www.thetroutoxford.co.uk**
Dir ***From A40 at Wolvercote roundabout (north of Oxford) follow signs for Wolvercote, through village to pub.***

The Trout was already ancient when Lewis Carroll, and later CS Lewis took inspiration here; centuries before it was a hospice for Godstow Nunnery, on the opposite bank of the Thames. It featured in several episodes of *Inspector Morse* and has long been a favourite with Oxford undergraduates. On a warm summer day, rush to bag a table on the terrace by the fast-flowing water and enjoy a pint and something from the all-pleasing menu.

Open all day, all week 11–11 Free House 20 portions/menu Wi-fi

WOODSTOCK

The Black Prince

Tel **01993 811530 | 2 Manor Road, OX20 1XJ**
Web **www.theblackprincewoodstock.com**
Dir ***North of Woodstock on A44, on outskirts of town.***

With a great location on the bank of the River Glyme, this dog-friendly ,16th-century inn has a lovely riverside garden, while inside you'll find stone walls, log fires and even a suit of armour. At lunchtime you can have sandwiches; bubble-and-squeak with bacon and eggs; or the pub's famous chicken and ham pie. Alternatively, there are pub classics of ham, egg and chips or fish and chips alongside daily specials.

Open all day, all week 12–11 Free House 8 portions/menu notice required

The Star Inn

Tel **01993 811373** | **22 Market Place, OX20 1TA**
Web **www.thestarinnwoodstock.co.uk**
Dir ***A44 Chipping Norton to town centre.***

Beer from Wells and Young and the Bedfordshire Brewery complements tapas-style dishes (patatas bravas, grilled tiger prawns) and pub classics (home-made steak and mushroom pie with mash or chips) at this classy, inviting, beamed and panelled old pub.

Open all day, all week Closed 25 Dec Charles Wells 12 portions/menu notice required

WOOLSTONE

The White Horse

Tel **01367 820726** | **SN7 7QL**
Web **www.whitehorsewoolstone.co.uk**
Dir ***Exit A420 at Watchfield onto B4508 towards Longcot signed Woolstone.***

This ancient, black-and-white timbered village pub appears as if on cue after an invigorating walk along the Ridgeway. It is said that Thomas Hughes (of *Tom Brown's Schooldays* fame) penned some of his works here. Upholstered stools line the traditional bar, and the fireplace conceals two priest holes. A weekday lunch could be pie of the day with potatoes and veg, or a super-food salad. For dinner, how about slow-braised ox cheeks, horseradish mash and onion sauce? .

Open all day, all week 11–11 Arkell's 12 from £14 notice required

WYTHAM

White Hart

Tel **01865 244372** | **OX2 8QA**
Web **whitehartwytham.com**
Dir ***From A34 (north-east of Oxford) follow Wytham signs.***

The White Hart's contemporary interior sits well with the big old fireplace and 400-year-old stone flags. They are as happy to serve a pint of real ale as a sit-down meal. In summer, dine on the Mediterranean-style terrace.

RUTLAND

BARROWDEN

The Exeter Arms

Tel **01572 747365** | **28 Main Street, LE15 8EQ**
Web **www.exeterarmsbarrowden.co.uk**
Dir ***From A47 turn at landmark windmill, village 0.75 mile south. 6 miles east of Uppingham and 17 miles west of Peterborough.***

A warm, friendly atmosphere prevails at this traditional country pub, which overlooks the village green and duck pond. Freshly prepared, home-cooked food is on offer, as well as regularly rotating real ales and a good selection of wines by the glass. Make the most of the considerable outside space in the attractive beer gardens.

Open 12–3 6–10 Wed to Thu (Tue 6–10 Fri to Sat 12–3 6–10.30 Sun 12–6) Closed 1 week Jan, 1 week Oct, Sun evening, Mon, Tue lunch Free House 12 portions/menu notice required

BRAUNSTON

The Blue Ball

Tel **01572 722135** | **6 Cedar Street, LE15 8QS**
Web **www.theblueballbraunston.co.uk**
Dir ***From Oakham north on B640. Left into Cold Overton Road, 2nd left into West Road, into Braunston Road (becomes Oakham Road). In village 2nd left into Cedar Street. Pub on left opposite church.***

The 17th-century thatched Blue Ball, a few miles from Rutland Water, is an excellent stopping-off point for cyclists and walkers, as well as diners and drinkers looking for a real country pub. Landlord Dominic Way looks after his ales, as locals in the beamed and cosy bar will testify. Seasonal and local ingredients go into classic pub fare and modern dishes such as pan-roasted duck breast, sautéed potatoes and braised red cabbage; wild mushroom and truffle risotto; or braised lamb shank with mash.

Open 12–2.30 6–11 (Fri 12–2.30 5–11 Sat 12–11 Sun 12–8) Closed 25 Dec, Mon (excluding bank holidays) Marston's 10 portions notice required

CLIPSHAM

The Olive Branch

 INN PICK OF THE PUBS

Tel **01780 410355** | **Main Street, LE15 7SH**
Web **www.theolivebranchpub.com**
Dir ***2 miles from A1 at B664 junction, north of Stamford.***

Never nurdled? Remedy the omission in this pretty, pantiled pub, while engaged with a pint of Grainstore from nearby Oakham, a sloe gin or a fruity cocktail flavoured with foraged berries. Worth highlighting are the superb Norfolk and Yorkshire coast shellfish, the sea bream, monkfish and turbot from Devon and Cornwall, and the deep-water white fish from Newhaven, all delivered daily. Ever-changing menus and blackboards offer a generous choice, ranging from ham hock terrine with duck egg mayo and roast pineapple, by way of beef bourguignon, roasted onions, mushroom purée, pancetta and bone-marrow mash, to hake with curried cauliflower fritter, coriander and wild rice.

Open all day, all week 8am–11pm (Sun 8am–10.30pm) Closed 25 Dec evening, 26 Dec evening and 1 Jan evening Free House 26 portions/menu

GREETHAM

The Wheatsheaf

Tel **01572 812325** | **1 Stretton Road, LE15 7NP**
Web **www.wheatsheaf-greetham.co.uk**
Dir ***From A1 follow signs for Oakham onto B668 to Greetham, pub on left.***

This 18th-century village pub is lovingly run by Carol and Scott Craddock. Carol notched up more than 20 years working in several renowned kitchens before coming here to put her wide experience to excellent use. She changes her modern British menu weekly, and cooks using locally sourced meats and high quality sustainable fresh fish; she makes bread daily, too. A typical dinner might feature pear, goats' cheese and spiced pecan salad, then crisp pork belly, mash, greens and mustard sauce. Rutland-brewed real ales are served in the bar.

Open 12–3 6–close (Fri to Sun all day) Closed 1st 2 weeks Jan, Mon (excluding bank holidays) Punch Taverns 14 from £15.50 portions/menu

LYDDINGTON

The Marquess of Exeter

Tel **01572 822477** | **52 Main Street, LE15 9LT**
Web **www.marquessexeter.co.uk**
Dir ***A1 north exit towards Leicester/A4. At roundabout onto A47 towards Leicester. At Uppingham roundabout onto A6003/Ayston Road. Through Uppingham to Stoke Road. Left into Lyddington, left into Main Street. Pub on left.***

Run by renowned local chef Brian Baker, this old village inn fits seamlessly into Lyddington's long, yellow-brown ironstone streetscape. Stylish, contemporary design works well together with traditional pub essentials, to wit, beams, flagstone floors and winter fires. Modern British menus offer main courses such as Brian's signature sharing dish of grilled rib of Derbyshire beef with frites and béarnaise sauce. Add a shady garden and the mix is complete for an enjoyable visit.

Open all day, all week 11–11 (Sat 11am to midnight Sun 12–10.30) Closed 25 Dec Marston's 13 from £14.50 portions/menu notice required

Old White Hart

Tel **01572 821703** | **51 Main Street, LE15 9LR**
Web **www.oldwhitehart.co.uk**
Dir ***From A6003 between Uppingham and Corby take B672. Pub on main street.***

This free house, opposite the village green, is constructed from honey-coloured sandstone like the surrounding cottages. Running the pub for over 20 years, owners Stuart and Holly East have built a good reputation for their food. Dishes could include crayfish thermidor and saddle of venison. On warm days customers take their pints of Nene Valley bitter or Aspall cider into the gardens or onto the covered patio. The inn also has a floodlit pétanque pitch.

Open all day, all week 12–11 (Sun 12–4 7–10.30) Closed 25 Dec, 26 Dec evening Free House 10 from £6 portions notice required

MANTON

The Horse and Jockey

Tel **01572 737335** | **2 St Marys Road, LE15 8SU**
Web **www.horseandjockeyrutland.co.uk**
Dir ***Exit A6003 between Oakham and Uppingham signed Rutland Water South Shore. 1st left in Manton into St Marys Road.***

Privately owned, this pleasing, stone-built village free house is a popular pitstop for cyclists and ramblers investigating the recreational tracks around Rutland Water. The innate charm of the traditional, stone-floored, beamed interior complements the well-kept Rutland-brewed beers and robust pub food.

MARKET OVERTON

The Black Bull

Tel **01572 767677** | **2 Teigh Road, LE15 7PW**
Web **www.theblackbullmarketoverton.co.uk**
Dir ***From Oakham take B668 to Cottesmore. Left signed Market Overton.***

The Black Bull occupies a lovely spot in the picturesque village of Market Overton. Once a coach house, the thatched pub offers a traditional atmosphere with real fires and sumptuous sofas, although walking boots, children and dogs are as welcome as diners. Menus feature hearty pub classics, so maybe kick off with chicken liver pâté with home-made chutney before moving on to steak and ale pie and chips; or pork sausages with creamy mash, onion gravy and buttered greens.

Open all year 12–3 5–12 (Sun 12–6) Closed Sun evening, Mon Free House 10 from £9 portions/menu Wi-fi notice required

NORTH LUFFENHAM

The Fox Country Pub

Tel **01780 720991** | **1 Pinfold Lane, LE15 8LE**
Web **www.thefoxrutland.co.uk**
Dir ***From A6003 follow Manton signs. Right signed Lyndon. Through Lyndon to North Luffenham. Pub on left. Or from A6121 follow North Luffenham signs.***

An attractive, 18th-century, double-fronted stone building in one of Rutland's oh-so-picturesque villages. Now in Jason Allen's caring hands and fully refurbished, the Fox welcomes all-comers at its locally-crafted oak bar, where stone-flagged floors are warmed by log-burners. Ample choice of refreshments includes four rotating real ales. Find a spot in the lounge for a relaxed snack or in the restaurant choose from the menu of home-cooked dishes such as beef and ale pie; carrot and lentil burger; and peanut posset with chocolate shortbread.

Open all year, all day 12–2.30 5.30–11 (Mon 5.30–11 Fri to Sun 12–11) Closed Mon lunch Free House 16 from £10.95 portions/menu Wi-fi notice required

OAKHAM

The Grainstore Brewery

Tel **01572 770065** | **Station Approach, LE15 6RE**
Web **www.grainstorebrewery.com**
Dir ***Adjacent to Oakham rail station.***

One of the best brew pubs in Britain, The Grainstore Brewery is housed in a three-storey Victorian grain store. William Davis and Peter Atkinson's brewing company uses the finest quality hops and ingredients to make the beers and ciders that can be sampled in the pub's taproom.

SOUTH LUFFENHAM

The Coach House Inn

Tel **01780 720866** | **3 Stamford Road, LE15 8NT**
Web **www.thecoachhouseinn.co.uk**
Dir ***On A6121, off A47 between Morcroft and Stamford.***

Horses were once stabled here while weary travellers enjoyed a drink in what is now a private house next door. This elegantly appointed, attractive stone inn offers a comfortable 40-cover dining room and a cosy bar serving Adnams, Morland and Greene King beers.

WING

King's Arms Inn

★★★★ INN

Tel 01572 737634 | Top Street, LE15 8SE
Web www.thekingsarms-wing.co.uk
Dir *1 mile off B6003 between Uppingham and Oakham.*

A traditional village inn with its own smokery

Lovers of smoked and cured fish and meats will want to visit Jimmy's Rutland Smokehouse at David and James Goss's 17th-century village inn, all stone walls, beams and flagstones. However, there's lots more than smoked produce to tempt the taste buds, as evidenced by starters of butternut squash and woodland mushroom risotto; and signature steamed mussels, then suet and puff pastry Big Pie; halibut with langoustine tails; baked duck egg and potato gnocchi en cocotte; braised Grasmere belly pork; and 28-day-aged rump steak. The 'lunch for less' menu suggests grilled fish of the day, chips and peas; and potato rösti, fried egg and Lincolnshire Poacher cheese, while children will no doubt head for Jimmy's pork sausages and mash; or mini-fish pie with vegetables. There are bar home-made snacks, such as biltong and home-smoked cashew nuts, and the pub makes its own sloe gin, elderflower vodka and mulled wine with fruits and berries foraged from nearby fields and hedgerows. Don't overlook its local real ales and ciders, and a bin-ends blackboard of fine and speciality wines. Highly appointed en suite guest rooms have been created in the Old Bake House and in Orchard House.

Open all year 12–3 6.30–11 (Mon 6.30–10 Fri 12–3 5–11 Sat all day Sun 12–3) Closed Sun evening, Mon lunch Free House 33 portions/menu notice required

STRETTON

The Jackson Stops Country Inn PICK OF THE PUBS

Tel **01780 410237 | Rookery Road, LE15 7RA**
Web **www.thejacksonstops.com**
Dir ***From A1 follow Stretton signs, 1st right into village.***

There can be few pubs in the country that have taken their name from a 'For Sale' sign. One change of ownership went on for so long locals dispensed with the old name in favour of the name of the estate agent. The long, low, stone-built partly thatched building dates from 1721, and inside you'll find stone fireplaces with log fires, quarry-tiled floors, scrubbed wood tables and five intimate dining rooms. In the beamed snug bar, real ales such as Grainstore Ten Fifty lift the heart, while the menu offers dishes like tian of prawn and crayfish; or steak, ale and shallot pie with a medley of roast root vegetables. Try the sticky toffee pudding and butterscotch sauce for afters.

Open all year 12–3 6–10.30 (Sun 12–3.30) Closed Sun evening, Mon Free House 10 from £11.50 portions/menu notice required

WHITWELL

The Noel @ Whitwell

Tel **01780 460347 | Main Road, LE15 8BW**
Web **www.thenoel.co.uk**
Dir ***Between Oakham and Stamford on A606, north shore of Rutland Water.***

The part-thatched village inn stands just a 15-minute stroll from the north shore of Rutland Water, so worth noting if you are walking or pedalling the lakeside trail and in need of refreshment. The friendly, smart bar and dining room both have a stylish modern feel and feature flagstone floors, heritage colours and warming winter log fires. Expect to find local Grainstore ales on tap and a wide-ranging menu with dishes like Thai green prawn curry and Moroccan vegetable couscous or fish and chips with mushy peas.

Open all year 12–3 6–close Closed Mon Enterprise Inns 10 portions/menu notice required

WING

King's Arms Inn – see opposite

SHROPSHIRE

ADMASTON

The Pheasant Inn at Admaston

Tel **01952 251989 | TF5 0AD**
Web **www.thepheasantadmaston.co.uk**
Dir ***M54 junction 6, A5223 north. At 4th roundabout left onto B5063 to Admaston. Pub on left.***

Dating from the 19th century, this lovely old country pub offers stylish interior decor and a real fire, which add character to the dining areas. The large enclosed garden is ideal for families and there is a good children's menu.

BASCHURCH

The New Inn

Tel **01939 260335 | Church Road, SY4 2EF**
Web **www.newinnbaschurch.com**
Dir ***8 miles from Shrewsbury, 8 miles from Oswestry.***

This really is a quintessential village inn. Well-kept regional ales such as Shropshire Gold or Hobsons Best Bitter are complemented by local cheeses, whilst the menu offers dishes like game faggots with leek and smoked bacon mash or a classic steak and ale pie. Grab a seat by the log burner or head for the garden.

Open Tue to Fri 12–3 6–11 (Sat 11–11 Sun 12–7) Closed 26 Dec, 1 Jan, Mon (except bank holidays) Free House 12 portions/menu

BISHOP'S CASTLE

The Castle  INN

Tel **01588 638403 | Market Square, SY9 5BN**
Web **www.thecastlehotelbishopscastle.co.uk**
Dir ***Between Lydham and Clun exit A488 to Bishop's Castle.***

In an elevated position off a quiet square, The Castle's beer garden offers panoramic views over Shropshire countryside. Dating from 1719, it's a haven of hospitality, warmed by log fires in the cooler months. Three bars serve an excellent choice of real ales such as Clun Pale, and the oak-panelled restaurant offers plates of sustainably produced south Shropshire food. A beer and cider festival is hosted in early July.

Open all day, all week Free House 12 from £11.95 portions/menu

The Three Tuns Inn PICK OF THE PUBS

Tel **01588 638797** | **Salop Street, SY9 5BW**
Web **www.thethreetunsinn.co.uk**
Dir ***From Ludlow take A49 through Craven Arms, left onto A489 to Lydham, A488 to Bishop's Castle, inn at top of town.***

The memorable old town of Bishop's Castle tumbles down steep hills on the fringe of Shropshire's Clun Forest. Traders from the time of King Charles I onwards have enjoyed the hospitality of The Three Tuns, where England's oldest brewery, licensed in 1642, continues to produce beers in its eye-catching tower brewery. The engaging warren of rooms is generally music and games machine free, although regular live music and morris dancing events prove popular, along with the beer festival held as part of the town's summer festival each July. Timbers, beams and redoubtable fireplaces add tremendous character, and menus include Three Tuns XXX beer-battered fish with hand-cut chips, mushy peas and tartare sauce.

Open all day, all week Star Pubs & Bars 10 portions/menu WiFi

BRIDGNORTH

Halfway House Inn ★★★ INN

Tel **01746 762670** | **Cleobury Road, Eardington, WV16 5LS**
Web **www.halfwayhouseinn.co.uk**
Dir ***M54 junction 4, A442 to Bridgnorth. Or M5 junction 4, A491 towards Stourbridge. A458 to Bridgnorth. Follow tourist signs on B4363.***

This 16th-century coaching inn was renamed in 1823 after the very young Princess Victoria stopped here en route between Shrewsbury and Worcester; when she asked where she was, came the diplomatic reply, 'halfway there ma'am'. The pub is renowned for a good selection of regional real ales, 40 malts and around 100 wines. A dinner menu might offer home-made chicken liver pâté; Shropshire beef with onions and mushrooms braised in Guinness and ale; or home-made chicken or lamb curry.

Open all week 4–11 (Fri to Sat 11am–11.30pm Sun 11–7) Closed 26 Dec Free House 10 from £13.95 portions/menu WiFi P *notice required*

The Kings Head and Stable Bar

Tel **01746 762141** | **Whitburn Street, WV16 4QN**
Web **www.thekingsheadbridgnorth.co.uk**
Dir ***Town centre.***

A splendid example of a heavily-timbered 17th-century coaching inn, built (or possibly rebuilt) after Bridgnorth's Great Fire in 1646. In the summer you can make the most of the weather in the small courtyard, while in the winter the three fires keep things cosy.

BUCKNELL

Baron at Bucknell

Tel **01547 530549** | **SY7 0AH**
Web **www.baronatbucknell.co.uk**
Dir ***From Bromfield on A49 onto A4113 towards Knighton. Through Leintwardine. Right to Bucknell. Cross rail line, left and follow brown signs for inn.***

A stone's throw from Ludlow in the lovely Shropshire Hills Area of Outstanding Natural Beauty, the Baron sits at the foot of Bucknell Mynd. It's beautifully peaceful and there are plenty of great walks if you need to work up an appetite. Good home-made food is what they promise here, and you can eat either in the charming restaurant or the airy conservatory. Start with roast sweet potato, beetroot, goats' cheese and pine nut salad, maybe, before moving on to game pie, or a warming chickpea casserole.

Open 6pm–10.30pm (Fri 12–3 6–11 Sat 12–11 Sun 12–6) Closed 2 weeks Jan, lunch Mon to Thu, Sun evening Free House portions/menu WiFi P

CARDINGTON

The Royal Oak

Tel **01694 771266** | **SY6 7JZ**
Web **www.at-the-oak.com**
Dir ***From Church Stretton on A49, take B4371 towards Much Wenlock. Through Hope Bowdler, left signed Cardington. Or from Much Wenlock, take B4371 towards Church Stretton. Turn right at Cardington sign.***

Reputedly the oldest continuously licensed pub in Shropshire and set in a conservation village, this free house can trace its roots to the 15th century. The rambling low-beamed bar with vast inglenook and comfortable beamed dining room are refreshingly undisturbed by music, TV or games machines. There's excellent cask ales and home-made dishes on the good-value menu that includes Shropshire Fidget pie – gammon cooked in spiced cider and apples with a puff pastry top.

Open all year 12–2.30 6–11 (Sat to Sun 12–11) Closed Mon (excluding bank holiday lunch) and Sun evening Nov to Mar Free House from £10.75 menus notice required

CHURCH STRETTON

The Bucks Head

Tel **01694 722898** | **42 High Street, SY6 6BX**
Web **www.thebucks-head.co.uk**
Dir ***12 miles from Shrewsbury and Ludlow.***

The small market town of Church Stretton is sandwiched between the Long Mynd and Wenlock Edge, and the charming old Bucks Head is where to stay to explore these impressive landscape features. The pub is known for comfort, well-kept ales, and for its restaurant.

CLEOBURY MORTIMER

The Hopton Crown

Tel **01299 270372** | **Hopton Wafers, DY14 0NB**
Web **www.hoptoncrown.co.uk**
Dir ***On A4117, 8 miles east of Ludlow, 2 miles west of Cleobury Mortimer.***

A delightful, creeper-clad, 16th-century coaching inn. Mail coaches used to take on extra horses here for the steep climb up the hill. Its period past is evident, with exposed beams, stonework and an inglenook fireplace.

CLUN

The White Horse Inn – see page 358

CRAVEN ARMS

The Sun Inn

Tel **01584 861239** | **Corfton, SY7 9DF**
Web **www.thesuninncorfton.co.uk**
Dir ***On B4368, 7 miles north of Ludlow.***

First licensed in 1613, this historic pub is close to the towns of Ludlow and Bridgnorth, and handy for the ramblers' paradise of Clee Hill and Long Mynd. Since 1997, landlord Norman Pearce has been brewing the Corvedale ales in what was the pub's old chicken and lumber shed, using local borehole water; Herefordshire's Gwatkin cider is another thirst-quenching option. Local produce appears in a delicious array of traditional dishes including vegetarian and vegan options.

Open all week 12–2 6–11 (Sun 12–3 7–11) Free House 6 from £10 portions/menu notice required

CRESSAGE

The Riverside Inn

Tel **01952 510900** | **Cound, SY5 6AF**
Web **www.theriversideinn.net**
Dir ***On A458. 7 miles from Shrewsbury, 1 mile from Cressage.***

This inn sits in three acres of gardens alongside the River Severn, offering its customers delightful river views. Originally a vicarage for St Peter's church in the village, the building also housed a girls' school and a railway halt before becoming a pub in 1878.

HODNET

The Bear at Hodnet

Tel **01630 685214** | **TF9 3NH**
Web **www.bearathodnet.co.uk**
Dir ***At junction of A53 and A442 turn right at roundabout. Inn in village centre.***

With old beams, open fireplaces and secret passages leading to the church, this black-and-white-timbered, former coaching inn was once known for its bear-baiting pit. Food includes prawn cocktail with rosemary and sea salt focaccia, and breaded whitebait.

CLUN

The White Horse Inn

Tel **01588 640305** | **The Square, SY7 8JA**
Web **www.whi-clun.co.uk**
Dir ***On A488 in town centre.***

Sixteenth-century inn on the ancient market square

In 'A Shropshire Lad', the poet A E Housman called Clun the 'Quietest place under the sun'. That was in 1896, but here in the beautiful Shropshire Hills, this gloriously unspoilt and unpretentious village inn with beams, aged wood and stone floors; still has huge charm. Claiming to be 'South Shropshire's premier real ale pub', the main bar is its heart and has three brews of its own, Citadel, Clun Pale and Loophole, while others from the county's many craft breweries complete the line-up. To the rear is a games room with pool table and dartboard. A variety of home-made, farmhouse-style food, sourced from very local suppliers, includes traditional suet puddings – a speciality – venison and red wine casserole; and parmesan and dill-crusted salmon, and a typical dessert of apple, Calvados and sultana crumble. Topside of beef is served on Sundays, with lamb, pork and chicken in rotation; for vegetarians there's a tasty nut roast. Regular events taking place here include live music, pool and poker nights, and the three-day Clun Valley Beer Festival on the first weekend in October. If you like poetry you can read some poems on display in the bar, and a surprisingly clean limerick, written about the White Horse.

Open all day, all week Free House portions/ menu notice required

IRONBRIDGE

White Hart ★★★★ INN

Tel 01952 432901 | The Wharfage, TF8 7AW
Web www.whitehartironbridge.com
Dir *In centre of Ironbridge, 200 yards from Bridge.*

Just 200 yards from the famous Georgian cast iron bridge, this modernised 18th-century inn occupies a lovely spot overlooking the River Severn. Drinkers make a beeline for the comfortable bar dispensing local ales like Shropshire Lad. Diners, meanwhile, are spoiled for choice, with a lunchtime bar menu offering pub classics such as home-baked ham, fried eggs and chips, and curried chicken. Alternatively, the pub's Number Ten restaurant offers dishes such as crispy duck leg, damson hoisin, spring onion and sesame; and tandoori spiced lamb keema, with cauliflower and onion masala.

Open all day, all week Free House 16 from £15 portions/menu notice required

LEEBOTWOOD

The Pound

Tel 01694 751477 | SY6 6ND
Web www.thepoundleebotwood.co.uk
Dir *On A49 between Church Stretton and Longnor.*

This thatched building – the oldest house in the village – dates back to 1457, although it didn't become an inn until 1823. It's a comfortable, relaxed place, and the bright, airy dining room has a contemporary feel while making the most of original features. Enjoy local ales such as Ludlow Gold or Stonehouse Station Bitter as you order daytime sandwiches or main meals like Penang chicken curry or steak and kidney pudding.

LITTLE STRETTON

The Green Dragon

Tel 01694 722925 | Ludlow Road, SY6 6RE
Web www.greendragonlittlestretton.co.uk
Dir *A49 from Shrewsbury towards Ludlow. 1 mile after Church Stretton right to Little Stretton. Pub in village centre.*

Close to the Long Mynd in the Shropshire Hills and backing on to Small Batch Valley, the 16th-century Green Dragon is in a prime location for walkers and campers but also convenient for the busy market town of Ludlow 14 miles away.

The Ragleth Inn

Tel 01694 722711 | Ludlow Road, SY6 6RB
Web www.theraglethinn.co.uk
Dir *From Shrewsbury take A49 towards Leominster. At lights in Church Stretton turn right. 3rd left into High Street. Continue to Little Stretton. Inn on right.*

This 17th-century country inn sits midway between Shrewsbury and Ludlow in beautiful countryside at the foot of the Long Mynd hills. Its pretty exterior overlooks a large beer garden and the food follows classic pub grub lines.

LUDLOW

The Charlton Arms ★★★★★ INN PICK OF THE PUBS

Tel 01584 872813 | Ludford Bridge, SY8 1PJ
Web www.thecharltonarms.co.uk
Dir *On B4361 from Ludlow towards Leominster (south of River Teme).*

Since taking over the pub a few years ago, Frenchman Cedric Bosi (brother of acclaimed London-based chef Claude) and his wife Amy have quickly established it as one of Ludlow's must-visit food pubs. Located on the town's iconic Grade I listed Ludford Bridge and a short walk from the castle, this smart, modernised stone-built pub has a lovely tiered terrace overlooking the River Teme. Inside, the airy dining area is relaxed and informal with scrubbed wooden floorboards and mismatched chairs. Whether it's dogs, children or muddy-booted walkers, everybody is made to feel welcome. Well-kept local ales such as Ludlow Gold keep beer drinkers happy and there are 14 wines by the glass. The food is excellent and the concise menu focuses on classy renditions of British classics.

Open all day, all week Free House 14 from £13 portions notice required

The Clive Arms ★★★★★

RESTAURANT WITH ROOMS | PICK OF THE PUBS

Tel **01584 856565 | Bromfield, SY8 2JR**
Web **www.theclive.co.uk**
Dir ***2 miles north of Ludlow on A49, between Hereford and Shrewsbury.***

A former farmhouse, this place has been a pub since the early 1900s. Today, it is a mix of contemporary style with original features still evident. The bar comprises two areas: an 18th-century lounge with log fire; and a more contemporary upper part that leads out to a courtyard with tables and parasols. You'll find Hobsons ales at the bar, plus ciders such as Robinsons Flagon, and 21 wines served by the glass. Lunchtime bar snacks might include a hot pork and apple sandwich; while a three-course choice in the evening could comprise game terrine, pickled walnuts and Melba toast; followed by roast vegetable Wellington, herbed potatoes, thyme and chestnut gravy. If there's still room try baked vanilla cheesecake. Restricted opening times on 25–26 December and 1 January.

Open all day, all week Free House 21 from £12 portions/menu notice required

MAESBURY MARSH

The Navigation Inn

Tel **01691 672958 | SY10 8JB**
Web **www.thenavigation.co.uk**
Dir ***From Shrewsbury take A5 to Mile End Services. A483 (Welshpool), 2nd left signed Knockin. Approximately 1.5 miles to Maesbury Marsh.***

Otherwise known as 'the Navy', this canal-side pub maximises the appeal of its red-brick and stone-built industrial heritage; the restaurant was a canal warehouse in the 18th century. Comfortable sofas, a wealth of beams, log fire and piano all add to the bar's appeal.

MARTON

The Lowfield Inn

Tel **01743 891313 | SY21 8JX**
Web **www.lowfieldinn.com**
Dir ***From Shrewsbury take B4386 towards Montgomery. Through Westbury and Brockton. Pub on right in 13 miles just before Marton.***

In a stunning location below the west Shropshire Hills, this pub combines the atmosphere of a friendly village local with a fierce support for microbreweries dotted along the England/Wales border – Monty's and Three Tuns beers are regularly stocked, as are a range of decent ciders. Modern British pub grub is offered – locally-made faggots; pork and leek sausages with mash, 'pie of the day' and 'curry of the day'. The eye-catching brick bar, comfy seating, slab floor, log-burner and duck pond add to the character of this village favourite.

Open all day, all week Free House 18 from £10 portions/menu

The Sun Inn

Tel **01938 561211 | SY21 8JP**
Web **www.suninn.org.uk**
Dir ***On B4386 (Shrewsbury to Montgomery road), in centre of Marton.***

Probably about 300 years old, the attractive, stone-built Sun Inn stands on a corner in a quiet hamlet, and Offa's Dyke Path runs nearby on its 177-mile route from Sedbury Cliffs on the Severn estuary to Prestatyn. The Gartell family runs this pub very much as a convivial local, with darts, dominoes, regular quiz nights and Hobsons real ales from Cleobury Mortimer. It's well respected as a dining venue, with the Gartells offering modern British dishes.

Open all year 12–2 7–11 Closed Sun evening, Mon, Tue, Wed lunch Free House 8 from £10.95 portions notice required

MUCH WENLOCK

Gaskell Arms ★★★ SMALL HOTEL

Tel **01952 727212 | High Street, TF13 6AQ**
Web **www.gaskellarms.co.uk**
Dir ***M6 junction 10A onto M54, exit at junction 4, follow signs for Ironbridge, Much Wenlock and A4169. Hotel at junction of A458 and High Street.***

This inn, originally part of the Much Wenlock estate, was bought by the Sheldon family 30 years ago, and it continues to change with the times. The stabling has been turned into accommodation, and modifications have revealed the best of its architectural features. Ponder then, as you relax with a pint of Worcestershire Way, how many four-horse carriages were welcomed outside the bay windows before the railways came. For the hungry, there's a menu of classic pub dishes.

Open all day, all week Free House from £12 portions/menu notice required

MUNSLOW

Crown Country Inn

★★★★ INN PICK OF THE PUBS

Tel **01584 841205** | **Craven Arms, SY7 9ET**
Web **www.crowncountryinn.co.uk**
Dir ***On B4368 between Craven Arms and Much Wenlock.***

The Grade II listed Crown has stood in its lovely setting below the limestone escarpment of Wenlock Edge since Tudor times. An impressive three-storey building, it's said to be haunted by a black-swathed figure known as Charlotte. The main bar retains its sturdy oak beams, flagstone floors and prominent inglenook fireplace, and on offer are beers from the Three Tuns Brewery, as well as local Munslow ciders. Owners Richard and Jane Arnold are well known for their strong commitment to good food, and meals based on top-quality local produce from trusted sources are served in the main bar, the Bay dining area, and the Corvedale restaurant, the former court room.

Open Tue to Sat 12–3.30 6.45–11 (Sun 12–3.30) Closed Christmas, Sun evening, Mon Free House 8 portions notice required

NEENTON

The Pheasant at Neenton

Tel **01746 787955** | **WV16 6RJ**
Web **www.pheasantatneenton.co.uk**
Dir ***On B4364 (Bridgnorth to Ludlow road).***

This 18th-century village pub was bought by the local community, restored to its former glory and reopened – it's now very much the hub of this picturesque village. Chef Mark Harris offers a varied menu themed around seasonal local ingredients, plus creative evening specials. A selection of pub classics includes fish and chips and delicious pies. There's an extensive wine list and several local ales including Hobsons Twisted Spire or Ludlow Gold.

Open all week 12–3 6–11 (Sat 12–11 Sun 12–9) Free House 16 from £9.95 portions/menu

NESSCLIFFE

The Old Three Pigeons

Tel **01743 741279** | **SY4 1DB**
Web **www.3pigeons.co.uk**
Dir ***Phone for detailed directions.***

The spirits of Sir Humphrey Kynaston and his horse Beelzebub are said to return occasionally to this ancient watering hole in deepest Shropshire; a local 'Robin Hood', he was outlawed by Henry VII and ultimately pardoned by Henry VIII. Red leather-clad armchairs, a forest of black beams and local real ales set the charming ambience, while the menu's broad range of pub dishes pleases all tastes and appetites. Vegetarians are also well catered for.

Open all day, all week 12–11 Free House 10 portions/menu notice required

NORTON

The Hundred House

★★★★ INN PICK OF THE PUBS

Tel **01952 580240** | **Bridgnorth Road, TF11 9EE**
Web **www.hundredhouse.co.uk**
Dir ***On A442, 6 miles north of Bridgnorth, 5 miles south of Telford centre.***

Lapped by astonishing gardens, this creeper-clad Shropshire brick inn dates in part to the 14th century. From its village location, lanes and paths filter down through verdant countryside into the depths of the Severn Gorge. Order a glass of local microbrewery beer and relax in the warren of lavishly decorated bars and dining rooms, replete with quarry-tiled floors, exposed brickwork, beamed ceilings and Jacobean oak panelling. Menus are rich in fish and game choices to accompany starters like black pudding, apple and chorizo stack with smoked cheese sauce and crispy onion rings. Move on to main dishes like rack of lamb with moussaka, harissa sauce and rich lamb jus; or smoked pheasant breast stuffed with walnut and fresh sage, and served with orange and red wine sauce.

Open all day, all week 10am–11pm Closed 25 Dec evening Free House 10 portions/menu notice required

OSWESTRY

The Bradford Arms

Tel **01691 830582 | Llanymynech, SY22 6EJ**
Web **www.bradfordarmshotel.co.uk**
Dir ***5.5 miles south of Oswestry on A483 in Llanymynech.***

Once part of the Earl of Bradford's estate, between Oswestry and Welshpool, this 17th-century coaching inn is ideally situated for golfing, fishing and walking, and is well known as a community pub serving first-class real ales. Eating in the spotless dining rooms and conservatory is a rewarding experience, with every taste catered for. A typical dinner menu might feature hunter's chicken; lamb casserole; or pork medallions.

Open all week 11.30–3 4.30–11.30 Free House portions/menu notice required

PAVE LANE

The Fox

Tel **01952 815940 | TF10 9LQ**
Web **www.brunningandprice.co.uk/fox**
Dir ***1 mile south of Newport, just off A41.***

Behind The Fox's smart exterior are spacious rooms and little nooks wrapped around a busy central bar, where there are plenty of Shropshire real ales demanding attention. Enjoy the gently rolling countryside and wooded hills from the lovely south-facing terrace.

PORTH-Y-WAEN

The Lime Kiln

Tel **01691 587590 | SY10 8LX**
Dir ***From Oswestry take A483 towards Welshpool. Right at Llynclys crossroads. Pub on right opposite Chads garage.***

An unassuming white-painted pub, with padded stools lining the counter in the homely bar, and cushioned wooden settles and leather sofas offering more relaxing seating. Expect pub classics on the menu, or look to the specials board for treats like slow-braised beef cheek with horseradish mash, cabbage and bacon, or lamb rump with mustard mash and pea purée.

Open all day, all week Sun to Thu 12–11, Fri to Sat 12-12 Free House menus notice required

PULVERBATCH

The White Horse Inn

Tel **01743 718247 | SY5 8DS**
Web **thewhitehorseinnpulverbatch.co.uk**
Dir ***From Shrewsbury at roundabout on B4380 into Longden Road signed Longden. Approximately 7 miles to Pulverbatch.***

Restored to its former glory, the 15th-century White Horse was a farmhouse until the 19th century. By the front door some old doggerel reads: "Cathercott upon the hill, Wilderly down in the dale, Churton for pretty girls, Pulverbatch for good ale".

RATLINGHOPE

The Bridges

Tel **01588 650260 | SY5 0ST**
Web **www.thebridgespub.co.uk**
Dir ***Phone for detailed directions.***

In the Shropshire Hills, this pub occupies an idyllic location beside the River Onny. The Bridges is also the tap house for the Three Tuns – the oldest licensed brewery in the UK, dating from 1642 – and stocks as many as nine of its beers including Rantipole and Cleric's Cure. Soak it up with one of the traditional dishes on the menu – perhaps home-made pie, mash and vegetables; vegetable chilli con carne; or home-made beef lasagne.

Open all day, all week The Three Tuns portions/menu

SHREWSBURY

The Boat House – see page opposite

Lion & Pheasant Hotel

★★★ TOWN HOUSE HOTEL

PICK OF THE PUBS

Tel **01743 770345 | 50 Wyle Cop, SY1 1XJ**
Web **www.lionandpheasant.co.uk**
Dir ***From south and east: pass abbey, cross river on English Bridge to Wyle Cop, hotel on left. From north and west: follow Town Centre signs onto one-way system to Wyle Cop. Hotel at bottom of hill on right.***

The handsome façade of this family-owned hotel graces medieval Wyle Cop, shortly before the street becomes the English Bridge over the River Severn. A coolly elegant look is evident throughout, from the ground floor public areas to the spacious, well-equipped bedrooms upstairs. Just off the reception is the wood-floored café-style bar, which leads to the flagstoned Inglenook Bar, serving locally brewed Salopian Shropshire Gold, an extensive choice of cocktails and gins and a full range of main meals and snacks. On the first floor is the split-level restaurant, where you'll find dishes like gin-cured salmon, tonic cucumber, citrus purée and coriander; pork fillet, beer-glazed pig's cheek, goats' cheese polenta, carrot, apricot and pork jus; and coconut pannacotta with macadamia crumb, lime and lemonade gel and mango salsa.

Open all day, all week Closed 25–26 Dec Free House 13 portions/menu Wi-fi P notice required

The Mytton and Mermaid

★★★★ INN PICK OF THE PUBS

Tel **01743 761220 | Atcham, SY5 6QG**
Web **www.myttonandmermaid.co.uk**
Dir ***M54 junction 7, follow Shrewsbury signs, at 2nd roundabout take 1st left signed Ironbridge and Atcham. In 1.5 miles hotel on right after bridge.***

Clough Williams-Ellis, creator of the Italianate Welsh village of Portmeirion, once owned this impressive Georgian former coaching inn. It stands on the banks of the River Severn, which you can watch sliding by from waterside benches in the garden, perhaps with a pint of Shropshire Gold or one of the dozen wines sold by the glass in the wood-floored bar. Diners have plenty to choose from, including meats, fish or meze sharing boards; pot pie of the day; Vietnamese bahn mi salad; duck with salt-baked celeriac, kale, beetroot, pear and poppy jus; and chargrills. Guest rooms are in the inn itself, in the courtyard and in the separate Bramble Cottage.

Open all day, all week 7am–11pm Free House 12 menus Wi-fi P notice required

SHREWSBURY

The Boat House

Tel **01743 231658 | New Street, SY3 8JQ**
Web **www.boathouseshrewsbury.co.uk**
Dir ***From A458 and A488 roundabout (north of River Severn) follow A488 (Porthill and Bishops Castle). 1st left into New Street. Pub on left by suspension footbridge.***

Riverside ambience and serious Shropshire fare

Paths from the medieval heart of the town drift through Quarry Park and across a footbridge to this half-timbered retreat beside a great loop of the River Severn at Shrewsbury. Lounge on the huge riverside terrace or make a base in the beamed, rambling, airy interior where real ales from Shropshire's best microbreweries, including Three Tuns and Ludlow Gold, should delight the most

discerning beer-lover. Dishes from the grill are specialities of the house, using the best of local produce. Otherwise, perhaps start with crispy calamari, chilli, lime, coriander and garlic aïoli; or courgette fries, then tuck into Moroccan-spiced lamb kebabs; and finish with glazed lemon tart.

Open all day, all week Enterprise Inns portions P

The Prince of Wales

Tel **01743 343301 | 30 Brynner Street, SY3 7NZ**
Web **www.theprince.pub**
Dir ***Phone for detailed directions.***

Tucked down the back streets of Belle Vue in the heart of Shrewsbury, The Prince of Wales is run by Victoria Payne who restored this friendly pub to its former glory. A rotating choice of guest ales has already won the pub several awards.

STIPERSTONES

The Stiperstones Inn

Tel **01743 791327 | SY5 0LZ**
Web **www.stiperstonesinn.co.uk**
Dir ***Phone for detailed directions.***

Built in the mid-16th century, the Stiperstones has been a pub since the 1840s and is full of charm and character. Set in the south Shropshire hills, in an Area of Outstanding Natural Beauty, it's ideally placed for walking the Stiperstones Ridge or the Long Mynd.

UPTON MAGNA

The Haughmond

Tel **01743 709918 | Pelham Road, SY4 4TZ**
Web **www.thehaughmond.co.uk**
Dir ***From A49 roundabout (north-east of Shrewsbury) take B5062 signed Newport. Right signed Upton Magna.***

This refurbished coaching inn has reclaimed its position at the heart of the community since Martin and Melanie Board took over. Local Salopian Shropshire Gold and The Haughmond Antler Ale are two of the regular beers on tap. The restaurant offers one lunch and two evening menus that showcase the best seasonal Shropshire ingredients, cleverly put together. The 'Tastes of The Haughmond' menu comprises seven small tastes from the seasonal à la carte with a few surprises! Wine flights are an optional delight. Booking recommended.

Open all day, all week Free House 10 from £13 portions Wi-fi

WELLINGTON

The Old Orleton Inn

Tel **01952 255011 | Holyhead Road, TF1 2HA**
Dir ***From M54 junction 7 take B5061 (Holyhead Road), 400 yards on left on corner of Haygate Road and Holyhead Road.***

Instead of a farmhouse becoming an inn – the usual story – this 17th-century coaching inn later became a farmhouse, before reverting. Real ales from Hobsons of Cleobury Mortimer join a monthly guest beer and real ciders. On the menu are Shropshire 'fidget' faggots; natural smoked haddock with Snowdonia Welsh rarebit; and carrot, cashew nut and cranberry Wellington.

Open all day, all week Closed 1st 2 weeks Jan Free House 13 portions Wi-fi *notice required*

WENTNOR

The Crown Inn

Tel **01588 650613 | SY9 5EE**
Web **www.crowninnwentnor.co.uk**
Dir ***From Shrewsbury A49 to Church Stretton, follow signs over Long Mynd to Asterton, right to Wentnor.***

Deep amid the Shropshire Hills, this inviting 16th-century timbered inn is popular with walkers who warm themselves at wood-burning stoves in winter and on the outside decking in the summer; here you can sup Three Tuns bitter and gaze at the Long Mynd's lofty ridge.

WISTANSTOW

The Plough Inn

Tel **01588 673251 | SY7 8DG**
Web **www.woodbrewery.co.uk/pubs/the-plough-inn**
Dir ***From A49 between Ludlow and Church Stretton onto A489 signed Newtown. Under railway bridge. 1st right, pub signed.***

Part of the neighbouring Wood's Brewery, which supplies real ales such as Shropshire Lad, The Plough has been part of village life since 1774. Menus tempt with dishes such as steak and ale pie, slow-roasted pork belly with cider apple sauce and mash, and Shropshire blue and creamed leek tart.

Open all day, all week Wood's Brewery 10 from £8.50 portions/menu Wi-fi *notice required*

SOMERSET

ASHCOTT

Ring O'Bells

Tel **01458 210232** | **High Street, TA7 9PZ**
Web **www.ringobells.com**
Dir ***M5 junction 23 follow A39 and Glastonbury signs. In Ashcott turn left, at post office follow church and village hall signs.***

Successfully run by the same family for more than 30 years, this independent free house dates in parts from 1750, and the interior reflects this with beams, split-level bars and a collection of bells and horse brasses. The pub is close to the Somerset Levels, the RSPB reserve at Ham Wall and the National Nature Reserve at Shapwick Heath. Local ales and ciders are a speciality, while good-value dishes and daily specials are all made on the premises.

Open all week 12–2.30 7–11 (Sun 12–2.30 7–10.30) Free House 8 from £8.50 portions/menu notice required

ASHILL

The Flying Fish

Tel **01823 480467** | **Windmill Hill, TA19 9NX**
Web **www.theflyingfishsomerset.co.uk**
Dir ***Exit A358 at Stewley Cross service station onto Wood Road. 1 mile to pub in Windmill Hill.***

Previously the Square & Compass, this pub overlooking the beautiful Blackdown Hills, changed hands and identity in 2018. Exmoor and St Austell ales head the refreshments list, while reasonably priced and freshly prepared meals combine pub classics with Caribbean dishes cooked by the Barbadian owners. Locally sourced sausages with mash and onion gravy sit alongside Jamaican jerk chicken with coconut rice and curried mutton. There's also a lovely garden and conservatory.

Open all year 12–3 5–11 (Sat 12–11 Sun 12–10 Mon 5–11) Closed Mon lunch Free House from £9 portions/menu notice required

AXBRIDGE

Lamb Inn

Tel **01934 732253** | **The Square, BS26 2AP**
Web **www.butcombe.com/pubs/the-lamb-hotel**
Dir ***10 miles from Wells and Weston-Super-Mare on A370.***

Parts of this rambling 15th-century building were once the guildhall, but it became an inn in 1830. The bars are heated by log fires and offer Butcombe ales; there's also a skittle alley and large terraced garden.

BABCARY

Red Lion ★★★★ INN

Tel **01458 223230** | **TA11 7ED**
Web **www.redlionbabcary.co.uk**
Dir ***North-east of Yeovil. Follow Babcary signs from A303 or A37.***

Rich colour-washed walls, heavy beams and simple wooden furniture characterise this beautifully appointed, thatched free house that has six en suite bedrooms. The bar offers a great selection of real ales, and you can dine here, in the restaurant or in the garden. The daily menus run from pub favourites to dishes like duck breast, potato and pancetta terrine. All bread is baked in-house and local suppliers are much used – they have a 24-hour 'port to plate' policy for the fish.

Open all week 12–3 6–12 Free House 12 portions/menu

BACKWELL

The Rising Sun ★★★★★ INN

Tel **01275 462215** | **91 West Town Road, BS48 3BH**
Web **www.ohhpubs.co.uk/the-rising-sun**
Dir ***Phone for detailed directions.***

A great base for exploring north Somerset, Backwell is a pleasant village with a fine church. The Rising Sun is a comfortable, family-friendly place, with a big garden and extensive play area for the kids. In the bar you'll find well-kept OHH Pale Ale and Butcombe Bitter, and the main menu might kick off with grilled mackerel fillet on toasted focaccia; followed by a pub classic like beer-battered haddock fillet with home-made chips.

Open all day, all week Closed 25 Dec Free House 20 from £9.95 portions/menu

BATH

The Bath Brew House

Tel **01225 805609 | 14 James Street West, BA1 2BX**
Web **www.thebathbrewhouse.com**
Dir ***A367 in central Bath, turn into James Street West, next to Odeon cinema.***

Since opening in 2013, this fine Georgian pub, set right in the centre of town, has served more than 1,000 different beers. There are always 12 craft beers on tap, and they brew their own on site, too – Gladiator best bitter, Emperor, and Sol Invictus.

The Blathwayt Arms – see below

The Chequers PICK OF THE PUBS

Tel **01225 360017 | 50 Rivers Street, BA1 2QA**
Web **www.thechequersbath.com**
Dir ***In city centre, near Royal Crescent and The Circus.***

A beautifully appointed gastro pub that's been serving customers since sedan-chair carriers first quenched their thirst here in 1776. A short walk from The Circus and the Royal Crescent, The Chequers' reputation for excellent ales and great food has made it a firm favourite; booking is advisable. Menus in the upstairs restaurant might feature dishes like rabbit terrine with carrot, sweetcorn, walnut and toast.

Open all day, all week 12–11 Enterprise Inns 26 from £14 portions notice required

The Garricks Head

Tel **01225 318368 | 7–8 St John's Place, BA1 1ET**
Web **www.garrickheadpub.com**
Dir ***Adjacent to Theatre Royal. Follow Theatre Royal brown tourist signs.***

Once the home of Beau Nash, the celebrated dandy, The Garricks Head is named after 18th-century theatrical powerhouse David Garrick and is adjacent to the Theatre Royal (pre-show menus available). The bar has a lot to commend it: a selection of natural wines from Europe, four real ales, Somerset ciders, and the largest selection of single malt whiskies in Bath. The food, mostly locally sourced, includes many pub classics such as steak and chips, and pie of the day.

Open all day, all week Closed 25–26 Dec Free House 20 from £9.95 portions/menu notice required

BATH

The Blathwayt Arms

Tel **01225 421995 | Lansdown, BA1 9BT**
Web **www.blathwaytarms.co.uk**
Dir ***2 miles north of Bath, next to Bath Racecourse.***

Classic country pub, traditional fare, interesting ales

Named after William Blathwayt, the 17th-century politician who established the War Office as an official government department. Blathwayt effectively became the country's first Minister for War; Dyrham Park, his National Trust country house, situated a few miles from the pub is known for its deer park. With its welcoming approach to dogs, children and muddy boots, this is a proper pub, where you can expect anything from a pint of Otter to a plate of Blathwayt steak and ale pie. Mulled wine is supped around wood-burners in winter,

while barbecues in summer are prepared in the large garden, which has a children's play area and overlooks Bath Racecourse.

Open all day, all week Free House 10 from £10 portions/menu notice required

The Hare & Hounds

Tel **01225 482682 | Lansdown Road, BA1 5TJ**
Web **www.hareandhoundsbath.com**
Dir ***Phone for detailed directions.***

Only a mile from Bath city centre, The Hare & Hounds sits high on Lansdown Hill with stunning views over the valley to Solsbury Hill. Happily, the feast for the eyes extends to the pub's food and drink. The welcome is warm, the staff and service friendly, and the food unpretentiously good. In summer, the terrace is much sought after for alfresco dining as you'd expect; typical dishes are honey-baked figs with goats' cheese; and venison shepherd's pie with spiced red cabbage.

Open all day, all week Star Pubs & Bars 31 from £12 portions/menu notice required

The Hop Pole PICK OF THE PUBS

Tel **01225 446327 | 7 Albion Buildings, Upper Bristol Road, BA1 3AR**
Web **www.bathales.co.uk**
Dir ***On A4 from city centre towards Bristol. Pub opposite Royal Victoria Park.***

A delightful pub in a great setting, just off the River Avon towpath and opposite Royal Victoria Park. Described as both 'a country pub in the heart of a city', and a 'secret oasis', it has a stripped-down, stylish interior and a spacious beer garden with a grapevine canopy. Bath Ales supplies many beers from its stable – here you'll find Barnsey, Gem and Special Pale Ale. Home-cooked food is the order of the day.

King William PICK OF THE PUBS

Tel **01225 428096 | 36 Thomas Street, BA1 5NN**
Web **www.kingwilliampub.com**
Dir ***At junction of Thomas Street and A4 (London Road), on left from Bath towards London. 15 minutes walk from Bath Spa rail station.***

A short stroll from the city centre on a busy main road, this unassuming Bath stone building offers a happy mix of destination dining inn and locals' pub. In the cosy snug and traditional bar, real ale buffs will generally find a regular Palmers ale, supplemented by guest beers from local microbreweries such as Stonehenge, Milk Street and Yeovil. The kitchen creates traditional dishes, with a contemporary twist, from locally produced seasonal ingredients. A winter dinner menu offers a starter of chicken and black pudding terrine, Waldorf salad and rosemary focaccia, then a main course of slow-cooked pork belly, white beans, sage pesto, chicory and cider syrup. Rhubarb sponge and stem ginger ice cream is one highly comforting end to an evening, matched by a carefully chosen wine list.

Open all week 12–3 5–close (Sat to Sun 12–close) Closed 25–26 Dec Free House 14 portions notice required

The Marlborough Tavern

PICK OF THE PUBS

Tel **01225 423731 | 35 Marlborough Buildings, BA1 2LY**
Web **www.marlborough-tavern.com**
Dir ***200 metres from west end of Royal Crescent.***

Just round the corner from the famous Royal Crescent, this 18th-century pub once refreshed foot-weary sedan-chair carriers. Today's clientele is more likely to need a break from the rigours of traipsing around Bath's shops, for which the Marlborough is handily placed. Butcombe and Box Steam Brewery's Piston Broke are the prime ales dispensed in the spotless bar; the wine selection comprising 30 sold by the glass offers something for everyone. The lunch menu pleases too by not straying far from popular and traditional pub classics, such as beer battered fish of the day with triple-cooked chips, mushy peas and tartare sauce. The must-book Sunday lunches might include roasted belly of pork with crackling, apple sauce and all the trimmings.

Open all day, all week 9am–11pm (25 Dec bookings only) Free House 30 from £12 portions/menu notice required

The Rising Sun Inn ★★★ INN

Tel **01225 425918 | 3–4 Grove Street, BA2 6PJ**
Web **www.therisingsunbath.co.uk**
Dir ***M4 junction 18, A46. Follow A4 and Bath signs at roundabout. At lights left into Bathwick Street. Over river bridge, 1st right into St Johns Road. Becomes Grove Street, pub on left.***

This Georgian pub is tucked away but well worth seeking out. Traditional but with fresh, modern decor and a peaceful courtyard garden, the atmosphere is friendly whether you just pop in for a pint or stop longer for the home-made food.

The Salamander

Tel **01225 428889 | 3 John Street, BA1 2JL**
Web **www.salamanderbath.co.uk**
Dir ***Phone for detailed directions.***

Just off Queen Square in the heart of Georgian Bath, this cosy, two-floor pub punches well above its diminutive size. Now owned by Cornwall's St Austell brewery, it has retained the range of beers from its time as a Bath Ales pub.

The Star Inn

Tel **01225 425072 | 23 Vineyards, BA1 5NA**
Web **www.star-inn-bath.co.uk**
Dir ***On A4, 300 metres from centre of Bath.***

Set amid glorious Georgian architecture and first licensed in 1760, the impressive Star Inn is one of Bath's oldest pubs and is of outstanding historical interest, with a rare and totally unspoiled interior, long famous for pints of Bass served from the jug.

BAWDRIP

The Knowle Inn

Tel **01278 683330 | TA7 8PN**
Web **www.theknowleinn.co.uk**
Dir ***M5 junction 23 or A39 from Bridgwater towards Glastonbury.***

This 16th-century pub on the A39 sits beneath the Polden Hills and has far-reaching views across Sedgemoor to the Quantocks and Blackdown Hills. The live music, skittles and darts are popular with locals, while the seafood specials and Mediterranean-style garden attract visitors from further afield.

BECKINGTON

Woolpack Inn

Tel **01373 831244 | BA11 6SP**
Web **www.oldenglish.co.uk**
Dir ***Just off A36 near junction with A361.***

This charming, stone-built coaching inn dates back to the 1500s. Standing in the middle of the village and a short drive from Bath, inside there's an attractive, flagstone floor in the bar and outside at the back, a delightful terraced garden.

BISHOP SUTTON

The Red Lion

Tel **01275 333042 | Sutton Hill, BS39 5UT**
Web **www.redlionbishopsutton.co.uk**
Dir ***Between Pensford and Clutton on A37 take A368 to Bishop Sutton.***

This has fast become a real little gem of a pub. In the bar, Bath Ales Gem single-handedly raises the flag for Somerset. The menus offer choices such as wild boar salami with fennel and apple salad; pappardelle pasta and venison ragù; pot roast belly of lamb; and salmon, crayfish and cod bake. There's also the 'classic stuff' such as thick slices of Walsh's ham, double fried egg, chips and chunky piccalilli; and a 12oz dry-aged (for a minimum of 31 days) T-bone steak.

Open all week 12–2.30 4.30–11 (Fri to Sun 12–12 Mon 5–11) Punch Taverns portions notice required

BISHOPSWOOD

Candlelight Inn

Tel **01460 234476 | TA20 3RS**
Web **www.candlelight-inn.co.uk**
Dir ***From A303 south-west of Newtown, right a crossroads signed Bishopswood and Churchinford. Pub on right in village.***

This rustic rural inn is tucked away deep in the Blackdown Hills. A 17th-century flint-built pub with wooden floors, crackling log fires and a warm and friendly atmosphere, locals gather here for tip-top pints of Exmoor or Branscombe ale drawn straight from the cask.

CATCOTT

The Crown Inn

Tel **01278 722288 | 1 The Nydon, TA7 9HQ**
Web **www.crowninncatcott.com**
Dir ***M5 junction 23, A39 towards Glastonbury. Turn left to Catcott.***

Originally a beer house serving local peat-cutters, this low-beamed, flagstoned pub in the Somerset Levels is perhaps 400 years old. The winter log fire takes the chill off Bristol Channel winds; in summer the half-acre beer garden is great for families and sun worshippers.

CHEW MAGNA

The Bear and Swan

★★★★★ INN PICK OF THE PUBS

Tel 01275 331100 | South Parade, BS40 8SL
Web www.ohhpubs.co.uk
Dir *A37 from Bristol. Turn right signed Chew Magna onto B3130. Or from A38 turn left on B3130.*

Chew Valley Lake is a real honeypot for anglers, birdwatchers and walkers, and so is this charming, early 18th-century pub, with oak-beams, scrubbed wooden floors, reclaimed furniture and assorted artefacts. In the restaurant, the main menu offers a good choice of fish, game, seafood, meats and vegetarian dishes, plus a specials board. Start with gin-cured salmon with celeriac remoulade, then perhaps a pub favourite: pan-fried calves' liver and bacon for instance, or rump of lamb with fondant potatoes, fennel and Mediterranean vegetables. To finish, maybe mango cheesecake with hazelnut praline. Culinary evenings are held monthly, and burger and steak nights twice weekly.

Open all day, all week 9am to midnight Fuller's 12 portions/menu Wi-fi P *notice required*

The Pony and Trap

PICK OF THE PUBS

Tel 01275 332627 | Knowle Hill, Newton, BS40 8TQ
Web www.theponyandtrap.co.uk
Dir *Take A37 south from Bristol. After Pensford turn right at roundabout onto A368 towards Weston-super-Mare. In 1.5 mile right signed Chew Magna and Winford. Pub 1 mile on right.*

Set on a low ridge above the Chew Valley, this appealing old country pub enjoys gorgeous views across pastures and woodland. North Somerset is where most of the produce is sourced; beer from Butcombe Brewery is equally local. The brother and sister team of Josh and Holly Eggleton have built a tremendous reputation for invigorating menus based on a mantra of field-to-fork simplicity. Start with rabbit terrine, celeriac remoulade, apple and Butcombe chutney; followed by fillet of brill with brown shrimp, celery, Savoy cabbage and seaweed butter. To finish, try the sticky ale pudding with salted caramel sauce and stout ice cream.

Open all year 12–2.30 7–11 (Fri to Sat 12–2.30 6–11 Sun 12–8) Closed Mon Free House 15 from £13.50 portions Wi-fi P

CHURCHILL

The Crown Inn

Tel 01934 852995 | The Batch, BS25 5PP
Dir *From Bristol take A38 south. Right at Churchill lights, left in 200 metres, up hill to pub.*

This gem of a pub was once a stop on what was then the Bristol to Exeter coach road. A good selection of real ales is served straight from the cask in the two flagstone-floored bars, where open fires blaze on cold days. Bar lunches include sandwiches, soups, salads and ploughman's, all made from the best local ingredients. In fact, the beef comes straight from the fields that can be seen from the pub's windows. Enjoy a meal in the beautiful gardens in warmer weather.

Open all day, all week 11–11 (Fri 11am–midnight) Free House from £5.75 portions Wi-fi P

CLAPTON-IN-GORDANO

The Black Horse PICK OF THE PUBS

Tel 01275 842105 | Clevedon Lane, BS20 7RH
Web www.blackhorseclapton.co.uk
Dir *M5 junction 19, A369 to Portishead. At roundabout left onto B3124. At 3rd roundabout left to Clapton-in-Gordano.*

The bars on one of the windows of this attractive, whitewashed inn near Bristol are a reminder that the Black Horse's Snug Bar was once the village lock-up. Built in the 14th century, the pub features low beams, flagstone floors, wooden settles, and old guns above the big open fireplace. Real ales served straight from the barrel include local Butcombe Bitter and Bath Ales Gem, whilst cider fans will rejoice at the sight of Thatchers Stan's. The small kitchen limits its output to traditional pub food served at lunchtimes only (Monday to Saturday). The repertoire includes hot and cold filled baguettes and rolls; home-made soup of the day; daily specials, and classics like sausage and mediterranean vegetable casserole.

Open all day, all week Enterprise Inns 8 Wi-fi P

CLUTTON

The Hunters Rest – see page 370

CLUTTON

The Hunters Rest

 INN

Tel 01761 452303 | King Lane, Clutton Hill, BS39 5QL
Web www.huntersrest.co.uk
Dir *On A37 follow signs for Wells through Pensford, at large roundabout left towards Bath, 100 metres right into country lane, pub 1 mile up hill.*

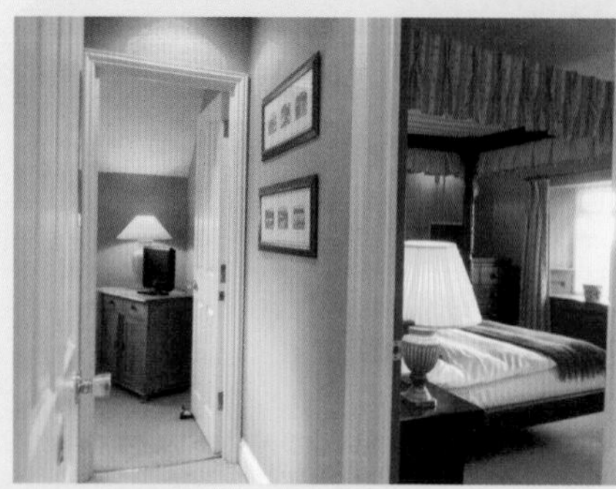

Traditional country inn with excellent views

PICK OF THE PUBS

Dating from 1750, The Earl of Warwick's former hunting lodge offers far-reaching views across the Cam Valley to the Mendip Hills and the Chew Valley towards Bristol. When the estate was sold in 1872, the building became a tavern serving the growing number of coal miners working in the area, but all the mines closed long ago and the place has been transformed into a popular and attractive inn. Paul Thomas has been running the place for more than 30 years, during which time he has established a great reputation for good home-made food, real ales – typically Butcombe and Otter and weekly changing local guest ale – and a well-stocked wine cellar. On the specials blackboard there's a selection of daily delivered, Brixham-landed fish – sea bass fillet, pea and ham risotto; or beer-battered cod being just two options perhaps. Finish with a popular dessert such as sticky toffee pudding; Bakewell tart; or chocolate and honeycomb cheesecake. In summer, you can sit out in the landscaped grounds, and if a longer visit is on the cards the inn has very stylish en suite bedrooms.

Open all day, all week Free House 10 from £10 portions/menu notice required

COMBE HAY

The Wheatsheaf Combe Hay

PICK OF THE PUBS

Tel **01225 833504** | **BA2 7EG**
Web **www.wheatsheafcombehay.co.uk**
Dir ***From Bath take A369 (Exeter road) to Odd Down, left at Park & Ride and immediately right towards Combe Hay. 2 miles to thatched cottage, turn left.***

Only 10 minutes' drive from Bath, this long, whitewashed pub in large terraced gardens overlooks the village and surrounding hills. First a farmhouse, it has been a pub for over 250 years, its rustic charm today enhanced by a country-chic look, massive wooden tables and open log fires. The real cider is from just down the lane and Butcombe, across the county to the west, brews the real ales. Bar snacks are available, while the concise menu might suggest pan-roasted halibut; roast venison loin; and home-made beef burger. Combe Hay appears in the 1952 Ealing Comedy, *The Titfield Thunderbolt*, with some scenes filmed on the long-closed railway line that once ran through the village.

Open 10.30–3 6–11 (Sun 11–5.30) Closed 25–26 Dec and 1st week Jan, Sun evening, Mon (excluding bank holidays) Free House 13 portions/menu

COMPTON DANDO

The Compton Inn

Tel **01761 490321** | **Court Hill, BS39 4JZ**
Web **www.thecomptoninn.co.uk**
Dir ***From A368 between Chelwood and Marksbury follow Hunstrete and Compton Dando signs.***

A former farmhouse, the Grade II listed Compton Inn has only been a pub since World War II, but it has been sympathetically restored. Located in picturesque Compton Dando, with its imposing church and hump-backed bridge crossing the River Chew, it is only a few miles from the bustling city of Bristol. It's an ideal bolt-hole to enjoy local ale and cider, and well-cooked dishes like Somerset faggots, spring onion mash and vegetables; or 12oz gammon steak and free-range eggs. For pudding try Bailey's crème brûlée.

Open all day, all week 12–11 (Sun to Mon 12–9.30) Star Pubs & Bars 10 from £10 portions/menu notice required

CORSTON

The Wheatsheaf

Tel **01225 872915** | **Wells Road, BA2 9HB**
Dir ***Phone for detailed directions.***

There's an enthusiastic new team at the refurbished Wheatsheaf, a cosy country pub with exposed walls, button-backed armchairs and a woodburner. Expect classic pub food and well-kept beer – Butcombe bitter, Sharp's Doom Bar and Fuller's London Pride.

Open 12–3 5–11 (Fri to Sat 12–11 Sun 12–9) Closed Mon Punch Taverns portions

CORTON DENHAM

The Queens Arms

★★★★★ INN PICK OF THE PUBS

Tel **01963 220317** | **DT9 4LR**
Web **www.thequeensarms.com**
Dir ***A303 follow signs for Sutton Montis, South Cadbury and Corton Denham. Through South Cadbury, 0.25 mile, left, up hill signed Corton Denham. Left at hill top to village, approximately 1 mile. Pub on right.***

Below the Blackdown Hills, just over the Dorset border in Somerset, stands this late 18th-century, stone-built, one-time cider house. Beneath the beams in the bar and separate dining room are grand open fireplaces, leather chairs and sofas, and old scrubbed tables set with tasteful china. The bar offers the pub's own ale, Legless Liz, alongside Otter and Exmoor beers, local farm ciders, apple juices and a remarkable range of bottled beers, gins, malts, world spirits and liqueurs; even the 60-bin wine list includes six champagnes. Owners Gordon and Jeanette Reid champion high-quality local produce – some from their own farm in Sutton Montis. The sheltered terrace and sunny garden are perfect for outdoor eating and drinking. Muddy boots and dogs are no problem here. In July, there's a beer festival.

Open all day, all week Free House 16 from £14 portions/menu notice required

See advertisement on page 373

CREWKERNE

The George Inn

Tel **01460 73650** | **Market Square, TA18 7LP**
Web **georgehotel.southcoastinns.co.uk**
Dir ***Phone for detailed directions.***

Situated in the heart of Crewkerne, The George has been welcoming travellers since 1541, though the present hamstone building dates from 1832. Thatchers Gold cider sits alongside the real ales in the bar, while the kitchen produces an array of popular dishes for bar snacks and more substantial meals from the daily specials board. Vegetarian and vegan meals are always available.

Open all day, all week Free House 8 portions/menu

The Manor Arms

Tel **01460 72901** | **North Perrott, TA18 7SG**
Web **www.manorarms.net**
Dir ***From A30 (Yeovil to Honiton) take A3066 towards Bridport. North Perrott 1.5 miles.***

On the Dorset–Somerset border, this 16th-century, Grade II listed pub and its neighbouring hamstone cottages overlook the green in the conservation village of North Perrott. The restored inn features an inglenook fireplace, flagstone floors and oak beams. Dogs and children are welcome, there's a fine beer garden for warmer days and plenty of rambling opportunities right on the doorstep. To accompany ales like Butcombe, and Ashton Press cider, expect wholesome, traditional food.

Open all year Tue to Sat 12–2 6–11 (Sun 12–3) Closed Mon, Sun evening Free House from £8.95 portions/menu

CROSCOMBE

The George Inn

Tel **01749 342306** | **Long Street, BA5 3QH**
Web **www.thegeorgeinn.co.uk**
Dir ***On A371 midway between Shepton Mallet and Wells.***

This 17th-century village pub has a traditional look with real hops, a large inglenook fireplace and family grandfather clock. In addition to a good range of local ales, including locally-made beer that's exclusive to the pub, there's eight real ciders too. Tempting food appears on the menu. The garden terrace incorporates an all-weather patio and children's area next to a function room, skittle alley and wood-fired pizza oven. There is a beer festival in mid-April.

Open all week 8–3 6–11 (Fri 8–3 5–12 Sat 8am–midnight Sun 8am–11pm) Free House 8 portions/menu notice required

DINNINGTON

Dinnington Docks

Tel **01460 52397** | **TA17 8SX**
Dir ***South of A303 between South Petherton and Ilminster.***

For over 250 years, this landmark pub, now owned by Matthew Mills, has stood on the ancient Fosse Way. Loud music, pool tables and fruit machines are out; in are silently evocative photographs and signage from a fictitious maritime and railway past, invented by a mischievous landlord 60 years ago. Good-quality cask ales and farm ciders, and freshly prepared traditional pub favourites feature. Classic-car owners meet here on the first Monday evening of the month.

Open all week 12–3 6–12 (Fri to Sun all day) Free House 10 from £11.50 portions notice required

DULVERTON

The Bridge Inn

Tel **01398 324130** | **20 Bridge Street, TA22 9HJ**
Web **www.thebridgeinndulverton.com**
Dir ***M5 junction 27, A361 towards Barnstaple. In Tiverton take A396 signed Dulverton. Left onto B3222 to Dulverton. Pub by river in village.***

Well-behaved dogs are welcome at this early-Victorian pub, and the resident canine, Milly, keeps a stash of gravy bones behind the bar for visiting dogs. Not only are dogs welcome, but well-behaved fans of award-winning cask ales, worldwide craft beers, sensibly priced wines and traditional pub food are also in luck. Favourites include fish pie and a selection of salads and burgers. Grazing plates, meaty and vegetarian, are designed as both main courses or for sharing.

Open all week 12–11 summer (winter Mon 12–3 Tue to Thu 12–3 6–11 Fri to Sun 12–11) Closed 25–26 Dec, 1 Jan Free House 12 from £11 portions/menu notice required

DUNSTER

The Luttrell Arms Hotel – see page 374

The Stags Head Inn

Tel **01643 821229 | 10 West Street, TA24 6SN**
Web **www.stagsheadinnexmoor.co.uk**
Dir ***From A39 take A396 to Dunster. Pub on right.***

Dunster Castle dominates this historic village, the Gateway to Exmoor National Park. The inn itself is 16th century, as a fresco in a bedroom depicting Henry VIII as the devil confirms. The bar stocks real ciders and ales, including Exmoor Ale brewed in Wiveliscombe. Sandwiches and a ploughman's are served at lunchtime, while the main menu presents slow-cooked lamb shank; a selection of pies; and pot roast chicken with fresh garden herbs. This small inn has limited seating, so reservations for dinner and Sunday lunch are definitely recommended.

Open all day, all week 12–11 Free House portions/menu notice required

EAST BOWER

The Bower Inn

Tel **01278 422926 | Bower Lane, TA6 4TY**
Web **www.thebowerinn.co.uk**
Dir ***M5 junction 23, A39 signed Glastonbury and Wells. Right at lights signed Bridgwater. Over motorway, left into Bower Lane to pub on left.***

The Bower Inn was converted from a family home to a restaurant in the 1980s, then following two years of closure, it attracted the attention of Peter and Candida Leaver, who purchased and renovated it. Business is good, both in the bar and the contemporary restaurant.

DUNSTER

The Luttrell Arms Hotel

★★★ HOTEL

Tel **01643 821555** | **High Street, TA24 6SG**
Web **www.luttrellarms.co.uk**
Dir ***From A39 (Bridgwater to Minehead), left onto A396 to Dunster (2 miles from Minehead).***

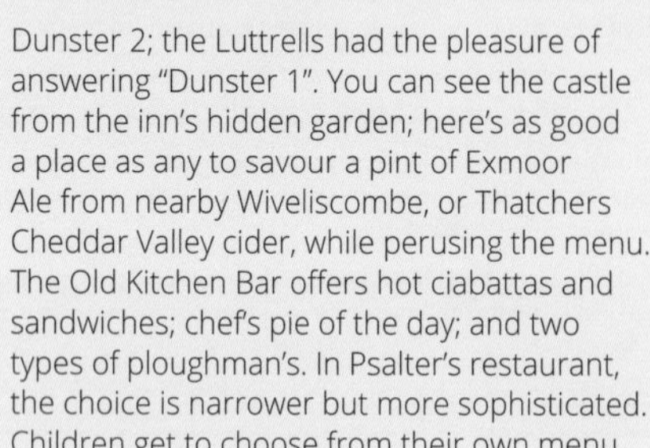

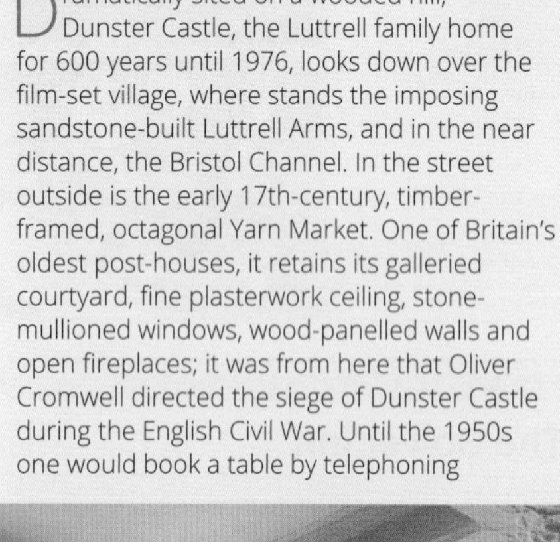

Ancient free house in memorable location

Dramatically sited on a wooded hill, Dunster Castle, the Luttrell family home for 600 years until 1976, looks down over the film-set village, where stands the imposing sandstone-built Luttrell Arms, and in the near distance, the Bristol Channel. In the street outside is the early 17th-century, timber-framed, octagonal Yarn Market. One of Britain's oldest post-houses, it retains its galleried courtyard, fine plasterwork ceiling, stone-mullioned windows, wood-panelled walls and open fireplaces; it was from here that Oliver Cromwell directed the siege of Dunster Castle during the English Civil War. Until the 1950s one would book a table by telephoning Dunster 2; the Luttrells had the pleasure of answering "Dunster 1". You can see the castle from the inn's hidden garden; here's as good a place as any to savour a pint of Exmoor Ale from nearby Wiveliscombe, or Thatchers Cheddar Valley cider, while perusing the menu. The Old Kitchen Bar offers hot ciabattas and sandwiches; chef's pie of the day; and two types of ploughman's. In Psalter's restaurant, the choice is narrower but more sophisticated. Children get to choose from their own menu.

Open all day, all week 8am–11pm *Free House* 12 *portions/menu*

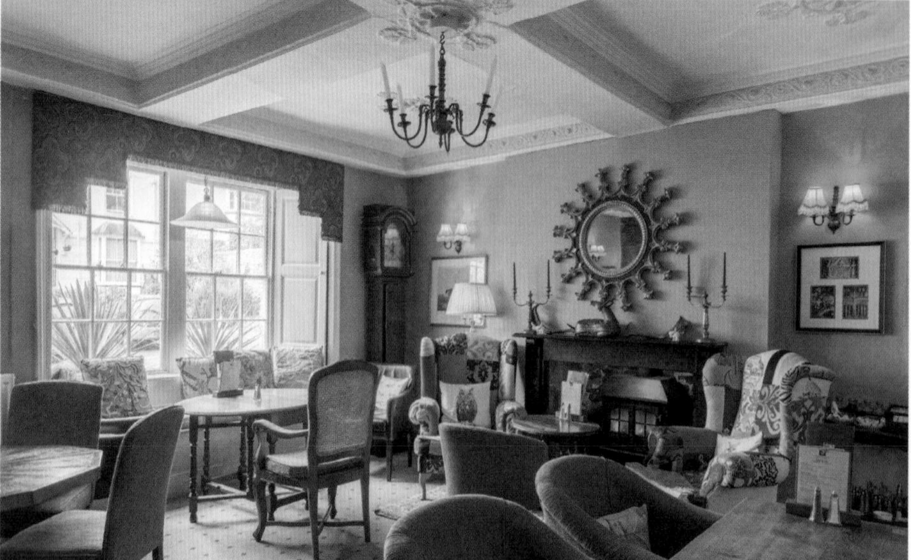

EAST HARPTREE

Castle of Comfort

Tel **01761 221321 | BS40 6DD**
Web **www.thecastleofcomfort.co.uk**
Dir ***On B3134.***

During Judge Jeffreys' time in the 17th century, prisoners from nearby Wells jail were taken to the Castle of Comfort for their last meal and a pint before being hanged at Gibbets Brow. Thankfully, modern-day visitors enjoy their time without the worry of being taken away.

EXFORD

The Crown Hotel **PICK OF THE PUBS**

Tel **01643 831554 | TA24 7PP**
Web **www.crownhotelexmoor.co.uk**
Dir ***From M5 junction 25 follow Taunton signs. Take A358 then B3224 via Wheddon Cross to Exford.***

A family-run, 17th-century coaching inn in the heart of Exmoor National Park, the Crown is a comfortable mix of elegance and tradition. The cosy bar is also very much the social hub of the village, where many of the patrons enjoy the range of Exmoor Ales from Wiveliscombe just down the road. The cuisine is based on Exmoor's profuse organic produce on the doorstep and the kitchen's close attention to sustainable sources. A typical selection from the bar menu could include ham hock and leek terrine with cider chutney and toasted brioche; pan-fried sea bass, spaghetti in tomato fondue with sauce vièrge; and creamy rice pudding with salted caramel with roasted pecans.

Open all day, all week 12–11 Free House 10 portions notice required

FAULKLAND

Tuckers Grave

Tel **01373 834230 | BA3 5XF**
Web **www.tuckersgraveinn.co.uk**
Dir ***From Bath take A36 towards Warminster. Right onto A366, through Norton St Philip towards Faulkland. In Radstock, left at crossroads, pub on left.***

Changing little since World War I, this 200-year-old cider house has an interior worth seeing, with no real bar to speak of, just a wonderful tap-room, small lounge bar and a few old settles. Real ales, and cider from Rich's of Highbridge, are drawn direct from the barrel. Coffee, tea and lunchtime sandwiches are available. The flower-bordered lawn is surrounded by open countryside. The pub's name refers to farm worker Edward Tucker, who died in 1747 and is buried nearby.

Open 11.30–3 6–11 (Sun 12–3 7–10.30) Closed 25 Dec, Mon lunch Free House

HASELBURY PLUCKNETT

The White Horse at Haselbury

PICK OF THE PUBS

Tel **01460 78873 | North Street, TA18 7RJ**
Web **www.thewhitehorsehaselbury.co.uk**
Dir ***Just off A30 between Crewkerne and Yeovil on B3066.***

This old pub was once a rope works and flax store, then a cider house. Owner Richard sources the majority of the produce for his French and British dishes from within a few miles – you'll get an idea of the cooking style from dishes such as a starter of lightly curried chicken and apricot terrine with celeriac and organic leaves; and roast grouse with Savoy cabbage and bacon, bread sauce and game chips. Guests who just want something simple, like a Dexter beefburger and hand-cut chips, are equally welcome. Real ales are from Otter, Palmers, Teignworthy and other breweries, with ciders from Burrow Hill and Thatchers.

Open all year 12–2.30 6.30–11 Closed Sun evening, Mon, Tue Free House 10 portions/menu notice required

5 SOMERSET PUBS WITH ACCOMMODATION

The following pubs are rated as part of the AA Guest Accommodation scheme (see page 10-11 for more information).

The Holcombe Inn ★★★★★ INN
Holcombe, *see page 376*

The Queens Arms ★★★★★ INN
Corton Denham, *see page 371*

The Hunters Rest ★★★★ INN Clutton, *see page 370*

The Litton ★★★★ INN Litton, *see page 377*

Red Lion ★★★★ INN Babcary, *see page 365*

HINTON ST GEORGE

The Lord Poulett Arms

PICK OF THE PUBS

Tel **01460 73149 | High Street, TA17 8SE**
Web **www.lordpoulettarms.com**
Dir ***2 miles north of Crewkerne, 1.5 miles south of A303.***

From its thatched roof and secluded garden to the wisteria-draped pergola tucked in next to an old Fives court, this handsome 17th-century village inn has that certain something. Inside, there's polished antique furniture, timeworn boarded floors, shiny flagstones and a vast fireplace pumping out the heat. The inner bar is popular with locals, not least because it dispenses pints of Butcombe and Otter ales, and West Country ciders. Food is several notches above pub grub, with starters such as Scotch egg and home-made chutney or home-cured pigeon bacon with pear and Blue Vinny risotto. Follow this with fish and chips, a Rubens burger or chargrilled monkfish with cinnamon roasted squash.

Open all day, all week 12–11 Closed 25 Dec Free House 20 from £14 menus

HOLCOMBE

The Holcombe Inn

★★★★★ INN PICK OF THE PUBS

Tel **01761 232478 | Stratton Road, BA3 5EB**
Web **www.holcombeinn.co.uk**
Dir ***On A367 to Stratton-on-the-Fosse, take concealed left turn opposite Downside Abbey signed Holcombe, take next right, pub 1.5 miles on left.***

A 17th-century, Grade II listed inn with views of nearby Downside Abbey, this is where to find some of the county's top locally-produced food, represented on the two AA-Rosette menus. Start with a pint of Bath Ales Gem in the log-fired, flagstone-floored bar, where local Orchard Pig cider is on tap and wines by the glass are plentiful. Linger a while in the evening, as the sunsets can be rather special here.

HOLTON

The Old Inn

Tel **01963 548416 | BA9 8AR**
Web **www.oldinnholton.co.uk**
Dir ***Exit A303 signed Wincanton. At roundabout left onto A371. At 2nd roundabout left, then right to Holton.***

In the safe hands of locally renowned chef Sue Bloxham, this sympathetically restored coaching inn is at the heart of this village near Wincanton. With Wessex produce well to the fore, you'll be assured of tip-top beers from local microbrewers.

HUISH EPISCOPI

Rose & Crown (Eli's)

Tel **01458 250494 | TA10 9QT**
Dir ***M5 junction 25, A358 towards Ilminster. Left onto A378. Huish Episcopi in 14 miles (1 mile from Langport). Pub near church in village.***

Locked in a glorious time-warp, this 17th-century thatched inn has been in the same family for over 150 years. Don't expect to find a bar counter, there's a flagstoned taproom where customers congregate. In the parlour rooms, you'll find a piano, dart board and pub games.

ILCHESTER

The Bull Inn

Tel **01935 840400 | The Square, BA22 8LH**
Web **www.bullinnilchester.com**
Dir ***From A303 between Sparkford and Ilminster take A37 signed Ilchester. At roundabout left onto B3151. Pub in village on left.***

Sitting in the heart of Ilchester's town square, the Bull is a traditional free house serving St Austell ales along with Thatchers cider. The menu is an unpretentious choice of pub favourites, meats are supplied by local butchers and fresh fish is delivered daily from Brixham. It's child-friendly, but note that the Bull opens at 3pm, and serves food from 4pm. There are big screen TVs for sporting events plus a pool table and a skittle alley.

Open all week 3pm to midnight Closed 25 Dec Free House 10 from £8 portions/menu

Ilchester Arms

Tel **01935 840220** | **The Square, BA22 8LN**
Web **www.ilchesterarms.com**
Dir ***From A303 take A37 signed Ilchester and Yeovil, left at 2nd Ilchester sign. Pub 100 yards on right.***

A handsome Georgian-fronted house, full of character, this pub proudly supports local producers, from ales to Orchard Pig cider, with Somerset meat and fish delivered daily from Devon appearing on the modern British menu.

Open all day, all week 7am–11pm Closed 26 Dec Free House 14 from £12 portions/menu notice required

ILMINSTER

The New Inn ★★★★ INN

Tel **01460 52413** | **Dowlish Wake, TA19 0NZ**
Web **www.newinn-ilminster.com**
Dir ***From Ilminster follow Kingstone and Perry's Cider Museum signs, in Dowlish Wake follow pub signs.***

Deep in rural Somerset, this 350-year-old stone-built pub is tucked away in the village of Dowlish Wake, close to Perry's thatched Cider Mill and Museum. Inside are two bars (serving Perry's Cider, of course) with wood-burning stoves and a restaurant, where menus of home-cooked food feature the best quality local produce. Try the signature dish of garlic and herb bass fillet.

Open all week 11.30–3 6–11 Free House 10 portions/menu notice required

KILVE

The Hood Arms

Tel **01278 741114** | **TA5 1EA**
Web **www.thehoodarms.co.uk/**
Dir ***From M5 junction 23/24 follow A39 to Kilve. Village between Bridgwater and Minehead.***

Just an ammonite's throw from Kilve's fossil-rich beach, the Quantock Hills rise up behind this family-run, 17th-century coaching inn. Real ales include Exmoor Gold and Otter Head, plus local ciders, any of which will happily accompany a ciabatta roll or something from the main menu, such as roast chump of lamb with dauphinoise potatoes, wilted greens and port jus.

Open 12–3 6–close Closed 25 Dec (varies), Mon, Sun evening Free House 10 portions/menu

KINGSDON

The Kingsdon Inn – see page 378

LITTON

The Litton   INN

Tel **01761 241554** | **BA3 4PW**
Web **thelitton.co.uk**
Dir ***Phone for detailed directions.***

The bar in this very stylish 'traditionally untraditional' pub is one solid piece of elm, reclaimed from an original ceiling beam. Modern British menus might offer roasted Cornish scallops; and butternut squash and sage risotto, with lemon posset to finish.

Open all day, all week Free House 25 from £12.50 portions/menu notice required

LONG ASHTON

The Bird in Hand

Tel **01275 395222** | **17 Weston Road, BS41 9LA**
Web **www.bird-in-hand.co.uk**
Dir ***Phone for detailed directions.***

Just to the west of Bristol, this pub's clean lines haven't smothered its former village-pub feel. To the left is the bar area, home of St Austell Tribute and guest ales; to the right the dining area. Here, with fish and shellfish delivered daily, meat sourced locally where possible, and much neighbourhood foraging, is a monthly-changing, modern British menu listing dishes like rib of beef, roast bone marrow, herb butter and triple-cooked chips. Home-made snacks include Scotch eggs and chicken Caesar croquettes.

Open all day, all week Free House 10 from £11 portions notice required

KINGSDON

The Kingsdon Inn

★★★★ INN

Tel 01935 840543 | TA11 7LG
Web www.kingsdoninn.co.uk
Dir *A303 onto A372, right onto B3151, right into village, right at post office.*

Former cider house with very good food

Once a cider house, this pretty thatched pub is furnished with stripped pine tables and cushioned farmhouse chairs, and there are enough open fires to keep everywhere well warmed. The three charmingly decorated, saggy-beamed rooms have a relaxed and friendly feel. Hosts Adam and Cinzia have a wealth of experience in some of the UK's most respected hotels and restaurants, and they have made food a key part of the Kingsdon's appeal. Menus make excellent use of seasonal, local and often organic produce – maybe start with bouillabaisse then crisp belly of cider braised Somerset pork, creamed potato, buttered baby red chard and broccolini with roasted apricot- and hibiscus-infused cooking juices.

Open all year 12–3 6–11.30 (Sun 12–4.30) Closed Sun evening Free House 15 portions

LONG SUTTON

The Devonshire Arms

★★★★ INN PICK OF THE PUBS

Tel 01458 241271 | TA10 9LP
Web www.thedevonshirearms.com
Dir *Exit A303 at Podimore roundabout onto A372. 4 miles, left onto B3165.*

Wisteria, acers and lavender surround the walled courtyard at the rear of this lovely pub; croquet, boules and Jenga can be played by all the family on the garden's terraced lawns. Ales include regulars such as Cheddar Potholer, Otter Bitter and Adam Henson's Rare Breed from Butcombe. Burrow Hill and village-pressed Harry's are the draught ciders. Locally sourced ingredients in modern British dishes have helped the inn achieve an AA Rosette.

Open all week 12–3 6–11 Closed 25–26 Dec Free House 10 from £13.95 menus

LOWER GODNEY

The Sheppey

Tel 01458 831594 | BA5 1RZ
Web www.thesheppey.co.uk
Dir *From Wells towards Wedmore on B3139. Through Bleadney. Left into Tilleys Drove to Godney. Or from Glastonbury and Street take B3151 to Meare, follow Godney signs.*

On the Somerset Levels and not far from Glastonbury, The Sheppey sits beside its eponymous river. There's around a dozen ales and craft beers, and 10 cider barrels sit atop the bar, so there's no danger of running out as happened in 1976! The modern menu offers twists on international dishes – Lyme Bay scallops, raisin purée, celeriac, cauliflower bhaji and sorrel oil; and hickory-smoked chicken, bulgur wheat pilaf, feta and mushroom ketchup.

Open all week 12–2.30 5.30–12 (Sat all day Sun 12–6.30) Free House portions/menu notice required

LOWER LANGFORD

The Langford Inn

Tel **01934 863059** | **BS40 5BL**
Web **www.langfordinn.co.uk**
Dir ***M5 junction 21, A370 towards Bristol. At Congresbury turn right onto B3133 to Lower Langford. Village on A38.***

Just outside Bristol, this acclaimed Mendips pub and restaurant serves decent pints of Butcombe ale in the bar, which is adorned with local memorabilia. Conveniently situated for nearby Bristol Airport.

MARTOCK

The Nag's Head Inn

Tel **01935 823432** | **East Street, TA12 6NF**
Web **www.thenagsheadmartock.wixsite.com/thenagsheadmartock**
Dir ***Phone for detailed directions.***

This 16th-century former cider house is set in a lovely hamstone street in a picturesque south Somerset village. The large rear garden is partly walled and has pretty borders and trees. Ales, wines and home-cooked food are served in both the public and lounge/diner bars, where crib, dominoes, darts and pool are available. A sample menu includes Cajun chicken, burgers, quiche and sizzling garlic butter rump steak. The pub also has a separate skittle alley. There's a poker evening on Monday, and Sunday evening is quiz night.

Open all week 12–3 6–11 (Fri to Sun 12–12) Free House portions/menu notice required

MELLS

The Talbot Inn

Tel **01373 812254** | **Selwood Street, BA11 3PN**
Web **www.talbotinn.com**
Dir ***A362 from Frome towards Radstock. Left signed Mells, Hapsford and Great Elm. Right at T-junction in Mells. Inn on right.***

In coaching days, this 15th-century inn was the stop before Wells. Perhaps some passengers mistakenly alighted here in Mells, a bonus for the innkeepers of the day. It has a main bar, snug and map rooms, all open for classic pub food and Talbot Ale. Across a cobbled courtyard is the Coach House Grill Room, where chef Pravin Nayar's fish and meats are grilled over a charcoal fire and, on Sundays, whole roast chickens and suckling pigs are carved at the table.

Open all day, all week 9am–11pm Free House 10 from £14 portions/menu

MIDFORD

The Hope and Anchor

Tel **01225 832296** | **Midford Road, BA2 7DD**
Web **www.hopeandanchormidford.co.uk**
Dir ***South of Bath on A367, left onto B3110 signed Midford. On left.***

Just 10 minutes from Bath, this welcoming pub is on the Colliers Way cycle path, a fairly gentle, pretty ride from the city. Parts of the building date back to the 17th century and it got its name when the nearby Somerset canal was first constructed.

MILVERTON

The Globe   INN

PICK OF THE PUBS

Tel **01823 400534** | **Fore Street, TA4 1JX**
Web **www.theglobemilverton.co.uk**
Dir ***On B3187.***

From the outside, the pub has all the character expected of a Grade II listed building, but the uncluttered interior is contemporary, with paintings by local artists, a wood-burning stove and a tranquil sun terrace providing for all seasons. Local real ales are one of the owner's passions, so expect tip-top local brews like Exmoor and Otter and heady cider from Sheppy's. The extensive menu makes good use of West Country produce and ranges from lunchtime sandwiches and ham, egg and chips, to evening specials such as spiced lamb and feta filo parcels with harissa and yogurt; or Creedy Carver duck breast with ratatouille and crushed new potatoes.

Open all year 12–3 6–11 (Fri to Sat 12–3 6–11.30) Closed Sun evening, Mon Free House 9 from £10.95 menus

MONKTON COMBE

Wheelwrights Arms

Tel **01225 722287 | Church Lane, BA2 7HB**
Web **www.wheelwrightsarms.co.uk**
Dir ***South-east of Bath, 2 miles from centre.***

Set on the slopes of the Avon Valley just outside Bath, this attractive village inn is handy for ramblers straying from the nearby Kennet & Avon Canal towpath walk. Sit in the lavender-scented garden with a Butcombe beer, or cosy up to the snug's log fire with a glass of Honey's cider. From the accomplished menu, start with crispy calamari, kimchi and chilli jam, perhaps followed by braised beef, ale and mushroom pie.

Open all day, all week Closed 26 Dec and 1 Jan evening Free House 10 from £14.50 portions notice required

MONTACUTE

The Kings Arms Inn

Tel **01935 822255 | 49 Bishopston, TA15 6UU**
Web **www.thekingsarmsinn.co.uk**
Dir ***From A303 onto A3088 at roundabout signed Montacute. Inn in village centre.***

The hamstone-built Kings Arms has stood in this picturesque village, at the foot of Mons Acutus (thus, supposedly, Montacute) since 1632. There are two restaurant areas, a bar/lounge and a large beer garden which has games for both adults and children. Seasonal dishes, based on locally sourced produce, appear on both the traditional bar menu and à la carte. Perhaps try confit rabbit, ham hock and trompette terrine; or braised beef cheek with parsnip and potato mash.

Open all day, all week 7.30am–11pm Closed 26 Dec, 1 Jan Greene King 11 portions/menu

The Phelips Arms

Tel **01935 822557 | The Borough, TA15 6XB**
Web **www.phelipsarms.co.uk**
Dir ***From Cartgate roundabout on A303 follow signs for Montacute.***

This 17th-century hamstone pub, with its beautiful walled garden, featured in the film *Sense and Sensibility* and the BBC drama series, *Wolf Hall*. Next to the National Trust-owned Montacute House, overlooking the village square, the pub serves well-kept Palmers beers and Thatchers cider. The main menu of pub favourites features shortcrust steak and ale pie and Thai green chicken curry. Afternoon tea is available too.

Open all year, all day Closed Mon Palmers from £10.50 portions/menu

NORTH CURRY

The Bird in Hand

Tel **01823 490248 | 1 Queen Square, TA3 6LT**
Web **www.birdinhandnorthcurry.co.uk**
Dir ***M5 junction 25, A358 towards Ilminster, left onto A378 towards Langport. Left to North Curry.***

Cheerful staff provide a warm welcome to this friendly 300-year-old village inn, which boasts large inglenook fireplaces, flagstone floors, and exposed beams. The place is very atmospheric at night by candlelight, and the blackboard menus feature local produce, including seasonal game and fish from the south coast. The à la carte menu always has two fresh fish dishes, steaks and a changing dessert board. A light bites/snack menu is available on some days along with a roast lunch on Sunday.

Open 12–3 6–11 (Sun 12–3) Closed 25 Dec evening and 26 Dec evening, Mon (except bank holidays) Free House 9 portions

NUNNEY

The George at Nunney

Tel **01373 836458 | Church Street, BA11 4LW**
Web **www.thegeorgeinnnunney.com**
Dir ***From A361 (between Shepton Mallet and Frome) follow Nunney signs. 0.5 mile to pub in village centre.***

With views of 14th-century moated castle ruins, and a babbling brook and waterfall directly opposite, this rambling inn has the added attractions of landscaped gardens and a winter log fire. The stylish interior merges contemporary with traditional.

OAKHILL

The Oakhill Inn

★★★★ INN

Tel 01749 840442 | Fosse Road, BA3 5HU
Web www.theoakhillinn.com
Dir *On A367 between Shepton Mallet and Stratton-on-the-Fosse.*

Mendips inn with a coveted AA Rosette

This smart stone-built inn stands on a corner in the middle of the village and from the landscaped garden you can see the village church and the Mendip Hills. Spacious yet cosy, old but contemporary, inside, the duck-egg blue interior features a display of over 20 clocks. The pub's own ale plus guests keep bar-top company with Worley's Red Hen and Mallets ciders. The award-winning food conforms to free-range, organic and local-sourcing principles so, even though the menus are brief, the dishes are certainly not short on quality. Consider a three-course meal of Wiltshire ham hock, soft boiled egg and watercress salad; slow-roast lamb rump, risotto and roast roots; and white chocolate cheesecake with raspberry coulis. The bar menu offers a good choice of sandwiches, steaks, pizzas, fish and chips and a ploughman's.

Open all week 12-3 5-11 (Sat to Sun 12-12)
Free House portions/menu
notice required

OVER STRATTON

The Royal Oak

Tel 01460 240906 | TA13 5LQ
Web www.royaloakoverstratton.co.uk
Dir ***Exit A303 at Hayes End roundabout (South Petherton). 1st left after Esso garage signed Over Stratton.***

With X-shaped tie-bar ends securing its aged hamstone walls, a thatched roof, blackened oak beams, flagstones, log fires, old church pews and settles, this 17th-century former farmhouse certainly looks like a textbook example of an English country pub. First licensed in the 1850s, the bar dispenses real ales from Hall & Woodhouse in Blandford, Dorset. Menus change every six weeks or so, with daily specials on offer; typically, expect coarse pork terrine with spiced chutney to start, followed by aubergine curry with pilau rice and crispy poppadum.

Open all week Mon 12-3 Tue to Fri 12-3 6-12 Sat 12-12 Sun 12-11 Hall & Woodhouse
portions/menu Wi-fi P notice required

PITNEY

The Halfway House

Tel 01458 252513 | TA10 9AB
Web www.thehalfwayhouse.co.uk
Dir ***On B3153, 2 miles from Langport and Somerton.***

A delightfully old-fashioned rural pub with open fires, books and traditional games, but no music or electronic games. This free house is largely dedicated to the promotion of quality brews, with an annual beer festival in March and cider festival in August. Eight to twelve top ales and ciders are served, including Teignworthy Reel Ale and Kingston Black cider. The home-cooked rustic fare is made using local ingredients. Sundays lunches stretch from 1 until 4.

Open all week 11.30-3 4-11 (Sat to Sun all day)
Free House 8 portions Wi-fi P

PORLOCK

The Bottom Ship

Tel **01643 863288 | Porlock Weir, TA24 8PB**
Web **www.shipinnporlockweir.co.uk**
Dir ***Phone for detailed directions.***

Enjoy superb views across the Bristol Channel to south Wales from the suntrap terrace of this thatched waterside pub, best enjoyed after an exhilarating coastal path stroll. Ales in the beamed bar all originate in the South West, and Rich's cider is also on tap.

The Ship Inn

Tel **01643 862507 | High Street, TA24 8QD**
Web **www.shipinnporlock.co.uk**
Dir ***A358 to Williton, then A39 to Porlock. 6 miles from Minehead.***

Reputedly one of the oldest inns on Exmoor, this 13th-century free house stands at the foot of Porlock's notorious hill. In the past it's attracted the sinister attentions of Nelson's press gang, but now its thatched roof and traditional interior provide a more welcoming atmosphere.

RADSTOCK

The Redan Inn

Tel **01761 258560 | Fry's Well, Chilcompton, BA3 4HA**
Web **www.theredaninn.co.uk**
Dir ***From Radstock on A367, at roundabout exit signed Wells and Chilcompton (B3139). In village of Chilcompton, right into Frys Well, inn on right.***

A historic inn in the centre of the village, halfway between Bath and Wells, the Redan Inn has been very stylishly refurbished to a high standard. The cosy bar mixes contemporary touches with period detail, with a wood-burner and well-kept real ales including Potholer from Cheddar Ales. The menus include whole roasted Cornish plaice; Moonbeams Farm duck with hispi cabbage; pub classics like gammon, egg and chips; or smoked shortrib from the charcoal barbecue, with Butcombe Bitter barbecue sauce.

Open all day, all week Free House 13 from £12.50 portions/menu Wi-fi notice required

RIMPTON

The White Post

Tel **01935 857525 | BA22 8AR**
Web **www.thewhitepost.com**
Dir ***From roundabout on A303 (south-west of Sparkford) take A359 signed Sherborne. Through West Camel and Marston Magna. Left onto B3148 signed Sherborne. Pub on right.***

Believed to be the country's only remaining pub to straddle two counties, it's only fair that one real ale and one cider – Butcombe and Orchard Pig, respectively – should come from Somerset and Dorset. Appearing on the thoroughly modern menus could be sea bass with samphire, crab tortellini, crab bisque, caviar and saffron mayo; lamb rump with confit Maris Piper potatoes, textures of onion, seared liver and roasted lamb sauce; and, requiring a deeper dig into the wallet, 50-day-hung, salt-chamber rib-eye with dripping-cooked chips and black-garlic ketchup.

Open all year 12–3 6–close Closed Sun evening and Mon Free House 10 portions/menu Wi-fi notice required

RODE

The Cross Keys

Tel **01373 830900 | 20 High Street, BA11 6NZ**
Web **www.thecrosskeysrode.co.uk**
Dir ***From A361 follow signs for Rode. On High Street.***

This delightful Grade II listed village inn dates back to the 17th century and it was once the site of a brewery. The building's support for local ales and ciders continues to this day, with Butcombe ale and Thatchers Gold cider on tap. With gluten-free menus, Friday steak night and lunchtime deals, the kitchen caters for everybody. Start with pork and black pudding croquettes before monkfish fillet, tarragon butter sauce and samphire. Canines and children are equally well looked after.

Open all year Mon 5.30–11 Tue to Thu 12–2.30 5.30–11 Fri 12–2.30 5–12 Sat 12–12 Sun 12–10 Closed Mon lunch Butcombe 10 portions/menu Wi-fi notice required

SHEPTON BEAUCHAMP

Duke of York

Tel **01460 240314** | **North Street, TA19 0LW**
Web **www.thesheptonduke.co.uk**
Dir ***North of A303 between Ilchester and Ilminster.***

Husband and wife team Paul and Hayley Rowlands have established a good reputation over the years at this 17th-century free house. The bar stocks good West Country ales and local ciders, and the restaurant's traditional menu pleases locals and tourists alike with confit chicken terrine with spiced gooseberry and fresh coriander, griddled cider and mustard sausages with red onion gravy and buttered mash, and pan-fried lamb's liver and bacon. Lunchtime sandwiches are also available. Gardens, a skittle alley, two steak nights a week and a Sunday carvery round off the attractions of this homely pub.

Open all year, all day Mon 5–11 Tue to Wed 3.30–11 Thu to Sun 12–12 Closed Mon lunch Free House 9 portions/menu notice required

SHEPTON MALLET

The Natterjack Inn ★★★★ INN

Tel **01749 860253** | **BA4 6NA**
Web **www.thenatterjackinn.co.uk**
Dir ***Between Castle Cary and Shepton Mallet on A371.***

This smart inn was originally called the Railway Hotel, which hosted passengers and goods yard workers on the Somerset and Dorset line for 100 years. Its current name is based in a legend that a live toad was added to the cider barrel before the bung was inserted.

The Three Horseshoes Inn

PICK OF THE PUBS

Tel **01749 850359** | **Batcombe, BA4 6HE**
Web **www.thethreehorseshoesinn.com**
Dir ***Take A359 from Frome to Bruton. Batcombe signed on right. Pub by church.***

Hidden away in the rural Batcombe Vale, this honey-coloured stone inn enjoys a peaceful position with a lovely rear garden overlooking the old parish church. The long, low-ceilinged main bar has exposed beams, a huge stone inglenook with log fire, and is tastefully decorated, with pale blue walls hung with old paintings. From gleaming handpumps on the bar come pints of local brews including Plain Ales Innocence. Menus draw on the wealth of fresh seasonal produce available, including surplus vegetables from local allotments. Lunches take in sandwiches, simply grilled south coast sardines; and locally-shot 'bunny' biryani. Choice at dinner extends to cottage pie with Westcombe Cheddar mash; slow-roasted Somerset pork belly; and home-smoked braised brisket. Desserts include local rhubarb crumble cake; or a board of local cheeses.

Open all week Mon to Fri 11–3 6–11 (Sat 11–11 Sun 12–10.30) Free House 8 portions/menu notice required

The Waggon and Horses

PICK OF THE PUBS

Tel **01749 880302** | **Old Frome Road, Doulting Beacon, BA4 4LA**
Dir ***1.5 miles north-east of Shepton Mallet. From Shepton Mallet take A37 north towards Bristol. At crossroads right into Old Frome Road (follow brown pub sign).***

With views towards Glastonbury Tor, this long, whitewashed building was a coaching inn in the 18th century, and its arched doorway once led into the blacksmith's forge. Beers include Butcombe and guest ales, with real ciders from Wilkins Farmhouse and Thatchers Gold. A bar menu lists lunchtime baguettes, jacket potatoes, ploughman's and cheesy chips, while among traditional, home-cooked mains are steak and ale pie; lasagne (beef or vegetarian) with chips and garlic bread; and a range of beef and gammon steaks. Friday night is (motor) Bike Night and the second Wednesday of the month is Acoustic Night.

Open all week Mon to Sat 12–2.30 6–11 (Sun 12–3) Free House portions/menu

SOMERTON

The White Hart ★★★★ INN

Tel **01458 272273** | **Market Place, TA11 7LX**
Web **www.whitehartsomerton.com**
Dir ***In village centre.***

Chic modern lines blend easily with old beams, wooden flooring, matchboarding and other timeless features to produce a quality dining pub where beer drinkers aren't left out. Bath Ales and Cheddar beers, together with farmhouse ciders ensure the place is a thriving local.

STANTON WICK

The Carpenters Arms

Tel 01761 490202 | BS39 4BX
Web www.the-carpenters-arms.co.uk
Dir ***From A37 at Chelwood roundabout take A368 signed Bishop Sutton. Right to Stanton Wick.***

Good food and local ale in peaceful hamlet

Well placed for visiting Bath, Bristol and Wells or, by the same token, if you're already in one of these cathedral cities, then this quiet hamlet is close enough to consider making for. A low-slung, stone-built, pantile-roofed free house overlooking the Chew Valley, it was converted from a row of miners' cottages, dating from when the Somerset coalfield was in production. Beyond the flower-hung porch, the rustic bar displays low beams, old pews, squashy sofas, and precision-cut logs stacked neatly in the large fireplace. An appealing music-free place, it's where a pint of local Butcombe Bitter, Cornish Doom Bar or a guest ale will always go down well, whether inside or on the attractively landscaped patio. The menus change regularly to make the best of West Country-sourced produce. Among the home-made desserts are treacle tart and clotted cream; and white chocolate and raspberry cheesecake. Not an overlong wine list, but a good range. If you have your walking boots, nearby Chew Valley Lake is an established wildlife haven.

Open all day, all week 11–11 (Sun 12–10.30) Closed 25–26 Dec Free House 10 from £12 portions/menu notice required

STOGUMBER

The White Horse

Tel **01984 656277** | **High Street, TA4 3TA**
Web **www.whitehorsestogumber.co.uk**
Dir ***From Taunton take A358 to Minehead. In 8 miles left to Stogumber, 2 miles into village centre. Right at T-junction and right again. Pub opposite church.***

This traditional free house on the edge of the Quantock Hills is ideally situated for walkers and visitors travelling on the West Somerset Steam Railway and who alight at Stogumber station. Formerly the village's Market Hall and Reading Room, the dining room is now the place to study a menu of home-cooked dishes such as Caribbean pork with apple, mango and ginger; steak and kidney pudding; or local gammon steak, egg and chips. Enjoy local ales such as Otter Bitter in the pretty courtyard garden.

Open all week 12–2.30 4.30–12 (Sat to Sun 12–12) Free House 10 from £9.50 portions/menu Wi-fi *notice required*

TAUNTON

The Hankridge Arms

Tel **01823 444405** | **Hankridge Way, TA1 2LR**
Web **www.thehankridgearms.com**
Dir ***M5 junction 25, A358 (Minehead). At roundabout take 2nd left into Heron Gate. At next roundabout 2nd left into Hankridge Way. With Sainsburys on left, pub on right at mini-roundabout.***

This 16th-century former farmhouse was rescued by Blandford brewery Hall & Woodhouse, whose expert attentions ensured that many of its original features remain. Starters on the wide-ranging menu include smoked haddock and spring onion fishcakes; and a deli board for two. Mains could be chicken curry; or sautéed breast of guinea fowl; washed down with a well-kept pint of hoppy Badger First Call ale. Mature gardens and a courtyard could, for some, be welcome relief following a shopping expedition in the retail park next door.

Open all week 11–3 5–11 (Sat 11–11 Sun 11–6) Closed 25 Dec Hall & Woodhouse 14 from £10 portions Wi-fi *notice required*

STREET

The King Alfred

Tel **01458 442421** | **38 Leigh Road, BA16 0HB**
Web **www.thekingalfredstreet.co.uk**
Dir ***Phone for detailed directions.***

Classic pub menu and a friendly welcome

A welcoming old pub with slate floors, exposed stone walls, old beams, mismatched furniture and a sunny beer garden. St Austell Tribute is always available, along with a regularly-changing selection of interesting guest ales and a range of ciders. A menu of traditional pub fare might feature classics like smoked salmon and prawn cocktail; steak and ale pie with gravy and mash; or honey and mustard seed glazed baked ham, eggs and chips. Beetroot, brie and walnut Wellington should please vegetarians. Choose a dessert from the blackboard. Close to Glastonbury and the Polden Hills, the village was home to the Quaker Clark family who manufactured boots and shoes. The company still has its headquarters there although there's no longer a factory – learn all about it at the Shoe Museum.

Open all week 12–3 5.30–11 (Sat 12–11 Sun 12–9) Free House from £9 portions/menu

TAUNTON *CONTINUED*

The Hatch Inn ★★★★ INN

Tel **01823 480245 | Village Road, Hatch Beauchamp, TA3 6SG**
Web **www.thehatchinn.co.uk**
Dir ***M5 junction 25, south on A358 for 3 miles. Left to Hatch Beauchamp, pub in 1 mile.***

Surrounded by splendid Somerset countryside, the pub dates back to the mid-1700s and prides itself on its friendly, community atmosphere and the quality of its wines and West Country beers. Wholesome home-made food is served, prepared from local produce, with a good choice of snacks and pub classics; at dinner you might find smoked haddock Scotch egg; or crispy haggis bon bons, followed by monkfish, chorizo and white bean stew; and wild mushroom risotto.

Open all year, all day 9–3 5–11 (Sat 12–12 Sun 12–4) Closed Sun evening; Mon Nov to Mar Free House 10 from £11 portions/menu notice required

TINTINHULL

The Crown and Victoria Inn

★★★★ INN PICK OF THE PUBS

Tel **01935 823341 | 14 Farm Street, BA22 8PZ**
Web **www.thecrownandvictoria.co.uk**
Dir ***1 mile south of A303. Adjacent to Tintinhull Garden (National Trust).***

Once ensconced in the tranquil garden of this 300-year-old village pub with a West Country real ale or cider, just relax and listen to the birdsong – or you could be nursing a glass of wine, of course, one of 10 available by the glass. Locally-sourced food featuring on the menus, much of it organic and free-range, might be garlic-fried chicken stuffed with ham, brie and grain mustard; confit duck leg and chorizo cassoulet with crispy cabbage; and roast tomato risotto with olive and hazelnut tapenade. Sunday roasts are joined by fresh fish and vegetarian options. For dessert, perhaps bread and butter pudding or vanilla ice cream. Accommodation comprises four doubles and a single.

Open all week 10–4 6–late Free House 10 portions/menu

WAMBROOK

The Cotley Inn

Tel **01460 62348 | TA20 3EN**
Web **www.cotleyinnwambrook.co.uk**
Dir ***Take A30 from Chard towards Yarcombe. At thatched roundhouse turn left to Wambrook. Pub on right.***

Situated in classic Somerset countryside, The Cotley makes an ideal watering hole for lovers of peace and quiet. Walkers with, or without, their dogs enjoy open fires in winter, and the raised terrace in summer with its views over the surrounding hills.

WATCHET

The Bell Inn

Tel **01984 631279 | 3 Market Street, TA23 0AN**
Web **www.the-bell-inn.co.uk**
Dir ***From A39 onto B3190 signed Watchet. Continue to town centre, into Swain Street. Left at end, 50 yards on left.***

Just 100 yards from the marina, The Bell Inn dates back to the 16th century and both Samuel Coleridge and William Wordsworth once stayed here. Its rich history is also evident from the serving hatch that still exists between the pub and the old foundry, where beer was passed directly to thirsty workers. These days, it's a lively community hub with live music and six skittles teams. Ales from Exmoor and Otter breweries and local Rich's cider accompany dishes like chilli con carne, burgers and home-made curry.

Open all day, all week Free House 12 from £8.70 menus

WEDMORE

The Swan

Tel **01934 710337 | Cheddar Road, BS28 4EQ**
Web **www.theswanwedmore.com**
Dir ***In village centre.***

Open fires, stripped wood floors and big mirrors now greet visitors to what in the early 1700s was a beer house, then by the 19th century had become a hotel. This free house stocks the bar with Cheddar Ales Potholer, Bath Ales Gem and Thatchers Gold cider.

WELLS

The Crown at Wells

Tel **01749 673457** | **Market Place, BA5 2RP**
Web **www.crownatwells.co.uk**
Dir ***On entering Wells follow signs for Hotels and Deliveries. Left at lights into Sadler Street, left into Market Place. For car park pass Bishop's Palace entrance, post office and town hall.***

The Crown is a 15th-century inn overlooking the Market Place in Wells and a stone's throw from the city's magnificent cathedral, Bishop's Palace and Vicar's Close – well-known for its starring role in the film *Hot Fuzz*. All dishes are freshly prepared and champion West Country produce, from the Brixham fish pie and mussels to the local pork belly and Somerset ploughman's. The pub also has its own wine shop.

Open all day, all week Free House 11 from £5.95 portions/menu notice required

The Fountain Inn

Tel **01749 672317** | **1 St Thomas Street, BA5 2UU**
Web **www.fountaininn.co.uk**
Dir ***In city centre, at A371 and B3139 junction. Follow signs for The Horringtons. Inn on junction of Tor Street and St Thomas Street.***

The tower of Wells Cathedral protrudes above the rooftops a short distance away from this attractive, three-storey pub with pretty window boxes. The interior is appealing, too, with a large open fire in the big, comfortable bar, interesting bric-à-brac and board games.

WEST BAGBOROUGH

The Rising Sun Inn

Tel **01823 432575** | **TA4 3EF**
Web **www.therisingsunbagborough.co.uk**
Dir ***Phone for detailed directions.***

This traditional, 16th-century village pub lies in an Area of Outstanding Natural Beauty. Found down a narrow lane, this old building was rebuilt around the original cob walls; inside the decor is smart and inviting.

WEST CAMEL

The Walnut Tree PICK OF THE PUBS

Tel **01935 851292** | **Fore Street, BA22 7QW**
Web **www.thewalnuttreehotel.com**
Dir ***Exit A303 between Sparkford and Yeovilton Air Base at crossroads signed West Camel.***

A handy location just half a mile from the A303 makes this an ideal pit stop for weary travellers driving to and from the West Country. The eponymous tree provides the terrace with welcoming dappled shade on warm sunny days, while inside the black-beamed, part-oak, part-flagstone-floored bar sets the scene. As well as a carefully chosen wine list, West Country-brewed Sharp's real ales (and Orchard Pig cider from Somerset) can accompany seasonal, locally sourced dishes in the comfortable, wood-panelled restaurant. Typical starters of spinach, wild mushroom and blue cheese tart; or fillet of smoked mackerel with red pepper and caper relish might precede main courses of pan-roasted smoked haddock loin, lentils, peas and bacon or Mauritian chicken curry. A two-course lunch menu is also available on weekdays.

Open 12–2.30 6–11 Closed 25–26 Dec, 1 Jan, Sun evening, Mon Free House portions

WEST HUNTSPILL

Crossways Inn PICK OF THE PUBS

Tel **01278 783756** | **Withy Road, TA9 3RA**
Web **www.crosswaysinn.com**
Dir ***M5 junctions 22 or 23 on A38.***

A family-run 17th century, tile-hung coaching inn ideally positioned for visitors to the Somerset Levels or walkers looking for a cosy respite from the rigours of the Mendip Hills. The bar offers an ever-rotating selection of excellent beers, often from microbreweries in Somerset, such as Exmoor and Cotleigh. The beer choice increases significantly during the pub's popular summer beer festival. Cider drinkers are spoiled for choice, too, with Thatchers on tap and Rich's Cider created at a local farm just a couple of miles away. The classic food here also tends to be very locally sourced, and check the specials board, one highlight is pie of the day.

Open all day, all week Closed 25 Dec Free House 16 portions/menu notice required

WEST MONKTON

The Monkton Inn PICK OF THE PUBS

Tel **01823 412414** | **Blundells Lane, TA2 8NP**
Web **www.themonkton.co.uk**
Dir ***M5 junction 25 to Taunton, right at Creech Castle for 1 mile, left into West Monkton, right at Procters Farm, 0.5 mile on left.***

Stone walls, polished floorboards, log fire, leather sofas and smart dining furniture – features that help paint a picture of this convivial pub. Landlords Peter and Val Mustoe's many years in South Africa are reflected in their menu, so you may well find bobotie, ostrich burger and Durban beef and Cape Malay curries there. But if you'd prefer braised lamb shank, chicken chasseur, or pan-fried sea bass, they could be there too. From Monday to Saturday all lunchtime mains are £10, including a drink. Monday is fish and chips night, and it's Thursday for steaks. Hot chocolate drinks include salted caramel, and mint. There's a children's play area in the beautiful garden.

Open all week 12–3 6–11 Enterprise Inns 10 portions/menu Wi-fi notice required

WINSCOMBE

The Woodborough Inn – see below

WINSFORD

The Royal Oak Exmoor

★★★★ INN

Tel **01643 851455** | **TA24 7JE**
Web **www.royaloakexmoor.co.uk**
Dir ***Follow Winsford signs from A396 (Minehead to Tiverton road).***

Previously a farmhouse and dairy, the Royal Oak is a stunningly attractive thatched inn in one of Exmoor's prettiest villages, huddled beneath the rising moors beside the River Exe. Inside, it's all big fires, comfy chairs and restful decor, perfect for enjoying good honest Exmoor beers and rich local produce from the seasonal bar and restaurant menus, including slow-braised lamb shank with pan-fried gnocchi and red wine jus.

Open all week 11–3 6–11 Free House 8 portions/menu Wi-fi

WINSCOMBE

The Woodborough Inn

Tel **01934 844167** | **Sandford Road, BS25 1HD**
Web **www.woodborough-inn.co.uk**
Dir ***M5 junction 21, A370 (Weston-super-Mare). At 2nd roundabout take A371 (Wells). Under motorway, in Banwell follow Winscombe signs. In Winscombe, under railway bridge, pub at crossroads on left.***

Cosy village hub

In the heart of Winscombe, this popular Tudor-style pub is particularly well placed for those walking the Strawberry Line Path from Shepton Mallet to Clevedon, which passes the door. A raised log-burner makes the bar a cosy place to enjoy international lagers, local ciders and a range of real ales from independent West Country brewers, such as Butcombe and Otter. After a starter, say, of lime, ginger and coconut king prawns, many different seasonal options present themselves, including perhaps rich brisket beef and stout stew; or butternut squash, spinach, sweet potato, sage and goats' cheese lasagne. The always-available 'Woody' classics include hand-battered haddock, chips and peas; and honey-glazed ham, free-range duck egg and chips.

Open all day, all week 10.30am–11pm (Sun 12–10.30) Free House 14 from £10 portions/menu notice required

WOOKEY

The Burcott Inn

Tel **01749 673874** | **Wells Road, BA5 1NJ**
Web **www.burcottinn.co.uk**
Dir ***2 miles from Wells on B3139.***

On the edge of a charming village, just two miles from the cathedral city of Wells, the age of this 300-year-old pub is confirmed by the low-beamed ceilings and flagstone floors. At the copper-topped bar, three real ales and Thatchers Gold are on handpull. Here, you can have a snack or a daily special, while in the restaurant typical dishes include garlic mushrooms; pan-fried tiger prawns; apricot chicken breast or poached salmon fillet. The large enclosed garden enjoys views of the Mendip Hills.

Open 12–2.30 6–11 (Sun 12–3) Closed 25–26 Dec, 1 Jan, Sun evening and Mon Free House from £9.70 portions/menu notice required

WOOKEY HOLE

Wookey Hole Inn

Tel **01749 676677** | **High Street, BA5 1BP**
Web **www.wookeyholeinn.com**
Dir ***Opposite Wookey Hole caves.***

Located opposite the famous caves, this inn is outwardly traditional, although the interior looks and feels very laid-back. Somerset and continental draught and bottled beers include Glastonbury Ales Love Monkey and fruity Belgian Früli; local Wilkins Farmhouse tempts cider-heads. The menu offers something for everyone.

WRAXALL

The Battleaxes ★★★★ INN

Tel **01275 857473** | **Bristol Road, BS48 1LQ**
Web **www.flatcappers.co.uk**
Dir ***Take A370 from Bristol towards Weston-super-Mare. Exit for B3130 signed Wraxall. Pub on left in village.***

Built in 1882, The Battleaxes was originally staff quarters for the many servants working for the Gibbs family, who owned the now National Trust-run Tyntesfield Estate. A great example of Gothic Revival architecture, the pub is owned by Flatcappers, a small local pub company.

YEOVIL

The Half Moon Inn ★★★ INN

Tel **01935 850289** | **Main Street, Mudford, BA21 5TF**
Web **www.thehalfmooninn.co.uk**
Dir ***A303 at Sparkford onto A359 to Yeovil, 3.5 miles on left.***

The exposed beams and flagstone floors retain the character of this painstakingly restored 17th-century village pub just north of Yeovil. Real ales are on tap to accompany the extensive menu of home-cooked food, which includes pub classics and main meals such as oven-roasted barbecue pork ribs; and smoked haddock, mash, mornay sauce and poached egg. Sandwiches, hot paninis and jackets are also available. The large cobbled courtyard is ideal for alfresco dining and spacious, well-equipped bedrooms are also available.

Open all day, all week Closed 25–26 Dec Free House portions/menu notice required

The Masons Arms ★★★★ INN

PICK OF THE PUBS

Tel **01935 862591** | **41 Lower Odcombe, BA22 8TX**
Web **www.masonsarmsodcombe.co.uk**
Dir ***A3088 to Yeovil, right to Montacute, through village, 3rd right after petrol station to Lower Odcombe.***

Once a cider house and bolt-hole for local quarry workers, this thatched, 16th-century pub serves an exclusive clutch of real ales – Drewers Broop, Winters Tale, Half Jack – all specially brewed on site. They also offer their own ales in bottles to take home and enjoy. Food is modern British and menus are seasonal and daily-changing. Mains include Masons Arms burger, served on a brioche bun with mature cheddar or Somerset Blue, burger sauce, fries, crispy onions and tomato salsa or perhaps a vegan option of Malaysian laksa curry with rice noodles, fresh turmeric, pumpkin, chickpeas and kohlrabi. Finish with lemon and lime posset with fennel and almond biscotti.

Open all week 12–3 6–12 Free House 8 from £12.50 portions/menu

STAFFORDSHIRE

ALSTONEFIELD

The George PICK OF THE PUBS

Tel **01335 310205** | **DE6 2FX**
Web **www.thegeorgeatalstonefield.com**
Dir ***7 miles north of Ashbourne, signed Alstonefield to left off A515.***

Located up above Dovedale, this pretty, stone-built pub offers a bar with a fire, historic artefacts, portraits of locals and a wide choice of real ales, including Banks's Sunbeam and Jennings Cumberland. There's an original simplicity about the dining room and snug, with their lime-plastered walls, farmhouse furniture, candlelight and fresh flowers. The kitchen's passion for locally sourced food is evident from the organic garden, source of abundant vegetables, salad leaves and herbs. A winter lunch menu might offer pheasant rillettes, celeriac remoulade, cornichons and toast; or smoked Scottish salmon, winter coleslaw and horseradish cream, followed by pappardelle, crème fraîche, woodland mushroom and roast squash; or a venison burger. Leave a space for apple and blackberry crumble with custard.

Open all week Mon to Fri 12–3 6–10 (Sat 12–11 Sun 12–6) Closed 25 Dec Marston's 10 portions

BARTON-UNDER-NEEDWOOD

The Waterfront

Tel **01283 711500** | **Barton Marina, DE13 8AS**
Web **www.waterfrontbarton.co.uk**
Dir ***Exit A38 onto B5016 towards Barton-under-Needwood. 1st left signed Barton Turn. 1st right into Barton Marina.***

Part of a purpose-built complex, this pub is constructed with reclaimed materials to resemble a Victorian canalside warehouse. The vaulted bar serves an extensive range of real ales, premium lagers, wines, cocktails and malts. Good value food is served in the restaurant, bar and lounge, as well as the terrace overlooking the marina. Children over five are welcome. A walk along the Trent & Mersey towpath leads to the nearby National Memorial Arboretum.

Open all day, all week Closed 25 Dec Free House 20 portions/menu notice required

CAULDON

Yew Tree Inn

Tel **01538 309876** | **ST10 3EJ**
Web **www.yewtreeinncauldon.co.uk**
Dir ***From either A52 or A523 follow brown tourist signs for 'Yew Tree Historical Inn'.***

This is a proper Aladdin's Cave of a pub with a collection of antiques and curios which includes Queen Victoria's stockings, a 3,000-year-old Grecian urn, penny-farthings and Victorian polyphons. It also features a motorcycle display room. Pull up a pew or settle on a grand settee to peruse the hearty menu.

Open all week 12–3 6–11 (Sat to Sun and bank holidays 12 to close) Free House 9 portions notice required

CHEADLE

The Queens at Freehay

Tel **01538 722383** | **Counslow Road, Freehay, ST10 1RF**
Web **www.queensatfreehay.co.uk**
Dir ***From Cheadle take A552 towards Uttoxeter. In Mobberley left, through Freehay to pub at next roundabout. Freehay also signed from B5032 (Cheadle to Denstone road).***

Surrounded by mature trees and well-tended gardens, this 18th-century, family-run pub and restaurant has a refreshing, modern interior and it's just four miles from Alton Towers. Marston's Pedigree is one of the beers on offer. With a good reputation for food, its main menu is supplemented by daily chef's specials on the fresh fish and meat boards. There are light bite options such as scampi and chips; and sausage, egg and chips too.

Open all week 12–3 6–11 (Sun 12–4 6.30–11) Closed 25–26, 31 Dec, 1 Jan Free House 10 from £11.95 portions

COLTON

The Yorkshireman PICK OF THE PUBS

Tel **01889 583977 | Colton Road, WS15 3HB**
Web **www.wine-dine.co.uk**
Dir ***From A51 roundabout in Rugeley follow rail station signs, under rail bridge, to pub.***

The pub's name derives from an erstwhile landlord, although the heritage of this edge-of-town pub opposite Rugeley's Trent Valley railway station is lost in the mists of time. These days it's a panelled and wood-floored dining pub with eclectic furnishings, including faux Stubbs paintings. Real ales come from Blythe Brewery and the seasonal menus, using top Staffordshire produce, are changed regularly, but maybe begin with Yorkshire crab, prawn and salmon cocktail; continue with a fillet of lemon sole stuffed with green beans and wrapped in Parma ham; and finish with traditional bread and butter pudding with vanilla custard.

Open all week 12–2 6–close (Sun 12–close) Free House 12 from £11 portions Wi-fi notice required

ELLASTONE

The Duncombe Arms – see page 392

GREAT BRIDGEFORD

The Mill at Worston

Tel **01785 282710 | Worston Lane, ST18 9QA**
Web **www.themillatworston.co.uk**
Dir ***M6 junction 14, A5013 signed Eccleshall. 2 miles to Great Bridgeford. Turn right signed Worston Mill. Or from Eccleshall on A5013 towards Stafford. 3 miles to Great Bridgeford, turn left to Mill.***

Documents can trace a mill on this site from 1279, but the building that occupies this rural spot beside the River Sow dates from 1814, when it was in daily use as a corn mill. Drop in for meals that range from ciabatta or baguette sandwiches, jacket potatoes and grills to home-made steak and ale pie, and roasted field mushrooms with Welsh rarebit, all washed down with a pint of Greene King IPA, perhaps. The pretty gardens make a great place for alfresco eating in the warmer months.

Open all day, all week Closed 26 Dec Free House 12 portions/menu Wi-fi notice required

See advertisement on page 393

KING'S BROMLEY

The Royal Oak

Tel **01543 473980 | Manor Road, DE13 7HZ**
Dir ***On A515.***

Overseeing the crossroads in the centre of the village, this is a true community pub. Owned by Marston's, you can expect big brand ales like Pedigree, Wainwright and Ringwood, as well as guests; bar snacks include sandwiches and jackets.

KNIGHTON

The White Lion at Knighton

Tel **01630 647300 | London Road, TF9 4HJ**
Web **www.thewhitelionatknighton.co.uk**
Dir ***From A51 or A53 onto B5026, at crossroads (junction with Bearstone Road), south of Knighton.***

This historic coaching inn has been welcoming travellers for more than 300 years. Eat in the restaurant or the 17th-century bar, with 10 to 15 local guest ales a month, most brewed from within 30 miles of the pub. The food is ethically produced and delivered with passion.

ROSETTES AND STARS

Stay the night

Many of the pubs in this guide have been inspected and rated for their hotel or guest accommodation by the AA.

To find out more about the accommodation ratings see pages 10–11.

Eat well

Rosette awards appear where the restaurant at the pub has been inspected for the quality of their cuisine.

To find out more about the Rosette award scheme see pages 12-13.

ELLASTONE

The Duncombe Arms ★★★★★ INN

Tel 01335 324275 | Main Road, DE6 2GZ
Web www.duncombearms.co.uk
Dir *From Ashbourne take A515 towards Lichfield. 1 mile, take A52 towards Leek. Approximately 1 mile left onto B5032 signed Ellastone. In village turn left, pub on left.*

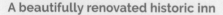

A beautifully renovated historic inn

It used to break Johnny and Laura Greenall's hearts to drive past the boarded-up, 1850s pub that had once been the hub of their village so, to cut a long story short, they bought it. The plan was to offer classic and modern British fine-dining in the warm, relaxed surroundings of a country pub, with rustic-chic decor, real fires and a spacious garden with views across the Dove Valley, and seamlessly blended classic and contemporary architecture. And that's what they've done, which is why it draws a convivial mix of loyal locals and visitors, to enjoy perhaps Marston's Pedigree, Duncombe Ale, a local guest, or one of the many wines by the glass from among the 160 bins. A policy of mixing pub classics with more adventurous modern British dishes leads to corned beef brisket; and honey-glazed ham with poached eggs at lunchtime and, in the evening, roast cod loin, brown shrimp and tenderstem broccoli; beef bourguignon pie; and Jerusalem artichoke with Colston Basset Blue Stilton beignet. Finish with tonka bean parfait, salted caramel and coffee crumble; or warm rice pudding, Armagnac prunes and candied peel.

Open all day, all week *Free House* 55 *from £16* *portions/menu* *notice required*

The Mill at Worston

Worston Lane, Great Bridgeford, Staffordshire ST18 9QA • **Tel:** 01785 282710
Website: www.themillatworston.co.uk • **Email:** info@themillatworston.co.uk

t is quite rare to stumble across a hidden gem as unique as *The Mill at Worston.* Nestled in some of our best Staffordshire countryside it sits beside the River Sow and has spectacular ounds, yet it is easily accessible, being just five minutes from junction 14 of the M6. The ıilding itself is a 200-year-old watermill and it has been tastefully converted retaining many atures from its milling days. Thus, the lounge is dominated by the impressive original 10-foot ıt wheel and full of character with enormous original beams spanning the ceiling and log ırning stoves providing warmth on autumn and winter evenings. *The Mill at Worston* is cask arque accredited and has four cask ales on rotation, featuring beers from many local microreweries including Titanic, Lymestone and Peakstones.

he Mill at Worston is an avid supporter of local sourcing, and nearby farms and suppliers feature rongly on their menu. Starters include grilled black pudding topped with poached egg laced ith a mustard dressing and oven-baked field mushroom filled with welsh rarebit and served ith rustic bread. For your main course our weekly specials currently feature such temptations ; salmon au poivre with sauté potatoes, chargrilled vegetables and chervil hollandaise and ıint glazed lamb cutlets with leek and potato cake, roast beetroot and spinach. If you've still ɔt room desserts start from £4.25 and include the highly recommended sticky toffee pudding ıade to The Mill's own recipe, or for those wanting something more adventurous why not y the raspberry and basil cheesecake? Alternatively, the cheeseboard features traditional ıvourites, along with more local produce. Service is friendly and attentive without being too ɔrmal, making *The Mill at Worston* the perfect place to relax with family and friends.

he Mill at Worston serves food all day, seven days a week from 12pm. The venue's restaurant is pen Wednesday to Saturday evenings from 6pm, and 12pm–4pm on Sundays when customers ın enjoy a traditional Sunday carvery. Reservations are advisable, especially at peak times.

Directions to *The Mill at Worston* and further information can be downloaded from www.themillatworston.co.uk.

LEEK

Three Horseshoes Country Inn

 INN

Tel **01538 300296** | **Buxton Road, Blackshaw Moor, ST13 8TW**
Web **www.3shoesinn.co.uk**
Dir ***On A53, 3 miles north of Leek.***

A family-run inn in the Peak District National Park, the Three Horseshoes offers breathtaking views of the moorlands, Tittesworth reservoir and rock formations from its attractive gardens. Inside this creeper-covered inn are ancient beams, gleaming brass, rustic furniture and wood fires in the winter, with a good selection of real ales. Visitors can choose from wide-ranging lunch and dinner menus of traditional British and signature dishes that use the best Staffordshire produce. Delicious afternoon teas are also available.

Open all day, all week Free House 12 from £10.95 portions/menu notice required

STAFFORD

The Holly Bush Inn – see opposite and see advertisement on page 396

STOURTON

The Fox Inn

Tel **01384 872614** | **Bridgnorth Road, DY7 5BH**
Web **www.fox-inn-stourton.co.uk**
Dir ***5 miles from Stourbridge town centre. On A458 (Stourbridge to Bridgnorth road).***

Stefan Caron has been running this late 18th-century inn for more than 40 years. In unspoilt countryside on an estate once owned by Lady Jane Grey, it retains the traditional style of an old country pub, with church pews in the bar. Black Country brewers Bathams and Wye Valley put on a double act. Menus range from chicken balti to pie of the day with peas and chunky chips. There's a large garden with a weeping willow, gazebo and attractive patio area.

Open all day, all week 11–11 Free House portions/menu notice required

SUMMERHILL

The Boat Inn

Tel **01543 361692** | **Walsall Road, WS14 0BU**
Web **www.theboatinnlichfield.com**
Dir ***A461 (Lichfield towards Walsall). At roundabout junction with A5 (Muckley Corner) continue on A461. 500 metres, U-turn on dual carriageway back to pub.***

Just four miles from Lichfield, this light, airy historic pub is on the banks of the Lichfield Canal. You'll find a good selection of real ales and excellent freshly made dishes, prepared in the open kitchen. The set lunch might start with artichoke risotto and smoked egg, followed by braised ox cheek and mash, while the à la carte menu could offer venison saddle and sausage with wild mushroom and potato terrine. The large, attractive beer garden is perfect on sunny days.

Open all year, all day 12–9.30 (Sun 12–8) Closed Mon and Tue Free House 13 portions/menu

SWYNNERTON

The Fitzherbert Arms – see page 397

TAMWORTH

The Globe Inn ★★★ INN

Tel **01827 60455** | **Lower Gungate, B79 7AT**
Web **www.theglobetamworth.com**
Dir ***M42 junctions 10 or 11 for Tamworth.***

The Globe's elegant restored frontage dates from a 1901 brewery rebuild. The interior, also revamped, still retains its period look, particularly the grand wooden bar and the fireplaces. Snacks include ciabattas and burgers, while the main menu is divided into grills and home comforts.

WALL

The Trooper

Tel **01543 480413** | **Watling Street, WS14 0AN**
Web **www.thetrooperwall.co.uk**
Dir ***Phone for detailed directions.***

The Trooper is a Victorian pub in the Roman village of Wall, built on the original line of Watling Street, now superseded by the A5. Open fires welcome you to the bar, where you'll find local ales including Black Country brewer Holden's Golden Glow.

STAFFORD

The Holly Bush Inn

Tel **01889 508234** | **Salt, ST18 0BX**
Web **www.hollybushinn.co.uk**
Dir ***From Stafford on A518 towards Weston. Left signed Salt. Pub on left in village.***

Ancient pub with second oldest licence in England

This thatched inn is situated in the village of Salt, which has been a settlement since the Saxon period. It is thought to be only the second pub in the country to receive, back in Charles II's reign, a licence to sell alcohol, although the building itself may date from 1190. When landlord Geoff Holland's son Joseph became a joint licensee six days past his 18th birthday, he was the youngest person ever to be granted a licence. The pub's comfortably traditional interior contains all the essential ingredients: heavy carved beams, open fires, attractive prints and cosy alcoves. The kitchen has a strong commitment to limiting food miles by supporting local producers, and to ensuring that animals supplying meat have lived stress-free lives. The main menu features dishes such as breaded whole-tail scampi; grilled pork chops with cheese, beer and mustard topping; and Greek lamb, namely roast shoulder with red wine, herbs and spices and Greek salad. Look to the blackboards for the day's vegetarian options and enjoy the seasonal puddings. During the warmer months, hand-made pizzas are cooked in a wood-fired brick oven. June and September are the months for beer and cider festivals.

Open all day, all week 12–11 (Sun 12–10.30) Closed 25–26 Dec *Admiral Taverns* 12 *from £7.95* *portions/menu*

THE HOLLY BUSH INN

SCRUMPTIOUS FOOD & QUAFFABLE ALES

The Holly Bush buys its fresh fish and meats as whole cuts dir from market and does all its own butchery and fishmongery, al practicing many other traditional cooking skills within its kitch such as home-smoking fish and dry-aging cuts of meats to develop taste and tenderness. The Holly Bush has also recen started growing some of its own fruit and vegetables within it garden.The family operated inn also rewards its customers wit preferred customer loyalty card scheme which offers 5p back every pound spent and other benefits such as a free bottle o house wine, when taken with a meal for two, on the card holder's birthday.

The Holly Bush Inn also offers promotional nights such as pizz pasta night which showcases fresh hand-crafted pizza, cooked its traditional wood-fired outdoor pizza oven and homemade pasta dishes.

SWYNNERTON

The Fitzherbert Arms

Tel 01782 796782 | ST15 0RA
Web **www.fitzherbertarms.co.uk**
Dir ***M6 junction 15, follow Eccleshall (A519) signs. At roundabout left onto A51 (Stone), 1st right signed Swynnerton. Pub in village centre.***

One for port fanciers – and much more

Reopened in 2016 by owners Tim Bird and Mary Mclaughlin, the interior is richly furnished with artefacts from the village smithy, including tables made from old anvils, blacksmith's furnace and water troughs, and it is warmed by three log fires. Real ales – Shropshire Gold, for example – are sourced within a 35-mile radius; while a house speciality is its collection of over 30 ports, including some fine vintages. Uncomplicated dishes of modern British food embrace pub favourites, seasonal specials and home-made puddings. Two people may want to share the 'Fitz' seafood trawler board, namely beetroot-cured salmon, smoked mackerel, horseradish pâté, salt cod and chorizo fishcake, spiced crab on toast, crispy squid with lime and chilli mayonnaise, and prawn and crayfish cocktail. Seasonal specials include braised shoulder of lamb; and pan-roasted venison haunch Stroganoff, while 'Fitz Favourites' are crispy buttermilk-fried chicken burger; 28-day aged prime 10oz sirloin steak; and smoked fish pie. Desserts, all home made, include coconut rum and raisin rice pudding with toasted almonds, and chocolate brownie with chocolate sauce and honeycomb ice cream. On Sundays there's roast sirloin of Rose County beef with all the usual extras. If you own a 'beautiful' car, you can join the Fitzherbert's car club.

Open all day, all week *Free House* *portions*

WETTON

The Royal Oak

Tel **01335 310287** | **DE6 2AF**
Web **www.royaloakwetton.co.uk**
Dir ***A515 from Ashbourne towards Buxton, left after 4 miles to Alstonfield. In Alstonfield follow Wetton sign.***

With its flagged floors, beams, open fire and outside tables with views to tree-studded pastures, this Peak District watering-hole continues to offer the most hospitable, time-honoured welcome to all. Popular with muddy-booted ramblers happy to sample beers from local producers and lunchtime baguettes, the menu also includes filling pub stalwarts like gammon steak with pineapple, peas and chips, and steak burgers topped with cheddar cheese and bacon.

Open all year, all day 12–11 Closed Mon to Tue in winter only Free House from £9.95 portions/menu notice required

WHITTINGTON

The Dog Inn

Tel **01543 432601** | **2 Main Street, WS14 9JU**
Web **doginnwhittington.com**
Dir ***From A51 between Lichfield and Tamworth follow Whittington signs.***

In the heart of the pretty village of Whittington, this whitewashed 18th-century pub with its open fire and separate restaurant appeals to local drinkers and diners. A traditional roast is served every Sunday lunchtime.

WRINEHILL

The Hand & Trumpet

Tel **01270 820048** | **Main Road, CW3 9BJ**
Web **www.brunningandprice.co.uk/hand**
Dir ***M6 junction 16, A351, follow Keele signs, 7 miles, pub on right in village.***

A deck to the rear of this relaxed country pub overlooks sizeable grounds. The pub has a comfortable interior with original floors, old furniture, open fires and rugs. Six cask ales and over 70 malt whiskies are offered, along with a locally sourced menu.

SUFFOLK

ALDRINGHAM

The Parrot and Punchbowl

Tel **01728 830221** | **Aldringham Lane, IP16 4PY**
Web **www.aldringhamparrot.com**
Dir ***On B1122, 1 mile from Leiston, 3 mile from Aldeburgh, on crossroads to Thorpeness.***

With its low ceilings, solid oak beams and open fire, it's not hard to imagine what this old pub was like when it was frequented by contraband smugglers in the 16th century. Suffolk-brewed Adnams ales and Aspall cider feature in the bar line-up, alongside a vast range of rums, gins and whiskies. Enjoy seasonal dishes in the restaurant or head out to the walled garden when the weather allows.

Open all year 11–2 6–11 (Sun 12–5) Closed Mon (Sep to Easter only) Enterprise Inns 15 from £10.50 portions/menu

BRANDESTON

The Queen

Tel **01728 685307** | **The Street, IP13 7AD**
Web **www.thequeenatbrandeston.co.uk**
Dir ***From A12 take B1078 (Clopton). Right signed Easton. Through Easton and Kettleburgh. Pub on right in Brandeston.***

When the current owners took over the old Queen's Head, they gave it a more modern look, a shorter name and a new lease of life. There's a reasonably priced wine list and real ales from mostly East Anglian breweries. The garden provides vegetables and herbs.

BROMESWELL

The Unruly Pig – see page 400

BUNGAY

The Castle Inn

Tel **01986 892283** | **35 Earsham Street, NR35 1AF**
Web **www.thecastleinn.net**
Dir ***From A143 into Broad Street (A144) signed Bungay. At junction right (around island), last exit into Earsham Street. Pub on left.***

Records going back over 400 years testify to The Castle Inn's roots as an alehouse – even if its name has changed several times. Today, the inn is known for simply cooked food based on fresh locally-sourced ingredients, and Suffolk ales from Earl Soham and Cliff Quay. Mussels in one form or another are likely to appear among the starters in the winter months, while the concise list of main courses will include well-aged beef, and perhaps a twice-baked brie soufflé.

Open Tue to Sat 12–10 Sun 12–4 Closed 1st 2 weeks Jan, Mon and Sun evening (Tue evening in winter) *Free House* *from £10* *portions/menu* Wi-fi *notice required*

BURY ST EDMUNDS

The Nutshell

Tel **01284 764867** | **17 The Traverse, IP33 1BJ**
Dir ***Phone for detailed directions.***

Measuring just 15ft by 7ft, this unique pub has been confirmed as Britain's smallest by Guinness World Records. It's certainly a tourist attraction and there's lots to talk about while you enjoy a drink – the mummified cat and the bar ceiling covered with paper money. There have been regular sightings of ghosts around the building, including a nun and a monk who apparently weren't praying! No food is available, though the pub jokes about its dining area for parties of two or fewer.

Open all day, all week *Greene King* Wi-fi *notice required*

The Old Cannon Brewery

★★★ INN PICK OF THE PUBS

Tel **01284 768769** | **86 Cannon Street, IP33 1JR**
Web **www.oldcannonbrewery.co.uk**
Dir ***From A14 junction 43 follow signs to Bury St Edmunds town centre, 1st left at 1st roundabout into Northgate Street, 1st right into Cadney Lane, left at end into Cannon Street, pub 100 yards on left.***

Brewing started at this Victorian pub over 160 years ago. Today it's just the same, an independent brewpub where you can see beer being brewed on a regular basis. Indeed, dominating the bar are two giant stainless steel brewing vessels, fount of Old Cannon Best Bitter, Gunner's Daughter and seasonal and special occasion beers.

Open all day, all week 12–11 (Sun 12–10.30) *Free House* *12* *from £8* *portions/menu* Wi-fi

CHILLESFORD

The Froize Inn

Tel **01394 450282** | **The Street, IP12 3PU**
Web **www.froize.co.uk**
Dir ***On B1084 between Woodbridge (8 miles) and Orford (3 miles).***

Nobody really knows what a froize is, or was. A savoury French pancake? Or Suffolk dialect for a friar? Anyhow, it's what this pantiled dining pub is called. No printed menus here, simply changing blackboards listing dishes and sharing boards based on the best local ingredients.

DENNINGTON

Dennington Queen

Tel **01728 638241** | **The Square, IP13 8AB**
Web **www.the denningtonqueen.co.uk**
Dir ***From Ipswich A14 to exit for Lowestoft (A12). Then B1116 to Framlingham, follow signs to Dennington.***

A 16th-century inn with bags of charm including open fires, a coffin hatch, a bricked-up tunnel to the neighbouring church and a ghost. Locally brewed Aspall cider accompanies real ales from Adnams, plus Black Sheep, Timothy Taylor and Sharp's ales. Suggestions from the modern British menu include Scotch egg with black pudding salad; crispy squid rings; and seared calves' liver, bacon, mash and onion gravy. A typical dessert might be lemon meringue roulade with raspberry coulis.

Open all week 12–3 6–11 *Free House* *from £8* *portions/menu* Wi-fi *notice required*

DUNWICH

The Ship at Dunwich

★★★★ INN PICK OF THE PUBS

Tel **01728 648219** | **St James Street, IP17 3DT**
Web **www.shipatdunwich.co.uk**
Dir ***North on A12 from Ipswich through Yoxford, right signed Dunwich.***

Dunwich was at one time a medieval port of some size and importance, but the original village was virtually destroyed by a storm in 1326. Further storms and erosion followed and now the place is little more than a hamlet beside a shingle beach. The Ship at Dunwich is a well-loved old smugglers' inn overlooking the salt marshes and sea; today it's popular with walkers and birdwatchers.

BROMESWELL

The Unruly Pig

Tel 01394 460310 | Orford Road, IP12 2PU
Web www.theunrulypig.co.uk
Dir *From A12 roundabout (north of Woodbridge) take A1152 through Melton. Over railway crossing. At roundabout take B1084 towards Orford. Pub on left.*

Stylish Suffolk pub with an enthusiastic kitchen team

Close to the National Trust's Sutton Hoo, Rendlesham Forest and the lovely medieval town of Woodbridge, The Unruly Pig is a 16th-century Suffolk inn. The style is a pleasing mixture of traditional and contemporary, with original oak beams, sloping ceilings, log-burners and an eclectic mix of pop and local art on the walls. In the cosy bar you'll find Adnams and award-winning ales, while in the wood-panelled dining rooms the monthly-changing menus offer a good choice – starters from the à la carte menu might feature raviolo of quail with tarragon and beetroot; or seared octopus with spicy sausage purée, apple and fennel. Mains range from the Unruly Burger in a Pump Street brioche bun, with Roquefort mayonnaise, dripping chips and onion rings, to hand-rolled farfalle pasta with mussels, cuttlefish, garlic, tomato and parsley. There is also a daily set menu as well as kids', vegetarian, dairy-free and gluten-free menus.

Open all week 12–3 6–10.30 (Sat all day Sun 12–10.30) *Punch Taverns* 60 *from £11* *portions/menu*

EARL SOHAM

Victoria

Tel **01728 685758 | The Street, IP13 7RL**
Web **www.earlsohamvictoria.co.uk**
Dir ***From A14 at Stowmarket take A1120 towards Yoxford, cross A140 at Stonham, through Pettaugh on A1120 to Earl Soham. Pub on right.***

Sandwiched amidst a range of cottages in a peaceful village above the Vale of Deben, this uncompromisingly unchanging country pub ticks all the right boxes for lovers of traditional locals. The licensee remains fiercely supportive of the microbrewery that started life in the pub's old chicken shed.

ELVEDEN

Elveden Inn ★★★★★ INN

PICK OF THE PUBS

Tel **01842 890876 | Brandon Road, IP24 3TP**
Web **www.elvedeninn.com**
Dir ***From Mildenhall take A11 towards Thetford. Left onto B1106, pub on left.***

Located on the Elveden Estate, home to a direct descendent of the Guinness family, this village inn offers a family-friendly atmosphere, blazing log fires in winter, a range of guest ales on tap, and a modern pub menu that brims with produce sourced from the estate farm and surrounding area. A meal could kick off with caramelised onion and mature cheddar croquettes with red pepper relish, followed by confit rabbit leg, sage and onion dauphinoise potato, roasted carrot and Dijon mustard sauce; or wild mushroom, vegetarian parmesan and chive risotto. Finish with the espresso crème brûlée; or try the sticky Guinness pudding with clotted cream and cinder toffee. Children can choose from their own selection of 'fawn-size' portions.

Open all day, all week Free House 30 from £13.95 portions/menu Wi-fi notice required

EYE

The White Horse Inn

★★★★ INN

Tel **01379 678222 | Stoke Ash, IP23 7ET**
Web **www.whitehorse-suffolk.co.uk**
Dir ***On A140 between Ipswich and Norwich.***

Midway between Norwich and Ipswich, this 17th-century coaching inn is set in lovely Suffolk countryside. The heavily timbered interior has an inglenook fireplace, two bars and a restaurant. An extensive menu is supplemented by lunchtime snacks, grills and daily blackboard specials. Try dishes such as ham hock terrine; rack of ribs; and grilled red mullet with a Parma ham crisp.

Open all day, all week 7am–11pm (Sat 8am–11pm Sun 8am–10.30pm) Free House portions/menu Wi-fi

FRAMLINGHAM

The Railway

Tel **01728 724760 | 9 Station Road, IP13 9EA**
Web **www.therailwayframlingham.co.uk**
Dir ***In village centre on B1116.***

The picturesque market town of Framlingham is the location for this dog-friendly pub. The Railway is stylish inside with a real fire in colder months, and a lovely enclosed garden at the rear is the perfect spot for alfresco eating and drinking.

The Station Hotel

Tel **01728 723455 | Station Road, IP13 9EE**
Web **www.thestationframlingham.com**
Dir ***Bypass Ipswich towards Lowestoft on A12. Approximately 6 miles, left onto B1116 to Framlingham.***

Built as part of the local railway in the 19th century, The Station Hotel has been a pub since the 1950s, long outliving the railway, which closed in 1962. During the last decade it has established a good reputation for its gutsy and earthy food listed on the ever-changing blackboard menu. Dishes may include smoked haddock kedgeree, and steamed steak and mushroom suet pudding. Several beers are supplied by Earl Soham Brewery and there's a beer festival in mid-July.

Open all week 12–2.30 5–11 (Sun 12–3 7–10.30) Free House from £10.50 portions Wi-fi

HAWKEDON

The Queen's Head

Tel **01284 789218 | Rede Road, IP29 4NN**
Web **www.hawkedonqueen.co.uk**
Dir ***From A143 at Wickham Street, between Bury St Edmunds and Haverhill, follow Stansfield sign. At junction left signed Hawkedon. 1 mile to village.***

Off-the-beaten track by the green in a picture-book village deep in rural Suffolk, The Queen's Head is worth seeking out for its classic 15th-century character and charm – inglenook fireplace, stone floors, head-cracking timbers and scrubbed wooden tables.

HOLBROOK

The Compasses

Tel **01473 328332 | Ipswich Road, IP9 2QR**
Web **www.compassesholbrook.com**
Dir ***From A137 south of Ipswich, take B1080 to Holbrook, pub on left. From Ipswich take B1456 to Shotley. At Freston Water Tower right onto B1080 to Holbrook. Pub 2 miles right.***

On the spectacular Shotley peninsula bordered by the rivers Orwell and Stour, this traditional 17th-century country pub offers a reasonably priced, traditional menu with plenty of choice, and food is served throughout the day.

INGHAM

The Cadogan ★★★★ INN

Tel **01284 728443 | The Street, IP31 1NG**
Web **www.thecadogan.co.uk**
Dir ***A14 junction 42, 1st exit onto B1106. At roundabout take 1st exit (A134). 3 miles to Ingham. Pub on right.***

A friendly and inviting pub with seven en suite bedrooms for those who want to stay longer, The Cadogan sits just four miles from the centre of Bury St Edmunds. The kitchen places an emphasis on seasonality and local produce; for something lighter there's grazing boards. Dinner menu options could be rabbit terrine, pickled quail egg, quince chutney and toast; or charred lamb belly, liver, parsley mash, carrots and gravy. Open all day, the pub has a large garden with a children's play area.

Open all day, all week Closed 25–26 Dec, 31 Jan evening Greene King 18 from £10 portions/menu notice required

IPSWICH

The Fat Cat

Tel **01473 726524 | 288 Spring Road, IP4 5NL**
Web **www.fatcatipswich.co.uk**
Dir ***From A12 take A1214 towards town centre, becomes A1071 (Woodbridge Road East). At mini-roundabout 2nd left into Spring Road.***

Good beer and conversation are the two main ingredients in this traditional free house. The Fat Cat is a mecca for beer aficionados, with a friendly atmosphere in the homely bar and a raft of real ales served in tip-top condition from the taproom behind the bar. The head-scratching choice – up to 18 every day – come from Adnams, Woodforde's and Crouch Vale and a host of local and national breweries. There are just simple bar snacks to accompany. Please note, children are not allowed inside or in the garden.

Open all day, all week Free House 8 notice required

LAXFIELD

The Kings Head (The Low House) PICK OF THE PUBS

Tel **01986 798395 | Gorams Mill Lane, IP13 8DW**
Web **www.lowhouselaxfield.com**
Dir ***On B1117.***

Known as The Low House by the locals, this unspoilt, thatched,16th-century alehouse behind All Saints Church is a rare Suffolk gem full of charm and character. Previously owned by the Adnams brewery, it became a free house under new owners in May 2018. Tip-top ales such as Earl Soham Victoria and Green Jack Golden Best are served straight from the barrel in the original taproom – this is one of the few UK pubs not to have a bar. Typical dishes are creamy garlic and Stilton chestnut mushrooms on toasted sourdough, followed by beef bourguignon with celeriac mash and vegetables. The pub holds seasonal beer festivals in the large garden.

Open all week 12–3 6–11 (Sat 8am–11pm Sun 8am–7pm) Free House 11 portions/menu notice required

MILDENHALL

The Bull Inn PICK OF THE PUBS

Tel **01638 711001** | **The Street, Barton Mills, IP28 6AA**
Web **www.bullinn-bartonmills.com**
Dir ***Exit A11 between Newmarket and Mildenhall, signed Barton Mills.***

With its fine roofline, dormer windows and old coaching courtyard, this rambling 16th-century building certainly looks like a traditional roadside inn. The charming interior blends original oak beams, wooden floors and big fireplaces with funky fabrics and bold colours. Study the menus in the bar, perhaps with one of the 14 wines by the glass, or an East Anglian real ale from Adnams, Wolf or Humpty Dumpty. Menus evolve with the seasons, with every effort made to reduce 'food miles' by sourcing locally. Try market fish in beer batter with double-cooked chips and crushed peas. Bar meals include classics like Newmarket sausages with mash and caramelised red onion gravy; and chicken curry with basmati rice.

Open all day, all week 8am–11pm Closed 24–26 Dec Free House 14 from £14 portions/menu notice required

MONKS ELEIGH

The Swan Inn

Tel **01449 744544** | **The Street, IP7 7AU**
Web **www.swaninnmonkseleigh.co.uk**
Dir ***On A1141 between Lavenham or Hadleigh. Pub in village centre.***

On a corner opposite the village green, this cream-washed inn is the only survivor from the four that were here a century ago. Lowish beams in the bar might catch any particularly tall guest distracted by thoughts of a pint of Brewers Gold, or Aspall cider. Traditional home-cooked meals sourced from local suppliers include Old Suffolk sausages with creamy mash, with banoffee pie or warm sticky toffee pudding to finish.

Open all year Tue to Thu 12–3 5–11 (Fri to Sat 12–11 Sun 12–10) Closed Mon Free House 12 portions/menu notice required

NAYLAND

Anchor Inn PICK OF THE PUBS

Tel **01206 262313** | **26 Court Street, CO6 4JL**
Web **www.anchornayland.co.uk**
Dir ***Take A134 from Colchester towards Sudbury for 3.5 miles, through Great Horkesley, at bottom of hill right into Horkesley Road. Pub on right after bridge.***

The inn, which enjoys a peaceful setting beside the alder-fringed meadows of the River Stour, is said to be the last remaining place from which press-gangs recruited their 'volunteers' in this area. Today's customers can rest easy, perhaps recovering from strolls around the idyllic village, which is close to the heart of 'Constable Country'. The Anchor is a light, airy destination where local and regional ales change monthly; the riverside decking and garden are ideal spots to tarry a while. The head chef presides over a progressive menu of pub favourites and modern European dishes, so anticipate smoked fish platter and smoked ribs (the inn has its own smokehouse); trio of Kerridge sausages and mash; battered 'catch of the day' with hand-cut chips, and home-made pies.

Open all week 11–11 (Sun 11–10.30) Free House 10 from £10.99 portions/menu notice required

NEWMARKET

The Packhorse Inn

★★★★★ INN PICK OF THE PUBS

Tel **01638 751818** | **Bridge Street, Moulton, CB8 8SP**
Web **www.thepackhorseinn.com**
Dir ***A14 junction 39, B1506 signed Newmarket. Left onto B1085 to Moulton.***

Those who seek out dining establishments with top notch food should head here, one of Suffolk's most highly acclaimed. Former banker and founder of Chestnut Inns, Philip Turner owns it, having reopened it following a six-month renovation and changing its name from the Kings Head in homage to the adjacent medieval, pedestrian-only bridge across the River Kennet. Just two miles from Newmarket Racecourse, this smart, family-friendly country pub and restaurant attracts all – locals, out-of-town race-goers and everyone in between – to its large dining and bar area. The emphasis in the concise but appealing, regularly changing menus is on quality, locally sourced food and drink, including game from shoots, lamb from Moulton, beers from Woodforde's and guest breweries, and Harry Sparrow cider from the Suffolk village of Aspall.

Open all day, all week Free House 25 from £14 portions notice required

PRESTON ST MARY

The Six Bells

Tel **01787 247440** | **The Street, CO10 9NG**
Web **www.thesixbellspreston.com**
Dir ***From Lavenham take A1141 towards Bury St Edmunds. Right into Preston Road signed Brettenham and Preston. At crossroads right. In Preston St Mary right into The Street to pub on right.***

This restored, charming Grade II listed pub is just outside Lavenham in a pretty village and is open from Wednesdays to Sundays. The huge garden is a bonus in the summer, and a good choice of ale is offered in the bar. In the dining room you'll find a daily-changing lunch and dinner menu, using strictly local and seasonal ingredients. Expect starters like beetroot, autumn vegetable and goats' curd salad, with mains taking in Blythburgh pork belly and faggot with chicory and apple.

Open all year, all day Closed Mon, Tue Free House 12 portions/menu notice required

REDE

The Plough

Tel **01284 789208** | **IP29 4BE**
Dir ***On A143 between Bury St Edmunds and Haverhill.***

Easily identified by an old plough and a weeping willow at the front, this part-thatched, 16th-century pub is tucked away on the pretty village green in Rede. On long-standing landlord Brian Desborough's ever-changing blackboard menu look for lamb braised in Rioja with vegetables and chorizo; and crab au gratin. The bar serves Fuller's, Adnams, Ringwood and Sharp's ales and 10 wines by the glass. At 128 metres above sea level, Rede is Suffolk's highest point – verified by Guinness World Records.

Open all week 11–3 6–12 (Sun 12–3) Admiral Taverns 10 portions notice required

SIBTON

Sibton White Horse Inn – see opposite

SNAPE

The Crown Inn PICK OF THE PUBS

Tel **01728 688324** | **Bridge Road, IP17 1SL**
Web **www.snape-crown.co.uk**
Dir ***A12 from Ipswich towards Lowestoft, right onto A1094 towards Aldeburgh. In Snape right at crossroads by church, pub at bottom of hill.***

Getting on for 600 years old and once the haunt of smugglers using the nearby River Alde, this village stalwart shelters beneath a most extraordinary saltbox pantile roof. Inside, there are vast old beams, mellow brick floors, cosy corners and an inglenook enclosed by the arms of a huge double settle. Folk musicians regularly take over this area for informal gigs; while the nearby Snape Maltings complex attracts international performers. Pre- or post-concert meals are available. The Crown's owners run their own livestock smallholding behind the pub, ensuring a very local supply chain. This is enhanced by locally sourced Limousin beef, seafood from Orford boats, game from nearby shoots, village vegetables and foraged specialities.

Open all week 12–3 6–11 Adnams 12 from £10.50 portions notice required

SIBTON

Sibton White Horse Inn

Tel 01728 660337 | Halesworth Road, IP17 2JJ
Web www.sibtonwhitehorseinn.co.uk
Dir *A12 at Yoxford onto A1120, 3 miles to Peasenhall. Right opposite butchers, inn 600 metres.*

Delightful, award-winning inn

Off the beaten track in the heart of the Suffolk countryside, yet, it's just five minutes from the A12 at Yoxford and 10 miles from the coast. This rustic 16th-century inn retains much of its Tudor charm and incorporates stone floors, exposed brickwork and ships' timbers believed to have come from Woodbridge shipyard. A free house, the bar with its raised gallery is the place to enjoy a pint of Adnams Southwold, Green Jack Trawlerboys or Woodforde's Once Bittern. There is a choice of dining areas to sample the award-winning food, while the secluded courtyard has a Mediterranean feel when the sun comes out. Owners Neil and Gill Mason are committed to producing high-quality food from fresh local ingredients – and to prove it they grow many of their own vegetables behind the pub. At lunch, you can order from the menu or from the selection of light bites and sandwiches while dinner offers restaurant fare. Children's portions are available at lunchtime, and six-year-olds and over are permitted in the evening.

Open 12–3 6.30–11 (Sun 12–3.30 6.45–10.30) Closed 26–27 Dec, Mon lunch, Tue lunch Free House 17 from £13 portions

Plough & Sail

Tel **01728 688413 | Snape Maltings, IP17 1SR**
Web **www.theploughandsailsnape.com**
Dir ***On B1069, south of Snape. Signed from A12.***

Twins Alex (front of house) and Oliver (chef) own this pantiled old inn at the heart of the renowned Snape Maltings complex; it's handy for cultural and shopping opportunities and close to splendid coastal walks. The interior is a comfy mix of dining and avant-garde destination pub.

SOMERLEYTON

The Duke's Head

Tel **01502 730281 | Slug's Lane, NR32 5QR**
Web **www.dukesheadsomerleyton.co.uk**
Dir ***From A143 onto B1074 signed Lowestoft and Somerleyton. Pub signed from B1074.***

On the edge of the village on the Norfolk–Suffolk border, this smart pub overlooks the Somerleyton Estate and was taken over in 2018 by Tara Smyth, who was manager here three years previously. A locally-sourced meal might include home-cured Old Spots ham, pickled mustard seeds and mustard mayo followed by beer-battered North Sea cod, chips and mushy peas. Wash it down with local Adnams ales.

Open all day, all week Closed 2 weeks in Jan Free House 18 from £13 portions/menu notice required

SOUTHWOLD

The Harbour Inn

Tel **01502 722381 | Blackshore Quay, IP18 6TA**
Web **www.harbourinnsouthwold.co.uk**
Dir ***From A12 (north of Blythburgh) take A1095 (Southwold). In Southwold right into York Road to Southwold Harbour.***

In contrast to pubs that don't tolerate wellies, in winter this one recommends them because it stands right by the water, sometimes in it. Inside are two snug bars, a nautically themed one with a wood-burner, and one where staff stoop to serve pints through a hatch.

The Randolph PICK OF THE PUBS

Tel **01502 723603 | 41 Wangford Road, Reydon, IP18 6PZ**
Web **www.therandolph.co.uk**
Dir ***A12 onto A1095 towards Southwold. Left into Wangford Road.***

This majestic pub was built in 1899 by Adnams Brewery, whose directors were pally with Lord Randolph Churchill, Sir Winston's father. Showing no real sign today of its late-Victorian origins, the light and airy bar is furnished with contemporary high-backed chairs and comfortable sofas. In the bar and restaurant, a concise modern British menu offers starters of Binham Blue mousse with pear, beetroot, walnut and rocket; or timbale of Bloody Mary- soused herrings with dill cream cheese. Mains include poached smoked haddock, cheese, spring onion and grain mustard sauce; steamed steak and kidney suet pudding; and Moroccan pot-roasted chicken with apricot couscous and pomegranate yogurt. Children can opt to select from their own menu.

Open all day, all week Adnams 9 from £11.50 portions/menu notice required

STOKE-BY-NAYLAND

The Angel Inn ★★★★★ INN PICK OF THE PUBS

Tel **01206 263245 | CO6 4SA**
Web **www.angelinnsuffolk.co.uk**
Dir ***From Colchester take A134 towards Sudbury, 5 miles to Nayland. Or from A12 between junctions 30 and 31 take B1068, then B1087 to Nayland.***

Serving ale since the 16th century, The Angel's doors open to reveal oak beams, quarry-tiled floors, log fires and a high-ceilinged dining area with a 52-foot well. As a free house it offers a range of ales, especially Suffolk brews, with alternatives including a dozen wines by the glass and a fair old gin selection. On the daily-changing restaurant menus look for pan-fried calves' liver and bacon; wild mushroom risotto; pig's cheek with slow-cooked pork belly; and pan-fried cod fillet. Children get their own menu. You'll find antique furniture in the individually styled rooms. Constable painted the village church several times, although not always in the right place!

Open all day, all week 11–11 (Sun 11–10.30) Free House 12 from £13 portions/menu notice required

The Crown ★★★ SMALL HOTEL

PICK OF THE PUBS

Tel **01206 262001** | **CO6 4SE**
Web **www.crowninn.net**
Dir ***Exit A12 signed Stratford St Mary and Dedham. Through Stratford St Mary 0.5 mile, left, follow signs to Higham. At village green left, left again, 2 miles, pub on right.***

Slap bang in the heart of Constable Country and handy for the timeless villages of Lavenham, Kersey and Long Melford, this 16th-century free house sits above the Stour and Box Valleys on the Suffolk/Essex border. The stylish dining areas are informal, and there's a great choice of local ales in the contemporary bar. These are matched by an award-winning cellar of some 250 bins; over 30 can be bought by the glass. Tasty seasonal and local produce underpins a modern British menu. Typical starters are curried pumpkin, crispy kale, toasted seeds; and roasted quail with lemon and herb stuffing. Children are welcome before 8pm. Dinner might feature roasted squash and chard quiche with salsa verde; or steak and kidney suet pudding with root vegetable crisps.

Open all day, all week 7.30am–11pm (Sun 8am–10.30pm) Closed 25–26 Dec Free House 32 from £11.50 portions/menu Wi-fi P

STOWMARKET

The Buxhall Crown

Tel **01449 736521** | **Mill Road, Buxhall, IP14 3DW**
Web **www.thebuxhallcrown.co.uk**
Dir ***B1115 from Stowmarket, through Great Finborough to Buxhall.***

The curious jigsaw that is an old country cottage and a Georgian farmhouse fit together seamlessly here, resulting in an appealing country pub set amidst the cornfields of deepest Suffolk. With a wealth of beams, log-burners and two contrasting areas in which to relax, indulge in a glass of Suffolk-brewed beer and find your bearings on an invigorating menu. Distinguished dishes from the carte may include slow-cooked belly of pork; seared king scallops; and noisettes of venison.

Open all year 12–3 7–11 (Sat 12–3 6.30–11) Closed Sun evening and Mon Free House 12 portions Wi-fi P notice required

STRADBROKE

The Ivy House

Tel **01379 384634** | **Wilby Road, IP21 5JN**
Dir ***Phone for detailed directions.***

Around the corner from Stradbroke's main street, this Grade II listed thatched pub dates from the Middle Ages. Real ales on hand pump and wine from the Adnams wine cellar are the draw here, and the weekly-changing menu makes good use of local and seasonal produce to offer both British and Asian-style dishes. Start with teriyaki-marinated chicken skewers with salsa; pan-fried calves' liver with Suffolk dry-cured bacon, mash and onion gravy to follow.

Open all week 12–3 6–11 Free House Wi-fi P

SWILLAND

Moon & Mushroom Inn

Tel **01473 785320** | **High Road, IP6 9LR**
Web **www.themoonandmushroom.co.uk**
Dir ***Take B1077 (Westerfield road) from Ipswich. Approximately 6 miles, right to Swilland.***

The delightful sight of firkins of East Anglian beer stillaged enticingly behind the bar welcomes drinkers to this 400-year-old free house. Diners, too, relish the prospect of indulging in home-cooked specials such as steamed venison suet pudding. In times gone by, the pub was reputedly a staging post for the dispatch of convicts to Australia, and the records do indeed show that a previous landlord was deported for stealing two ducks and a pig. Today's guests can linger longer in the cottagey interior or fragrant garden.

Open all year Tue to Sat and Sun lunch Closed Sun evening and Mon Free House from £10.95 portions/menu Wi-fi P notice required

THORPENESS

The Dolphin Inn

Tel **01728 454994** | **Peace Place, IP16 4NA**
Web **www.thorpenessdolphin.com**
Dir ***A12 onto A1094 and follow Thorpeness signs.***

Set in a conservation area, close to Suffolk's Heritage Coast, The Dolphin burnt down in 1995 but was back, better than ever, in 1998. You'll find real ales from Adnams, nearly 20 wines by the glass and a wide choice of bourbons and single malts in the bar.

TUDDENHAM

The Fountain

Tel **01473 785377** | **The Street, IP6 9BT**
Web **www.tuddenhamfountain.co.uk**
Dir ***From Ipswich take B1077 (Westerfield Road) signed Debenham. At Westerfield turn right for Tuddenham.***

Only three miles north of Ipswich, in a lovely village, this 16th-century country pub combines old fashioned hospitality with an informal bistro-style restaurant. The menu changes frequently, with an emphasis on local produce in dishes such as pan-seared scallops, celeriac and miso purée; and belly of pork, chorizo croquettes, braised apple and red cabbage. Wash it all down with pints of Adnams ale and Aspall cider.

Open all week 12–3 6–11 (Fri to Sat 12–11 Sun 12–8) Free House 9 portions/menu WiFi P

UFFORD

The Ufford Crown

Tel **01394 461030** | **High Street, IP13 6EL**
Web **www.theuffordcrown.com**
Dir ***Just off A12 between Woodbridge and Wickham.***

Step though the doors of this handsome property and you'll find a spacious restaurant, cosy bar, stylish lounge area and a terrace and garden, where there's plenty to keep children amused. Adnams and Earl Soham badges adorn the real ale pumps, with Aspall cider alongside.

WALBERSWICK

The Bell Inn ★★★ INN

Tel **01502 723109** | **Ferry Road, IP18 6TN**
Web **www.bellinnwalberswick.co.uk**
Dir ***From A12 take B1387 to Walberswick, after village green turn right into track.***

There's plenty of character here, with 600 years of history, oak-beamed ceilings, hidden alcoves, worn flagstone floors and open fires. Close to the Suffolk Coastal Path and the marshes, the pub has a family-friendly garden overlooking the beach. Firm favourites on the menu are deep-fried whitebait; shortcrust pastry pie of the day; and sticky toffee pudding with butterscotch sauce and toffee fudge ice cream. Well-behaved dogs are welcome.

Open all day, all week 11–11 Adnams 15 portions/menu WiFi P notice required

WESTLETON

The Westleton Crown

★★★ HOTEL PICK OF THE PUBS

Tel **01728 648777** | **The Street, IP17 3AD**
Web **www.westletoncrown.co.uk**
Dir ***A12 north, turn right signed Westleton just after Yoxford. Hotel opposite, on entering Westleton.***

This coaching inn is essentially 18th century, although some say its origins are considerably older. The pub retains plenty of character and rustic charm. In addition to winter real log fires, you'll find locally brewed ales, as well as a good wine list. The 'hearty' and 'sophisticated' food, to quote the Crown, is freshly prepared from top local produce, served in the cosy, dog-friendly bar, the elegant dining room, and the garden room.

WHEPSTEAD

The White Horse

PICK OF THE PUBS

Tel **01284 735760** | **Rede Road, IP29 4SS**
Web **www.whitehorsewhepstead.co.uk**
Dir ***From Bury St Edmunds take A143 towards Haverhill. Left onto B1066 to Whepstead. In Whepstead right into Church Hill, leads into Rede Road.***

Architectural evidence survives to prove that this now converted village inn was built as a farmhouse around 1600. Set back from the road beyond a half-moon-shaped front garden, smart and cosy rooms lead off from the heftily-beamed bar, where a copper-topped servery dispenses Suffolk ales, and a huge inglenook combats the winter chills. The work of local artists looks down on dining tables at which representative starters might include chargrilled king prawn kebabs; and smoked bacon and parmesan arancini; and mains may well take in free-range, corn-fed chicken breast with chorizo gnocchi; and paupiette of lemon sole with oak-smoked salmon. On a fine day the rear garden is a popular place to be.

Open 11.30–3 6–11 (Sun 11.30–4) Closed 25–26 Dec, Sun evening, Mon Free House 10 from £12.95 portions/menu P notice required

WOODBRIDGE

Cherry Tree Inn ★★★★ INN

Tel **01394 384627 | 73 Cumberland Street, IP12 4AG**
Web **www.thecherrytreepub.co.uk**
Dir ***Phone for detailed directions.***

The Cherry Tree Inn features a large central counter, and several distinct seating areas amidst the twisting oak beams. The focus on customer care manifests subtly in many ways: the availability of board games, children's play equipment in the large enclosed garden, wheelchair access, dog friendliness and free WiFi. Among the locally-sourced and home-cooked menu dishes, many gluten-free options are offered. The year sees around eight guest ales rotate, with Adnams and Aspall cider in permanent residence; plus a July beer festival.

Open all day, all week 10.30am–11pm Adnams 11 portions/menu notice required

SURREY

ABINGER

The Abinger Hatch

Tel **01306 730737 | Abinger Lane, RH5 6HZ**
Web **www.theabingerhatch.com**
Dir ***A25 from Dorking towards Guildford. Left to Abinger Common.***

Plenty of variety is the key here, from the children's choices to dishes based on local produce. Traditionally English from its beams to its flagstone floors, the pub enjoys a light and airy atmosphere. There's lots of space outdoors, with a spacious car park and a huge garden with outside service on summer weekends. A typical menu takes in classics like beer-battered fish and chips and pie of the day.

Open all day, all week Free House 22 from £12 portions/menu notice required

BRAMLEY

Jolly Farmer Inn

Tel **01483 893355 | High Street, GU5 0HB**
Web **www.jollyfarmer.co.uk**
Dir ***From Guildford take A281 (Horsham road). Bramley 3.5 miles south of Guildford.***

A 16th-century coaching inn steeped in character and history, this friendly family-run free house clearly has a passion for beer. You'll always find up to eight constantly-changing cask real ales on the counter. The pub offers a high standard of food all freshly cooked, with a daily specials board, featuring dishes such as chorizo and butter bean cassoulet; chicken and chilli gratin; vegan nut roast; and a selection of burgers.

Open all day, all week 11–11 Free House 16 portions/menu notice required

BROOK

The Dog & Pheasant

Tel **01428 682763 | Haslemere Road, GU8 5UJ**
Web **www.dogandpheasant.com**
Dir ***From Godalming take A286 towards Haslemere. Pub approximately 4.5 miles.***

Four open fires warm this picturesque 15th-century pub, where over the inglenook fire on Wednesday nights the chef grills steaks and fish. Sixteen wines are served by the glass and real ales are sourced from Surrey to Cornwall.

BUCKLAND

The Pheasant at Buckland

Tel **01737 221355 | Reigate Road, RH3 7BG**
Web **www.brunningandprice.co.uk/pheasant**
Dir ***West of Reigate, on A25.***

This pub began its life in the early 18th century and it has had several names over the years. Since 2015, The Pheasant has been in the hands of Brunning & Price, who have retained its traditional style with open fires, walls of local memorabilia and an extensive landscaped garden with three fire pits. A wide range of ales such as Surrey Hills Shere Drop is accompanied by a broad menu. Time a visit for the summer gin festival.

Open all day, all week Brunning & Price portions/menu notice required

CHIDDINGFOLD

The Crown Inn ★★★★★ INN

Tel **01428 682255** | **The Green, GU8 4TX**
Web **thecrownchiddingfold.com**
Dir ***On A283 between Milford and Petworth.***

Set by the village green, this beautifully appointed inn is one of the county's oldest buildings. It oozes charm and character, featuring ancient panelling, open fires, distinctive carvings, and comfortable bedrooms. In addition to the house beer, ales come from Surrey, Hampshire and London.

Open all day, all week *Free House* *12* *portions/menu*

The Swan Inn ★★★★ INN

PICK OF THE PUBS

Tel **01428 684688** | **Petworth Road, GU8 4TY**
Web **www.theswaninnchiddingfold.com**
Dir ***From A3 follow Milford/Petworth/A283 signs. At roundabout 1st exit onto A283. Slight right onto Guildford and Godalming bypass. Right into Portsmouth Road, left (continue on A283), to Chiddingfold.***

Rebuilt in the 1880s, the Swan today offers weary travellers a friendly and relaxed welcome. Located among the Surrey Hills, The Swan is typical of the coaching inns that once served customers travelling to or from the south coast. In the bar, temptations include local ales such as Upham Brewery's Punter, and from an international list, there are 14 wines served by the glass. The daily-changing menu has broad appeal; a typical meal might kick off with chicken and foie gras terrine, apricot chutney and pickled mustard seeds. That might be followed by a main course of crayfish linguine, chilli, garlic and spring onions. For dessert perhaps choose banana bread and butter pudding with poppy seed ice cream, or the carefully sourced cheeseboard.

Open all day, all week 10am–11pm (Sun 11–10.30) *Free House* *14* *from £14* *portions/menu*

COLDHARBOUR

The Plough Inn PICK OF THE PUBS

Tel **01306 711793** | **Coldharbour Lane, RH5 6HD**
Web **www.ploughinn.com**
Dir ***M25 junction 9, A24 to Dorking. A25 towards Guildford. Coldharbour signed from one-way system.***

Set in the heart of the Surrey Hills Area of Outstanding Natural Beauty, this charming 17th-century coaching inn has been brought bang up to date. Nearby Leith Hill, the highest point in south-east England at 965 feet, makes the pub a popular watering hole for walkers and cyclists needing sustenance after their exertions. The hill lends its name to the pub's own on-site craft brewery. The menu proffers good country fare sourced locally if possible, so start with apricot and game terrine, quince and plum chutney, walnut and fig toast and continue with 6oz beef fillet, sautéed potato, warm mushrooms, spinach salad; and finish with Black Forest chocolate roulade. Lighter lunches include artisan seeded baguettes.

Open all day, all week 12–close *Free House* *10* *from £13.95* *portions/menu* *notice required*

COMPTON

The Withies Inn

Tel **01483 421158** | **Withies Lane, GU3 1JA**
Web **www.thewithiesinn.com**
Dir ***Phone for detailed directions.***

This low-beamed inn has slumbered beside the wooded common for five centuries, maturing into a popular, cosy village local enhanced by an intimate restaurant area, where seasonal specials tumble from the menu. Start with seafood crêpe mornay; or paw paw with fresh crab; then escalope of veal Marsala; or grilled calves' liver with bacon and onions. After you've finished you could relax in the garden with a pint of TEA (Traditional English Ale) from the local Hogs Back Brewery.

Open all year 11–3 6–11 (Wed to Sat 11–11) Closed Sun evening *Free House* *12* *from £13.50* *portions* *notice required*

CRANLEIGH

The Richard Onslow

Tel **01483 274922 | 113–117 High Street, GU6 8AU**
Web **www.therichardonslow.co.uk**
Dir ***From A281 between Guildford and Horsham take B2130 to Cranleigh, pub in village centre.***

This grand old tile-hung pub stands at the heart of England's largest village. The updated interior retains its period appeal, particularly the original brick inglenook in the bar. The food emphasis is on top-notch seasonal produce.

DUNSFOLD

The Sun Inn

Tel **01483 200242 | The Common, GU8 4LE**
Dir ***A281 through Shalford and Bramley, take B2130 to Godalming. Dunsfold in 2 miles.***

This family-owned 17th-century inn ticks all the right boxes when it comes to a village pub, with roaring fires, beams and a fine vaulted ceiling. Dog-friendly to the point of having canine snacks on the bar, local ales are served alongside a menu of pub favourites that appeal to walkers and cyclists as well as locals. Look out for Wednesday pie night and occasional curry banquets.

Open all day, all week Free House 10 from £8.95 portions/menu notice required

EASHING

The Stag on the River

Tel **01483 421568 | Lower Eashing, GU7 2QG**
Web **www.stagontherivereashing.co.uk**
Dir ***From A3 southbound exit signed Eashing, 200 yards over river bridge. Pub on right.***

Located on the banks of the River Wey, this comfortable, well-appointed village inn takes full advantage of its location, with a large garden and separate patio. Fixtures on hand pump in the bar are Hogs Back TEA (Traditional English Ale) and their own Red Mist Ale, other local beers rotate. A seasonal menu might begin with home-made black pudding and pork Scotch egg followed by chicken and chorizo pie with sweet potato mash; or braised beef shin in red wine sauce.

Open all day, all week Closed 25 Dec Free House 12 portions/menu

EAST CLANDON

The Queens Head

Tel **01483 222332 | The Street, GU4 7RY**
Web **www.queensheadeastclandon.co.uk**
Dir ***4 miles east of Guildford on A246. Signed.***

With the North Downs Way (linking Farnham and the White Cliffs of Dover) nearby, you can expect fleece-clad backpackers alongside the locals here. Surrounding farms and suppliers contribute to the main course dishes – black pudding sausages and mash; and British steak ale and mushroom pie.

EFFINGHAM

The Plough

Tel **01372 303105 | Orestan Lane, KT24 5SW**
Web **www.plougheffingham.co.uk**
Dir ***Between Guildford and Leatherhead on A246.***

This little Surrey Hills pub is a popular stopping point for cyclists and walkers whether refuelling in the comfortable bar and dining room or the pretty garden and terrace. Monthly-changing menus offer contemporary and traditional favourites that cater for all appetites, whilst the slow-roasted meats served for Sunday lunch are worth a detour alone. The National Trust's Polesden Lacey and the Royal Horticultural Society's Wisley Gardens are nearby.

Open all week 11.30–3 5.30–11 (Fri to Sat 11.30–11 Sun 12–5) Young & Co's Brewery 20 from £12 portions/menu notice required

ELSTEAD

The Woolpack

Tel **01252 703106 | The Green, Milford Road, GU8 6HD**
Web **www.woolpackelstead.co.uk**
Dir ***A3 south, take Milford exit, follow signs for Elstead on B3001.***

Originally a wool exchange dating back to the 17th century, the tile-hung Woolpack displays weaving shuttles and other artefacts relating to the wool industry. The menu features Italian dishes, sandwiches and stone-baked pizzas. The surrounding common land attracts walkers and ramblers galore.

ENGLEFIELD GREEN

The Fox and Hounds

Tel **01784 433098** | **Bishopsgate Road, TW20 0XU**
Web **www.thefoxandhoundsrestaurant.com**
Dir ***M25 junction 13, A30 signed Basingstoke and Camberley. Right at lights onto A328 signed Englefield Green. With village green on left, left into Bishopsgate Road.***

Dating back to 1780, this pub is ideally situated next to the Bishopsgate entrance to Windsor Great Park. Enjoy a pint of Brakspear bitter in the stylish bar or a slap-up meal in the light and elegant conservatory restaurant. The locally sourced ingredients create a wide ranging choice of dishes, from Windsor Great Park venison to daily changing "Pie of the Day". Make sure you leave room for one of the home-made desserts. Summer barbecues are popular events.

Open all day, all week 8am–11pm (Sun 8–8) Free House 14 from £12 portions/menu Wi-fi P notice required

FARNHAM

The Bat & Ball Freehouse

PICK OF THE PUBS

Tel **01252 792108** | **15 Bat & Ball Lane, Boundstone, GU10 4SA**
Web **www.thebatandball.co.uk**
Dir ***From A31 (Farnham bypass) onto A325 signed Birdworld. Left at Bengal Lounge. At T-junction right, immediately left into Sandrock Hill Road. 0.25 mile left into Upper Bourne Lane. Follow signs.***

Down a long cul-de-sac and tricky to locate, you'll be pleased you persevered. A real community pub with terracotta floors, oak beams, a warming fire and cricketing memorabilia. The garden has a patio with picnic tables, a vine-topped pergola and a children's fort. Six frequently-changing real ales come from regional microbreweries, and ciders include local Hazy Hog. The menu is seasonal and local, with modern classics like espresso porter braised oxtail sitting alongside pub favourites such as the popular chicken and ham pie. A huge choice of ales and ciders can be experienced during the beer, cider and music festival during the second weekend in June.

Open all day, all week 11–11 (Sun 12–10.30) Free House 8 portions/menu Wi-fi P

The Wheatsheaf

Tel **01252 717135** | **19 West Street, GU9 7DR**
Web **www.thewheatsheaffarnham.co.uk**
Dir ***In town centre.***

This relaxed pub has had a stylish makeover, all pale grey paintwork and eclectic furnishings. Have a pint of local or craft beer, or check out the G&T Club. Local, sustainable food is the kitchen's motto, and as well as a selection of light lunches they offer a gluten-free menu.

FOREST GREEN

The Parrot Inn PICK OF THE PUBS

Tel **01306 775790** | **RH5 5RZ**
Web **www.brunningandprice.co.uk/parrot**
Dir ***B2126 from A29 at Ockley, signed Forest Green.***

Down in the Surrey Hills, overlooking the village green and cricket ground, stands this tile-hung village pub, with low-beamed ceilings, flagstone floors and huge brass fireplace. The bar, home to at least five real ales, some local, some regional, and more than 20 wines by the glass, leads to a sheltered, paved terrace. A tasty starter of parsnip and apple ginger soup could satisfyingly precede Sicilian fish stew of red mullet, king prawns and mussels; a 7oz fillet steak with Portobello mushrooms and peppercorn sauce; or, say, massaman aubergine, potato and okra curry. Finally, it shouldn't be too hard to resist dark Belgian chocolate torte, hazelnut brittle and sour cherry sorbet.

Open all day, all week Free House 22 from £10.95 portions/menu Wi-fi P

GUILDFORD

The Weyside

Tel **01483 568024** | **Millbrook, GU1 3XJ**
Web **www.theweyside.co.uk**
Dir ***From Guildford take A281 towards Shalford. Pub on right.***

Overlooking the River Wey, this is one humdinger of a pub. The decor, the furnishings, the accessorising – all have been conceived and applied by people who understand good interior design. There are plenty of places to eat and drink, not least on the waterside decking.

HAMBLEDON

The Merry Harriers

Tel **01428 682883** | **Hambledon Road, GU8 4DR**
Web **www.merryharriers.com**
Dir ***Phone for detailed directions.***

In the heart of the Surrey Hills, this 16th-century pub is only 12 miles from Guildford, but it makes the most of its rural position, even down to the herd of llamas in the adjacent field. Handpumps of locally brewed ales like Shere Drop and Loxhill Biscuit take pride of place in the bar and the kitchen keeps things simple whether it's the lunchtime sandwiches and platters or the main menu. A typical meal might include Thai green chicken curry; and a 1970s-inspired scampi in the basket.

Open all week 11.30–3 5.30–close Free House from £12.50 portions notice required

HASLEMERE

The Wheatsheaf Inn ★★★ INN

Tel **01428 644440** | **Grayswood Road, Grayswood, GU27 2DE**
Web **www.thewheatsheafgrayswood.co.uk**
Dir ***From Haslemere take A286 to Grayswood, approximately 1.5 miles.***

A distinctive Edwardian pub with enough vegetation to give Kew Gardens a run for its money. The hanging-basket festooned verandah, creeper-covered pergola and colourful garden just invite a lingering visit with a pint of Triple fff Alton's Pride to hand. Stay overnight in one of the comfy rooms and dine in to enjoy a pub classic or special from the wide-ranging menu. Perhaps, warmed brie with cranberry sauce then hake fillet in real ale batter with chips. There's also a selection of steaks, sandwiches and salads.

Open all week 11–3 6–11 (Sun 12–10.30) Closed 25 Dec Free House 8 from £9.95 portions/menu

HORLEY

The Fox Revived

Tel **01293 229270** | **Norwood Hill, RH6 0ET**
Web **www.brunningandprice.co.uk/foxrevived**
Dir ***From Horley follow signs for Charlwood. Through village, turn right into Norwood Hill Road, signed Newdigate. The Fox Revived at junction with Smalls Hill Road and Collendean Lane.***

A comfortable bar and a garden room with splendid views of the Surrey Hills are two reasons to visit The Fox Revived, with well-kept local ales like Surrey Hills Shere Drop and Hogsback TEA as further enticement should you need it. If you fancy taking in those views, stop for something to eat – maybe get things started with deep-fried Cornish brie, with main courses like fish pie or pork and leek sausages with mash, buttered greens and onion gravy.

Open all day, all week Mon to Sat 10.30am–11pm (Sun 10.30–10.30) Free House 25 from £11.95 portions/menu

HORSELL

The Red Lion

Tel **01483 768497** | **123 High Street, GU21 4SS**
Web **www.redlionhorsell.co.uk**
Dir ***In village centre.***

Less than a mile from Woking, this smart village pub is very much at the heart of the community, but it attracts diners from all over Surrey. The beautiful garden is a major draw in the summer, and real fires and sumptuous sofas and armchairs make it a cosy place in winter. Enjoy one of the 14 wines served by the glass or a pint of well-kept real ale before heading to the restaurant. Crispy fried sesame king prawns might precede pork belly, creamy mash and spiced plums.

Open all day, all week Star Pubs & Bars 14 from £12.95 portions/menu notice required

LALEHAM

The Three Horseshoes

Tel **01784 455014** | **25 Shepperton Road, TW18 1SE**
Web **www.threehorseshoeslaleham.co.uk**
Dir ***On B376.***

A wisteria-clad building, the Three Horseshoes describes itself as 'casual enough to be comfortable and smart enough to feel special'. You can pop in for a coffee or a drink, and they serve food all day. The lovely garden is ideal for alfresco dining, and in the winter it's relaxed and cosy with a real fire and comfy sofas. At lunchtime there are sandwiches and 'things on toast' as well as a range of pub classics, while in the evening you could share an oven-baked camembert before enjoying rotisserie chicken.

Open all day, all week *Fuller's* *16* *portions/menu* Wi-fi P *notice required*

LEIGH

The Plough

Tel **01306 611348** | **Church Road, RH2 8NJ**
Web **www.theploughleigh.com**
Dir ***Phone for detailed directions.***

Some parts of this appealing, architecturally mixed-up building date from the 15th century, whilst the popular locals' bar with its fire and traditional pub games is somewhat younger. Situated by a large green bordered by old houses and a medieval church, The Plough today is a cracking village pub. Beers from the Hall & Woodhouse list slake the thirst of walkers enjoying the Surrey Weald, whilst the pub grub menu includes their ever-popular home-made pies.

Open all day, all week 11–11 (Sun 12–11) *Hall & Woodhouse* *11* *portions/menu* Wi-fi P

The Seven Stars

Tel **01306 611254** | **Bunce Common Road, Dawes Green, RH2 8NP**
Web **www.7starsleigh.co.uk**
Dir ***South of A25 (Dorking to Reigate road).***

This 17th-century, tile-hung tavern is tucked away in the Mole Valley, its charm enhanced by the absence of screens and piped music. The older bar has an inglenook fireplace at one end and a log-burning stove at the other.

LONG DITTON

The George Evelyn PICK OF THE PUBS

Tel **020 8339 0785** | **64 Ditton Hill Road, KT6 5JD**
Web **www.thegeorgeevelyn.com**
Dir ***Phone for detailed directions.***

Formerly The Ditton, this renamed community local close to Hampton Court makes the most of its large south-facing beer garden, whether it's for children's entertainment or summer barbecues. Beers from local breweries like Surrey Hills, Hogs Back and Big Smoke Brew dominate the handpumps at the bar and there's a good choice of wines by the glass. A typical menu offers chilli and garlic king prawns, perhaps followed by a classic beef burger or creamy chicken pesto penne and vegetables. Make sure you leave a space for the sticky toffee pudding and warm toffee sauce or chocolate brownie. Live music backs a popular June beer and cider festival.

Open all day, all week Mon to Thu 12–11 (Fri to Sat 12–12 Sun 12–10) *Free House* *10* *portions/menu* Wi-fi P *notice required*

MICKLEHAM

Running Horses

Tel **01372 372279** | **Old London Road, RH5 6DU**
Web **www.therunninghorses.co.uk**
Dir ***M25 junction 9, A24 towards Dorking. Left signed Mickleham and B2209.***

Built in the 16th century, the inn had an important role as a coaching house, but it's also believed to have sheltered highwaymen. The inn's name dates to 1825, when two horses, Colonel and Cadland, running in the Derby at Epsom, passed the post together. They appear on the inn sign, and the bars are named after them. Food in the restaurant is rustic, crowd-pleasing fare from a seasonal menu.

Open all day, all week 12–11 (Sun 12–10.30) *Brakspear* *25* *portions/menu* Wi-fi

NEWDIGATE

The Surrey Oaks

Tel **01306 631200** | **Parkgate Road, RH5 5DZ**
Web **www.thesurreyoaks.com**
Dir ***From A24 follow signs to Newdigate, at T-junction turn left, pub 1 mile on left.***

This former wheelwright's shop is over 440 years old and still has wood fires burning in the inglenook fireplaces and original flagstones in the bar. At the bar counter you'll find Surrey Hills Shere Drop which is brewed just six miles from the pub. Much of the food on the seasonal menu is cooked in the wood-fired oven, including the steak burger and pizza. A separate list of daily specials features dishes based on supplies from the local butchers, fishmongers and gamekeepers.

Open all week 11.45–11 (Sun 12–10.30) Free House 22 portions notice required

RIPLEY

The Anchor – see page 416

SHAMLEY GREEN

The Red Lion

Tel **01483 892202** | **The Green, GU5 0UB**
Web **www.redlionshamleygreen.com**
Dir ***On B2128 between Guildford and Cranleigh.***

Film location scouts looking for a pub on a village green will find a prime candidate here. Although 17th century, it has been a pub only since the 1800s. Rich red ceilings and high-backed, red-upholstered settles help create that quintessential warm pubby feeling. A typical carte proposes prawn cocktail; chicken liver pâté; Greek spinach and feta pie; miso duck with peppers, chilli and jasmine rice. Sandwiches, jackets, and ploughman's add to the choices.

Open all day, all week Punch Taverns 11 from £10.95 portions/menu

SOUTH GODSTONE

Fox & Hounds

Tel **01342 893474** | **Tilburstow Hill Road, RH9 8LY**
Web **www.foxandhounds.org.uk**
Dir ***M25 junction 6, A22 to South Godstone. Right into Harts Lane. At T-junction right into Tilburstow Hill Road.***

Dating in part to 1368, the Fox & Hounds has been a pub since 1601. Allegedly, yet eminently believably, 17th-century pirate-turned-smuggler John Trenchman haunts the building, having been ambushed and fatally wounded nearby. The restaurant's large inglenook and the bar's real fire add to the old-world charm. Food-wise, there's plenty to choose from and landlady Ellie Conway travels to the south coast for her fish. A large garden features a pirate ship play area.

Open all year Tue to Fri 12–3 5–11.15 (Sat 12–11.15 Sun 12–10.15) Closed Mon (except bank holidays) Free House 14 from £9.95 portions/menu notice required

STOKE D'ABERNON

The Old Plough

Tel **01932 862244** | **2 Station Road, KT11 3BN**
Web **www.oldploughcobham.co.uk**
Dir ***From A245 into Station Road. Pub on corner.***

Contemporary decor and traditional lines blend easily at this dining inn in the Mole Valley. In earlier times it was the village courthouse; it also features in the Sherlock Holmes story 'The Adventure of The Speckled Band'. Locals and visitors alike enjoy the summer shade in the peaceful garden.

RIPLEY

The Anchor

Tel 01483 211866 | High Street, GU23 6AE
Web www.ripleyanchor.co.uk
Dir *M25 junction 10, A3 towards Guildford, then B2215 to Ripley.*

Modern food in a historic building

PICK OF THE PUBS

Award-winning chef Steve Drake (of Sorrel Restaurant in Dorking fame) bought his local pub with the aim of creating the sort of place he would want to eat and drink in on his day off. Built originally as an almshouse, The Anchor has been at the heart of village life since the 16th century. Its charmingly crooked red-brick and timber exterior conceals a soothingly contemporary interior, where you'll find a sophisticated modern British menu of very photogenic cuisine. The kitchen is run by Mike Wall-Palmer, who makes good use of local produce in creative dishes such as grilled mackerel escabeche with garlic and saffron mayonnaise; or cumin-braised mutton with lemon houmous and flatbread, followed by roast venison with swede purée, blackberries and kale; or tarragon gnocchi with curried cauliflower and Cornish gouda sauce. For dessert, there might be sticky beer cake and spiced apple ice cream, or ginger rice pudding, rhubarb jam and cinnamon popcorn. Bar snacks are great, too – try the black pudding Scotch egg or the puffed pork skin with apple sauce. Wash it down with a pint of Timothy Taylor or a guest ale from local breweries including Tillingbourne and Andwells, and make sure you look out for the whisky of the month.

Open Tue to Fri 12–3 5.30–11 (Sat to Sun 12–11) Closed 25–26 Dec, Mon Free House 14 from £16 portions

TANDRIDGE

The Barley Mow

Tel **01883 713770** | **Tandridge Lane, RH8 9NJ**
Web **www.barleymowtandridge.com**
Dir ***M25 junction 6 onto A22. At next roundabout onto A25 signed Oxted. At roundabout, turn right signed Tandridge. On main road through village.***

With its large landscaped garden and extensive food offering, landlords Stephen and Nicola Osborne have ensured that The Barley Mow is very much the village hub in Tandridge. A range of Badger ales including Fursty Ferret keeps the drinkers happy, with the family-friendly menus appealing to all ages and budgets. A bowl of home-made soup with warm, crusty bread might be one way to start and lead on to home-made pie of the week; or choose from a selection of steaks.

Open all week 12–11 (Sun 12–9) Hall & Woodhouse portions/menu notice required

THURSLEY

The Three Horseshoes

Tel **01252 703900** | **Dye House Road, GU8 6QD**
Web **threehorseshoesthursley.com**
Dir ***From A3 between Hindhead and Milford follow Thursley signs. Pub on left.***

Popular with walkers exploring the Devil's Punchbowl and Thursley Common, this lovely pub is in the village of Thursley. It's been sustaining guests since the 16th century, and was rescued from five years' closure by villagers who didn't want to lose the heart of their community.

TILFORD

The Duke of Cambridge

Tel **01252 792236** | **Tilford Road, GU10 2DD**
Web **www.dukeofcambridgetilford.co.uk**
Dir ***From Guildford on A31 towards Farnham follow Tongham, Seale, Runfield signs. Right at end, follow Eashing signs. Left at end, 1st right (signed Tilford Street). Over bridge, 1st left, 0.5 mile.***

Set among pine trees with a lovely garden and terrace, this attractive pub in the Surrey countryside welcomes all, children and dogs included. Expect Surrey ales and locally sourced food on their seasonal menus. The Garden Bar & Grill is a particular highlight in summer.

WEST CLANDON

The Onslow Arms

Tel **01483 222447** | **The Street, GU4 7TE**
Web **www.onslowarmsclandon.co.uk**
Dir ***On A247, south of railway line.***

Cyclists and ramblers, drinkers and diners all mix seamlessly at this vibrant and smart community local. The visually striking building retains much character, with a wealth of beams, huge open fire, squashy sofas and chairs set in a light, cool interior. Relax inside or on the sheltered terrace with a glass of local ale and choose from an all-day menu which offers a great mix of comfort meals and contemporary dishes.

Open all day, all week 11–11 (Fri to Sat 11am–11.30pm Sun 11–10.30) Closed 26 Dec Free House 18 portions/menu notice required

WINDLESHAM

The Half Moon

Tel **01276 473329** | **Church Road, GU20 6BN**
Web **www.thehalfmoonwindlesham.com**
Dir ***M3 junction 3, A322 follow Windlesham signs into New Road; right at T-junction into Church Road, pub on right.***

Family-owned since 1909, Helga and Conrad Sturt's slate-floored, low-beamed, 17th-century free house offers the traditional country pub experience, including locally brewed Hogs Back real ale and Lilley's Bee Sting pear cider from Somerset. There's plenty of choice at lunchtime, while dinner options include baked camembert with chilli jam; red Thai curry; calves' liver and smoked bacon with bubble-and-squeak; braised venison and ale ragout; and smoked trout salad. Go past the patio terrace to find the well-kept beer garden with its children's play area.

Open all day, all week 11–11 Free House 10 portions/menu notice required

EAST SUSSEX

ALFRISTON

George Inn

Tel **01323 870319 | High Street, BN26 5SY**
Web **www.thegeorge-alfriston.com**
Dir ***Phone for detailed directions.***

A network of smugglers' tunnels leads from the cellars of this splendid Grade II listed inn, which was first licensed to sell beer as far back as 1397. Set in a picturesque village with the South Downs Way passing its front door, the oak beams and inglenook fireplace add plenty of character to the bar, whilst the kitchen serves delights like chilli butter crevettes; paprika-spiced pork chops and king prawn and chorizo linguine.

Open all day, all week Closed 25–26 Dec Greene King 14 from £13.50 portions/menu Wi-fi notice required

The Star Inn ★★★★ INN

Tel **01323 870495 | High Street, BN26 5TA**
Web **www.thestaralfriston.co.uk**
Dir ***From A27, at Drusillas roundabout, follow Alfriston signs. Pub on right in High Street.***

Originally a hostelry for pilgrims making their way from Battle to Chichester, this timber-framed, 13th-century pub has a wealth of features including a lion figurehead from a 17th-century shipwreck. The heavy beams and real fires are still present and correct, with the 37 elegant bedrooms and restaurant offering more contemporary comforts. Order a pint of locally brewed Harvey's ale as you choose from a locally-sourced menu that includes pan-fried organic lamb's liver, mash, greens, bacon and roast onion gravy.

Open all day, all week Free House 10 portions/menu Wi-fi P

ASHBURNHAM PLACE

Ash Tree Inn

Tel **01424 892104 | Brownbread Street, TN33 9NX**
Web **www.ashtreeinn.com**
Dir ***From Eastbourne take A271 at Boreham Bridge towards Battle. Next left, follow pub signs.***

Deep in the Sussex countryside on the delightfully named Brownbread Street, the 400-year-old Ash Tree is a hub of local activity, hosting everything from quiz nights to cricket club meetings. It boasts a warm and bright interior, replete with stripped wooden floors, four fireplaces (two of them inglenooks), exposed beams and a friendly local atmosphere. Expect to find Harvey's ale on tap and traditional home-cooked meals created from locally caught fish and seafood and locally produced meat and game. Walkers and their dogs are welcome.

Open all year 12–4 7–11 (Sat 11.30am–midnight) Closed Mon pm (Sun pm winter) Free House 10 from £10 portions Wi-fi P notice required

BERWICK

The Cricketers Arms

PICK OF THE PUBS

Tel **01323 870469 | BN26 6SP**
Web **www.cricketersberwick.co.uk**
Dir ***At crossroads on A27 (between Polegate and Lewes) follow Berwick sign, pub on right.***

Previously two farmworkers' cottages dating from the 16th century, this flintstone Grade II listed building, in beautiful cottage gardens, is close to many popular walks – the South Downs Way runs along the crest of the chalk scarp between here and the sea. Three beamed, music-free rooms with stone floors and open fires are simply furnished with old pine furniture. The bar menu of home-made food includes garlic mushrooms with blue cheese or warm smoked salmon with saffron mayonnaise and granary bread as starters. Their home-made burger is an ever-popular main course, as are favourites such as local pork and herb sausages with double egg and chips; or poached smoked haddock with rarebit topping.

Open all week Mon to Fri 11–3 6–11 Sat 11–11 Sun 12–9 (Easter to Sep Mon to Sat 11–11 Sun 12–10.30) Closed 25 Dec Harvey's of Lewes 12 portions Wi-fi P notice required

BLACKBOYS

The Blackboys Inn

Tel **01825 890283 | Lewes Road, TN22 5LG**
Web **www.theblackboys.co.uk**
Dir ***From A22 at Uckfield take B2102 towards Cross in Hand. Or from A267 at Esso service station in Cross in Hand take B2102 towards Uckfield. Village 1.5 miles.***

Today visitors to this 14th-century pub enjoy two bars and a restaurant, vegetables from the garden, game from local shoots, and fish from Rye and Hastings. Outside are rambling grounds with resident ducks and an orchard.

BRIGHTON

The Basketmakers Arms

Tel **01273 689006 | 12 Gloucester Road, BN1 4AD**
Web **www.basket-makers-brighton.co.uk**
Dir ***From Brighton station main entrance 1st left (Gloucester Road). Pub on right at bottom of hill.***

Peter Dowd has run his Victorian back-street local with passion for over 30 years. Tucked away in the bohemian North Laine area, quirky customer messages left in vintage tins on the walls have made the pub a local legend. Expect a splendid selection of Fuller's and guest ales, around 100 malt whiskies and rarely seen vodkas, gins and bourbons. The menu lists good-value popular plates, and the specials board changes daily.

Open all day, all week 11–11 (Fri to Sat 11am–midnight Sun 12–11) Fuller's Wi-fi

The Chimney House

Tel **01273 556708 | 28 Upper Hamilton Road, BN1 5DF**
Web **www.chimneyhousebrighton.co.uk**
Dir ***From B2122 at Seven Dials roundabout into Dyke Road, right into Old Shoreham Road, 2nd left into Buxton Road, pub on right at end.***

Just north of Seven Dials in Port Hall, this convivial Brighton pub keeps the neighbours happy with locally brewed Harvey's and Dark Star Hophead ales. Close links with Sussex producers, growers and foragers means a menu that changes with the seasons. Main courses might include Saddlecombe Farm beef chuck with fermented turnip and wild garlic. Leave a space for innovative desserts such as sea buckthorn meringue pie.

Open all day 12–11 Closed 25–26 Dec, Mon Star Pubs portions/menu Wi-fi notice required

The Ginger Pig

Tel **01273 736123 | 3 Hove Street, Hove, BN3 2TR**
Web **www.gingermanrestaurants.com**
Dir ***From A259 (seafront) into Hove Street.***

Now refurbished, there's a grand old bar at the front of The Ginger Pig serving great cocktails and well-kept local ales like Dark Star. Very much a food pub, the emphasis is on seasonality here – they have established a strong reputation for game and seafood. The monthly-changing menu might offer starters including confit duck and ham hock rillettes; while for main course you could have cod fillet, whole plaice or braised lamb pie.

Open all day, all week Free House 20 from £13 portions/menu Wi-fi notice required

The Urchin

Tel **01273 241881 | 15–17 Belfast Street, BN3 3YS**
Web **www.urchinpub.co.uk**
Dir ***From A259 (coast road) into Hove Street (A2023). Right into Blatchington Road at lights. 4th right into Haddington Street, right into Malvern Street, left into Belfast Street to pub (one-way system).***

Now well established as part of Brighton's star-studded eating and drinking scene, this is a popular destination for enjoying a drink and the best seafood. Expect over 100 craft and speciality beers in addition to local real ales and wines.

CHELWOOD GATE

The Red Lion

Tel **01825 740836 | Lewes Road, RH17 7DE**
Web **www.redlionchelwood.co.uk**
Dir ***On A275.***

An attractive pub built in the early 1800s that includes among its famous visitors Prime Minister Harold Macmillan and President John F Kennedy. Although it is owned by Kent brewer Shepherd Neame, Harvey's of Lewes also gets a look in on the bar.

CHIDDINGLY

The Six Bells

Tel **01825 872227** | **BN8 6HE**
Dir ***East of A22 between Hailsham and Uckfield. Turn opposite Golden Cross pub.***

Inglenook fireplaces and plenty of bric-à-brac are to be found at this large free house, which is where various veteran car and motorbike enthusiasts meet on club nights; it's a popular walkers' pub too. Enjoy live music on Tuesday, Friday and Saturday evenings plus jazz at lunchtime on Sundays. The jury in the famous 1852 Onion Pie Murder trial sat and deliberated in the bar before finding the defendant, Sarah Ann French, guilty of poisoning her husband.

Open all week 10–3 6–11 (Fri to Sun all day) Free House portions

DANEHILL

The Coach and Horses – see below

DITCHLING

The Bull – see opposite

EAST CHILTINGTON

The Jolly Sportsman

Tel **01273 890400** | **Chapel Lane, BN7 3BA**
Web **www.thejollysportsman.com**
Dir ***From Lewes take A275, left at Offham onto B2166 towards Plumpton, into Novington Lane, after approximately 1 mile left into Chapel Lane.***

Isolated but well worth finding, this dining pub with a lovely garden, sits at the foot of the South Downs. Locally-sourced ales are on tap, and well-sourced, full-flavoured food shines on the contemporary daily-changing menus served throughout the pub, from calves' liver in bacon and shallot sauce, to haunch of local venison, cep and celeriac tart, squash purée, tenderstem broccoli and port sauce. Good value fixed-price and children's menus are also available.

Open Tue to Sat 12–3 5.45–11 (Sat all day in summer Sun 12–5) Closed 25 Dec, Sun evening and Mon Free House 14 portions/menu

DANEHILL

The Coach and Horses

Tel 01825 740369 | RH17 7JF
Web **www.coachandhorses.co**
Dir ***From East Grinstead, south through Forest Row on A22 to junction with A275 (Lewes road), right on A275, 2 miles to Danehill, left into School Lane, 0.5 mile, pub on left.***

PICK OF THE PUBS

Family-run country pub offering more than just beer

Dating from 1847 when it was a simple alehouse with stabling, today this is an attractive countryside inn. You'll find a sunny child-free terrace at the rear dominated by an enormous maple tree; children can play in the peaceful front garden, with views of the undulating South Downs. Understated and unspoilt, the pub's interior has retained the typical twin bar layout, with vaulted ceilings, wood-panelled walls and stone and oak flooring. The pub's dog lazing on a bar rug sets a friendly tone, along with locals supping weekly-changing guest ales from the likes of Long Man and Dark Star; local Danehill Black Pig cider is also popular. Dishes are traditionally English with ingredients sourced as locally as possible. There's also a good list of lighter lunches.

Open all week 12–3 5.30–11 (Sat to Sun 12–11) Closed 26 Dec Free House 8 from £11.75 portions/menu

DITCHLING

The Bull  INN

Tel 01273 843147 | 2 High Street, BN6 8TA
Web www.thebullditchling.com
Dir *From Brighton on A27 take A23, follow Pyecombe/Hassocks signs, then Ditchling signs, 3 miles.*

Eat, drink and admire the South Downs

One of the village's oldest buildings, now newly and sympathetically restored, has got the lot – gnarled old beams, bare floorboards, real fires, scrubbed candlelit tables and three bars and dining areas. And there's more – a garden with tables and parasols, night-time fire pits, twinkling lights and a wood-fired pizza oven. At nearby Plumpton Green is Bedlam, its very own solar-powered brewery, with hops grown on site; another 11 real ales join its Benchmark on the bar. Modern British food comes from the pub's kitchen garden, local farm estates and short-range fishing boats on the coast 20 minutes away. Should you stay here in one of the individually designed bedrooms, breakfast on home-made granola, yogurt and honey, or push the boat out with a full English. Lunch and dinner menus offer both small plates – rabbit ballotine and black pudding with baby leeks, for instance – and large ones, such as Madras-spiced monkfish, crispy mussels and pilau rice; hay-smoked venison haunch with chervil, chanterelles and kale; ham hock and chicken shortcrust pie; and 'cookhouse classics', perhaps steak, ale and mushroom pie. To finish, those with room to spare could surely manage home-made ice cream; or rhubarb citrus cheesecake with brown butter and Muscat.

Open all day, all week 8am–11pm (Sun 8am–10.30pm) Free House 25 from £13 portions/menu

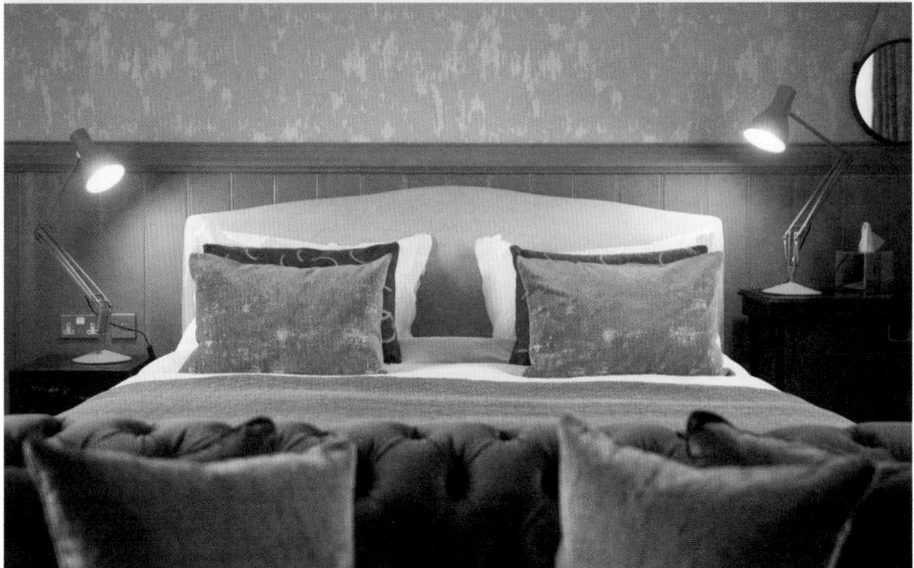

EAST DEAN

The Tiger Inn PICK OF THE PUBS

Tel **01323 423209** | **The Green, BN20 0DA**
Web **www.beachyhead.org.uk**
Dir ***From A259 between Eastbourne and Seaford. Pub 0.5 mile.***

Set beside the large sloping green in one of the prettiest old villages on the South Downs, it's just a short stroll along downland paths from the inn to the magnificent coastal walk at the renowned Seven Sisters cliffs. The pub was once the base for smugglers landing contraband and the interior recalls such heady days, with log fires, beams, stone floors and ancient settles. With a rotating selection of beers from local microbreweries, there is always something interesting on tap. The menu, too, is laden with local ingredients and fresh fish features in several choices; or look for game pie or beef Stroganoff. Steamed puddings lead the sweet choice.

Open all day, all week *Free House* *12* *portions/menu*

ERIDGE GREEN

The Nevill Crest and Gun

Tel **01892 864209** | **Eridge Road, TN3 9JR**
Web **www.brunningandprice.co.uk/nevillcrestandgun**
Dir ***On A26 between Tunbridge Wells and Crowborough.***

This uniquely named, tile-hung pub was built on land owned by the Nevill family, the Earls of Abergavenny. So the 'Crest' is easily explained; a cannon that once stood outside accounts for the 'Gun'. The location on the Kent-Sussex border is reflected by the real ales dispensed.

EWHURST GREEN

The White Dog

Tel **01580 830264** | **Village Street, TN32 5TD**
Web **www.thewhitedogewhurst.co.uk**
Dir ***On A21 from Tonbridge towards Hastings, left after Hurst Green signed Bodiam. Straight on at crossroads, through Bodiam. Over rail crossing, left for Ewhurst Green.***

This tile-hung village pub is either the first in, or the last out of the village, depending on which way you're travelling. Its age is more apparent from the interior, particularly the huge fireplace, old oak beams and stone floors. Four hand-pumps dispense regularly-changing, mostly Sussex real ales and some 20 wines are available by the glass. The seasonal menus show how dependent the kitchen is on the local area: for example, seared scallops with a piquillo pepper purée and chorizo; and pot-roasted wild rabbit.

Open all day, all week *Free House* *20* *from £12* *portions/menu* *notice required*

FLETCHING

The Griffin Inn PICK OF THE PUBS

Tel **01825 722890** | **TN22 3SS**
Web **www.thegriffininn.co.uk**
Dir ***M23 junction 10, A264 to East Grinstead, then A22, in Maresfield take A275. Village signed on left.***

The unspoilt village of Fletching overlooks the Ouse Valley, and this imposing Grade II listed inn has landscaped gardens with views over Ashdown Forest, the Sussex Downs and 'Capability' Brown-designed Sheffield Park Gardens. The 16th-century interior simply oozes charm, with beams, panelling, settles and log fires. Walkers and cyclists arriving to join destination diners will revel in the menu, created from the freshest of local produce. Look out for gambas crostini, garlic, chilli, white wine and parsley, or Devon crab cakes to start; follow with king prawn, chorizo and squid ink spaghetti; pan-roasted skate wing; or harissa lamb shank and buckwheat pie. On fine summer days, the barbecue is fired up and food can be served on the terrace.

Open all day, all week 12–11 (Sat 12–12) Closed 25 Dec *Free House* *16* *portions/menu* *notice required*

HARTFIELD

The Hatch Inn

Tel **01342 822363** | **Coleman's Hatch, TN7 4EJ**
Web **www.hatchinn.co.uk**
Dir ***A22 at Forest Row roundabout, 3 miles to Coleman's Hatch, right by church.***

Much-accoladed Ashdown Forest inn

The Hatch, built around 1430, is an eye-catching, clapboarded old inn on the site of one of the medieval gates into what was then dense woodland, that yielded valuable iron ore deposits and timber for charcoal. It was probably lived in by workers at a water-driven hammer mill at the foot of today's Kidd's Hill, named after the piratical Captain Kidd, who allegedly masterminded smuggling activities from here in the 18th century. With plenty of local suppliers to draw on, fresh seasonal produce is used in just about every dish on the daily-changing menus, complemented by an extensive wine list. So, lunchtime options could well be Shetland mussels with garlic cream and white wine sauce; beef and chilli meatballs with fettucine; Thai green chicken curry with fragrant jasmine rice; and goats' cheese and red onion marmalade tarte Tatin. It's a quite different menu in the evening, when white wine-poached pear and Roquefort salad with toasted pine nuts might appear as a starter, with mains including chargrilled Angus fillet steak with triple-cooked fries; new season's lamb, dauphinoise potatoes and roast vegetables; and roast fillet of monkfish with pancetta, chorizo and red lentil stew. Large garden areas look towards the forest.

Open all week 11.30–3 5.30–11 (Sat to Sun all day)
Free House 11 portions

GUN HILL

The Gun PICK OF THE PUBS

Tel **01825 872361** | **TN21 0JU**
Web **www.thegunhouse.co.uk**
Dir ***From Heathfield on A267 after Horam turn right into Chiddingly Road (signed Chiddingly). Follow to pub on left.***

Felons and miscreants were brought to face justice in this local courthouse centuries ago; today the rambling, steeply-roofed old inn welcomes discerning drinkers and diners. Located high in the Sussex Downs, extensive views reward those who sit in the tranquil tree-shaded garden with a Musket ale or Biddenden cider. Inside, lots of beams, wooden floors and open fireplaces picked out in old brick characterise an interior dressed with rustic furnishings. A beautifully panelled dining room is a particular draw. When surveying the menu, some get no further than the fish sharing platter with its king prawns, Shetland mussels, white anchovies, Gun smokie, fennel, radish and cucumber salad, coriander and garlic crème fraîche and crusty bread. Wood-fired sourdough pizzas are also much in demand.

Open all week 11.30–3 5.30–11 (Sun 11.30–10.30) Free House 14 from £12.50 menus WiFi

HARTFIELD

Anchor Inn

Tel **01892 770424** | **Church Street, TN7 4AG**
Web **www.anchorhartfield.com**
Dir ***On B2110.***

Although Winnie-the-Pooh never visited this nearly 550-year-old pub, a former manor house, his creator, A A Milne, who lived nearby, may occasionally have popped in. Locals today gather in the wooden-beamed front bar, perhaps to drink Harvey's or Larkins; the back bar, with its inglenook and library, feels more intimate. Dishes include peppered venison loin; honey-glazed pork belly; pan-fried sea bass; and Anchor fish pie. At the front is an attractive, gabled verandah, at the rear a large garden.

Open all day, all week Free House portions/menu WiFi *notice required*

The Hatch Inn – see page 423

HASTINGS AND ST LEONARDS

The Crown

Tel **01424 465100** | **64–66 All Saints Street, TN34 3BN**
Web **www.thecrownhastings.co.uk**
Dir ***From A259 in Hastings into Rock-A-Nore Road. Parking available at end. Walk along All Saints Street to pub on right.***

A relaxed atmosphere is the keynote here, with daily papers, open fires and board games for all the family; dogs are welcome too. Yet there's entertainment if you want it – The Crown hosts quiz nights, craft evenings, storytelling and exhibitions. The drinks choice embraces teas and coffees as well as Sussex ales, ciders and gins. Honestly-priced dishes are home-cooked from traceable sources – Romney Marsh lamb, local fish and seasonal vegetables.

Open all day, all week Free House 14 from £12 portions WiFi *notice required*

HEATHFIELD

Star Inn

Tel **01435 863570** | **Church Street, Old Heathfield, TN21 9AH**
Web **www.starinnoldheathfield.co.uk**
Dir ***From A265 between Cross in Hand and Broad Oak right onto B2096 signed Old Heathfield. Right signed Old Heathfield. At T-junction into School Hill. In Old Heathfield left into Church Street.***

Built as an inn for the stonemasons who constructed the 14th-century church, this creeper-clad stone building has a stunning summer garden that affords impressive views across the High Weald. Equally appealing is the atmospheric, low-beamed main bar with its rustic furnishings and huge inglenook fireplace.

ICKLESHAM

The Queen's Head

Tel **01424 814552** | **Parsonage Lane, TN36 4BL**
Web **www.queenshead.com**
Dir ***Between Hastings and Rye on A259. In Icklesham into Parsonage Lane. Pub on right.***

This 17th-century, tile-hung and oak-beamed pub enjoys magnificent views and has been in the same hands for more than 30 years. The traditional atmosphere has been preserved, with vaulted ceilings, inglenook fireplaces, split-level floors, church pews, antique farm implements, and a bar from the old Midland Bank in Eastbourne. Customers are kept happy with up to 10 real ales, beer festivals and wide-ranging menus.

Open all day, all week 11–11 (Sun 11–10.30) Closed 25–26 Dec Free House 12 from £10 portions/menu notice required

MAYFIELD

The Middle House PICK OF THE PUBS

Tel **01435 872146** | **High Street, TN20 6AB**
Web **www.mhmayfield.co.uk**
Dir ***East of A267, south of Tunbridge Wells.***

Once described as 'one of the finest examples of a timber-framed building in Sussex', this Grade I listed, 16th-century village inn dominates the high street, while its private chapel is regarded as 'one of the most magnificent in England'. Real ale drinkers do well; the handsome choice embraces half a dozen of the nation's favourite brewers. Meats, poultry, game and vegetables come from local farms and producers. Terraced gardens enjoy views of the rolling countryside.

Open all day, all week Free House 10 from £10 portions/menu

PILTDOWN

The Peacock Inn PICK OF THE PUBS

Tel **01825 762463** | **Shortbridge Road, TN22 3XA**
Web **www.peacock-inn.co.uk**
Dir ***Just off A272 (Haywards Heath to Uckfield road) and A26 (Uckfield to Lewes road).***

Mentioned in Samuel Pepys' diary, The Peacock Inn dates from 1567 and is well known for its food and warm welcome – and it's full of old-world charm, both inside and out. Long Man Best and a guest ale keep beer-lovers happy. For the hungry, there are starters such as baked camembert; shredded confit of duck salad; or Sussex smokie – smoked haddock with cream and mustard sauce; followed by steak, Guinness and mushroom pie; or wild mushroom risotto. Leave room for desserts such as tiramisù cheesecake with coffee ice cream, or winter berry brûlée and biscotti. The large rear patio garden is a delightful spot in summer.

Open all week 11–3 6–11 (Fri to Sun 11–11) Closed 25–26 Dec Free House 8 portions/menu

RINGMER

The Cock – see page 426

RYE

The George Tap

Tel **01797 222114** | **98 High Street, TN31 7JT**
Web **www.thegeorgeinrye.com**
Dir ***M20 junction 10, A2070 to Brenzett, A259 to Rye.***

This town centre inn can trace its origins back to 1575. Inside it offers a fascinating mix of old and new, with an exquisite original Georgian ballroom. In the bar, the draw is beers from Dark Star and Harvey's breweries and a tasty, light bar menu.

Mermaid Inn – see page 427

The Ypres Castle Inn

PICK OF THE PUBS

Tel **01797 223248** | **Gun Garden, TN31 7HH**
Web **www.yprescastleinn.co.uk**
Dir ***Behind church and adjacent to Ypres Tower.***

This pretty, weatherboarded inn has provided hospitality below the castle ramparts since 1640. Its relaxed and friendly bar atmosphere has perhaps something to do with the Sussex and Kentish cask ales, craft keg beers from further afield, a truly local farm cider, and German draught lagers. In the reading room you'll find children's games. Dishes on a sample menu include mussels in cider with sourdough bread; steak and kidney pudding; fisherman's pie; Goan vegetable curry; and whisky marmalade bread and butter pudding. The views of Romney Marsh from the beer garden are magnificent.

Open all year, all day 12–11 Closed Mon (Nov to Mar) Free House 10 from £10 portions notice required

RINGMER

The Cock

Tel **01273 812040** | **Uckfield Road, BN8 5RX**
Web **www.cockpub.co.uk**
Dir ***Just off A26 approximately 2 miles north of Lewes just outside Ringmer.***

White-painted, weatherboarded free house

Experts believe that the inn was built towards the end of the 16th century and it takes its name from the time when a cock-horse was a spare animal hitched up to provide extra pulling power, in this case for the long haul up to Tunbridge Wells. The famous nursery rhyme 'Ride a Cock-Horse to Banbury Cross' now makes sense. A mustering point for soldiers during the Civil War, the main bar is pretty much unaltered since Cromwell's time, with oak beams, flagstone floors and a lovely fire in the inglenook. Harvey's Best Bitter, the house real ale, is well supported by others, mostly from Sussex, but sometimes Kent. As far as eating is concerned, there's something for everyone, with ham, egg and chips; home-made steak and ale pie; and pan-fried liver and bacon with mash and onion gravy at the simpler end, and more adventurous specials, such as pheasant breast with bacon, mushrooms, parsnip purée and Savoy cabbage; sea bass fillet wrapped in Parma ham with watercress sauce; and sausage en croûte with dauphinoise potatoes, red cabbage, greens and cider gravy. Among vegetarian options is sweet potato, spinach and chickpea curry with rice, chutney and poppadom. Curry nights are held monthly.

Open all week 11–3 6–11.30 (Sun 11–11) Closed 26 Dec *Free House* 9 *from £10.50* *portions/menu* *notice required*

RYE

Mermaid Inn

★★★ ◎◎ HOTEL

Tel **01797 223065** | **Mermaid Street, TN31 7EY**
Web **www.mermaidinn.com**
Dir ***A259, follow signs to town centre, into Mermaid Street.***

Memorable seafood dishes in historic smugglers' inn

PICK OF THE PUBS

One of the most famous and photographed of England's ancient pubs, this venerable black and white timber-fronted building was a haunt of seafarers from the Cinque Port harbour. Its colourful history is reflected in ships' timbers for beams, a vast inglenook where the infamous Hawkshurst gang warmed themselves, a hidden priest hole, and huge open fireplaces carved from French stone ballast dredged from Rye harbour. Food is served in the bar, restaurant and under sunshades on the patio. Choose local mussels, beetroot, apple and ginger risotto; followed by south coast cod in beer batter; traditional steak and kidney pudding; or the sea food platter. Superb wines, local Harvey's beer and comfortable bedrooms complete the package.

Open all day, all week 12–11 Free House 15 from £11.50 portions/menu notice required

SALEHURST

Salehurst Halt PICK OF THE PUBS

Tel **01580 880620** | **Church Lane, TN32 5PH**
Web **www.salehursthalt.co.uk**
Dir ***0.5 mile from A21 (Tunbridge Wells to Hastings road). Exit at Robertsbridge roundabout to Salehurst.***

Built in the 1860s, when it was known as the Old Eight Bells. Legend puts the name change down to a church organist who commuted to the village from Bodiam, necessitating a new halt on the old Robertsbridge to Tenterden line. Today, the local hop crop is sold to Harvey's in Lewes, and returned as one of the ales sold by the pub – its traditional cellar is much prized for maintaining ale in top condition. The hop farm also supplies the pub's meats, including Buster's burgers. The landscaped garden has a wonderful terrace with beautiful views over the Rother Valley; here a wood-fired pizza oven runs almost continually during the summer, with orders taken at the garden counter.

Open all year, all day Closed Mon Free House 10 portions Wi-fi

THREE LEG CROSS

The Bull Inn

Tel **01580 200586** | **Dunster Mill Lane, TN5 7HH**
Dir ***From M25 exit at Sevenoaks toward Hastings, right at crossroads onto B2087, right onto B2099 through Ticehurst, right for Three Leg Cross.***

The Bull started life as a Wealden hall house in 14th century, reputedly one of the oldest dwellings in the country, and is set in a hamlet close to Bewl Water. The interior is crammed with oak beams, inglenook fireplaces, quarry-tiled floors, and a mass of small intimate areas in the bar. The extensive gardens include a duck pond, aviary and children's play area. Menus offer pub favourites ranging from bar snacks to hearty dishes such as steak and kidney suet pudding.

Open all day, all week 12–11 Free House from £10 portions/menu Wi-fi notice required

TICEHURST

The Bell in Ticehurst

★★★★ INN PICK OF THE PUBS

Tel **01580 200234** | **High Street, TN5 7AS**
Web **www.thebellinticehurst.com**
Dir ***From A21 follow signs for Ticehurst. Pub in village centre.***

This eye-catching gabled and tile-hung village centre inn is equally appealing inside, with heavy beams, a huge brick-and-timber inglenook, and rug-strewn bare boards in the main rooms. Quirky design touches abound, from the top hat lampshades and pillar of books in the bar, to the French horns for urinals in the Gents and the stuffed squirrel that appears to hold up a ceiling. Beers from Harvey's and local breweries populate the pumps. Menu choices are a cut above the ordinary; versatile mains typically cover aromatic pork belly with cauliflower purée and wild mushrooms, or catch of the day such as hake fillet, piquillo peppers, potatoes and chorizo.

Open all day, all week Free House 12 menus notice required

UCKFIELD

The Highlands Inn – see opposite

WARBLETON

The Black Duck

Tel **01435 830636** | **Church Hill, TN21 9BD**
Web **www.theblackduckpub.co.uk**
Dir ***From Heathfield take A265 towards Hawkhurst. Right onto B2096 signed Old Heathfield, right signed Warbleton.***

The Black Duck was so named by owners Gary and Nicola Kinnell to commemorate all those poor birds used as chimney sweeps in medieval times. The pub's tile-hung exterior and the scrubbed beams, timber framing inglenook fireplace and bread oven within are evidence of its venerable age, while a huge cellar keeps Harvey's beers in tip-top condition. The menu of popular pub fare is backed by a dozen specials every day, including several vegetarian options. There are lovely views from the beer garden.

Open all year 12–3 5.30–11 (Fri to Sat 12–11 Sun 12–6) Closed Sun evening, Mon Free House from £10 portions/menu

WILMINGTON

The Giants Rest

Tel **01323 870207** | **The Street, BN26 5SQ**
Web **www.thegiantsrest.co.uk**
Dir ***2 miles from Polegate on A27 towards Brighton.***

This traditional country pub is set back off the A27 in a pretty village close to the famous chalk figure of the Long Man of Wilmington. A family-owned Victorian free house, the pub is ideally situated for walkers exploring the South Downs Way.

WITHYHAM

The Dorset Arms PICK OF THE PUBS

Tel **01892 770278** | **Buckhurst Park, TN7 4BD**
Web **www.dorset-arms.co.uk**
Dir ***4 miles west of Tunbridge Wells on B2110 between Groombridge and Hartfield.***

Licensed over 250 years ago, the pub was named after the heads of the local landowning family, the Dukes and Earls of Dorset. The centuries-old building is a jigsaw of styles, with slender chimney stacks, sharp gables, white weatherboarding and worn tiles. The interior doesn't disappoint with its comfy period mix of flagstoned and oak-boarded floors, vast open fireplace and undulating beams. This is a true village local, with darts, and good Sussex and Kent ales from Harvey's and Larkins; wines served by the glass include three sparklers. The kitchen's output is also a major draw, with eggs, sausages and organic beef sourced from the Buckhurst Estate.

Open all day, all week 12–11 (Sun 12–10.30) Free House 15 portions notice required

UCKFIELD

The Highlands Inn

Tel 01825 762989 | Eastbourne Road, TN22 5SP
Web www.ridleyinns.co.uk
Dir *From roundabout (junction of A22 and A26) into Lewes Road signed Ridgewood. Pub on right.*

A relaxed family pub

The nearest real highlands are the South Downs, their highest point locally being 219-metre Firle Beacon, a few miles south of here. This Highlands, owned by the Ridley family, who also own The Cock at Ringmer, has a light and modern feel to its spacious, largely open-plan interior, and seating varying from chesterfield-style sofas to leather-clad armchairs, tartan-clothed banquettes and high stools. There's a big screen to watch the match if you're so inclined, while on hand-pump in the bar are resident Harvey's of Lewes, and a guest, such as Brighton-brewed Holler Boys, or Dark Star from Partridge Green, all rested for five days before serving; spirits are hand-measured, so no optics here. The menu is essentially home-made pub fare, with steaks, burgers, salads, 'funky fungi', Mexicana beef patties, and such favourites as pie of the day; and smoked Sussex haddock in cheddar with leek and mustard sauce. Vegetarian options include sweet potato, spinach, cauliflower and chickpea curry and rice. Treacle and ginger tart and custard, and chocolate and coconut torte are two of the desserts. A home-cooked children's menu and a choice of three roasts on Sunday complete the picture.

Open all day, all week 11–11 (Fri to Sat 11am–midnight Sun 11–10.30) Free House 11 portions/menu notice required

WEST SUSSEX

ALBOURNE

The Ginger Fox

Tel **01273 857888** | **Muddleswood Road, BN6 9EA**
Web **www.gingermanrestaurants.com**
Dir ***On A281 at junction with B2117.***

The South Downs look glorious from the beer garden, where children can play safely, and mums and dads can relax with a drink, maybe a pint of Bedlam, the real ale brewed up nearby Shaves Wood Lane. Local beef from Redlands Farm may be on the menu, specifically a fillet with spicy charred tomato ketchup and duck fat chips. Another possibility is wild brill with mushroom purée, lemon and herb gnocchi, Jerusalem artichoke fondants and truffle velouté.

Open all day, all week Closed 25 Dec Free House 20 from £15 menus Wi-fi notice required

AMBERLEY

The Bridge Inn – see opposite

ANGERMING

The Lamb at Angmering

Tel **01903 774300** | **The Square, BN16 4EQ**
Web **www.thelamb-angmering.com**
Dir ***From A27 onto A280 to Rustington, right into Water Lane. Pub in village centre.***

Rescued from closure in 2011 by the Newbon family, who have completely revitalised this lovely pub; its late 18th-century interior looks as good as promised by its white-painted exterior. It feels right too, not least thanks to a progression of Sussex breweries making their mark in the bar, and a carte offering slow-roast pork belly with braised cheek; and cod, Bombay potatoes and spinach. Typical light bites might be Welsh or buck rarebit; and a classic 10 oz sirloin steak.

Open all day, all week Free House 19 portions/menu Wi-fi

ASHURST

The Fountain Inn PICK OF THE PUBS

Tel **01403 710219** | **BN44 3AP**
Web **www.fountainashurst.pub**
Dir ***On B2135, north of Steyning.***

Paul McCartney loved this 16th-century listed building so much he filmed part of the video for 'Wonderful Christmas Time' here. Actor Laurence Olivier was also once a regular at this lovely pub with terrace views of the South Downs and the village duck pond. Wonky floorboards and inglenook fireplaces provide plenty of character, with local beers from Harvey's accompanying food that attracts walkers, cyclists and locals alike. At lunchtime there are light bites, but at lunch or dinner you could opt for Sussex pork belly fingers with apple purée, followed by pan-seared duck breast, fondant potato, Savoy cabbage, spinach and orange jus. Look out for live music events.

Open all day, all week 11–11 (Sun 11–10.30) Enterprise Inns 20 from £12 portions/menu Wi-fi notice required

BOSHAM

The Anchor Bleu

Tel **01243 573956** | **High Street, PO18 8LS**
Web **www.anchorbleu.co.uk**
Dir ***From A27 (south-west of Chichester) take A259. Follow Fishbourne signs, then Bosham signs.***

If you park your car opposite The Anchor Bleu, check the tide times at this 17th-century inn, as that area floods during most high tides. Flagstone floors, low beams, an open log fire, and two terraces, one overlooking Chichester Harbour, add to the charm.

AMBERLEY

The Bridge Inn

Tel 01798 831619 | Houghton Bridge, BN18 9LR
Web www.bridgeinnamberley.com
Dir *5 miles north of Arundel on B2139. Adjacent to Amberley rail station.*

Halfway along the South Downs Way

Next to this charming period pub is Houghton Bridge over the River Arun, while across the road is the fascinating Amberley Museum & Heritage Centre, once a busy chalk quarry. The pub has a long association with the museum's industrial heritage theme, since quarrymen and limekiln workers once slaked their thirsts here. Attracting people to the pub today are its candlelit bar's log fires, real ales from Harvey's brewery in Lewes and Long Man in Litlington, the sheltered garden with views of the South Downs countryside, and the extensive menu. This offers a broad range of dishes, among which you can expect prawn and crayfish cocktail; steak and kidney suet pudding; pan-fried sea bass with samphire and pea risotto; and Tunisian shakshouka, a spiced tomato, pepper and shallot stew. Vegetarians will find options too. Traditional roasts on Sundays usually include beef and pork, and sometimes a chicken or lamb dish. Before coffee, maybe order strawberry, basil and lime cheesecake with a gingernut base. Sandwiches, filled ciabattas and ploughman's lunches are available Monday to Saturday lunchtimes, and ploughman's all day Sunday. In addition to the South Downs Way, there are riverside and other downland walks right on the doorstep.

Open all day, all week 11–11 (Sun 12–9) Free House portions/menu notice required

BURGESS HILL

The Oak Barn

Tel **01444 258222 | Cuckfield Road, RH15 8RE**
Web **www.oakbarnrestaurant.co.uk**
Dir ***Phone for detailed directions.***

As its name suggests, this popular pub-restaurant occupies a 250-year-old barn that has been lovingly restored using salvaged timbers from wooden ships. Brimming with charm, the interior is rich in oak flooring, authentic wagon wheel chandeliers, and fine stained glass. Lofty raftered ceilings, a galleried restaurant, and leather chairs fronting a huge fireplace add to the atmosphere. Here, and in the bar and enclosed courtyard, you'll find sandwiches, pub classics and an à la carte menu at lunch and dinner. Sup a pint of Harvey's or Guinness and tuck into dishes created from seasonal British ingredients.

Open all day, all week 10am–11pm (Sun 11–11)
Free House 8 portions Wi-fi P

See advertisement below

BURPHAM

The George at Burpham

PICK OF THE PUBS

Tel **01903 883131 | Main Street, BN18 9RR**
Web **www.georgeatburpham.co.uk**
Dir ***Exit A27 1 mile east of Arundel signed Burpham, 2.5 miles, pub on left.***

Built in 1736, this popular pub stands opposite the 11th-century parish church. Head for the bar with its wood-burning stove, safe in the knowledge that Sussex-sourced real ales, soft drinks and even champagne are waiting. Bar snacks might include a hot smoked salmon and crème fraîche sandwich; and mains like potato gnocchi with spinach and wild mushroom sauce; house beefburger in a brioche bun with chips; a naked burger with poached egg and salad, or a haloumi burger with guacamole, sweet peppers and sweet potato fries. Puddings and Sussex cheeses tempt too. Booking is advisable.

Open all week 10.30–3 6–11 (Sat 10.30am–11pm Sun 10.30–5.30) Free House 10 from £12.95 portions/menu Wi-fi P *notice required*

CHARLTON

The Fox Goes Free

★★★★ INN

Tel 01243 811461 | PO18 0HU
Web www.thefoxgoesfree.com
Dir *A286, 6 miles from Chichester towards Midhurst.*

Friendly pub with William III, racing world and WI connections

Standing in unspoilt countryside at the foot of the South Downs, this lovely old brick and flint free house was a favoured hunting lodge of William III. With its three huge fireplaces, old pews and brick floors, the 17th-century building simply exudes charm and character. The pub, which hosted the first English Women's Institute meeting in 1915, lies close to the Weald and Downland Open Air Museum, where 50 historic buildings from around southern England have been reconstructed. Goodwood Estate is also close by, and the Fox attracts many customers during the racing season, the annual Festival of Speed and Revival. Away from the high life, you can watch the world go by from the solid timber benches and tables to the front, or relax in the lawned rear garden. Lest all this sounds rather extravagant, you'll find the Fox a friendly and welcoming drinkers' pub with a good selection of real ales that includes the eponymous Fox Goes Free bitter. Whether you're looking for a quick bar snack or something more substantial, the daily-changing menus offer something for every taste.

Open all day, all week 11–11 (Sun 12–11) Closed 25 Dec evening Free House 25 *from £12.50 portions/menu notice required*

CHICHESTER

The Bull's Head

Tel **01243 839895** | **99 Fishbourne Road West, PO19 3JP**
Web **www.bulls-head-fishbourne.co.uk**
Dir ***A27 onto A259, inn 0.5 mile on left.***

Only three minutes' walk from Chichester harbour, this traditional white-painted roadside pub with large open fire has been a hostelry since the 17th century. Its position just outside Chichester is perfect for anyone visiting Fishbourne Roman Palace and Bosham Harbour. Expect traditional home-cooked food.

The Earl of March

PICK OF THE PUBS

Tel **01243 533993** | **Lavant Road, Lavant, PO18 0BQ**
Web **www.theearlofmarch.com**
Dir ***On A286, 1 mile north of Chichester.***

The current Earl is the founder of the Festival of Speed and the Goodwood Revival, held on the nearby family estate of the Dukes of Richmond. In the pub in 1803 William Blake wrote the words to 'Jerusalem'; today's visitors can enjoy much the same memorable South Downs' views that influenced his verse. The excellent dishes, courtesy of Giles Thompson, former executive chef at London's Ritz Hotel, depend on local estates and the nearby English Channel. Taking the Earl's Menu, might see you enjoying a pan-fried pork fillet, white bean and wild mushroom cassoulet, cavolo nero, rösti and port wine jus. Plenty of bar and lighter meals are offered too.

Open all day, all week Enterprise Inns 24 portions/menu WI-FI

The George & Dragon Inn

★★★ INN

Tel **01243 785660** | **51 North Street, PO19 1NQ**
Web **www.thegeorgechichester.com**
Dir ***Near Chichester Festival Theatre. Phone for detailed directions.***

The George & Dragon stands next to the site of the original north walls' gatehouse in historic Chichester, and is well positioned near the Old Town Cross and cathedral. It dates from the early 18th century and today you'll find open fires, comfortable sofas and a courtyard to enhance the family-friendly feel. In the light and airy conservatory dining room, the menus reveal traditional pub favourites, house-smoked meats, cheeses and fish. All dishes are freshly prepared.

Open all day, all week Closed 25–26 Dec, 1 Jan Star Pubs & Bars 10 from £7.50 portions/menu WI-FI notice required

The Royal Oak ★★★★★ INN

PICK OF THE PUBS

Tel **01243 527434** | **Pook Lane, East Lavant, PO18 0AX**
Web **www.royaloakeastlavant.co.uk**
Dir ***2 miles north of Chichester. Exit A286 to East Lavant centre.***

At the foot of the South Downs, this 200-year-old whitewashed village inn near Chichester is a popular stopping point for walkers and for racegoers heading to Goodwood, a 10-minute drive away. The Royal Oak has retained much of its original character inside, with red-brick and flint walls, tiled and timbered floors and real fires. A modern 'field to fork' approach to pub cooking means a seasonal menu that might start with shallot tarte Tatin, Sussex honey and chilli dressing and Cerney Ash goats' cheese, followed by sea bream, Chardonnay and dill sauce, crushed baby potatoes, baby spinach or lamb shoulder, smoked almond crust, kale and celeriac dauphinoise.

Open all day, all week 7am–11pm Free House 16 from £14 portions WI-FI P

COMPTON

Coach & Horses

Tel **023 9263 1228** | **The Square, PO18 9HA**
Web **www.coachandhorsescompton.co.uk**
Dir ***On B2146, south of Petersfield. In village centre.***

Commanding the centre of a pretty South Downs' village, this 17th-century coaching inn is now run by Dave and Paul. They've updated the Victorian bar, with its two open fires, and as likely as not, you'll find Harvey's Sussex bitter in residence. The oldest part of the building is the beamed restaurant where you may take your pick from baguettes to banoffee tart, by way of chilli vegetable fritter; breast of duck with plum sauce; grilled fish of the day; or chickpea tagine.

Open Tue to Sun 12–11 Closed 26 Dec, 1 Jan, Mon Free House from £10 portions WI-FI notice required

CUCKFIELD

The Talbot

Tel **01444 455898 | High Street, RH17 5JX**
Web **www.thetalbotcuckfield.co.uk**
Dir ***B2036 into village centre.***

Once a staging post for travellers on the road between London and Brighton, The Talbot is still the hub in the historic village of Cuckfield. It's now a contemporary pub and restaurant that prides itself on making the most of the local larder, whether it's Dark Star ales or seasonal dishes such as crab arancini, watercress and lime mayonnaise; and roasted pork tenderloin, heritage carrots, white bean cassoulet and roasted apples.

Open all day, all week Free House 14 from £11.50 portions/menu notice required

DIAL POST

The Crown Inn

Tel **01403 710902 | Worthing Road, RH13 8NH**
Web **www.crown-inn-dialpost.co.uk**
Dir ***6 miles south of Horsham. Village signed from A24.***

Nicely positioned opposite the village green, with an excellent reputation for home-made, seasonal food, and well-kept ales: a house brew by Long Man and others from Hammerpot and Kissingate. Nearly everything is made from scratch – from soups, pâtés and home-ground steak burgers to puddings, ice creams and sorbets. The hand-crafted steak, kidney and local ale pies are hard to resist.

Open 12–3 6–11 (Sun 12–4) Closed Sun evenings (contact pub for Christmas opening times) Free House from £11 portions

DUNCTON

The Cricketers

Tel **01798 342473 | GU28 0LB**
Web **www.thecricketersduncton.co.uk**
Dir ***On A285, 3 miles from Petworth, 8 miles from Chichester.***

Named to commemorate its one-time owner John Wisden, the first-class cricketer and creator of the famous sporting almanac, this attractive whitewashed pub sits in beautiful gardens. Dating to the 16th century, with an inglenook fireplace, the inn has hardly changed over the years.

EARTHAM

The George

Tel **01243 814340 | PO18 0LT**
Web **www.thegeorgeeartham.com**
Dir ***From A283 (Petworth to Chichester Road) follow Eartham signs. Inn on right. Or from A27 follow Great Ballard and Eartham signs.***

Several inducements are at work at this appealing village pub – open fires, a pretty garden, a craft bar selling over 40 beers and lagers, first-rate English wines and an extensive gin menu. Typical dishes include cod fillet with cheese and potato croquette; sticky rib of beef with smoked bacon crumb; and, in season, whole roast partridge. The menu also includes a popular vegetarian section. Selsey crab and lobster appear on the ever-changing specials board in summer.

Open all year, all day Closed Mon Free House 12 portions

EAST GRINSTEAD

The Old Dunnings Mill

Tel **01342 821080 | Dunnings Road, RH19 4AT**
Web **www.olddunningsmill.co.uk**
Dir ***From High Street into Ship Street. At mini-roundabout right into Dunnings Road. Pub on right.***

A pub of two halves, parts of the ODM date from the 16th-century flour mill that inspired its name, the rest was added in the 1970s. As it's a Harvey's pub, you'll find their real ales in the bar. They hold June and September beer festivals.

ELSTED

The Three Horseshoes

Tel **01730 825746 | GU29 0JY**
Web **3hs.co.uk**
Dir ***A272 from Midhurst towards Petersfield, left in 2 miles signed Harting and Elsted, 3 miles to pub on left.***

This 16th-century former drovers' alehouse is one of those quintessential English country pubs that Sussex specialises in. Tucked below the steep scarp slope of the South Downs National Park, expect unspoilt cottage-style bars, brick and quarry tiled floors, low beams, latch doors, and a vast inglenook.

FERNHURST

The Red Lion

Tel **01428 643112 | The Green, GU27 3HY**
Web **www.red-lion-fernhurst.co.uk**
Dir ***Just off A286 midway between Haslemere and Midhurst.***

In the dimpled shade of a huge maple, this attractive stone-and-whitewashed inn overlooks a corner of the green in this peaceful village set in the wooded hills of the South Downs National Park. Cricketers from the nearby ground amble here to enjoy Fuller's beers and guest ales.

HENLEY

Duke of Cumberland Arms

PICK OF THE PUBS

Tel **01428 652280 | GU27 3HQ**
Web **www.dukeofcumberland.com**
Dir ***From A286 between Fernhurst and Midhurst take single-track road signed Nicholsons and Aspinals. Pub on right.***

In an absolutely delightful setting, this beautiful 16th-century pub, perched on a wooded hillside in the South Downs National Park is a real gem. Inside are flagstones, brick floors, scrubbed tables, and ales served straight from the barrels Harvey's and Langham breweries deliver them in. The first-rate menus impress at lunchtime with braised oxtail, horseradish mash, curly kale and red wine jus; or grilled south coast mackerel fillet open sandwich, while in the evening you might choose pig's head ballotine, smoked potato croquette, quail's egg and brown sauce to start, followed by Selsey crab thermidor; or an 8oz grain-fed sirloin steak, with roasted tomato, mixed leaf, peppercorn sauce and chunky chips.

Open all day, all week *Free House* 17 *portions* WIFI P

HEYSHOTT

Unicorn Inn **PICK OF THE PUBS**

Tel **01730 813486 | GU29 0DL**
Web **www.unicorn-inn-heyshott.co.uk**
Dir ***Phone for detailed directions.***

Enjoying stunning views of the South Downs from its beautiful, south-facing rear garden, this 18th-century free house is the perfect spot to relax with a pint of Adnams on a sunny day. The bar, with beams and a large log fire, is particularly atmospheric, while the subtly lit, cream-painted restaurant is where you can sample fresh fish from Selsey, or dishes like grilled pork belly with Stilton sauce; rib-eye steak; fish pie; or pheasant breast with apricot and date stuffing. Good sandwiches (perhaps roast beef and horseradish) and popular Sunday lunches complete the picture.

Open all year, all day Tue to Sat (Sun 12–4) Closed Sun evening and Mon (except bank holidays and summer) *Free House* *portions/menu* WIFI P *notice required*

HORSHAM

The Black Jug

Tel **01403 253526 | 31 North Street, RH12 1RJ**
Web **www.brunningandprice.co.uk/blackjug**
Dir ***Phone for detailed directions.***

This handsome, tile-hung and gabled pub has served the discerning clientele of Horsham town centre for around 200 years. With a trim garden and copious flower displays outside; the interior is a delightful mix of time-worn furniture and a warm atmosphere free of music and machines.

HORSTED KEYNES

The Crown Inn

Tel **01825 791609 | The Green, RH17 7AW**
Web **www.thecrownhorstedkeynes.co.uk**
Dir ***From A272 at North Chailey (east of Haywards Heath) take A275 towards East Grinstead. In Daneshill left signed Horsted Keynes.***

The Crown has been serving locals and travellers for more than 250 years. In 2003 a lightning strike caused serious damage, and large parts of the building were destroyed. Fortunately the oldest parts were untouched and the inn retains its cosy, relaxed feel.

HURSTPIERPOINT

The New Inn

Tel **01273 834608 | 76 High Street, BN6 9RQ**
Web **www.thenewinnhurst.com**
Dir ***In village centre.***

Despite its name, The New Inn actually dates back as far as 1450 and it has been a hub of the village ever since. Just off the A23 to the north of the South Downs National Park, this bustling village is also a short hop from Brighton. Whether it's one of the four areas in the pub or in the pretty beer garden, this friendly and lively pub is a great place to enjoy a glass of local Harvey's and enjoy a freshly prepared dish from the varied menu.

Open all day, all week Star Pubs & Bars 10 from £12.95 portions/menu Wi-fi

KINGSFOLD

The Dog and Duck

Tel **01306 627295 | Dorking Road, RH12 3SA**
Dir ***On A24, 3 miles north of Horsham.***

The Dog and Duck is a 16th-century family-run and family-friendly country pub serving enjoyable food like cottage pie, home-made curry and chicken and bacon pie, washed down with Dorset Best. There's plenty of children's play equipment in the huge garden and three very large fields that encourage canines and energetic owners to stretch their legs. The rest of the year sees the diary chock-full of celebratory events, including the charity fundraising beer festival, summer camp, hallowe'en party and firework display.

Open all year, all day Tue to Sat 12–9 (Sun 12–6) Closed Mon, Sun evening Hall & Woodhouse from £9.50 portions/menu P notice required

KINGSFOLD

The Owl at Kingsfold

Tel **01306 628499 | Dorking Road, RH12 3SA**
Web **www.theowl-kingsfold.co.uk**
Dir ***On A24, 4 miles north of Horsham.***

In a hamlet just 20 minutes from the sea

A traditional country free house with wooden beams, flagstone floors and log burners. It occupies a prominent roadside site in the village, with plenty of parking and a garden with views to the Surrey Hills; composer Ralph Vaughan Williams reputedly arranged the hymn 'Kingsfold' here. There are three real ales to choose from, while the frequently changing lunch menu might include Ardennes pâté with cranberry compôte; or filo-wrapped king prawns to start, followed by home-made chilli con carne; pork fillet with mustard, honey and

whisky cream sauce; or smoked cod loin with chorizo, potato and peas; a specials board adds to the choices.

Open all day, all week 11–11 Free House 12 from £11 portions/menu P

KIRDFORD

The Half Moon Inn

Tel **01403 820223 | Glasshouse Lane, RH14 0LT**
Web **www.halfmoonkirdford.co.uk**
Dir ***A281 from Horsham to Broadbridge Heath. A264 towards Guildford. At roundabout left into Stane Street signed Billinghurst. At 2nd rounabout 2nd exit onto A272 to Wisborough Green. Right to Kirdford.***

The kitchen's promise here is 'always local, always seasonal and always prepared from scratch'. The chef will even cook your favourite dish if it's phoned through a day in advance. Food aside, the Half Moon is still an idyllic village local with garden and picnic benches.

10 TOP SUSSEX PUBS WITH ACCOMMODATION

The following pubs are rated as part of the AA Guest Accommodation scheme (see page 10–11 for more information).

The Bull ★★★★★ INN Ditchling, East Sussex, *see page 421*
The Royal Oak ★★★★★ INN Chichester, West Sussex, *see page 434*
The Crab & Lobster ★★★★★ RESTAURANT WITH ROOMS Sidlesham, West Sussex, *see page 441*
The Halfway Bridge Inn ★★★★★ INN Lodsworth, West Sussex, *see page 438*
The Bell in Ticehurst ★★★★ INN Ticehurst, East Sussex, *see page 428*
The Horse Guards Inn ★★★★ INN Tillington, West Sussex, *see page 443*
The Fox Goes Free ★★★★ INN Charlton, West Sussex, *see page 433*
The White Hart ★★★★ INN South Harting, West Sussex, *see page 441*
The George & Dragon Inn ★★★ INN Chichester, West Sussex, *see page 434*
Mermaid Inn ★★★ HOTEL Rye, East Sussex, *see page 427*

LAMBS GREEN

The Lamb Inn

Tel **01293 871336 | RH12 4RG**
Web **www.thelambinn.org**
Dir ***6 miles from Horsham between Rusper and Faygate. 5 miles from Crawley.***

With its comfy sofas, inglenook fireplace and newly created, partly-covered garden with a wood-fired pizza oven, no wonder that it's more than just a popular village local. Its real ales all come from local microbreweries, and its home-made food, with vegetarian options, is, of course, locally sourced. Proof is the 21-day-aged Sussex beef, and the game, rabbits and venison shot by the pub's regulars. Whole roasted sea bass with chorizo and cherry tomatoes is a further option.

Open all week Mon to Thu 11.30–3 5.30–11 (Fri to Sat 11.30–11 Sun 12–10.30) Closed 25–26 Dec Free House 12 from £12 portions/menu Wi-fi notice required

LODSWORTH

The Halfway Bridge Inn

★★★★★ INN PICK OF THE PUBS

Tel **01798 861281 | Halfway Bridge, GU28 9BP**
Web **www.halfwaybridge.co.uk**
Dir ***Between Petworth and Midhurst, adjacent to Cowdray Estate and Golf Club on A272.***

This 17th-century traditional pub and contemporary dining inn stands roughly equidistant from Midhurst, home of the Cowdray Estate and British polo, and Petworth, with its National Trust mansion. Guests will find tastefully furnished rooms with beamed ceilings, log fires and peaceful patio and garden, while for those seeking a truly local pint there are real ales from Langham, brewed a mile away, and Sussex Gold from the Arundel Brewery. Lighter meals include open sandwiches, ciabattas and salads. From the mains selection there might be rolled belly of pork, bubble-and-squeak, kale and mustard cream sauce; or pan-fried fillet of sea trout, leek and chive crushed potato, buttered spinach and white wine cream sauce. Leave room for one of the tempting desserts, perhaps white chocolate rice pudding, rhubarb compôte and rhubarb syrup.

Open all day, all week 11–11 Free House 24 from £16.85 portions/menu Wi-fi

LODSWORTH

The Hollist Arms

Tel 01798 861310 | The Street, GU28 9BZ
Web www.thehollistarms.com
Dir ***From A272, halfway between Midhurst and Petworth, turn towards Lodsworth. In village, pub on left.***

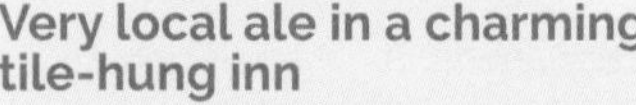

Very local ale in a charming tile-hung inn

The pretty Sussex village of Lodsworth, between Petworth and Midhurst, is where you'll find this characterful and welcoming 18th-century pub with its open fires and old beams. A great selection of beers, including some from the village's own Langham Brewery, accompanies the straightforward, seasonal menu of quality pub classics. You could choose a sharing plate, maybe the Hollist's houmous with pitta and crudités, or salt and pepper

squid, before getting stuck in to devilled crab salad with spinach, avocado, spring onion and chilli, or potted shrimps with picked cucumber and sourdough toast. Main courses range from ale-battered hake and chips to a 10oz Sussex sirloin, or confit duck leg with celeriac and potato dauphinoise.

Open all week 12–3.30 5–11 (Sat 12–12 Sun 12–10) Free House 12 from £12.50 portions/menu notice required

LOWER BEEDING

The Crabtree

Tel 01403 892666 | Brighton Road, RH13 6PT
Web www.crabtreesussex.com
Dir ***On A281 between Cowfold and Horsham, opposite South Lodge Hotel.***

Visit the family-run Crabtree and you'll be following in the footsteps of author and poet Hilaire Belloc who was often here. The inn, originally built in 1539, sits in beautiful countryside which is where the pub sources most of its produce. Trusty local companies supply meat from high welfare farms and the daily-caught fish and shellfish come via nearby Shoreham harbour. Start perhaps with confit duck and pear pastille, blackberry gel, apple crisp, followed by pan-fried monkfish with mussels and coriander and curry soup.

Open all day, all week Hall & Woodhouse 20 from £13 portions/menu

LURGASHALL

The Noah's Ark – see page 440

MAPLEHURST

The White Horse

Tel 01403 891208 | Park Lane, RH13 6LL
Web www.whitehorsemaplehurst.co.uk
Dir ***5 miles south-east of Horsham, between A281 and A272.***

This rural free house, owned by the same family for over 30 years, lies deep in the countryside. It offers a welcome haven free from music and fruit machines. Hearty home-cooked pub food, such as their popular chilli, plus an enticing selection of five real ales are served over what is reputed to be the widest bar counter in Sussex. Sip a pint of Harvey's Sussex Best Bitter or Weltons Pridenjoy whilst admiring the rolling countryside from the large, quiet, south-facing garden. Village-brewed cider is a speciality.

Open all year 12–2.30 6–11 (Sun 12–3) Closed Mon lunch (excluding bank holidays) Sun evening Free House 11 from £6.40 portions/menu notice required

LURGASHALL

The Noah's Ark

Tel **01428 707346** | **The Green, GU28 9ET**
Web **www.noahsarkinn.co.uk**
Dir ***B2131 from Haslemere follow signs to Petworth/Lurgashall. A3 from London towards Portsmouth. At Milford take A283 signed Petworth. Follow signs to Lurgashall.***

16th-century inn at the height of country chic

In a picturesque village beneath Blackdown Hill, this attractive 16th-century inn overlooks the cricket green. The pretty interior is full of old beams, a large inglenook fireplace, muted colours, pale wooden furniture and fresh flowers. In addition to the Greene King ales is a regularly changing guest, and the traditional British food with a contemporary twist uses seasonal ingredients carefully sourced from the best local suppliers. The menu is concise but enticing: crispy duck pancake with spring onion and cucumber salad; or smoked salmon with a courgette fritter and sour cream may precede chestnut mushroom Stroganoff; black tiger prawn and chorizo linguine; or battered haddock and chips.

Open all day, all week 11am–11.30pm (Sun 12–10 summer, Sun 12–8 winter) Greene King 30 from £13 portions/menu notice required

OVING

The Gribble Inn

Tel **01243 786893** | **PO20 2BP**
Web **www.gribbleinn.co.uk**
Dir ***From A27 take A259. After 1 mile left at roundabout, 1st right to Oving, 1st left in village.***

This charming 16th-century, thatched inn has its own microbrewery, and it is a peaceful spot to sup any of the own-brewed real ales on tap; any of the six ales can be taken away too. There are two open log fires, low beams and a pretty cottage garden. From the menu, enjoy traditional pub food. Summer and winter beer festivals are hosted, and there is a brewery tap bar. The inn is named after school teacher, Rose Gribble, who once lived in the building.

Open all day, all week Mon to Sat 11–11 (Sun 12–9) Free House 20 portions/menu

POYNINGS

Royal Oak PICK OF THE PUBS

Tel **01273 857389** | **The Street, BN45 7AQ**
Web **www.royaloakpoynings.pub**
Dir ***From A23 onto A281 signed Henfield and Poynings.***

Poynings is tucked well away in the South Downs National Park. It's not difficult to find this pink-painted village pub but should you fail you might regret it, especially after working up a thirst and an appetite walking in the nearby deep valley called Devil's Dyke. Inside, it's all oak floors, old beams and some undoubtedly welcome plush sofas. From a seasonal menu kick off with pan-fried wood-pigeon breast, or tempura king prawns, and continue with wild mushroom, thyme and pomegranate risotto; or a Sussex smokie of smoked haddock with a cheese gratin topping. Puddings are tempting too – perhaps, from a winter menu, poached pears in mulled wine. In summer, the wonderful garden offers barbecue facilities and fine downland views.

Open all day, all week 11–11 (Sun 12–10.30) Star Pubs And Bars 14 from £12 portions/menu notice required

ROWHOOK

The Chequers Inn

PICK OF THE PUBS

Tel **01403 790480** | **RH12 3PY**
Web **www.thechequersrowhook.com**
Dir ***From Horsham A281 towards Guildford. At roundabout take A29 signed London. In 200 metres left, follow Rowhook signs.***

A striking, 400-year-old higgledy-piggledy pub with a classic interior of flagstoned floor, low beams and blazing fire in the inglenook. The bar offers Firebird Heritage XX and Long Man Best Bitter on tap and an impressive wine list. You could snack on baked ciabatta, smoked bacon and Somerset brie, while Harvey's beer-battered fish and chips with mushy peas or home-made sausages with mashed potatoes and onion gravy are among the crowd-pleasing hot dishes. The kitchen often sources seasonal wild mushrooms and even truffles from the generous woodlands around the hamlet of Rowhook.

Open 11.30–3.30 6–11.30 (Sun 12–3.30) Closed 25 Dec, Sun evening and bank holidays evening Free House 10 from £11.50 portions Wi-fi

SHIPLEY

The Countryman Inn – see page 442

SIDLESHAM

The Crab & Lobster ★★★★★

 RESTAURANT WITH ROOMS

Tel **01243 641233** | **Mill Lane, PO20 7NB**
Web **www.crab-lobster.co.uk**
Dir ***A27 onto B2145 signed Selsey. 1st left after garage at Sidlesham into Rookery Lane to Crab & Lobster.***

On the banks of Pagham Harbour Reserve, the stylish 350-year-old Crab & Lobster prides itself on the coastal location. This sense of place extends to the ales from local breweries such as Arundel, as well as a menu featuring the latest catch from the Selsey fishing boats. Typical dishes on the inviting menu include salt and pepper fresh squid, kimchi, charred baby corn and pea purée; and the very popular dressed Selsey crab gratin. There are fabulous sea views from the bedrooms.

Open all day, all week Free House 24 from £17 portions Wi-fi

SLINDON

The Spur

Tel **01243 814216** | **BN18 0NE**
Web **www.thespurslindon.co.uk**
Dir ***From A27 take A29 signed Slindon.***

On top of the rolling South Downs, just outside the village of Slindon, this 17th-century pub is an ideal stopping-off point on a day out in the country. It has been praised for its friendly atmosphere and for generous portions of food. Outside, are large gardens and a courtyard, inside is an open-plan bar and restaurant, warmed by log fires. Daily-changing bar meals are marked up on the blackboard and may include home-made pies (four flavours on offer).

Open all week 11.30–3 6–11 (Sun 12–10) Closed 1 Jan Free House 12 from £10.95 portions/menu

SOUTH HARTING

The White Hart ★★★★ INN

Tel **01730 825124** | **The Street, GU31 5QB**
Web **www.the-whitehart.co.uk**
Dir ***From Petersfield take B2146 to South Harting.***

An engaging mix of beams and timber framing, log-burners, deep leather chairs and an eye-catching stone fireplace set the scene at this 16th-century inn at the heart of a pretty South Downs village. Beers come from Upham Brewery, and the tempting menu includes pub classics and ever-changing specials. Kick things off with a whole, baked camembert, before moving on to seared haunch of venison, butternut squash, crispy shallots and venison cottage pie.

Open all day, all week Free House 13 portions/menu Wi-fi

STEDHAM

Hamilton Arms/Nava Thai Restaurant – see page 443

SHIPLEY

The Countryman Inn

Tel 01403 741383 | Countryman Lane, RH13 8PZ
Web www.countrymanshipley.co.uk
Dir *A272 at Coolham into Smithers Hill Lane. 1 mile, left at T-junction.*

A real old fashioned, traditional pub that ticks all the boxes

Having run this traditional rural free house for around 30 years, Alan Vaughan and his family certainly know a thing or two about pleasing their customers. Surrounding the inn is the Knepp Castle Estate, 3,500 acres devoted to nature conservation through regeneration and restoration projects. In the pub's log fire-warmed bar, you'll find cask-conditioned beers from Sussex-brewed Harvey's, as well as ales from smaller microbreweries such as Hurst and Greyhound. Making their way to the kitchen are fish landed at Shoreham and Newhaven, the two closest ports; free-range meats from local farms; game from the Knepp Estate; vegetables and salads grown in the pub's own half-acre garden; and, through a 'swop shop' arrangement with villagers, unusual ingredients such as quince, kohlrabi or romanesco. Surplus garden produce can be purchased in the bar. Children are welcome in the restaurant at lunchtimes only, although the inn doesn't have a separate play area or family dining room. In the garden, weather permitting, an open-air kitchen serves grills, ploughman's and other snacks. In the pub's own farm shop you can buy free-range eggs and home-made preserves, pickles and relishes.

Open all week 11–3 6–10 Free House 18 from £12 portions

STEDHAM

Hamilton Arms/ Nava Thai Restaurant

Tel 01730 812555 | Hamilton Arms, School Lane, GU29 0NZ
Web www.thehamiltonarms.co.uk
Dir *Follow Stedham sign from A272 between Midhurst and Petersfield. Pub on left in vilage.*

Well known for the excellent Thai food

Opposite the village common, this country free house serves authentic Thai food, wine and beers – but if you prefer you can opt for English bar snacks and traditional ales. Thai food devotees will be spoilt for choice – the extensive menu features soups, salads and curries such as beef in coconut milk and bamboo shoots. For vegetarians the choice includes mushroom soup flavoured with lemongrass, lime leaves and chillies, perhaps followed by fried broccoli with garlic and oyster sauce. The pub is home to the Mudita Trust, a charity established 25 years ago to help abused and underprivileged children in Thailand.

Open all year, all day Closed Mon (excluding bank holidays) Free House 8 from £8.50 portions/menu

TILLINGTON

The Horse Guards Inn

★★★★  

Tel 01798 342332 | GU28 9AF
Web www.thehorseguardsinn.co.uk
Dir *From Petworth towards Midhurst on A272. 1 mile, right signed Tillington. Inn up hill opposite church.*

This 350-year-old inn's name recalls the day when Household Cavalry horses were rested in the parkland opposite. The tasteful interior features beams, stripped floorboards, open fires, antique furnishings, fresh flowers and candles. A fine range of real ales includes nearby Langham brews, and the compact, seasonal menu often incorporates goodies from Sussex hedgerows and seashores. Excellent steaks feature alongside main dishes such as Persian-style pork shoulder and potato curry, onion raita, kachumber salad and parsnip bhaji. Deckchairs, sheepskin-covered benches and even straw bales provide seating in the tree-shaded garden.

Open all day, all week Closed 25–26 Dec Enterprise Inns 16 from £14 portions/menu Wi-fi notice required

WALDERTON

The Barley Mow

Tel 023 9263 1321 | PO18 9ED
Web thebarleymow.pub
Dir *From Chichester take B2178 (East Ashling). Through East Ashling (road becomes B2146). In Funtington right into Hares Lane signed Walderton. At T-junction right. 0.5 mile to Walderton. Turn right at Walderton village sign, pub 100 yards on left.*

Famous locally for its skittle alley, this 18th-century pub is a favourite with walkers, cyclists and horse-riders. Its secluded, stream-bordered garden is a real sun-trap and inside is a log-fire-warmed bar. Booking is strongly advised for the popular Sunday carvery.

WARNINGLID

The Half Moon

Tel **01444 461227** | **The Street, RH17 5TR**
Web **www.thehalfmoonwarninglid.co.uk**
Dir ***1 mile from Warninglid and Cuckfield junction on A23 and 6 miles from Haywards Heath.***

This picture-perfect Grade II listed building dates from the 18th century and has been sympathetically extended to preserve its traditional feel. Look out for the glass-topped well as you come in. Enjoy a pint of Harvey's or a real cider while perusing the menu.

WEST ASHLING

The Richmond Arms 

Tel **01243 572046** | **Mill Road, PO18 8EA**
Web **www.therichmondarms.co.uk**
Dir ***Phone for detailed directions.***

Thatched flint cottages characterise this old village. The Richmond Arms is young by comparison, but this welcoming pub is drawing custom from far afield with its attractive combination of cheerful interiors, Harvey's beers, sumptuous wine carte and interesting menus. Dishes might be crispy, rare-cooked salmon tempura roll; slow-cooked hare lasagne; beef brisket with winter slaw; or BBQ pheasant with Kashmiri spices. Outside there's the WoodFired family-friendly bar with a vintage Citroën van that houses a wood-fired pizza oven, stoked up on Friday and Saturday evenings.

Open 11–3 6–11 Closed 23 Dec to 12 Jan, 23–30 Jul, Sun evening, Mon and Tue Free House 14 from £15.95 portions/menu

WEST DEAN

The Dean Inn

Tel **01243 811465** | **Main Road, PO18 0QX**
Web **www.thedeaninn.co.uk**
Dir ***Between Chichester and Midhurst on A286.***

Handy for race-goers to nearby Goodwood, this 200-year-old country dining inn occupies a tranquil spot in a village between the South Downs and Chichester. Drinkers revel in the choice of local real ales from the likes of Langham, Bedlam and Dark Star breweries. The kitchen team produces an arresting range of modern dishes, using local ingredients. Start with pan-fried pigeon, glazed shallots and raspberry gel before pork belly, celeriac mash, greens and red wine jus. Time a visit with the early May beer festival.

Open all week 11–3 5.30–10 (Sat 10am–11pm Sun 10–6.30) Free House 8 portions/menu notice required

WEST HOATHLY

The Cat Inn PICK OF THE PUBS

Tel **01342 810369** | **North Lane, RH19 4PP**
Web **www.catinn.co.uk**
Dir ***From East Grinstead centre take A22 towards Forest Row. Into left lane, into B2110 (Beeching Way) signed Turners Hill. Left into Vowels Lane signed Kingscote and West Hoathly. Left into Selsfield Road, straight on into Chapel Row, right into North Lane.***

A 16th-century tile-hung pub in a great walking area, set high on the Sussex Weald close to Ashdown Forest. In the old bar you'll find two inglenook fireplaces, oak beams, fine panelling and wooden floors, and the sort of buzzy atmosphere village pubs are so good at generating. Local breweries in Groombridge (Black Cat), Litlington (Long Man), Lewes (Harvey's) and Chiddingstone (Larkins) deliver the excellent beers. The menu tempts with an excellent choice of English or cosmopolitan flavours. Starters, for example, include a curried lamb Scotch egg, mango and butternut squash chutney, coriander and red onion salad; or harissa and dill mussels with beer bread. Follow on with something like wild skate wing, crushed potatoes, broccoli and caper butter. Youngsters over seven are welcome.

Open all day, all week 12–11.30 (Sun 12–10.30) Free House 12 from £10.50 portions

WEST WITTERING

The Lamb Inn

Tel **01243 511105** | **Chichester Road, PO20 8QA**
Web **www.thelambwittering.co.uk**
Dir ***From Chichester take A286 signed Witterings. At mini-roundabout right signed Wittering B2179. Pub on right.***

Just a mile from the beach at West Wittering and set in lovely rural surroundings, this pretty redbrick, tile-hung pub dates to the 19th century. They're serious about their food here and the menu offers a good selection of interesting dishes.

TYNE & WEAR

NEWCASTLE UPON TYNE

The Bridge Tavern

Tel **0191 261 9966 | 7 Akenside Hill, NE1 3UF**
Web **www.thebridgetavern.com**
Dir ***On A167 at Tyne Bridge.***

Built between the stanchions of the iconic Tyne Bridge, there has been an alehouse on this site for two hundred years. Today, there's a working microbrewery on site, brewing bespoke, never repeated ales available exclusively in the pub.

The Broad Chare

Tel **0191 211 2144 | 25 Broad Chare, Quayside, NE1 3DQ**
Web **www.thebroadchare.co.uk**
Dir ***Phone for detailed directions.***

The pub's own-label brew, The Writer's Block, is just one of several real ale choices at the polished oak bar here. Dog Dancer and Happy Daze ciders are here too, along with a choice of wines, world bottled beers and a quirky collection of whiskies.

Crown Posada

Tel **0191 232 1269 | 31 Side, NE1 3JE**
Web **sjf.co.uk/our-pubs/crown-posada**
Dir ***Phone for detailed directions.***

This glorious Grade II listed building is one of the most famous pubs in Newcastle. The façade is Victorian, there's an elaborately panelled entrance and original stained glass windows, and the music comes courtesy of a 1940s gramophone.

NORTH SHIELDS

The Staith House

Tel **0191 270 8441 | 57 Low Lights, NE30 1JA**
Dir ***Follow signs for North Shields Fishquay.***

John Calton used to dream of owning his own place on the North Shields fish quay. After working with some of Europe's top chefs, his dream finally came true. Regular tasting menus and a nine-course fish and seafood option are offered, or you can explore the best the region has to offer from the carte. Children are welcome until 7.30pm.

Open all day, all week Closed 25–26 Dec, 1st 2 weeks Jan Heineken 10 from £12.50 portions Wi-fi

WARWICKSHIRE

ALDERMINSTER

The Bell ★★★★ INN

PICK OF THE PUBS

Tel **01789 450414 | CV37 8NY**
Web **www.thebellald.co.uk**
Dir ***On A3400, 3.5 miles south of Stratford-upon-Avon.***

Part of the Alscot Estate, this striking Georgian coaching inn is set in the heart of a picturesque village. The interior is a refreshing mix of contemporary comforts and rustic charm, with beamed ceilings, blazing log fires and flagged floors combining with bold colours and stylish fabrics. Enjoy a pint of North Cotswold Windrush or the inn's locally-brewed Alscot Ale and nibble on a self-selected grazing platter. In the bar, sandwiches are served with hand-cut chips and salad, or you can try a Bell classic, perhaps the 8oz sirloin steak. Much of the produce is local, with vegetables and herbs harvested from Alscot's kitchen garden, and game reared on the estate.

Open all day, all week 9.30–3 6–11 (Fri to Sat 9.30am–11pm) Free House 12 portions/menu Wi-fi *notice required*

ALVESTON

The Baraset Barn PICK OF THE PUBS

Tel **01789 295510 | 1 Pimlico Lane, CV37 7RJ**
Web **www.barasetbarn.co.uk**
Dir ***Phone for detailed directions.***

The original flagstones reflect the Barn's 200 years of history, but now it's a light and modern gastro pub, the dramatic interior styled in granite, pewter and oak. Stone steps lead from the bar to the main dining area, while the open mezzanine level offers a good view of the glass-fronted kitchen. A sample of starters includes smoked haddock, leek and wholegrain mustard fishcake and spinach velouté and roast pumpkin and goats' cheese tart, roast figs and onion jam. Follow with roast breast of duck, plum and cherry purée, heritage carrots, confit duck rösti; or Moroccan spiced lamb rump, cauliflower couscous, smoked aubergine houmus and pomegranate.

Open all day 11–11 (Fri to Sat 11am to midnight Sun 12–6) Closed Mon (Jan), Sun evening Free House 16 portions/menu Wi-fi *notice required*

ARDENS GRAFTON

The Golden Cross PICK OF THE PUBS

Tel **01789 772420** | **Wixford Road, B50 4LG**
Web **www.golden-cross.co.uk**
Dir ***Phone for detailed directions.***

This traditional 18th-century country inn is the place to go to if you like faggots. The original recipe went missing but was then rediscovered. Eat them in the pastel-toned dining room with attractive plasterwork on the ceiling, or in the rug-strewn, flagstone-floored and heavily beamed bar. The seasonally-changing main menu of pub favourites is augmented by a daily-changing specials board; ingredients for the freshly prepared dishes are sourced from best quality local suppliers.

ARMSCOTE

The Fuzzy Duck 

INN PICK OF THE PUBS

Tel **01608 682635** | **Ilmington Road, CV37 8DD**
Web **www.fuzzyduckarmscote.com**
Dir ***From A429 (Fosse Way) north of Moreton-in-Marsh follow Armscote signs.***

In the picturesque hamlet of Armscote, a few miles south of Stratford-upon-Avon, this building once housed the local blacksmith before becoming a coaching inn in the 18th century. In the buzzy bar, contemporary furnishings combine with exposed beams, flagstone floors and original fireplaces to create a relaxed setting to enjoy local ales such as Purity Mad Goose. The seasonal menu majors on local produce and robust, innovative dishes. Try the smoked haddock rarebit tart; or warm, salt-baked beetroot salad; followed by slow-roast lamb shoulder with dauphinoise potatoes, cauliflower and cavolo nero; or butternut squash, sage and parmesan risotto. An attractive courtyard garden is a peaceful spot for alfresco dining but if the weather turns, you might be able to make use of the pub's quirky Hunter welly loan service.

Open all year 12–11 (Sun 12–5) Closed Sun evening, Mon Free House 11 from £12.50 portions/menu WI-FI P

ASTON CANTLOW

The King's Head

Tel **01789 488242** | **21 Bearley Road, B95 6HY**
Web **www.thekh.co.uk**
Dir ***Exit A3400 between Stratford-upon-Avon and Henley-in-Arden. Follow Aston Cantlow signs.***

Flanked by a huge spreading chestnut tree and oozing historic charm, this impressive Tudor building has been appointed in a modern style. Tastefully rustic, with lime-washed low beams, huge polished flagstones, old scrubbed pine tables and crackling log fires, it draws diners for innovative pub food.

BROOM

The Broom Tavern

Tel **01789 778199** | **32 High Street, B50 4HL**
Web **www.thebroomtavern.co.uk**
Dir ***From A46 onto B439 towards Bidford-on-Avon. Left into Victoria Road to Broom. In Broom left into High Street. Pub on right.***

Reputed to be one of Shakespeare's drinking haunts, The Broom Tavern is a timber-framed, 16th-century pub in a pretty village. This venerable inn has great charm and character, with log fires in winter and three sunny beer gardens for alfresco drinking in the summer. Chef-patron Fritz Ronneburg showcases the best local produce and offers locally-brewed ales including Purity Mad Goose. Everything is made on the premises and a typical meal might include 'CBLT' – griddled cod and crab, baby gem, roasted tomatoes and crab mayonnaise.

Open all week 12–3 5–11 (Fri to Sun all day) Free House 13 from £10.95 portions/menu WI-FI P *notice required*

EARLSWOOD

Bull's Head

Tel **01564 700368** | **7 Limekiln Lane, B94 6BU**
Web **www.bullsheadearlswood.co.uk**
Dir ***M42 junction 4, A34 signed Birmingham and Solihull. Left signed Chiswick Green. Through Chiswick Green, straight on at crossroads into Vicarage Road. Left at T-junction signed Earlswood. On right bend turn left into Salter Street. Pub on left.***

In a charming rural setting, the Bull's Head was built in the 18th century to house navvies constructing the Stratford-upon-Avon canal. Rumoured to be haunted by the ghost of a lime kiln worker, it comprises a cluster of whitewashed cottages. Popular with walkers, this Thwaites Brewery-owned pub retains much original charm courtesy of log fires and a large sun terrace. Enjoy a glass of Lancaster Bomber as you choose from an extensive menu offering pizzas, deli boards, salads and chargrilled steaks.

Open all day, all week The House of Daniel Thwaites 11 portions/menu notice required

EDGEHILL

Castle at Edgehill ★★★★ INN

Tel **01295 670255 | OX15 6DJ**
Web **www.castleatedgehill.co.uk**
Dir ***M40 junction 11, A422 towards Stratford-upon-Avon. 6 miles to Upton House, next right, 1.5 miles to Edgehill.***

In 1742, a man called Sanderson Miller built this curious castellated property to mark the centenary of the English Civil War's first major skirmish. In 1822, it became an alehouse; fast-forward a hundred years and it was acquired by the Hook Norton Brewery, whose real ales you'll find to this day in the bar. There are four dining areas including a glass-protected balcony with panoramic views. The modern menus are inviting.

Open all day, all week 11–11 (Sat 11am to midnight Sun 11–7) Hook Norton portions/menu notice required

ETTINGTON

The Chequers Inn PICK OF THE PUBS

Tel **01789 740387 | 91 Banbury Road, CV37 7SR**
Web **www.the-chequers-ettington.co.uk**
Dir ***Take A422 from Stratford-upon-Avon towards Banbury. Ettington in 5 miles, after junction with A429.***

Believed to have once been a courthouse, the white-painted children- and dog-friendly Chequers lies at the southern end of the village. A free house, it offers three real ales and a couple of real ciders, as well as 12 wines by the glass. Modern European temptations include pappardelle butternut squash with walnuts, spinach and shaved parmesan; pan-roasted cod fillet with crab and chorizo risotto; and rump and rib-eye steaks with hand-cut chips, sautéed button mushrooms and chargrilled beef tomato. Sundays offer more than just roasts; if you'd prefer, go instead for lightly battered cod and chips, or beef chilli con carne. The wine list will transport you around the world from France, Spain and Italy to New Zealand and Chile.

Open all year 12–3 5–11 (Sat 12–11 Sun 12–6) Closed Sun evening and Mon Free House 12 portions/menu notice required

FARNBOROUGH

The Kitchen at Farnborough

Tel **01295 690615 | OX17 1DZ**
Web **www.thekitchenfarnborough.co.uk**
Dir ***M40 junction 11 towards Banbury. Right at 3rd roundabout onto A423 signed Southam. 4 miles onto A423. Left onto single track road signed Farnborough. Approximately 1 mile, right into village, pub on right.***

This Grade II listed, 16th-century property on the National Trust-owned Farnborough Park Estate welcomes both dogs and wellies. The bar serves Purity Brewery ales, Cotswold Cider Company No Brainer and Sideburn, and plenty of wines by the glass.

GAYDON

The Malt Shovel

Tel **01926 641221 | Church Road, CV35 0ET**
Web **www.maltshovelgaydon.co.uk**
Dir ***M40 junction 12, B4451 to Gaydon.***

Richard and Debi Morisot's 16th-century village pub has a reputation for being friendly and reliable, qualities that have helped to make their venture a success. Another plus is the range of real ales, usually from Sharp's, Everards, Fuller's, Hook Norton, Timothy Taylor or Wadworth. Menu options include smoked haddock Welsh rarebit; beef casserole; goats' cheese and pesto cannelloni; and bread and butter pudding. A lunchtime snack could be chunky granary sandwiches, baguettes and hot paninis. Well-behaved children and dogs are welcome.

Open all week 11–3 5–11 (Fri to Sat 11–11 Sun 12–10.30) Enterprise Inns 11 from £7.95 portions notice required

HENLEY-IN-ARDEN

The Bluebell

Tel **01564 793049** | **93 High Street, B95 5AT**
Web **www.bluebell-henley.co.uk**
Dir ***Opposite police station on A3400 in town centre.***

This rambling, half-timbered coaching inn has fronted Henley's picturesque High Street for over 500 years. Behind the property is a secluded, lavender-scented garden, where beers from Purity can be enjoyed in the warmer months. The seasonal menus have gained the award of two AA Rosettes. Start with braised pig cheek, lobster bisque, apple and bacon followed by halibut, butter bean and chorizo cassoulet. Chocolate mousse cake and raspberry sorbet to finish.

Open all year, all day Closed Mon Free House 24 portions Wi-fi notice required

HUNNINGHAM

The Red Lion

Tel **01926 632715** | **Main Street, CV33 9DY**
Web **www.redlionhunningham.co.uk**
Dir ***From Leamington Spa take B4453, through Cubbington to Weston under Wetherby. Follow Hunningham signs (turn sharp right as road bends left towards Princethorpe).***

In the heart of rural Warwickshire, beside a 14th-century bridge, this 17th-century country pub's beer garden leads down to the River Leam and offers views of sheep and cows grazing. Inside, it's 'modern country-style' with different areas to eat in. Enjoy a pint of real ale as you choose from the appealing menu, which might start off with salt and pepper squid with aubergine caviar. Typical main courses include game pot pie and buttered Savoy cabbage or wild mushroom tortellini. Leave room for plum and port crumble.

Open all day, all week Mon to Sat 11–11 (Sun 11–10.30) Free House portions/menu Wi-fi notice required

ILMINGTON

The Howard Arms

★★★★★ INN PICK OF THE PUBS

Tel **01608 682226** | **Lower Green, CV36 4LT**
Web **www.howardarms.com**
Dir ***Exit A429 or A3400, 9 miles from Stratford-upon-Avon.***

Overlooking the lower green and pastures at the fringe of this charming north Cotswolds village, the 400-year-old Howard Arms is a great base for local walks and handy for the National Trust gardens at Hidcote. The flagstoned bar and open-plan dining room create a civilised, informal atmosphere; a crackling log fire ensures additional warmth for much of the year. Top notch beers from the likes of Purity wet the whistle; foodies will be rewarded with a stylish menu drawing on local, seasonal produce. Kick off with duck liver parfait, rabbit and apricot ballotine, plum jam and toast; leaving room for pub classics like ham, egg and chips or ploughman's, or modern dishes like pan-fried fillet of stone bass with polenta, kale and beetroot.

Open all day, all week Free House 15 from £14 portions Wi-fi notice required

KENILWORTH

The Almanack

Tel **01926 353637** | **Abbey End North, CV8 1QJ**
Web **www.thealmanack-kenilworth.co.uk**
Dir ***Exit A46 at Kenilworth and brown Castle sign, towards town centre. Left into Abbey Hill (B4104) signed Balsall Common. At roundabout into Abbey End. Opposite Holiday Inn.***

The Almanack has a bright, modern bar area with pale grey walls, comfortable armchairs, bar tables, herringbone parquet floors and mesh bar lighting. Metal screens divide the bar from the eatery; there's a chef's table here too.

LADBROKE

The Bell Inn – see page 450

LAPWORTH

The Boot Inn PICK OF THE PUBS

Tel **01564 782464 | Old Warwick Road, B94 6JU**
Web **www.lovelypubs.co.uk**
Dir ***Phone for detailed directions.***

A convivial, 16th-century coaching inn beside the Grand Union Canal. Beyond its smart interior is an attractive garden, on cooler days under a canopied patio with heaters. Free-house status means a good choice of real ales in the shape of Purity Pure UBU, Sharp's Doom Bar and Wye Valley HPA. But for many the draw is the brasserie-style food, and there's lots to choose from.

Navigation Inn

Tel **01564 783337 | Old Warwick Road, B94 6NA**
Web **www.navigationlapworth.co.uk**
Dir ***On B4439 (Old Warwick Road) between Lapworth and Rowington.***

Right by Bridge 65 on the Grand Union Canal, the Navigation has a long history of refreshing narrowboat crews, walkers and cyclists. Landlord and former brewery engineer Mark Ainley keeps his ales, lagers and ciders in optimum condition. Note to beer-hunters: unique to the pub is Coventry-brewed Lapworth Gold; also unique is Guinness on hand-pull, something Mark's expertise enabled him to devise. Fresh, home-made food is the order of the day.

Open all day, all week Enterprise Inns from £5.95 portions/menu

LEAMINGTON SPA (ROYAL)

The Drawing Board

Tel **01926 330636 | 18 Newbold Street, CV32 4HN**
Web **www.thedrawingboard.pub**
Dir ***Phone for detailed directions.***

Two levels of family- and dog-friendly, rug-strewn, timber-floored spaces, mismatched furniture, soft leather sofas, log-burners, framed vintage comics and shelves full of old children's annuals await you here. The drinks list, from five craft ales to 32 wines and way beyond, is impressive. So is the food, from tapas to pork belly with pork ballotine, Jerusalem artichokes and Savoy cabbage; and Korean-style short-rib of beef with Asian noodles and lotus root crisps.

Open all day, all week Closed 25 Dec Free House 18 from £10.95 portions/menu

The Moorings at Myton

Tel **01926 425043 | Myton Road, CV31 3NY**
Web **www.themoorings.co.uk**
Dir ***M40 junction 14 or 13, A452 towards Leamington Spa. At 4th roundabout after crossing canal, pub on left.***

This food-led pub beside the Grand Union Canal is a popular stop for boaters on England's arterial waterway. Diners may look forward to dishes created by Raymond Blanc protégé Charles Harris, whose ever-evolving Anglo-French menu relies on local suppliers for the ingredients. A sharing charcuterie board is a substantial starter, and mains include 28-day dry-aged Aberdeenshire steaks. Fruit ciders, an extensive wine list and beer from Warwickshire craft breweries slip down easily on the waterside terrace.

Open all day, all week Charles Wells 13 from £10 portions/menu notice required

LONG COMPTON

The Red Lion – see page 450

OFFCHURCH

The Stag at Offchurch

Tel **01926 425801 | Welsh Road, CV33 9AQ**
Web **www.thestagatoffchurch.com**
Dir ***From Leamington Spa take A425 towards Southam. At Radford Semele left into Offchurch Lane to Offchurch.***

The Stag is a charming thatched pub in a classic English village. Considerately modernised, it balances the feel of times long-gone with contemporary flourishes; diners, ramblers and locals all flock to the restaurant and bar. The imaginative menu offers plenty of choice.

OXHILL

The Peacock

Tel **01295 688060 | Main Street, CV35 0QU**
Web **www.peacockoxhill.com**
Dir ***From Stratford-upon-Avon take A422 towards Banbury. Turn right to Oxhill.***

This 16th-century, stone-built pub effortlessly combines its historic past with a relaxed modern atmosphere. Hand-pulled ales come from St Austell, Marston's and Wye Valley, and the food reflects the kitchen's focus on meats and vegetables from local farms, and fresh fish from Devon and Cornwall.

LADBROKE

The Bell Inn

Tel **01926 811224** | **Banbury Road, CV47 2BY**
Web **www.thebellinnladbroke.co.uk**
Dir ***Follow Ladbroke signs from A423 (south of Southam).***

Village pub run with flair

Originally one of four village pubs, only the attractive, white-painted Bell Inn has stood the test of time. Run with flair by husband and wife team Huw and Ruth Griffiths, it lies way back from the road, with a tree-shaded garden and tables to one side. Expert design skills are evident inside. Real ales change frequently, usually to include a local brew. Two fixed-price menus, one two-course, the other three, are available lunchtimes Wednesday to Friday, and Wednesday and Thursday evenings before 7pm. Or there's the main carte, which starts with pan-fried scallops; or beetroot-cured gravad lax, and moves on to pan-roasted partridge with pepper and Madeira cream; roast fillet of sea bass with crab mash; and Stilton, leek and broccoli tart. Grilled steaks and burgers also feature.

Open 12–3 5.30–11 Closed 1–16 Jan, Mon and Tue (Sun evening) Free House 15 portions/menu notice required

LONG COMPTON

The Red Lion ★★★★ INN

Tel **01608 684221** | **Main Street, CV36 5JS**
Web **www.redlion-longcompton.co.uk**
Dir ***On A3400 between Shipston on Stour and Chipping Norton.***

Cotswold character and award-winning cuisine

PICK OF THE PUBS

Explorers and ramblers in-the-know make a bee-line for the village's Red Lion pub. Its Georgian coaching inn origins bequeath an appealing mix of beams, stone-flags and honey-coloured stone, matchboarding, inglenook and log fires. The seasonal menu, complemented by daily specials, has a considered mix of classic and contemporary dishes, and may offer starters such as ham hock and leek terrine; or grilled whole sardines. Progress then with home-made steak and Hooky pie; or duck leg cassoulet, Cotswold sausage and cannellini beans. In summer, the shrubby beer garden is just the place to enjoy beers from Hook Norton and Wickwar breweries. Dogs are well-liked here, in fact pigs' ears are available as snacks for your four-legged friend; whilst well-appointed accommodation is on hand for those on short breaks.

Open all day, all week Free House 12 menus

PRESTON BAGOT

The Crabmill

Tel **01926 843342 | B95 5EE**
Web **www.brunningandprice.co.uk/crabmill**
Dir ***M40 junction 16, A3400 towards Stratford-upon-Avon. Take A4189 at lights in Henley-in-Arden. Left, 1.5 miles pub on left.***

Handy for a stroll in superb countryside alongside the Stratford-upon-Avon Canal, this carefully renovated former rural mill, where crab apples were perhaps mashed into cider, is a fine destination dining-pub presented in a modern rustic style. Comfy seating and light beams offer an informal interior.

STRATFORD-UPON-AVON

The One Elm PICK OF THE PUBS

Tel **01789 404919 | 1 Guild Street, CV37 6QZ**
Web **www.oneelmstratford.co.uk**
Dir ***From roundabout on A46 take A3400 (Birmingham Road) towards town centre. Pass Tesco, through lights, pub after mini-roundabout on left.***

Handy for the Avon, the popular canal and Stratford, the pub is named after a long-gone town boundary landmark. There's an almost continental feel, amplified by the chic, contemporary interior. Explore beyond the stylish, light interior and you'll find a secluded courtyard, the ideal retreat in which to sup beers from Purity, Church Farm and other carefully selected microbreweries in the area. The central, open-to-view kitchen offers a versatile menu of modern European dishes.

TANWORTH IN ARDEN

The Bell Inn

Tel **01564 742212 | The Green, B94 5AL**
Web **www.thebellattanworthinarden.co.uk**
Dir ***M42 junction 8, A435 signed Evesham. Left signed Portway and Tanworth (Penn Lane). To T-junction, left signed Tanworth. 1st right signed Tanworth. Inn in village centre.***

Older visitors might remember (or perhaps try to forget) a TV soap called *Crossroads*, many of whose outdoor scenes were shot in Tanworth, doubling as 'Kings Oak'. The pub overlooks the small village green and war memorial, and has stood here since the 17th century.

TEMPLE GRAFTON

The Blue Boar Inn ★★★ INN

Tel **01789 750010 | B49 6NR**
Web **www.theblueboar.co.uk**
Dir ***From A46 (Stratford to Alcester) turn left to Temple Grafton. Pub at 1st crossroads.***

The oldest part of this former ale house and now thriving village inn dates back to the early 1600s and includes a 35-foot deep well, now glassed over and illuminated, set into a flagstone floor and home to goldfish. There's a patio with views of the Cotswold Hills.

Open all day, all week 12–11.30 Marston's 10 from £9.95 portions/menu WIFI P notice required

WARWICK

The Rose & Crown PICK OF THE PUBS

Tel **01926 411117 | 30 Market Place, CV34 4SH**
Web **www.roseandcrownwarwick.co.uk**
Dir ***M40 junction 15 follow signs to Warwick. Pass castle car park entrance, up hill to West Gate, left into Bowling Green Street, 1st right, follow one-way system to T-junction, right into Market Place, pub visible ahead.***

Overlooking Warwick's market place, The Rose & Crown's outside tables are in pole position for people-watching while sinking that pint of Purity Gold or Harry Sparrow cider. The seasonally changing menus and daily specials rely on top quality ingredients – 28-day-aged beef from the Warwickshire butcher who holds The Queen's Royal Warrant, lamb from Cornwall, free-range chickens and sustainably managed fish. Try the salt and pepper squid, crunchy salad, lemongrass and chilli dressing; Devon crab and artichoke gratin with crusty bread; Cornish lamb chop and confit belly, mini moussaka, sautéed potatoes and salsa verde; and roasted monkfish, spring vegetables and mussels, with saffron and lemon sauce. Banoffee profiteroles with hot chocolate sauce are a great way to end a meal.

Open all day, all week 7am–11pm (Sat 8am to midnight Sun 8am–11pm) Closed 25 Dec Free House portions WIFI notice required

The Pheasant

~ Eating House ~

Tel: 01455 220 480 **Fax:** 01455 221 296

Website: www.thepheasanteatinghouse.com **Email:** thepheasant01@hotmail.c

A warm welcome greets you at this 17t century inn, idyllically situated beside a brook in the picturesque village of Withybrook.

The Pheasant is a popular freehouse, fu of character. An inglenook fireplace an farming implements add to the warm c atmosphere.

A chalkboard displays daily and season specials, complementing a wealth of food choices from an extensive menu. Examples of daily specials includes fres fish such as traditional cod and haddoc ranging to dover sole, lemon sole or lobster (preordered); local game; pasta and homemade pies. Vegetarian dishes also available. Outside the umbrella'd p area adjacent to the brook accommodat up to 100 people – perfect for a leisurel lunch or a thirst quenching pint of real after a walk in the beautiful surroundin countryside.

WELFORD-ON-AVON

The Bell Inn PICK OF THE PUBS

Tel **01789 750353** | **Binton Road, CV37 8EB**
Web **www.thebellwelford.co.uk**
Dir ***Phone for detailed directions.***

In pole position overlooking a small green, the Virginia creeper-covered Bell was where William Shakespeare had his last ever drink. Well, so legend has it. Allegedly, following a drinking session with dramatist Ben Jonson, the bard returned to Stratford-upon-Avon in the pouring rain and contracted fatal pneumonia. True? We'll never know. What we do know is that today this free house always has four real ales, including two locals, and that it has extensive menus, including one for gluten-free options. You'll find traditional lasagne with garlic bread; faggots with sage and onion gravy; fresh beer-battered haddock with crushed minted peas; and vegetarian options. Brunch is available at lunchtime, and Thursday is steak night.

Open all week 11.30–3 6–11 (Sat 11.30–11 Sun 12–10.30) Free House 16 portions/menu Wi-fi P notice required

WITHYBROOK

The Pheasant Eating House

Tel **01455 220480** | **Main Street, CV7 9LT**
Web **www.thepheasanteatinghouse.com**
Dir ***7 miles north-east of Coventry, on B4112.***

A warm welcome awaits at this 17th-century inn, idyllically situated beside the brook where withies were once cut for fencing. The Pheasant is cosy and full of character with an inglenook fireplace, farm implements and horse-racing photographs on display. The blackboard flags up specials, complementing a wealth of choices from the extensive main menu. Take your pick from a range of steak and chicken grills; a half roast duck with orange or plum sauce; and home-cooked lamb shank with root vegetables. Outside, the patio area is perfect for a leisurely lunch or a thirst-quenching pint of real ale after a walk in the beautiful countryside.

Open 11–3 6–11.30 (Sun and bank holiday 11–10) Closed 25–26 Dec, Mon (excluding bank holidays) Free House 16 portions/menu Wi-fi P notice required

See advertisement on opposite page

WEST MIDLANDS

BARSTON

The Malt Shovel at Barston

– see page 454

BIRMINGHAM

The High Field

Tel **0121 227 7068** | **22 Highfield Road, Edgbaston, B15 3DP**
Web **www.highfieldedgbaston.co.uk**
Dir ***Phone for detailed directions.***

The Peach Pubs Company renovated and extended this white-painted, early 20th-century Edgbaston villa to become a smart gastro pub. With two patios to catch plenty of sun, a leafy garden and a light, contemporary orangery, it's rapidly grown to be very popular.

The Old Joint Stock

Tel **0121 200 1892** | **4 Temple Row West, B2 5NY**
Web **www.oldjointstock.co.uk**
Dir ***Opposite main entrance to St Philip's Cathedral, just off Colmore Row.***

A pub with its own theatre and art gallery, the high-Victorian Gothic interior incorporates an immense domed ceiling, stately-home fittings and towering mahogany island bar. Pies take up a chunk of the menu, which also features grilled Loch Duart salmon and venison casserole with herb dumpling. Delicious desserts include vintage ale sticky toffee pudding.

Open all day, all week Fuller's 16 from £14 Wi-fi notice required

CHADWICK END

The Orange Tree PICK OF THE PUBS

Tel **01564 785364** | **Warwick Road, B93 0BN**
Web **www.orangetreepub.co.uk**
Dir ***3 miles from Knowle towards Warwick.***

Part of the small, Warwickshire-centred Lovely Pubs chain, The Orange Tree has a light, modern interior, wooden floors, log fires, old beams and antique mirrors. Wide-ranging menus group dishes according to type: 'grazing and sharing', 'hoof and fin', 'feather and fur' and 'pasta and flour'. Go for a 2-for-1 pizza deal (lunchtime and very early evening) Monday to Thursday.

BARSTON

The Malt Shovel at Barston

Tel **01675 443223** | **Barston Lane, B92 0JP**
Web **www.themaltshovelatbarston.com**
Dir ***M42 junction 5, A4141 towards Knowle. Left into Jacobean Lane, right at T-junction (Hampton Lane). Left into Barston Lane, 0.5 miles.***

Smart, busy inn down the country lanes

PICK OF THE PUBS

The Malt Shovel is an airy, well designed free house with modern soft furnishings and interesting artefacts. An early 20th-century, stylishly converted mill building, it sits comfortably in the countryside outside Solihull. Natural wood and pastel colours characterise the interiors and flowers decorate the unclothed tables in the tiled dining area. The bar is cosy and relaxed with winter log fires, and there's an attractive garden for outdoor dining; at weekends, the restaurant in the adjacent converted barn is opened. The extensive choice of modern British dishes makes the best of fresh seasonal ingredients, and, predictably, the daily fish specials board is popular with lovers of seafood – perhaps king prawn and chorizo risotto; or line-caught mackerel, free-range slow roast pork belly and buttered Savoy cabbage. As for desserts, you could easily be tempted by the lemon curd cheesecake with gin and lime glaze and a mint brandy snap; or chocolate truffles and petits fours. A board of English and European cheeses with grapes, celery, red onion chutney and artisan crackers will fill any remaining corners.

Open all day, all week *Free House* 17 *from £12.95* *portions/menu*

HAMPTON IN ARDEN

The White Lion Inn PICK OF THE PUBS

Tel **01675 442833 | 10 High Street, B92 0AA**
Web **www.thewhitelioninn.com**
Dir ***M42 junction 6, A45 towards Coventry. At roundabout take A452 towards Leamington Spa. At roundabout take B4102 towards Solihull. Approximately 2 miles to Hampton in Arden.***

Once a farmhouse, this 17th-century, timber-framed pub first acquired a drinks licence in the early 1800s. Its bright, modern interior is today furnished with wicker chairs and decorated with fresh flowers. Landlord Chris Roach and his partner FanFan draw on their considerable experience of working in or visiting restaurants, bistros and gastro pubs throughout England and France to present an ever-appealing combination of classic English pub grub and simple French bistro-style food. St Malo Black pudding or honey and mustard ham hock terrine would both make a good starter; a main of moules of the day and frites, or boeuf bourguignon could continue the Gallic approach; or go Italian with mushroom and pesto linguine. Real ales include St Austell Proper Job and Castle Rock Harvest Pale.

Open all day, all week noon–12.30am (Sun 12–10.30) Star Pubs & Bars 11 from £10.95 portions/menu notice required

SEDGLEY

Beacon Hotel & Sarah Hughes Brewery

PICK OF THE PUBS

Tel **01902 883380 | 129 Bilston Street, DY3 1JE**
Web **www.sarahhughesbrewery.co.uk**
Dir ***Phone for detailed directions.***

Home of the Sarah Hughes Brewery, the Beacon Hotel is a restored Victorian tap house that has barely changed in 150 years. The rare snob-screened island bar serves a simple taproom, with its old wall benches and a fine blackened range; a super cosy snug replete with a green-tiled marble fireplace, dark woodwork, velvet curtains and huge old tables; and a large smoke-room with an adjoining, plant-festooned conservatory. On a tour of the brewery you can see the original grist case and rare open-topped copper that add to the Victorian charm and give unique character to the brews. Flagship beers are Sarah Hughes Dark Ruby, Surprise and Pale Amber, with seasonal bitter and two guest beers from small microbreweries also available. Food in the pub is limited to filled cob rolls.

Open all week 12–2.30 5.30–11 (Sat 12–3 6–11 Sun 12–3 7–10.30) Free House notice required

WEST BROMWICH

The Vine

Tel **0121 553 2866 | Roebuck Street, B70 6RD**
Web **www.thevine.co.uk**
Dir ***M5 junction 1, follow West Bromwich/A41 signs. 1st left into Roebuck Street. Pub at end on corner.***

Beers from reliable, well-loved stalwarts such as Bathams and Holden's help this thriving, edge-of-town free house shine out. Equally adept at attracting customers to fill the surprisingly large open-plan interior and conservatory-style dining area is the remarkable menu created by Suki Patel, based around a pick 'n' mix of firm Indian favourites. Channa massala, saag aloo, curried goat, sheesh kebabs and mutter paneer all appear. The indoor barbecue is extremely popular, and there's also a range of traditional pub grub.

Open all week 11.30–2.30 5–11 (Fri to Sat 12–11 Sun 12–10) Free House from £5.95 notice required

WILTSHIRE

ALDBOURNE

The Blue Boar

Tel **01672 540237 | 20 The Green, SN8 2EN**
Web **www.theblueboarpub.co.uk**
Dir ***From Salisbury take B4192 to Aldbourne. Or M4 junction 14 take A338 to Hungerford, B4192 to Aldbourne and follow brown signs.***

This Wadworth-owned, 16th-century pub stands on the village green, itself distanced from traffic, with views of pretty houses, the church and a Celtic cross. It couldn't wish for a better location, so outdoor drinking and eating really are a particular pleasure.

The Crown Inn

Tel **01672 540214** | **The Square, SN8 2DU**
Web **www.thecrownaldbourne.co.uk**
Dir ***M4 junction 15, north on A419, signed Aldbourne.***

Walkers on the ancient Ridgeway, wondering whether to detour to this imposing coaching inn, will not be disappointed if they do. In the well-beamed old bar you'll find five real ales and home-prepared food, such as the 'hoppy one', namely kangaroo burgers, bacon and cheese in a brioche bun; slow-braised goose cassoulet, with French sausage and beans; battered Fowey cod with rustic fries; and goats' cheese and beetroot tortellini. They have movie nights on Mondays, quizzes on Tuesdays.

Open all day, all week 12–12 Enterprise Inns 16 from £10 portions/menu notice required

BERWICK ST JAMES

The Boot Inn

Tel **01722 790243** | **High Street, SP3 4TN**
Web **www.theboot.pub**
Dir ***From either A303 (Deptford to Winterbourne Stoke) or A36 (Deptford to Salisbury) take B3083 to Berwick St James. Pub in village centre.***

Here in their picturesque 16th-century property, formally trained chefs and landlords Giles and Cathy Dickinson aim to provide home-made, locally sourced, traditional British food and well-kept Wadworth beers. They say you won't find curry, chilli, lasagne or 'expensive gastro-pub concoctions'; instead, there are dishes like chicken liver and brandy pâté; rump of treacle-cured Stokes Marsh Farm beef with horseradish Yorkshire pudding; or garlic and rosemary slow-roasted leg of Wiltshire lamb. Finish with apple and blackberry crumble; or marmalade bread and butter pudding.

Open 12–3 6–11 (Fri to Sat 12–3 6–12 Sun 12–4) Closed 1–13 Feb, Sun evening and Mon Wadworth 9 portions/menu

BERWICK ST JOHN

The Talbot Inn

Tel **01747 828222** | **The Cross, SP7 0HA**
Web **www.talbotinnberwickstjohn.co.uk**
Dir ***From Shaftesbury take A30 towards Salisbury. Right to Berwick St John. Pub 1.5 miles.***

The Talbot Inn used to be three cottages, one of them the village shop, before becoming an alehouse in 1835. It dates from the 17th century and has the beams, low ceilings and huge inglenook fireplace so typical of its kind.

BISHOPSTONE

The Royal Oak

Tel **01793 790481** | **Cues Lane, SN6 8PP**
Web **www.helenbrowningsorganic.co.uk**
Dir ***M4 junction 15, A419 towards Swindon. At roundabout right into Pack Hill signed Wanborough. In Bishopstone left into Cues Lane. Pub on right.***

The delightful Royal Oak stands tucked away in a glorious village below the Wiltshire Downs, and you can expect a cracking community atmosphere, Arkell's ales, organic wines, roaring log fires and daily-changing menus. Almost 60 per cent of produce comes from Helen Browning's own organic farm, with the rest sourced from three other local organic farms and allotments. A three-course dinner could be Royal Oak charcuterie; fillet steak, salsa verde and chips; and sticky toffee pudding. The child-friendly garden has a wooden Wendy house and rope swing.

Open all day, all week Arkell's 12 from £14 portions/menu notice required

BOX

The Northey Arms

★★★★★ INN

Tel **01225 742333** | **Bath Road, SN13 8AE**
Web **www.ohhpubs.co.uk**
Dir ***A4 from Bath towards Chippenham, 4 miles. Between M4 junctions 17 and 18.***

This former station hotel, originally built by Brunel for the workers who were constructing Box Tunnel, has been transformed by Mark Warburton. The contemporary interior makes good use of wood and flagstone flooring, with high-backed oak chairs, leather loungers and handcrafted tables around the bar, where inviting sandwiches and pub classics hold sway. The main menu includes the pub's speciality fish dishes and great steaks. Comfortable bedrooms complete the picture.

Open all day, all week Closed 25 Dec Free House 16 portions/menu

The Quarrymans Arms

Tel **01225 743569 | Box Hill, SN13 8HN**
Web **www.butcombe.com/pubs/the-quarrymans-arms**
Dir ***On A4 between Box and Corsham, follow brown signs for pub.***

Superb views of the Box Valley can be enjoyed from this 300-year-old pub. A display of Bath stone-mining memorabilia bears witness to the years Brunel's navvies spent driving the Great Western Railway through Box Tunnel (spot the bar's replica fireplace) deep beneath the pub.

BRADFORD-ON-AVON

The George – see below

The Tollgate Inn – see page 458

BRINKWORTH

The Three Crowns PICK OF THE PUBS

Tel **01666 510366 | SN15 5AF**
Web **www.threecrownsbrinkworth.co.uk**
Dir ***From Swindon take A3102 to Royal Wootton Bassett, take B4042, 5 miles to Brinkworth.***

The Three Crowns is a thriving community pub, welcoming locals and their dogs, and families celebrating a special occasion. The village sits in rich farming countryside so expect lots of greenery inside and out, with the little village green at the front and the conservatory restaurant hosting some large pot-plants. Amiable staff greet you in the cosy, beamed bar, where ales include Butcombe Original. The menu has long been recognised for its ambition and variety. Expect starters like ham hock, mustard, piccalilli, pickled quail egg, apple and toast, perhaps followed by a main of seared scallops, crayfish and crab soup, linguine and herbs.

Open all day, all week Mon to Sat 11.30–11 Sun 12–11 Closed 26 Dec, 1 Jan afternoon Dawson Pubs 16 portions/menu notice required

BRADFORD-ON-AVON

The George   INN

Tel **01225 865650 | 67 Woolley Street, BA15 1AQ**
Web **www.thegeorgebradfordonavon.co.uk**
Dir ***From Trowbridge take B3105 to Bradford-on-Avon. Left at Woolley Grange Hotel into Woolley Street. Pub 500 yards.***

Where you'll be in very good hands

Owners Alexander Venables and Alison Ward-Baptiste were keen to open the sort of family- and dog-friendly dining pub they themselves would like to visit, with modern British food, comfortable rooms and delicious ales, and here they've achieved just that. Originally three Georgian houses, a complete refurbishment has resulted in a comfortably spacious interior. At the bar, cask beer drinkers declare their loyalty towards either Butcombe or Bath Ales. From the open-fronted kitchen come tip-top dishes, such as crab beignets; beef Wellington with red cabbage and dauphinoise potatoes; and grilled fillet of black bream with white wine mussel sauce. Luxurious accommodation includes two self-contained apartments. Alex runs a cycle club which sets off from the pub every Sunday morning.

Open all week 9.30–3 5.30–11 (Fri to Sat 9.30am–11pm Sun 9.30–5) Free House 10 portions/menu notice required

BRADFORD-ON-AVON

The Tollgate Inn

★★★★ INN

Tel 01225 782326 | Holt, BA14 6PX
Web www.tollgateinn.co.uk
Dir *M4 junction 18, A46 towards Bath, then A363 to Bradford-on-Avon, then B3107 towards Melksham, pub on right.*

Destination inn with a strong local following

Part Bath stone and part rendered, this 16th-century village inn is a popular destination, not least because it offers local real ales like Box Steam, and ciders such as Toodle Pip and Ashton Press, plus 19 wines by the glass from a wine list changed three times yearly. The kitchen makes good use of local produce, with free-range meats from nearby farms, and fish from day-boats out of Lyme Regis. Pheasant crispy parcels might precede pork belly, white bean and chorizo cassoulet; creamed leek, Stilton and spinach risotto; or pan-fried whole tiger prawns. Choosing from the list of home-made desserts could prove testing, but to start the ball rolling, there's bread and butter pudding, or chocolate brownie. Five luxury en suite rooms are individually styled.

Open all day 9am–11.30pm (Sun 9–4.30) Closed 25 Dec, Sun evening Free House 19 portions/ menu notice required

BURTON

The Old House at Home

★★★★★ INN

Tel 01454 218227 | SN14 7LT
Web www.ohhpubs.co.uk
Dir *On B4039 north-west of Chippenham.*

This ivy-clad, stone built free house (also known as OHH) dates from the early 19th century and is run by the Warburton family. Dad David has been here for years and still happily pulls pints of Maiden Voyage, Wadworth 6X and Thatchers Gold in the low-beamed bar. The finest seasonal ingredients are used to create impressive menu favourites. There are beautifully landscaped gardens, and six smart bedrooms are available in a stylish annexe.

Open all day, all week Free House 12 portions/ menu notice required

CALNE

The Lansdowne

Tel 01249 812488 | The Strand, SN11 0EH
Web www.lansdownestrand.co.uk
Dir *On A4 in town centre.*

Just 15 minutes from the M4 in the heart of Calne, this 16th-century former coaching inn was once home to the local brewery and the courtyard still retains the medieval brew house. Owned by Arkell's, the bar showcases that brewery's beers. The menu includes dishes like seared sea trout, smoked roe, cucumber, radish and sea vegetables; confit duck leg, celeriac purée, garlic mash, sour cherries and purple sprouting broccoli. Or from the lounge menu, favourites such as ham, egg and chips, and fish and chips.

Open all day, all week Arkell's from £12.50 menus notice required

The White Horse Inn

Tel **01249 813118 | Compton Bassett, SN11 8RG**
Web **www.whitehorse-comptonbassett.co.uk**
Dir ***M4 junction 16 onto A3102, after Hilmarton turn left to Compton Bassett.***

A stone-built, whitewashed village pub, named after the chalk figure cut out of a nearby hillside in 1870. The bar's log-burner keeps customers warm in winter, while a year-round attraction is the ever-changing roster of local and national real ales. The kitchen relies on local, seasonal ingredients for game, pistachio and apricot terrine; and home-made pie of the day.

Open all day, all week Free House 16 from £13.50 portions/menu notice required

COATE

The Sun Inn

Tel **01793 523292 | Marlborough Road, SN3 6AA**
Web **www.suninn-swindon.co.uk**
Dir ***M4 junction 15, A419 towards Swindon. At 1st roundabout take A459 signed Swindon and hospital. Left lane at lights. Pub on left before next roundabout.***

The third Sun public house on this site since 1685, today's pre-war building is close to Arkell's Swindon brewery, which bought its predecessor in 1891. With a large garden and playground, and with Coate Water Country Park nearby, it is understandably popular with families.

CORSHAM

The Methuen Arms

★★★★★ INN

Tel **01249 717060 | 2 High Street, SN13 0HB**
Web **www.themethuenarms.com**
Dir ***M4 junction 17, A350 towards Chippenham, at roundabout take A4 towards Bath. 1 mile after lights, at next roundabout sharp left into Pickwick Road, establishment 0.5 mile on left.***

A fine Georgian building of golden Bath stone, set in the lovely market town of Corsham. Full of period character, with all the flagstones, log fires and local prints you could wish for, it's also buzzing with contemporary spirit, especially in the three AA Rosette dining room, where chef Leigh Evans is providing extremely competent, precise cuisine using the finest local produce. Look out for dishes like the chicken glazed hake, with confit chicken wings, artichoke risotto, and chicken crumb; or fillet of halibut, served with Brixham crab, coconut rice, and fish broth. The stylish bedrooms are extremely well designed and comfortable. It's a great place to stay when exploring Bath and Somerset.

Open all day, all week Butcombe 18 from £15 menus

CORTON

The Dove Inn PICK OF THE PUBS

Tel **01985 850109 | BA12 0SZ**
Web **www.thedove.co.uk**
Dir ***5 miles south-east of Warminster. Exit A36 to Corton.***

A warm welcome is guaranteed at this bustling 19th-century pub, tucked away in the delightful Wylye Valley. The appealing à la carte menu features well-made pub classics. Typical starters include cayenne dusted whitebait with home-made aïoli and fresh lemon; and mussels in creamy white wine and garlic sauce. These might be followed by rolled pork belly stuffed with garlic, thyme and sage, served on Pommery mustard mash and purple sprouting broccoli. Fish and chips, and the famous Dove burger and chips are available to take away, traditionally wrapped in newspaper.

Open all day, all week Free House portions notice required

CRICKLADE

The Red Lion Inn ★★★★ INN

Tel **01793 750776 | 74 High Street, SN6 6DD**
Web **www.theredlioncricklade.co.uk**
Dir ***M4 junction 15, A419 towards Cirencester. Left onto B4040 into Cricklade. Right at T-junction (mini-roundabout) into High Street. Inn on right.***

Many awards, including an AA Rosette, have been bestowed upon this 17th-century pub, just off the Thames Path. The food is noteworthy not only because it's good, but for using locally foraged ingredients, rare-breed meats and sustainable fish. Start with curried crab and prawns on home-made fennel toast, followed perhaps by a steak from the grill, or Cornish mackerel fillets with crushed new potatoes and bacon. Some of the real ales are from the on-site microbrewery.

CRUDWELL

The Potting Shed

Tel **01666 577833** | **The Street, SN16 9EW**
Web **www.thepottingshedpub.com**
Dir ***On A429 between Malmesbury and Cirencester.***

Children and dogs are very welcome at this Cotswold dining pub where good ales, ciders and tempting menus are on offer. Two acres of grounds allow plenty of space for lawns, fruit trees and vegetable plots which supply fresh produce for the kitchen.

DONHEAD ST ANDREW

The Forester PICK OF THE PUBS

Tel **01747 828038** | **Lower Street, SP7 9EE**
Web **www.theforesterdonheadstandrew.co.uk**
Dir ***From Shaftesbury on A30 towards Salisbury. In approximately 4.5 miles left, follow village signs.***

A dog-friendly watering hole, this lovely 15th-century pub is an ideal place to put your feet up after a long walk with man's best friend (if you have one with you). Close to Wardour Castle in a pretty village, The Forester has warm stone walls, a thatched roof, original beams and inglenook fireplace. Local Donhead Craft Cider is a popular addition to the Butcombe and Otter ales served at the bar. An extension houses a restaurant with double doors opening onto the lower patio area. The pub has a reputation for excellent cooking at reasonable prices, and for its use of fresh West Country ingredients, especially seafood. Dishes are constructed with a mix of traditional and cosmopolitan flavours – crispy crumbed local pork with pickled winter vegetables, black pudding and piccalilli is typical. Follow with a main course of pan-fried Cornish cod fillet, squid ink, butternut squash and hollandaise. Special menus for children and vegetarians are available.

Open 12–2 6.30–11 Closed 25–26 Dec, Sun evening, Mon Free House 15 from £15 portions/menu notice required

EAST CHISENBURY

Red Lion Freehouse ★★★★★

 RESTAURANT WITH ROOMS

PICK OF THE PUBS

Tel **01980 671124** | **SN9 6AQ**
Web **www.redlionfreehouse.com**
Dir ***From A303 take A345 north. Exit at Enford. Left at T-junction towards East Chisenbury. Pub 1 mile on right.***

This ancient inn shares a sleepy hollow with other eye-catching thatched properties. Elements of the Tudor pub remain, with plenty of character from bare brick, log-burner and other rustic flourishes. At the bar, you'll find a rolling selection of beers from Stonehenge and Box Stream. Licensees Guy and Brittany Manning have a distinguished pedigree in the restaurant world and bring particular flair to the seasonal menus. Kick off with celeriac soup with partridge arancini, roasting juices and croûtons, then look for slow-cooked pork belly with parsnips, prunes, quince, crackling and roasting juices.

Open all year, all day Closed Mon to Tue Free House 27 from £20 portions/menu notice required

EAST KNOYLE

The Fox and Hounds – see page 462

EBBESBOURNE WAKE

The Horseshoe PICK OF THE PUBS

Tel **01722 780474** | **Handley Street, SP5 5JF**
Dir ***Phone for detailed directions.***

Dating from the 17th century, the family-run Horseshoe is a genuine old English pub. The original building has not changed much, and there's a lovely flower-filled garden. Beyond the climbing roses are two rooms adorned with simple furniture and country bygones, linked to a central servery where well-kept cask-conditioned ales are dispensed straight from their barrels – Bowman Ales Swift One, Otter Bitter and Palmers Copper Ale – plus real ciders too. Freshly prepared from local produce, the home-made pies are a firm favourite – try the wild boar and apricot steak or go for the steak and kidney.

Open 12–3 6.30–11 (Sun 12–4) Closed 26 Dec, Sun evening and Mon Free House portions

EDINGTON

The Three Daggers

 INN

Tel 01380 830940 | Westbury Road, BA13 4PG
Web www.threedaggers.co.uk
Dir *A36 towards Warminster, A350 to Westbury, A303 to Edington.*

Opened as the Paulet Arms in 1750 by Harry Paulet, the Lord of Edington Manor, locals quickly christened it The Three Daggers, after the family's coat of arms. The interesting menus might include Downland's black pudding Scotch egg, braised haricot beans and tomato sauce; lamb and rosemary pie; and dry-aged 28-day steaks from Stokes Marsh Farm. Next door there's a farm shop and a microbrewery with a viewing gallery.

Open all day, all week 10am–11pm Free House 14 portions/menu notice required

FONTHILL GIFFORD

The Beckford Arms – see page 463

FOXHAM

The Foxham Inn ★★★★ INN

Tel 01249 740665 | SN15 4NQ
Web www.thefoxhaminn.co.uk
Dir *M4 junction 17, B4122 (signed Sutton Benger). Onto B4069, through Sutton Benger. Right signed Foxham.*

This compact brick-built inn stands in a rural village close to the resurgent Wiltshire and Berkshire Canal. Real ales from the local Ramsbury brewery flow from the bar, but it's for the excellent cuisine that customers beat a path to the door. The accomplished menu offers an extensive range of dishes from lamb sweetbreads served with creamy Puy lentils; or terrine of smoked ham hock and pigeon breast with red onion marmalade. For mains, try duck breast with braised red cabbage and sauté potatoes with port wine sauce. There are equally fulfilling sweets to finish. Accommodation allows diners to rest easy after a classy repast.

Open 12–3 7–11 (Sun 12–3) Closed 1st 2 weeks Jan, Mon Free House 10 portions/menu notice required

FROXFIELD

The Pelican Inn

Tel 01488 682479 | Bath Road, SN8 3JY
Web www.pelicaninn.co.uk
Dir *On A4 midway between Marlborough and Hungerford.*

Contemporary free house near the canal

This 17th-century inn is a well-known landmark on the A4, once the main coach road between London and Bristol. Only 300 yards from lock gate 70 on the Kennet & Avon Canal, it is popular with the boating fraternity, walkers and cyclists. It changes its real ales frequently, although Falling Star from Wickwar has long been a favourite, with Andwells, Box Steam, Ramsbury or West Berkshire alongside. There are three inviting restaurant areas in which to eat traditional pub favourites, such as braised faggots and caramelised onion gravy: pan-fried lamb's liver and crispy bacon; Pelican fish pie; and the seasonal baked hake en papillote with buttered vegetables, plus steaks and burgers. Many of these, and snacks, are also available at lunchtime.

Open all day, all week 11–11 (Sun 12–10) Free House 12 from £12 portions/menu notice required

EAST KNOYLE

The Fox and Hounds

Tel **01747 830573** | **The Green, SP3 6BN**
Web **foxandhounds-eastknoyle.co.uk**
Dir ***From A303 follow Blandford/East Knoyle signs onto A350, follow brown pub signs.***

Traditional pub with lovely views

PICK OF THE PUBS

This partly thatched and half-timbered, rustic 15th-century inn makes the most of its stunning Blackmore Vale location. There are exceptional views from the patio beer garden and nearby East Knoyle village green across these Wiltshire and Dorset boundary-lands, where Sir Christopher Wren was born and the family of Jane Seymour (Henry VIII's third wife) were based. Hidden in a timeless village on a greensand ridge, the engaging exterior is well matched by the atmospheric interior, with lots of flagstone flooring, wood-burning fires and restful stripped wood furniture. Locals eager to partake of Thatchers Cheddar Valley cider or Hop Back Crop Circle rub shoulders with diners keen to make the acquaintance of the eclectic menu. Blackboard menus increase the choice, dependant entirely on the availability of the freshest local fare. Starters might include deep-fried rosemary and garlic crusted brie wedges with cranberry jelly. When it comes to main courses, good, wholesome pub grub is the order of the day. Desserts include lemon posset and gluten-free options are available.

Open all week 11.30–3 5.30–11 Free House 12 menus notice required

FONTHILL GIFFORD

The Beckford Arms

Tel 01747 870385 | SP3 6PX
Web **www.beckfordarms.com**
Dir ***From A303 (east of Wincanton) follow Fonthill Bishop sign. At T-junction in village right, 1st left signed Fonthill Gifford and Tisbury. Through Fonthill Estate arch to pub.***

Excellent food in elegant coaching inn with lovely garden

Just three minutes from the A303, this handsome 18th-century coaching inn is set on the edge of the beautiful rolling parkland of Lord Margadale's 10,000-acre Fonthill Estate. Once a stopping point for weary travellers on the way from London to the South West, this elegant dining pub is now a destination in its own right. You can eat wherever you want, either in the main bar with its huge fireplace and parquet floor or in the separate restaurant. In summer, head out into the rambling garden where hammocks hang between the trees, you can play pétanque and children can do what children do. In winter the huge open fire in the bar is used to spit-roast suckling pigs and warm mulled wine. Whatever the season, Keystone's Beckford Phoenix real ale is a permanent fixture in the bar, with other beers on tap and 12 wines available by the glass. An invigorating menu leads in with deep-fried ox tongue fritters, charred tenderstem, salsa verde and confit leeks as an eye-catching starter and then advances to traditional pub grub like beer-battered Cornish fish and chips; or Wiltshire ham and Westcombe Cheddar ploughman's.

Open all day, all week Closed 25 Dec Free House 12 from £12.50 portions/menu

GREAT BEDWYN

Three Tuns Freehouse

Tel **01672 870280 | 1 High Street, SN8 3NU**
Web **www.tunsfreehouse.com**
Dir ***Off A4 between Marlborough and Hungerford.***

On the edge of Savernake Forest, a few narrowboat lengths from the Kennet & Avon Canal, the lively, fire-warmed Three Tuns offers well-conditioned regional ales, carefully selected wines and gins galore. Chef/owner James Wilsey's hearty food is made largely in-house and on the day of your visit might include wild boar ragout and rigatoni; beetroot and red wine risotto; and cod and prawn fishcake with white wine velouté. Boules can be played in the garden.

Open 10–3 6–11 (Fri to Sat 10am–11pm Sun 10–6) Closed 25 Dec, Sun evening and Mon (excluding bank holidays) Free House 10 from £14 portions/menu notice required

HEYTESBURY

The Angel

Tel **01985 841790 | High Street, BA12 0ED**
Web **www.theangelatheytesbury.co.uk**
Dir ***A303 onto A36 towards Bath, 8 miles, Heytesbury on left.***

The Angel has stood on Heytesbury's High Street for over 400 years; but today features traditional and contemporary aspects of a village inn. Exposed brick, wooden flooring, beams and on-trend furnishings. You can choose to eat in the bar or restaurant.

HORNINGSHAM

The Bath Arms at Longleat

★★★★ INN PICK OF THE PUBS

Tel **01985 844308 | BA12 7LY**
Web **www.batharms.co.uk**
Dir ***Off B3092 south of Frome.***

Occupying a prime position at one of the entrances to Longleat Estate and the famous Safari Park, The Bath Arms dates back to the 17th century. An ivy-clad stone property, it features two beamed bars – one traditional with settles, old wooden tables and an open fire, and a bar for dining. In addition to sandwiches and sharing boards look out for main courses such as pan-fried sea bass with mussel, sweetcorn, potato and chive chowder; poached duck egg 'florentine' with buttered spinach on toasted muffin with hollandaise sauce; and pan-roast breast of Hayward Farm chicken wrapped in prosciutto stuffed with white apricot Stilton. Leave a space for elderflower and lime cheesecake and lemon sorbet or Eton Mess with Horningsham berry compôte and vanilla crème fraîche.

Open all day, all week 10am–11pm (Sun 10am–10.30pm) Free House 10 from £9.95 portions/menu notice required

KILMINGTON

The Red Lion

Tel **01985 844263 | BA12 6RP**
Web **www.theredlionkilmington.co.uk**
Dir ***On B3092 between Mere and Frome. 1 mile from National Trust Stourhead Gardens.***

A National Trust-owned building on the famous Stourhead Estate, The Red Lion has been a pub for around 350 years. The low-beamed, stone-flagged front bar is cosy and inviting, and children are welcome in the larger back bar. You'll find straightforward honest pub grub here.

LOWER CHICKSGROVE

Compasses Inn PICK OF THE PUBS

Tel **01722 714318 | SP3 6NB**
Web **www.thecompassesinn.com**
Dir ***On A30 (1.5 miles west of Fovant) 3rd right to Lower Chicksgrove. In 1.5 miles left into Lagpond Lane, pub 1 mile on left.***

The Compasses Inn was built in the 14th century and you can sense evidence of its history as soon as you walk through the low-latched door at the end of the cobbled path. Flagstone floors, low wooden beams and a roaring fire all help retain the timeless character of the pub but owner Ben Maschler has a rather more modern approach to the food and drink. The menu changes daily and is written around the freshest local ingredients. Pan-fried pigeon breasts, chorizo, lentils and sherry and walnut vinaigrette could be followed by fish pie with buttered greens, or Goan pork curry. Wash it down with a pint of Wiltshire-brewed Plain Ales Inntrigue.

Open all week 12–3 6–11 (Sat 12–11 Sun 12–10.30) Closed 25 Dec Free House 12 portions/menu

MALMESBURY

Kings Arms

Tel **01666 823383** | **29 High Street, SN16 9AA**
Web **www.thekahotel.co.uk**
Dir ***M4 junction 17, A429 to Malmesbury. Follow town centre signs. Pub on left in town centre.***

Tucked harmoniously into the streetscape close to Malmesbury Abbey, this old Arkell's brewery-owned inn offers two very different bars: separated by a covered walkway, one is within the main restaurant, the other is the contemporary Harry's Bar, formerly Bar 29. Sandwiches and more are available at lunchtime, while a typical dinner could be deep-fried crispy whitebait; chicken curry, basmati rice, poppadom and mango chutney; and tarte au citron.

Open all day, all week Arkell's 9 from £10 portions/menu notice required

The Vine Tree PICK OF THE PUBS

Tel **01666 837654** | **Foxley Road, Norton, SN16 0JP**
Web **www.thevinetree.co.uk**
Dir ***M4 junction 17, A429 towards Malmesbury. Turn left for village, after 1 mile follow brown signs.***

This atmospheric pub was once a mill; workers reputedly passed beverages out through front windows to passing carriages. Today, ramblers and cyclists exploring Wiltshire's charms are frequent visitors; the inn is situated on the official county cycle route. A large fireplace burns wood all winter in the bar, warming a wealth of old beams, flagstones and oak flooring. The pub is worth seeking out for its interesting modern British pub food and memorable outdoor dining.

MANTON

The Outside Chance

Tel **01672 512352** | **71 High Street, SN8 4HW**
Web **www.theoutsidechance.co.uk**
Dir ***From Marlborough take A4 towards Chippenham. Left signed Manton and The Outside Chance.***

When, in 2008, two racehorse owners acquired The Oddfellows Arms, the new name they chose became even more appropriate when Champion Jockey (now Sir) AP McCoy later joined them. The pub is full of sporting trophies and artefacts and there's a log fire in the fireplace.

MARDEN

The Millstream – see page 466

NEWTON TONY

The Malet Arms

Tel **01980 629279** | **SP4 0HF**
Web **www.maletarms.co.uk**
Dir ***8 miles north of Salisbury on A338, 2 miles from A303.***

In a quiet village on the River Bourne, this 17th-century inn was named after early Victorian lord of the manor, Sir Henry Malet. Fruit machine and piped music free, it has an enormous inglenook fireplace, and is bedecked with prints, trophies and myriad curiosities.

OAKSEY

The Wheatsheaf Inn – see page 467

OGBOURNE ST ANDREW

Silks on the Downs

Tel **01672 841229** | **Main Road, SN8 1RZ**
Web **www.silksonthedowns.com**
Dir ***M4 junction 15, A346 towards Marlborough. Approximately 6 miles to Ogbourne St Andrew. Pub on A346.***

A mile north of the bustling market town of Marlborough you'll find this pub, tucked away in rolling downland. The free house's name reflects the racing heritage of the Berkshire Downs (whose western boundary is on the border with Wiltshire).

PEWSEY

The Seven Stars Inn

Tel **01672 851325** | **Bottlesford, SN9 6LW**
Web **www.thesevenstarsinn.co.uk**
Dir ***From A345 follow Woodborough sign. Through North Newnton. Right to Bottlesford. Pub on left.***

Close to two of Wiltshire's famous white horses, this 16th-century free house lies in the heart of the Vale of Pewsey between Salisbury Plain and the Marlborough Downs, and is a 15-minute drive from the stone circles of Avebury. The bar maintains its original character.

MARDEN

The Millstream

Tel **01380 848490 | SN10 3RH**
Web **www.themillstream.co.uk**
Dir ***6 miles east of Devizes, north of A342.***

A family-run pub in the heart of Pewsey Vale

The Millstream is an attractive village pub near Devizes, with widely spaced tables in a large garden on the banks of the young Hampshire Avon. Inside, the three log fireplaces make for a cosy and romantic atmosphere in which to enjoy a Wadworth real ale or Thatchers cider, and perhaps duck leg confit with plum and ginger sauce; double-baked cheese soufflé; pork medallions with green peppercorn sauce; oven-roasted venison steak with wild mushrooms and Madeira sauce; home-made pie of the day; or butterbean and borlotti bean cassoulet with garlic bread. Fish arriving daily from St Mawes in Cornwall later appears on the specials board as, depending on the catch, baked crab pancakes with creamy crab sauce; whole baked megrim or lemon sole with lemon oil. Sunday roasts – topside of beef, loin of pork and chicken breast – are only part of the day's offering, as you could begin lunch with fried black pudding with Parma ham and toasted pecans; then wholetail Cornish scampi; or an 8oz venison burger with salad and chips; and end with strawberry and blueberry Eton Mess. The resident English pointers, Sophie and Francesca, are always pleased to welcome other dogs in the bar.

Open 11.30–3 6.30–11 (Sun 12–4) Closed 1st week Jan, Sun evening and Mon evening Wadworth from £9.95 portions/menu notice required

OAKSEY

The Wheatsheaf Inn

Tel **01666 575077** | **Wheatsheaf Lane, SN16 9TB**
Web **www.wheatsheafoaksey.co.uk**
Dir ***Phone for detailed directions.***

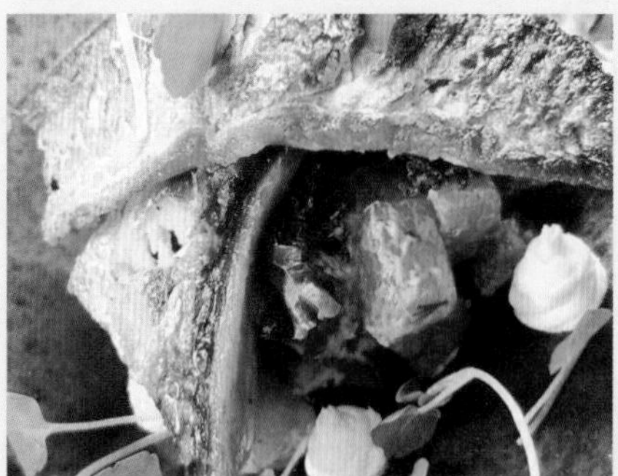

A great choice of cask ales and fine wines

A delightful, 700-year-old, golden Cotswold-stone village inn with a long pedigree as a public house, where regulars prop up the bar while their four-legged friends slumber on the floor. The bar is full of big beams, huge open fireplaces, scrubbed wooden tables, exposed stone walls and plenty of original features, so order a pint or a glass of wine while you check out the menu. Chef and landlord Mike delivers a great choice of hearty, locally-sourced dishes: for example, at lunchtime he might prepare chargrilled tandoori chicken strips with minted yogurt or steak and caramelised onion gourmet sandwiches. Then, in the evening, maybe pan-fried scallops or a honey and thyme baked camembert to share; followed by pub classics like home-baked Wiltshire ham with poached local farm eggs; or home-made chilli con carne and rice. Other choices might include herb-crusted salmon, baked new potatoes, samphire and prawn and garlic cream; or slow-cooked pork belly with creamy mash and apple purée. Finish with sticky toffee pudding or the chef's brûlée of the day. On Sundays, there's roast beef or lamb, a fish dish and a vegetarian option. The skittle alley can be hired.

Open all year, all day Closed Mon (except bank holidays) El Publican Partnerships 11 from £10 portions

PITTON

The Silver Plough PICK OF THE PUBS

Tel **01722 712266 | White Hill, SP5 1DU**
Web **www.silverplough-pitton.co.uk**
Dir ***From Salisbury take A30 towards Andover, Pitton signed. Approximately 3 miles.***

A traditional country village pub on the Clarendon Way, which links Salisbury with Winchester. Inside, its oak beams, old dark-wood bar, rustic furniture and adjoining rooms with log fires remain unchanged, although new landlords are now in charge of the beer pumps. It's a Hall & Woodhouse pub, so expect well-kept Badger Best, Fursty Ferret and Tanglefoot. On a traditional pub menu you'll also find the less traditional seared scallops with roast watermelon, cockles and peas; pan-roast duck breast with cavolo nero and turnips; and loin of cod on crab risotto. Also here is one of Wiltshire's few remaining skittle alleys.

Open all week 11–3 6–11 (Mon to Tue 11–3 6–10.30. All day 11–11 Sat and Sun in summer. Sun 12–5 in winter) Closed 25 Dec Hall & Woodhouse 15 portions/menu notice required

RAMSBURY

The Bell at Ramsbury

★★★★ INN PICK OF THE PUBS

Tel **01672 520230 | The Square, SN8 2PE**
Web **www.thebellramsbury.com**
Dir ***M4 junction 14, A338 to Hungerford. B4192 towards Swindon. Left to Ramsbury.***

From its strategic position in the centre of the village, this 17th-century coaching inn can keep an eye on the High Street. Just outside, on a little green, a lovely old tree provides shade for a couple of benches, while the light, spacious bar serves beers from its own brewery, including Flint Knapper, Ramsbury Gold and Farmers Best. The kitchen offers a selection of hearty meals, maybe salad of Jerusalem artichoke with hazelnut, mushroom ketchup and black truffle, then Creedy Carver duck breast with variations of carrot, smoked potato and turnip. As well as the bar and restaurant, you can also eat breakfast, light bites and lunches in Café Bella.

Open all day, all week 12–11 (Sun 12–10) Free House 12 portions/menu

ROWDE

The George & Dragon

★★★★ RESTAURANT WITH ROOMS

PICK OF THE PUBS

Tel **01380 723053 | High Street, SN10 2PN**
Web **www.thegeorgeanddragonrowde.co.uk**
Dir ***1 mile from Devizes, take A342 towards Chippenham.***

Narrowboaters on the nearby Kennet & Avon Canal can spend up to six hours negotiating the 29 locks of the Caen Flight – that's hard work, so no wonder they flock to this modernised 16th-century pub with its large open fireplaces, wooden floors, antique rugs and candlelit tables. The reward for the thirsty might be a pint of Butcombe or Bath Ales Gem; for the hungry, maybe a seafood platter featuring fish delivered daily from Cornwall. Other possibilities from the award-winning menu include, salmon tartare with avocado, lime and chilli on toasted rye; slow-roasted belly pork with borlotti beans and salsa verde; and pan-fried hake with prawn and whisky chowder.

Open all year 12–3 6–11 (Sat 12–4 6–11 Sun 12–4) Closed Sun evening Free House 10 from £16 portions/menu notice required

ROYAL WOOTTON BASSETT

The Angel ★★★★ INN

Tel **01793 851161 | 47 High Street, SN4 7AQ**
Web **www.theangelhotelwoottonbassett.co.uk**
Dir ***M4 junction 16, A3102 towards Royal Wootton Bassett. At 2nd roundabout left signed Royal Wootton Bassett. Pub on right after lights.***

Slap bang on the high street in Royal Wootton Bassett, this former coaching inn is a contemporary establishment with traditional bar serving a range of Arkell's ales and an oak-panelled dining room showcasing local produce. Sunday roasts are popular – booking is recommended.

SALISBURY

The Cloisters

Tel **01722 338102** | **83 Catherine Street, SP1 2DH**
Dir ***In city centre, near cathedral.***

Close to Salisbury's famous cathedral, the appropriately named Cloisters is a mid 18th-century pub with a beamed interior warmed by a pair of open fires. The menu will please everyone with its popular pub staples, from fish and chips to beef and ale pie. Doorstep sandwiches, baguettes and jacket potatoes are also available. The choice of ales includes Hop Back Summer Lightning and Butcombe Bitter.

Open all day, all week Enterprise Inns portions/menu notice required

The Wig and Quill

Tel **01722 335665** | **1 New Street, SP1 2PH**
Web **www.thewigandquill.com**
Dir ***On approach to Salisbury follow brown Old George Mall Car Park signs. Pub opposite car park.***

The roomy, beamed bar with open fires, flagstones and wood flooring of this old city pub is as welcoming as ever. Ales include 6X alongside newer Wadworth brews such as Swordfish. Menus proffer happy pub grub, served all day, every day. Sandwiches, salads and jacket potatoes with a range of fillings are on offer; lasagne with garlic bread; or trio of Cumberland sausages. The sheltered courtyard garden is a pleasantly restful spot in summer.

Open all day, all week 12–close Wadworth 9 from £9.95 portions/menu

SEMINGTON

The Lamb on the Strand

Tel **01380 870263** | **99 The Strand, BA14 6LL**
Web **www.thelambonthestrand.co.uk**
Dir ***1.5 miles east on A361 from junction with A350.***

This popular pub began life as a farmhouse in the 18th century, later developing into a beer and cider house. Food is always freshly prepared from locally sourced ingredients, and the Wiltshire Tapas menu offers an interesting mix of British and global treats.

SHERSTON

The Rattlebone Inn

Tel **01666 840871** | **Church Street, SN16 0LR**
Web **www.therattlebone.co.uk**
Dir ***M4 junction 17, A429 to Malmesbury. 2 miles after passing petrol station at Stanton St Quentin, turn left signed Sherston.***

With fine beer from Flying Monk Brewery, alley-skittles and a strong menu of both old-style and contemporary dishes, who would ever want to leave this character Cotswold village retreat? Not John Rattlebone, that's for sure; this Saxon warrior's name lives on as does his restless spirit that occasionally manifests itself here. The interior is one of beams, flagged floors, log-burners and golden stone; walled gardens enclose three boules pistes and sheltered patios, ideal for the July cider festival. Country bistro home cooking is the style.

Open all week 12–3 5–11 (Fri to Sat 12–12 Sun 12–11) Young & Co.'s Brewery 14 from £9.95 portions/menu notice required

SOUTH WRAXALL

The Longs Arms

Tel **01225 864450** | **BA15 2SB**
Web **www.thelongsarms.com**
Dir ***From Bradford-on Avon take B3109 towards Corsham. Approximately 3 miles, left to South Wraxall. Pub on left.***

This stunning-looking golden-stone pub commands the centre of a tiny village above the Avon Valley, just outside Bath. A log-burner, slab flooring and country prints welcome you to the airy bar; the cosy dining room is pleasingly cottagey in character. The cuisine is proudly British and seasonal. There's an on-site smokehouse, while the veg and herbs come from the grounds. The lavender-scented, secluded garden is a summer delight.

Open 12–3.30 6–11.30 (Sun 12–5) Closed 3 weeks Jan, 2 weeks Sep, Sun evening and Mon to Tue Wadworth 12 from £13.50 portions notice required

SWINDON

The Runner

Tel **01793 523903** | **Wootton Bassett Road, SN1 4NQ**
Web **www.runninghorsepub.co.uk**
Dir ***M4 junction 16, A3102 towards Swindon. At 2nd roundabout right signed town centre. Pub on right.***

Swindon's oldest brewery, Arkell's, owns this late 19th-century pub. A particular attraction is its riverside terrace, although a great gin selection, Tuesday poker, Thursday quiz, Sky TV and BT Sport, pool, darts and live entertainment also keep the footfall high. The Runner knows customers appreciate good value pub food, so steaks, hunter's chicken, hand-carved Wiltshire ham and eggs, home-made chilli con carne, are always on the menu. Children are welcome until 9pm.

Open all day, all week 11.30–11 (Sun 11.30–10.30) Arkell's 15 from £9.95 portions/menu Wi-fi P notice required

The Weighbridge Brewhouse

Tel **01793 881500** | **Penzance Drive, SN5 7JL**
Web **www.weighbridgebrewhouse.co.uk**
Dir ***M4 junction 16, follow Swindon Centre signs, then Outlet Car Park West signs.***

Built in 1906, the former Great Western Railway Weighhouse was transformed by experienced operator Anthony Windle into a stunning pub-restaurant concept, complete with microbrewery. Many fascinating original features have been retained and the old railway building boasts brick walls and lofty ceilings.

TOLLARD ROYAL

King John Inn ★★★★

RESTAURANT WITH ROOMS

Tel **01725 516207** | **SP5 5PS**
Web **www.kingjohninn.co.uk**
Dir ***On B3081 (7 miles east of Shaftesbury).***

This brick-built Victorian inn luxuriates in its location on Cranborne Chase deep in stunning countryside outside Shaftesbury. Its airy, open-plan bar and dining areas have a crisp country feel, featuring rugs on quarry tile flooring, pine tables, snug alcoves and winter log fires.

UPTON LOVELL

Prince Leopold Inn

Tel **01985 850460** | **BA12 0JP**
Web **www.princeleopold.co.uk**
Dir ***From Warminster take A36 towards Salisbury 4.5 miles, left to Upton Lovell.***

Built here just west of Salisbury Plain in 1878, the Leo was named after Victoria and Albert's popular, but sickly, eighth child, who lived at nearby Boyton Manor. There's a log fire, sofas and cameos of village life in the Victorian snug.

Open all year 12–3 6–11 (Sat 12–11 Sun 12–8) Closed Mon Free House 16 from £12 portions/menu Wi-fi P notice required

WANBOROUGH

The Harrow Inn

Tel **01793 791792** | **SN4 0AE**
Dir ***M4 junction 15, A419 towards Cirencester. Exit at next junction signed Cirencester and Oxford. Follow Wanborough sign from roundabout.***

This handsome, white-painted thatched inn dates back in part to 1747, and it retains plenty of original character including exposed beams and inglenook fireplace, the grate of which is Grade II listed. The pub offers a good range of ales such as Otter Bitter, which can be enjoyed with home-made parsnip and ginger soup; pheasant, chestnut and bacon terrine; puff-pastry steak and Otter pie; and braised ox cheeks with root vegetables and parsley and chive dumpling.

Open all day, all week 11.30–3 5–11 (Fri to Sat 11.30–12 Sun 11.30–11) Enterprise Inns 9 portions/menu Wi-fi P notice required

WARMINSTER

The George Inn ★★★★ INN

Tel **01985 840396** | **Longbridge Deverell, BA12 7DG**
Web **www.the-georgeinn.co.uk**
Dir ***Phone for detailed directions.***

A member of the expanding Upham Group, this 17th-century coaching inn overlooks the grassy banks of the River Wylye. Upham started out as a brewery, so it's their beers that you'll find alongside the guest ales. Food is served in the oak-beamed Smithy Bar and in the two restaurants, where menus open with smoked salmon and granary bread; and antipasti. They continue with beer-battered Atlantic cod, with chips, peas and chunky tartare sauce; slow-roasted pork belly, creamed potatoes and vegetables; or goats' cheese and caramelised onion quiche, new potatoes and salad.

Open all day, all week 11–11 (Sun 12–10.30) Closed 25 Dec from 3pm, 26 Dec (1 Jan open 11–3) Upham Group portions/menu Wi-fi notice required

WEST OVERTON

The Bell at West Overton

Tel **01672 861099 | Bath Road, SN8 1QD**
Web **www.thebellwestoverton.co.uk**
Dir ***4 miles west of Marlborough on A4.***

In coaching days, horses needed changing frequently; The Bell was once such staging post. Over 15 years here, Hannah McNaughton supervises front-of-house, and husband Andrew, with worldwide cooking experience behind him, runs the kitchen. Wiltshire ales take precedence on pumps in the bar, while the restaurant provides the perfect ambience for a starter of house-smoked salmon with courgette frittata, followed by slow-roast West Overton hoggett with hotpot potatoes, green beans and carrots.

Open all year 12–3 6–11 Closed Sun evening and Mon (excluding bank holidays) Free House 15 from £13.95 portions Wi-fi notice required

6 WILTSHIRE PUBS WITH ACCOMMODATION

The following pubs are rated as part of the AA Guest Accommodation scheme (see page 10-11 for more information).

The Methuen Arms ★★★★★ INN
Corsham, *see page 459*

The Northey Arms ★★★★★ INN Box,
see page 456

The Old House at Home ★★★★★
INN Burton, *see page 458*

The Three Daggers ★★★★★ INN
Edington, *see page 461*

The Bath Arms at Longleat ★★★★
INN Horningsham, *see page 464*

The Bell at Ramsbury ★★★★ INN
Ramsbury, *see page 468*

WOOTTON RIVERS

Royal Oak PICK OF THE PUBS

Tel **01672 810322 | SN8 4NQ**
Web **www.wiltshire-pubs.co.uk**
Dir ***3 miles south from Marlborough.***

This much expanded 16th-century thatched and timbered pub is perfectly situated for Stonehenge, Bath and Winchester and for exploring the ancient oaks of Savernake Forest. Only 100 yards from the Kennet & Avon Canal and the Mid Wilts Way, it has an interior as charming as the setting, with low, oak-beamed ceilings, exposed brickwork and wide open fireplaces. In the bar you'll find St Austell Tribute and local ale, Ramsbury Bitter. The daily-changing menus cover all manner of pubby favourites and beyond. Look for starters like fresh crab cocktail with lemon mayonnaise; or creamy goats' cheese with spiced beetroot and walnuts; then continue with roast topside of beef with Yorkshire pudding; Moroccan-spiced lamb pie; or pork and potato vindaloo.

Open all week 12–2.30 6–11 (Sun 12–10) Free House portions/menu Wi-fi notice required

WORCESTERSHIRE

ABBERLEY

The Manor Arms

★★★★★ INN

Tel **01299 890300 | WR6 6BN**
Web **www.themanorarms.co.uk**
Dir ***From Ombersley take A443 towards Tenbury. After Great Witley right onto B4202. Right into Netherton Lane. Pub on left in village.***

Narrow lanes and footpaths thread Worcestershire's secluded Abberley Hills. Several of these meet outside The Manor Arms, where satisfying meals and local beers awaits explorers. There's more than a hint of the old world here, with inglenook and rustic furniture creating a restful interior.

BAUGHTON

The Jockey Inn

Tel **01684 592153 | Pershore Road, WR8 9DQ**
Web **www.thejockeyinn.co.uk**
Dir ***Phone for detailed directions.***

After an extensive three-year programme of restoration and refurbishment, this smart, white-painted pub has reopened. The interiors are stylish, contemporary touches mixing comfortably with the log fires and beams of the old building.

BECKFORD

The Beckford

Tel **01386 881532 | Cheltenham Road, GL20 7AN**
Web **www.thebeckford.com**
Dir ***M5 junction 9, A46 towards Evesham, 5 miles to Beckford.***

Midway between Tewkesbury and Evesham, this rambling Georgian country inn has the Cotswolds beckoning just to the east and shapely Bredon Hill rising immediately to the north. The Beckford, now owned by the Wadworth brewery, is an enticing mix of contemporary comforts and traditional fixtures throughout.

BELBROUGHTON

The Queens

Tel **01562 730276 | 24 Queens Hill, DY9 0DU**
Web **thequeensbelbroughton.co.uk**
Dir ***Phone for detailed directions.***

The Queens is a charming 16th-century country pub set next to the old mill stream where scythes used to be made. Refurbished in 2016 by Janet Evans and Tim Balfour, it has a modern and light feel whilst retaining plenty of original features.

The Talbot

Tel **01562 730249 | Hartle Lane, DY9 9TG**
Web **www.thetalbotbelbroughton.co.uk**
Dir ***M5 junction 4, A491 towards Stourbridge. At lights left onto B4188 signed Belbroughton. Pub on right at T-junction in village.***

Believed to have been built in the late 17th or 18th century, the pub has oak timbers, open fires, soft furnishings and an enclosed garden with a covered patio. There are no geographical limits on real ale sourcing, with Cocker Hoop from Cumbria alongside Boondoggle from Hampshire.

BEWDLEY

The Hop Pole Inn

Tel **01299 401295 | Hop Pole Lane, DY12 2QH**
Web **www.thehoppolebewdley.co.uk**
Dir ***From Kidderminster take A456 towards Leominster. At roundabout take B4190 towards Bewdley. Pub on left.***

Over the years Louise and Daren Bale have lovingly nurtured and matured this destination dining pub, set close to the ancient Wyre Forest at the edge of Bewdley. Inside, shabby-chic meets comfy contemporary in a warmly welcoming environment.

Little Pack Horse

Tel **01299 403762 | 31 High Street, DY12 2DH**
Web **www.littlepackhorse.co.uk**
Dir ***From Kidderminster follow ring road and Safari Park signs. Then follow Bewdley signs over bridge, turn left, then right, right at top of Lax Lane.***

Close to an old ford through the River Severn, this timber framed inn in Bewdley's web of lanes has been catering for passing trade for over 480 years. It was a base for jaggers and their packhorses; the inside retains much character from those long-gone days.

BRANSFORD

The Bear & Ragged Staff

Tel **01886 833399 | Station Road, WR6 5JH**
Web **www.bearatbransford.co.uk**
Dir ***3 miles from Worcester or Malvern, clearly signed from A4103 or A449.***

Built in 1861 as an estate rent office and stables, this lovely old free house is easily reached from both Malvern and Worcester. The current owners have created a reputation for good food and beers, such as local Hobsons Twisted Spire and Cornish-brewed Sharp's Doom Bar.

BRETFORTON

The Fleece Inn

Tel 01386 831173 | The Cross, WR11 7JE
Web www.thefleeceinn.co.uk
Dir ***From Evesham follow signs for B4035 towards Chipping Campden. Through Badsey into Bretforton. Right at village hall, past church, pub in open parking area.***

An inn steeped in history

PICK OF THE PUBS

For more than 500 years this old inn remained in the same family, all descendants of an early 15th-century farmer called Byrd, who built himself this former longhouse. His last direct descendant was the Fleece's long-serving landlady, Lola Taplin, who on her death in 1977 bequeathed it to the National Trust, making it the first pub among a fair few it now owns or lets. Not licensed until 1848, this beautiful timbered building remains largely unchanged, thanks in particular to skilful restoration following a devastating fire in 2004. Two special things to look out for are a Jacobean pewter dinner service, reputedly Oliver Cromwell's, and big chalk-drawn 'witch circles' on the floor in front of each hearth, supposedly to prevent witches entering through the chimneys, a practice that Lola insisted should continue after her death. Ales change frequently and cider drinkers have a choice of home-brewed Ark or locally-produced ciders. Families will enjoy sunshine in the apple orchard, while children can let off steam in the play area. Folk music, Morris dancing, an annual asparagus festival and a beer and cider festival in the second half of October are events to catch.

Open all day, all week *Free House* 20 *from £9.50* *portions/menu* *notice required*

BROADWAY

Crown & Trumpet

Tel **01386 853202** | **14 Church Street, WR12 7AE**
Web **www.cotswoldholidays.co.uk**
Dir ***From High Street follow Snowshill sign. Pub 600 yards on left.***

Just behind the green in this internationally-known, picture-postcard village is the Crown & Trumpet, a traditional, 17th-century, mellow-stone inn. The classic beamed bar is just the place for a pint of Stroud Brewery's Tom Long or Stanway Brewery Broadway Artists, or you can take it out into the peaceful patio garden; a winter alternative is a glass of mulled wine or a hot toddy by the fire. Classic, home-made pub food is available at lunch and dinner. There's musical entertainment Thursdays, Fridays and Saturdays.

Open all week Enterprise Inns 9 from £8.95 portions/menu notice required

CLENT

The Vine Inn

Tel **01562 882491** | **Vine Lane, DY9 9PH**
Web **www.vineinnclent.com**
Dir ***Phone for detailed directions.***

Tucked into one of the valleys in the glorious Clent Hills, the Vine started life as a watermill at the dawn of the Industrial Revolution. Reborn as a pub in 1851, beers from Wye Valley, supplemented by cider and perry fresh from the Malvern Hills reward ramblers challenging the mini-mountain range that are the Clents. Recover in the tranquil wood-side gardens behind the flower basket-hung pub and consider a tempting menu that specialises in game and fresh fish.

Open all day, all week Star Pubs & Bars 15 from £10.95 portions notice required

CLIFTON UPON TEME

The Lion Inn and Restaurant

★★★★ INN

Tel **01886 812975** | **1 The Village, WR6 6DH**
Web **www.thelioninnclifton.co.uk**
Dir ***On B4204 between Worcester and Tenbury Wells. In centre of village.***

Overlooking the River Teme on an Anglo-Saxon settlement granted Royal Borough status by Edward III in 1377, The Lion Inn dates back to 1200 when it was used by travellers on the route between Worcester and Tenbury Wells.

DEFFORD

The Oak Inn

Tel **01386 750327** | **Woodmancote, WR8 9BW**
Web **www.theoakinndefford.com**
Dir ***On A4104 between Upton upon Severn and Pershore.***

Unspoilt Worcestershire countryside surrounds Defford. Beautifully maintained, the family-run Oak Inn dates to the 17th century and is friendly and informal. Local cask ales featuring in the cosy bar, and there's a quaint lounge with an inglenook fireplace, as well as a contemporary restaurant.

DROITWICH

The Chequers PICK OF THE PUBS

Tel **01299 851292** | **Kidderminster Road, Cutnall Green, WR9 0PJ**
Web **www.chequerscutnallgreen.co.uk**
Dir ***Phone for detailed directions.***

In a former life, Roger Narbett was the England football team chef; his soccer memorabilia can be found in the Players Lounge of this charming, traditionally decorated pub. Real ales such as Otter Bitter, Timothy Taylor and Wye Valley HPA are on offer in the bar, while the menus offer a wide choice, from sandwiches, deli platters and 'bucket food' to pub classics like fish and chips and shortcrust pie of the day. There are three beach huts on the patio which can be hired for parties and even have their own beach menu.

Open all day, all week Closed 25 Dec, 26 Dec evening and 1 Jan evening Free House 15 from £12.25 portions/menu notice required

The Honey Bee

Tel **01299 851620** | **Doverdale Lane, Doverdale, WR9 0QB**
Web **king-henrys-taverns.co.uk**
Dir ***From Droitwich take A442 towards Kidderminster. Left to Doverdale.***

Set in four and half acres of grounds, you can go fishing for carp in this pub's two lakes – and have your meal brought to you. The garden also has a great play area and there is a patio for outdoor drinking and dining.

ELDERSFIELD

The Butchers Arms

Tel **01452 840381** | **Lime Street, GL19 4NX**
Web **www.thebutchersarms.net**
Dir ***A417 from Gloucester towards Ledbury. After BP garage take B4211. In 2 miles take 4th left into Lime Street.***

The low-ceilinged, wooden-floored bar of the Block family's 16th-century pub (over 10s only) is so small it has room for just one cask of real ale, different every day. On the short, frequently-changing menu might be salt cod, Burford Brown egg, and chorizo and romesco sauce, as a starter; and, among the mains – Hereford beef fillet, St Austell Bay mussels and line-caught Cornish cod. To finish, chocolate ganache with salted caramel ice cream. A spacious garden awaits.

Open 12–3 7–11 Closed 1 weekend Aug, 25 Dec to 1st week Jan, Sun evening and Mon *Free House* 11 *from £17.50* WI-FI P

FLYFORD FLAVELL

The Boot Inn – see page 476

HARTLEBURY

The Tap House Hartlebury

Tel **01299 253275** | **Station Road, DY11 7YJ**
Web **www.thetaphousehartlebury.co.uk**
Dir ***From A449 follow station signs.***

Trains still call at the unmanned Hartlebury station, but don't buy a rail ticket; instead buy a beer in its former ticket office, now The Tap House (flagship of the neighbouring Hartlebury Brewing Company), whose bench seating and railway-style signage recall the old days. A full menu in the oak-panelled restaurant and bar lists grilled sea bass; peri peri chicken sizzler; and tagliatelle carbonara, as well as sharing platters, burgers and chargrills, salads and vegetarian options.

Open all day, all week *Free House* *from £8.95* *portions/menu* WI-FI P *notice required*

The White Hart

Tel **01299 250286** | **The Village, DY11 7TD**
Web **www.thewhitehartinhartlebury.co.uk**
Dir ***From Stourport-on-Severn take A4025 signed Worcester and Hartlebury. At roundabout take B4193. Pub in village centre.***

Owner and top chef Simon Diprose runs this traditional country pub which continues to go from strength to strength. His concise menus might begin with roast chicken and smoked bacon terrine; or spinach and watercress soup. Moving on to something more substantial there's salmon fillet with lightly spiced tomato risotto; or pan-fried pork fillet, creamy mash and onion gravy. Finish with lemon posset; or rich chocolate brownie. At lunchtime you could opt for just filled baps, a ploughman's or a burger and chunky chips.

Open all day, all week *Punch Taverns* 9 *from £10* *portions/menu* WI-FI P *notice required*

KEMERTON

The Crown Inn

Tel **01386 725020** | **High Street, GL20 7HP**
Web **www.thecrownkemerton.co.uk**
Dir ***In village centre.***

At the foot of Bredon Hill with its stunning views of the Malvern Hills, The Crown Inn is surrounded by fields, orchards and ancient paths, making it popular stopping point for Cotswold walkers. A friendly, vibrant village inn, the bar dispenses local Donnington Gold and Wye Valley Butty Bach ales, with Herefordshire-made Old Rosie keeping cider fans happy, perhaps with bar snacks of chorizo sausage roll or Scotch egg. Alongside sharing boards, enjoyable pub favourites include The Crown burger, steaks and seasonal specials.

Open all year, all day Closed Mon lunch *Free House* 15 *portions/menu* WI-FI P *notice required*

FLYFORD FLAVELL

The Boot Inn ★★★★ INN

Tel **01386 462658** | **Radford Road, WR7 4BS**
Web **www.thebootinn.com**
Dir ***A422 from Worcester towards Stratford. Turn right to village.***

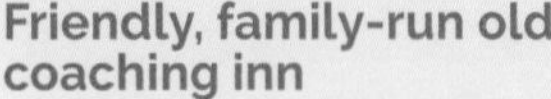

Friendly, family-run old coaching inn

Parts of this family-run, award-winning, traditional coaching inn can be traced back to the 13th century, and for evidence you need only to look at the heavy beams and slanting doorways. Keep an eye out too for the friendly ghost, age uncertain. There is a large, comfortable bar area and regulars like London Pride and Sharp's Doom Bar, and an extensive wine list complement the varied and imaginative menus which change every six weeks. You can eat from the lunchtime sandwich and bar snack menu, from the extensive specials board, or try a 'steak on the stone', The Boot's signature dish, but no matter which you choose, or indeed where – including the conservatory – only the best and freshest, mostly county-sourced, produce is used. Sundays are devoted to roasts – beef, pork and turkey are served, along with the specials menu. Gardens and a shaded patio area are especially suited to summer dining. The comfortable en suite bedrooms in the converted coach house are furnished in antique pine and equipped with practical goodies.

Open all day, all week *Punch Taverns* 8
portions/menu *notice required*

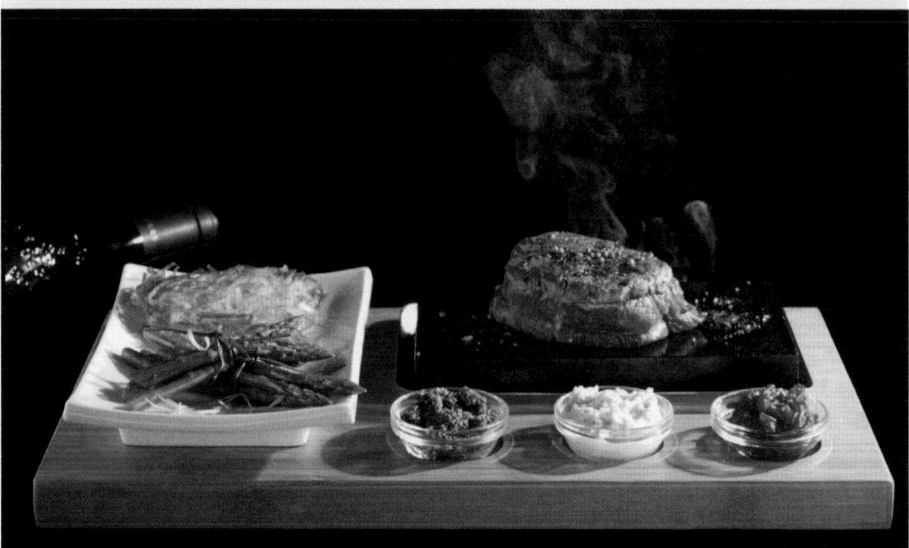

KEMPSEY

Walter de Cantelupe Inn

PICK OF THE PUBS

Tel **01905 820572** | **Main Road, WR5 3NA**
Web **www.walterdecantelupe.co.uk**
Dir ***4 miles south of Worcester city centre on A38. Pub in village centre.***

Just four miles from the centre of Worcester, this privately-owned free house commemorates a 13th-century bishop of that city. Whitewashed walls are bedecked with flowers in the summer, while the interior's wooden beams and stone floor testify to the inn's 17th-century origins. The daily blackboard menu might features soup with locally baked bread; a fillet of salmon with lemon and dill butter; and warm chocolate brownie with a scoop of ice cream make up a typical three-course selection. The walled and paved garden is fragrantly planted with clematis, roses and honeysuckle, and its south-facing aspect can be a real suntrap.

Open Tue to Fri 5.30–11 (Sat 12–2.30 5.30–11 Sun 12–3 6–9) Closed 25 to 26 Dec, 31 Dec, 1 Jan, Mon (except bank holidays) Free House from £8 portions

KNIGHTWICK

The Talbot at Knightwick

PICK OF THE PUBS

Tel **01886 821235** | **WR6 5PH**
Web **www.the-talbot.co.uk**
Dir ***Take A44 from Worcester towards Bromyard. In 8 miles right on B4197 to Knightwick.***

Sitting in the lee of wooded hills, parts of this rambling building date back 600 years. The peaceful village inn is home to the Teme Valley Brewery, which uses locally grown hops in a range of cask-conditioned ales. Winter sees huge log fires warm the timeless interior. From the seasonal menu, starters may include smoked pigeon Caesar salad, home-made pâtés and terrines of pork from pigs raised on site. Mains could be game cassoulet with locally shot muntjac venison, finishing with a cheeseboard with three local cheeses. Beer festivals are held here three times a year; farmers' markets every month.

Open all day, all week 7.30am–11.30pm Free House 12 portions

MALVERN

The Nag's Head

Tel **01684 574373** | **19–21 Bank Street, WR14 2JG**
Web **www.nagsheadmalvern.co.uk**
Dir ***Off A449.***

From this pub's garden, the looming presence of North Hill, northernmost top of the stunning Malvern Hills, takes the eye – if only momentarily – away from the panoply of delights at this enterprising free house.

The Wyche Inn ★★★★ INN

Tel **01684 575396** | **74 Wyche Road, WR14 4EQ**
Web **www.thewycheinn.co.uk**
Dir ***1.5 miles south of Malvern. On B4218 towards Malvern and Colwall. Off A449 (Worcester to Ledbury road).***

Start or end a walk in the Malvern Hills in this traditional, dog-friendly country inn, probably the highest in Worcestershire. Indeed, the views from various nearby high points are quite something; from Malvern Beacon, for instance, you can see seven counties. Beers come from Wye Valley among others, while home-cooked dishes include pie of the day, chicken curry and battered cod. Well-behaved pets are welcome in the bar, garden and the bedrooms.

Open all day, all week Free House 9 portions/menu

PEOPLETON

The Crown Inn

Tel **01905 840222** | **Main Street, WR10 2EE**
Web **www.crownpeopleton.co.uk**
Dir ***From A44 exit signed Peopleton. On Main Street.***

Overlooking the pretty St Nicholas church in the idyllic village of Peopleton, the 16th-century Crown Inn is packed with original character. Popular with villagers, walkers and cyclists alike, this family-run pub offers a broad choice of ales, wines and even has its own gin menu. Seasonally-changing menus include home-made sausage and black pudding Scotch egg, and pan-seared salmon supreme with sautéed kale, pea purée, chorizo, basil oil and salsa verde. There is a large beer garden at the rear and bank holiday beer festivals.

Open all day, all week Punch Taverns portions/menu notice required

PERSHORE

The Defford Arms

Tel **01386 750378** | **Upton Road, Defford, WR8 9BD**
Web **www.deffordarms.co.uk**
Dir ***From Pershore take A4104 towards Upton upon Severn. Pub on left in village.***

Neil, Les and Sue Overton said a firm 'no' to music, gambling machines and TV in favour of old-fashioned hospitality at the Defford Arms and it must surely contribute to the pub's continued success. It's in a great location too, so days out at Croome Park, the Three Counties Showground at Malvern, Cheltenham Racecourse or Pershore's plum festival could all include a welcome break here where traditional home-made food is order of the day.

Open all year Tue 12–2 6–9 Wed 12–2.30 6–9.30 Thu 12–2.30 6–10 Fri 12–2.30 6–11 Sat 12–2.30 6–11 Sun 12–4 Closed Sun evening and Mon Free House from £8.95 portions/menu notice required

POWICK

The Halfway House Inn

Tel **01905 831098** | **Bastonford, WR2 4SL**
Web **www.halfwayhouseinnpowick.co.uk**
Dir ***M5 junction 7, A4440 then A449.***

Standing halfway between Worcester and Malvern on the main road, this aptly named Georgian free house offers a range of bottled beers, winter log fires and a mature shady garden at the side. Steaks and seafood are a speciality, but the menu also features fresh, locally sourced dishes.

SEVERN STOKE

The Rose and Crown

Tel **01905 371249** | **Church Lane, WR8 9JQ**
Web **roseandcrownsevernstoke.co.uk**
Dir ***M5 junction 8, A38 (Malvern). In Severn Stoke, by war memorial, into Church Lane.***

Breaking a motorway journey to find a pleasant pub doesn't always pay off, but it should do at the 'Rosie'. Leave the M5 and it won't take long to reach this pretty, 500-year-old pub at the end of a lane leading to the village church.

WORCESTER

The Anchor Inn & Boathouse

Tel **01905 351094** | **54 Diglis Road, WR5 3BW**
Web **www.theanchorworcester.co.uk**
Dir ***Phone for detailed directions.***

Foodie pub with a waterside beer garden

A towpath leads from the city centre to this pub overlooking the picturesque Diglis Marina on the Worcester & Birmingham Canal, close to its junction with the River Severn. First-time visitors to the city should definitely make it part of their itinerary. Enjoy one of the five real ales or a real cider in the canalside garden; and dine on braised beef, mushroom and stout suet-crust pie; Moroccan chicken, fragrant couscous with chickpea tagine; or roast sweet potato and mushroom gnocchi.

Fish and shellfish from Devon is delivered weekly, ensuring continuing supplies of haddock, prawns, and lemon and Dover sole. Sunday roasts are all served with roast parsnips, cauliflower cheese, sautéed buttered vegetables, braised red cabbage and 'lashings' of meat gravy. Children and dogs are welcome.

Open all week Mon to Sat 10am–11pm (Sun 10am–10.30pm) portions/menu notice required

TENBURY WELLS

Pembroke House

Tel **01584 810301 | Cross Street, WR15 8EQ**
Web **www.pembrokehousetenbury.co.uk**
Dir ***Phone for detailed directions.***

This classic black and white timbered property was built as a farmhouse back in the 16th century, but it later became a cider house. With two restaurants and a beer garden, there are plenty of options. Real ales come from the likes of Hobsons and Wye Valley.

WORCESTER

The Anchor Inn & Boathouse – see opposite

Cardinal's Hat

Tel **01905 724006 | Friar Street, WR1 2NA**
Web **www.the-cardinals-hat.co.uk**
Dir ***In town centre.***

Reputedly the oldest watering hole in Worcester's historic heart and located near the cathedral, this fine Georgian building is a handsome example of an English city pub. Three beautiful period interiors impress with leaded windows, flagged floors, timber framing and oak panelling, stone fireplaces and chapel chairs.

The Old Rectifying House

Tel **01905 619622 | North Parade, WR1 3NN**
Web **theoldrec.co.uk**
Dir ***From A44 bridge over River Severn, into North Parade (one-way). Pub on right.***

Historically, the rear of this timbered, 18th-century building was used to rectify, or purify, gin on its arrival from the main part of the distillery on the other side of the Severn. The tastefully redesigned interior incorporates sofas in the bay windows overlooking the river.

EAST RIDING OF YORKSHIRE

BARMBY ON THE MARSH

The King's Head

Tel **01757 630705 | High Street, DN14 7HT**
Web **www.thekingsheadbarmby.co.uk**
Dir ***M62 junction 37 follow A614/Bridlington/York/Howden signs. Left at A63. At roundabout 1st exit onto A614/Booth Ferry Road towards Goole. At roundabout 4th exit on B1228/Booth Ferry Road. Left, through Asselby to Barmby on the Marsh.***

This 17th-century inn once served a ferry that crossed the rivers. Nowadays, this family-run village pub is a place that appeals to all tastes. Several members of the family are chefs and make the most of Yorkshire's burgeoning larder.

BEVERLEY

The Ferguson Fawsitt Arms & Country Lodge

Tel **01482 882665 | East End, Walkington, HU17 8RX**
Web **www.fergusonfawsitt.co.uk**
Dir ***M62 junction 38 onto B1230, left on A1034, right onto B1230, on left in centre of Walkington.***

Three miles from Beverley in the picturesque village of Walkington, there is a timeless quality to this Victorian pub named after two important local families. Parts of the pub used to form the village blacksmith's shop.

BRANTINGHAM

The Triton Inn

Tel **01482 667261 | Ellerker Road, Brantingham Road, HU15 1QE**
Web **www.thetritoninn.com**
Dir ***From A63 at South Cave follow Brantingham signs.***

Handy for the Wolds, the Humber Estuary and Beverley, this honeyed stone and pantiled building occupies a site where a pub has stood for many centuries. Today, it is a comfy mix of traditional pub and contemporary dining inn, a treasured community favourite.

FLAMBOROUGH

The Seabirds Inn

Tel **01262 850242** | **Tower Street, YO15 1PD**
Web **www.theseabirds.com**
Dir ***On B1255 east of Bridlington.***

Definitely one for fish lovers

Just under two miles east of this 200-year-old village pub is the distinctive chalk promontory of Flamborough Head and its famous 1806 lighthouse, which you can tour. A welcoming place, with inviting log fires in winter, the inn makes the most of the neighbouring North Sea with plenty of fish dishes, particularly haddock fillet Mornay; pan-seared sea bass; and luxury fish pie. In other respects, the menu sticks to staples like slow-cooked British beef in shortcrust pastry, with shallots and red wine gravy; chargrilled chicken breast with garlic butter; oven-roasted fresh salmon; and trio of sausages with mash and garden peas. Sunday lunchtime regulars are leg of lamb, topside of beef, pork loin and turkey crown, all with Yorkshire pudding, golden roast potatoes and seasonal vegetables.

Open all year 12–3 5.30–11 Closed Mon (winter)
Free House 9 portions/menu

GOODMANHAM

Goodmanham Arms

Tel **01430 873849** | **Main Street, YO43 3JA**
Web **www.goodmanhamarms.co.uk**
Dir ***From Market Place in Market Weighton into Londesborough Road signed Goodmanham. Right signed Goodmanham. Pub on right in village.***

In the pretty village of Goodmanham on the Wolds Way National Trail, this timeless red-brick inn is popular with walkers and cyclists refuelling on ales brewed by the pub's own All Hallows Brewery. Beers from other Yorkshire breweries also make regular appearances.

HUGGATE

The Wolds Inn ★★★ INN

Tel **01377 288217** | **YO42 1YH**
Web **www.woldsinn.co.uk**
Dir ***South off A166 between York and Driffield.***

Sixteenth century in origin, this family-run hostelry is, at 525 feet above sea level, the highest in the Yorkshire Wolds. Copper pans and gleaming brassware adorn the wood-panelled interior, and a typical meal in the charming restaurant could start with home-made pâté; or Yorkshire puddings; followed by loin of pork cooked in cider with crispy crackling; home-made steak pie or vegetarian sausages. Make sure you leave room for treacle sponge or fruit Pavlova.

Open all year 12–2 5.30–11 (Sun 12–10.30) Closed Mon (excluding bank holidays) Free House 14 from £9.50 portions/menu Wi-fi notice required

KILHAM

The Old Star

Tel **01262 420619** | **Church Street, YO25 4RG**
Web **www.theoldstarkilham.co.uk**
Dir ***From A614 (between Driffield and Bridlington) follow Kilham sign. Through Ruston Parva. Right at T-junction in Kilham, pub on right opposite church.***

This ancient pub stands opposite the church in a village at the heart of the Yorkshire Wolds. With open fires, log-burners, rustic decor and quirky artefacts to take the eye, it's a champion of local suppliers, with beers from microbreweries and cider from the village.

LOW CATTON

The Gold Cup Inn

Tel **01759 371354** | **YO41 1EA**
Web **www.goldcuplowcatton.com**
Dir ***1 mile south of A166 or 1 mile north of A1079, east of York.***

This charming, family-run free house is 300 years old but may not look it at first glance. Giveaways are the low beams and open fireplaces, wooden floors and wall-mounted coach lamps. Look out for choices like an 8oz fillet steak; cod goujons with chips and peas; and leek and Wensleydale potato cakes with spicy tomato relish. A paddock adjoining the large beer garden runs down to the River Derwent.

Open all year 12–2.30 6–11 (Sat to Sun 12–11) Closed Mon lunch Free House 11 portions/menu notice required

LUND

The Wellington Inn

Tel **01377 217294** | **19 The Green, YO25 9TE**
Web **www.thewellingtoninn.co.uk**
Dir ***On B1248 north-east of Beverley.***

Occupying a wonderfully rural location, this country pub is popular with locals and visitors alike. Inside is a unique blend of old and new; choose from the traditional pub menu or from the carte in the more formal restaurant.

NEWTON UPON DERWENT

The Half Moon Inn

Tel **01904 608883** | **Main Street, YO41 4DB**
Web **www.thehalfmoonnewton.co.uk**
Dir ***Phone for detailed directions.***

Located in a pretty village off the A1079 in the Vale of York, this charming free house dates back to 1743. Next to the Wolds Way and Five Parishes Circular Walk, the pub is a popular stop for walkers and Newton upon Derwent is famous for its barn owls. Well-kept Black Sheep and Tetley's beers are dispensed in the bar, where a typical menu might start with Yorkshire puddings filled with caramelised onion gravy and continue with a home-made steak and ale pie.

Open all week 5–11 (Sat to Sun 12–12) Free House 10 portions/menu

SANCTON

The Star

Tel **01430 827269** | **King Street, YO43 4QP**
Web **www.thestaratsancton.co.uk**
Dir ***2 miles south-east of Market Weighton on A1034.***

This stylishly modernised and extended old village pub stands at the heart of charming Sancton, close to Wolds Way. Beers from local microbreweries tempt ramblers to linger longer; more leisurely visits are rewarded by a reliable bar menu considerably enhanced by an evening restaurant choice. Smoked haddock risotto with a soft poached egg; Cumberland sausages with colcannon; and roast pumpkin tart, pickled walnuts and roast baby potatoes are typical of the satisfying dishes.

Open 12–3 6–11 (Sun all day) Closed 1st week Jan, Mon Free House 14 from £12.95 portions/menu

SOUTH DALTON

The Pipe & Glass Inn

INN PICK OF THE PUBS

Tel **01430 810246** | **West End, HU17 7PN**
Web **www.pipeandglass.co.uk**
Dir ***Just off B1248 (Beverley to Malton road). 7 miles from Beverley.***

This cute looking, pantiled former coaching inn dates from the 17th century. First and foremost, it's a friendly pub where it's perfectly okay to grab just a sandwich and a pint – try Two Chefs, the house beer – or settle in for a full-blown meal in the restaurant or garden-facing conservatory. Co-owner and chef James Mackenzie's seasonal modern British menus, including vegetarian, offer salt beef hash cake with Yorkshire rhubarb ketchup and fried quail egg; Barnsley lamb chop and belly boulangère with devilled kidneys and Chantenay carrots; and braised onion with wild mushrooms and mature cheddar rarebit, baby leeks and hazelnuts. Three new bedrooms have been added, making five in all.

Open all day 12–11 (Sun 12–10.30) Closed 2 weeks Jan, Mon (excluding bank holidays) Free House 15 portions/menu

SWANLAND

The Swan & Cygnet

Tel **01482 634571 | Main Street, HU14 3QP**
Web **www.swanandcygnet.co.uk**
Dir ***West of Hull.***

In the picture postcard village of Swanland surrounded by glorious East Yorkshire countryside, The Swan & Cygnet has a light and contemporary family-friendly dining pub. Jennings Cumberland Ale is one of three regular ales dispensed at the bar. Regional ingredients gets star billing on a menu that might start with east coast crab and chilli ravioli with shellfish bisque and continue with slow-roast belly pork, bubble-and-squeak, caramelised apple, black pudding and cider jus. Leave a space for rice pudding with fruit compôte.

Open all day, all week Marston's 8 portions/menu Wi-fi P notice required

THORNGUMBALD

The Camerton

Tel **01964 601208 | Main Street, HU12 9NG**
Web **www.thecamerton.com**
Dir ***From Hull take A1033 (signed Withernsea) to Thorngumbald.***

The unusual village name might be derived from Thorn (as shown in the Domesday Book) and from a Baron Gumbaud who settled in the area in the 13th century. This welcoming pub prides itself on traditional hospitality, good food and well-kept local real ales such as Theakston. A meal here might begin with smoked bacon, black pudding and wholegrain mustard bombs and continue with smoked haddock risotto. Root vegetable hotpot is one of the vegetarian options, whilst carnivores also get to choose from a separate grill menu.

Open all day, all week Star Pubs & Bars 24 portions/menu Wi-fi P

NORTH YORKSHIRE

AKEBAR

The Friar's Head

Tel **01677 450201 | Akebar Park, DL8 5LY**
Web **www.akebarpark.com**
Dir ***From A1 at Leeming Bar onto A684, 7 miles towards Leyburn. Entrance at Akebar Park.***

This 200-year-old pub lies in the heart of Wensleydale, known for its castles, abbeys and waterfalls. It overlooks beautiful countryside and has grounds where you can play bowls or croquet. Inside you'll find exposed beams and stonework, and hand-pulled Yorkshire ales at the bar.

ALDWARK

The Aldwark Arms

Tel **01347 838324 | YO61 1UB**
Web **www.aldwarkarms.co.uk**
Dir ***From York ring road take A19 north. Left into Warehill Lane signed Tollerton and Helperby. Through Tollerton, follow Aldwark signs.***

Successfully run by local boys, the Hardisty brothers, this friendly free house has an inviting atmosphere. Keen to include locally sourced, season produce on his menus, the chef offers the likes of Doreen's black pudding fritters with home-made apple and cider sauce.

ARKENDALE

The Blue Bell at Arkendale

Tel **01423 369242 | Moor Lane, HG5 0QT**
Web **www.thebluebellatarkendale.co.uk**
Dir ***A1(M) junction 47, A59 signed Green Hammerton and York. 1st left signed Boroughbridge and Walshford. At T-junction right on A168 (Boroughbridge). Left signed Arkendale. Pub on right.***

At the heart of a village of pantiled cottages and grassy verges; both contemporary and traditional styles blend seamlessly at this tastefully modernised country inn. Leather sofas and chairs cluster around a log-burning stove, and farmhouse kitchen-style furniture dots the tiled floor.

ARKENGARTHDALE

Charles Bathurst Inn

INN

Tel 0333 7000 779 | DL11 6EN
Web www.cbinn.co.uk
Dir *A1 onto A6108 at Scotch Corner, through Richmond, left onto B6270 to Reeth. At Buck Hotel right signed Langthwaite, pass church on right, inn 0.5 mile on right.*

PICK OF THE PUBS

Spectacular dale scenery at remote country inn

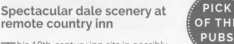

This 18th-century inn sits in possibly one of the North's finest dales, and takes its name from the son of Oliver Cromwell's physician who built it for his workers in what was once a busy lead mining area. In winter, it caters for serious walkers tackling The Pennine Way and the Coast to Coast route, and offers a welcome escape from the rigours of the moors, with many a tale being swapped over pints of Black Sheep Riggwelter or Rudgate's Jorvik Blonde. The 'Terrace Room' features handcrafted tables and chairs from Robert Thompson's craftsmen in nearby Kilburn, all with Thompson's unique hand-carved mouse hiding somewhere. English classics meet modern European dishes on a menu written up on the mirror hanging above the stone fireplace. The wine list is excellent, with well-composed tasting notes. From April to September the local outdoor game of quoits can be played. The bedrooms have fabulous views overlooking the Stang and Arkengarthdale and are finished to a high standard with exposed beams, cast-iron bed frames and warm colours.

Open all day, all week Closed 25 Dec *Free House* 12 *from £11.50* *portions/menu* *notice required*

ASKRIGG

The King's Arms

Tel **01969 650113 | Main Street, DL8 3HQ**
Dir ***From A1 exit at Scotch Corner onto A6108, through Richmond, right onto B6270 to Leyburn. Follow Askrigg signs to Main Street.***

This elegant, 18th-century coaching inn starred as the fictional Drover's Arms, vet James Herriot's favourite watering hole, in the BBC drama *All Creatures Great and Small*. Photographs of cast members can be seen in the oak-panelled bar with its big inglenook fireplace. Menus rely on top quality produce, including game from the surrounding moors, and fish fresh from Hartlepool. Look out for loin of local lamb; pan-fried salmon; or wild mushroom risotto.

Open all day, all week *Free House* *10* *portions/menu* *notice required*

BEDALE

The Castle Arms Inn

Tel **01677 470270 | Meadow Lane, Snape, DL8 2TB**
Web **www.castlearmsinn.uk**
Dir ***From A1(M) at Leeming Bar take A684 to Bedale. At crossroads in town centre take B6268 to Masham. Approximately 2 miles, turn left to Thorp Perrow Arboretum. In 0.5 mile left for Snape.***

In the sleepy village of Snape, this family-run 8th-century pub is a good starting point for walking and cycling, and visiting local stately homes, castles and film locations. The homely interior has exposed beams, flagstoned floors and real fires in the bar.

BIRSTWITH

The Station Hotel – see opposite

BOROUGHBRIDGE

The Black Bull Inn PICK OF THE PUBS

Tel **01423 322413 | 6 St James Square, YO51 9AR**
Dir ***A1(M) junction 48, B6265 east for 1 mile.***

Using a false name, highwayman Dick Turpin stayed at this ancient inn, which stands in a quiet corner of the market square and was one of the main stopping points for travellers on the long road between London and the North. Today, you have to turn off the A1(M), but it's well worth it to discover an inn built in 1258 that retains its ancient beams, low ceilings and roaring open fires, not to mention one that also gives houseroom to the supposed ghosts of a monk, a blacksmith, a cavalier and a small boy. Settle back and enjoy a pint of Timothy Taylor Boltmaker or a guest ale from the Rudgate's brewery. Expect a good choice of traditional pub food.

Open all day, all week 11–11 (Fri to Sat 11am–midnight Sun 12–11) *Free House* *11* *portions/menu*

The Crown Inn, Roecliffe
– see page 486

BROUGHTON

The Bull PICK OF THE PUBS

Tel **01756 792065 | BD23 3AE**
Web **www.brunningandprice.co.uk/bull**
Dir ***3 miles from Skipton on A59, on left.***

The Bull is traditional in style with open fires, flagged stone floors, good old furniture and lots of rugs and plants. The bar sits at the heart of things with an array of cask ales, shelves full of gins, whiskies and rum to welcome you as you walk through the door. There's also a list of around 50 or so wines. The kitchen's passion lies in fresh quality ingredients prepared and presented in a modern but unpretentious way. British dishes are complemented by more exotic influences from around the world and menus are updated on their website daily.

Open all day, all week 10am–11pm (Sun 10am–10.30pm) *Free House* *12* *portions/menu*

CALDWELL

Brownlow Arms

Tel **01325 718471 | DL11 7QH**
Web **brownlowarms.co.uk**
Dir ***From A1 at Scotch Corner take A66 towards Bowes. Right onto B6274 to Caldwell. Or from A1 junction 56 take B6275 north. 1st left through Mesonby to junction with B6274. Right to Caldwell.***

In the tiny village of Caldwell amidst the delightful rolling countryside between Barnard Castle and Darlington, this lovely stone inn is a great place to seek out. With 10 wines by the glass, plenty more bins and reliable Yorkshire real ales, time passes easily here.

BIRSTWITH

The Station Hotel

  INN

Tel **01423 770254** | **Station Road, HG3 3AG**
Web **www.station-hotel.net**
Dir ***Take A59 from Harrogate towards Skipton. Right into Chain Bar Lane signed Hampsthwaite. In Hampsthwaite at T-junction right signed Birstwith.***

Family-owned, Nidderdale country inn with spectacular scenery

Once serving the village railway station, this mid-Victorian inn offers a wide choice when it comes to places to visit, with Brimham Rocks, Fountains Abbey, Harrogate and great walks all close at hand. In the bar are Baa Baa, Boltmaker and Copper Dragon and other real ales, while a regularly-changing main menu is served throughout, the pick of the eating areas being the smart room that overlooks the garden.

Unfussy, yet full-flavoured food includes fish and chips; steak and ale pie; venison haunch with black pudding croquette; duck breast with brown butter fondant and cherry sauce; and pan-fried hake with shellfish bouillabaisse. Vegetarians are catered for with spiced pumpkin soup; and home-made falafel burger, while many dishes can be produced gluten- or dairy free. All guest bedrooms are en suite.

Open all day, all week Free House 14 from £12.95 portions/menu notice required

CARTHORPE

The Fox & Hounds PICK OF THE PUBS

Tel **01845 567433** | **DL8 2LG**
Web **www.foxandhoundscarthorpe.co.uk**
Dir ***Off A1, signed on both northbound and southbound carriageways.***

In the sleepy village of Carthorpe, the cosy Fox & Hounds has been a country inn for over 200 years, and the old anvil and other tools from its time as a smithy are still evident. The pub has an excellent reputation for its food, sourced from named suppliers and the daily delivery of fresh fish. A typical dinner could begin with duck filled filo parcels and plum sauce, followed by pan-fried fillets of sea bass and stir-fry vegetables, and ending with pear and almond tart with vanilla custard. There is a separate vegetarian menu. Beers include local Black Sheep, while the wine choice (all available by the glass) is global in scope. Home-made produce such as jams and chutneys are available to buy.

Open Tue to Sun 12–3 7–11 Closed 25 Dec and 1st 2 weeks Jan, Mon Free House from £10.95 portions

CHAPEL LE DALE

The Old Hill Inn

Tel **015242 41256** | **LA6 3AR**
Web **www.oldhillinningleton.co.uk**
Dir ***From Ingleton take B6255 towards Hawes, 4 miles, pub on right.***

Beautiful views of the Dales await visitors to this former farmhouse, later a drovers' inn, parts dating from 1615. When Winston Churchill stayed here on huntin', shootin', fishin' holidays, he no doubt enjoyed the bar, which these days serves eminent Yorkshire real ales like Black Sheep and Dent Aviator. A family of three chefs run the inn (one of whom makes sculptures from sugar).

Open Tue to Sun (in winter Tue to Thu open from 6.30) Closed 24–26 Dec, Mon (excluding bank holidays) Free House from £12.50 portions/menu

BOROUGHBRIDGE

The Crown Inn, Roecliffe

★★★★ RESTAURANT WITH ROOMS

Tel **01423 322300** | **Roecliffe, YO51 9LY**
Web **www.crowninnroecliffe.co.uk**
Dir ***A1(M) junction 48, follow Boroughbridge signs. At roundabout to Roecliffe.***

PICK OF THE PUBS

A destination pub par excellence

Built in 1568, the Crown was later a coaching inn, and in 2018 it was acquired by Joe and Sarah as the realisation of their long-shared dream. You can see why, for if you like stone-flagged floors, oak beams, roaring log fires, and some fashionably mismatched furniture, they're all here. The bar presents familiar North Yorkshire brewery pump badges like Black Sheep, Rudgate, Timothy Taylor and Wensleydale, although maybe it's the comprehensive wine list, with a good selection by the glass, that appeals. Meals are devised, cooked and presented to a high standard, so for dinner begin with the not-often-encountered consommé with poached quail's egg and gold leaf; or perhaps slow-cooked shin of beef, spelt risotto and truffle. From here one might opt for stone bass with seasonal greens, parisienne potatoes and tomato beurre blanc sauce; braised belly pork with Calvados-glazed apples, dauphinoise potatoes and mustard cream; or roast red pepper Moroccan couscous with curried yellow pepper dressing and tabbouleh salad. Maybe finish with pear Bakewell tart and toffee ice cream; or mandarin and mirin trifle. Or instead, cheese and biscuits and a glass of vintage port is a yet further option. Traditional Sunday lunches, as well as fish, vegetarian and children's options.

Open all day, all week Closed 31 Dec Free House 9 portions/menu notice required

CLAPHAM

The New Inn

Tel **01524 251203** | **LA2 8HH**
Web **www.newinn-clapham.co.uk**
Dir ***From A65 into Clapham. At T-junction right, over bridge, pub straight ahead.***

Set in the Yorkshire Dales beneath the three peaks of Pen-y-ghent, Ingleborough and Whernside, this is an ideal base for outdoor pursuits. The inn offers a bistro for relaxed dining, three bars, and seating outside overlooking the river and village.

COLTON

Ye Old Sun Inn PICK OF THE PUBS

Tel **01904 744261** | **Main Street, LS24 8EP**
Web **www.yeoldsuninn.co.uk**
Dir ***Approximately 3.5 miles from York, off A64.***

Since taking over this 17th-century country pub, Ashley and Kelly McCarthy have worked hard to transform it, adding a bar area and extending the dining area, allowing more space for the themed events, cookery demonstrations and classes that have proved so popular. In the dining room there's a deli where freshly baked bread, home-made jams and chutneys can be bought. A marquee overlooks rolling countryside and is used for large functions, like the summer beer festival and regular farmers' markets. Expect Yorkshire-style main courses such as slow-braised lamb shoulder or duo of local sausages. Finish with caramel apple crumble tart. All dishes come with a wine recommendation, or look to the handpumps – Rudgate Battle Axe and Timothy Taylor Landlord are among the choice of seven real ales.

Open all year 9.30–2 6–11 (Tue 6–11 Fri to Sun 9.30am–11pm) Closed Mon, Tue lunch Free House 18 portions/menu Wi-fi P

CRAYKE

The Durham Ox ★★★★★ A

RESTAURANT WITH ROOMS | PICK OF THE PUBS

Tel **01347 821506** | **Westway, YO61 4TE**
Web **www.thedurhamox.com**
Dir ***From A19 through Easingwold to Crayke. From market place left up hill, pub on right.***

They don't do things by halves here. Not only is this 300-year-old, hilltop pub-restaurant named after a 189-stone ox that was exhibited all over the country, but it also features a steel and cast-iron, charcoal-fired oven nicknamed Big Bertha, weighing in at over a ton. The ox was born in 1796 and, as the pub sign shows, he was a hefty beast. Inside, you'll find flagstone floors, exposed beams, oak panelling and winter fires – as well as Timothy Taylor Boltmaker from Keighley, and Treboom from York. Sandwiches and pub classics like game pie, and 'Ox' burger meet the need for something quick and easy, or if time is less of an issue you might want to work through the menu.

Open all day, all week 12–11.30 (Sun 12–10.30) Free House 10 from £10 portions/menu Wi-fi P *notice required*

CROPTON

The New Inn

Tel **01751 417330** | **YO18 8HH**
Web **www.newinncropton.co.uk**
Dir ***Phone for detailed directions.***

On the edge of the North York Moors National Park, this family-run free house is fortunate to have the acclaimed The Great Yorkshire Brewery at the bottom of the garden. Popular with locals and visitors alike, the pub is a draw to ale lovers.

EASINGWOLD

The New Inn

Tel **01347 824007** | **62–66 Long Street, YO61 3HT**
Web **www.thenewinnateasingwold.co.uk**
Dir ***In town centre.***

New it isn't, of course, having been a coaching stop in the 19th century. This inn on the aptly named Long Street, is owned by Yorkshire pub group, West Park Inns. The restaurant makes much of the fish and seafood available from the nearby coast.

EAST WITTON

The Blue Lion PICK OF THE PUBS

Tel **01969 624273 | DL8 4SN**
Web **www.thebluelion.co.uk**
Dir ***From Ripon take A6108 towards Leyburn.***

This well-maintained, 18th-century coaching inn, tucked away in an unspoilt estate village close to Jervaulx Abbey, once catered to drovers and travellers journeying through Wensleydale. The rural-chic interior oozes atmosphere and charm, and the classic bar, with its open fire and flagstone floor, is a beer drinker's haven where the best of the county's breweries present a pleasant dilemma. A blackboard displays imaginative but unpretentious bar meals, while a memorable meal in the candlelit restaurant may comprise smoked salmon and celeriac remoulade with crispy capers and lemon oil; slow-cooked pork belly with pickled apple pureé, black pudding Scotch egg and cider reduction; with yogurt and honey cheesecake with confit fig to round it all off.

Open all day, all week 11–11 Free House 12 portions

The Cover Bridge Inn

Tel **01969 623250 | DL8 4SQ**
Web **www.thecoverbridgeinn.co.uk**
Dir ***On A6108 between Middleham and East Witton.***

This magnificent little pub is at one end of an arched bridge on the River Cover, and probably dates back, in part, to 1670. Watch out for the cunning door-latch, which befuddles many a first-time visitor. The ancient interior rewards with wrinkled beams, a vast hearth and open log fires, settles and wholesome fodder, including home-made pies, daily specials, and their famous ham and eggs. Relax in the riverside garden with your choice from eight ales on tap, four of which are rotating guests.

Open all day, all week Free House portions/menu notice required

EGTON

The Wheatsheaf Inn

PICK OF THE PUBS

Tel **01947 895271 | YO21 1TZ**
Web **www.wheatsheafegton.com**
Dir ***Off A169, north-west of Grosmont.***

This modest old pub is popular with fishermen, as the River Esk runs along at the foot of the hill, and is a big draw for fly-fishers in particular. The pub sits back from the main road and would be easy to miss, but that would be a mistake as the welcoming main bar is cosy and traditional. There's a locals' bar too, but it only holds about a dozen people, so get there early.

EGTON BRIDGE

Horseshoe Hotel

Tel **01947 895245 | YO21 1XE**
Web **www.thehorseshoehotel.co.uk**
Dir ***From Whitby take A171 towards Middlesborough. Village signed in 5 miles.***

In beautiful grounds on the banks of the River Esk, this 18th-century village pub amply repays a short trip along minor roads. On entering its welcoming bar, notice the oak settles and tables, local artists' paintings, plates around the picture rails, and the in-house Horseshoe Blond ale, among other great beers. On the simple, but still varied menu are gammon and egg, Cajun chicken burger, wholetail Whitby scampi, steak and ale pie, and sandwiches and toasted paninis.

Open all week 11.30–3 6.30–11 (Sat 11.30–11 Sun 12–10.30) Free House portions/menu notice required

The Postgate

Tel **01947 895241 | YO21 1UX**
Web **www.postgateinn.com**
Dir ***Phone for detailed directions.***

In the Esk Valley within a stone's throw of the river, this is a typical North York Moors country inn; it played the part of the Black Dog in TV's *Heartbeat*. Being on the coast-to-coast trail, and known as a food destination, it is always very popular with walkers.

ELSLACK

The Tempest Arms

Tel **01282 842450** | **BD23 3AY**
Web **www.tempestarms.co.uk**
Dir ***A59 from Skipton towards Gisburn. At roundabout left onto A56. Pub on left.***

A local landmark, the Tempest dates to the early coaching days of the 17th century. Wood fires, comfy cushions, alcoves and dining spaces set the interior's comfortable mood, completed by a fine array of Yorkshire ales at the bar and a vast menu of pub food. A staple is the beer-battered haddock with chips, tartare sauce and mushy peas.

Open all day, all week Free House 16 from £10.95 portions/menu notice required

FELIXKIRK

The Carpenters Arms

Tel **01845 537369** | **YO7 2DP**
Web **www.thecarpentersarmsfelixkirk.com**
Dir ***From Thirsk take A170 towards Helmsley. Left signed Felixkirk, 2.25 miles to village.***

Felixkirk has no shops, making this Provenance Inns owned pub the village's only retail establishment. To the east are the Hambleton Hills and the North Yorks Moors National Park, while to the west are the Yorkshire Dales. Bare stonework, slate flooring and rich red walls characterise the interior. Food is locally sourced and seasonal.

GOATHLAND

Birch Hall Inn

Tel **01947 896245** | **Beck Hole, YO22 5LE**
Web **www.beckhole.info**
Dir ***9 miles from Whitby on A169.***

This delightful little free house has just two tiny rooms separated by a sweet shop; no more than 30 people plus two small dogs have ever fitted inside with the door closed! The main bar offers well-kept local ales to sup beside an open fire in winter, including the pub's house ale, Beckwatter. A basic menu is offered. In warm weather, food and drink can be enjoyed in the large garden, which has countryside views.

Open all year 11–3 7.30–11 (11–11 summer) Closed Mon evening and Tue Sep to Apr Free House

GRASSINGTON

Grassington House ★★★★★

 RESTAURANT WITH ROOMS

Tel **01756 752406** | **5 The Square, BD23 5AQ**
Web **www.grassingtonhouse.co.uk**
Dir ***A59 into Grassington, in town square opposite post office.***

Whoever commissioned this private house in 1760 chose the site well, for this elegant Georgian pub and restaurant stands imposingly in Grassington's cobbled square. Fresh local produce underpins the award-winning menu offering starters like corn-fed chicken liver pâté with apple jam and warm brioche, and mains such as spring lamb, shoulder and loin, crispy kale and rosemary dauphinoise. Dark Horse Hetton Pale Ale and other local beers are bar staples.

Open all day, all week Closed 25 Dec Free House 14 portions/menu notice required

GREAT HABTON

The Grapes Inn

Tel **01653 669166** | **YO17 6TU**
Dir ***From Malton take B1257 towards Helmsley. In Amotherby right into Amotherby Lane. After Newsham Bridge right into Habton Lane and follow pub signs. 0.75 mile to pub.***

A welcoming village pub between the Howardian Hills and the North Yorkshire Moors near the bustling market town of Malton. Enjoy a pint of Marston's EPA with the locals in the lively lounge bar, separated from the dining room – once the village post office – by a double-sided log-burner. Chef-proprietor Adam Myers has gained an enviable reputation in Ryedale for his chargrilled steaks, but other hearty options are fillet of pork stuffed with black pudding, potato and apple rösti and wild mushroom jus.

Open Tue to Fri 6pm–close (Sat 12–2 6–close Sun open all day) Closed from 2 Jan for 2 weeks, Mon Marston's 9 from £10.95 portions/menu

GREEN HAMMERTON

The Bay Horse Inn

Tel **01423 330338** | **York Road, YO26 8BN**
Web **www.bayhorsegreenhammerton.co.uk**
Dir ***A1 junction 47 follow signs for A59 towards York. After 3 miles, turn left into village, inn on right opposite post office.***

The Bay Horse's fire-warmed central bar retains its beams and other old features – from here other drinking and dining spaces are reached. The inn is known for authentic Indian curries, too many to more than hint at: Keralan beef, lamb passanda, and fish masala, for example, while vegetarian/vegan versions include kumbli palak aloo, and baingan palak aloo. Other options include a wide range of burgers, and fish and chips. Outside is a garden and patio area.

Open all week 12–11 (Sun 12–8) Greene King portions/menu notice required

GRINTON

The Bridge Inn PICK OF THE PUBS

Tel **01748 884224** | **DL11 6HH**
Web **www.bridgeinn-grinton.co.uk**
Dir ***Exit A1 at Scotch Corner onto A6108, through Richmond. Left onto B6270 towards Grinton and Reeth.***

Close to one of Yorkshire's finest old churches, known as the Cathedral of the Dales, this 13th-century riverside pub is located in Grinton, where two of the Yorkshire Dales' wildest and prettiest dales meet; Arkengarthdale and Swaledale collide in a symphony of fells, moors, waterfalls and cataracts. Lanes and tracks slope down from the heights, bringing ramblers and riders to appreciate the pub's range of northern beers; Jennings Brewery's Cocker Hoop being a case in point. Locals enjoy the bustling games room and beamed old bar serving baguettes and toasted ciabattas, while a more tranquil restaurant area caters for those after a more intimate meal experience. Expect traditional and familiar dishes with a modern twist, typically roast pheasant with a mushroom and onion tartlet, further enhanced by daily-changing specials.

Open all day, all week Jennings portions/menu

HARDRAW

The Green Dragon Inn

Tel **01969 667392** | **DL8 3LZ**
Web **www.thegreendragoninnhardraw.com**
Dir ***From Hawes take A684 towards Sedbergh. Right to Hardraw, approximately 1.5 miles.***

Entering the Bar Parlour is like stepping into a Tudor film-set, although parts of the inn are much older – 13th century in fact. Gravestones, forming part of the floor, were washed away from the neighbouring churchyard during floods. Regular live folk music events are big draws.

HAROME

The Star Inn PICK OF THE PUBS

Tel **01439 770397** | **YO62 5JE**
Web **www.thestaratharome.co.uk**
Dir ***From Helmsley take A170 towards Kirkbymoorside 0.5 mile. Turn right for Harome.***

On the fringe of the North Yorkshire Moors National Park, this 14th-century thatched gem sits in an idyllic village surrounded by wonderful walks. Although renowned as a foodie destination, the genuinely pubby bar is worth seeking out. Here you can relax with well-kept pints of Two Chefs whilst awaiting the call to dine. Chef-patron Andrew 's menus change frequently according to season; in autumn you might begin with smoked tartare of Harome venison, egg yolk, juniper mayonnaise, house-cured jerky; or Hartlepool haddock ravioli with wholegrain mustard and leek; mains might include butter-poached North Sea halibut with frogs' legs Kiev, roast hazelnut, parsnip, wood sorrel; or thyme-roasted fillet of Yorkshire beef with stout and oxtail pie, peppered swede purée, onion gravy and horseradish. Look out for specials and veggie choices.

Open all week 11.30–3 6.30–11 (Mon 6.30–11 Sun 12–11) Free House 20 from £17 portions/menu notice required

HARROGATE

The Fat Badger

Tel **01423 505681** | **Cold Bath Road, HG2 0NF**
Web **www.thefatbadgerharrogate.com**
Dir ***A59 to Harrogate. A661 3rd exit on roundabout to Harrogate. Left at roundabout onto A6040 for 1 mile. Right onto A61. Bear left into Montpellier Hill.***

In the heart of this spa town's Montpellier Quarter close to the famous Pump Rooms, The Fat Badger has the lofty ceilings, faux gas lamps and leather chesterfields that give the place an elegant, clubby feel. It's a relaxed setting to enjoy a cocktail, a glass of fizz or pint of real ale before choosing perhaps one of the sharing boards (cured and potted meats and smoked fish platter are just two); mussels marinière and frites; steak and Guinness pie; or weiner schnitzel and skinny fries.

Open all day, all week Free House 16 from £9 menus

HELPERBY

The Oak Tree Inn

Tel **01423 789189** | **Raskelf Road, YO61 2PH**
Web **www.theoaktreehelperby.com**
Dir ***A19 from York towards Thirsk. After Easingwold left signed Helperby. Approximately 5 miles to village.***

Depending on how you approach the village, the signs say either Helperby Brafferton or Brafferton Helperby, an apparent confusion which to locals probably makes perfect sense. This village inn has a spacious bar for informal dining, and a barn extension overlooking the rear courtyard for more formal meals. A Provenance Inn, The Oak Tree's menus offer seasonal Yorkshire produce and locally reared beef (burgers and steaks) cooked in the charcoal-fired oven. Also, on offer are home-made steak and ale pie, and a seafood platter.

Open all day, all week Free House portions/ menu notice required

HOVINGHAM

The Worsley Arms Hotel

★★★ SMALL HOTEL PICK OF THE PUBS

Tel **01653 628234** | **Main Street, YO62 4LA**
Web **www.worsleyarms.co.uk**
Dir ***On B1257 between Malton and Helmsley.***

This village hotel and pub form part of the Worsley family's historic Hovingham Hall Estate. Hambleton Stallion from nearby Thirsk, and Black Sheep from Masham are on tap in the Cricketers' Bar (the local team has played on the village green for over 150 years). You can eat here or in the restaurant; lunch and afternoon tea are also served in the walled garden. Lunchtime choices could include a selection of sandwiches; while the à la carte lists such dishes as grilled Barnsley chop, mint jelly fondant potato, heritage carrots, red wine jus; or heritage tomato tart and Yorkshire basil, Yellison goats' curd, roasted hazelnuts and heritage beetroot. The pub hosts regular wine evenings and a supper club.

Open all day, all week Free House 20 portions/ menu notice required

HUBBERHOLME

The George Inn

Tel **01756 760223** | **BD23 5JE**
Web **www.thegeorge-inn.co.uk**
Dir ***From Skipton take B6265 to Threshfield. B6160 to Buckden. Follow signs for Hubberholme.***

Stunningly located beside the River Wharfe in the Yorkshire Dales National Park, this 17th-century pub still has flagstone floors, stone walls, mullioned windows and an open fire. To check if the bar is open, look for a lighted candle in the window. Beers come from the Black Sheep and Yorkshire Dales breweries. For lunch, there's soup, sandwiches and baskets of chips; the traditional choices for an evening meal are based on locally sourced produce. Enjoy a drink on the terrace in the summer.

Open 12-3 6-10.30 (summer all day 12-11) Closed last 3 weeks Jan, Tue Free House portions

KETTLEWELL

King's Head ★★★★ INN

Tel **01756 761600 | The Green, BD23 5RD**
Web **www.thekingsheadkettlewell.co.uk**
Dir ***From A65 north of Skipton take B6265 signed Grassington. In Treshfield take B6160 to Kettlewell, right before river bridge. 1st left at maypole. Pub on left.***

The immense hearth and chimney breast are difficult to miss in the bar of this traditional family-run pub in the heart of the Yorkshire Dales; it's the perfect place to warm up on cold nights. Local beers include Dark Horse Hetton Pale Ale, and fresh, seasonal produce features on the modern British menus. Begin with seared pigeon breast with black pudding and a Scotch egg; follow with pork two ways with bubble-and-squeak croquette.

Open all day, all week Closed 2 weeks beginning Jan, 1 weekend Nov, 24–26 Dec Free House 10 from £14 portions/menu notice required

KILBURN

The Forresters Arms Inn

Tel **01347 868386 | The Square, YO61 4AH**
Web **www.forrestersarms.com**
Dir ***From Thirsk take A170, after 3 miles turn right signed Kilburn. At Kilburn Road junction, turn right, inn on left in village square.***

Next door to the famous Robert Thompson craft carpentry workshop, The Forresters Arms has fine examples of his early work, with the distinctive trademark mouse evident. It has log fires, cask ales and good food. There's a specials board and a selection of lunchtime sandwiches.

KIRKBY FLEETHAM

Black Horse Inn ★★★★★ INN

Tel **01609 749010 | Lumley Lane, DL7 0SH**
Web **www.blackhorseinnkirkbyfleetham.com**
Dir ***Signed from A1 between Catterick and Leeming Bar.***

Legend has it that Dick Turpin eloped with his lady from this pub in the Swale Valley, just off the vast village green; the inn was named after the outlaw's steed. The pub garden adjoins fields, and the interior, including seven, character bedrooms, is appointed to create a pleasing mix of tradition and comfort. No surprise then that locals and visitors are encouraged to tarry a while, to sup a grand Yorkshire pint and enjoy accomplished food that covers all the bases.

Open all day, all week Free House 10 from £9.95 portions/menu notice required

KIRKBYMOORSIDE

George & Dragon Hotel

PICK OF THE PUBS

Tel **01751 433334 | 17 Market Place, YO62 6AA**
Web **www.gdhotel-yorkshire.co.uk**
Dir ***Just off A170 between Scarborough and Thirsk. In town centre.***

A whitewashed coaching inn that's welcoming and dog-friendly. Affectionately known as the G&D, it's full of charm – from the log fire in the bar, the collection of local, historic photographs, to the fountain in the sheltered courtyard – and there are five well-kept, hand-pulled real ales on offer, including an in-house brew, plus continental lagers and an extensive wine list. At lunchtime, enjoy a baguette or panini in the bar, or Knight's Restaurant's menu offers a great selection of fish dishes – 'scaddock' (a combination of golden wholetail scampi and battered haddock); and Whitby Bay thermidor are just two. For meat eaters there's slow-braised shank of Yorkshire lamb; Holme farm venison steak; or steak and Stilton pie. The traditional Sunday lunch is extremely popular.

Open all day, all week 10.30am–11pm Free House 12 from £6.95 portions/menu

KIRKBY OVERBLOW

Shoulder of Mutton

Tel **01423 871205 | Main Street, HG3 1HD**
Web **www.shoulderofmuttonharrogate.co.uk**
Dir ***South from Harrogate on A61 towards Leeds, left for Kirkby Overblow.***

For those who might be wondering, Overblow is a corruption of oreblow, a reference to the village's iron-smelting past. Built of local stone in the 1880s, this traditional country pub still offers open log fires and the attraction of an enclosed garden.

KNARESBOROUGH

The General Tarleton Inn

★★★★★ ◎◎ RESTAURANT WITH ROOMS

PICK OF THE PUBS

Tel **01423 340284 | Boroughbridge Road, Ferrensby, HG5 0PZ**
Web **www.generaltarleton.co.uk**
Dir ***A1(M) junction 48 at Boroughbridge, take A6055 to Knaresborough. Inn 4 miles on right.***

Named in honour of General Banastre Tarleton, a hero of the American War of Independence, this 18th-century coaching inn retains its old beams and original log fires, while the sofas encourage guests to settle down with a pint of Black Sheep. East coast fish is delivered daily, and local vegetables arrive the day they've been picked, and seasonal game comes from nearby shoots. Food is served in the Bar Brasserie, the fine dining restaurant, or in the terrace garden and courtyard. Accompanying wines can be selected from a list of 150; 11 served by the glass.

Open all week 12–3 6–11 Free House 11 from £13.50 portions/menu Wi-fi P

LASTINGHAM

Blacksmiths Arms

Tel **01751 417247 | YO62 6TN**
Web **www.blacksmithsarmslastingham.co.uk**
Dir ***7 miles from Pickering and 4 miles from Kirkbymoorside. A170 (Pickering to Kirkbymoorside road), follow Lastingham and Appleton-le-Moors signs.***

With a cottage garden and decked outdoor seating area, this stone-built, 17th-century free house has a wonderful atmosphere. In the small front bar, pewter mugs and beer pump clips hang from the low beams, and copper cooking pans decorate the open range. A snug and two delightful dining rooms make up the rest of the interior. Enjoy home-cooked food, including roast topside of Yorkshire beef with Yorkshire pudding, with Theakston Best Bitter or a guest ale.

Open all day, all week Free House portions/menu Wi-fi *notice required*

LANGTHWAITE

The Red Lion Inn

Tel **01748 884218 | DL11 6RE**
Dir ***From A6108 between Richmond and Leyburn follow Reeth signs. In Reeth follow Langthwaite sign.***

Homely pub often used as a film and TV location

The Red Lion Inn is a traditional country community pub that has been owned by the same family for 54 years. It hosts a dart team in winter, a quoits team in summer, and offers only bar snacks, soup, pasties, hot drinks, ice cream, chocolate and sweets. There are some wonderful walks in this part of the Dales and relevant books and maps are on sale in the bar. In the tiny snug there are photographs relating to the various films and TV programmes filmed at this unusually photogenic establishment – they include *All Creatures Great and Small, A Woman of Substance* and *Hold the Dream.* You'll find real ales from the Black Sheep Brewery at the bar, including Baa Baa Pale Ale, and a monthly-changing guest.

Open all week 11–3 7–11 Free House 9 P

LEVISHAM

Horseshoe Inn ★★★★ INN

Tel **01751 460240** | **Main Street, YO18 7NL**
Web **www.horseshoelevisham.co.uk**
Dir ***A169, 5 miles from Pickering. 4 miles, pass Fox and Rabbit Inn on right. In 0.5 mile left to Lockton. Follow steep winding road to village.***

On the edge of the North York Moors National Park, this village pub is an ideal overnight stop while touring the area, perhaps by steam train from Levisham station. Charles and Toby Wood have created a welcoming atmosphere, especially apparent in the comfortable bar, with a roaring open fire, and real ales from Black Sheep and The Great Yorkshire Brewery. Local suppliers play a big part behind the scenes so that the kitchen can prepare good quality, hearty dishes.

Open all day, all week Free House 12 portions/menu Wi-fi P

LEYBURN

The Queens Head ★★★★ INN

Tel **01677 450259** | **Westmoor Lane, Finghall, DL8 1QZ**
Web **www.queensfinghall.co.uk**
Dir ***From Bedale follow A684 west towards Leyburn, just after pub and caravan park turn left signed Finghall.***

This pretty, 18th-century country inn with beams and open fires is set on a hillside above Wensleydale. The dining room overlooks Wild Wood – believed to be one of the inspirations for Kenneth Grahame's *Wind in the Willows*. Drinkers can quaff a pint of Theakston Black Bull Bitter by the fire and diners can create their own deli board while considering the menu, which demonstrates the kitchen team's passion for Dales produce.

Open all week 12–3 6–close Closed 26 Dec, 1 Jan Free House 10 portions/menu Wi-fi P notice required

Sandpiper Inn PICK OF THE PUBS

Tel **01969 622206** | **Market Place, DL8 5AT**
Web **www.sandpiperinn.co.uk**
Dir ***A1 onto A684 to Leyburn.***

The ivy-clad Sandpiper may only have been a pub for 30 years or so, but it's Leyburn's oldest building, dating to the 17th century. The bar and snug offer real ales from a small army of Yorkshire breweries, and some 100 single malts. The restaurant, distinguished by a huge stone lintel above an open fireplace, oak floors and candlelit tables, has an excellent reputation for modern British food. Such reputations require the finest ingredients, found in both traditional and international dishes such as pigeon with spinach risotto; and grilled red mullet with lobster and tiger prawn tagliatelle. For dessert, try one of the Sandpiper's own ice creams or sorbets.

Open 10.30–3 6–11 (Sun 12–2.30 6–10) Closed 2 weeks from 1st Jan, Mon and occasionally Tue Free House 10 £14 menus Wi-fi P

LITTON

Queens Arms

Tel **01756 770096** | **BD23 5QJ**
Web **www.queensarmslitton.co.uk**
Dir ***From Skipton north on B6265, through Threshfield and Kilnsey. Left signed Arncliffe and Litton.***

The whitewashed stone Queens in secluded Littondale radiates its 17th-century character and charm below the limestone crags of the Yorkshire Dales. Enjoy the views from the outside tables, perhaps while you contemplate climbing Pen-y-Ghent at the head of the dale.

LOW ROW

The Punch Bowl Inn – see opposite

MALHAM

The Lister Arms ★★★★ INN

PICK OF THE PUBS

Tel **01729 830444** | **BD23 4DB**
Web **www.listerarms.co.uk/food-drink**
Dir ***In village centre.***

For location alone, this handsome old coaching inn takes some beating, sitting as it does in some of Britain's most impressive cavern-riddled limestone scenery. A dense covering of creepers masks its stone walls, and the old mounting block from coaching days is still in situ. It's right on the village green, which presents much easier terrain for the fell-walkers, cavers and other outdoor types who drop in here for morning coffee or a pint.

Open all day, all week The House of Daniel Thwaites 12 from £12 portions/menu Wi-fi P

LOW ROW

The Punch Bowl Inn

★★★★ INN

Tel 0333 7000 779 | DL11 6PF
Web www.pbinn.co.uk
Dir *A1 from Scotch Corner take A6108 to Richmond. Through Richmond then right onto B6270 to Low Row.*

With Wainwright's Coast to Coast Walk on the doorstep

Refurbished it may have been, but it's still evident that this Grade II listed Swaledale pub is old, 17th century, in fact. Alongside open fires and antique furniture, the bar and bar stools were hand-crafted by Robert 'The Mouseman' Thompson's company, whose trademark is a discreetly placed carved mouse. Masham brewery Black Sheep's cask-conditioned ales are in the bar. The Lunch and Beyond Menu wends its way from home-made Scotch egg with spiced apple chutney, via steak and Blacksheep casserole, herb dumpling and horseradish mash, to Yorkshire parkin with apple compôte. An alternative menu, the Mirror, has suggestions such as creamy cauliflower and Stilton soup; sea bass with Asian spiced vegetables and poppadom; and roasted Mediterranean vegetables with brown lentils. Game comes from the surrounding moors, and fresh fish is delivered from Hartlepool six days a week. There's a traditional carvery every Sunday, and steak nights are held on the first and third Tuesdays of the month. If you stay over, perhaps for the Swaledale festival in late May, enjoy the views from one of the 11 bedrooms. The nearby market town of Richmond is famous for its castle and Georgian Theatre, Britain's oldest in its original form.

Open all day, all week 11am–midnight Closed 25 Dec *Free House* 12 *from £11.50* *portions/menu* *notice required*

MALTON

The New Malton

Tel **01653 693998 | 2–4 Market Place, YO17 7LX**
Web **www.thenewmalton.co.uk**
Dir ***In town centre opposite church.***

Overlooking the market place and the part-Norman parish church, the pub's rambling, split-level rooms, wooden floorboards and flagstones declare 18th-century origins. Weekly changing local ales spoil beer drinkers for choice. A comprehensive menu includes a not unexpected Yorkshire pudding and onion gravy. Other dishes include home-smoked venison hotpot; smoked haddock chowder, roast pork rump; and field and wild mushroom 'Kiev'. Vanilla crème brûlée with nutmeg shortbread would round off a meal well.

Open all day, all week Closed 25–26 Dec, 1 Jan Free House 9 portions/menu

MARTON (NEAR BOROUGHBRIDGE)

The Punch Bowl Inn

Tel **01423 322519 | YO51 9QY**
Web **www.thepunchbowlmartoncumgrafton.com**
Dir ***In village centre.***

A Provenance Inns group member, the 16th-century Punch Bowl commands a central location in the village. Its beamed, wood-floored bar and tap-room's generous seating includes a settle, and there's a log fire in each of the six eating areas. Kick of a good meal with pan-fried pigeon breast, black pudding, rosemary lentils and pickled blackberries; or monkfish scampi, then move onto to vension haunch, fondant potato, roast chestnuts and dates; or pan-fried salmon fillet, shellfish bisque, purple potatoes, spinach and samphire. Summer barbecues are held in the pleasant courtyard.

Open all day, all week Mon to Thu 12–3 5–11 (Fri to Sat 12–11 Sun 12–10.30) Provenance Inns & Hotels 14 portions/menu notice required

MASHAM

The Black Sheep Brewery

Tel **01765 680101 | Wellgarth, HG4 4EN**
Web **www.blacksheepbrewery.co.uk**
Dir ***Off A6108, 9 miles from Ripon and 7 miles from Bedale.***

Set up by Paul Theakston, a member of Masham's famous brewery family, in the former Wellgarth Maltings in 1992, the complex includes an excellent visitor centre and a popular bar and bistro. Don't miss the fascinating tour of the brewery. Next take in the wonderful views over the River Ure and surrounding countryside as you sup tip-top pints of Riggwelter and Best Bitter; then tuck into a plate of steak, Riggwelter and mash pie with a cheddar topping; roast vegetable curry; or a Wensleydale cheese sandwich.

Open all week 10–5 (Thu to Sat 10am–late) Closed 25–26 Dec (Mon in Jan and Feb) Black Sheep Brewery from £10.50 portions/menu notice required

The White Bear

Tel **01765 689319 | Wellgarth, HG4 4EN**
Dir ***Signed from A1 between Bedale and Ripon.***

Theakston Brewery's flagship inn stands just a short stroll from the legendary brewhouse and market square in Masham and provides the perfect base for exploring the Yorkshire Dales. Handsome and stylish, there's a snug taproom for quaffing pints of Old Peculier by the glowing fire, oak-floored lounges with deep sofas and chairs for perusing the daily papers, and an elegant dining room. Expect live music and 30 cask ales at the late June beer festival.

Open all day, all week Free House portions/menu notice required

MAUNBY

The Buck Inn

Tel **01845 587777 | YO7 4HD**
Web **www.thebuckinnmaunby.co.uk**
Dir ***A1(M) junction 50, A61 towards Thirsk. Left onto A671 (Northallerton). In South Otterington left signed Maunby. Or A1(M) junction 53, A684 towards Northallerton. At roundabout right onto A167 to South Otterington, right signed Maunby.***

The inn offers a warm and friendly welcome and a classic country pub atmosphere. Look out for a famous trainer exercising his horses, or the locals playing quoits in the garden.

MIDDLEHAM

The White Swan

Tel **01969 622093 | Market Place, DL8 4PE**
Web **www.whiteswanhotel.co.uk**
Dir ***From A1, take A684 towards Leyburn then A6108 to Ripon, 1.5 miles to Middleham.***

This Tudor coaching inn stands in Middleham's cobbled market square and, like the village, is steeped in the history of the turf, with several top horseracing stables located in the area. Oak beams, flagstones and roaring log fires all feature in the atmospheric bar, where you can quaff tip-top Black Sheep or Wensleydale ales. Using quality Yorkshire produce, the menu features modern Italian and English dishes – perhaps pappardelle al cinghiale (gorgonzola pasta parcels with wine and thyme sauce); coniglio (braised rabbit with vegetable risotto); a pizza; or a chargrilled rib-eye steak served plain or with red wine sauce.

Open all day, all week 8am–11pm (midnight at weekends) Free House 9 portions/menu notice required

MIDDLESMOOR

Crown Hotel

Tel **01423 755204 | HG3 5ST**
Dir ***Phone for detailed directions.***

This family-run free house dates back to the 17th century. It's an ideal spot for anyone following the popular Nidderdale Way, and there are great views towards Gouthwaite Reservoir from the village with its cobbled streets. Visitors can enjoy a good pint of local beer and food by the cosy, roaring log fire, or in the sunny pub garden. A large selection of malt whiskies is also on offer.

Open all year Nov to Apr Tue to Thu 7–11 Fri to Sun all day (May to Oct Tue to Thu 12–2 7–11 Fri to Sun all day) Closed all day Mon, Tue to Thu lunchtime (winter) Free House portions/menu

MOULTON

The Black Bull Inn

Tel **01325 377556 | DL10 6QJ**
Web **www.theblackbullmoulton.com**
Dir ***1 mile south of Scotch Corner off A1.***

An iconic Yorkshire dining pub for decades, The Black Bull Inn was bought and refurbished by Provenance Inns. With its stone-flagged floors, exposed brickwork and cosy corners, it's a great setting for some classic pub food. Seafood is a speciality here.

NEWTON ON OUSE

The Dawnay Arms

Tel **01347 848345 | YO30 2BR**
Web **www.thedawnayatnewton.co.uk**
Dir ***From A19 follow Newton on Ouse signs.***

The Dawnay Arms dates back to Georgian times. It sits on the banks of the River Ouse, and its garden runs down to moorings for those arriving by boat. The interior hosts Black Sheep and guest ales, and the well-chosen wine list also deserves mention.

NUN MONKTON

The Alice Hawthorn

PICK OF THE PUBS

Tel **01423 330303 | The Green, YO26 8EW**
Web **www.thealicehawthorn.com**
Dir ***From A59 between York and Harrogate follow Nun Monkton signs. Pub 2 miles on right.***

Located halfway between York and Harrogate, this Grade II listed pub overlooks a village green complete with duck pond, grazing cattle and England's tallest maypole. Inside, the pub has a contemporary interior and a snug bar where local beers take pride of place. Real fires blaze and the walls are hung with paintings of the champion Victorian racehorse after which the pub is named.

Open all year Wed to Sat 12–11 (Sun 12–8) Closed Mon and Tue Free House 10 portions/menu

OSMOTHERLEY

The Golden Lion

Tel **01609 883526 | 6 West End, DL6 3AA**
Web **www.goldenlionosmotherley.co.uk**
Dir ***Phone for detailed directions.***

Standing in Osmotherley, the 'Gateway to the North Yorkshire Moors', The Golden Lion is a 250-year-old sandstone building. The atmosphere is warm and welcoming with open fires, whitewashed walls, mirrors and fresh flowers. As well as some 45 single malt whiskies, there are always three real ales on offer. The extensive menu ranges from basic pub grub to more refined dishes – whole roast poussin with rosemary and garlic, green salad and chips, perhaps.

Open 12–3 6–11 Closed 25 Dec, Mon lunch, Tue lunch Free House portions/menu Wi-fi

PICKERING

Fox & Hounds Country Inn

PICK OF THE PUBS

Tel **01751 431577 | Sinnington, YO62 6SQ**
Web **www.thefoxandhoundsinn.co.uk**
Dir ***3 miles west of town, off A170 between Pickering and Helmsley.***

A friendly, 18th-century coaching inn on the edge of the North York Moors. In the wood-panelled bar, under oak beams and warmed by a double-sided log-burner called Big Bertha, a pint of Wainwright's, or Black Sheep Best could be waiting. Menus make full use of locally farmed produce, and might include starters like twice-baked Lincolnshire Poacher cheese soufflé, or confit duck leg with leek, chorizo and pine nut tart; followed by duo of Yorkshire lamb or pan-fried calves' liver with smoked bacon and mash.

Open all week 12–2 5.30–11 (Sat 12–2 6–11 Sun 12–2.30 5.30–10.30) Closed 25–27 Dec Free House 9 from £13.45 portions/menu Wi-fi P

The Fox & Rabbit Inn

Tel **01751 460213 | Whitby Road, Lockton, YO18 7NQ**
Web **www.foxandrabbit.co.uk**
Dir ***From Pickering take A169 towards Whitby. Lockton in 5 miles.***

On a wide ridge above wooded dales, the sound of steam trains may drift across pastures to this very traditional, limestone-built Yorkshire inn near Pickering. With beers sourced from nearby craft breweries and menu ingredients with a distinctly Yorkshire pedigree, the Wood brothers have an embarrassment of riches to offer their guests. Seasonally adjusted menus may offer Radford's sirloin steak with home-made chips; or spinach and ricotta cannelloni as filling mains, topped off with a chocolate brownie.

Open all day, all week Free House 13 portions/menu P *notice required*

The White Swan Inn

★★★ HOTEL **PICK OF THE PUBS**

Tel **01751 472288 | Market Place, YO18 7AA**
Web **www.white-swan.co.uk**
Dir ***From north: A19 or A1 to Thirsk, A170 to Pickering, left at lights, 1st right onto Market Place. Pub on left. From south: A1 or A1(M) to A64 to Malton roundabout, A169 to Pickering.***

At the heart of pretty Pickering, The White Swan Inn fronts the steep main street dropping to the beck and steam railway station. With open fires, flagstone floors, panelling and eclectic furnishings, this sturdy coaching inn oozes character, and the owners have skilfully combined good contemporary design to produce a stylish dining destination. Rare breed meats come from two top-quality butchers, and lobster and fish from Whitby take pride of place on the thoughtfully crafted menus. A starter of potted crab with celeriac remoulade or poached asparagus might be followed by roast shoulder of Tamworth pork with apple sauce, crackling, goose fat potatoes, Yorkshire pudding and gravy; or spring vegetable risotto with parmesan salad.

Open all day, all week Free House 19 from £12 portions/menu Wi-fi P *notice required*

RIPON

The Royal Oak

Tel **01765 602284** | **36 Kirkgate, HG4 1PB**
Web **www.royaloakripon.co.uk**
Dir ***In town centre.***

Built in the 18th century, this beautiful coaching inn is an ideal stop if exploring nearby Harrogate and York. Well-kept local cask ales from Timothy Taylor and Saltaire breweries can be enjoyed in the bar, as well as wines from a carefully chosen list. Menus offer a good selection of pub classics and more modern options.

SAWDON

The Anvil Inn PICK OF THE PUBS

Tel **01723 859896** | **Main Street, YO13 9DY**
Web **www.theanvilinnsawdon.com**
Dir ***1.5 miles north of Brompton-by-Sawdon, on A170 (8 miles east of Pickering and 6 miles west of Scarborough).***

The 18th-century, pantile-roofed Anvil stands in the middle of the village – its name is the first clue to its role as a forge until 1985. More clues are in the stone-walled, steeply pitched-ceilinged bar, particularly the furnace, bellows, tools and the anvil itself. Three Yorkshire cask ales are served in the bar, where adornment is provided by horse-brasses, bottles and whisky jugs, and seating choices include a red leather sofa and high bar chairs. Main courses include vegetable tagine with Mediterranean couscous; wholetail Whitby scampi and chips; and fillet of salmon with samphire and crispy seaweed. Wednesdays are steak nights, and on Thursdays you can choose from six curries.

Open 5–11 (Sat to Sun 12–11) Closed 25–26 Dec, 1 Jan, Mon and Tue Free House from £10.95 portions/menu

SCARBOROUGH

Downe Arms Country Inn

Tel **01723 862471** | **Main Road, Wykeham, YO13 9QB**
Web **www.downearmshotel.co.uk**
Dir ***On A170.***

A converted 17th-century farmhouse on the edge of the North Yorkshire Moors, within easy reach of the Scarborough coastline and Ryedale. Inside are lovely high ceilings, and large sash windows look down to the attractive stone village of Wykeham. Yorkshire ales populate the bar, and lunchtime plates represent excellent value. In the evening the charming restaurant is transformed into an intimate dining room, where themed evenings take place throughout the week. There's a carvery on Sundays.

Open all day, all week Free House 9 from £11 portions/menu notice required

SCAWTON

The Hare Inn PICK OF THE PUBS

Tel **01845 597769** | **YO7 2HG**
Web **www.thehare-inn.com**
Dir ***Exit A170 towards Rievaulx Abbey and Scawton. Pub 1 mile on right.***

It's hard to imagine what this whitewashed, pantile-roofed, 13th-century pub must have witnessed. Was it, as is believed, originally a monks' brewhouse? Did a witch live here? Does it have a ghost? Are tasting menus going out of fashion? Not here, say your hosts Liz and Paul Jackson in answer to the last question; indeed, there is no carte. You eat in the split-level, stone-walled dining room, choosing either the six- or eight-courser, for which he advises allowing three and four hours respectively. Among items on a sample full menu, all with beverage pairings, are cauliflower and Tunworth cheese; venison, beetroot and elderberries; mackerel, both oak-smoked and with shiso and soy; duck and hoi sin; milk and honey; and blackberry, ewes' milk and marigold.

Open Wed to Sat 6–9 Closed for annual holidays, dates vary (see The Hare Inn website for details), Sun to Tue and Wed lunch Free House 10

SETTLE

The Golden Lion ★★★★ INN

Tel **01729 822203 | Duke Street, BD24 9DU**
Web **www.goldenlionsettle.co.uk**
Dir ***Phone for detailed directions.***

Set in the heart of Settle's 17th-century market place, The Golden Lion has original inglenook fireplaces, wooden floors and a grand staircase lined with pictures that trace the town's history. Expect decent cask ales and a classic pub menu offering freshly prepared favourites. Typical examples include the ever-popular Settle pudding of beef steak and Thwaites ale. There's a beer festival in September.

Open all day, all week 8am–11pm The House of Daniel Thwaites 9 portions/menu notice required

SKIPTON

Devonshire Arms at Cracoe

Tel **01756 730237 | Grassington Road, Cracoe, BD23 6LA**
Web **www.devonshirearmsinn.co.uk**
Dir ***Phone for detailed directions.***

Close to the famous village of Grassington at the gateway to the Dales, and famed for its association with the Rhylstone Ladies WI calendar. This convivial and lovingly renovated 17th-century inn is favoured by Three Peaks ramblers who enjoy a rotating selection of real ales.

STILLINGTON

The Bay Tree

Tel **01347 811394 | Main Street, YO61 1JU**
Web **www.thebaytreeyork.co.uk**
Dir ***North of York on B1363, signed Helmsley. In village of Stillington, on Main Street.***

Some 10 miles from York and close to an Area of Outstanding Natural Beauty, the pub has forged a reputation for its food and a wide range of local ales and over 110 gins. Seasonal menus showcase local produce in dishes like home-made ham hock terrine, piccalilli and crispy egg; and grilled plaice fillets, champ potato, kale and parsley sauce. May and August beer and music festivals are held.

Open 12–2 5.30–11 (Sun 12–4 winter) Closed 2 weeks Jan, 2 weeks Sep, Mon and Tue Free House 13 from £8 portions/menu

THIRSK

Little 3

Tel **01845 523782 | 13 Finkle Street, YO7 1DA**
Web **www.littlethree.co.uk**
Dir ***Phone for detailed directions.***

The Little 3 depends on Yorkshire's many breweries for its constantly changing real ales; there are good wines too. Foodies should head upstairs for a 'world menu' listing lamb tagine; chicken milanese; vegetable tikka masala; and classics such as fish and chips; steak and ale pie; and chargrilled gammon, with sandwiches available most lunchtimes. There's plenty of seating in the large terraced garden. Local bands play live in the bustling bar on Thursday and Saturday evenings.

Open all day, all week 10 portions/menu

THORNTON LE DALE

The New Inn

Tel **01751 474226 | Maltongate, YO18 7LF**
Web **the-new-inn.com**
Dir ***A64 north from York towards Scarborough. At Malton take A169 to Pickering. At Pickering roundabout right onto A170, 2 miles, pub on right.***

Standing at the heart of a picturesque village complete with stocks and a market cross, this Georgian coaching house dates back to 1720. The old-world charm of the location is echoed inside the bar and restaurant, with real log fires and exposed beams.

THORNTON WATLASS

The Buck Inn PICK OF THE PUBS

Tel **01677 422461 | HG4 4AH**
Web **www.buckwatlass.co.uk**
Dir ***From A1 at Leeming Bar take A684 to Bedale, B6268 towards Masham. Village in 2 miles.***

Very much the heart of the local community, this traditional pub is welcoming and relaxed. You'll still see cricketing memorabilia in the Long Room, which overlooks the village green and cricket pitch (the pub is part of the boundary). You'll find up to five real ales in the bar with its open fire, including Theakston and a guest ale such as Gun Dog bitter. There are several separate dining areas and the menu ranges from sandwiches and light bites to traditional, freshly prepared pub fare. You might choose deep-fried whitebait or prawn cocktail to start, then mains of steak and ale pie; gammon steak with egg or pineapple, chips and peas; or Masham rarebit with home-made chutney. There's live jazz once a month.

Open all week 12–11 Free House 10 from £8.95 portions/menu notice required

TOPCLIFFE

The Angel at Topcliffe

Tel **01845 578000** | **YO7 3RW**
Web **www.theangelattopcliffe.co.uk**
Dir ***A1(M) junction 49, A168 to Topcliffe. Over river, pub on right.***

The Angel is a country pub offering the best Yorkshire's food and drink in relaxed surroundings. Spacious outdoor terraces are furnished with attractive parasol-shaded tables and chairs. The open-plan interior is equally appealing, with a mix of armchairs, alcove seats and stiff-backed chairs around dark wood tables. Hand-pulled Yorkshire ales include Theakston Best, while menus embrace sandwiches, hot and cold snacks, and classics such as haddock and chips; or steak and Guinness pie.

Open all day, all week Free House 13 portions/menu notice required

WELBURN

The Crown and Cushion

Tel **01653 618777** | **YO60 7DZ**
Web **www.thecrownandcushionwelburn.com**
Dir ***A64 from York towards Malton. 13 miles left to Welburn.***

Exposed stone walls and open log fires characterise the comfortable interior of this spacious yet homely village inn. It boasts a traditional tap room, a bar serving York Guzzler ale, and three separate dining areas. Menus are based on carefully sourced local produce, so expect top quality steaks and the likes of chicken liver parfait; fish pie; wild mushroom risotto; and swordfish steaks. Castle Howard is a mile down the road.

Open all week 12–3 5–11 (Fri to Sun all day from noon) Free House from £9.95 portions/menu notice required

WEST TANFIELD

The Bruce Arms

Tel **01677 470325** | **Main Street, HG4 5JJ**
Web **www.thebrucearms.com**
Dir ***On A6108 between Ripon and Masham.***

The stone-built inn is a comfy and traditional village pub, where Theakston ales and Yorkshire cider keep the regulars happy. Menus are firmly based on the very best local produce.

WEST WITTON

The Wensleydale Heifer

★★★★★ RESTAURANT WITH ROOMS

PICK OF THE PUBS

Tel **01969 622322** | **Main Street, DL8 4LS**
Web **www.wensleydaleheifer.co.uk**
Dir ***A1 to Leeming Bar junction, A684 towards Bedale for approximately 10 miles to Leyburn, then towards Hawes, 3.5 miles to West Witton.***

Built in 1631, this white-painted coaching inn is right in the heart of the Yorkshire Dales National Park. For a morning coffee, or a pint of Heifer Gold or Black Sheep real ale, head for the Whisky Lounge. Of the two dining areas, the Fish Bar, with sea-grass flooring, wooden tables and rattan chairs, is the less formal, while the restaurant is furnished with chocolate leather chairs and linen tablecloths. Start with beef, wild mushroom and truffle spring rolls; continue with roast Nidderdale lamb rump, garlic and herb mash plus roast confit garlic. There's loads of choice for vegetarians and vegans, and well as a lobster menu, a grill room menu and a fine choice of tapas and sandwiches.

Open all day, all week Free House from £18.50 portions/menu

WHITBY

The Magpie Café

Tel **01947 602058** | **14 Pier Road, YO21 3PU**
Web **www.magpiecafe.co.uk**
Dir ***Phone for detailed directions.***

The acclaimed Magpie Café has been the home of North Yorkshire's 'best-ever fish and chips' since the late 1930s. The excellent views of the harbour from the dining room, together with the prospect of fresh, sustainably fished seafood, prove a winning combination.

WIGHILL

The White Swan PICK OF THE PUBS

Tel **01937 832217** | **Main Street, LS24 8BQ**
Web **www.thewhiteswanwighill.co.uk**
Dir ***A64 onto A659 in Tadcaster. At crossroads (at lights) into Wighill Lane signed Wighill. Pub on right in village.***

New owner John Garside has injected new life into this appealing village pub which once appeared in TV's *Darling Buds of May*. Tall stools line the corner bar in the Snug, which stocks a real ale named after the pub, as well as Black Sheep, Moorhouse's and Timothy Taylor Landlord. Local ingredients from farms and producers close to the village drive the dishes emerging from the newly refurbished kitchen. Smoked haddock, wholegrain mustard and dill fishcake with wilted spinach might precede slow-braised lamb shoulder shepherd's pie topped with cheesy mashed potato and served with sautéed minted greens. A range of sandwiches and light bites are served from noon-3pm.

Open all year, all day Closed Mon Free House portions/menu Wi-fi P notice required

WOMBLETON

The Plough Inn

Tel **01751 431356** | **Main Street, YO62 7RW**
Web **www.theploughinnatwombleton.co.uk**
Dir ***From A170 between Helmsley and Kirkbymoorside follow signs to Wombleton.***

When he retired, the landlord bought this local, built a new kitchen and renovated the rest. The warm and genuine Yorkshire hospitality continues, with the serving of fine ales and good food – a tradition started in the 15th century when monks brewed beer for weary travellers.

18 YORKSHIRE PUBS WITH ACCOMMODATION

The following pubs are rated as part of the AA Guest Accommodation scheme (see page 10–11 for more information).

Grassington House ★★★★★ RESTAURANT WITH ROOMS Grassington, North Yorkshire, *see page 489*

The Pipe & Glass Inn ★★★★★ INN South Dalton, East Riding of Yorkshire, *see page 481*

Shibden Mill Inn ★★★★★ INN Halifax, West Yorkshire, *see page 506*

The Wensleydale Heifer ★★★★★ RESTAURANT WITH ROOMS West Witton, North Yorkshire, *see page 501*

Black Horse Inn ★★★★★ INN Kirkby Fleetham, North Yorkshire, *see page 492*

The Durham Ox ★★★★★ A RESTAURANT WITH ROOMS Crayke, North Yorkshire, *see page 487*

The General Tarleton Inn ★★★★★ RESTAURANT WITH ROOMS Knaresborough, North Yorkshire, *see page 493*

The Judge's Lodging ★★★★★ INN York, North Yorkshire, *see page 503*

The Woodman Inn ★★★★★ INN Kirkburton, West Yorkshire, *see page 508*

The Lister Arms ★★★★ INN Malham, North Yorkshire, *see page 494*

The Station Hotel ★★★★ INN Birstwith, North Yorkshire, *see page 485*

Charles Bathurst Inn ★★★★ INN Arkengarthdale, North Yorkshire, *see page 483*

Fox & Hounds Country Inn ★★★★ INN Pickering, North Yorkshire, *see page 498*

The Golden Lion ★★★★ INN Settle, North Yorkshire, *see page 500*

The Queens Head ★★★★ INN Leyburn, North Yorkshire, *see page 494*

Horseshoe Inn ★★★★ INN Levisham, North Yorkshire, *see page 494*

The Punch Bowl Inn ★★★★ INN Low Row, North Yorkshire, *see page 495*

The Windmill Inn ★★★★ INN Linton, West Yorkshire, *see page 508*

YORK

Blue Bell

Tel **01904 654904** | **53 Fossgate, YO1 9TF**
Dir ***At top of Fossgate (near The Shambles).***

This is York's smallest pub, although its vivid red-brick frontage gives its presence away. Serving customers since 1798, it was last refurbished in 1903, thus warranting a Grade II* listing for its hardly-touched interior. The taproom at the front is connected by a long corridor to the snug at the back, and the ales are expertly handled by the landlord. Groups are not permitted.

Open all day, all week Mon to Thu 11–11 (Fri to Sat 11am–midnight Sun 12–10.30) Punch Taverns 21 Wi-fi

The Judge's Lodging

★★★★★ INN

Tel **01904 638733** | **9 Lendal, YO1 8AQ**
Web **www.judgeslodgingyork.co.uk**
Dir ***Phone for detailed directions.***

Owning brewery Thwaites have tastefully upgraded this Grade I listed building, incorporating period features into a stunning period interior. Iron-railed steps sweep up to the grand entrance, and the tree-shaded terrace is a popular place to dine alfresco. The contemporary menu might offer glazed pork shank, winter broth of root vegetables, pearl barley and roast shallots; or spiced sweet potato and pumpkin burger; there's also a good range of small-plate dishes and sharing boards.

Open all day, all week The House of Daniel Thwaites 15 from £8.50 portions/menu Wi-fi *notice required*

Lamb & Lion Inn ★★★★ INN

Tel **01904 612078** | **2–4 High Petergate, YO1 7EH**
Web **www.lambandlioninnyork.com**
Dir ***From York Station, turn left. Stay in left lane, over Lendal Bridge. At lights left (Theatre Royal on right). At next lights pub on right under Bootham Bar (medieval gate).***

Sheltered by one of York's medieval city gates, this inn is a handy stop on a circuit of the city walls. The panorama from the elevated beer garden incorporates these historic features; relax here or settle into one of the cosy snugs in the very atmospheric Georgian interior.

Lysander Arms

Tel **01904 640845** | **Manor Lane, Shipton Road, YO30 5TZ**
Web **www.lysanderarms.co.uk**
Dir ***Phone for detailed directions.***

The pub stands on the former RAF Clifton airfield, where Westland Lysander aircraft were based until 1942. The long, fully air-conditioned bar incorporates a pool table, dartboard and large-screen TVs. Sandwiches, 'little plates' and salads are on offer, alongside mains such as pan-fried stone bass with sautéed wild mushrooms, wilted spinach and buttered new potatoes; and slow-braised lamb shoulder with cucumber and mint, couscous and pickled baby vegetables.

Open all day, all week Free House 8 from £9 portions/menu Wi-fi P

SOUTH YORKSHIRE

BRADFIELD

The Strines Inn

Tel **0114 285 1247** | **Bradfield Dale, S6 6JE**
Web **www.thestrinesinn.co.uk**
Dir ***North off A57 between Sheffield and Manchester.***

Although built as a manor house in 1275, most of the structure is 16th century; it has been an inn since 1771 – the public rooms contain artefacts from its bygone days. Locally brewed Acorn Yorkshire Pride shares bar space with ambassadors from the further-flung Marston's, Jennings and Wychwood. Traditional home-made food includes sandwiches, jackets potatoes, hot paninis, burgers, pie of the day, giant Yorkshire puddings, and home-made chilli. Outside there's a play area and an enclosure for peacocks, geese and chickens.

Open all day, all week 10.30am–11pm Closed 25 Dec Free House 10 from £8.25 portions/menu P *notice required*

CADEBY

The Cadeby Pub & Restaurant

Tel **01709 864009 | Main Street, DN5 7SW**
Web **www.cadebyinn.com**
Dir ***A1(M) junction 36, A630 signed Sheffield and Rotherham. At lights, right into Mill Lane signed Sprotbrough. Over River Don, 1st left into Nursery Lane. At T-junction left into Cadeby Road. Pub on left.***

With spectacular countryside all around, The Cadeby is a friendly village pub, lovingly restored and with a contemporary, quirky feel. A large selection of bottled beer joins Yorkshire-brewed real ales – usually Timothy Taylor Landlord and a selection of other bitters – plus guests from local breweries, speciality whiskies and gin lists. You can have afternoon tea, home-made pizza, or choose from the menu listing sandwiches, light bites and classic dishes.

Open all day, all week Free House 11 portions/menu

PENISTONE

Cubley Hall PICK OF THE PUBS

Tel **01226 766086 | Mortimer Road, Cubley, S36 9DF**
Web **www.cubleyhall.co.uk**
Dir ***M1 junction 37, A628 towards Manchester, or M1 junction 35a, A616. Hall just south of Penistone.***

On the edge of the Peak District National Park, Cubley Hall was built as a country house in the 18th century. It later became a children's home before being transformed into its current role in 1982. Following that, the massive, oak-beamed bar was converted into the restaurant and furnished with old pine tables, chairs and church pews, and the building was extended to incorporate a hotel, which was designed to harmonise with the original mosaic floors, ornate plaster ceilings, oak panelling and stained glass. Food-wise, take your pick from light bites, chalkboard specials and an extensive main menu, listing pub classics, a selection of 'proper big' burgers and home-made pizzas. The hall is reputedly haunted by friendly Florence Lockley, who married there in 1904 and is affectionately known as Flo.

Open all day, all week 7am–11.30pm Free House portions/menu notice required

SHEFFIELD

Broadfield Ale House

Tel **0114 255 0200 | 452 Abbeydale Road, S7 1FR**
Web **www.thebroadfield.co.uk**
Dir ***Phone for detailed directions.***

Silent movie-goers and steam railway passengers were among the first customers at the Broadfield, built just before Queen Victoria died. Millhouses and Ecclesall station no longer exists, but this distinctive pub on the Abbeydale Road is still very much in business.

The Fat Cat PICK OF THE PUBS

Tel **0114 249 4801 | 23 Alma Street, S3 8SA**
Web **www.thefatcat.co.uk**
Dir ***Phone for detailed directions.***

Built in 1832, it was known as The Alma Hotel for many years, then in 1981 it was the first Sheffield pub to introduce guest beers. The policy continues, with constantly changing (mainly microbrewery) guests from across the country, two hand-pumped ciders, unusual bottled beers, Belgian pure fruit juices and British country wines. The pub's own Kelham Island Brewery accounts for at least four of the 11 traditional draught real ales.

Kelham Island Tavern

PICK OF THE PUBS

Tel **0114 272 2482 | 62 Russell Street, S3 8RW**
Web **www.kelhamtavern.co.uk**
Dir ***Just off A61 (inner ring road). Follow brown tourist signs for Kelham Island.***

This 1830s backstreet pub was built to quench the thirst of steelmakers who lived and worked nearby, and it's become a gem of a busy, traditional local. The pub is in a conservation and popular walking area, where old buildings have been converted into stylish apartments, and The Kelham Island Museum around the corner tells the story of the city's industrial heritage.

The Sheffield Tap

Tel **0114 273 7558 | Platform 1B, Sheffield Station, Sheaf Street, S1 2BP**
Web **www.sheffieldtap.com**
Dir ***Access from Sheaf Street and from Platform 1B. (Note: limited access from Platform 1B on Fridays and Saturdays).***

For more than 30 years disused and derelict, the former Edwardian refreshment room and dining rooms of Sheffield Midland Railway Station have become a much praised Grade II listed free house. Food is limited to bagged bar snacks, and children are welcome until 8pm every day.

TOTLEY

The Cricket Inn PICK OF THE PUBS

Tel **0114 236 5256 | Penny Lane, S17 3AZ**
Web **www.cricketinn.co.uk**
Dir ***Follow A621 from Sheffield, 8 miles. Right into Hillfoot Road, 1st left into Penny Lane.***

Down a country lane bordered by wooded hills and pastures, this former farmhouse became a pub for the navvies building the nearby Totley railway tunnel in the late 1880s. Walkers and cyclists flock here, while dogs and children are made to feel welcome too. Chef Richard Smith co-runs it with the Thornbridge Brewery in Bakewell, which naturally enough provides the real ales. Dishes like braised beef shin and potato pie and wild mushroom and chestnut lasagne show the style, they also smoke their own fish and meats, and giant feasts are available for groups of eight and over. For dessert, try caramelised pear and white chocolate crumble. Summer barbecues are held in the field behind the pub and cricket is played next door.

Open all day, all week 11–11 Free House 10 portions/menu Wi-fi *notice required*

WEST YORKSHIRE

BRADFORD

New Beehive Inn

Tel **01274 721784 | 169–171 Westgate, BD1 3AA**
Web **www.newbeehive.co.uk**
Dir ***Phone for detailed directions.***

Dating from 1901, this classic Edwardian inn retains its period Arts and Crafts atmosphere with five separate bars and real gas lighting; it is on the national inventory list of historic pubs. Outside, with a complete change of mood, you can relax in the Mediterranean-style courtyard. The pub offers a good range of unusual real ales, such as Salamander Mudpuppy and Abbeydale Moonshine, and a selection of over 100 malt whiskies, served alongside some simple bar snacks. Regular live bands events too.

Open all day, all week Free House Wi-fi 

CALVERLEY

Calverley Arms

Tel **0113 255 7771 | Calverley Lane, LS28 5QQ**
Web **www.vintageinn.co.uk/restaurants/yorkshire/thecalverleyarmscalverley**
Dir ***Phone for detailed directions.***

Pleasantly located in the gently rolling countryside of the Aire Valley, with the popular Leeds & Liverpool Canal just across the fields, this very substantial village-edge inn makes the most of its situation, with lovely restful views from the leafy beer garden.

EMLEY

The White Horse

Tel **01924 849823 | 2 Chapel Lane, HD8 9SP**
Web **www.ossett-brewery.co.uk**
Dir ***M1 junction 38, A637 towards Huddersfield. At roundabout left onto A636, then right to Emley.***

On the old coaching route to Huddersfield and Halifax on the edge of the village, this refurbished 18th-century pub has views towards Emley Moor Mast and the surrounding countryside. The pub is popular with walkers, cyclists and locals – walking maps are available from the bar.

HALIFAX

Shibden Mill Inn

★★★★★ INN

Tel 01422 365840 | Shibden Mill Fold, HX3 7UL
Web www.shibdenmillinn.com
Dir *From A58 into Kell Lane. 0.5 mile, left into Blake Hill.*

Award-winning food in renovated mill

The Shibden Valley used to be an important wool production area, the waters of Red Beck powering this 17th-century former spinning mill until the industry collapsed in the late 1800s. Now it's a charming inn with open fires, oak beams, small windows and heavy tiles, happily enjoying a more civilised existence below overhanging trees in a wooded glen that makes Halifax just down the road seem a thousand miles away. The beer garden is extremely popular, not least with real ale fans: a brew called Shibden Mill, made especially for the inn, sits alongside the ever-reliable Black Sheep and three guest ales. With two AA Rosettes, the restaurant attracts those who enjoy excellent food prepared from trusted local growers and suppliers, and a seasonal menu which combines newly conceived dishes with old favourites. The Shibden's focus is on customer enjoyment and the menu leaves no room for disappointment. Gourmet dinners can be arranged – an ideal excuse to book one of the inn's luxury bedrooms.

Open all day, all week Closed 25–26 Dec evening and 1 Jan evening *Free House* 24 *portions/menu*

HARTSHEAD

The Gray Ox Inn

Tel **01274 872845** | **15 Hartshead Lane, WF15 8AL**
Web **www.grayoxinn.co.uk**
Dir ***M62 junction 25, A644 signed Dewsbury. Take A62, branch left signed Hartshead and Moor Top/B6119. Left to Hartshead.***

Originally a farmhouse that sold ale, this rural inn dating from 1709 occupies a commanding position overlooking the Calder Valley. Ales from Marston's, Jennings and a guest brewery are found in the bar, with its huge log fire. Fine locally-sourced dishes prepared by a five-strong kitchen team include monkfish pakora with cucumber and red onion salad, followed by roasted venison steak, shallot and carrot potato cake.

Open all week 12–3.30 6–12 (Sun 12–10.30) Marston's 12 from £12 portions/menu

HAWORTH

The Fleece Inn

Tel **01535 642172** | **67 Main Street, BD22 8DA**
Web **www.fleeceinnhaworth.co.uk**
Dir ***From B6142 in Haworth centre into Butt Lane. Left at T-junction into Main Street.***

Solidly planted on a steep cobbled road, this gritstone inn dates from the days when the Brontë sisters were writing in the village vicarage. The award-winning Yorkshire beers as reliable as the steam trains on the famous heritage railway at the foot of the hill.

The Old White Lion Hotel

Tel **01535 642313** | **Main Street, BD22 8DU**
Web **www.oldwhitelionhotel.com**
Dir ***A629 onto B6142, 0.5 mile past Haworth Station.***

This traditional family-run, 300-year-old coaching inn looks down onto Haworth's cobbled main street. There's a charming bar, and food is taken seriously and 'dispensed with hospitality and good measure'. Bar snacks include baguettes, salads and jackets, while a meal in the Gimmerton Restaurant might include dishes like pan-fried duck breast, fondant potato and brandy, orange and cherry sauce. Vegetarians are well catered for.

Open all day, all week 11–11 (Sun 12–10.30) Free House 9 portions/menu

ILKLEY

The Crescent Inn

Tel **01943 811250** | **Brook Street, LS29 8DG**
Web **www.thecrescentinn.co.uk**
Dir ***On corner of A65 (Church Street) and Brook Street.***

Part of a hotel dating back to 1861, The Crescent is a landmark building in the centre of Ilkley and it shares the site with its sister restaurant next door. The pub blends original Victorian features with contemporary decor including handcrafted furniture upholstered in local cloth. Choose from an ever-changing range of real ales from local breweries such as Saltaire Blonde. Unpretentious and enjoyable dishes on the menu include fish and chips, burgers, vegetarian dishes, nibbles and delicious home-made pies.

Open all day, all week Free House 15 portions/menu notice required

Friends of Ham

Tel **01943 604344** | **8 Wells Road, LS29 9JD**
Web **www.friendsofham.co.uk**
Dir ***From lights on A65 in Ilkley follow Ilkley Moor sign into Brook Street. At T-junction left onto B6382 signed Ben Rhydding. 1st right into Wells Road.***

This split-level charcuterie and bar occupies the skilfully adapted former editorial offices of the *Ilkley Gazette*. The inspiring choice of real ales from Yorkshire's finest microbreweries and beyond, and the range of carefully selected European wines are themselves newsworthy.

Ilkley Moor Vaults

Tel **01943 607012** | **Stockeld Road, LS29 9HD**
Web **www.ilkleymoorvaults.co.uk**
Dir ***From Ilkley on A65 towards Skipton. Pub on right.***

Known locally as The Taps, this traditional family pub has a pool table and retro arcade machine in the games room. Have a pint of local beer in front of the real fire, perhaps accompanied by something from the range of tasty bar snacks, or some loaded fries. Alternatively, go for one of the gourmet burgers or range of pub classics. There's a gluten-free choice, a function room and a leafy beer garden complete with 'igloos'.

Open all year 12–3 5–11 (Sat to Sun all day) Closed Mon (excluding bank holidays) Star Pubs & Bars 11 portions/menu notice required

KIRKBURTON

The Woodman Inn

★★★★★ INN

Tel **01484 605778** | **Thunderbridge Lane, HD8 0PX**
Web **www.woodman-inn.com**
Dir ***1.4 miles south-west of Kirkburton. From Huddersfield take A629 towards Sheffield. Follow brown Woodman Inn signs.***

Hidden in a charming hamlet of weavers' cottages in a secluded wooded valley, The Woodman Inn comes up trumps in any search for the perfect Yorkshire inn. Real ales are from county breweries, including the sublime Bradfield Farmers Blonde. Sup this in a long, cosy, log-fire warmed beamed room wrapped around the bar or in the restaurant, where rustic gastro pub-style food makes the most of Yorkshire's produce. Lamb and mutton pie is just one dish to try.

Open all day, all week *Free House* *14* *from £18* *portions/menu* *notice required*

LEEDS

The Cross Keys PICK OF THE PUBS

Tel **0113 243 3711** | **107 Water Lane, LS11 5WD**
Web **www.the-crosskeys.com**
Dir ***0.5 mile from Leeds Station: right into Neville Street, right into Water Lane. Pass Globe Road, pub on left.***

Built in 1802, The Cross Keys was a watering hole for local foundry workers and it's where steam engine inventor James Watt reputedly hired a room to spy on his competitor Matthew Murray. To learn Murray's trade secrets Watt bought drinks for his workers. Rescued from dereliction in the 21st century, this city-centre pub has a country-pub atmosphere, with hand-pulled pints from local microbreweries complementing food recreated from long lost recipes for traditional British dishes. The best seasonal produce goes into dishes such as ox cheek, mash, mushrooms and shallots with red wine jus, followed by sticky toffee pudding with butterscotch sauce.

Open all day, all week 12–11 (Fri to Sat 12–12 Sun 12–10.30) Closed 25–26 Dec, 1 Jan *Free House* *12* *portions/menu*

Friends of Ham

Tel **0113 242 0275** | **4–8 New Station Street, LS1 5DL**
Web **www.friendsofham.com**
Dir ***On one-way street to railway station.***

This quirky, on-trend bar in the shadow of Leeds railway station lifts experimentation well above the ordinary. It's a charcuterie proffering classic cured meats and rarely seen cheeses gleaned from far-and-wide. Add to this an extravagant selection of 14 draught, craft and cask keg beers; bottled ales and real ciders which change with a frequency that astonishes, as well as various wines and sherries and you have an upbeat location well worth seeking out. In the basement there's room to relax and mix-and-match to your heart's content.

Open all day, all week Closed 25–26 Dec, 1 Jan *Free House* *notice required*

LINTHWAITE

The Sair Inn

Tel **01484 842370** | **Lane Top, HD7 5SG**
Dir ***From Huddersfield take A62 (Oldham road) for 3.5 miles. Left just before lights at bus stop (in centre of road) into Hoyle Ing and follow sign.***

James Crabtree continues to brew the same legendary beers as did his late father. A Crabtree pint is much sought after by real ale drinkers, so even though the only food is crisps and nuts, the climb up to this old hilltop alehouse is worth it (and for the great jukebox music too). Three of its four small rooms are heated by old Yorkshire ranges. An outside drinking area overlooks the Colne Valley. Children and dogs are welcome.

Open all week 3–11 (Fri to Sun 12–11) *Free House* *9* *notice required*

LINTON

The Windmill Inn ★★★★ INN

Tel **01937 582209** | **Main Street, LS22 4HT**
Web **www.thewindmillinnlinton.co.uk**
Dir ***From A1 exit at Tadcaster/Otley junction, follow Otley signs. In Collingham follow Linton signs.***

Once the home of a long-forgotten miller, this pleasant village pub is made up of small beamed rooms that have been stripped back to bare stone, presumably the original 14th-century walls. A coaching inn since the 18th century, log fires, oak beams and copper-topped cast-iron tables set the scene for good pub food or seasonal menus in the bar, restaurant or award-winning beer garden. An annual beer festival is held in July and there are two spacious boutique B&B apartments.

Open all week 11–3 5–11 (Fri to Sat 11–11 Sun 12–10.30) Closed 1 Jan Heineken 12 from £11.95 portions/menu notice required

MARSDEN

The Olive Branch

Tel **01484 844487** | **Manchester Rd, HD7 6LU**
Web **www.olivebranch.uk.com**
Dir ***On A62 between Marsden and Slaithwaite, 6 miles from Huddersfield.***

Enter this traditional 19th-century inn on a former packhorse route above the River Colne and the Huddersfield Canal and you'll find yourself in a rambling series of rooms, fire-warmed in winter. The restaurant's brasserie-style food is exemplified by dishes like beetroot and grilled goats' cheese salad; and duo of lamb – roast rack and braised breast, with sticky red cabbage. Enjoy a pint of Greenfield Dobcross Bitter from Saddleworth on the sun deck and admire the views.

Open all year Tue to Sat 5.30pm–11pm (Sun 12–10.30) Closed Mon Free House portions/menu

RIPPONDEN

Old Bridge Inn

Tel **01422 822595** | **Priest Lane, HX6 4DF**
Web **www.theoldbridgeinn.co.uk**
Dir ***In village centre by church.***

An inn has stood by Ripponden's old bridge, and even earlier ford, since at least 1307. The lower bar is of cruck-frame construction and the top bar retains its wattle and daub walls. In addition to Timothy Taylor real ales and two guests, 14 wines are offered by the glass. Typical dishes are chickpea and potato curry with basmati rice; and Bolster Moor pork pie with mushy peas. Seating outside overlooks the River Ryburn. Booking for meals is recommended.

Open all week 12–3 5–11 (Fri to Sat 12–11.30 Sun 12–10.30) Closed 25 Dec Free House 14 from £8.95 portions

SHELLEY

The Three Acres Inn

PICK OF THE PUBS

Tel **01484 602606** | **HD8 8LR**
Web **www.3acres.com**
Dir ***From Huddersfield take A629 then B6116, turn left for village.***

For 51 years the Truelove family has owned and run this charming, turn-of-the-last-century inn. The inside is spacious, with exposed beams and large fireplaces, and feels very traditional, while the outside deck is the perfect place to sit on fine evenings with, say, a pint of Timothy Taylor. Food served in both bar and restaurant successfully fuses traditional English with international influences, thus a spring grill menu offers a pre-starter of Lindisfarne oysters; starters of Bolster Moor haggis Scotch egg; and Cullen skink; then ox cheek bourguignon; lobster thermidor; free-range Goan chicken, chargrills, salads and vegetarian options. Squeeze in chocolate and Amaretto délice to finish. It all makes a 10-minute detour from the M1 well worthwhile.

Open all day, all week Closed 25–26 Dec evening, 31 Dec lunch, 1 Jan evening Free House 19 from £17.95 portions/menu

SOWERBY BRIDGE

The Alma Inn

Tel **01422 823334** | **Cotton Stones, HX6 4NS**
Web **www.alma-inn.co.uk**
Dir ***Exit A58 at Triangle between Sowerby Bridge and Ripponden. Follow signs for Cotton Stones.***

An old stone inn set in a dramatically beautiful location at Cotton Stones with stunning views of the Ryburn Valley. Outside seating can accommodate 200 customers, while the interior features stone-flagged floors and real fires. The cosy bar serves several ales.

ISLE OF MAN AND CHANNEL ISLANDS

ISLE OF MAN

PEEL

The Creek Inn

Tel 01624 842216 | Station Place, IM5 1AT
Web www.thecreekinn.co.uk
Dir *On quayside opposite House of Manannan Museum.*

The family-run Creek Inn occupies a fine spot on the quayside, overlooked by Peel Hill. A real ale drinkers' paradise, it has locally brewed Okells ales with up to four changing guests. Bands play every weekend, and nightly during the TT and Manx Grand Prix, when the pub becomes the town's focal point. There's a huge selection of dishes on the menu, from local fish, steaks and burgers, to vegetarian options and salads, alongside sandwiches, hot baguettes and toasties.

Open all day, all week 10am–late Free House 12 portions/menu Wi-fi

PORT ERIN

Falcon's Nest Hotel

Tel 01624 834077 | The Promenade, Station Road, IM9 6AF
Web www.falconsnesthotel.co.uk
Dir *Follow coast road south from airport or ferry. Hotel on seafront, immediately after steam railway station.*

The Potts family has run the Falcon's Nest since 1984 and it's very much a part of life in Port Erin. The magnificent building overlooks the sheltered harbour and sandy beach, and this waterside location means local seafood dishes dominate the menu in the Victorian-style dining room. Local 'queenie' scallops turn up on the menu alongside a roast of the day, honey-roast Manx ham and many gluten-free options. A beer festival is held in early May.

Open all day, all week 11am to midnight (Fri to Sat 11am–12.45am) Free House portions/menu Wi-fi *notice required*

GUERNSEY

CASTEL

Fleur du Jardin PICK OF THE PUBS

Tel 01481 257996 | Kings Mills, GY5 7JT
Web www.fleurdujardin.com
Dir *2.5 miles from town centre.*

Named after a long-vanished breed of Guernsey cattle, this magnificent granite and golden stone property dates back over 500 years. You can see the evidence in the low, beamed ceiling, old fireplaces and stone features, cleverly complemented by contemporary decor and design. With the coast so close in all directions, fresh seafood, such as baked Guernsey crab, is an important part of the menu. Other contenders for your enjoyment include Thai red curry; a sizzling chicken, beef or king prawn platter; and specials, such as slow-braised lamb shank, and wild mushroom risotto. After the short walk from Vazon Bay, head for the bar and its ever-changing selection of island and mainland beers, real cider from nearby Castel and carefully selected wines.

Open all day, all week Free House 12 portions/menu Wi-fi *notice required*

ST PETER PORT

The Pickled Pig ★★★ HOTEL

Tel 01481 721431 | Duke of Normandie Hotel, Lefebvre St, GY1 2JP
Web www.dukeofnormandie.com
Dir *From harbour roundabout into St Julians Avenue, 3rd left into Anns Place, continue to right, up hill, left into Lefebvre Street, archway entrance on right.*

Part of the Duke of Normandie Hotel, The Pickled Pig attracts a happy mix of Guernsey locals and hotel residents. You can be served your refreshments out in the suntrap courtyard beer garden in warmer weather. The lunch and dinner menus proffer traditional pub favourites, plus the likes of lamb curry; pan-roasted chicken supreme with bubble-and-squeak; and beef and ale pie. At least 80% of the Pickled Pig's produce is sourced locally, including beef from Meadow Court Farm, just a short drive away.

Open all day, all week 11am–11.30pm Free House 14 from £12 portions/menu Wi-fi *notice required*

JERSEY

ROZEL

The Rozel Pub & Dining

Tel 01534 863438 | La Vallee de Rozel, JE3 6AJ
Web www.chateau-la-chaire.co.uk
Dir *From St Helier to St Martin. At T-junction in St Martin (opposite church) turn right, 1st left signed Rozel Bay. At next T-junction right signed Rozel Bay. Pub on left as entering village.*

Now refurbished inside and out, The Rozel is a short stroll from Château la Chaire, its sister property, just inland from Rozel Bay in Jersey's north-eastern corner. A popular community pub, it offers sandwiches, sharing platters and salads as well as traditional mains.

ST AUBIN

Old Court House Inn

Tel 01534 746433 | St Aubin's Harbour, JE3 8AB
Web www.oldcourthousejersey.com
Dir *From Jersey Airport, right at exit, left at lights, 0.5 mile to St Aubin.*

Overlooking the stunning bay at St Aubin's Fort, this old inn's medieval origins are testified by the wizened beams and mellow stone walls. The cellars here were once allegedly used to hide contraband, although the restaurant itself is housed in the original court house building.

ST BRELADE

The Portelet Inn

Tel 01534 741899 | La Route de Noirmont, JE3 8AJ
Web www.randalls-jersey.co.uk
Dir *Phone for detailed directions.*

Parts of this cliff-top building date back to the 16th century. Over time it's developed into a mini theme park for all the family. Children let off steam while parents sup their pints of international beer or relax with a glass of Prosecco on adult-only balconies.

ST MARTIN

Royal Hotel

Tel 01534 856289 | La Grande Route de Faldouet, JE3 6UG
Web www.randalls-jersey.co.uk/the-royal
Dir *2 miles from Five Oaks roundabout towards St Martin. Pub on right next to St Martin's Church.*

A friendly local in the heart of St Martin, this former coaching inn prides itself on offering quality food and drink. A roaring log fire in the spacious lounge warm winter visitors, and there's a sunny beer garden to enjoy during the summer months.

ST MARY

St Mary's Country Inn

Tel 01534 482897 | La Rue des Buttes, JE3 3DS
Web www.liberationgroup.com
Dir *Phone for detailed directions.*

Jersey's Liberation Brewery owns this appealing country inn with smart, contemporary interior. The menu offers imaginative food at reasonable prices. Choice on the wine list extends to half-litre carafes and plenty by the glass. There's a delightful seating area outside.

SCOTLAND

SCOTTISH ISLANDS

ABERDEEN

ABERDEEN

Old Blackfriars

Tel **01224 581922 | 52 Castle Street, AB11 5BB**
Web **www.belhavenpubs.co.uk/pubs/aberdeenshire/old-blackfriars**
Dir ***From rail station right into Guild Street left into Market Street, at end right into Union Street. Pub on right on corner of Marishal Street.***

Situated in Aberdeen's historic Castlegate, this traditional city-centre pub stands on the site of property owned by Blackfriars Dominican monks. Inside, you'll find stunning stained glass, plus well-kept real ales and a large selection of malt whiskies. The pub is renowned for good food.

ABERDEENSHIRE

ABOYNE

The Boat Inn

Tel **01339 886137 | Charleston Road, AB34 5EL**
Web **www.theboatinnaboyne.co.uk**
Dir ***A93 from Aberdeen to Aboyne. Left in Aboyne centre into Charleston Road.***

Dating from 1720, this roadside inn stands by the River Dee at the spot where a ferry once operated. Mounted antlers, animal skins and hats adorn the walls of the modernised, log fire-warmed rooms. You'll find a rotating selection of real ales, many local, plus locally distilled spirits (vodka, gin and rum), plus whisky, of course. Lunch and dinner menus depend extensively on local estates and suppliers for dishes such as beef and haggis pie; and Highland-reared sirloin steak.

Open all day, all week Closed 25–26 Dec, 1 Jan Free House portions/menu notice required

BALMEDIE

The Cock & Bull Bar & Restaurant

Tel **01358 743249 | Ellon Road, Blairton, AB23 8XY**
Web **www.thecockandbull.co.uk**
Dir ***11 miles north of city centre, on left of A90 between Balmedie junction and Foveran.***

A cast-iron range warms the bar in this creeper-clad, stone-built coaching inn, standing quite alone in open farmland north of Aberdeen. Conversation is easily stimulated by local artist Irene Morrison's paintings, assorted hanging artefacts and good beer. Affordably priced food in the restaurant uses Marine Stewardship Council-approved white fish and Peterhead-landed shellfish; and beef and pork from the region's stock farms. A seasonal menu might list ham hock terrine with pineapple salsa; braised ox cheek; or fillet of hake with mussels and samphire. Great wines and whiskies as well.

Open all day, all week 10am–11.30pm (Sun 12–7.30) Closed 26–27 Dec , 2–3 Jan Free House portions/menu notice required

KILDRUMMY

Kildrummy Inn ★★★★  

Tel **01975 571227 | AB33 8QS**
Web **www.kildrummyinn.co.uk**
Dir ***Take A944 from Aberdeen, left onto A97 (Strathdon). Inn on right.***

Brothers-in-law David Littlewood and Nigel Hake, together with their wives, have fulfilled their long-held ambition to own an inn. Thanks to David's expert cooking and Nigel's amiable hospitality, they have swiftly achieved a reputation for attentive service, highly praised modern Scottish food and excellent accommodation. There are over 50 malts from some of Scotland's smaller distilleries to choose from. A sample dinner menu lists beef two ways – sirloin and featherblade – horseradish, mash, roots, glazed pearl onions and jus; loin of venison with pommes dauphine, sticky red cabbage and barley jus; and North Sea cod, langoustines and shellfish bisque.

Open 6pm–late (Sun 12–2.30 6–late) Closed Jan, Tue Free House 12 from £20 portions notice required

NETHERLEY

The Lairhillock Inn PICK OF THE PUBS

Tel 01569 730001 | AB39 3QS
Web www.lairhillock.co.uk
Dir *From Aberdeen take A90. Right towards Durris on B9077 then left onto B979 to Netherley.*

A 15-minute drive from Aberdeen city centre brings you to this generously beamed inn, part of the scenery in rural Deeside for over 200 years. It's a charmingly rambling place full of nooks and crannies; in winter, wood smoke drifts up from the unusual, slab-mounted central fire grate. In the bar, Timothy Taylor Landlord is usually accompanied by two guest real ales, while the menu majors on Scottish produce, with a starter of Cullen skink. Unsurprisingly, Aberdeen Angus steaks have a high profile alongside roasted pumpkin and wild mushroom risotto; puff pastry pie of the day; and pork and herb meatballs served with spaghetti in rich tomato and basil sauce. There's a light, bright conservatory with garden views, candlelit tables and gleaming brass and copper lamps.

Open all day, all week Closed 25–26 Dec, 1–2 Jan Free House portions/menu notice required

OLDMELDRUM

The Redgarth

Tel 01651 872353 | Kirk Brae, AB51 0DJ
Web www.redgarth.com
Dir *From A947 (Oldmeldrum bypass) follow signs to Golf Club/Pleasure Park. Inn east of bypass.*

Built in 1928 as a house, The Redgarth has been a thriving family owned business for over 28 years. A cask-conditioned ale, such as Highland Scapa Special or Jarl, or a tot of the village's own Glen Garioch malt whisky, might precede haggis-stuffed mushrooms with coarse grain mustard dip; haggis stuffed chicken breast with whisky sauce; or catch of the day. Grills are well represented and vegetarians will very likely find a sweet potato, leek and red onion flan, or spinach stuffed cannelloni on the menu.

Open all week 11–3 5–11 (Fri to Sat 11–3 5–11.45 Sun all day) Closed 25–26 Dec, 1–3 Jan Free House from £11.95 portions/menu Wi-fi

STONEHAVEN

The Marine Hotel

Tel 01569 762155 | Shore Head, AB39 2JY
Web www.marinehotelstonehaven.co.uk
Dir *On harbour side.*

Fine views over Stonehaven's lovely harbour are just some of the advantages of this comfortable hotel. They've got their own brewery, Six°North, brewing Belgian-style beer, and they offer a rotating choice of six real ales and 12 craft beers in the cosy bar. Upstairs, the stylish restaurant has a contemporary look, and serves a great selection of seasonally-changing dishes. You might start with local crab; deep fried goats' cheese; or duck liver pâté. Mains could be slow-cooked venison haunch; or a 10oz Aberdeen Angus steak.

Open all day, all week Closed 25 Dec, 1 Jan Free House from £13.95 portions/menu Wi-fi *notice required*

The Ship Inn ★★★ INN

Tel 01569 762617 | 5 Shorehead, AB39 2JY
Web www.shipinnstonehaven.com
Dir *From A90 follow signs to Stonehaven, then signs to harbour.*

Overnight guests will surely testify that the Ship has one of the best locations in town – it overlooks the almost circular harbour, once an important centre of the herring trade. In the bar, you'll find real ales from Inveralmond, Orkney and elsewhere, plus over 100 malts. Seafood is served in the bar, the air-conditioned restaurant, and on the outdoor terrace, all with harbour views. Typical dishes are Cullen skink; venison and black pudding Scotch egg; sea bass with chorizo and herb risotto; and steak and Guinness pie.

Open all day, all week Free House from £10 portions/menu Wi-fi

ANGUS

FORFAR

The Drovers Inn

Tel **01307 860322 | Memus, DD8 3TY**
Web **www.the-drovers.com**
Dir ***North of Forfar from A90 follow Memus signs. Through Justinhaugh, follow Memus signs.***

Secluded but convenient for the A90, this charming pub retains much of its character from when it was a drovers' stop-over. Three shapely dormer windows project from its slate roof and there's an attractive vaulted interior. The bar's regularly changing real ales might include Northern Light from Orkney, while a fine collection of malts waits alongside. A typical meal might start with Arbroath smokie tartlet and continue with pan-roasted loin of venison.

Open all day, all week 12–11 (Fri to Sat 12–12 Sun 12.30–late) Closed 26 Dec Free House portions/ menu Wi-fi P notice required

ARGYLL & BUTE

ARDUAINE

The Bistro at Loch Melfort Hotel PICK OF THE PUBS

Tel **01852 200233 | PA34 4XG**
Web **www.lochmelfort.co.uk**
Dir ***On A816, midway between Oban and Lochgilphead.***

Seafood lovers flock to this modern bar and bistro, part of the Loch Melfort Hotel, next door to National Trust Scotland's Arduaine Garden. It's not just the langoustines, scallops and mussels they come for – the views over Asknish Bay towards Jura, Scarba and Shuna are a real treat, too. Enjoy Fyne Ales from Cairndow, and perhaps Ayrshire ham and lentil soup; a warm Argyll pork loin, home-made apple sauce sandwich; Loch Fyne oysters; home-made Scottish beef burger; or Easdale game pie. If sitting outside is out of the question, you relax in front of the fire and watch the waves crashing against the rocks. Sailors can moor free of charge from April to October, hang up their oilskins and freshen up with a shower.

Open all week 11–10 Closed Oct to Easter Free House 8 portions/menu Wi-fi P

ARROCHAR

Village Inn

Tel **01301 702279 | Shore Road, G83 7AX**
Web **www.villageinnarrochar.co.uk**
Dir ***From Arrochar take A814 towards Helensburgh. Inn in 1 mile.***

On the east shore of Loch Long you'll find the Village Inn. There's a large beer garden and superb views of the 'Arrochar Alps'. Ideally located for the hills and trails of the National Park, the friendly inn is popular with locals and visitors alike.

CAIRNDOW

Cairndow Stagecoach Inn

★★★ INN

Tel **01499 600286 | PA26 8BN**
Web **www.cairndowinn.com**
Dir ***North of Glasgow take A82, left onto A83 at Arrochar. Through Rest and be Thankful to Cairndow. Follow signs for inn.***

On the upper reaches of Loch Fyne, this old coaching inn offers plenty of fine views of mountains, magnificent woodlands and rivers. Sample one of many malt whiskies in the friendly bar by the roaring fire, or idle away the time in the loch-side garden watching the oyster-catchers while sipping the local Fyne Ales. The menu in the candlelit Stables Restaurant could offer steak and Fyne Ale pie; and pan-fried venison steaks. Accommodation is available. You should also look out for Britain's tallest tree (Ardkinglas Grand Fir).

Open all day, all week Free House portions/ menu Wi-fi P notice required

CRINAN

Crinan Hotel PICK OF THE PUBS

Tel **01546 830261 | PA31 8SR**
Web **www.crinanhotel.com**
Dir ***From M8, at end of bridge take A82, at Tarbert left onto A83. At Inveraray follow Campbeltown signs to Lochgilphead, follow signs for A816 to Oban. 2 miles, left to Crinan on B841.***

This romantic retreat enjoys a stunning location with fabulous views across the Sound of Jura. The hotel stands at the north end of the Crinan Canal, which connects Loch Fyne to the Atlantic Ocean. For over two hundred years this hostelry has been caring for the community needs of this tiny fishing village, and welcoming travellers. Relax with a drink in the pub, restaurant or seafood bar, which extends to the patio overlooking the fishing boats. The Westward Restaurant's cuisine is firmly based on the freshest seafood – it's landed daily just 50 metres from the hotel. Look out for jumbo prawns, lobsters and oysters, as well as meat, seafood stew or vegetarian options.

Open all day, all week 11–11 Closed 25 Dec Free House 8 portions/menu notice required

INVERARAY

George Hotel

Tel **01499 302111 | Main Street East, PA32 8TT**
Web **www.thegeorgehotel.co.uk**
Dir ***On A83.***

Although built back in 1770 by the Duke of Argyll as two private houses, the George has been, since 1860, a hotel owned by the Clark family. Occupying a prime spot in this historic conservation town, it still has the original flagstone floors and four alluring log and peat fires. More than 100 whiskies and a range of Fyne Ales from up the road at Cairndow are complemented by a menu that includes dressed Mull of Kintyre crab, Scottish smoked hake, and haggis, neeps and tatties.

Open all day, all week 11am–1am Closed 25 Dec Free House 11 portions/menu notice required

LUSS

The Inn on Loch Lomond

★★★★ INN

Tel **01436 860201 | G83 8PD**
Web **www.innonlochlomond.co.uk**
Dir ***12 miles north of Balloch.***

This roadside inn sits on Loch Lomond's western shore, and first opened its doors in 1814. Today, it incorporates Mr C's Fish & Whisky Bar where the menu might feature haggis, neeps and tatties; Cullen skink; and roast salmon and haddock fishcakes. A little shy of 200 whiskies are available, but if you prefer ale, there's Loch Lomond or Sharp's Doom Bar. Live folk music on Fridays and Saturdays throughout the summer.

Open all day, all week 11–11 (Fri to Sat 11am–midnight) Free House portions/menu notice required

OBAN

Cuan Mor

Tel **01631 565078 | 60 George Street, PA34 5SD**
Web **www.cuanmor.co.uk**
Dir ***Phone for detailed directions.***

Cuan Mor means 'big ocean', clearly a reference to the Atlantic, which stretches a finger called the Firth of Lorn towards Oban. Restaurant and bars make effective use of reclaimed Ballachulish slate and timbers from the old lighthouse pier. There is a constantly changing selection of Scottish real ales and 100 or so single malts and special blends – read the Brewery Bar's Whisky Bible for guidance. As you overlook Oban Bay enjoy Isle of Mull scallops, or braised Moroccan-style lamb.

Open all day, all week Free House 16 portions/menu notice required

The Lorne

Tel **01631 570020 | Stevenson Street, PA34 5NA**
Web **www.thelornebar.co.uk**
Dir ***Phone for detailed directions.***

Handy for both Oban's train station and the Mull ferry terminal, The Lorne is a family-friendly haven with a sheltered and heated beer garden – an ideal spot to enjoy a freshly brewed coffee or a Fyne Ales pint of beer. The menu offers a good choice of pub classics, like burgers, as well as steaks and lamb shank. The 'feast for a fiver' is great value and there are some small plates for smaller appetites. It has a busy programme of pub quizzes, DJ nights and live music.

Open all day, all week Free House 12 portions/menu notice required

PORT APPIN

The Pierhouse Hotel & Seafood Restaurant

★★★ SMALL HOTEL PICK OF THE PUBS

Tel **01631 730302 | PA38 4DE**
Web **www.pierhousehotel.co.uk**
Dir ***A828 from Ballachulish to Oban. In Appin right at Port Appin and Lismore ferry sign. After 2.5 miles left after post office, hotel at end of road by pier.***

The piermaster once lived in this distinctive whitewashed building on the shores of Loch Linnhe and the grand views across the channel of water called the Lynn of Lorne to the islands of Lismore and Mull have not changed. Belhaven ales, 50 malt whiskies and dishes like the langoustine platter and Highland game pie help to make the Ferry Bar a popular spot in this pretty little fishing village. In the AA Rosette-award-winning, loch-facing restaurant, a three-course dinner might begin with West Coast scallops, then roast saddle of Scottish venison; or seared salmon fillet and langoustine-baked fishcake. For dessert, try the clotted cream and lemon cheesecake. Stay overnight in an individually designed bedroom with superb views.

Open all week 11–11 Closed 25–26 Dec Free House from £10 portions/menu

STRACHUR

Creggans Inn PICK OF THE PUBS

Tel **01369 860279 | PA27 8BX**
Web **www.creggans-inn.co.uk**
Dir ***A82 from Glasgow, at Tarbet take A83 towards Cairndow, left onto A815 to Strachur.***

Set between the woods and the water, visitors to this centuries-old, loch-side hotel can look forward to the astounding view across Loch Fyne. The reputation of the area's produce is well-established; this is matched by beers from the Fyne microbrewery at the head of the loch. Take a pint and a seat on the terrace while considering the menu's daily-changing dishes. Eat outside, dine in the bistro-style MacPhunn's bar or the more formal Loch Fyne dining room; try Ramsay haggis, creamy mash, buttered neeps and whisky sauce; or West Coast fillet of salmon, crushed potato, spinach with white wine and prawn sauce.

Open all day, all week 11–11 Free House from £13.50 portions/menu

TARBERT

West Loch Hotel

Tel **01880 820283 | PA29 6YF**
Web **www.westlochhotel.com**
Dir ***On A83 south-west of Tarbert.***

On an arm of the Atlantic, this former coaching inn is now a family-run hotel, bar and restaurant. With open fires on chilly nights, real-ale drinkers enjoy brews from the Arran, Colonsay and Fyne breweries, while malt whisky fanciers can range the alphabet from Aberlour to Tobermory, and gin lovers from Arran to Tiree. Locally landed fish and seafood includes haddock, salmon, North Atlantic prawns, scallops and langoustines, while meats and game come from the Ardlamont Estate across Loch Fyne.

Open all day, all week Free House 8 portions/menu notice required

TAYVALLICH

Tayvallich Inn

Tel **01546 870282 | PA31 8PL**
Web **www.tayvallichinn.com**
Dir ***From Lochgilphead take A816 then B841, B8025.***

Established for over 30 years, the inn stands in a picturesque fishing village overlooking the natural harbour of Tayvallich Bay at the head of Loch Sween. There are unrivalled views, particularly from the outside decking area. Fresh seafood features strongly.

EAST AYRSHIRE

SORN

The Sorn Inn PICK OF THE PUBS

Tel **01290 551305 | 35 Main Street, KA5 6HU**
Web **www.sorninn.com**
Dir ***A70 from south; or A76 from north onto B743 to Sorn.***

Stage coaches travelling between Edinburgh and Kilmarnock changed horses at the Sorn Inn, and travellers would grab some basic refreshment. It's all very different today in this smart gastro pub, where fine dining/brasserie-style fusion food is the big attraction. Particularly popular are seasoned cuts of aged Scotch beef, available in both the Chop House and the Restaurant, maybe even more so when enhanced with a slice of black pudding or haggis. Look too for smoked Ayrshire bacon carbonara; pan-fried fillets of sea bass; and spaghetti cauliflower with capers and chilli, while chargrills and daily blackboard specials widen the choice. Dogs are welcome in the bar. Sorn, by the way, is Gaelic for kiln.

Open 12–2.30 6–10 (Fri 12–2.30 6–12 Sat 12–12 Sun 12–10) Closed 2 weeks Jan, Mon Free House 12 from £16.95 portions/menu Wi-fi P notice required

12 TOP SCOTTISH PUBS WITH ACCOMMODATION

The following pubs are rated as part of the AA Guest Accommodation scheme (see page 10-11 for more information).

Killiecrankie House Hotel ★★★ SMALL HOTEL Killiecrankie, Perth & Kinross, *see page 536*

The Bonnie Badger ★★★★★ RESTAURANT WITH ROOMS Gullane, East Lothian, *see page 534*

The Bridge Inn ★★★★ INN Ratho, Edinburgh, *see page 525*

Kildrummy Inn ★★★★ INN Kildrummy, Aberdeenshire, *see page 516*

The Ship Inn ★★★★ INN Elie, Fife, see *page 526*

The Inn on Loch Lomond ★★★★ INN Luss, Argyll & Bute, *see page 519*

Meikleour Arms ★★★★ INN Meikleour, Perth & Kinross, *see page 535*

Moorings Hotel ★★★★ HOTEL Fort William, Highland, *see page 529*

The Inverkip ★★★ INN Inverkip, Inverclyde, *see page 533*

The Ship Inn ★★★ INN Stonehaven, Aberdeenshire, *see page 517*

Cairndow Stagecoach Inn ★★★ INN Cairndow, Argyll & Bute, *see page 518*

The Pierhouse Hotel & Seafood Restaurant ★★★ SMALL HOTEL Port Appin, Argyll & Bute, *see page 520*

SOUTH AYRSHIRE

SYMINGTON

Wheatsheaf Inn

Tel **01563 830307** | **Main Street, KA1 5QB**
Web **www.thewheatsheafsymington.co.uk**
Dir ***Off A77 between Ayr and Kilmarnock.***

Close to the Royal Troon Golf Course and one of Scotland's oldest churches, this charming 17th-century free house has a welcoming atmosphere. Log fires burn in every room of the former coaching inn and the interior is decorated with the work of local artists.

DUMFRIES & GALLOWAY

BARGRENNAN

House O'Hill Hotel

Tel **01671 840243** | **DG8 6RN**
Web **www.houseohill.co.uk**
Dir ***From Newton Stewart take A714 towards Girvan, 8 miles. Hotel signed.***

At the fringe of loch-speckled Galloway Forest and beautiful Glen Trool, this contemporary, homely little hotel makes the most of its setting in Europe's first Dark Sky Park, attracting cyclists and ramblers on the Southern Upland Way by offering local microbrewery beers.

BLADNOCH

The Bladnoch Inn

Tel **01988 402200** | **DG8 9AB**
Web **www.bladnochinn.co.uk**
Dir ***A714 south of Wigtown to Bladnoch. Inn at roundabout by river bridge.***

This traditional country inn is in the heart of the Machars peninsula. At lunchtime, starters include haggis fritters; duck and orange pâté; and garlic mushrooms. Traditional pub favourites make up the mains' choices – home-made chicken curry; pork and leek sausages with mash and honey-roast vegetables; beer-battered fish, pea purée and fries; and macaroni cheese. A carvery is available on Sundays.

Open all day, all week Free House 15 portions/menu Wi-fi P notice required

ISLE OF WHITHORN

The Steam Packet Inn

Tel **01988 500334 | Harbour Row, DG8 8LL**
Web **www.thesteampacketinn.biz**
Dir ***From Newton Stewart take A714, then A746 to Whithorn, then to Isle of Whithorn.***

Run by the Scoular family for over 30 years, this lively quayside pub stands in a picturesque village at the tip of the Machars peninsula. Sit in one of the comfortable bars and enjoy a real ale while glancing out of the picture windows to watch the fishermen at work. The menu includes extensive seafood choices – perhaps salmon and fishcake kebabs, or smoked haddock fillet wrapped with black pudding and bacon.

Open all day, all week 11–11 (Sun 12–11) Closed 25 Dec Free House 12 from £9.95 portions/ menu

KIRKCUDBRIGHT

Selkirk Arms Hotel

Tel **01557 330402 | Old High Street, DG6 4JG**
Web **www.selkirkarmshotel.co.uk**
Dir ***M74 and M6 to A75, halfway between Dumfries and Stranraer on A75.***

In 1794, when dining at what today is a tastefully appointed town house, Robert Burns reputedly penned and delivered 'The Selkirk Grace'. In the bar, Sulwath Brewery's eponymous ale celebrates the occasion. A good choice of dishes is offered in both the homely lounge and bistro.

NEW GALLOWAY

Cross Keys Hotel

Tel **01644 420494 | High Street, DG7 3RN**
Web **www.thecrosskeys-newgalloway.co.uk**
Dir ***At north end of Loch Ken, 10 miles from Castle Douglas on A712.***

This 17th-century coaching inn sits in a stunning location at the top of Loch Ken on the edge of Galloway Forest Park, a superb area for walking, fishing, birdwatching, golf, watersports and photography. Part of the hotel was once the police station and in the beamed period bar the food is served in restored, stone-walled cells. The weekly-changing dinner specials might include deep-fried goats' cheese with caramelised onion relish; minted shoulder of lamb, creamy mash and seasonal vegetables; and home-made Galloway steak pie and chips.

Open all year 6.30pm–11pm Closed Sun Free House 9 from £11.75 notice required

PORTPATRICK

The Crown Hotel

Tel **01776 810261 | 9 North Crescent, DG9 8SX**
Web **www.crownhotelportpatrick.com**
Dir ***A77 into Portpatrick. At seafront turn right. Hotel on right.***

With views across Portpatrick's pretty harbour and the Irish Sea to Ulster's Mountains of Mourne, this hotel forms an integral part of the historic seafront. The terrace is perfect for a beer – try the town brewery's Fog Horn. If you expect seafood, you'll have come to the right place, because options include fresh local crab claws, and West Coast scallops in smoked bacon. Also noteworthy is the Galloway venison casserole.

Open all day, all week Free House 8 portions/ menu notice required

SANDHEAD

Tigh Na Mara Hotel

Tel **01776 830210 | Main Street, DG9 9JF**
Web **tighnamarahotel.co.uk**
Dir ***A75 from Dumfries towards Stranraer. Left onto B7084 to Sandhead. Hotel in village centre.***

Tigh na Mara means 'house by the sea', which seems appropriate asr this family-run village hotel is set in the tranquil seaside village of Sandhead and boasts breathtaking views of the Sands of Luce. Dishes on the menu make good use of top-quality local ingredients.

DUNDEE

BROUGHTY FERRY

The Royal Arch Bar

Tel 01382 779741 | 285 Brook Street, DD5 2DS
Web www.royal-arch.co.uk
Dir *On A930, 3 miles from Dundee at Broughty Ferry rail station.*

This long-established, street-corner inn is a pleasing mix of locals' saloon bar, complete with stained-glass windows and an eye-catching Victorian gantry and bar, and a well-maintained art deco lounge long ago converted from the inn's stables. Dispensed from this bar are quality Scottish beers such as from local Brewing 71, as well as over 50 malt whiskies; satisfying pub meals can include the impressive Broughty Burger. There's a pavement terrace canopy for all-weather alfresco eating and drinking. Beer, cider and sausage festivals are held.

Open all day, all week *Free House* 30 *portions* Wi-fi

DUNDEE

Speedwell Bar

Tel 01382 667783 | 165–167 Perth Road, DD2 1AS
Web www.mennies.co.uk
Dir *From A92 (Tay Bridge), A991 signed Perth/A85/ Coupar Angus/A923. At Riverside roundabout 3rd exit (A991). At lights left into Nethergate signed Parking/South Tay Street. Becomes Perth Road. Pass university. Bar on right.*

This fine example of an unspoiled Edwardian art deco bar is worth visiting for its interior alone; all the fitments in the bar and sitting rooms are beautifully crafted mahogany – gantry, drink shelves, dado panelling and fireplace. As well as the cask-conditioned ales, 157 whiskies and imported bottles are offered. A kitchen would be good, but since the pub is listed this is impossible. Visitors are encouraged to bring their own snacks from nearby bakeries.

Open all day, all week 11am to midnight *Free House* 18 Wi-fi

EDINBURGH

EDINBURGH

The Bow Bar

Tel 0131 226 7667 | 80 The West Bow, EH1 2HH
Web www.thebowbar.co.uk
Dir *Phone for detailed directions.*

If there is one free house that reflects the history and traditions of Edinburgh's Old Town, it's The Bow Bar. With a startling number of malt whiskies (310 to date), nine real ales poured from traditional tall founts and 50 bottled beers, the focus may be on liquid refreshment but the snacks do include haggis and bridies (meat pastries). In January and July, the pub holds 10-day long beer festivals. Tables from old train carriages and a church gantry add to the unique atmosphere.

Open all day, all week Closed 25–26 Dec *Free House* Wi-fi

The Café Royal PICK OF THE PUBS

Tel 0131 556 1884 | 19 West Register Street, EH2 2AA
Web www.caferoyaledinburgh.co.uk
Dir *Off Princes Street, in city centre.*

Designed by local architect Robert Paterson and a listed building, The Café Royal (now owned by Greene King) is a glorious example of Victorian and Baroque, with an interior seemingly frozen in time. Elegant stained glass and fine late Victorian plasterwork dominate the building, as do irreplaceable Doulton ceramic murals in the bar and restaurant. They serve local ales such as Kelburn Ca'Canny and Goldihops, wine, coffee and fresh oysters in the bar and restaurant.

Open all day, all week *Greene King* 9 *from £11* Wi-fi *notice required*

Doric Tavern

Tel 0131 225 1084 | 15–16 Market Street, EH1 1DE
Web www.the-doric.com
Dir *In city centre opposite Waverly Station and Edinburgh Dungeons.*

There's been a dining inn on this site, close to the Royal Mile and the Scottish National Gallery, since at least 1823. As such it's the oldest food-inn in Edinburgh, and it proudly continues to offer top-quality Scottish sourced produce. Award-winning Scottish beers are the mainstay here, including brews from Caledonian and micros like Cairngorm.

The Guildford Arms

Tel **0131 556 4312 | 1–5 West Register Street, EH2 2AA**
Web **www.guildfordarms.com**
Dir ***Opposite Balmoral Hotel at east end of Princes Street.***

Arrive at Edinburgh Waverley railway station and head straight here. Worthy of study are the bar's magnificent Jacobean-style ceiling, and 10 blue porcelain-handled real ale hand-pumps bearing the Stewart family crest. April and October beer festivals, and monthly brewery weekends underscore their commitment to the products of malted barley. The galleried restaurant offers dishes such as fish chowder; and 21-day aged, 8oz Tweed Valley rib-eye or sirloin steaks. Burgers and sandwiches are there too. Please note, under fives are not allowed in the bar.

Open all day, all week Closed 25–26 Dec, 1 Jan Free House 14 from £9.95 portions

Halfway House

Tel **0131 225 7101 | 24 Fleshmarket Close, EH1 1BX**
Dir ***From Royal Mile (close to crossroads with north and south bridges) into Cockburn Street. Into Fleshmarket Close, or take flight of steps off Cockburn Street on right. From Waverley station, take Market Street exit and cross road. Fleshmarket Close is opposite.***

Hidden down one of the Old Town's 'closes' (an historic alleyway, often with a flight of steps and enclosed by tall buildings), the cosy interior of this pub is adorned with railway memorabilia and throngs with locals, tourists, lawyers, students and beer aficionados supping interesting ales from Stewart's or StrathBraan, Scottish microbreweries. Mop up the ale with some traditional Scottish bar food made from fresh, local produce – Cullen skink; stovies and oatcakes; or haggis, tatties and neeps perhaps.

Open all day, all week Free House

The Scran & Scallie

PICK OF THE PUBS

Tel **0131 332 6281 | 1 Comely Bank Road, EH4 1DR**
Web **www.scranandscallie.com**
Dir ***On B900, in Stockbridge area, opposite Inverleith Park and Botanical Gardens.***

Readers from south of the Scottish border might like to know that 'scran' is food and 'scallie' is a scallywag. Here you'll find original features blending harmoniously with trendy Scandinavian influences, reclaimed furniture and Isle of Bute fabrics. Modern seasonal dishes and regional classics feature – maybe dressed Newhaven crab; Highland Wagyu beefburger and chips; and Jerusalem artichoke and pearl barley risotto. Sunday roasts may be served alongside 'forgotten' dishes like sheep's heid Scotch broth. Among 'Yer puddins', find treacle tart and mascarpone.

Open all day, all week noon to 1am Closed 25 Dec Free House 38 portions/menu notice required

The Shore Bar & Restaurant

Tel **0131 553 5080 | 3 Shore, Leith, EH6 6QW**
Web **www.fishersbistros.co.uk**
Dir ***Phone for detailed directions.***

This old pub, at the heart of Leith's bustling waterfront, welcomes guests to a memorable wood-boarded and mirrored interior. Locals and visitors are drawn here by the excellent Scottish seafood, meat and game for which the place is famous. Enjoy live jazz four times a week.

Whiski Bar & Restaurant

Tel **0131 556 3095 | 119 High Street, EH1 1SG**
Web **www.whiskibar.co.uk**
Dir ***Phone for detailed directions.***

If you find yourself on Edinburgh's famous Royal Mile and in need of sustenance and a wee dram, then seek out this highly acclaimed bar at number 119. Choose from over 300 malt whiskies (all available by the nip) and tuck into some traditional Scottish food. Served all day, the menu makes good use of Scottish beef and daily deliveries of seafood. Typically, try Cullen skink, or Haggis tower with neeps and mash. The Whiski is famous for its fiddle music.

Open all day, all week 11am–1am (Sat and Sun 9am–1am) Closed 25 Dec Free House 9 portions/menu notice required

RATHO

The Bridge Inn ★★★★ INN

PICK OF THE PUBS

Tel 0131 333 1320 | 27 Baird Road, EH28 8RA
Web www.bridgeinn.com
Dir *From Newbridge at B7030 junction, follow signs for Ratho and Edinburgh Canal Centre.*

The tree-lined Union Canal between Edinburgh and the Falkirk Wheel runs past this waterside inn. The menu offers dishes based on local produce, including from the pub's kitchen garden, and from its own chickens, ducks and Saddleback pigs, the latter providing a rich supply of pork loin, fillet, belly and sausages. Typical dishes on the menu are starters of seared wood pigeon, crispy lamb haggis, butternut and burnt onion; and Cullen skink, followed by sea bass fillets, lightly spiced sweet potato purée, chorizo, scallop and sauce vièrge; or beetroot and borlotti bean risotto. Guest Scottish cask ales may include Trade Winds from Cairngorm Brewery, Dark Island from Orkney and beers from Arran. The pub has two renovated barges which can provide Sunday lunch, afternoon tea and dinner cruises.

Open all day, all week 11–11 (Fri to Sat 11am–midnight) Closed 25 Dec Free House portions/menu notice required

FALKIRK

BO'NESS

Corbie Inn

Tel 01506 825307 | 82–84 Corbiehall, EH51 0AS
Web www.corbieinn.co.uk
Dir *M9 junction 5, A905 signed Bo'ness. Follow Bo'ness signs at next roundabout. Follow A904 signs.*

You'll find the Corbie Inn on the foreshore at Bo'ness, beside the Bo'ness and Kinneil Railway. Restored, refurbished (and in some places rebuilt) it's a cosy and very friendly little place, where you can tuck into good home-cooked bar meals and pub grub.

FIFE

BURNTISLAND

Burntisland Sands Hotel

Tel 01592 872230 | Lochies Road, KY3 9JX
Web www.burntislandsands.co.uk
Dir *Towards Kirkcaldy, Burntisland on A921. Hotel on right before Kinghorn.*

Once a highly regarded girls' boarding school, this small hotel stands only 50 yards from an award-winning sandy beach. Visitors can expect reasonably priced meals, available throughout the day, including internationally themed evenings. There is a patio garden and children can play with the rabbits.

CULROSS

Red Lion Inn

Tel 01383 881280 | Low Causeway, KY12 8HN
Web www.redlionculross.co.uk
Dir *From A985 between Crombie and Kincardine follow Culross signs. Pub in village centre.*

Culross is the most complete example in Scotland of a 17th- and 18th-century burgh, its old, whitewashed buildings and cobbled streets a fascinating time-warp. The step-gabled Red Lion's ceilings were painted by Stirling artist Douglas Cadoo and depict scenes from *Kidnapped* by Robert Louis Stevenson. If you're planning on a meal, haggis, whisky and cream creggans make a good starter; these could be followed by rotisserie chicken in barbecue sauce. A sorbet or a crumble might well tick the dessert box.

Open all day, all week Free House 8 menus notice required

ELIE

The Ship Inn ★★★★ INN

PICK OF THE PUBS

Tel 01333 330246 | The Toft, KY9 1DT
Web www.shipinn.scot
Dir *A915 and A917 to Elie. From High Street follow signs to Watersport Centre and The Toft.*

Overlooking Elie Bay, the beer garden of this coastal pub is on the beach itself and there is an outside bar and barbecue throughout the summer. With its bay views, the light and airy upstairs restaurant has a seaside feel and a gallery space showcasing Scottish artists. In winter, grab a sofa or armchair next to the open fire, perhaps with a glass of Crail Ale in hand. Scottish produce, particularly local shellfish and seafood, drives the menu. Typical dishes include grilled Queenie scallops with lemon pollen; and Scottish lamb hotpot, and chop, braised red cabbage, roast baby carrots. Time a visit between May and September and you might well see the pub's cricket team play a match on the beach, all depending on the tide of course.

Open all day, all week Closed 25 Dec Free House 12 from £9.50 portions/menu Wi-fi notice required

ST ANDREWS

Hams Hame Pub & Grill

Tel 01334 474371 | The Old Course Hotel, Golf Resort & Spa, KY16 9SP
Web www.oldcoursehotel.co.uk
Dir *M90 junction 8, A91 to St Andrews.*

Part of a famous complex, this pub is over the road from the Old Course's 18th green. This being one of the 19th holes in the hotel, your fellow diner or drinker might well be a golfing legend, sharing your enjoyment of some of Scotland's best breweries and menus showcasing its finest produce. Freshly landed North Sea fish and seafood is a given, other dishes include mac and cheese; build your own gourmet burger; gammon steak; Highland beef rib-eye; and goats' cheese and beetroot salad.

Open all day, all week Free House portions/menu Wi-fi notice required

The Jigger Inn PICK OF THE PUBS

Tel 01334 474371 | The Old Course Hotel, Golf Resort & Spa, KY16 9SP
Web www.oldcoursehotel.co.uk
Dir *M90 junction 8, A91 to St Andrews.*

Golfing history is an all-embracing experience at this former stationmaster's lodge on the now long-disused railway line from St Andrews to Leuchars. It's in the grounds of the Old Course Hotel, Golf Resort & Spa, which sits alongside the world-famous Old Course Golf Course of St Andrews. Belhaven brewery supplies the appropriately named Jigger Ale, brewed exclusively for both the pub and its sister golfing resort in Wisconsin, USA. Available all day is seafood landed in nearby fishing villages, carefully selected pork, lamb, beef, game and poultry reared by award-winning Scottish producers, and seasonal fruit and vegetables from local farms. Main courses include fish and chips; Cullen skink; rib-eye steak with grilled Portobello mushrooms and peppercorn sauce; and the Jigger Inn burger with Mull cheese, Ayrshire bacon and fries.

Open all day, all week 11–11 (Sun 12–11) Free House 8 P

GLASGOW

GLASGOW

Bon Accord

Tel 0141 248 4427 | 153 North Street, G3 7DA
Web www.bonaccordpub.com
Dir *M8 junction 19 merge onto A804 (North Street) signed Charing Cross.*

Visitors from all over the world come to the 'Bon', Paul McDonagh and son Thomas's acclaimed alehouse and malt whisky bar to sample some of the annual tally of a 1,000-plus different beers, over 40 ciders, or the 350-strong malts collection.

The Pot Still

Tel 0141 333 0980 | 154 Hope Street, G2 2TH
Web www.thepotstill.co.uk
Dir *Phone for detailed directions.*

Finding a pub in Glasgow that serves whisky is hardly unusual, but not many boast over seven hundred on their shelves. Add to this a range of Scottish and German ales which you can enjoy with one of Pot Stills "proper pies" and it's a must for any whisky lover. The team are passionate about their whiskies and gain satisfaction from matching customers to the appropriate dram from the extensive selection. It's not just Scottish whisky, either, they provide an array of the spirit from around the world. AA Pub of the Year for Scotland 2018–19.

Stravaigin PICK OF THE PUBS

Tel **0141 334 2665 | 26–30 Gibson Street, G12 8NX**
Web **www.stravaigin.com**
Dir ***From A804 into Woodlands Road. At mini-roundabout take 2nd exit into Eldon Street. Over river, inn on right.***

In a busy street near the university, this popular place has an extended street-level café bar and basement restaurant. It offers a long list of wines by the glass and real ales such as Argyll-brewed Fyne Chip 71. Expect innovative fusion food cooked from top-quality, seasonal Scottish ingredients. Typically available on the carte are smoked haddock beignet or Stravaign's own haggis, both meat and vegetarian versions; roast wood pigeon or seared sea trout. They churn their own ice creams and sorbets.

Open all day, all week Closed 25 Dec, 1 Jan Free House 27 portions/menu Wi-fi

Ubiquitous Chip

PICK OF THE PUBS

Tel **0141 334 5007 | 12 Ashton Lane, G12 8SJ**
Web **www.ubiquitouschip.co.uk**
Dir ***In West End of Glasgow, off Byres Road. Beside Hillhead subway station.***

From opening day in 1971, the Chip has drawn inspiration from regional Scottish dishes, with people's aunties, grannies and even folklore a constant source of inspiration. The main dining area opens into a vine-covered courtyard, while upstairs is the brasserie-style restaurant with its fine-dining menu. Lighter choices are offered in the various bars, mezzanine and roof terrace. There are several drinking areas – the traditional Big Pub, serving real ales, nearly 30 wines by the glass and more than 150 malt whiskies, and the Corner Bar which serves cocktails across a granite slab reclaimed from a mortuary; The Wee Pub (the smallest in Scotland) is a great place to chat with a dram.

Open all day, all week 11am–1am Closed 25 Dec, 1 Jan Free House 29 portions/menu Wi-fi *notice required*

WEST on the Green PICK OF THE PUBS

Tel **0141 550 0135 | Templeton Building, Glasgow Green, G40 1AW**
Web **www.westbeer.com**
Dir ***Phone for detailed directions.***

'Glaswegian heart, German head' is the strapline this buzzy brewpub and restaurant uses as it's the only UK brewery producing beers in accordance with Germany's Purity Law of 1516, which means no additives, colourings or preservatives. It occupies the old Winding House of a former carpet factory, modelled by its Victorian architect on the Doge's Palace in Venice. Look down into the brewhouse from the beer hall and watch the brewers making artisanal lagers and wheat beers, including GPA, St Mungo, Dunkel and Hefeweizen. Brewery tours are conducted on selected days of the week. The all-day menu has a German flavour too, offering reibeküchen; spätzle; currywurst; and jägerschnitzel; you can also choose from grills, burgers and other British pub grub. October's Fridays are Oktoberfest beer festival days.

Open all day, all week Closed 25–26 Dec, 1–2 Jan Free House 11 from £6.50 portions/menu Wi-fi *notice required*

HIGHLAND

ACHILTIBUIE

Summer Isles Hotel & Bar

PICK OF THE PUBS

Tel **01854 622282 | IV26 2YG**
Web **www.summerisleshotel.com**
Dir ***Take A835 north from Ullapool for 10 miles, Achiltibuie signed on left, 15 miles to village. Hotel 1 mile on left.***

With its wonderful views of Badentarbat Bay and the Summer Isles, this highly praised hotel is a comforting presence in a truly beautiful place. Real ales come from the An Teallach brewery on a croft a few miles to the south at Dundonnell, and the seafood couldn't be fresher – scallops and lobster come from the bay itself. The bar serves coffee, snacks, lunch, afternoon tea and evening meals, and there's formal dining as well.

CAWDOR

Cawdor Tavern

Tel 01667 404777 | The Lane, IV12 5XP
Web www.cawdortavern.co.uk
Dir *Between Inverness and Nairn, take A96 onto B9006, follow Cawdor Castle signs. Tavern in village centre.*

Scottish innkeeping at its best

PICK OF THE PUBS

The Tavern is tucked away in the heart of Cawdor's pretty conservation village; nearby is the castle where Macbeth held court. Pretty, wooded countryside slides away from the pub, offering umpteen opportunities for rambles and challenging cycle routes. Exercise over, repair to this homely hostelry to enjoy the welcoming mix of fine Scottish food and island microbrewery ales that makes the pub a destination in its own right. There's an almost baronial feel to the bars, created from the Cawdor Estate's joinery workshop in the 1960s. The lounge bar's wonderful panelling came from Cawdor Castle's dining room as a gift from a former laird; log fires and stoves add winter warmth, as does the impressive choice of Orkney Brewery beers and Highland and Island malts. An accomplished menu balances meat, fish, game and vegetarian options, prepared in a modern Scottish style with first class Scottish produce. Settle in the delightful restaurant beneath wrought iron Jacobean chandeliers – alternatively, alfresco drinking and dining is possible on the colourful patio area at the front of the Tavern during the warmer summer months.

Open all day, all week 11–11 (Sat 11am–midnight Sun 12.30–11) Closed 25 Dec, 1 Jan *Free House* 9 *portions/menu* *notice required*

APPLECROSS

Applecross Inn

Tel **01520 744262 | IV54 8LR**
Web **www.applecrossinn.co.uk**
Dir ***From A87 onto A890 signed Lochcarron. Left onto A896, through Lochcarron. Two alternatives routes to Applecross signed in Tornapress.***

Dating from the early 1800s, this former hotel has views across the sea towards the Isles of Raasay and Skye, and it's a magnificent setting to enjoy one of the 50 malt whiskies on offer. Scottish produce and seafood from local fishermen drive the menu. Whole local prawns in garlic butter might precede Applecross Bay dressed crab salad or Scottish lamb rump with wild mushrooms and pancetta lardons. The inn is now home to the Applecross Brewing Company, which offers its ales on tap at the bar.

Open all day, all week *Free House* *from £12* *portions/menu* Wi-fi *notice required*

CAWDOR

Cawdor Tavern – see opposite

FORT WILLIAM

Moorings Hotel ★★★★ HOTEL

Tel **01397 772797 | Banavie, PH33 7LY**
Web **www.moorings-fortwilliam.co.uk**
Dir ***From A82 in Fort William follow signs for Mallaig, left onto A830 for 1 mile. Cross canal bridge, 1st right signed Banavie.***

The historic Caledonian Canal and Neptune's Staircase, the famous flight of eight locks, runs right beside this modern hotel and bistro. On clear days it has panoramic views towards Ben Nevis, best savoured from the Upper Deck lounge bar and the bedrooms. Food, served in the lounge bar and the Moorings Café and bistro features local fish and seafood, with other choices such as steak and ale pie, and rib-eye of Highland beef. There is access to the canal towpath from the gardens.

Open all day, all week Closed 24–26 Dec *Free House* *8* *from £9.95* *portions/menu* Wi-fi *notice required*

GAIRLOCH

The Old Inn PICK OF THE PUBS

Tel **01445 712006 | IV21 2BD**
Web **www.theoldinn.net**
Dir ***Just off A832, near harbour at south end of village.***

Specialising in freshly landed local seafood, Highland game, Scottish real ales and live folk music, The Old Inn is set below the majestic Torridon Mountains, just inland from Gairloch's little harbour. Several beers are brewed on site, and some from other Scottish micros also appear. Specialising in local seafood and game, the pub also smokes its own meats, fish and cheese, and bread is baked in-house. Start with a seafood chowder, followed by haggis stack, neeps, potatoes, Drambuie cream and oatcakes; or the steak and ale hotpot. Specials might well include seafood risotto; langoustine and calamari platter; venison steak; and home-made game casserole. There are always vegetarian and vegan dishes available and special dietary requirements can be catered for.

Open all day, all week 12–12 Closed Nov to Feb *Free House* *from £12.95* *portions/menu* Wi-fi *notice required*

GLENCOE

Clachaig Inn

Tel **01855 811252 | PH49 4HX**
Web **clachaig.com**
Dir ***Follow Glencoe signs from A82. Inn 3 miles south of village.***

In the heart of Glencoe, against a backdrop of spectacular mountains, this famous Highland inn has welcomed climbers, hill-walkers, skiers, kayakers and intrepid travellers for over 300 years. Real ales, over 300 malt whiskies, and good food are served in all three bars.

GLENUIG

Glenuig Inn

Tel **01687 470219** | **PH38 4NG**
Web **www.glenuig.com**
Dir ***From Fort William on A830 towards Mallaig through Glen Finnan. Left onto A861, 8 miles to Glenuig Bay.***

Renowned for its green credentials – running on 100% renewable energy, with a gold award from the Green Tourism Business Scheme – Glenuig Inn is also a great base for exploring the stunning scenery of Scotland's west coast, with a fabulous setting right by the beach on the Sound of Arisaig. It's open all year, and has a locally sourced Scottish seasonal menu including gluten free and vegetarian dishes, plus real ales and organic wines. It is dog-friendly throughout.

Open all day, all week 12–9 Free House 9 portions/menu Wi-fi

INVERGARRY

The Invergarry Hotel

Tel **01809 501206** | **PH35 4HJ**
Web **www.invergarryhotel.co.uk**
Dir ***At junction of A82 and A87.***

A real Highland atmosphere pervades this roadside inn set in glorious mountain scenery between Fort William and Fort Augustus. Relax by the crackling log fire with a wee dram or a pint of Belhaven IPA, then tuck into a good meal. Perhaps try baked filo parcel stuffed with haggis, bashit neeps, roasted shallot with malt whisky and thyme mayonnaise to start; followed by a 10oz rib-eye Scottish beefsteak with hand-cut chips. There are, of course, excellent walks from the front door. Please note, booking is required for dinner.

Open all day, all week Free House portions/menu Wi-fi

KYLESKU

Kylesku Hotel PICK OF THE PUBS

Tel **01971 502231** | **IV27 4HW**
Web **www.kyleskuhotel.co.uk**
Dir ***A835, A837 and A894 to Kylesku. Hotel at end of road at Old Ferry Pier.***

This 17th-century coaching inn sits at the centre of the North West Highlands Global Geopark. Surrounded by lochs, mountains and wild coast, it's a glorious location. Views from the bar and restaurant are truly memorable – you may catch sight of seals, dolphins, otters, eagles and terns. The fishing boats moor at the old ferry slipway to land the creel-caught seafood that forms the backbone of the daily-changing menu. So settle down with a pint of organic Black Isle beer, and ponder your choice of the morning's catch, perhaps starting with seared hand-dived king scallops; or home-cured salmon gravad lax with pickled cucumber and oaties. Next, you could go for Glendhu langoustines, either hot or cold. Gluten-free and vegetarian menus also available.

Open all day, all week Closed Dec to Jan Free House 25 from £14.95 portions/menu Wi-fi

ROSETTES AND STARS

Stay the night

Many of the pubs in this guide have been inspected and rated for their hotel or guest accommodation by the AA.

To find out more about the accommodation ratings see pages 10–11.

Eat well

Rosette awards appear where the restaurant at the pub has been inspected for the quality of their cuisine.

To find out more about the Rosette award scheme see pages 12-13.

PLOCKTON

The Plockton Hotel

Tel 01599 544274 | Harbour Street, IV52 8TN
Web www.plocktonhotel.co.uk
Dir *A87 towards Kyle of Lochalsh. At Balmacara follow Plockton signs, 7 miles.*

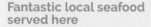

Fantastic local seafood served here

With the mountains on one side and the deep blue waters of Loch Carron on the other, this lovely village is well known for its whitewashed cottages and, of all things, palm trees. Dating from 1827, this original black fronted building is thought to have been a ships' chandlery before it was converted to serve as the village inn. Run by Alan and Mags Pearson, the couple have inherited a successful legacy from Alan's parents who were in charge for two decades. The hotel specialises in seafood – including freshly landed fish and locally caught langoustines (mid afternoon you can watch the catch being landed) – supplemented by Highland steaks and locally reared beef. Lunchtime features light bites and toasted paninis, as well as a good range of hot dishes. Daily specials, written up on the blackboard, add to the tempting choices. There are four Scottish real ales on tap, and a fine range of malts is available to round off that perfect Highland day, perhaps accompanied by one of the 'basket' meals served every evening from 9pm to 10pm – try the breaded scampi tails.

Open all day, all week 11am–midnight (Sun 12–11) Closed 25 Dec, 1 Jan Free House from £9.50 portions/menu

LEWISTON

The Loch Ness Inn

Tel **01456 450991 | IV63 6UW**
Web **www.staylochness.co.uk**
Dir ***Phone for detailed directions.***

Close to the waymarked Great Glen Way, this place is a hive of activity and there's always an event of some kind going on. The modern menu is based on top Scottish ingredients – Scottish seafood chowder or haggis and clapshot in an oatcake bowl, followed by Black Isle rib-eye steak; or east coast haddock. All this will build an appetite for a loch-side ramble to famous Urquhart Castle. Unusually, a range of Scottish distilled gins is available at the bar.

Open all day, all week Closed 25 Dec Free House 12 portions/menu notice required

LOCHINVER

The Caberfeidh

Tel **01571 844321 | Main Street, IV27 4JY**
Web **www.thecaberfeidh.co.uk**
Dir ***A837 to Lochinver. Pub on right.***

Meaning 'stag's antlers' in Gaelic, The Caberfeidh is run by experienced chef-hoteliers Colin Craig and Lesley Cornfield. Its waterfront location is reflected in the menus, which display a strong sense of place with an emphasis on seasonal produce including wild game and locally caught fish and shellfish. Start, perhaps, with Lochinver whole creel-caught langoustines moving on to Highland sirloin steak or wild Highland venison moussaka. As opening times vary throughout the year, please check the exact times with the pub.

Open times vary throughout the year Closed Mon in winter Free House 14 from £14.50 portions notice required

NORTH BALLACHULISH

Old Ferry Bar at Loch Leven Hotel **PICK OF THE PUBS**

Tel **01855 821236 | Old Ferry Road, PH33 6SA**
Web **www.lochlevenhotel.co.uk**
Dir ***Off A82, north of Ballachulish Bridge.***

A gin distillery and 'Gin School' can be found in the grounds of this hotel pub, and the bar stocks some of their own spirits, distilled just 10 metres away. Enjoy a craft G&T or pint of River Leven real ale on the sundeck with one of the best views from a pub anywhere in Britain, or on chillier days sit beside the open fire. The well-stocked bar serves over 60 malt whiskies, 50 gins, a wide selection of beers and boasts a carefully selected cocktail list. The location is extraordinary, near the foot of Glencoe and with Munro peaks rising above azure sea lochs.

Open all day, all week 12–11 (Thu to Sat 12–12 Sun 12.30–11) Free House 8 from £11.95 menus notice required

PLOCKTON

The Plockton Hotel – see page 531

Plockton Inn & Seafood Restaurant

PICK OF THE PUBS

Tel **01599 544222 | Innes Street, IV52 8TW**
Web **www.plocktoninn.co.uk**
Dir ***A87 towards Kyle of Lochalsh. At Balmacara follow Plockton signs, 7 miles.***

Owned and run by Mary Gollan, her brother Kenny and his partner Susan Trowbridge. The Gollans were born and bred in the village and the pub was originally built by their great-grandfather. In the bar you'll find winter fires, Plockton real ales from the village brewery, and a selection of over 50 malt whiskies. A meal in the reasonably formal Dining Room or more relaxed Lounge Bar is a must, with a wealth of freshly caught local fish and shellfish, West Highland beef, lamb, game and home-made vegetarian dishes on the menu, plus daily specials. The public bar is alive on Tuesdays and Thursdays with music from local musicians.

Open all day, all week Free House portions/menu notice required

SHIELDAIG

Shieldaig Bar & Coastal Kitchen PICK OF THE PUBS

Tel 01520 755251 | IV54 8XN
Web www.tighaneilean.co.uk
Dir *Exit A896.*

Remote enough to make its Inverness postcode look totally inappropriate, the Shieldaig Bar & Coastal Kitchen is part of the famous Tigh an Eilean (House of the Island) Hotel. Here, the majestic Torridon Mountains meet the western seas and Upper Loch Torridon is just round the corner. From a croft at the magical-sounding Little Loch Broom, the An Teallach Brewery supplies real ales to the traditional bar, where live music and ceilidhs add a weekend buzz.

TORRIDON

The Torridon Inn PICK OF THE PUBS

Tel 01445 791242 | IV22 2EY
Web www.thetorridon.com/inn
Dir *From Inverness take A9 north, then follow signs to Ullapool. Take A835 then A832. In Kinlochewe take A896 to Annat. Pub 200 yards on right after village.*

The waters of Loch Torridon and the striking mountains on the other side are neighbours to this bustling inn. It makes it a convenient base to walk, mountaineer, kayak or rock climb, but the cosy comfortable atmosphere and good home-cooked food very much appeal to the less active too. Painstakingly converted from old farm buildings, a stable block and buttery, the inn has a good range of Highlands and Islands beer on tap, often from Skye and An Teallach breweries. A cosy interior with wood fires and bright decor as well as an airy conservatory-diner is a restful place to consider a fine Scottish menu, much of it from the west coast area. Venison burgers and local fish and chips are always popular. There's a specials board and seafood is a speciality.

Open all day, all week Closed Jan Free House portions/menu Wi-fi P notice required

INVERCLYDE

INVERKIP

The Inverkip ★★★ INN

Tel 01475 521478 | Main Street, PA16 0AS
Web www.inverkip.co.uk
Dir *Just off A78, near Inverkip Marina.*

Run by the Hardy family for over 30 years, The Inverkip is a smart building on the main street of a small farming community. Settle down with a sharing board of local charcuterie, or maybe a bowl of Shetland mussels, and then enjoy pork belly with creamy mash, tatties and apple purée, or Ayrshire ham hock macaroni and cheese. There's a fine Scottish cheeseboard or, if you prefer, a dessert such as bramble and apple toasted oatmeal crumble. Vegetarian and gluten-free menus are also available.

Open all day, all week Closed 25 Dec, 1 Jan Free House 9 portions/menu Wi-fi P

NORTH LANARKSHIRE

CUMBERNAULD

Castlecary House Hotel

Tel 01324 840233 | Castlecary Road, G68 0HD
Web castlecaryhotel.com
Dir *A80 onto B816 between Glasgow and Stirling. 7 miles from Falkirk, 9 miles from Stirling.*

Castlecary House Hotel is located close to the historic Antonine Wall and the Forth and Clyde Canal. Meals plough a traditional furrow but more formal fare is available in Camerons Restaurant, where high tea is also served on Sundays. Live music every Saturday evening.

EAST LOTHIAN

GULLANE

The Bonnie Badger

★★★★★ RESTAURANT WITH ROOMS

Tel **01620 621111 | Main Street, EH31 2AB**
Web **bonniebadger.com**
Dir ***Exit A1 towards North Berwick at Bankton junction onto A198. Continue through Longniddry and Aberlady. On left in Main Street.***

Having reopened in December 2018 after extensive renovations, The Bonnie Badger is an extremely stylish and charming hotel, restaurant and bar. The food is a 'modern take on pub classics' inspired by Tom Kitchin's passion for the very best quality local produce. Typical dishes from the à la carte are starters of pumpkin soup and crowdie cheese ravioli; and home-cured salmon and rye bread, followed by steak pie and bone marrow; hake, shellfish and lemon; or spelt and lentil burger with chips. For pudding, how about treacle tart and clotted cream,; or meringue, sea buckthorn and yogurt?

Open all day, all week Free House 38 from £12.50 portions/menu notice required

The Old Clubhouse

Tel **01620 842008 | East Links Road, EH31 2AF**
Dir ***A198 into Gullane, 3rd right into East Links Road, pass church, on left.***

Established in 1890 as the home of Gullane Golf Club, this building has had a chequered past, but since the Campanile family took over 25 years ago it hasn't looked back. Roaring winter fires and walls crammed with golfing memorabilia make a good first impression, and the menu delivers a list of international favourites including pork katsu curry; haggis, neeps and tatties; posh mac and cheese; and quinoa veggie burger. For dessert, maybe banoffee pie.

Open all day, all week Closed 25 Dec, 1 Jan Free House 9 portions/menu notice required

LONGNIDDRY

The Longniddry Inn

Tel **01875 852401 | Main Street, EH32 0NF**
Web **www.longniddryinn.com**
Dir ***On A198 (Main Street), near rail station.***

This combination of a former blacksmith's forge and four cottages on Longniddry's Main Street continues to be a popular spot. Held in high esteem locally for friendly service and good food, it offers an extensive menu featuring the likes of roast chicken platter; pan-fried lamb's liver, crispy bacon, mash, vegetables and onion gravy; Mexican enchiladas; spaghetti carbonara; and haddock mornay. In warmer weather why not take your pint of Belhaven Best, glass of wine or freshly ground coffee outside.

Open all day, all week Closed 26 Dec, 1 Jan Punch Taverns portions/menu

WEST LOTHIAN

LINLITHGOW

Champany Inn – The Chop and Ale House

PICK OF THE PUBS

Tel **01506 834532 | Champany, EH49 7LU**
Web **www.champany.com**
Dir ***2 miles north-east of Linlithgow at junction of A904 and A803.***

Spread across a collection of buildings, some dating from the 16th century, Champany Corner is within striking distance of Edinburgh. Have a glass of Thistly Cross farmhouse cider from Dunbar, and take in the menu. Entirely separate from the restaurant in a former bar is the Chop and Ale House, where starters include smoked salmon rillettes; and home-smoked chorizo with apricot and mango chutney. Although the inn is big on Aberdeen Angus steaks and burgers, there's plenty more choice, including best-end-of-neck lamb chops; haddock in home-made batter; and charcoal-grilled peri-peri chicken. For pudding, hot malted waffles are served with maple syrup and whipped cream.

Open all week 12–2 6.30–10 (Fri to Sun 12–10) Closed 25–26 Dec, 1 Jan Free House 8 portions/menu

MEIKLEOUR

Meikleour Arms ★★★★ INN

Tel 01250 883206 | PH2 6EB
Web www.meikleourarms.co.uk
Dir *From A93 north of Perth, approximately 12 miles take A984 signed Caputh and Dunkeld to Meikleour.*

Country pub with stylish accommodation

Built in 1820 as a stopover for mail coaches, later becoming a fishing lodge, it is owned and run by Meikleour Estate, one of the oldest in east Scotland, which farms, manages forests and offers salmon fishing on the Tay and Isla. In 2017, it underwent a complete renovation and now has luxury accommodation. The inn's own Lure of Meikleour real ale inhabits the bar, as does an extensive wine list; with one of the pub's owners coming from Bordeaux expect some good clarets, as well as wines from off-the-beaten-track vineyards elsewhere. Eat in the traditional flagstone-floored bar, the woodland-themed stone barn, the more intimate private dining room, or in the garden. The restaurant serves country food, including venison from estate woods, beef from Aberdeenshire, white fish from the east coast, mussels from Shetland and rod-caught trout from local lochs. All homemade are haggis with fondant neeps and tatties; crispy Saddleback pork belly salad; Shetland moules frites; steak and ale pie; and kedgeree with smoked haddock, cod and quail eggs. For dessert, orange crème brûlée, or poached spiced pear with glazed vanilla rice pudding. Dogs are welcome in dedicated areas of the restaurant, in some of the bedrooms and all four guest cottages.

Open all day, all week 11–11 *Free House* 12 *from £12.95* *menus*

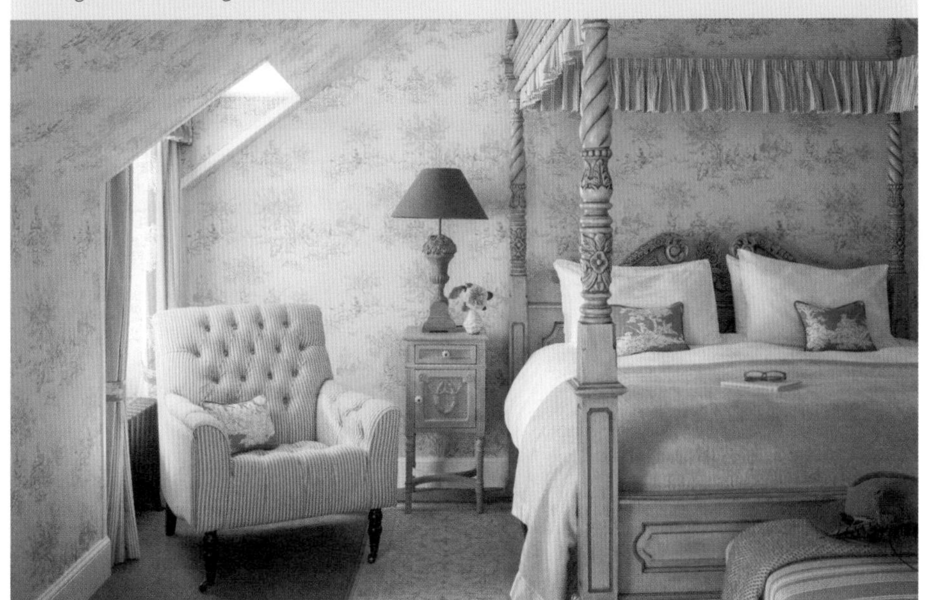

The Four Marys

Tel **01506 842171 | 65–67 High Street, EH49 7ED**
Web **www.thefourmarys.co.uk**
Dir ***M9 junction 3 or junction 4, A803 to Linlithgow. Pub in town centre.***

This eye-catching building at the heart of Linlithgow has only been a pub since 1981, but its pedigree stretches back a further 500 years to when royalty lived at the nearby palace. The eponymous Marys were ladies-in-waiting to Linlithgow-born Mary, Queen of Scots. Low ceilings, striking dressed-stone walls, and period and antique furnishings give the pub a real sense of atmosphere and history. The real ales offered are frequently rotated, and hearty pub grub includes steak and Belhaven ale pie, a selection of burgers, and fish and chips.

Open all day, all week Belhaven/Greene King 17 portions/menu notice required

MIDLOTHIAN

DALKEITH

The Sun Inn PICK OF THE PUBS

Tel **0131 663 2456 | Lothian Bridge, EH22 4TR**
Web **thesuninnedinburgh.co.uk**
Dir ***On A7 towards Galashiels, opposite Newbattle Viaduct.***

This family-run former coaching inn is an expert blend of old and new. The fireplace, oak beams and exposed stone walls are original, while the fine wooden floor owes much to the 21st century. Food in the more formal restaurant is modern British, offering pub classics with a strong Scottish accent. Noteworthy dishes include braised daube of Perthshire venison, horseradish and chive mash, red wine cabbage and roast quince; grilled John Dory, crab and samphire risotto, roasted salsify and brown shrimp butter sauce; and 'Sun Inn pig on a plate', featuring pork fillet wrapped in Parma ham, sausage roll, crisp black pudding, creamed mash and apple sauce.

Open all day, all week Closed 26 Dec, 1 Jan Free House 19 portions/menu notice required

ROSLIN

The Original Rosslyn Inn

Tel **0131 440 2384 | 2–4 Main Street, EH25 9LE**
Web **www.theoriginalrosslyninn.co.uk**
Dir ***From City of Edinburgh bypass exit at Straiton onto A701 signed Peebles and City Centre. At 2nd roundabout left onto B7006 signed Roslin. At crossroads in Roslin, inn on corner on left.***

Just eight miles from central Edinburgh and a short walk from Rosslyn Chapel, this family-run village inn has been in the Harris family for over 40 years. Robert Burns stayed here in 1787 and wrote a two verse poem for the landlady about his visit.

MORAY

FORRES

The Old Mill Inn

Tel **01309 641605 | Brodie, IV36 2TD**
Web **www.oldmillinnspeyside.co.uk**
Dir ***Between Nairn and Forres on A96.***

Situated on the Scottish Riviera, officially recorded as one of the sunniest and driest places in the UK, this former watermill has acquired windows, panelling and a beautiful door from a demolished stately home across the Moray Firth. There's an ever-changing selection of Scottish real ales.

PERTH & KINROSS

KILLIECRANKIE

Killiecrankie House Hotel

★★★ SMALL HOTEL PICK OF THE PUBS

Tel **01796 473220 | PH16 5LG**
Web **www.killiecrankiehotel.co.uk**
Dir ***Take B8079 north from Pitlochry. Hotel in 3 miles.***

This white-painted Victorian hotel stands at the Pass of Killiecrankie, the gateway to The Highlands. This magnificent gorge is famed for the battle in 1689, when the Jacobites routed the forces of King William III; today it is a stronghold for red squirrels and a renowned birdwatching area. There are walks beside rivers and lochs, and countless hill walks, including on the majestic Ben Vrackie that rises behind the hotel. Standing in a four-acre estate, the hotel retains plenty of character, blended successfully with modern comforts.

The cosy, panelled bar is a popular haunt, while the snug sitting room opens on to a small patio. Arm yourself with a Scottish beer such as Blessed Thistle as you study a menu that makes the most of Scotland's diverse produce.

Open all day, all week Closed 3 Jan to 19 Mar Free House 11 from £12 portions/menu

MEIKLEOUR

Meikleour Arms – see page 535

PITLOCHRY

Moulin Hotel PICK OF THE PUBS

Tel **01796 472196** | **11–13 Kirkmichael Road, Moulin, PH16 5EH**
Web **www.moulinhotel.co.uk**
Dir ***From A9 at Pitlochry take A924. Moulin 0.75 mile.***

Dating from 1695, this welcoming inn, located on an old drovers' road at the foot of Ben Vrackie, is a popular base for walking and touring. Locals are drawn to the bar for the excellent home-brewed beers, with Moulin Ale of Atholl, Braveheart and Light, and Belhaven Best served on hand pump. The interior boasts beautiful stone walls and lots of cosy niches, with blazing log fires in winter; while the courtyard garden is lovely in summer. Menus offer the opportunity to try something local such as mince and tatties; or Vrackie Grostel (sautéed potatoes with smoked bacon lightly herbed and topped with a fried egg). A specials board broadens the choice further. 25 wines by the glass and more than 30 malt whiskies are available.

Open all day, all week 12–11 (Fri to Sat 12–11.45 Sun 12–11) Free House 25 from £10.95 portions/menu notice required

SCOTTISH BORDERS

ALLANTON

Allanton Inn

Tel **01890 818260** | **TD11 3JZ**
Web **www.allantoninn.co.uk**
Dir ***From A1 at Berwick take A6105 for Chirnside (5 miles). At Chirnside Inn take Coldstream Road for 1 mile to Allanton.***

It's the brightly coloured soft furnishings, local artwork, fresh flowers and open log fire that catch the eye in this 18th-century coaching inn. Seeking attention too are the carefully chosen, mostly Scottish, real ales and the weekly nominated gin from the 40-plus in stock. To sample the fish caught off Eyemouth, such as smoked mackerel fillet with rhubarb compôte, you could opt for the seafood platter. Or try Berwickshire venison salami with smoked venison haunch, smoked pheasant and houmous.

Open all day, all week 12–11 Free House 10 from £11 portions/menu

JEDBURGH

The Ancrum Cross Keys

Tel **01835 830242** | **The Green, Ancrum, TD8 6XH**
Web **www.ancrumcrosskeys.com**
Dir ***From Jedburgh take A68 towards St Boswells. Left onto B6400 to Ancrum.***

The delightfully large garden bordering the idyllic Ale Water is a huge factor in the favour of this 200-year-old pub,. Others are the Front Bar which serves ales from the Scottish Borders Brewery including Foxy Blonde and Dark Horse.

KELSO

The Cobbles Freehouse & Dining PICK OF THE PUBS

Tel **01573 223548** | **7 Bowmont Street, TD5 7JH**
Web **www.thecobbleskelso.co.uk**
Dir ***A6089 from Edinburgh to Kelso, right at roundabout into Bowmont Street. Pub in 0.3 mile.***

Tucked away in a corner of the town's rather fine square stands this modernised 19th-century coaching inn. For the last few years it has taken on the role as the brewery tap for the Tempest Brewing Co. The ales are always perfectly on song in the log fire-warmed bar. The kitchen's AA Rosette was awarded for its skilfully prepared mix of cuisines – British pub classics, Pacific Rim and modern European.

Open all day, all week 11.30–11 Closed 25 Dec Free House 9 portions/menu notice required

KIRK YETHOLM

The Border Hotel

Tel **01573 420237 | The Green, TD5 8PQ**
Web **www.borderhotel.co.uk**
Dir ***From A698 in Kelso take B6352 for 7 miles to Kirk Yetholm.***

On the village green, at the northern end of the Pennine Way, this part-thatched former coaching inn dates from 1750. The menu features local game and meats, worth considering accompanied by a Hadrian Border Brewery beer. Try a home-made burger, or perhaps gammon steak with honey-sautéed pineapple chunks; or breaded Whitby scampi with salad and chips. The stone-flagged bar has a log fire, and the conservatory dining room overlooks the patio and garden.

Open all day, all week Closed 25–26 Dec Free House portions/menu Wi-fi notice required

LILLIESLEAF

The Plough Inn, Pub & Restaurant

Tel **01835 870220 | 15 Main Street, TD6 9JD**
Web **www.theploughinnlilliesleaf.co.uk**
Dir ***From A7 north of Hawick, turn left onto B6400 signed Lilliesleaf.***

The centre of village life for over 100 years, this refurbished pub reopened in 2016 with a new restaurant and is thriving once more. In a great location for exploring the Scottish Borders, it's cosy in the winter, with log fires, and a garden for the warmer weather. Dogs are welcome in the bar, and the restaurant has a pleasantly rustic feel. The menu changes monthly and uses local produce in creatively prepared dishes.

Open all year Wed to Thu 5–10 (Fri to Sat 5–12 or 1am Sun 12–10) Closed Mon and Tue Free House 10 portions Wi-fi notice required

MELROSE

Burts Hotel PICK OF THE PUBS

Tel **01896 822285 | Market Square, TD6 9PL**
Web **www.burtshotel.co.uk**
Dir ***From A68 north of St Boswells take A6091 towards Melrose, approximately 2 miles right signed Melrose and B6374, follow to Market Square.***

The Henderson family has owned this 18th-century hotel for around four decades. Overlooking the market square, its age dictates listed-building status, which restoration, extension and upgrades have all respected in the Hendersons' quest for a modern hotel. After a day out, settle in with one of the 90 single malts, or a pint of Caledonian Deuchars IPA. A meal in the restaurant might begin with herb-crusted hen's egg, confit tomato, spinach and Isle of Mull cheese sauce, followed by harissa-marinated rump of Borders lamb, with lightly spiced couscous, yogurt, and courgette Charlotte. Light lunch specials may list breaded fishcakes with sweet chilli and lime sauce.

Open all week 12–2.30 5–11 Free House 10 portions/menu Wi-fi

ST BOSWELLS

Buccleuch Arms

Tel **01835 822243 | The Green, TD6 0EW**
Web **www.buccleucharms.com**
Dir ***On A68, 10 miles north of Jedburgh. Inn on village green.***

This charming old coaching inn dating from 1836 overlooks the village green. An attractive brick and pink stone building, it houses a large and comfortable lounge warmed, when needed, by a log fire, while for warmer days there's an immaculate garden. Extensive menus in both the Blue Coo Bistrot and the rustic Huntsman Bar specialise in beef, especially Aberdeen Angus steaks and traditional prime Scotch rib-eyes and sirloins; half a dozen beef-based 'coo' burgers; monkfish, crab tian and bisque; Mexican pozole and butternut squash and feta tortelloni. Roasted duck breast, breaded scampi and salads, pulled pork tacos, risottos and pastas broaden the choice and check the blackboard for specials.

Open all day, all week 12–11 Closed 25 Dec Free House 20 from £12 portions/menu notice required

SWINTON

The Wheatsheaf at Swinton

PICK OF THE PUBS

Tel **01890 860257 | Main Street, TD11 3JJ**
Web **www.eatdrinkstaywheatsheaf.com**
Dir ***From Edinburgh A697 onto B6461. From East Lothian A1 onto B6461.***

This welcoming place has an impressive reputation for both their beer and their food. In the bar you'll find Belhaven IPA, draught Peroni and Scottish Borders Brewery bottled beers. Plus there's a whisky map and tasting notes to study before choosing your single malt. There are two dining rooms, one overlooking the village green, and in both the menus feature home-made, locally-sourced food. Dinner might kick off with grilled langoustine, garlic and lemon butter, or chicken and black pudding terrine with spicy chutney and pickled vegetables, before moving on to roast partridge with saffron fondant potato and bramble jus; or pan-seared cod fillet with langoustine. Desserts might feature sticky toffee pudding or red fruit Pavlova.

Open all week 4–11 (Sat 12–12 Sun 12–11) Free House 18 from £14.95 portions notice required

STIRLING

CALLANDER

The Lade Inn

Tel **01877 330152 | Kilmahog, FK17 8HD**
Web **www.theladeinn.com**
Dir ***From Stirling take A84 to Callander. 1 mile north of Callander, left at Kilmahog Woollen Mills onto A821 towards Aberfoyle. Pub immediately on left.***

In the heart of the Trossachs National Park, the family-owned Lade Inn is known for its own real ales and for its 16-day beer festival from late August to mid-September. There is also an on-site shop selling bottled ales from microbreweries throughout Scotland. The home-cooked menu offers many allergen-free dishes. Typical choices are crispy battered haggis balls; Aberdeenshire pork and leek sausages; and beer-battered North Sea haddock. The garden with its three ponds and bird-feeding station appeals greatly to families.

Open all day, all week Mon to Thu 12–11 (Fri to Sat noon to 1am Sun 12.30–10.30) Free House 9 portions/menu notice required

KIPPEN

Cross Keys Hotel

Tel **01786 870293 | Main Street, FK8 3DN**
Web **www.kippencrosskeys.com**
Dir ***10 miles west of Stirling, 20 miles from Loch Lomond off A811.***

The 300-year-old Cross Keys offers seasonally changing menus and a good pint of cask ale. The pub's welcoming interior, warmed by three log fires, is perfect for resting your feet after a walk in nearby Burnside Wood, or you can sit in the garden when the weather permits. The menus feature sweet-cured herring and toasted oats; venison burger, straw fries and relish; and roasted pork belly, mustard mash, sweet red cabbage and apple sauce. Dogs are welcome in the top bar.

Open all week 12–3 5–11 (Fri 12–3 5–1am Sat noon–1am Sun 12–12) Closed 25 Dec, 1 Jan Free House 10 from £12 portions/menu notice required

The Inn at Kippen

Tel **01786 870500 | Fore Road, FK8 3DT**
Web **www.theinnatkippen.co.uk**
Dir ***From Stirling take A811 to Loch Lomond. 1st left at Kippen station roundabout, 1st right into Fore Road. Inn on left.***

The vista from this white-painted village free house is stunning, stretching across the Forth Valley to the Highlands. At the foot of the Campsie Hills, this popular inn welcomes all comers, including children and dogs. In the winter months you'll be warmed by real fires in the stylish bar, whilst summer visitors can settle in the pretty garden with a pint from Loch Lomond ales. Menus feature the best regional produce.

Open all day, all week Free House 9 from £10.95 portions/menu notice required

SCOTTISH ISLANDS

▶ COLL

ARINAGOUR

Coll Hotel PICK OF THE PUBS

Tel **01879 230334 | PA78 6SZ**
Web **www.collhotel.com**
Dir ***Ferry from Oban. Hotel at head of Arinagour Bay, 1 mile from Pier (collections by arrangement).***

The Coll Hotel is the Iisland's only inn, so come here to mingle with the locals, soak in the atmosphere, and enjoy pints of Fyne Ale and malt whiskies. Famed for its seafood, you'll find dishes such as Inverawe smoked halibut; Hebridean seafood casserole; or locally caught pan-fried scallops with hazelnut butter, roasted cherry tomatoes, spinach and sauté potatoes. Among the non-fish options, try the Argyll venison fillet.

Open all day, all week Free House from £15 portions/menu Wi-fi notice required

▶ ISLAY

PORT CHARLOTTE

The Port Charlotte Hotel

Tel **01496 850360 | Main Street, PA48 7TU**
Web **www.portcharlottehotel.co.uk**
Dir ***A846 from Port Askaig towards Bowmore. Right onto A847, through Blackrock. Take unclassified road to Port Charlotte.***

This sympathetically restored Victorian hotel is perfectly positioned on the west shore of Loch Indaal. Islay ales and whiskies make a great way to warm up before enjoying menus with a seafood focus – perhaps fillet of cod, lemon and basil risotto with pickled asparagus, or whole plaice, crushed new potatoes, baby leeks and caper noisette.

Open all day, all week Closed 24–26 Dec Free House 9 from £11.95 portions/menu Wi-fi notice required

▶ MULL

DERVAIG

The Bellachroy Hotel – see opposite

▶ ORKNEY

STROMNESS

Ferry Inn

Tel **01856 850280 | John Street, KW16 3AD**
Web **www.ferryinn.com**
Dir ***Opposite ferry terminal.***

With its prominent harbour-front location, the Ferry Inn has long enjoyed a reputation for its beer. The pub has racking for a further 10 local ales on top of the four handpulls on the bar and although these change regularly, look out for the island's own Scapa Special, Dark Island and Orkney IPA. There's an appealing menu that may include seafood chowder followed by a prime Orkney steak; or grilled hot smoked Orkney salmon.

Open all day, all week Free House from £10 portions/menu Wi-fi

▶ SKYE

CARBOST

The Old Inn and Waterfront Bunkhouse

Tel **01478 640205 | IV47 8SR**
Web **www.theoldinnskye.co.uk**
Dir ***From Skye Bridge follow A87 north. Take A863, then B8009 to inn.***

A charming, 200-year-old island cottage on the shores of Loch Harport, very popular among the walking and climbing fraternity. Bag a table on the waterside patio and savour the breathtaking views. Inside, open fires welcome winter visitors, and live Highland music is a regular feature most weekends. The menu includes daily home-cooked specials with numerous fresh fish dishes.

EDINBANE

The Edinbane Inn

Tel **01470 582414 | Old Dunvegan Road, IV51 9PW**
Web **www.edinbaneinn.co.uk**
Dir ***Off A850.***

Some original features of this 150-year-old building have been retained, especially in the stone-walled bar. Most real ales come from the Skye brewery in Portree, while the guest ale will be from the mainland.

DERVAIG (MULL)

The Bellachroy Hotel

Tel 01688 400225 | PA75 6QW
Web www.thebellachroy.co.uk
Dir *Take ferry from Oban to Craignure. A849 towards Tobermory. Left at T-junction onto B8073 to Dervaig.*

Dishes from sea and moorland

Look out for sea eagles while travelling the seven miles from Tobermory's brightly painted houses to the whitewashed cottages of Dervaig, and Mull's oldest hotel, dating from 1608. Overlooking the pretty inlet of Loch Cuin is the bar, which a sign suggests is known as the Bear Pit. The chefs here take full advantage of produce from the isle's coastal waters and surrounding moors, as shown by starters like smoked trout and smoked salmon salad; and house-smoked venison. Further options might involve crab or mackerel, for example, or maybe salt beef brisket bun with mustard mayo, gherkin, slaw and fries; or roast cauliflower korma with rice and flatbread. Bramley apple and custard millefeuille with oat crumble is a tasty dessert, Isle of Mull cheeses with oatcakes and chutney another. Children and vegetarians have dedicated menus.

Open all day, all week Closed Mon and Tue Nov to Mar Free House 12 from £13.50 portions/menu P notice required

ISLEORNSAY

Hotel Eilean Iarmain

PICK OF THE PUBS

Tel 01471 833332 | IV43 8QR
Web www.eileaniarmain.co.uk
Dir *A851, A852 right to Isleornsay harbour.*

In a magnificent coastal location towards the southern end of the Isle of Skye, where waterside tables served from the Am Praban bar overlook the Sound of Sleat to the horizon bristling with shapely peaks. Step inside to find tartan carpets and antlers in the hallway, whilst elsewhere the decor is mainly cotton and linen chintzes with traditional furniture. Bar meals are served in a relaxed atmosphere, with winter log fires, and it's the ideal place to meet the local Gaelic-speaking community; the island's native tongue is woven into ballads and songs by local musicians who regularly perform here, perhaps fortified by island beers and a considered selection of malts, some very local indeed. The menu is a mix of modern dishes and traditional favourites.

Open all day, all week 11am–11.30pm (Thu and Sat 11am–12.30am Fri 11am–1am Sun noon–11.30) Free House from £13 portions/menu Wi-fi P notice required

SOUTH UIST

LOCHBOISDALE

The Polochar Inn

Tel 01878 700215 | Polochar, HS8 5TT
Web polocharinn.com
Dir *B888 west from Lochboisdale. Hotel at end of road.*

Standing virtually alone overlooking the Sound of Eriskay and a prehistoric standing stone, this is the former change-house for the ferry to Barra. It serves Hebridean real ales and specialises in local seafood and meats. The beer garden is ideal for dolphin watching and admiring beautiful sunsets.

WALES

ISLE OF ANGLESEY

ABERFFRAW

The Crown

Tel **01407 840222 | Bodorgan Square, LL63 5BX**
Web **www.thecrownaberffraw.co.uk**
Dir ***From A4080 into village and Bodorgan Square.***

Close to the superb beaches on south-west Anglesey's rugged and spectacular coastline, the origins of this timeless inn predate the former Seion Chapel next door and it's now the last public house in the village.

BEAUMARIS

The Bull – Beaumaris

★★★★★ INN PICK OF THE PUBS

Tel **01248 810329 | Castle Street, LL58 8AP**
Web **www.bullsheadinn.co.uk**
Dir ***From Britannia Road Bridge follow A545. Inn in town centre.***

This 15th-century pub is just a stone's throw from the gates of Beaumaris' medieval castle. The bar transports drinkers back to Dickensian times with settles and antique furnishings. The Coach Restaurant in the former stables, serves a good range of modern global dishes.

Open all day, all week Closed 25 Dec Free House 20 portions/menu

RED WHARF BAY

The Ship Inn

Tel **01248 852568 | LL75 8RJ**
Web **www.shipinnredwharfbay.co.uk**
Dir ***Phone for detailed directions.***

Wading birds flock here to feed on the extensive sands of Red Wharf Bay, making the Ship's waterside beer garden a birdwatcher's paradise. In the Kenneally family's hands for over 40 years, this traditional free house proffers carefully tended real ales, including the pub's own brewed by Conwy, and Facer's Bulkeley. Local fish and seafood feature in dishes such as Menai mussels marinière. Otherwise plump for excellent Welsh beef in the steak and ale pie.

Open all day, all week Free House portions/menu

BRIDGEND

KENFIG

Prince of Wales Inn

Tel **01656 740356 | CF33 4PR**
Web **www.princekenfig.co.uk**
Dir ***M4 junction 37 into North Cornelly. Left at crossroads, follow signs for Kenfig and Porthcawl. Pub 600 yards on right.***

Thought to be one of the most haunted pubs in Wales, this 16th-century stone-built free house was formerly the seat of local government for the lost city of Kenfig. It is also the only pub in Britain to have held a Sunday school continuously from 1857 to 2000.

CARDIFF

CREIGIAU

Caesars Arms PICK OF THE PUBS

Tel **029 2089 0486 | Cardiff Road, CF15 9NN**
Web **www.caesarsarms.co.uk**
Dir ***M4 junction 34, A4119 towards Llantrisant/Rhondda. Approximately 0.5 mile right at lights signed Groesfaen. Through Groesfaen, past Dynevor Arms pub. Next left, signed Creigiau. 1 mile, left at T-junction, pass Creigiau Golf Course. Pub 1 mile on left.***

The Caesars Arms has a lot to offer. Vegetable gardens, polytunnels and a smallholding all form part of this enterprise, supplying a huge variety of greens, rare breed pork, honey, smoked meats and fish to the adjoining farm shop, as well as to the kitchen of the country pub and brasserie itself. The chefs pride themselves in offering a progressive, modern menu combined with some old favourites. Sea bream, turbot or red mullet may feature, while Welsh game, beef and lamb satisfy the meat-eaters, and free-range chicken and duck come from Madgetts Farm in the Wye Valley. An extensive wine list ensures that finding the perfect companion to your chosen main meal will be a breeze.

Open 12–2.30 6–12 (Sat 12–2.30 5–12 Sun 12–4) Closed 25–26 Dec, Sun evening Free House portions/menu notice required

GWAELOD-Y-GARTH

Gwaelod-y-Garth Inn

Tel **029 2081 0408 | Main Road, CF15 9HH**
Web **www.gwaelodinn.co.uk**
Dir ***M4 junction 32, north on A470, left at next exit, at roundabout right, 0.5 mile. Right into village.***

On the wooded flank of Garth Hill, high above Taffs Well, the views are great; across the vale, for example, is Castell Coch, built in Victorian Gothic Revival style. The Gwaelod, meaning 'foot of the mountain', has its own brewery, nicknamed 'The Brew with a View'.

PENTYRCH

Kings Arms

Tel **029 2089 0202 | 22 Church Road, CF15 9QF**
Web **www.kingsarmspentyrch.co.uk**
Dir ***M4 junction 32, A470 (Merthyr Tydfil). Left onto B4262 signed Radyr then Pentyrch. Right at roundabout for Pentyrch. Or M4 junction 34, A4119 (dual carriageway) signed Llantrisant and Rhondda. Into right lane, right at lights signed Groes Farm. Left to Pentyrch.***

In a leafy village on the outskirts of Cardiff, this Grade II listed pub is full of traditional features, from the flagstoned snug to the exposed lime-washed walls and log fire of the lounge, and there are lovely landscaped gardens.

CARMARTHENSHIRE

ABERGORLECH

The Black Lion

Tel **01558 685271 | SA32 7SN**
Web **www.blion.co.uk**
Dir ***A40 east from Carmarthen, then B4310 signed Brechfa and Abergorlech.***

This attractive 16th-century village pub in the pretty Cothi Valley is run by Lyn and Phil Kane. You can eat from the Welsh-sourced menu in the flagstoned bar or restaurant; the evening menu offers starters like slow-cooked Welsh pork belly with hot and sour rhubarb, followed by Capestone free-range lemon chicken, buttery crushed potatoes and watercress.

Open all year, all day 12–11 (Sun 12–10) Closed Mon
Free House portions/menu Wi-fi
notice required

LLANDDAROG

Butchers Arms

Tel **01267 275330 | SA32 8NS**
Web **www.butchersofllanddarog.co.uk**
Dir ***From A48 between Carmarthen and Cross Hands follow Llanddarog/B4310 signs. Pub adjacent to church.***

David and Mavis James's more than 30 years in this pretty village pub surely make them Old Favourites; as it happens, this is also the term David uses for some of his dishes – beef and ale pie or boiled ham and chips, for example.

LLANDEILO

The Angel Hotel

Tel **01558 822765 | Rhosmaen Street, SA19 6EN**
Web **www.angelbistro.co.uk**
Dir ***In town centre adjacent to post office.***

This gabled inn commands a position at the fringe of the Brecon Beacons National Park. Popular as both a locals' pub and as an intimate place to dine in Y Capel Bach Bistro, an 18th-century gem tucked away at the rear of the hotel.

LLANDOVERY

The Castle

Tel **01550 720343 | Kings Road, SA20 0AP**
Web **castle-hotel-llandovery.co.uk**
Dir ***On A40 in town centre.***

Set in a coaching inn once used by Lord Nelson on his journey to meet the fleet at Pembroke, The Castle is well positioned for exploring the Brecon Beacons National Park. Family-run by chefs, it's no surprise that food is top of the agenda.

The Kings Head

Tel **01550 720393 | 1 Market Square, SA20 0AB**
Web **www.kingsheadcoachinginn.co.uk**
Dir ***M4 junction 49, A483 through Ammanford, Llandeilo onto A40 to Llandovery. Pub in town centre opposite clock tower.***

Once the home of the Llandovery Bank, this 17th-century inn overlooks the town's cobbled market square. Step inside and the exposed beams and crooked floors are a reminder of the pub's heritage, with beers from the Gower and Evans Breweries representing the Principality.

LLANFALLTEG

The Plash Inn

Tel **01437 563472 | SA34 0UN**
Web **www.theplashinn.co.uk**
Dir ***From A40 in Llanddewi Velfrey follow sign for Llanfallteg. 2 miles, pub on left.***

Hidden in the beautiful Taf Valley on the Carmarthenshire–Pembrokeshire border, The Plash (it means 'house on the mud') was built in the 1870s as a railway inn and it stayed in the same family for 60 years until the line was closed by Mr Beeching in the 1960s. Log fires in the winter and a lovely sunny beer garden means it's a popular spot all year round, whether it's for a pint of local real ale or a tasty dish chosen from the menu, that showcases fresh and local produce.

Open all week 5–11 (Sun 3–9) Free House portions/menu notice required

LLANLLWNI

Belle @ Llanllwni

Tel **01570 480495 | SA40 9SQ**
Web **www.bellevueinn.co.uk**
Dir ***Midway between Carmarthen and Lampeter on A485.***

This cosy and welcoming roadside inn, on the A485, is surrounded by countryside and has stunning views – it's a great place to dine alfresco on a sunny day. There are two rotating ales here to enjoy along with Westons Stowford Press and local Welsh ciders. Expect excellent ingredients including locally reared meats. Menus could include seared pork fillet, Parma ham, Savoy cabbage and gratin potatoes; or Welsh beef lasagne with triple-cooked chips. There is a seasonal specials board and themed evenings.

Open 12–3 5.30–11 Closed 25–26 Dec, Mon (excluding bank holidays) Free House 9 from £10.50 portions/menu notice required

LLANSTEFFAN

Inn at the Sticks

Tel **01267 241066 | High Street, SA33 5JG**
Web **www.innatthesticks-llansteffan.com**
Dir ***A40 onto B4312 to Llansteffan. In centre of village, opposite church.***

Overlooked by Llansteffan's historic castle on the banks of the Towy Estuary, the Inn at the Sticks was for centuries an important resting place for pilgrims heading to nearby St Davids. Regionally-brewed ales like Buckleys Best and The Rev. James accompany dishes such as pan-fried pigeon, broccoli, wild garlic pesto and Madeira jus. Regular live music plus an August Bank Holiday festival.

NANTGAREDIG

Y Polyn PICK OF THE PUBS

Tel **01267 290000 | SA32 7LH**
Web **www.ypolyn.co.uk**
Dir ***From A48 follow signs to National Botanic Garden of Wales. Then follow brown signs to Y Polyn.***

Y Polyn is a former tollhouse, now well established as a destination pub for lovers of Welsh food, and handily placed for exploring Carmarthen and the National Botanic Garden of Wales. The bounty of west Wales is at the forefront of the uncomplicated, tempting dishes. Starters include the famous Y Polyn fish soup with gruyère, rouille and croûtons; or venison ragù, pappardelle, pangritata and parmesan; follow that with roast rack of Welsh lamb, spiced lamb and potato terrine, onion, garlic and thyme purée and curly kale, maybe, or pork belly, caramelised endive, black pudding, apple purée, buttered mash and crackling. The warm pear frangipane tart and stem ginger ice is a winner. The excellent beers come from local breweries.

Open all year all week 12–4 7–11 Closed Sun evening and Mon Free House 12 from £16.50 portions

PENDINE

Springwell Inn

Tel **01994 453274 | Marsh Road, SA33 4PA**
Web **www.springwellinn.com**
Dir ***A40 from Carmarthen to St Clears, onto A4066 to Pendine.***

In the coastal village of Pendine, this 500-year-old pub offers far-reaching beach views and is only four miles from Laugharne. Traditional with a cosy lounge warmed by a real fire in winter, the bar and restaurant offer pub classics, as well as main courses such as Gwendraeth Valley gammon steak with pineapple and egg. The Sunday lunch carvery is a popular option and children can choose from their own menu.

Open all day, all week Free House 12 menus notice required

PUMSAINT

The Dolaucothi Arms

Tel **01558 650237 | SA19 8UW**
Dir ***On A482 between Lampeter and Llandovery. From Llandeilo or Llandovery take A40.***

Set in the rolling green Cothi Valley, The Dolaucothi Arms is owned by the National Trust. Choose an armchair in the cosy lounge bar, or sit at a large table in the main bar where Welsh real ales and ciders are on tap.

CEREDIGION

ABERAERON

The Harbourmaster

PICK OF THE PUBS

Tel **01545 570755 | Pen Cei, SA46 0BT**
Web **www.harbour-master.com**
Dir ***In Aberaeron follow Tourist Information Centre signs. Pub adjacent.***

Close to the harbour mouth, fabulous sunsets illuminate the pastel colours of the quayside buildings crowding in around the old port. The food is an easy medley of traditional and contemporary dishes. Bar menus might highlight crispy cockles with chilli vinegar; or Cardigan Bay crab with chilli and garlic linguine. The restaurant menu majors on seafood, but also carries braised pork cheeks with turnip purée, salt baked turnip, cavolo vero and cider. Beers are from first-rate microbreweries, the real cider comes from the Ebbw Valley.

Open all day, all week 10am–11.30pm Closed 25 Dec Free House 21 from £10.50 portions/menu Wi-fi P

ABERYSTWYTH

The Glengower

Tel **01970 626191 | 3 Victoria Terrace, SY23 2DH**
Web **www.glengower.co.uk**
Dir ***Phone for detailed directions.***

Literally a stone's throw from the beach, the sun terrace at 'The Glen' – as it's affectionately known by the locals – offers fabulous views across Cardigan Bay where you might possibly spot one of the friendly local dolphins.

PENRHIWLLAN

The Daffodil Inn

Tel **01559 370343 | SA44 5NG**
Web **www.thedaffodilinn.co.uk**
Dir ***On A475, 4 miles east of Newcastle Emlyn.***

An inn since the 16th century, The Daffodil is close to Newquay beach and Llandysul canoeing centre, and is popular with walkers and cyclists stopping off for a glass of Abbot Ale or Stowford Press cider. Diners can eat in the bar or in the restaurant with its valley views and open kitchen. Seasonal Welsh produce is represented by ingredients like Glamorgan sausages and Milford Haven hake.

Open all year 11.45–3.30 5.30–11 Closed Mon (Oct to Easter) Free House from £9.95 portions/menu Wi-fi P *notice required*

PONTRHYDFENDIGAID

The Black Lion Hotel

Tel **01974 831624 | SY25 6BE**
Web **www.blacklionhotel.co.uk**
Dir ***On B4343 north of Tregaron.***

Walkers, cyclists, fishermen and nature lovers attracted by the nearby ruined abbey at Strata Florida and the other local scenic delights, visit here and enjoy its Welsh-farmhouse-like interior, where Llandeilo brewery Evan Evans satisfies the many real-ale drinkers among them.

TREGARON

Y Talbot ★★★★ INN

PICK OF THE PUBS

Tel **01974 298208 | The Square, SY25 6JL**
Web **www.ytalbot.com**
Dir ***On B4343 in village centre.***

Right on the main square, this former drovers' pub is full of charm and character, from the 250-year-old beams to the inglenook fireplaces, the ideal setting for real ales from different Welsh breweries. With a wealth of local produce and a head chef who trained with Marco Pierre White and worked at The Ritz, it's hardly surprising that Y Talbot has earned AA Rosettes for dishes like roast Welsh lamb and roast wood pigeon.

Open all day, all week Free House from £10.50 portions/menu Wi-fi P *notice required*

CONWY

ABERGELE

The Kinmel Arms PICK OF THE PUBS

Tel **01745 832207 | The Village, St George, LL22 9BP**
Web **thekinmelarms.co.uk**
Dir ***From A55 junction 24a to St George. East on A55, junction 24. 1st left to Rhuddlan, 1st right into St George. 2nd right.***

This 17th-century pub is set in a secluded hamlet between the coastal plain and the beautiful Elwy Valley. The original sandstone frontage and mullion windows disguise a contemporary, slightly quirky interior, which features a log-burning stove and an eclectic choice of decor. While beers from local microbreweries and Welsh cider quench a walker's thirst; hungry guests are rewarded with a stylish menu, where local produce is the baseline for dishes that can include mains like beef, kidney and mushroom pie with bone marrow gravy. Finish with a dark chocolate sphere filled with textures of passionfruit and chocolate.

Open all week Free House 15 portions/menu notice required

COLWYN BAY

Pen-y-Bryn PICK OF THE PUBS

Tel **01492 533360 | Pen-y-Bryn Road, LL29 6DD**
Web **www.brunningandprice.com/penybryn**
Dir ***1 mile from A55. Follow signs to Welsh Mountain Zoo. Establishment at top of hill.***

A self-guided walk from the pub makes the most of the wooded hills and lanes here above Colwyn Bay. Alternatively, grab a seat in the garden and appreciate the views across to the gigantic headlands of The Little and Great Orme hills jutting out into silvery Liverpool Bay. Beer festivals are regularly held, complementing the already generous selection of real ales, many from north Wales breweries. Daily-changing menus offer a liberal choice, from sandwiches upwards. Mains cover all the bases: Sicilian fish stew; slow-braised lamb shoulder; and roasted squash, leek and chestnut Wellington are typical quality choices on the all-day menu.

Open all day, all week 12–11 (Sun 12–10.30) Brunning & Price 14 from £11.75 portions/menu

CONWY

The Groes Inn ★★★★★ INN

PICK OF THE PUBS

Tel **01492 650545 | Ty'n-y-Groes, LL32 8TN**
Web **www.groesinn.com**
Dir ***Exit A55 to Conwy, left at mini rounabout by Conwy Castle onto B5106, 2.5 miles inn on right.***

This 450-year-old, creeper-smothered inn – the first licensed house in Wales – overlooks the sweeping Conwy estuary. Rambling, oak-beamed rooms are full of ancient settles, log fires, military hats and historic cooking utensils. Study the nicely balanced menu over a leisurely Welsh Black beer from Llandudno's Great Orme brewery. Main dishes might include Welsh lamb cutlets with root vegetable dauphinoise, wilted spinach, roast cherry tomatoes, redcurrant and rosemary gravy.

Open all day, all week 11–9 J W Lees portions/menu notice required

DOLWYDDELAN

Elen's Castle Hotel

Tel **01690 750207 | LL25 0EJ**
Web **www.hotelinsnowdonia.co.uk**
Dir ***5 miles south of Betws-y-Coed, follow A470.***

First opened it as a coaching inn around 1880, these days it boasts an old-world bar with a wood-burning stove and an intimate restaurant with mountain views. Sample dishes include sweet potato and spinach curry; local Welsh chops with new potatoes and seasonal vegetables; and deep-filled shortcrust Welsh Black beef pie.

Open times vary seasonally Closed 1st 2 weeks Jan, some week days in winter Free House portions/menu notice required

LLANDUDNO

The Cottage Loaf

Tel **01492 870762 | Market Street, LL30 2SR**
Web **www.the-cottageloaf.co.uk**
Dir ***From A55 onto A470, then A456. Into Mostyn Street, left into Market Street.***

This welcoming pub attracts visitors all year round. A former bakery, it only became a pub in 1981 and much of its interior is made up of salvaged materials from a ship-wrecked coal schooner.

LLANDUDNO JUNCTION

The Queens Head

Tel **01492 546570 | Glanwydden, LL31 9JP**
Web **www.queensheadglanwydden.co.uk**
Dir ***A55 onto A470 towards Llandudno. At 3rd roundabout right towards Penrhyn Bay, 2nd right into Glanwydden, pub on left.***

Appealing village free house

PICK OF THE PUBS

A few sympathetic improvements apart, 2018's new owners have left this former wheelwright's cottage as the charming village pub it's always been, with low beams, winter log fires and masses of summer garden colour. Welsh real ales tend to come from nearby places like Conwy and Porthmadog, or even as far away as Caerphilly. For a cychwyn, or starter, maybe deep-fried Perl-Wen brie with cranberry, clementine and ginger chutney, and then 'from the sea' (o'r môr) monkfish, king prawn and coconut Goan curry; or 'from the land' (o'r tir), chargrilled Welsh sirloin steak; butternut squash, spinach and aubergine lasagne in rich tomato ragù; a traditional classic, or a daily special. A sheltered terrace runs around the building, so there should always be a place in the sun.

Open all day, all week 12–10.30 Free House 15 portions/menu notice required

LLANELIAN-YN-RHÔS

The White Lion Inn

Tel **01492 515807 | LL29 8YA**
Web **www.whitelioninn.co.uk**
Dir ***A55 junction 22, left signed Old Colwyn, A547. At roundabout 2nd exit onto B5383 signed Betwys-yn-Rhos. In 1 mile turn right into Llanelian Road, follow to village. Pub on right.***

Incredibly, parts of this attractive family-run inn are reputed to date back over 1,200 years. It still retains a slate floor and oak-beamed ceiling, and there is an old salt cellar by the inglenook fireplace. The food is traditional, home cooked, and wherever possible locally sourced. Look out for grilled fillet of plaice; chicken curry; tart of the week, baby potatoes and salad; or braised steak in Guinness gravy. Sandwiches, hot baguettes and jacket potatoes are also available. Dogs are allowed in the snug.

Open all year 11.30–3 6–11 (Sat 11.30–4 5–11.30 Sun 12–10.30) Closed Mon (excluding bank holidays and school summer holidays) Free House 15 portions/menu Wi-fi notice required

LLANNEFYDD

The Hawk & Buckle Inn

Tel **01745 540249 | LL16 5ED**
Web **www.thehawkandbuckle.com**
Dir ***Phone for detailed directions.***

From high in the north Wales hills, this lovingly restored 17th-century coaching inn enjoys spectacular views across the local countryside to Blackpool Tower and beyond. The real ale selection includes Heavy Industry and Purple Moose Glaslyn Ale, while a regularly changing menu uses the best of fresh local produce. Here's just a sample of what you might find – grilled salmon fillet with sweet chilli sauce; vegetable or beef lasagne; beef and ale pie; or gammon steak with fried egg, grilled pineapple, peas and chips.

Open all day, all week 6–11 Free House portions/menu Wi-fi notice required

DENBIGHSHIRE

GRAIGFECHAN

Three Pigeons

Tel **01824 703178 | LL15 2EU**
Web **www.threepigeonsinn.co.uk**
Dir ***A949 from Ruthin towards Mold. Right onto B5429 signed Graigfechan.***

In centuries past drovers broke their journeys here on their way to market, and their livestock would graze on the adjacent field. The interior of this 1777 building is warm and traditional, with oak beams, open fires and brassware. Local brews are served in jugs straight from casks, a practice that nostalgic regulars appreciate. Rosie's Triple D (Drovers at Dafarn Dywyrch) cider is local too. In the restaurant, enjoy rump of lamb and minted mash; and home-made pie of the day.

Open all year 12–3 5–11 (Sat to Sun 12–11) Closed Mon (excluding bank holiday), Tue lunch (winter only) Free House 10 portions/menu notice required

RUTHIN

The White Horse

Tel **01824 790218 | Hendrerwydd, LL16 4LL**
Web **www.whitehorserestaurant.co.uk**
Dir ***From Ruthin A494 (Mold road). Left at Llanbedr-Dyffryn-Clwyd onto B5429 (Llandyrnog). Right signed Gellifor. At crossroads in Hendrerwydd, pub on left. Or from Denbigh, A525 (Ruthin road). Left onto B5429 to Llandyrnog. Left to Hendrerwydd.***

Surrounded by the sublime scenery of the Clwydian hills, this pretty, whitewashed pub really is the 'charming and friendly retreat from the world' owners Lucy and Jason Stock set out to create. Modern British food is locally sourced – extra-mature Welsh steak, roast vine tomatoes, grilled flat mushrooms and hand-cut chips; and roasted shoulder of Gellifor pork with sautéed Jersey Royals and creamed Savoy cabbage. Real ales, such as Porthmadog's Purple Moose, come from local microbreweries.

Open all year 12–2 5–11 (Sat to Sun 12–11) Closed Mon and Tue Free House portions/menu notice required

ST ASAPH

The Plough Inn

Tel **01745 585080 | The Roe, LL17 0LU**
Web **www.ploughsa.com**
Dir ***Exit A55 at Rhyl and St Asaph signs, left at roundabout, pub 200 yards on left.***

The bar here is a quirky blend of modern and traditional, with open fires, blackboard menus, an unusual trompe l'oeil bar and real ales from north Wales; the restaurant, though very modern, retains a vaulted ceiling from its days as a ballroom. Dine here on Welsh cask ale-battered haddock with chips and mushy peas; cauliflower, spinach and chickpea curry; or pie of the day. There's live music on Friday and Saturday nights, as well as a cocktail bar and a wine shop.

Open all day, all week Free House 10 portions/menu

FLINTSHIRE

CILCAIN

White Horse Inn

Tel **01352 740142 | CH7 5NN**
Dir ***From Mold take A541 towards Denbigh. After approximately 6 miles turn left.***

This 400-year-old pub is the last survivor of the five originally to be found in this lovely hillside village, which was the bustling centre of the local gold-mining industry in the 19th century. Today, the White Horse is popular with walkers, cyclists and horse-riders. Food here is home made by the landlord's wife using the best quality local ingredients, and is accompanied by a good range of local real ales.

Open all year 12–11 (Sun 12–10.30 Mon 5–11) Closed Mon lunch Free House 8 portions notice required

HAWARDEN

The Glynne Arms

Tel **01244 569988 | 3 Glynne Way, CH5 3NS**
Web **www.theglynnearms.co.uk**
Dir ***From North Wales Expressway junction 36a onto B5125 to Hawarden. Pub in village centre.***

This fine-looking old coaching inn is owned by Charlie and Caroline Gladstone. Charlie's great-great grandfather was 19th-century prime minister Sir William Ewart Gladstone, who married into Hawarden Castle's Glynne dynasty. Meat, fruit and vegetables come from the couple's Estate Farm Shop down the road.

MOLD

Glasfryn PICK OF THE PUBS

Tel **01352 750500 | Raikes Lane, Sychdyn, CH7 6LR**
Web **www.brunningandprice.co.uk**
Dir ***From Mold follow signs to Theatr Clwyd, 1 mile from town centre.***

This imposing dining pub enjoys magical views over the Alyn Valley towards the Clwydian Range Area of Outstanding Natural Beauty. There's beer from Purple Moose Brewery and Timothy Taylor, and typical dishes are a starter of pheasant, rabbit and prune faggot with celeriac purée and wild mushroom gravy; and Sicilian fish stew with salmon, prawns, mussels, squid and red mullet served with aïoli. Beer festivals in March and October coincide with national food weeks.

Open all day, all week *Brunning & Price* *16* *portions/menu* Wi-fi P

NORTHOP

The Celtic Arms

Tel **01352 840423 | Northop Country Park, CH7 6WA**
Web **www.thecelticarms.co.uk**
Dir ***A55 junction 33a (westbound), left into Northop Country Park. Or A55 junction 33 (eastbound) through Northop. At lights left (signed A5126) into Connah's Quay Road, right signed Northop Country Park.***

Transformed into a stylish free house in 2015, this former golf clubhouse is set in the beautiful surroundings of Northop County Park. The long bar has areas at each end for drinking and eating. Children eat well here and there's an outdoor play area, too.

GWYNEDD

ABERDYFI

Penhelig Arms – see page 552

BEDDGELERT

Tanronnen Inn ★★★★ INN

Tel **01766 890347 | LL55 4YB**
Web **www.tanronnen.co.uk**
Dir ***In village centre opposite river bridge.***

Originally part of the Beddgelert Estate, this stone building was the stables for the passing coach trade in 1809. By the end of the 19th century it had two letting bedrooms and was serving meals for visitors; so setting the style of today's operation The inn has two attractive small bars serving Robinsons ales, a large lounge with open fire, and a dining room, open to non-residents, in which to enjoy a wide range of home-cooked meals on a daily-changing menu.

Open all day, all week *Robinsons* *portions/menu* P

BRITHDIR

Cross Foxes

Tel **01341 421001 | LL40 2SG**
Web **www.crossfoxes.co.uk**
Dir ***At junction of A470 and A487, 4 miles from Dolgellau.***

Grade II listed the Cross Foxes may be, but what an interior! It's true that traditional Welsh materials like slate and stone are used in the design, but the effect is light years from being Welsh Traditional. In the impressive bar you'll find regional real ales and ciders, and in the café a multiplicity of teas (including one from Wales), fresh coffees and finger sandwiches. Dishes in The Grill dining room might be potted laver cockles; and Welsh lamb, potato and ale pie.

Open all day, all week *Free House* *from £9.95* *portions/menu* Wi-fi P *notice required*

CAERNARFON

Black Boy Inn – see page 552

ABERDYFI

Penhelig Arms

★★★★★ INN

Tel **01654 767215 | Terrace Road, LL35 0LT**
Web **www.penheligarms.com**
Dir ***On A493, west of Machynlleth.***

Small hostelry with a big reputation

This popular waterside inn has been serving travellers and locals since 1870 and offers spectacular views over the mountain-backed tidal Dyfi Estuary. Aberdyfi is a charming little resort, a favourite with golfers and watersports enthusiasts. Music and TV-free, the wood-panelled and log-fire-warmed Fisherman's Bar is a cosy and friendly bolt-hole to enjoy Brains real ales and bar meals such as gourmet burgers and bloomer sandwiches. The waterfront restaurant offers a more brasserie-style experience with views over the estuary and menus showcasing the abundant Welsh seafood (a Penhelig speciality) and Welsh beef and lamb. The kitchen team emphasises the freshness of ingredients and fuse local and cosmopolitan influences in a style of cooking that allows natural flavours to shine through. The short wine list is attractively priced and complements the excellent food.

Open all day, all week *Brains* *25* *portions/menu*

CAERNARFON

Black Boy Inn

★★★★ INN

Tel **01286 673604 | Northgate Street, LL55 1RW**
Web **www.black-boy-inn.com**
Dir ***A55 junction 9 onto A487, follow signs for Caernarfon and Victoria Docks. Within town walls between castle and Victoria Dock.***

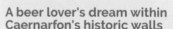

A beer lover's dream within Caernarfon's historic walls

Full of character, this ancient gabled inn, built around 1522, is one of the oldest in Wales. Its fire-warmed, low-ceilinged rooms remain in place thanks to beams rescued from old ships. In the largely Welsh-speaking bar, 20 taps feature cask and keg beers from some of the leading independent breweries, favourites being Camden Town and Flying Dog, the far more local Purple Moose in Porthmadog, and Llandudno's Great Orme. Meat and other products are generally locally sourced, and dishes from the long menu might include deep-fried fishcake; chef's special lamb pie; mozzarella and sundried tomato chicken breast; and slow-cooked blade of beef. The well-proportioned bedrooms are ideal for those wishing to stay and explore Snowdon, the Lleyn Peninsula or ride on the Welsh Highland Railway.

Open all day, all week Closed 25 Dec *Free House* *10* *from £8.50* *portions/menu*  *notice required*

LLANBEDR

Victoria Inn ★★★★ INN

Tel **01341 241213 | LL45 2LD**
Web **www.vic-inn.co.uk**
Dir ***On A496 between Barmouth and Harlech.***

Fascinating features for pub connoisseurs are the circular wooden settle, ancient stove, grandfather clock and flagged floors in the atmospheric bar of the Victoria. Home-made food is served in the lounge bar and restaurant, complemented by a range of Robinsons traditional ales.

Open all day, all week 11–11 (Sun 12–10.30)
Robinsons 10 portions/menu
notice required

MALLWYD

Brigands Inn

Tel **01650 511999 | SY20 9HJ**
Web **www.brigandsinn.com**
Dir ***At junction of A470 and A458.***

A splendid 15th-century coaching inn set in the beautiful Dovey Valley, and reputed to have been the meeting place of the infamous 'red-headed brigands of Mawddwy'. It's full of character, with beams, open fireplaces and stylish decor. It's a dog-friendly place, too.

PENNAL

Glan yr Afon/Riverside

Tel **01654 791285 | Riverside Hotel, SY20 9DW**
Web **www.riversidehotel-pennal.co.uk**
Dir ***3 miles from Machynlleth on A493 towards Aberdovey. Pub on left.***

In the glorious Dyfi Valley, this family-run inn has slate floors, modern light oak furnishings and bold funky fabrics. There's a wood-burning stove pumping out heat in winter, Dark Side of the Moose ale on tap, and a good range of modern pub food. Relax and opt for a starter of warm duck and orange salad; then chicken breast wrapped in pancetta with green vegetable risotto; or spiced Mediterranean fish stew. There's a riverside garden with views to the hills.

Open 12–3 6–11 (Sat to Sun all day) Closed 25–26 Dec, 2 weeks Jan, Mon, Tue (Nov to Mar) Free House 12 from £9.50 portions/menu Wi-fi
notice required

TUDWEILIOG

Lion Hotel

Tel **01758 770244 | LL53 8ND**
Web **www.lionhoteltudweiliog.co.uk**
Dir ***A487 from Caernarfon onto A499 towards Pwllheli. Right onto B4417 to Nefyn, through Edern to Tudweiliog.***

Family-run pub offering good-value dining

Standing at a tangent to the road, fronted by a garden with tables and chairs, the 300-year-old Lion has been run by the Lee family for the past 40 years or so. The bar features an extensive list of whiskies, alongside real ales from Big Bog, Cwrw Llyn and Purple Moose breweries, all Welsh of course. Typical pub meals include classics like spare ribs in barbecue sauce; lamb or chicken balti; sweet chilli, prawn and cod fishcakes; and leek and mushroom crumble. Ample parking and a children's play area both help to make it popular with the many families holidaying in the beautiful Lleyn Peninsula.

Open all week 11–3 6–11 (summer all day)
Free House from £9.50 portions/menu
notice required

WAUNFAWR

Snowdonia Parc Brewpub & Campsite

Tel **01286 650409 | LL55 4AQ**
Web **www.snowdonia-park.co.uk**
Dir ***Phone for detailed directions.***

In the heart of Snowdonia, a short drive from Mount Snowdon, this popular walkers' pub is located at Waunfawr Station on the Welsh Highland Railway. There are steam trains on site (the building was originally the stationmaster's house), plus a microbrewery and campsite. Home-cooked food ranges from chicken, leek and ham pie to vegetable curry or roast Welsh beef with all the trimmings. All real ales served are brewed on the premises. The Welsh Highland Railway Rail Ale Festival is held in mid-May.

Open all day, all week 11–11 (Fri to Sat 11am–11.30pm) Free House portions/menu notice required

MONMOUTHSHIRE

ABERGAVENNY

Clytha Arms PICK OF THE PUBS

Tel **01873 840206 | Clytha, NP7 9BW**
Web **www.clytha-arms.com**
Dir ***From A449 and A40 junction (east of Abergavenny) follow Old Road Abergavenny and Clytha signs.***

This converted dower house stands on the edge of parkland with captivating views from the garden embracing the lush and shapely Vale of Gwent. The main bar is full of character, with old pews, tables and rustic furnishings, as well as a wood-burning stove. The ever-changing range of real ales number more than 300 in any given year. Grazers can sift through a list of 20 tasty tapas dishes, or choose a simple ploughman's with Welsh cheeses. The restaurant menu delights with its flavour combinations; some dishes, such as cockles with bacon and laverbread, can be served as either a starter or a main course.

Open 12–3 6–12 (Fri to Sat 12–12 Sun 12–9) Closed 25 Dec, Mon lunch Free House 12 portions/menu

LLANGATTOCK LINGOED

The Hunters Moon Inn

Tel **01873 821499 | NP7 8RR**
Web **www.hunters-moon-inn.co.uk**
Dir ***Phone for detailed directions.***

In a peaceful village on the Offa's Dyke Path, the Hunters Moon dates back to the 13th century and is now run by three generations of the Bateman family who have returned it to its former glory.

LLANGYBI

The White Hart Village Inn

Tel **01633 450258 | NP15 1NP**
Web **www.thewhitehartllangybi.co.uk**
Dir ***M4 junction 25 onto B4596 (Caerleon road), through Caerleon High Street, straight over roundabout into Usk Road, continue to Llangybi.***

With 11 fireplaces, a 'warm' welcome is assured at this picturesque inn. Oliver Cromwell based himself here during local Civil War campaigns; so add a priest hole, Tudor plasterwork and a mention in T S Eliot's poem 'Usk' and this is a destination to savour.

LLANTRISANT

The Greyhound Inn PICK OF THE PUBS

Tel **01291 672505 | NP15 1LE**
Web **www.greyhound-inn.com**
Dir ***M4 junction 24, A449 towards Monmouth, exit at 1st junction signed Usk. In Usk left into Twyn Square follow Llantrisant signs. 2.5 miles, under A449 bridge. Inn on right.***

Set between the Rivers Usk and Wye, this 17th-century Welsh longhouse has been an inn since 1845. The cosy main bar serves three lounges, while the Stable Bar is popular with the locals, not least for the chance to play darts, crib or dominoes. The tiled floor also means muddy boots, children and dogs are not a problem. A typical menu offers duck spring rolls with hoisin sauce or grilled goats' cheese to start, followed by grill options, and old favourites like steak and kidney pie, fresh battered plaice, or chilli. Vegetarians have plenty of choice, and desserts are listed on the daily-changing blackboard.

Open all day, all week 11–11 Closed 25 Dec, 1 Jan Free House 10 from £10.95 portions/menu notice required

LLANVAIR DISCOED

The Woodlands Tavern Country Pub & Dining

PICK OF THE PUBS

Tel **01633 400313 | NP16 6LX**
Web **www.thewoodlandstavern.co.uk**
Dir ***5 miles from Caldicot and Magor.***

In the heart of the beautiful village of Llanvair Discoed, near the Roman fortress town of Caerwent, this charming pub was originally known as the Kings Arms. At the foot of Gray Hill and Wentwood forest, the Woodlands Tavern occupies an enviable spot in lovely countryside that's popular with walkers, cyclists and fishermen. A good selection of Welsh ales, such as Wye Valley or Felinfoel, is matched by the varied menu that includes baguettes, jacket potatoes, pub classics and daily fish specials. Deep-fried brie with dressed leaves and home-made chutney might lead on to rack of lamb with grain mustard mash and red wine sauce.

Open 12–3 6–12 (Sat all day Sun 12–4) Closed 25–26 Dec, 1 Jan, Sun evening, Mon and Tue Free House 10 portions/menu

PANTYGELLI

The Crown

Tel **01873 853314 | Old Hereford Road, NP7 7HR**
Web **www.thecrownatpantygelli.com**
Dir ***Phone for detailed directions.***

A charming family-run free house dating from the 16th century, The Crown has fine views of Skirrid known also as Holy Mountain. Walkers and cyclists love it, but it's a genuine community pub too, serving Bass, Rhymney, Wye Valley HPA and guest real ales.

PENALLT

Inn at Penallt ★★★★ INN

Tel **01600 772765 | NP25 4SE**
Web **www.innatpenallt.online**
Dir ***From Monmouth take B4293 to Trellech. Approximately 2 miles, left at brown sign for inn. At next crossroads left. Right at war memorial.***

Narrow, winding lanes drop steeply from tiny Penallt's trim village green into the River Wye's famous gorge, which strikes along the foot of thick woodlands close to this appealing stone inn. It's family and dog-friendly and a favourite stop with ramblers on the area's many footpaths. The inn welcomes both drinkers seeking beers and ciders made just a few miles away and diners keen to sample the generous larder of Monmouthshire and the southern Marches.

RHYD-Y-MEIRCH

Goose and Cuckoo Inn

Tel **01873 880277 | Upper Llanover, NP7 9ER**
Web **www.thegooseandcuckoo.co.uk**
Dir ***From Abergavenny take A4042 towards Pontypool. Turn left after Llanover, follow signs for inn.***

Popular with walkers, this friendly, whitewashed pub in the Brecon Beacons National Park has a garden with views of the Malvern Hills and a traditional interior with flagstoned bar area and a wood-burning stove.

TAL-Y-COED

Warwicks country pub

Tel **01600 780227 | NP7 8TL**
Web **www.warwickscountrypub.org**
Dir ***From A40 in Monmouth take B4233 signed Rockfield. Through Rockfield. Approximately 5 miles to pub on right.***

Halfway between Abergavenny and Monmouth on the B4223, this wisteria-clad family-run pub occupies a lovely spot in the pretty hamlet of Tal-y-Coed. Surrounded by stunning countryside, it's a popular haunt for Offa's Dyke walkers, who can refuel with a glass of Otter Bitter by the open fire or in the sunny garden. Chef Mark Edwards keeps things simple and his menus have broad appeal. Beer-battered black pudding might precede a main course of a trio of Rawlings award-winning sausages, served with mash and onion gravy.

Open all year 12–2.30 6–11 (Wed 6.30–10.30 Sat 12–11 Sun 12–10) Closed Mon and Tue Free House portions/menu notice required

TINTERN PARVA

The Anchor Inn

Tel **01291 689582 | Chapel Hill, NP16 6TE**
Web **theanchortintern.co.uk**
Dir ***Take A466 north from Chepstow to Tintern. Approximately 4 miles. Pub adjacent to Tintern Abbey ruins.***

Great views of Tintern Abbey

By the River Wye, with fine views of the world-famous Tintern Abbey, this stone-built inn, once the abbey grainstore, dates back to the 12th century. Sympathetically restored and developed, this ancient building now offers more room, a garden terrace and a reconfigured restaurant with a centrepiece real log fire. In the newly expanded bar area, locally brewed ales from Kingstone in Tintern itself and Wye Valley stand shoulder to shoulder with up to three local ciders. Once the ferryman's cottage and boat house, the restaurant showcases local produce in burgers and grilled steaks and chicken; beef, ale and mushroom pie; local pork and leek sausages; fish pie with vegetables; and three-bean chilli with rice. Finish with cherry and apple oat crumble. Best views of the abbey are from the Orangery.

Open all day, all week 10am–11pm *Free House* 9 *from £10* *portions/menu*

TREDUNNOCK

Newbridge on Usk ★★★★★

RESTAURANT WITH ROOMS

PICK OF THE PUBS

Tel **01633 410262 | NP15 1LY**
Web **www.celtic-manor.com**
Dir ***M4 junction 24 follow Newport signs onto B4237. Right at Toby Carvery onto B4236 to Caerleon. Right over bridge, through Caerleon to mini-roundabout. Straight ahead into Usk Road towards Llangybi. In approximately 4 miles right signed Tredunnock. Through Tredunnock, down hill, inn car park on left.***

The River Usk swings lazily beneath the eponymous bridge beside this country inn in deepest Monmouthshire. From the gardens are restful views across to the forested heights of Wentwood and riverside knolls; the Usk Valley Walk passes nearby. The interior is a pleasing blend of traditional beamed ceilings, snug corners and rustic ambience with modern touches and furnishings adding a certain élan. Beers from Brain's Cardiff brewery are the ales of choice, or Welsh cider may hit the spot. The fresh, zingy menu is influenced by the availability of premium products from local suppliers. Starters may include mackerel, pepper and crayfish terrine, leading to roasted Madgett's Farm duck breast with salt-baked swede and garlic barley; or pan-roasted brill with curried lentils, carrot and coconut.

Open all day, all week 12–12 *Free House* 12 *portions/menu* Wi-fi

TRELLECH

The Lion Inn PICK OF THE PUBS

Tel **01600 860322 | NP25 4PA**
Web **www.lioninn.co.uk**
Dir ***From A40 south of Monmouth take B4293, follow Trellech signs. From M8 junction 2, straight across roundabout, 2nd left at 2nd roundabout, B4293 to Trellech.***

Built in 1580 as a brewhouse and inn by a former sea captain, the Lion consists of two rooms, both with open fires; one is a traditional bar, the other a restaurant. In the bar you'll find Wye Valley Butty Bach and Felinfoel Double Dragon, and a number of local ciders including Raglan Cider Mill Snowy Owl. In the restaurant there are bar snacks, baguettes, ploughman's, light meals and a range of main dishes, typically home-made lasagne;

locally sourced faggots; and wild mushroom, brie and cranberry Wellington. There are beautiful views from the suntrap courtyard, and look out for the beer festival in June and the cider festival in August.

Open all day, all week 12–11 (Thu to Sat 12–12 Sun 12–10.30) Free House portions notice required

TRELLECK GRANGE

Fountain Inn

Tel **01291 689303 | NP16 6QW**
Web **www.fountaininntrellech.co.uk**
Dir ***From M48 junction 2 follow Chepstow then A466 and Tintern signs. In Tintern turn by George Hotel for Raglan. Bear right, inn at top of hill, 2 miles from A466.***

A fine old inn dating from 1611 in lovely countryside, with a garden overlooking the Wye Valley. The owners' passion for real ales and ciders is evident both in the great bar line-up, and at the September beer festival. The pub offers several curries; and Welsh Black beef, Welsh lamb and roasted ham, all with fresh vegetables, roast potatoes, Yorkshire pudding and beer gravy. There is also a fresh fish menu.

Open all year Tue to Sun all day Closed Mon Free House 9 portions/menu notice required

USK

The Nags Head Inn

Tel **01291 672820 | Twyn Square, NP15 1BH**
Web **www.nagsheadusk.co.uk**
Dir ***On A472.***

Fronting Usk's old market place, parts of this inn date from the 15th century. Three generations of the Key family have run it, lovingly caring for the flower-filled baskets above the pavement parasols in summer, and maintaining the interior of the beams, polished tables, rural artefacts and horse-brasses. Take your pick of the Brains and Buckley's ales at the bar while perusing the menu. You'll find 'local and seasonal' are watchwords for most of the classic dishes.

Open all week 10.30–2.30 5–11 Closed 25 Dec Free House 9 portions/menu

The Raglan Arms

PICK OF THE PUBS

Tel **01291 690800 | Llandenny, NP15 1DL**
Web **www.raglanarms.co.uk**
Dir ***From Monmouth take A449 to Raglan, left in village. From M4 take A449 exit. Follow Llandenny signs on right.***

Whether eating in, or just enjoying a pint brewed just three miles away, visitors are sure of a warm welcome at this stone-built, 19th-century pub. At the heart of a small village tucked between Tintern Forest and the Usk Valley, this neat inn continues to receive praise for its varied and frequently changing menu. The head chef and his team use high quality ingredients for the imaginative menu; the pub is keen to reduce food miles and most suppliers are within a nine-mile radius. So try a starter of laverbread cake with smoked bacon, garlic and cockles, then follow on with saddle of Brecon venison, Welsh black pudding and sweet and sour pickled beetroot. Finish with chocolate and almond praline tart.

Open Wed to Sat 12–3 6.30–11.30 (Sun 12–2.30 Tue evening) Closed 27 Dec for a few days, Sun evening, Mon, Tue lunchtime Free House portions/menu

NEWPORT

CAERLEON

The Bell at Caerleon

Tel **01633 420613 | Bulmore Road, NP18 1QQ**
Web **www.thebellinncaerleon.co.uk**
Dir ***M4 junction 25, B4596 signed Caerleon. In Caerleon before river bridge right onto B4238 signed Christchurch. Left into Bulmore Road (follow brown pub sign).***

Close to an ancient Roman burial ground (believed by some to be the location of King Arthur's Camelot), this 17th-century coaching inn has stood here on the banks of the River Usk for more than 400 years.

NEWPORT

The Ridgeway Bar & Kitchen

Tel **01633 266053 | 2 Ridgeway Avenue, NP20 5AJ**
Web **www.storyinns.com**
Dir ***M4 junction 27, B4591 towards Newport. At roundabout 1st left into Fields Park Road. 1st left into Ridgeway Avenue.***

Set in a quiet suburb of Newport, and just a couple of minutes from the M4, the Ridgeway was given a New England-style makeover a few years ago. There's a breezy coastal atmosphere, beautiful tiled floors and clever contemporary touches.

▶ PEMBROKESHIRE

AMROTH

The New Inn

Tel **01834 812368 | SA67 8NW**
Dir ***A48 to Carmarthen, A40 to St Clears, A477 to Llanteg then left, follow road to seafront, turn left. 0.25 mile on left.***

Originally a farmhouse, this 16th-century inn has been family run for over 40 years. The pub has old-world charm with beamed ceilings, a flagstone floor, a Flemish chimney and an inglenook fireplace. It is close to the beach, with views towards Saundersfoot and Tenby from the dining room upstairs. Welsh beef features on the menu, and home-made dishes are popular.

Open all day, all week Mar to Oct 11–11 (Oct to Mar evenings and weekends only) Free House portions/menu Wi-fi

ANGLE

The Old Point House

Tel **01646 641205 | East Angle Bay, SA71 5AS**
Web **www.theoldpointhouseangle.co.uk**
Dir ***From Pembroke take B4320 signed Monkton and Hundleton. Right signed Angle. At T-junction left signed West Angle Bay. 1st right at pub sign on wall into narrow lane. Follow lane round bay to pub.***

It's all angles round here – Angle village, Angle Bay, Angle RNLI. Indeed, the 15th-century Old Point has been the lifeboatmen's local since 1868, when their boathouse was built nearby. The track from the village skirts the foreshore and occasionally gets cut off by high spring tides.

BOSHERSTON

St Govans Country Inn

Tel **01646 661311 | SA71 5DN**
Dir ***From Pembroke take B4319 signed Castlemartin, then follow Bosherston and brown pub signs.***

Surrounded by breathtaking scenery on the Pembrokeshire coast, the pub is just a mile from the stunning beaches of Broadhaven South and Barafundle Bay. Enjoy pints of Evan Evans Cwrw and Gower Gold as you choose from a menu.

DALE

Griffin Inn

Tel **01646 636227 | SA62 3RB**
Web **www.griffininndale.co.uk**
Dir ***From end of M4 onto A48 to Carmarthen. A40 to Haverfordwest, B4327 to Dale. In Dale (with sea on left) pub on corner by slipway.***

Fresh lobster, crab, razor clams, scallops, sea bream – seafood is a big attraction at this historic, tucked-away pub. But first, order a Welsh ale – try the seasonal Cwrw Haf – or cider, and enjoy it in the quarry-tiled bar, in the glass-fronted extension, or on the rooftop terrace. If you're eating fish, staff will take you through the extensive menu. A traditional bar menu offers Welsh lamb broth; beef and stout pie; and spicy prawn and mango curry.

Open all week Apr to Sep all day (winter opening times vary) Closed Nov Free House portions/menu Wi-fi *notice required*

LETTERSTON

The Harp Inn

Tel **01348 840061 | 31 Haverfordwest Road, SA62 5UA**
Dir ***On A40, 10 miles from Haverfordwest, 4 miles from Fishguard.***

Formerly a working farm, this 15th-century free house has been owned by the Sandall family since 1981, the building has a stylish conservatory restaurant where diners can enjoy local favourites like Welsh fillet steak; Welsh mussels; venison Roquefort; and whole sea bass. Alternatively, the bar lunch menu offers classic pub meals including crispy battered cod and chips, and there are two real ales on tap plus guest ales in the summer.

Open all day, all week Free House portions/menu Wi-fi *notice required*

LITTLE HAVEN

St Brides Inn

Tel **01437 781266 | St Brides Road, SA62 3UN**
Web **www.saintbridesinn.co.uk**
Dir ***From Haverfordwest take B4341 signed Broad Haven. Through Broad Haven to Little Haven.***

An ideal stop for walkers on the nearby Pembrokeshire Coast Path as it runs through the seaside village of Little Haven, the St Brides Inn has the added attraction of an indoor ancient well, as well as a pretty floral beer garden. Dishes, where possible, are produced using locally-sourced ingredients, including seafood and fish caught nearby. Home-made vegetarian and vegan options are also on offer. Enjoy a pint of local ale or a warming coffee on a colder day.

Open all day, all week Free House 15 portions/ menu notice required

11 WELSH PUBS WITH ACCOMMODATION

The following pubs are rated as part of the AA Guest Accommodation scheme (see page 10–11 for more information).

The Groes Inn ★★★★ INN Conwy, Conwy, *see page 548*

The Nags Head Inn ★★★★★ INN Montgomery, Powys, *see page 562*

Newbridge on Usk ★★★★★ RESTAURANT WITH ROOMS Tredunnock, Monmouthshire, *see page 556*

Penhelig Arms ★★★★★ INN Aberdyfi, Gwynedd, *see page 552*

The Bear ★★★★ INN Crickhowell, Powys, *see page 560*

Black Boy Inn ★★★★ INN Caernarfon, Gwynedd, *see page 552*

Y Talbot ★★★★ INN Tregaron, Ceredigion, *see page 547*

The Hand at Llanarmon ★★★★ INN Llanarmon Dyffryn Ceiriog, Wrexham, *see page 567*

The Fox and Hounds ★★★★ INN Barry, Vale of Glamorgan, *see page 566*

Inn at Penallt ★★★★ INN Penallt, Monmouthshire, *see page 555*

The Old Black Lion ★★★★ INN Hay-On-Wye, Powys, *see page 563*

PORTHGAIN

The Sloop Inn

Tel **01348 831449 | SA62 5BN**
Web **www.sloop.co.uk**
Dir ***Take A487 north-east from St Davids for 6 miles. Left at Croesgooch for 2 miles to Porthgain.***

Located in the beautiful harbour village of Porthgain, The Sloop Inn is especially enticing on a cold winter's day. The walls and ceilings are packed with pictures and memorabilia from nearby shipwrecks. With ales like Felinfoel and The Rev. James on the pump, the varied menu includes breakfasts, snacks, pub favourites, steaks and fresh fish. Just the place to call into when out for one of the amazing nearby walks.

Open all day, all week 9.30am–11pm (winter 11.30–10) Closed 25 Dec evening Free House portions/ menu

ROSEBUSH

Tafarn Sinc

Tel **01437 532214 | Preseli, SA66 7QT**
Web **www.tafarnsinc.cymru**
Dir ***Phone for detailed directions.***

Built to serve the railway that no longer exists, this large red corrugated-iron free house stands testament to its rapid construction in 1876. This idiosyncratic establishment refuses to be modernised and boasts wood-burning stoves, a sawdust floor, and a charming garden.

ST DOGMAELS

Webley Waterfront Inn (Gwesty'r Webley)

Tel **01239 612085 | Poppit Sands, SA43 3LN**
Web **www.webleyhotel.co.uk**
Dir ***A484 from Carmarthen to Cardigan, then to St Dogmaels, right in village centre to Poppit Sands on B4546.***

This long-established family business is spectacularly situated at the start of the Pembrokeshire Coast National Park, a haven for birdwatchers and watersports enthusiasts. The inn offers outstanding views across the River Teifi and Poppit Sands to Cardigan Bay, which supplies the daily catch for the menu.

STACKPOLE

The Stackpole Inn PICK OF THE PUBS

Tel **01646 672324 | SA71 5DF**
Web **www.stackpoleinn.co.uk**
Dir ***From Pembroke take B4319, follow Stackpole signs, approximately 4 miles.***

This traditional inn is a walker's delight, set in pristine gardens at the heart of the National Trust's Stackpole Estate and close to the spectacular Pembrokeshire coastal path. Popular with cyclists, fishermen and climbers, as well as those who simply prefer to relax, once inside, you'll find a slate bar, ceiling beams made from estate-grown ash trees, and a wood-burning stove set within the stone fireplace. There's always a guest beer to accompany two Welsh ales, a couple of real ciders and a varied wine list. Chef Mark Dowding oversees the creation of menus that use the best local produce from the surrounding countryside and fish from the coast.

Open all year all week 12–3 6–11 (summer 12–11) Closed Sun evening (winter) Free House 12 portions/menu

TENBY

Hope and Anchor

Tel **01834 842131 | St Julians Street, SA70 7AX**
Dir ***A478 or A4139 into Tenby. Into High Street, becomes St Julians Street. Pub on left.***

Heading down towards the harbour and the beach at Tenby and you can't miss the blue Hope and Anchor pub. Traditionally a fishing pub it has remained popular with locals for years and years. They offer a choice of rotating guest ales.

POWYS

BEGUILDY

The Radnorshire Arms

Tel **01547 510634 | LD7 1YE**
Dir ***8 miles from Knighton on B4355 towards Newtown.***

Tucked away in the Teme Valley, this centuries-old black and white timber framed pub started life as a drovers' inn and it retains an old-world charm with mind-your-head beams, inglenook fireplace and wood-burner. Sup on pints of local Ludlow Best or Stonehouse Station Bitter and choose between the bar menu with its pub classics or the main menu. Typical dinner choices include leek and crab tartlet; and venison haunch steak with braised red cabbage, herb mash and red wine sauce.

Open all year 12–2 6–11 Closed Mon Free House from £9.50 portions/menu notice required

BRECON

The Usk Inn PICK OF THE PUBS

Tel **01874 676251 | Talybont-on-Usk, LD3 7JE**
Web **www.uskinn.co.uk**
Dir ***6 miles east of Brecon, just off A40 towards Abergavenny and Crickhowell.***

Well-positioned on the picturesque Abergavenny to Brecon road, not far from the village centre, The Usk Inn opened in the 1840s just as the Brecon to Merthyr railway line was being built alongside it. Expect a choice of guest ales at the bar, along with ciders and popular wines. Dishes are based on carefully sourced ingredients.

COEDWAY

The Old Hand and Diamond Inn

– see opposite

CRICKHOWELL

The Bear ★★★★ INN

PICK OF THE PUBS

Tel **01873 810408 | Brecon Road, NP8 1BW**
Web **www.bearhotel.co.uk**
Dir ***On A40 between Abergavenny and Brecon.***

This imposing white-painted inn, dating from the 15th century, has been run by the Hindmarsh family for over 40 years. The rug-strewn, antique-laden bar offers sandwiches and baguettes and Welsh real ales take the lead at the pumps. Alternatively, dine in the original D Restaurant, or at a table in the restored former kitchen. Head chef Padrig Jones makes good use of local Welsh produce, as in a starter of Welsh rarebit on toasted ciabatta with watercress salad, followed by home-made faggots with onion gravy; or Cornish fish pie. Finish with sticky toffee pudding with caramel sauce and rich clotted cream.

Open all day, all week Closed 25 Dec Free House 10 from £12.95 portions/menu notice required

COEDWAY

The Old Hand and Diamond Inn

Tel **01743 884379 | SY5 9AR**
Web **www.oldhandanddiamond.co.uk**
Dir ***From Shrewsbury take A458 towards Welshpool. Right onto B4393 signed Four Crosses. Coedway approximately 5 miles.***

One for all the family

On the Powys--Shropshire border, this 17th-century inn retains much of its original character, with exposed beams and an inglenook fireplace. Its reputation for good quality food owes much to local farmers who supply excellent meats, including lamb and mutton from rare-breed Jacob sheep. Enjoy local Shropshire Lad and guest real ales in the bar, while choosing from an extensive menu that lists grilled lamb chop and shepherd's pie; Stilton, pepper, mushroom and onion pudding; and steak, mushroom and ale pie. Among the desserts are fresh fruit Pavlova and banoffee pie. The beer garden has plenty of seating and a children's play area.

Open all day, all week 11am–1am *Free House* *from £7* *portions*

DEFYNNOG

The Tanners Arms

Tel **01874 638032 | LD3 8SF**
Web **www.tannersarmspub.com**
Dir ***From Brecon take A40 towards Llandovery. Left onto A4067 to Defynnog.***

Overlooking open countryside, this 17th-century inn derives its name from the tannery that was once in business up the road. In the foothills of the Brecon Beacons National Park, it makes a good stopping point for exploring this mountain area.

GLASBURY

The Harp Inn

Tel **01497 847373 | HR3 5NR**
Web **www.theharpinn.co.uk**
Dir ***In village centre on B4350, approximately 3.5 miles from Hay-on-Wye.***

A pub since the 17th century, this comfortable inn overlooks the River Wye and is just a few miles from Hay-on-Wye itself. In the bar, grab a table and enjoy a pint of one of several local real ales, including Mayfields Glasbury Undaunted specially brewed for the pub. The tempting menu offers a range of curries; steak and ale pie; and mixed bean casserole. There's also a specials board to watch out for. Regular music events take place.

Open all year 12–3 6–12 (Sun 12–3 7–11 Mon 6–11) Closed Mon lunch *Free House* *portions/menu* Wi-fi *notice required*

HAY-ON-WYE

The Old Black Lion – see page 563

The Three Tuns

Tel **01497 821855 | 4 Broad Street, HR3 5DB**
Web **www.three-tuns.com**
Dir ***In town centre.***

Hay's oldest licensed house reveals its 16th-century origins in its three cruck timber frames, later largely encased in stone, a huge central inglenook chimney and a dog-leg staircase. On the Italian-inspired menu start with Sicilian chickpea soup, then Chianti-slow-roasted beef brisket.

Open all day, all week Closed 25 Dec *Free House* *portions/menu* Wi-fi

LLANDRINDOD WELLS

The Laughing Dog

Tel **01597 822406 | Howey, LD1 5PT**
Dir ***From A483 between Builth Wells and Llandrindod Wells follow Howey signs. Pub in village centre.***

All you'd expect from a thriving village local, from pub games in the fire-warmed bar to real ales from respected Welsh microbreweries such as Rhymney and Cwm Rhondda. Originating as a drovers' stopover some 300 years ago and reputedly haunted, this pub is located in superb walking countryside. The varied menu combines the best of Welsh ingredients with influences from Europe and further afield. Dishes include lamb cawl with leeks, root vegetables, pearl barley and thyme; and Glamorgan sausages, bubble-and-squeak with red wine and onion gravy.

Open Tue to Thu 6–10 (Fri 5.30–11 Sat 12–11 Sun 12–2) Closed 1 Jan, Mon, Sun evenings, Tue to Fri lunch Free House from £10.95 portions/menu notice required

LLANFYLLIN

Cain Valley Hotel

Tel **01691 648366 | High Street, SY22 5AQ**
Web **www.cainvalleyhotel.co.uk**
Dir ***From Shrewsbury and Oswestry follow signs for Lake Vyrnwy onto A490 to Llanfyllin. Hotel on right.***

A watering hole since the 17th century, this hotel offers the choice of an oak-panelled lounge bar and a heavily beamed restaurant. Lovers of mild ale will find The Rev. James in the bar along with Westons Stowford Press cider.

LLANGYNIDR

The Coach & Horses

Tel **01874 730245 | Cwmcrawnon Road, NP8 1LS**
Web **www.thecoachandhorsesinn.com**
Dir ***Take A40 from Abergavenny towards Brecon. At Crickhowell left onto B4558 to Llangynidr (Note: narrow river bridge), or from Beaufort take B4560 through Brynmawr to Llangynidr.***

Surrounded by the Brecon Beacons, this early 18th-century free house is a popular meeting place for car club members. Wye Valley Butty Bach is a bar staple, while on the menu steak and Stogs stew with dumplings features real ale Betty Stogs, a Cornish folklore character.

MONTGOMERY

The Nags Head Inn

★★★★★ INN

Tel **01686 640600 | Garthmyl, SY15 6RS**
Web **www.nagsheadgarthmyl.co.uk**
Dir ***On A458 between Welshpool and Newtown Powys.***

It's great when you come across a property like The Nags Head, where a traditional coaching inn has been brought up to date for modern travellers. Abbie and her team are to be commended for their efforts, welcoming all guests whether for a drink in the comfortable bar area with its open fires, dining in the restaurant or on the terrace, or staying in one of the luxurious well-equipped rooms. As an independent inn they showcase a range of local breweries to ensure the perfect pint is always on tap. Wines come locally from Tanners in Shrewsbury and the spirits selection is ever expanding. The food is a highlight and sees the kitchen team showcase the best local produce in imaginative takes on the classics.
AA Pub of the Year for Wales 2018–19.

Open all day, all week Free House 8 portions/menu notice required

OLD RADNOR

The Harp PICK OF THE PUBS

Tel **01544 350655 | LD8 2RH**
Web **www.harpinnradnor.co.uk**
Dir ***Old Radnor signed from A44 between Kington and New Radnor.***

With magnificent views across the Radnor Valley, this stone-built Welsh longhouse dates from the 15th century. Open the plain wooden door and you step into a cosy lounge and bars with original oak beams, crackling log fires, semi-circular wooden settles and slate floors; books, board games and hop bines complete the warm, traditional appeal. The food focus is on fresh and seasonal produce, and local sourcing is highlighted on the concise, refreshingly no-frills menu.

HAY-ON-WYE

The Old Black Lion

★★★★  INN

Tel **01497 820841** | **HR3 5AD**
Web **www.oldblacklion.co.uk**
Dir ***From B4348 in Hay-on-Wye into Lion Street. Inn on right.***

Historic inn on English–Welsh border

Near Lion Gate, one of the original entrances to this old walled town, parts of this charming, mainly 17th-century inn could well date from the 1300s. During the English Civil Wars, Oliver Cromwell may have stayed here when his Roundheads laid siege to Hay Castle. The timbered main bar is furnished with scrubbed pine tables, and dining tables and easy chairs are in the Den, overlooking the garden; both these inviting areas have log-burners, making meals outside a real pleasure. The inn has a long-standing reputation for its locally sourced, freshly cooked food, prepared for daily menus by award-winning chef Mark Turton, among whose delights are roast lamb rack; pan-seared salmon; 21-day-matured local rib-eye steak; and crispy belly pork. Vegetarian options include spinach and roasted squash hash. Sunday alternatives to roasts include grey mullet; and goats' cheese and vegetable parcel. Every Friday evening there's live jazz in the bar. En suite guest rooms are spread between the main building, the Coach House and the Cottage. Hay is famous as the official National Book Town of Wales, and is home to a renowned annual literary festival; it also holds a Dark Skies Festival each October.

Open all day, all week 8am–11pm *Free House*
from £13 *portions/menu*

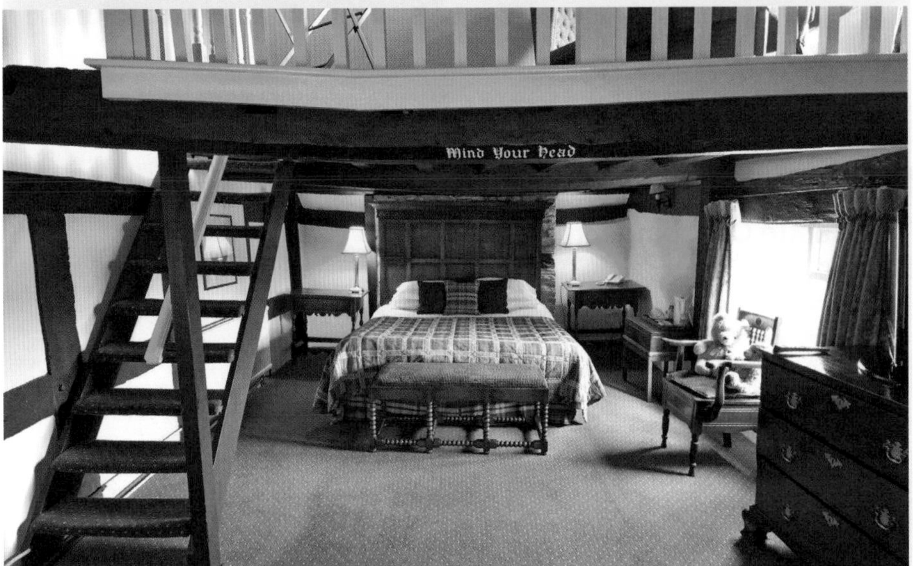

PAINSCASTLE

The Roast Ox Inn

Tel **01497 851398** | **LD2 3JL**
Web **www.roastox.co.uk**
Dir ***From Hay-on-Wye take B4351, through Clyro to Painscastle.***

In stunning countryside close to Hay-on-Wye and Brecon, the Roast Ox is traditional through and through. Expect rustic brick floors, stone walls, old fireplaces and a classic pub atmosphere alongside local Wye Valley Butty Bach ale tapped straight from the barrel. Head for the dining room, originally a blacksmith's workshop, for home-cooked and locally sourced fodder.

Open all year all week Closed Mon to Tue (Jan to Mar) Free House 8 from £10.95 portions Wi-fi *notice required*

TALYBONT-ON-USK

Star Inn

Tel **01874 676635** | **LD3 7YX**
Web **www.thestarinntalybont.com**
Dir ***Take A40 from Brecon toward Crickhowell. 6 miles to pub in town centre.***

The Star has a great deal going for it. The Monmouthshire & Brecon Canal runs past its back door, there are beer festivals in mid-June and mid-October, and the ever-changing real ales feature over 500 guest brews a year. In addition to pub classics, the menu may tempt with braised Welsh lamb shank in red wine; or a 10oz rib-eye steak.

Open all week 5–close (Sat to Sun 12–close) Free House 10 portions/menu Wi-fi

TRECASTLE

The Castle Coaching Inn

PICK OF THE PUBS

Tel **01874 636354** | **LD3 8UH**
Web **www.castle-coaching-inn.co.uk**
Dir ***On A40, west of Brecon.***

This Georgian coaching inn makes an ideal base. Two real ales on tap change weekly, ensuring a pint in tip-top condition; wines and a good selection of Scottish and Irish whiskies are also served. Some guests prefer to stay in the bar to eat where there is additional bar food. Outside, the peaceful terrace and garden beckon.

RHONDDA CYNON TAF

PONTYPRIDD

Bunch of Grapes – see opposite

SWANSEA

LLANGENNITH

Kings Head ★★★★ INN

Tel **01792 386212** | **SA3 1HX**
Web **www.kingsheadgower.co.uk**
Dir ***M4 junction 47, follow signs for Gower A483, 2nd exit at roundabout, right at lights onto B495 towards Old Walls, left at fork to Llangennith, pub on right.***

Situated close to Rhossili Bay's magnificent beach, this 17th-century village inn has old beams, exposed stonework and a large open fire. The bar serves a weekly rotating list of real ales from the Gower Brewery, co-founded by landlord Chris Stevens. Expect home-made food, from Vietnamese, Goan and Thai curries to pizzas and gourmet burgers. Comfortable and stylish accommodation is available. A beer and cider festival is held on the last weekend of October.

Open all day, all week 9am–11pm (Sun 9am–10.30pm) Free House from £8.95 portions/menu

LLANMADOC

Britannia Inn – see opposite

REYNOLDSTON

King Arthur Hotel

Tel **01792 390775** | **Higher Green, SA3 1AD**
Web **www.kingarthurhotel.co.uk**
Dir ***Just north of A4118, south-west of Swansea.***

Sheep graze on the village green opposite this charming inn, set in a pretty village at the heart of the Gower Peninsula. Inside you'll find real log fires, bare wood floors and walls decorated with nautical memorabilia. Eat in the restaurant, main bar or family room, where choices range from pub favourites such as cod fillet in beer batter through to healthy salads. Well-kept local ales and 11 wines served by the glass, accompany.

Open all day, all week (25 Dec 11–2) Free House 11 portions/menu Wi-fi *notice required*

PONTYPRIDD

Bunch of Grapes

Tel **01443 402934 | Ynysangharad Road, CF37 4DA**
Web **www.bunchofgrapes.org.uk**
Dir ***From A470 onto A4054 (Pentrebach Road to Merthyr road) into Ynysangharad Road.***

PICK OF THE PUBS

A gastro pub in the true sense of the word

Fondly known as The Bunch, it's owned by Nick Otley, founder of the well respected, but now closed, Otley Brewing Company. Cask ale is king here, clues being the impressive line-up of real ale, craft keg and real cider pumps on the bar, with imported European and American bottles and kegs adding to the repertoire. The wine list is no also-ran, casting its net worldwide. At lunchtime, the menu takes a pub-grub approach with,

typically, a Breconshire rump steak with garlic mushrooms, hand-cut chips and peppercorn sauce. In the evening, you might be seduced by pan-fried hake with pea velouté, roasted fennel and samphire; or warm mixed bean and pea salad, chickpea mash, and spring onion and mint salsa. Themed beer weekends, cider festivals, cheese nights and food-themed weeks are held monthly.

Open all day, all week *Free House* 9
portions/menu

LLANMADOC

Britannia Inn

Tel **01792 386624 | SA3 1DB**
Web **www.britanniainngower.co.uk**
Dir ***Phone for detailed directions.***

Pub, restaurant and beer garden on the Gower

After years of experience in cooking and hospitality, literally around the world, Martin and Lindsey Davies returned to Wales, their home territory, more than 13 years ago, to apply their skills at the Britannia. The pub's whitewashed and flower-bedecked exterior features a terrace with lovely views. Inside, chunky, modern wooden furniture and beamed ceilings provide a welcoming ambience. Martin's fixed-price lunch menu is indicative of the quality fare, with a focus on regional dishes, on offer: salt marsh lamb; Glamorgan leek

sausages; and Welsh rarebit with Swansea smoked salmon, for example. Real ale drinkers will find Gower Gold, a changing Welsh brew and the ubiquitous Doom Bar. In 1956, the Gower was the first part of the UK to be designated an Area of Outstanding Natural Beauty.

Open all day, all week *Enterprise Inns*
portions/menu *notice required*

VALE OF GLAMORGAN

BARRY

The Fox and Hounds

★★★★ INN

Tel **01446 781287 | Llancarfan, CF62 3AD**
Web **www.fandhllancarfan.co.uk**
Dir ***Phone for detailed directions.***

Beautiful countryside surrounds the little village of Llancarfan, and the church houses medieval paintings dating back to the 15th century. There's a light and airy restaurant and an ornate glass-roofed canopy that means you can eat outside even if it happens to be raining.

COWBRIDGE

Cross Inn PICK OF THE PUBS

Tel **01446 772995 | Church Road, Llanblethian, CF71 7JF**
Dir ***Take B4270 from Cowbridge towards Llantwit Major, pub 0.5 mile on right.***

This 17th-century former coaching inn is set in a picturesque corner of the Vale of Glamorgan, just a few miles from the splendid Heritage Coast. A family-run pub, Cross Inn has a cosy restaurant and comfortable, characterful bar with welcoming log fires and a properly convivial atmosphere. The chefs take great pride in developing daily menus of essentially British food with European influences. Expect choices on the frequently changing restaurant menu to include pub favourites along with specials from the board featuring a variety of locally sourced fish, meat and game. The traditional Sunday lunch is always popular. An ideal starting and finishing point for walkers.

Open all day, all week Mon to Tue 5.30–9.30, Wed to Fri 11.30–3 5.30–11, Sat 11.30–11, Sun 11–10 Free House portions/menu Wi-fi

Victoria Inn

Tel **01446 773943 | Sigingstone, CF71 7LP**
Web **www.victoriainnsigingstone.com**
Dir ***From Llantwit Major north on B4270. Right to Sigingstone.***

This inn is tucked away along country lanes, with the captivating coastline of the Bristol Channel just a short hop away. The eye-catching exterior beckons villagers and explorers into a cottagey, beamed interior with lots of prints, brass and antiques. The locally sourced menu, which is strong on seafood dishes, may start with prawn cocktail, or deep-fried breaded brie wedges with mild cranberry salsa; followed by the inn's popular fish pancake; or home-made steak and kidney pie.

Open all week 11.45–3 6–11.30 (Fri to Sun all day) Free House 10 menus Wi-fi *notice required*

EAST ABERTHAW

Blue Anchor Inn PICK OF THE PUBS

Tel **01446 750329 | CF62 3DD**
Web **www.blueanchoraberthaw.com**
Dir ***From Barry take A4226, then B4265 towards Llantwit Major. Follow signs, turn left for East Aberthaw. 3 miles west of Cardiff Airport.***

Trading since 1380 – thus undoubtedly one of the oldest pubs in Wales – the Blue Anchor has, since 1941, been run by four generations of the Coleman family. Its name comes from the blue marl (mud) which coated the anchors of vessels in the nearby Bristol Channel. A warmly traditional warren of small, low-beamed rooms with open fires includes a large inglenook. Wadworth 6X and Wye Valley Hereford Pale Ale are among the four house beers, with a guest alongside. In the bar and upstairs restaurant starters include home-cured whisky and treacle salmon; and spiced salt beef with Dijon mustard and pickled onions. For the next course, try deep-fried fillet of line-caught cod; honey-glazed, slow-cooked belly pork; fragrant Thai green chicken curry; or roasted butternut squash gnocchi. There's sheltered seating outside.

Open all day, all week 11–11 (Sun 12–10.30 25 Dec 12–2) Free House 9 menus Wi-fi *notice required*

PENARTH

The Pilot

Tel **029 2071 0615 | 67 Queens Road, CF64 1DJ**
Dir ***Phone for detailed directions.***

Set on a hillside with great views across the waters of Cardiff Bay, The Pilot has certainly seen immense changes in the years since it originated as a dock-workers' pub. Transformed like the harbour and docklands at its feet, the pub is now a popular destination. With craft beers from the respected VOG Brewery and ciders from Gwynt y Ddraig to slake a thirst, attention can turn to the ever-changing dishes on the chalkboard. Pub classics mix with modern British dishes – perhaps pan-seared scallops, squash purée and truffle salad; and an 8oz Welsh rib-eye.

Open all day, all week *Brains* *17* *from £10* *portions/menu* *notice required*

WREXHAM

GRESFORD

Pant-yr-Ochain PICK OF THE PUBS

Tel **01978 853525 | Old Wrexham Road, LL12 8TY**
Web **www.pantyrochain-gresford.co.uk**
Dir ***From Chester towards Wrexham on A483 take A5156 signed Nantwich (dual carriageway). 1st left into Old Wrexham Road. Pub 500 yards on right.***

Just outside Wrexham, set in a country estate of gentle hills, woods and meres, this astonishing Tudor manor house stands at the end of a long, sweeping drive. Timber framed gables overlook award-winning gardens, whilst the interior retains many period features. Brick fireplaces, nooks and crannies, alcoves and quiet corners all help to create an Edwardian country house atmosphere. Splendid real ales from breweries like Stonehouse and Weetwood head up a great selection of ales, with real ciders adding local colour. From the kitchen emerge contemporary British dishes. Starters chime in with pigeon breast with blackberry and juniper jus, which might be followed by sea bass fillets with crab risotto and langoustine bisque; or game suet pudding with mash and red wine gravy.

Open all day, all week 11.30–11 (Sun 11.30–10.30) *Free House* *22* *portions/menu*

LLANARMON DYFFRYN CEIRIOG

The Hand at Llanarmon

★★★★ INN PICK OF THE PUBS

Tel **01691 600666 | LL20 7LD**
Web **www.thehandhotel.co.uk**
Dir ***Exit A5 at Chirk follow B4500 for 11 miles. Through Ceiriog Valley to Llanarmon Dyffryn Ceiriog. Pub straight ahead.***

This 16th-century free house and inn, set in the remote Ceiriog Valley, in the shadow of the Berwyn Mountains, was once a rest stop for drovers and their flocks on the old road from Anglesey to London. The cosy interior has original oak beams, plum-coloured walls, large fireplaces and mix-and-match furniture, and the well-stocked bar offers Weetwood Cheshire Cat and Station real ales and plenty of malt whiskies, including a Welsh one. Everything is freshly prepared on the premises – except the steak and ale, and chicken and gammon pies from McArdle's of Chirk. To follow, try tiramisù with stewed forest berries; or sticky toffee pudding with caramel sauce.

Open all day, all week *Free House* *from £10.50* *portions/menu* *notice required*

West Arms

Tel **01691 600665 | LL20 7LD**
Web **www.thewestarms.co.uk**
Dir ***Exit A483 or A5 at Chirk, take B4500 to Ceiriog Valley for 6 miles to Llanarmon. Pub on right.***

A favourite former pit-stop of those old Welsh drovers, for whom herding sheep to distant markets was a thirsty business. It's no wonder Nicky and Mark Williamson found taking over here in 2018 irresistible. With the Berwyn Mountains as a backdrop, its 15th-century origins are evident from its slate flags, low beams and inglenook. Enjoy rainbow trout smoked two ways, or local game terrine, then Berwyn-raised organic lamb, or Welsh rib-eye steak.

Open all day, all week *Free House* *15* *from £15* *portions/menu* *notice required*

ROSSETT

The Golden Lion

Tel **01244 571020 | Chester Road, LL12 0HN**
Web **www.thegoldenlionrossett.co.uk**
Dir ***From Chester take A483 towards Wrexham, left onto B5102 signed Rossett, left onto B5445, pub on left in Rossett.***

Haunted by the ghost of a murderous ploughman, this village centre pub in the northern Welsh Marches is an engaging mix of old and new. Lots of beams, trusses and eclectic furnishings offer great character within. The regularly-changing fare has much for seafood fans, a good vegetarian choice and may feature cottage pie or a fillet steak; platters and bar nibbles prove popular too. Dogs are very welcome in the bar, and outside is an immense, tree-shaded beer garden.

Open all day, all week Sun to Wed 12–11 (Thu 12–11.30 Fri to Sat 12–12) *Hydes Brewery* *16* *from £9.95* *portions/menu* *notice required*

Location index

Recommend a pub

We're always on the lookout for great pubs. If you've visited a pub that you feel warrants an entry in the AA Pub Guide, please drop us a line at **pubs@theAA.com**

We are interested in the quality of the food, the selection of drinks and the overall ambience of the establishment. Please be sure to mention the full address of the pub including postcode wherever possible. We'll only use your communication for considerting pubs for the guide and will not use your details for any other purpose.

Feedback

Alternatively, there may be a pub in the guide you've visited that you'd like to praise further (or not, as the case may be). Please let us know at **pubs@theAA.com**

Feedback from readers helps to keep our guide accurate and up to date. However, if you have a complaint to make about your visit, we do recommend that you discuss the matter with the pub management there and then, so that they have a chance to put things right before your visit is spoilt.

Please note that AA Media does not undertake to arbitrate between you and the pub management, or to obtain compensation or engage in protracted correspondence.

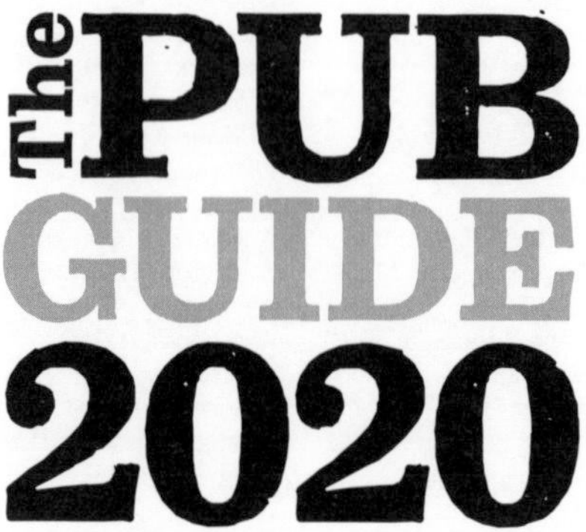